THE PAYROLL SOURCE

APA AMERICAN PAYROLL ASSOCIATION

# American Payroll Association

2008 Edition

By Michael P. O'Toole, Esq.
Senior Director of Publications and Government Relations, APA

In the preparation of this text, every effort has been made to offer the most current, correct, and clearly understandable information possible. Nonetheless, inadvertent errors can occur, and tax rules and regulations are constantly changing.

This text is intended to provide authoritative information in regard to the subject matter covered and can be used as a training tool. As such, it is not an evaluation device upon which to base performance reviews and/or promotions.

This material is distributed with the understanding that the publisher and author are not engaged in rendering legal, accounting, or other professional services. If legal advice or other professional assistance is required, the service of your attorney or certified public accountant should be sought. Readers are encouraged to consult with appropriate professional advisors for advice concerning specific matters before making decisions affecting their individual operations. The publisher disclaims any responsibility for positions taken by practitioners in their individual cases or for any misunderstanding on the part of readers. The information in this text is current as of February 1, 2008.

*Please visit our Web site at www.americanpayroll.org*

ISBN: 978-1-934951-00-2

Printed in the United States

## ABOUT THE AUTHOR

The author of *The Payroll Source*® is Michael P. O'Toole, Esq. As an employment law expert and munici-pal court judge, his background includes more than 25 years as a writer and editor of payroll and employ-ment law books, loose-leaf guides, and newsletters. Michael has served as Managing Editor of Payroll and Employment Law Publications for Prentice Hall Information Services and Warren Gorham Lamont, includ-ing WGL's *Payroll Guide* (now published by RIA).

Currently, Michael is the Senior Director of Publications and Government Relations for the American Payroll Association. He has been with APA for 15 years. As such he oversees APA staff who are responsible for APA resource materials and newsletters, the APA website, representation of the membership in Washington, DC, and technology services. He is also a frequent presenter and author on technical payroll compliance issues for APA.

Michael received his Bachelor of Arts degree from Syracuse University and a Juris Doctor from the Syracuse University College of Law. He was admitted to practice law in New York in 1977, and has served as Acting Village Justice for Tuckahoe, NY since 1991.

Michael lives in Tuckahoe, NY with his wife Roseann and his daughters, Jessica and Sara, without whose patience and understanding *The Payroll Source* would not have been possible.

# ACKNOWLEDGEMENTS

The publisher and author would like to offer their special appreciation to Michael Casey, MAAT, CPP for his work in creating the Review Questions and Exercises appearing at the end of each section of *The Payroll Source*, as well as the Answer Key.

The publisher and author would also like to thank the following individuals for their invaluable contributions as members of a panel of reviewers who provided this book with a payroll practitioner's insight and perspective:

Ruth Chobit, Boston College, Chestnut Hill, MA

Kay C. Tucker, CPA, The Tucker Company, Houston, TX

Bernardita, C. Gonzalez, Esq., American Payroll Association, New York, NY

Brent R. Gow, CPP, Starbucks Coffee Company, Seattle, WA

Lisbeth Green, L.K. Green & Associates, Santa Clara, CA

Vickie Majors, CPP, IBM, Hermitage, TN

James Medlock, CPP, American Payroll Association, San Antonio, TX

Mary Jo Maley, CPP, American Payroll Association, San Antonio, TX

Rena Pirsos, J.D., American Payroll Association, New York, NY

Maureen F. Brown, CPP, CGBA, Gemini Consulting, Inc., Leesburg, VA

Diana Robertson, CPP, Northrop Grumman, Herndon, VA

Nola Wills, CPP, Harbor America, Inc., Houston, TX

The author would like to offer his special thanks to John J. Cervini, Jr., the American Payroll Association's Manager of Production Purchasing, and Debbie Cervini, Production Coordinator, for their effort in the production of *The Payroll Source*.

# TABLE OF CONTENTS

## SECTION 1: THE EMPLOYER-EMPLOYEE RELATIONSHIP

## SECTION 2: FEDERAL AND STATE WAGE-HOUR LAWS

# Table of Contents

## SECTION 4: HEALTH, ACCIDENT, AND RETIREMENT BENEFITS

## SECTION 5: PAYING THE EMPLOYEE

## SECTION 6: WITHHOLDING TAXES

# Table of Contents

## SECTION 8: DEPOSITING AND REPORTING WITHHELD TAXES

## SECTION 9:  OTHER DEDUCTIONS FROM PAY

## SECTION 10:  RECORDKEEPING AND RECORD RETENTION

## Table of Contents

## SECTION 11: PAYROLL ACCOUNTING

## SECTION 13: MANAGING A PAYROLL DEPARTMENT

## SECTION 14: PAYROLL FOR U.S. EMPLOYEES ABROAD AND ALIENS IN THE U.S.

## SECTION 15: PREPARING FOR THE CPP EXAM

## Table of Contents

# SECTION 1: THE EMPLOYER-EMPLOYEE RELATIONSHIP

## TABLE OF CONTENTS

# SECTION 1: THE EMPLOYER-EMPLOYEE RELATIONSHIP

Perhaps the most basic decision an employer must make when hiring a worker to perform a service is whether the worker is an employee. Not all workers are employees, and the employer's determination affects the entire relationship between the employer and the worker. Hiring employees gives the employer the benefits of controlling the methods and results of the work to be done, having full-time workers who work only for the employer, and having workers who have been trained by the employer.

The employer-employee relationship also brings obligations—income and employment tax withholding, unemployment insurance contributions, workers' compensation premiums, etc. This section examines the criteria that determine whether a worker is an employee, as well as the employer's obligations once the employer-employee relationship is established and the penalties resulting from misclassification of a worker as a nonemployee.

This section also outlines an employer's obligation to determine whether a newly hired employee is eligible to work in the United States under U.S. immigration laws and the requirement to report new hires to state government agencies to aid in their effort to enforce child support obligations and prevent fraud in obtaining unemployment compensation, workers' compensation, and public assistance.

## 1.1  Importance of the Determination

Under the Internal Revenue Code (IRC), an employer must withhold income, social security, and Medicare taxes from employees' wages, and it must match the withheld social security and Medicare taxes with employer funds. Under the Federal Unemployment Tax Act (FUTA), covered employers must pay a certain percentage based on each employee's wages to support federal and state unemployment insurance programs (public sector employers are exempt).

Most states and many local governments also require income tax withholding from employees' wages, and all states require most employers to pay "contributions" based on their employees' earnings into state unemployment insurance funds. A few states also require employers to withhold unemployment insurance taxes from employees' wages. Several states require employers to withhold amounts from employees' wages to fund state disability insurance benefit payments and make contributions to the disability plan out of their own funds. Most companies have their own list of benefits and other entitlements they provide to employees as well (e.g., retirement plan, vacations, sick pay, health insurance, etc.).

While this is not meant to be an exhaustive listing of all the obligations that face an employer once the employer-employee relationship is established, it provides some idea of why the initial determination of a worker's status is so important, and why many employers use workers who are not employees to perform services for them.

## 1.2  Employee vs. Independent Contractor

Most of the problems employers have in regard to worker classification arise when determining whether a worker is an employee or an independent contractor. It is often much less expensive for a business to use independent contractors to provide services because the taxing and reporting requirements are much less costly than they are for employees. So long as the independent contractor provides the employer with a valid Taxpayer Identification Number (TIN), the employer's only obligations are to give the contractor a Form 1099-MISC (see Appendix page A-261) at the end of the year stating how much the contractor was paid for the services rendered (if the total was at least $600) and to send a copy of the form to the Internal Revenue Service (see Section 8.12-1 for more details).

**WATCH OUT** Several states have expanded their new hire reporting requirements to include reporting of independent contractors. See pages 1-36 — 1-41 for the new hire reporting requirements of individual states. If states in which an employer operates require reporting of independent contractors, the accounts payable department must be notified to ensure compliance.

Social security and Medicare taxes need not be withheld from an independent contractor's payments or matched by the employer. No federal or state unemployment insurance taxes are required, and employee benefits do not have to be funded, paid, or administered on their behalf.

Because misclassification of workers as independent contractors rather than employees has led to substantial losses in revenue for the federal government and the failure to properly credit earnings for social security and unemployment benefit purposes, the IRS is focusing more resources on payroll tax audits for worker misclassification. Therefore, employers should be sure their human resources and payroll departments are familiar with the tests for determining whether a new hire is an employee or an independent contractor.

# 1.2-1 Common Law Test

While there is no uniform definition of an employee under all payroll laws, most workers can be classified as either employees or independent contractors once the "common law test" has been applied. The IRS, for example, relies on the common law test in making worker status determinations for the purposes of federal income tax withholding and the withholding and payment of employment (social security, Medicare, and federal unemployment) taxes. (Other tests and exceptions are discussed later in this section.)

**Right to control is the key.** Under the common law test, if the employer has the *right to control what work will be done and how that work will be done*, then an employer-employee relationship exists and the worker is a common law employee. This is true regardless of whether the employer actually exercises the right on a regular basis.[1] However, if an individual is subject to the control or direction of another only as to the results to be accomplished, and not as to the details by which those results are accomplished, the individual would not be an employee under the common law test. It makes no difference what the worker is called by the employer. An "agent" or "contractor" is still an employee if the employer controls the work to be done.[2]

**IRS looks to identify key control factors**. The IRS has sought to streamline the process for determining whether a worker is an employee or an independent contractor by identifying those factors that most clearly indicate the degree of control or independence in the relationship of the worker and the business. Evidence of the degree of control and independence can be grouped into three general types or categories: behavioral control, financial control, and the type of relationship between the parties.[3]

*Behavioral control.* Factors that determine behavioral control, which is the right to direct and control the details and means by which the worker performs the work to be done, include:

- *Level of instructions the business gives the worker*—Evidence that a worker is subject to detailed instructions about when, where and how to work tends to show the worker is an employee. Even if no such instructions are given, the right to control through instructions may be sufficient evidence of employment status. The important thing is whether the business has the right to control the details of the worker's performance or has instead given up that right.

- *Level of training provided to the worker*—an employment relationship is indicated where the business provides periodic or ongoing training regarding particular procedures to be followed and methods to be used in performing the work. Independent contractors generally rely on their own methods.

---

1.      IRS Reg. §31.3121(d)-1(c)(2); §31.3306(c)-2; §31.3401(c)-1(b).
2.      IRS Reg. §31.3121(d)-1(c)(2); §31.3401(c)-1(e).
3.      IRS Pub. 15-A, Employer's Supplemental Tax Guide; Training 3320-102, 3-97.

*Financial control.* Factors that must be considered when determining whether the business has the right to direct and control the economic aspects of the worker's job include:

- *Whether the worker has unreimbursed business expenses*—Independent contractors are more likely to have unreimbursed business expenses than employees. The IRS considers fixed ongoing costs that are incurred whether or not work is being performed as particularly important. However, employees may also have unreimbursed business expenses in connection with their employment.

- *Whether the worker has a substantial investment in the work*—While it is not required, independent contractors often have a significant financial investment in the facilities they use to perform services for a business.

- *Whether the worker's services are available to the public*—Evidence that the worker offers his or her services to the public at large (e.g., business cards, phone listing, marketing materials) indicates independent contractor status, although employees can work for more than one employer at a time.

- *How the worker is paid*—Employees generally are paid by the hour, week, or month, while independent contractors are usually paid by the job. However, some independent contractors, such as lawyers or accountants, are customarily paid by the hour.

- *Whether the worker can realize a profit or incur a loss*—All this financial evidence helps determine whether a worker has the opportunity to make a profit or suffer a loss. If so, independent contractor status is indicated.

**Type of relationship.** There are several factors that generally indicate how the worker and the business perceive their relationship to each other and their intent regarding the right to direct and control the manner and means of the worker's activities. These factors include:

- *Whether there is a written agreement*—A written contract may indicate the type of relationship the parties intended to create.

- *Whether employee-type benefits are provided*—If the business provides the worker with benefits usually provided to employees, such as paid vacations, health and life insurance, sick pay, or a retirement plan, an employment relationship is indicated.

- *The term of the relationship*—If a worker is hired with the expectation that the relationship will continue indefinitely rather than for a specific period or project, this is generally evidence that the intent was to create an employment relationship.

- *Whether the worker's services are an important aspect of the business's regular operations*—If a worker provides services that make up a key aspect of the entity's regular business activity, it is likely that the business will have the right to direct and control the worker's activities.

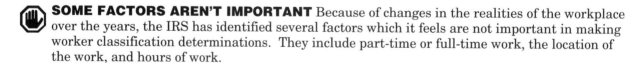 **SOME FACTORS AREN'T IMPORTANT** Because of changes in the realities of the workplace over the years, the IRS has identified several factors which it feels are not important in making worker classification determinations. They include part-time or full-time work, the location of the work, and hours of work.

**Example 1**: Fred is an experienced plumber who agreed to perform full-time services for The Building Group, Inc. at its construction sites. He uses his own tools and performs the work in the order designated by TBG, according to their specifications. TBG supplies all Fred's materials, frequently inspects his work, pays him on a piecework basis, and carries workers' compensation insurance on him. Fred does not advertise his services or hold himself out as available to perform similar services for other companies. Fred is an employee of TBG.

***Example 2***: Rusty's Auto Sales, Inc. provides a garage with two bays and a lift for Harold to perform car repair services. Harold brings his own tools and supplies and does all of Rusty's body work and painting. Harold also solicits business from insurance adjusters and others. Harold hires his own helpers, can fire them for poor performance, and sets their work hours. He can determine the prices for work done and is compensated by a percentage of the gross revenue from work done in the repair shop. Harold is also responsible for any collected charges. Harold is an independent contractor whose helpers are his employees, not those of Rusty's.

***Example 3***: Lisa, a computer programmer, loses her job after a layoff at Overbyte, Inc. However, Overbyte agrees to pay Lisa a flat amount to complete a one-time project to create a new product. The length of time for completion of the project is unclear, and there is no guaranteed minimum payment for the job. The only instructions Overbyte gives Lisa are the project specifications. Lisa and Overbyte agree in writing that Lisa is considered to be an independent contractor, is required to pay federal and state taxes, receives no benefits from Overbyte, and will receive a 1099-MISC from Overbyte. Lisa works at home and is not required or allowed to attend meetings of the software development group. Lisa is an independent contractor.

***Example 4***: Anne rents a taxi cab from Greenfield Cab Co. for $150 per day. Anne pays the cost of maintaining and operating the cab, and she keeps all fares she receives from her riders. Although she receives the benefit of Greenfield's radio communications equipment, dispatcher, and advertising, these items benefit both parties. Anne is an independent contractor.

**Managers are employees, too.** Federal payroll tax laws apply to all levels of employees, including supervisors, managers, and other executives. A corporation's officers, as well, are generally covered, unless they perform only minor services and neither receive nor are entitled to any compensation. Keep in mind, however, that managerial employees are most likely exempt from coverage under other employment-related laws, such as the Fair Labor Standards Act and the National Labor Relations Act. Members of a corporation's Board of Directors are not employees of the corporation with respect to services performed as a director.

**Length of employment makes no difference.** So long as an individual meets the common law test for employment status, a part-time or temporary employee is covered under the federal payroll tax laws. The number of hours or days worked makes no difference. (See Section 1.4 for the proper treatment of workers hired through a temporary help agency.)

***Example:*** Rose, a proofreader and copy editor, works on a part-time basis for Book Jacket, Ltd. on their premises and is paid by the page. Her work is reviewed by a production editor, and she can be discharged or can quit at any time. She also works for other publishers as time permits, since her hours at Book Jacket vary greatly. Rose is an employee of Book Jacket, although she may be an employee or independent contractor in her other jobs, depending on the circumstances.

# 1.2-2 Reasonable Basis Test

Even though a worker meets the definition of an employee under the common law test, an employer may treat a worker as an independent contractor exempt from federal payroll tax laws if it has a "reasonable basis" for doing so, as determined by §530 of the Revenue Act of 1978.[4] The reasonable basis may consist of one or more of the following, as well as any other reasonable basis:

- court decisions, published IRS rulings, IRS technical advice sent to the employer, or a private letter ruling from the IRS indicating that the worker (or workers in similar situations) is not an employee;

---

4.     P.L. 95-600, as amended.

- a past IRS audit of the employer (not one of its workers) that did not result in a finding of taxes owed or a penalty attributable to the employer's treatment of the worker (or workers in similar situations) as an independent contractor; or

- a longstanding, recognized practice in a significant segment of the employer's industry of treating workers in similar situations as independent contractors.

**Consistent treatment is a must.** In order to take advantage of the "safe harbor" provided by the reasonable basis test, the employer must treat the worker whose status is in question (and all similarly situated workers) consistently as an independent contractor and must file all federal tax and information returns for the period in question based on that treatment. The treatment must have been consistent since 1978 by the employer and/or its predecessor.[5]

*Example:* A worker who receives a W-2 form reporting income earned in a year or is asked to complete a Form W-4 providing the number of withholding allowances is not being consistently treated as an independent contractor, and the employer cannot use the §530 safe harbor.

The application of the reasonable basis test was clarified for periods beginning after December 31, 1996 by the Small Business Job Protection Act of 1996. Under these amendments to Section 530:

- Audits begun after December 31, 1996 may not be relied on unless they include an employment classification audit of the worker involved or a similarly situated worker.

- In making a "significant segment" determination, the IRS cannot require an employer to show that more than 25% of its industry treated similarly situated workers as independent contractors.

- In making a "longstanding recognized practice" determination, the IRS cannot require the employer to show the practice continued for more than 10 years or that it was in existence before 1978.

- There does not have to be an initial determination that the worker is an employee under the common law test before Section 530 can be applied.

- If an employer changes its treatment of a worker for employment tax purposes from an independent contractor to an employee, the employer may still claim Section 530 protection for the periods before the change in treatment.

- In determining whether two workers hold substantially similar positions, the IRS must take into account the relationship between the employer and the workers.

- Once an employer offers sufficient proof that it reasonably treated a worker as an independent contractor under Section 530 and complied with all information requests from the IRS, the burden of proving that the worker is an employee is up to the IRS.

*Failure to file Forms 1099-MISC in one year no bar to §530 relief in later years.*[6] An employer may be entitled to tax relief under §530 for a subsequent tax year even if it failed to file Forms 1099-MISC for workers it treated as independent contractors in an earlier year. So long as the employer is otherwise entitled to §530 relief for the subsequent year and files the appropriate returns for that year treating the workers as independent contractors, the IRS will not deny the employer relief from income and employment tax withholding obligations for those workers.

---

5.    Rev. Proc. 85-18, 1985-1 CB 518.
6.    ILM 200211037, 1-14-02.

*Example 1:*  After examining Ulloa, Inc.'s employment tax liability for 2006, the IRS determined that several of Ulloa's workers, whom Ulloa considered to be independent contractors, were employees for federal income tax purposes.  Ulloa did not file 2006 Forms 1099-MISC for the workers, but it did file 2007 Forms 1099-MISC for payments made to them in 2007.  Ulloa is not entitled to §530 tax relief for 2006 because of its failure to file Forms 1099-MISC for that year.  However, such relief is available to Ulloa for 2007 because the forms were filed for that year, if it can show a reasonable basis for treating the workers as independent contractors during that year.

*Example 2:*  After examining Morrissey Co.'s employment tax liability for 2006, the IRS determined that several of Morrissey's workers were employees for federal income tax purposes, rather than independent contractors.  Morrissey filed Forms 1099-MISC for the workers for 2006, but not for 2007.  Forms 1099 for payments made during 2008 were not yet due at the time of the audit. Morrissey is not entitled to §530 relief for 2007, but if it timely files Forms 1099-MISC for 2008, it may be entitled to §530 relief for 2008.

*Example 3:*  After examining Grant Corp.'s employment tax liability for 2006, the IRS determined that several of Grant's workers who had been treated as independent contractors were actually employees for federal income tax purposes.  Grant filed Forms 1099-MISC for about half of those workers for 2006, and was considering whether it should file Forms W-2 or 1099-MISC for 2007 at the time of the audit.  Grant is not entitled to §530 relief for 2006 as to the workers for whom it did not file Forms 1099-MISC, but if it timely filed Forms 1099-MISC for those workers for 2007, it may be entitled to such relief for 2007.

**Notice of Section 530 must be provided by IRS**.  Before a worker classification audit can begin, the IRS employee conducting the audit must give the employer written notice of the availability of the Section 530 safe harbor protections (see page 1-8).[7]  If the audit does not begin with worker classification issues, the notice does not have to be provided until such issues are brought up.

**IRS auditors must be "liberal" in applying Section 530**.  The IRS training manual on worker classification audits requires examiners to "liberally construe" employers' claims that they have a reasonable basis for treating a worker as an independent contractor.  They also must consider whether the safe harbor applies even if the employer does not raise the issue.

 **WATCH OUT**  Employers that make payments to workers covered by the Section 530 "reasonable basis" test must report those payments to the workers on Form 1099-MISC (see Section 8.12-1) in Box 7.  Section 530 workers must pay their own social security and Medicare taxes (but not their employer's share) when they file their personal income tax return (Form 1040).  The instructions for recipients of Form 1099-MISC tell such workers to report the amount in Box 7 on the "Wages, salaries, tips, etc." line of Form 1040 and to complete and attach Form 8919, *Uncollected Social Security and Medicare Tax on Wages* (see Appendix page A-398).  Form 8919 was introduced by the IRS in November 2007 in an effort to clarify the social security and Medicare tax payment and reporting obligations of common law employees who are treated as independent contractors under Section 530.

---

7.    Publication 1976, Independent Contractor or Employee?

# SECTION 530 RELIEF REQUIREMENTS

**YOUR** business has been selected for an employment tax examination to determine whether you correctly treated certain workers as independent contractors. However, you will not owe employment taxes for these workers if you meet the **relief requirements** described below. If you do not meet these **relief requirements**, the IRS will need to determine whether the workers are independent contractors or employees and whether you owe employment taxes for those workers.

**Section 530 Relief Requirements:**
To receive relief, you must meet all three of the following requirements:

## I. Reasonable Basis

First, you had a reasonable basis for not treating the workers as employees. To establish that you had a reasonable basis for not treating the workers as employees, you can show that:

- You reasonably relied on a court case about Federal taxes or a ruling issued to you by the IRS; or

- Your business was audited by the IRS at a time when you treated similar workers as independent contractors and the IRS did not reclassify those workers as employees. You may not rely on an audit commenced after December 31, 1996, unless such audit included an examination for employment tax purposes of whether the individual involved (or any other individual holding a substantially similar position) should be treated as your employee; or

- You treated the workers as independent contractors because you knew that was how a significant segment of your industry treated similar workers; or

- You relied on some other reasonable basis. For example, you relied on the advice of a business lawyer or accountant who knew the facts about your business.

If you did not have a reasonable basis for treating the workers as independent contractors, you do not meet the **relief requirements**.

## II. Substantive Consistency

In addition, you (and any predecessor business) must have treated the workers, and any similar workers, as independent contractors. If you treated similar workers as employees, this relief provision is not available. If you are paying an individual who is providing services as a test proctor or room supervisor assisting in the administration of college entrance or placements examinations, the substantive consistency requirement does not apply with respect to services performed after December 31, 2006, (and remuneration paid with respect to such services). The provision applies if the individual (1) is performing the services for a tax-exempt organization, and (2) is not otherwise treated as an employee of such organization for purposes of employment taxes.

## III. Reporting Consistency

Finally, you must have filed all required federal tax returns (including information returns) consistent with your treatment of each worker as not being employees. This means, for example, that if you treated a worker as an independent contractor and paid him or her $600 or more, you must have filed Form 1099-MISC for the worker. Relief is not available for any year and for any workers for whom you did not file the required information returns.

*The IRS examiner will answer any questions you may have about your eligibility for this relief.*

**Technical services specialists get special treatment.** Section 530 specifically excludes from the reasonable basis test technical services specialists who work under a "three-party" arrangement involving the worker, a technical services firm, and the firm's client. The status of such workers must be determined under the common law test, and they can be independent contractors or employees of either the technical services firm or the client company. "Technical services specialists" include engineers, drafters, designers, computer programmers, systems analysts, and other similarly skilled workers.[8]

**IRS's role is strictly limited by law.** Section 530 specifically prohibits the IRS from issuing any regulations or rulings "clarifying the employment status of individuals for purposes of the employment taxes."[9]

**Schools may treat exam proctors as independent contractors.** Under the Pension Protection Act of 2006, tax-exempt organizations may treat proctors or room supervisors who help administer college entrance or placement examinations as independent contractors under §530 beginning in 2007 if the proctors are not otherwise common law employees of the institution.[10]

**Form SS-8: IRS makes the status determination.** An employer can get a definitive ruling from the IRS as to a newly hired worker's status as an employee or an independent contractor by completing Form SS-8, *Determination of Worker Status for Purposes of Federal Employment Taxes and Income Tax Withholding* (see Appendix page A-51). A ruling can be applied to a class of workers whose employment status is in question if the form is completed for one person who is representative of the class. Form SS-8 contains a series of questions designed to determine the extent of the employer's right to control the result and means of the work being performed by application of the factors considered by the IRS. Call 1-800-829-3676 (1-800-TAX FORM) to order a copy of the form or go to the IRS website at www.irs.gov.

Employers whose principal place of business or office is located in the eastern half of the U.S. should send the completed form to:

> Internal Revenue Service
> SS-8 Determinations
> 40 Lakemont Road
> Newport, VT 05855-1555

Employers whose principal place of business or office is located in the western half of the U.S. should send the completed form to:

> Internal Revenue Service
> SS-8 Determinations
> P.O. Box 630
> Stop 631
> Holtsville, NY 11742-0630

While waiting for the IRS to respond to the Form SS-8 (which could take from several weeks to six months), the employer should treat the worker(s) in question as an employee, with all appropriate wages and taxes reported and/or withheld (see Sections 6, 7, and 8). This helps the employer avoid penalties and interest assessments if the IRS finds an employer-employee relationship. If the IRS rules the worker is an independent contractor, the employer is not entitled to a refund of any employment taxes paid.

In 2004, the Treasury Inspector General for Tax Administration (TIGTA) reported the results of a review it conducted of the SS-8 program. TIGTA found that there is no mechanism in place to follow up once employment status determinations are made using the form, and it recommended that compliance be made one of the goals of the program and that follow-up procedures be instituted to identify and measure

---

8.     IRS Notice 87-19, 1987-1 CB 455; Pub. Law 95-600, §530(d).
9.     P.L. 95-600, §530(b).
10.     P.L. 109-280, §864; P.L. 95-600, §530(f).

compliance. The report also recommended that a system of quality review be implemented to help ensure consistency among examiners and between processing sites.[11]

**Specific industry guidelines.** In 1994, the IRS issued guidelines to help its field personnel and industry members make determinations of employee/independent contractor status in the television commercial production and professional video communication industries (not including feature film or network television production). The nonbinding guidelines grew out of meetings between the IRS and industry representatives and are designed to identify the significant factors in determining the degree of the employer's right to control in the industry and the standards for determining whether these factors are met.

In 1997, the IRS issued worker classification guidelines for limousine drivers. In 1998, it finalized guidelines for moving van operators, as well as the garment manufacturing, hardwood timber, and furniture manufacturing industries. Other industry groups and workers for whom guidelines are being developed include physical therapists, home delivery services, and drywall contractors.

**Disputes can be heard by Tax Court**. The Tax Court has jurisdiction to determine whether the IRS has been correct in finding during an audit that one or more workers are employees or that the employer cannot claim the protection of Section 530 regarding its treatment of them. The Tax Court can also decide the amount of employment taxes and/or additions to tax and penalties due if it finds a misclassification of employees. Assessment and collection of the taxes is suspended pending a decision by the Tax Court, and both parties are bound by the court's decision.[12] Under guidance issued by the IRS, there must be an IRS "Notice of Determination" of employment status arising out of an audit to give the court jurisdiction, not merely a finding made in the context of a private letter ruling or Form SS-8 (see page 1-9).

The employer is the only party that can seek review by the Tax Court, not employees or third parties. The "Notice of Determination" sent to the employer by the IRS will advise the employer of the chance for Tax Court review. The Notice is sent after the employer has exhausted the internal IRS appeals process or has decided not to use that process. The employer has 90 days after the Notice is mailed to seek Tax Court review. Otherwise, the employer can pay the assessed tax first and then seek a refund. If the refund claim is denied or the IRS has not responded within 6 months the employer can seek review in federal district court or the Court of Federal Claims.[13]

# 1.3 Employment Status Determined by Law

The status of some workers is determined by law, specifically the Internal Revenue Code, regardless of what their classification would be under the common law or reasonable basis test. This means that some workers who would be considered independent contractors under one of these tests are nevertheless "statutory employees" for certain purposes. And some workers who would be considered employees under one of these tests are treated as "statutory nonemployees" under the IRC.

## 1.3-1 Statutory Employees

Statutory employees are workers who, while they are not employees under the common law, are treated as employees for certain employment tax purposes. Payments made by an employer to statutory employees are not subject to federal income tax withholding, but are subject to withholding for social security and Medicare taxes. Also, the employer must pay the employer's share of social security and Medicare taxes and, in some instances, federal unemployment tax (FUTA).[14] Statutory employees fall into four categories.

---

11.   TIGTA 2004-30-055, 3-5-04.
12.   IRC §7436; Chief Counsel Notice CC-2001-044, 10-4-01; Ewens and Miller, Inc. v. Commissioner, 117 T.C. No. 22, No. 13069-99 (12-11-01); Charlotte's Office Boutique, Inc. v. Commissioner, 425 F.3d 1203 (9 CA, 2005).
13.   IRS Notice 2002-5, 2002-3 IRB 320; IRS Notice 98-43, 1998-2 CB 211.
14.   IRC §3121(d)(3); IRS Reg. §31.3121(d)-1(d).

**Agent-drivers or commission-drivers.**[15] The driver must be engaged in distributing meat, vegetables, fruits, baked goods, beverages (other than milk), or laundry or dry-cleaning services. The driver must also be paid on a commission basis, or the difference between the sales price of the goods or services and the price paid by the driver.

**Full-time life insurance salespersons.**[16] The salesperson's principal business activity must be selling life insurance and/or annuity contracts, primarily for one life insurance company. Generally, the salesperson will use office space made available by the company and will not have to pay for the use of stenographic assistance, telephones, forms, rate books, or advertising materials.

 **WATCH OUT** Employers are exempt from paying FUTA tax on the earnings of a full-time life insurance salesperson only if all the earnings are from commissions.[17] If any part of the earnings consist of salary payments, all the earnings are subject to FUTA tax.

**Homeworkers.**[18] The homeworker must work away from the employer's premises, according to specifications provided by the employer, and with goods or materials provided by the employer that must be returned to the employer or someone designated by the employer. Also, the homeworker must be paid at least $100 in cash wages during the year before the wages become subject to social security and Medicare taxes. The earnings of a homeworker who is not an employee under the common law test are not subject to FUTA tax. Homeworkers are not to be confused with domestic employees who perform household duties in the employer's home. They are governed by a totally different set of rules.

**Traveling or city salespersons.**[19] The salesperson's principal business activity must be working full-time for the employer soliciting orders from wholesalers, retailers, contractors, or operators of hotels, restaurants, or similar establishments who either resell or use the merchandise in their own businesses. If the salesperson occasionally solicits orders on behalf of another company, he or she is still a statutory employee, but only with respect to the primary employer.

**General requirements.**[20] Workers who fall into one of the above categories must also meet some general requirements before qualifying as statutory employees.

1. They must agree with the employer that all services are to be performed personally by the worker.

2. They must not make a substantial investment in business equipment or facilities (other than transportation).

3. Their work must be part of a continuing relationship with the employer, rather than a single transaction.

## 1.3-2 Statutory Nonemployees

Certain categories of workers, while they may qualify as employees under the common law test, are nevertheless treated under the IRC as independent contractors for federal income tax withholding and social security, Medicare, and FUTA tax purposes. They are known as statutory nonemployees. The earnings of statutory nonemployees are not subject to federal income tax withholding or social security, Medicare, or FUTA taxes regardless of their status under the common law test, so long as certain conditions are met.[21] There are two categories of statutory nonemployees.

---

15.   IRC §3121(d)(3)(A); §3306(i); IRS Reg. §31.3121(d)-1(d)(3)(i).
16.   IRC §3121(d)(3)(B); §3306(i); IRS Reg. §31.3121(d)-1(d)(3)(ii).
17.   IRC §3306(c)(14); §3306(i); IRS Reg. §31.3306(c)(14)-1.
18.   IRC §3121(d)(3)(C); §3306(i); IRS Reg. §31.3121(d)-1(d)(3)(iii).
19.   IRC §3121(d)(3)(D); §3306(i); IRS Reg. §31.3121(d)-1(d)(3)(iv)
20.   IRC §3121(d); IRS Reg. §31.3121(d)-1(d)(4).
21.   IRC §3508; IRS Prop. Reg. §31.3508-1.

**Qualified real estate agents.** This exemption applies to salespersons who are licensed real estate agents performing services in connection with the sale of real property, including advertising or showing the property, making appraisals, and recruiting, training, or supervising other real estate sales agents.

**Direct sellers.** This exemption applies to individuals who sell consumer products on a buy-sell or deposit-commission basis to be resold in the home or someplace other than a permanent retail establishment. It also applies to individuals who sell the products themselves in the home or someplace other than a permanent retail establishment. The exemption also applies to workers engaged in delivering or distributing newspapers or shopping news (including any directly related services).

**General requirements.** Real estate agents or direct sellers who meet these criteria must also meet two general requirements before their earnings are considered exempt from payroll tax laws.

1. Most of their compensation must be directly related to sales or other work output rather than the number of hours worked.

2. Their work must be performed under a written contract providing that the individual will not be treated as an employee for federal income, social security, Medicare, or FUTA tax purposes.

# 1.4 Temporary Help Agency Employees

To meet short-term staffing needs, many employers make use of workers hired through temporary help agencies rather than hiring the workers themselves. The temporary workers are hired, screened, and trained by the temporary help agency to provide services for client firms. They are employees of the temporary help agency, which has the sole right to hire and fire them. The agency is responsible for complying with any payroll, benefits, and human resources requirements.

The client company's only obligation is to pay the agency a fee for the temporary workers' services as required by its contract with the agency. Although it may have the contractual right to refuse any worker sent by the agency or to request certain workers who may have done a good job in the past, these rights do not make the workers employees of the client company.

> *Example:* Sara, the president of TaxPrepCo, needs extra data processors to handle electronic filing of tax returns in March and April. She contracts with Short-Temps, Inc., which has supplied her with such workers in the past, and asks for several workers who performed well previously. Short-Temps has trained the workers and provides them to several tax preparation services as needed, reviewing their performance with some input from the client firms. The data processors are employees of Short-Temps.

>  **WATCH OUT** Employers should make sure they are dealing with a financially secure and reputable temporary help agency before entering into a contract, since the agency's financial failure could lead to the client company becoming liable for any withholding or employment taxes that remain unpaid.

# 1.5 Leased Employees

Another avenue for employers to pursue when looking to lower their expenses for payroll and benefits is that of leasing employees from an employee leasing company. Under a leasing arrangement, the leasing company hires, trains, and qualifies workers for a client company, which pays a fee to the leasing company to cover the cost of payroll, benefits, etc. Although the client company may have the right to hire and fire the workers, set wage levels, and supervise their work, the workers generally are employees of the leasing company, which is responsible for all withholding and employment taxes as well as the administration and funding of any benefits it wishes to provide.

**WATCH OUT** The leasing company's treatment as the employer of the leased employees stems from its control over the payment of the employees' wages and benefits.[22] The more control the client company retains, the greater the likelihood that it may be considered the employer rather than the leasing company.

In a legal memorandum from its Chief Counsel, IRS said that in order for IRS to establish that a client company is liable for unpaid employment taxes due on wages paid to employees it leased from a leasing company or a professional employer organization, the Service would have to show that the client company was either the common law employer, co-employer with the leasing company, or statutory employer controlling the payment of wages.[23] This determination would have to be made based on the facts and circumstances in each case, including the language of the agreement between the client company and the leasing company or PEO. But be careful, because even though IRS's position is that a PEO is not in control of the payment of wages unless the PEO first receives funds from the client, the agreement between the client and the PEO will determine whether funds have to be provided to the PEO before employees are paid.

**Wage bases restart with leasing agreement.** In 2000, the IRS Chief Counsel ruled that where a leasing company provides employees to a client company, and those same employees worked as employees of the client company earlier in the same calendar year before the leasing agreement was signed, the leasing company must apply separate social security and federal unemployment tax (FUTA) wage bases to the wages it pays to those employees. It cannot take into account the wages paid to the employees by the client company earlier in the year.[24]

**Employment status issues lead to benefit plan relief from IRS.** Because of the difficulties that often are encountered when determining whether "worksite employees" are employees of the client organization (CO) or the leasing company, the IRS issued guidance describing steps that may be taken to ensure the qualified status of defined contribution retirement plans maintained by leasing companies, and professional employer organizations (PEOs).[25]

*Exclusive benefit rule noncompliance could cause plan disqualification.* If the CO, not the PEO, is the employer of the worksite employees under the common law test, a plan maintained by the PEO that benefits worksite employees of the CO will not satisfy the "exclusive benefit rule." Under this rule, a qualified pension, profit-sharing, or stock bonus plan must be established and maintained by an employer for the exclusive benefit of the employer's employees and their beneficiaries (see Section 4-6.1). A retirement plan that provides benefits for individuals who are not employees of the employer maintaining the plan violates the exclusive benefit rule. Therefore, if the CO, not the PEO, is the employer, a plan maintained by the PEO that benefits worksite employees of the CO will not satisfy the exclusive benefit rule.

*Relief from plan disqualification.* Under Revenue Procedure 2002-21, if a PEO has a "PEO retirement plan" in existence on May 13, 2002 that benefits worksite employees, the PEO has the option of either converting its plan to a multiple employer plan or terminating it. If the PEO timely satisfies the requirements, the IRS will not disqualify the pre-existing retirement plan solely on the grounds that it violates or has violated the exclusive benefit rule for plan years beginning before the "compliance date" (the last date of the first plan year of the PEO retirement plan beginning on or after January 1, 2003).

*Termination option.* If a PEO chooses this option, it must take binding action (e.g., board of directors resolution, partnership vote) on or before the "PEO decision date" (120 days after the first day of the plan year beginning on or after January 1, 2003), providing that the plan will be terminated on or before the compliance date. Also before the PEO decision date, the PEO must notify each CO that has worksite employees with accrued benefits in the PEO's retirement plan that the CO has the option of either transferring assets and liabilities attributable to those employees to its own retirement plan (by the compliance date) or of spinning off those assets and liabilities to a separate plan and terminating it (by the compliance date). The CO

---

22. IRC §3401(d)(1); IRS Reg. §31.3401(d)-1(f); General Motors Corp. v. U.S., No. 89-CV-73046-DT (ED Mich. 12-20-90), 67 AFTR2d 520.
23. ILM 200415008, 4-9-04.
24. ILM 200017041, 3-3-00.
25. Rev. Proc. 2002-21, 2002-19 IRB 911; Rev. Proc. 2003-86, 2003-50 IRB 1211.

must provide notice of the selected option by a date specified by the PEO. If it does not, the PEO must treat the CO as having chosen the spinoff and termination option. In any event, the PEO must implement the choice made or deemed made by each CO on or before the compliance date.

*Conversion option.* If a PEO chooses this option, it must adopt plan amendments necessary to convert its plan to a "multiple employer retirement plan" on or before the PEO decision date. The effective date of the plan amendments must be no later than the first day of the first plan year beginning after the compliance date. Also before the PEO decision date, the PEO must notify each CO that has worksite employees with accrued benefits in the PEO's retirement plan that the CO has the option of adopting the multiple employer retirement plan by the effective date of the plan conversion, as well as the options available under the termination option (described above). If the CO does not provide notice of the selected option by the date specified by the PEO, the PEO must treat the CO as having chosen the spinoff and termination option (as above).

**Small companies reap most of the benefits.** Employee leasing has been especially attractive to smaller employers—those with fewer than 100 workers. They often cannot obtain low group health insurance rates, while a leasing company with a larger work force may be eligible for lower rates. Also, smaller companies often find it too costly to staff their own payroll, compensation, or benefits departments or to hire a payroll service bureau, while a larger leasing company faces fewer such obstacles.

Larger businesses may also take advantage of employee leasing, especially when setting up new facilities in new locations or when looking to hire a group of workers with specialized skills (e.g., engineers, systems analysts). Whether an employer will benefit from employee leasing depends on whether the fee charged by the leasing company would be less than the cost of the payroll, benefits, and human resources responsibilities attached to those employees.

 **WATCH OUT** Employers should make sure that they are dealing with a financially secure and reputable leasing company before entering into a contract, since the leasing company's financial failure could lead to the client company becoming liable for any withholding or employment taxes that remain unpaid. (But see footnote 22 for a court ruling that where the leasing company was the employer, the client had no employment tax liability when the leasing company went bankrupt).

**States may have different rules.** While in most instances leased employees are treated the same under state income tax withholding and unemployment insurance laws as they are under federal payroll tax laws, some state laws may place more responsibility on the client company depending on how much control it retains. A check of the applicable state law is necessary before negotiating a lease agreement.

# 1.6 Employees Under Other Federal and State Laws

The Internal Revenue Code is not the only law that requires compliance based on the existence of an employer-employee relationship. Other federal and state laws governing minimum wages and overtime pay, unemployment insurance, and disability insurance have their own definitions of employee status that determine an employer's responsibilities.

# 1.6-1 Federal Wage-Hour Law

The federal Fair Labor Standards Act regulates minimum wage rates, overtime pay, child labor, and equal pay for employees covered by the law (see Section 2 for details). The FLSA broadly characterizes an employee as any individual who works for an employer. In interpreting this definition, the federal courts have steered away from a technical or legal approach, choosing instead to look at the "economic facts" in each case. Using such an approach, the courts and the U.S. Department of Labor's Wage and Hour Division will find an employer-employee relationship where the worker is "economically dependent" on the employer.

Factors the courts and the DOL consider when making an employment status determination include:

- how much control the employer has over how the work is performed;

- whether the worker has the chance to make a profit or risks a loss based on how skillfully the work is performed;

- whether the worker invests in tools or materials required to perform the work or hires helpers;

- whether the work requires a special skill;

- how permanent the working relationship is; and

- whether the work performed is an integral part of the employer's business operation.[26]

## 1.6-2 State Wage-Hour Laws

Most states have laws similar to the FLSA regulating minimum wage rates, overtime pay, maximum hours, and child labor. An individual who is an employee for FLSA purposes would generally satisfy the test for employment status under state law, although some states exempt FLSA-covered employees from state wage-hour requirements. Employers should check the state laws in those states where they have workers to make sure of their status.

## 1.6-3 State Income Tax Withholding Laws

In general, states that require withholding of state income tax follow the common law test used by the IRS in determining whether an employer-employee relationship exists (see Section 1.2-1). Therefore, where the employer has the right to control what work will be done and how it will be done, state income tax withholding will most likely be required.

**What about nonresident employees?** Most states that have an income tax apply it to residents and also to nonresidents who are employed in the state. To prevent employees who live in one state and work in another from being subject to double taxation, some states have entered into "reciprocity agreements" that require employers to withhold only for their employees' states of residence. Other states allow residents to claim a state income tax credit for taxes paid to other states or localities. Where employees live in one state and work in two or more states, an allocation of the work may need to be made. Employers should check the income tax withholding requirements of the states where they do business. [For more information on state laws governing the taxation of nonresident employees, see Table 3.1 in *APA's Guide to State Payroll Laws*.]

## 1.6-4 State Unemployment Insurance Laws

Because the aim of state unemployment insurance laws is to provide benefits for individuals who are out of work through no fault of their own, their definition of the employer-employee relationship is often more inclusive than the definition used under the Internal Revenue Code or the Federal Unemployment Tax Act. While many states use the common law test that determines employee status under FUTA, more than half use what is known as the "ABC test."

Under the ABC test, a worker is an independent contractor only if:

*Absence of control*—the worker is free from control or direction in performing the work both by agreement and in reality;

---

26.    Real v. Driscoll Strawberry Associates, Inc., 603 F.2d 748 (9 CA 1979).

*Business is unusual and/or away*—the work is performed outside the usual course of the company's business or away from any of the employer's facilities; and

*Customarily independent contractor*—the worker is customarily engaged in an independent trade, occupation, or business.

The application of the ABC test makes it tougher for a company to exclude its workers from coverage under state unemployment insurance contribution laws. Some states apply only two of the three conditions. See Table 1.1 for a chart showing state rules on determining employee status for unemployment insurance contribution purposes. [For more information on the determination of employment status under state unemployment insurance laws, see Table 8.1 in *APA's Guide to State Payroll Laws*.]

Table 1.1

| EMPLOYMENT STATUS DETERMINATIONS UNDER STATE UNEMPLOYMENT INSURANCE LAWS | | | |
|---|---|---|---|
| **State** | **Rule** | **State** | **Rule** |
| Alabama | Common Law | Montana | AC |
| Alaska | ABC | Nebraska | ABC |
| Arizona | Common Law | Nevada | ABC |
| Arkansas | ABC | New Hampshire | ABC |
| California | Common Law | New Jersey | ABC |
| Colorado | AC | New Mexico | ABC |
| Connecticut | ABC | New York | Common Law |
| Delaware | ABC | North Carolina | Common Law |
| Dist. of Col. | Common Law | North Dakota | Common Law |
| Florida | Common Law | Ohio | ABC |
| Georgia | ABC | Oklahoma | AB or AC |
| Hawaii | ABC | Oregon | ABC |
| Idaho | AC | Pennsylvania | AC |
| Illinois | ABC | Puerto Rico | ABC |
| Indiana | ABC | Rhode Island | ABC |
| Iowa | Common Law | South Carolina | Common Law |
| Kansas | ABC | South Dakota | Common Law |
| Kentucky | Common Law | Tennessee | ABC |
| Louisiana | ABC | Texas | Common Law |
| Maine | ABC | Utah | Common Law |
| Maryland | ABC | Vermont | ABC |

| EMPLOYMENT STATUS DETERMINATIONS UNDER STATE UNEMPLOYMENT INSURANCE LAWS | | | |
|---|---|---|---|
| **State** | **Rule** | **State** | **Rule** |
| Massachusetts | ABC | Virginia | AB or AC |
| Michigan | Common Law | Washington | ABC |
| Minnesota | Common Law | West Virginia | ABC |
| Mississippi | Common Law | Wisconsin | AC |
| Missouri | Common Law | Wyoming | AC |

 **MAKE THAT CALL** Employers that are unsure as to whether a worker is an employee or independent contractor for state unemployment insurance purposes can call their state employment security agency for an answer (see Section 7.4 for a directory of state employment security agencies).

## 1.6-5 State Disability Insurance Laws

In those states that require employer withholding from employees' wages to fund state disability insurance benefit payments (California, Hawaii, New Jersey, New York, Rhode Island, plus Puerto Rico), employment status is determined under the same test the state uses for its unemployment insurance law. (See Section 7.3 for more on these laws).

## 1.7 Worker Misclassification: Enforcement and Penalties

Employers that misclassify employees as nonemployees or independent contractors face substantial financial penalties as the result of not withholding income tax, failing to withhold and pay employment taxes, and failing to file the correct reports and returns with the IRS, SSA, and state government agencies. The IRS has begin to increase its enforcement efforts concerning misclassification in recent years after realizing billions of dollars in revenue were being lost.

## 1.7-1 IRS Penalties

The Internal Revenue Code provides special tax assessments for unintentionally misclassifying an employee as an independent contractor:[27]

- For not withholding federal income tax, the tax assessed is 1.5% of wages paid. This assessment is doubled to 3% if the employer failed to file an information return (Form 1099-MISC, see Appendix page A-261) for the worker with the IRS.
- For not withholding the employee's share of social security and Medicare taxes, the tax assessed is 20% of the employee's share. This assessment is doubled to 40% if the employer failed to file an information return (Form 1099-MISC, see Appendix page A-261) for the worker with the IRS. The employer's share of social security and Medicare taxes must also be paid.

If the employer intentionally misclassifies the worker as an independent contractor even after determining an employer-employee relationship exists (e.g., a Form SS-8 indicating employee status), these special assessments do not apply and the employer is liable for the full amount of federal income tax that should have been withheld and 100% of the employee's and employer's share of social security and Medicare

---

27. IRC §3509(a); §3509(b); IRS Prop. Reg. §31.3509-1(a) - (c).

taxes.[28]  Remember that the employer is also subject to all other penalties that can be assessed for failing to file returns or pay taxes (see Sections 6 and 8).

 **STATE PENALTIES TOO!**  The failure to withhold and pay over state income taxes because of worker misclassification will result in back tax assessments and penalties at the state level.

# 1.7-2  IRS Enforcement Efforts

The IRS uses several different programs in trying to detect worker misclassifications.  The 1099 Matching Program targets those individuals who file only one Form 1099-MISC with their personal tax return.  A person receiving payments from only one company may well be an employee rather than an independent contractor.

The IRS also will try to spot employees who receive Forms W-2 and 1099-MISC from the same employer in one year.  This situation often occurs when a business brings back retired employees as independent contractors (e.g., consultants).  While a worker can lawfully be an employee and an independent contractor for the same business entity in the same year (e.g., a production employee who runs a lawn-care company on the weekends and has his employer as a client), an IRS tax examiner will closely examine the facts in such situations if they are uncovered during an employment tax audit.  The IRS also uses its regular audit routine to detect improper employment status designations, but too few employment tax returns are examined to make this a valuable enforcement tool.  Under its Employment Tax Examination (ETE) Program, the IRS assigns revenue examiners to concentrate on employers suspected of worker misclassification, often based on leads from other federal and state government agencies.

In 1995 the IRS came under increasing criticism, especially from small business owners, regarding its allegedly inconsistent and sometimes "overzealous" enforcement of worker classification requirements.  In response, the Service acted on several fronts.  The IRS issued a training manual in 1996 for its examiners to guide them in making worker classification determinations, in which it emphasized that hiring workers as independent contractors is a legitimate choice for businesses.

At about the same time, the Service announced the release of its Worker Classification Settlement Program, which allows examiners and businesses to resolve worker classification cases as early in the enforcement process as possible.  Under the CSP, the examiner must first determine whether the business is entitled to Section 530 relief.  If so, there is no assessment and the business can continue to treat the workers in question as independent contractors.  If the business wishes to begin treating the workers as employees, it can agree to do so in the future (no later than the beginning of the next year) without giving up its claim to Section 530 relief for earlier periods.

If the examiner finds that the business is wrongfully treating employees as independent contractors, one of two graduated CSP settlement offers can be made.  If the business has met the reporting consistency requirement of Section 530 but clearly has no reasonable basis for its treatment of the workers as independent contractors or has been inconsistent in its treatment of the workers, the offer will be a full employment tax assessment under §3509.  If the business has met the reporting consistency requirement and can reasonably argue that it met the reasonable basis and consistency of treatment tests, the offer will be an assessment of 25% of the employment tax liability for the audit year under §3509.  Under each offer, the business must agree to treat the workers as employees in the future.

When an employer does not agree with the CSP terms, it may request an early referral of its case to IRS's Office of Appeals.  If an agreement still cannot be reached, the case will be returned to the District Office, where the worker classification and §530 issues will be handled separately from other issues in the case.[29]  (See Section 1.2-2 for information on Tax Court proceedings involving employment tax and worker classification issues.)

**IRS shares information with state agencies.**  In November 2007, 29 state workforce (unemployment) agencies signed a memorandum of understanding (MOU) with the Internal Revenue Service to share the

---

28.    IRC §3509(c); IRS Reg. §31.3509-1(d)(4).
29.    Rev. Proc. 99-28, 1999-29 IRB 109.

results of employment tax examinations in an effort to increase employer compliance with federal and state employment tax requirements. The agreements are the first result of the Questionable Employment Tax Practice (QETP) initiative.[30]

The QETP initiative is a collaborative, nationwide program seeking to identify employment tax schemes and illegal practices and increase voluntary compliance with employment tax rules and regulations. The IRS, U.S. Department of Labor, National Association of State Workforce Agencies, Federation of Tax Administrators, and state workforce agencies of California, Michigan, New Jersey, New York, and North Carolina worked together to develop the QETP initiative and endorse the MOU as a tool to help increase employment tax compliance at the federal and state levels.

*Participating states.* The following 29 states have signed agreements with the IRS: Arizona, Arkansas, California, Colorado, Connecticut, Hawaii, Idaho, Kentucky, Louisiana, Maine, Massachusetts, Michigan, Minnesota, Nebraska, New Hampshire, New Jersey, New York, North Dakota, Ohio, Oklahoma, Rhode Island, South Carolina, South Dakota, Texas, Utah, Vermont, Virginia, Washington, and Wisconsin.

*What will happen?* Under the MOU, the following actions will take place:

- The IRS and participating state workforce agencies will exchange employment tax information for civil cases, which primarily involve attempts to evade or inappropriately reduce employment tax liabilities.

- The IRS and the states may exchange information using either actual employment tax reports or a template compatible with federal and state information that the QETP oversight team has developed.

- The IRS and the states may participate in coordinated enforcement efforts. The MOU will allow the IRS and the state workforce agencies to share independently conducted examination results or work side-by-side on an examination.

- The IRS and the states will strive to be consistent with their examination results, reducing the chances that states might classify a worker as an employee while the IRS classifies the worker as an independent contractor, or vice versa.

- The IRS and the states will share employment tax training opportunities and materials.

- The IRS and the states will share outreach opportunities with the business community whenever practical.

**Reclassification can mean retroactive benefits as well**. Payment of back employment taxes is not the only thing that employers who misclassify employees as independent contractors have to worry about. In 1996, a federal appeals court held that Microsoft Corporation, which had agreed to reclassify "freelancers" as employees after an IRS employment tax audit, also had to include the misclassified workers in its §401(k) plan and §423 employee stock purchase plan.[31] Upon rehearing the case (in part because of a brief submitted by the APA), the court reaffirmed its earlier decision regarding the employee stock purchase plan, but it said the §401(k) plan administrator had to make the initial determination as to whether the reclassified employees were entitled to participate in that plan.[32]

In 1999, the court ruled that the class of employees eligible to participate in the employee stock purchase plan could not be limited to workers hired before the initial reclassification, but had to include workers hired later as temporary employees who were converted into the reclassified positions.[33]

---

30. IR-2007-184, 11-6-07.
31. Vizcaino v. Microsoft Corporation, 97 F.3d 1187 (3 CA 1996).
32. Vizcaino v. Microsoft Corporation, 120 F.3d 1006 (9 CA, 1997); cert. denied, 118 S.Ct. 899 (1999).
33. Vizcaino v. Microsoft Corporation, 173 F.3d 713 (9 CA, 1999); reh. den. 184 F.3d 1070 (9 CA, 1999).

But all may not be lost for employers that fear the costly consequences of a reclassification, and, as usual, thoughtful planning beforehand is the key. In a legal memorandum issued to one of its field offices after the *Vizcaino* decision, the IRS said that employers can write their retirement plan eligibility rules:

- to cover only employees who are common law employees in the employer's payroll records; and

- to exclude other individuals even if a court or administrative agency later determines that such individuals are common law employees and not independent contractors.[34]

A federal district court in New York deferred to the determination of an administrative committee for an employer's benefit plans that sales representatives were not eligible for benefits, despite rejecting the employer's claim that the individuals were independent contractors rather than employees. The committee had denied the sales representatives' claims for benefits because they were paid through accounts payable and the plan limited eligibility to employees paid on the "regular payroll" and required employee contributions through payroll deductions. The court said the committee's determination was reasonable because it was consistent with the plans' contribution language.[35]

## 1.7-3 FLSA Complaints Filed With the Department of Labor

Workers who feel they are being improperly treated as independent contractors and are not being paid the minimum wages or overtime pay they are entitled to may file a complaint with the U.S. Department of Labor's Wage and Hour Division. More than 75% of the audits conducted by Division investigators are the result of individual complaints. And each complaint can result in a full-blown audit of the employer's classification practices.

Huge backpay and damage awards can result because the misclassified worker's recollection will support a claim of overtime hours worked if the employer has no documented record of hours worked. The DOL may also file suit for the equivalent of two years' wages owed (three if the misclassification was willful) and damages on behalf of other workers who were misclassified. FLSA violations carry substantial civil fines as well (see Section 2.9).

## 1.7-4 State Unemployment Agencies

Many employers' misclassification problems begin when someone who has been treated as an independent contractor stops receiving work and files a claim for unemployment benefits. When the person is denied benefits because there were no eligible earnings, the claimant's charge that he or she was actually an employee will often lead to a full-scale investigation of the employer's employment status determinations.

A finding of misclassification can lead to the assessment of penalties for both failure to report wages and to pay unemployment insurance contributions. It can also mean a reduction in the credit the employer receives against federal unemployment taxes owed for state taxes paid in full and on time.

## 1.8 Proof of the Right to Work in the U.S.

Once an employer hires a worker as an employee, the employee must prove his or her identity and right to work in the United States. The Immigration Reform and Control Act of 1986 (IRCA) makes it illegal for an employer to knowingly hire or continue to employ an unauthorized worker.[36] Employers must comply with this requirement by verifying the identity and right to work of all employees hired after November 6, 1986.

---

34. TAM, 7-28-99; Tax Analysts Doc. 2000-14434.
35. Administrative Committee of the Time Warner, Inc. Benefits Plans v. Biscardi, No. 99 CIV 12270, 2000 U.S. Dist. LEXIS 16707 (SD N.Y., 11-17-00).
36. P.L. 99-603, as amended by P.L. 100-525; P.L. 101-649; P.L. 104-208; 8 U.S.C. §1324a; IRCA Regs. 8 CFR Part 274a; 28 CFR Part 44.

## Section 1: The Employer-Employee Relationship

**Employers can protect themselves.** Employers will not be penalized under IRCA if they have acted in good faith, even though they may have employed an unauthorized worker after accepting a fraudulent document offered as proof of the right to work. Employers can protect themselves by:

- having employees fill out Section 1 of Form I-9, *Employment Eligibility Verification* (see Appendix page A-34), on their first day of work;

- making sure employees provide original documentary evidence of their identity and eligibility to work within 3 business days of the date of hire;

- making sure the documents establishing the employee's identity and eligibility to work appear genuine within 3 business days of the date of hire;

- properly completing the employer's portion of Form I-9 (Section 2) within 3 business days of the date of hire;

- keeping completed I-9 forms for at least 3 years from the date of hire or 1 year from the date of termination, whichever is longer; and

- presenting Form I-9 on request to an inspector from U.S. Citizenship and Immigration Services or the Department of Labor.

**INS becomes USCIS.** On March 1, 2003, the employment eligibility-related functions of the Immigration and Naturalization Service (INS) transitioned to the Bureau of Citizenship and Immigration Services (BCIS), an agency that is part of the Department of Homeland Security. On August 23, 2004, BCIS became United States Citizenship and Immigration Services. Employers deal with USCIS on employment eligibility issues in the same way they dealt with INS. The Internet website for USCIS is www.uscis.gov.[37]

**Documents prove identity and/or work authorization.** All newly hired employees must show evidence of their identity and right to work in the U.S. They can do this by presenting any of a number of documents listed on Form I-9 (one from List A or one each from List B and List C):[38]

*List A—Documents proving both identity and work authorization*

1. U.S. passport (expired or unexpired);

2. Permanent Resident Card or Alien Registration Receipt Card (green card)—USCIS Form I-551, that contains a photograph, fingerprint, and signature of the bearer (the name was changed from Alien Registration Receipt Card to Permanent Resident Card by regulation in 1998);

   **WATCH OUT** Old green cards (Form I-151) are no longer valid proof of immigrant status, identity, and employment eligibility. Lawful permanent resident aliens should have Form I-551, which has the bearer's photograph, signature, and fingerprint.

3. Unexpired foreign passport with a temporary I-551 stamp reading "processed for I-551. Temporary Evidence of Lawful Admission for permanent residence. Valid until ____ Employment Authorized";

4. Unexpired Employment Authorization Document that contains a photograph, USCIS Form I-766, I-688, I-688A, I-688B;

5. An unexpired foreign passport with an unexpired Arrival-Departure Record, Form I-94, bearing the same name as the passport and containing an endorsement of the alien's nonimmigrant status, if that status authorizes the alien to work for the employer.

---

37.    69 FR 60938, 10-13-04.
38.    IRCA Reg. 8 CFR §274a.2; Form I-9.

**EAD UPGRADED** In 2004, USCIS issued a new version of the Employment Authorization Document (EAD), Form I-766. The new EAD has more security features to prevent counterfeiting and fraud, including a magnetic strip, a two-dimensional barcode, and several features that can be used in forensic examination to determine its authenticity.

*List B—Documents Proving Identity Only*

1. Driver's license or ID card issued by a state or U.S. possession with a photograph or identifying information including name, date of birth, sex, height, color of eyes, and address;

2. ID card issued by federal, state, or local government agency or entity with a photograph or identifying information in No. 1.

3. School ID card with a photograph;

4. Voter's registration card;

5. U.S. Military card or draft record;

6. Military dependent's ID card;

7. U.S. Coast Guard Merchant Mariner Card;

8. Native American tribal document;

9. Canadian driver's license;

10. For persons under age 18:

    a. school record or report card;

    b. clinic, doctor, or hospital record;

    c. day care or nursery school record.

*List C—Documents Proving Work Authorization Only*

1. U.S. social security card issued by SSA, if it does not say the card is not valid for employment;

2. Certification of Birth Abroad issued by the Department of State, Form FS-545 or Form DS-1350;

3. Original or certified copy of a birth certificate with an official seal issued by a state or local government agency or a U.S. possession;

4. Native American tribal document;

5. U.S. Citizen ID Card, Form I-197;

6. ID Card for Use of Resident Citizen in the U.S., Form I-179;

7. Unexpired employment authorization document issued by DHS (other than those in List A).

 **BE CAREFUL** Specific documents cannot be demanded by the employer (e.g., social security card, driver's license, passport). An employee can provide any document(s) on the lists to prove identity and work authorization.

# Section 1: The Employer-Employee Relationship

**Documentation changes still pending**. The Illegal Immigration Reform and Immigrant Responsibility Act of 1996 reduced the number of documents that USCIS must accept as proof of eligibility to work in the U.S., and set September 30, 1997 as the deadline for regulations implementing those changes to be issued. On that day, an interim rule removed documents 2, 3, 8 and 9 from List A and narrowed the instances when document 4 would be acceptable.[39]

Within a week, Public Law 105-54 was enacted extending the deadline for issuing regulations to March 30, 1998. On February 2, 1998, proposed regulations were issued that would implement a significant reduction in the types of documents that employees could offer to prove their identity and work authorization, as well as make other changes.[40] Those proposed rules have not yet been finalized.

**Revised Form I-9 issued in 2007.** In November 2007, USCIS released an updated version of Form I-9, as well as a revised *Handbook for Employers* (Publication M-274) containing instructions for completing Form I-9. USCIS revised Form I-9 to bring it into compliance with the 1997 interim rule.

**Previous forms no longer valid.** Employers must use the new Form I-9, which has a date of June 5, 2007, beginning on December 27, 2007.[41]

**Completing the Form I-9.** Ensure that the employee fully completes Section 1 of Form I-9 at the time of hire – when the employee begins work. Review the employee's document(s) and fully complete Section 2 of the Form I-9 within 3 business days of hire. If a person is hired for less than 3 business days, Sections 1 and 2 of the Form I-9 must be fully completed at the time of hire – when the employee begins work.

Form I-9 DOES NOT need to be completed for persons who are:

- hired before November 7, 1986, who are continuing in their employment and have a reasonable expectation of employment at all times;
- employed for casual domestic work in a private home on a sporadic, irregular, or intermittent basis;
- independent contractors; or
- providing labor to you who are employed by a contractor providing contract services (e.g., employee leasing or temporary agencies).

*Section 1.* Have the employee complete Section 1 at the time of hire (when he or she begins to work) by filling in the correct information and signing and dating the form. Ensure that the employee prints the information clearly. If the employee cannot complete Section 1 without assistance or if he or she needs the Form I-9 translated, someone may assist him or her. The preparer or translator must read the form to the employee, assist him or her in completing Section 1, and have the employee sign or mark the form in the appropriate place. The preparer or translator must then complete the Preparer/Translator Certification block on the form.

  **BE CAREFUL** Providing a social security number on Form I-9 is voluntary for all employees unless the employer is participating in USCIS's E-Verify Program (see page 1-30), which requires an employee's social security number for employment eligibility verification. Employers may not, however, ask an employee to provide specific documents with the employee's social security number on it.

*Section 2.* The employee must present an original document or documents that establish identity and employment eligibility within 3 business days of the date employment begins. Some documents establish both identity and employment eligibility (List A). Other documents establish identity only (List B) or employment authorization only (List C). The employee can choose which document(s) he or she wants to present from the Lists of Acceptable Documents.

---

39. 62 F.R. 51001, 9-30-97.
40. 63 F.R. 5287, 2-2-98
41. 72 FR 65974, 11-26-07.

Examine the original document or documents the employee presents and then fully complete Section 2 of Form I-9. Employers must examine one document from List A, or one from List B and one from List C. Record the title, issuing authority, number, and expiration date (if any) of the document(s); fill in the date of hire and correct information in the certification block; and sign and date the Form I-9. Employers must accept any document from the Lists of Acceptable Documents presented by the individual which reasonably appear on their face to be genuine and to relate to the person presenting them. Employers may not specify which document an employee must present.

**WATCH OUT** An employer participating in the E-Verify Program may only accept List B documents that have a photograph.

In certain circumstances, employers must accept a receipt in lieu of a listed document if one is presented by an employee.[42] A receipt indicating that an individual has applied for initial work authorization or for an extension of expiring work authorization is not acceptable proof of employment eligibility on Form I-9. Receipts are never acceptable if employment lasts less than 3 business days.

Receipts and other documents that serve as proof of temporary employment eligibility that employers can accept are:

1. Receipts for the application of a replacement document where the document was lost, stolen, or destroyed. The employee must present the replacement document within 90 days from the date of hire.

2. The arrival portion of a Form I-94 with an attached photo and a temporary I-551 stamp, which is a receipt for a List A document. When the stamp expires, or if the stamp has no expiration, one year from date of issue, the employee must present the Form I-551 Permanent Resident Card.

3. The departure portion of the Form I-94 with a refugee admission stamp, which is a receipt for a List A document. The employee must present, within 90 days from date of hire, Form I-766, or a List B document and an unrestricted social security card.

When the employee provides an acceptable receipt, the employer should record the document title in Section 2 of the Form I-9 and write the word "receipt" and any document number in the "Document #" space. When the employee presents the actual document, the employer should cross out the word "receipt" and any accompanying document number, insert the number from the actual document presented, and initial and date the change.

**Minors (individuals under age 18).** If a person under the age of 18 cannot present a List A document or an identity document from List B, Form I-9 should be completed in the following way:

- a parent or legal guardian must complete Section 1 and write "Individual under age 18" in the space for the employee's signature;
- the parent or legal guardian must complete the "Preparer/Translator Certification" block;
- the employer should write "Individual under age 18" in Section 2, List B, in the space after the words "Document #"; and
- the minor must present a List C document showing his or her employment eligibility. The employer should record the required information in the appropriate space in Section 2.

**Employees with disabilities (special placement).** If a person with a disability, who is placed in a job by a nonprofit organization or as part of a rehabilitation program, cannot present a List A document or an identity document from List B, Form I-9 should be completed in the following way:

- A representative of the nonprofit organization, a parent or a legal guardian must complete Section 1 and write "Special Placement" in the space for the employee's signature;

---

42.    IRCA Reg. 8 CFR §274a.2b(1)(vi)(B), (C).

# Section 1: The Employer-Employee Relationship

- The representative, parent or legal guardian must complete the "Preparer/Translator Certification" block;
- The employer should write "Special Placement" in Section 2, List B, in the space after the words "Document #"; and
- The employee with a disability must present a List C document showing his or her employment eligibility. The employer should record the required information in the appropriate space in Section 2.

**Future expiration dates.** Future expiration dates may appear on the employment authorization documents of aliens, including, among others, permanent residents and refugees. USCIS includes expiration dates even on documents issued to aliens with permanent work authorization. The existence of a future expiration date:

- does not preclude continuous employment authorization;
- does not mean that subsequent employment authorization will not be granted; and
- should not be considered in determining whether the alien is qualified for a particular position.

**Reverifying employment authorization for current employees.** When an employee's work authorization expires, the employer must reverify his or her employment eligibility. Use Section 3 of Form I-9, or, if Section 3 has already been used for a previous reverification or update, use a new Form I-9. When using a new form, write the employee's name in Section 1, complete Section 3, and retain the new form with the original. The employee must present a document that shows either an extension of the employee's initial employment authorization or new work authorization. If the employee cannot provide the employer with proof of current work authorization (e.g. any document from List A or List C, including an unrestricted social security card), that individual cannot continue to be employed.

**Note:** List B identity documents, such as a driver's license, should not be reverified when they expire.

To maintain continuous employment eligibility, an employee with temporary work authorization should apply for new work authorization at least 90 days before the current expiration date. If USCIS fails to adjudicate the application for employment authorization within 90 days, then the employee will be authorized for employment on Form I-766 for a period not to exceed 240 days.

**Reverifying or updating employment authorization for rehired employees.** When rehiring an employee, the employer must ensure that he or she is still authorized to work. Employers may do this by completing a new Form I-9 or by reverifying or updating the original form by completing Section 3. When rehiring an employee who has previously completed a Form I-9, the employer may *reverify* on the employee's original Form I-9 (or on a new Form I-9 if Section 3 of the original has already been used) if:

- rehiring the employee within three years of the initial date of hire; and
- the employee's previous grant of work authorization has expired, but he or she is currently eligible to work on a different basis or under a new grant of work authorization than when the original Form I-9 was completed.

To reverify, the employer must:

- record the date of rehire;
- record the document title, number and expiration date (if any) of any document presented;
- sign and date Section 3; and
- when reverifying on a new Form I-9, write the employee's name in Section 1.

When rehiring an employee who has previously completed a Form I-9, the employer may *update* on the employee's original Form I-9 or on a new Form I-9 if:

- the employer rehired the employee within three years of the initial date of hire; and
- the employee is still eligible to work on the same basis as when the original Form I-9 was completed.

To update, the employer must:

- record the date of rehire;
- sign and date Section 3; and
- when updating on a new Form I-9, write the employee's name in Section 1.

Employers always have the option of completing Sections 1 and 2 of a new Form I-9 instead of completing Section 3 when rehiring employees.

**Spanish version.** Form I-9 is available in English and Spanish. However, only employers in Puerto Rico may have employees complete the Spanish version for their records. Employers in Puerto Rico may use either the Spanish or the English version of Form I-9 to verify employees. Employers in the 50 states, the District of Columbia, and other territories may use the Spanish version as a translation guide for Spanish-speaking employees, but must complete the English version and keep it in their records.

**Penalties.**[43] Employers that knowingly hire unauthorized aliens face civil penalties of $250 - $2,000 for each worker hired for a first offense, $2,000 - $5,000 for a second offense, and $3,000 - $10,000 for more than two offenses. Employers that fail to comply with the verification requirements can be fined $100 - $1,000 for each person for whom proper verification was not required. Employers that engage in a pattern and practice of violating the hiring and/or verification requirements face criminal penalties of up to $3,000 and/or six months in jail. Where the verification violation is minor and future compliance is expected, a warning notice explaining the nature of the violation may be issued in lieu of a fine.

Under the Illegal Immigration Reform and Immigrant Responsibility Act of 1996, certain minor, unintentional, technical, and procedural violations made during the verification process are not considered compliance failures if the employer makes a good faith attempt to correct them during the 10-day period normally allotted for making corrections after being notified by USCIS. In 1998, proposed rules implementing the good faith exception were issued.[44] The employer must make any corrections to sections 2 or 3 and ensure that the employee, preparer, or translator make any corrections to section 1. All such corrections must be initialed and dated. The rules also outline situations that would not be considered good faith, such as technical or procedural mistakes committed to avoid verification, making knowingly false corrections, preparing a Form I-9 knowing the form contains false information, and corrections made after receiving previous notices of violations.

In 2007, U.S. Immigration and Customs Enforcement (ICE) began using a new strategy for combating unlawful employment of illegal aliens. Because it found that administrative fines did not deter unscrupulous employers that viewed them simply as a cost of doing business, ICE now often pursues more serious criminal charges. For example, a felony conviction for harboring illegal aliens can result in a 10-year prison sentence. ICE has found these criminal sanctions to be a far greater deterrent to illegal employment schemes than administrative sanctions.

**What constitutes 'knowingly' hiring unauthorized aliens?** Under IRCA (8 U.S.C. §1324a(a)(2)), it is unlawful for an employer, after hiring an alien, to continue to employ the alien in the U.S. "knowing" the alien is (or has become) unauthorized with respect to such employment. An employer can violate this section by having either actual or constructive knowledge (i.e., the employer knew or should have known) that an employee is unauthorized to work. In 2007, ICE issued final regulations describing safe harbor procedures for employers that receive a "no-match" letter from the Social Security Administration (SSA) or DHS. Employers that follow these procedures will not be considered to have "constructive knowledge" that an employee is unauthorized to work in the U.S. just because they received a no-match letter.[45]

---

43. IRCA Reg. 8 CFR §274a.9; §274a.10.
44. 63 F.R. 16909, 4-7-98.
45. 72 F.R. 45611, 8-15-07.

**FEDERAL COURT PUTS REGS ON HOLD** A federal district court in California issued an order stopping ICE's regulations from taking effect as scheduled in September 2007 and barring SSA from mailing out no-match letters to employers for 2006 W-2s because the letters refer to the new regulations and employers' duties under the safe harbor procedures.[46] DHS then asked the court to delay a final decision until it could answer some of the court's concerns and reissue the regulations in March 2008.

Employers annually send the SSA millions of Forms W-2 (*Wage and Tax Statement*) in which the combination of employee name and social security number (SSN) does not match SSA records. In some of these cases, SSA sends a "no-match" letter that informs the employer of this fact (see Section 8.13-1). ICE sends a similar letter after it has inspected an employer's Forms I-9 during an audit and has unsuccessfully attempted to confirm, in agency records, that an immigration status or employment authorization document presented or referenced by the employee in completing the Form I-9 was assigned to that person.

*Constructive knowledge: examples added.*[47] The final regulations amend the definition of "constructive knowledge" by adding examples of information available to an employer indicating that an employee could be an alien not authorized to work in the U.S.:

- Written notice from SSA that the combination of name and SSN submitted for an employee does not match SSA records; and
- Written notice from ICE that the immigration status or employment authorization document presented or referenced by the employee in completing Form I-9 was assigned to another person, or that there is no agency record that the document was assigned to anyone.

*Employer's obligations explicitly stated.* The final regulations explicitly state that if the employer fails to take reasonable steps after receiving such information, and if the employee is in fact an unauthorized alien, then the employer may be found to have constructive knowledge of that fact, although that would depend on the "totality of the circumstances" in the particular case.

*Safe harbor.* The final regulations describe the steps an employer should take after receiving a no-match letter to avoid the risk that ICE might find that the employer had constructive knowledge that the employee was not authorized to work in the U.S.:[48]

Step 1. A reasonable employer must check its records promptly (i.e., within 30 days) after receiving a no-match letter, to determine whether the discrepancy results from a typographical, transcribing, or similar clerical error in the employer's records or in its communication to the SSA or ICE. If there is such an error, the employer must correct its records, inform the relevant agencies (in accordance with the letter's instructions, if any; otherwise in any reasonable way), and verify that the name and number, as corrected, match agency records – in other words, verify with the relevant agency that the discrepancy has been resolved – and make a record of the manner, date, and time of verification.

Step 2. If such actions do not resolve the discrepancy, the reasonable employer must promptly ask the employee to confirm that the employer's records are correct. If they are not correct, the employer must take the actions needed to correct them, inform the relevant agencies, and verify the corrected records with the relevant agency. If the records are correct according to the employee, the reasonable employer must ask the employee to pursue the matter personally with the relevant agency.

A discrepancy will be considered resolved only if the employer verifies with SSA or DHS, as the case may be, that the employee's name matches an SSN assigned to that name in SSA's records, and the number is valid for work or is valid for work with DHS authorization (and verifies such authorization with DHS) or that DHS records indicate that the immigration status or employment authorization document was assigned to the employee. Employers should make a record of the manner, date, and time of any such verification, as SSA may not provide any written documentation.

---

46.    American Federation of Labor v. Chertoff, No. C 07-04472 CRB (ND Cal., 10-10-07).
47.    8 CFR §274a.1(l)(1)(iii)(B), (C).
48.    8 CFR §274a.1(l)(2)(i) – (iii).

<u>Step 3.</u> If the discrepancy is not resolved within 90 days of receipt of the no-match letter, the safe harbor procedure requires the employer and employee to complete a new Form I-9 as if the employee were newly hired, with certain restrictions:

- If an employer tried to resolve the discrepancy described in the no-match letter for the full 90 days, the employer and employee have an additional three days to complete a new Form I-9.
- No document containing the SSN or alien number that is the subject of the no-match letter, and no receipt for an application for a replacement of such a document, can be used to establish employment authorization and/or identity.
- No document without a photograph can be used to establish identity (or both identity and employment authorization).

**KEEP BOTH FORMS** If a new Form I-9 is completed, it must be retained by the employer with the employee's prior Form(s) I-9 under the general Form I-9 recordkeeping requirements.[49]

*Employer choices.* If the discrepancy referred to in the no-match letter is not resolved, and if the employee's identity and work authorization cannot be verified, then the employer must choose between terminating the employee or facing the risk that ICE may find that the employer had constructive knowledge that the employee was an unauthorized alien. An employer that follows procedures other than the safe harbor procedures described in the final regulations runs the risk that ICE may not agree and may find that the employer has constructive knowledge of the employee's status as an unauthorized alien.

*Actual knowledge.* The final regulations do not preclude ICE from finding that an employer had actual knowledge that an employee was an unauthorized alien. An employer with actual knowledge cannot avoid liability by following the procedures described in the final regulations.

*Information received outside of no-match letters.* The safe harbor procedures do not extend to information received by employers from sources other than no-match letters. For example, the regulations do not apply to SSA or DHS new hire verifications done through the Social Security Number Verification Service (SSNVS – see Section 6.2-1) or the E-Verify program operated by USCIS (see page 1-30).

**Leasing companies and temporary help agencies.** Employers using leased employees and temporary help agency referrals should make sure the agency assumes the responsibility of the employer under IRCA in the language of the lease agreement or temporary agency contract. Otherwise, the employer may be responsible for complying with IRCA regarding those employees.

**Electronic Forms I-9.** Rules were issued in 1996 allowing employers to generate paper Forms I-9 electronically if the form is legible, there are no changes to the name, content, or sequence of the data elements, no additional data elements or language are inserted, and the paper meets the standards for retention and production for inspection.[50] Employers can also download a fillable electronic Form I-9 from www.uscis.gov. In 2004, the Immigration and Nationality Act was amended to allow employers to accept electronic signatures on Form I-9 and to store the form in an electronic format. This allows employers to implement a system for completing Form I-9 electronically and to save on the space they previously needed to store paper Forms I-9. The amendment was to take effect on April 28, 2005, or earlier if USCIS issued implementing regulations that took effect before that date.[51] On April 29, 2005, implementing regulations were still being developed, so ICE issued interim guidelines for employers that wanted to make use of the electronic completion and/or storage options.

In June 2006, ICE issued an interim rule establishing standards for electronic signatures and the electronic retention of Form I-9.[52]

---

49.     8 CFR §274a.1(l)(2)(iii)(B).
50.     IRCA Reg. 8 CFR §274a.2.(a)(2).
51.     Pub. Law No. 108-390.
52.     71 F.R. 34510, 6-15-06.

*Electronic recordkeeping standards.* To reduce the burden on employers, ICE has adopted standards that closely follow the widely accepted electronic storage standards and requirements used by the IRS for tax records (see Section 10.2). The standards are technology-neutral and allow businesses the flexibility to keep employment authorization records in the same manner they use for other business records. If an electronic I-9 records system is IRS-compliant, it will also be ICE-compliant.

*Electronic signatures.* If an employer uses an electronic Form I-9, the attestations in the form must be completed using a system for capturing an electronic signature that meets the following standards:[53]
- includes a method to acknowledge that the attestation has been read by the person providing the signature;
- attaches the signature to, or logically associates it with, an electronically completed Form I-9;
- affixes the signature at the time of the transaction;
- creates and preserves a record verifying the identity of the person producing the signature; and
- provides a printed confirmation of the transaction, at the time of the transaction, to the person providing the signature.

Electronic signatures can be accomplished using various technologies including, but not limited to, electronic signature pads, personal identification numbers (PINs), biometrics, and "click to accept" dialog boxes.

*Electronic creation and retention.* An employer's electronic Form I-9 generation or storage system must include:[54]
- reasonable controls to ensure the integrity, accuracy, and reliability of the electronic generation or storage system;
- reasonable controls to prevent and detect the unauthorized or accidental creation, alteration, deletion, or deterioration of an electronically completed or stored Form I-9;
- an inspection and quality assurance program that produces regular evaluations of the electronic system;
- a retrieval system with an indexing system that permits searches by any data element; and
- the ability to reproduce legible and readable hardcopies.

All documents reproduced by an electronic retention system must show a high degree of legibility and readability when displayed on a video display terminal or when printed on paper, microfilm, or microfiche. This means the reader must be able to identify all letters and numbers individually and as words or complete numbers.[55]

An electronic creation or storage system must not be subject to an agreement restricting the federal government's access to and use of the system. The system must also remain available as long as it contains records subject to USCIS inspection.[56]

*Records inspections.* At the time of an inspection, the employer must:[57]
- retrieve and reproduce (including printed copies on request) only the Forms I-9 retained electronically, along with specifically requested supporting documentation, plus the associated audit trails showing who accessed the system and what actions they performed on the system during the specified time period;
- provide the inspector with the resources (e.g., hardware and software, personnel, and documentation) needed to locate, retrieve, read, and reproduce the requested records; and
- provide on request any reasonably available or obtainable electronic summary file, such as a spreadsheet, containing the information fields on the electronically stored Forms I-9.

*Documentation.* Upon request by an inspector, employers must make available documentation of the business processes that:[58]

---

53. IRCA Reg. 8 CFR §274a.2(h).
54. IRCA Reg. 8 CFR §274a.2(e)(1).
55. IRCA Reg. 8 CFR §274a.2(e)(2).
56. IRCA Reg. 8 CFR §274a.2(e)(3), (4).
57. IRCA Reg. 8 CFR §274a.2(e)(8).
58. IRCA Reg. 8 CFR §274a.2(f).

- create, modify, and maintain the stored Forms I-9;
- establish the authenticity of the stored Forms I-9, such as audit trails.

*Security.* Employers that create and store Forms I-9 and supporting documentation electronically must implement an effective records security program that:[59]
- ensures that only authorized personnel have access to the electronically stored records;
- provides for backup and recovery of records;
- ensures that employees are trained to minimize the risk of unauthorized or accidental changes or deletions of electronically stored records;
- ensures that whenever the electronic record is touched, a secure and permanent record is created that establishes the date of access, the identity of the person who accessed the records, and the action taken by that person.

*Paper vs. electronic I-9 process.* An employer in compliance with current recordkeeping and retention requirements is not required to take any additional or different action to comply with the interim rule, which merely offers an additional option. The interim rule does not require any employer to use an electronic recordkeeping system. Nor does it make any change in the current paper Form I-9 process.

An employer can use a combination of paper and electronic methods to fulfill its obligations. For example, an employer can complete a paper Form I-9 and then scan it to retain the form electronically. Employers that copy documents provided by employees to prove their identity and work authorization must retain those copies with the Forms I-9; under the interim rule, the copies can be retained as electronic images rather than on paper.

*Effective date.* The interim rule was effective on June 15, 2006, the date it was published. Because the effective date of the underlying statute authorizing electronic retention of Form I-9 was April 28, 2005, forms created between that date and June 15, 2006, do not have to comply with the interim rule.

**Employment verification pilot programs**. The Illegal Immigration Reform and Immigrant Responsibility Act of 1996 contained three verification pilot programs.

Each pilot used an automated confirmation system through which employers match information provided by new employees on Form I-9 against existing information contained in the Social Security Administration's or USCIS's database to confirm the employee's employment eligibility. The pilots were conducted in select states and originally, each was scheduled to last up to four years. The three pilots were the Basic Pilot, the Citizen Attestation Pilot, and the Machine Readable Document Pilot. In mid-2003, the Citizen Attestation Pilot and the Machine Readable Document Pilot expired and were not renewed. In December 2003, the Basic Pilot Program Extension and Expansion Act extended the Basic Pilot for 5 more years (through November 2008) and broadened its reach to all the states by December 1, 2004.[60] In 2007, the Basic Pilot Program became the E-Verify Program.

**General rules**. Employers may request that E-Verify apply to all their hiring in each state where the program will take place, or that it be limited to hiring in one or more states, or to one or more places of hiring within a state.

**E-Verify Program.** The E-Verify Program involves verification checks of the SSA and DHS databases, using an automated system to verify the employment authorization of all newly hired employees. Participation in E-Verify is voluntary, and it is free to participating employers other than some federal entities and previous serious violators of the IRCA requirements. The program falls under the jurisdiction of USCIS's Systematic Alien Verification for Entitlements (SAVE) Program.

E-Verify is available on the Internet using a Web-based access method. This allows employers to use the system from any personal computer with access to the Internet. Once an employer has registered and com-

---

59.    IRCA Reg. 8 CFR §274a.2(g).
60.    Basic Pilot Program Extension and Expansion Act of 2003, P.L. 108-156; 69 F.R. 75997, 12-20-04.

pleted the Web-based tutorial, it can immediately begin using the Web-based access method of the program. To register, go to www.dhs.gov/E-Verify and follow the instructions. Following are some enhancements that E-Verify offers:

*Participants register on the Internet.* Persons interested in using E-Verify need to register on the Internet and sign a Memorandum of Understanding (MOU) with the SAVE Program and the SSA. This gives the user access to the automated Verification Information System (VIS), which checks the SSA and USCIS databases to verify employment authorization. Instructions are provided for completing, signing, and submitting the MOU to the SAVE Program. Individuals will receive confirmation of his or her company's participation in E-Verify via e-mail, and, at the same time, will be provided with a user ID and temporary password.

*Internet training.* E-Verify is extremely user-friendly and has mouse-over text helpers to provide hints while entering your queries, e.g., entering complex surnames. New users must complete the Web-based tutorial (WBT). Once the WBT is completed, the system is immediately available for performing verification queries.

*New user types.* Three user types have been created for E-Verify. You determine your user type after registering. Depending on the user type you select, you will be able to perform different functions, e.g., perform queries, manage your account, and view reports. You will only be able to access information relating to your company site. Following is a description of each user type:

- Program Administrator – The Program Administrator is to be located at each of your company's sites. This user is responsible for: creating and managing user accounts at its site for the Corporate Administrator and the General User; unlocking user accounts; updating site information; and viewing reports. Since the Program Administrator may be the only person at your site using the system, he or she also may have the capability to perform queries. The person registering your company is automatically defaulted as a Program Administrator.
- General User – A general user can perform verification queries, view user reports, and update his or her personal user profile information, e.g., name change, new phone or fax number, etc.
- Corporate Administrator – Corporate Administrators can manage multiple company accounts, view reports for multiple company sites, as well as create and administer company and user accounts. However, they cannot perform verification inquires unless they register to participate in E-Verify.

*View and print reports.* All users have the capability to view and print their own reports. These reports provide statistics on the queries performed by the user(s) within the company.

*Internet resources.* E-Verify's Resources section includes a variety of resources available to assist employers with the verification process and other immigration-related matters. Some of the resources available include:

- The Web-Based Tutorial
- The E-Verify User Manual
- A Guide to Selected Travel and Identity Documents
- E-Verify Notices to be posted in the employer's hiring area
- Spanish and English versions of the E-Verify Notice of Tentative Nonconfirmation and Basic Pilot Referral Notices

*Designated agent.* An employer may choose a Designated Agent to conduct E-Verify on its behalf. The Designated Agent and the employer must sign an MOU and an Agency Agreement allowing the agent to carry out the employer's responsibilities under the MOU.

To receive information on E-Verify, or on becoming a Designated Agent, please call the SAVE Program toll free at (888) 464-4218, or fax your request for information to (202) 272-8744 or 8745, or write to the Department of Homeland Security, SAVE Program, 20 Massachusetts Ave., NW, ULLICO Building 4th Floor, Washington, DC 20529.

*Photo screening tool available.* In September 2007, USCIS launched a photo-screening tool as an enhancement of E-Verify. The photo tool can be used when a new employee presents an Employment Authorization Document (EAD) or Permanent Resident Card ("green card") to prove work authorization and identity when completing a Form I-9. It allows the employer to compare identical photos – the individual's photo on the EAD or green card against the image stored in USCIS's databases. The tool is designed to help an employer determine whether the document presented reasonably relates to the individual presenting it and contains a valid photo.

Employers already participating in E-Verify will be trained on the system enhancement through a mandatory refresher tutorial that launched automatically on September 17, 2007. Employers registering after that date will learn how to use the photo tool through an updated E-Verify manual, tutorial, and memorandum of understanding.

*Program rules.* Employees to be verified must be new hires after the MOU has been signed and their I-9 forms must be completed before the employer initiates a query through the system. The program may not be used to pre-screen job applicants or to reverify the employment eligibility of employees whose employment eligibility document has expired. Form I-9 requirements remain the same, except that all "List B" identity documents must contain a photograph. Verification inquiries must be made by the employer within three days of hire and cannot be selective—all employees subject to verification at an employer site must be verified.

The inquiries go to SSA's database for confirmation. If SSA cannot confirm work authorization status, the inquiry immediately is sent to USCIS for confirmation. Generally, confirmation or nonconfirmation takes only a few seconds. If more information is needed, the employer is asked to tell the employee to contact SSA or USCIS to provide the needed information.

If a "tentative nonconfirmation" is received by the employer, it must notify the employee. If the employee does not contest the tentative nonconfirmation, it will be considered a final nonconfirmation. If the employee does contest, he or she must contact the appropriate agency office within 10 working days for verification of status. If an employer receives a final nonconfirmation from SSA or USCIS, the employer can terminate the employee and will not be subject to civil or criminal liability so long as the employer acts in good faith reliance on the information provided through the confirmation system.

**ICE partners with businesses to reduce employment of illegal aliens.** In August 2006, ICE announced a new best business practice initiative called the ICE Mutual Agreement between Government and Employers (IMAGE) program. The IMAGE program is designed to build cooperative relationships between the government and businesses in targeted sectors to strengthen hiring practices and reduce the unlawful employment of illegal aliens. It also seeks to accomplish greater industry compliance and corporate due diligence through enhanced federal training and education of employers.

*IMAGE program: employer benefits.* ICE will:
- provide training and education to IMAGE partners on proper hiring procedures, fraudulent document detection, and anti-discrimination laws.
- share data with employers on the latest illegal schemes used to circumvent legal hiring requirements.
- review hiring and employment practices of IMAGE partners and work collaboratively with them to correct isolated, minor compliance issues that are detected.

A participating company can:
- become "IMAGE-certified," a distinction that ICE believes will become an industry standard.
- reduce unauthorized employment and identity theft.
- better protect the integrity of its workforce by helping ensure that employees are who they represent themselves to be.

*IMAGE program: employer duties.* A company must agree to a Form I-9 audit by ICE and adhere to a series of best practices:

- use the Basic Pilot employment verification program for all new hires;
- establish an internal training program on completing employment verification forms, detecting fraudulent documents, and using the Basic Pilot program;
- permit the Form I-9 and Basic Pilot processes to be conducted only by individuals who have received this training;
- arrange for annual Form I-9 audits by neutral parties;
- establish a procedure for reporting to ICE any violations or discovered deficiencies;
- establish a protocol for responding to no-match letters from the Social Security Administration;
- establish a tip line for employees to report activity relating to the employment of unauthorized aliens, and a protocol for responding to such tips;
- establish safeguards against use of the verification process for unlawful discrimination;
- establish a protocol for assessing adherence to these best practice guidelines by contractors and subcontractors; and
- submit an annual report to ICE tracking results and assessing the effect of participation in the IMAGE program.

**Will E-Verify become mandatory?** In 2006 and 2007, the U.S. House and Senate each passed immigration reform bills that were very different in their approaches toward border security and employment of unauthorized aliens. However, both bills would have required employers to use an expanded version of the E-Verify program to verify all new hires and possibly current employees as well. Be sure to look for any developments in this area in *Payroll Currently*, APA's biweekly payroll compliance membership newsletter.

**States try to fill the immigration reform gap.** When Congress failed to act together to get an immigration reform bill enacted into law in 2006 and again in 2007, several states and localities tried to fill the gap by enacting their own legislation and executive orders.

These laws make use of various tactics to deter the hiring of unauthorized aliens, including:

- requiring public employers and government contractors to participate in the E-Verify program (Georgia, Minnesota, Oklahona);
- denying business licenses to employers that employ unauthorized workers (Arizona, Tennessee);
- denying a business expense deduction for wages paid to unauthorized employees (Georgia);
- requiring an affirmation by the employer that it has examined the work status of all new hires and has not altered their supporting documentation (Colorado);
- imposing its own monetary penalties for hiring unauthorized aliens (West Virginia);
- fining employers that provide false records concerning an employee's work authorization (West Virginia);
- sharing information among state agencies to confirm legal work status (West Virginia); and
- requiring employers to withhold state income tax from independent contractors who fail to provide documentation verifying their work eligibility (Oklahoma).

# 1.9 New Hire Reporting

Since 1997, payroll practitioners have been required to report information regarding newly hired and rehired employees to state agencies. This information may be used to facilitate the collection of child support and/or to uncover fraud and abuse in unemployment compensation, workers' compensation, and public assistance (welfare) benefit programs.

**Federal new hire reporting requirement.** Under the Personal Responsibility and Work Opportunity Reconciliation Act of 1996, employers were required to comply with a federal new hire reporting requirement beginning October 1, 1997.[61] The states that did not have a new hire reporting law in existence on

---

61.    P.L. 104-193.

August 22, 1996 were required to establish an automated State Directory of New Hires by October 1, 1997 that can accept new hire information provided by employers. States with new hire reporting laws already in existence at that time had until October 1, 1998 to comply, but they had to begin transferring new hire information received from employers to the National Directory of New Hires by October 1, 1997. All states have laws mandating new hire reporting and setting out the procedures to be followed.

*Reporting requirement.*[62] For each newly hired employee, the employer must provide the following information to the state directory:

- the employee's name, address, and social security number; and
- the employer's name, address, and federal employer identification number (EIN).

Employers with employees only in one state must report newly hired employees to that state, either on paper, magnetically or electronically. Employers with employees in 2 or more states that report new hires magnetically or electronically may designate one state where they have employees as the state to which they will report all their new hires. Multistate employers that wish to file all their new hire reports with one state must designate that state to the Secretary of Health and Human Services. Employers can notify HHS in one of several ways: in writing on an HHS form or a letter that can be mailed or faxed, or on the Internet. Regardless of the method used, the following information must be provided:

- employer's name, address, phone number, and federal Employer Identification Number
- the state to which the employer will report new hires and the date on which multistate reporting will begin
- other states in which the employer has employees
- employer contact information (name, title, phone number, e-mail address, fax number)
- FEIN, name, state and zip code of any subsidiary of the employer with a different FEIN for which the employer will be reporting new hires

Completed forms and letters should be mailed to: Department of Health and Human Services, Administration for Children and Families, Office of Child Support Enforcement, Multistate Employer Notification, P.O. Box 509, Randallstown, MD 21133; or faxed to 410-277-9325. Employers can make their designation on the Internet at the OCSE World Wide website: http://www.acf.dhhs.gov or download a copy of the form to complete later.

 **REMINDERS SENT TO MULTISTATE EMPLOYERS** In March 2006, the OCSE mailed letters to 89,000 multistate employers to remind them of their new hire reporting responsibilities after identifying more than 63,000 multistate employers that were reporting all their newly hired employees to one state, but that were not registered with HHS. In addition, information maintained on 26,000 registered multistate employers needed to be updated as the result of a merger, acquisition, or other change.

Federal government employers must report new hires to the National Directory of New Hires. The reporting requirements do not apply to employees of federal or state agencies performing intelligence or counterintelligence functions if the head of the agency determines that such reporting would endanger the employee or compromise an ongoing agency mission.

In general, employers must report newly hired employees within 20 calendar days of the date of hire. If an employer reports new hires magnetically or electronically, it must send 2 transmissions per calendar month which are 12 - 16 days apart. States can establish their own time frames for reporting new hires, but they can be no longer than the federal requirements. Multistate employers that submit reports twice monthly must submit information for a newly hired employee as soon as possible after the date of hire, but no later than the next semimonthly pay period. All states can accept multistate new hire reports.

---

62.    42 U.S.C. §653A(a) - (c).

Some states may require employers to report more information than the elements required by federal law. But the Office of Child Support Enforcement said that multistate employers do not have to report the required elements for every state in which they have employees—only those required by the state the employer has selected for new hire reporting purposes.[63]

An employee's date of hire is considered to be the first day services are performed for wages by the employee, and employees who work for as little as one day must be reported. The federal reporting requirement does not apply to independent contractors, but some states do require such reporting. Multi-state employers that choose to report all new hires to a state that does not require reporting of independent contractors do not have to report newly hired independent contractors in any state. Also, employees who are rehired after being laid off or return to work after a leave of absence do not need to be reported as a new hire if they were not removed from payroll records and do not have to complete a new Form W-4.

Temporary help agencies that pay wages to the employees they refer are responsible for reporting them as new hires. If the agency merely refers individuals for jobs, and they are paid by the client, the client is the employer and must report the new hires. Labor unions and hiring halls must report their own newly hired employees, but not individuals who are referred for employment.

*Reporting format and method.* Employers can report new hires on the employee's Form W-4 or an equivalent form containing the required information, and can transmit the report by first class mail, fax, magnetically, electronically, or over the Internet. Using the employee's Form W-4 to meet the new hire reporting requirement entails a burden not previously faced by employers, since the employer identifying information does not otherwise need to be placed on a Form W-4 unless the form is being submitted upon written request to the IRS (see Section 6.3-1). Because Form W-4 cannot be altered to include additional information (see section 6.3-1), the IRS advises that employers should use a copy of the original form if other information will be written on the form (e.g., date of birth) before it is filed for new hire reporting purposes.

*Penalties for failure to report new hires.*[64] States have the option to set a civil penalty of up to $25 for a failure to comply with the new hire reporting requirements, with a $500 maximum if the failure to comply is the result of a conspiracy between the employer and the employee.

*Information processing.*[65] The state has 5 business days to enter information reported by employers into the State Directory of New Hires data base, and 2 business days from the date of entry to transmit a child support withholding order (if one is in effect against the employee) to the employee's employer containing the periodic amount to withhold (including any past due amounts). Within 3 business days from the date of entry, the state must furnish new hire information to the National Directory of New Hires so it can be matched with records from other state directories. In addition to enforcement of child support obligations, states can use new hire information to aid in administration of their unemployment compensation, workers' compensation, and certain other government benefit programs to cut down on fraud and abuse.

Table 1.2 summarizes many of the provisions in the individual state new hire reporting laws. Since all states require employers filing new hire reports magnetically or electronically to report twice monthly from 12-16 days apart, this information is not included for each state in the table. [For more information on state new hire reporting requirements for employees and independent contractors, see Tables 5.1 and 5.2 of *APA's Guide to State Payroll Laws.*]

---

63. OCSE-AT-98-06, 3-2-98.
64. 42 U.S.C. §653A(d).
65. 42 U.S.C. §653A(e) - (h).

Table 1.2

| STATE NEW HIRE REPORTING REQUIREMENTS | | | | | | | |
|---|---|---|---|---|---|---|---|
| State | Who Must Report | Employees To Report | What to Report | When to Report | How to Report | Late Report Penalty | Contact Information |
| Alabama | All employers | New hires, rehires and recalls | Federal elements; date of hire, state ID number | Within 7 days of hire, rehire, or recall | W-4 or equivalent; mail, fax, mag media or electronically | $25 | 334-353-8491<br><br>http://dir.alabama.gov/nh |
| Alaska | All employers | New hires and rehires | Federal elements | Within 20 days of hire | W-4 or equivalent, mail, fax, mag media or electronically | $10; $100 for conspiracy | 877-269-6685 907-269-6089<br><br>www.childsupport.alaska.gov/FAQ/FAQ_New.Hires.asp |
| Arizona | All employers | New hires and rehires | Federal elements | Within 20 days of hire | W-4 or equivalent, mail, fax, mag media or electronically | No penalty | 888-282-2064 602-340-0555<br><br>www.az-newhirereporting.com/az-newhire/default.asp |
| Arkansas | All employers | New hires and rehires | Federal elements | Within 20 days of hire or rehire | W-4 or equivalent, mail, fax, mag media or electronically, e-mail | No penalty | 800-259-2095 501-376-2125<br><br>www.ar-newhirereporting.com/ar-newhire/default.asp |
| California | All employers | New hires and rehires; contractors over $600 | Federal elements; date of hire; state EIN; date, dollar amount, expiration date of contract | Within 20 days of hire or rehire; or after $600 minimum is met or contract is signed, whichever is earlier | W-4 or equivalent, state form DE 34; mail, fax, mag media or electronically | $24, $490 for conspiracy | 916-651-6945<br><br>www.edd.ca.gov/taxrep/taxner.htm |
| Colorado | All employers | New hires and rehires | Federal elements | Within 20 days of hire or rehire or 1st payroll after hire | W-4 or equivalent, mail, fax, mag media or electronically | No penalty | 303-297-2849 800-696-1468<br><br>www.newhire.state.co.us/newhire/do |
| Connecticut | All employers | New hires and rehires; contractors if contract exceeds $5,000 for calendar year | Federal elements; state EIN | Within 20 days of hire or rehire | W-4 or equivalent, mail, fax, Internet, or electronically | No penalty | 860-263-6310<br><br>www1.ctdol.state.ct.us/newhires/index.asp |
| Delaware | All employers | New hires and rehires | Federal elements | Within 20 days of hire or rehire | W-4 or equivalent, mail, fax, mag media or electronically | $25, $500 for conspiracy | 302-577-7171<br><br>www.dhss.delaware.gov/dcse/nhr.html |
| District of Columbia | All employers | All new hires and rehires | Federal elements; date of birth, salary, date of hire; UI ID number: optional: health ins. availability, employer contact, employee's gender | Within 20 days of hire or rehire | W-4 or equivalent, mail, fax, mag media, e-mail, Internet or electronically | $25, $500 for conspiracy | 877-846-9523<br><br>https://newhirereporting.com/dc-newhire/ |

## STATE NEW HIRE REPORTING REQUIREMENTS

| State | Who Must Report | Employees To Report | What to Report | When to Report | How to Report | Late Report Penalty | Contact Information |
|---|---|---|---|---|---|---|---|
| Florida | All employers | All new hires and rehires | Federal elements; date of hire; date of birth (optional) | Within 20 days of hire or rehire | W-4 or equivalent, mail, fax, mag media or electronically | No penalty | 888-854-4791 850-656-3343 https:// newhirereporting. com/fl-newhire/ default.asp |
| Georgia | All employers | All new hires and rehires | Federal elements; date of birth, UI ID# or UBI ID# | Within 10 days of hire or rehire | W-4 or equivalent, mail, fax, mag media or electronically | Written warning | 888-541-0469 404-525-2985 https:// newhirereporting. com/ga-newhire/ default.asp |
| Hawaii | All employers | All new hires and rehires | Federal elements | Within 20 days of hire or rehire | W-4 or equivalent, mail, fax, mag media or electronically | $25, $500 for conspiracy | 808-692-7029 http://hawaii.gov/ ag/csea/main/pis/ locate#NDNH |
| Idaho | All employers | All hires and rehires | Federal elements; date of hire; UI ID | Within 20 days of hire or rehire | W-4 or equivalent, mail, fax, phone, mag media, e-mail, Internet or electronically | No penalty | 800-627-3880 https://cl.idaho. gov/applications/ newhire/Default. aspx |
| Illinois | All employers | All new hires | Federal elements; optional: date of hire; alternate address for income withholding orders | Within 20 days of hire | W-4 or equivalent, mail, fax, mag media, Internet or electronically | $15, $500 for conspiracy | 800-327-4473 www.ides.state.il. us/employer/new hire/general.asp |
| Indiana | All employers | All new hires | Federal elements; date of hire | Within 20 days of hire | W-4 or equivalent, mail, fax, mag media, Internet or electronically | $500 for conspiracy | 866-879-0198 317-612-3028 https:// newhirereporting. com/in-newhire/ default.asp |
| Iowa | All employers | All hires and rehires; independent contractors over $600 | Federal elements; date of birth; health insurance; address to send income withholding orders; start date of contract; payor's phone number | Within 15 days of hire, rehire, or contract | W-4 or equivalent, mail, fax, phone, mag media or electronically | Contempt of court | 877-274-2580 https://dhssecure. dhs.state.ia.us/ epay |
| Kansas | All employers | All new hires and rehires | Federal elements | Within 20 days of hire | W-4 or equivalent, mail, fax, e-mail, Internet or electronically | No penalty | 888-219-7801 913-296-1716 www.dol.ks.gov/ ui/html/newhires_ BUS.html |
| Kentucky | All employers | All new hires, rehires and job refusals | Federal elements; state EIN | Within 20 days of hire or rehire | W-4 or equivalent, mail, fax, mag media or electronically | $250 for 3rd and later offenses | 800-817-2262 www.newhire-usa. com/ky/ |

## STATE NEW HIRE REPORTING REQUIREMENTS

| State | Who Must Report | Employees To Report | What to Report | When to Report | How to Report | Late Report Penalty | Contact Information |
|---|---|---|---|---|---|---|---|
| Louisiana | All employers | All new hires and rehires | Federal elements; occupation | Within 20 days of hire or rehire | W-4 or equivalent, mail, fax, Internet phone, mag media or electronically | $25; $500 for conspiracy | 888-223-1461 www.dss.state.la.us/departments/dss/New_Hire_registry.html |
| Maine | All employers | All new hires and rehires | Federal elements; date of birth; UI or UBI number | Within 7 days of hire or rehire | W-4 or equivalent, mail, fax, phone, mag media or electronically | Written warning, then $200 per month | 207-624-7880 www.maine.gov/dhhs/OIAS/dser/employer/index.html |
| Maryland | All employers | All new hires | Federal elements; date of hire; medical benefits availability; starting wage; UI ID | Within 20 days from hire | W-4 or equivalent, mail, fax, mag media or electronically | $20, $500 for conspiracy | 888-634-4737 410-281-6000 https://newhirereporting.com/md-newhire/default/asp |
| Massachusetts | All employers | All new hires and rehires; contractors over $600 | Federal elements; date of hire or contract | Within 14 days of hire, rehire or contract | W-4 or equivalent, mail, fax, mag media or electronically; Internet required if employer has 25 employees or contractors | $25; $500 for conspiracy | 617-626-4154 www.mass.gov/?pageID=mg2homepage&L=1&L0=Home&sid=massgov2 |
| Michigan | All employers | All new hires | Federal elements | Within 20 days of hire | W-4 or equivalent, mail, fax, Internet mag media or electronically | No penalty | 800-524-9846 http://mi-newhire.com/MI-Newhire/default.aspx |
| Minnesota | All employers | All new hires, and rehires; government contractors | Federal elements; optional: date of birth; date of hire; state of hire | Within 20 days of hire or rehire | W-4 or equivalent, mail, fax, phone, mag media or electronically | $25, $500 for conspiracy | 800-672-4473 651-227-4661 https://newhirereporting.com/mn-newhire/default.asp |
| Mississippi | All employers | All new hires and rehires; independent contractors paid on a recurring basis | Federal elements; date of hire; date of birth; state EIN; date contractor begins services | Within 15 days of hire or rehire; date of contract for contractors | W-4 or equivalent, mail, fax, e-mail, or Internet | $25, $500 for conspiracy | 800-241-1330 404-808-9016 https://newhirereporting.com/ms-newhire/default.asp |
| Missouri | All employers | All new hires | Federal elements | Within 20 days of hire or rehire | W-4 or equivalent, mail, fax, or electronically | $25, $350 for conspiracy | 800-585-9234 800-859-7999 www.dss.mo.gov/cse/newhire.htm |

| STATE NEW HIRE REPORTING REQUIREMENTS | | | | | | | |
|---|---|---|---|---|---|---|---|
| **State** | **Who Must Report** | **Employees To Report** | **What to Report** | **When to Report** | **How to Report** | **Late Report Penalty** | **Contact Information** |
| Montana | All employers | All new hires and rehires | Federal elements; date of hire; optional: date of birth; medical insurance availability | Within 20 days of hire or rehire | W-4 or equivalent, mail, fax, phone, mag media, Internet or electronically | No penalty | 888-866-0327 406-444-9290 www.dphhs.mt.gov/csed/relatedtopics/employerinformation.shtml |
| Nebraska | All employers | All new hires and rehires | Federal elements; date of hire or rehire | Within 20 days of hire or rehire | W-4 or equivalent, mail, fax, Internet, mag media or electronically | $25 | 888-256-0293 402-691-9957 https://newhirereporting.com/ne-newhire/default.asp |
| Nevada | All employers | All new hires | Federal elements | Within 20 days of hire or rehire | W-4 or equivalent, mail, fax, mag media or electronically | $25 | 888-639-7241 775-684-8685 https://uitax.nvdetr.org/crphtml/new_hire_info.htm |
| New Hampshire | All employers | All new hires and rehires; contractors over $2,500 | Federal elements; UI ID; optional: date of hire; work state | Within 20 days of hire or rehire | W-4 or equivalent, W-9 for contractors, mail, fax, mag media or electronically | $25, $500 for conspiracy | 800-803-4485 603-229-4371 www.nh.gov/nhes/documemts/newhire.pdf |
| New Jersey | All employers | All new hires, rehires and contractors | Federal elements; date of birth; optional: date of hire | Within 20 days of hire or rehire; every 15 days on mag media | W-4 or equivalent, mail, fax, electronically, or Internet | $25, $500 for conspiracy | 888-624-6339 877-654-4737 https://newhirereporting.com/nj-newhire/default.asp |
| New Mexico | All employers | All new hires | Federal elements | Within 20 days of hire or rehire | W-4 or equivalent, mail, fax, or electronically | $20, $500 for conspiracy | 888-878-1607 505-995-8230 https://newhirereporting.com/nm-newhire/default.asp |
| New York | All employers | All new hires and rehires | Federal elements | Within 20 days of hire or rehire | W-4 or equivalent, mail, fax, Internet, mag media or electronically | $20, $450 for conspiracy | 800-972-1233 800-225-5829 www.tax.state.ny.us/wt/newhire.htm |
| North Carolina | All employers | All new hires and rehires | Federal elements; state EIN | Within 20 days of hire or rehire | W-4 or equivalent, mail, fax, phone, e-mail, mag media or electronically | $25, $500 for conspiracy | 888-514-4568 https://newhirereporting.com/nc-newhire/default.asp |

## STATE NEW HIRE REPORTING REQUIREMENTS

| State | Who Must Report | Employees To Report | What to Report | When to Report | How to Report | Late Report Penalty | Contact Information |
|---|---|---|---|---|---|---|---|
| North Dakota | All employers | All new hires | Federal elements | Within 20 days of hire | W-4 or equivalent, mail, fax, mag media, e-mail, Internet or electronically | $20, $250 for conspiracy | 800-755-8530 701-328-3582<br><br>www.nd.gov/ dhs/services/ childsupport/ empinfo/newhire |
| Ohio | All employers | All new hires and rehires; independent contractors | Federal elements; date of birth; date of hire; date payments begin to contractors; length of time contractor will perform services | Within 20 days of hire or rehire; or engagement/ re-engagement of a contractor; or contractor resumes providing services. | W-4 or equivalent, mail, fax, mag media, e-mail, Internet or electronically | $25, $500 for a conspiracy | 888-872-1490 614-221-5330<br><br>https:// newhirereporting. com/oh-newhire/ default.asp |
| Oklahoma | All employers | All new hires | Federal elements; date of hire; state of hire | Within 20 days of hire | W-4 or equivalent, mail, fax, Internet, mag media or electronically | No penalty | 800-317-3785 405-557-7133<br><br>www.okdhs.org/ programsandservices /cse/buspart/emp/ newhire/ |
| Oregon | All employers | All new hires and rehires | Federal elements | Within 20 days of hire or rehire | W-4 or equivalent, mail, fax, mag media | No penalty | 503-378-2868<br><br>http://dcs.state.or. us/employers |
| Pennsylvania | All employers | All new hires and rehires | Federal elements; date of hire; employer contact information | Within 20 days of hire or rehire | W-4 or equivalent, mail, fax, or mag media | Written warning, $25 for later violations, $500 for conspiracy | 888-724-4737<br><br>www.panewhires. com |
| Rhode Island | All employers | All new hires and rehires | Federal elements; health insurance; wage withholding address; optional: date of birth; date of hire; state of hire | Within 14 days of hire or rehire | W-4 or equivalent, mail, fax, phone, e-mail, mag media or electronically | $20, $500 for con- spiracy | 888-870-6461<br><br>www.rinewhire. com |
| South Carolina | All employers | All new hires and rehires | Federal elements; optional: date of birth; date of hire; employer phone number | Within 20 days of hire | W-4 or equivalent, mail, fax, mag media or electroni- cally | $25 for second offense, $500 for conspiracy | 888-454-5294 803-898-9235<br><br>www.state.sc.us/ dss/csed/newhire. htm |
| South Dakota | All employers | All new hires and rehires | Federal elements | Within 20 days of hire or rehire | W-4 or equivalent, mail, fax, mag media or electronically | Civil proceeding for a petty offense | 888-827-6078 605-626-2942<br><br>www.state.sd.us/ applications/ LD01DOL/ frameset.asp?navid =305&filtertype=1 |
| Tennessee | All employers | All new hires and rehires | Federal elements; date of hire | Within 20 days of hire or rehire | W-4 or equivalent, mail, fax, mag media | $20, $400 for conspiracy | 888-715-2280<br><br>www.tnnewhire. com |

| | | | **STATE NEW HIRE REPORTING REQUIREMENTS** | | | | |
|---|---|---|---|---|---|---|---|
| **State** | **Who Must Report** | **Employees To Report** | **What to Report** | **When to Report** | **How to Report** | **Late Report Penalty** | **Contact Information** |
| Texas | All employers | All hires and rehires | Federal elements; optional: date of birth; date of hire; salary; payroll address to mail notice to withhold child support | Within 20 days of hire or rehire | W-4 or equivalent, mail, fax, or electronically | $25; $500 for conspiracy | 888-839-4473<br><br>https://portal.cs. oag.state.tx.us/ wps/portal/ employerhome |
| Utah | All employers | All new hires and rehires | Federal elements; optional: date of hire; job title; work status | Within 20 days of hire or rehire | W-4 or equivalent, mail, fax, mag media | $25, $500 for conspiracy | 801-526-4361<br><br>http://jobs.utah. gov/ui/employer/ login.aspx |
| Vermont | All employers | All new hires and rehires | Federal elements | Within 20 days of hire or rehire | W-4 or equivalent, mail, fax, phone, mag media or electronically | $500 for conspiracy | 800-786-3214 802-241-2194<br><br>https://uipublic. labor.vermont.gov/ OnlineNewhire/ pages/newhirehome. aspx |
| Virginia | All employers | All new hires | Federal elements | Within 20 days of hire | W-4 or equivalent, mail, fax, mag media or electronically | No penalty | 800-979-9014 804-771-9733<br><br>https:// newhirereporting. com/va-newhire/ default.asp |
| Washington | All employers | All hires and rehires | Federal elements; date of birth | Within 20 days of hire or rehire | W-4 or equivalent, mail, fax, mag media or electronically | $25; $500 for conspiracy | 800-562-0479<br><br>www1.dshs. wa.gov/newhire/ |
| West Virginia | All employers | All hires and rehires | Federal elements; payroll address (if different); optional: date of birth; income information | Within 14 days of hire or rehire | W-4 or equivalent, mail, fax, phone, mag media or electronically | $25, $500 for conspiracy | 877-625-4669 304-346-9513<br><br>https:// newhirereporting. com/wv-newhire/ default.asp |
| Wisconsin | All employers | All new hires and rehires | Federal elements; date of birth; date of hire | Within 20 days of hire or rehire | W-4 or equivalent, mail, fax, mag media or electronically | $25, $500 for conspiracy | 888-300-4473<br><br>www.newhire-usa. com/wi/ |
| Wyoming | All employers | All new hires | Federal elements; optional: date of birth; date of hire | Within 20 days of hire or rehire | W-4 or equivalent, mail, fax, mag media or electronically | No penalty | 800-970-9258 307-638-1675<br><br>https:// newhirereporting. com/wy-newhire/ default.asp |

# 1.10 Review Questions and Exercises

## Review Questions

1. List the factors used in determining whether a business has the right to control the financial aspects of a worker's activities.

2. What are the four categories of statutory employees? *Ins. Sales, homeworker,*

3. What are the two categories of statutory nonemployees? *re agents,*

4. Compare a temporary help agency employee and a leased employee.

5. When leasing an employee or using a temporary help agency, aside from looking at the cost, what should you know about the overall company that you are dealing with to avoid having to pay any withholding or employment taxes?

6. What are the three parts of the ABC test, and what is the test used to determine?

7. What is Form I-9 used for?

8. When a client company hires leased employees, who is responsible for withholding and/or paying federal income, social security, Medicare, and FUTA taxes?

9. What factors do the courts and the Department of Labor consider when making an employment status determination under the FLSA?

10. Why would many employers rather use workers who are not employees to perform services for them?

11. What does a social security card prove in terms of an employee's work authorization status under IRCA?

12. Which factors are considered not to be important by the IRS in making a worker classification determination because of changes in the workplace over the years?

13. What information must be reported by an employer for each new hire under the federal new hire reporting requirement?

14. When must employers report newly hired employees under the federal new hire reporting requirement?

15. What is the name of the program employers can use to verify the employment authorization status of new hires with U.S. Citizenship and Immigration Services?

## True or False Questions

_____ 1. If the employer has the right to control what work will be done and how that work will be done, an employer-employee relationship exists.

_____ 2. Full-time life insurance salespersons are always considered statutory employees and are never subject to FUTA tax.

_____ 3. Workers hired through a temporary help agency are not employees of the client company.

## Section 1: The Employer-Employee Relationship

_F_ 4. Telemarketers working under the direction of a company are usually independent contractors.

_T_ 5. An accountant who provides bookkeeping and payroll services to several local businesses and works at her own office is an independent contractor.

_T_ 6. The responsibility for determining the employment status of an individual who performs services rests with the employer.

_T_ 7. If an independent contractor timely provides the employer with a correct Taxpayer Identification Number, there will be no backup withholding.

_F_ 8. ? The IRS usually relies on the reasonable basis test in making employment status determinations.

_F_ 9. Managers and executives are excluded from the employer-employee relationship for tax purposes.

_T_ 10. Length of employment makes no difference in determining employment status.

_T_ _F_ ~~11.~~ Technical services specialists are specifically excluded from the "reasonable basis" test.

_T_ 12. Under the ABC test, one of the determining factors is whether the worker in question is free from control or direction in performing the work both by agreement and in reality.

_F_ 13. Part-time employees are not covered under the federal payroll tax laws even if they meet the common law test for employment status.

_T_ 14. "Reciprocity agreements" require employers to withhold state income tax only for their employees' states of residence.

_F_ 15. Employers can demand specific documents to prove an employee's eligibility to work in the U.S.

_____ 16. Employers who claim Section 530 status for their workers because a significant segment of their industry classifies similar workers the same way must show that at least 50% of the industry treats these workers as independent contractors.

_____ 17. An employer that changes its classification of a worker from independent contractor to employee may still claim Section 530 protection for the period before the change in treatment.

_T_ 18. An IRS agent conducting an employment tax audit must give the employer written notice of the availability of the Section 530 protections.

_T_ 19. Under the federal new hire reporting requirements, multistate employers must report a new hire to the state in which the employee works.
*one state to report all hires.*

## Multiple Choice Questions

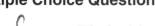

C 1. Which of the following forms may be completed and submitted to the IRS to determine the employment status of an individual for federal income and employment tax purposes?

    a.    Form SS-4
    b.    Form SS-5
    c.    Form SS-8
    d.    Form W-9

b 2. Which of the following forms must be submitted to an independent contractor (who is paid at least $600) after the end of the year for services performed during that year?

    a.    Form W-2
    b.    Form 1099-MISC
    c.    Form 1096
    d.    Form SS-8

a 3. All of the following types of evidence support an employer's treatment of a worker as an independent contractor under the "reasonable basis" test EXCEPT:

    a.    Place of work
    b.    Court decisions
    c.    Private letter rulings
    d.    Past IRS employment tax audits

b 4. All of the following criteria would be typical of an independent contractor EXCEPT:

    a.    Works off site
    b.    Paid by the hour
    c.    Furnishes own tools
    d.    Sets own work hours

c 5. Each of the following individuals would be classified as an employee EXCEPT:

    a.    Controller of a company
    b.    College professor
    c.    Attorney (solo practitioner)
    d.    City police officer

b 6. All of the following workers are statutory employees EXCEPT:

    a.    Full-time life insurance salespersons
    b.    Qualified real estate agents
    c.    Homeworkers
    d.    Traveling or city salespersons

(c) d 7. Full-time life insurance salespersons paid solely by commission are exempt from:

    a.    Social security and Medicare taxes
    b.    Social security tax only
    (c.)    FUTA tax
    d.    Social security, Medicare, and FUTA taxes

8. If an employer fails to withhold social security and Medicare taxes and does not file a Form W-2 or a Form 1099 for an individual, what penalty may the IRS impose?

    a. 10% of the employee's share of social security and Medicare taxes
    b. 20% of the employee's share of social security and Medicare taxes
    c. 40% of the employee's share of social security and Medicare taxes
    d. 100% of the employee's share of social security and Medicare taxes

9. How long must an employer retain a Form I-9 for a terminated employee who worked for the employer for more than four years?

    a. 1 year after termination
    b. 3 years after termination
    c. 7 years after termination
    d. Does not have to keep terminated employees' I-9 forms

10. Which of the following situations describes one of the general requirements that must be met for workers to be considered statutory employees?

    a. They have a continuing relationship with the employer
    b. They have a substantial investment in the business equipment
    c. They are licensed real estate agents
    d. Most of their compensation is related to sales

11. Each of the following goals is a reason why states might require employers to report newly hired employees EXCEPT:

    a. to detect welfare fraud
    b. to detect unemployment compensation fraud
    c. to locate individuals who have not claimed state lottery winnings
    d. to locate noncustodial parents subject to a child support withholding order

12. Which of the following individuals are statutory nonemployees?

    a. homeworkers
    b. full-time life insurance salespersons
    c. newspaper deliverers
    d. traveling salespersons

# SECTION 2: FEDERAL AND STATE WAGE-HOUR LAWS

## TABLE OF CONTENTS

# SECTION 2: FEDERAL AND STATE WAGE-HOUR LAWS

Most people are familiar with the terms "minimum wage," "overtime pay," "child labor," "exempt employee," and "nonexempt employee" from their own work experiences, regardless of whether they have worked in a payroll environment. These terms, and the requirements and restrictions they imply, are found in the various federal and state laws regulating employees' wages and hours.

This section begins with a detailed discussion of the basic law in this area, the Fair Labor Standards Act, explaining its requirements governing minimum wages, overtime pay, child labor, etc., as well as how the law is enforced and how costly violations can be. Following is a summary of the special wage-hour laws that govern businesses working under contracts with the federal government. At the end of this section are several tables providing information on state wage-hour requirements, including minimum wage, overtime pay, etc.

## 2.1 Federal Wage-Hour Law (Fair Labor Standards Act)

Perhaps the most basic of all payroll and employment laws is the Fair Labor Standards Act of 1938 (FLSA), also known as the Federal Wage-Hour Law.[1] The FLSA does the following:

- sets the minimum wage and overtime rates employees must receive for their work;

- requires recordkeeping by employers;

- places restrictions on the types of work children can do and the hours they can work; and

- mandates equal pay for equal work.

Almost as important is what the FLSA does not do. The FLSA does not:

- require employers to provide paid vacations, sick days, jury duty leave, holidays, lunch breaks, or coffee breaks;

- regulate how often employees must be paid, or when they must be paid after termination of employment (either voluntarily or involuntarily); or

- restrict the hours that employees over 16 years of age may be required to work.

These areas may be governed by another federal law or regulation, but in most instances they are handled by the individual states.

 **BUT WAGES MUST BE PAID BY PAYDAY** While the FLSA does not require that wages be paid within a certain amount of time after services are performed, federal courts have ruled that wages are "unpaid" unless they are paid on the employees' regular payday. Payment beyond that date violates the FLSA's minimum wage and overtime pay requirements, the courts said, although overtime pay may lawfully be delayed until it can be correctly calculated.[2] On a related issue, a federal appeals court said that delaying payday by one day for each of 5 weeks while changing from a weekly current to a biweekly lagged pay schedule does not violate the FLSA's

---

1.   29 U.S.C. §201 - §219.
2.   W-H Reg. 29 CFR §778.106; Biggs v. Wilson, 1 F.3d 1537 (9 CA, 1993); Seneca Coal & Coke Co. v. Lofton, 136 F.2d 359 (10 CA, 1943); Boyd v. Runyon, 1996 U.S. Dist. LEXIS 8272 (D Kan.); Brooks v. Village of Ridgefield Park, N.J., 978 F. Supp. 613 (D N.J., 1997), aff'd 185 F. 3d 130 (3 CA, 1999); Mathis v. About Your Smile, P. C., No. 02-CV-597, 2002 U.S. Dist. LEXIS 15572 (ED Pa., 8-14-02).

minimum wage and overtime provisions and may not violate the prompt payment requirement if the change is intended to be permanent, does not unreasonably delay payment, and is made for a legitimate business purpose.[3]

**DOL enforcement.** The Federal Wage-Hour Law (except for the equal pay provisions) is administered and enforced by the Wage and Hour Division of the U.S. Department of Labor's Employment Standards Administration (see Section 2.9 for details). The equal pay provisions are enforced by the Equal Employment Opportunity Commission.

## 2.2 Federal/State Relationship

All employers and payroll practitioners must be aware not only of the FLSA, but of the state wage-hour laws in states where they operate. There are two reasons for this:

1. Areas left unregulated by the FLSA are most likely regulated by all states to one degree or another.

2. Even where the FLSA has an applicable provision, the employer must comply with a state law covering the same issue if the state law is more favorable to the employee.[4] (However, there are several states that exempt employers and employees covered by the FLSA from state law coverage.)

*Example 1:* The FLSA requires overtime pay at 1½ times an employee's regular rate of pay for all hours physically worked over 40 in a workweek. In addition to this requirement, California requires the same overtime premium for hours physically worked over 8 in a workday (with some exceptions allowing 10-hour workdays in a 4-day workweek). Therefore, a California employee working 11 hours a day for 4 days in a workweek would be entitled to overtime pay for 12 hours (3 hours per day), since the state law is more beneficial to the employee.

*Example 2:* The minimum hourly wage under the FLSA at the beginning of 2008 is $5.85, while the Connecticut minimum hourly wage is $7.65. Employees covered by the Connecticut law must be paid at least $7.65 an hour.

*Example 3:* The FLSA does not restrict the hours that can be worked by 16- and 17-year-olds in non-hazardous jobs, but Michigan limits 16 and 17-year-olds to a 48-hour workweek (with certain exceptions). Despite the FLSA, a 17-year-old Michigan employee may not work more than 48 hours in a week.

## 2.3 Employer and Employee Coverage

The FLSA provides for broad coverage of employers and employees to meet its stated goal of eliminating "conditions detrimental to the maintenance of the minimum standard of living necessary for health, efficiency, and general well-being of workers."[5] Businesses with as few as one employee may be covered by the law if the tests for coverage are met. Under the FLSA, there are two types of coverage—enterprise coverage and individual employee coverage.

**Enterprise coverage.** Under the enterprise coverage test,[6] all the employees of a business are covered and protected by the FLSA if:

---

3. Rogers v. City of Troy, 148 F. 3d 52 (2 CA, 1998).
4. FLSA §18(a).
5. FLSA §2(a).
6. FLSA §3(s).

1.  at least two employees of the business are employed in jobs closely related and directly essential to interstate commerce or the production of goods for interstate commerce (including employees who handle, sell, or otherwise work on goods or materials that have been moved in or produced for interstate commerce), and

2.  the business has annual gross sales of at least $500,000.

Certain businesses (and all their employees) are specifically covered by the FLSA regardless of annual sales volume. They include:

*   hospitals
*   nursing homes
*   elementary and secondary schools and colleges (whether public or private)
*   public (government) agencies

**Individual employee coverage.** Under the individual employee coverage test, an employee is covered by the FLSA if he or she is engaged in interstate commerce or in the production of goods for interstate commerce.[7] It does not matter if the business is not a covered enterprise, so long as the employee's job is in interstate commerce.

 **WHAT IS INTERSTATE COMMERCE?** Basically, interstate commerce is any trade, transportation, or communication between one state and another state (or states) or between a state and a foreign country.

Both of these tests for FLSA coverage, as well as the definition of interstate commerce, have been interpreted rather broadly by the Wage and Hour Division and the courts, so that nearly all businesses are covered by the FLSA unless a specific exemption applies. One of the few remaining exemptions from the FLSA is for "Mom and Pop" shops, where the only employees are the owner and immediate family members.[8]

 **BE CAREFUL** Those employers that are not covered by the FLSA (e.g., their annual sales volume may be less than $500,000) may still be subject to state wage-hour requirements, which may be more generous to employees. Those employers that were covered by the FLSA until the sales volume threshold was raised to $500,000 on April 1, 1990 must pay the minimum wage in effect on March 31, 1990—$3.35 an hour.

## 2.4 Exempt and Nonexempt Employees

Not all employees of covered enterprises or who work in interstate commerce are entitled to the protections of the FLSA. When human resources and payroll staff members speak of an "exempt" or "nonexempt" employee, they are referring to the employee's status under the FLSA. Exempt employees are those who do not have to be paid the required minimum wage or overtime payments, and the employer does not have to keep certain records detailing their work. The most well-known of these exemptions is the "white collar exemption" for executive, administrative, professional, and outside sales employees, but there are also narrower exemptions that apply to retail and service establishment employees, hotel and restaurant employees, and others. Nonexempt employees must be paid at least the minimum wage for all hours worked, and an overtime premium for hours worked over 40 in a workweek.

---

7.    FLSA §6(a); W-H Reg. 29 CFR §776.0 - §776.21.
8.    FLSA §3(s)(2).

## 2.4-1 White Collar Exemption

Bona fide administrative, executive, professional, and computer-related professional employees, as well as outside sales employees, are exempt "white collar" employees under the FLSA. This means they are not covered by the minimum wage, overtime, and certain recordkeeping requirements of the law.[9] The tests for determining exempt status measure the actual duties and responsibilities of the employee, not the job title. The determination also depends on:

- the employee's primary duty;
- the employee's level of discretionary authority; and
- whether a minimum salary requirement is met.

**DOL finalizes long-awaited revision of white collar exemption rules.** On April 23, 2004, the DOL's Wage and Hour Division finalized sweeping changes to the regulations defining who is exempt as a "white collar" employee.[10] The regulations updated salary levels used in determining exempt status for the first time since 1975, while the duties tests received their first overhaul since 1949. The DOL hopes the new rules will make it easier for employers to properly classify employees as exempt or nonexempt, thus avoiding potentially costly misclassification lawsuits, and will help employees understand when they are due overtime pay.

The regulations provide that, in general, any employee earning less than $455 a week ($23,660 a year) is a nonexempt employee entitled to overtime pay, whether he or she is paid on an hourly or salary basis. Employees paid a salary above that level have to meet a revamped and streamlined duties test in order to be classified as an exempt executive, administrative, or professional employee. Employees earning more than $100,000 a year have to meet only one prong of one of the revamped duties tests to qualify as exempt.

Below you will find tables that provide brief comparisons between the salary and duties tests for administrative, executive, professional, and computer employees under the previous DOL regulations and the new, final regulations.

| COMPARING THE DUTIES TEST FOR ADMINISTRATIVE EMPLOYEES | | |
|---|---|---|
| Salary level | Previous short test $250 per week | New standard test $455 per week |
| Duties .................... | Whose primary duty consists of the performance of office or non-manual work directly related to management policies or general business operations of the employer or the employer's customers; and Which includes work requiring the exercise of discretion and independent judgment. | Whose primary duty is the performance of office or non-manual work directly related to the management or general business operations of the employer or the employer's customers; and Whose primary duty includes the exercise of discretion and independent judgment with respect to matters of significance. |

---

9.   FLSA §13(a)(1).
10.   69 F.R. 22122, 4-23-04; 29 CFR Part 541.

## COMPARING THE DUTIES TEST FOR EXECUTIVE EMPLOYEES

| Salary level | Previous short test $250 per week | New standard test $455 per week |
|---|---|---|
| Duties ..................... | Whose primary duty consists of the management of the enterprise in which he is employed or of a customarily recognized department or subdivision thereof; and<br>Who customarily and regularly directs the work of two or more other employees. | Whose primary duty is management of the enterprise in which the employee is employed or of a customarily recognized department or subdivision thereof;<br>Who customarily and regularly directs the work of two or more other employees; and<br>Who has the authority to hire or fire other employees or whose suggestions and recommendations as to the hiring, firing, advancement, promotion, or any other change of status of other employees are given particular weight. |

## COMPARING THE DUTIES TEST FOR PROFESSIONAL EMPLOYEES

| Salary level | Previous short test $250 per week | New standard test $455 per week |
|---|---|---|
| Duties ..................... | Whose primary duty consists of the performance of work requiring knowledge of an advanced type in a field of science or learning customarily acquired by a prolonged course of specialized instruction and study; and<br>Which includes work requiring the consistent exercise of discretion and judgment; or<br>Whose primary duty consists of the performance of work requiring invention, imagination, or talent in a recognized field of artistic endeavor. | Whose primary duty is the performance or work requiring knowledge of an advanced type (defined as work which is predominantly intellectual in character, and which includes work requiring the consistent exercise of discretion and judgment) in a field of science or learning customarily acquired by a prolonged course of specialized intellectual instruction; or<br>Whose primary duty is the performance of work requiring invention, imagination, originality, or talent in a recognized field of artistic or creative endeavor. |

## COMPARING THE DUTIES TESTS FOR COMPUTER EMPLOYEES

| Salary Level | Previous short test $250 per week | Section 13(a)(17) $27.63 an hour | New standard test $455 per week or $27.63 an hour |
|---|---|---|---|
| Duties... | Employed as a computer systems analyst, computer programmer, software engineer, or other similarly skilled worker in the computer software field.<br><br>Primary duty of performing work requiring theoretical and practical application of highly-specialized knowledge in computer systems analysis, programming, and software engineering; and<br><br>Whose work requires the consistent exercise of discretion and independent judgment. | Employee who is a computer systems analyst, computer programmer, software engineer, or other similarly skilled worker whose primary duty is:<br>(A) application of systems analysis techniques and procedures, including consulting with users to determine hardware, software, or system functional applications;<br>(B) design, development, documentation, analysis, creation, testing, or modification of computer systems or programs, including prototypes, based on and related to user or system design specifications;<br>(C) design, documentation, testing, creation, or modification of computer programs related to machine operating systems; or<br>(D) a combination of (A), (B), and (C), the performance of which requires the same level of skills. | The exemptions apply to only to a computer employee whose primary duty consists of:<br>(1) The application of systems analysis techniques and procedures, including consulting with users, to determine hardware, software, or system functional specifications;<br>(2) The design, development, documentation, analysis, creation, testing, or modification of computer systems or programs, including prototypes, based on and related to user or system design specifications;<br>(3) The design, documentation, testing, creation, or modification of computer programs related to machine operating systems; or<br>(4) A combination of the aforementioned duties, the performance of which requires the same level of skills. |

**State laws and union contracts.**[11] As noted elsewhere in this section, the FLSA does not preempt state laws and collective bargaining agreements that require higher minimum wages or overtime pay than the FLSA. Also, state laws that do not follow the new federal regulations in defining exempt white collar employees take precedence over the DOL regulations where they are more favorable to the employee whose status is being determined. [For more information on state overtime pay requirements and exemptions, see Tables 1.2 and 1.3 of *APA's Guide to State Payroll Laws*]. The white collar regulations reinforce that principle and also make it clear that union contracts cannot waive or reduce the FLSA's protections for employees.

---

11.    W-H Reg. 29 CFR §541.4.

Following are detailed explanations of the white collar exemption requirements under the new regulations for each category of exempt employee. These changes took effect on August 23, 2004.

**Job titles do not determine exempt status.**[12] Just because an employee has a position with a title that sounds important, that is not enough to establish the employee's status as an exempt employee. The exempt/nonexempt status of an employee is determined by the employer only on the basis of whether the employee's status and duties meet the requirements established by the DOL's regulations.

**Administrative employees – general rule.** To qualify as an exempt administrative employee, each of the following tests must be met:[13]

1.  The employee's primary duty must be the performance of office or nonmanual work directly related to the management or general business operations of the employer or the employer's customers;

2.  The employee's primary duty must include the exercise of discretion and independent judgment regarding matters of significance; and

3.  The employee must be paid at least $455 a week on a salary or fee basis, not including board, lodging, or other facilities.

*Directly related to management or general business operations.* In order to meet this requirement, the employee must perform work directly related to assisting with the running or servicing of the business, as distinguished from working on a production line in a manufacturing facility or selling products in a retail or service establishment.[14] The type of work that qualifies includes, among others, work in these functional areas:

| | |
|---|---|
| tax | personnel management |
| finance | human resources |
| accounting | employee benefits |
| budgeting | labor relations |
| auditing | public relations |
| insurance | government relations |
| quality control | computer network, Internet, and data base administration |
| purchasing | legal and regulatory compliance |
| procurement | research |
| advertising | safety and health |
| marketing | |

*Exercising discretion and independent judgment.*[15] The exercise of discretion and independent judgment involves evaluating and comparing different courses of conduct, and then making a decision after considering the various possibilities and outcomes. Whether an employee's work involves matters of significance is determined by the facts and circumstances in each case. Factors to be considered when determining whether an employee exercises discretion and independent judgment in matters of significance include:

*   whether the employee has authority to formulate, affect, interpret, or implement management policies or operating practices;
*   whether the employee carries out major assignments in conducting the operations of the business;
*   whether the employee's work affects business operations to a substantial degree, even though the employee only works in one area of the business;
*   whether the employee has authority to negotiate and commit the employer in matters that have a significant financial impact;

---

12. W-H Reg. 29 CFR §541.2.
13. W-H Reg. 29 CFR §541.200.
14. W-H Reg. 29 CFR §541.201.
15. W-H Reg. 29 CFR §541.202.

- whether the employee can waive or deviate from employer policies and procedures without prior approval;
- whether the employee provides consultation or expert advice to management;
- whether the employee is involved in planning long- or short-term business objectives;
- whether the employee investigates and resolves matters of significance on behalf of management; and
- whether the employee represents the employer in handling complaints, arbitrating disputes, or resolving grievances.

Exercising discretion and independent judgment implies that the employee operates free from immediate or direct supervision, but it does not mean that the employee's decisions are not subject to review or approval at a higher level or that they may not be reversed or modified. The decisions made by an exempt administrative employee may consist of recommendations for action rather than actually taking action. At larger employers, the fact that several employees perform the same work or work of the same significance to the employer does not mean that the work of each of them does not involve the exercise of discretion and independent judgment on matters of significance.

The exercise of discretion and independent judgment does not include clerical or secretarial work, recording or tabulating data (even if the employee is called a statistician), or other mechanical, repetitive, recurrent, or routine work.

*Risk of financial loss not determinative.* Even though the employee's failure to perform adequately will result in a significant financial loss for the employer, that does not mean the employee exercises discretion and independent judgment. Therefore, a messenger carrying a large sum of money for delivery does not exercise discretion and independent judgment just because his company stands to lose a great deal if the money is not delivered. The same holds true for an employee who operates very expensive equipment and whose negligence would be very costly for the employer.

*Applying procedures in manuals not enough.*[16] The exercise of discretion and independent judgment has to be more than the use of skill in applying well-established techniques, procedures, or specific standards found in manuals or other sources within narrowly defined limits to determine the correct response to a situation. However, the use of manuals or guidelines relating to highly scientific, financial, legal, or other highly complex matters that can be understood only by those with advanced or specialized knowledge does not affect an employee's exempt status.

**Administrative employees – examples.**[17] The following types of employees are included as examples in the regulations, mainly because of the troublesome issues involved in making the determination of the employee's exempt status.

*Insurance claims adjusters.* Insurance claims adjusters, whether they work for an insurance carrier or another company, generally meet the duties requirements for the administrative exemption if their duties include:

- interviewing insureds, witnesses, and physicians;
- inspecting property damage;
- reviewing factual information to prepare damage estimates;
- evaluating and making recommendations regarding whether claims are covered;
- determining liability and the total value of a claim;
- negotiating settlements; and
- making recommendations regarding litigation.

*Financial services employees.* Employees in the financial services industry whose primary duty is selling financial products do not qualify for the administrative exemption. However, other employees in the financial services industry generally meet the duties requirements for the administrative exemption if their duties include:

---

16.    W-H Reg. 29 CFR §541.202(e); §541.704.
17.    W-H Reg. 29 CFR §541.203.

- collecting and analyzing information regarding the customers' income, assets, investments, or debts;
- determining which financial products best meet customers' needs and financial circumstances;
- advising customers regarding the advantages and disadvantages of different financial products; and
- marketing, servicing, or promoting the employer's financial products.

*Team leaders.* An employee who leads a team of other employees assigned to complete one or more major projects for an employer generally meets the duties test for the administrative exemption, even if the employee does not have direct supervisory authority over the other team members. Examples of "major projects" include purchasing, selling, or closing all or part of a business, negotiating a real estate transaction or collective bargaining agreement, or designing and implementing productivity improvements.

*Executive assistants.* An executive assistant or administrative assistant to a business owner or senior executive of a large employer generally meets the duties requirements for the administrative exemption if the employee has been delegated authority regarding matters of significance and performs the work without specific instructions or prescribed procedures.

*Human resource managers.* Human resource managers who formulate, interpret, or implement employment policies generally meet the duties requirements for the administrative exemption, while personnel clerks who screen applicants to determine if they meet the minimum qualifications for employment do not, even though they may reject applicants who fail to meet the minimum standards. If a human resource manager handles the initial screening as well as final hiring decisions or recommendations, all the work is exempt work since the initial screening work is directly and closely related to the employee's exempt functions.

*Purchasing agents.* Purchasing agents with authority to bind the company on significant purchases generally meet the duties test for the administrative exemption even if they have to consult with top management in some instances.

*Inspectors and graders.* Work performed by inspectors, examiners, or graders generally does not meet the duties test for the administrative exemption because they normally perform specialized work involving well-established techniques and procedures that may be set forth in manuals or other sources. They have some leeway in performing their work, but only within narrowly prescribed limits.

For similar reasons, public sector inspectors or investigators (e.g., fire prevention, building construction, health or sanitation, environmental or soil specialists) also generally do not meet the duties tests for the administrative exemption. Also, their work is not directly related to the management or general business operations of their employer.

*Retail store buyers.* Buyers who evaluate reports on competitors' pricing to set their employer's prices generally meet the duties requirements for the administrative exemption. Employees who merely gather information regarding competitors' prices do not qualify for the exemption.

**DOL and courts issue interpretations.** Several months after the regulations were finalized, the Wage and Hour Division began issuing opinion letters interpreting the rules as they related to specific fact situations presented by specific employers, hopefully providing further guidance as to how the Division would act in applying the new rules. Soon after, the federal courts also began issuing decisions interpreting the new rules.

*Paralegals.*[18] The Division said that paralegals are not exempt administrative employees because their primary duty does not involve the exercise of discretion and independent judgment. Paralegals apply particular knowledge and skills in preparing assignments but do not exercise discretion and independent judgment despite having some leeway in reaching conclusions. They also are prohibited from practicing law, which shows they don't have the authority to exercise independent judgment in legal matters.

---

18.   W-H Op. Ltr, FLSA2005-54, 12-16-05.

*Nurse supervisors.*[19] A nurse supervisor was an exempt administrative employee because she used discretion in finding nurses to meet emergency needs and had to match patient needs with nurses' skills, which was her main task.

*Insurance claims adjusters.*[20] Claims adjusters are exempt administrative employees where they use discretion to determine whether the loss is covered, set reserves, decide where to lay blame, and negotiate with the insured party or his or her lawyer. The use of estimating software by auto damage adjusters did not negate their exercise of discretion because it could not always be used and was not of much help in total loss situations.

*Technology support specialists.*[21] "Information technology support specialists" (ITSS) are not exempt administrative employees. Their primary duty (75% of their time) consists of installing, configuring, testing, and troubleshooting computer applications, networks, and hardware. Maintaining a computer system and testing by systematic routines to determine whether a piece of computer equipment or a computer application is working properly according to specifications designed by others are examples of work that lacks the discretion and independent judgment needed for the administrative exemption. These duties do not involve, with respect to matters of significance, the comparison and evaluation of possible courses of conduct, and acting or making a decision after the various possibilities have been considered.

**Academic administrative employees.**[22] There is a separate administrative exemption for employees:

1.  whose primary duty is performing administrative functions directly related to academic instruction or training in an educational establishment; and

2.  who are paid a salary or fee of at least $455 a week, not including board, lodging, or other facilities, or a salary at least equal to the entrance salary for teachers in the educational establishment where they are employed.

To qualify under this separate exemption, the employee's work must be related to the academic operations and functions of the school rather than its general business operations. Employees engaged in academic administrative functions include:

*   superintendent of an elementary or secondary school system;
*   assistant superintendents responsible for curriculum, quality and methods of instruction, testing learning potential, establishing academic and grading standards, and other aspects of the teaching program;
*   principal or vice-principal of an elementary or secondary school system;
*   department heads in post-secondary educational institutions;
*   academic counselors; and
*   other employees with similar responsibilities.

**Executive employees – general rule.**[23] To qualify as an exempt executive employee, each of the following tests must be met:

1.  The employee's primary duty must be management of the enterprise in which the employee is employed or of a customarily recognized department or subdivision of the enterprise;

2.  The employee must customarily and regularly direct the work of two or more other employees;

---

19.    Goff v. Bayada Nurses, Inc., 424 F.Supp. 2d 816 (ED Pa., 3-24-06).
20.    In re Farmers Insurance Exchange, No. 05-35080, 2006 U.S. App. LEXIS 26671 (9 CA, 10-26-06); Millington v. Morrow County Board of Commissioners, No. 2:06-cv-347, 2007 U.S. Dist. LEXIS 74348 (SD Ohio, 10-4-07).
21.    W-H Op. Ltr., FLSA2006-42, 10-26-06.
22.    W-H Reg. 29 CFR §541.204.
23.    W-H Reg. 29 CFR §541.100.

3.  The employee must have the authority to hire or fire other employees, or particular weight must be given to the employee's recommendations as to the hiring, firing, advancement, promotion, or other change of employment status of other employees; and

4.  The employee must be paid a salary of at least $455 per week, not including board, lodging, or other facilities.

*Business owner.*[24] Also qualifying as an exempt executive employee is any employee who owns at least a bona fide 20% equity interest in the employer and is actively engaged in its management. The salary requirements do not apply to such employees.

*Management.*[25] Management includes activities such as:

*[handwritten: CEO's that don't make more than 25K — Ann]*

*   interviewing, selecting, and training employees;
*   setting and adjusting employees' pay rates and work hours;
*   directing the work of employees;
*   maintaining production or sales records for use in supervision of employees;
*   appraising employee's performance for the purpose or recommending promotions or other changes in status;
*   handling employee complaints and grievances;
*   disciplining employees;
*   planning employees' work;
*   determining techniques to be used;
*   dividing the work among employees;
*   determining the types of materials, supplies, machinery, equipment, or tools to be used;
*   determining the types of merchandise to be bought, stocked, and sold;
*   controlling the flow and distribution of materials or merchandise and supplies;
*   providing for the safety and security of the employees or the property;
*   planning and controlling the budget; and
*   monitoring or implementing legal compliance measures.

*Department or subdivision.*[26] A customarily recognized department or subdivision must have a permanent status and a continuing function, rather than being a mere collection of employees assigned to a specific job or series of jobs. When a business has more than one facility, the employee in charge of each facility may be considered in charge of a recognized subdivision of the business.

A recognized department or subdivision does not have to be physically within the employer's establishment and may move from place to place. An exempt executive employee can work in more than one location as long as other factors show the employee is in charge of a recognized unit with a continuing function. The same is true if an employee draws and supervises workers from a pool or supervises a team of employees drawn from other recognized units.

*Two or more other employees.*[27] The phrase "two or more other employees" means two or more full-time employees or their equivalent. For example, one full-time and two half-time employees, or four half-time employees, are equivalent to two full-time employees. The number of work hours in a workweek that constitutes a full-time equivalent is determined by the employer's policy (e.g., 40, 37.5, or 35 hours a week). Hours worked by an employee cannot be credited more than once for different executive employees, but a full-time employee can be credited as a half-time employee for both executives.

24.  W-H Reg. 29 CFR §541.101.
25.  W-H Reg. 29 CFR §541.102.
26.  W-H Reg. 29 CFR §541.103.
27.  W-H Reg. 29 CFR §541.104; W-H Op. Ltr. FLSA2006-35, 9-21-06.

**CONTRACTORS DON'T COUNT**  The term "employee" does not include independent contractors for purposes of the executive employee exemption, so someone who manages two independent contractors but no employees would not qualify as an exempt executive. Such employees could, however, be classified as exempt administrative employees if the other requirements for that exemption are met.

The supervisory responsibilities can be spread among two or more employees, but each one must direct the work of two or more other full-time employees or the equivalent. Therefore, a department with five full-time employees could have up to two exempt managers. An employee who assists the manager of a department and supervises two or more employees when the manager is absent does not meet this requirement. This means that an employee who supervises only on a short-term basis, such as during a lunch break or while a manager is on vacation, does not meet the requirement of customarily and regularly managing two or more other employees. On the other hand, the manager does not have to be physically present with the employees being supervised.

*Particular weight.*[28]  The factors to be considered in determining whether an employee's employment status recommendations are given particular weight include:

- whether it is part of the employee's job duties to make such recommendations, as shown by job descriptions and/or performance reviews;
- the frequency with which such recommendations are made or requested; and
- the frequency with which such recommendations are relied upon.

An employee's suggestions and recommendations may still be found to have particular weight even if a higher level manager's recommendation has more importance and the employee does not have the authority to make the ultimate decision as to the employee's change in status.

*Concurrent duties.*[29]  Performance of both exempt and nonexempt duties in the same workweek does not disqualify an employee from the executive exemption so long as the employee's primary duty meets the test for the executive exemption. Generally, executive employees decide when to perform nonexempt duties and still remain responsible for the success of operations under their management while performing the nonexempt work. On the other hand, nonexempt employees are generally directed by a supervisor to perform any exempt work or they perform the exempt work during defined time periods. An employee whose primary duty is production work or routine, recurrent, or repetitive tasks cannot qualify as an exempt executive even if they perform some exempt work, such as directing the work of other employees occasionally or providing input on performance issues from time to time.

> **Example 1:**  An assistant manager in a retail establishment may perform work such as serving customers, cooking food, stocking shelves, and cleaning without losing the executive exemption if the assistant manager's primary duty is management.

> **Example 2:**  A working supervisor whose primary duty is performing nonexempt work on a production line in a manufacturing plant does not become exempt merely because the working supervisor occasionally has some responsibility for directing the work of other nonexempt employees when the exempt manager is unavailable.

**DOL and courts issue interpretations.**  Several months after the regulations were finalized, the Wage and Hour Division began issuing opinion letters interpreting the rules as they related to specific fact situations presented by specific employers, hopefully providing further guidance as to how the Division would act in applying the new rules. Soon after, the federal courts also began issuing decisions interpreting the new rules.

---

28.   W-H Reg. 29 CFR §541.105.
29.   W-H Reg. 29 CFR §541.106.

*Supervision of 2 full-time employees.*[30] A federal district court ruled that an employee must direct the equivalent of 80 subordinate hours per workweek 80% of the time in order to satisfy the requirement that an executive employee must customarily and regularly direct the work of two or more other employees.

*High-ranking police and fire officers.*[31] The Wage and Hour Division said that police lieutenants, police captains, and fire battalion chiefs qualified as exempt executive employees because they perform traditional management functions, such as supervising employees, performing employee appraisals, and imposing discipline. Even though they did not have the final decision on hiring, firing, and promotions, their recommendations were given significant consideration.

*Nurse supervisors.*[32] A nurse supervisor was an exempt executive employee because her "main function" was to oversee caseload management activity and see that health services were delivered according to her employer's standards. She also assisted with interviewing and selecting employees, maintained production records, handled employee complaints, and disciplined employees.

*Retail chain store managers.*[33] Managers at coffee shops operated by Starbucks were exempt executive employees, despite performing the job duties of nonexempt, hourly "baristas" for a sizable portion of their time. Their primary duty was the performance of significant managerial functions, such as ordering and controlling inventory, deciding whom to interview and hire, training and scheduling employees, and monitoring labor costs—all of which were critical to the successful operation of their stores. The fact that they, as managers for a multi-store chain, were required to conform to the company's desire for standardization and uniformity and were visited often by regional managers did not detract from the discretion they exercised as the highest-ranking store employees.

**Professional employees – general rule.**[34] To qualify as an exempt professional employee, each of the following tests must be met:

1. The employee's primary duty must be the performance of work:
   a. requiring advanced knowledge in a field of science or learning customarily acquired by a prolonged course of specialized intellectual instruction (learned professional exemption); or
   b. requiring invention, imagination, originality, or talent in a recognized field of artistic or creative endeavor (creative professional exemption); and
2. The employee must be paid at least $455 a week on a salary or fee basis, not including board, lodging, or other facilities.

*Work requiring advanced knowledge.*[35] Work requiring advanced knowledge is work that is predominantly intellectual and includes work requiring the consistent exercise of discretion and independent judgment. Such work does not include the performance of routine mental, manual, mechanical, or physical work. An employee performing work requiring advanced knowledge generally uses that knowledge to analyze, interpret, or make deductions from varying facts or circumstances.

*Field of science or learning.* A field of science or learning includes the traditional professions of law, medicine, theology, accounting, actuarial computation, engineering, architecture, teaching, various types of physical, chemical, and biological sciences, pharmacy, and other similar occupations that have a recognized professional status. These occupations are distinguished from the mechanical arts or skilled trades where the knowledge can be of a fairly advanced type but is not in a field of science or learning.

*Customarily acquired by a prolonged course of specialized intellectual instruction.* The learned professional exemption is restricted to professions where specialized academic training is a standard prerequisite for entrance into the profession. The best evidence that an employee meets this requirement is possession of the appropriate

---

30.  Perez v. RadioShack Corp., 386 F.Supp. 2d 979 (ND Ill., 9-9-05).
31.  W-H Op. Ltr., FLSA2006-5, 3-10-06.
32.  Goff v. Bayada Nurses, Inc., 424 F. Supp. 2d 816 (ED Pa., 3-24-06).
33.  Mims v. Starbucks Corp., No. H-05-0791, 2007 U.S. Dist. LEXIS 9 (SD Tex., 1-2-07).
34.  W-H Reg. 29 CFR §541.300.
35.  W-H Reg. 29 CFR §541.301.

academic degree. But the word "customarily" means that the exemption is also available to employees in such professions who have substantially the same knowledge level and perform the same work as degreed employees, but who attained the knowledge through a combination of work experience and intellectual instruction.

Therefore, the learned professional exemption is available to lawyers who did not go to law school but were eligible to take a state bar exam because of their work experience as a law clerk. However, the exemption is not available for occupations that customarily may be performed with the general knowledge obtained from a college degree in any field, with the knowledge gained from an apprenticeship, or with training in the performance of routine mental, manual, mechanical, or physical processes. The learned professional exemption also does not apply to occupations in which most employees have acquired their skill by experience rather than by advanced specialized intellectual instruction.

**Learned professionals – examples.**[36] DOL's regulations contain several examples of professions that may not be thought of as among the traditional professions, but whose employees may qualify as learned professional exempt employees depending on the level of specialized advanced instruction they need to acquire.

*Nurses.* Nurses who are registered by the appropriate state examining board generally meet the duties requirements for the learned professional exemption. However, licensed practical nurses and other similar health care employees generally do not qualify because having a specialized advanced academic degree is not a standard requirement for entry into such occupations.

*Registered or certified medical technologists.* Registered or certified medical technologists who have successfully completed three years of academic or pre-professional study in an accredited college or university plus a fourth year of professional course work in a school of medical technology approved by the Council of Medical Education of the American Medical Association generally meet the duties requirements for the learned professional exemption.

*Dental hygienists.* Dental hygienists who have successfully completed four years of pre-professional and professional study in an accredited college or university approved by the Commission on Accreditation of Dental and Central Auxiliary Educational Programs of the American Dental Association generally meet the duties requirements for the learned professional exemption.

*Physician assistants.* Physician assistants who have successfully completed four years of pre-professional and professional study, including graduation from a physician assistant program accredited by the Accreditation Review Commission on Education for the Physician Assistant, and who are certified by the National Commission on Certification of Physician Assistants generally meet the duties requirements for the learned professional exemption.

*Accountants.* Certified public accountants generally meet the duties requirements for the learned professional exemption, and other accountants who perform similar duties but who are not CPAs may meet the duties requirements. But accounting clerks, bookkeepers, and other similar employees who perform a great deal of routine work generally will not qualify as exempt professionals.

*Chefs.* Executive chefs and sous chefs who have attained a four-year specialized academic degree in a culinary arts program generally qualify as exempt learned professionals. However, the exemption is not available to cooks who perform mainly routine mental, manual, mechanical, or physical work.

*Paralegals.* Paralegals and legal assistants generally do not qualify as exempt learned professionals, since most specialized paralegal programs are two-year associate degree programs from a community college or equivalent institution. However, the exemption is available to paralegals who possess an advanced specialized degree in another professional field and apply the advanced knowledge in that field in performing their duties as a paralegal. One example would be an engineer who is hired by a law firm as a paralegal to provide expert advice on patent or product liability cases.

---

36.   W-H Reg. 29 CFR §541.301(e).

*Athletic trainers.* Athletic trainers who have successfully completed four academic years of pre-professional and professional study in a specialized curriculum accredited by the Commission on Accreditation of Allied Health Education Programs and who are certified by the Board of Certification of the National Athletic Trainers Association Board of Certification generally meet the duties requirements for the learned professional exemption.

*Funeral directors or embalmers.* Licensed funeral directors and embalmers who are licensed by and working in a state that requires successful completion of four academic years of pre-professional and professional study, including graduation from a college of mortuary science accredited by the American Board of Funeral Service Education, generally meet the duties requirements for the learned professional exemption.

**Creative professionals.**[37] To qualify for the creative professional exemption, an employee's primary duty must involve work requiring invention, imagination, originality, or talent. Therefore, the exemption does not apply to work that can be produced by a person with general manual or intellectual ability and training. The work must also be performed in a field of artistic or creative endeavor, including music, writing, acting, and the graphic arts.

The work performed by creative professionals is distinguished from work that depends primarily on intelligence, diligence, and accuracy. While the duties performed by such employees vary greatly, the exemption depends on the extent of the invention, imagination, originality, or talent exercised by the employee, which makes it necessary to determine the exemption on a case-by-case basis. This test is generally met by the following employees:

- actors, musicians, composers, conductors, and soloists;
- painters who are given only the subject matter of the painting;
- cartoonists who are told only the title or underlying concept of a cartoon;
- essayists, novelists, short-story writers and screenplay writers who choose their own subjects and hand in a finished piece of work; and
- people holding more responsible positions in advertising agencies.

This test generally is not met by copyists, animators of motion picture cartoons, or retouchers of photographs.

*Journalists.* Journalists may meet the duties requirements for the creative professionals exemption. Employees of newspapers, magazines, television, and other media are not exempt creative professionals if they only collect, organize, and record information that is routine or already public, or if they do not contribute a unique interpretation or analysis to a news product. So, reporters who rewrite press releases or write standard recounts of public information by gathering facts on routine public events are not exempt creative professionals. They also don't qualify if their work product is subject to substantial control by their employer.

However, journalists may qualify as exempt creative professionals if their primary duty is:

- performing on the air in radio, television, or other electronic media;
- conducting investigative interviews;
- analyzing or interpreting public events;
- writing editorials, opinion columns, or other commentary; or
- acting as a narrator or commentator.

**Chefs.** Chefs can be creative professionals if their primary duty is using their originality and talent to create or design unique dishes and menu items. The exemption is only for original chefs, such as those who work at gourmet establishments.

---

37.    W-H Reg. 29 CFR §541.302.

**Teachers.**[38] Someone working for an educational institution whose primary duty is teaching, tutoring, instructing, or lecturing students at that institution is an exempt professional employee. The salary requirements for the exemption do not apply. Exempt teachers include:

- regular academic teachers;
- kindergarten or nursery school teachers;
- teachers of gifted or disabled children;
- teachers of skilled and semi-skilled trades and occupations;
- teachers of driver education;
- aircraft flight instructors;
- home economics teachers;
- vocal or instrumental music instructors; and
- teachers who also spend a considerable amount of time directing students in extracurricular activities, such as sports, drama, or journalism.

While possession of a teaching certificate is clear evidence identifying an individual as being within the scope of the exemption for teaching professionals, a teacher who is not certified may qualify for the exemption if the individual is employed as a teacher by the employing school or school system.

**Lawyers.**[39] Any employee who holds a valid license to practice law and is engaged in the practice of law is an exempt professional. The salary requirements for the professional employee exemption do not apply.

**Physicians.**[40] Any employee who holds a valid license to practice medicine and is engaged in the practice of medicine is an exempt professional. The exemption applies to physicians and other practitioners practicing in the field of medical science and healing or any of the medical specialties practiced by physicians or practitioners. The exemption also applies to any employee who holds the requisite academic degree for the general practice of medicine and is engaged in an internship or resident program pursuant to the practice of the profession. The employee does not have to be licensed when the program begins to qualify for the exemption.

The salary requirement does not apply to physicians engaged in the practice of medicine. This exception from the salary requirement does not apply to nurses, nurse practitioners, physician assistants, therapists, technologists, sanitarians, dieticians, social workers, psychologists, psychometrists, or members of other professions that service the medical profession.

**DOL and courts issue interpretations.** Several months after the regulations were finalized, the Wage and Hour Division began issuing opinion letters interpreting the rules as they related to specific fact situations presented by specific employers, hopefully providing further guidance as to how the Division would act in applying the new rules. Soon after, the federal courts also began issuing decisions interpreting the new rules.

*Respiratory therapists.*[41] The Wage and Hour Division advised that a hospital's respiratory therapists did not qualify as exempt learned professional employees because their job does not customarily require an advanced specialized degree. Only 12% of accredited RT programs are at the baccalaureate level, and individuals can be licensed and certified as an RT after only two years of specialized instruction leading to an associate's degree.

*Nonexempt employees teaching part-time.*[42] Full-time nonexempt employees of a community college who taught continuing education courses at night did not become exempt professional employees because their primary duty was not teaching, but performing their nonexempt duties, which were more important to the college.

---

38.  W-H Reg. 29 CFR §541.303.
39.  W-H Reg. 29 CFR §541.304(a)(1), (d).
40.  W-H Reg. 29 CFR §541.304; §541.600(e).
41.  W-H Op. Ltr., FLSA2006-26, 7-24-06.
42.  W-H Op. Ltr., FLSA2005-29, 8-26-05.

*Pre-school teachers.*[43] Instructors in the Head Start program are exempt professional employees because they are teachers employed by an educational institution. They engage in a wide variety of behavioral and academic activities, giving lessons on typical school subjects, developing methods to assist struggling students, conducting parent conferences, and making home visits.

*Social workers and caseworkers.*[44] The Division said that social workers for a private nonprofit social services agency may qualify as exempt learned professionals, but that the agency's caseworkers do not. The social workers need a master's degree in an aspect of social work and two years' experience beyond that. They also make independent decisions about the course of a client's therapy and develop treatment plans using a variety of therapeutic approaches. Caseworkers, however, need only a bachelor's degree in the social sciences, not specialized academic training.

*Substitute teachers.*[45] A school district's substitute teachers were exempt teaching professionals even if they did not have a teaching certificate or a bachelor's degree, so long as their primary duty was teaching.

*Physician assistants and nurse practitioners.*[46] A federal appeals court ruled that physician assistants and nurse practitioners paid on an hourly basis were not exempt professional employees. First, they were not exempt professionals because they were paid on an hourly basis rather than a salary basis. There is an exception to the salary basis requirement for employees who hold a license to practice medicine and who actually practice medicine, but the court deferred to the DOL, which has consistently ruled that PAs and RNs must be paid on a salary basis because they are not engaged in the practice of medicine.

*Newspaper reporters.*[47] A federal district court held that newspaper reporters were not exempt creative professional employees because their primary duty depended mainly on their intelligence, diligence, and accuracy, as opposed to invention, imagination, and talent. They covered only local news, and the majority of their articles were rewrites of press releases and community events announcements.

*Part-time professors.*[48] A university professor who qualifies as an exempt teacher is not subject to the general salary requirement for other professional employees, so the professor's compensation may be subject to deductions if the professor works less than a full day, without losing the exemption.

**Blue collar workers and first responders are not exempt.**[49] The white collar exemptions do not apply to manual laborers or other "blue collar" workers whose work involves performing repetitive operations with their hands, physical skill, and energy. Such employees gain the skills and knowledge they need through apprenticeships and on-the-job training, not through a course of specialized intellectual instruction that qualifies an employee as an exempt learned professional.

Therefore, non-management production line employees and non-management employees in maintenance, construction, and similar occupations such as carpenters, electricians, mechanics, plumbers, iron workers, craftsmen, operating engineers, longshoremen, construction workers, and laborers must be paid at least the minimum wage and overtime pay under the FLSA. They are not exempt no matter how much they earn.

The white collar exemptions also do not apply to the following employees, no matter their rank or pay level:

| | |
|---|---|
| police officers | park rangers |
| detectives | firefighters |
| deputy sheriffs | paramedics |
| state troopers | emergency medical technicians |
| highway patrol officers | ambulance personnel |

---

43. Ramos v. Lee County School Board, No. 2:04-cv-308-FtM-33SPC, 2005 U.S. Dist. LEXIS 21770 (MD Fla., 9-29-05).
44. W-H Op. Ltr., FLSA2005-50, 11-4-05.
45. W-H Op. Ltr., FLSA2005-39, 10-13-05.
46. Belt v. EmCare, Inc. 444 F.3d 403 (5 CA, 2006); cert. den. (2006) 127 S. Ct. 349.
47. Wang v. Chinese Daily News, Inc. 435 F.Supp. 2d 1042 (CD Calif., 6-7-06).
48. W-H Op. Ltr., FLSA2005-34, 9-23-05.
49. W-H Reg. 29 CFR §541.3.

| investigators | rescue workers |
|---|---|
| inspectors | hazardous material workers |
| correctional officers | similar employees |
| probation officers | |

who perform work such as:

- preventing, controlling, or extinguishing fires of any type;
- rescuing fire, crime, or accident victims;
- preventing or detecting crimes;
- conducting investigations or inspections for violations of law;
- performing surveillance;
- pursuing, restraining, and apprehending suspects;
- detaining or supervising suspected and convicted criminals, including those on probation or parole;
- interviewing witnesses;
- interrogating and fingerprinting suspects;
- preparing investigative reports; or
- other similar work.

These categories of employees are not exempt executive employees because their primary duty is not management. Therefore, a police officer or firefighter whose primary duty is to investigate crimes or fight fires is not an exempt executive merely because the employee directs the work of other employees in conducting an investigation or fighting a fire. These employees are not exempt administrative employees either because their primary duty is not the performance of work directly related to the management or general business operations of their employer. Finally, they are also not exempt professional employees because their work does not require advanced knowledge customarily acquired by a prolonged course of specialized instruction. While some of these employees may be required to have college degrees, a specialized academic degree is not a standard prerequisite.

**Computer-related professional employees.**[50] The definition of exempt professional employees includes highly skilled computer professionals working as systems analysts, programmers, software engineers, or in similar positions who meet the other requirements for professional employee status.

To satisfy the duties test for the computer professional exemption, the employee's primary duty must consist of one or more of the following:

1. the application of systems analysis techniques and procedures, including consulting with users, to determine hardware, software, or system functional specifications;

2. the design, development, documentation, analysis, creation, testing, or modification of computer systems or programs, including prototypes, based on and related to user or system design specifications;

3. the creation, design, documentation, testing, or modification of computer programs related to machine operating systems; or

4. a combination of these duties, the performance of which requires the same level of skills.

Highly skilled computer professionals who meet the primary duty test must be paid a salary or fee of at least $455 per week to qualify for the professional employee exemption. The professional employee exemption also applies to hourly paid computer professionals if they are paid at least $27.63 an hour.[51] Hourly paid computer professionals making less than this amount are not exempt from the FLSA, regardless of their professional duties.

---

50. W-H Reg. 29 CFR §541.400-§541.402.
51. FLSA §13(a)(17); W-H Reg. 29 CFR §541.400(b); DOL Field Assistance Bulletin 2006-3, 12-14-06.

The computer professional exemption is not available to employees engaged in the manufacture or repair of computer hardware and related equipment. Employees whose work is highly dependent on the use of computers and computer software programs but who are not engaged in systems analysis and programming or similar computer-related occupations also do not qualify for the computer professional exemption.

On the other hand, some computer employees, whether they qualify or not for the computer professional exemption, may qualify as an exempt executive or administrative employee. A senior or lead computer programmer who supervises two or more other programmers in a recognized department of the employer may be an exempt executive employee. Systems analysts and programmers can meet the duties requirements for the administrative exemption if their primary duty consists of planning, scheduling, and coordinating activities required to develop systems to solve complex problems of the employer or the employer's customers.

*Technology support specialists.*[52] "Information technology support specialists" (ITSS) are not exempt computer professional employees because the primary duty of installing, configuring, testing and troubleshooting computer applications, networks, and hardware is not the equivalent of any of the three types of primary duties needed to satisfy the exemption.

**Outside sales employees.**[53] To qualify as an exempt outside sales employee, each of the following tests must be met:

1. The employee's primary duty must be:
   a. making sales of tangible or intangible items such as goods, insurance, stocks, bonds, or real estate; or
   b. obtaining orders or contracts for services or the use of facilities; and
2. The employee must customarily and regularly work away from the employer's place or places of business in performing the employee's primary duty.

In determining an outside sales employee's primary duty, work that is performed incidental to and in conjunction with the employee's own outside sales or solicitations is regarded as exempt outside sales work. This includes incidental deliveries and collections, and it also includes promotional work so long as it is related to the employee's own sales and not sales made by someone else. Other work that furthers the employee's sales efforts also is exempt work, including writing sales reports, updating or revising catalogs, planning itineraries, and attending sales meetings or conferences.

 **NO SALARY TEST** There is no salary requirement to qualify as an exempt outside sales employee.

*Sales of facilities and services.* Obtaining orders for the use of facilities includes selling time on radio, television, or other electronic media, soliciting advertising for newspapers and other publications, and soliciting freight for railroads and other transportation facilities. The outside sales exemption also applies to employees who sell or take orders for a service that may be performed for the customer by someone other than the employee taking the order.

*Away from the employer's place of business.* The outside sales exemption applies only to employees who work away from the employer's place of business, generally at the customer's place of business or the customer's home, if the employee is selling door-to-door. Sales made by telephone, mail, or the Internet do not qualify as outside sales unless such means are used merely to supplement personal calls. Any fixed site used by a sales employee as a headquarters or for telephone solicitations is considered one of the employer's places of business.

However, an outside sales employee does not lose the exemption by displaying samples in hotel sample rooms while traveling from city to city. Such rooms are not considered the employer's places of business. The same holds true if the sales employee displays the employer's products at a trade show, even if selling actually occurs, rather than just sales promotion, so long as the trade show lasts only one or two weeks.

---

52.    W-H Op. Ltr., FLSA2006-42, 10-26-06.
53.    W-H Reg. 29 CFR §541.500 - §541.504; §541.701.

*Customarily and regularly.* The term "customarily and regularly" means a frequency that must be greater than occasional but less than constant. Tasks performed customarily and regularly are performed each workweek rather than on an isolated or one-time basis.

*Drivers who sell.* Drivers who both deliver and sell products qualify as outside sales employees only if their primary duty is making sales. In making this determination, incidental work related to the employee's own sales, including loading, driving, or delivering products, is exempt outside sales work. The factors to be considered in determining a driver's primary duty include:

- a comparison of the driver's duties with those of other truck drivers and sales employees;
- possession of a selling or solicitor's license if one is required by local law;
- whether there are customary or contractual arrangements concerning amounts of products to be delivered;
- the driver's job description;
- the employer's qualifications for hiring for the driver's position;
- sales training;
- attendance at sales conferences;
- method of payment; and
- the proportion of earnings directly attributable to sales.

Drivers who may qualify as exempt outside sales employees include:

- a driver who is the only contact between the employer and the customer, calls on customers and takes orders, delivers products to the customer when the order is taken or at a later time, and is paid in relation to the amount of products sold;
- a driver who obtains or solicits orders from someone who has the authority to commit the customer for purchases;
- a driver who calls on prospects along the driver's route to solicit sales of the employer's products; and
- a driver who solicits additional sales from established customers even thought the initial sale was made by someone else.

Drivers who generally would not qualify as exempt outside sales employees include:

- a driver whose primary duty is to deliver products sold through vending machines and to keep the machines stocked, in good repair, and in good locations for sales;
- a driver who calls regularly on established customers and delivers some of the employer's products at each call, the amount of which is determined by how much the customer sold since the last delivery and is not due to the driver's solicitation efforts; and
- a driver primarily engaged in delivering products to customers and performing promotional activities, such as placing advertising materials, putting prices on goods, arranging products on shelves, in coolers, or in cabinets, rotating stock, and otherwise servicing display cases, unless such work helps further the driver's own sales efforts.

**DOL and courts issue interpretations.** Several months after the regulations were finalized, the Wage and Hour Division began issuing opinion letters interpreting the rules as they related to specific fact situations presented by specific employers, hopefully providing further guidance as to how the Division would act in applying the new rules. Soon after, the federal courts also began issuing decisions interpreting the new rules.

*Mortgage loan officers.*[54] Mortgage loan officers qualified as exempt outside sales employees because there primary duty was the sale of mortgage loan packages and they met clients at the clients' homes on a recurring basis. The activities they performed at the employer's office or in their own homes were incidental to their outside sales activities, so they also qualified as exempt outside sales work.

---

54.    W-H Op. Ltr., FLSA2006-11, 3-31-06.

*Real estate salespersons.*[55] A federal district court ruled that real estate salespersons who sold homes at a subdivision site to which they were assigned by their employer were not exempt outside sales employees because the entire subdivision site was the employer's place of business. The fact that the site was separate from the employer's home office in another city did not mean the employees were working away from the employer's place of business, the court said.

The DOL disagreed with this reasoning, pointing out that it has long said that real estate salespersons working from a model home on a tract from which parcels of land are sold, whether or not they are improved, who leave the model home to show homes and engage in other sales activities are making sales "away from" the employer's place of business—even if all the property shown to prospects is within the tract on which the model home is located.[56]

However, the DOL concluded that the outside sales exemption does not apply to employees who sell time-shares on site at resorts because they are not engaged away from the employer's place or places of business. Resorts in which timeshares are sold are generally maintained on a permanent basis as a location of the employer and are staffed with the personnel necessary to maintain the resort facilities.[57]

**Work under different exemptions.**[58] An employee whose primary duty involves a combination of work from two or more exemptions qualifies as an exempt employee. The work that is exempt under one category of exempt employees does not defeat the exemption under any other category.

A federal appeals court has affirmed that the "combination exemption" does not relieve an employer of the burden to establish the other requirements of the exemptions whose duties are combined. Accordingly, an employee whose primary duties combined elements of the administrative and outside sales exemptions, but who did not meet the other requirements for those exemptions, was a nonexempt employee.[59]

**Determining an employee's primary duty.** Under each of the white collar exemptions, an employee qualifies as exempt only if the employee's primary duty is the performance of exempt work as defined in that particular exemption. "Primary duty" means the principal, main, major, or most important duty that the employee performs. The determination of an employee's primary duty is based on all the facts underlying an employee's particular situation, but the major emphasis must be on the character of the employee's job as a whole.

Factors that are considered when making such a determination include:

- the relative importance of the exempt duties when compared to other duties performed by the employee;
- the amount of time spent performing exempt work;
- the employee's relative freedom from supervision; and
- the relationship between the salary paid the employee and the wages paid to other employees for the kind of nonexempt work performed by the employee.

*Percentage of time spent on exempt work.* The amount of time spent on exempt work can be useful in determining an employee's primary duty, but it is not the sole factor. An employee who spends more than 50% of his or her time performing exempt work will generally satisfy the primary duty test. But time is not the only test, and nothing requires that exempt employees spend more than 50% of their time performing exempt work. Such employees may still meet the primary duty requirement if other factors support that result.

---

55.   Billingslea v. Brayson Homes, Inc., No. 1:04-CV-00962-JEC, 2006 U.S. Dist. LEXIS 11707 (ND Ga., 3-7-06).
56.   W-H Op. Ltr., FLSA2007-1, 1-25-07; FLSA2007-2, 1-25-07.
57.   W-H Op. Ltr., FLSA2007-4, 1-25-07.
58.   W-H Reg. 29 CFR §541.708; Pinillia v. Northwings Accessories Corp., No. 07-21564-CIV, 2007 U.S. Dist. LEXIS 83842 (SD Fla., 11-13-07).
59.   IntraComm, Inc. v. Bajaj, 492 F.3d 285 (4 CA, 7-5-07).

*Example:* Assistant managers in a retail store who perform exempt work such as supervising other employees, ordering merchandise, managing the budget, and authorizing bill payment may have management as their primary duty even if they spend more than 50% of their time performing nonexempt work such as working at the cash register. But if they are closely supervised and earn only a little more than nonexempt employees working at the cash register, then they would not meet the primary duty requirement.

**Work that is 'directly and closely related' to exempt work.**[60] Work that would normally be considered nonexempt work is actually exempt work if it is "directly and closely related" to the performance of exempt work. "Directly and closely related" means tasks that are related to exempt work and that contribute to or facilitate the performance of exempt work. Such work includes:

- routine work without which exempt employees cannot properly perform their jobs;
- recordkeeping;
- monitoring and adjusting machinery;
- taking notes;
- using a computer to create documents or presentations;
- opening the mail to read it and make decisions; and
- using a photocopier or fax machine.

Occasional tasks that cannot practicably be performed by nonexempt employees and that help an exempt employee carry out exempt functions and responsibilities are exempt work. Here are the factors to consider when determining whether such work is exempt work:

- whether the same work is performed by the exempt employee's subordinates;
- can the work be delegated to a nonexempt employee;
- whether the exempt employee performs the task occasionally or frequently; and
- whether there is an industry practice for the exempt employee to perform the nonexempt work.

**Trainees are not exempt.**[61] The white collar exemptions do not apply to employees who are training for a job in one of these categories and are not performing the duties of an administrative, executive, professional, computer professional, or outside sales employee.

**Emergency nonexempt work does not cause exemption to be lost.**[62] An exempt employee does not lose the exemption because the employee performs nonexempt work because of an emergency that threatens employees' safety, may cause a disruption of the employer's operations, or may cause serious damage to the employer's property. Emergencies do not include things that are not beyond the employer's control or for which the employer can reasonably provide in the ordinary course of business, and they must occur rarely and be events that could not have been anticipated.

Following are some examples showing the distinction between emergency exempt work and routine nonexempt work.

- a mine superintendent who helps get workers out who are trapped after an explosion is still an exempt executive;
- assisting nonexempt employees during busy periods is not exempt work;
- replacing a nonexempt employee during the first day or a partial day of the nonexempt employee's illness may be exempt work depending on the size of the establishment and the department, the nature of the industry, the consequences of failing to replace the nonexempt employee, and whether the employee's place could be filled promptly with another nonexempt employee; and
- regular cleaning and repair of equipment is not emergency work, even if it is needed to prevent fire or explosion, unless the need for the repair is caused by an accident that the employer could not anticipate.

---

60. W-H Reg. 29 CFR §541.703; §541.707.
61. W-H Reg. 29 CFR §541.705.
62. W-H Reg. 29 CFR §541.706.

**Salary requirement.**[63] As noted in the discussions of the individual exemptions for administrative, executive, and professional employees, an employee must be paid on a salary basis at least $455 per week, exclusive of board, lodging, or other facilities. Administrative and professional employees can also be paid on a fee basis for a single job, which must equate to at least $455 per week if the employee worked 40 hours. The salary or fee basis requirement is $380 if the employee works in American Samoa for an employer other than the U.S. government.

 **EQUIVALENT AMOUNTS** The salary requirement is met if the employee is paid a salary of at least $910 biweekly, $985.83 semimonthly, or $1,971.66 monthly.

**Highly compensated employees.**[64] An employee with total annual compensation of at least $100,000 is an exempt "white collar" employee if the employee customarily and regularly performs one or more of the exempt duties of an exempt administrative, executive, or professional employee. The employee's compensation must include a salary of at least $455 a week. Total annual compensation may also include commissions, nondiscretionary bonuses, and other nondiscretionary compensation earned during a 52-week period. Total annual compensation does not include board, lodging, and other facilities, payments for medical insurance, payments for life insurance, contributions to retirement plans, and the cost of other fringe benefits.

*'Catch-up payment.'* If the employee's compensation has not reached $100,000 by the last pay period of the 52-week period, the employer can make one final payment to bring the total annual compensation up to $100,000. The payment must be made during the last pay period of the 52-week period or within one month after the end of the period. Any such "catch-up" payment can only count toward the prior year's total annual compensation for purposes of the highly compensated employee exemption. If such a payment is not made, then the employer must determine whether the employee qualifies as exempt under one of the tests for the specific exemptions.

*'Partial-year employment.'* An employee who does not work a full year because the employee was hired after the year began or leaves employment before the year ends can still qualify for the highly compensated employee exemption. To qualify, the employee must receive a pro rata portion of the $100,000 minimum based on the number of weeks the employee was employed. A "catch-up" payment to qualify the employee may be made within one month of the employee's separation from employment.

*'52-week period.'* It is up to the employer to choose the 52-week period as the year for determining an employee's total annual compensation. It can be any 52-week period, such as a calendar year, fiscal year, or an anniversary of hire year. If the employer does not choose a year, the calendar year period will be used.

*Not for production workers.* The highly compensated employee exemption applies only to employees whose primary duty involves office or nonmanual work. Therefore, non-management production line workers and non-management workers in maintenance, construction, and similar occupations who perform work involving repetitive operations with their hands, physical skill, and energy are not exempt under this exemption no matter how much they are paid. This includes carpenters, electricians, plumbers, mechanics, iron workers, craftsmen, operating engineers, longshoremen, construction workers, and laborers.

**White collar exempt employees must be paid on a salary or fee basis.**[65] For those exempt employees who must be paid on a salary basis, the general rule is that they must be paid their guaranteed salary in any workweek in which they do any work regardless of the quality or quantity of the work performed. It generally does not matter how many days or hours they work, but they do not have to be paid for any workweeks in which they do no work at all. An exempt employee is not paid on a salary basis if deductions from the employee's full salary are made for absences caused by the employer or by the operating requirements of the business. So long as the employee is ready, willing, and able to work, deductions may not be made for time when work is not available.

---

63.     W-H Reg. 29 CFR §541.600.
64.     W-H Reg. 29 CFR §541.601.
65.     W-H Reg. 29 CFR §541.602; W-H Op. Ltr., FLSA 2005-7, 1-7-05.

**PLANNED SALARY REDUCTIONS OK** Even though exempt employees' salaries cannot be reduced because of variations in the quantity of work performed, a federal appeals court said it was lawful for an employer to prospectively reduce an exempt employee's salary to accommodate the employer's business needs. In this case, a retailer generally reduced the work hours and salaries of its pharmacists each year during periods when business is generally anticipated to be slow. The court said that was lawful because the employer wasn't changing salaries so often that the exempt employees were really being paid an hourly wage.[66]

*Employees performing same duties may not have same status.* The DOL advised a hospital that it may pay one nurse practitioner as a nonexempt employee without jeopardizing the exempt status of the other nurse practitioners. Having some employees within the same job classification who perform the same exempt duties as others but who are paid on a different (hourly) basis does not affect the exempt status of other employees paid on a salary basis. The FLSA's white collar exemptions are not based upon a job title or job classification, but upon the salary and duties of each individual employee.[67]

There are several exceptions from the prohibition against deductions from an employee's salary. They include:

*Absences for personal reasons.* Deductions from an exempt employee's pay may be made for absences of one or more full days for personal reasons, other than sickness or disability (e.g., inclement weather). But such deductions may not be made for partial day absences.

*Absences for sickness or disability.* Deductions from an exempt employee's pay may be made for absences of one or more full days caused by sickness or disability (including work-related accidents) if the employee is receiving pay under the employer's sick or disability pay plan or under a state disability insurance law or workers' compensation law. Such deductions can also be made if the employee has not yet qualified for the employer's plan and after the employee has exhausted available leave under the plan.

In order for an employer to deduct from an exempt employee's salary for full days due to sickness or disability, the deduction must be made under a bona fide sickness or disability plan. In order to be a bona fide plan, the employer's plan must provide for a reasonable amount of paid sick leave. Where an employer's plan provided for one paid sick/personal day per year but also allowed employees to use their 1-3 weeks of vacation time as sick leave (an employee had to work one year to be eligible for one week of paid vacation), the Wage and Hour Division said the plan was bona fide and the employer could dock exempt employees who were out sick for one or more full days and were out of sick and vacation leave or had not yet become eligible for the leave without losing their exempt status.[68]

*Jury duty, witnesses, military leave.* An employer cannot make deductions from an exempt employee's pay for absences caused by jury duty, attendance as a witness, or temporary military leave, but the employer can offset any amounts received as jury fees, witness fees, or military pay for a week against the employee's salary for that week without losing the exemption. Also, the employee does not have to be paid if he or she does not do any work during the week.

*Safety rule infractions.* Deductions from an exempt employee's pay may be made for penalties imposed in good faith for violations of safety rules of major significance. Such rules include those relating to the prevention of serious danger in the workplace or to other employees, such as rules prohibiting smoking in explosive plants, oil refineries, and coal mines.

*Workplace conduct rule violations.* Employers can impose unpaid disciplinary suspensions of one or more full days for violations of workplace conduct rules if the suspensions are imposed in good faith under a written policy applied to all employees. Therefore, an exempt employee can be suspended without pay for three days for violating a written policy prohibiting sexual harassment, or for six days for violating a written

---

66. In re Wal-Mart Stores, Inc., 395 F.3d 1177 (10 CA, 2005); In re Wal-Mart Stores, Inc., No. 96-civ-91139-ZLW-CBS, 2007 U.S. Dist. LEXIS 5019 (D Colo., 1-23-07).
67. W-H Op. Ltr., FLSA2005-20, 8-19-05.
68. W-H Op. Ltr., FLSA2006-32, 9-14-06.

policy prohibiting workplace violence, but the same employee cannot be suspended for 4.5 days for violating a written policy prohibiting employee theft.

*Initial and terminal weeks.* An employer is not required to pay an exempt employee's full salary in the first or last week of employment. Instead, the employer may pay a proportionate part of the employee's full salary for the time actually worked during those weeks. The employer can pay an hourly or daily equivalent of the employee's full salary for the time actually worked. This does not mean that the employer can pay a proportionate part of the weekly salary if the employee occasionally works a few days per week.

**Deducting from leave banks for partial day absences is OK.**[69] Without affecting an employee's exempt status, an employer may deduct from the employee's accrued leave account for partial day absences, so long as the employee's full guaranteed salary is paid for the workweek when the deductions are taken.

**Motion picture employees.**[70] The salary basis requirement does not apply to an employee in the motion picture production industry who is paid at a base rate of at least $695 per week, exclusive of board, lodging, and other facilities. Such employees can be paid a proportionate amount of their base rate based on the number of days they work in any week in which they do not work a full week (based on a week of not more than six days). Exempt employees in motion picture production can also be paid a daily rate if the employee is in a job category that does not have a weekly base rate and the daily base rate would provide at least $695 if six days were worked or if the employee is in a job category with a weekly base rate of at least $695 and the daily base rate is at least one-sixth of the weekly base rate.

 **CONDITIONAL BONUSES CAN AFFECT EXEMPT STATUS** In an opinion letter, the Wage and Hour Division said that pharmacists participating in an employer's incentive programs would not be exempt because the programs' incentive payments would be deducted from the pharmacists' final paycheck if they didn't work for the employer for a minimum length of time.[71]

*Family and Medical Leave Act provides an exception*[72] Under the Family and Medical Leave Act of 1993 (see Section 4.2), employers must grant employees up to 12 weeks of unpaid leave for the birth or adoption of a child, to care for a seriously ill family member, or because the employee is seriously ill. This leave may be taken intermittently rather than all at once, and in blocks of less than one day. Under FMLA and FLSA regulations, an exempt employee does not lose his or her exemption merely because the employer provides unpaid FMLA leave of less than a day. For this exception to the salary basis test to apply, the employer and the employee must be covered by the FMLA and the leave must qualify as FMLA leave. If not, the FLSA's docking restrictions remain in effect.

The DOL said the FMLA exception for intermittent leave did not apply where a state law allowed employees to take up to 24 hours of unpaid leave to participate in a child's school activities or to accompany a child or elderly relative to routine medical or dental care. The employer could make deductions from an exempt employee's pay in such circumstances only for full-day absences because the leave was for personal reasons other than sickness or disability.[73]

For nonexempt employees paid by the fluctuating workweek method (see Section 2.6-4), the employer can pay such employees on an hourly basis and pay only for the hours the employee works during the period during which intermittent or reduced schedule FMLA leave is taken. During such periods (including weeks during which no leave is taken), the employee must be compensated at 1½ times the employee's regular rate of pay for hours worked over 40 in a workweek. The regular rate is determined by dividing the employee's weekly salary by the employee's average schedule of hours worked during weeks in which FMLA leave is not taken. If the employer chooses to use this method of payment, it must do so for all employees being paid by the fluctuating workweek method. Without a conversion to hourly pay, no deduction for intermittent FMLA leave can be taken.

---

69.     69 F.R. 22178, 4-23-04; W-H Op. Ltr., FLSA2005-7, 1-7-05.
70.     W-H Reg. 29 CFR §541.709.
71.     W-H Op. Ltr., 2-20-01.
72.     W-H Reg. 29 CFR §825.206; 29 CFR §541.602(b)(7).
73      W-H Op. Ltr., FLSA2007-6, 2-8-07.

*Public sector employers get a break.* Recognizing that this definition of salary basis is particularly burdensome in the public sector, where tax revenues are used to pay employees' salaries and laws often prevent the payment of employees for hours not worked, DOL regulations ease the burden.[74] Under these rules, the exemption will not be lost where a public sector (government) employer is required by law, regulation, or principals of public accountability to reduce an employee's pay for absences for personal reasons or for absences of less than one workday due to sickness or injury and where accrued leave is not used by an employee because:

- permission to use the leave was not asked for or was denied;
- the employee's accrued leave has been exhausted; or
- the employee chooses to use leave without pay.

If the reduction is due to a budget-required furlough, the employee remains exempt except during the week of the furlough. This exemption, however, does not apply to the ban on improper deductions.

**DOL and courts issue interpretations.** Several months after the regulations were finalized, the Wage and Hour Division began issuing opinion letters interpreting the rules as they related to specific fact situations presented by specific employers, hopefully providing further guidance as to how the Division would act in applying the new rules. Soon after, the federal courts also began issuing decisions interpreting the new rules.

*Accountants paid a percentage of fees.*[75] The Division said that accountants who were paid a percentage of the fees charged by their company for individual transactions were not compensated on a fee basis, so they were not exempt professional employees. The compensation scheme was more like a piecework arrangement than a fee arrangement because a fee is generally paid for a unique job, rather than for a series of jobs repeated over and over again for which payments on an identical basis are made over and over again.

*Threats to dock pay.*[76] When an employer installed card readers to track employees' coming and going from their manufacturing plant and told exempt employees that timesheet comparisons to the card reader reports could result in "pay adjustments," this did not change the status of the company's exempt employees. A federal appeals court said there was no "significant likelihood" of pay deductions since no exempt employee's pay had been docked and the reports were pulled about once a month, but only in response to a concern about a particular employee's absenteeism.

*Breakage deductions.*[77] The Division said that an employer's policy to deduct from exempt employees' salaries or seek reimbursement from them for breakage, loss, or destruction of property would violate the FLSA's requirement that exempt employees' salaries be paid "free and clear."

*Deductions from bonuses.*[78] Any compensation beyond an exempt employee's salary is a matter of agreement between the employer and employee, and the prohibition against improper deductions from an exempt employee's salary does not apply to such additional compensation. Accordingly, an employer can take deductions for bad checks and other cash shortages from bonus payments to exempt managers without affecting their exempt status.

*Work hour requirements.*[79] The Division said that an employer can require exempt employees to work a minimum number hours per week and to make up work time lost due to personal absences of less than a day if it does not dock the pay of employees who fail to comply with the policies. The employer also could not suspend exempt employees as a possible penalty for failing to comply, since the attendance rule is not a "workplace conduct rule."

---

74.   W-H Reg. 29 CFR §541.710; W-H Op. Ltr., FLSA2005-16, 4-11-05.
75.   W-H Op. Ltr., FLSA2005-24, 8-26-05.
76.   Whisman v. Ford Motor Co., No. 04-3877, 2005 U.S. App. LEXIS 23284 (6 CA, 10-26-05).
77.   W-H Op. Ltr., FLSA2006-7, 3-10-06.
78    W-H Op. Ltr., FLSA2006-24NA, 11-3-06.
79.   W-H Op. Ltr., FLSA2006-6, 3-10-06.

*Using tip credit as salary.*[80] An employer cannot count an exempt administrative employee's tips as a credit toward the minimum salary requirement of $455 per week. A tip credit can only be taken against a portion of an hourly employee's tips toward the minimum wage. Also, a tip is an employee's property and is not compensation paid by the employer.

*Salary paid in foreign currency.*[81] The Division said that amounts paid to an employee in U.S. dollars and in foreign currency may be combined in order to satisfy the salary requirement for an exempt employee. The employer must use the generally available exchange rate in effect at the time of payment in the vicinity where the employee is working.

*Part-time exempt employees.*[82] The Division explained that an employee holding a part-time position must still be paid a salary of at least $455 to qualify as an exempt white collar employee, subject to limited exemptions for teachers, lawyers, and physicians who are not governed by the general salary requirement.

*Requirement to report 40 hours.* Where exempt employees were required to report at least 40 hours per week to receive their full salary and would receive less if they entered fewer than 40 hours, the employees did not lose their exempt status because the employer had a process to correct the underpayments once the employees corrected their time-entry errors.[83]

**Effect of improper docking of pay.**[84] In general, an employer that makes improper deductions from the pay of exempt employees does not intend to pay those employees on a salary basis and will lose the exemption for them. The factors the DOL will consider when determining whether an employer has an actual practice of making improper deductions include:

- the number of improper deductions, especially when compared to the whole number of employee infractions resulting in discipline;
- the time period during which the improper deductions were made;
- the number and geographic location of employees whose pay was improperly reduced;
- the number and geographic location of managers who made the improper deductions; and
- whether the employer has a clearly communicated policy permitting or prohibiting improper deductions.

If the facts show that the employer has an actual practice of making improper deductions, the employer will lose the exemption for the time period when the improper deductions were made, but only for employees in the same job classification and working for the same managers responsible for the improper deductions.

*Example:* If a manager routinely docks the pay of exempt engineers at a company facility for partial-day personal absences, then all engineers working at that facility whose pay could have been docked by that manager would lose the exemption. Engineers working at other facilities or for other managers at the same facility would remain exempt.

*Exemption not lost for isolated deductions.* On the other hand, improper deductions that are isolated or inadvertent will not result in loss of the exemption for the employees whose pay was docked if the employer reimburses the employees for the improper deductions.

*Safe harbor provision.* If an employer:

- has a clearly communicated policy prohibiting improper pay deductions;
- includes a complaint mechanism;
- reimburses employees for any improper deductions; and
- makes a good faith commitment to comply in the future;

---

80.   Chao v. Fossco, Inc., No. 03-3360-CV-S-JCE, 2006 U.S. Dist. LEXIS 23400 (WD Mo., 4-13-06).
81.   W-H Op. Ltr., FLSA2006-17, 5-23-06.
82.   W-H Op. Ltr., FLSA2006-10NA, 6-1-06.
83.   Acs v. Detroit Edison Co., 444 F.3d 763 (6 CA, 4-14-06).
84.   W-H Reg. 29 CFR §541.603.

the employer will not lose the exemption for any employees unless the employer willfully violates the policy by continuing to make improper deductions after getting employee complaints. If an employer fails to reimburse employees for any improper deductions or continues to make improper deductions after employees have complained, the exemption is lost during the time period in which the improper deductions were made for employees in the same job classifications and working for the same managers who made the improper deductions.[85] The employer can best protect itself with a written policy prohibiting improper deductions that was distributed to employees before any improper deductions were made, either at the time of hire, in an employee handbook, or on a company Intranet.

**Payment on an hourly, daily, or shift basis.**[86] An employer may compute an exempt employee's earnings on an hourly, daily, or shift basis without losing the exemption if the employment agreement also includes a guarantee of at least the minimum weekly required amount regardless of the number of hours, shifts, or days worked, and a reasonable relationship exists between the guaranteed amount and the amount actually earned.

The reasonable relationship test is met if the weekly guarantee is roughly equivalent to the employee's usual earnings at the assigned hourly, daily, or shift rate for the employer's normal workweek.

> *Example:* An exempt employee who is guaranteed compensation of at least $500 a week for any week in which the employee works, and who normally works four or five shifts each week, may be paid $150 per shift without violating the salary basis requirement.

Where disabled exempt employees are able to work part-time while recuperating from an illness or injury, the Wage-Hour Division approved an employer's plan guaranteeing the employees their full hourly rate (calculated as a pro-rata share of their pre-disability salary) for all hours the employees anticipated working during a week, whether or not the employees actually worked that number of hours, and a reduced amount for hours the employees do not anticipate working during a week because of their disability. However, the Division did not approve a plan where the recuperating employees would be paid the discounted disability pay and were to be paid at their full hourly rate only for hours actually worked. In this situation, there was no reasonable relationship between the weekly guarantee of $250 ($455 as of August 23, 2004) and the employee's actual normal earnings.[87]

**Extra compensation is OK.**[88] An employer can provide an exempt employee with additional compensation without violating the salary basis requirement, so long as the employee is guaranteed the required amount on a salary basis. Such additional compensation can be calculated and paid on any basis, including:

- commissions on sales;
- straight time or time-and-a-half pay for hours worked beyond the normal workweek;
- shift differential;
- flat sum; or
- paid time off.

**Employers can track exempt employees' hours.**[89] An employer can require exempt employees to track and record the hours they work without losing the exemption, even though such recordkeeping is not necessary under the FLSA. Employers can also require exempt employees to work a specified schedule.

**What employers need to do to comply with the regulations.** Nearly all employers in the U.S. are affected by the DOL's revised white collar exemption regulations, and their human resources and payroll departments will need to perform some or all of the following tasks to remain in compliance.

---

85. Baden-Winterwood v. Lifetime Fitness, No. 2:06-cv-99, 2007 U.S. Dist. LEXIS 49777 (SD Ohio, 7-10-07).
86. W-H Reg. 29 CFR §541.604(b).
87. W-H Op. Ltr., FLSA2004-5, 6-25-04.
88. W-H Reg. 29 CFR §541.604(a).
89. 69 F.R. 22178, 4-23-04; W-H Op. Ltr., FLSA2005-5, 1-7-05; W-H Op. Ltr., FLSA 2005-16, 4-11-05.

*Find employees earning less than $23,660 annually.* Employers need to identify all their employees who earn less than $23,660 annually, and then determine if any of them are salaried employees who are currently being treated as exempt. For any such employees, the employer will have to decide whether to raise their salaries to keep their exempt status (if their primary duty qualifies for exemption under the new rules) or to reclassify them as nonexempt and pay them overtime.

*Find employees earning $100,000 or more annually.* Employers should identify all their employees who earn at least $100,000 annually. While they will probably fit under one of the white collar exemptions as defined in the new rules, the status of any who are not currently classified as exempt should be re-examined to see if they meet the new highly compensated employee exemption test.

*Use job analyses to revamp job descriptions.* A new job analysis for each position needs to be conducted, focusing on duties that may fit under the white collar exemptions. This should be followed by revising individual job descriptions based on the results of the job analyses.

*Make status changes in payroll system.* If the exempt/nonexempt status of any employees is changed as a result of the job analyses and revised job descriptions, make sure that the changes are entered into the payroll system.

*Take advantage of new pay docking rules.* If an employer wants to take advantage of the new pay docking rules, including the safe harbor, it will have to design a new discipline policy that complies with the rules and make sure it is communicated to all employees. A model salary basis policy can be found on the DOL website at www.dol.gov/esa/regs/compliance/whd/fairpay/modelpolicy_pf.htm

*Watch out for union contract obligations.* Even though employers may have employees who can be classified as exempt, the employees may be covered by a collective bargaining agreement that requires overtime pay. If that is the case, the employer must follow the contract.

*Tell employees in advance.* Employers should communicate with employees in advance of conducting job analyses and revising job descriptions so they know what is coming and why it is being done. An employee's exempt/nonexempt status can be a very sensitive issue, and a change from getting overtime pay to not getting overtime pay, or vice versa, can trigger emotional reactions. Some one-on-one communications and reassurance of value to the employer will be necessary in many situations.

# 2.4-2 Retail and Service Industry Exemption

Employees in retail or service industries are exempt from the overtime pay requirements of the FLSA if:

1. their regular rate of pay on a weekly basis (hourly rate plus commissions) is at least 1½ times the federal minimum wage in effect; and
2. more than half of their pay for a representative period (at least one month) comes from commissions.[90]

**Example:** Employee Erica sells beds and mattresses for The Big Sleep Co., a furniture retailer, and is compensated by both salary and commissions. Her compensation for a 6-week period covering August and September 2008, working a different number of hours each week, looked like this:

---

90. FLSA §7(i); W-H Reg. 29 CFR §779.410 - §779.421.

| Week | Salary | Commission | Total | Hours | Regular Rate |
|------|--------|-----------|-------|-------|-------------|
| 1st | $250 | $310 | $560 | 45 | $12.44 |
| 2nd | $250 | $250 | $500 | 50 | $10.00 |
| 3rd | $250 | $330 | $580 | 55 | $10.55 |
| 4th | $250 | $300 | $550 | 52 | $10.58 |
| 5th | $250 | $250 | $500 | 48 | $10.42 |
| 6th | $250 | $360 | $610 | 55 | $11.09 |
| Total | $1,500 | $1,800 | $3,300 | | |

Erica is exempt from the overtime pay requirements of the law for each of the six weeks because her regular rate of pay was more than 1.5 times the minimum hourly rate in effect during each of those weeks ($6.55 x 1.5  = $9.83) and more than one-half her total compensation came from commissions ($3,300.00 x 0.5  = $1,650.00).

**What about service charges in hotels and restaurants?** The Wage and Hour Division has ruled that waiters and waitresses in hotels and restaurants may qualify for the overtime exemption granted to retail and service industry commission salespersons.[91] For the exemption to apply, the "commission" received by employees must consist of service charges added to customers' bills. Tips or gratuities that are optional for the customer do not qualify as commissions, and employees receiving such tips must be paid overtime according to the law.

If the employee does receive compensation from service charges, then the overtime exemption will apply if the employee's regular rate of pay each week is more than 1½ times the applicable minimum hourly wage and the employee's compensation from service charges makes up more than one-half of the employee's total compensation for a representative period of at least a month.

**Employees can sell products related to retail goods.** At an automobile dealership, an employee who earned commissions on service contracts and insurance he sold to customers who bought vehicles was exempt under the retail industry exemption. A federal appeals court said the exemption applies to any employee of a retail establishment who meets the compensation requirements, not only those employees who sell the retail goods.[92]

## 2.4-3 Public Sector Exempt Employees

While the FLSA generally applies to employees of the federal, state, and local governments and their agencies and political subdivisions, there are several exemptions in addition to those that apply generally. On the state and local government level, employees who are not subject to state or local civil service laws are exempt from the FLSA if they are:[93]

- publicly elected officials;
- persons selected by an elected official to be members of the official's personal staff, if they are directly supervised by the official;
- persons appointed by an elected official to serve in a policymaking position;
- persons who are immediate advisors to an elected official on the constitutional or legal powers of the office; and
- persons employed by a state or local legislative branch, other than a legislative library or a school board.

---

91.  W-H Div. Sp. Op. (WH-379), 3-26-76.
92.  Gieg v. DRR, Inc., 4076 F.3d 1038 (9 CA, 2005).
93.  FLSA §3(e)(2)(C); W-H Reg. 29 CFR §553.10 - §553.12.

## 2.4-4 Other Exempt Employees

The following table shows employees who may be exempt from the minimum wage and/or overtime pay requirements of the FLSA if certain conditions are met (X = full, P = partial, N = narrow):[94]

Table 2.1

| MISCELLANEOUS FLSA EXEMPTIONS | | | |
|---|---|---|---|
| **Employee Job Description** | **Minimum Wage Exemption** | **Overtime Exemption** | **Full Minimum Wage & Overtime Exemption** |
| Employees covered by collective bargaining agreements (union contracts)—FLSA §7(b) | | X | |
| Tobacco employees—FLSA §7(m) | | P | |
| Local transit employees engaged in charter activities—FLSA §7(n) | | N | |
| Employees of seasonal amusement or recreational establishments, organized camps, or religious or nonprofit educational conference centers—FLSA §13(a)(3) | | | X |
| Fishing employees (including first processing at sea)—FLSA §13(a)(5) | | | X |
| Farm workers (depends on duties and size of employer)—FLSA §13(a)(6), (b)(12) - (b)(16) | | X | X |
| Small local newspaper employees—FLSA §13(a)(8) | | | X |
| Switchboard operators for small public telephone companies—FLSA §13(a)(10) | | | X |
| Seamen on foreign vessels—FLSA §13(a)(12) | | | X |
| Seamen on American vessels—FLSA §13(b)(6) | | X | |
| Casual baby sitters or home companions for individuals who cannot take care of themselves—FLSA §13(a)(15) | | | X |
| Motor carrier employees—FLSA §13(b)(1) | | X | |
| Employees of interstate railroads and airlines—FLSA §13(b)(2), (b)(3) | | X | |
| Announcers, news editors, and chief engineers of small radio and television stations—FLSA §13(b)(9) | | X | |

---

94.    FLSA §6; §7; §13.

| MISCELLANEOUS FLSA EXEMPTIONS | | | |
|---|---|---|---|
| Employee Job Description | Minimum Wage Exemption | Overtime Exemption | Full Minimum Wage & Overtime Exemption |
| Salespersons and mechanics in auto dealerships (also salespersons in trailer, boat, or aircraft dealerships)—FLSA §13(b)(10) | | X | |
| Local delivery drivers and driver's helpers—FLSA §13(b)(11) | | X | |
| Taxicab drivers—FLSA §13(b)(17) | | X | |
| Firefighters and police officers in very small towns—FLSA §13(b)(20) | | X | |
| Live-in domestic workers—FLSA §13(b)(21) | | X | |
| Motion picture theater employees—FLSA §13(b)(27) | | X | |
| Couples employed by a nonprofit educational institution to work with orphaned children—FLSA §13(b)(24) | | X | |
| Employees of small logging operations—FLSA §13(b)(28) | | X | |
| News carriers who deliver newspapers directly to the consumer—FLSA §13(d) | | | X |
| Homeworkers making evergreen wreaths—FLSA §13(d) | | | X |
| Employees working in a foreign country—FLSA §13(f) | | | X |
| Cotton and sugar service and processing employees—FLSA §13(h) - (j) | | P | |
| Learners, apprentices, students, handicapped workers, and messengers—FLSA §13(a)(7); §14(a) | P | X | |
| Local bulk petroleum distributor employees —FLSA §7(b)(3) | | P | |
| Outside buyers of poultry or dairy products in their natural state—FLSA §13(b)(5) | | X | |
| Employees of amusement or recreational establishments in a national park or forest—FLSA §13(b)(29) | | P | |

The U.S. Supreme Court upheld the DOL regulation that extends the FLSA's companionship services exemption (FLSA §13(a)(15)) to individuals employed by a third party. The Court said the regulation (29 C.F.R. §552.109(a)) was valid and enforceable.[95]

---

95.    Long Island Care at Home, Ltd. v. Coke, 127 S.Ct. 2339 (2007).

# 2.5 Minimum Wage

The federal minimum wage, which had been $5.15 per hour since 1997, was increased in three stages by the Fair Minimum Wage Act of 2007. On July 24, 2007, the federal minimum wage became $5.85 per hour. On July 24, 2008, it will rise to $6.55 per hour, and finally to $7.25 per hour on July 24, 2009.[96]

All covered employees who are not otherwise exempt must be paid at least the minimum wage for all hours worked. Employees may be paid on a piecework, salary, or commission basis, so long as the wages at least equal the minimum hourly rate.

**Lower "opportunity" wage for teenagers.** The minimum wage for newly hired employees under the age of 20 is $4.25 per hour for the first 90 consecutive calendar days after they are hired, unless the employee is covered by a state law requiring a higher minimum wage.[97] The 90-day period begins on the first day of work and continues to run regardless of any breaks in service, including the employee's resignation or termination. If the employee reaches age 20 during the 90-day period, the employee must be paid at least the federal minimum wage in effect as of the employee's birthday. Employers may not terminate a current employee or reduce any current employee's hours, wages, or benefits in order to hire a teenage employee at the opportunity wage. Employers that violate this prohibition are treated as violating the ban on discrimination against employees who file a complaint under the FLSA (see page 2-62).

**Minimum wage required if any covered work is done.** In any workweek in which employees do some work that is covered by the FLSA and some that is not covered, they must be paid at least the minimum wage for all work done during that workweek. The two types of work cannot be segregated during the workweek.

**Determinations based on workweek.** In determining whether an employee has been paid the minimum wage, the Wage and Hour Division uses the workweek as the basic unit of time. Therefore, an employee's pay cannot be averaged over any longer period to determine whether there has been compliance with the minimum wage requirement.[98]

*Example:* For 35 hours work in one workweek during May 2008, employee Linda is paid $200.00—$4.75 below the minimum in effect at that time (35 x $5.85 = $204.75). For the same number of hours worked in the next workweek, Linda is paid $220.00—$15.25 above the minimum ($220.00 - $204.75 = $15.25). Even though Linda's average weekly wage for the two weeks ($210.00) exceeds the minimum required for a 35-hour workweek, the employer violated the minimum wage requirement for the first week.

**Wages other than cash included in minimum wage calculation.** In addition to wages paid in cash or check, employees may be paid in noncash forms as well. They may be paid partly in room, board, or other facilities provided by the employer. These facilities may be used by employers to bring the cash wages below the minimum wage rate, but only if all the following tests are met:

1. The employee must actually benefit from the facilities and accept them voluntarily.

2. The facilities must be supplied regularly to the employee or regularly supplied by other employers in a similar business.

3. The facilities must primarily benefit the employee, not the employer.

4. The employer can deduct only the reasonable cost of the facilities from the employee's wages and cannot make a profit from providing the facilities.[99]

---

96.   FLSA §6(a)(1).
97.   FLSA §6(g).
98.   W-H Reg. 29 CFR §776.4
99.   FLSA §3(m); W-H Reg. 29 CFR §531.33.

These tests need not be considered if the deductions for facilities do not bring the employee's wages below the statutory minimum for the workweek.

At least one federal court has ruled that an employer could use the average cost of meals in determining the amount it deducts from employees' wages and that the deductions could be taken regardless of whether the employees actually accept the meals. The court said the requirement in the regulations that the employees accept the meals voluntarily was beyond the Department of Labor's authority and was invalid.[100] A federal appeals court ruled that Florida strawberry growers had to reimburse Mexican immigrant workers for their transportation costs in traveling from Mexico to Florida and their expenses related to obtaining proper visas because the expenses were incurred primarily for the employers' benefit, and the employees' payments constructively reduced the laborers' wages below the federal minimum wage.[101]

**Taxes are part of wages.** Money required to be withheld from an employee's pay for income, social security, and Medicare taxes is included when determining whether an employee has been paid the minimum wage. Therefore, an employee making the minimum wage can still have taxes taken out of his or her paycheck.

**Uniforms.** One particularly troublesome area is the cost of employee uniforms. Where employees are required to wear uniforms that cannot be used as regular "street clothing" and their cost and maintenance would put the employee below the minimum hourly wage, the employer must pay for the purchase, cleaning, and repair of the uniforms. If the "uniform" can be worn off the job, the employer need not reimburse, even if the employee's wages go below the minimum.

Where employee uniforms require ironing, dry cleaning, or other special treatment, employees must be reimbursed for uniform maintenance costs that reduce their wages below the minimum wage. However, where the employer notifies employees that the employer will launder or clean uniforms at no cost to the employee, the employer is not required to reimburse employees who nevertheless choose to clean the uniforms at their own expense. And an employer is not required to reimburse employees for uniform maintenance at all when uniforms are "wash and wear," can be routinely washed and dried with other garments, and do not require ironing or other special treatment.

**Training wages.** Where time spent by employees in employer-provided training is considered hours worked (see Section 2.7-6), a state law (or the employer) cannot require the employee to reimburse the employer for the wages paid during the training period, where the employee resigns within a certain time period after completing the training, if the reimbursement would bring the wages received "free and clear" by the employee below the minimum wage required by the FLSA. Wages are not considered paid by the employer and received by the employee when the employee is required to give back a portion of the wages if certain conditions are not met.[102]

 **WATCH OUT FOR GARNISHMENTS** Although deductions for court-ordered garnishments or attachments and wage assignments may bring the employee's wages below the minimum wage, employers are bound by the limits of the federal Consumer Credit Protection Act and state laws when making such deductions (see Section 9 for details).

## 2.5-1  Tips and the Tip Credit

Under the FLSA, employers are required to pay "tipped employees" only $2.13 per hour in wages, so long as the employee's tips are enough to make up the remainder of the minimum hourly wage then in effect ($5.85 per hour through July 23, 2008; $6.55 per hour effective July 24, 2008; $7.25 per hour effective July 24, 2009).[103] This means that the employer can take a "tip credit" of up to 3.72 ($5.85 - $2.13) through July 23, 2008; $4.42 ($6.55 - $2.13) effective July 24, 2008; and $5.12 ($7.25 - $2.13) effective July 24, 2009.

---

100.  Herman v. Collis Foods, Inc., 176 F.3d 912 (6 CA, 1999).
101.  Arriaga v. Florida Pacific Farms, LLC, 305 F.3d 1228, 2002 U.S. App. LEXIS 18737 (11 CA, 2002).
102.  W-H Op. Ltr., FLSA2005-18, 5-31-05.
103.  FLSA §3(m), (t); W-H Reg. 29 CFR §531.50-§531.60.

If the employee's tips do not bring the employee's total wages up to the current minimum wage, the employer must make up the difference. "Tipped employees" are employees who work in an occupation in which they regularly receive more than $30 a month in tips.

**Conditions to be met.** For employers to take advantage of the tip credit, they must meet the following conditions:

1. The tipped employee must actually receive at least as much in tips as the credit taken by the employer.

2. The employee must be informed about the tip credit provisions of the law before the credit is taken.

3. All tips received by the employee must be kept by the employee, although tip pooling may be required among employees who are customarily and regularly tipped (not janitors, dishwashers, salad makers, managers, etc.).

4. Credit card tips must be given to the employee by the next payday, although the credit card company's percentage charge for the use of the card may be deducted from the tip.

*Example:* If a tip left on a credit card bill is $10 and the credit card company charges the business owner 5% for the use of its credit cards, the employee must receive at least 95% of the tip, or $9.50 ($10 x .95 = $9.50).

*More on credit card fees and tips.*[104] While an employer may deduct charges imposed by credit card companies attributable to credit card tips, it may not deduct any portion of its general administrative costs incurred for accepting credit card payments, such as dedicated phone lines or time spent processing credit card transactions. For administrative simplicity, the employer can use a standard deduction amount where the credit card fees were both over and under that amount but the employer received no more than the actual credit card fee over a period of time. Where a credit card charge is uncollectible, the employer can recover the tip from the employee, but any recovery may not reduce the tips retained by the employee below any tip credit claimed by the employer.

5. The tip credit may not be increased for overtime hours worked that are paid at a premium rate (see section 2.6).

*Uniform costs can't come out of tips.* The Wage and Hour Division said that an employer's proposals to use its servers' tips to pay for cleaning their uniforms were unlawful.[105] Under the first proposal, the restaurant would enter into voluntary agreements with its servers under which the first $15 of tips received in each workweek would become the employer's property, and would be used to pay the actual cleaning cost. If the actual laundering cost is less than $15, the difference would be returned to the employee. The restaurant would guarantee that, with tips, the servers would be paid at least the minimum wage, plus applicable overtime.

The FLSA's tip credit rules do not apply to a tipped employee unless all tips received by the employee are retained by him/her (although valid tip pooling arrangements are allowed). Thus, tips must become the property of the employee who receives them free and clear, and any arrangement whereby a tipped employee agrees that part of his or her tips becomes the property of the employer violates the tip credit provisions of the FLSA.

Under the other proposals, the restaurant would deduct the actual cost of laundering the servers' shirts and aprons from the servers' earnings if those earnings (direct wages paid by the employer and tips received by the server) are at least the hourly minimum wage after the deduction.

---

104. W-H Op. Ltr., FLSA2006-1, 1-13-06; Gillis v. Twenty-Three East Adams Street Corp., No. 04 C 4012, 2006 U.S. Dist. LEXIS 12994 (ND Ill., 3-6-06).
105. W-H Op. Ltr., FLSA2006-21, 6-9-06.

The FLSA defines a tipped employee's wage rate as the cash amount paid (at least $2.13 an hour), plus an amount of tips sufficient to bring the employee to the minimum wage. Therefore, even if the tips received by an employee exceed the maximum tip credit the employer needs to claim toward payment of the minimum wage, these excess tips are not wages for FLSA purposes. In this situation, a server paid $2.13 an hour in direct wages by the employer would still be considered to be paid no more than the minimum wage.

However, if the employer claims the full tip credit allowed (and the employee receives that amount in tips) and the employer pays direct wages at a rate that exceeds the minimum required, the employer would be allowed to accept from the tipped employee a payment for uniform cleaning that did not exceed the amount of the direct cash wage received in that workweek in excess of the required minimum. For example, if the employer during October 2008 pays $3.13 per hour in direct wages and claims the full tip credit ($4.42 per hour), the tipped employee's regular rate of pay would be $7.55 per hour, and the employee could deduct each week for uniform maintenance up to $1.00 per hour for each day worked by the server in the workweek.

**Service charges.** Where service charges are automatically added to customers' bills and then turned over to employees, these amounts are not tips and are considered wages when determining whether the minimum wage has been paid.[106]

 **WATCH OUT FOR STATE LAWS** Some states have laws prohibiting the use of tip credits or providing for lower tip credit amounts than the FLSA. Where the result of applying these laws is more favorable to employees than the FLSA, they must be followed by employers operating in those states. The employer must figure the minimum wage required under both federal and state law and then apply the one providing the higher cash payment to the employee. See Table 2.4 for a chart providing information on state tip credit laws.

*Example:* As of June 2008, the minimum hourly wage in Idaho is $5.85 and the maximum tip credit is $2.50. Under the FLSA at that time, the minimum hourly wage is $5.85 and the maximum tip credit is $3.72. Under Idaho law, the net minimum wage that must be paid is $3.35 ($5.85 − $2.50 = $3.35). The FLSA requires a net minimum hourly rate of $2.13. Because the Idaho net minimum wage is higher, Idaho employers must pay $3.35 an hour to tipped employees, rather than the $2.13 required by the FLSA.

## 2.5-2 Equal Pay for Equal Work

In 1963, the minimum wage provisions of the FLSA were amended by the Equal Pay Act to require equal pay for men and women doing equal work under similar working conditions. "Equal work" means jobs requiring equal skill, effort and responsibility. The law exempts earnings measured under a seniority system, merit system, system using quantity or quality of production to determine wages, or factor other than sex.

The Equal Pay Act is enforced by the Equal Employment Opportunity Commission, which handles employee complaints and conducts investigations. Violations of the EPA are considered violations of the minimum wage and overtime sections of the FLSA, and employers cannot reduce the wages of any employee to comply with the law.

## 2.6 Overtime Pay Requirements

The general rule under the FLSA is that all covered employees must be paid at least 1½ times their "regular rate of pay" for all hours physically worked over 40 in a workweek.[107] In other words, they must receive an overtime premium of one-half their regular rate of pay for all overtime hours worked.

*Example:* Employee Jared generally works a 40-hour week at an hourly rate of $12 an hour. In a week when Jared works 46 hours, his total weekly earnings are determined as follows:

---

106.    W-H Div. Sp. Op. 1-17-68; WH-305, 1-15-75.
107.    FLSA §7(a)(1).

| | |
|---|---|
| Regular earnings: | 46 hours x $12 per hour = $552.00 |
| Overtime hours: | 46 hours – 40 hours = 6 hours |
| Overtime premium rate: | $12.00 per hour x 0.5 = $6.00 |
| Overtime premium pay: | $6.00 per hour x 6 hours = $36.00 |
| Total weekly earnings: | $552.00 + $36.00 = $588.00 |

*[handwritten: 40×12 = 480; 6×18 = 108; 46 = $588]*

For tipped employees, the employer cannot take an increased tip credit for overtime hours worked. For example, if during November 2008, the employer is taking the full tip credit of $4.42 per hour and paying the employee a cash wage of $2.13 an hour, the cash wage for overtime hours is $5.41 [($6.55 x 1.5) – $4.42 = $5.41].

Several questions must be answered, however, before the calculation determining the overtime pay owed can be applied. They include:

- What is a workweek and why is it important?

- What constitutes hours physically worked under the FLSA?

- What payments to an employee are considered wages for the purposes of determining overtime?

- What is the employee's regular rate of pay?

**Help available from DOL.** The U.S. Department of Labor has launched a new Web resource at www.dol.gov/elaws/otcalculator.htm to help employers understand how to calculate overtime pay under the FLSA. Compute overtime pay in a sample pay period based on information you provide such as the primary method of pay, additional compensation paid in the form of bonuses, commissions and shift differentials, and information relating to the hours employees worked.

The calculator totals the hours worked during the sample pay period and, based on the user's input, calculates the overtime due for any overtime hours worked. Because it is an educational tool, the advisor also provides links to definitions and detailed information on overtime pay requirements. The advisor does not collect any personally identifying information. In addition, information provided about pay and hours worked is not saved by the advisor after overtime is calculated.

## 2.6-1 The Workweek

As was mentioned in the discussion of the minimum wage requirements (see Section 2.5), the basic unit for determining the proper wages due employees is the workweek. The employer is responsible for establishing its workweek—a regularly recurring period of 168 hours (7 consecutive 24-hour periods).[108] The workweek does not have to be the same as a calendar week or begin at the start of a day.

*Example:* The Early Morning Bagel Co. establishes a workweek that begins at 2:00 a.m. Wednesday and ends at 2:00 a.m. the next Wednesday to accommodate its early morning shifts. Such a workweek is lawful under the FLSA.

Employers may also establish different workweeks for different facilities or groups of employees, so long as each workweek remains fixed once it is established. It does not matter what the pay period is (e.g., weekly, biweekly, semimonthly) or whether the end of the workweek coincides with the end of the pay period. Each workweek stands alone. The workweek can be changed, but only if the change is intended to be permanent. Frequent changes may be seen by the Wage and Hour Division as an attempt to avoid FLSA obligations. As one example, the Division said an employer violated the FLSA by continually rotating employees

---

108.    W-H Reg. 29 CFR §778.103 - §778.106.

between day and evening shifts that had different workweeks, so that a regular workweek was never established for those employees.[109]

**Why is the workweek so important?** In general, the workweek is the longest period for which an overtime determination can be made. Generally, periods of longer than a workweek cannot be averaged to determine the hours worked in a workweek.

> *Example:* Jerry worked 35 hours in Week 1, 38 in Week 2, and 45 in Week 3. Although Jerry's average hours worked per workweek for the 3-week period were below 40 (39.3), he still is owed overtime pay for the workweek in which he worked 45 hours.

The Wage and Hour Division rejected an employer's proposed schedule that would have had employees working four 9-hour days and one 8-hour day in the first week of a biweekly pay period, and four 9-hour days in the second week. The employees would be paid for 40 hours for each week, with 4 hours from the first week "banked" and then added to the hours worked during the second week. The Division said the plan violated the FLSA because the Act does not allow averaging an employee's hours over 2 workweeks.[110]

**Exemption for hospitals and nursing homes.** The FLSA contains an exemption to the workweek standard for hospitals and nursing homes that is designed to give them more flexibility in scheduling.[111] The law allows such employers to use a 14-day period rather than the workweek for determining overtime compensation. And the extended period can be used for different groups of employees as the employer sees fit.

All of the following conditions must be met for the exemption to apply:

1. There must be an agreement or understanding between the employer and the employees before work is performed that the 14-day period will be used.

2. If the agreement or understanding is not in writing, the employer must keep some special record of it.

3. The employer must pay employees covered by the agreement or understanding at least 1½ times their regular rate of pay for all hours worked over 8 in a day or 80 in the 14-day period, whichever would result in higher pay for the employee.

> *Example:* Jack, a nonexempt hospital employee, has agreed with the hospital to work on a 14-day work period basis, and his regular rate of pay is $12 an hour. Jack works 5 days at 8 hours each and 4 at 10 hours each during the 14-day period.
>
> | | |
> |---|---|
> | Total hours worked: | (5 x 8) + (4 x 10) = 80 |
> | Hours over 8 per day: | (10 - 8) x 4 = 8 |

Even though Jack's total hours for the 14-day work period did not exceed 80, he is entitled to overtime pay for the 8 hours worked over 8 in a day. Jack's total earnings are determined as follows:

| | |
|---|---|
| Regular earnings: | $12/hour x 80 hours = $960 |
| Overtime premium rate: | $12/hour x .5 = $6 |
| Overtime premium pay: | $6 x 8 hours = $48 |
| Total earnings: | $960 + $48 = $1,008 |

**When workweeks are changed.** While the FLSA encourages employers to establish permanent workweeks, a change may be necessary to meet changing business needs. But if a change is made, the employer must be careful when determining hours worked where the new and old workweeks overlap.[112]

---

109.  W-H Div. Op. Ltr., 2-16-01.
110.  W-H Div. Op. Ltr., 7-21-97.
111.  FLSA §7(j); W-H Reg. 29 CFR §778.601.
112.  W-H Reg. 29 CFR §778.301 - §778.302.

Several steps must be taken to ensure that the employee receives all overtime pay to which he or she is entitled:

1. Add the overlapping days to the old workweek.

2. Calculate the overtime hours and pay due for the old and new workweeks on this basis.

3. Add the overlapping days to the new workweek.

4. Calculate the overtime hours and pay due for the old and new workweeks on this basis.

5. Pay the employee the greater amount from step 2 or step 4.

*Example:* Goode Company used a workweek running from 7:00 a.m. Monday to 7:00 a.m. the next Monday. They are permanently changing their workweek to run from 7:00 a.m. Sunday to 7:00 a.m. the following Sunday. Employee Dave works from 9:00 a.m. to 5:00 p.m. (8 hours per day) according to the two-week schedule in the following chart. The change takes effect on the Sunday falling during the first week in the chart:

| Mon | Tue | Wed | Thu | Fri | Sat | Sun |
|-----|-----|-----|-----|-----|-----|-----|
|     | 8   | 8   |     | 8   | 8   | 8   |
| 8   | 8   | 8   |     | 8   | 8   |     |

Sunday of Week 1 is the overlapping day of the old and new workweeks. Adding the hours worked on that day to the previous workweek gives Dave 40 hours worked in Week 1 and 40 hours worked in Week 2. Adding the hours worked on that day to the new workweek gives Dave 32 hours worked in Week 1 and 48 hours worked in Week 2. While the total hours worked for the two-week period are the same under either alternative, because the new workweek would give Dave 8 hours of overtime, it must be used in calculating Dave's earnings.

## 2.6-2 Hours Worked

Because the FLSA requires overtime pay only for hours physically worked over 40 in a workweek, hours that employees are paid for but during which no actual work is done do not have to be counted when calculating the number of hours worked.[113] Therefore, paid time off for illness, jury or witness duty, holidays, vacations, etc., need not be added when determining whether the 40-hour threshold has been met. However, payments for hours not worked cannot be offset against any overtime pay due for hours actually worked over 40 during the same workweek.

*Example:* Employee Chrissy worked 12 hours a day for 4 days in a workweek and was paid 8 hours' holiday pay for another day. Because she actually worked 48 hours during the workweek, Chrissy is entitled to overtime pay for 8 hours, and the holiday pay she received cannot be offset against that obligation.

**No maximum hour limitation.** So long as the employer pays the required overtime premium for all hours physically worked over 40 in a workweek, the FLSA places no limit on the number of hours an employee may be required to work (see Section 2.8 for restrictions applying to minors under age 16). But employers should check the laws in the states where they operate for any maximum hours restrictions that may apply. [For more information on state maximum hour restrictions for minors, see Table 1.4 of *APA's Guide to State Payroll Laws*].

---

113. W-H Reg. 29 CFR §778.102.

# 2.6-3 Regular Rate of Pay

The required overtime pay under the FLSA is 1½ times the employee's "regular rate of pay." In general, the regular rate of pay is an hourly pay rate determined by dividing the total regular pay actually earned for the workweek by the total number of hours worked.[114] The calculation of the regular rate of pay is sometimes difficult when other types of payments besides cash wages need to be included in determining the regular rate. Also, employees are often paid on a basis other than an hourly rate.

**What is included in the regular rate?** The following payments, in addition to hourly or contract wages, must be considered when calculating an employee's regular rate of pay:

*Shift differentials:* A shift differential is an amount added to an hourly rate to compensate an employee for working an evening, late night, or other undesirable shift.

> *Example:* Karen's normal hourly rate is $11, but she receives a $.50 per hour shift differential for working the midnight to 8 a.m. shift. During a workweek when she works 44 hours on the late shift, her regular rate for that week is $11.50 an hour.

*Nondiscretionary bonuses:* Any contractual or agreed-upon bonus or incentive related to production, efficiency, attendance, quality, or some other measure of performance must be included in the calculation of the regular rate of pay for the workweek during which it was earned.[115] The calculation is made by adding the bonus to the employee's other regular earnings for the workweek and dividing the total by the number of hours worked during the workweek.

> *Example:* Anne exceeded her production quota for the week at the What's It Widget Co., earning a $24 bonus in addition to her normal hourly rate of $9. Anne worked 43 hours during the workweek, so her regular rate of pay would be:
>
> $9.00/ hour x 43 hours = $387.00
> $387.00  + $24.00 = $411.00
> $411.00 ÷ 43 = $9.56

 **VENDOR BONUSES COUNT TOO** A nondiscretionary bonus paid by an employer to an employee for selling a vendor's products must be included in the employee's regular rate of pay, even if the amount and nature of the bonus are determined by the vendor and the money for the bonus is paid to the employer by the vendor.[116]

The Wage and Hour Division said that where a company pays an annual bonus on the same date each year if the company has exceeded certain goals related to a return on assets, return on equity, deposit growth, and efficiency, the bonus is nondiscretionary because the criteria for paying the bonus are announced by the employer well in advance of the payment.[117]

The Division reached the same conclusion with regard to team bonuses promised to employees as an incentive for increased or sustained productivity goals that are set at the beginning of the year and are made known to the employees.[118]

If bonuses are not determined each week, but at some later date (e.g., after a month or after a specific production goal has been reached), they must be allocated when finally determined to the workweeks during which they were earned.[119] If they cannot be tied specifically to work done during each workweek, they may

---

114.    W-H Reg. 29 CFR §778.102.
115.    FLSA §7(e)(3); W-H Reg. 29 CFR §778.208 - §778-210.
116.    W-H. Op. Ltr., FLSA2005-4NA, 7-5-05; DOL Field Operations Handbook, ¶32b07
117.    W-H Op. Ltr., FLSA2006-9NA, 5-11-06.
118.    W-H Op. Ltr., FLSA2006-5NA, 4-27-06.
119.    W-H Reg. 29 CFR §778.209.

be allocated evenly to each workweek or each hour worked during the period for which the bonus was paid, whichever method better fits the actual work situation.

> ***Example:*** For a six-month period covering 26 workweeks, employee Arnie exceeded his production quota at Little Rock Saxophone Mfg. Co. and earned a bonus of $1,950. Because no weekly production records were kept (monthly totals only) and Arnie worked 44 hours each week during the six-month period, Little Rock Saxophone allocated an equal amount of the bonus to each workweek and calculated the overtime due as follows:

| | |
|---|---|
| Bonus allocated to each workweek: | $1,950 ÷ 26 = $75 |
| Bonus allocated to each hour worked: | $75 ÷ 44 = $1.70 |
| Extra overtime pay for each workweek: | .5 x $1.70 x 4 = $3.40 |
| Total extra overtime earnings: | 26 x $3.40 = $88.40 |

If a nonexempt employee is paid a bonus for remaining on the job after a layoff or plant shutdown (a "stay bonus"), the bonus must be allocated to the time during which the employee had to work to earn the bonus, and the employee's regular rate of pay must be allocated accordingly. If the bonus is paid on a deferred basis and the employee earns interest until it is paid, the interest is not wages and should not be taken into consideration when calculating the employee's regular rate of pay.[120]

Fortunately, the regulations issued under the FLSA provide a procedure that keeps employers from having to recompute the overtime pay due for the period for which the bonus is being paid.[121] If, before the work is performed, a contract or bonus plan provides that the bonus will be paid as a "percentage of total earnings" (the employee's straight time and overtime earnings), the bonus will satisfy the overtime requirements and no recomputation will be necessary. Paying a straight dollar amount as an incentive would not eliminate the recalculation requirement, since the percentage of straight time and overtime earnings would be different.[122]

> ***Example:*** Under a bonus plan designed by Al's Auto Insurance Co., claims adjusters are paid a 10% bonus of all regular and overtime earnings once they process a certain number of claims in a week. Such a plan satisfies the overtime requirements of the FLSA.

Where the bonus is based on a percentage of total wages earned in a previous year, the bonus payments need not be considered as compensation for the bonus calculation for the year in which they are actually paid.[123]

> ***Example:*** Early in 2007, the What's It Widget Co. pays Anne a nondiscretionary bonus as a percentage of her wages earned in 2006. When it comes time to calculate Anne's bonus for 2007, which will be paid in 2008, the amount of the 2006 bonus paid in 2007 is not added to Anne's wages earned in 2007 in making the calculation.

Similarly, recalculation would not be necessary where a bonus is based on the ratio of an employee's total gross earnings, including overtime pay, to the employer's total labor costs as part of a bonus plan based on labor cost savings.[124]

*Payments in a form other than cash:* If payments to an employee are made in the form of goods or services rather than cash, the reasonable cost to the employer or the fair market value of the goods or services must be included when determining the regular rate of pay.[125]

*Retroactive pay:* If retroactive pay is awarded for a period during which overtime hours were worked, the regular rate of pay is also increased for that period. This is true whether the retroactive pay is in the form of an hourly increase or a lump-sum payment that must be allocated to the weeks or hours worked in the same manner as a nondiscretionary bonus.

---

120.   W-H Op. Ltr., FLSA2005-47, 11-4-05.
121.   W-H Reg. 29 CFR §778.210; W-H Op. Ltr., FLSA 2006-8NA, 5-11-06; FLSA 2006-4NA, 2-17-06.
122.   W-H Op. Ltr., FLSA2004-11, 9-21-04.
123.   W-H Op. Ltr., FLSA2005-22, 8-26-05.
124.   W-H Div. Op. Ltr., 2-5-01.
125.   W-H Reg. 29 CFR §778.116.

*On-call pay:* Pay received for compensable on-call time (see Section 2.7-4) must be included in the employee's total earnings when computing the regular rate of pay.

*Supplemental disability payments:* A federal court of appeals ruled that supplemental payments designed to bring the wage of a partially disabled worker up to the employee's predisability wage level must be included in determining the employee's regular rate of pay.[126]

*Sick leave buyback payments.* A federal appeals court ruled that a city's payments to firefighters under its sick leave buyback program should have been included in determining the firefighters' regular rate of pay for overtime purposes. The court said the payments were similar to a nondiscretionary bonus since they were determined under a formula based on how much unused sick leave a firefighter had earned, and were clearly part of their compensation for employment.[127]

**What is not included in the regular rate of pay?** The FLSA exempts several types of payments to employees from inclusion in the regular rate of pay for overtime purposes:

*Gifts:* Amounts paid to employees as gifts at Christmas or other special occasions are not included in employees' regular rate of pay so long as the amount does not depend on hours worked, production, or efficiency.[128] The amount may differ for each employee if it is based on a percentage of salary or length of service.

*Paid time off and reimbursed expenses:* Payments received for time not worked because of holidays, illness, vacations, jury duty, bereavement, or the failure of the employer to provide sufficient work (not layoffs or reduced work schedules) need not be included in employees' regular rate of pay. The same exclusion applies to reimbursements for employees' business-related expenses incurred on behalf of or for the convenience of the employer.[129]

*Discretionary bonuses:* Bonuses paid for services performed need not be included in employees' regular rate of pay if the employer has the discretion whether to pay the bonus and to determine the amount.[130] The employer's discretion must also be exercised at or near the end of the period during which the services were performed. In order to be considered discretionary, the bonus must not be paid pursuant to a promise made in advance, a contract, or some other agreement.

**Example:** The owner of Jerry's Sporting Goods, Inc. decides at the end of its fiscal year that, because business has been so good, he will give his employees a bonus equal to 2 weeks' pay. In succeeding years, Jerry sometimes decides not to provide such a bonus or to provide a lower bonus if business has not been so good. In other years, the bonus is the same or higher than that offered in the first year. Because the bonus is not promised in advance to employees each year and Jerry decides if the bonus will be awarded and how large it will be, the bonus is discretionary and need not be included in the employees' regular rate of pay during the fiscal year.

*Volunteer work counted toward group's bonus.* Where an employer encouraged its employees to perform volunteer work with unrelated charitable organizations (e.g., Habitat for Humanity), partly by offering to include the volunteer work as part of a matrix for determining group bonuses, the Wage and Hour Division said the employer did not have to pay nonexempt employees for the hours spent volunteering outside of normal working hours. The time is not compensable even though it is taken into account in determining the group bonus, so long as no employee is denied any part of the bonus for failure to participate in the volunteer work and the group could still qualify for the full bonus without performing the volunteer work. The Division also said the employees could receive small promotional items for engaging in volunteer work without turning that time into compensable time.[131]

---

126.   Local 246 Utility Workers Union of America v. Southern California Edison Co., 83 F.3d 292 (9 CA, 1996).
127.   Acton v. City of Columbia, 436 F.3d 969 (8 CA, 2006).
128.   FLSA §7(e)(1); W-H Reg. 29 CFR §778.212.
129.   FLSA §7(e)(2); W-H Reg. 29 CFR §778.216 - §778.224; W-H Op. Ltr. FLSA 2004-3, 5-13-04.
130.   FLSA §7(e)(3); W-H Reg. 29 CFR §778.211.
131.   W-H Op. Ltr., FLSA2006-4, 1-27-06.

*Benefit plan contributions:* Employer contributions to profit-sharing, thrift or savings (e.g., §401(k)), or other employee benefit plans (e.g., retirement, life insurance, health insurance) are excluded from employees' regular rate of pay.[132] However, in 2001 a federal appeals court ruled that an employer's contributions to a cafeteria plan may have to be included in calculating the employees' regular rate of pay because the employees could elect to receive the entire amount of the employer's contribution in cash instead of using it to purchase benefits. This option meant that the plan may not be a "bona fide" employee benefit plan, the court said.[133]

In an opinion letter issued in 2003, the DOL identified a two-part test for determining whether an employer's cafeteria plan contribution qualifies as part of a bona fide benefits plan:

- No more than 20% of the employer's contribution is paid out in cash (applied on a plan-wide basis); and
- The cash is paid under circumstances that are consistent with the plan's overall primary purpose of providing benefits (e.g., the plan allows cash payments instead of medical insurance coverage only if the employee shows they have other coverage).[134]

 **NO OVERTIME PAY OFFSET** While the payments mentioned in the preceding paragraphs are not included in an employee's regular rate of pay for determining overtime pay due, they also cannot be used as an offset against any overtime pay due.

An employer's contributions to an employee stock purchase plan (ESPP) do not have to be included in the participating employees' regular rate of pay because the ESPP qualified as a bona fide thrift or savings plan. Even though the employer's contributions exceeded the amount that the employees contributed, the Wage and Hour Division said the plan qualified because it met the other requirements for a bona fide savings plan, participation was voluntary, employees' salaries were not influenced by their decision to participate, and the employer's contributions were preset and did not depend on the employees' performance or hours worked.[135]

The DOL also ruled that a $100 decrease in monthly health insurance premiums for employees who do not smoke does not have to be included in the employees' regular rate of pay. The increased employer contribution qualifies for exclusion from the regular rate of pay as a contribution to an employee benefit plan, and the fact that two groups of employees (smokers and nonsmokers) receive different contribution levels does not change this analysis.[136]

> *Example:* Employee Sam Noel receives a Christmas gift of $100 from his employer that does not have to be included in his regular rate of pay for the week in which he received it. During that week, his regular rate of pay was $14 an hour and he worked 45 hours. Therefore, Sam was due an overtime premium of $35 (overtime premium rate of $7 ($14 x .5) x 5 overtime hours). Since the gift cannot be used to offset the overtime premium, Sam's gross pay for the week was $765 ($14 x 45 hours = $630; $630 + $100 (gift) + $35 (overtime premium pay) = $765).

*Stock options:* Any income an employee gets from employer-provided grants or rights provided under a stock option, stock appreciation right, or employee stock purchase program is not included in the employee's regular rate of pay if all the following criteria are met:[137]

- Grants must be made pursuant to a program whose terms and conditions are communicated to participating employees either at the beginning of their participation in the program or at the time of the grant.

---

132. FLSA §7(e)(3), (e)(4); W-H Reg. 29 CFR §778.213 - §778.215.
133. Madison v. Resources for Human Development, Inc., 39 F.Supp. 2d 542 (ED Pa., 1999); remanded by 233 F.3d 175 (3 CA, 2000).
134. W-H Op. Ltr., 7-2-03.
135. W-H Op. Ltr., FLSA2006-8, 3-10-06.
136. W-H Op. Ltr., FLSA2004-17, 10-28-04.
137. FLSA §7(e)(8), (h)(1)

- Grants or rights based on performance must be based on:
  - meeting previously established performance criteria (e.g., hours of work, efficiency, or productivity) of any business unit consisting of at least 10 employees or of a facility;
  - length of service or a minimum schedule of hours or days of work; or
  - the past performance (including any criteria) of one or more employees in a given period if the determination is in the sole discretion of the employer and not based on any prior contract.

- Exercise of such grants or rights must be voluntary.

- Stock options and stock appreciation rights must not be exercisable until at least six months after the grant (unless they become exercisable because of the employee's death, disability, or retirement, or a change in corporate ownership, or other circumstances allowed in the regulations) and cannot be exercised for less than 85% of the fair market value of the stock at the time of the grant.

- The "value or income derived from" the grants or rights cannot be credited toward any minimum wages or overtime pay due to the employee.

*Overtime compensation:* Overtime premiums paid (they can be more or less than 1½ times the regular rate) for hours worked over 8 in a day or in excess of the employee's normal working hours (40 or less) for the workweek or because the employer has a policy of including paid hours for time not worked (e.g., vacation or sick time) in calculating overtime need not be included in the employee's regular rate of pay.[138] They also may be offset against any overtime due the employee for the workweek, so long as the premiums are paid during the same workweek.[139]

*Premium pay for extra days worked:* Extra pay provided to an employee for working on a Saturday, Sunday, holiday, or other regular day of rest (but not for working more than 40 hours in the workweek) need not be included in the employee's regular rate of pay if it is at least 1½ times the rate for similar work done during the normal workweek.[140] Such pay may also be used to offset any overtime pay due the employee for the workweek.

*Premium pay under a union contract for extra hours:* Another type of pay that need not be included when computing an employee's regular rate of pay is premium pay for work outside the employee's regular workday (no more than 8 hours) or workweek (no more than 40 hours) established by a valid collective bargaining agreement. The exclusion is valid if the premium pay is at least 1½ times the contractual rate for work done during the regular workday or workweek.[141] Such premium pay may also be used to offset any overtime pay due the employee for the workweek, but not to offset overtime pay due for workweeks other than the workweek when the premium pay was earned.[142]

## 2.6-4 Special Problems in Regular Rate Determinations

Here are some of the unique situations that can arise when determining an employee's regular rate of pay for overtime purposes:

**Employees working at more than one rate.** When an employee is paid at two or more different rates by an employer for doing two or more different jobs during the workweek, the regular rate of pay must take into account the different rates.[143] This is done by adapting the general regular rate formula so that a "weighted average" is calculated: total regular pay from all jobs ÷ total hours worked = regular rate of pay.

---

138. FLSA §7(e)(5); W-H Reg. 29 CFR §778.201; §778.202.
139. Bell v. Iowa Turkey Growers Corp., 407 F. Supp. 2d 1051 (SD Iowa, 2006).
140. FLSA §7(e)(6); W-H Reg. 29 CFR §778.203; §778.205.
141. FLSA §7(e)(7); W-H Reg. 29 CFR §778.204; §778.206; §778.207.
142. Howard v. City of Springfield, 274 F.3d 1141 (7CA, 2001); Herman v. Fabri-Centers of America, Inc., No. 01-3080, 2002 U.S. App. LEXIS 21632 (6 CA, 10-17-02).
143. W-H Reg. 29 CFR §778.115.

*Example:* George works as a copy editor for 8 hours a day from Monday through Friday for $12 an hour. In the same week, he works an extra 12 hours (4 on Thursday and 8 on Saturday) as a proofreader for $9 an hour. His regular rate of pay for the workweek is $11.31 [(40 x $12) + (12 x $9)] ÷ 52 = $11.31.

To avoid having to make this calculation, many employers merely use the highest rate paid during the week as the regular rate when determining overtime due. While not required under the FLSA, this method is lawful because the employee would get an amount greater than the law guarantees. Using the lowest rate paid during the week is prohibited by the FLSA, since that rate is lower than the regular rate of pay when the higher rates are taken into account.

In general, the employer cannot automatically use the rate paid during the overtime hours as the basis for calculating overtime pay due, as it may be lower than the regular rate of pay. There is an exception, however, where the employee agrees in advance and several other conditions are met:[144]

- the employee's average hourly earnings for the workweek (not including overtime pay and other earnings excluded from the regular rate) equal or exceed the minimum wage;

- extra overtime pay is paid on other forms of earnings that are included in the regular rate, such as nondiscretionary bonuses;

- the hourly rate used to determine the overtime rate equals or exceeds the minimum wage and is the rate actually paid for such work during nonovertime hours;

- the hours of work for which overtime is paid qualify as overtime hours; and

- the number of overtime hours is at least the number of hours worked in excess of the FLSA maximum (40 in a workweek).

**Salaried nonexempt employees.** It is important to remember that not all salaried employees are exempt from the FLSA's overtime requirements. Only those employees whose salaries exceed a certain level and who meet the duties and responsibilities tests for exemption are classified as exempt. All other salaried employees must be paid overtime. The regular rate of pay for such employees is determined by dividing the employee's salary by the number of hours the salary is intended to compensate.[145]

The easiest way to accomplish this is to calculate the employee's yearly salary and then divide by the number of hours to be compensated in a year. For employees who normally work a 40-hour-per-week schedule, the number of hours worked in a year is 2,080 (1,820 if the employee normally works 35 hours per week). According to Wage and Hour Division personnel, employers should not use a different number of hours for this calculation in years when there are more than 260 work days, because the FLSA bases its overtime requirements on hours worked during a workweek and a salaried, nonexempt employee's regular rate of pay is determined by the number of hours for which the employee's salary is intended to compensate during that workweek.

*Example 1:* Sara works 35 hours per week and is paid a biweekly salary of $1,200.

| | |
|---|---|
| Yearly salary: | $1,200 x 26 = $31,200 |
| Hours worked in a year: | 52 x 35 = 1,820 |
| Regular rate of pay: | $31,200 ÷ 1,820 = $17.14 per hour |

*Example 2:* Bill works 40 hours per week and is paid a monthly salary of $1,800.

| | |
|---|---|
| Yearly salary: | $1,800 x 12 = $21,600 |
| Hours worked in a year: | 52 x 40 = 2,080 |
| Regular rate of pay: | $21,600 ÷ 2,080 = $10.38 per hour |

---

144.   FLSA §7(g); W-H Reg. 29 CFR §778.415 - §778.421; W-H Op. Ltr., FLSA2006-10, 3-10-06.
145.   W-H Reg. 29 CFR §778.113.

**Workweeks of less than 40 hours.** For many employees, the standard workweek is less than 40 hours—often 35 or even 32 hours. For instance, in Example 1 above, Sara worked 35 hours per week and had a regular rate of pay of $17.14 per hour. If Sara works more than 40 hours in a workweek, she must be paid at her regular rate of pay of $17.14 for all hours worked, plus an overtime premium of $8.57 for all hours worked over 40.

But what if Sara works more than 35 hours but no more than 40 hours in a workweek? Under the FLSA, does she have to be paid anything beyond her regular salary for those hours? Most of the courts that have addressed this situation have ruled that it is not a violation of the FLSA's minimum wage or overtime provisions if the employee is not paid for such "gap" time, so long as the employee receives at least the minimum wage for the total number of hours worked.[146] In Sara's situation, her biweekly salary of $1,200 equates to $600 per week. If she worked 40 hours in a week, she would still be paid well in excess of the minimum wage for the week ($600 ÷ 40 = $15 per hour).

In the "gap" time situation, the courts may look to what the agreement is between the employer and the employee regarding the hours worked between the employee's normal workweek and a 40-hour workweek, rather than the FLSA, in determining whether any extra pay is due the employee.[147]

**Computing the regular rate and overtime for pieceworkers.** Under a piece-rate system, the basic method for determining the regular rate of pay is to add the weekly piece-rate earnings to any other earnings for the workweek (e.g., production bonuses, waiting time pay) and then divide the total by the number of hours worked in the workweek. Where pieceworkers are paid at piece rates or a guaranteed hourly minimum, the guaranteed minimum becomes the regular rate of pay in weeks where it is paid because the employee's piece-rate earnings failed to reach the minimum.

There are two acceptable methods for calculating the overtime due pieceworkers under the FLSA:[148]

*Method 1:* Once the regular rate of pay is determined, the pieceworker must be paid, in addition to the piecework earnings for the workweek, an amount equal to one-half the regular rate times the number of hours worked over 40 in the workweek.

> *Example:* Brad receives $1 for each doll he assembles, plus a $0.25 bonus per doll for each doll over 352 he assembles in a regular 46-hour workweek. In one workweek, Brad assembled 420 dolls.

| | |
|---|---|
| Regular piecework earnings: | $1.00 x 420 dolls = $420.00 |
| Production bonus: | $0.25 x 68 dolls = $17.00 |
| Total piecework earnings: | $420.00 + $17 = $437.00 |
| Regular rate of pay: | $437.00 ÷ 46 = $9.50 |
| Overtime premium rate: | $9.50 x .5 = $4.75 |
| Overtime premium pay: | $4.75 x 6 = $28.50 |
| Total earnings for workweek: | $437.00 + $28.50 = $465.50 |

*Method 2:* If employees agree before the work is performed, they may be paid at a rate not less than 1½ times the regular piece rate for each piece made during the overtime hours. (Other conditions must also be met that help guarantee that pieceworkers are not taken advantage of by their employers.)

> *Example:* Sally receives $2.50 for each figurine she paints. In one 45-hour workweek, she painted 140 figurines in the first 40 hours and 18 in the next 5 hours.

---

146. U.S. v. Klinghoffer Brothers Realty Corp., 285 F.2d 487 (2 CA, 1961); Monahan v. County of Chesterfield, 95 F.3d 1263 (4 CA, 1996); O'Brien v. Encotech Construction, No. 00-CV-1133 (ND Ill., 3-23-04); Sherman v. Premium Concrete Cutting, Inc., No. 01 C 7263 (ND Ill., 7-6-04); Ladegaard v. Hard Rock Concrete Cutters, Inc., No. 00 C 5755 (ND Ill., 8-17-04).
147. Monahan v. County of Chesterfield, 95 F.3d 1263 (4 CA, 1996).
148. FLSA §7(g); W-H Reg. 29 CFR §778.111; §778.418.

Regular piecework earnings (40 hours):      $2.50 x 140 figurines = $350.00
Overtime piecework rate:      $2.50 x 1.5 = $3.75
Overtime piecework earnings (5 hours):    $3.75 x 18 figurines = $67.50
Total earnings for workweek:    $350.00 + $67.50 = $417.50

**Tipped employees**. If a tipped employee is being paid less than the minimum wage by an employer because the employer is taking some or all of the allowable tip credit (see Section 2.5-1), the full minimum wage is used in determining the employee's regular rate of pay (plus any other payments from the employer that would normally be included in the regular rate).

*Example 1:* Rene is a waiter whose employer pays him $2.13 per hour during August 2008 and takes the full tip credit of $4.42. In one workweek, Rene works 45 hours and collects $142.50 in tips. His total pay for the week is calculated as follows:

| | | | |
|---|---|---|---|
| Cash wages without tip credit: | | $2.13 x 45 = | $95.85 |
| | | | |
| Tip credit: $4.42 x 45 = | $198.90 | | |
| Tips received: | $142.50 | | $142.50 |
| Tip credit make-up: | $56.40 | | $56.40 |
| Regular rate of pay: | | $6.55 | |
| Overtime premium rate: $6.55 x .5 = | | $3.28 | |
| Overtime premium pay: | | $3.28 x 5 = | $16.40 |
| Total pay: | | | $311.15 |

*Example 2:* Belinda is a waitress whose employer pays her $3.00 per hour and takes a tip credit of $3.55. She also receives $1.00 for each cheesecake her customers order. During one workweek in October 2008, Belinda works 50 hours, sells 15 cheesecakes, and collects $200.00 in tips. Her total pay for the week is calculated as follows:

| | | |
|---|---|---|
| Cash wages without tip credit: | $3.00 x 50 = | $150.00 |
| Cheesecakes sold: | $1.00 x 15 = | $15.00 |
| | | |
| Tips received: | | $200.00 |

Tips are greater than tip credit ($3.55 x 50 = $177.50), so no tip credit make-up is necessary.

| | | |
|---|---|---|
| Regular hourly pay: | $6.55 x 50 = $327.50 | |
| Total regular pay: | $327.50 + $15.00 = $342.50 | |
| Regular rate of pay: | $342.50 ÷ 50 = $6.85 | |
| Overtime premium rate: | $6.85 x .5 = $3.43 | |
| Overtime premium pay: | $3.43 x 10 = | $34.30 |
| Total pay: | | $399.30 |

**Fluctuating workweeks.** Some employers may find it advantageous to enter into agreements with their employees to pay them a fixed weekly salary even though their hours may vary from week to week because of the availability of materials, production schedules, etc. The FLSA allows such arrangements, so long as the employees receive one-half of the regular hourly rate for the week for each hour of overtime worked during that week and the fixed weekly salary is high enough to ensure that even when the employees work a great number of hours their straight time pay (fixed weekly salary) will not fall below the minimum hourly wage.[149]

*Example:* George agrees to a fixed salary of $400 per week and generally works between 35 and 50 hours per week, with a different amount worked each week. In a week where George works 47 hours:

---

149.    W-H Reg. 29 CFR §778.114.

| | |
|---|---|
| Regular rate of pay: | $400 ÷ 47 = $8.51 |
| Overtime premium rate: | $8.51 x .5 = $4.26 |
| Overtime premium pay: | $4.26 x 7 = $29.82 |
| Total earnings for the week: | $400 + $29.82 = $429.82 |

In a week where George works 43 hours:

| | |
|---|---|
| Regular rate of pay: | $400 ÷ 43 = $9.30 |
| Overtime premium rate: | $9.30 x .5 = $4.65 |
| Overtime premium pay: | $4.65 x 3 = $13.95 |
| Total earnings for the week: | $400 + $13.95 = $413.95 |

If, in an emergency situation, the fixed weekly wage is insufficient to pay the statutory minimum to an employee because a great number of hours had to be worked, the fluctuating workweek plan would not be declared invalid by the Wage and Hour Division, but the employer would have to make sure that the statutory minimum was paid for the week.

An employer may not make full-day deductions from the salary of a nonexempt employee paid under the fluctuating workweek method when the employee has exhausted available sick leave or has not earned enough leave to cover the absence. The employer may take disciplinary deductions for willful absences or tardiness, or for infractions of major safety rules, if they do not cut into the required minimum wage or overtime compensation. Frequent or consistent deductions would call into question the validity of the employer's fluctuating workweek plan overall.[150]

There is nothing limiting the use of the fluctuating workweek method to employers using a 7-day workweek. Employers of law enforcement personnel who have a 28-day work period (see Section 2.6-5) are not precluded from using the fluctuating workweek method if the conditions for its use are met.

**Belo-type constant wage plans.** A plan similar to the fluctuating workweek plan was approved by the U.S. Supreme Court and later made part of the FLSA and its regulations.[151] The plans are called Belo plans after the name of the company involved in the High Court's decision, and they guarantee a fixed salary for irregular hours that includes a set amount of overtime pay. To qualify:

- the plan must be agreed to by the employee through an individual contract or collective bargaining agreement;

- the employee must work irregular hours (with workweeks fluctuating above and below 40 hours);

- the contract must guarantee a straight time rate of at least the statutory minimum and an overtime rate of at least 1½ times the regular rate; and

- the weekly guarantee must be for not more than 60 hours of work.

*Example:* A Belo plan guarantees Bernie $475 per week for 45 hours, with a straight time hourly rate of $10 ($10 x 45) and an overtime premium rate of $5 ($10 x .5), plus time-and-a-half for hours worked over 45. Bernie will receive $475 no matter how many hours he works each week up to 45, and will receive $15 ($10 x 1.5) for each hour worked over 45.

**Overtime prepayment plan.** The DOL has ruled that an employer can pay anticipated overtime compensation to employees before an employee has worked the overtime hours, under certain circumstances.[152] Under the employer's plan considered by the DOL, employees are paid for 40 hours work even though they worked fewer hours in most weeks, in order to provide them with a stable wage payment. Excess pay is considered an advance against future overtime hours, and is offset at time-and-a-half the employee's regular rate

---

150.   W-H Op. Ltr., FLSA2006-15, 5-12-06.
151.   Walling v. A.H. Belo Corp. (1942) 62 S.Ct. 1223, 316 U.S. 624; FLSA §7(f); W-H Reg. 29 CFR §778.402 - §778.414.
152.   W-H Op. Ltr., FLSA2005-3, 1-7-05.

then in effect when the overtime is worked. If the employee works more overtime hours than the employer has advanced, the employer pays time-and-a-half for the extra hours on the next payday.

While the DOL acknowledged that overtime pay due an employee must normally be paid at the time of the employee's regular payday, it will not object if the employer pays anticipated overtime compensation in advance. The employer must maintain for each employee of the amount of pay to the employer's credit. At no time may the employer owe the employee overtime compensation past the next payday. The plan cannot be applied to an employee who is paid a set salary for a fluctuating workweek.

**Daylight saving time issues.** Employers must consider the effect that the change from standard time to daylight saving time and back again can have on employees who are working overnight shifts. For most of the U.S., daylight saving time goes into effect at 2:00 a.m. on the second Sunday in March beginning in 2008 (except for American Samoa, Arizona (other than inside the Navajo nation), Guam, Hawaii, Puerto Rico, and Virgin Islands). Because the clocks are set forward one hour at that time, employees whose shift includes the changeover will work one less hour than usual during that shift.

If the employee is paid for the full shift, the employer need not count the extra paid hour as an hour worked for overtime purposes and need not include the extra pay when determining the employee's regular rate of pay for the workweek. The extra pay also cannot be credited against any overtime pay due the employee. When the clocks are turned back one hour to standard time at 2:00 a.m. on the first Sunday in November, the same employee will work one extra hour during that shift. The employee must be paid for the extra hour, and the hour must be counted for regular rate of pay and overtime calculations.

*Example 1:* Keith works on the midnight to 8:00 a.m. shift assembling toys for Acme Toy Co. for $8.50 an hour. Acme's workweek runs from Monday through Sunday. Keith works the following hours during the week of March 3 – 9, 2008:

| Mon | Tue | Wed | Thru | Fri | Sat | Sun |
|-----|-----|-----|------|-----|-----|-----|
| 0   | 8   | 8   | 8    | 8   | 8   | 7   |

If Acme wishes to pay Keith for the hour he did not work on Sunday, March 9, when the clocks were advanced, his total pay would be calculated as follows:

| | |
|---|---|
| Total hours physically worked: | 47 |
| Regular earnings: | $8.50 x 47 = $399.50 |
| Overtime premium rate: | $8.50 x .5 = $4.25 |
| Overtime premium pay: | $4.25 x 7 = $29.75 |
| Pay for extra hour: | $8.50 |
| Total earnings for the workweek: | $399.50 + $29.75 + $8.50 = $437.75 |

*Example 2:* Keith is still working the same shift for the same wage during the week of October 27 – November 2, 2008. Here are the hours he worked during that week:

| Mon | Tue | Wed | Thru | Fri | Sat | Sun |
|-----|-----|-----|------|-----|-----|-----|
| 0   | 8   | 8   | 8    | 8   | 8   | 9   |

Keith's total pay for the workweek would be calculated as follows:

| | |
|---|---|
| Total hours physically worked: | 49 |
| Regular earnings: | $8.50 x 49 = $416.50 |
| Overtime premium rate: | $8.50 x .5 = $4.25 |
| Overtime premium pay: | $4.25 x 9 = $38.25 |
| Total earnings for the workweek: | $416.50 + $38.25 = $454.75 |

## 2.6-5 Compensatory Time Off

Because the workweek is the FLSA's basic unit of time used in determining whether overtime pay is due an employee, employers generally cannot "pay" overtime earned in one workweek by giving the employee time off from work in another workweek, even if 1½ hours off are given for each overtime hour worked. Employers also cannot "average" the hours worked in consecutive workweeks to avoid paying overtime (see Section 2.6-1).

But there are exceptions to the general rule. One narrow exception allows employers to provide time off within the same pay period to keep their overtime cash costs down. There is also a broader exception for state and local government employers.

**Time off in the same pay period.** When employees are paid either biweekly, semimonthly, or monthly, the employer can give them at least 1½ hours off for every hour of overtime worked, so long as the time off is given within the same pay period that the overtime is worked and the overtime premium is paid for the actual overtime hours worked.[153]

> **Example:** Lloyd repairs televisions for $12 an hour and is paid biweekly. If Lloyd works 45 hours in the first week of the pay period, he is due $570 [(45 x $12) + (5 x $6)]. To keep Lloyd's biweekly pay at $960 (80 x $12), he can be given 7½ hours off during the second week of the pay period. Therefore, he works 32½ hours in the second week, for which he earns $390 (32.5 x $12). His total pay for the pay period is $960 ($570 + $390 = $960).

The plan becomes more complicated for employees paid on a semimonthly or monthly basis because such periods cannot be broken down evenly into workweeks, but it still can be used. Also, while the plan is most easily applied to hourly paid employees, salaried employees can fit under the plan if their salary is docked for working less than the normal workweek (in effect making the employee an hourly paid employee).

**Public sector employers can provide comp time instead of cash.** If certain conditions are met, state and local government employers can give their nonexempt employees at least 1½ hours of paid compensatory time off for each hour of overtime worked rather than paying a premium rate for the overtime.[154] These conditions are discussed in the following paragraphs.

*Agreement before work.*[155] In order to give compensatory time off instead of cash to public sector employees, there must be an agreement between the employer and the employees or their collective bargaining representative before any work is done. For employees hired before April 15, 1986, no new agreement is necessary if a compensatory time off policy was in effect at that time. The employer may agree to different plans with different employees. Agreements that are not part of collective bargaining agreements do not have to be in writing, but a written record of them must be kept by the employer.

*Reasonable period of time to take time off.*[156] Once they request it, employees must be allowed to take compensatory time owed to them within a reasonable period of time, considering the employer's work schedule, emergency staffing requirements, and available substitutes.

An employer can refuse an employee's request to use comp time at a specific time if granting the request would "unduly disrupt" the employer's operations by making it unreasonably difficult to provide needed services to the public.[157] Several federal courts have ruled that requiring one police officer to work overtime or requiring a replacement from another shift or precinct in order to allow another officer to use comp time during the time requested does not constitute an "undue disruption."[158]

---

153. DOL Field Operations Handbook ¶32j16b.
154. FLSA §7(o), (p); W-H Reg. 29 CFR §553.1 - §553.233.
155. W-H Reg. 29 CFR §553.23.
156. W-H Reg. 29 CFR §553.25.
157. FLSA §7(o); W-H Reg. 29 CFR §553.25
158. Heitman v. City of Chicago, No. 04 C 3304, 2207 U.S. Dist. LEXIS 67684 (ND Ill., 9-11-07); Canney v. Town of Brookline, No. 98-11955-MEL, 2000 U.S. Dist. LEXIS 16279 (D Mass., 10-9-00); Debraska v City of Milwaukee, 131 F. Supp. 2d 1032 (ED Wis., 2000).

On the other hand, other federal courts have said that the FLSA does not require a public sector employer to authorize the use of comp time on a date specifically requested by an employee, but only that comp time be permitted within a reasonable time after the employee's request. These courts also ruled that the employer could not be forced to pay another employee overtime so that the employee who made the comp time request could get his requested day off.[159]

*Employees can be required to use comp time.*[160] The U.S. Supreme Court ruled that a public sector employer may, without a preexisting agreement, require its employees to use accrued compensatory time. The Court rejected the argument that, because the FLSA expressly grants employees authority to use compensatory time (subject to certain limitations), it implies that no other methods of spending comp time are permitted.

The Court said this argument was "unpersuasive" and that the law should instead be read as guaranteeing that, at the very minimum, an employee will get to use accrued comp time unless doing so would disrupt the employer's operations. The FLSA imposes a restriction on an employer's efforts to *prohibit* the use of comp time when an employee requests to do so, but it "says nothing about restricting an employer's efforts to *require* employees to use comp time," the Court reasoned.

 **NO COMP TIME FOR STRAIGHT TIME WORKED** Public sector employees cannot be given compensatory time off for hours worked up to 40 hours in a workweek. They must be paid in cash for all such hours.[161] However, the FLSA does not prohibit the use of compensatory time for non-overtime hours so long as the employee's regular rate of pay is at least equal to the federal minimum wage for all hours worked. Therefore, a part-time public employee could be given comp time off for extra non-overtime hours so long as the employee was paid at least the minimum wage for all hours actually worked.[162]

*Payment on termination.*[163] If employment is terminated for any reason, the employee must be paid for all compensatory time owed at the rate of pay then in effect for the employee or the average rate over the employee's last three years of employment, whichever is higher. If the employer pays cash for accrued compensatory overtime at any other time, the overtime pay must be based on the employee's regular rate when the payment is made.

*Maximum compensatory time accrual.*[164] Public employees can accumulate up to 240 hours of compensatory time off (160 overtime hours worked). Any overtime worked beyond that point must be compensated for in cash, with the employee getting at least 1½ times the regular rate of pay for those overtime hours.

*Exceptions to overtime requirements.* Not all work done by public employees must be included when determining whether overtime pay or compensatory time off is due. If they work occasionally on a part-time basis for the same public agency in a different job, the hours in that job can be excluded from the overtime calculation.[165] It is important to note that the part-time job cannot be regular or in the same field as the employee's regular job. Also, volunteer work by an employee for a public agency would not be hours worked for the purposes of calculating overtime, unless the work is the same type of work normally done by the employee for the same agency.[166]

Another exception exists for employees who substitute for or "trade time" with one another.[167] If the employees work for the same public agency in the same capacity and the agreement is entered into voluntarily, the hours worked by the substituting employee need not be included in overtime calculations. The regulations note that each employee will be credited as if he or she had worked his or her normal work schedule for that shift and the originally scheduled hours will count as hours worked in determining overtime due to the employees.[168]

---

159.   Mortensen v. County of Sacramento, 368 F.3d 1082 (9 CA 2004); Houston Police Officers' Union v. City of Houston, 330 F.3d 298 (5 CA, 2003), cert. den. 124 S.Ct. 300 (2003).
160.   Christensen v. Harris County, 120 S. Ct. 1655 (2000).
161.   W-H Op. Ltr., FLSA2004-10, 9-20-04.
162    W-H Op. Ltr., FLSA2007-9, 5-14-07.
163.   W-H Reg. 29 CFR §553.27.
164.   W-H Reg. 29 CFR §553.21; §553.22.
165.   FLSA §7(p)(2); W-H Reg. 29 CFR §553.30.
166.   FLSA §3(a)(4); W-H Reg. 29 CFR §553.100 - §553.106.
167.   FLSA §7(p)(3); W-H Reg. 29 CFR §553.31.
168.   Senger v. City of Aberdeen, 466 F.3d 670 (8 CA, 2006); cert. den. No. 06-1093 (U.S. S. Ct., 5-14-07).

Still another exception applies to time spent by a public sector court reporter in preparing a court transcript.[169] Such time is not considered hours worked for the purpose of calculating overtime and payments for such work are not included in determining the employee's regular rate of pay if:

- the work is performed outside the employee's regular working hours; and

- the employee is paid for preparing the transcript at a per-page rate that at least equals the maximum rate established by state or local law, the maximum rate established by a judicial or administrative officer in effect on July 1, 1995, or the rate negotiated between the employee and the party requesting the transcript (other than the presiding judge).

*Public safety, emergency response, and seasonal employees.*[170] The maximum number of compensatory overtime hours that can be accrued is 480 (320 overtime hours worked) for employees engaged in public safety, emergency response, and seasonal activities. This exception covers law enforcement officers and firefighters, emergency medical personnel, and seasonal workers whose jobs are subject to regularly recurring periods of peak demand.

Public safety employees are also covered by another exception to the FLSA's overtime requirements. Where firefighters have a work period lasting from 7-28 consecutive days, no overtime pay or compensatory time off is due until the ratio of the number of hours worked to the number of days in the work period exceeds the ratio of 212 hours to 28 days (171 hours to 28 days for law enforcement officers). The firefighter exemption also includes paramedics, emergency medical technicians, rescue workers, ambulance personnel and hazardous materials workers who are trained and engage in fire prevention and suppression or respond to emergency situations.[171] This exception allows public employers to spread hours worked for public safety employees over the entire work period, thus saving on overtime costs. Table 2.2 shows the maximum hours that can be worked in a work period before overtime pay is due for firefighters and law enforcement officers.

It is up to the employer or the collective bargaining agreement with the employees' union to establish the work period, and it need not coincide with the employees' duty cycle, which may occur at a different cycle than the work period.[172]

Table 2.2

| MAXIMUM HOURS FOR POLICE OFFICERS AND FIREFIGHTERS | | |
|:---:|:---:|:---:|
| Work Period (days) | Fire Protection | Law Enforcement |
| 28 | 212 | 171 |
| 27 | 204 | 165 |
| 26 | 197 | 159 |
| 25 | 189 | 153 |
| 24 | 182 | 147 |
| 23 | 174 | 141 |
| 22 | 167 | 134 |
| 21 | 159 | 128 |
| 20 | 151 | 122 |
| 19 | 144 | 116 |

---

169. FLSA §7(o)(6).
170. FLSA §7(o)(3)(A); W-H Reg. 29 CFR §553.24.
171. FLSA §3(y); §7(k); W-H Reg. 29 CFR §553.210 - §553.233.
172. Franklin v. City of Kettering, Ohio, 246 F. 3d 531 (6 CA, 2001).

| MAXIMUM HOURS FOR POLICE OFFICERS AND FIREFIGHTERS | | |
|:---:|:---:|:---:|
| **Work Period (days)** | **Fire Protection** | **Law Enforcement** |
| 18 | 136 | 110 |
| 17 | 129 | 104 |
| 16 | 121 | 98 |
| 15 | 114 | 92 |
| 14 | 106 | 86 |
| 13 | 98 | 79 |
| 12 | 91 | 73 |
| 11 | 83 | 67 |
| 10 | 76 | 61 |
| 9 | 68 | 55 |
| 8 | 61 | 49 |
| 7 | 53 | 43 |

There is also a complete minimum wage and overtime exemption for public safety employees in very small towns (see Section 2.4-4).

# 2.7 Compensable Time Issues

Under the FLSA, employees must be compensated for all hours worked. This does not mean all hours spent doing productive work. It means all hours during which the employee is under the employer's control, even if the time is unproductive, so long as the time spent is for the employer's benefit.[173] Following is a discussion of some of the problem areas in determining what is working time.

# 2.7-1 Unauthorized Overtime

The FLSA's definition of "employ" is to "suffer or permit to work." This means that if the employer allows an employee to do work, the time spent working is compensable time and must be considered when calculating overtime due. This is true even if the employer does not ask the employee to do the work or in general forbids such work. Time spent working at home or at some other site away from the work site is also working time. Merely having a rule against unauthorized work is not enough. The rule must be consistently enforced (e.g., through disciplinary action) whenever possible.[174]

Where a hospital employee failed to record her alleged overtime work on her timesheets or anywhere else and failed to inform her managers that she was working at home "off the clock," a federal district court said she failed to prove that she actually worked the overtime hours.[175]

> ***Example:*** Zoe works a 40-hour week as a data processor and is not paid for her lunch hour. Because of an increase in invoices that must be processed and the resulting pressure from her supervisor, Zoe begins working on them during the last half of her lunch hour, despite a rule in the company handbook prohibiting such work. Unless her supervisor or another manager specifically forbids her from working on her lunch hour and backs it up with a threat of discipline, her time spent is working time.

---

173.   W-H Reg. 29 CFR §785.7.
174.   FLSA §3(g); W-H Reg. 29 CFR §785.11 - §785.13.
175.   Slattery v. HCA Wesley Rehabilitation Hospital, 83 F.Supp.2d 1224 (D Kan., 2000).

## 2.7-2 Meal and Rest Periods

Employers do not have to consider meal periods as working time if the employee is relieved of all duties and responsibilities. Generally, the meal period must be at least 30 minutes long to be considered nonwork time, although the Wage and Hour Division and the courts have allowed shorter time periods where the employees are relieved of all duties or special conditions have prevailed.[176] The employer does not have to allow the employee to leave the employer's premises, so long as the employee is free to pursue personal interests rather than work during the meal period. Where an employer required employees to remain at their off-premises work sites during their lunch break to provide security for the sites, the lunch periods were working time since the employees performed valuable services for the benefit of their employer. If they had not stayed at the work sites, the employer would have had to pay other employees to provide the needed security.[177] But where employees are completely relieved from duty, lunchroom facilities are readily available, and employees agreed in order to end their workday earlier, the Wage and Hour Division ruled that a 15-minute lunch period was a bona fide meal period that did not have to be considered working time.[178]

According to the Wage and Hour Division, paying employees for the first 15 minutes of a 30-minute meal period does not automatically convert the remaining 15 minutes into a compensable break period, so long as the employees are completely relieved from duty during the entire period. The payments are also excluded from the employees' regular rate of pay and cannot be counted toward any overtime pay due the employees.[179]

Rest periods or coffee breaks, however, which are generally shorter than meal periods, must be paid for as worktime. They help promote employee efficiency and are primarily for the benefit of the employer.[180] Such breaks are not required under the FLSA, but may be required under state law.

## 2.7-3 Travel Time

Whether time spent traveling by an employee is compensable worktime depends on the type of travel and its purpose. Most of the rules governing travel time are contained in the Portal-to-Portal Act of 1947 and are applicable to employees covered by the FLSA.[181]

**Travel from home to work.** In general, the time an employee spends going from home to work and from work to home is not worktime, whether the employee reports to a fixed location or to different job sites. A contract or custom of the employer may require payment for home-to-work travel time, but the time is not hours worked for the purpose of calculating overtime due unless that is separately agreed to.

There are some instances when travel from home to work is considered worktime:

1. If an employee who is already home from work is called out on an emergency call and must travel a substantial distance to get there.

2. If an employee has a special assignment for one day in another city and travels outside the regular workday to get there and back (although time spent traveling from home to a railroad station or airport would not be compensable).

Even where the employer required members of its work crews to commute together to and from its oil and gas wells and they had to meet at a convenience store and load their personal safety equipment in one car, the time spent commuting was not compensable.[182]

---

176. W-H Reg. 29 CFR §785.19; Myracle v. General Electric Co., 33 F.3d 55 (6 CA, 1994).
177. Reich v. Southern New England Telecommunications Corp., 121 F.3d 58 (2 CA, 1997).
178. W-H Div. Op. Ltr., 9-25-00.
179. W-H Div. Op. Ltr., 12-3-96.
180. W-H Reg. 29 CFR §785.18.
181. Portal-to-Portal Act §4; W-H Reg. 29 CFR §785.33 - §785.41.
182. Smith v. Aztec Well Servicing Co., 462 F.3d 1274 (10 CA, 2006).

**Travel as part of job.** Time spent traveling as part of an employee's daily work activity is compensable worktime, including travel from one job site to another or travel from a designated meeting place to a job site.[183]

**Travel to and from home in a company vehicle.** Use by an employee of an employer's vehicle for commuting and other incidental travel is not part of the employee's principal activities and is not compensable time if the vehicle is used within the normal commuting area for the employer's business or establishment and its use is subject to an agreement between the employer and the employee or the employee's collective bargaining representative.

**Travel away from home.** Travel by an employee who will be away from home overnight is worktime only during those periods that coincide with the employee's regular working hours (e.g., 9 a.m.-5 p.m.). Such time is counted as hours worked even if it occurs on a non-working day (e.g., Saturday or Sunday between 9 a.m. and 5 p.m.). Travel outside regular working hours as a passenger in a plane, train, boat, bus, or automobile is not hours worked.

> *Example:* Edgar's employer operates on a Sunday through Saturday workweek, and Edgar is regularly scheduled to work from 8:00 a.m. to 5:00 p.m. Monday through Friday, with one hour off for lunch (usually 1:00 p.m. to 2:00 p.m.). One week, Edgar must travel on Sunday from 10:00 a.m. to 4:00 p.m. (EST) to go from Atlanta to San Francisco for a Monday meeting and then work his regularly scheduled 40 hours from Monday through Friday. He is entitled to 5 hours of overtime pay for the week because his travel time (minus one hour for his regular lunch break) must be added to his regular work hours for a total of 45 hours worked for the week.

If the employee uses his or her own car rather than available public transportation for travel away from home, the employer can count as hours worked either the time spent driving or the time that would have been spent on public transportation during regular working hours. An employee riding with the driver would be entitled to pay only for those hours that fall during the passenger's regular working hours (minus meal periods).

## 2.7-4 On-Call Time

Problems determining compensable time often arise when employees are required to be "on-call" so they are available to handle emergencies. Employees who must be on-call on the employer's premises or close enough to seriously curtail their use of the time for their own purposes must be paid for the time spent on-call. But employees who merely have to leave word where they can be reached are not working while on call.[184]

On-call time questions have increased in recent years with the increased use of pagers or cellular phones to notify employees of work assignments. If employees are required to carry a pager or a cell phone and stay within a certain radius of the work site while on-call, but they are not otherwise limited in conducting personal affairs, their on-call time is probably not compensable. The greater the restrictions are in terms of response time, geography, frequency of calls, and personal activities, the more likely that the on-call time is compensable worktime.

Nurses who were required to carry a pager or a cell phone or leave a number where they could be reached while on call were not working during that time because they were not required to remain at the hospital, they were generally not called in more than once per shift, and the main restriction placed on them was that they could not use alcohol or mind altering drugs during such times.[185] On the other hand, electronic technicians who were on call 15 hours a day (24 hours on weekend days) had to be paid for all their on-call time because they had to respond to alarms within 10-15 minutes and their pagers were not always reliable, so they had to stay at or near their homes, severely restricting their personal activities. They also had to respond to 3-5 alarms per night at 45 minutes per response, which severely disrupted their sleep habits.[186]

---

183.  Burton v. Hillsborough County, No. 05-10247, 2006 U.S. App. LEXIS 12207 (11 CA, 5-18-06); cert. den. No. 06-315 (U.S. S. Ct., 11-6-06).
184.  W-H Reg. 29 CFR §785.17.
185.  Reimer v. Champion Healthcare Corp., 258 F. 3d 720 (8CA, 2001); Wisnewski v. Champion Healthcare Corp., No. A3-96-72, 2000 U.S. Dist. LEXIS 12734 (D N.D., 1-11-00).
186.  Pabst v. Oklahoma Gas & Electric Co., 228 F. 3d 1128 (10 CA, 2000).

Power plant employees who were required to live on site and remain within walking distance of the plant during off hours on their "duty" shift days were entitled to be compensated for those hours because of the restrictions on their movements and personal activities.[187]

**Sleeping time.** Employees who are on duty for shifts of less than 24 hours must be paid for all time on duty, even though they may sleep or engage in other personal activities when not busy. Where a shift is 24 hours or more, actual meal periods and sleeping periods of at least 8 hours may be excluded from worktime if the employer and employee agree beforehand. The employer must provide adequate sleeping facilities, and only 8 hours may be excluded, even if a longer sleeping period is agreed to. If the sleeping period is interrupted for work, time spent working is hours worked, and if the employee cannot get at least 5 hours of uninterrupted sleep, the entire sleeping period is working time.[188]

**Employees living on the employer's premises.**[189] Employees who live on the employer's premises permanently or for extended periods of time are not considered to be working during all the time spent on the employer's premises. Such employees generally have enough time for eating, sleeping, entertaining, and other times when they have no duties and can leave the employer's premises. Because it is difficult to clearly determine the exact hours worked under such an arrangement, the DOL will accept any reasonable agreement between the employees and the employer as compliant with the FLSA if all the relevant facts are taken into consideration in the agreement.

In applying this regulation, the DOL said that residential employees of a group home who were required to remain at the home during the sleeping hours of 10:00 p.m. to 6:00 a.m. did not have to be paid for those hours unless they were awakened and called to work, and the agreement between the home and the employees provided for such payments.[190] In upholding the agreement, the DOL also noted that the employees were free to leave the home and pursue activities of their own other than during sleep time and some other paid duty time in the mornings and on weekends.

## 2.7-5 Waiting Time

Whether time spent waiting is compensable worktime depends on whether the employee is "engaged to be waiting" or "waiting to be engaged."[191] Time spent "engaged to be waiting" is compensable worktime because it is usually short, spent on the employer's premises, and insufficient for the employee to use for his or her own purposes. Such time includes waiting for minor repairs so a machine will be operable, waiting for assignments, or waiting for a customer to arrive.

Conversely, time spent "waiting to be engaged" is not worktime because the employee is freed from all duties and responsibilities for a definite period of time and has enough time to pursue personal business before returning to work. Even if the employee remains on the employer's premises, the waiting time is not worktime.

## 2.7-6 Time Spent at Meetings and Training Sessions

Attendance at lectures, meetings, seminars, and training sessions is worktime unless all the following conditions are met:

1. the meeting, lecture, etc., is held outside of the employee's regular working hours;

2. attendance is voluntary (not a condition of employment);

---

187. Brigham v. Eugene Water & Electric Bd., 357 F.3d 931 (9 CA, 2004).
188. W-H Reg. 29 CFR §785.20 - §785.22; Herman v. Palo Group Foster Home, 183 F.3d 468 (6 CA, 1999); W-H Op. Ltr.,8-13-02.
189. W-H Reg. 29 CFR §785.23.
190. W-H Op. Ltr., 7-27-04.
191. W-H Reg. 29 CFR §785.14 - §785.16.

3.  the meeting, lecture, etc., is not directly related to the employee's job; and

4.  the employee does not perform any productive work for the employer while attending.[192]

Employees did not have to be paid for time spent in classroom training and testing to obtain licenses required by the state and to meet continuing education requirements. Even though the training was clearly related to the employees' job, the regulations allow such training to be uncompensated since it was provided by an independent institution and enabled the employees to work for any insurance company, making it primarily for the benefit of the employee, not the employer. The training was also voluntary because the state imposed the licensing requirement, not the employer.[193]

A federal appeals court reached the same conclusion when it held that campus police officers were not entitled to overtime pay for time they spent training to become emergency medical technicians. While EMT certification was an employer-imposed requirement to complete the officers' probationary period, the university could just as easily have made it a precondition of hire, the court said, and it should not be held liable for overtime pay simply because it decided to hire the officers on a probationary basis until they completed the required training.[194] Another federal court said that EMT training time was compensable where the employer-provided training included material that was not included in corresponding courses offered by independent educational institutions.[195]

**Remedial education exemption.** The FLSA contains a partial overtime pay exemption for employees receiving remedial education. An employer may employ a worker for up to 10 hours over the 40-hour workweek without having to pay overtime, if the extra hours are spent in a remedial education program. Straight time pay is all that must be provided for the extra hours. To qualify, the program must be for employees who have not graduated from high school or attained an eighth grade level of education and must provide reading and other basic skills at an eighth grade level or below. The program also may not include any job specific training. Because of these restrictions, the employer must keep accurate records of the hours spent by employees in remedial education and what they were paid for that time.[196]

The Wage and Hour Division said that time employees spent studying English outside regular work hours is not compensable where the employer developed a training program to teach its employees basic English words and phrases, and they wanted to study after going home. The study arrangement was voluntary and was outside work hours, and the employees were not performing productive work during that time. The Division also said the studying was not directly related to their job because the training is general and designed to improve their English-speaking skills, not help them work more efficiently, since their jobs did not require English proficiency.[197]

## 2.7-7 Preliminary and Postliminary Activities

The Portal-to-Portal Act of 1947 provides that activities which are "preliminary or postliminary" to an employee's principal work activity are not compensable worktime unless a contract or custom of the employer makes them compensable.[198] This means that time spent by employees to get ready for work or to get ready to leave work is not worktime unless the activities engaged in are essential to the employee's principal work activity.

Where employees were given a certain amount of time to leave the employer's premises after their shifts or be "locked-in" while the employer carried out its collection procedures for the day's receipts, the time they spent locked in the warehouse was not compensable work time since their presence was not essential to their principal work activity and both the employer and the employees benefitted from the safety aspects of the procedures.[199]

---

192.  W-H Reg. 29 CFR §785.27 - §785.32.
193.  W-H Div. Sp. Op. Ltr., 9-15-97.
194.  *Bienkowski v. Northeastern University*, 285 F.3d 138 (1 CA, 2002).
195.  *Haszard v. American Medical Response Northwest, Inc.*, 237 F. Supp. 2d 1151 (D Ore., 2001).
196.  FLSA §7(q); W-H Reg. 29 CFR §778.603.
197.  W-H Op. Ltr., FLSA2006-5, 3-10-06.
198.  Portal-to-Portal Act §4; FLSA §3(o); W-H Reg. 29 CFR §785.24 -§785.26.
199.  *Richardson v. Costco Wholesale Corp.*, 169 F. Supp. 2d 56 (D Conn., 2001).

The Portal-to-Portal Act has no effect once an employee has begun his or her first principal activity and before the end of the employee's last principal activity for the workday under the DOL's "continuous workday" rule.[200]  An employee's principal activity includes all activities that are "integral and indispensable" to the principal activity.

**Changing clothes.**  If an employee must change clothes ("donning and doffing") while at work at the beginning and end of a shift, the time spent changing clothes is worktime if changing clothes is integral and indispensable to the employee's principal activity.[201]   In the context of a poultry processing plant, the U.S. Supreme Court ruled that the time spent by production employees in putting on protective gear was integral and indispensable to their principal activity of cutting and bagging meat.  Therefore, time spent walking to and from the production area to change clothes and waiting to take off protective gear at the end of a shift was also compensable worktime under the continuous workday rule.[202]

However, the Supreme Court did not disturb lower court findings in the case that time spent donning basic "non-unique" protective gear, such as hard hats, hairnets, boots, ear plugs, or safety glasses, or time spent changing clothes or washing up, was not compensable under the FLSA.

Also, time spent by police officers changing into and out of police uniforms at the beginning and end of their shifts was not compensable worktime, even though they were required to show up for the beginning of their shift with their uniform on.[203]

**Security procedures.**  Time spent by workers at a nuclear power plant and an airport construction site passing through security checkpoints and going through security procedures at the beginning and the end of the workday was not compensable work time.  While such activities may be indispensable because they are required before and after the employees begin and end their workday, they are not integral to the employee's principal activities.[204]

**Cleaning up.**  If the demands of the job or state or federal law make showering or otherwise cleaning up after work integral and indispensable to employee's principal activity (e.g., use of caustic chemicals while working), the time spent cleaning up is compensable worktime.

**De minimis time.**  Where time worked by an employee after regular working hours is so insignificant that it cannot be definitely measured, the time is considered de minimis and need not be counted as worktime.  To avoid employer abuses, this rule applies only where the time period is indefinite and lasts no more than a few seconds or minutes.  And no part of an employee's regular working hours (or other measurable working time) can be disregarded, no matter how small.[205]

**Time clock differences.**  Where time clocks or other mechanical or automated devices are used to record hours worked, employees will often punch in or log in early and punch out or log out late.  The time before and after work is not compensable if the employee is not working during that time.  However, the Wage and Hour Division will closely scrutinize an employer's records if there are large differences between the clock records and actual hours worked.[206]

**Rounding differences.**  The Wage and Hour Division has accepted the practice of rounding off an employee's worktime, especially where time cards are used, to the nearest tenth (6 minutes) or quarter (15 minutes) of an hour.  The practice must be used consistently, however, so that employees are compensated, over a period of time, for all time actually worked.

---

200.    29 CFR §790.6(a), (b).
201.    Steiner v. Mitchell, (1956) 350 U.S. 247.
202.    IBP, Inc. v. Alvarez, No. 03-1238 (U.S. S.Ct., 11-8-05).
203.    Martin v. City of Richmond, No. C 06-06146 CRB, 2007 U.S. Dist. LEXIS 61442 (ND Cal.,8-10-07).
204.    Gorman v. Consolidated Edison Corp., No. 05-6546-cv, 2007 U.S. App. LEXIS 12450 (2 CA, 5-30-07); Bonilla v. Baker Concrete Construction, Inc., No. 06-12515, 2007 U.S. App. LEXIS 12431 (11th CA, 5-30-07), cert. den. No. 07-554 (U.S. S.Ct., 12-10-07).
205.    W-H Reg. 29 CFR §785.47.
206.    W-H Reg. 29 CFR §785.48.

## 2.7-8 Receiving Medical Attention

Any time spent by an employee waiting for or receiving medical attention on the employer's premises or at the employer's direction during regular working hours is compensable worktime. Also, compulsory medical exams and counseling sessions are compensable whenever they occur.[207] The same is true for mandatory drug and alcohol testing.[208]

However, the time employees using sick leave must spend to obtain medical verification of their illnesses under the employer's paid sick leave policy is not compensable "hours worked," since the time spent on sick leave is primarily for the benefit of the employee, not the employer.[209]

## 2.8 Child Labor Restrictions

The FLSA prohibits the employment of any "oppressive child labor" in connection with interstate commerce. It also prohibits the delivery or shipping of any goods produced by an establishment that used oppressive child labor within 30 days of their initial shipment. Oppressive child labor is the employment of any child under age 18 in violation of the child labor restrictions of the FLSA and regulations issued under it.[210] Here are the minimum age restrictions under the FLSA:

**Minors under age 18.**[211] No minor under age 18 can work in a job that has been declared hazardous by the Wage and Hour Division. Most of the jobs declared hazardous are in dangerous industries, such as mining, logging, woodworking, meat packing, and construction, or involve dangerous machinery. Some minors age 16 and 17 are exempt from these restrictions under certain student learner or apprentice programs. Employees age 16 and 17 can also load materials into, but not operate or unload material from, scrap paper balers and paper box compactors that are considered safe for 16- and 17-year-olds and that cannot be operated while being unloaded. There is also an exception for minors under 18 who are exempt from compulsory school attendance and who work with wood products under the supervision of an adult relative or member of the same religious sect, so long as no power-driven woodworking machines are used and the minor is protected from flying wood particles, noise, and saw dust.

**Minors age 14 and 15.**[212] Minors age 14 and 15 can work in a limited number of nonhazardous jobs in retail, food service, and gasoline service establishments. They cannot work during school hours and are limited to working 3 hours a day and 18 hours a week when school is in session (8 hours a day and 40 a week when school is not in session). They also can work only between 7 a.m. and 7 p.m. (7 a.m. and 9 p.m. from June 1 through Labor Day).

**Minors under age 14.**[213] Employment is generally prohibited, unless the minor is working for a parent, and even those jobs cannot be hazardous or in mining or manufacturing.

**Exceptions.** The minimum age and hours restrictions are greatly relaxed for agricultural occupations, especially where the minor is employed by his or her parents. Also, minors working as actors or performers in the movies, television, theater, or radio are exempt, as are news carriers and homeworkers making Christmas wreaths.[214]

Wage and Hour Division regulations exempt minors 14 and 15 years of age who work as "professional sports attendants" from the maximum hours restrictions of the FLSA, so long as the work is performed outside school hours.[215] Ballboys/girls, batboys/girls, etc., are not limited in their hours of work or to certain times of the day if they perform traditional sports attendant duties (e.g., putting out and taking in field equipment, running errands for players, supplying balls to the umpire).

---

207.    W-H Reg. 29 CFR §785.43, W-H Div. Sp. Op. Ltr., 9-15-97.
208.    W-H Div Op. Ltr., 1-26-98; Sehie v. City of Aurora, 432 F.3d 749 (7 CA, 2005).
209.    W-H Op. Ltr., FLSA2005-3NA, 5-16-05.
210.    FLSA §3(l); §12; W-H Reg. 29 CFR §570.2; §570.50 - §570.120.
211.    FLSA §13(c); W-H Reg. 29 CFR §570.51 - §570.68.
212.    W-H Reg. 29 CFR §570.119.
213.    W-H Reg. 29 CFR §570.126.
214.    FLSA §13(c), (d); W-H Reg. 29 CFR §570.122 - §570.126.
215.    29 CFR §570.35(b).

Under the Drive for Teen Employment Act of 1998, 17-year-olds can drive on public roadways as part of their jobs up to one-third of their workday and 20% of their workweek, subject to certain restrictions on the type of worktime driving. Also, they can drive only during daylight hours, cannot have any moving violations on their driver's license, must have taken a state-approved driver's education course, and cannot drive a vehicle exceeding 6,000 pounds of gross vehicle weight. The employer must instruct the employees to wear seat belts while driving for the employer.[216]

**Age certificates.** Employers can protect themselves from child labor violations by getting from the minor proof of age in the form of an age certificate approved or recognized by the Wage and Hour Division. Employers should request an age certificate for all prospective employees who claim to be at or near the required age for employment to protect themselves against later charges, should the minor's documents prove to be false.[217] When the minor terminates employment, the employer should give the certificate to the minor.

 **WATCH STATE LAWS** Many states have child labor laws that are more restrictive than the FLSA as to what jobs minors can do and what hours they can work. Employers must comply with the more restrictive law when covered by both federal and state law.

## 2.9  Enforcement and Penalties

As was mentioned at the beginning of this section, the FLSA is administered and enforced by the Wage and Hour Division of the U.S. Department of Labor's Employment Standards Administration. The Division investigates employee complaints of violations or takes up investigations on its own, and can sue to gain compliance or seek damages from employers that have violated the law.[218] Employees may also sue to collect any back minimum wages or overtime due.

 **DOL OFFERS PHONE HELP** The Department of Labor has established a National Call Center, a toll-free service offering live operator assistance. Employers and employees can get answers to their questions on pay, overtime, and child labor at 866-4-US-WAGE.

In addition to making it unlawful to violate any provision of the law, the FLSA also makes it unlawful to discriminate against or discharge an employee because the employee files a suit or testifies in enforcement proceedings brought by the Division.[219] This is true regardless of whether the suit or claim is successful.[220] The federal courts are split as to whether the prohibition also applies to internal complaints within the employee's organization.[221] The Portal-to-Portal Act, however, protects employers if they have relied in good faith on a written interpretation of the FLSA by the Division or an administrative practice or enforcement policy of the Division.[222]

 **WATCH OUT FOR HOT GOODS** Employers that move goods through interstate commerce that have been produced in an establishment where there were minimum wage, overtime, or child labor violations are in violation of the FLSA unless they relied on a written statement from the producer of the goods that they were produced in compliance with the law.[223]

216.  FLSA §13(c)(6); P.L. 105-334; W-H Reg. 29 CFR §570.52.
217.  FLSA §3(l)(2); W-H Reg. 29 CFR §570.5 - §570.12; §570.121.
218.  FLSA §16; W-H Reg. 29 CFR §579.1 - §579.5; §580.1 - §580.18.
219.  FLSA §15(a).
220.  Sapperstein v. Hager, 188 F.3d 852 (7 CA, 1999).
221.  Lambert v Ackley, 180 F.3d 997 (9 CA, 1999); cert. den. 120 S. Ct.936 (2000); Valerio v. Putnam Associates, Inc. 173 F.3d 35(1 CA, 1999); Coyle v. Madden, No. 03-4433 (ED Pa., 12-17-03)—internal complaints support retaliation claim; Ball v MemphisBar-B-Q Co., Inc., 228 F.3d 360 (4 CA, 2000); Nicolaou v. Horizon Media, Inc., No. 01 Civ. 0785 (BSJ) (SD N.Y., 9-23-03); Chennisi v. Communications Construction Group, LLC, No. 04-4826, 2005 U.S. Dist. LEXIS 2274 (ED Pa., 2-17-05); Boateng v. Terminix International Co. Ltd., No. 07-617, 2007 U.S. Dist. LEXIS 65466 (ED Va., 9-4-07)—informal complaints don't support retaliation claim.
222.  Portal-to-Portal Act §10.
223.  FLSA §12(a); §15(a)(1).

**Wage and Hour investigations.** According to the Wage and Hour Division, a significant majority of its investigations is triggered by employee complaints of violations. Others may be conducted as follow-ups after promises to cure violations or after massive reports of serious violations in an industry. Division compliance officers are empowered to inspect all applicable records kept by an employer (for more on record-keeping required by the FLSA, see Section 10.1).[224] If a compliance officer believes that a violation has been committed, an attempt at settlement or "conciliation" will be made.

If no agreement can be reached, the compliance officer will notify the employer that it owes back wages to all employees affected by the alleged violations. At this point, if the back wage assessment is not paid, either the affected employees or the Division can bring a lawsuit to enforce payment, but once the Division brings suit, the employees can no longer do so.

**Backpay and damages.** A wage suit may be brought by an employee or the Division under the FLSA to recover back minimum wages and overtime due, plus an equal amount in "liquidated damages" for willful violations of the law.[225] This provision is designed to encourage compliance with the law by making the penalties for noncompliance costly. Employers cannot claim they did not know the provisions of the FLSA. Employers' violations are willful if the employer knew or should have known it was acting unlawfully, although a good faith belief that it was in compliance may keep an employer from having to pay liquidated damages.[226] However, the U.S. Supreme Court ruled in 1999 that state employees cannot sue their employer in state court for violations of the FLSA because that would violate the state's sovereign immunity from lawsuits inherent in the U.S. constitution.[227] In an earlier decision involving a different federal law, the High Court said that private suits against states cannot be brought in federal court. The result is that state employees cannot bring individual suits to enforce the FLSA against their employer. Their remedies seem to be limited to filing complaints with the Wage and Hour Division, which can sue on their behalf.

Where an employee claims that he or she was fired or demoted for assisting in an FLSA investigation, the court may award reinstatement and promotion of the employee, as well as damages for wages lost. The federal appeals courts are split over the issue of whether punitive damages can also be awarded for unlawful retaliation against an employee.[228] In any suit by an employee where the court finds an FLSA violation, the court will award attorneys' fees and court costs to the employee (such an award is unavailable in suits brought by the Division).[229]

 **RECORDS A KEY**  In any investigation or lawsuit for backpay and back overtime, records proving the hours worked and earnings of the employees involved are important to both the employer's and employees' positions. If accurate documentation has not been maintained by the employer, the employees' calculations will be accepted, most likely leading to a victory for the employees and an award of damages against the employer.

**Compulsory arbitration.** It has become increasingly common for employers to require prospective employees to sign agreements to submit any future dispute with the employer to arbitration and give up their right to file a lawsuit. Several federal appeals courts said they would enforce such an agreement, so long as the arbitration procedure seemed fair and would provide an adequate remedy for FLSA violations.[230] One court refused to enforce such an agreement where claims had to be brought in a shorter time period than under the FLSA and the employees were required to pay for half the costs of the arbitration.[231]

---

224.  FLSA §11(a).
225.  FLSA §16(b); §16(c).
226.  Portal-to-Portal Act §11.
227.  Alden v. Maine, 119 S.Ct. 2240 (1999).
228.  Travis v. Gary Community Mental Health Center, Inc., 921 F.2d 1500 (11 CA, 1993); Snapp v. Unlimited Concepts, Inc.,208 F. 3d 928 (11 CA, 2000).
229.  FLSA §16(b).
230.  Floss v. Ryan's Family Steak Houses, Inc., 211 F. 3d 306 (6 CA, 2000), cert. den. 121 S.Ct. 763 (2005); Carter v. Countrywide Credit Industries, Inc., 362 F. 3d 294 (5 CA, 2004).
231.  Bailey v. Ameriquest Mortgage Co., Civil No. 01-545 (JRT/FLN), 2002 U.S. Dist. LEXIS 1343 (D Minn., 1-23-02).

Another court denied enforcement where the employer provided nearly half the funding for the arbitration service that was to be used and the procedures to be followed showed a structural bias toward the employer.[232]

**Statute of limitations.**[233] Complaints can be filed with the Division for minimum wages and overtime due up to two years earlier (three years if the violation was willful).

**Injunctions.**[234] In addition to suing to collect minimum wages and overtime due employees, the Secretary of Labor can go to court for an order (injunction) prohibiting an employer from committing further violations of the FLSA or requiring the employer to comply with an order to pay backpay. Employers that violate such an order can be held in contempt of court and face stiff fines and/or imprisonment.

**Civil and criminal penalties.**[235] In addition to the damages that can be awarded to employees for violations of the FLSA, employers can be fined and/or its officers jailed for their unlawful acts. Employers that repeatedly or willfully violate the minimum wage and overtime provisions of the law can be fined up to $1,100 for each violation. Child labor violations can bring fines of up to $11,000 for each violation that causes the death or serious injury of a minor. The amount of the fines will depend on the size of the employer and the seriousness of the violations. Employers that willfully violate the FLSA can be fined up to $10,000 and the officers imprisoned for up to 6 months for second and later offenses.

# 2.10 Public Contracts Laws

Several other federal laws regulate the minimum wages and overtime pay that must be paid to employees who are working for employers performing under contracts with the federal government. They are also administered and enforced by the Wage and Hour Division.

## 2.10-1 Walsh-Healey Public Contracts Act

The Walsh-Healey Public Contracts Act[236] governs the wages and hours of employees of manufacturers and dealers furnishing the federal government with materials, supplies, and equipment under contracts exceeding $10,000. The Act requires covered employees to be paid 1½ times their basic (regular) rate of pay for all hours physically worked over 40 in a workweek. They also must be paid the prevailing minimum wage for work in the same or similar industries in the locality where the goods are manufactured or furnished. Learners, apprentices, beginners, and handicapped workers may be employed at rates below the minimum under special certificates issued by the Labor Secretary.

The Wage and Hour Division has broad powers to investigate alleged violations of the Act and may order employers to make payments of back wages and overtime pay due employees. Employers may also have to pay damages for breach of contract and can be barred from receiving a government contract for up to three years.

## 2.10-2 Davis-Bacon Act

Under the Davis-Bacon Act,[237] the Secretary of Labor sets prevailing minimum wage standards for laborers and mechanics working on federally financed construction contracts of $2,000 or more. The prevailing wages are based on wages for similar workers in the locality where the project is to take place.

---

232. Walker v. Ryan's Family Steak Houses, Inc., 289 F.Supp.2d 916 (MD Tenn., 2003).
233. Portal-to-Portal Act §6.
234. FLSA §17.
235. FLSA §16(a), (e); W-H Reg. 29 CFR §578.3; §579.5.
236. 41 U.S.C. §35 - §45.
237. 40 U.S.C. §276a - §276a-7.

In contrast to the industry-wide wage determinations issued under the Walsh-Healey Act, Davis-Bacon wage determinations set standards for specific job classifications. A certain level of fringe benefits may also be required to be paid if they are not already required by another federal or state law.

In determining the overtime due employees covered by the Davis-Bacon Act, the regular rate is the hourly rate plus fringe benefits unless the total is greater than that required by the Secretary of Labor. If that is the case, the employer can subtract the amount of fringes actually being paid or the amount required by the Secretary, whichever is greater, to calculate the regular rate. Violators can be barred from government contracts for up to three years.

## 2.10-3 Contract Work Hours and Safety Standards Act

The Contract Work Hours and Safety Standards Act[238] requires contractors with the federal government (not those already covered by Walsh-Healey or Davis-Bacon) to pay employees overtime of at least 1½ times their "basic rate" for hours worked over 40 in a workweek. Overtime must be paid only for work covered by the contract (Walsh-Healey applies to both covered and uncovered work).

The basic rate is the same as the employee's regular rate under the FLSA. Violators are subject to liquidated damages of $10 per day for each employee working in violation of the Act. Such amounts can be withheld from amounts owed the contractor under its contract with the federal government.

## 2.10-4 Service Contract Act

The McNamara-O'Hara Service Contract Act[239] applies to employers that contract with the federal government to provide services to a federal agency. It applies to contracts over $2,500 and requires that employees be paid prevailing minimum wages and fringe benefits based on the wages and benefits for similar employment in the locality or on a collective bargaining agreement (the Secretary of Labor decides), but no less than the minimum wage under the FLSA.

Nonservice employees and employees working on contracts of up to $2,500 must be paid the minimum wage required by the FLSA. Fringe benefits not included in the regular rate under the FLSA are also not included in the basic rate for overtime purposes under the Service Contract Act. Violations can result in employers being barred from federal government contracts for up to three years.

## 2.10-5 Copeland Anti-Kickback Act

The Copeland Anti-Kickback Act[240] protects the wages due employees of contractors and subcontractors on federally-financed construction contracts. Under the Act, employers are prohibited from forcing employees to surrender or "kick back" compensation to which the employees are lawfully entitled.

Contractors should note that the coverage for the Anti-Kickback Act is broader than that of the Davis-Bacon Act in two respects:

- It covers all employees actually working on a covered contract, rather than just mechanics and laborers, and

- It covers all construction contracts financed in whole or in part by federal funds regardless of the dollar amount, rather than those contracts in excess of $2,000.

---

238.   40 U.S.C. §327.
239.   41 U.S.C. §351 et seq.
240.   40 U.S.C. §3145.

## 2.11 State Wage-Hour Charts

The following pages contain several charts containing minimum wage, overtime pay, tip credit, and meal and rest period requirements for each state, where applicable. The information provided is current as of January 1, 2005. Employers should check the states where they do business for any changes since then.

 **BE CAREFUL** Where the state law requirements in these charts are less favorable to an employee than the requirements in the FLSA, they apply only to those employees who are not covered by the FLSA. Where the state requirements are more favorable to an employee than the FLSA, they apply to all employees covered by the state law, even if they are also covered by the FLSA.

## 2.11-1 State Minimum Wage Rates

Table 2.3 shows the minimum hourly wage rates for each of the states that requires payment of a minimum wage. In those states without a minimum wage rate, the federal hourly minimum of $5.85 ($6.55, effective July 24, 2008; $7.25, effective July 24, 2009) applies to employees covered by the Federal Wage-Hour Law. This also holds true where the state minimum wage is lower than the federal minimum. Where the state minimum wage is higher than the federal minimum, the state minimum applies to all employees covered by the state provisions. In most states, the types of employees who are exempt from the minimum wage requirements are similar to those who are exempt from the FLSA. States may also have lower rates for teenage employees, similar to the FLSA opportunity wage. [For more information on state minimum wage rates, see Table 1.1 of APA's Guide to State Payroll Laws.]

Table 2.3

| STATE MINIMUM WAGE RATE CHART AS OF JANUARY 1, 2008 | | | |
|---|---|---|---|
| **State** | **Minimum Wage** | **State** | **Minimum Wage** |
| Alabama | No provision | Montana | $6.25; $6.55, eff. 7-24-08; $4.00 if annual gross sales are $110,000 or less |
| Alaska | $7.15 | Nebraska | $5.85; $6.55, eff. 7-24-08; $7.25, eff. 7-24-09 |
| Arizona | $6.90 | Nevada | $6.33; $5.85 if employer provides health benefits |
| Arkansas | $6.25 | New Hampshire | $6.50; $7.25, eff. 9-1-08 |
| California | $8.00 | New Jersey | $7.15 |
| Colorado | $7.02 | New Mexico | $6.50; $7.50, eff. 1-1-09 |
| Connecticut | $7.65 | New York | $7.15 |
| Delaware | $7.15 | North Carolina | $6.15; $6.55, eff. 7-24-08; $7.25, eff. 7-24-09 |
| Dist. of Col. | $7.00 | North Dakota | $5.85; $6.55, eff. 7-24-08; $7.25, eff. 7-24-09 |
| Florida | $6.79 | Ohio | $7.00; federal rate if annual gross receipts of $255,000 or less |
| Georgia | $5.15 | Oklahoma | $5.85; $6.55, eff. 7-24-08; $7.25, eff. 7-24-09 |
| Hawaii | $7.25 | Oregon | $7.95 |
| Idaho | $5.85; $6.55, eff. 7-24-08; $7.25, eff. 7-24-09 | Pennsylvania | $7.15; $7.25, eff. 7-24-09 |

| STATE MINIMUM WAGE RATE CHART AS OF JANUARY 1, 2008 | | | |
|---|---|---|---|
| **State** | **Minimum Wage** | **State** | **Minimum Wage** |
| Illinois | $7.50; $7.75, eff. 7-1-08; $8.00, eff. 7-1-09; $8.25, eff. 7-1-10 ($0.50 lower during first 90 calendar days of job) | Rhode Island | $7.40 |
| Indiana | $5.85; $6.55, eff. 7-24-08; $7.25, eff. 7-24-09 | South Carolina | No provision |
| Iowa | $7.25 | South Dakota | $5.85; $6.55, eff. 7-24-08; $7.25, eff. 7-24-09 |
| Kansas | $2.65 | Tennessee | No provision |
| Kentucky | $5.85; $6.55, eff. 7-1-08; $7.25, eff. 7-1-09 | Texas | $5.85; $6.55, eff. 7-24-08; $7.25, eff. 7-24-09 |
| Louisiana | No provision | Utah | $5.85; $6.55, eff. 7-24-08; $7.25, eff. 7-24-09 |
| Maine | $7.00 | Vermont | $7.68 |
| Maryland | $6.15 | Virginia | $5.85; $6.55, eff. 7-24-08; $7.25, eff. 7-24-09 |
| Massachusetts | $8.00 | Washington | $8.07 |
| Michigan | $7.15; $7.40, eff. 7-1-08 | West Virginia | $6.55; $7.25, eff. 7-1-08 |
| Minnesota | $6.15 (large employers) $5.25 (small employers) | Wisconsin | $6.50 |
| Mississippi | No provision | Wyoming | $5.15 |
| Missouri | $6.65 | | |

## 2.11-2 State Tip Credits

Table 2.4 shows the amount of tips received by an employee that can be applied by the employer as a tip credit against the minimum wage in each state. For tipped employees covered by both the state and federal wage-hour laws, the law guaranteeing the employee the highest net minimum wage (after applying the tip credit) must be followed. See Section 2.5-1 for more details on how the tip credit is applied. [For more information on state tip credit requirements, see Table 1.1 of *APA's Guide to State Payroll Laws.*]

Table 2.4

| STATE TIP CREDITS AGAINST THE MINIMUM WAGE | | | |
|---|---|---|---|
| **State** | **Tip Credit Maximum** | **State** | **Tip Credit Maximum** |
| Alabama | No provision | Montana | No tip credit |
| Alaska | No tip credit | Nebraska | $3.72; $4.42, eff. 7-24-08; $5.12, eff. 7-24-09 |
| Arizona | $3.00 | Nevada | No tip credit |
| Arkansas | $3.62 | New Hampshire | $3.57; $3.99, eff. 9-1-08 |
| California | No tip credit | New Jersey | $5.02 |
| Colorado | $3.02 | New Mexico | $4.37, $5.37, eff. 1-1-09 |
| Connecticut | 29.3% of minimum wage ($2.24); 8.2% of minimum wage for bartenders ($0.63) | New York | $2.55 |

| STATE TIP CREDITS AGAINST THE MINIMUM WAGE | | | |
|---|---|---|---|
| **State** | **Tip Credit Maximum** | **State** | **Tip Credit Maximum** |
| Delaware | $4.92 | North Carolina | $3.72 ; $4.42, eff. 7-24-08; $5.12, eff. 7-24-09 |
| Dist. of Col. | $4.23 | North Dakota | 33% of minimum wage ($1.93; $2.16, eff. 7-24-08; $2.39, eff. 7-24-09) |
| Florida | $3.02 | Ohio | $3.50 |
| Georgia | No minimum applicable | Oklahoma | 50% of minimum wage ($2.92) |
| Hawaii | $0.25 | Oregon | No tip credit |
| Idaho | $2.50 | Pennsylvania | $4.32; $4.42 eff. 7-24-09 |
| Illinois | 40% of minimum wage ($3.00); $3.10, eff. 7-1-08; $3.20, eff. 7-1-09; $3.30, eff. 7-1-10 | Puerto Rico | No tip credit |
| Indiana | $3.02; $4.42, eff. 7-24-08; $5.12, eff. 7-24-09 | Rhode Island | $4.51 |
| Iowa | 40% of minimum wage ($2.90) | South Carolina | No provision |
| Kansas | 40% of minimum wage ($1.06) | South Dakota | $3.72; $4.42, eff. 7-24-08; $5.12, eff. 7-24-09 |
| Kentucky | $3.72; $4.42, eff. 7-1-08; $5.12, eff. 7-1-09 | Tennessee | No provision |
| Louisiana | No provision | Texas | $3.72; $4.42, eff. 7-24-08; $5.12, eff. 7-24-09 |
| Maine | 50% of minimum wage | Utah | $3.72; $4.42, eff.7-24-08; $5.12 eff. 7-24-09 |
| Maryland | 50% of minimum wage ($3.075) | Vermont | $3.96 |
| Massachusetts | $5.37 | Virginia | Up to employer |
| Michigan | $4.50; $4.75, eff. 7-1-08 | Washington | No tip credit |
| Minnesota | No tip credit | West Virginia | 20% of minimum wage ($1.31; $1.45, eff. 7-1-08) |
| Mississippi | No provision | Wisconsin | $4.17 |
| Missouri | 50% of minimum wage ($3.32) | Wyoming | $3.02 |

# 2.11-3 State Overtime Pay Requirements

Table 2.5 shows the overtime pay requirements for states that require premium pay for hours worked over certain daily or weekly maximums. The requirements summarized in this table are generally applicable within the state to employees covered by the state's wage-hour law (exemptions in most states are similar to those under the FLSA). Different provisions may apply to specific industries (e.g., health care, hotels and restaurants, resorts) or to public sector (government) employers. So employers must check the states where they do business for any possible exceptions or variations from the general rules. [For more information on state overtime pay requirements, see Table 1.2 of *APA's Guide to State Payroll Laws*.]

Table 2.5

| STATE OVERTIME PAY REQUIREMENTS (GENERAL ONLY—CHECK YOUR STATE LAW FOR EXCEPTIONS) | | | |
|---|---|---|---|
| **State** | **Overtime Pay Required** | **State** | **Overtime Pay Required** |
| Alabama | No general provision | Montana | 1½ times regular rate after 40-hour week |
| Alaska | 1½ times regular rate after 8-hour day, 40-hour week (10-hour day, 4-day week if agreed to) | Nebraska | No general provision |
| Arizona | No general provision | Nevada | 1½ times regular rate after 8-hour day or 40-hour week (10-hour day, 4-day week if agreed to) |
| Arkansas | 1½ times regular rate after 40-hour week | New Hampshire | 1½ times regular rate after 40-hour week |
| California | 1½ times regular rate after 8-hour day, 40-hour week in most industries, and for 1st 8 hours worked on 7th consecutive day worked in a workweek; check specific wage orders for other rules and exceptions | New Jersey | 1½ times regular rate after 40-hour week |
| Colorado | 1½ times regular rate after 12-hour day or 40-hour week | New Mexico | 1½ times regular rate after 40-hour week |
| Connecticut | 1½ times regular rate after 40-hour week | New York | 1½ times regular rate after 40-hour week |
| Delaware | No provision | North Carolina | 1½ times regular rate after 40-hour week |
| Dist. of Col. | 1½ times regular rate after 40-hour week | North Dakota | 1½ times regular rate after 40-hour week |
| Florida | No general provision | Ohio | 1½ times regular rate after 40-hour week |
| Georgia | No general provision | Oklahoma | No provision |
| Hawaii | 1½ times regular rate after 40-hour week | Oregon | 1½ times regular rate after 40-hour week (10-hour day in some industries) |
| Idaho | No provision | Pennsylvania | 1½ times regular rate after 40-hour week |
| Illinois | 1½ times regular rate after 40-hour week | Puerto Rico | 1½ times regular rate after 8-hour day, 40-hour week except under contract, custom, nature of work |
| Indiana | 1½ times regular rate after 40-hour week | Rhode Island | 1½ times regular rate after 40-hour week |
| Iowa | No provision | South Carolina | No provision |
| Kansas | 1½ times regular rate after 46-hour week | South Dakota | No provision |
| Kentucky | 1½ times regular rate after 40-hour week | Tennessee | No provision |
| Louisiana | No provision | Texas | No provision |
| Maine | 1½ times regular rate after 40-hour week | Utah | No general provision |
| Maryland | 1½ times regular rate after 40-hour week | Vermont | 1½ times regular rate after 40-hour week |
| Massachusetts | 1½ times regular rate after 40-hour week | Virginia | No general provision |
| Michigan | 1½ times regular rate after 40-hour week | Washington | 1½ times regular rate after 40-hour week |
| Minnesota | 1½ times regular rate after 48-hour week | West Virginia | 1½ times regular rate after 40-hour week |
| Mississippi | No provision | Wisconsin | No general provision |
| Missouri | 1½ times regular rate after 40-hour week | Wyoming | No provision |

# 2.11-4 State Meal and Rest Period Requirements

Many states require that employers give employees a certain amount of time off from work during their work shift for rest or meals after a certain number of hours has been worked. These requirements are found only in state wage-hour laws, not in the FLSA. Table 2.6 provides the generally applicable meal and rest period requirements in each state where they exist. Employers in those states should check the state law for exceptions in times of emergency, details on mid-shift break times, or for different restrictions in certain industries (e.g., agriculture). [For more information on state meal and rest period requirements, see Table 1.2 of *APA's Guide to State Payroll Laws*.]

Table 2.6

| STATE MEAL AND REST PERIOD CHART | | | |
|---|---|---|---|
| **State** | **Meal and/or Rest Period Required** | **State** | **Meal and/or Rest Period Required** |
| Alabama | Minors under 16: 30 minutes meal or rest after 5 hours | Montana | No provision minutes rest after 5 hours |
| Alaska | Minors: two 30 minute rest periods in 6-hour shift (after first 1.5 hours and before last hour of shift) | Nebraska | Manufacturing employees: 30-minute meal period in an 8-hour shift |
| Arizona | No provision | Nevada | 30-minute meal period in an 8-hour shift; 10 minutes rest for each 4 hours (more rest periods for shifts over 7 hours) |
| Arkansas | No provision | New Hampshire | 30-minute meal period after 5 hours |
| California | 30-minute meal period after 5 hours; 30 minutes more after 10 hours; 10 minutes rest after 4 hours | New Jersey | Minors under 18: 30-minute lunch period during shift of 5 or more hours |
| Colorado | Retail, food and beverage, health care, construction, service industries: 30-minute meal period after 5 hours; 10 minutes rest during 4-hour shift | New Mexico | 30-minute meal period during 6-hour shift |
| Connecticut | 30-minute meal period during 7½-hour shift (after first 2 hours and before last 2 hours of shift) | New York | 30 minutes for noon meal from 11 a.m.-2 p.m. (60 in factory); another 20 minutes from 5 p.m.-7. p.m. if shift starts before 11 a.m. and goes after 7 p.m.; 45 minutes during shift of at least 6 hours starting between 1 p.m. and 6 a.m. (60 in factory) |
| Delaware | 30-minute meal period during 7½-hour shift (after first 2 hours and before last 2 hours of shift); Minors: 30 minutes rest during shift of 5 or more hours | North Carolina | Minors under 16: 30-minute rest period during shift of 5 or more hours |
| Dist. of Col. | No provision | North Dakota | 30-minute meal period after 5 hours |
| Florida | Minors: 30-minute meal period after 4 hours | Ohio | Minors: 30 minutes rest after 5 hours |
| Georgia | No provision | Oklahoma | Minors under 16: 1-hour cumulative rest period during 8-hour shift; 30-minute rest period after 5 hours work |

## STATE MEAL AND REST PERIOD CHART

| State | Meal and/or Rest Period Required | State | Meal and/or Rest Period Required |
|---|---|---|---|
| Hawaii | Minors under 16: 30-minute meal or rest period in 5-hour shift | Oregon | 30-minute meal period during 6-8 hour shifts, from 2nd-5th hour if shift is 7 hours or less, 3rd-6th hour if shift is more than 7 hours; 10 minutes rest each 4 hours; minors: 30-minute meal or rest period before 5 hours and 1 minute of shift |
| Idaho | No provision | Pennsylvania | Minors: 30-minute rest period after 5 hours work |
| Illinois | 20-minute meal period during first 5 hours of 7½-hour shift; Minors under 16: 30- minute meal period during 5 hour shift | Puerto Rico | 1-hour meal period after 3rd and before 6th hour of shift unless agreed otherwise; minors 14-17: 1-hour meal period in 4-hour shift |
| Indiana | Minors: 30-minute rest break during 3rd-5th hour of shift lasting at least 6 hours | Rhode Island | 20-minute meal period during 6-hour shift; 30 minutes during 8-hour shift, with some exceptions |
| Iowa | Minors under 16: 30-minute rest period during 5-hour shift | South Carolina | No provision |
| Kansas | No provision | South Dakota | No provision |
| Kentucky | Reasonable meal period within 3-5 hours after shift starts; 10-minute rest each 4 hours; minors: 30-minute meal period after 5 hours | Tennessee | 30-minute meal period or rest during shift of 6 hours (not during first hour of shift) |
| Louisiana | Minors: 30-minute meal period after 5 hours | Texas | No provision |
| Maine | 30-minute period after 6 hours | Utah | Minors: 30-minute meal period after 5 hours; 10 minutes rest each 4 hours |
| Maryland | Minors: 30-minute rest for 5 hours' work | Vermont | Reasonable opportunity to eat and use toilet facilities. |
| Massachusetts | 30-minute meal period after 6 hours | Virginia | Minors: 30-minute meal period during 5-hour shift |
| Michigan | Minors: 30-minute meal and rest period during 5-hour shift | Washington | 30-minute meal period within 2-5 hours after shift starts and after 3 hours' overtime; 10 minutes rest each 4 hours |
| Minnesota | Sufficient time to eat a meal during shift of at least 8 hours; adequate time to visit restroom in each 4 hours of work; reasonable time to express breast milk (doesn't need to be paid) | West Virginia | 20 minutes for 6 hours; minors: 30-minute lunch period for 5 hours work |
| Mississippi | No provision | Wisconsin | 30-minute meal period near middle of shift of 6 hours |
| Missouri | No provision | Wyoming | No provision |

# 2.11-5 Directory of State Wage and Hour Agencies

Following is a list of the state agencies, with their address and phone number, that administer the various state wage and hour laws and regulations. When you have a question that involves whether your company policy is lawful under a particular state law, the state wage and hour agency is usually a good place to start.

**Alabama**
Department of Labor
100 North Union St.
PO Box 303500
Montgomery, Al 36130-3500
334-242-3460
www.alalabor.state.al.us

**Alaska**
Department of Labor and Workforce Development
Labor Standards and Safety Division
Wage and Hour Administration
1111 West Eighth St., Rm 302
P. O. Box 21149
Juneau, AK 99802-1149
(907) 465-4842
www.labor.state.ak.us/lss/whhome.htm

**Arizona**
Industrial Commission
Labor Department
800 West Washington St.
Phoenix, AZ 85007-9070
(602) 542-4515
www.ica.state.az.us/divisions/labor/index.html

**Arkansas**
Department of Labor
Employment Standards Division
Wage and Hour Section
10421 West Markham
Little Rock, AR 72205
(501) 682-4500
www.ark.org/labor/divisions/labor_standards_
p1.html#hour

**California**
Department of Industrial Relations
Division of Labor Standards Enforcement
455 Golden Gate Avenue, 9th Fl.
San Francisco, CA 94102
415-703-4810
www.dir.ca.gov/dlse/dlse.html

**Colorado**
Department of Labor and Employment
Division of Labor
Labor Standards Office
633 17th St., Ste. 200
Denver, CO 80202-3660
(303) 318-8441
www.coworkforce.com/LAB/

**Connecticut**
Department of Labor
Wage and Workplace Standards Division
200 Folly Brook Blvd.
Wethersfield, CT 06109
(860) 263-6790
www.ctdol.state.ct.us/wgwkstnd/wgemenu.htm

**Delaware**
Department of Labor
Division of Industrial Affairs
Office of Labor Law Enforcement
4425 N. Market St., 3rd Floor
Wilmington, DE 19802
(302) 761-8200
www.delawareworks.com/industrialaffairs/
services/LaborLawEnforcement.shtml

**District of Columbia**
Department of Employment Services
Office of Wage-Hour
Office of Labor Standards
64 New York Avenue, NE, Room 3812
Washington, DC 20002
(202) 671-1880
http://does.ci.washington.dc.us/does/cwp/
view,a,1232,q,537799.asp

**Florida**
Agency for Workforce Innovation
107 East Madison St.
Caldwell Bldg.
Tallahassee, FL 32399-4120
(850) 245-7105
www.floridajobs.org/

**Georgia**
Department of Labor
Sussex Bldg.
148 International Blvd., NE, Ste. 600
Atlanta, GA 30303-1751
(866) 487-9243
www.dol.state.ga.us/

**Hawaii**
Department of Labor and Industrial Relations
Wage Standards Division
830 Punchbowl St., Rm. 340
Honolulu, HI 96813
(808) 586-8777
http://hawaii.gov/labor/wsd/index.shtml

**Idaho**
Department of Labor
Wage and Hour Division
317 West Main St.
Boise, ID 83735-0910
(208) 332-3579
http://cl.idaho.gov/portal/ICL/alias__jobservice/
tabID__4523/DesktopDefault.aspx

**Illinois**
Department of Labor
Fair Labor Standards Division
160 North LaSalle, Ste. C1300
Chicago, IL 60601-3150
(312) 793-2800
www.state.il.us/agency/idol/

**Indiana**
Department of Labor
Wage and Hour Division
402 West Washington St., Rm. W195
Indianapolis, IN 46204
(317) 232-2655
www.in.gov/labor/wagehour/wagehourlaws.htm

**Iowa**
Iowa Workforce Development
Division of Labor Services
1000 East Grand Ave.
Des Moines, IA 50319-0209
(515) 281-5387
www.iowaworkforce.org//labor

**Kansas**
Department of Labor
Office of Employment Standards
401 SW Topeka Blvd.
Topeka, KS 66603
(785) 296-4062
www.dol.ks.gov/ES/HTML/laws_RES.html

**Kentucky**
Department of Labor
Division of Employment Standards,
Apprenticeship and Training
1047 U.S. 127 South, Ste. 4
Frankfort, KY 40601-4381
(502) 564-3070
www.labor.ky.gov/ows/employmentstandards/

**Louisiana**
Department of Labor
1001 North 23rd St.
P.O. Box 94094
Baton Rouge, LA 70804-9094
(225) 342-3111
www.ldol.state.la.us/

**Maine**
Department of Labor
Bureau of Labor Standards
Wage and Hour Division
45 State House Station
Augusta, ME 04333-0045
(207) 624-6400
www.maine.gov/labor/labor_laws/wagehour.html

**Maryland**
Department of Labor, Licensing and Regulation
Employment Standards Service
1100 N. Eutaw St., Rm. 607
Baltimore, MD 21201-2357
(410) 767-2357
www.dllr.state.md.us/labor/emps.html

**Massachusetts**
Office of the Attorney General
Fair Labor and Business Practices Division
100 Cambridge St.
Boston, MA 02114
(617) 727-3465
www.ago.state.ma.us

**Michigan**
Department of Labor and Economic Growth
Wage and Hour Division
7150 Harris Dr.
P.O. Box 30476
Lansing, MI 48909
(517) 335-0400
www.michigan.gov/cis/0,1607,7-154-27673---,00.
html

**Minnesota**
Department of Labor and Industry
Labor Standards Division
443 Lafayette Rd. N.
St. Paul, MN 55155-4306
(651) 284-5005; (800) 342-5354
www.doli.state.mn.us/laborlaw.html

**Mississippi**
Employment Security Commission
1520 West Capital St.
Jackson, MS 39203
(601) 965-4347
http://mdes.ms.gov/wps/portal/#null

**Missouri**
Department of Labor and Industrial Relations
Division of Labor Standards
Wage and Hour Section
P.O. Box 449
3315 West Truman Blvd.
Jefferson City, MO 65102-0449
(573) 751-3403
www.dolir.state.mo.us/ls/wagehour

**Montana**
Department of Labor and Industry
Employment Relations Division
Labor Standards Bureau
Wage and Hour Unit
1805 Prospect Avenue
P.O. Box 6518
Helena, MT 59604-6518
(406) 444-5600
http://erd.dli.state.mt.us/laborstandard/
wagehrlaws.asp

**Nebraska**
Nebraska Workforce Department
Labor and Safety Standards Division
State Office Bldg.
301 Centennial Mall South
P.O. Box 95024
Lincoln, NE 68509-5024
(402) 471-4712 or (402) 471-2239
www.dol.state.ne.us/

**Nevada**
Department of Business and Industry
Office of Labor Commissioner
555 East Washington Avenue, Ste. 4100
Las Vegas, NV 89101
(702) 486-2650
www.laborcommissioner.com

**New Hampshire**
Department of Labor
Inspection Division
95 Pleasant St.
P.O. Box 2076
Concord, NH 03302-2076
(603) 271-6294
www.labor.state.nh.us/wage_hour.asp

**New Jersey**
Department of Labor and Workforce Development
Division of Wage and Hour Compliance
225 E. State St.
P.O. Box 389
Trenton, NJ 08625-0389
(609) 292-2305
http://lwd.dol.state.nj.us/labor/wagehour

**New Mexico**
Department of Workforce Solutions
Division of Labor Relations
Wage and Hour Bureau
501 Mountain Rd.
Albuquerque, NM 87102
(505) 222-4667
www.dws.state.nm.us/dws-wagehour.html

**New York**
Department of Labor
Division of Labor Standards
State Office Campus
Building 12, Rm. 185A
Albany, NY 12240
(518) 457-2730
www.labor.state.ny.us/workerprotection/
laborstandards/workprot/lsdists.shtm

**North Carolina**
Department of Labor
Wage and Hour Bureau
1101 Mail Service Center
Raleigh, NC 27699-1101
919-807-2796
www.nclabor.com/wh/wh.htm

**North Dakota**
Department of Labor
Wage and Hour Division
State Capitol Bldg.
600 East Blvd. Ave., Dept. 406
Bismarck, ND 58505-0340
(701) 328-2660
www.state.nd.us/labor/services/wage-hour/

**Ohio**
Department of Commerce
Division of Labor and Worker Safety
Wage and Hour Bureau
77 South High St., 22nd Floor
Columbus, OH 43215
(614) 644-2239
http://198.234.41.198/w3/webwh.nsf?Opendatabase

**Oklahoma**
Department of Labor
Employment Standards
Wage and Hour Unit
4001 North Lincoln Blvd.
Oklahoma City, OK 73105-5212
(405) 528-1500
www.state.ok.us/~okdol/wh/index.htm

**Oregon**
Bureau of Labor and Industries
Wage and Hour Division
800 N.E. Oregon St., Ste. 1045
Portland, OR 97232
(503) 731-4200 or (971) 673-0761
www.boli.state.or.us/BOLI/WHD/index.shtml

**Pennsylvania**
Department of Labor and Industry
Bureau of Labor Law Compliance
Labor and Industry Bldg., Rm. 1700
Seventh and Forster Sts.
Harrisburg, PA 17120
(717) 787-5279
www.dli.state.pa.us/landi/site/default.asp

**Puerto Rico**
Department of Labor and Human Resources
Prudencio Rivera Martinez Building
505 Munoz Rivera Ave.
Hato Rey, PR 00918
(787) 754-5353/5740
www.dtrh.gobierno.pr

**Rhode Island**
Department of Labor and Training
Division of Labor Standards
1511 Pontiac Ave.
Cranston, RI 02920
(401) 462-8550
www.dlt.ri.gov/ls

**South Carolina**
Department of Labor, Licensing and Regulation
Labor Programs
P.O. Box 11329
Columbia, SC 29210-1329
(803) 896-4300
www.llr.state.sc.us/labor.asp

**South Dakota**
Department of Labor
Division of Labor and Management
Kneip Bldg.
700 Governors Drive
Pierre, SD 57501-2291
(605) 773-3681
www.state.sd.us/applications/LDO1dol/frameset.
asp?navid=0filtertype=1

**Tennessee**
Department of Labor and Workforce Development
Division of Labor Standards
710 James Robertson Pkwy., 8th Fl.
Andrew Johnson Tower
Nashville, TN 37243
(615) 741-2858
www.state.tn.us/labor/-wfd/isdiv.html

**Texas**
Texas Workforce Commission
Labor Law Department
101 East 15th St.
Austin, TX 78778-0001
(800) 832-9243
www.twc.state.tx.us/customers/bemp/bemp.html

**Utah**
Labor Commission of Utah
Antidiscrimination and Labor Division
P.O. Box 146630
Salt Lake City, UT 84114-6630
(801) 530-6801
http://laborcommission.utah.gov/

**Vermont**
Department of Labor
Division of Unemployment Insurance and Wages
Wage and Hour Program
National Life Bldg., Drawer 20
Montpelier, VT 05620-3401
(802) 828-0267
www.labor.vermont.gov/

**Virginia**
Department of Labor and Industry
Powers-Taylor Bldg.
13 South 13th St.
Richmond, VA 23219-4101
(804) 371-2324
www.doli.state.va.us/

**Washington**
Department of Labor and Industries
Employment Standards Program
P.O. Box 44000
Olympia, WA 98504-4400
(360) 902-5316
www.lni.wa.gov/

**West Virginia**
Division of Labor
Wage and Hour Section
State Capitol Complex
Building 6, Rm. B749
Charleston, WV 25305
(304) 558-7890
www.wvlabor.org/home.htm

**Wisconsin**
Department of Workforce Development
Division of Equal Rights
Labor Standards Bureau
1 South Pinckney St., Rm. 320
P.O. Box 8928
Madison, WI 53702-8928
(608) 266-6860
www.dwd.state.wi.us/er/labor_
standards_bureau/default.htm

**Wyoming**
Department of Employment
Labor Standards Office
1510 East Pershing Blvd., West Wing
Cheyenne, WY 82002
(307) 777-7261
http://wydoe.state.wy.us/doe.asp?ID=3

## 2.12 Review Questions and Exercises

### Review Questions

1. What are five areas regulated by the Fair Labor Standards Act?

2. Under the FLSA, what are the differences between enterprise coverage and individual employee coverage?

3. What is the basic difference between exempt and nonexempt employees?

4. What is the time limit for filing an FLSA complaint with the Wage and Hour Division?

5. A plan similar to the fluctuating workweek plan was approved by the U.S. Supreme Court and later made part of the FLSA and its regulations. What is this plan called, and what does it provide?

6. What is the meaning of the term "compensable time?"

7. The "white collar" exemption from the FLSA is made up of what categories of employees?

8. What questions must be answered before overtime pay can be calculated?

9. What is the "regular rate of pay" and how is it determined?

10. Company B hires a computer systems analyst and agrees to pay him $25 an hour. If this person works over 40 hours in a week, is the employee due overtime pay?

11. What must an employee's primary duty be to qualify for the administrative employee exemption under the FLSA?

12. What conditions must be met for an employer to take advantage of the tip credit?

13. Attendance at lectures, meetings, seminars, and training sessions is considered work time unless certain conditions are met. What are these conditions?

14. What restrictions does the FLSA place on employers regarding the employment of minors under 18?

15. What penalty can be assessed for violations of the FLSA's child labor restrictions?

## Section 2: Federal and State Wage-Hour Laws

**True or False Questions**

_____ 1. The Federal Wage-Hour Law always overrides any state wage-hour law.

_____ 2. The basic unit for determining the proper wages due employees is the workweek.

_____ 3. Hospital workers are covered by the FLSA regardless of the hospital's annual volume of revenue.

_____ 4. The job title is a strong factor in determining whether an employee is covered by the FLSA.

_____ 5. Employers that enter into an agreement with their employees to pay them a fixed weekly wage even though their hours vary from week to week are operating under a fluctuating workweek.

_____ 6. FLSA wages include the fair market value of perquisites such as board and lodging.

_____ 7. The FLSA requires overtime pay at 1½ times the employee's regular hourly rate of pay.

_____ 8. The FLSA requires overtime pay for hours worked on Sunday.

_____ 9. Employers are required by the FLSA to give rest periods to employees.

_____ 10. The time spent by employees during bona fide meal periods is considered working time.

_____ 11. The FLSA requires employers to pay employees for hours not worked because of illness.

_____ 12. The FLSA does not require that an employee's preliminary and postliminary activities be counted as time worked.

_____ 13. To determine gross earnings, the total overtime earnings are subtracted from the total regular earnings.

_____ 14. The FLSA is commonly known as the Federal Wage-Hour Law.

_____ 15. Sharon works in Oregon, where the minimum hourly wage in January 2008 is $7.95. At that time, Sharon must be paid at least the federal minimum hourly wage of $5.85 if she is covered by both the state wage-hour law and the FLSA.

_____ 16. "Mom and Pop" shops whose only employees are immediate family members are excluded from coverage under the FLSA.

_____ 17. Exempt employees do not have to be paid the required minimum wage or overtime payments.

_____ 18. The Portal-to-Portal Act of 1947 generally states that travel time spent commuting from home to work and work to home is not considered compensable work time.

_____ 19. Seamen working on foreign ships are fully exempt from the FLSA's minimum wage and overtime requirements.

_____ 20. Taxicab drivers are exempt from the minimum wage and overtime requirements of the FLSA.

_____ 21. For a 40-hour workweek, Paul is paid $200. This is a violation of the FLSA.

_____ 22. Wages other than cash are included in the minimum wage calculation if they primarily benefit the employer.

_____ 23. In January 2008, the FLSA requires employers to pay tipped employees a cash wage of $2.13 per hour.

_____ 24. For the purpose of determining whether the minimum wage has been paid, service charges automatically added to a customer's bill are classified as tips.

_____ 25. A mechanic must be reimbursed for the cost of laundering his work clothes if the clothes are required by the employer.

## Multiple Choice Questions

_____ 1. What government agency enforces the Equal Pay Act?

    a. National Labor Relations Board
    b. Equal Employment Opportunity Commission
    c. Wage and Hour Division
    d. Federal Consumer Group

_____ 2. Which of the following conditions of employment is governed by the FLSA?

    a. The frequency of pay for employees
    b. Recordkeeping requirements
    c. Hours worked by employees over the age of 16
    d. Lunch and rest break requirements

_____ 3. In January 2008, what wage must hourly paid computer professionals exceed to be exempt from the overtime requirements of the FLSA?

    a. $4.25 per hour
    b. $10.00 per hour
    c. $29.967 per hour
    d. $27.63 per hour

_____ 4. What is the FLSA salary test for outside salespersons?

    a. $425 per workweek
    b. $250 per workweek
    c. $455 per workweek
    d. There is no salary minimum

_____ 5. What is the maximum number of hours a nonexempt employee can work in a workweek under the FLSA before overtime premium pay is due?

    a. 40
    b. 55
    c. 80
    d. 168

_____ 6. Barbara is an hourly paid employee making $7.48 per hour. She is scheduled to work 35 hours a week. For the past week, Barbara worked 43 hours. Under the FLSA, what is the minimum she must receive as gross pay?

    a. $261.80
    b. $332.86
    c. $310.42
    d. $321.64

_____ 7. Which of the following laws established minimum wage and overtime standards in the U.S.?

    a. Civil Rights Act
    b. Fair Labor Standards Act
    c. Age Discrimination in Employment Act
    d. Federal Insurance Contributions Act

_____ 8. Sam's regular workweek consists of 40 hours and he is paid biweekly. If Sam works 38 hours in week one and 43 hours in week two, how many overtime hours must he be paid for?

    a. 0
    b. 1
    c. 1.5
    d. 3

_____ 9. Employees covered by collective bargaining agreements may be exempt from which provisions of the FLSA?

    a. Minimum wage requirements
    b. Overtime pay requirements
    c. Minimum wage and overtime pay requirements
    d. Child labor restrictions

_____ 10. Which of the following areas is not governed by the Portal-to-Portal Act?

    a. Travel time
    b. Equal pay for equal work
    c. De minimis time
    d. Preliminary and postliminary activities

## Problems

1. David, a nonexempt hospital employee, has agreed with the hospital to work on a 14-day work period basis, and his regular rate of pay is $10 an hour. David works 5 days at 9 hours each and 4 days at 10 hours each during the 14-day period. Calculate his gross pay for the period.

2. Joe, a nonexempt employee, receives an hourly wage of $9 for a 40-hour workweek. During one workweek he worked 47 hours. Calculate his total earnings for the workweek.

3. Bob, a nonexempt employee, receives an hourly wage of $12 for a 35-hour workweek. In one week, in addition to his regular hours he worked 7 hours on Saturday. Calculate his total earnings for the workweek.

4.  Teri is a nonexempt employee whose normal hourly rate is $10, but she receives a $1 per hour shift differential for working the midnight to 8 a.m. shift. During one workweek she works 45 hours on the late shift. Calculate her total earnings for the workweek.

5.  George, a nonexempt employee, received a production bonus of $38 for a workweek in addition to his regular hourly rate of $10. George worked 44 hours during the workweek. Calculate his total earnings for the workweek.

6.  Susan, a nonexempt employee, received a Christmas bonus of $100 from her employer that does not have to be included in her regular rate of pay for the week in which it is received. During that week, Susan worked 48 hours and her hourly rate of pay was $9.50. Calculate her total earnings for the workweek.

7.  Eric, a nonexempt employee, is paid a shift differential for working different shifts. For 3 days during the workweek he works 8 hours a day for $10 an hour. On 2 other days, he works 10 hours a day for $12 an hour. Calculate Eric's total earnings for the workweek.

8.  Joe, a nonexempt employee, is paid a salary of $520 a week for a workweek consisting of 40 hours. Overtime is paid at 1½ times the regular rate of pay. Last week Joe worked 49 hours. Calculate his total earnings for the week.

9.  Margie's annual salary is $23,400, and she is paid every Friday. Margie is a nonexempt employee who normally works 40 hours per workweek. In one workweek, Margie worked 48 hours. Calculate her total earnings for the workweek.

10. Jim is a nonexempt employee who is paid a monthly salary of $1,500 and normally works 40 hours per workweek. Last week Jim worked 49 hours. Calculate his total earnings for the workweek.

11. Sandra works 32 hours per week, is a nonexempt employee, and is paid a semimonthly salary of $1,000. In one workweek, Sandra worked 42 hours. Calculate her total earnings for the week.

12. Tony is a nonexempt employee who works 35 hours per week and is paid a monthly salary of $2,500. During a certain workweek, Tony worked 43 hours. Calculate his total earnings for the workweek.

13. John, a production worker, is paid $0.50 per unit under a piece-rate system. During one workweek, John produced 840 units in 46 hours. Calculate his total earnings for the workweek.

14. Mark works under the piece-rate system and receives $2 for each component he produces. He also receives a bonus of $0.50 for each component over 300 in a workweek. In one workweek, Mark produced 326 components in 43 hours. Calculate his total earnings for the workweek.

15. Debbie agreed with her employer prior to the performance of any work that she would be paid 1½ times the regular piece rate for any work produced during overtime hours. Debbie is paid $0.30 for each unit she produces. In one workweek, she produced 1,560 units in the first 40 hours and 212 in the next 4 hours. Calculate her total earnings for the workweek.

# SECTION 3: TAXABLE AND NONTAXABLE COMPENSATION

## TABLE OF CONTENTS

# SECTION 3: TAXABLE AND NONTAXABLE COMPENSATION

In general, the Internal Revenue Code (IRC) provides that all compensation an employee receives from an employer, no matter what form it takes, constitutes wages subject to federal income and employment taxes. Such compensation is excluded from wages and exempt from taxation only where the IRC provides a specific exclusion. This section provides an explanation of many different types of compensation an employee may receive beyond cash wages and salary and whether they are classified as taxable wages under the IRC. The methods by which these different types of compensation are calculated, taxed, and reported are also discussed so that a clear picture of the rules regarding employee compensation is provided.

## 3.1 Gross Income and Wages Under the IRC

The IRC uses the term "gross income" as the starting point for determining a taxpayer's federal tax bill, and it broadly defines the term as including "compensation for services, including fees, commissions, fringe benefits, and similar items."[1] The individual withholding and employment tax sections of the IRC are also worded broadly, in that they define wages as "all remuneration for employment, including the cash value of all remuneration (including benefits) paid in any medium other than cash."[2]

What this means is that wages and benefits (whether they are called fringe benefits or "perks" or something else) are generally included in income and subject to income and employment tax withholding, deposit, and reporting requirements unless the IRC says otherwise. The Code does not define the term "fringe benefit," although the Code and the IRS Regulations include several examples of both included and excluded fringe benefits:

- employer-provided cars
- flights on employer-provided aircraft
- free or discounted commercial flights
- vacations
- discounts on property or services
- employer-paid memberships in country clubs or other social clubs
- tickets to entertainment or sporting events
- qualified tuition reductions
- dependent care assistance
- no-additional-cost services
- working condition fringes
- qualified transportation fringes
- qualified moving expense reimbursements
- de minimis fringes[3]

## 3.1-1 Income and Employment Taxes Defined

In general, when employee compensation is described as "taxable," this means:

- it is subject to federal income tax and the employer must withhold the tax from the employee's pay and remit it to the Internal Revenue Service; and

---

1. IRC §61(a)(1).
2. IRC §3121(a); §3306(b); §3401(a).
3. IRS Reg. §1.61-21(a).

- it is subject to social security and Medicare taxes under the Federal Insurance Contributions Act (FICA), as well as federal unemployment tax under the Federal Unemployment Tax Act (FUTA)—these taxes are often referred to as employment taxes.

Because many types of employee compensation are subject to one or more but not all of these taxes (i.e., subject to federal income tax withholding but not social security or Medicare tax), references to them throughout this book will be as specific as possible.

## 3.1-2 Fair Market Value

When noncash fringe benefits or perks are provided by an employer to its employees, the amount of the benefit is defined as its fair market value, or what it would cost an individual to purchase the benefit on the open market in an "arm's length transaction."[4] This means that the relationship between the employer and the employee, the employee's subjective perception of the value of the benefit, or the actual cost of the benefit to the employer should not enter into the calculation of the benefit's fair market value.

The amount of the benefit the employer must include as income to the employee is the amount by which the fair market value exceeds the amount the employee paid for the benefit after taxes plus any amount the law specifically excludes:[5]

$$IFBA = FMV - (EPA + AEL)$$

IFBA = Includable Fringe Benefit Amount
FMV = Fair Market Value
EPA = Employee-Paid Amount
AEL = Amount Excluded by Law

***Example:*** Harry's employer pays for Harry's parking space in a commercial parking lot next to the employer's premises. The employer's cost for the space is $300 per month in 2008 which is the same fee charged to all monthly payers. Harry pays nothing for the parking space and has access to it everyday. Up to $220 per month of employer-provided parking is excluded from income by law in 2008 (see Section 3.2-1). Harry's taxable income from the parking benefit is determined as follows:

IFBA = $300 - ($0 + $220)
IFBA = $300 - $220
IFBA = $80 per month

 **SPECIAL RULES** Some fringe benefits are valued using special valuation rules other than the general fair market value rule (e.g., personal use of employer-provided cars, group-term life insurance). See the applicable sections discussing these benefits for details.

**Benefits for dependents included.** In addition to employer-provided benefits used by employees, benefits provided to their dependents are also included in the employees' income unless specifically excluded.

## 3.2 Fringe Benefits Under the Internal Revenue Code

As was mentioned in Section 3.1, certain employer-provided fringe benefits are specifically mentioned in the Internal Revenue Code and IRS Regulations and defined as either taxable or nontaxable.

---

4.     IRS Reg. §1.61-21(b)(2).
5.     IRS Reg. §1.61-21(b)(1).

## 3.2-1 Nontaxable Fringe Benefits

Once certain conditions are met, IRC §132 exempts certain fringe benefits from inclusion in income. They are therefore not subject to federal income tax withholding or social security, Medicare, or FUTA taxes. They include:

- no-additional-cost services;
- qualified employee discounts;
- working condition fringes;
- de minimis fringes;
- qualified transportation benefits;
- on-premises athletic facilities;
- qualified retirement planning services; and
- qualified moving expense reimbursements.

**No-additional-cost services.** An employer may offer free services to its employees without including the fair market value of those services in the employees' income if the following conditions are met:[6]

1. The free service is one that is regularly offered for sale to customers (not employees) in the normal course of the employer's "line of business" in which the employee works. There is an exception where companies have written "reciprocal agreements" providing free services to employees of the other employer covered by the agreement and neither employer incurs substantial additional cost in providing the benefit.

2. The employer bears no substantial additional cost (including lost revenue and additional labor) in providing the service to the employee.

3. The term employee includes current and former employees who left because of retirement or disability and their widow(er)s, spouses, and dependent children. For the purposes of air transportation, the term employee also includes a parent of an employee.

4. The service is available on equal terms to each member of a group of employees whose classification does not discriminate in favor of highly compensated employees.

Highly compensated employees include any employee who:[7]

- was a 5% owner of the employer's stock or capital (if not a corporation) at any time during the current or preceding year; or

- for 2008, received more than $105,000 in compensation from the employer during the preceding year (indexed annually to the next lowest multiple of $5,000).

If the employer wishes, it can limit the employees fitting under the second definition to those in the top-paid 20% of employees.

*Example:* John is a cashier for the Out of Town Inn Corp., which owns hotels around the U.S. While on vacation, he and his wife and children stay for free at a company-operated hotel where there is space available. The free hotel rooms are a no-additional-cost service, even though he also receives housekeeping services incidental to the room.

---

6.   IRC §132(b), (h), (i), (j); IRS Reg. §1.132-1(b)(3); §1.132-2; §1.132-8.
7.   IRC §414(q); IRS Temp. Reg. §1.414(q)-1T.

**Qualified employee discounts.** An employer may offer discounted goods or services to its employees without adding the fair market value of the discounts to the employees' income if the following conditions are met:[8]

1. The discount on goods cannot exceed the gross profit percentage when the goods are sold to customers (not employees). The gross profit percentage is:

   (total sales - cost of goods sold) ÷ total sales

2. The discount on services cannot exceed 20% of the price at which the services are offered to customers. If the discount exceeds 20%, the excess is taxable income to the employee.

3. The goods or services must be offered for sale to customers in the employer's line of business in which the employee normally works.

4. The discount is available on equal terms to each member of a group of employees whose classification does not discriminate in favor of highly compensated employees (for a definition, see the discussion earlier in this section on no-additional-cost fringes).

5. Real estate, whether for investment purposes or not, does not qualify for the employee discount. Neither does personal property normally held for investment, such as stocks, bonds, or currency.

6. The term employee includes current and former employees who left because of retirement or disability and their widow(er)s, spouses, and dependent children.

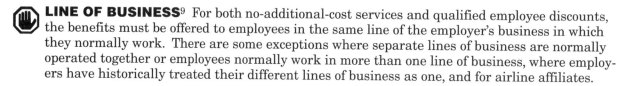 **LINE OF BUSINESS**[9] For both no-additional-cost services and qualified employee discounts, the benefits must be offered to employees in the same line of the employer's business in which they normally work. There are some exceptions where separate lines of business are normally operated together or employees normally work in more than one line of business, where employers have historically treated their different lines of business as one, and for airline affiliates.

**Working condition fringes.** An employer may offer certain work-related property or services to employees without including their fair market value in the employees' income if the following conditions are met:[10]

1. The employee's use of the property or services must relate to the employer's trade or business.

2. The employee would be able to take a business deduction on his or her personal tax return if the employee paid for the benefit (but see exception for reimbursements of business-related club dues and spousal travel expenses).

3. The term "employee" means a current employee, partner, director, or independent contractor performing services for the employer.

4. The employer must maintain the required records to substantiate the business deductions. Where the benefit is in the form of cash, the employer must require beforehand that the payment be used for a business activity, that the employee verify that the payment was used for that purpose, and that any excess be returned to the employer within a reasonable period of time.

---

8.  IRC §132(c), (h), (j); IRS Reg. §1.132-1(b)(3); §1.132-3; §1.132-8.
9.  IRC §4977; IRS Reg. §1.132-4; IRS Temp. Reg. §54.4977-1T.
10. IRC §132(d), (j); IRS Reg. §1.132-1(b)(2); §1.132-5.

Working condition fringes may include the following:

- business use of a company car or airplane
- chauffeur or bodyguard provided for security protection (see Section 3.4-22)
- dues and membership fees for professional organizations (such as the APA)
- an employee's subscriptions to business periodicals
- job-related education
- goods used for product testing by employees
- use of a demonstration automobile by a full-time car salesperson
- outplacement services

The nondiscrimination rules that apply to no-additional-cost services and qualified employee discounts do not generally apply to working condition fringes. In the area of product testing, however, if the employer limits the benefit to a group consisting mainly of highly compensated employees (for a definition, see the discussion earlier in this section on no-additional-cost fringes), it must be able to justify the limitation.[11]

*Tax preparation services are not a working condition fringe.* The value of employer-provided personal income tax preparation services is taxable to the employees receiving it for federal income tax withholding, as well as social security, Medicare, and FUTA taxes. The value is not excluded as a working condition fringe benefit because the employee could not deduct the cost of the services as a business expense, even though it might be deductible as a personal miscellaneous deduction.[12]

*Employer-provided cell phones: personal use is taxable.*[13] In 2007, the IRS Office of Chief Counsel wrote a letter to the U.S. House of Representatives discussing the tax treatment of employer-provided cell phones. The letter explained that cell phones are "listed property" under IRC §280F(d)(4)(A)(v), which includes items obtained for use in a business that lend themselves easily to personal use. The letter then said that an employer can exclude the value of an employee's business use of an employer-provided cell phone from the employee's gross income if the employer requires the employee to keep records that distinguish business from personal phone charges.

The employer must include the value of any personal use of the cell phone in the employee's wages. Personal use includes individual personal calls, as well as a pro rata share of monthly service charges. If the employee uses the cell phone exclusively for business, the value of all use is excluded from the employee's income as a working condition fringe benefit.

To ensure that an employee's business use of the employer-provided cell phone is excludable from gross income, the employee must keep a record of each call and its business purpose. For example, if the employee receives a monthly itemized statement, the employee should identify each call as personal or business.

*Special rule for club dues and spousal travel expenses.* The Omnibus Budget Reconciliation Act of 1993 amended the Internal Revenue Code to disallow a business deduction under §162 for membership dues paid to a club organized for business, pleasure, recreation, or other social purposes and for travel expenses paid for a spouse, dependent, or other individual accompanying the taxpayer. Despite this disallowance, amounts paid or reimbursed by an employer for club dues and/or spousal travel expenses may still qualify as a working condition fringe benefit for the employee to the extent the employee can substantiate the business purpose of the dues or expenses.[14] For a more detailed explanation of the rules regarding club dues and spousal travel expenses, see Sections 3.2-6 and 3.3-5, respectively.

**De minimis fringes.** An employer may provide certain property or services of small value to employees without including the value in the employees' income if the following conditions are met:[15]

---

11. IRS Reg. §1.132-5(q).
12. FSA 200137039, 6-19-01.
13. INFO 2007-0030, released 9-28-07.
14. IRS Reg. §1.132-5(s), (t).
15. IRC §132(e); IRS Reg. §1.132-1(b); §1.132-6; §1.132-7.

1. The value of the benefit is so small that accounting for it would be unreasonable or impracticable.

2. The employer must take into account the frequency with which it provides the benefit to all its employees in making this determination.

3. The term employee means anyone to whom the benefit is provided.

De minimis fringes may include the following:

- occasional typing of personal letters by company personnel
- occasional personal use of the company copier (no more than 15% of its total use)
- occasional parties and picnics for all employees
- occasional tickets to sporting events or the theater
- traditional holiday gifts (e.g., turkeys, candy) with a small value (no cash or cash equivalents)
- coffee and doughnuts provided to employees
- occasional use of company telephones for local personal calls
- occasional meals, supper money, or cab fare for employees who must work late (cannot be based on the number of hours worked and must be provided to enable the employee to work overtime)
- cab fare for employees working other than their usual shift and in unsafe circumstances ($1.50 per one-way commute must be included in income)
- operation by the employer of an eating facility on or near the employer's premises (e.g., company cafeteria) if the facility does not operate at a loss (i.e., revenue from employees must at least equal the cost of operating the facility).

The nondiscrimination rules that apply to no-additional-cost services and qualified employee discounts do not apply to de minimis fringe benefits except for eating facilities provided on or near the employer's premises.

*No specific dollar maximum.* The IRS has never set a specific dollar maximum on the value of a de minimis fringe benefit before it becomes taxable. Each benefit is evaluated in relation to the circumstances at the organization where it is provided. In an internal legal memorandum, the IRS did state plainly that a noncash award with a fair market value of $100 would not qualify as a de minimis fringe because an award of that size was not so small that the employer would have difficulty accounting for it.[16] However, this does not mean that all noncash awards or fringes with a value less than $100 automatically qualify as de minimis.

*Gift certificates and gift cards are not excludable.* Other than occasional meal money or cab fare, cash and cash equivalents do not qualify as de minimis fringes. Gift certificates and gift cards generally would not qualify as de minimis fringes since they are considered cash equivalents, even if the property or service bought with the gift certificate or gift card (if provided in kind) would qualify as a de minimis fringe benefit.[17]

The IRS reinforced its stance in this area in 2004 when it ruled that a holiday gift coupon with a face value of $35 that was redeemable for merchandise at several local grocery stores was not a de minimis fringe benefit, even though the coupons could only be used once and any unused portion was forfeited.[18] The employer distributed the coupons after it changed its prior holiday gift policy of distributing hams, turkeys, and gift baskets, but the IRS said that a cash equivalent, like a gift card, is not excludable from income even though the property bought with the card might be excludable as a de minimis fringe. The cards have a "readily ascertainable" value that can easily be accounted for.

*Meal allowances and supper money.* Because many employers have had difficulty applying the rules regarding meals and meal allowances provided to employees who work beyond their normal working hours, the IRS issued a Coordinated Issue Paper addressing the subject.[19] The IRS emphasized that in determining whether a benefit is provided on an occasional basis, it will consider the availability, regularity, and rou-

---

16. ILM 200108042, 12-20-00.
17. IRS Reg. §1.132-6(c).
18. TAM 200437030, 4-30-04.
19. All Industries—Meal Allowance, Coordinated Issue Paper, 4-15-94.

tine with which the benefit is provided, as well as whether the benefit is provided under an existing employer policy or collective bargaining agreement rather than at the employer's discretion.

When making this determination, the IRS will analyze the payments on an individual employee basis, rather than a group basis. This same individualized procedure will then be used to determine whether the value of the meal allowance is small enough to qualify as de minimis. If meal allowances must be included in an employee's income because they do not meet the definition of a de minimis fringe, their entire value is subject to federal income tax withholding and social security, Medicare, and FUTA taxes.

*In-kind meals treated differently.* The value of meals furnished to an employee for the benefit of the employer on the employer's business premises is excluded from the employee's income (see Section 3.3-6), and if the meal is provided at an employer-operated eating facility, the employee will be considered to have paid an amount equal to the direct operating costs of the facility attributable to the meal.[20] This exclusion does not apply to meal allowances or supper money, only to meals furnished in-kind.

*Tax filing services.*[21] Also qualifying as a de minimis fringe benefit is an employer's electronic filing of an employee's tax return and the value of income tax return preparation services provided to an employee at a Volunteer Income Tax Assistance (VITA) site sponsored by the employer. The IRS said the value of transmitting a completed income tax return is too small to require accounting for it, while sponsoring the VITA site merely made more available something the employees would have been entitled to anyway. However, if the employer pays for the services of an independent tax return preparer, those payments are not de minimis since they are not available to employees without charge. (See the discussion of working condition fringe benefits for more on employer-provided tax preparation services.)

**Qualified transportation fringes.** An employer may provide certain transportation fringe benefits to its employees without including the fair market value of the benefits in their income.[22] They include:

1. Transportation between home and work in a commuter highway vehicle provided by the employer (e.g., vanpool) if:

- the vehicle seats at least 6 adults other than the driver;
- at least 80% of the vehicle's mileage can be expected to be for commuting; and
- at least one-half of the vehicle's seating capacity (excluding the driver) is used by employees.

The excluded benefit is limited to a value of $115 per month in 2008.

2. Transit passes, vouchers, tokens, or fare cards, or reimbursement for them by the employer, for up to $115 per month in 2008.

3. Parking provided on or near the employer's premises or at a "park and ride" facility from which the employee uses mass transportation, a vanpool, or a carpool or any other means to get to work, up to a value of $220 per month in 2008. Parking "on or near the employer's premises" includes parking on or near a work location where the employee works for the employer, but not if the value of parking provided by the employer or reimbursement for the employee's parking cost is otherwise excluded from income as a working condition fringe benefit or an employee business expense reimbursed under an accountable plan.

*Exclusion limits.* Up to $115 per month (for 2008) is excluded from income for employer-provided transit passes and transportation in a commuter highway vehicle. The $115 limit applies whether the benefits are provided separately or are combined. Up to $220 per month (for 2008) is excluded from income for qualified parking provided by the employer, and it is not reduced if combined with other qualified transportation fringes. Each limit is adjusted annually for inflation to the next lowest multiple of $5.[23]

---

20. IRC §119; §132(e)(2); IRS Reg. §1.119-1.
21. PLR 9442003, 7-11-94.
22. IRC §132(f); IRS Reg. §1.132-9; IRS Notice 94-3, 1994-1 CB 327.
23. IRC §132(f)(2), (6); IRS Reg. §1.132-9, Q & A 7; Pub. L. 105-178, §9010(b)(1), (2), (c)(1), (2).

*For employees only.*[24] Qualified transportation fringe benefits may be provided only by employers to employees. The definition of employee in this context does not include partners, independent contractors, or 2% shareholders of an S corporation.

*Public sector included.* The rules governing qualified transportation fringes apply to government employers as well as the private sector. This extends to parking provided to law enforcement officers who travel from home to work in vehicles provided by the law enforcement agency unless the vehicle is a qualified non-personal use vehicle (see Section 3.2-2).

*Written plan not needed.*[25] The law does not require that an employer's qualified transportation fringe benefit plan be in writing (but see the requirements for a compensation reduction election below).

*Cash reimbursement and substantiation.*[26] Qualified transportation fringe benefits include cash reimbursements to an employee for expenses incurred for a vanpool and qualified parking. (The term does not include cash advances.) Reimbursements for a transit pass are qualified only if a voucher or similar item that can be exchanged for a transit pass is not "readily available" for direct distribution to the employee by the employer. A voucher is "readily available" if the employer can obtain it without paying more than the employee and without incurring a significant administrative cost (i.e., the fee paid to the provider of the voucher). The determination of significant administrative cost is made for each type of voucher, not all vouchers as a whole. Administrative costs are significant if the average annual costs incurred by the employer for a voucher (disregarding delivery charges imposed by the provider up to $15 per order) are more than 1% of the average annual value of the vouchers for a mass transit system.

> **Example:** Metro Transit sells mass transit vouchers to employers in the metropolitan San Francisco area worth $85 each. A number of different transit operators in the area accept the vouchers. Metro Transit adds a charge of $.50 on each voucher to cover its operating costs, plus a $15 delivery charge for each delivery. Angela's Cookie Co. buys vouchers from Metro Transit and distributes the vouchers to its employees who use mass transit. Because the added cost of the voucher is only .59% of the value of the voucher ($.50 ÷ $85 = .59%), and the delivery charge is not more than $15, the vouchers are qualified transportation fringes and any reimbursement of employees' mass transit costs would not be a qualified transportation fringe.

In determining whether the employer's administrative costs in obtaining transit vouchers exceed 1% of their value, only the fees paid by the employer to the voucher provider are considered, not any of the employer's internal administrative costs incurred in distributing the vouchers. However, the employer can consider certain nonfinancial restrictions on the purchase of vouchers in determining if the vouchers are "readily available," including: advance purchase requirements, purchase quantity requirements, and limitations on the available denominations. If multiple transit system vouchers are available for direct distribution to employees, the employer must consider the lowest cost voucher for purposes of determining whether the voucher provider fees cause vouchers to not be "readily available" under the 1% rule. However, if multiple vouchers are required to meet the transit needs of employees in a particular area, the employer has the option of averaging the costs applied to vouchers from each system in making this determination.

Employers that make cash reimbursements must establish a bona fide reimbursement arrangement to establish that their employees have actually incurred transportation expenses. What constitutes a bona fide reimbursement arrangement depends on the particular facts and circumstances, including the methods of payment utilized. Sufficient substantiation procedures include having the employee provide a parking receipt or a used transit pass and certify that the parking or transit pass was used by the employee. Certification of both the type and amount of the expenses is acceptable where a receipt is not normally provided (e.g., metered parking or used transit passes that are not returned to the user). The certifications do not meet the requirement if the employer has reason to doubt them. Certifications can be provided only after the expense has been incurred. Substantiation within 180 days after an expense has been paid meets the requirement that substantiation occur within a reasonable period of time. There is no substantiation

---

24.     IRS Reg. §1.132-9, Q & A 5, 24
25.     IRS Reg. §1.132-9, Q&A 6.
26.     IRS Reg. §1.132-9, Q&A 16-19.

requirement if the employer distributes transit passes, so employees who receive them do not have to certify that they were or will be used to get to work. Reimbursements can be made to employees for costs incurred in more than one month, as long as the reimbursement for each month is calculated separately and does not exceed the applicable monthly limit for any month.

 **WATCH OUT** The IRS ruled that where an employer reduces its employees' wages in return for parking provided by the employer and then "reimburses" the employees so that their net pay is the same as before the reduction in wages, the "reimbursements" are taxable income to the employees.[27] Because the parking was treated as provided by the employer rather than paid for by the employee, the "reimbursement" is not excludable because the employee has not incurred an expense for the parking that can be reimbursed.

*Use of electronic media for mass transit may be nontaxable.* In 2006, the IRS issued guidance describing situations where employer-provided transportation benefits provided through smartcards, debit or credit cards, or other electronic media are excluded from gross income.[28] The ruling is effective January 1, 2009, but may be relied on before that date.

Excluded from income:
- *Smartcards.* If the fare media value stored on the smartcards is useable only as fare media for the applicable transit system and the amount allocated to each employee's smartcard is within the limit for exclusion, the smartcard qualifies as a transit system voucher.
- *Terminal-restricted debit cards.* A terminal-restricted debit card qualifies as a transit system voucher if it can be used only at merchant terminals at points of sale where only fare media for the applicable transit system can be purchased and the amount allocated to each employee's debit card each month is within the limit for exclusion.
- *MCC-restricted debit cards.* Generally, an MCC- (merchant category code) restricted debit card does not qualify as a transit system voucher because it is possible that the card may be used to purchase items other than transit passes. However, where a voucher exchangeable only for fare media is not readily available, a bona fide reimbursement arrangement for transit passes may be established by facts and circumstances. For example:

1. with respect to expenses paid using the card, the employer receives periodic statements providing information on the purchases made with the card, including the identity of the seller, and the date and amount of the transactions;
2. for the first month an employee uses the card, he/she must certify that the card was used only to purchase fare media;
3. the employer does not require monthly certifications with respect to recurring items if the item described in the periodic statement matches with respect to seller and time period items that have previously been substantiated as transit pass expenses;
4. the employer requires annual recertification from each employee that the card was used only to purchase fare media;
5. prior to remitting an amount as reimbursement for transit pass expenses for an employee, the employer examines the periodic statements describing card transactions in combination with employee certifications; and
6. the employer provides funds to be electronically allocated to the cards only as reimbursements for substantiated transit pass expenses incurred and substantiated in this fashion.

---

27. Rev. Rul. 2004-98, 2004-42 IRB 664.
28. Rev. Rul. 2006-57, 2006-47 IRB 911; IRS Notice 2007-76, 2007-40 IRB 735.

Not excluded from income:
- **MCC-restricted debit cards.** Where the employer provides the cards in advance, requiring its employees to certify that they will use them exclusively to purchase transit passes, the arrangement does not constitute a bona fide reimbursement arrangement. The arrangement provides for advances rather than reimbursements and relies solely on employee certifications provided before the expense is incurred. Those certifications, standing alone, do not provide the substantiation of expenses incurred necessary for there to be a bona fide reimbursement arrangement.

*Salary reduction plans.*[29] Qualified transportation fringe benefits can be provided under a "compensation reduction arrangement" that offers employees a choice between cash compensation and the transportation fringes. An employee can choose the transportation fringe by making a "compensation reduction election" in which the employee chooses between a fixed amount of compensation to be received at a specified future date and a fixed amount of qualified transportation fringes to be provided with respect to a specific future period. The election amount may not exceed the aggregate monthly maximum for that year ($335 for 2008), and the election must be made before the employee is able currently to receive the taxable compensation.

The election must be made in writing or in another form, such as electronic, that includes, in a permanent and verifiable form, the information required to be in the election (the date of the election, the amount of the compensation to be reduced, and the period for which the benefit will be provided). The compensation reduction amount must be a fixed dollar amount or a fixed percentage of compensation. The election may be automatically renewed for subsequent periods. The election must be irrevocable after the beginning of the period for which the qualified transportation fringes will be provided. However, unused amounts can be carried over to any subsequent months, including months in later years, but cannot be used for any other purpose and cannot be refunded to the employee.

 **NEGATIVE ELECTION OK** An employer may provide that a compensation reduction election will be deemed to have been made if the employee does not elect to receive cash compensation in place of the qualified transportation fringe, provided that the employee receives adequate notice that the reduction will be made and gets an adequate opportunity to choose to receive the cash compensation instead of the qualified transportation fringe.

*Determining the value of qualified parking.*[30] "Qualified parking" is access to parking provided by the employer on or near the employer's premises or at a "park and ride" lot from where the employee commutes to work. Qualified parking means parking for which the employer pays (either to the operator or by reimbursing the employee) or provides on premises it owns or leases. Generally, the value of parking provided by an employer to an employee is based on the cost an individual would incur in an arm's length transaction to obtain parking at the same site. Another spot in the same lot or in the same general location can be used if the cost of the exact spot is not ascertainable.

Reimbursement for parking costs incurred at a nontemporary work location away from the employer's premises is a qualified transportation fringe to the extent the reimbursement does not exceed the statutory monthly limit. The IRS said that parking at a nontemporary work location (i.e., a location where the employee is not expected to work for less than a year) should be treated the same as parking on or near the business premises of the employer.[31]

*Rules for vanpools using a "commuter highway vehicle."*[32] For vanpools operated by an employer (i.e., the employer owns, leases, or pays a nonemployee third party to operate and maintain the van), the transportation provided may be valued using all the facts and circumstances or one of the special valuation rules used to value an employee's personal use of a company-provided vehicle (automobile lease valuation rule, vehicle cents-per-mile rule, and commuting valuation rule—see Section 3.2-2), but only if the special valuation rule

29.    IRS Reg. §1.132-9, Q&A 11-15.
30.    IRS Reg. §1.61-21(b)(2); IRS Reg. §1.132-9, Q&A 20.
31.    ILM 200105007, 9-28-00.
32.    IRS Reg. §1.132-9, Q&A 21.

is used for all employees sharing the van. If the vanpool is operated by an employee independent of the employer, cash reimbursements to the employee are excluded up to $115 per month in 2008.

If an employee gets a qualified parking space because of membership in a car or vanpool, the individual to whom the space is assigned—the "prime member"—must bear any tax consequences. If no such assignment is made, the employer must designate an employee as the prime member. Members of a van pool cannot add their exclusions together to relieve the prime member of any tax consequences of the parking benefit.

> *Example:* Employees Alice, Gary, and Linda are members of a car pool in 2008 with access to employer-provided parking worth $240 a month. Their employer designates Linda as the prime member of the car pool. Linda may not use Gary's and Alice's exclusions to increase her exclusion limit. Therefore, her employer must include $20 per month in Linda's income ($240 - $220).

*Determining the value of transit passes.* The value of a transit pass, fare card or voucher is its purchase price, not the face amount of the pass.

> *Example:* Chad Paper Co. provides transit passes with a face amount of $125 to each of its employees for each month during 2008. The passes can be bought by any individual for $115. The value of the transit passes is $115 each, and as such there is no taxable income for the employees.

*Determining the excess amount included in income.*[33] Based on the general formula for determining the fringe benefit amount that is included in income, the amount of a qualified transportation fringe that is included in income is the amount by which the fair market value of the benefit exceeds the exclusion amount plus any amount paid by the employee for the benefit. This amount is subject to federal income tax withholding and social security, Medicare, and FUTA taxes.

> *Example:* Advertime, Inc. pays for a parking space in a nearby commercial parking lot for employee Erica in 2008, and the fair market value of the space is $325 per month. Erica pays Advertime $75 each month for the space. The amount included in Erica's income each month is determined as follows:
>
> IFBA = FMV - (EPA + AEL)
> IFBA = $325 - ($75 + $220)
> IFBA = $30

*Exclusion applies on a monthly basis.*[34] The value of a qualified transportation fringe benefit must be calculated on a monthly basis to determine whether any part of the benefit is included in income. If the value for any month is less than the exclusion amount ($115 or $220 in 2008), the unused portion cannot be carried over and added to any other month. Reimbursements to employees may be made in subsequent months, so long as the value of the benefit is calculated on a monthly basis. A "month" is defined as a calendar month or any "substantially equivalent period applied consistently."

In the case of a transit pass, the monthly limit applies to the transit passes provided by the employer to the employee in a month for all months for which the transit passes are distributed. Transit passes can be provided in advance for 2-12 months, and the monthly value of a pass that is valid for more than one month (e.g., an annual pass) may be calculated by dividing the total value of the pass by the number of months for which it is valid.

> *Example:* Arnold purchases monthly commuter train passes worth $125 each for three months in 2008, after which his employer reimburses him $375. Because the value of the reimbursed expenses exceeded the exclusion amount by $10 each month ($125 benefit per month - $115 monthly exclusion amount), the employer must include $30 in Arnold's income when he is reimbursed.

---

33.    IRS Reg. §1.132-9, Q&A 8.
34.    IRS Reg. §1.132-9, Q&A 9.

*Benefits from more than one employer OK.*[35] An employee may receive qualified transportation fringe benefits up to the applicable monthly limit from more than one employer, although entities under common control are treated as a single employer.

*Withholding on and reporting excess benefits.*[36] Employers are governed by the general rules for withholding on and reporting the value of qualified transportation fringe benefits included in an employee's gross income (see Section 3.5). This means that noncash benefits (e.g., transit passes, parking) can be treated as paid on a pay period, monthly, quarterly, semiannual, or annual basis so long as this is done by December 31 of the year they are provided. The special accounting rule is also available when accounting for noncash transportation benefits (not reimbursements). Cash reimbursements in excess of the exclusion limits must be deemed paid when actually paid to the employee. Whichever form the benefits take, they must be calculated on a monthly basis to determine whether they exceed the statutory exclusions.

There is a special set of rules governing the situation where transit passes are provided in advance to an employee who terminates employment before the beginning of one or more months for which the pass is valid.

- The value of transit passes provided in advance to an employee for any month after the employee terminates employment is included in the employee's wages for income tax purposes.
- The value of transit passes provided in advance to an employee is not subject to federal income tax withholding or social security, Medicare or FUTA taxes if the passes are not distributed more than 3 months in advance and when they were distributed there was no established date for the employee's termination before the last month for which the transit passes are provided.
- If there is an established termination date for the employee when the transit passes are distributed up to 3 months in advance and the employee does terminate before the last month for which the transit passes are provided, the value of the passes provided for the months after the employee terminates is subject to federal income tax withholding and social security, Medicare and FUTA taxes.
- If the employer distributes transit passes in advance to the employee for more than 3 months, the value of the passes for the months after the employee terminates is subject to federal income tax withholding and social security, Medicare and FUTA taxes regardless of whether there was an established date of termination for the employee when the passes were distributed.

*Qualified nonpersonal use vehicles.* Employees who are provided with "qualified nonpersonal use vehicles" by their employer are not taxed on any of the value of the use of the vehicle since it is not likely to be used for personal travel (see Section 3.2-2). This working condition fringe benefit includes employer-provided parking for such a vehicle up to any amount, even if it exceeds the limit applicable to parking provided as a qualified transportation fringe.

**On-premises athletic facilities.** An employer may allow its employees to use an on-premises gym or other athletic facility free of charge without including the fair market value of the use in the employees' income if the following conditions are met:[37]

1. The athletic facility is located on the employer's premises, whether leased or owned by the employer.

2. The athletic facility is operated by the employer through its employees or another entity.

3. Substantially all use of the athletic facility is by employees, their spouses, and their dependent children. The term employee includes current and former employees who left because of retirement or disability, as well as their widow(er)s.

4. The athletic facility is not a resort or other residential facility.

---

35.    IRS Reg. §1.132-9, Q&A 10.
36.    IRS Reg. §1.132-9, Q&A 9, 22.
37.    IRC §132(i)(4); IRS Reg. §1.132-1(b)(3), (e).

The nondiscrimination rules that apply to no-additional-cost services and qualified employee discounts do not apply to on-premises athletic facilities.

**Qualified retirement planning services.** Employers can provide retirement planning services to their employees and the employees' spouses without the value of the services being included in the employees' income or subject to social security, Medicare, or FUTA tax.[38] Qualified retirement planning services include retirement planning advice or information provided by an employer maintaining a qualified retirement plan – a §401(a), §401(k), §403(b), simplified employee pension (SEP), §408(p) SIMPLE, or §501(c)(18)(D) plan, but not a §457 plan.

Retirement planning advice or information can include advice and information outside the plan itself, such as retirement income planning and how the employer's plan fits into the employee's overall retirement income plan. The exclusion does not apply to services that may be related to retirement planning, such as tax preparation, accounting, or brokerage services. The exclusion applies to highly compensated employees and their spouses only if the retirement planning services are available on the same terms to each member of the group of employees who are normally provided education and information about the employer's qualified retirement plan.

**Qualified military base realignment and closure fringe.**[39] Certain payments made to offset the adverse effects on housing values as a result of a military base realignment or closure are not included in income, but they are limited to certain maximum amounts.

**Qualified moving expense reimbursements.** The Omnibus Budget Reconciliation Act of 1993 made significant changes in the rules regarding the taxation of employer-reimbursed moving expenses. The current rules severely curtail the types of moving expenses that are deductible and classify reimbursements for those that remain deductible as a nontaxable fringe benefit under IRC Section 132(g). For full details on the tax treatment of job-related moving expenses, see Section 3.3-2.

# 3.2-2 Personal Use of Employer-Provided Vehicles

One of the most common fringe benefits provided to employees is use of a company-owned or company-leased vehicle. When the vehicle is used for business-related purposes, the value of the use is excluded from income as a working condition fringe benefit (see Section 3.2-1). All other use of the vehicle is generally considered taxable income to the employee—unless an exception applies.

There are several exceptions to the personal use rule. They are:

**De minimis fringe benefit.** If the employee uses a company car mainly for the employer's business, infrequent and brief side trips for personal reasons are considered de minimis fringe benefits whose value is excluded from income.

**Qualified nonpersonal use vehicle.** If a company-provided vehicle is unlikely to be used for personal travel because of its special design, use of the vehicle by an employee is excluded from income. Such vehicles include: marked and unmarked police cars; ambulances or hearses; delivery trucks with only a driver's seat; moving vans; school buses; passenger buses seating at least 20; animal control vehicles; dump trucks; qualified utility repair vehicles; and trucks with a loaded weight of over 14,000 pounds.[40]

**Automobile salespeople.** Use of a demonstration vehicle by a full-time automobile salesperson or sales manager within the sales area of the dealership is excluded from income as a working condition fringe benefit if the personal use of the vehicle is substantially restricted (e.g., no one else can use the vehicle, no vacation trips, no storage of personal possessions).[41] To qualify for the exclusion, managers must manage the

---

39.    IRC §132(n); see also §1013 of the Demonstration Cities and Metropolitan Development Act of 1966 (42 U.S.C. §3374).
40.    IRC §274(i); IRS Reg. §1.132-5(h); IRS Temp. Reg. §1.274-5T(k)—ILM 200051041, 10-27-00.
41.    IRC §132(1);(3); IRS Reg. §1.132-5(o).

sales staff rather than parts and maintenance or general operations, and they must have meaningful customer contact, including substantial promotion and negotiation. They do not have to be paid on a commission basis, however. The restriction on vehicle use to the sales area of the dealership permits a limitation of the greater of a 75-mile radius of the dealership or the employee's actual commuting distance.[42]

The IRS has issued guidance on optional simplified methods for determining whether the use of demonstration automobiles provided by automobile dealerships to their salespersons can be fully or partially excluded from income and how to value any taxable amount. The simplified methods are structured sequentially so that if the use by an employee does not qualify for full exclusion, it may still be accounted for under the partial exclusion method. But employers may choose to use the partial exclusion method without first attempting to satisfy the requirements of the full exclusion method. In fact, an employer may choose to apply different optional methods on an employee-by-employee basis.[43]

*Simplified method for full exclusion.* In order to use the simplified full exclusion method, the employer must have in place and communicate to each full-time automobile salesperson allowed the use of a demonstration automobile a qualified written policy that:
- Prohibits the use of the vehicle outside of normal business hours by individuals other than full-time salespeople.
- Prohibits the use of the vehicle for personal vacation trips.
- Prohibits use outside of the sales area in which the employer's sales office is located.
- Prohibits storage of personal possessions in the vehicle.
- Limits the total use (by mileage) of the vehicle by the salesperson outside normal working hours to commuting between the salesperson's home and the dealer's sales office plus an additional average of 10 miles or less per day.

The employer must maintain the following records to satisfy the requirements for the full exclusion for any month:

- A copy of the written policy on vehicle use and evidence that it was communicated to the employee (e.g., a copy of a poster, letter, or electronic communication notifying the employee of the policy, or a statement signed by the employee acknowledging receipt of the written policy).
- Records establishing that the salesperson's personal use (by mileage) was calculated at least once each calendar month, including the following: records identifying each demonstration automobile assigned to each salesperson during the period: records identifying the total mileage for each demonstration automobile assigned to a salesperson during the period; records supporting the total use outside of normal working hours under the "simplified out/in method" for each day the automobile is used (i.e., records showing the "out mileage" on the automobile at the end of the working hours of the salesperson using the automobile and the "in mileage" at the beginning of that salesperson's working hours on the next working day); and records identifying the round trip commuting mileage of each salesperson assigned a demonstration automobile from the salesperson's home to the dealer's office during the period.

*Simplified method for partial exclusion.* Where a full-time salesperson (otherwise satisfying the requirements for the full exclusion) exceeds the average 10 miles per day of personal use or does not provide records with respect to the business use of a demonstration automobile, the employer will generally be able to account for the use of the vehicle by using the simplified partial exclusion method. In order to use this method, the following conditions must be met:

- The employer must have a written policy limiting the use of the demonstration automobile that prohibits use of the vehicle outside of normal business hours by individuals other than full-time salespeople, prohibits use of the vehicle for personal vacation trips, and prohibits storage of personal possessions in the vehicle.
- The employer must reasonably believe that the full-time automobile salesperson has complied with that policy.

---

42.    ITA 1994-15, 10-24-94.
43.    Rev. Proc. 2001-56, 2001-51 IRB 590.

- The employer must account for the nondeductible personal use of any full- time automobile salesperson by including in the employee's gross income at least monthly the appropriate amount from the table below and must maintain records necessary to support that accounting, namely records supporting the determination of the value of the use of the demonstration automobiles. The employer must also maintain records showing that appropriate amounts were timely included in an employee's wages (e.g., copies of wage statements). Finally, the employer must maintain a copy of its written policy on demonstration automobile use and evidence that the policy was communicated to the employee (see earlier discussion).

| Value of the Demonstration Automobile | Daily Inclusion Amount |
|---|---|
| 0 – $14,999 | $3 |
| $15,000 – $29,999 | $6 |
| $30,000 – $44,999 | $9 |
| $45,000 – $59,999 | $13 |
| $60,000 – $74,999 | $17 |
| $75,000 and above | $21 |

*Inclusion of the value when no exclusion applies.* If an employee using a demonstration automobile is not a full-time salesperson, then the full and partial exclusions discussed here do not apply and the employer may either include in the employee's wages each month the full value of the demonstration automobile or exclude from the employee's income a portion of the value attributable to business use. If a full-time salesperson does not qualify for either the full or partial income exclusion, then the full value of the demonstration automobile must be included in the employee's wages at least monthly.

The amount to be included in gross income is the greater of $3 per day or the pro rata portion (the full value of the demonstration automobile, divided by 365) of the amount specified in the annual lease value table (see the discussion later in this section of the annual lease valuation method), rounded to the nearest dollar. In order to use the full inclusion method, the employer must maintain records supporting the determination of the value of the demonstration automobile provided to the employee by any "reasonable method," as well as evidence that the amount was timely included in the employee's wages.

**Accounting for vehicle use.** If an employee uses a company-provided vehicle for both business and personal travel, the employee must account to the employer for the business use. This is done by substantiating the usage (e.g., mileage), the time and place of the travel, and the business purpose of the travel. Written records made at the time of each business use are the best evidence. Any use of a company-provided vehicle that is not substantiated as business use is defined by the IRC to be personal use and is included in income.

Another option for employers is to treat all employee use of a company-provided car as personal use by including the value of all use in the employee's income. Employers doing this risk overpaying social security, Medicare, and FUTA taxes, however, if some of the vehicle use was nontaxable and the employee's income does not exceed the social security or FUTA wage bases.

**Valuation methods.** Employers can determine the fair market value of taxable personal use of a company-provided vehicle by using either a general valuation method or one of three special valuation (i.e., safe-harbor) methods.

*General valuation method.*[44] Under the general valuation method, the fair market value of a company-provided vehicle is the price an individual would pay to lease the same or a comparable vehicle in an arm's length transaction in the same geographic area for the same length of time. A cents-per-mile lease rate cannot be used unless it can be shown such a lease was available for that type of car at that time and in that

---

44.    IRS Reg. §1.61-21(b)(4).

area. Because an employee's use of the vehicle is generally mixed between business and personal use, it is most likely more advantageous to use one of the special valuation methods.

As car phones have become more popular, the issue of their inclusion in the value of a company-provided car has drawn the attention of the IRS. Such phones are not included in a vehicle's fair market value if they are necessary to the employee's carrying on the employer's business. Any specialized equipment in the car is also not included in the employee's income if it is not susceptible to personal use.

*Special valuation methods.* There are three special valuation methods for determining the fair market value of the personal use of a company-provided vehicle: commuting valuation; vehicle cents-per-mile valuation; and annual lease valuation. Here are some general rules that apply:[45]

1. If either the vehicle cents-per-mile or annual lease valuation method is used by the employer, it must be used for all subsequent years that the vehicle is provided to any employee, although the employer may switch to the commuting valuation method in any year it applies.

2. Neither the employer nor the employee may use a special valuation method unless at least one of the following is met:

    a. the employer reports the value of the benefit as wages by January 31 of the next year;
    b. the employee includes the value of the benefit in income within the prescribed time;

    c. the employee is not a control employee (see the discussion of the commuting valuation method following); or

    d. the employer demonstrates a good faith effort to treat the benefit correctly for reporting purposes.

3. The same special valuation method need not be used for all company-provided vehicles or all employees.

4. If an employer uses a special valuation method, the employee must use the same rule or the general valuation method on his or her personal income tax return.

5. If a single company-provided vehicle is used by more than one employee, the employer must use the same special valuation method for all the employees using that vehicle and must allocate the vehicle's use based on the facts of the situation.

*Commuting valuation method.*[46] This method allows an employer to value an employee's personal commuting use of an employer-provided vehicle at $1.50 per one-way commute and $3.00 per round trip if the following conditions are met:

1. The vehicle is owned or leased by the employer and is provided to the employee for use in connection with the employer's trade or business.

2. The employer, for noncompensatory business reasons, requires the employee to commute to and/or from work in the vehicle.

**CARPOOLS AND VANPOOLS OK** Employer-provided vehicles used to transport at least three employees to and from work in an employer-sponsored carpool or vanpool arrangement satisfy these two requirements.[47]

---

45.    IRS Reg. §1.61-21(c); IRS Reg. §1.61-21(d)(7), (e)(5).
46.    IRS Reg. §1.61-21(f).
47.    IRS Pub. 15-B, Employer's Tax Guide to Fringe Benefits.

3.  The employer has a written policy prohibiting the employee (and the employee's spouse and dependents) from using the vehicle for personal use other than commuting or de minimis personal errands, and the policy is enforced.

4.  The employee is not a control employee. In the private sector, a control employee is an employee who:

    - is a corporate officer earning at least $90,000 in 2008 (indexed annually to the next lowest multiple of $5,000);
    - is a director;
    - earns at least $185,000 in 2008 (indexed annually to the next lowest multiple of $5,000); or
    - is a 1% owner.

In the public sector, a control employee is an employee who:

    - is an elected official; or
    - earns more than a federal employee at Executive Level V ($139,600 in 2008).

Instead of using these definitions, the employer may choose to treat all its highly compensated employees (see Section 3.2-1 for a definition) as control employees for purposes of using the commuting valuation method.

*Annual lease valuation method.*[48] Under this method, the fair market value of an employee's personal use of a company-provided car is determined by multiplying the annual lease value of the car (as found in Table 3.1 following) by the percentage of personal miles driven. Here are the steps the employer must take:

1.  The employer must determine the fair market value of the car as of the first day it was made available to any employee for personal use. For employer-owned vehicles, this is the total cost of the car to an individual in an arm's length transaction (including sales tax and title fees.) For employer-leased vehicles, the value can be determined by using a nationally recognized pricing source, such as the "blue book," and it is recalculated after four full calendar years. If the vehicle is transferred to another employee, the annual lease value may be recalculated based on the car's fair market value on January 1 of the calendar year of the transfer.

2.  Find the car's fair market value in the Table 3.1. The car's annual lease value can be found directly to the right.

---

48.    IRS Reg. §1.61-21(d).

Table 3.1

| IRS ANNUAL LEASE VALUE TABLE | | | |
|---|---|---|---|
| Automobile Fair Market Value | Annual Lease Value | Automobile Fair Market Value | Annual Lease Value |
| $     0-999 | $   600 | $22,000-22,999 | $ 6,100 |
| 1,000-1,999 | 850 | 23,000-23,999 | 6,350 |
| 2,000-2,999 | 1,100 | 24,000-24,999 | 6,600 |
| 3,000-3,999 | 1,350 | 25,000-25,999 | 6,850 |
| 4,000-4,999 | 1,600 | 26,000-27,999 | 7,250 |
| 5,000-5,999 | 1,850 | 28,000-29,999 | 7,750 |
| 6,000-6,999 | 2,100 | 30,000-31,999 | 8,250 |
| 7,000-7,999 | 2,350 | 32,000-33,999 | 8,750 |
| 8,000-8,999 | 2,600 | 34,000-35,999 | 9,250 |
| 9,000-9,999 | 2,850 | 36,000-37,999 | 9,750 |
| 10,000-10,999 | 3,100 | 38,000-39,999 | 10,250 |
| 11,000-11,999 | 3,350 | 40,000-41,999 | 10,750 |
| 12,000-12,999 | 3,600 | 42,000-43,999 | 11,250 |
| 13,000-13,999 | 3,850 | 44,000-45,999 | 11,750 |
| 14,000,14,999 | 4,100 | 46,000-47,999 | 12,250 |
| 15,000-15,999 | 4,350 | 48,000-49,999 | 12,750 |
| 16,000-16,999 | 4,600 | 50,000-51,999 | 13,250 |
| 17,000-17,999 | 4,850 | 52,000-53,999 | 13,750 |
| 18,000-18,999 | 5,100 | 54,000-55,999 | 14,250 |
| 19,000-19,999 | 5,350 | 56,000-57,999 | 14,750 |
| 20,000-20,999 | 5,600 | 58,000-59,999 | 15,250 |
| 21,000-21,999 | 5,850 | | |

For vehicles having a fair market value in excess of $59,999, the annual lease value = (0.25 x the auto's fair market value) + $500.

3. Calculate the percentage of personal miles driven during the year (personal miles driven ÷ total miles driven).

4. Calculate the fair market value of the employee's personal use of the car that must be included in the employee's income (annual lease value x percentage of personal miles driven).

*Example:* Employee Gilbert drives an employer-provided car that he uses for both business and personal driving. Gilbert drove 17,000 miles during the year—12,300 business miles and 4,700 personal miles. The car's fair market value is $16,200. The amount of the car's fair market value that must be included in Gilbert's income for the year is calculated as follows:

ALV of $16,200 car (from table)  =   $4,600

% of personal miles = 4,700 ÷ 17,000 = .2765  =   27.65%

FMV of personal use = $4,600 x .2765   = $1,271.90

If the employee has the car for less than a year but it is available for use for at least 30 consecutive days, the annual lease value (ALV) must be prorated for that period by using the following formula:

prorated ALV = ALV x (number of days available ÷ 365)

If the car is available to the employee for periods of less than 30 consecutive days during the year, the employer should treat the car as being available for 30 days to avoid harsher valuation rules (unless the availability is 7 or fewer days per year).

 **FUEL NOT INCLUDED** The annual lease value does not include the value of employer-provided fuel. The employer may determine the value by using the actual cost of the fuel or an IRS-approved rate of 5.5 cents ($.055) per mile in 2008 (indexed periodically).

*Company fleet valuation.* Where a company has a fleet of at least 20 vehicles, it may use the average fair market value of the vehicles to determine their annual lease value. There are certain limitations, including recalculating the value at least once every two years. Also, the fair market value of any of the vehicles in the fleet may not exceed a certain amount on the day the vehicle is first provided for use by the employee. For 2008, the maximum value for passenger cars is $19,900 and for passenger trucks or vans (including SUVs or mini-vans) with a truck chassis it is $20,800. These amounts are indexed annually for inflation.

*Vehicle cents-per-mile method.*[49] Under this method, the fair market value of an employee's personal use of a company-provided vehicle is determined by multiplying the IRS's standard business mileage rate by the number of personal miles driven. The business standard mileage rate in 2008 is $.505 (50.5 cents) per mile (indexed annually).[50] To use this method for standard passenger automobiles, the following conditions must be met:

1.  The employer must expect the employee to regularly use the vehicle while conducting the employer's business, or the vehicle must actually be driven at least 10,000 miles annually (including personal use) and be used primarily by employees.

2.  The fair market value of the car cannot exceed $15,000 for cars placed in service in 2008 (indexed annually). The maximum values of cars placed in service in earlier years are:

| before 1/1/90 | $12,800 | in 1994 | $14,700 | in 1999 | $15,500 | in 2004 | $14,800 |
| in 1990 | $13,200 | in 1995 | $15,200 | in 2000 | $15,400 | in 2005 | $14,800 |
| in 1991 | $13,400 | in 1996 | $15,400 | in 2001 | $15,400 | in 2006 | $15,000 |
| in 1992 | $13,900 | in 1997 | $15,700 | in 2002 | $15,300 | in 2007 | $15,100 |
| in 1993 | $14,200 | in 1998 | $15,600 | in 2003 | $15,200 | | |

 **DIFFERENT MAXIMUM FOR TRUCKS, VANS** If the company-provided vehicle is a passenger truck or van (including SUVs and mini-vans) with a truck chassis, the maximum fair market value for vehicles placed in service in 2008 is $15,900 ($16,100 in 2007).

---

49.    IRS Reg. §1.61-21(e).
50.    Rev. Proc. 2006-49, 2006-47 IRB 936.

3.  If the employee pays for fuel, the mileage rate is reduced by 5.5 cents ($.055) per mile for 2008 (indexed periodically).

**Example:** Employee Margaret drives a qualifying car 16,000 miles during 2008, including 7,600 personal miles. If Margaret's employer pays for the gasoline for the car, the fair market value of her personal use of the car is calculated as follows:

FMV of personal use  =        7,600 personal miles x $0.505 =        $3,838.00

If Margaret pays for the car's gasoline, the fair market value of her personal use of the car is calculated as follows:

FMV =                         7,600 x ($0.505 - $0.055) = 7,600 x $0.45 = $3,420.00

**Recordkeeping.**[51] It is very important that employers and employees maintain adequate records to determine the business and personal use of a company-provided vehicle. The employee should log the business use of the vehicle for each trip including the date, business purpose of the trip, and mileage. However, if the employee's business or personal mileage is the same for each period during a year (e.g., each week, month, etc.), adequate records kept during one period can be used to project totals for the entire year.

An employer can avoid these substantiation requirements by enforcing a written policy against personal use of vehicles it provides to employees, by meeting the rules governing the commuting valuation method, or by considering all employee use of the vehicles as personal use.

# 3.2-3 Personal Use of Employer-Provided Aircraft

The value of employee business travel in a company-owned airplane or helicopter is excluded from the employee's income as a working condition fringe benefit. But if the travel is primarily personal, the value is included in the employee's income. Travel that combines business and personal purposes must be allocated to each. The value of the employee's personal air travel can be determined by either the general valuation rule or the non-commercial flight valuation rule (flights on commercial aircraft are governed by different rules, see Section 3.2-4).

**General valuation rule.**[52] The value of a personal flight on an employer-provided aircraft where the employer also provides the pilot is the amount an individual would pay in an arm's length transaction to charter a comparable aircraft and pilot for a comparable flight. If more than one employee is on the flight, the value is allocated among them. If the employer does not provide the pilot, the value would be the amount paid to lease a comparable aircraft for the same time in the same area.

**Non-commercial flight valuation rule.**[53] The value of a personal flight where the employer provides the aircraft and the pilot is calculated by using an aircraft multiple based on the weight of the aircraft and a cents-per-mile rate known as the Standard Industry Fare Level (SIFL). Here is the formula:

[(SIFL x mileage) x weight-based aircraft multiple] + terminal charge = value

The formula varies depending on whether the employee taking the flight is a control employee (see Section 3.2-2). Also, the SIFL and the terminal charges are revised twice a year by the U.S. Department of Transportation. If an employer uses the non-commercial flight valuation rule to value any flight provided to an employee, it must use the rule to value all eligible flights provided to employees during the calendar year, although the employees can use the general valuation rule even if the employer does not.

---

51.    IRS Temp. Reg. §1.274-5T.
52.    IRS Reg. §1.61-21(b)(6), (b)(7).
53.    IRS Reg. §1.61-21(g); LTR 9840015, 6-29-98.

In 2007, the IRS proposed regulations modifying the consistency rule to permit an employer to value the entertainment use of aircraft by "specified individuals" under the general valuation rule, while valuing flights for other employees and for specified individuals not traveling for entertainment under either the general valuation rule or the SIFL formula. The consistency rule continues to apply for valuing the entertainment use of aircraft by non-specified individuals and with respect to non-entertainment flights.

Specified individuals are those subject to the requirements of §16(a) of the Securities Exchange Act (e.g., directors and officers, owners of more than 10% of a company's stock) or who would be subject if the employer were a publicly traded company subject to the securities laws. While the regulations were not finalized by the end of 2007, they may be relied on by employers.[54]

The SIFL rates and the terminal charge used to calculate the value of personal flights on employer-provided or commercial aircraft for purposes of federal income, social security, Medicare and FUTA taxes are as follows:

| Time Period | SIFL Rates Per Mile | | Terminal Charge |
|---|---|---|---|
| 01/01/07 - 06/30/07 | Up to 500 miles | $0.2075 | $37.92 |
| | 501 - 1500 miles | $0.1582 | |
| | Over 1500 miles | $0.1521 | |
| 07/01/07 – 12/31/07 | Up to 500 miles | $0.2074 | $37.91 |
| | 501 – 1500 miles | $0.1581 | |
| | Over 1500 miles | $0.1520 | |

| Maximum Certified Takeoff Weight | Control Employee | Non-control Employee |
|---|---|---|
| 6,000 lbs. or less | 0.625 | 0.156 |
| 6,001 - 10,000 lbs. | 1.25 | 0.234 |
| 10,001 - 25,000 lbs. | 3.00 | 0.313 |
| More than 25,000 lbs. | 4.00 | 0.313 |

***Example:*** Miriam is a non-control employee taking a 3,000 mile flight on November 14, 2007 in an aircraft with a maximum certified takeoff weight of 30,000 pounds

(500 x $.2074 = $103.70); (1000 x $.1581 = $158.10); (1500 x $.1520 = $228.00)
$103.70 + $158.10 + $228.00 = $489.80
$489.80 x .313 = $153.31
$153.31 + $37.91 = $191.22 (amount to include as taxable income)

*Seating capacity exception.* When at least 50% of the regular seating capacity in an employer-provided aircraft is occupied by individuals flying on the employer's business, the value of the flight for an employee flying for personal use is zero.

## 3.2-4  Free or Discounted Commercial Flights

Under the commercial flight valuation rule, the value of a space available or stand-by flight for relatives of airline employees when they do not qualify for the no-additional-cost service exclusion (see Section 3.2-1) is 25% of the airline's highest unrestricted coach fare in effect for that particular flight. This means that 25% of the fare must be included in the employee's income and is subject to federal income tax withholding and social security, Medicare, and FUTA taxes. An employer using the commercial flight valuation rule for any flight must use the rule to value all eligible flights taken during the calendar year.[55]

---

54.    IRS Prop. Reg. §1.61-21(g)(14)(iii); §1.274-9; §1.274-10; IRS Notice 2005-45, 2005-24 IRB 1228.
55.    IRS Reg. §1.61-21(h).

## 3.2-5  Discounts on Property or Services

Qualified employee discounts qualify as nontaxable fringe benefits.  But employee discounts on goods or services normally sold to customers that do not qualify for the exclusion must be included in the employee's income.[56]  These include:

- residential or commercial real estate bought for any purpose;
- personal property of a kind normally held for investment, such as stocks, bonds, or currency;
- discounts on property or services sold primarily to employees and their families, such as through a company store;
- discounts on the sale of services that exceed 20% of the sales price to customers who are not employees;
- discounts on the sale of goods that exceed the gross profit percentage earned on the goods when sold to customers who are not employees; and
- discounts provided to an employee by another employer under a written reciprocal agreement with the employee's employer.

## 3.2-6  Club Memberships

**Deduction disallowed.**  The Omnibus Budget Reconciliation Act of 1993 amended IRC §274(a) to deny a business deduction for "amounts paid or incurred for membership in any club organized for business, pleasure, recreation, or other social purpose."[57]  The disallowance of the deduction beginning January 1, 1994 left employers unsure of whether they were required in every case to include reimbursements or payments of club dues on behalf of employees in the employees' income for federal income tax withholding and social security, Medicare, and FUTA tax purposes, especially when the reimbursements were business-related. And even where the reimbursements were included in employees' income, employers were unsure whether they could still take a wage expense deduction for the reimbursements.

**Club dues may be a working condition fringe.**  Regulations issued by the IRS provide that the denial of the deduction to the employer under Section 274 for the employer's payment of an employee's club dues does not preclude the payment from qualifying as a working condition fringe benefit for employees.[58]

These employer reimbursements or payments qualify as working condition fringe benefits to the extent:

- the employer does not treat them as wages;
- the expenses would be deductible by the employee had Section 274(a)(3) not been added by OBRA '93; and
- the employee substantiates the expenses.

In essence, the employer can exclude the club dues payments or reimbursements from the employee's income to the extent they are business-related and the employee substantiates the business portion of them. The exclusion applies even if the employee's use of the club is primarily personal, so long as the business use can be substantiated.  This rule applies to all employers, even those who are exempt from federal taxation and are not subject to the deduction disallowance of §274(a)(3).

An employer can avoid the deduction disallowance of Section 274(a)(3) by treating employer-paid club dues as employee compensation.  If the employer chooses to do this, the employer-paid amount is fully included in the employee's income and is subject to federal income tax withholding and social security, Medicare, and FUTA taxes.

---

56.   IRC §132(c)(4); IRS Reg. §1.132-3(a)(2), (a)(3).
57.   IRC §274(a)(3); (e)(4).
58.   IRS Reg. §1.132-5(s).

***Example 1:*** Acme Printing Co. provides employee Eileen with a country club membership valued at $20,000, and Acme does not treat the payment of the business-related portion of the dues as wages. Eileen substantiates that the club was used 40% for business purposes. The business use of the club, $8,000 ($20,000 x .40), is considered a working condition fringe benefit, even though Acme does not get a business deduction for the dues. Eileen's personal use of the club, $12,000 ($20,000 - $8,000), must be included in gross income and is subject to federal income tax withholding and social security, Medicare, and FUTA taxes. Acme can deduct the amount of dues attributed to Eileen's personal use of the club as a wage deduction.

***Example 2:*** Assume the same facts as in Example 1, except that Acme treats the $20,000 club dues payment as compensation to Eileen. Even though Eileen can substantiate that she used the club 40% for business purposes, the business use is not considered a working condition fringe benefit because the deduction disallowance now applies to Eileen. The entire $20,000 must be included in Eileen's income, it is subject to federal income tax withholding and social security, Medicare, and FUTA taxes, and she gets no deduction for the business use of the club.

**What's a club?**[59] Clubs organized for business, pleasure, recreation, or other social purpose include (but are not limited to):

- country clubs
- golf and athletic clubs
- airline clubs
- hotel clubs
- clubs operated to provide meals under circumstances that are conducive to business discussion

There are several types of organizations that are exempt from the definition of a club, so long as their principal purpose is not to conduct entertainment activities for members or guests or to provide access to entertainment facilities for members or guests. The exemption applies to:

- business leagues
- trade associations
- chambers of commerce
- boards of trade
- real estate boards
- professional organizations (e.g., bar associations, medical associations, APA)
- civic or public service organizations (e.g., Kiwanis, Lions, Rotary, Civitan)

 **BE CAREFUL** Remember that payments or reimbursements of dues for organizations that do not meet the definition of club under §274(a)(3) must still be included as income to the employee unless the employee substantiates the business purpose and the amount of the dues.

# 3.3 Additional Employer-Provided Benefits

Although not specifically mentioned in the Internal Revenue Code as fringe benefits, several other employer-provided benefits deserve special attention because of the frequency with which they are offered and the complex rules that govern their taxation and reporting.

## 3.3-1 Life Insurance

One of the more popular benefits offered employees is employer-provided life insurance. The most common type of insurance is group-term life insurance, which most often provides a death benefit payable in a lump sum to the employee's designated beneficiary. Special rules in the IRC govern the taxation of employ-

---

59.     IRS Reg. §1.274-2(a)(2)(iii).

er-provided group-term life insurance coverage.[60]  Other types of life insurance, such as whole life or split-dollar life insurance, are also discussed in this section.

**Group-term life insurance.**  The value of employer-provided group-term life insurance up to $50,000 is excluded from an employee's income.  The value of coverage in excess of $50,000, minus any amount paid for the coverage by the employee after taxes, must be included in the employee's income.  The value of the excess coverage is subject to social security and Medicare taxes, but is not subject to federal income tax withholding or federal unemployment (FUTA) tax.  At their option, employers may withhold federal income tax on the value.

The employee must pay the federal income tax owed with his or her personal income tax return.  The value must be reported on the employee's Form W-2 in Boxes 1, 3, 5, and 12 (with Code C), and on the employer's reporting Forms 940 (Part 2, Lines 3 and 4) and 941 (Lines 2, 5a, and 5c).

*Exceptions.*  The value of group-term life insurance over $50,000 is not included in an employee's income when:

- the beneficiary is the employer;
- the beneficiary is a charitable organization; or
- the employee terminates employment during the year because of a permanent disability.

*Nondiscrimination testing.*  The tax benefits of group-term life insurance (no inclusion in income below $50,000, valued at a special low rate above that amount) are not available to an employer's "key" employees if the insurance plan is discriminatory in favor of such employees.

Key employees include—employees who, at any time during the plan year, are:[61]

- corporate officers whose annual compensation is greater than $150,000 for 2008 (indexed annually to the next lowest multiple of $5,000); limited to 50 officers, but in companies with fewer than 500 employees, no more than 10% (but no less than 3 employees) may be treated as officers;
- 5% owners; or
- 1% owners whose annual earnings are greater than $150,000.

A group-term life insurance plan is not discriminatory if one of the following tests is met:

1.  At least 70% of all employees benefit from the plan;

2.  At least 85% of employees participating in the plan are not key employees;

3.  All participants belong to a classification that the IRS has determined to be nondiscriminatory; or

4.  The plan is part of a qualified cafeteria plan (see Section 4.5).

*Calculating excess group-term life insurance.*  The value of group-term life insurance in excess of $50,000 must be included in income.  It is determined by using IRS Section 79 Table I and the uniform premiums it provides, rather than the actual cost to the employer.  Table I lists the value of each $1,000 of group-term life insurance coverage per month, broken down in five-year age brackets.[62]

---

60.    IRC §79; §3121(a)(2)(C); §3306(b)(2)(C); IRS Reg. §1.79-1 - §1.79-3; IRS Temp. Reg. §1.79-4T.
61.    IRC §416(i)(1).
62.    IRS Reg. §1.79-3(d)(2).

| IRS TABLE I—UNIFORM PREMIUMS | |
|---|---|
| Fair Market Value of GTL Insurance<br>Per $1,000 of Excess Benefit Per Month | |
| Under Age 25 | $0.05 |
| Age 25-29 | 0.06 |
| Age 30-34 | 0.08 |
| Age 35-39 | 0.09 |
| Age 40-44 | 0.10 |
| Age 45-49 | 0.15 |
| Age 50-54 | 0.23 |
| Age 55-59 | 0.43 |
| Age 60-64 | 0.66 |
| Age 65-69 | 1.27 |
| Age 70 and above | 2.06 |

Here are the steps an employer must take in computing the monthly value of excess group-term life insurance to include in an employee's income.

1. Determine the total amount of the employee's group-term life insurance coverage under the employer's plan (including coverage purchased by both the employer and the employee). Most plans figure coverage as a multiple of the employee's base salary, which may increase during the year if the employee gets a raise. That is why many employers use the employee's base salary as of January 1 of each year as the base amount for determining life insurance coverage. Many companies also have a maximum amount of employer-provided coverage.

2. Calculate the excess benefit over $50,000.

3. Divide the excess insurance amount by $1,000.

4. Determine the employee's age as of December 31 of the calendar year during which the benefit is taxable.

5. Use IRS Table I to calculate the fair market value of one month of excess insurance per $1,000 and multiply it by the answer obtained from Step 3.

6. Deduct any after-tax contributions by the employee from the value of the insurance.

7. Add the excess amount to the employee's income, withhold and pay social security and Medicare taxes, and report the amount as required.

***Example:*** Valerie was born April 23, 1950. Her employer's nondiscriminatory group-term life insurance plan provides her with coverage equal to 2 x her annual salary as of January 1, and her salary as of 1-1-08 was $65,000. Her employer's plan has a maximum coverage amount of $125,000. Valerie contributes $25 per month in after-tax dollars toward the insurance premiums.

Step 1:  2 x $65,000 = $130,000
maximum coverage amount = $125,000
Valerie's coverage = $125,000

Step 2: $125,000 - $50,000 = $75,000

Step 3: $75,000 ÷ $1,000 = 75

Step 4: Valerie will be 58 years old on 12-31-08

Step 5: $.43 x 75 = $32.25

Step 6: $32.25 - $25.00 = $7.25 per month of taxable income in 2008

If Valerie did not pay anything for the group-term life insurance, or paid with only pre-tax dollars, the entire $32.25 would be included in her income each month.

*Former employees.* Group-term life insurance provided to former employees is generally subject to federal income, social security and Medicare taxes on the same basis as when provided to current employees (i.e., the excess over $50,000 of coverage). For excess coverage provided to former employees, however, the employer is relieved of the responsibility of collecting and paying the former employee's share of social security and Medicare taxes, so long as the coverage was provided after the employment relationship ended. A "former employee" is an individual with a continuing relationship with the employer (e.g., a retiree) after employment ends. The employer is required to include the uncollected social security and Medicare taxes on the ex-employee's Form W-2 in Box 12 with Code "M" and "N" respectively (see Section 8.8-3).[63]

 **BE CAREFUL** Social security and Medicare taxes that were not collected from a former employee while he or she was an employee remain the responsibility of the employer.

*Dependent group-term life insurance.* Group-term life insurance coverage may be provided to an employee's dependents (spouse and/or children) as well as the employee. If so, the value of up to $2,000 of coverage is not included in the employee's income because it is a de minimis fringe benefit. If the coverage exceeds $2,000, its entire value must be included in the employee's income after being calculated using IRS Table I and the age of each covered dependent. If the dependent's age is not known, the employee's age is used in the calculation. If the difference between the Table I value of the dependent life insurance and the amount paid by the employee in after-tax dollars is considered de minimis, then there is no income for the employee.[64] Unlike group-term life insurance on the life of an employee, the value of dependent group-term life insurance included in the employee's income is subject to federal income tax withholding, as well as social security and Medicare taxes, minus any amount paid by the employee with after-tax dollars. The amount included in the employee's income is not subject to FUTA tax, however.

**Whole-life insurance.** An employer may purchase individual whole-life or straight-life insurance policies for employees (usually done for key managers) or pay the premiums on policies already owned by the employees. A straight-life policy provides two types of benefits:

- *Death benefit*—A benefit is payable at the death of the insured employee equal to the face amount of the policy.
- *Savings*—A portion of each premium payment is applied toward the savings segment of the policy. As premiums are paid, this "cash surrender value" of the policy increases. Employees may be allowed to borrow against the cash surrender value or withdraw from it. A return is also earned from the insurance carrier which may be reflected as additional increases in the cash surrender value, additional insurance coverage, or a payout of cash dividends.

If the proceeds of the policy are payable to the employee's designated beneficiary, the value of the straight-life policy that is paid for by the employer is included in income and subject to federal income tax withholding.[65] If the employer is the sole beneficiary of the policy or the employee pays the premiums with after-tax dollars, the value of the policy is not included in income. If the insurance coverage is part of a plan

---

63.   IRC §3102(d).
64.   IRS Notice 89-110, 1989-2 CB 447; IRS Reg. §1.61-2(d)(2)(ii)(b); §1.132-6(e)(2); §31.3401(a)(14)-1; TAM 200502040, 1-14-05.
65.   IRS Reg. §1.61-2(d)(2)(ii).

intended to benefit employees or their dependents, the value of the policy is not subject to social security, Medicare, or FUTA tax.[66]

*Calculating taxable income.* If the proceeds of the policy are payable to the employee's beneficiary, the amount included in the employee's income is the sum of:

- the increase in the policy's cash surrender value for the year (if the employee has a vested right to the cash value), and

- the "reasonable net premium cost" of the current life insurance protection (the death benefit payable minus the cash surrender value at the end of the year).

**Split-dollar life insurance.** In 2003, the IRS issued final regulations on the income and employment tax consequences of split-dollar life insurance plans.[67] Under these plans, an employer and an employee join in the purchase of a life insurance contract on the life of the employee subject to a contractual allocation of policy benefits between the two parties. The regulations apply to any split-dollar life insurance arrangement entered into after September 17, 2003, as well as to any such arrangement entered into on or before that date that is materially modified after that date.

**Definition of split-dollar life insurance arrangement.**
*General rule.* The regulations define a split-dollar life insurance arrangement as any arrangement (that is not part of a group-term life insurance plan) between an owner of a life insurance contract and a non-owner of the contract under which either party pays all or part of the premiums, and one of the parties paying the premiums is entitled to recover a portion of those premiums and the recovery is to be made from, or is secured by, the proceeds of the life insurance contract.

*Special rule.* A special rule applies in the case of an arrangement (that is not part of a group-term life insurance plan) entered into in connection with the performance of services. Under this special rule, a split-dollar life insurance arrangement is any arrangement between an owner and a non-owner of a life insurance contract under which the employer pays, directly or indirectly, all or any portion of the premiums and the beneficiary of all or any portion of the death benefit is designated by the employee or is any person whom the employee would reasonably be expected to name as beneficiary.

*Note:* As in the case of the general rule, the special rule is not intended to cover the purchase of an insurance contract where the only parties to the arrangement are the policy owner and the life insurance company acting only in its capacity as insurer of the contract.

**Owners and non-owners.** The regulations provide rules for determining the owner and the non-owner of the life insurance contract.

*Owner.* The owner is the person named as the policy owner. If two or more individuals are designated as the policy owners, then the first-named person generally is treated as the owner of the entire contract. However, in the employment context, the employer is treated as the owner of the contract if, at all times, the only economic benefit available to the employee under the arrangement is the value of current life insurance protection (these are known as "non-equity" arrangements).

*Non-owner.* The non-owner is any person other than the owner of the life insurance contract having any direct or indirect interest in the arrangement (other than a life insurance company acting only in its capacity as issuer of the life insurance contract). For example, an employee whose spouse is designated by the employee as the beneficiary of a life insurance contract owned by the employer has an indirect interest in the contract and, therefore, would be treated as a non-owner.

---

66.     IRC §3121(a)(2)(C); §3306(b)(2)(C); IRS Reg. §31.3121(a)-1; §31.3306(b)-1.
67.     IRS Reg. §1.61-2(d)(2)(ii)(A); §1.61-22; §1.7872-15; §31.3121(a)-1(k); §31.3306(b)-1(l); §31.3401(a)-1(b)(15).

*Special attribution rules.* The regulations provide attribution rules for compensatory split-dollar life insurance arrangements. Under these rules, the employer will be treated as the owner of the life insurance contract if the contract is owned by certain specified parties (e.g., a member of the employer's controlled group).

**Mutually exclusive regimes.** The regulations provide two mutually exclusive regimes for taxing split-dollar life insurance arrangements, the economic benefit regime and the loan regime.

*Loan regime.* Under the loan regime, the non-owner of the life insurance contract is treated as loaning premium payments to the owner of the contract. Except for specified arrangements, the loan regime applies to any split-dollar loan.

*Economic benefit regime.* A special rule requires the economic benefit regime to apply (and the loan regime not to apply) to any split-dollar life insurance arrangement entered into in connection with the performance of services where the employee is not the owner of the life insurance contract.

*Accounting.* The regulations require both the owner and the non-owner of a split-dollar life insurance arrangement to "fully and consistently account for all amounts under the arrangement." For example, if an employer pays premiums on a contract owned by the employee and the payments are not split-dollar loans, the employee must include the full amount of the payments in gross income at the time they are paid by the employer to the extent that the employee's rights to the life insurance contract are substantially vested.

Also, to the extent that an owner's repayment obligation is waived, cancelled, or forgiven at any time under an arrangement that prior to the cancellation of indebtedness was treated as a split-dollar loan, the owner and non-owner must account for the amount waived, cancelled, or forgiven "in accordance with the relationship between the parties." Thus, if the arrangement were in a compensatory context, the owner of the contract (the employee) and the non-owner (the employer) would account for the amount as compensation.

*Special transfer rule.* The regulations include a rule regarding the treatment of a transfer of a life insurance contract under a split-dollar life insurance arrangement from an owner to a non-owner when payments under the arrangement have been treated, prior to transfer, as split-dollar loans. Under the rule, the economic benefit regime applies to the split-dollar life insurance arrangement from the date of the transfer, and the payments made (both before and after the transfer) are not treated as split-dollar loans on or after the date of transfer. The transferor of the life insurance contract must fully take into account all economic benefits provided under the split-dollar life insurance arrangement.

**Taxation under the loan regime.** A payment made pursuant to a spilt-dollar life insurance arrangement is a split-dollar loan and the owner and non-owner are treated, respectively, as borrower and lender if:

- the payment is made either directly or indirectly by the non-owner to the owner;
- a reasonable person would expect the payment to be repaid in full to the non-owner (with or without interest); and
- the repayment is to be made from, or is secured by, either the policy's death benefit proceeds or its cash surrender value.

**Taxation under the economic benefit regime.**
*Non-equity split-dollar life insurance arrangements.* Under a non-equity split-dollar life insurance arrangement, the owner is treated as providing current life insurance protection to the non-owner. The amount of the current life insurance protection provided to the non-owner for a taxable year equals the excess of the average death benefit of the life insurance contract over the total amount payable to the owner under the split-dollar life insurance arrangement. The total amount payable to the owner is increased by the amount of any outstanding policy loan. The cost of the current life insurance protection provided to the non-owner in any year equals the amount of the current life insurance protection provided to the non-owner multiplied by the "life insurance premium factor," published in IRS guidance.

***Example:*** Assume that employer R is the owner of a $1,000,000 life insurance contract that is part of a split-dollar life insurance arrangement between R and employee E. Under the arrangement, R pays all of the $10,000 annual premiums and is entitled to receive the greater of its premiums or the cash surrender value of the contract when the arrangement terminates or E dies. Assume that through year 10 of the arrangement R has paid $100,000 of premiums and that in year 10 the cost of term insurance for E is $1.00 for $1,000 of insurance and the cash surrender value of the contract is $200,000. In year 10, E must include in compensation income $800 ($1,000,000 - $200,000 payable to R, or $800,000, multiplied by .001 (E's "premium rate factor")). If, however, E paid $300 of the premium, E would include $500 in compensation income.

*Equity split-dollar life insurance arrangements.* The owner and the non-owner also must account fully and consistently for any right in, or benefit of, a life insurance contract provided to the non-owner under an equity split-dollar life insurance arrangement. For example, where the insurance contract is owned by the employer, the employee must include in gross income the value of any interest in the cash surrender value of the contract provided to the employee during a taxable year.

**Valuing economic benefits.** The regulations provide guidance on the valuation of economic benefits (including the valuation of an interest in policy cash value) under a split-dollar life insurance arrangement for federal income and employment tax purposes. The value of the economic benefits provided to the employee for a taxable year equals:

(1) the cost of any current life insurance protection provided to the employee,
(2) the amount of policy cash value to which the employee has current access, and
(3) the value of any other economic benefits provided to the employee.

*Current term life insurance protection.* The cost of current life insurance protection provided to the employee for a taxable year equals the amount of the current life insurance protection multiplied by the life insurance premium factor provided in IRS guidance (see p. 3-32).

*Current access to policy cash value.* The employee has current access to any portion of the policy cash value that is directly or indirectly accessible by him or her and inaccessible to the employer or the employer's general creditors.

For example, an employee has current access to policy cash value if he or she can directly or indirectly make a withdrawal from the policy; borrow from the policy; make a total or partial surrender of the policy; anticipate, assign, alienate, pledge, or encumber the policy cash value; or if the policy cash value is available to the employee's creditors by attachment, garnishment, levy, execution, etc.

*Other economic benefits.* The value of all other economic benefits provided to the employee – including any benefit, right, or feature of the life insurance contract (other than current life insurance protection and policy cash value) – must be taken into account.

**Taxation of amounts received under the life insurance contract.** Any amount received under the life insurance contract (other than an amount received on account of death) and provided, directly or indirectly, to the non-owner is treated as though paid by the insurance company to the owner and then by the owner to the non-owner. This rule applies to a policy owner dividend, the proceeds of a specified policy loan, a withdrawal, or the proceeds of a partial surrender. The non-owner (and the owner for employment tax purposes) must take the amount into account as a payment of compensation.

| TABLE 2001 INTERIM TABLE OF ONE-YEAR TERM PREMIUMS FOR $1,000 OF LIFE INSURANCE PROTECTION | | | | | |
|---|---|---|---|---|---|
| Attained Age | Section 79 Extended and Interpolated Annual Rates | Attained Age | Section 79 Extended and Interpolated Annual Rates | Attained Age | Section 79 Extended and Interpolated Annual Rates |
| 0 | $0.70 | 34 | 0.98 | 67 | 15.20 |
| 1 | 0.41 | 35 | $0.99 | 68 | 16.92 |
| 2 | 0.27 | 36 | 1.01 | 69 | 18.70 |
| 3 | 0.19 | 37 | 1.04 | 70 | $20.62 |
| 4 | 0.13 | 38 | 1.06 | 71 | 22.72 |
| 5 | 0.13 | 39 | 1.07 | 72 | 25.07 |
| 6 | 0.14 | 40 | 1.10 | 73 | 27.57 |
| 7 | 0.15 | 41 | 1.13 | 74 | 30.18 |
| 8 | 0.16 | 42 | 1.20 | 75 | 33.05 |
| 9 | 0.16 | 43 | 1.29 | 76 | 36.33 |
| 10 | 0.16 | 44 | 1.40 | 77 | 40.17 |
| 11 | 0.19 | 45 | 1.53 | 78 | 44.33 |
| 12 | 0.24 | 46 | 1.67 | 79 | 49.23 |
| 13 | 0.28 | 47 | 1.83 | 80 | 54.56 |
| 14 | 0.33 | 48 | 1.98 | 81 | 60.51 |
| 15 | 0.38 | 49 | 2.13 | 82 | 66.74 |
| 16 | 0.52 | 50 | 2.30 | 83 | 73.07 |
| 17 | 0.57 | 51 | 2.52 | 84 | 80.35 |
| 18 | 0.59 | 52 | 2.81 | 85 | 88.76 |
| 19 | 0.61 | 53 | 3.20 | 86 | 99.16 |
| 20 | 0.62 | 54 | 3.65 | 87 | 110.40 |
| 21 | 0.62 | 55 | 4.15 | 88 | 121.85 |
| 22 | 0.64 | 56 | 4.68 | 89 | 133.40 |
| 23 | 0.66 | 57 | 5.20 | 90 | 144.30 |
| 24 | 0.68 | 58 | 5.66 | 91 | 155.80 |
| 25 | 0.71 | 59 | 6.06 | 92 | 168.75 |
| 26 | 0.73 | 60 | 6.51 | 93 | 186.44 |
| 27 | 0.76 | 61 | 7.11 | 94 | 206.70 |
| 28 | 0.80 | 62 | 7.96 | 95 | 228.35 |
| 29 | 0.83 | 63 | 9.08 | 96 | 250.01 |
| 30 | 0.87 | 64 | 10.41 | 97 | 265.09 |
| 31 | 0.90 | 65 | 11.90 | 98 | 270.11 |
| 32 | 0.93 | 66 | 13.51 | 99 | 281.05 |
| 33 | 0.96 | | | | |

# 3.3-2 Moving Expenses

When employees are relocated from one workplace to another or move to begin a new job, the employer often pays for the costs of the move, either directly or by reimbursing the employee for moving expenses. Generally, if an employer reimburses an employee or pays a third party directly for moving expenses that qualify for a tax deduction, the amount reimbursed or paid is not included in the employee's income.[68] All other amounts paid or reimbursed must be included in income and are subject to federal income tax withholding and social security, Medicare, and FUTA taxes. The following paragraphs explain the current rules governing the tax treatment of job-related moving expenses.

**Initial tests of deductibility—distance and time.** Before any expenses of a job-related move can be considered deductible and reimbursements for them excluded from income, two tests must be met:[69]

*Distance test.* The new workplace must be at least 50 miles farther from the employee's old residence than the previous workplace was (e.g., if the employee's old job was 15 miles from his old residence, the new job must be at least 65 miles from the old residence). If there was no previous workplace, the new workplace must be at least 50 miles from the employee's old residence. The distance measured by this test is the shortest of the most commonly used routes between the two points.

*Time test.* During the 12-month period immediately following the move, the employee must work full-time for at least 39 weeks in the general location of the new workplace. This requirement does not apply if the employee cannot meet it because of death, disability, involuntary termination of employment (except for willful misconduct), or transfer for the employer's benefit.

If the employer reasonably believes the employee will meet these two tests, payments made to a third party or reimbursements made to the employee for expenses related to the move are not included in income so long as the expenses themselves meet the tests for deductibility.

**Deductible moving expenses.**[70] There are only two types of deductible moving expenses—transportation and in-transit storage of household goods and personal effects, and traveling from the old residence to the new residence (including lodging but not meals).

*Transportation of household goods.* All reasonable expenses incurred in packing and moving household goods and personal effects to the new residence and storing and insuring them while in transit are deductible. Storage costs constitute "in-transit" expenses if they are incurred within 30 days after the goods and effects are moved from the old residence and before delivery to the new residence. The employer can reimburse the employee for the expenses or pay a moving company directly.

*Expenses of traveling from old home to new home.* All reasonable expenses incurred while traveling from the employee's old home to the new home, such as transportation and lodging during the trip, are deductible. However, there is no longer any deduction allowed for meal expenses while traveling to the new residence. The mileage rate for moving expenses is $.19 per mile for 2008.

*Members of household are included.* The deduction for an employee's moving expenses includes amounts spent on transporting and storing household goods and personal effects belonging to members of the employee's household who live in both the old and new residences. Their reasonable expenses in traveling from the old home to the new home are also deductible to the employee.

---

68.    IRC §82; §132(a)(6); §132(g); §217; §3401(a)(15); §3121(a)(11); §3306(b)(9).
69.    IRC §217(c); (d); IRS Reg. §1.217-2(c); (d).
70.    IRC §217(b).

**REASONABLE EXPENSES ONLY**[71] Moving expenses are deductible only to the extent they are reasonable under all the circumstances related to the move. This means the shortest and most direct routes must be taken when traveling and conventional modes of transportation must be used. If not, any excess expenses incurred are not deductible. Also, lodging expenses incurred while traveling must not be "lavish or extravagant."

*Foreign move storage rule.*[72] If an employee's move to a new workplace outside the U.S. otherwise qualifies for a deduction, the cost of moving household goods and personal effects to and from storage and storing them while the employee is in the new workplace is a deductible moving expense. The move can be from the U.S. to a foreign country, from one foreign country to another, or within a foreign country (so long as the 50-mile distance test is met). A move from a foreign country to the U.S. is a domestic move.

**Qualified moving expense reimbursements are nontaxable fringe benefits.** The amounts paid or reimbursed by the employer are a nontaxable fringe benefit under IRC §132(g) to the extent the moving expenses qualify for a deduction and if the employee did not deduct them in a previous year.[73] If the employer does not reimburse the employee for the full amount of the qualified moving expenses, the employee can deduct the excess expenses from gross income on his or her personal income tax return.[74]

The Conference Report on OBRA '93 expressed the intent of the House and Senate conferees that reimbursed moving expenses should be subject to the same rules relating to accountable plans that govern reimbursement of employee business expenses (see Section 3.3-5).[75] This means that employees must substantiate the amount and business purpose of the expenses, as well as return any amounts paid by the employer in excess of the substantiated expenses within a reasonable period of time.

 **BE CAREFUL** While qualified moving expense reimbursements are excluded from income only to the extent the employee did not deduct the expenses in a previous year, the Conference Report for OBRA '93 says that an employer should exclude such reimbursements from the employee's income unless the employer has "actual knowledge" that the employee deducted the expenses previously. The employer has no obligation to determine whether the employee deducted the expenses.[76]

**Nondeductible moving expenses and nonqualified reimbursements.** Employer payments or reimbursements for expenses other than transportation of household goods or traveling from the employee's old home to the new home are included in the employee's income for federal income tax withholding and social security, Medicare, and FUTA tax purposes. Reimbursements for or payment of the following common nondeductible expenses are included in the employee's income:

- cost of meals while traveling from the old home to the new home
- pre-move househunting expenses
- temporary living expenses after starting work in the new location
- real estate expenses incurred by the employee in selling a residence in the prior location and/or buying one in the new location

Where an employee sells his or home through a relocation company acting as the employer's agent and the employer pays expenses related to the home (e.g., taxes, maintenance, insurance) before the employee transfers the "benefits and burdens of ownership," the amounts paid by the employer are taxable income to the employee.[77]

---

71.  IRS Reg. §1.217-2(b)(2).
72.  IRC §217(h); IRS Reg. §1.217-2(h)(2); (h)(3).
73.  IRC §132(a)(6); §132(g).
74.  IRC §62(a)(15).a
75.  H. Rept. 103-213, p. 592.
76.  H. Rept. 103-213, p. 592.
77.  Rev. Rul. 2005-74, 2005-51 IRB 1153.

**Reporting moving expense reimbursements.**[78] Moving expense reimbursements or payments that qualify as a nontaxable fringe benefit should not be reported in Box 1, 3, or 5 of the 2008 Form W-2, *Wage and Tax Statement* (see Appendix page A-60). Qualified moving expenses paid by an employer to a third party (e.g., a moving company) on behalf of an employee and services that an employer furnishes in kind to an employee are not reported at all on the employee's Form W-2. Qualified moving expense reimbursements paid directly to an employee must be reported in Box 12, preceded by Code "P."

Qualified moving expense reimbursements and payments, no matter who they are paid to, are not reported on the employer's Form 941. However, they must be reported on Form 940 in Part 2, Lines 3 and 4.

Amounts reimbursed by an employer that do not qualify as a nontaxable fringe benefit are wages and must be included as such in Boxes 1, 3, and 5 of Form W-2 (enter amounts withheld in Boxes 2, 4, and 6), but not in Box 12. Such amounts must also be reported on Form 941 on Lines 2, 5a, and 5c, and on Form 940 in Part 2, Line 3.

Through tax year 1997, employers were required to report any moving expense reimbursements or payments made on an employee's behalf on Form 4782, *Employee Moving Expense Information*. The form was provided to the employee and broke down the reimbursements and payments based on who the payment was made to and whether it was qualified or nonqualified. In tax year 1998, however, the IRS eliminated Form 4782 as unnecessary, although employers are free to provide similar information to their employees if they feel it would be helpful.

If the amount of the qualified moving expense reimbursements paid directly to an employee (as reported on Form W-2, Box 12, preceded by Code "P") is less than the amount of the employee's qualified moving expenses paid directly by the employee, the employee can deduct the remaining qualified expenses from gross income by completing and attaching Form 3903, *Moving Expenses* (see Appendix page A-346), to his or her personal income tax return. Form 3903 is used for both domestic and foreign moves.

> *Example:* Linda is transferred by her employer from San Antonio, Texas to New York City during 2008. Linda easily meets the distance test for a deductible move, and her employer expects her to work at least 39 weeks in New York. Linda is reimbursed in 2008 for the following relocation expenses:
>
> To move and store household goods and personal effects
>
> | | |
> |---|---|
> | Employer pays mover directly | $7,500 |
>
> Travel from San Antonio to New York City
>
> | | |
> |---|---|
> | Mileage cost (1,400 miles at $.19 per mile) | 266 |
> | Hotel | 450 |
> | Meals | 125 |
>
> Premove househunting and temporary living expenses
>
> | | |
> |---|---|
> | Hotel (15 days) | 1,100 |
> | Meals | 375 |
> | Car rental | 300 |

---

78.  IRS Announcement 97-77, 1997-33 IRB 58; Form W-2 Instructions.

Real estate expenses

| | |
|---|---|
| Realtor's commission | 12,000 |
| Attorneys' fees | 2,000 |
| Appraisal fees | 500 |
| | |
| Relocation bonus | 5,000 |
| Total | $29,630 |

See below for a completed Form W-2 for this example

## Form W-2 Wage and Tax Statement 2008

| | | |
|---|---|---|
| **22222** Void ☐ | **a** Employee's social security number 333-44-5555 | For Official Use Only ▶ OMB No. 1545-0008 |

| **b** Employer identification number (EIN) | **1** Wages, tips, other compensation 21400.00 | **2** Federal income tax withheld 5350.00 |
|---|---|---|
| **c** Employer's name, address, and ZIP code | **3** Social security wages 21400.00 | **4** Social security tax withheld 1326.80 |
| | **5** Medicare wages and tips 21400.00 | **6** Medicare tax withheld 310.30 |
| | **7** Social security tips | **8** Allocated tips |
| **d** Control number | **9** Advance EIC payment | **10** Dependent care benefits |
| **e** Employee's first name and initial: Linda | Last name | Suff. | **11** Nonqualified plans | **12a** See instructions for box 12 Code P 716.00 |
| | **13** Statutory employee ☐ Retirement plan ☐ Third-party sick pay ☐ | **12b** |
| | **14** Other | **12c** |
| | | **12d** |
| **f** Employee's address and ZIP code | | |

| **15** State Employer's state ID number | **16** State wages, tips, etc. | **17** State income tax | **18** Local wages, tips, etc. | **19** Local income tax | **20** Locality name |
|---|---|---|---|---|---|
| | | | | | |

Department of the Treasury—Internal Revenue Service

Copy A For Social Security Administration — Send this entire page with Form W-3 to the Social Security Administration; photocopies are **not** acceptable.

For Privacy Act and Paperwork Reduction Act Notice, see back of Copy D.

Cat. No. 10134D

**Do Not Cut, Fold, or Staple Forms on This Page — Do Not Cut, Fold, or Staple Forms on This Page**

**Special rules for military personnel.** When the types of deductions for job-related moving expenses were restricted by OBRA '93, there was some concern over the effect of the restrictions on the exclusion from income of certain allowances provided to American military personnel on active duty who move because of a military order and incident to a permanent change of station. These allowances include:

- a dislocation allowance to partially reimburse expenses incurred in relocating a household;
- a temporary lodging expense to help offset the cost of temporary lodging (up to 10 days) within the U.S.;
- a temporary lodging allowance to help defray higher living costs (up to 60 days) outside the U.S.; and
- a moving-in housing allowance to offset costs associated with occupying leased quarters outside the U.S.

The IRS has since clarified that these allowances are considered "subsistence or quarters allowances" and are excluded from gross income.[79] The regulations also clarified that no deduction is allowed for any expenses incurred during a move to a new permanent duty station to the extent the expenses are reimbursed through an excludable allowance.

# 3.3-3 Educational Assistance

One of the most popular benefits provided by employers is employer-paid educational assistance, whereby the employer pays for or reimburses the cost of educational courses attended by an employee. Different taxation rules apply depending on whether the courses are job-related, and there are special rules for employees of educational institutions who receive tuition reductions when they or their spouses and dependents take courses offered by their employer.

**Job-related education.**[80] Employer-paid education that is related to the employee's current job is excluded from income as a working condition fringe benefit if the following conditions are met:

1. The courses must not be necessary to meet the minimum education requirements of the current job.

2. The courses are not taken to qualify the employee for a promotion or transfer to a different type of work.

3. The education must be related to the employee's current job and must help maintain or improve the knowledge and skills required for that job (e.g., refresher or update courses). If the requirements change while the employee is working, employer-paid education designed to meet them is a working condition fringe.

*What about graduate courses?* For the most part, the IRS does not consider graduate-level education to be job-related under the test explained above, either because the employee is taking the courses to qualify for a promotion or transfer to a different job, or the education is a minimum requirement for the employee's current job. However, in 2005 the Tax Court ruled that expenses incurred by a salesperson in pursuing a Master's degree in business administration (MBA) were deductible as job-related education.[81]

The court said the salesperson could deduct the expenses from his income because he was not required to get an MBA to keep his job and the degree actually enhanced and maintained the skills he already used in his job, rather than qualifying him for a new trade or business. He had already begun to receive expanded work assignments before enrolling in the MBA program, and the promotions he received while taking courses were not conditioned on working toward or getting the degree. The court also distinguished this case from one where an individual pursues a course of study to obtain a professional license or certification, or where the individual's duties were technical before enrolling in a graduate program and managerial afterward.

While this case involved an employee deducting graduate-level education expenses where his employer had a policy of not paying for its employees' education, the same rationale should apply to exclude employer reimbursements of such expenses from an employee's income if the facts and circumstances are similar.

**Non job-related education.**[82] The Economic Growth and Tax Relief Reconciliation Act of 2001 (EGTRRA) extended the income exclusion for up to $5,250 a year of nonjob-related educational assistance provided by an employer to an employee through the end of 2010, when EGTRRA itself expires. Under

---

79.   IRS Reg. §1.61-2(b); §1.217-2(g)(6).
80.   IRC §132(d); IRS Reg. §1.162-5.
81.   Allemeier v. Commissioner, T.C. Memo 2005-207, 2005 Tax Ct. Memo LEXIS 208 (8-31-05).
82.   IRC §127; §3121(a)(18); §3306(b)(13); §3401(a)(18); IRS Reg. §1.127-1; §1.127-2; §31.3121(a)(18)1; §31.3306(b)(13)-1; §31.3401(a)(18)-1.

IRC §127, the educational assistance must be provided through an Educational Assistance Program (EAP). EGTRRA also expanded the exclusion to graduate-level courses beginning after December 31, 2001.

Employer-provided educational assistance for non job-related graduate-level courses that began after June 30, 1996, and before January 1, 2002, must be included in income. Such assistance, as well as all assistance of more than $5,250 for any nonjob-related education, is subject to federal income tax withholding and social security, Medicare, and FUTA taxes.

According to the IRS, a graduate-level course is any course taken by an employee who has a bachelor's degree or is receiving credit toward a more advanced degree, if the course can be taken for credit in a program leading to a law, business, medical, or other advanced academic or professional degree. At the same time, the IRS defined the date that a course begins as the first regular day of class for the course. That is the first day on which regular classes generally begin for courses offered during that term (e.g., semester or session). The date on which the employee registers for a course does not determine when the course begins.[83]

Educational Assistance Programs must meet the following requirements to satisfy §127:

*For the benefit of employees only.* The program must be for the exclusive benefit of the employer's employees, including employees on military leave, individuals who are self-employed, and employees who are retired, disabled, or laid-off. The program may not provide benefits to an employee's spouse or other dependents. The IRS has broadly interpreted the definition of employee by clarifying that employers may continue to provide educational assistance to employees under their EAP after an employee has terminated, regardless of the reason for the termination, so long as the benefits are provided as a result of the employee's employment with the employer.[84] Examples of such EAPs include:

- a plan that provides educational assistance benefits to employees based on hours of service and that allows participants to use the assistance while employed or after termination, whether voluntary or involuntary; and

- a plan that provides educational assistance benefits to former employees who were terminated because of corporate downsizing.

*Separate written plan.* The EAP must be a separate written plan that provides only educational assistance benefits.

*No discrimination allowed.* The EAP may not discriminate in favor of highly compensated employees (for a definition, see the discussion of no-additional-cost fringe benefits at Section 3.2-1). In testing the program, employees covered by a collective bargaining agreement need not be counted if non job-related educational assistance was the subject of bargaining between the union and the employer.

*Benefits limited for owners.* No more than 5% of the educational assistance provided in any year may go to shareholders or owners owning more than 5% of the stock or capital of the employer.

*Not part of a cafeteria plan.* The EAP cannot provide employees with a choice between educational assistance benefits and other compensation, so they cannot be offered as part of a salary reduction arrangement or a cafeteria plan (see Section 4.5-1).

*Notification of employees.* Employers must provide reasonable notification of the availability and terms of the program to eligible employees.

*Benefits can be tied to course grade.* The EAP can require successful completion of a course or the attainment of a specific grade in determining reimbursement under the program.

---

83.    IRS Notice 96-68, 1996-2 CB 236.
84.    Rev. Rul. 96-41, 1996-2 CB 8.

*Qualified assistance only.* The EAP may not include payment for: tools or supplies (except for books) the employee can keep after the course ends; meals, lodging, or transportation; or education involving sports, games, or hobbies unless it involves the business of the employer or is a required part of a degree program.

*Substantiation required.* Employees receiving employer-provided educational assistance must be able to substantiate that the assistance qualifies under §127.

**Educational assistance reporting requirements for tax credits eased for employers**. Employers received an unwanted surprise when the Taxpayer Relief Act of 1997 became law. As part of the new Hope Scholarship and Lifetime Learning tax credits and the deduction for interest paid on student loans, new IRC §6050S was enacted.[85] Section 6050S required the reporting of certain education-related receipts and payments, including: employer payments to employees, independent contractors, and scholarship recipients (e.g., employees' children) for courses taken at institutions of higher education; the receipt of more than $600 in interest on a student loan; and the receipt of tuition and related expenses by institutions of higher education.

After an outcry from the business community regarding the employer-provided educational assistance reporting requirements, §6050S was amended as part of the IRS Restructuring and Reform Act of 1998. The reporting requirement is now limited to businesses making reimbursements or payments of education expenses "under an insurance arrangement."

 **WATCH OUT** Even though employers are not required to report educational assistance provided to employees that is not included in the employees' income, they may want to track those payments because employees may ask for that information in filing their personal income tax returns for the year. If an employee claims the Hope Scholarship or Lifetime Learning credit on Form 1040, the credit cannot be applied to expenses for which the employee has already received a nontaxable reimbursement from the employer.

**Tuition reduction.**[86] Employees of educational institutions may receive reductions in tuition from their employer for courses at that school or another educational institution without including the amount of the reduction in income. The assistance is limited to employees taking undergraduate courses, as well as graduate teaching and research assistants, although the reduction must not represent a payment for services rendered to the educational institution.

Individuals eligible for tuition reduction assistance include current employees, retired or disabled employees, and their widow(er)s, spouses, and dependent children, but they do not include domestic partners of employees. The reduction is available to highly compensated employees (see Section 3.2-1 for a definition) if it does not discriminate in their favor.

**Scholarships and fellowships.**[87] Qualified scholarships and fellowship grants, including tuition payments and related expenses, are excluded from an individual's income if the individual is a candidate for a degree at an educational institution. The exclusion does not apply to any part of the scholarship or fellowship grant that represents payment for teaching, research, or other services rendered to the educational institution as a condition for receiving the scholarship. Tuition and related expenses are defined as tuition, fees, books, supplies, and equipment required for enrollment and courses of instruction.

The restriction on providing teaching, research, or other services in return for the scholarship payments does not apply to any amount received under the National Health Service Corps Scholarship Program or the Armed Forces Health Professions Scholarship and Financial Assistance Program.

The IRS has ruled that scholarships awarded to degree candidates under a program that requires recipients to perform 10 hours of community service per week during the school year (20 hours per week in the summer) are qualified under §117. The community service requirement does not require the performance of substantial services that would make the scholarship compensation subject to taxation.[88]

---

85.    IRC §6050S.
86.    IRC §117(d); §132(h); §3121(a)(19); §3306(b)(16); §3401(a)(19); LTR 200137041, 6-20-01.
87.    IRC §117(a) - (c); §3121(a)(19); §3306(b)(16); §3401(a)(19); IRS Reg. §1.117-1; IRS Prop. Reg. §1.117-6.
88.    PLR 9645021, 8-12-96.

The IRS also ruled that grants paid by a hospital to participants in a research training program were not wages because the focus of the program was on training, not research services.[89] And it said that stipends paid by an educational organization to participants in fellowship training programs to develop the skills and qualifications required for leadership roles in the field were not wages paid in connection with the performance of services, but "disinterested grants" to enable development, training, and study.[90]

Employer-sponsored scholarship programs can also provide grants to employees' spouses and children without resulting in income to the employees. The principal purpose of the grants must be to educate the recipients and not to provide extra compensation or other incentives to employees.[91] If the grants or scholarships are awarded by a private foundation established by the employer, the following criteria must be met to show that the primary purpose of the grant program is to provide education:
- the program must not be used for employee recruitment or an inducement to stay with the employer;
- an independent committee must make the grant awards based on objective standards unrelated to the employee's employment;
- there must be identifiable minimum standards of eligibility;
- grants must continue even if the employee terminates employment;
- the courses of study cannot be limited to those that would benefit the employer or the foundation;
- the terms of the grant must give recipients the chance to get an education in their individual capacities for their personal benefit; and
- the number of grants awarded in a year do not exceed 25% of the children or spouses who applied for grants and were considered by the selection committee, or 10% of the children or spouses who were eligible for grants, whether or not they applied.

## 3.3-4 Group Legal Services

Through June 30, 1992, employer-paid group legal services insurance provided under a separate, written plan of the employer was excluded from the employee's income up to $70. To qualify, the plan could not discriminate in eligibility in favor of highly compensated employees and had to be for the exclusive benefit of employees and their spouses and dependents.[92] With the exclusion expiring on July 1, 1992, all group legal services payments are included in the employee's income and are subject to federal income tax withholding and social security, Medicare, and FUTA taxes. Several bills have been introduced in Congress to reinstate this exclusion, but none has been enacted into law.

## 3.3-5 Employee Business Travel Expense Reimbursements

One of the more complex areas regarding the taxability of payments to employees is when employers reimburse business travel expenses incurred by their employees. In general, if the reimbursement is made under an "accountable plan," the amount is excluded from income and is not subject to federal income tax withholding or social security, Medicare, or FUTA taxes. If the reimbursement is made under a "nonaccountable plan" or exceeds the amount substantiated by the employee, the reimbursement or the excess amount is included in income and is subject to federal income tax withholding and social security, Medicare, and FUTA taxes.[93]

**Travel must be "away from home" and "temporary."** Before a determination regarding the employer's reimbursement plan is made, an initial determination must be made as to whether the expenses themselves qualify for deduction as a travel expense. Employer reimbursements of employee business travel expenses can be excluded from income only if the expenses are incurred while the employee is temporarily

89. LTR 200010033, 12-9-99; LTR 20042027, 7-25-00; LTR 200226005, 3-3-02; LTR 200607017, 3-7-05.
90. LTR 200113020, 12-27-00.
91. Rev. Proc. 76-47, 1976-2 CB 670; TAM 9408001, 9-27-93.
92. IRC §120; §3121(a)(17); §3306(b)(12).
93. IRC §62(a)(2)(A), (c); §162(a)(2); §274(d); IRS Reg. §1.62-2; §1.274(d)-1; IRS Temp. Reg. §1.274-5T.

away from home on the employer's business.[94] To qualify as "away from home," the employee must be away overnight from his or her regular or principal place of business.

*Possible exception to the "away from home" requirement.*[95] In 2007, the IRS announced that it will amend its regulations to provide that the costs of a taxpayer's lodging not incurred in traveling away from home are personal expenses but may be deductible if they qualify as deductible expenses under IRC §162 (business expenses). Pending the issuance of the amended regulations, an employer's reimbursement of an employee's lodging expenses that are not incurred while the employee is traveling away from home and that an employer provides to the employee or requires the employee to obtain will not be taxable income to the employee if three conditions are met:

- the lodging is on a temporary basis;
- the lodging is necessary for the employee to participate in or be available for a bona fide business meeting or function of the employer; and
- the expenses are otherwise deductible by the employee, or would be deductible if paid by the employee, under §162.

To qualify as "temporary" travel away from home, the employee must be away from home for no more than one year.[96] The IRS has adopted a "realistic expectation" test that focuses on whether employment in a single location is realistically expected to last for more or less than one year, rather than on the actual length of employment at a temporary location:

- if employment away from home in a single location is realistically expected to last (and does in fact last) for one year or less, the employment will be treated as temporary in the absence of facts and circumstances indicating otherwise;

- if employment away from home is expected to last for more than one year or there is no realistic expectation that the employment will last for one year or less, the employment will be treated as indefinite, regardless of whether it actually exceeds one year; and

- if employment away from home is realistically expected not to exceed one year, the employment will be treated as temporary (in the absence of facts and circumstances indicating otherwise) until the date the taxpayer's realistic expectation changes.

**Example 1:** Employee Joan is regularly employed in New York City. In 2007, Joan accepted work with her employer in Buffalo, N.Y., which is 400 miles from New York City. Joan realistically expected the work in Buffalo to be completed in 6 months and planned to return to New York City at that time. In fact, the employment lasted 10 months, after which time Joan returned to New York City. Because Joan realistically expected that the work in Buffalo would last only 6 months, it did in fact last less than one year, and Joan had always intended to return to New York City at the end of her employment in Buffalo, this employment is temporary. Thus, reimbursements for Joan's travel expenses by her employer are excluded from income if they are paid under an accountable plan.

**Example 2:** The facts are the same as in Example 1, except Joan realistically expected the work in Buffalo to be completed in 18 months, but in fact it was completed in 10 months. Joan's employment in Buffalo is indefinite because she realistically expected that the work there would last longer than one year, even though it actually lasted less than one year. Reimbursements for Joan's travel expenses paid by her employer are included in income regardless of the employer's reimbursement plan.

---

94.   IRC §162(a)(2); IRS Reg. §1.162-2.
95.   IRS Notice 2007-47, 2007-24 IRB 1393.
96.   Rev. Rul. 93-86, 1993-2 CB 71.

***Example 3:*** The facts are the same as in Example 1, except that Joan realistically expected the work in Buffalo to be completed in 9 months. After 8 months, however, Joan was asked to remain for 7 more months (for a total actual stay of 15 months). Therefore, Joan's employment in Buffalo is temporary for 8 months, and indefinite for the remaining 7 months. Reimbursements for Joan's travel expenses incurred during the first 8 months are excluded from income if the employer reimburses her under an accountable plan, but the remainder of the reimbursements must be included in income.

Despite the insistence of the IRS that commuting expenses are not deductible and that reimbursements for them are taxable wages subject to withholding, a federal appeals court ruled that an employer was not required to withhold income, social security, or Medicare tax from reimbursements paid to employees for airline tickets to Anchorage, AK when the employees were on their way to work at the North Slope oil fields. The court did not rule that the payments were not subject to federal income tax, but that they were not subject to withholding for federal income and employment taxes because the expenses were ordinary and necessary to the business of the employer.[97]

**Reimbursements for daily transportation expenses.**[98] In 1999, the IRS ruled that reimbursements for an employee's daily transportation expenses are not included in the employee's income if:

- the expenses are incurred in going between the employee's residence and a temporary work location outside the metropolitan area where the employee lives and normally works;
- the employee has one or more regular work locations away from the employee's residence and the expenses are incurred in going between the employee's residence and a temporary work location in the same trade or business, regardless of the distance; or
- the employee's residence is his or her principal place of business and the expenses are incurred in going between the employee's residence and another work location in the same trade or business, regardless of whether the other work location is regular or temporary and regardless of the distance.

The determination of whether a work location is temporary is governed by the same rules that generally apply to temporary travel away from home (i.e., is the employment expected to last no more than one year and in fact lasts no longer than one year). Qualifying expenses include not only mileage, but incidental expenses such as parking fees and tolls as well.

***Example 1:*** Employee Jenny has been assigned to perform services at the office of Acme Scooter Co., and the assignment is expected to be completed in approximately 36 months. Jenny plans to spend about 95% of her total available time on site. Employment at Acme Scooter's office is not realistically expected to last for one year or less, so their office is not a temporary work location. Jenny's expenses incurred in going between her residence and the client's office are nondeductible commuting expenses, and reimbursements of these expenses are wages included in income.

***Example 2:*** Employee Jon has been assigned to oversee three separate teams of employees, with each team assigned to perform services on site for a different client of Millennium Tools, Inc. Each of the projects is planned to be completed within 9 or 10 months, and the starting date for each project will be staggered two or three months to give Jon time to complete the planning of each project before he begins the next. During these planning phases he will spend essentially all of his available time at the project site. After the planning phase, his time will be divided approximately equally between the three cases, spending one to five days at a time on site for each. The three projects will be completed within an overall time frame of 15 to 20 months. Employment at each of the work locations is realistically expected to last for one year or less, therefore, the offices of Millennium Tools' clients are temporary work locations unless and until the realistic expectation changes. Reimbursement for Jon's expenses incurred in going between his residence and these clients' offices are not included in income.

---

97.   HB&R, Inc. v. U.S., 229 F. 3d 688 (8 CA, 2000).
98.   Rev. Rul. 99-7, 1999-1 CB 361; ILM 199948016, 9-3-99; ILM 199948018, 9-3-99; ILM 199948019, 9-3-99; ILM 200018052, 3-10-00.

**Example 3:** Same facts as in Example 2, but Jon will work with smaller teams. Because he will be more involved in the day-to-day work at each site, he will divide his time approximately equally among the projects. Each of the projects is expected to take 1.5 years to complete. Employment at each of the work locations is not realistically expected to last for one year or less, and therefore the clients' offices are not temporary work locations. Jon's expenses incurred in going between his residence and these clients' offices are nondeductible commuting expenses, and any reimbursements of these expenses are wages included in income.

**Example 4:** Employee Cheryl routinely carries an "inventory" of eight projects at a time for Millennium Tools' clients. Each project can be completed with the application of 75 to 150 staff days. Since each project is budgeted to require 18 to 24 months, Cheryl will work for a few days each month on site on each project. She first performs planning activities, and she may ask the client for further information. While waiting for responses, she works on other projects. After counting additional time to develop and research complex issues with respect to the client, and to meet with the client, she is frequently assigned to each project for two years. Employment at each of the work locations is not realistically expected to last for one year or less, so the clients' offices are not temporary work locations. Cheryl's expenses incurred in going between her residence and these clients' offices are nondeductible commuting expenses, and any reimbursements of these expenses are wages included in income.

**Example 5:** Employee Yolanda is a technical specialist, and she is used on site either in a consulting role for smaller projects or as a team member for larger projects. She generally spends 100 to 120 days per year on the larger projects, with an estimated "cycle" time from beginning to end of 10 to 18 months. The balance of her available time is spent on smaller cases, and this may be spent on site or in her office. For those projects at which employment is realistically expected to last for one year or less, the clients' offices are temporary work locations unless and until the realistic expectation changes. Reimbursements of Yolanda's expenses of going between her residence and these offices are not included in income. With respect to those projects at which employment is not realistically expected to last for one year or less, the clients' offices are not temporary work locations. Yolanda's expenses incurred in going between her residence and these clients' offices are nondeductible commuting expenses, and any reimbursements of these expenses are wages included in income.

**Example 6:** Employee Nancy is assigned to six projects, each of which is expected to last for more than one year. During the course of the year, three of the projects are unexpectedly completed. Because employment at each of the work locations is expected to last for more than one year, employment at each of the locations is not temporary. This is the case regardless of whether employment actually exceeds one year. Nancy's expenses of going between her residence and these locations are nondeductible commuting expenses, and any reimbursements of these expenses are wages included in income.

**Example 7:** Employee Juan is given a six-month assignment on a long-term project, and more than a year after completing the six-month assignment, he is unexpectedly reassigned to the project for a seven-month period. Since the initial six-month assignment is realistically expected to last for one year or less, the employee's employment with respect to that phase of the project is temporary. Juan's expenses of going between his residence and this location are deductible business expenses, and reimbursements for those expenses are not included in his income.

**Example 8:** Employee Keith is assigned to perform services at a client's office for a period exceeding one year, and Webcast Services, Inc. pays a mileage allowance based on the lesser of (1) the distance from the employee's residence to the assignment or (2) the distance from the employer's regular office to the assignment. Employment at the client's office is not realistically expected to last for one year or less, and therefore the client's office is not a temporary work location. The employee's expenses incurred in going between his residence and this client's office are nondeductible commuting expenses, and any reimbursements of these expenses are wages included in income.

Complications can arise when there are breaks in the employee's service or the employee provides services during recurring but infrequent trips.[99] While no general guidance has been issued on these subjects, the IRS has stated that short breaks of 2-3 weeks are not significant and would not stall the application of the 1-year limit on temporary assignments. The Service also stated that a break of at least 7 months is significant and that 2 work assignments separated by a 7-month break are treated separately in applying the 1-year limitation. Where the employee makes infrequent but recurring trips to a work location on an assignment that is expected to last more than a year, employment at the location will be treated as temporary if the employee works in the location no more than 35 days in a calendar year. If the employee realistically expects to spend less than 35 days at a work location in a calendar year but that expectation changes during the year, the assignment will no longer be considered temporary for at least the remainder of that calendar year.

**Reimbursements under an accountable plan.**[100] To be an accountable plan, an expense reimbursement or advance payment program must meet the following conditions.

*Business connection.* Advances, allowances, or reimbursements have a business connection only if the employee's expenses are incurred in connection with the performance of services as an employee of the employer. Such expenses include transportation, meals and lodging, phone calls, tips, laundry, and taxi fares incurred while away from home overnight on business. They do not include personal expenses.

*Substantiation.* The employee must substantiate his or her business expenses by providing the employer with evidence of the amount, time, place, and business purpose of the expenses within a reasonable period of time after they are paid or incurred. The most popular method of providing such substantiation is an expense report accompanied by receipts showing the amounts of each expense (other than tips and other small amounts). Generally, expenses over $75 (plus all lodging expenses), must be supported by receipts or other documentary evidence.[101] This rule does not apply to transportation expenses where such evidence is not readily available. (Exceptions for "deemed substantiation" are discussed later in this section.)

In substantiating hotel expenses, an employee cannot merely provide credit card records that show a total amount paid for the hotel stay, plus the employee's own expense report. A copy of the itemized hotel bill must also be provided. The IRS said the credit card statement or receipt was insufficient because it did not break down the hotel charges so that deductible and nondeductible expenses could be determined.[102]

In 1997, the IRS issued optional rules under which employees of some federal government agencies can substantiate business expenses with an account book or expense log without also providing receipts or bills for individual expenses. The Service is also considering whether to expand this optional method to other employers. Under these rules, employees must give their employer an expense log or similar record detailing the amount, time, place and business purpose of the expenses within a reasonable amount of time after incurring them. They also must keep their receipts or paid bills for expenses in excess of $75 and all lodging expenses for 4 years after submitting the expense voucher and produce them if requested by the employer or the IRS. Employers have to approve the expenses, tell employees about their recordkeeping requirements, periodically audit a representative sample of expense vouchers, submit their reimbursement policies for review by an independent government authority, and either collect any excess reimbursements or treat the excess as paid under a nonaccountable plan.[103]

*IRS approves electronic and Web-based reimbursement plans.* In two rulings, the IRS examined employers' expense reimbursement plans that relied on electronic and Web-based reporting and substantiation. The first employer's plan required employees to submit electronic or paper expense reports within 30 days of incurring a business expense, supported by electronic or paper receipts showing the amount, time, place, and character of each expense. For expenses over $75 and all lodging expenses where the electronic receipt did not provide an itemized list of the expenses, the employees were required to provide paper receipts showing

---

99.   ILM 200025052, 4-26-00; ILM 200027047, 5-10-00; ILM 200026025, 5-31-00.
100.  IRS Reg. §1.62(c) - (g).
101.  IRS Notice 95-50, 1995-2 CB 333; IRS Temp. Reg. §1.274-5T(c)(2)(iii).
102.  LTR 200103015, 10-16-00.
103.  Rev. Proc. 97-45, 1997-2 CB 499.

such information. The IRS said the electronic and/or paper documents submitted to the employer constituted adequate substantiation.[104]

The second employer had Internet access to all its employees' charges on company credit cards, and the employees created electronic expense reports by adding detail to the charges appearing on the website in a 40-character field. The IRS said the employer's digital receipt system meets the substantiation requirements of an accountable plan if the employees' entries contain:

- a description of each expense and its business purpose; and
- for each entertainment expense, the name and business relationship of the person entertained, plus the date, place, and duration of and participants in any business discussion that took place before or after the entertainment.

The IRS also noted that the employer had to require paper receipts and expense reports for expenses over $75 and lodging expenses that are not itemized on the electronic receipt provided by the merchant, as well as expenses paid without using the company credit card.[105]

*Returning excess amounts.* In general, amounts paid by the employer that exceed amounts spent by the employee must be returned to the employer within a reasonable period of time. There are exceptions for situations where a per diem or mileage allowance exceeds actual expenses.

The IRS provides two safe-harbor methods for requiring substantiation and the return of excess amounts within a reasonable period of time.

- Under the *fixed-date method*, if an advance is provided no more than 30 days before an expense was incurred, the expense is substantiated by the employee within 60 days of being paid or incurred, and the excess amount is returned to the employer within 120 days of when the expense was paid or incurred, the reasonable period requirement is met.

- Under the *periodic statement method*, the employer can issue a periodic statement to the employee (at least quarterly) detailing amounts that have been paid and not substantiated and require the employee to either substantiate the excess amount or return it to the employer within 120 days of receiving the statement.

**50% meal deduction impacts employer, not employees.**[106] OBRA '93 amended the Internal Revenue Code to disallow a business deduction for 50% of business meal and entertainment expenses. The IRS later clarified that Congress did not intend for the partial deduction disallowance to result in income to employees. Therefore, reimbursements or advances for employees' business meal or entertainment expenses are not included in income for federal income tax withholding or social security, Medicare, or FUTA tax purposes, so long as all the other requirements of an accountable plan are met.

**Payments under a nonaccountable plan.** If an employer's reimbursement plan fails to meet any single requirement just mentioned, it is a nonaccountable plan and payments made under the plan are subject to federal income tax withholding and social security, Medicare, and FUTA taxes. On the other hand, if an employer has an accountable plan and one employee fails to substantiate his or her expenses, the plan does not become nonaccountable for all other employees. Also, if an employer has elements of both accountable and nonaccountable plans in its reimbursement plan, the IRS will allow the elements to be treated separately.[107]

The IRS insists that the reimbursements be matched against specific expenses incurred by the employee in order to be excluded from income. In a 2005 ruling, the Service said that amounts paid to motor vehicle service technicians who provided and maintained their own tools were wages since the amounts were based

---

104. Rev. Rul. 2003-106, 2003-44 IRB 936.
105. LTR 200433010, 4-27-04.
106. IRC §274(n)(1); IRS Reg. §1.62-2(h)(1).
107. IRS Reg. §1.62-2(i).

on an estimate of their hourly tool expenses rather than their actual expenses.[108] In 2007, the IRS said that where an employer recharacterized part of its employee service technicians' wages as tool expense reimbursements, this was an abuse of the accountable plan rules because the employer did not require adequate substantiation of the expenses or their connection to the work being done for the employer, and there were no actual reimbursements because the employees were paid the same regardless of the amount treated as expenses.[109]A federal appeals court used similar reasoning in ruling that reimbursement amounts paid to couriers were wages because the amounts were based on the amount customers were charged, not the couriers' expenses.[110] In another courier situation, the IRS concluded that payments made to the drivers and labeled as "equipment rentals" were wages because there was no written plan for reimbursing the drivers, no mileage records were kept, there were no records of the equipment's rental value, and the payments bore no relationship to any mileage or rental expenses.[111]

> **Example 1:** Employee George, an architect, receives $200 a day from his employer, Blueprints, Inc., of which $50 is designated as reimbursement for travel expenses when George is working away from home. Because George gets $200 a day whether he is traveling on business or not, the reimbursement designation is not a true reimbursement for business expenses and all payments to George are treated as made under a nonaccountable plan.

> **Example 2:** Financial Help Corp. reimburses its employees for business travel expenses while away from home under a plan requiring the employees to substantiate their expenses with receipts within 14 days of returning home. FHC also gives its employees $50 a month as an allowance to spend on office supplies, without requiring substantiation or return of amounts provided in excess of actual expenses. The monthly office expense allowance program is a nonaccountable plan that the IRS would treat separately from the travel expense reimbursement plan. All payments made under the office supplies plan are included in the employees' income when paid.

> **Example 3:** Employee Joan receives an expense allowance before traveling on behalf of her employer and is required to substantiate her expenses and return any excess within a reasonable period of time. When she returns the excess, however, the employer pays her a "bonus" equal to the excess amount. The employer has not properly required the return of excess amounts and must treat the entire expense allowance as wages subject to federal income tax withholding and social security, Medicare, and FUTA taxes.

> **Example 4:** Employee David receives a $2,500 advance from East Virginia Coal Co. on March 27 for a business trip to begin on April 10. David actually spends only $2,000 on his trip, which ends on April 20. David is required by EVCC to substantiate his expenses within 60 days of returning from his trip and to return any excess amounts within 120 days of returning. David submits an expense report and receipts substantiating his expenses on May 28, but does not return the $500 excess until October 1. When the 120-day period ends, EVCC must treat the $500 excess as income to David, and no adjustment can be made when he finally returns the excess amount.

 **WATCH OUT FOR CONTINUING OR PERMANENT ADVANCES** It has been customary formany employers to provide employees who regularly travel with continuing expense advances. Under such arrangements, employees are given a fixed amount and then reimbursed after each trip for whatever they spent so that their continuing advance remains fixed. These plans are generally nonaccountable since they do not provide amounts reasonably calculated to match anticipated expenses or do not require the return of excess amounts.

---

108. Rev. Rul. 2005-52, 2005-35 IRB 423.
109. ILM 200745018, 8-2-07.
110. Shotgun Delivery, Inc. v. U.S., 269 F.3d 969 (9 CA, 2001).
111. FSA 200132002, 2-3-01.

*Example 5:* Even though Acme Training, Inc. does not expect that any of its customer representatives will spend more than $500 in any quarter on business travel, it provides them with an advance of $1,500. After they substantiate a travel expense, Acme reimburses them for the amount they spent, providing a continuing advance of $1,500. Because the advance is not calculated to match anticipated expenses and is paid without regard to whether business expenses will be incurred within a reasonable period, the continuing advance program is a nonaccountable plan and all amounts paid must be included as wages when paid.

**What about frequent flyer miles?** One of the most talked-about fringe benefit issues of the last 20 years has been the taxability of frequent flyer miles earned from employee business travel but then used by employees to get free personal travel benefits from airlines. Several regulation projects on the issue have been opened and closed since 1985, with the IRS coming to no conclusion as to the valuation, taxability, or reportability generated by frequent flyer miles or other airline benefits, such as penalty payments or free flights for employees who are denied seating on overbooked flights.

In 2002, the IRS announced that it will not assert that an employee has taxable income because he or she received or used frequent flyer miles or other in-kind promotional benefits that were earned while flying on the employer's business. The IRS acknowledged that there are many technical and administrative issues relating to frequent flyer miles on which no official guidance has ever been provided, and for that reason, the IRS has not pursued a tax enforcement program for frequent flyer miles. The IRS's position does not apply to travel or other promotional benefits that are converted to cash, to compensation that is paid in the form of travel or other promotional benefits, or in other circumstances where these benefits are used to avoid paying taxes.[112]

**Deemed substantiation and per diem allowances.**[113] Rather than requiring employees to substantiate the actual expenses they incur while traveling on business away from home, employers may provide reimbursement in the form of a per diem allowance for each day of travel. The amount of the per diem allowance is deemed substantiated so long as it does not exceed IRS-established federal per diem rates and the employee substantiates the time, place, and business purpose of the expenses. The lodging per diem does not include an amount for lodging taxes, which can be claimed as a miscellaneous expense.

If the per diem plan meets all other requirements of an accountable plan, a per diem allowance may be used to substantiate expenses incurred if the allowance:

1.  is paid for ordinary and necessary business expenses incurred, or reasonably expected to be incurred, by an employee for, lodging, meals and incidentals while traveling away from home;

2.  is reasonably calculated not to exceed the amount of the expenses or expected expenses; and

3.  is paid at the applicable federal per diem rate or other IRS-approved rate or is paid under a flat rate or stated schedule in accord with normal business practices.

 **WHAT ARE INCIDENTALS?** Beginning in 2003, the IRS adopted the definition of incidental expenses as it applies to federal government employees. That means that incidental expenses now include: fees and tips for porters, baggage carriers, bell staff, housecleaning staff, stewards and stewardesses on ships, and hotel servants in foreign countries; transportation between places of lodging or business and places where meals are taken, if meals can be obtained at the temporary duty site; and the mailing costs for filing travel vouchers and paying employer-sponsored charge card billings. They do not include expenses for laundering, cleaning, and pressing of clothing, lodging taxes, taxi and limousine fares, telegrams, telephone calls, or facsimile charges.

To meet the requirement that employees be required to return amounts in excess of those substantiated to the employer within a reasonable period of time, a per diem allowance arrangement must require employees to return any amounts provided for days or miles not substantiated within a reasonable period of time. The

---

112.   IRS Ann. 2002-18, 2002-10 IRB 621.
113.   IRS Reg. §1.62-2(f); Rev. Proc. 2007-63, 2007-42 IRB 809.

arrangement does not have to require employees to return amounts in excess of the deemed substantiation amount for days or miles for which time, place, and business purpose have been substantiated.

Under the per diem allowance method, the amount deemed substantiated is the lesser of the per diem allowance or the federal per diem rate for the area the employee is traveling to (i.e., the locality of travel). The federal per diem rate is a combination of the federal lodging expense rate and the meal and incidental expense (M&IE) rate for the locality of travel. The federal per diem rates for localities of travel in the continental U.S. (CONUS) beginning October 1, 2007 range from $109 to $381 for more than 500 locations listed in IRS Publication 1542, Per Diem Rates (the rate is $109 for locations not listed). The lodging rates range from $70 to $317, and there are six M&IE rates ($39, $44, $49, $54, $59 and $64). There are other rates for locations outside the continental U.S. (OCONUS) that are under U.S. control. The CONUS, OCONUS, and foreign location rates can be found on the Internet at www.gsa.gov/Portal/gsa/ep/contentView.do?contentId=1 7943&contentType=GSA_BASIC.

 **EMPLOYERS CAN CHOOSE EFFECTIVE DATE** Beginning with the fourth quarter of 2000, the General Services Administration decided to issue new per diem rates to coincide with the beginning of the federal government's fiscal year, October 1. For the fourth quarter of each year, employers can use either the rates that have been in effect since January 1, or the new rates that took effect October 1, but cannot switch between them.[114]

*M&IE-only per diem allowance.* An employer may provide a per diem allowance to employees that covers only meal and incidental expenses, but only if:

1. the employer reimburses the employee for actual lodging expenses;
2. the employer actually provides the lodging;

3. the employer pays the provider of the lodging directly;

4. the employer reasonably expects that there will be no lodging expenses; or

5. the allowance is completed on a basis similar to that used for calculating the employee's wages or other compensation.

If an M&IE per diem allowance is used, the amount deemed substantiated is the lesser of the per diem allowance or the federal M&IE rate for the locality of travel.

*Incidentals-only per diem deduction.*[115] The IRS has also provided an optional method for computing the deductible costs of incidental expenses paid or incurred while traveling away from home by employees who do not incur meal costs and who are not reimbursed for the incidental expenses. Instead of using actual expenses, employees who do not incur meal expenses while traveling away from home may deduct $3 per day for each calendar day (or partial day) they are away from home, effective October 1, 2007. This amount will be deemed substantiated if the employee substantiates the time, place, and business purpose of the travel for that day.

*Special transportation industry rules.* For employers in the transportation industry who provide per diem allowances for meal and incidental expenses only, there is a special M&IE rate of $52 for any locality of travel in CONUS. For OCONUS travel, the rate is $58. If the special rate is used for an employee, it must be used for all covered travel by that employee during the calendar year. Employees are in the transportation industry if they move people or goods by vehicle, plane, ship, or train, regularly travel away from home, and generally travel to different localities of travel during each trip.

---

114.   Rev. Proc. 2007-63, 2007-42 IRB 809.
115.   IRS Reg. 1.62-2(e)(2); §1.274-5(j)(3), (m); Rev. Proc. 2007-63, 2007-42 IRB 809.

*High-low substantiation method.* A simpler method of calculating per diem allowances is allowed by the IRS, whereby one federal per diem rate is established for high-cost localities of travel and another rate for all other locations within CONUS. Under this high-low substantiation method, the employer may use the high-low per diem rate instead of the individual federal per diem rate of the locality of travel, so long as the allowance is for lodging, meal, and incidental expenses, not just meals and incidentals, and the travel is within CONUS.

For the high-cost localities listed in Table 3.2, the federal per diem rate is $237, effective October 1, 2007. These localities all have a federal per diem rate of $194 or more for all or a portion of the year. For all other CONUS localities of travel, the federal per diem rate under the high-low substantiation method is $152. If the high-low substantiation method is used to reimburse an employee for business travel, it must be used for the employee's expenses for the entire calendar year, with limited exceptions for travel where no lodging expenses are incurred or for travel outside CONUS. The employer may also reimburse the employee for actual expenses rather than use the high-low substantiation method.

The high-cost per diem includes $58 for meals, while the low-cost per diem includes $45 for meals. While these amounts cannot be used to reimburse employees who are not incurring lodging expenses, the employer uses these amounts to determine how much it can deduct for employee meal expenses on its corporate income tax return, since only 50% of such expenses are deductible.

 **EMPLOYER CAN CHOOSE EFFECTIVE DATE** Employers that used the general per diems for the first 9 months of the year cannot switch to the high-low method for those employees until the following January 1. Employers that used the high-low method for the first 9 months of the year must use it for the remainder of the year, although they can switch to the new rates and localities during that period as long as they do it for all employees reimbursed under the high-low method.

 **WATCH OUT** The chart of high-cost localities at Table 3.2 refers only to cities with high combined lodging and M&IE rates. It is not a complete list of the cities that have the highest M&IE rate ($64). Several low-cost localities have 2008 M&IE rates of $64. On the other hand, several of the high-cost localities have M&IE rates of $39 or $44. Employers that pay meal and incidental expense allowances but not lodging per diems must use the actual M&IE rates on the CONUS rate schedule.

Table 3.2

| HIGH-COST LOCALITIES | |
|---|---|
| **Key City** | **County and Other Defined Location** |
| Arizona | |
| Phoenix/Scottsdale (1/1-3/31)<br>Sedona (3/1-4/30) | Maricopa<br>City limits of Sedona |
| California | |
| Napa<br>Palm Springs (1/1-4/30)<br>San Diego<br>San Francisco<br>Santa Barbara<br>Santa Monica<br>South Lake Tahoe (12/1-3/31)<br>Yosemite National Park | Napa<br>Riverside<br>San Diego<br>San Francisco<br>Santa Barbara<br>City limits of Santa Monica<br>El Dorado<br>Mariposa |

| HIGH-COST LOCALITIES | |
|---|---|
| **Key City** | **County and Other Defined Location** |
| Colorado | |
| Aspen (12/1-4/30)<br>Crested Butte/Gunnison (12/1-3/31)<br>Silverthorne/Breckenridge (12/1-3/31)<br>Steamboat Springs (12/1-2/29)<br>Telluride (10/1-3/31)<br>Vail | Pitkin<br>Gunnison<br>Summit<br>Routt<br>San Miguel<br>Eagle |
| District of Columbia | |
| Washington, D.C. | Washington, D.C. (also the cities of Alexandria, Falls Church, and Fairfax, and the counties of Arlington and Fairfax, in Virginia; and the counties of Montgomery and Prince George's in Maryland) |
| Florida | |
| Fort Lauderdale (10/1-4/30)<br>Fort Walton Beach/DeFuniak Springs (6/1-7/31)<br>Key West<br>Miami (10/1-2/29)<br>Naples (2/1-3/31)<br>Palm Beach (1/1-3/31)<br><br><br>Stuart (2/1-3/31) | Broward<br>Okaloosa and Walton<br><br>Monroe<br>Miami-Dade<br>Collier<br>Boca Raton, Delray Beach, Jupiter, Palm Beach Gardens, Palm Beach, Palm Beach Shores, Singer Island, and West Palm Beach<br>Martin |
| Illinois | |
| Chicago | Cook and Lake |
| Maryland | |
| Baltimore<br>Cambridge/St. Michaels (4/1-8/31)<br>Ocean City (6/1-8/31) | Baltimore City<br>Dorchester and Talbot<br>Worcester |
| Massachusetts | |
| Boston/Cambridge<br>Martha's Vineyard (7/1-8/31)<br>Nantucket (10/1-11/30 and 6/1-9/30) | Suffolk, City of Cambridge<br>Dukes<br>Nantucket |
| Nevada | |
| Incline Village/Crystal Bay/Reno/<br>Sparks (6/1-8/31) | Washoe |
| New York | |
| Floral Park/Garden City/Glen Cove/<br>    Great Neck/Roslyn<br>Manhattan<br><br>Queens<br>Saratoga Springs/<br>    Schenectady (7/1-8/31)<br>Tarrytown/White Plains/New Rochelle/<br>    Yonkers | Nassau<br><br>Boroughs of Manhattan, Brooklyn, the Bronx and Staten Island<br>Queens<br><br>Saratoga and Schenectady<br>Westchester |

| HIGH-COST LOCALITIES | |
|---|---|
| **Key City** | **County and Other Defined Location** |
| Pennsylvania | |
| Philadelphia | Philadelphia |
| Rhode Island | |
| Jamestown/Middletown/Newport (10/1-11/30 and 2/1-9/30) | Newport |
| Providence | Providence |
| Utah | |
| Park City (1/1-3/31) | Summit |
| Virginia | |
| Loudoun County | Loudoun |
| Virginia Beach (6/1-8/31) | City of Virginia Beach |
| Washington | |
| Seattle | King |
| Wisconsin | |
| Lake Geneva (6/1-9/30) | Walworth |

*Example:* Employee Alex is reimbursed by his employer under the high-low substantiation method. Before he traveled from Boston to Washington, D.C. in June 2008, his employer gave him a 7-day advance of $1,855 (7 x $265, the employer's per diem rate). Alex's business in Washington took only 4 days, after which he returned to Boston. Alex substantiated the 4 days of business travel and was required to return $795 ($265 x 3 days). Under the high-low substantiation method, Washington, D.C. is a high-cost locality of travel, so the federal per diem rate is $237. Therefore, if Alex is not required to return amounts in excess of the federal per diem rate, his employer will have to include $112 in his income [4 days x ($265 - $237) = 4 days x $28 daily excess].

*Meals provided to the employee.* The federal per diem rates allocable to meals and incidental expenses do not have to be reduced where some of the employee's meals will be provided at no cost to the employee while on the road, so long as the employer reasonably expects the employee to incur meal expenses.

*Prorated per diems.* Where the employer provides employees with a per diem allowance or an M&IE allowance and less than a full day of travel (12:01 a.m. to 12:00 midnight) will be involved (e.g., a 3½-day trip), the allowance must be prorated. Under federal travel regulations, the employer can allocate three-quarters of the allowance to each partial day during which the employee is traveling away from home on business. Employers can also use any other consistently applied method that is in accordance with reasonable business practice.

*Mileage allowances.* An employer may reimburse its employees for local travel or transportation expenses while away from home through a mileage allowance. The amount of the allowance up to the federal business standard mileage rate is deemed substantiated, so long as the employee substantiates the time, place, and business purpose of the travel.[116] For 2008, the business standard mileage rate is $.505 (50.5 cents) per mile.

---

116.   Rev. Proc. 2007-70, 2007-50 IRB 1162.

**Example:** In 2008, Titanic Frozen Foods provides its sales reps with a mileage allowance of $.525 per mile and does not require them to return amounts in excess of the amount deemed substantiated, although they must return amounts advanced for unsubstantiated miles. Employee Nancy receives an allowance for 800 miles of business travel. She travels 500 miles on business, which she substantiates. Nancy must return $157.50 to Titanic, representing the amount of the allowance for unsubstantiated miles (300 x $.525). She may keep the $10.00 that represents the amount advanced in excess of the deemed substantiation amount [500 x ($.525 - $.505)], but it must be included in her wages. On Nancy's 2008 Form W-2, Titanic must include the $10.00 excess amount in Boxes 1, 3 and 5 and the amount represented by the IRS-approved rate—$252.50 (500 miles x $.505)—in Box 12 preceded by Code "L."

*Flat rate or stated schedule.* An allowance for business expenses paid on a regular and objective basis (e.g., days or hours away from home, number of miles traveled) is paid at a flat rate or stated schedule. For instance, a cents-per-mile payment to truck drivers traveling away from home to cover expenses incurred while driving is an allowance paid at a flat rate or stated schedule.

*Fixed and variable rate allowance.*[117] Another type of mileage allowance that can be used as a basis for reimbursing employees for their business-related automobile expenses is a fixed and variable rate (FAVR) allowance. A FAVR allowance uses a flat rate or stated schedule that combines periodic fixed and variable rate payments, and it relieves employees of the need to keep a record of their actual expenses.

The amount of the FAVR must be based on costs from the geographic area where the employee drives the car on business (the base locality), must reflect retail prices paid by consumers, and must be reasonably and statistically defensible in estimating the employee's actual expenses. A FAVR allowance has two components:

1. a periodic fixed payment covering projected fixed costs, such as depreciation, insurance, registration, and license fees; and
2. a periodic variable payment covering projected operating costs, such as fuel, oil, tires, and routine maintenance and repairs.

The payments are based on the cost of a standard automobile selected by the employer. The cost may not exceed 95% of the dealer's sticker price plus state and local taxes, and may not exceed $27,500 in 2008.

To qualify as part of an accountable plan, the employee must be required to return any portion of a periodic variable payment that relates to unsubstantiated business miles or a periodic fixed payment that relates to a time when the employee was not covered by a FAVR allowance. If this is not done, the FAVR allowance will not be deemed substantiated to the employer for those payment amounts.

Here are several other conditions that apply to a FAVR allowance:

1. The annual business mileage must be at least 6,250 miles, and the percentage of business use may not exceed 75%

2. Control employees are not eligible, although the definition is somewhat narrower than under the commuting valuation method (see Section 3.2-2).

3. Management employees may not make up the majority of employees subject to a FAVR allowance at any point during the year.

4. At least 5 employees must be covered by a FAVR allowance during the year.

For details on the complex requirements of the FAVR allowance, see IRS Rev. Proc. 2007-70, 2007-50 IRB 1162.

---

117.   Rev. Proc. 2007-70, 2007-50 IRB 1162.

**Taxation and reporting requirements.**[118] Employer reimbursements for actual, substantiated employee business expenses under an accountable plan are not included in an employee's income and are not subject to federal income tax withholding or social security, Medicare, or FUTA taxes or reporting on the employee's Form W-2. Employer reimbursements under a nonaccountable plan must be included in the employee's income when determined to be made under a nonaccountable plan and are subject to federal income tax withholding and social security, Medicare, and FUTA taxes, as well as reporting as wages or other compensation on the employee's Form W-2. The employee can take a deduction for unreimbursed amounts actually spent as business expenses on his or her personal tax return, subject to the 50% limit for meal and entertainment expenses and the 2% floor for miscellaneous deductions.

Under an accountable per diem or mileage allowance plan, amounts provided to an employee that are less than or equal to the IRS-approved rate (federal per diem rate, high-low substantiation rate, or business standard mileage rate) are not included in the employee's income and are not subject to federal income tax withholding or social security, Medicare, or FUTA taxes. They are not reported on the employee's Form W-2 as wages or other compensation (but see the next paragraph).

Amounts provided to an employee that exceed the IRS-approved rate are treated as if provided under a nonaccountable plan and are included in the employee's income and are subject to federal income tax withholding and social security, Medicare, and FUTA taxes. They also must be reported in Boxes 1, 3 and 5 of the employee's Form W-2. The amount reimbursed up to the IRS-approved rate must be reported in Box 12, preceded by Code "L." For details on Form W-2 reporting requirements, see Section 8.8-3.

The rules for determining when to treat taxable portions of reimbursements, advances, or per diem allowances as wages subject to federal income tax withholding and social security, Medicare, and FUTA taxes are as follows:

*Nonaccountable plans.* Amounts paid to an employee under a plan that does not meet the requirements for business connection, substantiation, or return of excess amounts must be included in the employee's wages when they are paid and are subject to federal income tax withholding and social security, Medicare, and FUTA taxes at that time.

*Accountable plans.* If amounts paid to an employee under an accountable plan are not substantiated within a reasonable period of time, or amounts exceeding the substantiated amount are not returned within a reasonable period of time, such amounts must be included in the employee's wages in the first payroll period following the end of the reasonable period. Where the accountable plan is a per diem or mileage allowance arrangement, the timing of the inclusion of excess amounts as wages depends on whether the arrangement provides for reimbursements or advances.

If an employee is reimbursed under an accountable per diem or mileage allowance plan in excess of the IRS-approved rate, the excess must be included in the employee's wages when the reimbursement is paid. If the employee is advanced an amount that exceeds the amount deemed substantiated under the IRS-approved rate, the excess must be included in the employee's wages by the first payroll period after the employee substantiates the time, place, and business purpose of the expenses. If an employee who receives an advance fails to substantiate days or miles of travel within a reasonable period of time or does not return the portion of the advance relating to those unsubstantiated days or miles within a reasonable period of time, the unreturned portion of the advance is subject to federal income tax withholding and social security, Medicare, and FUTA taxes in the first payroll period following the end of the reasonable period.

> ***Example:*** Under an accountable per diem allowance arrangement, Employee Tom is reimbursed $150 per day for business travel expenses. When Tom returns from a business trip from his home in Kansas City, Mo. to Buffalo, N.Y., in June 2008, he substantiates 5 days of business travel. The federal per diem rate for Buffalo in June is $140. Tom is reimbursed $750 for his trip, and he is not required to return the amount in excess of the federal per diem rate. Tom's employer must include $50 [(5 x $150) - (5 x $140)] in Tom's wages for the payroll period during which the reimbursement was paid and withhold and pay federal income, social security, Medicare, and FUTA taxes on that amount.

---

118.  IRS Reg. §1.62-2(h); Rev. Proc. 2007-70, 2007-50 IRB 1162; Rev. Proc. 2007-63, 2007-42 IRB 809.

*Pattern of abuse.*[119] If an employer regularly fails to comply with the requirements for reimbursing or advancing amounts paid or incurred by employees for business expenses, the IRS will consider this a "pattern of abuse" and will treat all payments as being made under a nonaccountable plan.

The IRS explained that:
- where an expense allowance arrangement has no mechanism or process to determine when an allowance exceeds the amount that may be deemed substantiated, and
- the arrangement routinely pays allowances in excess of the amount that may be deemed substantiated without requiring actual substantiation of all the expenses or repayment of the excess amount,
- then the failure of the arrangement to treat the excess allowances as wages for employment tax purposes shows a pattern of abuse that causes all payments made under the arrangement to be treated as made under a nonaccountable plan.[120]

**Spousal travel expenses.** Under IRC amendments made by the Omnibus Budget Reconciliation Act of 1993, travel expenses of a spouse, dependent, or other person (not including business associates) accompanying an individual on a business trip are not deductible as a business deduction unless:

- the spouse, dependent, or other person is also an employee of the employer providing the reimbursement;

- the travel of the spouse, dependent, or other person is for a bona fide business purpose; and

- the expenses would otherwise be deductible as a business expense by the spouse, dependent, or other person.[121]

The disallowance of the deduction left employers unsure of whether they were required in every case to include reimbursements or payments of "spousal travel expenses" on behalf of employees in the employees' income for federal income tax withholding and social security, Medicare, and FUTA tax purposes, especially when the reimbursements were business-related. And even where the reimbursements were included in employees' income, employers were unsure whether they could still take a wage expense deduction for the reimbursements.

*Spousal travel expense reimbursements may be a working condition fringe.* Regulations issued by the IRS provide that the denial of the deduction to the employer under Section 274 for the employer's payment of an employee's spousal travel expenses does not preclude the payment from qualifying as a working condition fringe benefit for the employee under certain circumstances.[122]

These employer reimbursements or payments qualify as working condition fringe benefits only if:

- the employer does not treat them as wages;
- the expenses would be deductible by the employee had Section 274(m)(3) not been added by OBRA '93; and
- the employee substantiates the expenses.

In essence, the employer can exclude the spousal travel expense payments or reimbursements from the employee's income if the employee can show that there was a legitimate business purpose for the spouse's, dependent's, or other individual's presence on the trip and the employee substantiates the expenses. This rule applies to all employers, even those who are exempt from federal taxation and are not subject to the deduction disallowance of §274(a)(3). If the travel does not qualify as a working condition fringe benefit, the

---

119.   IRS Reg. §1.62-2(k); Rev. Proc. 2006-41, 2006-43 IRB 777.
120.   Rev. Rul. 2006-56, 2006-46 IRB 874.
121.   IRC §274(m)(3).
122.   IRS Reg. §1.132-5(t).

employer-paid amounts must be included in the employee's income and are subject to federal income tax withholding and social security, Medicare, and FUTA taxes.

*Employer may get a wage deduction.* An employer can avoid the deduction disallowance by treating employer-paid spousal travel expenses as employee compensation. If the employer chooses to do this, the employer-paid amount is fully included in the employee's income and is subject to federal income tax withholding and social security, Medicare, and FUTA taxes.

# 3.3-6 Employer-Provided Meals and Lodging

**Employer-provided meals.** Generally, the value of meals furnished in kind by an employer to an employee is excluded from the employee's income and is not subject to federal income tax withholding or social security, Medicare, or FUTA tax if:

- the meals are furnished on the employer's business premises; and
- they are furnished for the convenience of the employer.[123]

Under an amendment added by the IRS Restructuring and Reform Act of 1998, all meals furnished to employees on the business premises of the employer are treated as furnished for the convenience of the employer if more than half of the employees who are furnished such meals are provided with them for the convenience of the employer.[124]

*What is "for the convenience of the employer?"* [125] Meals are furnished for the convenience of the employer if they are provided for a "substantial noncompensatory business reason of the employer." Meals furnished as a means of providing additional compensation to an employee are not provided for the employer's convenience. Here are some examples of noncompensatory business reasons for employer-provided meals:

- meals furnished to an employee during working hours so the employee can handle emergency calls during his or her meal period;
- meals furnished to an employee because the employer's business allows only a short meal period (e.g., 30-45 minutes) and the employee could not be expected to eat elsewhere during that time (e.g., employer's peak business hours occur during the employee's meal period);
- meals furnished to an employee because there are no eating facilities in the employer's vicinity; and
- meals furnished to restaurant or food service employees for each meal period they work.

Generally, meals furnished during nonworking hours are not provided for the convenience of the employer. While there are some exceptions (i.e., meals furnished to restaurant employees immediately before or after the meal period, meals furnished to an employee immediately after working hours because the employee's work kept him or her from eating during working hours), meals furnished on nonworking days do not qualify for the exclusion.

*Special rules for meals furnished with a charge.*[126] Sometimes, an employer provides meals to employees for a fee. The taxability of the subsidized amount depends on several factors. If the employee has a choice whether or not to purchase the meals, the meals are not furnished for the convenience of the employer. If the employee must pay the meal charge (e.g., through a salary reduction) whether or not the employee eats the meal, then a determination of whether the meals are furnished for the convenience of the employer must be made according to the rules just explained.

---

123. IRC §119(a); §3121(a)(19); §3306(b)(14); IRS Reg. §1.119-1(a).
124. IRC §119(b)(4).
125. IRS Reg. §1.119-1(a)(2).
126. IRS Reg. §1.119-1(a)(3); LTR 9602001, 9-15-95.

*What is the employer's business premises?* [127] The employee's place of employment is the employer's business premises for purposes of the meals and lodging exclusion.

*Hospitality industry initiatives.* Much of the controversy and confusion regarding the issue of employer-provided meals has arisen in the hospitality industry. In 1999, a federal appeals court ruled that a casino/hotel operator could deduct 100% of the cost of free meals provided to its employees and did not have to include the value of the meals in the employees' income. In its ruling, the court said the employer's policy requiring employees to stay on the employer's premises during their shifts was a substantial noncompensatory business reason under §119 for providing the meals. Despite its opposition to the employer's claims and its victories in the lower courts, the IRS decided not to appeal the decision and withdrew proposed training materials for its agents on the application of §119 to employer-provided meals in the hospitality industry as well as a related settlement initiative.[128]

**Employer-provided lodging.** The value of employer-provided lodging is excluded from the employee's income if:

- the lodging is furnished on the employer's business premises (including a camp provided by the employer near the work site, if it is in a remote area of a foreign country);
- the lodging is furnished for the employer's convenience; and
- the employee is required to accept the lodging as a condition of employment.[129]

Where an employee was provided housing in a condominium community in a fairly remote area of a foreign country near the employer's premises, the value was included in the employee's income because the condominiums were available to the general public and the units rented by the employer did not meet the definition of a "camp."[130]

A separate exclusion applies to the value of qualified campus lodging provided to employees of educational institutions and academic health centers, with certain limitations based on the rent the employee is paying in comparison to the average rental paid for such lodging.[131]

**Cash allowances not excluded.** The exclusion for meals and lodging does not apply to cash allowances for meals or lodging rather than meals or lodging furnished in kind, although such allowances may be excluded as an advance or reimbursement for business-related employee expenses (see Section 3-3.5). Also, if the employee has the choice of receiving cash or the in-kind meals or lodging, the value is not excluded from the employee's income.[132]

**Contract or state law not determinative.** When determining whether employer-provided meals or lodging are furnished for the convenience of the employer, the provisions of an employment contract or state statute characterizing the meals or lodging are not determinative. All the facts and circumstances must be considered when making a decision.[133]

## 3.3-7 Adoption Assistance

The Small Business Job Protection Act of 1996 added IRC §23 and §137 relating to adoption expenses. While §23 allows individuals to take an income tax credit for qualified adoption expenses, §137 excludes from an employee's income employer-provided adoption assistance that is furnished under an adoption

127.   IRS Reg. §1.119-1(c).
128.   Boyd Gaming Corp. v. Commissioner, 177 F.3d 1096 (9 CA, 1999); Ann. 99-77, 1999-34 IRB 243.
129.   IRC §119(a), (c); §3121(a)(19); §3306(b)(14); IRS Reg. §1.119-1(b), (d).
130.   Nielsen v. Commissioner, T.C. Summary Op. 2007-53, No. 18883-04S (4-2-07).
131.   IRC §119(d).
132.   IRS Reg. §1.119-1(e).
133.   IRC §119(b)(1); IRS Reg. §1.119-1(b).

assistance program in connection with the employee's adoption of an eligible child. The income exclusion is subject to the following limitations and requirements:[134]

**Dollar limitation**. The maximum exclusion for qualified adoption expenses in 2008 is $11,650 per eligible child (adjusted annually for inflation) over all taxable years related to the particular adoption. The limitation is not applied on an annual basis. The maximum exclusion includes amounts connected with an unsuccessful attempt to adopt a child before successfully finalizing the adoption of another child. The $11,650 limitation applies both to married individuals and to unmarried individuals adopting an eligible child. An unmarried couple that seeks to adopt an eligible child must apply the dollar limitation to the couple's combined qualified adoption expenses. The maximum exclusion for the year applies to adoptions of a child with special needs regardless of the amount of qualified adoption expenses, so long as the adoption is finalized.

**Income limitation**. The amount that can be excluded from gross income is phased out for individuals with modified adjusted gross income of more than $174,730 (adjusted annually for inflation) until it is totally lost to individuals with a modified adjusted gross income of at least $214,730. A taxpayer's modified adjusted gross income is equal to adjusted gross income without applying the adoption assistance exclusion, deductions for tuition or interest on education loans, the foreign earned income or foreign housing exclusion (see Section 14.1-4), or the exclusion for income from Puerto Rico, Guam, American Samoa, or the Northern Mariana Islands.

*Example 1*: In 2008, Sherman Shoe Corp. pays $11,650 of qualified adoption expenses on behalf of employee Sylvia under its adoption assistance program. Sylvia and her husband do not reach the income limitation in either 2008 or 2009. In 2008, Sylvia can exclude $11,650 from gross income. In 2009, SSC pays another $2,000 of qualified adoption expenses on Sylvia's behalf in relation to the same eligible child. Sylvia must include the entire $2,000 in her gross income in 2009.

*Example 2*: In 2008, Sherman Shoe Corp. pays $12,000 of qualified adoption expenses on behalf of employee Marina under its adoption assistance program ($6,000 for an unsuccessful attempt to adopt an eligible child, and $6,000 for the final adoption of an eligible child). Marina and her husband do not reach the income limitation in 2008. In 2008, Marina can exclude $11,650 from gross income, but she must include the remaining $350 provided on her behalf.

**Adoption of an eligible child**. An eligible child is an individual who is under age 18 or is physically or mentally incapable of caring for himself or herself when the adoption assistance is provided. A child with special needs is an eligible child who a state has determined cannot or should not be returned to the parents' home and cannot be placed for adoption without adoption assistance because of a specific factor or condition. A child with special needs must be a citizen or resident of the United States.

**Qualified adoption expenses**. Qualified adoption expenses include reasonable and necessary adoption fees, court costs, attorneys' fees, travel expenses (including meals and lodging) while away from home, and other expenses directly related to the legal adoption of an eligible child. Qualified expenses do not include any expenses incurred in violation of federal or state law, in carrying out any surrogate parenting arrangement, or in connection with the adoption of a child of the employee's spouse.

**Adoption assistance program requirements**. Following are several requirements that must be met for an adoption assistance program before employer-provided adoption assistance can be excluded from an employee's income:

*Separate written plan*. The adoption assistance program must be a separate written plan established for the exclusive benefit of the employer's employees, although it may be a part of an employer's comprehensive employee benefit plan.

---

134.   IRC §23(a) - (h); §137(a) - (e); IRS Notice 97-9, 1997-2 IRB 35; IRS Pub. 968, Tax Benefits for Adoption; IRS Announcement 97-64, 1997-26 IRB 9; Rev. Proc. 2007-66, 2007-45 IRB 970.

*No discrimination allowed.* The program may not discriminate in favor of highly compensated employees (for a definition, see the discussion of no-additional-cost services at Section 3.2-1) or their dependents.

*Benefits limited for owners.* No more than 5% of the adoption assistance provided in any year may go to shareholders or owners owning more than 5% of the stock, capital, or profits interest of the employer on any day during the year.

*No funding required.* The program is not required to be funded.

*Notification of employees.* Employers must provide reasonable notification of the availability and terms of the program to eligible employees.

**Military programs qualify.** Adoption reimbursement programs relating to members of the Armed Forces or the Coast Guard are treated as qualified adoption assistance programs under §137.

**Program can be in cafeteria plan.** An adoption assistance program that meets the requirements of §137 may be offered as a qualified benefit through an employer's cafeteria plan.

**Withholding and reporting obligations.** The IRS has ruled that employer-provided adoption assistance that meets the requirements of §137 is not subject to federal income tax withholding, even if assistance exceeds the maximum dollar limitation. However, these amounts are subject to social security, Medicare, and FUTA taxes. Qualified adoption assistance must therefore be reported in Boxes 3 and 5 of the employee's Form W-2, and the amounts withheld for social security and Medicare taxes reported in Boxes 4 and 6. The assistance must also be reported in Box 12, with code "T" (see Section 8.8-3). This includes amounts in excess of the maximum exclusion amount, as well as adoption benefits paid or reimbursed from an employee's pre-tax contributions to a cafeteria plan. Employees who receive qualified adoption assistance must file Form 8839, *Qualified Adoption Expenses*, with their personal income tax return to determine the nontaxable and taxable portion of the assistance. The employee may also need to make an adjustment to his or her Form W-4, *Employee's Withholding Allowance Certificate* (see Section 6.3-1), for additional withholding to avoid penalties for underpayment of tax.

**Foreign adoptions.** If the eligible child is not a citizen or resident of the U.S., the exclusion for employer-paid adoption assistance is available only if the adoption becomes final. Adoption assistance provided by the employer before the year in which the adoption becomes final is excluded from the employee's income in the year in which the adoption becomes final. Therefore, employer-paid adoption assistance provided in a year before a foreign adoption becomes final is included in the employee's income in the year the assistance is provided, and the employee must include it on his or her personal income tax return. The employer must comply with the employment tax withholding, payment, and reporting requirements discussed earlier for the year the assistance was provided. The employee can claim an exclusion from income for the assistance in the year the adoption becomes final.

In 2005, the IRS established safe harbors for determining the finality of an adoption of a foreign-born child.[135] The guidance applies to qualified adoption expenses paid or incurred in connection with the adoption of a foreign-born child who has received an "immediate relative" (IR) visa from the Department of State. Because IR visas are only issued to foreign-born children who enter the U.S. pursuant to a decree of adoption or guardianship issued by a "competent authority" of a foreign country, the guidance does not apply where the child is a citizen or resident of the U.S. at the time the adoption proceedings commence.

For federal income tax purposes, the adoption of a foreign-born child will be treated as final, if the child receives an IR2, IR3, or IR4 (simple adoption) visa:

- in the taxable year in which the competent authority enters a decree of adoption, or

---

135.    Rev. Proc. 2005-31, 2005-26 IRB 1374.

- in the taxable year in which a home state court enters a decree of re-adoption or the home state otherwise recognizes the decree of the foreign-sending country, if that taxable year is one of the next two taxable years after the taxable year in which the competent authority enters the decree.

If the child receives an IR4 (guardianship or legal custody) visa, the adoption is treated as final:

- in the taxable year in which a home state court enters a decree of adoption.

*Re-adoption expenses.* Re-adoption is defined as an adoption or other recognition proceeding under home state law occurring after the entry of a foreign-born child into the U.S. under an IR visa. Otherwise qualified expenses paid or incurred in connection with a re-adoption satisfy the requirement that expenses be "reasonable and necessary" for purposes of determining whether the expenses are qualified adoption expenses.

**Coordinating the exclusion and the credit**. An employee may claim an income exclusion and a tax credit in connection with the adoption of an eligible child, but cannot claim both for the same expense. Also, an employee may not claim a credit for any expense that has been reimbursed by the employee's employer, whether or not the reimbursement is paid under a qualified adoption assistance program.

# 3.4  Other Payments

This section provides explanations of other types of payments an employer may make to an employee and a discussion of their inclusion or exclusion from income.

## 3.4-1  Advances and Overpayments

Salary advances (prepaid wages) and overpayments must be included in the employee's income for the payroll period when received and are subject to federal income tax withholding and social security, Medicare, and FUTA taxes at that time. The appropriate tax treatment of repaid advances or overpayments depends on the type of tax involved and when the money is repaid to the employer.[136]

**Federal income tax withheld**. If the employee repays the advance or overpayment during the same year the money was received, the employer excludes the amount from the employee's income when reporting on Form W-2. The employee will then receive any excess income tax withheld as a tax refund when filing his or her personal tax return. If the employee repays the advance or overpayment in a later year, the amount of the repayment cannot be excluded from the employee's income for that year or any year. The employee may be able to take a deduction from income or a tax credit on his or her personal tax return for the repayment, subject to certain restrictions. While the employee's Form W-2 for the year of the repayment would be unaffected by the repayment, the employer should give the employee a separate receipt showing the repayment.

**Social security and Medicare taxes**. If the employee repays the advance or overpayment after the employer has filed its Form 941 for the quarter during which the overpayment was made (whether during the same or a later year), the employer must refund any overwithheld social security and Medicare taxes to the employee. The employer must keep a receipt noting the date and amount of the employee's repayment, as well as written evidence of the refund paid to the employee.

A written statement should also be obtained from the employee to the effect that the employee will not seek a refund of the social security and Medicare taxes directly from the IRS. This must be obtained before the employer can claim a credit or refund of the employee's and employer's shares of overpaid social security and Medicare taxes (see Section 8.6 for details on how this is accomplished). If the repayment is made in a year after the advance or overpayment was made, the repayment will not reduce the employee's social security or Medicare wages for the year of repayment. If the repayment results in an overpayment of social security or

---

136.  PLR 9103031, 10-23-90; Rev. Rul. 70-177, 1970-1 CB 214; Rev. Rul. 79-311, 1979-2 CB-25; SCA 1998-026, 12-23-98.

Medicare taxes for the earlier year (i.e., the employee's wages for the earlier year did not reach the social security wage base even after considering the repayment), the employee must be issued a Form W-2c, *Corrected Wage and Tax Statement*, for that year.

 **BE CAREFUL** If an employee repays an advance or overpayment in a later year and requests a refund of overpaid social security and Medicare taxes, the employer must take into account any applicable wage bases for these taxes for the year in which the advance or overpayment was made. If the employee's earnings exceed the applicable wage base even after the repayment is taken into consideration, neither the employee nor the employer is due a refund.

**Federal unemployment tax**. The employer may also be able to claim a refund of overpaid FUTA tax once the employee repays the advance or overpayment, but only if, after the repayment, the employee earned less than $7,000 during the year. The FUTA wage base is $7,000, so if the employee's earnings exceed that amount after taking into consideration the repayment, the employer is still liable for the maximum amount of FUTA tax and is not entitled to a refund.

**Good idea to get gross repayments for prior year overpayments**. Because an employer cannot collect the prior year's federal income tax withheld from an employee making a repayment in a subsequent year, employers can better protect themselves with a policy that requires the employee to repay the gross amount of the overpayment, rather than the net amount after taxes had been withheld. At the employer's option, the gross amount can be reduced by the amount of social security and Medicare tax overwithheld, or the employer can issue a separate check to the employee refunding the overwithheld amount.

*Example 1 — Repayment Made in Same Calendar Year*: Yuome, Inc. hired Fred on April 3, 2008 at a salary of $3,000 per month. Fred also received a sign-on bonus of $1,000 that he was required to repay if he left Yuome within one year of being hired. When Fred resigned from Yuome on November 30, 2008, he repaid the net sign-on bonus of $673.50 to the company. Since Fred received the bonus and repaid it in the same year (2008), Yuome will reduce Fred's taxable income and social security and Medicare wages, as well as withheld federal income, social security, and Medicare taxes.

|  | 2008 Payments | 2008 Repayment | 2008 Net Payments | 2008 Form W-2 |
|---|---|---|---|---|
| Federal Wages | $25,000.00 | $1,000.00 | $24,000.00 | $24,000.00 |
| Soc. Sec. Wages | $25,000.00 | $1,000.00 | $24,000.00 | $24,000.00 |
| Medicare Wages | $25,000.00 | $1,000.00 | $24,000.00 | $24,000.00 |
| FIT Withheld | $4,510.00 | $250.00 | $4,260.00 | $4,260.00 |
| SS Withheld | $1,550.00 | $62.00 | $1,488.00 | $1,488.00 |
| Med. Withheld | $362.50 | $14.50 | $348.00 | $348.00 |
| Net Pay | $18,577.50 | $673.50 | $17,904.00 |  |

Yuome filed corrections for the payments on Form 941 by attaching Form 941c for the fourth quarter of 2008. Fred's employer also recovered the employer share of social security and Medicare taxes through Form 941c. If the repayment had been for an amount overpaid in the same quarter as the correction, a Form 941c would not have been required.

***Example 2 — Repayment Made in a Subsequent Calendar Year:*** Yuome, Inc. hired Fred on July 3, 2007 at a salary of $3,000 per month. Fred also received a $1,000 sign-on bonus that he was required to repay if he left the company within 1 year of being hired. Fred resigned on March 29, 2008 and repaid the net sign-on bonus of $673.50 to Yuome. Since Fred resigned and repaid only the net amount of his sign-on bonus, the company will not be able to take an adjustment for the federal income tax withheld from the sign-on bonus on its Form 941 for the first quarter of 2008. Yuome must request an additional repayment from Fred for $250 to recapture the federal income tax withheld from the sign-on bonus.

| | 2007 Payments | 2008 Payments | 2008 Repayment | 2007 Form W-2c | 2008 Form 941 |
|---|---|---|---|---|---|
| Federal Wages | $19,000.00 | $9,000.00 | $1,000.00 | N/A[1] | N/A[1] |
| Soc. Sec. Wages | $19,000.00 | $9,000.00 | $1,000.00 | ($1,000.00) | ($1,000.00) |
| Medicare Wages | $19,000.00 | $9,000.00 | $1,000.00 | ($1,000.00) | ($1,000.00) |
| FIT Withheld | $3,450.00 | $1,595.00 | $250.00 | N/A[2] | N/A[2] |
| SS Withheld | $1,178.00 | $558.00 | $62.00 | ($62.00)[3] | ($124.00)[4] |
| Med. Withheld | $275.50 | $130.50 | $14.50 | ($14.50)[3] | ($29.00)[4] |
| Net Pay | $14,096.50 | $6,716.50 | $673.50 | | |

[1]. Will only show as a deduction on Fred's personal income tax return for the amount of the repayment.

[2]. Fred can claim a deduction on his 2008 personal income tax return for the repayment. Yuome cannot claim a credit or refund from the IRS for prior year federal income tax withheld. Yuome must request this repayment from Fred.

[3]. Yuome will claim the applicable social security and Medicare taxes on the amount Fred repaid as an adjustment when filing Form 941c with its first quarter 2008 Form 941. To claim this amount, Fred must sign a statement that he has not and will not request a refund of the social security and Medicare taxes from IRS.

[4]. Yuome files corrections for the repayments in 2008 on Form 941 by attaching Form 941c. Yuome will recover the employee and employer shares of social security and Medicare taxes through Form 941c.

By requesting only the net amount of the repayment from Fred, Yuome will recover only $826.50 of the sign-on bonus ($673.50 from Fred and $153.00 from the IRS). Yuome loses $250 by requesting the net amount rather than the gross amount.

***Example 3 — Repayment Made in a Subsequent Calendar Year (Gross-Up):*** On December 15, 2007, Alice received a net relocation bonus of $10,000 from Yuome, Inc., resulting in a gross-up amount of $14,847.81. Alice, who earns $3,000 per month, was required to repay the gross amount if she left Yuome within 1 year of being hired. Alice resigned from Yuome on May 31, 2008 and repaid her gross relocation bonus, even though she received a net check of $10,000. The employer refunds Alice the employee social security and Medicare taxes withheld from the gross-up amount—$1,135.85

| | 2007 Payments | 2007 Relo. Bonus | 2008 Payments | 2008 Repayment | 2007 Form W-2c | 2008 Form 941 |
|---|---|---|---|---|---|---|
| Federal Wages | $16,347.81 | $14,847.81 | $15,000.00 | $14,847.81 | N/A[1] | N/A[1] |
| Soc. Sec. Wages | $16,347.81 | $14,847.81 | $15,000.00 | $14,847.81 | ($14,847.81) | ($14,847.81) |
| Medicare Wages | $16,347.81 | $14,847.81 | $15,000.00 | $14,847.81 | ($14,847.81) | ($14,847.81) |
| FIT Withheld | $3,976.39 | $3,711.95 | $2,657.00 | | N/A[2] | N/A[2] |
| Soc. Sec. Withheld | $1,013.56 | $920.56 | $930.00 | | ($920.56)[3] | ($1,841.12)[4] |
| Med. Withheld | $237.04 | $215.29 | $217.50 | | ($215.29)[3] | ($430.58)[4] |
| Net Pay | $11,120.82 | $10,000.00 | $11,195.50 | $14,847.81 | | |

[1]. Will only show as a deduction on Alice's personal income tax return for 2008. Alice can claim $14,847.81 since that was the amount repaid to Yuome.

[2]. Alice can claim a deduction on her personal income tax return for the repayment. Yuome cannot claim a refund from the IRS for prior year federal income tax withheld.

[3]. Yuome must repay Alice the applicable social security and Medicare taxes on the amount she repaid. The company will claim this amount as an adjustment when filing Form 941c with the second quarter 2008 Form 941. For Yuome to take this adjustment, Alice must sign a statement that she has hot and will not request a refund of the social security and Medicare taxes from the IRS.

[4]. Yuome takes adjustments for the repayment in 2008 on Form 941 by attaching Form 941c. Yuome will recover the employee and employer shares of social security and Medicare taxes.

By requesting the gross amount to be repaid, Yuome does not lose any portion of the refund made to Alice. The company would have lost in excess of $3,711 if it asked Alice to repay only the net amount of $10,000.

For information on the treatment of advances against commissions paid to salespersons, see Section 3.4-18.

## 3.4-2 Awards and Prizes

Awards and prizes provided to employees for outstanding achievement, money-saving suggestions, etc., are generally included in the employees' income and are subject to federal income tax withholding and social security, Medicare, and FUTA taxes.[137] There are exceptions for certain noncash awards that comply with several restrictions.

**Length of service or safety achievement awards.**[138] Employers do not include awards for length of service or safety achievement in an employee's income if the amount of the award is deductible to the employer as a business expense. The extent to which the award is deductible to the employer depends on whether the award meets several general and specific requirements and whether it is granted under a qualified or nonqualified plan.

*General requirements.* To qualify as deductible to the employer, a length of service or safety achievement award must be an award of "tangible personal property," which does not include cash or cash equivalents, stocks, bonds, vacations, meals, lodging, or tickets to theater or sporting events. Also, the award must be presented in a "meaningful presentation" that need not be elaborate but must emphasize the employee's achievement (e.g., presentation by a supervisor at a gathering of employees). Finally, the award must not be "dis-

---

137.   IRC §74(a); IRS Reg. §1.74-1(a).
138.   IRC §74(c); §274(j); IRS Prop. Reg. §1.74-2; §1.274-8.

guised compensation," which might be shown by an award made at the time of a salary review or by an award that cost the employer much less than its fair market value.

*Specific length of service award requirements.* To qualify as a deductible achievement award, a length of service award must not be presented for less than five years on the job and must not have been awarded to the same employee within the last four years. Retirement awards are length of service awards, although they may also be considered de minimis fringe benefits (e.g., a gold watch for 25 years of service.)

*Specific safety award requirements.* Safety awards will not qualify as deductible achievement awards if the employer has already presented them to 10% of its eligible employees during its taxable year or if they are presented to managers, administrators, professional employees, or clerical employees.

*Qualified plan awards.* Achievement awards that meet the general requirements are awarded under a qualified plan if the employer has a written plan that does not discriminate in favor of highly compensated employees (see Section 3.2-1 for a definition). The average cost of all qualified plan awards presented by the employer during its tax year (except those costing the employer $50 or less) may not exceed $400, or none of them will be considered qualified plan awards. The total deduction allowed to the employer for qualified plan awards granted to one employee is $1,600 per year.

*Nonqualified plan awards.* The employer is limited to a total deduction of $400 per employee per year for awards that are not granted under a qualified plan but that meet the general and specific requirements for deductibility.

*Excess included in income.* If the achievement award exceeds the limit on the employer's deductibility, the amount that must be included in the employee's income is the greater of (1) the difference between the employer's cost and the deduction limitation and (2) the difference between the award's fair market value and the deduction limitation. If the award is given before the required number of years of service, the entire amount is taxable and included in income.

**Civic and charitable awards.**[139] Awards for civic, charitable, religious, or educational achievement are excluded from income if the recipient did not actively seek the award, the award is not conditioned on performing future services, and the recipient turns the award over to a governmental or charitable organization designated before the award is used by the recipient (e.g., if the award is money, before the recipient spends, deposits, or invests it).

The designation of the governmental unit or charitable organization should be made before the award is to be presented by the employer to avoid the possibility of use of the award by the recipient. The designation should be made in writing and given to the employer. If the award is unexpected and the recipient cannot make the appropriate designation before receiving the award, the recipient must return the award to the employer and provide the designation before using the award. Under these circumstances the employer should provide written acknowledgement of the designation to the recipient.

**Prizes for retail salespeople.**[140] Noncash prizes awarded to retail salespeople paid solely on a commission basis for exceeding quotas or selling the most goods receive special treatment. Employers do not have to withhold federal income tax from such prizes, although they must be reported as income to the salespeople on their Forms W-2. The prizes are subject to social security, Medicare, and FUTA taxes, however.

## 3.4-3 Back Pay Awards

When employees win lawsuits or settlements against their employer for alleged violations of federal and state employment laws (e.g., wage-hour, anti-discrimination, labor-management), the amounts awarded are often considered to be back pay for wages unlawfully denied. As such, the IRS has generally ruled that they are subject to federal income tax withholding and social security, Medicare, and FUTA taxes.

---

139.   IRC §74(b); IRS Reg. §1.74-1(b); IRS Prop. Reg. §1.74-1(b) - (e); Rev. Proc. 87-54, 1987-2 CB 669.
140.   IRC §3402(j); IRS Reg. §31.3402(j)-1.

The basic rules governing the taxability of back pay awards and other damages received in employment-related lawsuits are contained in IRC §104(a), which was amended by the Small Business Job Protection Act of 1996 to exclude from income only damages received on account of personal physical injuries or physical sickness.[141] The amended section also specifically includes in income all awards for punitive damages (except in limited situations in wrongful death lawsuits) as well as awards for emotional distress damages beyond the amount attributed to medical care for the emotional distress. Even before the amendment, which added the word "physical" as well as the restrictions on punitive and emotional distress damages, the U.S. Supreme Court had ruled that back pay and liquidated (punitive) damages recovered under the Age Discrimination in Employment Act were taxable income.[142]

After the Supreme Court decision and the amendment of §104(a), the IRS clarified its position on damages awarded in employment discrimination lawsuits.[143] It said that back pay received in satisfaction of an employment discrimination claim is included in gross income because it is not received on account of personal physical injuries or physical sickness. As a result, back pay is wages subject to federal income tax withholding and social security, Medicare, and FUTA taxes, and should be reported as such on Form W-2 (see Section 8.8-3). The IRS also said that emotional distress damages received to satisfy such a claim must be included in gross income to the extent that they exceed damages for medical care attributable to the emotional distress. Employers should report punitive and emotional distress damages on Form 1099-MISC in Box 3 (see Section 8.12-1).

 **CONSTITUTIONAL QUESTION** In 2006, a federal appeals court ruled that the limited exclusion from income in §104(a) for physical injury and sickness was unconstitutional and that damages for emotional injury and injury to reputation were also not income but merely a nontaxable "return of capital." Later in the year, however, the court agreed to rehear the case and then, in 2007, reversed its original decision and ruled that §104(a) is constitutional.[144]

With the different rulings from the IRS, there is still a great deal of uncertainty for employers in this area over what damage awards are actually "wages" subject to federal income tax withholding, social security, Medicare and FUTA taxes, and Form W-2 reporting. The uncertainty stems from court decisions that have defined wages more narrowly than the IRS. In one case, a federal appeals court ruled that there should be no withholding from an award of pay that would have been earned had a job applicant not been discriminated against because of age. The court said that no employment relationship had existed, so the award could not have been for "wages" as defined under the income tax withholding and employment tax sections of the IRC.[145] In reaching its conclusion, the court rejected an earlier IRS Revenue Ruling that found such an award to be taxable wages.[146]

In another case, a federal district court ruled that an award made in a suit for wrongful termination brought under the Family and Medical Leave Act was not subject to withholding or employment taxes under federal or state law. The court relied on the fact that damages were awarded for the time period after the employee was terminated, therefore, the award could not represent wages for services performed.[147] This court also rejected earlier IRS Revenue Rulings that reached an opposite conclusion, finding that they contradicted the plain language of the law.

 **STRICT INTERPRETATIONS** In each of these cases, the court relied heavily on language in IRC §3401(a) requiring federal income tax withholding on wages "for services performed by an employee for his employer" and §3121(a) requiring FICA withholding from "all remuneration for employment." Both courts said that neither of these definitions can be stretched to cover situations where no employment relationship had existed or where it had ended because of a termination.

---

141. IRC §104(a).
142. Commissioner v. Schleier, 115 SCt 2159 (1995).
143. Rev. Rul. 96-65, 1996-2 CB 6.
144. Murphy v. IRS, 460 F.3d 79 (DC CA, 2006); rev., No. 05-5139 (DC CA, 7-3-07)..
145. Newhouse v. McCormick & Co., 157 F. 3d 582 (8 CA, 1998).
146. Rev. Rul. 78-176, 1978-1 CB 303.
147. Churchill v. Star Enterprises, 3 F. Supp. 2d 622 (ED Pa., 1998); see also Lisec, et al. v. United Airlines, 11 Cal. Rptr.2d 689 (Cal. Ct. of App., 1992).

In most instances, taxable back pay awards should be treated as wages in the year paid rather than the year earned for income withholding and employment tax purposes. This is the position of the IRS and the U.S. Supreme Court, which upheld the agency's position as reasonable.[148] Other amounts awarded by a court, such as interest and court costs, are not included in an employee's wages if they are distinguished from the back pay award.

**What about attorneys' fees?** The issue of whether attorneys' fees should be included in an employee's income when they are part of award in an employment lawsuit has caused controversy over the years. The issue generally arises when the employee has a contingent fee arrangement with the attorney, meaning that if the employee is awarded damages, the attorney is paid a prearranged percentage of the award.

Some courts have ruled that the entire amount of the award is income to the employee, including the attorneys' fees, and that the employee can then deduct the attorneys' fees on his or her personal income tax return. The U.S. Supreme Court agreed with these decisions, finding that the portion of the award earmarked for attorneys' fees cannot be excluded from income just because it was assigned in advance to the attorneys.[149] Those deductions are subject to certain restrictions, however, that can greatly reduce the net amount of the award.

*New 'above-the-line' deduction.* Recognizing the problems that were being caused by the different court decisions, a provision was added to the American Jobs Creation Act of 2004 that allows the employee to take an "above-the-line" deduction for attorneys' fees and court costs paid by or on behalf of the employee in connection with any lawsuit brought for "unlawful discrimination," up to the amount of the award included in the employee's gross income. "Above-the-line" deductions from gross income are not subject to the restrictions placed on itemized miscellaneous deductions. The new rule applies to attorneys' fees and court costs paid or incurred on or after October 22, 2004 in connection with judgments or settlements awarding damages that are entered into after that date.[150]

*Unlawful discrimination defined.* Unlawful discrimination is an act that is made unlawful under any federal, state, or local law that provides for the enforcement of civil rights or that regulates any aspect of the employment relationship, including claims for wages, compensation, or benefits, or that prohibits discharge, discrimination, or other forms of retaliation against an employee for taking actions permitted by law.

 **WATCH OUT** This new provision allowing the "above the-line" deduction does not alter the treatment of a damages award paid to an employee as gross income or an employer's reporting responsibilities with regard to payments made to current or former employees, or their attorneys, under a judgment or settlement of an employment-related lawsuit. (See Section 8.12-1.)

**Reporting back pay awards.** The IRS has ruled that taxable back pay awards should be reported on the employer's current quarterly Form 941, and on the employee's Form W-2 for the year the award was paid, in Boxes 1, 3 and 5.[151] If the employer did not include the back pay on the employee's W-2 form in the year the award was paid, the employer should issue a Form W-2c, *Corrected Wage and Tax Statement* (see Section 8.10), to add the amount of the back pay award to the wages previously reported. (For information on reporting payments of the "gross proceeds" of an award to an employee's attorney, see Section 8.12-1.)

**Different rules for SSA reporting.**[152] Publication 957, Reporting Back Pay and Special Wage Payments to the Social Security Administration, details the special rules that apply to the reporting of back pay awards. For social security coverage and benefit purposes, all back pay, whether or not awarded under a statute, is wages except amounts specifically designated otherwise, such as compensatory damages, interest, penalties, and legal fees. The determination of when the back pay is credited as earnings, however, depends on whether the back pay is awarded under a statute or not. All back pay except that awarded under a statute is treated as wages for allocation purposes in the year it is paid.

---

148.    Rev. Rul. 89-35, 1989-1 CB 290; FSA 200029001, 2-1-00; U.S. v. Cleveland Indians Baseball Co., 121 S.Ct. 1433 (2001).
149.    Commissioner v. Banks, 125 S. Ct. 826 (2005).
150.    IRC §62(a)(19); §62(e).
151.    Rev. Rul. 72-268, 1972-1 CB 313; Rev. Rul. 55-203, 1955-1 CB 114.
152.    IRS Pub. 957, Reporting Back Pay and Special Wage Payments to the Social Security Administration.

*Back pay under a statute.* Back pay under a statute is a payment by an employer pursuant to an award, determination, or agreement approved by a court or government agency responsible for enforcing a federal or state law that protects an employee's right to employment or wages.

Examples of such laws include:

- Age Discrimination in Employment Act
- Americans with Disabilities Act
- Civil Rights Act
- Equal Pay Act
- Fair Labor Standards Act
- Family and Medical Leave Act
- National Labor Relations Act
- State minimum wage laws
- Other state laws that protect rights to employment and wages

Back pay awards resulting from negotiated out-of-court settlements constitute back pay under a statute if the award is court-approved and is intended to comply with the provisions of a federal or state law that restores an employee's right to employment or wages. The fact that a court-approved settlement agreement contains a clause whereby the defendant does not admit discrimination does not change the nature of the back pay award as back pay awarded under a statute.

 **LOCAL LAWS DON'T COUNT** Payments awarded under local laws, ordinances, or regulations are not back pay awarded under a statute.

Payments for back wages that are negotiated between an employer and employee (or employee's attorney) without an award, determination, or approval by a court or government agency are not considered made under a statute. Neither are delayed wage payments and retroactive pay increases required by a collective bargaining agreement.

*Reporting back pay awarded under a statute.* The SSA credits back pay awarded under a statute as wages for allocation purposes to an individual's earnings record in the period it should have been paid. Wages not credited to the proper year may result in lower social security benefits or the failure to qualify for benefits. Unless the employer notifies SSA of the proper allocation of the back pay, it will be posted to the employee's earnings record in the year it is reported on Form W-2. Therefore, to meet the needs of both the IRS and SSA, employers should not prepare Forms W-2 or W-2c to allocate the back pay awarded under a statute to earlier years for social security wage purposes. Employers should prepare a special report and send it to:

Social Security Administration
Office of Central Operations
Metro West
Attn: Back Pay (DERO) Analyst Staff
300 North Greene Street
Baltimore, MD 21202

The following information should be included in the special report, which should be submitted to the SSA at the same time or after the employer files the Form W-2 (or magnetic media) with SSA for the year in which the statutory back pay was paid to the employee:

1. Employer's name, address, and employer identification number (EIN)

2. A signed statement citing the federal or state law under which the payment was made (without this, the SSA will not make the allocation to earlier periods)

3. The name and telephone number of a contact person

4. List of employees receiving the payment and the following specific information for each:

- tax year in which the back pay was paid and reported;
- social security number;
- name as shown on the employee's social security card;
- back pay award amount, excluding any amounts that are specifically designated as damages, penalties, interest, or legal fees;
- periods for which the back pay was awarded (beginning and ending dates—month and year);
- total amount of other wages paid subject to social security and/or Medicare tax and reported on that same year's Form W-2 (excluding any backpay included in that W-2); and
- the amount that should be allocated to each reporting period, including any amount to be allocated (if applicable) to the tax year in which the award payment was made (without such a showing, the SSA will make an allocation by dividing the payment by the number of months or years it covers).

*Special situations.* For periods before January 1, 1978 (state and local employers before January 1, 1981), wage amounts must be shown by calendar quarters. For all tax years, the Social Security and/or Medicare Qualified Government Employment (MQGE) wages (where applicable) must be shown separately and identified. For tax years 1991 and later, the social security and Medicare wages must be listed separately.

In a cover letter, include the following information:

- name and address of the employer;
- statute under which the employer paid the back pay;
- name and telephone number of the employer contact; and
- signature of the reporting official.

 **FOR QUESTIONS** Employers with questions concerning back pay under a statute should contact their local SSA office. State or local government employers covered by an agreement under Section 218 of the Social Security Act that have questions about statutory back pay awards made before January 1, 1987 should contact their state social security administrator's office.

*Format for SSA report.* The SSA requests that information in the special back pay report regarding employee names and social security numbers, award amounts and periods, other social security and Medicare wages paid, and amounts allocated be reported in the format shown below.

Format for Report (Under Covering Letter) to Request SSA to
Allocate Back Pay Under a Statute Wages

**EMPLOYER'S EIN: XX-XXXXXXX**
**TAX YEAR IN WHICH AWARD PAYMENT WAS PAID: 2003**

| (1) SSN AND EMPLOYEE NAME | (2)[1] AWARD AMOUNT AND PERIOD(S) | (3) [2,3] OTHER SOC. SEC./ MED. WAGES PAID IN AWARD YEAR | | (4)[3] ALLOCATION | | |
|---|---|---|---|---|---|---|
| | | SOC. SEC. | MED./MQGE | YEAR | SOC.SEC. | MED./MQGE |
| XXX-XX-XXXX HELEN T. SMITH | $100,000.00 1/2000-12/2003 | $40,000.00 | $40,000.00 | 2000 | $20,000.00 | $20,000.00 |
| | | | | 2001 | 25,000.00 | $25,000.00 |
| | | | | 2002 | 27,000.00 | 27,000.00 |
| | | | | 2003 | 28,000.00 | 28,000.00 |
| XXX-XX-XXXX SAM W. EVANS | 30,000.00 7/89-12/91 | 0.00 | 0.00 | 1989 | | 6,000.00 |
| | | | | 1990 | | 12,000.00 |
| | | | | 1991 | | 12,000.00 |
| XXX-XX-XXXX ROLAND S. ADAMS | 15,000.00 7/80-12/81 | 0.00 | 0.00 | 9/80 | 3,500.00 | |
| | | | | 12/80 | 3,500.00 | |
| | | | | 1981 | 8,000.00 | |

**(EXPLANATION OF EXAMPLES:)**

Helen T. Smith—The back pay award, excluding interest, was $100,000 for the periods 1/2000-12/2003. In 2003 this employee was also paid $40,000 in other wages. (Her W-2 for 2003 reported $87,000 for Social Security and $140,000 for Medicare. The SSA allocation will result in posted wages of $68,000 for Social Security and $68,000 for Medicare for 1997.)

Sam W. Evans—The back pay award was $30,000 for the periods 7/89-12/91. This employee was hired in 1989 and was subject to MQGE only. He was no longer employed by this governmental employer in 2003. (His W-2 for 2003 reported $30,000 for Social Security and $30,000 for Medicare. After the SSA allocation, he will not have any posted wages for 2003.)

Roland S. Adams—The back pay award was $15,000 for the periods 7/80-12/81. He was no longer employed by this State and local employer in 2003. (His W-2 for 2003 reported $15,000 for Social Security and $15,000 for Medicare; after the SSA allocation, he will not have any posted wages for 2003.)

NOTE:
1. Exclude amounts specifically designated as damages, penalties, etc.
2. Exclude the amount of back pay, if any, included in that amount.
3. For periods before January 1, 1978 (and for state and local government (Section 218) employers before January 1, 1981), show the wage amounts by calendar quarters. The social security and/or Medicare Qualified Government Employment (MQGE) wages (where applicable) must be shown separately FOR ALL YEARS. (Wages subject ONLY to MQGE would be shown in the Medicare/MQGE column; no wages would be shown in the Soc. Sec. column.) For tax years 1991 and later, the social security and Medicare wages must be listed separately.

## 3.4-4 Bonuses

Amounts paid to employees as bonuses in addition to their usual compensation must be included in the employees' income and are subject to federal income tax withholding and social security, Medicare, and FUTA taxes.[153]

**Signing bonuses.**[154] In 2004, the IRS ruled that bonuses paid by employers to employees for signing a contract are wages subject to federal income tax withholding and social security, Medicare, and FUTA taxes. In the ruling, the IRS used the example of a baseball club that negotiates the first contract between the club and a baseball player and includes in the contract a signing bonus that the player will receive when he reports to spring training. Once the player reports, however, the bonus is not contingent on the player's future performance of services. The IRS said the bonus is part of the compensation paid to the player as remuneration for employment because it could not be separated from the employer-employee relationship, revoking earlier rulings that it said were decided incorrectly.

As part of the same ruling, the IRS applied similar logic in finding that bonuses received by employees because they are employed on the ratification date of a union contract are wages subject to federal income tax withholding and social security, Medicare, and FUTA taxes. The bonus was paid regardless of whether the employees were employed before or after the ratification date, so long as they were employed on that date, and the bonus was the same for all employees, regardless of salary, seniority, job title, or whether the employee voted for or against ratification. The IRS said none of that mattered, since the bonuses were paid as part of a bargain that established the terms and conditions of the employment relationship.

**Contract cancellation payments.**[155] The IRS ruled that a payment made by an employer to an employee in return for cancellation of the employee's rights under an employment contract is wages subject to federal income tax withholding and social security, Medicare, and FUTA taxes. In this situation, the contract itself did not provide for any payments in the event of a cancellation of the contract.

The IRS said that employment includes the establishment, maintenance, furtherance, alteration, or cancellation of the employer-employee relationship. Therefore, the cancellation payment was part of the compensation paid by the employer as remuneration for employment, regardless of what the payment was called or whether the employee was still employed when the payment was made. In issuing its ruling, the IRS revoked earlier rulings that had found such payments not to be wages.

In a case involving payments made to college professors in return for relinquishing their rights to tenure, a federal appeals court ruled that the payments were made to the professors in exchange for giving up their legally protected tenure rights, not as remuneration for services rendered, so the payments were not wages subject to social security and Medicare taxes.[156]

Other courts have reached a different conclusion, finding that such payments are similar to severance and early retirement payments that are based on length of service, not just the relinquishment of tenure rights.[157]

**Push money exception.** When a manufacturer pays a bonus to salespeople working for a retailer to get them to "push" its products, the bonus is not wages because it is being paid by a third party, not the employer, for services performed for the third party.[158] (But see the discussion of third-party commission payments made to salespeople in Section 3.4-5.) The payments are not subject to federal income tax withholding or social security, Medicare, or FUTA taxes. The bonus is taxable income to the salespeople, however, and must be reported on their personal income tax return.

---

153. IRS Reg. §31.3121(a)-1(c); §31.3306(b)-1(c); §31.3401(a)-1(a)(2).
154. Rev. Rul. 2004-109, 2004-50 IRB 958.
155. Rev. Rul. 2004-110, 2004-50 IRB 960.
156. North Dakota State University v. U.S., 255 F.3d 599 (8 CA, 2001), affirming 84 F.Supp.2d 1043 (D N.D., 1999).
157. Appoloni v. U.S., 450 F.3d 185 (6 CA, 2006), cert. den. No. 06-334 (U.S. S.Ct., 1-16-07); University of Pittsburgh v. U.S., 507 F.3d 165 (3 CA, 2007).
158. Rev. Rul. 70-337, 1970-1 CB 191; Rev. Rul. 70-331, 1970-1 CB 14.

## 3.4-5 Commissions

Commissions on sales of goods or insurance premiums are subject to federal income tax withholding and social security, Medicare, and FUTA taxes when paid to an employee (or a former employee entitled to deferred or renewal commissions).[159] This is true whether or not the employee was directly involved in selling the products.

Full-time life insurance salespeople are governed by special rules applicable to statutory employees (see Section 1.3-1). Commissions paid to them are not subject to federal income tax withholding, but they are subject to social security and Medicare taxes when paid. The commissions are excluded from wages for FUTA tax purposes only if the salesperson is paid solely by commission.

**Third-party commission payments**. Where commissions are paid by a third-party manufacturer directly to an employer's salespersons at the employer's request, rather than to the employer for distribution to the salespersons, the commissions are wages because they are compensation for services performed for the employer. However, because the manufacturer has control of the payment of the commissions, the manufacturer is responsible for withholding and/or paying federal income, social security, Medicare, and FUTA taxes on the commissions. If the commissions are paid to the employer for distribution to the salespersons, the employer is responsible for all withholding and payment of income and employment taxes.[160]

## 3.4-6 Conventions

If an employee's attendance at a convention, conference, or seminar is related to the employee's job and the employee accounts for his or her expenses in attending, any reimbursement by the employer up to the full amount of the expenses is excluded from the employee's income as a working condition fringe benefit (see Section 3.2-1). The employee's attendance is job-related if the employee will benefit as an employee from attending. There are special requirements that must be met before reimbursements for expenses incurred while attending conventions outside North America, in Caribbean countries, or on cruise ships will be considered excluded.[161]

## 3.4-7 Death Benefits

The Small Business Job Protection Act of 1996 repealed the income exclusion for up to $5,000 in death benefits paid upon an employee's death to his or her estate or beneficiaries.[162] Such benefits must be reported on Form 1099-R (see Section 8.12-2), whether they are paid under a plan or not.[163] The benefits are not subject to social security or Medicare taxes.

## 3.4-8 Dependent Care Assistance Programs

Many employers now provide some type of dependent care assistance program for their employees, whether it is an on-site or off-site day care facility or reimbursement for the employees' expenses in obtaining their own dependent care. Amounts spent by the employer on behalf of employees under a dependent care assistance program are excluded from the employees' income and are not subject to federal income tax withholding or social security, Medicare, or FUTA taxes under the following conditions and limitations:[164]

---

159.  IRS Reg. §31.3121(a)-1(c); §31.3306(b)-1(c); §31.3401(a)-1(a)(2).
160.  LTR 9647003, 7-31-96; Rev. Rul. 57-145, 1957-1 CB 332; Rev. Rul. 54-171, 1954-2 CB 348.
161.  IRC §274(h); IRS Reg. §1.162-2(d).
162.  Small Business Job Protection Act of 1996, §1402.
163.  Rev. Rul. 86-109, 1986-2 CB 196.
164.  IRC §129; §3121(a)(18); §3306(b)(13); §3401(a)(18).

**Exclusion limitation.** The excluded amount of dependent care assistance cannot exceed $5,000 in a year ($2,500 for married individuals filing separately) or the employee's earned income for the year, whichever is less. Payments above these limits are subject to federal income tax withholding and social security, Medicare, and FUTA taxes.[165]

**Dependent care must be "necessary."** For the income exclusion to apply, the dependent care assistance program must pay for or provide services that are necessary so that the employee receiving the benefit can work. Also, the dependent must be a child under age 13 or other dependent who cannot care for herself or himself.[166]

**When expenses are incurred.** An employer's dependent care expenses are treated as incurred when the care is provided, not when payments are made to the employee or a third party.[167]

> *Example*: Employee Alan has child care expenses of $10,000 in 2007, but his employer reimburses him only $7,500, waiting until 2008 to provide the other $2,500. Alan's employer must withhold during 2007 for the full $5,000 by which Alan's expenses exceed the excludable limits, even though the final reimbursement is not paid until 2008. Alan has a taxable benefit of $5,000 for 2007.

**Written plan.** The dependent care assistance program must be a separate, written plan of the employer and it must be designed solely for the employees' benefit.[168]

**No discrimination.** The program must not discriminate in favor of highly compensated employees (see Section 3.2-1 for a definition) in terms of contributions, benefits, or eligibility. No more than 25% of the assistance provided during the year may benefit shareholders or owners owning more than a 5% interest in the employer. The average benefits provided to nonhighly compensated employees must be at least 55% of the average benefits provided to highly compensated employees.[169]

**Notification.** Eligible employees must receive reasonable notification of the availability and terms of the program.[170]

 **NONCOMPLYING PLAN STILL OK FOR SOME** Even though a dependent care assistance program may not meet the requirements regarding nondiscrimination, notification, or a written plan, the program remains qualified for nonhighly compensated employees.[171]

**Annual statement.** The employer must give the employee a statement each year by January 31 showing the dependent care expenses incurred by the employer during the previous year.[172] This can be accomplished by reporting the assistance in Box 10 of the employee's Form W-2.

**Valuing the benefit.**[173] Where the employer reimburses employees for their expenses, the value of benefits provided under a dependent care assistance program is the amount reimbursed during the year, and any amount reimbursed after the year for assistance provided during the previous year.

> *Example:* Harold receives quarterly child care reimbursements of $2,400 from his employer. Harold paid $9,600 for child care during 2008, and he was reimbursed for $7,200 in 2008 and $2,400 in January 2009. The value of Harold's 2008 dependent care benefit is $9,600, even though only $7,200 was reimbursed during 2008.

---

165. IRC §129(a)(2)(A); §129(b).
166. IRC §21(b); §129(e)(1).
167. IRC §129(a)(2)(B).
168. IRC §129(d)(1).
169. IRC §129(d)(2), (d)(8).
170. IRC §129(d)(6).
171. IRC §129(d)(1).
172. IRC §129(d)(7).
173. IRS Notice 89-111, 1989-2 CB 449; IRS Notice 90-66, 1990-2 CB 350

Where the assistance is in the form of an actual day care facility (either off-site or on the employer's premises), the value is what the employee would have to pay for the same care in an arm's length transaction (minus any amount paid by the employee in after-tax dollars). The employer can also use a safe-harbor method that estimates the value as 125% of the direct costs of operating the facility (including food, supplies, transportation, insurance, labor, and management fees). The value per employee is figured as follows:

125% of direct costs ÷ number of dependents at capacity ÷ number of days facility is open x number of days employee's dependent used the facility

*Example:* Eastbridge Clothiers provides an on-site child care facility for its employees' use. Its direct operating costs for the facility in 2008 were $90,000, and the number of children it could care for at any one time was 30. The facility was open for 250 days during 2008. Employee Janice brought her son to the child care facility on 225 days during 2008. The value of Janice's use of the child care facility is determined as follows:

direct costs x 125% = $90,000 x 1.25 = $112,500

$112,500 ÷ children at capacity = $112,500 ÷ 30 = $3,750

$3,750 ÷ number of days open = $3,750 ÷ 250 = $15

$15 x days used by child = $15 x 225 = $3,375

**Reporting the benefit.** Once the benefit is valued, the employer must include the value of the benefit on the employee's Form W-2 in Box 10, with the taxable amounts in Boxes 1, 3, and 5 as necessary (see Section 8.8-3 for more details on W-2 reporting).

## 3.4-9 Directors' Fees

Fees paid to nonemployee directors of a corporation for services performed as directors are not wages subject to federal income tax withholding and social security, Medicare, and FUTA taxes.[174] The director is responsible for reporting such payments on his or her personal tax return and for paying self-employment tax (see Section 6.7-5). The employer must report the fees paid to the director on a Form 1099-MISC (see Section 8.12-1 for details).

## 3.4-10 Disaster Relief Payments

The Victims of Terrorism Tax Relief Act added IRC §139, which provides that gross income does not include any amount received by an individual as a qualified disaster payment.[175] The term "qualified disaster payment" means any amount paid to or for the benefit of an individual:

- to reimburse or pay reasonable and necessary personal, family, living, or funeral expenses incurred as a result of a qualified disaster;
- to reimburse or pay reasonable and necessary expenses incurred for the repair or rehabilitation of a personal residence or repair or replacement of its contents to the extent that the need for such repair, rehabilitation, or replacement is attributable to a qualified disaster; or
- by a federal, state, or local government (or government agency or instrumentality) in connection with a qualified disaster in order to promote the general welfare.

---

174.   IRS Reg. §31.3121(d)-1(b); §31.3306(i)-1(e); §31.3401(c)-1(f).
175.   P.L. No. 107-134; IRC §139(a)-(f).

A "qualified disaster" includes:

- a disaster that results from a terrorist or military action;
- a Presidentially declared disaster;
- a disaster resulting from any event the Secretary of the Treasury determines to be of a catastrophic nature; or
- a disaster that is determined by a federal, state, or local authority to warrant assistance from the federal, state, or local government (or a government agency or instrumentality).

**Employer's disaster relief payments to employees may be tax-free.**[176] The IRS explained how this new section applies in a hypothetical disaster situation involving employer payments to employees: An area within a state is affected by a flood that is a Presidentially declared disaster. An employer makes grants to its employees who are affected by the flood, regardless of the employees' length or type of service. The grants pay or reimburse employees for medical, temporary housing, and transportation expenses they incur as a result of the flood that are not compensated for by insurance or otherwise.

The employer does not require employees to provide proof of actual expenses to receive a grant payment. The employer's program, however, contains requirements to ensure that the grant amounts will be reasonably commensurate with the amount of unreimbursed reasonable and necessary medical, temporary housing, and transportation expenses that employees incur as a result of the flood. The grants are not intended to indemnify all flood-related losses or to reimburse the cost of nonessential, luxury, or decorative items and services.

The grants made by the employer to its employees do not qualify as gifts because any amounts transferred by an employer to or for the benefit of an employee do not qualify (see Section 3.4-13). Nor are they excluded from the employees' income under the general welfare exclusion, because the employer is a nongovernmental entity.

Here, however, the grants are reasonably expected to be commensurate with the unreimbursed reasonable and necessary personal, living, or family expenses that the employer's employees incur as a result of a flood that is a qualified disaster. Additionally, they are paid to compensate individuals for expenses that are not compensated for by insurance or otherwise. Therefore, the employer's grants are qualified disaster relief payments that are excluded from the gross income of its employees. As such, they are not subject to federal income, social security, Medicare, or FUTA tax or to any information reporting requirement.

## 3.4-11 Employer-Paid Taxes (Grossing-Up)

When an employer pays an employee's taxes, the amount paid is an employer-provided benefit. The taxes paid on the employee's behalf are also taxable income to the employee. To resolve the never-ending pyramiding situation that would result from such payments (i.e., each payment of taxes results in more wages and more taxes), the IRS has approved a procedure commonly known as "grossing-up" to calculate the gross payment the employee must receive when the employer pays the employee's taxes.[177]

Gross amount of earnings = $\dfrac{\text{Desired net payment}}{100\% - \text{Total tax }\%}$

*Example 1:* Generosity, Inc. wants to give employee Linda a $6,000 year-end bonus in 2008. To ensure that Linda receives $6,000, Generosity agrees to pay her federal and state income and social security and Medicare taxes on the bonus, which is treated as supplemental wages (see Section 6.4-4). Here is how the employer would calculate the gross payment to Linda and the amounts that must be withheld, assuming Linda has been paid $50,000 so far in 2008 and the state supplemental wage withholding rate is 3.5%:

176.   Rev. Rul. 2003-12, 2003-3 IRB 283.
177.   Rev. Proc. 81-48, 1981-2 CB 623; Rev. Rul. 86-14, 1986-1 CB 304.

Total tax % =  25% FIT + 3.5% SIT + 6.2% SS + 1.45% Med.

Total tax % = 36.15%

Gross-up rate = 100% - 36.15% = 63.85%

Gross earnings = $6,000 ÷ 63.85% = $9,397.02

FITW = 25% x $9,397.02 = $2,349.26
SITW = 3.5% x $9,397.02 = $328.90
SS  = 6.2% x $9,397.02 = $582.62
Med. = 1.45% x $9,397.02 = $136.26

To check:
$9,397.02 - $2,349.26 - $328.90 - $582.62 - $136.26 = $6,000

The following example involves a situation where the employee's bonus will push her year-to-date wages above the social security wage base for the year.

**Example 2:**  Assume the same facts as in Example 1, except that, at the time the bonus is paid, Linda has already been paid $100,000 during 2008.  Here is how the employer would calculate the gross payment to Linda and the amounts that must be withheld:

Social security wage base for 2008 = $102,000; Tax rate = 6.2%

Amount of bonus subject to SS tax = $102,000 - $100,000 = $2,000

SS tax on $2,000 = $2,000 x .062 = $124.00

Total amount for gross-up calculation = $6,000 + $124 = $6,124

Total tax % = 25% FITW + 3.5% SIT + 1.45% Med. = 29.95%

Gross-up rate = 100% - 29.95% = 70.05%

Gross earnings on $6,124 = $6,124 ÷ 70.05% = $8,742.33

FITW = 25% x $8,742.33 = $2,185.58
SITW = 3.5% x $8,742.33 = $305.98
SS  = 6.2% x $2,000.00 = $124.00
Med. = 1.45% x $8,742.33 = $126.76

To check:
$8,742.33 - $2,185.58 - $305.98 - $124.00 - $126.76 = $6,000

The following two examples involve situations where the bonus itself or the resulting amount after grossing-up a bonus results in the employee receiving more than $1,000,000 in year-to-date supplemental wages. Supplemental wages in excess of $1,000,000 in one year must be taxed at a flat rate of 35% (see Section 6.4-4 for more details).  The following formula can be used to calculate the gross earnings and taxes:

X = gross earnings

Desired net = X − [.25 ($1,000,000 − YTD supplemental wages)] − [.35 (X − ($1,000,000 − YTD supplemental wages)] - .035X - .0145X

**Example 3:** Assume the same facts as in Example 1, except that, at the time the bonus is paid, Linda has already been paid $997,000 during 2008. To keep its gross-up costs down, Linda's employer decides to tax only the amount above $1,000,000 at the 35% flat rate, rather than the entire bonus. Here is how the employer would calculate the gross payment to Linda and the amounts that must be withheld:

$6,000 = X – [.25 ($1,000,000 - $997,000)] – [.35 (X - $1,000,000 - $997,000)] - .035X - .0145X

$6,000 = X - .25($3,000) - .35(X - $3,000) - .035X - .0145X

$6,000 = X - $750 - .35X + $1,050 - .035X - .0145X

$6,000 + $750 - $1,050 = X - .35X - .035X - .0145X

$5,700 = .6005X

$9,492.09 = X

FITW = (25% x $3,000) + [35% x ($9,492.09 - $3,000)]
FITW = $750 + (35% x $6,492.09) = $3,022.23
SITW = 3.5% x $9,492.09 = $332.22
Med. = 1.45% x $9,492.09 = $137.64

To check:
$9,492.09 - $3,022.23 - $332.22 - $137.64 = $6,000

**Example 4:** Assume the same facts as in Example 1, except that, at the time the bonus is paid, Linda has already been paid $993,000 during 2008. Here is how the employer would calculate the gross payment to Linda and the amounts that must be withheld:

$6,000 = X – [.25 ($1,000,000 - $993,000)] – [.35 (X - $1,000,000 - $993,000)] - .035X - .0145X

$6,000 = X - [.25 ($7,000)] – [.35 (X - $7,000)] - .035X - .0145X

$6,000 = X - $1,750 - .35X + $2,450 - .035X - .0145X

$6,000 + $1,750 - $2,450 = X - .35X - .035X - .0145X

$5,300 = .6005X

$8,825.98 = X

FITW = 25% x $7,000 + [35% x ($8,825.98 - $7,000)
FITW = $1,750 + (35% x $1,825.98) = $2,389.09
SITW = 3.5% x $8,825.98 = $308.91
Med. = 1.45% x $8,825.98 = $127.98

To check:
$8,825.98 - $2,389.09 - $308.91 - $127.98 = $6,000

The following example involves a situation where an employee who participates in a §401(k) plan (see Section 4.6-2) receives a bonus that the employer wants to gross-up. The §401(k) plan deferral is based only on the bonus amount, not the taxes paid by the employer.

***Example 5:*** Assume the same facts as in Example 1.  Also, Linda has elected to defer 5% of her wages into Generosity, Inc.'s §401(k) plan, so she should end up with a net payment of $5,700 ($6,000 x 5% = $300; $6,000 - $300 = $5,700).

Amount deferred into §401(k) plan = $6,000 x 5% = $300

Amount subject to SS and Medicare taxes = $6,000

Amount subject to federal and state income taxes = $5,700

SS tax on $300 = $300 x 6.2% = $18.60

Medicare tax on $300 = $300 x 1.45% = $4.35

Total amount for gross-up calculation = $5,700 + $18.60 + $4.35 = $5,722.95

Total tax % = 25% FITW + 3.5% SITW + 6.2% SS + 1.45% Med. = 36.15%

Gross-up rate = 100% - 36.15% = 63.85%

Gross earnings subject to FITW and SITW = $5,722.95 ÷ .6385 = $8,963.12

Gross earnings subject to SS and Medicare taxes = $8,963.12 + $300 = $9,263.12

FITW = 25% x $8,963.12 = $2,240.78
SITW = 3.5% x $8,963.12 = $313.71
SS = 6.2% x $9,263.12 = $574.31
Med. = 1.45% x $9,263.12 = $134.32
§401(k) deferral = $300

To check:
$9,263.12 - $2,240.78 - $313.71 - $574.31 - $134.32 - $300 = $5,700

## 3.4-12 Equipment Allowances

Where an employer pays an allowance to employees who use their own tools or heavy equipment on the job, the allowance is not included in the employee's wages and is not subject to federal income tax withholding or social security, Medicare, or FUTA taxes.  But the employer must be sure to keep the allowance payment separate from the employee's wages.  The exclusion is not allowed if the allowance is paid to all employees regardless of whether they use the employer's tools or their own.[178]

**Special rule for pipeline construction industry.**[179]  The IRS has clarified that payments to employees for equipment they are required to provide as a condition of employment in the pipeline construction and repair industry are wages for federal employment tax purposes, unless such amounts are paid under an accountable plan (see Section 3.3-5). The IRS ruling involved welders and heavy equipment mechanics who provide welding and mechanics rigs, respectively, and laborers who provide pickup trucks for their own use in performing their jobs, and who incur expenses in connection with the operation and maintenance of these vehicles while doing so.

At the same time, the IRS provided employers in the pipeline construction industry an optional deemed substantiation method for reimbursing certain employee business expenses, namely rig-related expenses incurred by employees who are required to use their own welding or mechanics rigs as a condition of employment.  In 2008, an amount of up to $15 per hour will be deemed substantiated under an accountable

---

178.    Rev. Rul. 65-187, 1965-2 CB 382.
179.    Rev. Rul.  2002-35, 2002-23 IRB 1067; Rev. Proc. 2002-41, 2002-23 IRB 1098; Rev. Proc. 2007-66, 2007-45 IRB 970.

plan in cases to which it applies (up to $9 per hour if the employer provides fuel or otherwise reimburses fuel expenses). These amounts are adjusted annually for inflation.

## 3.4-13 Gifts

Gifts provided to employees must be included in the employees' income and are subject to federal income tax withholding and social security, Medicare, and FUTA taxes unless they can be excluded as a de minimis fringe benefit (see Section 3.2-1) or as a gift between relatives that is not based on the employer-employee relationship.[180] Gifts excluded as de minimis fringe benefits include Christmas or other holiday gifts of small value, so long as they do not consist of cash or a cash equivalent. Gift certificates and gift cards do not meet this test since they are considered cash equivalents, even if the property or service bought with the gift certificate or gift card (if provided in kind) would qualify as a de minimis fringe benefit.[181]

## 3.4-14 Golden Parachute Payments

When companies change ownership, key executives are often provided with "golden parachutes" to soften their landing should they be terminated by the new owner. The IRC contains special rules governing the taxation of such payments.[182] Under these rules, a "parachute payment" is compensation paid to an officer, shareholder, or highly compensated employee (see Section 3.2-1 for a definition) only after a change in corporate ownership or control that is at least three times the employee's average compensation during the five most recent tax years. An "excess parachute payment" is the portion of the parachute payment that exceeds the employee's five-year average compensation.

The entire parachute payment is wages and is subject to federal income tax withholding and social security and Medicare taxes. The excess parachute payment is also subject to a 20% excise tax the employer must withhold. The FUTA tax rules were not amended to reflect the changes relating to parachute payments. The employer must report the payment on Form W-2, with the withheld excise tax entered in Box 12, preceded by Code "K" (for details, see Section 8.8-3).

> *Example:* Employee Jack receives a parachute payment of $1,000,000 after Softwear Clothing is bought and Jack is asked to resign as president. Jack's average compensation for the last 5 years was $300,000. The entire $1,000,000 parachute payment is subject to federal income tax withholding and social security (up to the applicable wage limit) and Medicare taxes, while 20% of the excess payment of $700,000 ($140,000) must also be withheld to pay excise taxes.

## 3.4-15 Guaranteed Wage Payments

In some industries, most notably those that have been able to increase productivity and reduce staffing by using new technologies, employers have entered into agreements with employees and their representatives to pay employees an annual income or guarantee them a job even when no work is available. Payments provided under such guaranteed annual wage (GAW) plans are wages subject to federal income tax withholding and social security, Medicare, and FUTA taxes.

## 3.4-16 Jury Duty Pay

The tax treatment of wages received from an employer for time an employee spends on jury duty depends on the employer's policy in providing such wages.[183]

---

180.    IRC §102(c); IRS Prop. Reg. §1.102-1(f).
181.    IRS Reg. §1.132-6(c).
182.    IRC §280G; IRS Prop. Reg. §1.280G-1.
183.    IRC §61(a); §62(a)(13); IRS Reg. §1.61-2(a).

1. If the employer pays an employee his or her regular wages in addition to jury duty pay received from the government unit involved, the wages are subject to federal income tax withholding and social security, Medicare, and FUTA taxes.

2. If the employer pays an employee the difference between the employee's regular pay and the jury duty pay, only that difference is subject to federal income tax withholding and social security, Medicare, and FUTA taxes.

3. If the employer pays an employee wages for time spent on jury duty but requires the employee to turn over the jury duty pay to the employer, only the difference between the amount paid and amount turned over is subject to federal income tax withholding and social security, Medicare, and FUTA taxes. The employee may deduct the amount turned over on his or her personal income tax return.

In cases where the employee is allowed to keep the jury duty pay, it must be included in income on the employee's personal tax return. If a juror is paid at least $600 by a state or political subdivision, that amount is not considered wages, but must be reported on Form 1099-MISC in Box 3 as "other income." The juror compensation from the state or political subdivision is not subject to federal income tax withholding or social security, Medicare and FUTA taxes.

# 3.4-17 Leave-Sharing Plans

Under an employer's leave sharing plan, employees donate a certain number of paid leave days, which are then "deposited" in a leave bank. Employees who participate in the plan and have medical emergencies can then use paid days from the bank when their own paid leave has been exhausted. The plan may restrict the number of days that can be deposited or used for medical emergencies.

Compensation paid to employees using paid days from the leave bank is wages subject to federal income tax withholding and social security, Medicare, and FUTA taxes. Employees who donate paid leave days and then do not use any of the banked days do not receive wages related to the amount of leave they donated, but they also cannot deduct the compensation donated from their income.[184]

In 2006, the IRS relied on the rules governing medical emergency leave-sharing plans when it announced that an employee who deposits leave in an employer-sponsored leave bank under a "major disaster leave-sharing plan" does not have wages or compensation with respect to the deposited leave, provided that the plan treats payments made by the employer to the employees using the leave as wages for purposes of federal income tax withholding and social security, Medicare, and FUTA taxes.[185] In addition, the employee who donated the leave may not claim an expense, charitable contribution, or loss deduction on account of the deposit of the leave or its use by the recipient.

Under a "major disaster leave-sharing plan," employees may deposit leave in an employer-sponsored leave bank for use by other employees who have been adversely affected by a Presidentially-declared disaster. A leave donor must be a current employee whose voluntary written request to deposit leave has been approved by the employer. A leave recipient must be a current employee for whom the employer has approved an application to receive leave under the plan.

A "major disaster leave-sharing plan" is defined as a written plan that meets the following requirements:
1. The plan allows an employee (i.e., leave donor) to deposit accrued leave in an employer-sponsored leave bank for use by other employees who have been adversely affected by a major disaster. For purposes of the plan, an employee is considered to be adversely affected by a major disaster if the disaster has caused severe hardship to the employee or a family member of the employee that requires the employee to be absent from work.

---

184.   Rev. Rul. 90-29, 1990-1 CB 11; LTR 200720017, 2-9-07.
185.   Notice 2006-59, 2006-28 IRB 60; LTR 200720017, 2-19-07.

2. The plan does not allow an employee to deposit leave for transfer to a specific leave recipient.
3. The amount of leave that may be donated by an employee in any year generally does not exceed the maximum amount of leave that an employee normally accrues during the year.
4. A leave recipient may receive paid leave (at his or her normal rate of compensation) from leave deposited in the leave bank. Each leave recipient must use this leave for purposes related to the major disaster.
5. The plan adopts a reasonable limit, based on the severity of the disaster, on the time after the major disaster occurs during which an employee may deposit leave in the leave bank and a leave recipient must use the leave received from the leave bank.
6. A leave recipient may not convert leave received under the plan into cash in lieu of using the leave. However, a leave recipient may use leave received under the plan to eliminate a negative leave balance that arose from leave that was advanced to him or her because of the effects of the major disaster. A leave recipient also may substitute leave received under the plan for leave without pay used because of the major disaster.
7. The employer must make a reasonable determination, based on need, as to how much leave each approved leave recipient may receive under the leave-sharing plan.
8. Leave deposited on account of one major disaster may be used only for employees affected by that major disaster. Except for an amount so small as to make accounting for it unreasonable or administratively impracticable, any leave deposited under a major disaster leave-sharing plan that is not used by leave recipients by the end of the employer-specified limit must be returned within a reasonable period of time to the leave donors (or, at the employer's option, to those leave donors who are still employed by the employer) so that the donors will be able to use the leave. The amount of leave returned to each leave donor must be in the same proportion as the amount of leave donated by the leave donor bears to the total amount of leave donated on account of that major disaster.

**Leave time donated to charity.**[186] Near the end of 2001, some employers adopted leave-based donation programs, under which employees forego vacation, sick, or personal leave in exchange for employer contributions to charitable and veterans' organizations described in IRC §170(c). The IRS responded by saying that payments made in exchange for an employee's personal, sick, or vacation time before January 1, 2003 would not constitute wages for that employee and should not be reported on the employee's Form W-2. At the end of 2002, however, after considering comments on this policy, the IRS announced it was not going to extend this treatment to payments made on or after January 1, 2003.

In 2005, Hurricane Katrina devastated a large area of the Gulf Coast region of the U.S. The IRS once again ruled that leave foregone by employees under employer leave donation programs would not result in taxable wages for the employees so long as the employer donated the amount of the leave to a charitable organization for the relief of victims of Hurricane Katrina before January 1, 2007.[187]

In situations other than these, however, the value of the leave surrendered under an employer's leave donation program is income to the employee who surrenders it and wages for purposes of income tax withholding and social security and Medicare taxes. The payment to the charity equals the value of the leave surrendered, less the withheld taxes. On the other hand, employees who do not participate in the leave donation program do not have income merely because they have the ability to participate in it.[188]

## 3.4-18 Loans to Employees

Loans made to employees by their employer at interest rates below the applicable federal interest rate are below-market, compensation-related loans. The amount representing the difference between the interest charged to the employee and the applicable federal interest rate must be included in the income of the employee on any day in which the combined amount of all outstanding loans between the employer and the employee is more than $10,000.

---

186.   IRS Notice 2001-69, 2001-46 IRB 491; IRS Notice 2003-1, 2003-2 IRB 257
187.   IRS Notice 2005-68, 2005-40 IRB 622.
188.    LTR 200601005, 9-29-05.

The taxable amount is not subject to federal income tax withholding, but must be reported on the employee's Form W-2. The taxable amount is subject to social security, Medicare, and FUTA taxes. If the employer forgives the debt, or for any other reason the employee is not expected to repay the loan, the entire balance of the loan becomes income subject to federal income tax withholding and social security, Medicare, and FUTA taxes in the year the debt is forgiven. Loans made to employees in connection with a job-related relocation to facilitate the purchase of a new residence (e.g., mortgage or bridge loans) may be tax exempt if the move qualifies for the moving expense deduction (see Section 3.3-2).[189]

Where an employer loans money to an employee at the applicable federal interest rate to purchase employer stock pursuant to an exercise of a nonstatutory stock option and then reduces the principal of the loan when the stock's value declines, the amount of the reduction in principal is compensation income to the employee. The income is wages and is subject to federal income tax withholding and social security, Medicare, and FUTA taxes.[190]

Where a hospital offers to forgive tuition loans made to nursing students who work at the hospital for two years upon graduation, the amount of the loans becomes income only at the point they are forgiven. When the loans are initially made to the students, there is no employment relationship with the hospital, but there certainly is one when they have worked for the hospital for two years and the loans are forgiven. At that point, the forgiven amount must be included in the nurses' income and is subject to federal income tax withholding, social security and Medicare taxes, and FUTA tax.[191]

**Draws against commissions.** Salespeople often receive compensation in the form of advances that are later subtracted from (or drawn against) earned commissions. Such amounts are not loans and are wages if the employee is not legally obligated to repay them under an agreement with the employer. If, however, the employee signs an agreement acknowledging the indebtedness and the loan otherwise qualifies under the rules for compensation-related loans to employees, the advance is not wages and is not subject to federal income tax withholding or social security, Medicare, or FUTA taxes.[192]

# 3.4-19 Military Pay

**Supplemental military pay.** Compensation paid to employees while on military duty that represents the difference between the employee's regular pay and the pay provided by the state or federal government is referred to as supplemental (or differential) military pay. The tax treatment of supplemental military pay is governed by the circumstances of the employee's military service.[193]

1.  If the supplemental military pay is provided while the employee is on temporary assignment with the state National Guard or the Armed Forces Reserve, it is wages subject to federal income tax withholding and social security, Medicare, and FUTA taxes.

2.  If the supplemental military pay is provided while the employee is on active service with the U.S. Armed Forces or on an indefinite assignment with the state National Guard, the IRS treats the employment relationship as broken and the compensation is not subject to federal income tax withholding or social security, Medicare, or FUTA taxes.

*Reporting supplemental military pay.* If the supplemental military pay is considered wages, it must be reported on the employee's Form W-2. If the employment tax relationship no longer exists, the payments are reported on Form 1099-MISC in Box 3, "Other Income," if they are at least $600.

*Other benefits while on military leave.* According to the IRS, employer-provided medical coverage and employer contributions to health benefits plans are not included in the income of an employee on military

---

189.   IRC §7872; IRS Prop. Reg. §1.7872-1; IRS Temp. Reg. §1.7872-5T.
190.   Rev. Rul. 2004-37, 2004-11 IRB 583.
191.   LTR 200452027, 12-23-04.
192.   Rev. Rul. 68-239, 1968-1 CB 414; Rev. Rul. 68-337, 1968-1 CB 417.
193.   Rev. Rul. 69-136, 1969-1 CB 252; Rev. Rul. 68-238, 1968-1 CB 420.

leave and are not reported on Form W-2 or 1099-MISC. Also, the tax treatment of employer-provided group-term life insurance is the same as it is for employees who are not on military leave.

 **WATCH OUT** Any vacation pay earned or accrued before the employee goes into active service is considered taxable wages no matter when it is paid.

Employees who have entered active military service can continue deferrals from any supplemental military pay paid by their employer into a defined contribution retirement plan under §401(k), §403(b), or §457 (see Section 4.6 for details on these and other retirement plans). Such amounts have to be reported on Form W-2 in Box 12 with the appropriate code (see Section 8.8-3).[194] Employees returning from active service can also make retroactive deferrals for the time spent in the service when they made no deferrals. See section 8.8-3 for the rules on reporting such deferrals.

Detailed information on the tax and reporting rules governing supplemental military pay can be found on the IRS website at www.irs.gov/newsroom/article/0,,id=129833,00.html.

**Combat zone pay.**[195] Under IRC §112, pay received by U.S. military personnel while serving in a "combat zone" or while hospitalized as a result of such service is excluded from income with certain limitations. The exclusion applies to any compensation received by U.S. military personnel for a month, limited to the highest rate of basic pay for enlisted personnel, any part of which was spent in a combat zone or in a hospital as result of combat zone service. The exclusion applies only to federal income tax, not to social security and Medicare taxes. The exclusion for pay received during periods of hospitalization does not apply after 2 years from the date specified by the President as the last day of hostile activities in the combat zone.

*Definition of "service" and "combat zone."* The income exclusion for combat zone pay applies only to military personnel actively serving in a combat zone. The individual must be actually serving in the U.S. Armed Forces, which includes time absent from duty because of sickness, wounds, leave, or imprisonment by the enemy. However, the date and place of payment are irrelevant—the time and place of entitlement to the compensation determine whether the exclusion applies (e.g., payment for leave accrued during combat zone service but taken afterward is excluded).

A combat zone is an area designated as such by the President in an Executive Order, from the date of the designation to the date specified by the President as the last day of combatant activities in the zone. Service outside the combat zone may qualify for the exclusion if the service is in direct support of military activity in the zone and the individual is entitled to special pay for "duty subject to hostile fire or imminent danger." Military personnel who are present in a combat zone may not qualify for the exclusion if they are there on leave from a duty station outside the combat zone, for their own personal convenience, or passing through or over the zone while traveling between two points outside the zone.

*Only military pay is excluded.* The exclusion for combat zone pay applies only to compensation provided by the U.S. Armed Forces, with an exception for military personnel paid by another U.S. agency or international organization who are on active duty status when assigned to the agency or organization. Compensation paid by private employers cannot be excluded under §112 even if the payment is made to supplement the individual's military pay or is labeled as compensation for active service. Likewise, compensation paid to civilian employees of any federal government agency, including the Armed Forces, is not excluded. Severance pay provided to an individual in exchange for an agreement to leave the armed services is not excluded, even if the severance is paid while the individual is in a combat zone.

 **NEW REPORTING REQUIREMENT** Beginning with the 2005 Form W-2, military employers that pay nontaxable combat pay to U.S. military personnel must report the amount on Form W-2 in Box 12 with Code "Q".

---

194. IRS Reg. §1.401(k)-1(e)(8); §1.403(b)-3(b)(4)(ii); §1.457-4(d)(1).
195. IRC §112; IRS Reg. §1.112-1.

## 3.4-20 Outplacement Services

Services provided by employers to help employees find a new job after a layoff or reduction in force are excluded from income as a working condition fringe benefit (see Section 3.2-1) if:

1. The employer derives a substantial business benefit from providing the outplacement services (e.g., a positive corporate image, an attractive benefit that encourages new hires).

2. The employee does not have the choice of accepting cash rather than the outplacement services (e.g., a higher severance payment if the services are not used).

3. The employees would be able to deduct the cost of the outplacement services as a business expense on their personal tax returns.[196]

## 3.4-21 Retroactive Wage Payments

Retroactive wage payments are treated as wages when they are made and are subject at that time to federal income tax withholding and social security, Medicare, and FUTA taxes at current rates and under current wage limits.

## 3.4-22 Security Provided to Employees

Security provided to employees who carry large sums of money or jewelry, have access to confidential information, or have jobs involving matters of national security may be excluded from income as a working condition fringe. To qualify, the employer must have a "bona fide business-oriented security concern" caused by terrorist activity or threats of death, kidnapping, or serious injury against the employee's life because of his or her employment status.

Also, the security must be provided as part of an overall security program designed to protect the employee on a 24-hour basis that has been justified by an independent security study. Where the employee is provided with a vehicle that is used for both business and personal purposes, the personal use is income to the employee, but security devices placed in the vehicle are not, even though they help protect the employee during times of personal use.[197]

**Security for spouses and dependents.**[198] If the employee's use of a vehicle qualifies as a working condition fringe benefit because of business-oriented security concerns, the value of the use of the vehicle by the employee's spouse or dependents at the same time is not included in the employee's income. The value of other security provided to the employee's spouse and dependents is not included in income only if the spouse and dependents independently qualify for the security under the same rules as the employee.

**Chauffeurs and bodyguards.**[199] If a business-oriented security concern requires that an employee be provided with a vehicle and a bodyguard/chauffeur, the entire value of the bodyguard/chauffeur's services is excluded from the employee's income. The bodyguard/chauffeur must be trained in evasive driving techniques for the services to be excluded under this provision. (See Section 3.2-1 for other rules regarding chauffeur services as a working condition fringe benefit.)

---

196. Rev. Rul. 92-69, 1992-2 CB 51.
197. IRS Reg. §1.132-5(m)(1), (2).
198. IRS Reg. §1.132-5(m)(3).
199. IRS Reg. §1.132-5(m)(5).

## 3.4-23 Severance or Dismissal Pay

Severance or dismissal pay, which is provided to employees because they were terminated involuntarily through no fault of their own (e.g., downsizing, plant closing, company relocation, etc.), must be included in the terminated employee's income and is subject to federal income tax withholding and social security, Medicare, and FUTA taxes.[200] These amounts are generally subject to taxation when paid because they are not subject to the special timing rules applicable to nonqualified deferred compensation, but they may be subject to the requirements of IRC §409A depending on how large the amounts are and over what time period they are paid (see Section 4.6-10).

Several ex-employees have claimed that severance pay received after signing a waiver of their right to sue the employer under anti-discrimination laws should not be included in income because it was paid as a "settlement" of a personal injury claim. The IRS and the courts have refused to accept this argument, ruling that such a general waiver, entered into before any claim of discrimination is made, cannot be considered a personal injury settlement.[201] See also Section 3.4-3 on back pay awards and Section 3.4-26 on supplemental unemployment benefits.

## 3.4-24 Stocks and Stock Options

To promote company loyalty and increase efficiency and productivity, employers often compensate employees or provide incentives in the form of company stock or an option to buy company stock at a fixed price. New and expanding companies often offer these types of compensation to retain key employees by giving them an ownership interest in the developing company. The tax consequences of such compensation depend on several variables, such as the form of the compensation and the conditions attached to receiving it.

**Employer stock as compensation.** If an employer pays employees with company stock instead of cash as compensation for services rendered, the fair market value of the stock when transferred to the employee without restrictions is wages subject to federal income tax withholding and social security, Medicare, and FUTA taxes.[202] (For details on stock provided as part of a qualified employee stock ownership plan, see Section 4.6-8).

**Stock options.** Options to buy company stock at a favorable price can take several forms, including incentive stock options, employee stock purchase plans, and nonqualified stock options. Incentive stock options and employee stock purchase plans are considered "statutory options," while nonqualified stock options are also known as "nonstatutory options."

**Incentive stock options.** An incentive stock option (ISO) gives an employee the opportunity to buy the employer corporation's stock at a fixed price for a certain period of time. To qualify for favorable tax treatment (i.e., no income tax withholding, no income recognized until stock is sold), the following conditions must be met:[203]

1. The plan containing the option must be approved by the corporation's shareholders.

2. The employer must require the option to be exercised within 10 years of being granted.

3. The option price must at least equal the fair market value of the stock when the option was granted.

---

200. IRS Reg. §31.3401(a)-1(b)(4); see also Associated Electric Cooperative, Inc. v. U.S., 226 F.3d 1322 (Fed. CA, 2000).
201. PLR 9331007, 5-5-94; Taggi v. U.S., 35 F.3d 93 (2 CA, 1994); Abrahamsen v. U.S., 228 F.3d 1360 (Fed. CA, 2000); cert. denied (U.S. S.Ct., 4-2-01).
202. IRS Reg. §31.3121(a)-1(e); §31.3306(b)-1(e); §31.3401(a)-1(a)(4).
203. IRC §421; §422; IRS Reg. §1.421-2; §1.422-1 to 1.422-5; §1.424.1 to §1.424-4.

4. The option must not be transferrable before the employee's death.

5. The employee must not own more than 10% of the employer's voting stock, unless the option price is at least 110% of the stock's fair market value and the option must be exercised within 5 years of being granted.

6. The employee must not sell the stock within 2 years of the option being granted or within 1 year of exercising the option. An early sale will be treated as a "disqualifying disposition," and the difference between the option price and the exercise price (or the sale price if lower) is included in the employee's ordinary income.

7. The employee must exercise the option while employed by the employer or within 3 months after terminating employment (1 year if the employee stopped working because of permanent and total disability).

8. No more than $100,000 worth of stock options (using the value of the stock when the option is granted) can become exercisable for the first time in any year by each employee. The excess will be treated as a nonqualified stock option.

*Favorable tax treatment.* If an employee exercises an option under a qualified incentive stock option plan and complies with the holding periods before selling the stock, no income is realized at the time the option is exercised and the income realized by the employee at the time of sale is taxed at capital gain rates and is generally not subject to federal income tax withholding or social security, Medicare, or FUTA taxes. If an employee buys stock under an incentive stock option plan and sells it before the holding period ends, the ordinary income that is realized is not subject to federal income tax withholding or social security, Medicare, or FUTA taxes, although the income must be reported on the employee's Form W-2.

**Employee stock purchase plans.** Similar qualifying conditions are placed on employee stock purchase plans (ESPP), under which employees are given the opportunity to buy the employer corporation's stock at a discount. There are some differences, however. The option must be made available to all employees, except for recently hired, part-time, temporary, and highly compensated employees (see Section 3.2-1 for a definition). The discount can be no more than 15% of the value of the stock, which is measured when the option is granted if the maximum exercise period is 27 months. It is measured when the option is exercised if the maximum exercise period is longer (up to 5 years). Employees holding more than 5% of the employer's voting stock are ineligible, and no more than $25,000 worth of options can be exercised in any year by each employee.[204] Also, the employee cannot sell the stock less than 2 years after the option is granted or less than 1 year after the option is exercised, and the employee must be employed by the employer at all times from the date the option is granted until no more than 3 months before the option is exercised.

If an employee exercises an option under a qualified employee stock purchase plan and complies with the holding periods before selling the stock, the employee does not have any income when the option is exercised. When the stock is sold, the employee has ordinary income equal to the lesser of: (1) the difference between the option price and the fair market value of the stock on the day the option was granted; or (2) the difference between the option price and the fair market value of the stock on the day of sale. The employee also has capital gain income equal to the difference between the fair market value of the stock on the day of sale and the option price plus any amount included in the employee's gross income because of the sale.

**No employment taxes upon exercise or sale.** Despite the fact that under §421(a) no income is recognized when an employee exercises a statutory stock option, in the 1990s the IRS took the position that the excess of the fair market value of the stock over the exercise price is subject to social security, Medicare, and FUTA taxes when the option is exercised.[205]

---

204. IRC §423; IRS Reg. §1.423-1; PLR 9650005, 9-4-96.
205. PLR 9243026, 7-24-92; FSA 199926034, 7-2-99.

In 2001 the IRS proposed rules that would have solidified this position, but it pulled back in 2002 after receiving a great deal of negative comments from the business community, including APA. At that point, the IRS said it would not assess social security, Medicare, or FUTA taxes or require federal income tax withholding on the spread at exercise or sale of a statutory stock option until at least two years after issuing final regulations.[206]

Before any final regulations could be issued, a provision was added to the American Jobs Creation Act of 2004 that said any gain on account of the exercise of a statutory stock option after October 22, 2004 or the sale of stock acquired pursuant to such exercise is excluded from social security, Medicare, and FUTA wages.

Also, federal income tax withholding is not required on any income resulting from a disqualifying disposition of such stock nor when compensation is recognized in connection with an ESPP discount.[207]

**Reporting required after stock transfer.**[208] When a corporation transfers legal title to stock to an employee who has exercised an incentive stock option, the employer must furnish a written statement to the employee. Similarly, when a corporation transfers legal title to stock that has been acquired by an employee in exercising an option under an employee stock purchase plan, the employer must furnish a statement to the employee. In the case of an ESPP, the statement is required for "the first transfer of legal title" to the stock, even if that transfer is not to the employee – for example, where the employee does not take legal title immediately but directs an agent of the corporation to transfer the stock to another party. For an incentive stock option, the written statement provided to the employee must include the following information:

- The name, address and employer identification number (EIN) of the corporation transferring the stock;
- The name, address, and Taxpayer Identification Number (SSN if transferred to an employee) of the person to whom the share or shares of stock were transferred;
- The name and address of the corporation the stock of which is the subject of the option (if other than the corporation transferring the stock);
- The date the option was granted;
- The date the shares were transferred to the employee exercising the option;
- The fair market value of the stock at the time the option was exercised;
- The number of shares of stock transferred pursuant to the option;
- The type of option under which the transferred shares were acquired; and
- The total cost of all the shares.

For the transfer of an option granted under an employee stock purchase plan, the written statement provided to the employee must include the following information:

- The name and address of the corporation whose stock is being transferred;
- The name, address, and TIN of the transferor;
- The date the stock was transferred to the transferor;
- The number of shares to which title was transferred; and
- The type of options under which the transferred shares were acquired.

The statement must be furnished by January 31 of the year following the year for which the statement is required. A 30-day extension may be granted by the IRS if an application is submitted by January 31 that explains the reason for the extension. The statement may be provided to the employee electronically if the employee consents to that form of delivery. The rules governing electronic delivery are the same as those governing the electronic delivery of Form W-2 to employees. (See Section 8.8-2.) The penalty for not providing the statement or for providing a statement with incorrect information is $50 per statement, up to a maximum of $100,000 in one year ($100 per statement with no maximum if the employer intentionally disregards the statement requirement).

---

206. IRS Prop. Reg. §31.3121(a)-1(k); §31.3306(b)-1(l); §31.3401(a)-1(b);. IRS Notice 2002-47, 2002-28 IRB 97.
207. IRC §421(b); §423(c); §3121(a)(22); §3306(b)(19).
208. IRC §6039; IRS Reg. §1.6039-1.

The Tax Relief and Health Care Act of 2006 amended §6039 to require an employer to file an information return with the IRS, in addition to providing the employee statement, beginning in 2007.[209] The time and form for filing the information return with IRS will be set by the Treasury Secretary and the IRS in regulations. Employers that fail to comply are subject to same penalties that apply to a failure to file other information returns.

Because no regulations regarding the time and form for filing the information return with the IRS had been issued by the end of 2007, the IRS waived the reporting requirement for 2007 stock transfers.[210]

**Nonqualified stock options.** A nonqualified (nonstatutory) stock option gives an employee the opportunity to buy the employer corporation's stock at a fixed price for a certain period of time, without the conditions placed on incentive stock options. When the option is exercised, the employee receives income equal to the excess of the value of the stock when the option is exercised over the price paid by the employee. This income is subject to federal income tax withholding and social security, Medicare, and FUTA taxes at the time of exercise. The income must be reported in Boxes 1, 3, and 5 of the employee's Form W-2. The employer must also report the income in Box 12 preceded by Code V.[211] When the stock is sold, any increase in the stock's value over the value when the option was exercised is taxed as capital gain.[212]

*Payment for cancelled options was income.* A payment made to an employee for stock options that were cancelled after a corporate merger was regular income, the Tax Court ruled. The court upheld the IRS's reliance on IRC §83(a), which provides that when property is transferred to a taxpayer in connection with the performance of services, the excess fair market value of the property over the amount, if any, paid for it is includible in gross income. Here, the employee obtained the stock options as part of her employment, and because she paid nothing to obtain the stock options and nothing at the time of their cancellation, the entire payment was taxable as ordinary income.[213]

*How to withhold.* If an employer must withhold federal income and/or social security, Medicare, and FUTA taxes when an employee exercises a nonqualified stock option, the income should be treated as supplemental wages (see Section 6.4-4). The employer can withhold from other wages payable to the employee at the same time, by holding on to a certain number of shares, or by asking the employee to make a payment equal to the withholding amount, which can be made through a broker from proceeds of the sale (i.e., a cashless exercise).

*When to deposit withheld amounts.* In a memorandum establishing guidelines for its tax examiners, the IRS announced that the exercise of nonqualified stock options does not give rise to constructive payment of wages until the settlement date – that is, the day on which the shares of stock are available in the employee's brokerage account.[214] This is typically three business days after the exercise date (the date the employee notifies the broker). "FICA and income tax withholding provisions do not impose a withholding obligation on the employer until wages are actively or constructively paid. It has been argued that the shares (or the value of the shares) are not available to the exerciser of the options until settlement date, and therefore no active or constructive payment of wages takes place until that time." For more information on the payroll tax deposit rules once actual or constructive payment has taken place, see Section 8.2-1.

A cashless nonstatutory option exercise program generally works as follows. The employee notifies a designated broker that he or she would like to exercise the employee's option to buy stock at a reduced exercise price under the option agreement. The employee further instructs the broker to immediately sell enough of the stock (at full market value) to cover the exercise price, the taxes imposed on the income (the difference between the value of the stock and the price the employee paid), or both. The stock that the employee buys is generally delivered to the employee's brokerage account three days after the exercise process begins.

---

209. IRC §6039(a); §6724(d)(1)(B)(xix); P.L. 109-432, §403.
210. IRS Notice 2008-8, 2008-3 IRB 276.
211. IRS Ann. 2002-108, 2002-49 IRB 952; Palahnuk v. U.S., 70 Fed. Cl. 87 (Ct. of Fed. Cl., 2006), aff'd No. 2006-5069 (Fed. CA, 2-12-07); Cidale v. U.S., No. 05-51372 (5 CA, 1-9-07); Racine v. Commissioner, 493 F. 3d 777 (7 CA, 7-3-07)..
212. IRC §83; IRS Reg. §1.83-7; Rev. Rul. 67-257, 1967-2 CB 359.
213. Buckley v. Commissioner, T.C. Summary Op. 2003-69, No. 5696-02S (6-9-03).
214. Memorandum for Industry Directors, LMSB, 3-14-03.

During that time, the broker sells some shares according to the employee's instructions. By the time the stock actually gets to the employee's account, it is a reduced amount of stock (purchased shares less sold shares), together with cash proceeds remitted by the broker to the employer, which adjusts the proceeds as necessary and deposits them as taxes.

**Nonqualified stock option transfers as part of a divorce.**[215] In 2004, the IRS issued guidance on the income and employment tax consequences of the transfer of nonqualified stock options to a former spouse in connection with a divorce. In the IRS example used to illustrate the guidance, a husband is employed by a corporation that issues nonstatutory stock options to him as part of his compensation. The stock options' fair market value cannot be determined at the time they are granted to the husband, and no amount is included in his gross income when he receives them.

Under state law, stock options earned by a spouse are marital property subject to equitable division between the spouses in the event of divorce. Under their divorce settlement, the husband transfers to his wife one-third of the nonstatutory stock options issued to him by his employer. Several years later, the wife exercises all of the stock options and receives stock with a fair market value in excess of the exercise price.

The IRS ruled that the nonstatutory stock options transferred to the wife are property within the meaning of §1041, which means there is no income recognized when he transfers these interests to his wife. Furthermore, the husband is not required to include in gross income any income resulting from his wife's eventual exercise of the stock options.

However, when the wife exercises the options, she must include in income the excess of the fair market value of the stock over the exercise price as if she were the person who performed the services. The same conclusions apply if the husband and wife live in a community property state and all or some of these income rights are community property subject to division between them as part of their divorce.

The IRS ruled that the transfer of interests in nonstatutory stock options from an employee spouse to a non-employee spouse in connection with divorce does not result in a payment of wages for social security, Medicare, and FUTA tax purposes. However, the nonstatutory stock options are subject to social security, Medicare, and FUTA taxes at the time of exercise by the non-employee spouse to the same extent as if the options had been retained by the employee spouse and exercised by him.

To the extent social security, Medicare, and FUTA taxation applies, the wages are the wages of the employee spouse; the employee portion of social security and Medicare taxes is deducted from the property and payments made to the non-employee spouse when the wages are taken into account for social security and Medicare tax purposes. For purposes of the social security and FUTA wage bases, the wages are credited to the employee spouse. The IRS also ruled that the income recognized by the non-employee spouse with respect to the exercise of the nonqualified stock options is subject to federal income tax withholding as wages. The employer can use the supplemental wage flat rate to determine the amount to withhold.

Social security and Medicare wages and taxes withheld, if applicable, are reportable on Form W-2 in Boxes 3-6 with the name, address, and social security number of the employee spouse. However, no amount is included in Box 1 or Box 2 of the employee's Form W-2 with respect to these payments. Income derived from the exercise of the nonstatutory stock options by the non-employee spouse is reportable in Box 3 as "other income" on Form 1099-MISC with the name, address, and social security number of the non-employee spouse. Income tax withholding with respect to these payments is included in Box 4, "federal income tax withheld." Income tax withholding on payments to the non-employee spouse is included on Form 945, filed by the employer. The social security and Medicare taxes are reported on the employer's Form 941, and the FUTA tax is reported on the employer's Form 940.

---

215.  Rev. Rul. 2004-60, 2004-24 IRB 1051.

## 3.4-25 Strike Benefits

Strike and lockout benefits paid by a union to its members to provide them with money to pay bills during the strike generally are not wages and are not subject to federal income tax withholding or social security, Medicare, or FUTA taxes. However, if the union pays members an hourly wage for picketing activity, the payments are wages.[216]

## 3.4-26 Supplemental Unemployment Benefits

Many employers in industries with strong unions and substantial plant closings or reductions in force have entered into agreements providing for supplemental unemployment benefits (SUBs) for their laid-off workers. SUBs are paid in addition to a laid-off employee's state unemployment compensation benefits. The tax treatment of such payments depends on several factors.

Whether the SUB plan provides for a trust or another method for making payments, the payments are subject to federal income tax withholding (unless there is some reason to exclude them from gross income altogether). The payments are excluded from wages subject to social security, Medicare, and FUTA taxes if:[217]

- benefits are paid only to unemployed former employees who are laid off by the employer;
- eligibility depends on meeting certain prescribed conditions after termination of employment (e.g., eligibility for state unemployment compensation);
- the amount of benefits payable is based on state unemployment compensation and the employee's straight-time pay;
- the duration of benefits is affected by the fund level and the employee's seniority;
- the benefits are not attributable to the rendering of particular services; and
- no employee has any right to benefits until the employee is qualified and eligible to receive benefits.

According to the IRS, the crucial factor is the link between SUB pay and state unemployment compensation, since SUB pay is designed to supplement unemployment benefits. Because the receipt of lump-sum SUB pay would allow employees to receive the same amount of benefits regardless of the length of time spent unemployed, lump-sum payments lack a sufficient link to state unemployment compensation and are not excluded from income for social security, Medicare, and FUTA tax purposes.

**Court decision causes confusion.**[218] Payments to permanently laid-off employees under a reduction-in-force program qualified as supplemental unemployment benefits under IRC §3402(o)(2) and therefore were not wages for FICA-tax purposes, the U.S. Court of Federal Claims ruled, even though the program payments did not meet the factors that the IRS considers crucial in making this determination. CSX Corporation, the parent company of a group of railroads, implemented a major reduction in its workforce between 1984 and 1990. This workforce reduction was accomplished by (1) job layoffs, (2) reductions in hours of work and rates of pay, and (3) permanent separations from employment.

The question for the court was whether the payments CSX made pursuant to its reduction-in-force program were wages for FICA-tax purposes. CSX argued that the payments were supplemental unemployment benefits, and that such benefits are not subject to taxation under FICA. Section 3402(o)(2) defines supplemental unemployment benefits as: "amounts which are paid to an employee, pursuant to a plan to which the employer is a party, because of an employee's involuntary separation from employment (whether or not such separation is temporary), resulting directly from a reduction-in-force, the discontinuance of a plant or operation, or other similar conditions, but only to the extent such benefits are includible in the employee's gross income."

---

216. Rev. Rul. 75-475, 1975-2 CB 406; Rev. Rul. 68-539, 1968-2 CB 422; Rev. Rul. 68-424, 1968-2 CB 419.
217. IRC §3402(o); IRS Reg. §31.3402(o)-1; Rev. Rul. 90-72, 1990-2 CB 211; Rev. Rul. 60-330, 1960-2 CB 46; Rev. Rul. 58-128, 1958-1 CB 89; Rev. Rul. 56-249, 1956-1 CB 488; see also PLR 9449002, 7-22-94; PLR 9734035, 5-22-97.
218. CSX Corp. Inc. v. U.S., 52 Fed. Cl., 2002 U.S. Claims LEXIS 73 (Ct. of Fed. Cl., 2002).

The court agreed with CSX that supplemental unemployment benefits meeting this definition are not "wages." The court then found that the payments made to laid-off employees met the definition of supplemental unemployment benefits, while payments made to employees whose full-time positions were eliminated did not, because they were "on standby" and obliged to remain subject to recall on an as-needed basis. In a later decision involving the same parties, the court reaffirmed its earlier finding that payments made to employees who voluntarily separated from employment could not qualify as SUB pay or be excluded from social security, Medicare, or FUTA tax.[219]

In another subsequent decision, the court ruled that payments made under a "forced transfer" provision of the program did not qualify as SUB pay and were wages subject to social security, Medicare, and FUTA taxes.[220]

The IRS has since reasserted its traditional position that, in order to be excluded from income subject to social security, Medicare, and FUTA taxes, payments to laid-off employees must be tied to the employees' eligibility for state unemployment compensation benefits and the amounts the employees will receive.[221]

 **WHAT SHOULD EMPLOYERS DO?** Employers that have had layoffs over the last several years are often puzzled at what to do in reaction to the CSX decision. Because of the uncertainty surrounding what will happen if and when the decision is appealed by the IRS, employers can best protect themselves by withholding and/or paying social security, Medicare, and FUTA taxes on severance payments to laid-off employees and then filing refund claims, which the IRS will hold in abeyance until a final decision is made by a higher court.

**Union-provided supplemental pay.** Collective bargaining agreements sometimes allow new employees or employees performing certain jobs to receive lower pay than other employees to create more jobs for union members while allowing employers to remain competitive with nonunion companies. Where the union provides supplemental pay to these lower-paid employees from a common trust funded by special dues payments from union members, the supplemental payments are not wages subject to federal income tax withholding or social security, Medicare, or FUTA tax.[222]

# 3.4-27 Tips

Generally, tips or gratuities provided voluntarily by customers are taxable wages to the employee receiving them. Because of the special nature of tip income, with the employee's wages being provided to a great extent by customers rather by the employer, there are special rules that apply.

 **SERVICE CHARGES ARE NOT TIPS** Where the customer is required to pay a service charge added to the bill, that is not a tip. When it is turned over to the employee, it is regular wages.

**Employees must report tip income to employer.** Employees who receive at least $20 a month in cash tips must report their tip income to their employer at least once a month by the 10th of the next month (more frequently if the employer requires it). The easiest way is for the employer to provide them with Form 4070, *Employee's Report of Tips to Employer* (see Appendix page A-348), although the employer may use its own form.[223]

---

219. CSX Corp., Inc. v. U.S., No. 95-858T, 2003 US Claims LEXIS 321 (Ct. of Fed. Cl., 10-31-03).
220. CSX Corp., Inc. v. U.S., No 95-858T, 2006 US Claims LEXIS 173 (Ct. of Fed. Cl., 6-27-06).
221. LTR 200322012, 2-12-03.
222. PLR 9416027, 1-18-94.
223. IRC §6053(a).

**Electronic tip reporting.** IRS regulations allow employers to establish electronic systems for their tipped employees to use in reporting tips to their employer.[224] Employers can select the type(s) of electronic systems to be used by their employees (e.g., phone or computer). Whatever system is used, it must:

- ensure that the information received is the information transmitted by the employee;
- document each time the system is accessed that results in transmission of a tip report;
- make it reasonably certain that the person transmitting the report is the employee identified in the transmission; and
- produce a hard copy for the employer to provide to the IRS during an audit.

The electronic tip report must contain exactly the same information that must be reported on a paper tip report, along with the employee's electronic signature. The signature must identify the employee providing the report and verify the transmission, and it can be in any form that satisfies these conditions. The record retention requirements that apply to an employer's automatic data processing systems (see Section 10.2) also apply to electronic tip reporting systems. The employee can meet his or her substantiation requirements if the employee reports tips on a daily basis through the employer's electronic system and keeps a hard copy of the daily record based on those entries (e.g., a weekly printout from the employer's system showing the daily amount of tips reported).

**Withholding on tip income.** Tip income is subject to federal income tax withholding and social security, Medicare, and FUTA taxes if the employee reports more than $20 in tips for the month. Tip income for which no withholding is required is still income to the employee, who must report it on his or her personal tax return. Income, social security, and Medicare taxes on tip income should be withheld from the employee's regular wages, either by combining the amounts or using the supplemental wage method (see Section 6.4-4).

Where the taxes to be withheld exceed the wages available, the employee can be asked to provide the employer with enough funds to satisfy the withholding obligation. If that is not done, or the amount provided is not enough, the employer should withhold taxes in the following priority: social security and Medicare taxes on regular wages; federal income tax on regular wages; social security and Medicare taxes on tips; federal income tax on tips. The uncollected amount of social security and Medicare taxes must be reported on the employee's Form W-2 in Box 12 with Codes "A" and "B" respectively (see Section 8.8-3 for details). Withheld amounts must be reported in Boxes 4 and 6 respectively. The employer must pay its full share of social security and Medicare taxes even if the employee's share was not fully collectable.[225]

**When tips are deemed paid.** Tips are deemed paid to the employee when the employee furnishes the required report to the employer. If no report is furnished, the tips are paid when received from the customer (or from the employer if they are credit card tips or are otherwise required to be turned over to the employer initially).[226]

**Special rules for employer share of FICA taxes on unreported or underreported tips.**[227] What happens when an employee fails to report or underreports the amount of tips received? In that case, the employer is liable only for the employer share of social security and Medicare (FICA) taxes, while the employee is liable for the employee share. Under IRC §3121(q), for purposes of the employer share of the taxes, the tips that were not reported or were underreported are deemed paid when the employer receives a notice and demand for the social security and Medicare taxes from the IRS.

The law does not require that a notice and demand take any particular form, but such a document must:

- contain the words "notice and demand" and "section 3121(q)";
- state the amount of tips received by the employee or employees; and

---

224.    IRS Reg. §31.6053-1; §31.6053-4.
225.    IRC §3121(a)(12); §3306(s); §3401(a)(16); §3402(k); IRS Reg. §31.3121(a)(12)-1; §31.3401(a)(16)-1; §31.3402(k)-1.
226.    IRC §3121(q); §3401(f); IRS Reg. §31.3401(f)-1.
227.    Rev. Rul. 95-7, 1995-1 CB 185.

- state the period to which the tips relate.

To compute the employer share of social security and Medicare taxes, the employer must use the rates and wage bases in effect *in the year in which the tips were actually received by the employee.*

*Deposit rules.* The employer must deposit the social security and Medicare taxes owed as a result of the notice and demand according to the general rules for making deposits of employment taxes (see Section 8.2-1). The taxes owed are deemed to accumulate on the date of the notice and demand, which requires the employer to make the calculation as to the amount owed before its next deposit due date, which could be the next day for large employers who have already accumulated more than $100,000 in total withheld income and employment tax liability. The IRS said it intends to notify employers at least 30 calendar days before it issues a notice and demand for employer social security and Medicare taxes on unreported tips.

*Reporting requirements.* The employer reports its liability for the social security and Medicare taxes by making an adjustment on the employer's Form 941, *Employer's Quarterly Federal Tax Return* (see Section 8.3), for the quarter in which the notice and demand is made. The employer should include the amount of the adjustment on on line 7g (after being notified by the IRS to do so) and in either the Record of Federal Tax Liability (Line 15) or on Schedule B depending on whether the employer is a monthly or semiweekly depositor.

To explain the adjustment, the employer must attach a copy of the notice and demand and Form 941c, *Supporting Statement to Correct Information* (see Section 8.6). The employer should write "3121(q)" in the top margin of the Form 941c. This must be a separate Form 941c with no other adjustments on it. Parts I and II of the form should not be completed. In Part III, Column (a), the employer should enter "3121(q)" and the year to which the notice and demand applies (put different years on different lines). Columns (b), (c), and (d) should not be completed. In Column (e), the employer should enter the total tips for the year as shown on the notice and demand, with the employer share of the social security tax on that amount placed in Column (f). In Part IV, Column (a), enter the same information as in Part III, Column (a). Column (b) should be left blank. In Column (c), enter the total tips for the year as shown on the notice and demand, with the employer share of the Medicare tax on that amount placed in column (d).

*Limitations period on assessment of taxes.* In general, the IRS must assess any employer taxes remaining owed within 3 years after April 15 of the year following the year in which the notice and demand is made. This rule holds true if the employer files a Form 941 with the adjustment for the employer share of the social security and Medicare taxes owed, whether or not the adjustment is correct or the form is filed after the due date. However, if the Form 941 with the adjustment is not filed until after April 15 of the year following the year in which the notice and demand is made, the IRS has 3 years after the date the return was filed to assess any taxes owed. If a false or fraudulent Form 941 is filed for the quarter in which the adjustment is required, or no Form 941 is filed for that quarter, the employer share of the social security and Medicare taxes can be assessed at any time.

*No interest if there is timely payment.* The employer is not subject to interest on the liability for the employer share of the social security and Medicare taxes if the taxes are paid by the due date of the Form 941 for the quarter during which the notice and demand is made. Interest will accrue on late payments from the due date of the return.

*Employees must pay their share.* Employees who fail to report or underreport their tip income to their employer must pay their share of social security and Medicare taxes by completing Form 4137, *Social Security and Medicare Tax on Unreported Tip Income*, and filing it with their personal income tax return. In doing so, they must use the tax rates and wage bases applicable to the year in which the tips were actually received.

**Tax credit for restaurant employers.** For businesses providing, delivering, or serving food or beverages for consumption, OBRA '93 introduced a business tax credit (taken on the employer's corporate income tax return) for the employer's share of social security and Medicare taxes paid on employees' tips treated as paid by the employer under §3121(q). The credit is available only for taxes paid on tips exceeding any amount treated as wages (the "tip credit") in meeting the minimum wage required by the Fair Labor Standards Act before the minimum wage was increased in July 2007 (see Section 2.5-1).[228] Therefore, the minimum wage for purposes of the FICA tax credit for restaurant employees is $5.15 per hour.

> *Example:* Tad's House of Tacos pays its tipped employees an hourly wage of $2.13 an hour. The business tax credit for Tad's share of social security and Medicare taxes applies only to the taxes paid on the employees' tips above the $3.02 to reach $5.15 an hour, which is the minimum wage for FICA business tax credit purposes.

The Small Business Job Protection Act of 1996 clarified that the credit is available whether or not the tips were reported by the employee to the employer.[229] The credit is taken on Form 8846, *Credit for Employer Social Security and Medicare Taxes Paid on Certain Employee Tips* (see Appendix page A-395).

**When tips are allocated.**[230] Food and beverage establishments with more than 10 employees must "allocate" tips if the amount of tips reported by employees for a payroll period is less than 8% of the establishment's gross sales subject to tips for that period. The difference between the amount reported by the employees and 8% must be allocated to the employees and reported on the employees' W-2 forms, although the amount allocated is not subject to federal income tax withholding or social security, Medicare, or FUTA taxes.

No allocation is made for any employee whose reported tips equal at least 8% of the employee's prorated share of the establishment's gross revenue if the employer allocates tips based on the "gross receipts" method just described. The employer can also choose to allocate tips among all tipped employees based on a "good faith agreement" with at least two-thirds of its tipped employees at each establishment owned by the employer. The agreement should provide for allocated tip amounts that approximate the actual distribution of tips among the tipped employees, and the employer is not liable for amounts incorrectly allocated.

Amounts allocated to each employee must be reported to the employee in Box 8 of Form W-2, but not Boxes 1, 3 or 5. The amounts for all employees must also be reported (along with information supporting the allocated amounts) to the IRS by the last day of February of the year after the year for which the return is made, on Form 8027, *Employer's Annual Return of Tip Income and Allocated Tips* (see Appendix page A-358). A Form 8027 must be filed for each establishment owned by the employer. If more than one Form 8027 is being filed, they must be accompanied by a Form 8027-T, *Transmittal of Employer's Annual Return of Tip Income and Allocated Tips* (see Appendix page A-365).

**Expensive tip audits lead to employer-IRS agreements.** In the early 1990s, the IRS stepped up enforcement efforts designed to collect the employer's share of social security and Medicare taxes on unreported tip income in the restaurant industry. Tipped employees were interviewed to determine whether tips had been underreported, and the employer was assessed its share of employment taxes on the underreported amounts, along with penalties and interest.

In 1994, the IRS designed an alternative to tip audits—the Tip Rate Determination Agreement (TRDA). Employers entering into a TRDA would agree on a certain tip percentage with the IRS based on the charge tips it reported and a formula used by the IRS to determine cash tips. The TRDA also required that a minimum of 75% of the employees at each establishment agree to report at least the percentage of tips agreed on in the TRDA. Employees who did not agree were reported annually to the IRS, greatly increasing their chances for an audit. Employers who did not enter into a TRDA could face a tip audit for all years back to 1988. While entering into a TRDA greatly reduced an employer's risk of a tip audit, many employers felt that it was still an onerous burden. They were also concerned because the social security and Medicare taxes collected from employers were not being credited to individual employee accounts in most instances.

Employer dissatisfaction with the TRDA led to a suggested alternative that was adopted by the IRS in May 1995. It was scheduled to expire on May 31, 2005, but has been extended indefinitely. The Tip

---

228.   IRC §45B.
229.   Pub. L. 104-188, §1112.
230.   IRC §6053(c); IRS Reg. §31.6053-3.

Reporting Alternative Commitment (TRAC) requires hospitality and restaurant employers to educate their tipped employees so they understand that all tips must be reported. It also requires employers to record charge tips for individual employees, establish a method for regularly recording cash tips on an employee-by-employee basis, include all recorded tips on the employees' Form W-2, and to allocate tips to 8% when applicable.

Employers can be assessed the employer's share of social security and Medicare taxes on unreported tips based on data gathered by the IRS from individual employee tax returns and employee audits. In return, the employer is protected from most tip audits while "on TRAC," and any employment taxes paid by the employer are matched by an employee's social security wage history, since all assessments are based on reported tips or individual employee tax returns or audits. Each employer's IRS District Director will evaluate and approve the employer's program.

*Expansion of tip agreements to other industries.* In 2000, the IRS simplified and expanded both of its tip reporting compliance agreements, making them available to all industries where tipping is customary. The IRS is also allowing employers in the food and beverage industry to design their own program through emTRAC (Employer's Tip Reporting Alternative Commitment).[231] In 2007, the IRS announced an updated Gaming Industry Tip Compliance Agreement under which a gaming industry employer and the IRS agree on minimum tip rates for tipped employees in specified jobs, a minimum level of participation by the employer's tipped employees, and reduced compliance burdens for the employer and enforcement burdens for the IRS. Employers and employees that meet the reporting requirements under the agreement are deemed to have met the tip reporting requirements under IRC §6053.[232] All these efforts are part of IRS's Tip Rate Determination/Education Program (TRD/EP) to enhance tax compliance through education and voluntary compliance agreements. In 2004, the IRS extended the program indefinitely.[233]

*Another tip reporting program for the restaurant industry.*[234] In 2006, the IRS issued guidance on a new tip reporting procedure, the Attributed Tip Income Program (ATIP), for the food and beverage industry. ATIP is a pilot program that attributes tip income to employees by applying a "formula tip rate" to a restaurant's gross receipts for a period of time determined by the employer. The employer then allocates the total tips to the employees participating in the program using a reasonable method, such as hours worked by an employee in relation to the total hours worked. Employers may elect to participate in ATIP on a calendar year basis for each of the three calendar years beginning on or after January 1, 2007. To qualify for ATIP:

- at least 20% of the establishment's gross receipts must be charged receipts that reflect a charged tip;
- at least 75% of tipped employees must agree to participate in the program; and
- the employer must report attributed tips on employees' Forms W-2 and pay taxes using the formula tip rate, which is defined as the charged tip rate (determined based on information from the establishment's Form 8027) minus 2%.

Participating employers will benefit under ATIP because the IRS will not initiate an "employer-only" §3121 examination while the employer is participating and in many cases employers will not have to receive and process tip records from participating employees. To enroll, employers simply check the designated ATIP box on Form 8027. Simplified filing is provided for small establishments not required to file Form 8027.

Participating employees elect to participate in ATIP by signing an agreement with their employer to have their tip income computed under the program and reported as wages. They will also benefit from the program because they do not have to keep a daily tip log or other tip records, and the IRS will not initiate a tip examination while the employer and employee are participating in ATIP.

---

231. IRS Announcement 2001-1, 2001-2 IRB 277; IRS Notice 2001-1, 2001-2 IRB 261.
232. Rev. Proc. 2007-32, 2007-22 IRB 1322.
233. IR-2004-117, 9-16-2004.
234. Rev. Proc. 2006-30, 2006-31 IRB 110.

*IRS wins court battle over FICA assessments.* The U.S. Supreme Court has ruled that the IRS acted reasonably in requiring employers to pay the employer's share of social security and Medicare taxes on unreported tips, even where the individual employees' share of the taxes is not determined.[235] The restaurant had argued that the aggregate estimation method is unreasonable because it will sometimes include tips that should not count in calculating the social security and Medicare taxes the employer owes, such as on employee income outside the "wages band" (under $20 a month or over the social security wage base). The estimate can also overstate the total amount of tips because (1) customers who pay with cash rather than credit cards tend to leave smaller tips; (2) some customers leave no tip at all; (3) some customers write a high tip on the credit card slip, but ask for some cash back, leaving a lower net amount; and (4) some restaurants deduct the credit card company fee from the tip, leaving the employees with a lower net amount.

The Court said that these considerations did not make the IRS's aggregate estimating method unreasonable, even though its application may sometimes put restaurants in an awkward position. A restaurant owner is free to present evidence that an assessment is inaccurate in a particular case. The restaurant in this case failed to convince the Court that individualized employee assessments inevitably lead to a more reasonable assessment of employer liability, because they are based on estimates themselves. The Court also rejected the argument that IRS's aggregate estimation method may be used coercively to force a restaurant to enter its TRAC program, finding that such a general possibility was not enough to make use of the method unlawful in all cases.

# 3.4-28 Uniform Allowances

If an employer pays for the cost of purchasing and maintaining an employee's uniform either through an advance or a reimbursement, the amount paid is not wages if the uniform is required as a condition of employment and cannot be worn as street clothes (e.g., uniforms worn by police officers, firefighters, nurses). Also, the employee must be required to account to the employer for the amount spent on the uniform and return any excess amounts advanced by the employer.[236]

# 3.4-29 Vacation Pay

Payments provided to an employee as vacation leave are taxable wages subject to federal income tax withholding and social security, Medicare, and FUTA taxes whether the employee takes the leave or receives extra compensation for not taking it. Where the employee does not take the leave, the extra compensation may be treated as supplemental wages (see Section 6.4-4).[237]

# 3.4-30 Wages Paid After Death

The tax treatment and reporting obligations for wages paid after an employee's death depend on when the wages are paid in relation to the employee's death.

**Employee dies before cashing paycheck.** If an employee dies after receiving a paycheck but before cashing it, the employer should reissue the check to the employee's personal representative for the same net amount, since income and employment taxes were properly withheld. The wages and amounts withheld must be reported on the deceased employee's Form W-2.

 **CHECK STATE LAWS** Before reissuing the deceased employee's paycheck, the employer must check state law for any requirements regarding who can receive the check, how much can be paid, etc. (see Section 5.6).

235.   Fior D'Italia, Inc. v. U.S., 122 S.Ct. 2117 (2002).
236.   IRC §62(c); IRS Reg. §1.62-2; §1.274-5T(f)(2); §31.3121(a)-3; §31.3306(b)-2; §31.3401(a)-4.
237.   IRS Reg. §31.3121(a)-1(g); §31.3306(b)-1(h); §31.3401(a)-1(b)(3).

**Wages paid after employee dies and in the same year.** Wages paid to a deceased employee's estate or legal representative after the employee dies but in the year of death are not subject to federal income tax withholding. They are subject to social security, Medicare, and FUTA taxes, however. Therefore, the employer must report the social security and Medicare wages and the amounts withheld on the deceased employee's Form W-2 in Boxes 3-6. The amount of taxable income should be reported only in Box 3 (Other) of Form 1099-MISC in the name of the beneficiary of the payment (see Section 8.12-1 for details on Form 1099-MISC).

**Wages paid after the year of death.** Wages paid to a deceased employee's estate or legal representative after the year of the employee's death are not subject to federal income tax withholding or social security, Medicare, or FUTA taxes and should be reported only in Box 3 (Other) of Form 1099-MISC in the name of the beneficiary of the payment.[238]

# 3.5 Withholding and Reporting Rules for Employer-Provided Benefits

After determining that a benefit provided to its employees is taxable income subject to federal income tax withholding and social security, Medicare, and FUTA taxes, the next step for the employer is to properly withhold, pay, and report on the benefit and the taxes withheld to the IRS and SSA. Because of the special nature of fringe benefits paid in a form other than cash, the rules differ for cash fringe benefits and noncash fringe benefits.

## 3.5-1 Withholding on Cash Fringe Benefits

If a fringe benefit that must be included in an employee's income is provided by the employer in cash (e.g., bonus, severance pay, vacation pay), the employer must withhold any federal income, social security, or Medicare tax due when the benefit is paid.[239] (See Section 6.1 for information on when wages are considered paid.) The employer's share of social security, Medicare, and FUTA taxes also must be determined at the same time. If the full amount is not withheld, the employer becomes liable for paying the taxes.

## 3.5-2 Withholding and Reporting on Noncash Fringe Benefits

Fringe benefits provided in a form other than cash are known as "noncash fringe benefits" and are accorded special treatment by the IRS (e.g., personal use of an employer-provided car, a trip awarded to a top performer).[240] The employer may treat the benefit as being paid on a pay period, quarterly, semiannual, annual, or other basis, but no less frequently than annually. The rules do not require the employer to make the same election for all its employees, and they allow the employer to change its election at any time so long as all benefits provided in a calendar year are treated as paid by December 31 of that year.

An employer may also treat the value of a single fringe benefit as being paid on several dates during the calendar year. The employees do not have to be told of the employer's election, and neither does the IRS. Employers should be careful in choosing when to treat fringe benefits as having been paid. If they are not treated as paid until at or near the end of the year, the employer runs the risk of not having enough regular wages for the employee from which to withhold. If this happens, the employer is liable for the uncollected social security and Medicare taxes as well as its own share.

---

238.  IRC §691(a)(1); §3121(a)(14); §3306(b)(15); Rev. Rul. 86-109, 1986-2 CB 196; Rev. Rul. 71-525, 1971-2 CB 356; Form W-2 Instructions.
239.  IRS Reg. §31.3402(a)-1(b).
240.  IRS Announcement 85-113, 1985-31 IRB 31.

*Example:* Employee Walter's personal use of a company-provided car is valued quarterly by his employer, while employee Peter's personal use of a company car is recognized twice a year. The employer also treats both employees' personal use of the employer's private airplane as having been paid annually on November 30. All of the above treatments are permissible under IRS rules.

**Exception for investment property.** The liberalized rules regarding when an employer must treat noncash fringe benefits as paid do not apply to personal property that is normally held for investment (e.g., stocks, bonds) or real property. Such property must be considered paid when transferred to the employee.

**Withholding methods.** The employer may use one of two methods to withhold federal income, social security, and Medicare taxes from noncash fringe benefits:

1. Add the included fringe benefit amount to the employee's regular wages for a payroll period (imputing) and calculate withholding on the total. The fringe benefit amount may be spread over several payroll periods.

2. Treat the included fringe benefit amount as supplemental wages and withhold federal income tax on the amount from regular wages at the applicable supplemental wage rate of 25% or 35% (see Section 6.4-4 for more on supplemental wages).

**Imputing noncash fringes to determine withholding.** In most situations involving fringe benefits, taxes are not or cannot be withheld when the benefit is provided to the employee. Therefore, the taxable value of the benefit must be added to a regular wage payment. The total withheld taxes are then determined and subtracted, along with the fringe benefit amount, from the original total to reach the employee's net pay. For examples of calculating withholding taxes on imputed income, see Section 6.4-3 on alternative withholding methods.

**Depositing withheld amounts.** Once the employer determines the date on which it will treat the taxable noncash fringe benefit as paid, it must withhold applicable taxes on that date and then deposit them according to the applicable federal deposit rules (see Section 8.2-1). To meet its deposit obligations, the employer may estimate the included fringe benefit amount if its value is not yet certain (e.g., an allocation of the benefit among several employees has not yet been made).

If the employer underestimates the included fringe benefit amount or for some other reason does not withhold and deposit enough taxes, it must pay the employee's share of social security and Medicare taxes. It can collect the tax from the employee at a future date by deducting it from the employee's after-tax wages before the next April 1.[241]

**Reporting requirements.** During the year, the employer should report the taxable value of fringe benefits on the quarterly reporting form (Form 941) for the period in which they are considered paid. The actual value of all such fringe benefits (not estimates) must be reported no later than on the employer's Form 941 for the fourth quarter and on the employee's Form W-2 (both due by January 31 of the following year). See Section 8 for full details.

**Special accounting rule.** Employers have another option for reporting noncash fringe benefits. They may treat fringe benefits provided during November and December of one year (or any shorter period during those two months) as being paid during the next year. This gives employers additional time to value noncash fringe benefits. There are some restrictions that apply to an employer's use of the rule.

1. The rule applies only to noncash fringes *provided* during November and December, not all benefits the employer treats as paid during those two months.

2. While the employer does not have to formally elect to use the special accounting rule, it must notify employees of its decision during the period beginning with the employee's last paycheck of the calendar year and ending with the employee's receipt of the Form W-2 for that year.

---

241. IRS Pub. 15, Circular E, Employer's Tax Guide.

3. The employer can choose to use the special accounting rule for some benefits and not others, but if the rule is used for one benefit, it must be used for all employees receiving that benefit.

4. The employer can use different ending dates during November and December for each benefit.

5. An employee can use the special accounting rule on his or her personal tax return only if the employer uses it, and must use the rule if the employer uses it.

6. The special accounting rule may not be used if the noncash fringe benefit is personal property normally held for investment or real property. The rule also cannot be used to value such benefits as reimbursed moving expenses or group-term life insurance.

*Application to special valuation rules.* If an employer is using the special accounting rule to value noncash fringes, benefits considered provided in the following year are also considered provided in that year for purposes of any special valuation rules the employer is using to value benefits (e.g., annual lease method, vehicle cents-per-mile method).[242]

**Election not to withhold on company-provided vehicle use.**[243] One final withholding option for employers is whether to withhold federal income tax on the value of an employee's personal use of a company-provided vehicle. The employer can make the choice to withhold from some employees and not others. Affected employees must be notified in writing of the election not to withhold by the employer by January 31 of the year for which the election is made or within 30 days after the employee first gets the vehicle (whichever is later). The employer can change its decision not to withhold by notifying the employee in writing again. If the employer elects not to withhold, it must still include the value of the employee's personal use of the car on the employee's Form W-2 in Boxes 1, 3, and 5.

 **NO OPTION ON FICA** The option to not withhold federal income tax from an employee's personal use of a company car does not extend to the employee's share of social security and Medicare taxes.

## 3.6  Review Questions and Exercises

### Review Questions

1. What conditions must be satisfied for the employer to use the vehicle cents-per-mile method in determining the fair market value of the personal use of a company-provided vehicle?

2. How do you define a de minimis fringe benefit?

3. An employee's personal use of a company-provided vehicle generally is a taxable benefit. What are the 3 special valuation methods that can be used to determine the taxable amount?

4. a. An employee earns $30,000 per year, and the company provides group-term life insurance of three times the employee's salary. How much of the insurance coverage is subject to taxation?

   b. Using the above example, if the employee is 46 years old as of December 31, 2008, what rate is used to compute the imputed monthly income for 2008?

5. What is the maximum amount of group-term life insurance an employer can provide an employee's dependents without its value being taxable to the employee?

---

242.   IRS Reg. §1.61-21(c)(7).
243.   IRC §3402(s); IRS Announcement 85-113, 1985-31 IRB 31.

6. When an employee travels on business for his or her employer and receives an advance to pay business-related expenses, what are the general rules for determining when the advance is taxable to the employee and when is it not?

7. If an employee receives a bonus of $2,000 when her year-to-date earnings are $50,000, and the employer pays the taxes, are the taxes considered taxable income? What method is used to determine the amount of taxes the employer will pay?

8. During cutbacks or reductions in force (RIFs), employers sometimes provide outplacement services for employees who will be terminated. Under what circumstances is the value of these services not taxable income to the employee?

9. Who is a control employee for purposes of using the commuting method of valuation of personal use of a company car?

10. Name the two types of deductible moving expenses.

11. What is the difference between an "accountable plan" and a "nonaccountable plan" in relation to the tax treatment of an employee's business travel expense reimbursements?

12. In regards to substantiating employee business expenses, what does the IRS mean by a "pattern of abuse?"

13. For employers to exclude the value of a length of service award from an employee's income, what is the minimum length of service for which the award can be given?

14. With regard to bonuses, what is meant by the "push money exception?"

15. What conditions and limitations must be satisfied for employer-provided dependent care assistance to be excluded from an employee's income?

16. What is meant by the term "golden parachute" payments?

## True or False Questions

_____ 1.    The Internal Revenue Code specifically defines the term "fringe benefits."

_____ 2.    An employer may not discriminate in favor of highly compensated employees when providing no-additional-cost services.

_____ 3.    Qualified employee discounts may be offered to employees in any line of the employer's business.

_____ 4.    An employer may provide transit passes valued at up to $115 in a month to its employees in 2008 without including the fair market value of the benefits in their income.

_____ 5.    The value of an employee's personal use of a company-provided vehicle is taxable income to the employee.

_____ 6.    When an employer-provided vehicle is used for business-related purposes, it is a working condition fringe benefit.

_____ 7.    Cellular phones in company-provided cars must be included in the vehicles' fair market value if they are necessary to the employer's business.

_____ 8. When valuing vehicles, if the employer uses a special valuation method, the employee must also use the same rule or the general valuation method.

_____ 9. The annual lease method for valuing vehicles includes the value of employer-provided fuel.

_____ 10. When an employee uses a company aircraft for business and personal use, the cost of travel for personal use is excluded from the employee's income.

_____ 11. Qualified employee discounts qualify as nontaxable fringe benefits.

_____ 12. The value of employer-provided group-term life insurance up to $50,000 is excluded from an employee's federal taxable income.

_____ 13. Employers are not required to withhold federal income tax on excess group-term life insurance coverage.

_____ 14. In order for a moving expense reimbursement to be excluded from income, the employee must work full time for the same employer in the general vicinity of the new job location for at least 39 consecutive weeks.

_____ 15. A $25.00 check with a note attached saying "Buy a Christmas turkey with this." is excluded from taxable earnings as a de minimis fringe.

_____ 16. If an employee terminates employment during the year because of a permanent disability, then the value of group-term life insurance over $50,000 is not included in the employee's income.

_____ 17. Scholarships and fellowships are included in an individual's income even if the individual is a candidate for a degree at an educational institution

_____ 18. If a meal and incidental expense (M+IE) per diem allowance is used, the amount deemed substantiated is the lesser of the per diem allowance or the federal M+IE rate for the locality of travel.

_____ 19. Employee business travel expense reimbursements under a nonaccountable plan are subject to income withholding and employment taxes.

_____ 20. Salary advances (prepaid wages) must be included in the employee's income for the payroll period in which they are received.

_____ 21. When an employee's wife regularly uses a company car to go shopping, the value of this employee fringe benefit is included in the employee's gross income.

_____ 22. A car salesman who receives a $1,000 award for having the top sales for the month will have this amount included in his income.

_____ 23. Gifts provided to an employee by his or her employer are excluded from income.

_____ 24. Death benefits paid to an employee's estate or beneficiary upon the death of the employee are excluded from income up to $5,000.

_____ 25. Dismissal pay is included in a terminated employee's income and is subject to federal income tax withholding and social security, Medicare, and FUTA taxes.

_____ 26.    The cost of traveling from Boston to Germany for a trip that is for both business and pleasure may be deducted in full as a travel expense.

_____ 27.    To qualify for the travel expense deduction, the employee must be away from home for at least 24 hours.

_____ 28.    If the employee does not maintain adequate records of miles driven, the standard business mileage rate cannot be used in reimbursing the employee for local business travel.

_____ 29.    If an employee works at two or more jobs during the same day, the cost of transportation from one job to the other may be treated as a deductible expense.

_____ 30.    Wages paid to a deceased employee's estate or legal representative after the employee dies but in the year of death are subject to social security, Medicare, and FUTA taxes.

## Multiple Choice Questions

_____ 1.    All of the following benefits are nontaxable fringe benefits EXCEPT:

   a.    No-additional-cost services
   b.    Qualified employee discounts
   c.    Employer-paid membership fees to an athletic club
   d.    De minimis fringes

_____ 2.    All of the following benefits are working condition fringe benefits EXCEPT:

   a.    Business use of a company car or airplane
   b.    Dues and membership fees to professional organizations
   c.    Goods used for product testing by employees
   d.    Dependent care assistance

_____ 3.    All of the following benefits are de minimis fringe benefits EXCEPT:

   a.    Occasional tickets to sporting events
   b.    Subscriptions to business periodicals
   c.    Traditional holiday gifts (e.g., turkeys, candy)
   d.    Occasional personal use of company telephones

_____ 4.    All of the following data elements are recordkeeping requirements for the business use of company-provided vehicles EXCEPT:

   a.    Date of the trip
   b.    Business purpose of the trip
   c.    Mileage for the trip
   d.    Car phone use for the trip

_____ 5.    The business standard mileage rate for 2008 is:

   a.    50.5 cents per mile
   b.    42.5 cents per mile
   c.    44.5 cents per mile
   d.    48.5 cents per mile

_____ 6.  The IRS-approved rate for employer-provided fuel for 2007 is:

    a.  5 cents per mile
    b.  5.5 cents per mile
    c.  7.5 cents per mile
    d.  9 cents per mile

_____ 7.  An employer must withhold on group-term life insurance in excess of $50,000 for which of the following taxes?

    a.  Social security and Medicare taxes only
    b.  Social security, Medicare and federal income taxes
    c.  Social security, Medicare and FUTA taxes
    d.  Social security, Medicare, federal income, and FUTA taxes

_____ 8.  Which of the following conditions need not be met for job-related educational assistance to be excluded from income?

    a.  Courses are not taken to qualify the employee for a promotion or transfer
    b.  Courses must be related to the employee's current job
    c.  Must be covered by an Educational Assistance Program
    d.  Course must not be necessary to meet the minimum education requirement of the job

_____ 9.  Under the "fixed-date" method for substantiating business travel expenses, an advance can be provided no more than how many days before an expense is incurred?

    a.  10 days
    b.  15 days
    c.  20 days
    d.  30 days

_____ 10.  For what travel expenses may an employer use the high-low per diem rate instead of the individual federal per diem rate of the locality of travel?

    a.  Lodging, not just meals and incidentals, and the travel is within CONUS
    b.  Lodging, meals and incidental expenses, not just meals and incidentals, and the travel is within CONUS
    c.  Meals and incidental expenses, and the travel is outside CONUS
    d.  None of the above

_____ 11.  Which of the following expenses is a deductible moving expense?

    a.  The cost of moving household goods
    b.  Expenses for temporary living quarters in the new location
    c.  The cost of fixing up the employee's old residence for sale
    d.  Pre-move househunting expenses

_____ 12.  David has child and dependent care expenses of $6,500 during 2008, and his employer reimburses him in full during the same year.  How much of the reimbursement is taxable to David for 2008?

    a.  $1,500
    b.  $5,000
    c.  $6,500
    d.  None of it is taxable

_____ 13. An employee who regularly earns $400 per week is called to jury duty and is given $150 per week in jury duty pay. The employer makes up the difference between the jury duty pay and the employee's regular pay. What amount is subject to federal income tax withholding and social security, Medicare, and FUTA taxes?

    a. $150
    b. $250
    c. $400
    d. None of the above

_____ 14. All of the following items incurred while on travel are travel expenses EXCEPT:

    a. The cost of meals
    b. The cost of lodging
    c. Transportation costs
    d. Cost of entertaining clients

_____ 15. All of the following expenses incurred while on travel qualify as a travel expense EXCEPT:

    a. Dry cleaning of suit
    b. Gift purchased for a prospective customer
    c. Meals
    d. Tips

_____ 16. All of the following payments are classified as wages subject to federal income tax withholding EXCEPT:

    a. Gift certificates for a local supermarket provided at the end of the year.
    b. Deceased worker's wages paid to the worker's estate or legal representative
    c. Bonuses
    d. Backpay awards

_____ 17. Emma, a sales representative, receives a $1,500 bonus in December 2008 for outstanding performance. The bonus is supplemental wages subject to federal income tax withholding at a flat 25% rate; the social security tax rate is 6.2%; and the Medicare tax rate is 1.45%. Assuming there are no state or local taxes and that Emma has earned $85,000 during the year so far, what is the amount Emma must be paid to guarantee her a net bonus of $1,500.

    a. $2,227.17
    b. $2,096.44
    c. $2,800.76
    d. $2,295.33

## Problems

1. An employee uses a company car 40% for personal use in 2008. The car has a fair market value of $12,000. Using the IRS Annual Lease Value Table, calculate the taxable compensation for the employee's personal use of the car.

2. Tom uses a company car 70% for business purposes each month of 2008. The car has a fair market value of $14,500. Tom drives the car 12,000 miles during 2008. Calculate the value of the personal use of the vehicle using the cents-per-mile method.

## Section 3: Taxable and Nontaxable Compensation

3. Bill was born on March 17, 1969 and earns $35,000 per year. His company provides group-term life insurance coverage at two times each employee's annual salary. Calculate the monthly taxable value of Bill's group-term life insurance coverage for 2008.

4. Assume the same facts as in Problem No. 3, except that Bill's salary increases by $3,000 on May 1, 2008 and at the same time he begins contributing $2 per month in after-tax dollars toward the insurance coverage. Recalculate the monthly taxable value of Bill's group-term life insurance coverage for May - December 2008.

5. You are instructed to issue a bonus to employee Sean in the net amount of $4,500 and to tax it as supplemental wages. The following tax rates apply: FIT - 25%, SIT - 5%, Social Security - 6.2%, Medicare - 1.45%.

   a. Calculate this check if Sean is $15,000 short of reaching the social security wage limit.

   b. Calculate this check if Sean is $1,500 short of reaching the social security wage limit.

6. Joan has been granted a bonus of $6,000 net in 2008. Perform the gross-up for tax purposes. Use 25% for FIT, 3.5% for SIT, 6.2% for social security, and 1.45% for Medicare. The bonus will not put Joan over the social security wage limit. Please determine the amount for the following:

   a. Gross-up
   b. FIT
   c. SIT
   d. Social Security
   e. Medicare
   f. Net check

7. Wilfred accepts a new job in 2008 with the same employer that requires him to move from Chicago, IL to Austin, TX. Wilfred easily meets the distance test for a job-related move, and his employer expects him to work at least 39 weeks in Austin during the next 12 months. Wilfred's employer reimburses him in 2008 for the following expenses for his move from Chicago:

   | | |
   |---|---|
   | Moving, packing, and storage charges | $ 2,800 |
   | Travel expenses during the move (includes $150 for meals) | 1,500 |
   | Pre-move househunting expenses (includes $300 for meals) | 1,400 |
   | Temporary living expenses (includes $400 for meals) | 1,200 |
   | Selling expenses of old residence | 9,700 |
   | Relocation bonus | 4,000 |
   | Total | $20,600 |

   How much of the reimbursement is a nontaxable qualified moving expense reimbursement for Wilfred?

# SECTION 4: HEALTH, ACCIDENT, AND RETIREMENT BENEFITS

## TABLE OF CONTENTS

# SECTION 4: HEALTH, ACCIDENT, AND RETIREMENT BENEFITS

In the previous section, we discussed many of the different ways in which employees are compensated and whether those payments are subject to federal income, social security, Medicare, and FUTA taxes. In this section, we will deal separately with some of the most important benefits offered by employers—health insurance, sick and disability pay, and retirement benefits.

These benefits have become standard at most mid-size and large companies, and have become even more important to employees as health care costs continue to rise and solid retirement plans are needed to supplement social security benefits. The rules governing the tax treatment of these benefits are detailed and complex, and promise to become even more so.

## 4.1 Health Insurance

Most mid-size and large employers provide some type of health or medical insurance for their employees, who consider it one of the most important benefits of their employment (although they are generally required to help pay for it). This section covers contributions to and benefits from health insurance plans that pay or reimburse employees for their medical expenses. Insurance plans designed to replace an employee's salary while he or she is ill or injured are discussed later.

## 4.1-1 Types of Health Insurance Plans

There are several types of health care plans offered by employers to their employees. They can generally be categorized as one of the following:

*Traditional health insurance plans.* Under a traditional health insurance plan, the employer either purchases an insurance policy from a third-party insurance carrier or self-insures and pays claims to employees or health care providers from its own insurance fund. Where the employer buys insurance coverage from a third-party insurance carrier, the employer (or the employer and the employee) pays premiums to the insurer, which then reimburses the employee for medical expenses incurred or makes payments directly to the health care provider (doctor or hospital). Some of the premium costs may be paid to the employer by the employee before the employer pays the third-party insurance carrier. This is a traditional fee-for-service arrangement.

Many mid-size and large employers choose self-insurance rather than purchasing a policy from an insurance company because such plans are less regulated than third-party plans and give the employers more direct control over plan reserves and health care cost containment. In doing so, they pay benefits out of their own insurance funds and either administer the plan themselves or contract with a third-party administrator to do it. Self-insured employers may also purchase "stop-loss" insurance from an insurance carrier to pay claims once the employer has paid out a certain amount in benefits during the year, thus limiting the employer's liability in the event of catastrophic medical expenses. Employers may also limit their liability through participation in "minimum premium plans," which combine third-party insurance and self-insurance. The employer pays a portion of a calculated premium to the insurer to cover administrative costs and the insurer's profit, while placing other funds in an account to cover benefit claims. If the benefit claims exceed the calculated premium, the employer's liability is limited to the amount of the premium. If not, the employer gets to keep the difference.

*Health maintenance organizations (HMOs).* An HMO is a health care system that provides health care but does not directly pay for it, as does a health insurance carrier. The HMO provides these health care services on a prepaid basis with employers contributing to the plan on behalf of employees choosing the HMO option. (Employees also may be required to contribute if contributions are required from employees for non-HMO plans.) While HMOs may be attractive to employees because they generally do not involve deductibles or complex claim forms, they limit members to using HMO doctors and hospitals.

There are two types of health maintenance organizations. Under the traditional scheme, the HMO has its own health care facility or facilities, and patients (e.g., employees and their families) have to go there to receive medical services. The other type of HMO is the Individual Practice Association, under which physicians sign up with a health care group and patients have the option of choosing their own physicians among those in the group, rather than being required to go to the HMO facility and seeing the first available physician.

Another product being offered by many HMOs is the Point-of-Service (POS) plan. The POS option allows covered employees and their dependents to use non-HMO health care providers, with the inclusion of deductibles and insurance copayments. Employees and their dependents must select a primary care physician from the POS network, who acts as a gatekeeper and oversees the delivery of all health care services. But the employee can choose a physician contrary to the primary care physician's recommendation or go initially to a physician outside the network subject to deductibles and reduced levels of reimbursement. Some HMOs also offer "open access" POS plans, which do not require an employee to choose a primary care physician from the POS network.

*Preferred provider organizations (PPOs).* A PPO is a health care delivery system that gives participants a choice of a higher level of benefits and lower out-of-pocket costs if they use doctors who are part of the PPO's "network." If they use nonnetwork providers, the employees' costs, in terms of deductibles and copayments, are significantly higher. Participants may or may not have to choose a "primary care physician," who must approve or authorize all of their health care before the higher level of benefits is provided. Under some PPO plans, employees may have the option of paying a higher premium that reduces the higher nonnetwork deductibles and copayments, which can be attractive to employees who expect to incur a significant amount of nonnetwork expenses during the plan year.

## 4.1-2 Tax Treatment of Contributions and Benefits

**Employer-paid premiums excludable from income.** Generally, contributions made by an employer to an accident or health insurance plan providing insurance for its employees and their spouses and dependents are not wages and are not subject to federal income tax withholding or social security, Medicare, and federal unemployment (FUTA) taxes.[1] On the other hand, contributions made by employees from their wages for health insurance must be included in their income for income tax withholding and employment tax purposes unless the contributions are made through a valid salary reduction plan under IRC §125 (see the discussion of cafeteria plans at Section 4.5).

 **DEPENDENT DEFINITION WILL STAY THE SAME**[2] In 2004, the American Jobs Creation Act amended the definition of dependent under IRC §152 to promote uniformity in applying the definition. In doing so, however, the new definition would have made employer-provided health insurance taxable for employees in certain situations where a dependent under the prior definition would not be a dependent under the new definition (e.g., a 24-year-old graduate student earning more than the annual exemption amount whose parents pay more than half of his or her support). The IRS said that this is not what Congress intended and announced that its regulations would be amended to make sure that the prior definition of dependent continues to apply in this area.

The rules are not so clear when an employer (without a §125 plan) gives its employees a choice whether to receive a portion of their compensation as wages or have the amount paid by the employer to a health insurance carrier to cover premiums. The IRS's position is that such amounts must be included in the employees'

---

1.   IRC §106(a); IRS Reg. §1.106-1.
2.   IRS Notice 2004-79, 2004-49 IRB 898.

income and are subject to federal income tax withholding and social security, Medicare and FUTA taxes no matter what choice is made. A federal district court, however, said such salary reduction amounts are not included in income because there is no basis for distinguishing between amounts paid by an employer above and beyond an employee's salary for health insurance and amounts paid pursuant to a salary reduction plan.[3]

The IRS has also ruled that, where an employer reduces its employees' salaries, uses those amounts to pay for health insurance premiums, and then reimburses the employees for the amount of the salary reduction, the reimbursements are not excluded from income.[4]

Where an employer's plan would allow the employer to convert a retired employee's unused sick time into a cash equivalent that the employer would then use to purchase additional medical insurance coverage for the retiree, the amount converted would not be income to the retired employee, according to the IRS.[5]

However, where the employee has the option to receive a portion of accumulated sick leave as a cash payment or to apply it to continued participation in the employer's health plan, the contribution cannot be excluded from gross income under §106 because the contribution is considered an employee contribution.[6]

**Insurance benefits excludable from income.** Benefits received by an employee under an accident or health insurance plan that directly or indirectly reimburses the employee for medical expenses incurred by the employee and his or her spouse and dependents (by paying the employee or the medical care provider) are also not included in the employee's income. To qualify for this exclusion, the employee's expenses must be for medical care, defined by the Internal Revenue Code as "the diagnosis, cure, mitigation, treatment, or prevention of disease, or for the purpose of affecting any structure or function of the body."[7]

The IRS said that the definition of "medical care" for purposes of determining whether a reimbursement for employee medical expenses is excludable from income is somewhat broader than the definition for purposes of calculating the itemized deduction for medical expenses on an individual's personal tax return. Therefore, the IRS ruled that employer reimbursements of employee expenses for nonprescription drugs, either directly through a health insurance plan or indirectly through a health flexible spending account (FSA, see Section 4.5-7) or health reimbursement arrangement (HRA, see Section 4.1-6), are excludable from the employee's income. The IRS distinguished an earlier ruling in which it had concluded that expenses incurred for nonprescription drugs did not qualify as deductible medical expenses.[8]

In other rulings, the IRS ruled that the following procedures and equipment qualify as medical care under IRC §213(d)(1):

- radial keratotomy surgery to improve eyesight;[9]
- participation in a weight-loss program as treatment for a specific disease diagnosed by a physician, including obesity;[10]
- breast reconstruction surgery after a mastectomy as a treatment for cancer;[11]
- laser eye surgery to correct myopia;
- bandages to cover torn skin on an injured leg and crutches to enhance mobility while the leg heals;[12]
- blood sugar test kit for a diabetic to monitor blood sugar levels;
- annual physical exam performed by a physician;

---

3. PLR 9406002; Express Oil Change, Inc. v. U.S., 25 F.Supp.2d 1313 (ND Ala, 1996); aff'd 162 F.3d 1290 (11 CA, 1998).
4. Rev. Rul. 2002-3, 2002-3 IRB 316; Rev. Rul. 2002-80, 2002-49 IRB 925.
5. LTR 200222019, 2-27-02.
6. LTR 200704005, 1-26-07.
7. IRC §105; §213(d)(1).
8. Rev. Rul. 2003-102, 2003-38 IRB 559, distinguishing Rev. Rul. 2003-58, 2003-22 IRB 959; IR-2003-108, 9-3-03.
9. LTR 200226003, 3-7-02
10. Rev. Rul. 2002-19, 2002-16 IRB 779.
11. Rev. Rul. 2003-57, 2003-22 IRB 959.
12. Rev. Rul. 2003-58, 2003-22 IRB 959.

- full-body electronic scan performed by a technician at a clinic; and
- pregnancy test kit used to determine whether an individual is pregnant.[13]

The IRS has also ruled that the cost of tuition for a medically handicapped child to attend a school with a program designed "to enable [the child] to compensate for and overcome her diagnosed medical conditions" was a medical expense under §213.[14]

The following procedures and items do not qualify as medical care, according to the IRS:

- teeth-whitening procedure performed by a dentist to whiten teeth discolored by age;
- dietary supplements, such as vitamins, that are purchased to improve general good health; and
- diet foods purchased as part of a weight-loss program, which substitute for other food that would normally be consumed to satisfy normal nutritional requirements.

 **PLASTIC SURGERY, SEX CHANGE OPERATIONS ARE NOT MEDICAL CARE** The exclusion for medical care expenses does not apply to plastic or "cosmetic" surgery that is designed to improve a person's appearance without promoting the proper function of the body or preventing or treating an illness or disease. There are exceptions where the surgery is needed to correct a deformity, treat a disfiguring disease, or heal a personal injury suffered during an accident or other trauma.[15] Relying on the same statutory language, the IRS ruled that the costs associated with "gender reassignment surgery" also do not qualify as deductible medical expenses under IRC §213(d)(9).[16]

The exclusion for reimbursed medical care expenses applies only up to the amount actually spent or incurred by the employee. Any reimbursements in excess of that amount are taxable income to the employee. Any amounts reimbursed for an employee's expenses incurred before the plan initially takes effect must be included in the employee's income.[17]

**Social security, Medicare, and FUTA requirements.** To exclude employer contributions from employment taxes (social security, Medicare, and FUTA), the payments must be made under a plan. A plan can be shown by one of the following:

1. the plan is written or is otherwise made known to employees;

2. the plan is referred to in an employment contract (e.g., collective bargaining agreement) involving the employees;

3. employees contribute to the plan;

4. employer contributions are made to a fund that is separate from the employer's salary account; or

5. the employer is required to make the contributions.[18]

Once the existence of a plan is established, the social security, Medicare, and FUTA tax exclusion for employer contributions will apply if the plan is set up to benefit employees and their dependents. Payments to the plan by an employer will not be excluded if the plan benefits dependents only.[19]

---

13.  Rev. Rul. 2007-72, 2007-50 IRB 1154.
14.  LTR 200729019, 4-10-07.
15.  IRC §213(d)(9).
16.  ILM 200603025, 10-14-05.
17.  Rev. Rul. 2002-58, 2002-38 IRB 541.
18.  Social Security Handbook, §1311; §1312.
19.  IRC §3121(a)(2); §3306(b)(2); IRS Reg. §31.3121(a)(2)-1; §31.3306(b)(2)-1.

**Living together is not enough.**[20]  Health insurance plan contributions and benefits are not excluded from income if made or received on behalf of an employee's "life partner," "nonspouse cohabitant," or domestic partner unless that person is recognized as a spouse under state law.  If the employee's domestic partner is of the same sex as the employee, the partner does not qualify as the employee's spouse for federal tax purposes, regardless of state law.  The partner may qualify as a dependent of the employee if the partner receives more than half of his or her support from the employee, lives with the employee, and the relationship does not violate local law.[21]

 **WHAT ABOUT THE STATES?**  In 2000, Vermont enacted a state law allowing same-sex couples to enter into a "civil union" that provides all the same state benefits that are provided to a married couple.  Health insurance premiums paid by an employer to cover an employee's civil union partner are not taxable to the employee for state purposes in Vermont, but remain subject to federal income, social security, and Medicare taxes.  Other states where "domestic partner benefits" are not subject to state income tax include California, Connecticut, District of Columbia, Massachusetts, New Hampshire, New Jersey, Oregon, and Washington.

**Employer-paid physical exams.**  The fair market value of a physical examination that is paid for by the employer is not excluded from income as a working condition fringe benefit (see Section 3.2-1), but it is excluded as an employer-paid medical care expense.[22]

**Nondiscrimination requirements.**[23]  Where an employer provides health insurance for its employees through a third-party insurance company, there are no nondiscrimination requirements.  The plan may be tailored to favor highly compensated employees or to benefit only them without losing the exclusion for employer contributions and reimbursements.

However, an employer that is self-insured and reimburses its employees' medical expenses from its own funds may not discriminate in favor of highly compensated employees, in terms of either benefits or eligibility.  This is true whether the employer administers the plan itself or pays a third party to administer it, since the insurance risk is not shifted to the administrator.  If the plan is discriminatory, amounts paid to highly compensated employees must be included in their income.

For purposes of this nondiscrimination test, highly compensated employees include:

- the 5 highest-paid officers;
- an owner of more than 10% of the employer's stock; and
- the top-paid 25% of employees.

In order to be nondiscriminatory in terms of eligibility, the self-insured plan must benefit:

- at least 70% of all employees;
- at least 80% of all employees who are eligible to participate in the plan (if at least 70% of all employees are eligible to participate); or
- a classification of employees that the Secretary of the Treasury finds not to be discriminatory.

In terms of benefits, a self-insured plan is nondiscriminatory if all the benefits provided to highly compensated employees are provided for all other participating employees.  Plans may have limits on benefits, but they must be uniform for all participants when based on employer contributions and must not be proportionately based on employee compensation.

If the plan is discriminatory, only those reimbursements and benefits that discriminate in favor of highly compensated employees are taxable, and only to the highly compensated employees receiving them.

---

20.  PLR 9034048, 5-29-90; LTR 9603011, 10-18-95.
21.  LTR 9850011, 12-11-98; LTR 200108010, 11-17-00.
22.  IRS Reg. §1.105-11(g); §1.132-5(a); PLR 9040051, 7-10-90.
23.  IRC §105(h); IRS Reg. §1.105-11.

Other participants receive their benefits tax-free. The determination of the taxable amount depends on where the discrimination occurred.

If a highly compensated employee receives a reimbursement or benefit other participants are not entitled to or that otherwise discriminates in favor of the highly compensated employee, the full value is taxable to the employee. If the plan is discriminatory in terms of eligibility, the taxable amount of reimbursements received by a highly compensated employee is determined by the following formula:

$$\text{taxable amount} = \text{amount paid to HCE} \times \frac{\text{all amounts paid to HCEs}}{\text{all amounts paid to employees}}$$

Benefits that are included in highly compensated employees' income because they are not provided to non-highly compensated employees are not taken into account when using this formula.

> ***Example***: Green Food, Inc. (GFI) has a self-insured medical plan. Only the 5 highest paid officers are eligible for dental benefits, and the plan otherwise fails the eligibility test for nondiscrimination regarding its other benefits. During 2008, employee Anne is one of the 5 highest paid officers and she receives $300 in dental benefits. The other 4 receive a total of $700 in dental benefits. In addition, Anne was reimbursed for $4,500 of medical expenses, a benefit that was available to all participants in the discriminatory plan. GFI's medical plan paid out a total of $51,000 in medical and dental benefits to all employees in 2008, including $31,000 to the 5 highest paid officers.
>
> For 2008, because dental benefits are available only to the 5 highest paid officers, Anne received a taxable dental benefit of $300. In computing the amount of Anne's medical benefit that is taxable, the dental benefits paid by the plan are excluded since they are not available to nonhighly compensated employees. Therefore, her taxable income is calculated as follows:
>
> $$\text{medical taxable amount} = \$4{,}500 \times \frac{\$31{,}000 - (\$300 + \$700)}{\$51{,}000 - (\$300 + \$700)}$$
>
> $$\text{medical taxable amount} = \$4{,}500 \times .6$$
>
> $$\text{medical taxable amount} = \$2{,}700$$
>
> $$\text{medical and dental taxable amount} = \$2{,}700 + \$300 = \$3{,}000$$

Although these discriminatory reimbursements are taxable income to the highly compensated employees receiving them, they are not subject to federal income tax withholding or social security, Medicare, and FUTA taxes.[24]

**Reimbursements that exceed expenses.** For health insurance plans involving a third-party insurer, as well as for nondiscriminatory self-insured plans, reimbursements for employees' medical expenses are not included in income up to the amount of those expenses. Any amounts reimbursed in excess of expenses are considered income to the extent they can be linked to employer-paid premiums. If the employee pays the premiums with after-tax dollars, payments from the plan are tax-free.

**Payments for loss of a limb or disfigurement.** Payments received by employees or their dependents under an employer-financed accidental death and dismemberment plan (usually part of a life insurance plan) for the permanent loss or loss of use of a body part or function or for permanent disfigurement are not included in the employees' income. The payments must not be related to time lost from work, only to the permanent loss or disfigurement.[25]

---

24. IRC §3121(a)(2)(B), (a)(4); §3306(b)(2)(B), (b)(4); §3401(a)(20); IRS Reg. §31.3121(a)(2)-1(a)(3); §31.3306(b)(2)-1(a)(3); §31.3401(a)(19)-1.
25. IRC §105(c); IRS Reg. §1.105-3.

## 4.1-3 Medical Savings Accounts

The Health Insurance Portability and Accountability Act of 1996 established a pilot project that allows employees of small employers who are covered by an employer-sponsored high deductible health insurance plan to make tax deductible contributions to a Medical Savings Account (MSA) or to have the employer make contributions on the employee's behalf that are not included in the employee's income. In 2000, these accounts were renamed "Archer MSAs."

**Covered employers.**[26] Employers are eligible to provide MSAs for their employees if they employed no more than 50 employees during either of the two preceding calendar years. Employers that were not in existence during the full second preceding year do not count that year, and employers that were not in existence for the full preceding year determine their coverage based on the average number of employees the employer reasonably expects to employ in the current year.

If a small employer ceases to be a small employer because it exceeds the 50-employee limit in the preceding and second preceding year, the employer and its employees can continue to establish MSAs and contribute to them (this is true for new employees and those who did not have an MSA before) through the year following the first year in which the employer has more than 200 employees. Thereafter, only employees who already have MSAs can contribute to them or have the employer contribute on their behalf.

**Eligible employees and qualifying health plans.**[27] In order to be eligible to make contributions to an MSA (or to have the employer make contributions on his or her behalf), the employee must be covered only by a high deductible health insurance plan, with certain limited exceptions. An eligible employee can have additional coverage for accidents, disability, dental care, vision care, long-term care, insurance for a specified disease or illness, or insurance that pays a fixed amount for a period of hospitalization.

For 2008, a high deductible health plan is a plan with an annual deductible of $1,950-$2,900 for individual coverage and $3,850-$5,800 for family coverage (i.e., anything other than individual coverage). For family coverage, the plan must provide that no benefits are payable, no matter which family member incurs expenses, until the family as a whole incurs medical expenses exceeding $3850. Maximum out-of-pocket expenses can be no more than $3,850 for individual coverage and $7,050 for family coverage. Out-of-pocket expenses include deductibles, co-payments, and other amounts the employee must pay for covered benefits, but not premiums. These amounts are indexed for inflation to the nearest multiple of $50.

**Tax treatment of and limitations on contributions to an MSA.**[28] Contributions to an MSA can be made either by the employee or the employer, but not both. Employee contributions to an MSA are deductible from income and employer contributions are excludable from income and not subject to federal income tax withholding or social security, Medicare or FUTA tax, with certain limitations. The deduction cannot exceed the employee's compensation received from the employer sponsoring the high deductible health plan. The maximum annual contribution that can be made to an MSA by an employee or an employer is 65% of the plan deductible for individual coverage and 75% of the plan deductible for family coverage. The contribution limit is determined separately for each month, based on the employee's status and coverage as of the first day of the month. Employer contributions in excess of the maximum are included in income. The exclusion from income for employer contributions does not apply if the health plan is provided by the employer for an individual who has elected coverage under COBRA (see Section 4.1-5).

*Example*: Employee Gwen has individual coverage in 2008 under a high deductible health plan with an annual deductible of $2,000. The annual MSA contribution limit is $1,300 (65% of $2,000) and the monthly contribution limit is $108.33 ($1,300 ÷ 12). If Gwen is eligible under the plan for only the first 9 months of the year, the contribution limit for 2008 is $975 (9 x $108.33).

---

26.    IRC §220(c)(4).

27.    IRC §220(c)(1), (c)(2), (c)(5), (g); Rev. Rul. 97-20, 1997-1 CB 77.

28.    RC §106(b); §220(b); §3121(a)(5); §3306(b)(17); §3401(a)(21).

If the employer contributes to its employees' MSAs, it must contribute the same amount for each employee, based on either the dollar amount or the percentage of the applicable deductible.[29] This rule is applied separately to part-time employees covered by the plan (i.e., employees who customarily work less than 30 hours per week). Employers that fail to comply with this "comparability rule" for a certain period face an excise tax penalty equal to 35% of the total amount contributed by the employer to MSAs during that period. If the employer has reasonable cause for failing to comply, the IRS may waive part or all of the penalty if it feels the full penalty would be excessive.

> *Example:* Fly By Night Airlines (FBNA) maintains two high deductible health plans. Plan A has a deductible of $2,000 for single coverage and $4,000 for family coverage, while Plan B has a deductible of $2,200 for single coverage and $4,400 for family coverage. FBNA contributes $1,000 for single coverage and $1,600 for family coverage for its full-time employees in Plan A. To comply with the comparability rule, FBNA would have to offer its full-time employees in Plan B either the same dollar contributions (i.e., $1,000 for single coverage and $1,600 for family coverage) or an equal percentage contribution of $1,100 for single coverage ($1,000 ÷ $2,000 = $1,100 ÷ $2,200) and $1,760 for family coverage ($1,600 ÷ $4,000 = $1,760 ÷ $4,400). FBNA could make different or no contributions for its part-time employees who are covered under either plan.

While the annual contribution limit is determined using monthly data, the employer's contribution for the year can be made in one or more payments during the year. Contributions to an MSA must be made in cash, and not in the form or stock or other personal property.[30]

**MSAs cannot be part of a cafeteria plan**. Employers can provide a high deductible health plan as part of a cafeteria plan, and it can be used in conjunction with an MSA. However, the MSA must be established outside the cafeteria plan, because a cafeteria plan is not permitted to provide for contributions to an MSA. Outside of the cafeteria plan context, an employee will not be subject to taxation merely because the employee has a choice between employer contributions to an MSA and other employer-provided accident or health coverage.[31]

**Tax treatment of earnings and distributions**.[32] Earnings on amounts in an MSA are not included in income until there is a distribution of those earnings. Distributions from an MSA are excluded from income if they are for medical expenses incurred by the employee or his or her dependents and are included in income if used for any other purpose. The person for whom the expenses are incurred must be covered by the high deductible health plan and must not have other coverage that would make the individual ineligible for an MSA Distributions that are included in income are subject to an additional 15% tax unless made after age 65, disability, or death.

Covered medical expenses are generally the same as those described in Section 4.1-2, in the discussion of employer-paid health insurance, but they do not include premiums for insurance other than long-term care insurance, premiums for health care continuation coverage under COBRA, or premiums for health care coverage while an individual receives unemployment insurance benefits.[33] MSA trustees or custodians are not required to determine whether MSA distributions are used for medical expenses. The MSA account holder should make that determination.

**Information reporting requirements**. Employer contributions to an employee's MSA must be reported in Box 12 of the employee's Form W-2, *Wage and Tax Statement* (see Section 8.8-3), preceded by Code "R." The employee must also report such contributions on his or her personal income tax return. Employee contributions to a medical savings account are subject to federal income tax withholding and social security and Medicare taxes, and must be reported as such in Boxes 1, 3, and 5 of Form W-2. The employee can take a deduction for the contributions on his or her personal income tax return, subject to the limitations discussed

---

29.   IRC §4980E.
30.   IRC §106(b)(3); IRS Notice 96-53, 1996-2 CB 219.
31.   IRC §125(f); IRS Notice 96-53, 1996-2 CB 219.
32.   IRC §220(e), (f).
33.   IRC §220(d)(2).

earlier. Plan trustees must report distributions from an MSA on Form 1099-SA, *Distributions From an HSA, Archer MSA, or Medicare Advantage MSA* (see Appendix page A-287). They must report contributions to an MSA on Form 5498-SA, *HSA, Archer MSA or Medicare Advantage MSA Information* (see Appendix page A-352).

**Length of pilot project**.[34] MSAs are authorized as a pilot project that will expire on December 31, 2007. The ability to establish MSAs would have ended sooner if the number of individuals contributing to an MSA exceeds certain limits, but this did not happen, and 2006 is not a cut-off year. After the pilot project ends, eligible individuals who made or received MSA contributions can continue to do so while they are eligible, and distributions from MSAs can continue to be made. Also, employees can establish MSAs after the end of the project if their employer has a high deductible health plan and other employees have already established MSAs under it. If the statutory limits are reached early, the IRS will make an announcement by October 1 of the relevant year stating the applicable cut-off date. MSA trustees and custodians must report by August 1 of each year the number of MSAs established by July 1 of that year. The number of MSAs established must be reported on Form 8851, *Summary of Medical Savings Accounts*.

## 4.1-4 Long-Term Care Insurance

Under the Health Insurance Portability and Accountability Act of 1996, long-term care insurance contracts are generally treated as accident and health insurance contracts.[35] Therefore, amounts received under such contracts are excluded from income as amounts received for personal injuries and sickness and reimbursements for medical expenses. If the contract makes per diem payments (i.e., a certain amount of coverage is paid for each day of care); the excludible amount will be capped at $270 per day in 2008 (indexed for inflation), although excess amounts will be excluded to the extent of the actual cost of care.

Employer-provided coverage under a long-term care insurance contract is excluded from income to the same extent as employer-provided accident and health insurance coverage, but there are several restrictions:

- Long-term care coverage is not subject to the COBRA health care continuation requirements (see Section 4.1-5);[36]
- Long-term care coverage is not a qualified benefit that can be offered as part of a cafeteria plan under IRC §125 (see Section 4.5-1);[37] and
- Long-term care coverage that is provided as part of a flexible spending arrangement is included in the employee's income (see Section 4.5-7).[38]

To qualify, a long-term care insurance contract must provide only for coverage of qualified long-term care services, such as necessary diagnostic, preventive, treating, mitigating, and rehabilitative services, plus maintenance or personal care services that are required by a chronically ill individual.[39] The services must be provided under a plan of care prescribed by a licensed health care practitioner. A chronically ill individual is someone who is unable to perform at least 2 activities of daily living (e.g., eating, toileting, bathing, dressing, continence, transferring) or has a severe cognitive impairment requiring substantial supervision.

## 4.1-5 COBRA Health Insurance Continuation

The Consolidated Omnibus Budget Reconciliation Act of 1985 requires health plan sponsors to provide employees and their beneficiaries with the opportunity to elect continued group health coverage for a given time period should their coverage be lost due to certain "qualifying events."[40] The requirements apply to

---

34. IRC §220(i), (j); IRS Notice 96-53, 1996-2 CB 219.
35. IRC §7702B(a), (d).
36. IRC §4980B(g).
37. IRC §125(f).
38. IRC §106(c).
39. IRC §7702B(c); IRS Notice 97-31, 1997-21 IRB 5.
40. IRC §4980B; IRS Reg. §54.4980B-1—§54.4980B-10.

employers with 20 or more employees on a typical business day (part-time employees must be converted to full-time equivalents for this determination). The time period for continued group coverage is generally 18 or 36 months depending on the qualifying event, and an option to switch to individual coverage must be provided before the continued group coverage expires.

**Type of coverage required.** The continuation coverage must be the same as that provided to similarly situated beneficiaries (i.e., employees, spouses, and dependents) under the health insurance plan who have not suffered a qualifying event. If such coverage is changed in any way during the continuation period for the similarly situated beneficiaries, the changes must also be applied to beneficiaries receiving continuation coverage.

 **WHAT ABOUT CAFETERIA PLANS?** Employees who have opted to purchase health care coverage under an employer's cafeteria plan, including flexible spending arrangements (see Section 4.5), are eligible for COBRA continuation coverage at the level of coverage they are receiving at the time of a qualifying event.

**Qualified beneficiaries entitled to coverage.** The term "qualified beneficiary" means the spouse and/or dependents of an employee covered by the plan on the day before a qualifying event occurs as well as children born to or adopted by the covered employee during the period of continuation coverage. The term also includes the employee if the qualifying event causing a loss of coverage is the employee's termination or a reduction in hours worked.

**Qualifying events.** A qualifying event is any of the following that would result in the loss of group health insurance coverage (which includes increased premiums caused by the event) for a qualified beneficiary:

- death of the covered employee;
- the covered employee's termination of employment (for reasons other than gross misconduct) or reduction in hours worked;
- divorce or separation of the covered employee;
- entitlement of the covered employee to Medicare benefits (upon enrolling in the program);
- a dependent child losing that status; and
- bankruptcy proceedings that cause a retired covered employee or the employee's dependents to lose coverage.

The IRS clarified that, where an employee eliminates the health coverage of a spouse after a divorce decree has been issued but before the date of the divorce, the COBRA qualifying event occurs on the date of the divorce, and the group health plan must make continuation coverage available as of that date.[41]

**Period of coverage.** The following maximum periods of continuation coverage apply once group coverage would have been lost because of a qualifying event:

- where the qualifying event is the employee's termination or reduction in work hours—18 months (24 months if the reason for absence from employment is the employee's military service);[42] but if another qualifying event occurs during the 18-month period (other than the commencement of bankruptcy proceedings), the period is extended to 36 months;
- where the qualifying event is the employer's bankruptcy—the life of the retiree or the retiree's spouse; but once the retiree dies, the period of continuation coverage for the retiree's spouse and children is 36 months from the retiree's death;
- where the qualifying event is the employee's termination or reduction in work hours and a qualified beneficiary (employee or dependent) is disabled under the Social Security Act at any time during the first 60 days of continued coverage—29 months for all qualified beneficiaries entitled to continued coverage because of the same qualifying event (36 months if another qualifying event (other than bankruptcy) occurs during the 29-month period);

---

41. Rev. Rul. 2002-88, 2002-52 IRB 995.
42. 38 USC §4317(a)(1)(A).

- where the qualifying event is the covered employee's death, divorce, separation, or entitlement to Medicare, or a dependent child's loss of dependent child status—36 months.

Continuation coverage ends before these maximum coverage periods are reached if:

- the employer ceases to provide group health coverage to its employees;
- the required premium for the continuation coverage is not paid within 30 days of the due date;
- the qualified beneficiary becomes covered under any other group health plan which does not impose pre-existing condition restrictions on the beneficiary (unless the restriction does not apply to the beneficiary or the beneficiary satisfies the conditions of the restriction); or
- the qualified beneficiary becomes entitled to Medicare benefits, unless the employer's bankruptcy is the qualifying event.

For children born to or adopted by the covered employee during the period of continued coverage, their period of coverage ends at the same time as for other family members.

The U.S. Supreme Court ruled that COBRA coverage could not be denied to an otherwise eligible employee or family member because he or she is already covered under another group health plan when the COBRA election is made (e.g., a terminated employee who is covered under his spouse's health plan). The Court said the language allowing COBRA coverage to be cut off if an employee becomes covered under another plan after COBRA coverage is elected cannot be used to deny COBRA coverage before an election has been made. The IRS adopted this conclusion in its COBRA regulations.[43]

**Premium requirements.** The group health plan can require the employee or other qualified beneficiary to pay a premium for the continuation coverage of up to 102% of the group premium paid for similar coverage under the plan by the employer and its employees. The individual can choose to pay the premiums in monthly installments. The maximum premium increases to 150% for disabled qualified beneficiaries after the 18th month of their continuation coverage, whether the maximum coverage period becomes 29 or 36 months. The first premium payment may not be required earlier than 45 days after the qualified beneficiary elects continuation coverage (see discussion of elections following).

**Election and notice provisions.** Employees and other qualified beneficiaries who wish to take advantage of continued group health plan coverage must make an election of such coverage. The election period must last for at least 60 days and can begin no earlier than the date on which coverage was terminated because of the qualifying event (which may be later than the date of the qualifying event itself). The election period also cannot end before 60 days after the qualified beneficiary receives notice of the termination of coverage, if the notice was received after the date coverage was terminated.

An election of continuation coverage by an employee or other qualified beneficiary is generally binding on other qualified beneficiaries who would have lost coverage without the election, unless the election specifically provides otherwise. Once continuation coverage is elected, other qualified beneficiaries who are subject to the election may elect a different type of coverage if more than one type is available. The failure to elect continuation coverage, however, does not affect the right of other qualified beneficiaries to elect such coverage.

There are also several notice requirements under COBRA that apply to employers, group health plans, plan administrators, employees, and qualified beneficiaries:[44]

- When an employee and his or her spouse first become covered under a group health plan, the plan must provide a written general notice of the COBRA continuation coverage rights within 90 days after the employee and spouse first become covered under the plan. The information required to be in the notice can be put into the summary plan description (SPD) if the SPD is provided to the employee within the general notice time limit. The general notice can also be provided electronically if delivery meets the standards established under ERISA.

---

43. Geissal v. Moore Medical Corp., 118 S.Ct. 1869 (1998); IRS Reg. §54.4980B-7, Q&A 2.
44. 29 CFR §2590.606-1 to §2590.606-4.

- Where the qualifying event is the employee's death, termination, reduction in hours, or entitlement to Medicare, or the employer's bankruptcy, the employer must notify the plan administrator of the qualifying event within 30 days after the qualifying event occurs or the coverage is lost (unless a multiemployer plan provides a longer period).
- Where the qualifying event is the employee's divorce or separation, or a dependent child's loss of dependent child status, the employee or qualified beneficiary must notify the plan administrator of the qualifying event within 60 days after the qualifying event occurs or the coverage is lost. The 60-day time limit also does not run until the employer has met its requirement to provide a general notice of COBRA continuation coverage rights to the qualified beneficiaries. The plan must establish reasonable procedures for beneficiaries to furnish these notices, and the procedures may require the completion of a specific form if the form is easily accessible at no cost. If no such procedures are provided, notice is deemed to have been provided if information identifying the qualifying event is provided to someone who usually handles employee benefit matters.
- Where a qualified beneficiary is determined to have been disabled under the Social Security Act at the time of the employee's termination or reduction in hours, any qualified beneficiary affected by the qualifying event must notify the plan administrator of the determination within 60 days (and before the end of the original 18-month period of continued coverage) and within 30 days of any determination that the qualified beneficiary is no longer disabled.
- Once it becomes aware of a qualifying event, the plan administrator has 14 days to notify qualified beneficiaries of their rights concerning continuation coverage (unless a multiemployer plan provides a longer period), and notification of an employee's spouse serves as notification of dependent children living with the spouse. The notice must contain contact information for plan and COBRA administrators, plus information on how continuation coverage rights can be exercised, premium payment requirements, the consequences of not electing coverage, and possible extensions of the coverage period.

**Penalties for noncompliance.** Employers that fail to comply with the COBRA continuation coverage requirements are subject to a tax of $100 per day of noncompliance for each qualified beneficiary (maximum of $200 per day per family affected by the same qualifying event). The tax will not be imposed if the failure to comply is due to reasonable cause and is corrected within 30 days of when the noncompliance was discovered or should have been discovered.

For unintentional failures which are due to reasonable cause and not willful neglect, the maximum penalty for a single employer plan during a taxable year is the lesser of 10% of the amount paid by the employer for group health plans during the preceding taxable year or $500,000. For multiemployer plans, the maximum penalty is the lesser of 10% of the amount the plan trust paid to obtain medical care during the taxable year or $500,000.

**FMLA/COBRA interaction.** Employers have raised serious questions about the effect on their COBRA obligation to provide continuation coverage caused by the requirements imposed by the Family and Medical Leave Act (FMLA—see Section 4.2). The IRS answered many of these questions in its final COBRA regulations.[45]

*Is there a qualifying event when an employee does not return to work after FMLA leave?* The FMLA leave in itself does not constitute a qualifying event. A qualifying event would occur with respect to a covered employee or qualified beneficiary when the employee does not return to work at the end of the FMLA leave and the employee or beneficiary would therefore lose coverage before the end of the maximum coverage period (generally 18 months).

 **NO PLAN, NO COVERAGE** Even if the above conditions are met, there is no qualifying event if the employer eliminates group health coverage for the class of employees that would have included the covered employee had he or she not taken FMLA leave.

---

45.    IRS Reg. §54.4980B-10.

*When does a qualifying event occur under these circumstances?* If the conditions described above are met, the qualifying event occurs on the last day of FMLA leave, and the maximum continuation coverage period is measured from that date. However, if the plan provides that coverage is lost at a later date and that COBRA continuation coverage does not begin until that later date, the maximum coverage period is also measured from that later date.

> **Example 1:** Employee Jane is covered by Ace Bandaid Co.'s group health plan on January 31. She begins FMLA leave on February 1, and her last day of leave is 12 weeks later on April 25. She does not return to work at the end of her leave and will lose her group health coverage on April 26. Jane experiences a qualifying event on April 25 and the maximum coverage period (18 months) is measured from that date.

> **Example 2:** Employee Peter and his spouse are covered by Pharmaceutical, Inc.'s group health plan on August 15. Peter begins FMLA leave on August 16 and informs Pharmaceutical on September 28 (less than 7 weeks later) that he will not be returning to work. Under FMLA regulations, Peter's last day of FMLA leave is September 28. Peter and his spouse will lose their group health coverage on September 29. They experience a qualifying event on September 28 and the maximum coverage period is measured from that date.

*What happens if the employee does not pay the required premium while on FMLA leave or declines coverage while on leave?* The rules described earlier still apply. A lapse of coverage under a group health plan during FMLA leave is irrelevant in determining whether a qualifying event has occurred.

*Can continuation coverage be conditioned on the repayment of employer-paid premiums by employees who do not return to work after FMLA leave?* Even if recovery of premiums is permitted under FMLA regulations in such circumstances, the right to COBRA continuation coverage cannot be conditioned on the employee's reimbursement of the premiums.

*How do state laws requiring longer family or medical leaves with health coverage affect these rules?* State or local laws that require group health plan coverage to be maintained for a longer period of time than under the FMLA are disregarded for purposes of determining when a qualifying event occurs under COBRA.

# 4.1-6 Health Reimbursement Arrangements

In 2002, the IRS issued guidance describing a new type of employer-provided health benefit referred to as a health reimbursement arrangement (HRA) and providing illustrative guidance on administering this benefit.[46]

Generally, an HRA is an arrangement that:

- Is paid for solely by the employer and not provided pursuant to a salary reduction election or under a §125 cafeteria plan;
- Reimburses the employee for medical care expenses incurred by the employee and the employee's spouse and dependents; and
- Provides reimbursements up to a maximum dollar amount for a coverage period, with any unused portion of the maximum dollar amount at the end of the coverage period carried forward to increase the maximum reimbursement amount in subsequent coverage periods.

**Benefits under an HRA.** Coverage and reimbursements of medical care expenses of an employee and the employee's spouse and dependents under an HRA are generally excluded from the employee's gross income. To qualify for exclusion:

---

46.     IRS Notice 2002-45, 2002-28 IRB 93; Rev. Rul. 2002-41, 2002-28 IRB 75; IRS Notice 2006-69, 2006-31 IRB 107.

- An HRA may only reimburse expenses for medical care as defined in IRC §213(d). (See section 4.1-2 for information on the definition of "medical care.")
- Each medical care expense submitted for reimbursement must be substantiated. The employee must provide substantiation from an independent third party verifying the expenses, or a third party can provide substantiation directly to the employer (e.g., an insurance carrier provides an explanation of benefits). If an HRA allows an employee to self-certify or self-substantiate medical expenses or copayments, then all reimbursements made under the HRA for any employee are included in the employees' income.
- An HRA may not reimburse a medical care expense attributable to a medical expense deduction for a prior taxable year, or that is incurred before the date the HRA is in existence, or that is incurred before the employee is first enrolled in the HRA.

Note that no person may have the right to receive cash or any benefit under the arrangement other than the reimbursement of medical care expenses. If any person has such a right currently or for any future year, then all distributions to all persons under the arrangement in the current tax year are included in gross income, even amounts paid to reimburse medical care expenses.

The IRS further explained this principle in a revenue ruling using the following examples:[47]

*Example:* If an HRA provides for a cash payment equal to all or a portion of the unused reimbursement amount available at the end of the plan year or upon termination of employment, if earlier, then no amounts paid under the plan are considered reimbursements for medical care expenses or excludable from income.

*Example:* If an HRA pays a death benefit of all or a portion of the unused reimbursement amount without regard to medical care expenses, then no amounts paid under the arrangement are considered to be reimbursements for medical care expenses or excludable from income.

*Example:* An employer adopted an "option plan" that was supposedly separate from its HRA. Employees who elected to participate in the option plan before the beginning of the plan year would forfeit any unreimbursed amounts in the employee's HRA at the end of the plan year, but they could elect to transfer all or a portion of the forfeited amount to one of several retirement plans or take it as a cash payment. Employees who didn't elect to participate in the option plan would have their unreimbursed amounts carried forward to use in future plan years. The option plan converts unreimbursed amounts to cash or other benefits without regard to medical care expenses, and the option plan and the HRA constitute one plan despite the employer's efforts to separate them. Therefore, no amounts paid under the HRA or the option plan to any person are considered reimbursements for medical care expenses or excludable from income.

Note also that arrangements formally outside the HRA that provide for an adjustment of an employee's compensation will be considered in determining whether the arrangement is an HRA and whether the amounts are eligible for exclusion.

*Example:* If, in the year an employee retires, an employee receives a bonus in an amount related to that employee's maximum reimbursement amount remaining in an HRA at the time of retirement, or if an employer provides severance pay only to employees who have reimbursement amounts remaining in an HRA at the time of termination of employment, then no amounts paid under the arrangement are considered to be reimbursements for medical care expenses.

**Coverage under an HRA.** Medical care expense reimbursements under an HRA are excluded from the employee's gross income if the reimbursements are provided to current and former employees (including retired employees), their spouses and dependents, and the spouses and dependents of deceased employees. An HRA may continue to reimburse former employees or retired employees for medical care expenses after termination of employment or retirement (even if the employee does not elect COBRA continuation coverage). For example, an HRA:

---

47. Rev. Rul. 2005-24, 2005-16 IRB 892.

- May have a provision that reimburses a former employee for medical care expenses only up to an amount equal to the unused reimbursement amount remaining at termination or retirement.
- May provide that the maximum reimbursement amount available after retirement or other termination of employment is reduced for any administrative costs of continuing such coverage.
- May or may not provide for an increase in the amount available for reimbursement of medical care expenses after the employee retires or otherwise terminates employment.

*Payments to beneficiaries other than employee's spouse and dependents.*[48] In 2006, the IRS ruled that amounts paid to an employee or any other person under an HRA are not excludable from the employee's income if the plan permits amounts to be paid as medical benefits to a designated beneficiary other than the employee's spouse or dependents. The effective date of the ruling (August 14, 2006) is delayed until 2009 for HRA provisions created before August 14, 2006 that allow qualified medical expenses of a beneficiary other than the employee's spouse or dependents to be reimbursed after the death of the employee and any surviving spouse and dependents.

**Reimbursements can be paid with debit, credit cards.**[49] In 2003 and 2006, the IRS issued guidance on the use of debit and credit cards to make it easier for employers to reimburse employee medical expenses under an HRA. Using several factual scenarios, the IRS said that the following elements would help ensure that the reimbursements are excludable from the employees' income.

*Enrollment procedures.*
- Employees issued a debit or credit card certify on enrollment in the HRA (and each plan year after that) that the card will only be used for eligible medical care expenses, that any expenses paid for with the card have not been otherwise reimbursed, and that the employee will not seek reimbursement under any other health plan.

- Employees agree to keep documentation for any expense paid with the card (e.g., invoices and receipts).

- The card is only accepted at merchants and service providers authorized by the employer.

- The card is automatically cancelled when the employee terminates employment.

*Substantiation procedures.*
- For copayments, recurring expenses, and purchases with real-time substantiation and verification by a third party, the charge is considered fully substantiated and no further review or submission of a receipt is needed. This rule also applies if the dollar amount of a transaction equals an exact multiple of up to 5 times the dollar amount of the copayment for the specific service. If the plan has multiple copayments for the same service (e.g., prescription drugs), the maximum amount deemed substantiated is 5 times the exact multiple of the highest copayment.

- Where the merchant's system collects information about the items purchased using inventory control information, compares it against a list of items, the purchase of which qualifies as medical expenses, and approves use of the card only for the medical expenses covered under the HRA, the approved amounts are considered substantiated and no further review is necessary. The merchant must request another payment method for non-medical expenses and expenses above the HRA coverage limit. Employers can expand their list of authorized merchants and service providers to those without health care-related merchant category codes if they use the inventory information approval system.

---

48.   Rev. Rul. 2006-36, 2006-26 IRB 353.
49.   Rev. Rul. 2003-43, 2003-21 IRB 935, IRS Notice 2006-69, 2006-31 IRB 107; IRS Notice 2007-2, 2007-2 IRB 254.

**TRANSITION RELIEF FOR CERTAIN MERCHANTS** Through December 31, 2007, super-markets, grocery stores, discount stores, wholesale clubs, mail order vendors, and Web-based vendors were relieved from the inventory information approval system requirement for merchants without health care-related merchant category codes, so long as all medical expense purchases are substantiated and the correction procedures discussed below are put in place. After December 31, 2008, HRA debit and credit cards cannot be used at stores with the "drug stores or pharmacies" merchant category code unless they have an inventory information approval system or at least 90% of their gross receipts during the preceding year consisted of qualified medical expenses.

- In all other cases, the employer requires that merchant or service provider receipts be provided by the employee describing the service or product, date of the service or sale, and the amount of the purchase.

*Correction procedures.*
- Where there has been an improper payment, the employer withholds the amount from the employee's wages (to the extent allowed by law) and denies the employee access to the card until the amount has been repaid.

- If this does not work, the employer treats the improper payment as it would any other business debt.

Where the employer does not require substantiation of all medical expenses, but relies only on reviewing a sampling of a small percentage of reimbursements under a certain threshold, the IRS said that all payments made with a debit or credit card would not be excludable from the employees' income.

**No debit or credit card reporting required.** In general, fees paid by a company for medical services must be reported on Form 1099-MISC if they exceed $600 (see Section 8.12-1). Early in 2003, the IRS provided guidance as to when expense reimbursements under an HRA made through debit or credit cards or other electronic media are excludable from gross income (see Section 4.5-7). In that guidance, the IRS stated that payments made to medical service providers through debit and credit cards must be reported by the employer on Form 1099-MISC.

This ruling got quite a reaction from the business community because of the problems involved in reprogramming systems to make such reporting possible. Therefore, a provision was added to the Medicare reform bill enacted in December 2003 exempting payments for medical care under an HRA from this general reporting requirement.[50] Even though the exemption applied specifically to payments made after December 31, 2002, the IRS later clarified that the reporting requirement in the 2003 revenue ruling would not apply to payments made before January 1, 2003.[51]

**HRAs and cafeteria plans.** Employer contributions to an HRA may not be attributable to salary reduction or provided under a §125 cafeteria plan (see Section 4.5 for more on cafeteria plans). However, an HRA is not considered to be paid pursuant to salary reduction merely because it is provided in conjunction with a cafeteria plan. In such a case, all the facts and circumstances are considered in determining whether the salary reduction is attributable to the HRA. The mere fact that an employee may participate in the HRA only if the employee participates in a specified accident or health plan funded by a salary reduction election does not necessarily mean that the salary reduction is attributable to the HRA. However, if the salary reduction election for a coverage period exceeds the actual cost of the accident or health plan coverage for that period, then the salary reduction is attributable to the HRA.

For any coverage period, for purposes solely of determining whether a salary reduction election exceeds the cost of coverage, the actual cost of the specified accident or health plan coverage for the coverage period may be determined using the rules for determining the applicable COBRA premium (see Section 4.1-5).

---

50.     Pub. L. 108-173, §1203.
51.     IRS Notice 2004-16, 2004-9 IRB 527.

*Example:* Assume that an employer offers an HRA and an employee who participates in the HRA must also participate in the corresponding employee-only or family coverage option in a high-deductible accident and health plan. If the applicable COBRA premium for the high-deductible accident and health coverage would be $2,100 for the employee-only coverage and $4,500 for family coverage if such coverage were offered separately from the HRA, then the annual maximum allowable salary reduction in this case would be $2,100 for employee-only coverage and $4,500 for family coverage in order for the salary reduction to be treated as not attributable to the HRA.

An arrangement is not treated as an HRA if it interacts with a cafeteria plan in such a way as to permit employees to use salary reduction indirectly to fund the HRA. Therefore, where an employee who participates in an HRA has a choice among two or more accident or health plans to be used in conjunction with the HRA (or a choice among various maximum reimbursement amounts credited for a coverage period) and there is a correlation between the maximum reimbursement amount available under the HRA for the coverage period and the amount of salary reduction election for the specified accident and health plan, then the salary reduction is attributed to the HRA even if the amount of salary reduction election is equal to or less than the actual cost of the other accident or health coverage.

*Example:* Assume an employer offers a reimbursement arrangement plus other specified accident or health coverage, with the actual cost for family coverage for the specified accident or health plan being $4,500 and the employee having a choice to reduce salary by $2,500 or $3,500 to fund this coverage. An employee who elects family coverage and $2,500 salary reduction receives a $1,000 maximum reimbursement amount under the reimbursement arrangement for the coverage period, and an employee who elects family coverage and $3,500 salary reduction receives a $2,000 maximum reimbursement amount under the reimbursement arrangement for the coverage period. In this case, although the maximum allowable salary reduction is not exceeded, a portion of the salary reduction is attributed to the reimbursement arrangement because the increase in salary reduction election is related to a larger maximum reimbursement amount in the reimbursement arrangement for the coverage period. This arrangement is not an HRA and is subject to §125.

*Example:* Assume an employer provides a reimbursement arrangement in conjunction with another accident or health plan. Employees participating in the reimbursement arrangement are reimbursed up to $1,000 each year for substantiated medical care expenses, and unused amounts remaining at the end of the year are carried forward for reimbursements in later years. The employee share of the annual premium for the other accident or health plan is $1,500. Employees have a choice either to use amounts in the reimbursement arrangement to pay for the premium for the other accident or health plan or to pay that premium pursuant to a salary reduction election. Under this plan, the reimbursement arrangement does not reimburse any portion of the premium paid by salary reduction. Because an employee may use the reimbursement arrangement to pay a portion of the premium instead of electing to salary reduce, the reimbursement arrangement is indirectly funded pursuant to salary reduction and does not meet the definition of an HRA.

**HRAs and FSAs**. If the amount credited to a reimbursement arrangement is directly or indirectly based on the amount forfeited under a §125 flexible spending account (FSA), then the arrangement will be treated as funded by salary reduction (see Section 4.5-7 for more on FSAs). For purposes of making this determination, facts and circumstances taken into consideration include the manner in which salary reduction is implemented for other accident and health plans offered by the employer. Because an HRA is paid for solely by the employer and not pursuant to salary reduction, the following restrictions on health FSAs under §125 are not applicable to HRAs:

- The prohibition against a benefit that defers compensation by permitting employees to carry over unused elective contributions or plan benefits from one plan year to another plan year;
- The requirement that the maximum amount of reimbursement must be available at all times during the coverage period;
- The mandatory 12-month period of coverage; and
- The limitation that medical expenses reimbursed must be incurred during the period of coverage (except as otherwise provided).

As a result, the maximum reimbursement amount for a coverage period (not including amounts carried forward from previous coverage periods) need not be available at all times during the coverage period. Also, an HRA may specify a coverage period for a reimbursement amount that is less than a year. Although claims incurred during one coverage period may be reimbursed in a later coverage period, an unreimbursed claim may be reimbursed in a later coverage period only if the individual was covered under the HRA when the claim was incurred. Additionally, the maximum reimbursement amount credited under the HRA in the future (not including amounts carried forward from previous coverage periods) may be increased or decreased.

A medical care expense may not be reimbursed from a §125 health FSA if the expense has been reimbursed or is reimbursable under any accident or health plan. Generally, if coverage is provided under both an HRA and a §125 health FSA for the same medical care expenses, amounts available under an HRA must be exhausted before reimbursements may be made from the FSA. However, a §125 health FSA will not violate this rule if coverage is provided under both an HRA and a §125 FSA and the FSA reimburses a medical care expense that is not reimbursable by the HRA. But in no case may an employee be reimbursed for the same medical care expense by both an HRA and a §125 FSA.

Before a §125 health FSA plan year begins, the plan document for the HRA may specify that coverage under the HRA is available only after expenses exceeding the dollar amount of the §125 FSA have been paid.

> *Example:* If an employer sponsors a §125 health FSA and an HRA, both of which provide coverage for the same medical care expenses, and the HRA plan document includes a provision that the HRA is not available for reimbursements of medical care expenses that are covered by the §125 health FSA until after expenses exceeding the dollar amount of the §125 FSA have been paid, then those medical care expenses may be reimbursed first from the §125 health FSA and then from the HRA when the amount available under the §125 FSA is exhausted.

**Nondiscrimination rules applicable to HRAs**. Section 105(h), which sets forth nondiscrimination rules for self-insured medical expense reimbursement plans, also applies to HRAs (see Section 4.1-2).

**COBRA continuation coverage.** An HRA is a group health plan generally subject to the COBRA continuation coverage requirements (see Section 4.1-5). If an individual elects COBRA continuation coverage, an HRA complies with these requirements by providing for the continuation of the maximum reimbursement amount for an individual at the time of the COBRA qualifying event and by increasing that maximum amount at the same time and by the same increment that it is increased for similarly situated non-COBRA beneficiaries (and by decreasing it for claims reimbursed). An HRA complies with the COBRA requirements for calculating the applicable premium if the applicable premium is the same for qualified beneficiaries with different total reimbursement amounts available from the HRA (and otherwise also satisfies the requirements of §4980B).

> *Example:* If the annual additional reimbursement amount credited under an HRA is $1,000 and the maximum reimbursement amount remaining for two similarly situated qualified beneficiaries at the time of their qualifying events is $500 and $5,000, then the applicable premium is the same for each individual.

The plan rules for an HRA may provide for continued reimbursements after a COBRA qualifying event regardless of whether a qualified beneficiary elects continuation coverage.

> *Example:* An HRA might allow reimbursements up to the unused maximum reimbursement amount following termination of employment. In such a situation, an HRA subject to COBRA must still comply with the COBRA continuation coverage requirements.

If a qualified beneficiary elects COBRA continuation coverage in addition to the continued reimbursement amount already available, an HRA complies with the COBRA requirements by increasing the maximum reimbursement amount at the same time and by the same increment that it is increased for similarly situated non-COBRA beneficiaries (and by decreasing it for claims reimbursed).

**Administering an HRA.** *Scenario #1*: An employer sponsors a medical plan for its employees with a $2,000 annual deductible for employee-only coverage and a $4,000 annual deductible for family coverage, except that certain preventive care benefits (e.g., annual physicals and well-baby visits) are covered without regard to the plan's deductible. The medical plan is paid for in part by salary reduction elections under the employer's cafeteria plan; the election form provides that salary reduction elections are used only to pay for the medical plan. To participate in the medical plan, an employee must make a $1,000 annual salary reduction election for employee-only coverage or a $3,500 annual salary reduction election for family coverage.

The employer also sponsors an HRA that reimburses the medical care expenses of all participating employees and their spouses and dependents up to an annual maximum amount that is fixed on January 1 of each year. The HRA is available only to employees who participate in the medical plan. It meets the non-discrimination requirements of §105(h). The HRA is paid for by the employer. Employees do not make any salary reduction election to pay for it. The HRA operates on a calendar year basis. Employees have no right to receive cash or any benefit other than reimbursement for medical care expenses under the HRA.

Expenses reimbursable under the HRA are any medical care expenses that would be covered by the medical plan but for the plan's deductible, limited to expenses that are "usual, customary, and reasonable," or any other similar dollar limitation imposed by the medical plan. Only expenses that are substantiated are reimbursed.

The maximum reimbursement amount for the first year in which an employee participates in the HRA is $1,000 for an employee who has employee-only coverage under the medical plan and $2,000 for an employee who has family coverage under the medical plan. Unused reimbursement amounts from one year are carried forward for use in later years. Therefore, in each year after the first year, the maximum reimbursement amount under the HRA equals $1,000 for an employee who has employee-only coverage under the medical plan and $2,000 for an employee who has family coverage under the medical plan, increased by the unused amount from the previous year. If an employee retires or otherwise terminates employment, any unused reimbursement amount remaining in the HRA is unavailable thereafter.

A qualified beneficiary who elects COBRA continuation coverage may only elect the HRA in conjunction with the medical plan. However, a qualified beneficiary may choose to elect COBRA continuation coverage for only the medical plan. The COBRA applicable premium in that case is $1,800 for employee-only coverage and $4,500 for family coverage.

*Scenario #2*: The facts are the same as in Scenario #1, except that any portion of the maximum reimbursement amount under the HRA that is not applied to reimburse medical care expenses before an employee retires or otherwise terminates employment continues to be available for medical care expenses incurred by the former employee or his/her spouse and dependents. However, the maximum reimbursement amount is not increased unless COBRA continuation coverage is elected.

*IRS analysis:* The HRA in Scenario #1 is an employer-provided accident and health plan used exclusively to reimburse expenses incurred for medical care as defined under §213(d). Under the HRA, no benefits other than reimbursements for medical care expenses are available either in the form of cash or other benefits at any time.

For purposes of determining whether any part of the salary reduction for the medical plan is attributable to the HRA, the applicable premium for COBRA continuation coverage may be used as the actual cost of the medical plan. Here, the actual cost of the medical plan for one year is $1,800 for employee-only coverage and $4,500 for family coverage. The amount of salary reduction election for employee-only coverage ($1,000) is less than $1,800 and the amount of salary reduction election for family coverage ($3,500) is less than $4,500. Also the cafeteria plan election form states that salary reduction elections are used only to pay for the medical plan. Therefore, here the HRA reimbursement amounts are not attributable to the salary reduction contributions made to pay for the medical plan.

In Scenario #2, the employer provides accident and health coverage under the HRA for former employees. This coverage is provided based on the former employee's prior employment relationship with the employer.

The HRA is used to reimburse the former employee only for medical care expenses of the former employee or his/her spouse or dependents. Neither the former employee nor his/her spouse or dependents receive any other benefits from the HRA at any time.

Employer-provided coverage and medical care expense reimbursements made under the HRA that allows unused amounts to be carried forward, as described in Scenarios #1 and #2, are excluded from gross income under §106 and §105, respectively.

# 4.1-7 Health Savings Accounts

In December 2003, President Bush signed into law the Medicare Prescription Drug, Improvement, and Modernization Act of 2003.[52] While most of the public attention on this law focused on the prescription drug benefit it creates for Medicare beneficiaries, the law also creates a new type of tax-favored savings vehicle that is designed to help employees save for medical expenses while they are employed and into retirement.

Effective for taxable years beginning after December 31, 2003, the legislation creates health savings accounts (HSAs). In general, HSAs are tax-exempt trusts or custodial accounts created exclusively to pay for the qualified medical expenses of the account holder and his or her spouse and dependents. They are subject to rules similar to those applicable to IRAs.

**HSAs are for eligible individuals in a high deductible health plan.** HSAs may be established by individuals who are covered by a high deductible health plan (HDHP), which is defined as a plan with an annual deductible of at least $1,100 for 2008 in the case of self-only coverage or $2,200 in the case of family coverage, and that has an out-of-pocket expense limit of no more than $5,600 for 2008 in the case of self-only coverage and $11,200 in the case of family coverage. These amounts are adjusted for inflation annually to the nearest multiple of $50.

In the case of family coverage, a plan is an HDHP only if, under the terms of the plan and without regard to which family member or members incur expenses, no amounts are payable from the HDHP until the family has incurred annual covered medical expenses in excess of the minimum annual deductible. Note that an HDHP can have a smaller deductible or none at all for preventive care (e.g., first dollar coverage for preventive care), including:

- periodic health evaluations;
- routine prenatal and well-child care;
- child and adult immunizations;
- tobacco cessation programs;
- obesity weight-loss programs; and
- various screening services.

*Example 1:* A plan provides coverage for Rafael and his family. The plan provides for the payment of covered medical expenses of any member of Rafael's family if the member has incurred covered medical expenses during 2008 in excess of $1,100 even if the family has not incurred covered medical expenses in excess of $2,200. If Rafael incurred covered medical expenses of $1,500 in a year, the plan would pay $400. Thus, benefits are potentially available under the plan even if the family's covered medical expenses do not exceed $2,200. Because the plan provides family coverage with an annual deductible of less than $2,200, it is not an HDHP.

*Example 2:* Same facts as in Example 1, except that the plan has a $5,000 family deductible and provides payment for covered medical expenses if any member of Rafael's family has incurred covered medical expenses during 2008 in excess of $2,200. The plan satisfies the requirements for an HDHP with respect to the deductibles.

---

52. Pub. L. 108-173, §1201; IRC §223; IRS Notice 2004-2, 2004-2 IRB 269; IRS Notice 2004-23, 2004-15 IRB 725; Rev. Rul. 2004-38, 2004-15 IRB 717; Rev. Proc. 2004-22, 2004-15 IRB 727; IRS Notice 2004-43, 2004-27 IRB 10; IRS Notice 2004-50, 2004-33 IRB 196; IRS Notice 2005-83, 2005-49 IRB 1075.

Generally, an individual is not eligible to establish an HSA if the individual is covered under an HDHP and another health plan as an individual, spouse, or dependent. If the employee has a choice between an HDHP and another health plan and chooses the HDHP, the employee is an eligible individual. There is an exception to this restriction on other coverage if it is provided by "permitted insurance." Permitted insurance is insurance under which substantially all of the coverage relates to liabilities incurred under workers' compensation laws, tort liabilities, liabilities relating to ownership or use of property (e.g., auto insurance), insurance for a specified disease or illness, and insurance that pays a fixed amount per day (or other period) of hospitalization. In addition, an individual does not lose eligibility for an HSA if the individual has coverage outside an HDHP for accidents, disability, dental care, vision care, or long-term care.

*Prescription drug plans.* Applying these rules, the IRS said that individuals are not eligible to make contributions under an HSA if they are covered by their health plan or another plan for prescription drug benefits before the annual HDHP deductible has been met. But, because many employers and health insurers were unable to modify their plans to meet this requirement, the IRS provided transition relief for 2004 and 2005 that allows otherwise eligible individuals to contribute to an HSA if the reason why they are ineligible is prescription drug coverage.

*State law coverage mandates.* The IRS announced other transition relief to deal with the situation where a state law requires coverage for certain benefits either without a deductible or with a lower deductible than the minimum for an HDHP. Through renewal periods of 12 months or less beginning before January 1, 2006, plans are treated as HDHPs if the only reason they would not qualify for such treatment is state-mandated benefits, and employees covered by such plans can contribute to an HSA.

*Spousal coverage issues.*[53] An employee who otherwise qualifies as an eligible individual does not fail to be an eligible individual merely because the employee's spouse has non-HDHP family coverage, if the spouse's non-HDHP does not cover the employee. In that situation, the employee may contribute to an HSA. The maximum amount that the employee could contribute to an HSA is based on whether the employee has self-only or family HDHP coverage.

*Riders and optional benefits.*[54] If an employee is covered by a rider or optional benefit that does not satisfy the requirements for permitted coverage, then the employee is not eligible to make contributions to an HSA, even if the employee is covered by a policy that satisfies the requirements.

**Network plans can be HDHPs.** A network plan (e.g., PPO or POS plan) is a plan that generally provides more favorable benefits for services provided by its network of providers than for services provided outside the network. In the case of a plan using a network of providers, the plan does not fail to be an HDHP solely because the out-of-pocket expense limits for services provided outside the network exceed the maximum annual out-of-pocket expense limits allowed for an HDHP. In addition, the plan's annual deductible for out-of-network services is not taken into account in determining the annual contribution limit. Rather, the annual contribution limit is determined by reference to the deductible for services within the network.

**Contributions up to maximum not included in income.**[55] Contributions to an HSA made by or on behalf of an eligible individual up to the maximum annual contribution limit are deductible by the individual. In addition, employer contributions (including salary reduction contributions made through a cafeteria plan) are excludable from gross income and wages for income tax withholding and social security, Medicare, and FUTA tax purposes if the employer reasonably believes at the time the contribution is made that it will be excludable from the employee's income. Both the employer and the employee can contribute to the employee's HSA. All contributions are aggregated for purposes of the maximum annual contribution limit. Also, contributions to Archer MSAs reduce the annual contribution limit for HSAs. Contributions by an employer to an HSA for an employee are included in the gross income of the employee to the extent they exceed the annual limit or if they are made on behalf of an employee who is not an eligible individual. In addition, an excise tax of 6% for each taxable year is imposed on the account beneficiary for excess individual and employer contributions.

---

53. Rev. Rul. 2005-25, 2005-18 IRB 971.
54. LTR 200704010, 1-25-06.
55. IRC §106(d); §125(d)(2)(D); §3306(b)(18); §3401(a)(22).

An employer that contributes to an employee's HSA is only responsible for determining the following with respect to an employee's eligibility and maximum annual contribution limit on HSA contributions:

- whether the employee is covered under an HDHP (and the deductible) or low deductible health plan or plans (including FSAs and HRAs) sponsored by that employer; and
- the employee's age (for catch-up contributions – see the discussion below); note that the employer may rely on the employee's representation about his or her date of birth.

**HSAs and cafeteria plans.**  Both an HSA and an HDHP can be offered as options under a cafeteria plan (see Section 4.5-1), so an employee may elect to have amounts contributed as employer contributions on a salary reduction basis.

The following requirements for health FSAs (see Section 4.5-7) under a cafeteria plan do not apply to HSAs:

- the prohibition against a benefit that defers compensation by permitting employees to carry over unused elective contributions or plan benefits from one plan year to another;
- the requirement that the maximum amount of reimbursement must be available at all times during the coverage period; and
- the mandatory 12-month coverage period.

A cafeteria plan may permit an employee to revoke an election during a coverage period with respect to a qualified benefit and make a new election for the remaining portion of the period under certain circumstances. Because the eligibility requirements and contribution limits for HSAs are determined on a month-to-month basis, rather than on an annual basis, an employee who elects to make HSA contributions under a cafeteria plan may start or stop the election or increase or decrease the election at any time as long as the change is effective prospectively (i.e., after the request for the change is received). If an employer places additional restrictions on the election of HSA contributions under a cafeteria plan, the same restrictions must apply to all employees.

An employer can permit employees to elect an HSA mid-year if it is offered as a new benefit under the employer's cafeteria plan if the election for the HSA is made on a prospective basis. However, the HSA election does not permit a change or revocation of any other coverage under the cafeteria plan unless the change is otherwise permitted under the change of status rules. Therefore, while an HSA may be offered to and elected by an employee mid-year, the employee may have other coverage under the cafeteria plan that cannot be changed, which may prevent the employee from being an eligible individual.

If an employee elects to make contributions to an HSA through the employer's cafeteria plan, the employer may contribute amounts to an employee's HSA to cover qualified medical expenses incurred by an employee that exceed the employee's current HSA balance, up to the maximum amount elected by the employee. While any accelerated contribution made by the employer must be equally available to all participating employees throughout the plan year and must be provided to all participating employees on the same terms, the employee must repay the amount of the accelerated contribution by the end of the plan year.  However, once an accelerated contribution is made, the employer cannot recoup any amount that the employee has not repaid if the employee terminates employment during the year.

> *Example:* On January 2, 2008, an employer makes the maximum annual contribution to its employees' HSAs, in the expectation that the employees will work for the entire calendar year 2008. On February 1, 2008, one employee terminates employment. The employer may not recoup from that employee's HSA any portion of the contribution previously made to the employee's HSA.

**Maximum annual contribution.**  The maximum annual contribution that can be made to an HSA is the maximum deductible permitted under an Archer MSA high deductible plan, as adjusted for inflation. For 2008, the amount of the maximum high deductible is $2,900 in the case of self-only coverage and $5,800 in the case of family coverage.

In the case of individuals who are married to each other, if either spouse has family coverage, both are treated as having family coverage. The contribution limit for the spouses is divided equally between the spouses unless they agree on a different division. The family coverage limit is reduced further by any contribution to an Archer MSA. However, both spouses may make the catch-up contributions for individuals age 55 or over (see discussion following) without exceeding the family coverage limit.

*Contribution limitation and part-year coverage.*[56] A full year's contribution can be made to an HSA for a partial year's coverage, provided the employee maintains the high deductible plan for at least 12 months after the last month of the partial year. Failure to meet this condition results in a loss of the deduction and a 10% penalty, unless the failure is due to the employee's death or disability.

*Example:* Employee Henry enrolls in a high deductible health plan in December 2008 and is otherwise an eligible individual in that month. Henry was not an eligible individual in any other month in 2008. Henry may make HSA contributions as if he had been enrolled in the plan for all of 2008. Henry ceases to be covered under a high deductible health plan in June 2009, so an amount equal to the HSA deduction attributable to treating Henry as an eligible individual for January through November 2008 is included in income in 2009. In addition, a 10% additional tax applies to the amount included.

**Catch-up contributions.** Individuals age 55 and older (including those who reach age 55 by the end of the taxable year) can make additional "catch-up" contributions to an HSA until they are enrolled in Medicare. The additional allowable contribution is:

| Calendar Year | Allowable Catch-Up Contribution |
|---|---|
| 2005 | $600 |
| 2006 | $700 |
| 2007 | $800 |
| 2008 | $900 |
| 2009 and beyond | $1,000 |

However, contributions, including catch-up contributions, cannot be made once an individual is eligible for Medicare.

**Rollovers.** Amounts can be rolled into an HSA from an Archer MSA (see Section 4.1-3) or from another HSA.

**Transfer from an HRA or FSA.**[57] Beginning in 2007, employers can make a one-time transfer of the balance in an employee's HRA or FSA to an HSA ("qualified HSA distribution"). The maximum transfer is the lesser of the HRA or FSA balance on the date of transfer or September 21, 2006. Transfers must be made by January 1, 2012 (see Section 4.5-7). Qualified HSA distributions are excluded from gross income and wages for employment tax purposes, are not taken into account in applying the maximum deduction limitation for other HSA contributions, and are not deductible. Such distributions are treated as rollover contributions.

If the employee is not an eligible individual with coverage under an HDHP at any time during the 12-month period beginning with the month of the HSA distribution, then the HSA distribution is included in the employee's gross income and the employee is subject to an additional tax equal to 10% of the distribution unless the reason for the employee's ineligibility is the employee's death or disability.

If the employer makes a qualified HSA distribution for any employee, it must make them for all eligible individuals. If not, the employer violates the requirement to make comparable contributions for its employees (see discussion below).

---

56.    IRC §223(b)(8).

57.    IRC §106(e); IRS Notice 2007-22, 2007-10 IRB 670.

**Transfer from an IRA.**[58] Eligible individuals are permitted a one-time contribution to an HSA of amounts distributed from an IRA ("qualified HSA funding distribution"), up to the applicable maximum deductible contribution limit for the type of coverage they have at the time of the contribution. Amounts contributed under this provision are not includible in income (ordinarily, amounts distributed from an IRA for medical expenses are taxable income, while amounts distributed from an HSA for this purpose are not) and are not subject to the 10% tax on early distributions, so long as the employee remains an eligible individual for at least 12 months.

If the employee does not remain an eligible individual for 12 months after the contribution for a reason other than death or disability of the employee, the amount of the contribution is included in the employee's income, and there is an additional tax equal to 10% of the contribution. The provision does not apply to simplified employee pensions (SEPs) or to SIMPLE retirement accounts.

 **NO COBRA COVERAGE REQUIREMENT** Like Archer MSAs, HSAs are not subject to COBRA continuation coverage.

**Comparable contributions required.**[59] If an employer makes contributions to employee HSAs, the employer must make available comparable contributions on behalf of all employees in the same category with comparable coverage during the same period. Contributions are considered comparable if they are either of the same amount or the same percentage of the deductible under the plan. The comparability rule is applied separately to part-time employees (i.e., employees who are customarily employed for fewer than 30 hours per week). The comparability rule does not apply to amounts rolled over from an employee's HSA, health care FSA, or Archer MSA, to salary reduction contributions made through a cafeteria plan, or to after-tax contributions.

*Lower paid workers can get more.*[60] Beginning in 2007, employers can make additional contributions to nonhighly compensated employees' HSAs. The comparable contribution rules continue to apply to these contributions, so that the employer must make comparable contributions on behalf of all nonhighly compensated employees with comparable coverage during the same period.

> ***Example:*** An employer is permitted to make a $1,000 contribution to the HSA of each nonhighly compensated employee for a year without making contributions to the HSA of each highly compensated employee.

*Coverage under the comparability provision.* Contributions to the HSAs of certain individuals are not taken into account in determining whether an employer's contributions to the HSAs of its employees satisfy the comparability rules. Specifically, contributions to the HSAs of independent contractors, sole proprietors, and partners are not taken into account under the comparability rules. In addition, the comparability rules do not apply to amounts rolled over from an employee's HSA or Archer Medical Savings Account (MSA) or to after-tax employee contributions.[61]

The categories of employees who must be taken into account for comparability testing are current full-time employees (i.e., working at least 30 hours per week), current part-time employees (i.e., working less than 30 hours per week), and former employees (except for former employees with coverage under the employer's HDHP because of an election under a COBRA continuation provision).[62] The comparability rules apply separately to each of the categories of employees. If an employer contributes to the HSA of any employee in a category of employees, the employer must make comparable contributions to the HSAs of all comparable participating employees within that category. Therefore, an employer cannot contribute to the HSAs of only management employees.

---

58. IRC §408(d)(9).
59. IRC §4980G; IRS Reg. §54.4980G-1-5
60. IRC §4980G(d).
61. IRS Reg. §54.4980G-2; 54.4980G-3, Q&A-1—3.
62. IRS Reg. §54.4980G-3, Q&A-5—9.

Employees who are included in a unit of employees covered by a bona fide collective bargaining agreement are not comparable participating employees, if health benefits were the subject of good faith bargaining between the employees and the employer.[63]

Comparable participating employees are eligible individuals who have the same category of HDHP coverage – i.e., self-only or family coverage. Family HDHP coverage can be subdivided into the following additional categories of HDHP coverage: self plus one, self plus two, and self plus three or more. An employer's contribution with respect to the self plus two category may not be less than the employer's contribution with respect to the self plus one category, and the employer's contribution with respect to the self plus three or more category may not be less than the employer's contribution with respect to the self plus two category.[64]

The comparability rules apply to a category of employees only if an employer contributes to the HSA of any employee within the category. For example, an employer that makes comparable contributions to the HSAs of all full-time employees who are eligible individuals, but does not contribute to the HSA of any employee who is not a full-time employee, satisfies the comparability rules. At the same time, an employer can make contributions to the HSAs of full-time employees with single coverage under an HDHP, while not contributing at the same rate for full-time employees with family coverage. An employer can also limit its contributions to the HSAs of employees with coverage under the employer's HDHP, rather than coverage under another HDHP, but if it contributes to the HSA of any employee who has coverage under another HDHP, it must make contributions for all such employees.

An employer making comparable contributions to former employees must take reasonable actions to locate any missing comparable participating former employees (e.g., certified mail, IRS Letter Forwarding Program, SSA Letter Forwarding Service).

*Employees with HSAs and Archer MSAs.*[65] The comparability rules apply separately to employees with HSAs and those with Archer MSAs. If an employee has both an HSA and an Archer MSA, the employer can contribute to one, but not both.

**Calculating comparable contributions.** Section 4980G mandates the use of a calendar year for comparability testing purposes (rather than a plan year). The determination of whether the rate of interest used by an employer is reasonable will be based on all the facts and circumstances. Note, however, that if an employer calculates interest using the federal short-term rate as determined by the Secretary of the Treasury, then the employer will be deemed to be using a reasonable rate.

*Procedures for making comparable contributions.* There are several ways an employer can comply with the comparability requirement.[66]

Pay-as-you-go basis. An employer may comply with the comparability rules by contributing amounts at one or more times for the calendar year to the HSAs of employees who are eligible individuals, if contributions are the same amount or the same percentage of the HDHP deductible for employees who are eligible individuals with the same category of coverage and are made at the same time.

If an employer makes comparable HSA contributions on a pay-as-you-go basis, it must do so for each comparable participating employee who is an employee during the time period used to make contributions. For example, if an employer makes HSA contributions each pay period, it must do so for each comparable participating employee who is an employee during the pay period. The pay periods do not have to be the same for all comparable participating employees, however. Contributions for comparable participating employees who are paid at different intervals (e.g., biweekly vs. monthly) are considered to be made at the same time.

---

63.   IRS Reg. §54.4980G-3, Q&A-6.
64.   IRS Reg. §54.4980G-1, Q&A-2.
65.   IRS Reg. §54.4980G-3, Q&A-13.
66.   IRS Reg. §54.4980G-4, Q&A-2—6, 12.

Look-back basis. An employer may also satisfy the comparability rules by determining comparable contributions for the calendar year at the end of the calendar year, taking into account all employees who were eligible individuals for any month during the calendar year and contributing the correct amount (a percentage of the HDHP deductible or a specified dollar amount for the same categories of coverage) to the employees' HSAs by April 15th of the following year.

If an employer makes comparable contributions on a look-back basis, it must do so for each employee who was a comparable participating employee for any month during the calendar year.

Pre-funded basis. In addition, an employer may make all of its contributions to the HSAs of employees who are eligible individuals at the beginning of the calendar year. An employer that makes comparable HSA contributions on a pre-funded basis will not fail to satisfy the comparability rules because an employee who terminates employment prior to the end of the calendar year has received more HSA contributions on a monthly basis than employees who worked the entire calendar year.

If an employer makes HSA contributions on a pre-funded basis, it must do so for all employees who are comparable participating employees at the beginning of the calendar year. And an employer that makes HSA contributions on a pre-funded basis must make comparable HSA contributions for all employees who are comparable participating employees for any month during the calendar year, including employees hired after the date of the initial funding.

Special situations. If an employee has not established an HSA at the time the employer funds its employees' HSAs, the employer complies with the comparability rules by contributing comparable amounts to the employee's HSA when the employee establishes it, taking into account each month that the employee was a comparable participating employee.

If an employer determines that the comparability rules are not satisfied for a calendar year, the employer may not recoup from an employee's HSA any portion of its contribution because an account beneficiary's interest in an HSA is nonforfeitable. However, an employer may make additional HSA contributions to satisfy the comparability rules. An employer may contribute up until April 15th following the calendar year in which the non-comparable contributions were made. *Note:* An employer that makes additional HSA contributions to correct non-comparable contributions must also contribute reasonable interest.

In proposed regulations issued in 2007, the IRS provides a means for employers to comply with the comparability requirements with respect to:

- employees who have not established an HSA by December 31, or
- employees who may have established an HSA but not notified the employer of that fact.[67]

By January 15 of the following calendar year, the employer must provide all such employees written notice that each eligible employee who, by the last day of February, both establishes an HSA and notifies the employer that he or she has established it will receive a comparable contribution to the HSA. If an eligible employee then establishes an HSA and notifies the employer by the end of February, the employer must contribute to the HSA by April 15 comparable amounts (taking into account each month that the employee was a comparable participating employee) plus reasonable interest.

The notice may be delivered electronically. The proposed regulations provide sample language that employers may use as a basis in preparing their own notices. The notice is timely if the employer issues the notice no earlier than 90 days before the employer makes its first HSA contributions for a calendar year and no later than January 15 of the following calendar year.

Employers may rely on these proposed regulations before final regulations are issued, or they can rely on previously published proposed regulations which provide that an employer is not required to make comparable contributions for a calendar year to an employee's HSA if the employee has not established one by December 31.

---

67.    IRS Prop. Reg. §54.4980G-4, Q&A-14 and 16.

*Acceleration of employer contributions.*[68] For any calendar year, an employer may accelerate part or all of its contributions for the entire year to the HSAs of employees who have incurred qualified medical expenses exceeding the employer's HSA contributions at that time.

If an employer accelerates contributions for this reason:

- these contributions must be available on an equal and uniform basis to all eligible employees throughout the calendar year; and
- the employer must establish reasonable uniform methods and requirements for accelerating contributions and determining medical expenses.

An employer is not required to contribute reasonable interest on either accelerated or nonaccelerated HSA contributions.

*Impermissible contribution methods.*[69] Employers cannot use the following as a basis for making comparable contributions to employees' HSAs:

- The amount the employees contribute to their HSAs;
- The employee's participation in health assessments, disease management programs, or wellness programs;
- The employee's age or length of service; or
- The employee's eligibility to make catch-up contributions.

*Exception to the comparability rules for cafeteria plans.*[70] The comparability rules do not apply to HSA contributions that an employer makes through a cafeteria plan. However, the nondiscrimination rules in IRC §125 apply to HSA contributions (including matching contributions) made through a cafeteria plan (see Section 4.5-6).

Unlike the cafeteria plan nondiscrimination rules, the comparability rules are not based on discrimination in favor of highly compensated or key employees. Therefore, an employer that maintains an HDHP only for highly compensated or key employees and makes HSA contributions through a cafeteria plan only for those eligible employees does not violate the comparability rules, but may violate the cafeteria plan nondiscrimination rules.

*Penalty for not making comparable contributions.*[71] If the employer's contributions to its employees' HSAs do not satisfy the comparability requirement, the employer is subject to an excise tax equal to 35% of all amounts the employer contributed to its employees' HSAs during the calendar year. The penalty may be waived to the extent the failure to comply was due to reasonable cause and not willful neglect.

**Distributions can be tax-free.** Distributions from an HSA for qualified medical expenses of the employee and his or her spouse or dependents are excluded from gross income (see Section 4.1-2 for a definition of expenses for medical care) if they are not covered by insurance or otherwise. Distributions from an HSA that are not for qualified medical expenses are included in gross income. Distributions included in gross income are subject to an additional 10% tax unless made after death, disability, or the individual reaches the age of Medicare eligibility (i.e., 65).

Distributions from an HSA to an employee's spouse or dependents are excluded from gross income even if they are not eligible individuals, so long as the distribution is made for a qualified medical expense that is not reimbursed by another health plan. If both the employee and the employee's spouse have HSAs, distributions from one HSA can be used to pay the other individual's qualified medical expenses if both HSAs don't reimburse the same expenses.

---

68.    IRS Prop. Reg. §54.4980G-4, Q&A-15.
69.    IRS Reg. §54.4980G-4, Q&A-8—11.
70.    IRS Reg. §54.4980G-5, Q&A-1—3.
71.    IRC §4980G; IRS Reg. §54.4980G-1, Q&A-4; §54.4980G-5, Q&A-4.

If administration and account maintenance fees (e.g., flat administrative fees) are withdrawn from the HSA, the withdrawn amounts are not treated as a taxable distribution and are not included in the account beneficiary's gross income. At the same time the withdrawn amounts do not increase the maximum annual HSA contribution limit. For example, if the maximum annual contribution limit is $2,900, and a $25 administration fee is withdrawn from the HSA, the annual contribution limit is still $2,900, not $2,925.

Generally, health insurance premiums are not qualified medical expenses except for qualified long-term care insurance, COBRA health care continuation coverage, and health care coverage while an individual is receiving unemployment compensation benefits. Also, for individuals over age 65, Medicare premiums and the employee share of premiums for employer-provided health insurance can be paid from an HSA, but not premiums for Medigap policies.

Employers are not required to determine whether HSA distributions are used for qualified medical expenses. Employees who establish HSAs make that determination and should maintain records of their medical expenses sufficient to show that the distributions have been made exclusively for qualified medical expenses and are therefore excludable from gross income.

 **DEBIT AND CREDIT CARDS CAN BE USED** Employers can provide eligible individuals with debt, credit, or stored-value cards to receive distributions from an HSA for qualified medical expenses. For guidance on how to ensure that such distributions are excluded from employees' gross income, see Section 4.1-6).

**Interaction of HSAs with other FSAs and HRAs.**[72] In 2004, the IRS issued guidance clarifying how health flexible spending arrangements (FSAs) and health reimbursement arrangements (HRAs) interact with HSAs. An employee who is covered by an HDHP and a health FSA or HRA that pays or reimburses medical expenses is generally not eligible to make contributions to an HSA. However, the IRS ruled that the employee is eligible to make contributions to an HSA for periods he or she is covered under certain specified types of employer-provided plans that reimburse employee medical expenses. In addition, combinations of these arrangements will not disqualify the employee from being eligible to make contributions to an HSA.

The guidance also clarifies that an employee may not be reimbursed for the same medical expense by more than one plan or arrangement. However, if the employee has available an HSA, a health FSA, and an HRA that pay or reimburse the same medical expense, the health FSA or HRA may pay or reimburse the medical expense before any distribution is taken from the HSA, so long as the employee certifies to the employer that the expense has not been reimbursed and that he or she will not seek reimbursement under any other plan or arrangement (including the HSA).

*Limited-purpose health FSA or HRA.* An employee is eligible to make contributions to an HSA if he or she is covered under a limited-purpose health FSA that pays or reimburses benefits for "permitted coverage" (but not through insurance or for long-term care services) or a limited-purpose HRA that pays or reimburses benefits for "permitted insurance" (for a specific disease or illness that provides a fixed amount per day (or other period) of hospitalization) or "permitted coverage" (but not for long-term care services). In addition, the limited-purpose health FSA or HRA may pay or reimburse preventive care benefits. Here, the employee is eligible to make contributions to an HSA because the limited-purpose health FSA or HRA provides only HSA-compatible benefits whether or not the HDHP deductible has been satisfied.

*Suspended HRA.* An employee is eligible to make contributions to an HSA if he or she is covered under a suspended HRA, pursuant to an election made before the beginning of the HRA coverage period, that does not pay or reimburse any medical expense incurred during the suspension period except preventive care, permitted insurance, and permitted coverage (if otherwise allowed to be paid or reimbursed by the HRA). Here, the employee is eligible to make contributions to an HSA during the suspension period because he or she has elected to forego health reimbursements for the coverage period. When the suspension period ends, the employee is no longer eligible to make such contributions.

---

72.    Rev. Rul. 2004-45, 2004-22 IRB 971.

If an HSA is funded through salary reduction under a cafeteria plan during the suspension period, the terms of the salary reduction election must indicate that the salary reduction is used only to pay for the HSA offered in conjunction with the HRA and not to pay for the HRA itself. In other words, the mere fact that an employee participates in an HSA funded pursuant to a salary reduction election does not necessarily mean that the salary reduction is attributable to the HRA.

*Post-deductible health FSA or HRA.* An employee is eligible to make contributions to an HSA if he or she is covered under a post-deductible FSA or HRA that does not pay or reimburse any medical expense incurred before the minimum annual HDHP deductible has been satisfied. The deductible for the HRA or health FSA need not be the same as the deductible for the HDHP, but in no event may the HDHP or other coverage provide benefits before the minimum annual HDHP deductible has been satisfied. Where the HDHP and the other coverage do not have identical deductibles, contributions to the HSA are limited to the lower of the deductibles. In addition, although the deductibles of the HDHP and the other coverage may be satisfied independently by separate expenses, no benefits may be paid before the minimum annual HDHP deductible has been satisfied.

*Retirement HRA.* Before retirement, an employee is eligible to make contributions to an HSA if he or she is covered under a retirement HRA that pays or reimburses medical expenses incurred after retirement (but not expenses incurred before retirement). After retirement, when the retirement HRA may pay or reimburse medical expenses, the employee is no longer eligible to make contributions to an HSA.

**Example 1:** Employee Brad is covered by an HDHP (with an 80%-20% coinsurance feature above the deductible) and also by a health FSA and HRA. The health FSA and HRA pay or reimburse medical expenses incurred before the minimum annual HDHP deductible has been satisfied. In addition, the health FSA and HRA pay or reimburse medical expenses that are not limited to the exceptions for permitted insurance, permitted coverage, or preventive care (e.g., co-payments, coinsurance, expenses not covered due to the deductible, and other medical expenses not covered by the HDHP). Brad is not entitled to Medicare benefits and may not be claimed as a dependent on another person's tax return. Brad is not eligible to make contributions to an HSA. The result is the same if Brad is covered by a health FSA or HRA sponsored by his or her spouse's employer.

**Example 2:** Same facts as Example 1, except that the health FSA and HRA are limited-purpose arrangements that pay or reimburse only vision and dental expenses (which are permitted coverage) and preventive care. In that situation, Brad is eligible to make contributions to an HSA.

**Example 3:** Same facts as Example 1, except that the health FSA and HRA only pay or reimburse medical expenses (including the employee's 20% coinsurance responsibility for expenses above the deductible) after the minimum annual HDHP deductible has been satisfied. In this situation, Brad is eligible to make contributions to an HSA.

**Example 4:** Same facts as Example 1, except that the employee is not covered by a health FSA. The employer's HRA only pays or reimburses medical expenses incurred after the employee retires. Brad is eligible to make contributions to an HSA before retirement, but not after.

**Effect of FSA grace period on HSA eligibility.**[73] At the end of 2005, The IRS issued guidance clarifying that an individual participating in a health flexible spending arrangement (health FSA) who is covered by a grace period for incurring medical expenses after the end of the plan year (see Section 4.5-7) is generally not eligible to contribute to an HSA until the first day of the first month following the end of the grace period. However, an employer may amend its cafeteria plan document to enable a health FSA participant to become HSA-eligible during the grace period.

Normally, an employee participating in a health FSA that reimburses the employee for medical expenses is not an HSA-eligible individual. But, as explained earlier, an employee who is otherwise eligible for an HSA may be covered under a limited purpose health FSA or a post-deductible FSA, or a combination of both, and remain eligible to contribute to an HSA.

---

73.    IRS Notice 2005-86, 2005-49 IRB 1075.

*Options available to an employer.* An employer may adopt either of the following two options, which will affect participants' HSA eligibility during the cafeteria plan grace period:

General purpose health FSA during grace period. An employer amends its cafeteria plan document to provide a grace period but takes no other action with respect to the general purpose health FSA. Because a health FSA that pays or reimburses all qualifying medical expenses constitutes impermissible "other coverage" for HSA eligibility purposes, an individual who participates in the health FSA (or a spouse whose medical expenses are eligible for reimbursement under the health FSA) for the immediately preceding cafeteria plan year and who is covered by the grace period, is not eligible to contribute to an HSA until the first day of the first month following the end of the grace period. But see the exception to this FSA grace period rate below.

Mandatory conversion from health FSA to HSA-compatible health FSA for all participants. An employer amends its cafeteria plan document to provide for both a grace period and a mandatory conversion of the general purpose health FSA to a limited-purpose or post-deductible FSA (or combined limited-purpose and post-deductible health FSA) during the grace period. The amendments do not permit an individual participant to elect between an HSA-compatible FSA or an FSA that is not HSA-compatible. The amendments apply to the entire grace period and to all participants in the health FSA who are covered by the grace period. Coverage of these participants by the HSA-compatible FSA during the grace period does not disqualify participants who are otherwise eligible individuals from contributing to an HSA during the grace period.

*Transition relief.* For cafeteria plan years ending before June 5, 2006, an employee participating in a general purpose health FSA that provides coverage during a grace period will be eligible to contribute to an HSA during the grace period if the following requirements are met:

(1) If not for the coverage under a general purpose health FSA described in clause (2), the individual would be an "eligible individual" during the grace period (in general, covered under an HDHP and not covered under any impermissible other health coverage); and

(2) Either
  (A) the individual's (and the individual's spouse's) general purpose health FSA has no unused contributions or benefits remaining at the end of the immediately preceding cafeteria plan year, or
  (B) in the case of an individual who is not covered during the grace period under a general purpose health FSA maintained by the employer of his/her spouse, the individual's employer amends its cafeteria plan document to provide that the grace period does not provide coverage to an individual who elects HDHP coverage.

*Exception to FSA grace period rule.*[74] Coverage under a health FSA during the "grace period" is disregarded in determining the employee's ability to make tax deductible HSA contributions during that period if the balance in the FSA at the end of the plan year is zero, or if the entire remaining balance in the FSA at the end of the year is contributed to an HSA under IRC §106(e) discussed earlier in this section.

The zero-balance exception only applies to health FSA coverage during a grace period following a plan year. Therefore, health FSA coverage during the plan year is not disregarded, regardless of whether the health FSA balance is reduced to zero during the plan year by a qualified HSA distribution or otherwise.

**Reporting requirements.**[75] Employer contributions, including salary reduction contributions through a cafeteria plan, are required to be reported on the employee's Form W-2. They must be reported in Box 12 with Code "W". Employer contributions that are not excludable from income also must be reported in Boxes 1, 3 and 5, with the taxes withheld reported in Boxes 2, 4, and 6 (see Section 8.8-3 for detailed instructions on Form W-2 reporting). Such amounts would also have to be reported on Forms 941 and 940.

---

74.    IRC §223(c)(1)(iii); IRS Notice 2007-22, 2007-10 IRB 670.
75.    IRC §6051(a)(12); Form W-2 Instructions.

An employee's contributions that are not made by salary reduction must be reported in Box 1 as wages and are subject to federal income tax withholding and social security and Medicare taxes. The employee can deduct the contributions, up to the annual contribution limit, on the employee's personal tax return.

 **HSAs AREN'T ERISA PLANS**[76] The U.S. Labor Department's Employee Benefits Security Administration concluded that HSAs are personal health care savings vehicles rather than a form of group health insurance, so generally they will not constitute ERISA-covered employee welfare benefit plans. EBSA also ruled that employer contributions to employees' HSAs does not result in ERISA coverage where employee establishment of an HSA is completely voluntary and the employer's involvement is otherwise limited to making sure that tax requirements are met and picking the HSA providers with which employees can establish HSAs.

## 4.2 Family and Medical Leave Act

One of the major pieces of social legislation to be enacted during the 1990s was the Family and Medical Leave Act (FMLA). In general, the FMLA guarantees employees (in workplaces with 50 or more employees) 12 weeks of unpaid leave in a year to be with a newborn or newly adopted child, to take care of a seriously ill child, spouse, or parent, or to care for themselves if they are seriously ill. The law also guarantees continuation of employees' health benefits while on leave.[77]

**Employer and employee coverage.**[78] The FMLA applies to private sector employers with 50 or more employees, including part-timers and employees on leave or suspension, but not laid-off employees. The definition of employee is the same as that under the Fair Labor Standards Act (see Section 1.6-1). An employee at a facility with less than 50 employees may still be eligible for the leave benefits if the employer has at least 50 employees working within a 75-mile radius of the facility. Public sector (government) employers are also covered by the FMLA, with each state or political subdivision of a state considered a covered public agency. A public sector employee is eligible for leave benefits if the public agency has 50 employees working within a 75-mile radius of the employee's worksite.

 **COVERAGE LOOPHOLE** While all employers with 50 employees are covered by the FMLA, an employee is not eligible for leave benefits if fewer than 50 employees are employed by the employer within 75 miles of the employee's worksite when leave is requested. Therefore, it is possible for an employer to have several hundred or thousand employees who are ineligible for leave even though the employer is technically covered by the FMLA (e.g., a fast food chain with 40 stores, each employing 30-35 employees, and no store is within 75 miles of another, would have no eligible employees).[79] The 75-mile distance is measured by surface miles, using surface transportation over public roads or waterways along the shortest route from the employee's worksite.[80] A federal appeals court ruled that an employee's "worksite" means just that – the place where the employee works – not the employer's headquarters or regional office from where the employee is assigned or reports.[81]

To be eligible for leave benefits, employees must also have been employed by the employer for at least 12 months (not necessarily consecutively) and have worked at least 1,250 hours within the previous 12-month period. "Hours worked" are determined on the same basis as under the Fair Labor Standards Act (see Section 2.6-2), and exempt employees who have worked for the employer for at least a year are deemed to have met the 1,250-hours requirement unless the employer can prove otherwise.

---

76. EBSA Field Assistance Bulletin 2004-01, 4-7-04.

77. Public Law 103-3; 29 USC §2601-2654.

78. FMLA §101; FMLA Reg. 29 CFR §825.104 - §825.111.

79. FMLA Reg. 29 CFR §825.111.

80. 29 CFR §829.111(b); Bellum v. PCE Constructors, Inc., 407 F.3d 734 (5 CA, 2005), cert. den. 126 S.Ct. 1150 (2006); Hackworth v. Progressive Casualty Ins. Co., 468 F.3d 722 (10 CA, 2006), cert. den. No. 06-1300 (U.S. S. Ct., 5-29-07).

81. Harbert v. Healthcare Services Group, Inc., 391 F.3d 1140 (10 CA, 2005); Hackworth v. Progressive Casualty Ins. Co., 468 F.3d 722 (10 CA, 2006), cert. den. No. 06-1300 (U.S. S. Ct., 5-29-07).

The federal courts have ruled that an employee's accrued vacation time, short-term disability leave, and unexcused absences can be used to complete the 12-month employment requirement,[82] but they are split when it comes to whether work hours lost by an employee that were later compensated after successful pursuit of a grievance or lawsuit counted as hours worked in meeting the 1,250-hours requirement.[83] Where a participating nurse worked 48 hours in two consecutive weekends and was compensated for 68 hours of work under a special incentive program, the extra 20 hours for which she was compensated did not count as hours worked toward FMLA eligibility.[84] Federal appeals courts have ruled that previous periods of employment before a break in service can be counted in determining whether the 12-month employment requirement was met, with no limit on the length of the break.[85]

The Department of Labor has issued guidance on the FMLA eligibility of reemployed members of the military in light of their entitlement under the Uniformed Services Employment and Reemployment Rights Act (USERRA) to the same rights or benefits they would have had if they had remained continuously employed. The DOL said that, in determining whether a military veteran meets the FMLA eligibility threshold, the months actually employed and the hours actually worked for the employer must be combined with the months and hours that would have been worked during the 12 months prior to the start of the requested leave but for the military service.[86]

 **EXPATRIATES ARE NOT COVERED** The FMLA applies only to employees who work within the U.S. or any of its territories and possessions. Employees who are employed in foreign countries are not counted for purposes of determining employer coverage or employee eligibility.[87]

**Types of leave guaranteed.**[88] Eligible employees are entitled to 12 weeks of unpaid leave within 12 months after the birth of a child or the placement of an adopted or foster child. They are also entitled to 12 weeks of unpaid leave within a 12-month period to care for a child, spouse, or parent with a "serious health condition" or because of the employee's own serious health condition that makes it impossible for the employee to continue working.

It is up to the employer to decide what constitutes a 12-month period (e.g., calendar year, fiscal year, year beginning on employee's anniversary date). If the employer fails to make its decision clear, the 12-month period applied is the one most favorable to the employee.[89] Where both spouses are employed by the same employer, they are entitled to a total of 12 weeks' leave to care for a newborn or newly adopted child or a seriously ill parent. They are each entitled to 12 weeks' leave to care for a sick child or the other spouse, and they must be allowed to take that leave simultaneously, according to a federal district court.[90]

 **CALIFORNIA AND WASHINGTON REQUIRE PAID FAMILY LEAVE** California is the first state to provide workers with paid family and medical leave under its Paid Family Leave initative. Eligible employees can collect up to 6 weeks of wage replacement benefits (about 55% of their salary) during a 12-month period for taking time off from work to care for a seriously ill child, spouse, parent, or domestic partner, or for the birth, adoption, or foster care placement of a child. The benefits are funded entirely by employees through increased contributions to the state disability insurance (SDI) fund. (See Section 7.3 for information on the amount of the employees' contribution.) Washington enacted similar legislation in 2007 that guarantees 5 weeks of paid leave under similar circumstances beginning October 1, 2009. As of the end of 2007, the funding mechanism for the program had not yet been worked out.

---

82. Ruder v. Maine General Medical Ctr., 204 F. Supp. 2d 16 (D Me., 2002); Babcock v. BellSouth Advertising and Publishing Corp., 348 F.3d 73 (4 CA, 2003)

83. Plumley v. Southern Container, Inc., 303 F. 3d 364 (1 CA, 2002)—such time did not count; Savage v. Chicago Transit Authority, No. 06C1407, 2007 U.S. Dist. LEXIS 17605 (ND Ill., 3-9-07)—such time did count.

84. Mutchler v. Dunlop Memorial Hosp., 485 F.3d 854 (6 CA, 2007).

85. Rucker v. Lee Holding Co., 471 F.3d 6 (1 CA, 2006); O'Connor v. Busch's, Inc., 492 F. Supp. 2d 736 (Ed Mich., 2007).

86. DOL Memorandum, 7-22-02.

87. FMLA Reg. 29 CFR §825.105(b).

88. FMLA §102; §103; FMLA Reg. 29 CFR §825.112 - §825.118; §825.200 - §825.202.

89. Bachelder v. America West Airlines, Inc., 259 F.3d 1112 (9 CA, 2001).

90. Werner v. Ford Motor Co., No. 1:06cv092 (SD Ohio, 4-13-07).

**Employer can require employee to take leave.** A federal district court ruled there is nothing in the FMLA that prohibits an employer from requiring an employee to take unpaid leave if the employee has a serious health condition that makes him unable to perform the functions of his position. The court said that guaranteeing an employee's right to ask for such leave does not prevent the employer from putting an employee on FMLA leave in this situation.[91] On the other hand, the employer may not require the employee to work while on FMLA leave.[92]

**Serious health condition defined.**[93] Under final regulations interpreting and implementing the FMLA, a serious health condition is an "illness, injury, impairment, or physical or mental condition" involving *inpatient* care in a health care facility (including any period of incapacity or subsequent treatment related to the inpatient care) or *continuing treatment* (two or more times during the absence from work) by a health care provider. The continuing treatment generally must involve a period of incapacity (e.g., inability to work or attend school) of at least three consecutive calendar days (not workdays) and includes subsequent treatment by or under the supervision of a health care provider. But it does not include consecutive partial days of incapacity.[94]

Continuing treatment that can be initiated without a visit to a health care provider, such as the taking of over-the-counter medicine, bed rest, drinking fluids, or exercise, does not qualify as continuing treatment for purposes of FMLA leave. Treatment also does not include routine physical, dental, or eye examinations. Exceptions to the three-day requirement for a period of incapacity include treatment for chronic conditions (e.g., asthma or diabetes) or any incapacity caused by pregnancy or for prenatal care.

 **WHAT ABOUT THE FLU?** While at first glance it may not seem that the flu is the type of illness Congress had in mind when it passed the FMLA, at least two federal appeals courts have ruled that the flu can be a "serious health condition" entitling an employee to the protection of the Act. In each case, the court found that the broad definition of "serious health condition" does not exclude the flu where the employee is unable to work for at least 3 days and is being treated by a health care provider.[95]

**Intermittent leave.**[96] An employee who needs to take leave because of an illness suffered by the employee or the employee's child, spouse, or parent on an intermittent or occasional basis may do so. This may be done by taking off several days or weeks at a time or by working reduced hours. Intermittent FMLA leave taken as reduced hours may be deducted from an exempt employee's salary without converting the employee into a nonexempt employee under the FLSA (see Section 2.4-1). However, an employer did not have to treat an employee's chronic lateness for work as intermittent FMLA leave where there was no medical reason for her behavior (e.g., no doctor's appointments, medical treatments, or other medical necessities).[97]

When an employee takes a full week of intermittent leave under the FMLA, a holiday falling within that week counts toward the amount of FMLA leave used by the employee.[98]

**Designation as paid or unpaid leave.**[99] Employers can require eligible employees to use any paid vacation, personal, sick, medical, or family leave as part of the 12-week guaranteed leave if that does not violate any existing contract between the employer and employees' representative. Under the regulations, the employer must make its designation of leave as paid or unpaid FMLA leave known to the employee within 2 business days of receiving notice from the employee that a leave will be taken or having enough information to make the deci-

---

91.   Moss v. Formosa Plastics Corp., 99 F. Supp. 2d 737 (MD La., 2000).

92.   Arban v. West Publishing Corp., 345 F. 3d 390 (6 CA, 2003).

93.   FMLA Reg. 29 CFR §825.114; Jones v. Denver Public Schools, 427 F.3d 1315 (10 CA, 2005).

94.   Russell v. North Broward Hospital, 346 F. 3d 1335 (11 CA, 2003).

95.   Miller v. AT&T, 250 F.3d 820 (4 CA, 2001); Rankin v. Seagate Technologies, Inc., 246 F.3d 1145 (8 CA, 2001).

96.   FMLA §102(b); FMLA Reg. 29 CFR §825.203 - §825.206.

97.   Brown v. Eastern Maine Medical Ctr., No. 06-60-P-H, 2007 U.S. Dist. LEXIS 76967 (D Me., 10-15-07).

98.   Mellen v. Trustees of Boston Univ., 504 F.3d 21 (1 CA, 2007).

99.   FMLA §102(d); FMLA Reg. 29 CFR §825.207 - §825.208; Brotherhood of Maintenance of Way Employees vs. CSX Transportation, Inc., No. 03 C 9419, 2005 U.S. Dist. LEXIS 37950 (ND Ill., 12-28-05).

sion. In any event it cannot make the decision after the leave has ended unless the employee was absent for an FMLA reason and the employer did not learn of the reason until the employee returned to work, or the employer has been unable to confirm that the leave qualifies under the FMLA. The employer's notice to the employee that leave is being designated as paid or unpaid FMLA leave may be oral or written. If the notice is oral, it must be confirmed in writing by the next payday (or by the following payday if the first payday is less than a week after the oral notice is given). The written notice may take any form, including a notation on the employee's pay stub.

A separate section of the regulations provides that, if an employer does not designate leave taken by an employee as FMLA leave, the leave does not count against the employee's FMLA leave entitlement. However, the U.S. Supreme Court said this part of the regulation was invalid because it gives certain employees more than the 12 weeks of leave guaranteed by the FMLA. In that case, the employee was given 30 weeks of unpaid leave with 6 months' paid medical benefits, and she was discharged when she didn't return to work after the leave period ended. She claimed she was entitled to another 12 weeks of FMLA leave because her employer had not designated any part of the 30-week leave as FMLA leave, but the Court said such a penalty would not comply with the intent of Congress to require employers to provide 12 weeks of leave in a 12-month period and would be disproportionate to the $100 fine contained in the law for notice violations.[100]

**Notice requirements for employees.**[101] When an employee requests leave to care for a newborn or newly adopted child, he or she must give the employer 30 days' notice or as much as can be given under the circumstances. The same requirement applies to leave because of serious medical conditions where the medical treatment is foreseeable. Unforeseen medical events require whatever notice is possible under the circumstances. A stricter company requirement was thrown out by a federal appeals court.[102] If the required notice is not provided, the employer can deny the leave request for up to 30 days after notice is provided, but only if the event making the leave necessary was clearly foreseeable. If an employer's benefit plan, a state law, or a collective bargaining agreement allow for a shorter notice period, the 30-day notice period does not apply.

**Benefits continue during leave.**[103] Health insurance benefits the employee enjoyed before the leave must be continued during the FMLA leave on the same basis. For example, if the employee was required to pay part of any health insurance premiums before the leave, the employer can require the payments during the leave. Changes to the plan occurring during the leave apply to the employee on FMLA leave (e.g., increased premium charges or co-payments). Employees who fail to pay can lose their coverage after 30 days, unless the employer's plan contains a longer grace period, but coverage must be restored when they return to work.

Before dropping the employee from coverage, the employer must provide written notice to the employee that the payment has not been received, at least 15 days before coverage will be ceased. Coverage may be ceased retroactively to the payment due date if the employer's health benefit plan includes such a provision. If an employee does not return to work after an FMLA leave for any reason other than the continuation or onset of a serious illness (or some other reason beyond the employee's control), the employer may act to recover any health premiums it paid on the employee's behalf during the leave. An employee must be back at work for at least 30 days before being considered to have "returned to work." If the employee uses paid leave, premiums are paid under the method normally used during any paid leave.

 **FMLA/COBRA INTERACTION** Employers have raised many questions regarding the effect of their FMLA obligations on requirements under the Consolidated Omnibus Budget Reconciliation Act of 1985 to provide continued health insurance coverage for employees and beneficiaries who lose their group coverage. For a discussion of answers provided by the IRS to some of the questions that have been raised, see Section 4.1-5.

---

100.   FMLA Reg. 29 CFR §825.700(a); Ragsdale v. Wolverine World Wide, Inc., 122 S.Ct. 1155 (2002).
101.   FMLA §102(e); FMLA Reg. 29 CFR §825.302 - §825.304; §825.312.
102.   Cavin v. Honda of America Mfg., Inc., 346 F 3d 713 (6 CA, 2003).
103.   FMLA §104(c); FMLA Reg. 29 CFR §825.209 - §825.213.

**Job guarantee upon return from leave.**[104] Employees returning from leave are entitled to their previous job or one that is "equivalent," with no loss of pay or benefits accruing before the leave (with a limited exemption for highly paid employees). The reinstatement must occur as soon as the employee returns from leave even if the employee returns before his or her anticipated return date.[105] The employee is not entitled to accrue any benefits or seniority during an unpaid FMLA leave, but any pay or benefit increases or improvements that do not depend on seniority must be made effective upon the employee's return to work. Also, leave time, whether paid or unpaid, must be treated as continued service under pension and retirement plans for vesting and qualification purposes.

An employer may deny reinstatement to "key employees" if it is necessary to prevent "substantial and grievous" economic injury to the employer's operations. A key employee is an employee paid on a salary basis (see Section 2.4-1) who is among the highest paid 10% of all the employees within 75 miles of the employee's worksite when the FMLA leave is requested. An employer contemplating a denial of reinstatement must tell the employee when leave is requested that the employee is a key employee and what will happen if the employer determines that the employee's reinstatement would cause the employer serious economic injury. The employer must notify the employee in writing of its determination as soon as it is made, either in person or by certified mail.

**Recordkeeping requirements.** In general, the FMLA requires employers to keep basic payroll records regarding hours worked, rate of pay, and deductions from wages, as well as records detailing the dates and amount of FMLA leave taken and copies of notices and documents related to FMLA leave. The records must be provided to U.S. Department of Labor officials on request. For details on these recordkeeping requirements, see Section 10.3-5.

**Enforcement.**[106] The FMLA is administered and enforced by the Department of Labor's Wage and Hour Division, which can investigate complaints brought by employees. Employees may also sue employers to recover lost wages and benefits as well as for reinstatement and promotion. Successful employees are entitled to additional liquidated damages (equal to the actual damages) unless the employer acted in good faith when it violated the FMLA, plus attorneys' fees, expert witness fees, and court costs.

*State employees' right to sue.* Despite the express coverage of state and local government employers in the FMLA, several federal appeals courts had ruled that employees could not sue their government employers because of the states' immunity from lawsuits under the U.S. Constitution. In 2003, however, the U.S. Supreme Court upheld the employees' right to sue after finding that Congress had properly tailored the protections and remedies of the FMLA to correct the effects of longstanding unconstitutional discrimination against women by all employers, including state and local governments.[107]

Since the *Hibbs* decision, several federal courts have limited it by ruling that it applies only to employees who exercise their rights under the FMLA's family care leave provisions, but not to state employees alleging interference with their rights under the law's personal medical leave provisions. The courts said the state government was immune from such suits.[108]

*Individual supervisors can be sued.* A federal district court ruled that the definition of an "employer" subject to suit under the FMLA includes individual government employees. The court said the definition of employer includes both individuals and public agencies, so it must include individuals in public agencies, although it acknowledged that there is a split among the courts on this issue.[109]

**Retaliation for exercise of FMLA rights prohibited.** Employers are prohibited from retaliating against employees because they tried to enforce their FMLA rights or from interfering with employees'

---

104.    FMLA §104(a), (b); FMLA Reg. 29 CFR §825.214 - §825.219.

105.    Hoge v. Honda of America Mfg., Inc., 2004 U.S. App. LEXIS 19384 (6 CA, 2004).

106.    FMLA §106; §107; FMLA Reg. 29 CFR §825.400 - §825.401.

107.    Nevada Department of Human Resources v. Hibbs, (2003) 123 S.Ct. 1972.

108.    Touvell v. Ohio Dept. of Mental Retardation and Developmental Disability, 422 F.3d 392 (6 CA, 2005); Toeller v. Wisconsin Dept. of Corrections, 461 F. 3d 871 (7 CA, 2006); Brockman v. Wyoming Dept. of Family Services, 342 F. 3d 1159 (10 CA. 2003).

109.    Carter v. U.S. Postal Service, 157 F.Supp.2d 726 (WD Ky., 2001).

attempts to exercise their FMLA rights.[110] This prohibition applies to former employees who seek to be rehired but are rejected because they took FMLA leave when they had previously worked for the employer.[111] The ban on retaliation also applies to employees who are not yet eligible for leave but who will need leave after their projected eligibility date (e.g., a pregnant employee who notifies her employer before she is FMLA-eligible that she will need FMLA leave after she is FMLA-eligible).[112] Employees also cannot waive their right to FMLA leave or to be free from retaliation for asserting their rights under the FMLA, either prospectively or retroactively.[113]

**FMLA vs. other federal and state laws.**[114] Several states have laws requiring family and/or medical leave in a similar fashion to the FMLA. Employers covered by both the FMLA and state law must comply with the law that provides the greatest benefits and protection to the employee requesting leave. The FMLA must also be considered by employers in conjunction with other federal and state civil rights laws, such as the Civil Rights Act and the Americans with Disabilities Act. Regulations issued by the Wage and Hour Division do not address all the interrelationships between the FMLA and employee benefit plans, especially regarding tax issues and the FMLA's effect on cafeteria plans and flexible spending arrangements (see Section 4.5). Employers with questions in this area should contact the IRS.

**Interaction of FMLA and cafeteria plans.** Because of the confusion surrounding the effect of the FMLA on IRC §125 cafeteria plans, the IRS issued regulations in 2001. The regulations do not interpret the FMLA but instead provide guidance on the cafeteria plan rules that apply to employees in circumstances where the FMLA and the Labor Department's regulations also apply.

*Employee is responsible for premiums during leave.*[115] Under the FMLA regulations, an employee is entitled to continue group health plan coverage during FMLA leave, whether or not provided under a cafeteria plan (including a health flexible spending arrangement). Under the IRS regulations, an employee making premium payments under a cafeteria plan who chooses to continue group health plan coverage while on FMLA leave is responsible for the share of group health premiums that the employee was paying while working, such as amounts paid under a salary reduction agreement. The employer must continue to contribute the share of the cost of the employee's coverage that the employer was paying before the employee started FMLA leave.

The employer must also allow an employee on unpaid FMLA leave to revoke coverage or to continue coverage but without continuing to pay the employee's share of the premiums for the period of the leave. The employer does not have to allow the employee to revoke coverage during the leave if the employer pays the employee's share of the health insurance premiums (including a health FSA). The employee also has the right to reinstatement of health coverage after unpaid FMLA leave (including a health FSA) if the coverage had terminated during the leave period because the employee revoked coverage or did not pay the premiums. And employees on FMLA leave must be allowed to revoke or change cafeteria plan elections under the same terms and conditions that are available to employees who are working and are not on FMLA leave.[116]

*Payment options.*[117] A cafeteria plan may offer, on a nondiscriminatory basis, one or more of the following three payment options to employees continuing group health plan coverage while on unpaid FMLA leave, subject to certain limitations. The options offered must be at least as favorable as those offered to employees who are not on FMLA leave.

<u>Pre-pay.</u> Under the pre-pay option, the plan may permit—but may not require—the employee to pay the amounts due for the FMLA leave period before the leave begins. Pre-paid contributions may be made on a

---

110. FMLA §105; FMLA Reg. 29 CFR §825.220.
111. Smith v. BellSouth Telecommunications, Inc., 273 F.3d 1303 (11 CA, 2001).
112. Beffert v. Pennsylvania Department of Public Welfare, No. 05-43, 2005 U.S. Dist. LEXIS 6681 (ED Pa., 4-18-05).
113. Taylor v. Progress Energy, Inc., 415 F.3d 364 (4 CA, 2005), reaff'd 493 F.3d 454 (4 CA, 2007).
114. FMLA §401; FMLA Reg. 29 CFR §825.701 - §825.702.
115. IRS Reg. §1.125-3, Q&A-2.
116. IRS Reg. §1.125-3, Q&A-1.
117. IRS Reg. §1.125-3, Q&A-3.

pre-tax salary reduction basis from any taxable compensation (including the cashing out of unused sick days or vacation days), or on an after-tax basis.

Pay-as-you-go. This option permits employees to pay their share of the premium on the same schedule as payments made if the employee were not on leave or under any other payment schedule permitted by the FMLA regulations (e.g., a COBRA payment schedule). Contributions under this option are generally made by the employee on an after-tax basis, but they may be made pre-tax to the extent that the contributions are made from taxable compensation (including the cashing out of unused sick days or vacation days) due the employee during the leave period, and provided that all cafeteria plan requirements are met.

Catch-up. If the catch-up option is used, the employer and the employee must agree in advance of the coverage period that: the employee elects to continue health coverage while on unpaid FMLA leave; the employer will assume responsibility for advancing payment of the premiums on the employee's behalf during the leave period; and the advanced amounts will be paid by the employee when the employee returns to work. However, if the employee fails to make required premium payments while on FMLA leave and the employer chooses to continue the coverage during that period, the employer can use the catch-up option to recoup the employee's share of premiums when the employee returns to work, even without the prior agreement of the employee. Contributions under the catch-up option may be made on a pre-tax salary reduction basis from any available taxable compensation after the employee returns from FMLA leave, or they may be made on an after-tax basis.

 **WATCH OUT FOR RESTRICTIONS** The pre-pay option cannot be the sole option offered to employees on FMLA leave, but it can be included as an option even if it is not offered to employees on unpaid non-FMLA leave. The catch-up option can be the sole option offered only if the catch-up option is the only option offered to employees on unpaid non-FMLA leave. If the pay-as-you-go option is offered to employees on unpaid non-FMLA leave, the option must also be offered to employees on unpaid FMLA leave. The employer may also offer employees on FMLA leave the pre-pay option and/or the catch-up option.

*What about employees on paid FMLA leave?* [118] If an employee is on paid FMLA leave (e.g., the employee is using sick or vacation pay during the leave) and the employer requires that the employee continue group health plan coverage while on FMLA leave, the employee's share of the premiums must be paid by the method normally used during any paid leave. Therefore, the premiums would be paid by pre-tax salary reduction if they were paid using that method before the FMLA leave began.

*Rules for health FSAs.* [119] A health flexible spending arrangement (FSA, see Section 4.5-7) offered under a cafeteria plan is governed by the generally applicable rules concerning employees who take FMLA leave. Therefore, employees must be allowed to continue coverage under a health FSA while on FMLA leave and use the payment options discussed earlier in this section. Employees on unpaid FMLA leave must be allowed to either revoke coverage or to continue coverage but discontinue paying premiums for the leave period. Employees must be allowed to reinstate health FSA coverage upon returning to work from unpaid FMLA leave, and the employer can require reinstatement if it also requires such reinstatement after an unpaid non-FMLA leave.

If the employee continues coverage during an unpaid FMLA leave (or the employee continues it for an employee who stops paying premiums), the full amount of the elected health FSA coverage, minus any prior reimbursements, must be available to the employee at all times. If an employee's health FSA coverage terminates during the FMLA leave, the employee is not entitled to reimbursement for claims incurred during the period when coverage was terminated, even if the employee's coverage is later reinstated. Upon reinstatement of coverage, the employee can resume coverage at the prior level for the year and make up the unpaid premiums or resume coverage at a reduced level and resume payments at the level in effect before the FMLA leave. If the employee chooses the reduced level of coverage for the remainder of the year, the coverage is prorated to account for the period during which no premiums were paid.

---

118.   IRS Reg. §1.125-3, Q&A-4.
119.   IRS Reg. §1.125-3, Q&A-6.

***Example 1:*** Employee Natalie elects $1,200 of coverage under her employer's health FSA, with an annual premium of $1,200. She elects to pay the premiums through pre-tax salary reductions of $100 per month. Natalie paid the first 3 months' premiums and had no medical expenses before taking FMLA leave from April-June. She paid no premiums while on leave and her coverage was terminated. Natalie returns from FMLA leave on July 1 and elects to be reinstated in the FSA at that time.

Natalie must be given the choice of resuming coverage at $1,200 and making up the $300 in unpaid premiums or resuming a reduced level of coverage with premium payments at the pre-FMLA leave level. If Natalie elects to resume full-year coverage, her coverage for the rest of the year will be $1,200 and her monthly premiums will be $150 ($100 + ($300 ÷ 6 months). If Natalie chooses prorated coverage, her coverage for the rest of the year will be $900 ($1,200 - $300 (3 months' coverage)) and she will resume paying $100 per month in premiums.

***Example 2:*** Assume the same facts as in Example 1, except that Natalie had $200 in medical expenses in February for which she was reimbursed. If Natalie chooses full-year coverage when she returns from FMLA leave, her coverage for the rest of the year will be $1,000 ($1,200 - $200) and her monthly premiums will be $150. If Natalie chooses prorated coverage, her coverage for the rest of the year will be $700 ($1,200 prorated for 9 months - $200) and she will resume paying $100 per month in premiums.

***Example 3:*** Assume the same facts as in Example 1, except that Natalie elects to continue her health FSA coverage while on FMLA leave and chooses the catch-up payment option. She also chooses to pay the $300 in missed premiums on an equal basis over the last 6 months of the year. Natalie's monthly premium payments for the rest of the year will be $150 ($100 + ($300 ÷ 6 months).

*Effect of FMLA leave on non-health benefits.*[120] The FMLA does not require an employer to maintain an employee's non-health benefits (e.g., life insurance) during FMLA leave. An employee's entitlement to benefits other than group health benefits under a cafeteria plan while on FMLA leave is determined by the employer's established policy for providing such benefits when the employee is on non-FMLA leave. Therefore, an employee who takes FMLA leave is entitled to revoke an election of non-health benefits under a cafeteria plan to the same extent employees taking non-FMLA leave are permitted to make such revocations (see Section 4.5-4).

*Effect of leave extending to the next year.*[121] Under general cafeteria plan rules, an employee cannot defer compensation from one year to the next. This means that an employee who elects to pre-pay health insurance premiums for an FMLA leave spanning two cafeteria plan years can pay on a pre-tax basis only for the premiums due in the first year. Another payment option must be chosen for the premiums due during the second year.

# 4.3 Sick Pay

One of the more vexing payroll issues is the tax treatment of "sick pay." Sick pay can take many forms, but its essential purpose is to replace the wages of an employee who cannot work because of an illness or injury. The tax treatment of such payments depends on several variables, including who makes the payments, who bears the insurance risk, who paid the premiums on any insurance involved, and whether the employee is temporarily or permanently unable to work.

---

120. IRS Reg. §1.125-3, Q&A-7.
121. IRS Reg. §1.125-3, Q&A-5.

**WORKERS' COMPENSATION IS DIFFERENT** This section deals with payments to employees who cannot work because of non job-related injuries or illnesses. When an employee suffers a work-related injury or illness, payments are made from a state-sponsored or privately insured workers' compensation fund. The payroll aspects of workers' compensation benefits are discussed in Section 4.4.

## 4.3-1 Sick Leave Pay

Most employers provide their employees with paid "sick leave" or "sick days" so they will receive their regular salaries for brief absences from work due to illness or injury. Payments are made from the regular payroll account and are taxable wages subject to federal income tax withholding and social security, Medicare, and FUTA taxes when paid. Under most such policies, employees who exceed the allotted number of sick days are forced to take unpaid leave for the excess days or to use other available paid leave (e.g., vacation, personal days).

## 4.3-2 Sick Pay Under a Separate Plan

When employees are absent from work due to illness or injury for more than a few days but are expected to return to work at some point, they generally receive wage replacement income through their employer's sick pay plan, in the form of either short-term or long-term disability payments. The payments may be made by the employer, an agent of the employer, or a third-party insurance company.

**How much is taxable?** Whether payments to an employee under a sick pay or disability plan are taxable income to the employee depends on how the plan benefits are funded.[122] Any benefits provided that are attributable to employee contributions made after taxes had been withheld from an employee's wages are not taxable income.

Benefits that are attributable to employer contributions or to employee pre-tax contributions through a cafeteria plan (see Section 4.5) are taxable income to the employee and may be subject to federal income tax withholding and social security, Medicare, and FUTA taxes (see discussion following). Where the employer and the employee both contribute to the premiums for the disability insurance plan, the taxable portion of benefits received is the amount attributable to the employer-funded portion of the premiums.[123] Where the employer and employee both contribute to a group insurance policy, special rules for determining the amount of benefits included in the employee's income apply. If the employer knows the net premiums paid for at least 3 policy years, the formula for calculating the employee's taxable amount is as follows:

employee's sick pay x $\dfrac{\text{employer-paid premiums for last 3 years}}{\text{total premiums for last 3 years}}$

***Example:*** Employee Jim was injured in a non job-related accident on February 29, 2008 and was out of work until January 1, 2009. Jim received payments of $2,000 per month while out of work from his employer's insurance company. During the 3 policy years before 2008, Jim's employer contributed $28,000 in net premiums to insure its employees, while the employees paid $12,000 in after-tax dollars. The amount of Jim's monthly sick pay that is included in income is:

taxable sick pay = $2,000 x [$28,000 ÷ ($28,000 + $12,000)]

taxable sick pay = $2,000 x ($28,000 ÷ $40,000)

taxable sick pay = $2,000 x .7

taxable sick pay = $1,400

---

122. LTR 200613023, 12-14-05.
123. IRC §104(a)(3); §105(a); §3121(a)(2)(A); §3306(b)(2)(A); IRS Reg. §1.104-1(d); §1.105-1; §31.3121(a)(2)-1; §31.3306(b)(2)-1; Rev. Rul. 2004-55, 2004-26 IRB 1081.

**Responsibility for income withholding and employment taxes.** Once it is determined that payments under a sick pay or disability plan are taxable income in whole or part to an employee, the next step is to determine the federal income tax withholding and social security, Medicare, and FUTA tax responsibilities related to the taxable portion of the payments. See IRS Publication 15-A, *Employer's Supplemental Tax Guide*, for more information on taxation and reporting of sick pay.

*Payments made by employer.* Where the employer's sick pay plan is self-insured (i.e., the employer bears the insurance risk) and the employer makes the payments, the employer must withhold federal income tax based on the employee's most recent Form W-4, *Employee's Withholding Allowance Certificate* (see Section 6.3-1 and Appendix page A-91). The employer must also pay its share of social security and Medicare taxes, withhold the employee's share of those taxes, and pay FUTA tax for all payments made within 6 calendar months after the end of the last month during which the employee worked for the employer.[124] If the employee returns to work during the six-month period, a new six-month period would begin if the employee later leaves again on disability leave.

> **Example:** Employee Eileen receives serious injuries in a weekend, non job-related softball game on July 5, 2008 and does not return to work until April 20, 2009. Eileen does not contribute to the premiums for her employer's disability plan. Her employer must withhold federal income tax from payments it makes to her under its disability plan for the entire time she is absent from work. The employer must also pay social security, Medicare, and FUTA taxes and withhold Eileen's share of social security and Medicare taxes on payments made until January 31, 2009, up to the applicable social security and FUTA wage bases (6 calendar months after the end of the month during which she last worked for the employer).

*Payments made by employer's agent.* Where the employer contracts with a third party to administer its disability plan and pays the third party on a cost-plus-fee basis while retaining the insurance risk (i.e., no premiums are paid to the third party), payments made to disabled employees by the third party are treated as if made by the employer. The third-party agent may treat the payments as supplemental wages (see Section 6.4-4) for federal income tax withholding purposes and withhold at a flat 25% rate if it is not an agent that also pays regular wages to the employee (the rate is 35% if the employee's year-to-date supplemental wages exceed $1 million). The employer retains its responsibility for social security, Medicare, and FUTA tax withholding and payment unless it enters into an agreement with the agent providing that the agent will be responsible for employment taxes.[125]

*Payments made by a third party who is not an agent.* Where the employer contracts with a third-party insurer to make disability payments to its employees and the third party bears the risk of insuring the employees (i.e., it is paid a premium by the employer and/or the employees), it assumes a greater role in the area of tax responsibility. The third party is not required to withhold federal income tax from payments made to a disabled employee unless the employee requests a certain amount be withheld by furnishing the third party with Form W-4S, *Request for Federal Income Tax Withholding From Sick Pay* (see Section 6.3-3 and Appendix page A-97). If the employee provides Form W-4S, the third party must begin withholding with the first payment made at least 8 days after the form is provided. Through Form W-4S, the employee requests that a flat dollar amount be withheld from each payment. The minimum amount that can be withheld is $20 per week, and after withholding, the employee must receive at least $10. The third-party payer may also voluntarily allow employees receiving sick pay to request that a specific percentage be withheld rather than a flat dollar amount. The minimum is 10%. No matter which withholding method is used, if the amount requested to be withheld reduces the net sick payment to below $10, no federal income tax should be withheld from that payment. If a payment is smaller or larger than a regular payment (e.g., the employee receives a raise), the amount withheld must be changed in the same proportion as the payment.[126]

---

124.   IRC §3121(a)(4); §3306(b)(4); IRS Reg. §31.3121(a)(4)-1; §31.3306(a)(4)-1.
125.   IRS Reg. §31.3401(a)-1(b)(8); IRS Temp. Reg. §32.1(e)(3).
126.   IRC §3402(o); IRS Reg. §31.3402(o)-3.

***Example:*** Employee Ken receives $250 per week in sick pay from Back-to-Work Insurance Co., a third-party insurer, and files a Form W-4S asking that $50 per week be withheld for federal income tax. After being out 4 full weeks, Ken returns to work on Wednesday of the next week (having been absent on sick leave Monday and Tuesday). For the week in which Ken returns to work, he is entitled to $100 in sick pay:

$$\text{sick pay} = \frac{\text{number of days on sick leave in week}}{\text{number of days in week}} \times \$250$$

$$\text{sick pay} = \frac{2}{5} \times \$250 = \$100$$

Because Ken receives only 40% of his weekly sick pay ($250 x .40 = $100), the amount of federal income tax withheld from his sick pay should be 40% of the regular withholding amount, or $20 ($50 x .40 = $20). Therefore, his net sick pay for the partial week on sick leave is $80 ($100 - $20).

 **PRACTICAL PROBLEM** While IRS regulations provide that third-party payers are to withhold from sick pay based on an employee's Form W-4S or a substitute form with identical provisions, Form W-4S does not provide a percentage withholding option. It calls for a specific dollar amount.

The third party must withhold and pay over the employee's share of social security and Medicare taxes for each payment made within 6 months after the end of the last month the employee worked for the employer. The third party is also responsible for the employer's share of social security and Medicare, as well as FUTA, unless it transfers the liability for these taxes back to the employer. To do this, the third party must:

1.  withhold and timely deposit the employee's share of social security and Medicare taxes;

2.  notify the employer of the payments on which social security and Medicare taxes were withheld and deposited, within the time allowed for the third party to make the deposit; and

3.  provide a statement to the employer by January 15 following the year during which payments were made providing each employee's name and social security number, the amount of sick pay paid to the employee, and the amount of federal income, social security, and Medicare taxes withheld from the sick pay (a similar statement must be furnished to each employee by the employer by January 31).[127]

 **SPECIAL RULE FOR MULTIEMPLOYER PLANS** If a third-party insurer makes payments to employees under an insurance contract with a multiemployer plan governed by a collective bargaining agreement, special notification timing rules apply. If the third party timely withholds and deposits the employee's share of social security and Medicare taxes and gives the plan the required notice of the payments on which such taxes were withheld, then the plan must pay the employer's share of social security and Medicare taxes and FUTA tax. However, if the plan provides notice to the employee's employer within 6 days after the plan receives notice from the third party, the employer must pay the employer's share of social security and Medicare taxes and FUTA tax.

To aid the third party in properly meeting its withholding, depositing, and reporting responsibilities, the employer should be prepared to provide the third party with the following information, which can be relied on by the third party.[128]

---

127.    IRC §6051(f); IRS Reg. §31.6051-3(a); IRS Temp. Reg. §32.1(e).
128.    IRS Temp. Reg. §32.1(e)(4).

1. the total wages paid by the employer to the employee during the calendar year before the third party begins making payments (helps determine whether social security and FUTA tax wage bases have been met);

2. the last date on which the employee worked for the employer (helps determine how long the third party is responsible for social security, Medicare, and FUTA taxes); and

3. the employee contributions made to the disability plan after taxes have been withheld, expressed as a percentage of total contributions (helps determine how much of each disability payment is taxable).

**Depositing withheld taxes.**[129] The general rules for depositing withheld income and employment taxes (see Sections 7.1-5 and 8.2) apply to sick pay, although the liability for depositing may vary depending on who is responsible. Where the employer or the employer's agent makes the payments, withholding is required when the payments are made and the liability to deposit begins at that time. Where a third-party insurer makes the payments and transfers the liability for FUTA and the employer's share of social security and Medicare taxes to the employer, the employer is liable for the employment taxes when it is notified timely by the third party as to the amount of the payments made and employee social security and Medicare taxes withheld and deposited.

If the third party does not transfer social security and Medicare tax liability to the employer, it becomes liable for depositing those taxes (along with the employee's share of social security and Medicare and any withheld income taxes) when payment is made to the employee. The third party should make the deposit using its own name and employer identification number (EIN), not the employer's.

If the third party properly transfers the responsibility for the employer's share of social security, Medicare, and FUTA taxes to the employer, it must deposit only the employee's share of social security, Medicare, and withheld income taxes, using its own name and EIN.

**Reporting responsibilities.**[130] Once again, the responsibilities for reporting income and employment taxes withheld and deposited depend on the sick pay agreement and who made the payments to employees.

*Employer makes payments.* Where disability payments are made by the employer under a self-insured plan:

- the employer must report all taxable amounts on its quarterly Form 941 on Lines 2, 5a, and 5c, with the amount of income tax withheld on Line 3 (see Section 8.3 for full details on Form 941 reporting);

- the taxable amounts must also be reported to the employee on Form W-2 in Boxes 1, 3, and 5 (nontaxable amounts attributable to employee contributions in Box 12, preceded by Code "J"), and the amounts withheld on lines 2, 4, and 6 (see Section 8.8 for details on Form W-2 reporting); and

- all payments must be reported on Form 940 in Part 2, Line 3, with exempt payments reported in Part 2, Line 4, and Box 4e "other" should be checked (see Section 7.1-5 for full details on Form 940 reporting).

*Employer's agent makes payments.* Generally, the employer retains the responsibility for reporting disability payments when its third-party agent administers the payments, and the employer's name and EIN are used on all forms. However, if the agency agreement shifts the responsibility from the employer to the agent, the agent should use its own name and EIN on reporting forms. The agency agreement must be filed with the IRS using Form 2678, *Employer / Payer Appointment of Agent* (see Appendix page A-337).

---

129. IRS Pub. 15-A, Employer's Supplemental Tax Guide
130. IRS Pub. 15-A, Employer's Supplemental Tax Guide

*Third-party insurer makes payments.* The employer and the third party each have reporting responsibilities when the third party bears the insurance risk and makes the benefit payments. If the third party does not properly transfer the liability for the employer's share of social security, Medicare, and FUTA taxes to the employer:

- it must report the taxable amount of sick pay on its quarterly Form 941 on Lines 2, 5a, and 5c, with the amount of income tax withheld on Line 3 (see Section 8.3 for full details on Form 941 reporting);

- the taxable amounts must also be reported by the third party to the employee on Form W-2 in Boxes 1, 3, and 5 (nontaxable amounts attributable to employee contributions in Box 12, preceded by Code "J"), and the amounts withheld in Boxes 2, 4, and 6 (see Section 8.8 for full details on Form W-2 reporting), with the third party's name, address, and EIN instead of the employer's information;

- the checkbox "third-party sick pay" must be checked off in Box 13 of Form W-2; and

- all payments must be reported on Form 940 in Part 2, Line 3, with exempt payments reported in Part 2, Line 4, and Box 4e "other" should be checked.

If the third party properly transfers the employment tax liability to the employer, the rules regarding each reporting form become quite complex for each party involved.

*Form 941.* The employer must include taxable third-party sick pay on Lines 2, 5a, and 5c, and then report on Line 7b the employees' share of social security and Medicare taxes withheld and deposited by the third party. The third party must include social security and Medicare taxable sick pay payments on Lines 5a and 5c (not Line 2) and the amount of federal income tax it withheld from sick pay on Line 3. It must then subtract on Line 7b the employer's share of social security and Medicare taxes.

*Forms W-2 and W-3.* Generally, the employer prepares the actual Form W-2 for third-party sick pay received by its employees, using either a separate W-2 for sick pay only or combining it with the employee's regular wages on one form. The Form W-2 must contain the employer's name, address, and EIN, as well as the employee's name, address, and social security number. The taxable third-party sick pay must be included in Boxes 1, 3, and 5, and the taxes withheld in Boxes 2, 4, and 6. Any sick pay that was nontaxable because it was attributed to employee contributions to premiums is included in Box 12, preceded by Code "J." In Box 13, the employer should mark the checkbox "Third-party sick pay." The employer should complete Boxes b, c, e, f, g, 1-6, and 14 of Form W-3.

*"Recap" Forms W-2 and W-3.* The third party must prepare third-party sick pay recap Forms W-2 and W-3 that reflect all sick pay payments made to employees of the third party's clients. These forms are needed to reconcile wages shown on the third party's Form 941 that will not be shown on its regular Forms W-2 and W-3. On the recap Form W-2, the third-party uses its own name, address, and EIN, and in Box e it must write "Third-party sick pay recap" instead of the employee's name. It must include the total taxable third-party sick pay payments in Box 1, the amount subject to social security and Medicare taxes in Boxes 3 and 5 respectively, and the taxes withheld in Boxes 2, 4, and 6. The recap Form W-2 should then be attached to a recap Form W-3, of which only Boxes b, e, f, g, 1-6, and 13 are completed (Box 14 is for the employer). The third party must write "Third-Party Sick Pay Recap" in Box 13. The recap forms should not be filed on magnetic media or electronically.

 **W-2 TRANSFER OPTION** The employer and the third-party payer have the option of agreeing that the third party will be the employer's agent solely for purposes of preparing Forms W-2 for sick pay. Under such an agreement, the third party provides actual Forms W-2 to each employee, and the employer must prepare recap Forms W-2 and W-3 to aid in its wage reconciliation. The third party also does not have to provide the employer with the annual sick pay statement mentioned earlier in our discussion of withholding responsibilities.[131]

---

131.   IRS Reg. §31.6051-3(c).

*Form 940.* Form 940 must be prepared by the employer once employment tax liability is transferred, with all sick pay reported in Part 2, Line 3, and exempt sick pay in Part 2, Line 4 with Box 4e "other" checked.

## 4.3-3 Permanent Disability Benefits

The treatment of payments made under a disability plan where the employee is not expected to return to work is somewhat different than for payments to employees who are temporarily disabled. Payments to totally and permanently disabled employees are income to the employees and are subject to federal income tax withholding by the party making the payments to the extent the employer paid the premiums or the employee paid the premiums with pre-tax dollars. Amounts paid under a definite plan or system on or after the employment relationship has been terminated because of death or disability retirement are not subject to social security, Medicare, or FUTA tax.[132] (The plan must not be set up for the benefit of employees' dependents only.) However, such amounts are subject to employment taxes if they would have been paid even if the employment relationship would not have been terminated for such a reason. One example is a payment to a disabled former employee for unused vacation time that would have been made regardless of the reason for termination. Such a payment is subject to social security, Medicare, and FUTA taxes.

Also exempt from social security and Medicare taxes are payments made under a plan to an employee who is receiving disability insurance benefits under Section 223(a) of the Social Security Act.[133] For this exemption to apply, the employee must have been entitled to the social security disability benefits before the calendar year in which the payments under the plan are made, and the employee must perform no services for the employer during the period for which the payments under the plan are made. The payments made under the plan are not exempt from FUTA tax, however.

## 4.4 Workers' Compensation Insurance

The workers' compensation system may not appear to have anything to do with payroll, but actually it can have an effect in two distinct areas, benefits and premiums. Workers' compensation is a form of insurance employers are generally required to buy to insulate them against lawsuits brought by employees who are hurt or become ill while working.

## 4.4-1 Benefit Payments

Payments received as workers' compensation benefits are not included in an employee's gross income and are not subject to any employment taxes.[134] This exemption applies only to amounts received as compensation for injuries or illnesses suffered on the job, and only to amounts that do not exceed the benefits provided under the applicable state or federal workers' compensation law.

The exclusion is not limited to benefits paid by a state workers' compensation agency, but may include some employer payments (most often in the public sector). To be excluded, the payments must be made under a federal, state, or local law or regulations issued by a political subdivision, such as a sewer district or school board, that are "in the nature of a workmen's compensation act." This exclusion also applies to federal income and employment taxes.[135]

Some employers arrange with their employees to pay them all or part of their salary while they are receiving workers' compensation benefits, in return for which the employees turn over their workers' compensation benefits to the employer. Under such an arrangement, any amount paid to the employee in excess of the employee's workers' compensation benefits is wages subject to federal income tax withholding and social security, Medicare, and FUTA taxes.[136]

---

132. IRC §3121(a)(13); §3306(b)(10); IRS Reg. §31.3121(a)(13)-1; §31.3306(b)(10)-1; IRS Pub. 15-A, Employer's Supplemental Tax Guide.
133. IRC §3121(a)(15); IRS Reg. §31.3121(a)(15)-1.
134. IRC §104(a)(3); §3121(a)(2)(A); §3306(b)(2)(A); IRS Reg. §1.104-1(b).
135. IRS Reg. §31.3121(a)(2)-1(d).
136. Rev. Rul. 56-83, 1956-1 CB 79.

## 4.4-2 Premium Payments

The payroll department plays a central role in determining an employer's workers' compensation premiums. The premium an employer pays for workers' compensation insurance, whether the insurer is a state fund or a private insurance carrier or the employer is self-insured, is generally based on the type of business the employer engages in and the size of its payroll (but see the discussion on classification exceptions following).

Each state has its own workers' compensation law setting premium rates and benefits, assigning classification codes, and determining what types of employee compensation are included in calculating premiums.

These differences can increase the administrative burden on the payroll department, especially for employers with operations in a number of states. The states can be broken down into 4 categories in their approach to workers' compensation insurance.

**National Council states.** The large majority of states (39 states plus the District of Columbia) are called National Council states for purposes of workers' compensation because they adhere to the uniform classification codes (see discussion following) in the *Basic Manual for Workers' Compensation,* which is published by the National Council on Compensation Insurance. These states are listed below:

| | | | |
|---|---|---|---|
| Alabama | Idaho | Minnesota | Oklahoma |
| Alaska | Illinois | Mississippi | Oregon |
| Arizona | Indiana | Minnesota | Rhode Island |
| Arkansas | Iowa | Montana | South Carolina |
| Colorado | Kansas | Nebraska | South Dakota |
| Connecticut | Kentucky | Nevada | Tennessee |
| Dist. of Columbia | Louisiana | New Hampshire | Utah |
| Florida | Maine | New Mexico | Vermont |
| Georgia | Maryland | North Carolina | Virginia |
| Hawaii | Massachusetts | Ohio | Wisconsin |

**Non-National Council states.** There are 7 states that use independent workers' compensation manuals (California, Delaware, Michigan, New Jersey, New York, Pennsylvania, and Texas), although many of the classification codes they use are identical to those used in National Council states.

**Monopolistic states.** There are 4 states (North Dakota, Washington, West Virginia, and Wyoming) that administer workers' compensation premiums and benefits solely through a state fund, prohibiting employers from purchasing insurance from a private insurance carrier. The premiums are deposited and reported in much the same way as an employment tax.

**Competitive state funds.** Twelve National Council states (Arizona, California, Colorado, Idaho, Maryland, Michigan, Montana, New York, Oklahoma, Oregon, Pennsylvania, and Utah) allow private insurance carriers to compete with a state workers' compensation fund. Where an employer's workers' compensation needs are handled through the state fund, premiums are deposited and reported in much the same way as an employment tax.

**Classification codes.** Employers are assigned "classification codes" based on the type of business they carry on (manufacturing, mining, construction, restaurant, etc.), although different codes are needed for certain employees. A dollar value is then assigned to the code and it is multiplied by the employer's total payroll allocated to the code (minus certain exceptions, such as overtime premiums) to determine the employer's workers' compensation premium. The payroll department can affect the amount of the premium in two major ways:

- finding employees who may be assigned a less costly classification code than that assigned to the employer as a whole; and
- making sure compensation that can be excluded from total payroll is in fact excluded.

**Classification code exceptions.** While an employer's business generally determines its classification code, and the more dangerous the business the higher the dollar value assigned to that code, some employees may be assigned a different and less costly code because of the duties they perform. Employees who work exclusively in an office, outside salespeople, and drivers and their helpers may be assigned a "standard exception classification." Such classifications generally carry a significantly lower dollar value than other employee classifications. Therefore, the payroll department must be very careful if asked to determine an employee's qualifications for such an exception.

**Included and excluded payroll.** Certain types of employee compensation can be excluded when an employer determines the total payroll figure that must be used to calculate its workers' compensation premium. Because a lower total payroll figure necessarily means a lower premium, the payroll department should be on the lookout for employee compensation that can be excluded from total payroll.

The most important exclusion from total payroll is money paid as overtime premiums—the 50% extra per hour that an employee earns for working beyond the normal workweek (100% where the employee is paid double time). But remember that only the overtime premium is excluded, not the entire amount earned for working overtime. Other exclusions that apply generally throughout the states include:

- reimbursed travel expenses
- third-party sick pay
- reimbursed moving expenses
- tips
- personal use of company-provided vehicle
- group-term life insurance over $50,000
- severance pay
- educational assistance payments
- employer contributions to group pension or insurance plans, other than employee elective deferrals

 **WATCH OUT FOR THE STATES** Because workers' compensation insurance is a matter of state law, each state has its own formulas for determining insurance premiums and its own list of payments to employees that are included and excluded from an employer's total payroll. Therefore, the payroll department must be aware of the inclusions and exclusions in the states where the employer has employees.

# 4.5 Cafeteria Plans

An increasingly popular benefit offered by mid-size and large employers is the "cafeteria plan," which gives employees a choice from a "menu" of cash compensation and nontaxable (qualified) benefits. Many people use the term "flexible benefit plan" to describe a cafeteria plan, but a flexible benefit plan is any plan that offers employees a choice of benefits, while a cafeteria plan is a specific type of flexible benefit plan authorized by §125 of the Internal Revenue Code.

In 2007, the IRS issued a comprehensive set of proposed regulations to replace earlier proposed and temporary rules that needed to be updated to reflect changes in §125 that had been enacted over the years. The new proposed regulations are scheduled to take effect January 1, 2009, but may be relied on by employers before that date. The material in the following subsections is based on §125 and these new proposed regulations.

These regulations clarify that when employees may elect between taxable and nontaxable benefits, this ability to elect results in gross income to the employees unless the election is made under a cafeteria plan that satisfies the requirements of IRC §125 and the regulations.[137] The amount included in income is the value of the taxable benefit with the greatest value that the employee could have elected to receive, even if the employee elects to receive only nontaxable benefits, and it is included in the year the employee would have actually received the taxable benefit. Reasons that a plan would fail to satisfy the §125 requirements include:

---

137.    IRS Prop. Reg. §125-1(b)(1).

- offering nonqualified benefits;
- not offering an election between at least one permitted taxable benefit and at least one qualified benefit;
- deferring compensation;
- failing to comply with the uniform coverage rule or use-or-lose rule;
- allowing employees to revoke elections or make new elections during a plan year, except as provided in the regulations;
- failing to comply with substantiation requirements;
- paying or reimbursing expenses incurred for qualified benefits before the effective date of the cafeteria plan or before a period of coverage;
- allocating experience gains (forfeitures) other than as expressly allowed in the regulations; and
- failing to comply with grace period rules.

# 4.5-1 What Benefits Can Be Offered

Basically, a cafeteria plan provides participants a choice among permitted taxable (cash) and nontaxable (qualified) benefits. The plan must contain at least one of each, and usually contains several qualified benefits.[138] Qualified nontaxable benefits include any benefit not included in an employee's wages under the IRC except for:[139]

- scholarships and fellowships
- nontaxable fringe benefits under IRC §132 (working condition fringes, no-additional-cost services, de minimis fringes, qualified employee discounts, qualified transportation fringes, and qualified moving expense reimbursements)
- educational assistance
- meals and lodging furnished for the benefit of the employer
- employer contributions to Archer MSAs
- long-term care insurance, except for long-term care insurance or services purchased with funds from a Health Savings Account offered as a qualified benefit
- group-term life insurance on the life of anyone other than an employee, whether the insurance is included in income or not
- Health Reimbursement Arrangements that allow any unused amount to be carried over to the next coverage period to increase the maximum reimbursement amount
- Elective deferrals to a §403(b) plan

A plan that offers any of these nonqualified benefits is not a cafeteria plan, and allowing employees to elect them will result in income to the employees.

Some examples of qualified benefits are:

- coverage under accident and health insurance plans (medical, dental, vision, sick pay, etc.) other than long-term care insurance plans
- coverage under dependent care assistance plans
- group-term life insurance on the lives of employees (even where the benefit exceeds $50,000, although the excess is subject to federal income tax and social security and Medicare taxes)
- qualified adoption assistance
- premiums for COBRA continuation coverage
- accidental death and dismemberment insurance
- long-term and short-term disability coverage
- a §401(k) plan
- contributions to Health Savings Accounts

---

138.   IRC §125(a); §125(d)(1); IRS Prop. Reg. §1.125-1(b)(4).
139.   IRC §125(f); IRS Prop. Reg. §1.125-1(q).

**Premium-only plans.** These plans, known as POPs or premium conversion plans, are used by employers who require their employees to contribute toward benefits, usually health insurance. A POP plan generally does not offer a "menu" of benefits to choose from. It merely allows employees to pay for their share of the benefit costs on a pre-tax basis through a salary reduction in the amount of the required contribution. They are permissible under §125.[140]

**Deferred compensation.**[141] The rules governing cafeteria plans generally prohibit the inclusion of any plan providing for or allowing the deferral of compensation. A cafeteria plan violates this rule if it allows employees to:

- carry over unused contributions or benefits from one plan year to another (e.g., purchased vacation days); or
- use contributions from one plan year to purchase benefits the employer will provide in a later plan year.

There is an exception, however, for cash or deferred arrangements under IRC §401(k) (see Section 4.6-2), which allows an employee to contribute part of his or her salary to a pension or profit sharing plan on a pretax basis. Employee after-tax and employer matching contributions under such a plan are also permitted as part of a cafeteria plan. Another exception applies to contributions made by an educational institution for postretirement group-term life insurance. (To be eligible, all the contributions must be made before retirement and the insurance must have no cash surrender value at any time.) There is also an exception for amounts remaining in a health savings account (see Section 4.1-7) at the end of a calendar year.

*Health plan benefits relating to more than one year.*[142] An accident and health insurance policy may include certain benefits without violating the prohibition against deferred compensation.

- credit toward the deductible for unreimbursed covered expenses incurred in prior periods;
- reasonable lifetime maximum limit on benefits;
- level premiums;
- premium waiver during disability;
- guaranteed renewability of coverage, without further evidence of insurability (but not guaranty of the amount of premium upon renewal);
- coverage for a specified accidental injury;
- coverage for a specified disease or illness, including payments at initial diagnosis of the specified disease or illness, and progressive payments of a set amount per month following the initial diagnosis (sometimes referred to as progressive diagnosis payments); and
- payment of a fixed amount per day (or other period) of hospitalization.

*Benefits under a long-term disability policy relating to more than one year.* A long-term disability policy paying disability benefits over more than one year does not violate the prohibition against deferring compensation.

*Mandatory two-year election for vision or dental insurance.* When a cafeteria plan offers vision or dental insurance that requires a mandatory two-year coverage period, but not longer, the mandatory two-year coverage period does not result in deferred compensation if the premiums for each plan year are paid no less frequently than annually and the cafeteria plan does not use salary reduction or flex-credits relating to the first year of a two-year election to apply to vision or dental insurance for the second year of the two-year election.

*Using salary reduction amounts to pay premiums for the first month of the next plan year.* Salary reduction amounts from the last month of one plan year of a cafeteria plan may be applied to pay premiums for health insurance during the first month of the immediately following plan year, if done on a uniform and consistent basis with respect to all participants (based on the usual payroll interval for each group of participants).

---

140.   IRS Prop. Reg. §1.125-1(b)(4)(ii).
141.   IRC §125(d)(2); IRS Prop. Reg. §1.125-1(b)(5); (o).
142.   IRS Prop. Reg. §1.125-1(p).

*Special rule for purchased paid time off.*[143] While a cafeteria plan may offer employees the option of purchasing additional paid time off (vacation, sick, or personal days) with pre-tax dollars, the leave becomes taxable when taken and is subject to several restrictions related to the ban on deferred compensation.

- First, the plan must prohibit employees from carrying over to a later year any purchased days off that go unused at the end of a plan year.

- Second, the plan must prohibit employees from receiving cash for such unused purchased days off after the end of the plan year. Employees may "cash out" purchased days off they do not think they will use, but they must do so before the end of the plan year.

- Third, purchased days off may not be used until all an employee's regular paid time off has been used.

Also, a plan that only offers the choice of cash or paid time off is not a cafeteria plan under §125.

> *Example:* Employee Andria has accrued 10 vacation days under her employer's vacation policy and purchases 3 more under a cafeteria plan. By the end of the year, Andria has used 11 vacation days. Because her accrued vacation leave must be used first when determining whether she will forfeit any purchased vacation days, Andria has 2 purchased vacation days that remain unused at the end of the year. Andria must forfeit the 2 unused days or take cash for them before the end of the year.

*Supplemental plans with renewable premiums are OK.* An employer can allow its employees to purchase additional coverage for specific diseases through its cafeteria plan, even though the coverage is provided through individual policies with guaranteed renewability, premium waivers during periods of disability, and a progressive benefit payment until a stricken employee reaches age 65. The IRS said that none of these provisions constituted deferral of compensation because no unused salary reduction amounts from previous years are being used to fund benefits in later years.[144]

## 4.5-2 How Cafeteria Plans Are Funded

Cafeteria plans and other flexible benefit plans are generally funded by either or both of the following mechanisms:

**"Flex dollars" or "flex credits."**[145] Under this option, each employee is provided with a certain amount of "flex dollars" or "flex credits," which the employee can then use to buy selections from the plan menu or elect to receive them in cash.

**Salary reduction.**[146] In this scenario, employees use part of their own salary to purchase their benefit selections through pre-tax or after-tax deductions. Purchasing qualified benefits through pre-tax deductions can provide employees with increased take-home pay.

Salary reduction contributions to a cafeteria plan are considered to be employer contributions because the employees are electing to have a portion of their salary contributed to the plan by the employer.

*Advantages of pre-tax benefit contributions.* When employers require or allow employees to contribute a portion of the cost of certain benefits they provide, those contributions may be made pre-tax or after-tax. A pre-tax contribution is one that is made from an employee's wages before the tax on those wages is calculated, while an after-tax contribution is made after the tax is calculated. A pre-tax contribution will result in higher take-home pay for the employee.

---

143.   IRS Prop. Reg. §1.125-1(o)(4).
144.   TAM 199936046, 5-19-99.
145.   IRS Prop. Reg. §1.125-1(r)(3).
146.   IRS Prop. Reg. §1.125-1(r)(1)-(2).

***Example:*** Employee Richard earns $700 per week in 2008, claims single and 1 withholding allowance on his Form W-4, and contributes $30 per week to his employer's cafeteria plan for medical and dental insurance. Using the wage-bracket method, Richard's federal income tax withholding is $76.00. The social security tax rate is 6.2%, the Medicare tax rate is 1.45%, and the state tax rate is 5% (assume the state treats pre-tax contributions the same as the IRC). If Richard's contribution is pre-tax, his net pay would be figured as follows:

| | |
|---|---|
| Regular wages: | $700.00 |
| Medical and dental: | - 30.00 |
| Taxable wages: | $670.00 |
| | |
| FITW | -76.00 |
| SS ($670 x 6.2%) | - 41.54 |
| Med. ($670 x 1.45%) | - 9.72 |
| SITW ($670 x 5%) | - 33.50 |
| Net pay: | $509.24 |

If Richard's contribution is after-tax, his net pay would be figured as follows:

| | |
|---|---|
| Regular (taxable) wages: | $700.00 |
| FITW | -81.00 |
| SS ($700 x 6.2%) | - 43.40 |
| Med. ($700 x 1.45%) | - 10.15 |
| SITW ($700 x 5%) | - 35.00 |
| Medical and dental: | - 30.00 |
| Net pay: | $501.45 |

A cafeteria plan can require employees to use pre-tax deductions rather than after-tax deductions to pay the employees' share of any qualified benefit offered under the plan. The plan can also pay reasonable cafeteria plan administrative fees through salary reduction amounts, which are excluded from the employees' income.

For information on the effect of the Family and Medical Leave Act health benefit guarantees on cafeteria plan health benefit payment options, see Section 4.2.

**Automatic deferrals (i.e., "negative elections") are OK.**[147] Salary deferrals used to purchase group health coverage under a §125 cafeteria plan are not included in the employee's income where the employer uses an automatic enrollment process that reduces the employee's salary to pay for a portion of the coverage unless the employee makes a choice to receive the amount in cash. If the employer limits the ability to choose cash to those employees who already have other health care coverage, then §125 applies only to such employees, since employees without other coverage do not have a choice between the salary reduction or the cash.

**After-tax employee contributions.** Cafeteria plans may offer employees the chance to purchase benefits with after-tax contributions, including health insurance for someone other than the employee's spouse or dependents.

***Example:*** Employee George elects salary reduction to pay for health insurance under his employer's plan for himself and his ex-spouse, who is not considered George's dependent. If the coverage for George's spouse is valued at $3,000, George's employer includes $3,000 in his income. No benefit payments or reimbursements under the plan are included in George's income or that of his ex-spouse. The result is the same if the $3,000 cost of the ex-spouse's coverage is paid by George outside the cafeteria plan.

---

147.  IRS Prop Reg. §1.125-2(b); Rev. Rul. 2002-27, 2002-20 IRB 925.

# 4.5-3 What the Cafeteria Plan Document Must Contain

A cafeteria plan must have a written document laying out the particulars of the plan and it must be intended to be a permanent plan.[148] The plan document must contain:

- a description of the benefits available under the plan, including each benefit's period of coverage;
- the plan's rules for becoming eligible to participate, including the requirement that all plan participants be employees;
- procedures governing participants' elections under the plan (e.g., when elections can be made, how long they are effective, when may they be revoked);
- the manner in which contributions are made, such as salary reduction or nonelective employer contributions;
- the maximum amount of employer contributions (including salary reductions) available to any participant;
- a definition of the plan year;
- if the plan offers paid time off, the ordering rule for using nonelective and elective paid time off;
- the plan's provisions complying with any additional requirements for flexible spending arrangements (see Section 4.5-7);
- the plan's grace period provisions, if there is a grace period; and
- the plan's provisions for HSA distributions from a health FSA, if the plan allows such distributions.

Written plans are also required for self-insured medical reimbursement plans, dependent care assistance programs, adoption assistance programs, and §401(k) plans offered as benefits under a cafeteria plan, and this requirement can be satisfied by meeting the written cafeteria plan requirements or having separate written plans for each of these benefits that are incorporated by reference to them.

If there is no written cafeteria plan or the written plan does not satisfy any of these individual requirements, the plan is not a cafeteria plan, and an employee's election between taxable and nontaxable benefits will result in income for the employee.

# 4.5-4 Benefit Elections

Generally, employees must make irrevocable benefit elections under a cafeteria plan before the benefit becomes available or the plan year begins, whichever comes first.[149] Changes or revocations during the plan year can be allowed by the cafeteria plan only under limited circumstances.

**Regs allow election revocations because of status changes.**[150] IRS regulations clarify a cafeteria plan's right to permit employees to revoke or change an election during a plan year based on a change in status. The change can be made in writing or electronically. (Rules governing election changes and revocations based on cost or coverage changes are discussed later in this section.)

The changes in status that allow a cafeteria plan to permit an employee (not a spouse or dependent) to revoke or change a benefit election during a plan year include:[151]

- *marital status changes*—marriage, divorce, death of spouse, legal separation, or annulment;

- *changes in the number of dependents*—birth, adoption, placement for adoption, or death of a dependent;

---

148.  IRC §125(d)(1); IRS Prop. Reg. §1.125-1(c).

149.  IRS Prop. Reg. §1.125-2(a).

150.  IRS Reg. §1.125-4. (a)-(e), (i); IRS Prop. Reg. §1.125-2(a)(4), (5).

151.  IRS Reg. §125-4(c)(2).

- *employment status changes* *(applies to employee, spouse, or dependent)*—termination or commencement of employment, strike or lockout, starting or ending an unpaid leave of absence, change in worksite, change from full-time to part-time, exempt to nonexempt, or salaried to hourly status;

- *change in dependent status*—any event that causes an employee's dependent to become covered or lose coverage (e.g., attainment of a certain age, student status);

- *residence change*—a change in the place of residence of the employee, spouse, or dependent; or

- *adoptions*—the commencement or termination of an adoption proceeding.

Furthermore, the regulations provide that an election change can be made only if the status change results in the employee, spouse, or dependent gaining or losing eligibility for coverage under the plan (or a benefit option under the plan) and the election change corresponds with the effect on eligibility. For dependent care assistance or adoption assistance benefits, the plan can also allow an election change if the change in status affects dependent care or adoption expenses.

If the change in status is the employee's divorce, annulment, legal separation, death of a spouse or dependent, or a dependent losing eligibility for coverage, the employee's election to cancel accident or health insurance coverage for any individual other than the spouse or dependent for whom coverage ceased fails to correspond with the change in status and cannot be allowed. If an employee, spouse, or dependent gains coverage under a family member plan as a result of a change in marital or employment status, the employee's election to cease or decrease coverage for that individual corresponds with the change in status only if that individual actually becomes covered or gets increased coverage under the family member plan.

Employees can elect to either increase or decrease group-term life insurance or disability income coverage in the event of a qualifying change in status.

**Example 1**: Employee Susan, a single parent, elects family health coverage under her employer's cafeteria plan to cover herself and her 21-year-old daughter, Charlotte, who is in her senior year of college. When Charlotte graduates from college during the year, Susan wants to revoke her election of family coverage and make a new election for single coverage because the health plan does not cover dependents over 19 who are not full-time students. The cafeteria plan may permit this election change since Charlotte's loss of eligibility is a change in status and Susan's new election is consistent with that status change.

**Example 2**: Employee Steve has elected family health coverage under his employer's cafeteria plan to cover himself, his wife Amy, and their son Mel. The other options under the employer's plan are no coverage, employee-only coverage, and employee-plus-one-dependent coverage. During the year, Steve and Amy divorce, and Amy becomes ineligible for coverage under the plan, while Mel does not. Steve wants to revoke his original election and elect employee-only coverage. Steve's revocation of his original coverage is consistent with the divorce, which was a change in status that ended Amy's coverage. But the plan cannot permit Steve to elect employee-only coverage, since Mel did not lose coverage and such a change would not be consistent with the change in status. The plan may permit Steve to elect employee-plus-one-dependent coverage. If Amy is employed and elects coverage for Mel under her employer's plan, then Steve may be permitted to elect employee-only coverage under his employer's plan.

**Example 3**: Titanic Corp. provides group-term life insurance coverage to its employees through a cafeteria plan. Employees can elect coverage up to $50,000 and pay for it through the cafeteria plan. Employee Juan, who is married and has a child, elects $10,000 of group-term life insurance coverage before the plan year. During the plan year, Juan and his wife are divorced. Because the divorce is a change in status, the cafeteria plan may allow Juan to either increase or decrease his group-term life insurance coverage.

***Example 4***:   Employee Tim has employee-only indemnity coverage under his employer's cafeteria plan and elects salary reduction contributions of $600 to fund his FSA. His wife, Joanne, also has employee-only coverage under her employer's health plan. Joanne then resigns from her job and loses her coverage, and Tim wants to elect family coverage and increase his FSA contribution. Joanne's resignation from her job is a qualified change in status, and Tim's election changes are consistent with that change in status, so the cafeteria plan may permit Tim's changes.

***Example 5:***   Employee Rene has one child, Maria. Rene's employer has a cafeteria plan that includes a dependent care flexible spending account. Before the year begins, Rene elects to have his salary reduced by $4,000 to fund the FSA. When Maria turns 13 during the year, Rene can change his election to cancel dependent care coverage for Maria because this change in status affected his dependent care expenses.

*Special exceptions.* The regulations include several exceptions to the change in status requirements to comply with mandates in other laws governing the availability of health insurance coverage.

COBRA—If an employee, spouse, or dependent becomes eligible for continued health coverage under the employer's group health plan under COBRA (see Section 4.1-5) or a similar state law, the employee may elect to increase payments under the employer's cafeteria plan to pay for the continuation coverage.

Medical support orders—If a court or agency has issued an order requiring accident or health coverage for an employee's child, the cafeteria plan can change the employee's election to include coverage for the child if the order requires coverage under the employee's plan. On the other hand, the cafeteria plan can allow the employee to cancel coverage for the child if the order requires the former spouse to provide the coverage.

Medicare or Medicaid eligibility—If an employee, spouse, or dependent who is covered under an employer's group plan becomes entitled to coverage under Medicare or Medicaid, the cafeteria plan may permit the employee to revoke coverage for that person. If the employee, spouse or dependent loses their Medicare or Medicaid coverage, the cafeteria plan can allow the employee to elect to cover or increase their coverage under the plan.

Special enrollment rights under HIPAA—If an employee has a right to enroll in an employer's group health plan or to add coverage for a family member under the Heath Insurance Portability and Accountability Act because other health coverage was lost or a person becomes the spouse or dependent of the employee, the cafeteria plan may permit the employee to make a conforming election under the plan to make the payments for the increased coverage on a pre-tax basis.

Elective deferrals under a CODA—The regulations make it clear that a cafeteria plan may permit an employee to change or revoke elections regarding elective deferrals to a §401(k) plan (see Section 4.6-2) or employee contributions governed by §401(m) in accordance with those sections. The election revocation restrictions of §125 do not apply in such situations.

FMLA leave changes—An employee on FMLA leave may revoke or change an existing cafeteria plan election of group health plan coverage for the remaining portion of the period of coverage on the same basis as employees not on FMLA leave.

**Rules for cost-driven changes.**[152] Under the regulations, election changes also may be made to reflect significant cost or coverage changes for all types of qualified benefits provided under a cafeteria plan during the plan year. For example:

- If the cost of a qualified benefits plan increases or decreases during a period of coverage and the plan's terms require employees to make a corresponding change in their payments, the plan may automatically make a prospective increase or decrease in the affected employees' elective contributions for the plan.

---

152.   IRS Reg. §1.125-4(f).

- If the cost of a benefit package option significantly increases or significantly decreases during a period of coverage, then a cafeteria plan may allow employees to make a corresponding change in election under the cafeteria plan. Such changes may include choosing the option with the decrease in cost for employees with no coverage or revoking an election for coverage with a cost increase and either choosing coverage under a benefit package option with similar coverage or dropping coverage if no such option is available.

- The cost change provisions apply in the case of dependent care assistance only if the cost change is imposed by a dependent care provider who is not a relative of the employee.

- If the coverage under a plan is significantly lessened or ends during a period of coverage, the cafeteria plan may allow affected employees to revoke their elections and make a new election for coverage under another benefit package option providing similar coverage. If coverage is lost (not just lessened), the employee may be allowed to drop coverage if no similar option is available. Accident and health coverage is significantly lessened only if there is an overall reduction in coverage to participants generally (i.e., the loss of one doctor would not be significant in most cases).

- If a cafeteria plan adds a new benefit package option (such as a new HMO option) or significantly improves an existing one, then the plan may permit employees to elect that option and make a corresponding election change with respect to other benefit package options. A change in dependent care provider is treated as similar to the addition of a new HMO option under an accident or health plan. Where the dependent care provider is a relative of the employee making the election, however, the coverage change rules apply but the cost change rules do not.

- If an employee's spouse or dependent makes an election change during an open enrollment period – where that individual's employer has a different plan year – then a cafeteria plan may permit the employee to make a corresponding election change. This rule also applies to changes in the plan of a spouse's or dependent's employer permitted under the new proposed regulations, so that if a spouse's employer adds a new HMO option to its group health plan, and the spouse elects to enroll the family in that new option, then a cafeteria plan may permit the employee to drop family coverage.

- If the employee or the employee's spouse or dependent loses coverage under a group health plan sponsored by a governmental or educational institution, the employer's cafeteria plan may allow the employee to elect coverage under that plan. Plans sponsored by a governmental or educational institution include a state children's health insurance program (SCHIP), a state health benefits risk pool, a medical care program of an Indian tribal government, or a foreign government group health plan.

The change in cost or coverage rules do not apply to health flexible spending accounts (see Section 4.5-7).

*Example 1:* Widgets, Inc. has a cafeteria plan under its union contract that offers indemnity health insurance and a health FSA. After mid-year contract renegotiations, the premiums and office visit co-payments for the indemnity insurance are reduced and an HMO option is added. The cafeteria plan may automatically decrease the amount of salary reduction contributions of plan participants by an amount corresponding to the decrease in premiums, but it may not permit employees to change their FSA elections to reflect the reduction in co-payment amounts. The plan may also allow employees to change their elections and elect the improved indemnity plan or the new HMO option, but not to change their FSA elections to reflect different HMO co-payments.

*Example 2:*  Employee George elects employee-only coverage for 2008 under his employer's calendar year cafeteria plan, while his wife Jean has elected similar coverage under her employer's cafeteria plan, which has a plan year beginning on September 1. For the plan year beginning on September 1, 2008, Jean wants to elect no coverage under her employer's plan. George's employer's cafeteria plan can allow him to change his election prospectively to family coverage effective September 1, 2008 if he certifies that Jean will elect no coverage under her employer's cafeteria plan for the plan year beginning on that date and George's employer has no reason not to believe him.

*Example 3:*  Gigantic Corp. has a cafeteria plan offering health coverage under either an indemnity plan or an HMO. Employee Samantha elects HMO coverage before the plan year at a premium cost of $100 per month. Sometime during the plan year, Samantha switches to the indemnity plan, with a premium of $140 per month. Because both plans were offered before the beginning of the plan year and neither one had a cost change during the year, Samantha's change from the HMO to the indemnity plan does not qualify under the change in cost or coverage rules. While the health plan can allow Samantha to change her coverage, the cafeteria plan cannot permit her to make an election change to reflect the increased premium. She may pay the difference in premium cost with after-tax dollars.

*Example 4:*  Employee Jim is married to Pat, and they have one child, Adam. Jim's employer has a cafeteria plan with a dependent care FSA. Adam attends the employer's on-site day care facility, and Jim elects to reduce his salary by $3,000 during the upcoming year to fund coverage. During the year, Jim finds a new dependent care provider and wants to revoke his FSA election. The availability of the new provider (whether it's a household employee, a relative of Jim or Pat, or another person) is a significant change in coverage, so the cafeteria plan may allow Jim to revoke his earlier election and make a new one to reflect the cost of the new child care provider.

**Election rules for salary reduction contributions to HSAs.**[153]  Contributions may be made to a Health Savings Account through a cafeteria plan. A cafeteria plan offering HSA contributions through salary reduction may permit employees to make prospective salary reduction elections or change or revoke salary reduction elections for HSA contributions at any time during the plan year, effective before salary becomes currently available. If a cafeteria plan offers HSA contributions as a qualified benefit, the plan must:

- specifically describe the HSA contribution benefit;
- allow a participant to prospectively change his or her salary reduction election for HSA contributions on a monthly basis (or more frequently); and
- allow a participant who becomes ineligible to make HSA contributions to prospectively revoke his or her salary reduction election for HSA contributions.

**Optional election for new employees.**[154] A cafeteria plan may give new employees 30 days after their hire date to make elections between cash and qualified benefits. The election is effective as of the employee's hire date. However, salary reduction amounts used to pay for such an election must be from compensation not yet currently available on the date of the election. The written cafeteria plan must provide that any employee who terminates employment and is rehired within 30 days after terminating employment (or who returns to employment following an unpaid leave of absence of less than 30 days) is not a new employee eligible for this election.

## 4.5-5  Who Can Participate in the Plan

Cafeteria plan participation must be restricted to employees (including former employees but not self-employed individuals), and the plan must be maintained for their benefit. The plan may not be maintained solely for the benefit of former employees. Employees include common law employees, leased employees, and full-time life insurance salesmen. All employees who are treated as employed by a single employer under IRC §414 are treated as employed by a single employer for purposes of §125. Although an employee's spouse

---

153.   IRS Prop. Reg. §1.125-2(c).
154.   IRS Prop. Reg. §1.125-2(d).

and dependents cannot participate in the plan in the sense of making elections or buying benefits, they may benefit from the employee's selection of benefits (e.g., through family medical coverage or the right to choose among several death benefit options the employee had purchased).[155]

# 4.5-6 Nondiscrimination Testing

To qualify for favorable tax treatment for all cafeteria plan participants, the plan must not discriminate in terms of eligibility, contributions, or benefits in favor of highly compensated individuals, or participants, or key employees.[156] These special classifications are defined as follows:

*Highly compensated individuals.*[157] They include individuals who are:

- corporate officers;
- shareholders owning more than 5% of the voting power or value of the employer's stock;
- highly compensated (based on facts and circumstances of the situation); and
- a spouse or dependent of one of the above.

*Highly compensated participants.* They are highly compensated individuals who participate in the cafeteria plan.

*Highly compensated.* For 2008, the term "highly compensated" means any individual or participant who for the preceding year was paid more than $105,000 by the employer (indexed annually to the next lowest multiple of $5,000). The employer can limit this group to the top-paid 20% of its employees for the preceding year.[158]

*Key employees.*[159] They include:

- corporate officers whose annual compensation is greater than $150,000 for 2008 (indexed annually to the next lowest multiple of $5,000); limited to 50 officers, but in companies with fewer than 500 employees, no more than 10% (but no less than 3 employees) may be treated as officers;
- 5% owners; and
- 1% owners whose annual earnings are greater than $150,000.

Employees who meet this definition for the preceding plan year are key employees for cafeteria plan nondiscrimination testing purposes. The annual compensation amount to be used is the one that applied for the specific calendar year before the plan year began.

**Nondiscrimination tests** There are three main nondiscrimination tests that cafeteria plans must satisfy to qualify for preferential tax treatment. See Section 4.5-8 for the tax treatment of discriminatory plans.

*Eligibility test.*[160] Under the eligibility test, the cafeteria plan's participation requirements must meet these conditions:

- the plan benefits a group of employees that qualifies as a reasonable classification established by the employer (job catagories, types of compensation, location, etc.);
- employees may not be required to have more than 3 years' employment with the employer before becoming eligible for the plan;
- all employees must be covered by the same length of employment requirement;

---

155. IRS Prop. Reg. §1.125-1(a)(1), (g).
156. IRC §125(b), (c); IRS Prop. Reg. §1.125-7.
157. IRC §125(e); IRS Prop. Reg. §1.125-7(a)(3).
158. IRC §125(e); IRS Prop. Reg. §1.125-7(a)(9).
159. IRC §125(b)(2); §416(i)(1); IRS Prop. Reg. §1.125-7(a)(10).
160. IRC §125(b), (c), (g)(3); IRS Prop. Reg. §1.125-7(b).

- employees must be eligible to participate no later than the first day of the first plan year after they meet the length of employment requirement, unless they leave employment before that date; and
- the group of employees who are eligible for benefits satisfies the safe harbor percentage test or the unsafe harbor percentage component of the facts and circumstances test for nondiscriminatory classifications under IRS Reg. §1.410(b)-4(c).

*Contributions and benefits test.*[161] Under the contributions and benefits test, the cafeteria plan is not discriminatory where either qualified (nontaxable) benefits and total benefits, or employer contributions for such benefits do not discriminate in favor of highly compensated participants. This requirement must be met with respect to both benefit availability and benefit selection. In other words, each participant must have an equal opportunity to select nontaxable (qualified) benefits, and highly compensated participants must not disproportionately select nontaxable benefits while other employees select taxable benefits.

*Concentration test.*[162] Under the concentration test, a cafeteria plan is not discriminatory if the qualified (nontaxable) benefits provided to key employees do not exceed 25% of such benefits provided to all employees under the plan.

**Special health benefits test.**[163] There is a special nondiscrimination test for cafeteria plans that offer health insurance as a benefit option. They are nondiscriminatory if:

- employer contributions under the plan (including pre-tax salary reductions) on behalf of each participant equal 100% of the health benefit costs (premiums) for the majority of similarly situated highly compensated employees or equal or exceed 75% of the health benefit costs for the similarly situated participant with the highest health benefit costs; and

- excess contributions or benefits bear a uniform relationship to the participant's compensation.

**Separate tests allowed for new employees.**[164] If employees with less than three years of employment can participate in the employer's cafeteria plan, the plan can test for nondiscrimination as if there were two separate plans – one for employees with less than three years on the job and one for employees with at least three years experience. If the employer treats the cafeteria paln as two plans for testing purposes, it must do so for both the eligibility and contributions and benefits tests.

On the other hand, an employer with more than one cafeteria plan can aggregate them into a combined plan for nondiscrimination testing purposes, as long as it does so for both the eligibility and contributions and benefits tests.[165]

**Tests must be performed at year-end.**[166] Nondiscrimination testing must be performed as of the last day of the plan year, using all non-excludible employees who were employed by the employer for at least one day during the plan year.

**Union contract exception.**[167] Cafeteria plans that are the result of collective bargaining between an employer and a union are exempt from the nondiscrimination tests.

---

161.   IRS Prop. Reg. §1.125-7(c).
162.   IRS Prop. Reg. §1.125-7(d).
163.   IRC §125(g)(2); IRS Prop. Reg. §1.125-7(e).
164.   IRS Prop. Reg. §1.125-7(g).
165.   IRS Prop. Reg. §1.125-5(h).
166.   IRS Prop. Reg. §1.125-5(j).
167.   IRC §125(g)(1).

## 4.5-7 Flexible Spending Arrangements

Many cafeteria plans offer another type of benefit program known as a flexible spending arrangement or FSA (they are also referred to as flexible spending accounts or reimbursement accounts).[168] FSAs give employees the chance to pay for certain covered health care, dependent care, and adoption expenses with pre-tax dollars provided through salary reduction. As the employees incur covered expenses, they are reimbursed up to the amount that will be contributed during the plan year through salary reduction.

By using pre-tax dollars to fund the FSA, the employee reduces his or her out-of-pocket expenses by the amount of the taxes that are saved. Other than the rules governing cafeteria plans in general, there are specific requirements that FSAs must meet.

The cafeteria plan is permitted to specify any interval for employees' salary reduction contributions. The interval specified in the plan must be uniform for all participants.[169]

**Coverage requirements.** To qualify as an FSA, the benefit program must provide coverage under which:

- specified expenses incurred by employees may be reimbursed up to certain maximums and subject to other reasonable conditions; and

- maximum reimbursement amounts cannot be substantially more than the total salary reduction and employer non-elective contributions (flex-credits) for the employee's coverage; less than 500% of the total salary reduction and employer flex-credits is allowed as a maximum reimbursement amount.

**Health care FSA rules.**[170] Health care FSAs providing for medical, dental, or vision care benefits are governed by the following rules:

*Elections cover a full plan year.* Because a health FSA cannot allow an employee to be covered only when expenses are expected to be incurred, it must require employees to elect coverage and determine funding amounts for a full plan year before the plan year begins. Therefore, employees must determine how many flex credits or pre-tax dollars to contribute to the FSA before each plan year begins.

*No deferred compensation—"use it or lose it."* Because cafeteria plans cannot allow compensation to be deferred beyond the plan year, the general rule is that any amount in a health FSA that remains unused at the end of the plan year (or the end of a grace period if applicable) is forfeited by the employee (i.e., use-it-or-lose-it). It may not be used for the reimbursement of another benefit or carried over to a later year. This means employees must be very careful in estimating covered medical care and dependent care expenses when making a fund election before the beginning of each plan year.

> **Example:** Employee Brent joins his employer's health FSA, and before 2007 begins, he elects to contribute $900 to the plan during the year through a salary reduction plan. During 2007, Brent is reimbursed for $750 of substantiated, uninsured medical expenses. The remaining $150 ($900 - $750) is not given back to Brent and cannot be used toward next year's plan premium; it reverts to the plan.

Under a special exemption, if all the premiums paid into an employer's health FSA during a plan year exceed the FSA's reimbursements of claims and administrative costs, the excess may be used to reduce employees' required premiums for the next plan year or returned to the employees as a dividend or premium refund. The excess (i.e., experience gain) must be allocated on a uniform basis, which can be the coverage levels selected by employees. The excess may not be allocated based on the participants' individual claims experience, since that would violate the use-it-or-lose-it requirements.

---

168.   IRS Prop. Reg. §1.125-5.
169.   IRS Prop. Reg. §1.125-5(g)(2).
170.   IRS Prop. Reg. §1.125-5(k).

*Plan can allow a "grace period" up to 2½ months.* Cafeteria plans can add a grace period of up to 2½ months after the end of a plan year. This means that unused amounts in FSAs may be paid or reimbursed to plan participants for qualified expenses incurred during the grace period. For calendar year plans, this change allows employers to give employees until March 15 to spend amounts they contributed to their FSAs during the previous year before they lose amounts that are not spent.[171] The grace period can be applied to some benefits and not others.

If the cafeteria plan is amended to provide a grace period (there is no requirement that it do so), the grace period must apply to all participants in the cafeteria plan. Expenses for qualified benefits incurred during the grace period may be paid or reimbursed from benefits or contributions remaining unused at the end of the immediately preceding plan year, as if the expenses had been incurred in the immediately preceding plan year. During the grace period, a cafeteria plan may not permit unused benefits or contributions to be cashed out or converted to any other taxable or nontaxable benefit. The grace period does not apply to paid time off and elective deferrals to a §401(k) plan.

To the extent any unused benefits or contributions from the immediately preceding plan year exceed the expenses for the qualified benefit incurred during the grace period, those remaining unused benefits or contributions may not be carried forward to any subsequent period (including the subsequent plan year) and are forfeited under the "use-it-or-lose-it" rule. Employers may continue to provide a "run-out" period after the end of the grace period, during which expenses for qualified benefits incurred during the cafeteria plan year and the grace period may be paid or reimbursed.

> **Example 1:** Woods Hole Mfg. has a cafeteria plan with a plan year ending on December 31, 2008. During 2008, Woods Hole amended the plan document to allow all participants to apply unused amounts in their FSAs remaining at the end of the plan year to qualified expenses incurred during the grace period immediately following that plan year. The grace period adopted by Woods Hole ends on March 15, 2009. Employee Tony timely elected salary reduction of $1,000 for a health FSA for the 2008 plan year. As of December 31, 2008, Tony has $200 remaining in his health FSA. Tony timely elected salary reduction of $1,500 for the 2009 plan year. During the grace period from January 1 to March 15, 2009, Tony incurs $300 of unreimbursed medical expenses. The unused $200 from the plan year ending December 31, 2008 is applied to pay or reimburse $200 of Tony's $300 of medical expenses incurred during the grace period. Therefore, as of March 16, 2009, Tony has no unused benefits or contributions remaining for the 2008 plan year. The remaining $100 of medical expenses incurred between January 1 and March 15, 2009 is paid or reimbursed from Tony's health FSA for the 2009 plan year. As of March 16, 2009, Tony has $1,400 remaining in the health FSA for the plan year ending December 31, 2009.

> **Example 2:** Assume the same facts as in Example 1, except that Tony incurs $150 of medical expenses during the grace period. As of March 16, 2009, Tony has $50 of unused benefits or contributions remaining for the plan year ending December 31, 2008. The unused $50 cannot be cashed-out, converted to any other taxable or nontaxable benefit, or used in any other plan year (including the plan year ending December 31, 2009). The unused $50 is subject to the "use-it-or-lose-it" rule and is forfeited. As of March 16, 2009, Tony has the entire $1,500 he elected in the health FSA for the plan year ending December 31, 2009.

*Uniform coverage throughout coverage period.* The maximum amount of reimbursement from a health FSA (i.e., the total of the employee's salary reduction and flex-credits for the plan year) must be available to the employee at all times during the plan year. The amount available is reduced each time the employee submits a claim for reimbursement. It does not matter how much the employee has paid into the FSA when the claim is made, and the premium payment schedule cannot be accelerated because of the employee's claims or because the employee separates from employment.

---

171.    IRS Prop. Reg. §1.125-1(e), (f); IRS Notice 2005-42, 2005-23 IRB 1204.

**Example:** Employee Ralph selects coverage under a health care FSA requiring premium payments of $1,200 in monthly salary reductions of $100. By March, Ralph has contributed $300 in salary reductions and has not requested any reimbursements. If he submits a medical expense claim for $1,000 in March, he must be reimbursed for the entire amount. The employer cannot accelerate Ralph's salary reductions to make up the difference between the premiums paid and the claim. If Ralph resigns from his job in June after having paid $600 in premiums, the employer cannot collect the $400 difference between the reimbursement and the premium payments, and is out the $400.

Reimbursement is deemed to be available at all times if it is paid at least monthly or when the total amount of the claims submitted is at least a specified, reasonable amount (e.g., $50).[172]

When an employee is no longer a participant in the FSA, the plan must pay the employee any amount the employee previously paid through salary reduction to the extent the previously paid amount relates to the period from the date the employee no longer participates in the FSA through the end of the plan year.[173]

*12-month period of coverage.*[174] Generally, a health care FSA must provide coverage for a period of at least 12 months, with limited exceptions (e.g., short first plan year, new employees). Employees cannot change or revoke elections made before the plan year unless they have undergone a change in status that would allow an election change or revocation in general under a cafeteria plan (see Section 4.5-4). The plan may allow employees who leave employment during the period of coverage to revoke their benefit elections, and may provide that employees who stop making premium payments will have their FSA coverage terminated. However, if a separated employee continues to make premium payments for the rest of the period of coverage, the plan must continue to make reimbursements during the period up to the maximum amount.

*Reimbursements must be for medical expenses.* Employee reimbursements under a health care FSA are excludable from income only if the expenses are "medical expenses" under IRC §213(d). For details on the definition of "medical expenses" for FSA purposes, see Section 4.1-2. A health FSA can limit plan reimbursements to certain types of medical expenses rather than reimbursing all §213(d) medical expenses (e.g., no reimbursements for over-the-counter drugs).

*Prohibited reimbursements.* Health care FSAs can only reimburse medical expenses incurred during the coverage period (including the grace period, if the plan provides for one). They cannot reimburse premiums paid for medical insurance under the employer's health plan (which can be paid on a pre-tax basis through the general cafeteria plan), for another health plan of the employer, or for a health plan maintained by the employer for the employee's spouse or dependents. They also cannot reimburse premiums paid for long-term care insurance or expenses for long-term care services.

*Claims substantiation.* Medical expenses may be reimbursed only if the employee provides two written statements: (1) from an independent third party (e.g., doctor, hospital) stating the amount incurred and (2) from the employee stating the expense has not yet been reimbursed and is not reimbursable under any other health coverage. Reimbursements of future or anticipated expenses cannot be made.

As an alternative, the third party may provide the required substantiation directly to the employer (e.g., an insurance carrier provides an explanation of benefits showing the medical expenses incurred and which of them have been paid or are unreimbursable). If a health FSA allows an employee to self-certify or self-substantiate medical expenses or copayments, then all reimbursements made under the FSA for any employee are included in the employees' income.[175]

---

172. IRS Prop. Reg. §1.125-5(d)(2).

173. IRS Prop. Reg. §1.125-5(d)(3).

174. IRS Prop. Reg. §1.125-5(e).

175. IRS Prop. Reg. §1.125-6(b); IRS Notice 2006-69, 2006-31 IRB 107.

*Claims incurred.* Reimbursement can only be made for medical expenses actually incurred during the period of coverage, including COBRA coverage. Medical expenses are incurred when the medical care is provided, not when the employee is billed or pays for the care. The reimbursement itself may take place after the period of coverage.

*Limiting health FSA enrollment to health plan participants.*[176] At the employer's option, a cafeteria plan is permitted to provide that only those employees who participate in one or more specified employer-provided health plans may participate in a health FSA.

*Coordination with HIPAA requirements.*[177] Under certain conditions, benefits under a health FSA are treated as "excepted benefits" under the Health Insurance Portability and Accountability Act. If those conditions are met, the FSA is not subject to the group market portability provisions of HIPAA. Therefore, the health plan does not have to issue a certificate of creditable coverage for the FSA to employees leaving the plan. Also, coverage that consists solely of coverage under a health FSA does not constitute creditable coverage. Benefits under a health FSA are excepted benefits if:

- the maximum benefit payable to the employee for the year does not exceed the greater of 2 times the employee's salary reduction election for the year or the amount of the employee's salary reduction for the year plus $500;
- the employee has other coverage available under a group health plan of the employer; and
- the other coverage is not limited to excepted benefits.

*FSA benefits followed transferred employees after asset sale.*[178] The IRS ruled that in an asset sale, transferred employees who have elected to participate in health FSAs under the seller's cafeteria plan may continue to exclude the salary reduction amounts and medical expense reimbursements from gross income without interruption and at the same level of coverage after becoming employees of the buyer. This is true either when the seller agrees to continue its existing health FSA for the transferred employees or when the buyer agrees to adopt a continuation of the seller's health FSA for the transferred employees.

In addition, there is no loss of eligibility for coverage. Therefore, transferred employees continue to be subject to their existing FSA elections and may not change those elections during the remainder of the plan year of the asset sale (unless a change of status occurs which permits an election change).

**Using debit and credit cards for payments and reimbursements.**[179] A health FSA paying or reimbursing employee medical expenses through a debit, credit, or stored value card must meet all of the following requirements:

- Before any participating employee receives the card, the employee agrees in writing:
    — to use the card only to pay for medical expenses of the employee or his or her spouse or dependents,
    — that the employee will not use the debit card for any medical expense that has already been reimbursed,
    — that the employee will not seek reimbursement under any other health plan for any expense paid for with the card, and
    — that the employee will acquire and retain sufficient documentation (including invoices and receipts) for any expense paid with the card.
- The card includes a statement providing that these agreements are reaffirmed each time the employee uses the card.

---

176. IRS Prop. Reg. §1.125-5(g)(1).
177. 62 F.R. 67687, 12-29-97.
178. Rev. Rul. 2002-32, 2002-23 IRB 1069.
179. IRS Prop. Reg. §1.125-6(d); Rev. Rul. 2003-43, 2003-21 IRB 935; IRS Notice 2006-69, 2006-31 IRB 107; IRS Notice 2007-2, 2007-2 IRB 254.

- The amount available through the card equals the amount elected by the employee for the health FSA for the cafeteria plan year, and is reduced by amounts paid or reimbursed for medical expenses incurred during the plan year.
- The card is automatically cancelled when the employee ceases to participate in the health FSA.

*Limiting card use to appropriate providers.* The employer must also limit use of the debit or credit card to:

- physicians, dentists, vision care offices, hospitals, and other medical care providers (as identified by the merchant category code);
- stores with the merchant category code for Drugstores and Pharmacies if, on a location-by-location basis, 90% of the store's gross receipts during the prior taxable year consisted of items that qualify as medical expenses; and
- stores that have implemented an appropriate inventory information approval system explained below.

*Correction procedures after improper payments.* The employer must follow all of the following correction procedures for any improper payments using the debit or credit card:

- Until the amount of the improper payment is recovered, the debit card must be de-activated and the employee must request payments or reimbursements of medical expenses through other methods (e.g., by submitting receipts or invoices showing the employee incurred a medical expense);
- The employer demands that the employee repay the plan an amount equal to the improper payment;
- If the employee fails to repay the amount of the improper charge, the employer withholds the amount of the improper charge from the employee's pay or other compensation, to the full extent allowed by applicable law;
- If any portion of the improper payment remains outstanding, the employer offsets the amount of the improper payment against a reimbursement for a later substantiated expense claim; and
- If, after applying all these procedures, the employee remains indebted to the employer for improper payments, the employer treats the improper payment as it would any other business indebtedness.

*Substantiation procedures.*[180] Medical expenses may be substantiated using the following methods if incurred at physicians, pharmacies, dentists, vision care offices, hospitals, other medical care providers (as identified by the merchant category code) and at stores with the Drug Stores and Pharmacies merchant category code, if, on a store location-by-location basis, 90% of the store's gross receipts during the prior taxable year consisted of items which qualify as medical expenses.

*Matching copayments.* If an employer's health plan has copayments in specific dollar amounts, and the dollar amount of the transaction at a medical care provider equals an exact multiple of not more than five times the dollar amount of the copayment for the specific service (e.g., pharmacy benefit copayment, copayment for a physician's office visit), then the charge is fully substantiated without the need for submission of a receipt or further review. If a health plan has multiple copayments for the same benefit, (e.g., tiered copayments for a pharmacy benefit), exact matches of multiples or combinations of up to five copayments are similarly fully substantiated without the need for submission of a receipt or further review.

If the dollar amount of the transaction is not an exact multiple of the copayment (or an exact match of a multiple or combination of different copayments for a benefit in the case of multiple copayments), the transaction must be treated as conditional pending confirmation of the charge, even if the amount is less than five times the copayment.

If the dollar amount of the transaction at a medical care provider equals a multiple of six or more times the dollar amount of the copayment for the specific service, the transaction must be treated as conditional

---

180. IRS Prop. Reg. §1.125-6(e).

pending confirmation of the charge by the submission of additional third-party information, such as merchant or service provider receipts.

The copayment schedule required under the accident or health plan must be independently verified by the employer. Statements or other representations by the employee are not sufficient. Self-substantiation or self-certification of an employee's copayment in connection with copayment matching procedures through debit or credit cards or otherwise does not constitute substantiation.

Recurring medical expenses. Automatic payment or reimbursement satisfies the substantiation rules for payment of recurring expenses that match expenses previously approved as to amount, medical care provider, and time period (e.g., for an employee who refills a prescription drug on a regular basis at the same provider and in the same amount). The payment is substantiated without the need for submission of a receipt or further review.

Real-time substantiation. If an independent third party provides, at the time and point of sale, information to verify to the employer (including electronically by e-mail, the Internet, intranet, or telephone) that the charge is for a medical expense, the expense is substantiated without the need for further review.

Other medical expenses paid or reimbursed through a health FSA debit or credit card. All other charges to the card must be treated as conditional, pending substantiation of the charge through additional independent third-party information describing the goods or services, the date of the service or sale and the amount of the transaction. All such card payments must be substantiated, regardless of the amount of the payment.

*Inventory information approval system.*[181] An inventory information approval system meeting certain requirements may be used to substantiate payments made using a debit card, including payments to merchants and service providers that do not meet the 90% medical expense requirement. Transactions using this system are fully substantiated without the need for submission of a receipt by the employee or further review.

When an employee uses the card, the payment card processor's or participating merchant's system must collect information about the items purchased using the inventory control information (for example, stock keeping units (SKUs)). The system compares the inventory control information for the items purchased against a list of items that qualify as medical expenses. The medical expenses are totaled and the merchant's or payment card processor's system approves the use of the card only for the amount of the medical expenses eligible for coverage under the health FSA.

If the transaction is only partially approved, the employee is required to pay for the additional amounts, resulting in a split-tender transaction. The merchant or service-provider must also request additional payment from the employee if the employee does not have sufficient health FSA coverage to purchase the medical expense items. Any attempt to use the card at non-participating merchants or service-providers must fail.

Where the employer does not require substantiation of all medical expenses, but relies only on reviewing a sampling of a small percentage of reimbursements under a certain threshold, the IRS said that all payments made with a debit or credit card would not be excludable from the employees' income.

**Special dependent care assistance rules.**[182] Similar rules apply to dependent care assistance FSAs, as well as the rules that generally apply to dependent care assistance programs (see Section 3.4-8). However, dependent care FSAs are not subject to the uniform coverage rule requiring the maximum amount of reimbursement to be available at all times. The risk of employer loss is not present in dependent care FSAs.

Employees can be reimbursed up to $5,000 of dependent care expenses each plan year but only up to the amount they have paid in premiums. Eligible expenses under dependent care FSAs include nonmedical expenses that allow an employee to keep working and provide for a dependent's protection and well-being (not just children).

---

181.    IRS Prop. Reg. §1.125-6(f).
182.    IRS Prop. Reg. §1.125-5(d)(5); §1.125-5(i); §1.125-6(a)(4).

A dependent care assistance FSA may not reimburse employees for expenses other than dependent care expenses, so if the employee has less dependent care expenses than salary reductions, reimbursements for other expenses cannot be used to make up the difference.

**Use of debit cards for dependent care assistance programs.**[183] An employer may use a debit card program to provide benefits under a dependent care assistance program (DCAP), including a dependent care FSA. However, dependent care expenses may not be reimbursed before they are incurred. For this purpose, dependent care expenses are treated as having been incurred when the dependent care services are provided, not when the expenses are formally billed or paid by the employee. Thus, if a dependent care provider requires payment before the dependent care services are provided, those expenses cannot be reimbursed at the time of payment through the use of a payment card program.

An employer offering a DCAP or dependent care FSA may nevertheless adopt the following method to provide reimbursements for dependent care expenses through a debit card program: At the beginning of the plan year or on enrollment in the DCAP, the employee pays initial expenses to the dependent care provider and submits to the employer or plan administrator a statement from the provider substantiating the dates and amounts for the services. After the employer or plan administrator receives the substantiation, but not before the date the services are provided as indicated by the statement from the provider, the plan makes available through the debit card an amount equal to the lesser of:

- the previously incurred and substantiated expense, or
- the employee's total salary reduction amount to date.

The amount available through the card may be increased in the amount of any additional dependent care expenses only after such expenses have been incurred. The amount on the card may then be used to pay for subsequent dependent care expenses.

Subsequent card transactions that have been previously approved as to the dependent care provider and time period may be treated as substantiated without further review if they are for an amount equal to or less than the previously substantiated amount. If there is an increase to the previously substantiated amount or a change in the dependent care provider, the employee must submit a statement or receipt from the provider substantiating the new claimed expense before amounts relating to the increased amount or new provider may be added to the card.

*Example:* Pete's Publishing Co. sponsors a dependent care FSA that is offered through its cafeteria plan. Salary reductions for participating employees are made on a weekly basis, and they are available for dependent care coverage on a weekly basis. As a result, the amount of available dependent care coverage equals the employee's salary reduction amount minus claims previously paid from the plan. Pete's has adopted a debit card program for its dependent care FSA. Employee Fran is a participant and has elected $5,000 of dependent care coverage. Pete's reduces Fran's salary by $96.15 on a weekly basis to pay for coverage under the dependent care FSA ($5,000 ÷ 26 = $96.15).

At the beginning of the plan year, Fran is issued a debit card with a balance of zero. Fran's childcare provider, ABC Daycare Center, requires a $250 advance payment at the beginning of the week for dependent care services that will be provided during the week. The dependent care services provided for Fran by ABC qualify for reimbursement. However, because the services have not yet been provided as of the beginning of the plan year, Fran cannot be reimbursed for any of the amounts until the end of the first week after the services have been provided. Fran submits a claim for reimbursement that includes a statement from ABC with a description of the services, the amount due for the services, and the dates the services will be provided. Pete's increases the balance of Fran's payment card to $96.15 after the services have been provided, which is the lesser of Fran's salary reduction to date or the incurred dependent care expenses. Fran uses the card to pay ABC $96.15 on the first day of the next week and pays ABC the remaining balance due for the week ($153.85) by check.

---

183.    IRS Prop. Reg. §1.125-6(g); IRS Notice 2006-69, 2006-31 IRB 107.

To the extent that this card transaction and each subsequent transaction is with ABC and is for an amount equal to or less than the previously substantiated amount, the charges are fully substantiated. Fran does not need to submit a statement from the provider and the employer does not need to perform any further review. However, the subsequent amount may not be made available on the card until the end of the week when the services have been provided.

*Coordination with dependent care tax credit.* Employees participating in a dependent care FSA must reduce any dependent care tax credit they receive dollar for dollar by any amounts they contribute to the FSA. So they should consult with a tax advisor before making an election to participate in a dependent care FSA.

**Adoption assistance FSAs.**[184] Rules similar to those governing dependent care assistance FSAs govern adoption assistance FSAs, which also must meet the rules that generally apply to adoption assistance programs under IRC §137 (see Section 3.3-7).

An adoption assistance FSA may not reimburse employees for expenses other than adoption expenses, so if the employee has less adoption expenses than salary reductions, reimbursements for other expenses cannot be used to make up the difference.

**HSA-compatible FSAs.**[185] To be eligible to contribute to a Health Savings Account (HSA), an individual must be covered only under a high deductible health plan (HDHP – see Section 4.1-7). A general purpose health FSA is not an HDHP and an individual covered by a general purpose health FSA is not eligible to contribute to an HSA. However, an individual covered by an HDHP does not fail to be an eligible individual merely because the individual is also covered by a limited-purpose health FSA or post-deductible health FSA or a combination of the two.

*Limited-purpose health FSA.* A limited-purpose health FSA is a health FSA that only pays or reimburses permitted coverage benefits, such as vision care, dental care, or preventive care.

*Post-deductible health FSA.* A post-deductible health FSA is a health FSA that only pays or reimburses medical expenses for preventive care or medical expenses incurred after the minimum annual HDHP deductible is satisfied. No medical expenses incurred before the annual HDHP deductible is satisfied may be reimbursed by a post-deductible FSA, regardless of whether the HDHP covers the expense or whether the deductible is later satisfied.

**Qualified HSA distributions.**[186] A health FSA in a cafeteria plan is permitted to offer employees the right to elect qualified HSA distributions described in §106(e) (see Section 4.1-7). No qualified HSA distribution may be made in a plan year unless the employer amends the health FSA written plan with respect to all employees, effective by the last day of the plan year, to allow a qualified HSA distribution. In addition, an HSA distribution must meet all of the following requirements:

- No qualified HSA distribution has been previously made on behalf of the employee from this health FSA;
- The employee elects to have the employer make a qualified HSA distribution from the health FSA to the HSA of the employee;
- The distribution does not exceed the lesser of the balance of the health FSA on:
  — September 21, 2006; or
  — the date of the distribution;
- Balances as of any date are determined on a cash basis, without taking into account expenses incurred but not reimbursed as of a date, and applying the uniform coverage rule;
- The distribution is made no later than December 31, 2011; and
- The employer makes the distribution directly to the trustee of the employee's HSA.

---

184. IRS Prop. Reg. §1.125-5(j).
185. IRC §223(c)(2)(C); IRS Prop. Reg. §1.125-5(m).
186. IRS Prop. Reg. §1.125-5(n).

A qualified HSA distribution does not alter an employee's irrevocable benefit elections or constitute a change in status. If a qualified HSA distribution is made to an employee's HSA, even if the balance in a health FSA is reduced to zero, the employee's health FSA coverage continues to the end of the plan year. Unused benefits and contributions remaining at the end of a plan year (or at the end of a grace period, if applicable) must be forfeited.

**FSA experience gains or forfeitures.**[187] An FSA experience gain (i.e., a forfeiture under the use-or-lose rule) with respect to a plan year (plus any grace period following the end of a plan year), equals the amount of the employer contributions, including salary reduction contributions, and after-tax employee contributions to the FSA minus the FSA's total claims reimbursements for the year. Experience gains (or forfeitures) may be:

- Retained by the employer maintaining the cafeteria plan;
- Used to reduce required salary reduction amounts for the immediately following plan year, on a reasonable and uniform basis;
- Returned to the employees on a reasonable and uniform basis; or
- Used to defray expenses to administer the cafeteria plan.

If not retained by the employer or used to defray expenses of administering the plan, the experience gains must be allocated among employees on a reasonable and uniform basis. It is permissible to allocate these amounts based on the different coverage levels of employees under the FSA. Experience gains allocated in compliance with these requirements are not a deferral of compensation. However, in no case may the experience gains be allocated among employees based (directly or indirectly) on their individual claims experience. Experience gains may not be used as contributions directly or indirectly to any deferred compensation benefit plan.

## 4.5-8 Tax Treatment of Cafeteria Plans

If a flexible benefit plan qualifies as a §125 cafeteria plan, certain tax benefits are available to employees who participate in the plan.[188]

**Employer contributions.** Employer contributions to a qualified cafeteria plan are excluded from the employee's income and are not subject to federal income tax withholding or employment taxes to the extent the contributions relate to nontaxable benefits selected by the employee. Employer contributions made to purchase taxable benefits must be included in the employee's income and are subject to federal income tax withholding and social security, Medicare, and FUTA taxes to the same extent as if they were made outside the plan.

**Pre-tax contributions.** Pre-tax contributions (salary reductions) made by an employee to a qualified cafeteria plan are excluded from the employee's income. They are not subject to federal income tax withholding or social security, Medicare, and FUTA taxes whether the benefits purchased are taxable or nontaxable (qualified) benefits. Any taxable benefits purchased become taxable when they become "currently available" to the employee. Pre-tax contributions do not reduce the amount of the taxable benefit that must be included in the employee's income. Pre-tax contributions made by an employee are considered to be employer contributions when determining the taxable value of a benefit.

 **401(k) PLAN EXCEPTION** While pre-tax contributions to a §401(k) cash or deferred arrangement (see Section 4.6-2) are not subject to federal income tax withholding, they are subject to social security, Medicare, and FUTA taxes.

---

187. IRS Prop. Reg. §1.125-5(o).
188. IRS Prop. Reg. §1.125-7(m)(1).

**Group-term life insurance.**[189] In addition to offering up to $50,000 of nontaxable group-term life insurance on the life of an employee, a cafeteria plan may offer coverage above $50,000 as a qualified benefit. The cafeteria plan regulations provide that the entire amount of salary reduction and employer flex-credits used by an employee to pay for group-term life insurance coverage on the life of the employee is excluded from the employee's gross income, regardless of whether the amount of coverage exceeds $50,000.

In determining the cost of excess group-term life insurance that must be included in income, the regulations adopt the general rule that the includible amount is the Table I cost of the excess coverage (minus all after-tax contributions by the employee for group-term life insurance coverage) – see Section 3.3-1 for details on calculating the cost of excess group-term life insurance.

*Example 1:* Employee Courtney, age 42, elects salary reduction of $200 to pay for $150,000 of group-term life insurance on her own life through her employer's cafeteria plan. The $200 salary reduction is excluded from her income. Courtney has $100,000 in excess group-term life insurance ($150,000 - $50,000), and the Table I cost of the excess is $120 per month for a person age 40-44 ($1.20 per $1,000 of coverage X 100 = $120). The amount included in Courtney's income is $120.

*Example 2:* Assume the same facts as in Example 1, except that Courtney elects a salary reduction of $100 and makes an after-tax contribution of $100 for the group-term life insurance. The $100 salary reduction is excluded from her income. The Table I cost of $120 for $100,000 of excess group-term life insurance is reduced by Courtney's $100 after-tax contribution. The amount included in Courtney's income is $20.

**After-tax contributions.** Contributions toward benefits that are made with after-tax dollars are included in the employee's income and are subject to federal income tax withholding and social security, Medicare, and FUTA taxes. The benefits purchased, however, are excluded from the employee's income.

For information on the relationship between cafeteria plans and the Family and Medical Leave Act, see Section 4.2.

**Cash.** If employees choose to take cash instead of purchasing benefits with their flex dollars, the payments are wages and are subject to federal income tax withholding and social security, Medicare, and FUTA taxes. The same holds true for purchased vacation days that are cashed out because the employee feels they will not be used before the year ends.

**Discriminatory plans.**[190] Cafeteria plans that discriminate in favor of highly compensated individuals, employees, or participants, or key employees are not disqualified and do not have negative tax consequences for other participants. But those highly compensated participants and key employee participants lose the tax benefits of the plan and are subject to tax (including federal income tax withholding and social security, Medicare, and FUTA taxes) on the combination of the taxable benefits with the highest total value they could have selected for the plan year.

*Example:* Barbara, a highly compensated participant in her employer's cafeteria plan, has the opportunity to select benefits costing $2,500. The benefits offered include $500 in cash and $3,500 in various qualified benefits. Barbara elects to receive $300 in cash and $2,200 in qualified benefits. If the plan is discriminatory, Barbara will have $500 (the total cash she could have taken) included in her taxable income—the total of the taxable benefits she could have elected to receive. The $200 she did not receive in cash will be allocated to the qualified benefits she did choose in proportion to their cost.

---

189.   IRS Prop. Reg. §1.125-1(k).
190.   IRS Prop. Reg. §1.125-7(m)(2).

**Taxation of qualified HSA distributions.**[191] A qualified HSA distribution from the health FSA covering the participant to his or her HSA is a rollover to the HSA and thus is generally not includible in gross income. However, if the participant is not an eligible individual (as defined in section 223(c)(1)) at any time during a testing period following the qualified HSA distribution, the amount of the distribution is includible in the participant's gross income and he or she is also subject to an additional 10% tax (with certain exceptions).

 **WATCH OUT FOR THE STATES** Not all states and localities treat cafeteria plans the same as the federal government for purposes of income tax withholding, unemployment insurance contributions, or state disability insurance contributions. (See Table 4.1 in Section 4.7 for a chart of state tax treatments of elective deferrals to a cafeteria plan.) Employers must check the states where they operate for the rules that apply.

## 4.5-9 Reporting Requirements

Generally, pre-tax contributions to a cafeteria plan need not be reported by an employer on its quarterly Form 941 or an employee's Form W-2 as taxable wages. On the employer's annual Form 940, such contributions are included in Part 2, Line 3 in total payments and then in Part 2, Line 4 as an exempt payment, and Box 4a should be checked. Taxable contributions and benefits are reported as they would be if they were provided outside the cafeteria plan.

**Cash or deferred arrangements.** While pre-tax contributions to a §401(k) cash or deferred arrangement (see Section 4.6-2) are not subject to federal income tax withholding, they are subject to social security, Medicare, and FUTA taxes.[192] Therefore, they must be reported on the employee's Form W-2 in Boxes 3 and 5, respectively, with the amounts withheld reported in Boxes 4 and 6. The elective deferrals must also be reported in Box 12, preceded by Code "D." On Form 941, the employer must report the pre-tax contributions on Lines 5a and 5c, since they are subject to social security and Medicare taxes.

**Dependent care assistance.** If an employee contributes to a dependent care assistance FSA through either pre-tax contributions or flex credits, the employer must report the amounts on the employee's Form W-2 in Box 10, with the excess over $5,000 reported as well in Boxes 1, 3, and 5.

The amount reported on Form W-2 is the total amount of cash reimbursement furnished to the employee during the calendar year. However, if the employer does not know the actual total amount of cash reimbursement at the time the Form W-2 is prepared, then the employer may report a reasonable estimate of the total amount. The amount an employee elects to contribute for the year (plus any employer matching contributions) is considered a reasonable estimate.

In 2005, the IRS clarified that an employer that amends its cafeteria plan to provide a grace period for dependent care assistance may continue to rely on these rules by reporting in Box 10 of Form W-2 the salary reduction amount elected by the employee for the year for dependent care assistance (plus employer matching contributions).[193]

> *Example:* An employer amends its calendar year cafeteria plan to permit a grace period for dependent care assistance until March 15 of the subsequent year. An employee elects salary reduction of $5,000 for dependent care assistance for the 2008 calendar year and $5,000 for the 2009 calendar year. The employee has $500 of dependent care contributions remaining unused at the end of the 2008 plan year, which is available to reimburse dependent care expenses incurred during the grace period. For the 2008 calendar year, the employer should report in Box 10 of Form W-2 the $5,000 salary reduction amount elected by the employee for 2008. Similarly, for the 2009 calendar year, the employer should report in Box 10 of Form W-2 the $5,000 salary reduction amount elected by the employee for 2009.

191. IRS Prop. Reg. §1.125-5(n)(2).
192. IRC §3121(v)(1)(A); §3306(r)(1)(A).
193. IRS Notice 2005-61, 2005-39 IRB 607.

**Form 5500 reporting requirement suspended.**[194] In 2002, the IRS suspended the requirement under IRC §6039D that employers offering a cafeteria plan to their employees file Form 5500, *Annual Return/Report of Employee Benefit Plan*, along with Schedule F. The suspension applies to all plan years for which the returns have not been filed, including years before 2001, so there is no need to request relief from the DOL or IRS for the failure to file. During the suspension period, the IRS is reviewing the reporting requirements and electronic filing options, and any future reporting requirements will apply only to plan years beginning after further guidance is issued.

**No debit or credit card reporting required.** In general, fees paid by a company for medical services must be reported on Form 1099-MISC if they exceed $600 (see Section 8.12-1). Early in 2003, the IRS provided guidance as to when expense reimbursements under an FSA made through debit or credit cards or other electronic media are excludable from gross income (see Section 4.5-7). In that guidance, the IRS stated that payments made to medical service providers through debit and credit cards must be reported by the employer on Form 1099-MISC.

This ruling got quite a reaction from the business community because of the problems involved in reprogramming systems to make such reporting possible. Therefore, a provision was added to the Medicare reform bill enacted in December 2003 exempting payments for medical care under an FSA from this general reporting requirement.[195]

Even though the exemption applied specifically to payments made after December 31, 2002, the IRS later clarified that the reporting requirement in the 2003 revenue ruling would not apply to payments made before January 1, 2003.[196]

# 4.6 Retirement and Deferred Compensation Plans

Along with medical insurance, one of the most important benefits employers generally provide is a plan to ensure that their employees will have a source of income after retirement. Many different types of plans are used to provide retirement income, but they are all based on the same general premise—funds are contributed by the employer and/or the employee under a plan that invests the money and returns the contributions and investment gains to the employee upon retirement.

This section discusses the more common plans offered by employers and whether contributions to and payments from the plans are taxable income and subject to federal income tax withholding and social security, Medicare, and FUTA taxes. It also includes information on any contribution caps associated with the various plans, as well as nondiscrimination requirements.

## 4.6-1 Qualified Pension and Profit-Sharing Plans (IRC §401(a))

While both pension and profit-sharing plans may be aimed at providing employees with retirement income, they approach that goal in different fashions. A pension plan provides a benefit that is determinable when the employee retires and is payable over a period of years, usually the employee's life, and the employer's contributions to the plan are not based on its profits. A profit-sharing plan, however, is designed to allow employees to participate in company profits as a retirement planning vehicle, with employer contributions based on a formula selected by the employer.

Pension plans can be categorized as either defined benefit plans or defined contribution plans.

**Defined benefit plans.** A defined benefit plan is designed to provide a certain level of benefits during the employee's retirement that is generally based on the employee's age, compensation level, and length of

---

194.    IRC §6039D; IRS Notice 2002-24, 2002-16 IRB 785.
195.    Pub. L. 108-173, §1203.
196.    IRS Notice 2004-16, 2004-9 IRB 527.

service. Using those factors, a retiring employee will be able to calculate the monthly benefit he or she will receive. The employer is required to make contributions to the plan that, when invested, will be sufficient to provide the level of benefits earned by the employee.

Other characteristics of a defined benefit pension plan include:

- plan formulas are geared to retirement benefits and not contributions;
- the employer's contributions are actuarially determined (based on the employee's earnings, age, and life expectancy);
- certain benefits are insured by the federal government through the Pension Benefit Guaranty Corporation;
- early termination of the plan is subject to special rules; and
- contributions and benefits forfeited by employees who leave before vesting help the employer reduce its future contributions.

*Payroll implications.* While defined benefit plans are generally administered through a company's benefits department, the payroll department must maintain accurate records of hours worked, compensation earned, and dates of birth and hire for the plan administrator and plan actuary.

**Defined contribution plans.** A defined contribution plan contains individual accounts for each employee, with a set amount being contributed into the account by the employer (and sometimes the employee) periodically. The employee's retirement benefit depends on the amount of money in his or her account at retirement, which is determined by the contribution amounts and any investment gains or losses. Under one of the simplest types of defined contribution plans, the money purchase pension plan, the employer is required to contribute an amount each year based on each employee's compensation for the year.

Other highlights of defined contribution plans include:

- the plan provides for a contribution formula involving the employer and/or the employees;
- employer contributions are usually made annually (sometimes more often);
- knowing how much is in their individual accounts makes the plan easy to understand for employees;
- no need for actuarial calculations; and
- annual reports must be filed with the IRS and the Department of Labor.

*Profit-sharing plans.* A profit-sharing plan is a defined contribution plan to which the company agrees to make "substantial and recurring" contributions, although they may be discretionary to some degree. Amounts contributed to the plan are invested for eventual distribution to participants or their beneficiaries either at retirement, after a fixed number of years, or after a specified event occurs (death, disability, separation from employment).

Employer contributions are determined by a formula that may not require the existence of current or accumulated net profits for a contribution to be made, depending on the discretion allowed the employer by the plan. Other plans use a strict formula that requires contributions of a certain amount if profits reach a specified level.

**Annual compensation and contribution limits.** Defined benefit and defined contribution plans may not base benefit accruals or contributions on an employee's compensation in excess of the "annual compensation limit."[197] The annual compensation limit for 2008 is $230,000 (indexed annually to the next lowest multiple of $5,000). The annual compensation limit also applies when determining the amount of an employee's annual compensation that may be taken into account in applying certain nondiscrimination tests to retirement plans.

---

197. IRC §401(a)(17); IRS Reg. §1.401(a)(17)-1.

Annual contributions and other "additions" to defined contribution plans are also limited. Under IRC §415(c)(1)(A), the total of all employer and employee contributions on behalf of an employee to a qualified defined contribution plan cannot exceed the lesser of $46,000 in 2008 (indexed annually) or 100% of the employee's compensation for the year (up to the annual compensation limit).

*Post-termination payments generally not 'compensation.'*[198] Amounts received following severance from employment are generally not considered "compensation," but there is an exception for certain payments made by the later of:

- 2½ months following severance from employment, or
- the end of the limitation year that includes the date of severance from employment.

Payments covered by the exception include payments for overtime, shift differentials, commissions, and bonuses that would have been payable if employment had not terminated. Payments with respect to accrued bona fide sick, vacation, or other leave that would have been available for use by the employee if employment had not terminated are not included in compensation unless the plan specifically includes such payments.

Compensation does not include amounts paid after severance from employment that are severance pay or parachute payments, even if they are paid within the allowable period following termination.

The general rule that post-severance payments are not compensation does not apply to employer payments to an individual in qualified military service up to the amount the individual would have received if he or she was still working for the employer. In other words, employees may continue to contribute to their employers' retirement plans while performing qualified military service. However, the IRS has ruled that supplemental pay from an employer to an employee in active service with the U.S. Armed Forces or on an indefinite assignment with the state National Guard is not wages for federal income tax withholding and employment tax purposes (see Section 3.4-19).

There is also an exception to the post-severance timing rule for compensation paid to a permanently and totally disabled participant, provided certain conditions are met.

**Many compensation and contribution limits changed by EGTRRA.**[199] As part of efforts to enhance the ability of employees to save for retirement, the Economic Growth and Tax Relief Reconciliation Act of 2001 increased the annual compensation and contribution limits for defined benefit and defined contribution plans. Some of the limits were set by EGTRRA for several years, with built-in increases before being adjusted for inflation, while others were set just for 2002 before annual adjustments took effect. Still other limits were unaffected by EGTRRA at all. The new amounts are summarized below, and those that apply to specific types of plans (e.g., §401(k) plans) are explained more fully in the section dealing with that plan.

 **NO "SUNSET" AFTER 2010** Under EGTRRA, the increases in the annual compensation and contribution limits and the establishment of "catch-up" contributions for older employees (see discussion below) were scheduled to expire after 2010 and revert to their pre-2002 levels. However, the Pension Protection Act of 2006 repealed this "sunset" provision.[200]

---

198.   IRS Reg. §1.415(c)-2(e).
199.   P.L. 107-16.
200.   P.L. 109-280, §811.

| Type of Limit | New Limit and Inflation Adjustment |
|---|---|
| Annual benefit limit for defined benefit plans | $185,000 in 2008; to the next lowest multiple of $5,000 |
| Annual compensation limit | $230,000 in 2008; to the next lowest multiple of $5,000 |
| Annual additions to defined contribution plan limit | $46,000 in 2008; to the next lowest multiple of $1,000 |
| Elective deferral limit for 401(k), 403(b), 457(b), 408(k) SEP plans | $15,500 in 2008; to the next lowest multiple of $500 |
| Elective deferral limit for 408(p) SIMPLE plans | $10,500 in 2008; to the next lowest multiple of $500 |
| Annual IRA contribution limit | $5,000 for 2008; to the next lowest multiple of $500 beginning in 2009 |
| Highly compensated employee definition | $105,000 in 2008; to the next lowest multiple of $5,000 |
| Annual compensation minimum for 408(k) SEP plan eligibility | $500 in 2008; to the next lowest multiple of $50 |

**"Catch-up" contributions.** Under EGTRRA, beginning in 2002, employees who are eligible to make elective salary deferrals to defined contribution plans and who would be at least 50 years old by the end of the plan year can defer an additional amount to the plan as a "catch-up" contribution if the plan allows such contributions. In July 2003, the IRS issued final regulations providing guidance on how employers and plan administrators should handle catch-up contributions.[201] The regulations apply to §401(k), §403(b), SIMPLE, SEP, and state and local government §457 plans.

*Eligibility for catch-up contributions.* Under the regulations, an employee is a catch-up eligible participant if the employee is otherwise eligible to make elective deferrals under the plan and is age 50 or older. An employee who will reach age 50 before the end of a calendar year is deemed to be age 50 as of January 1 of that year. This means that all participants who will reach age 50 during a calendar year are treated the same beginning January 1 of that year, without regard to whether the participant survives to his or her 50th birthday or terminates employment during the year and without regard to the employer's choice of plan year.

*Maximum catch-up contribution amounts.* Catch-up contributions have annual limits (the "applicable dollar amount") based on a calendar year, depending on the type of plan involved. The limits are set by EGTRRA, which also provides for inflation adjustments after a certain period of time. For §401(k), §403(b), §457, and simplified employee pension plans, the limit is $5,000 in 2008 and is adjusted annually for inflation to the next lowest multiple of $500. For SIMPLE plans, the limit is $2,500 in 2008, with annual adjustments to the next lowest multiple of $500. The catch-up contribution maximum is the lesser of the "applicable dollar amount" or the employee's compensation for the year reduced by any other elective deferrals made during that year.

> **Example 1:** Employee Rita is eligible to make elective deferrals under her employer's §401(k) plan, which does not limit deferrals except to comply with statutory elective deferral (§401(a)(30)) and annual addition (§415) limits. In 2008, Rita is 52 years old. The plan also provides that a catch-up eligible participant can defer amounts in excess of the annual elective deferral limit up to the applicable dollar catch-up limit for the year. Rita defers $20,500 from her salary into the plan in 2008. Rita's $5,000 in elective deferrals in excess of the $15,500 limit for 2008 do not exceed the catch-up limit for 2008 ($5,000).

*Determination of catch-up contribution.* Elective deferrals made by a catch-up eligible participant are treated as catch-up contributions if they exceed any "otherwise applicable limit," to the extent they do not exceed the maximum dollar amount of catch-up contributions permitted under §414(v). However, a participant need not have made elective deferrals in excess of an otherwise applicable limit in order to be a catch-up eligible participant. This means that a plan providing for $5,000 of catch-up contributions in 2008 may allow a participant who is at least age 50 to make elective deferrals in an amount projected to exceed the otherwise applicable limit by up to $5,000 at any time during 2008.

---

201. IRC §414(v); IRS Reg. §1.414(v)-1.

Under the regulations, catch-up contributions are determined by reference to three types of limits:

- A statutory limit is a limit contained in the Internal Revenue Code on elective deferrals or annual additions permitted to be made under the plan or contract.

- An employer-provided limit is a limit on the elective deferrals an employee can make under the plan that is contained in the terms of the plan, but that is not a statutory limit.

- The actual deferral percentage (ADP) limit (see Section 4.6-2) is the highest dollar amount of elective deferrals that may be retained in the plan by a highly compensated employee after ADP testing.

**Example 2:** Employee Matt is a highly compensated employee who is 51 years old in 2008 and participates in his employer's 401(k) plan. The maximum annual deferral limit is $15,500. After application of the special nondiscrimination rules applicable to 401(k) plans, the maximum elective deferral Matt may make for the year under the plan is $8,000. Under EGTRRA, Matt is able to make additional catch-up contributions of $5,000, for a total of $13,000 of elective deferrals.

The amount of elective deferrals in excess of an applicable limit is generally determined as of the end of a plan year by comparing the total elective deferrals for the plan year with the applicable limit for the plan year. For a limit that is determined on the basis of a year other than a plan year (e.g., the statutory limit on elective deferrals), the determination of whether elective deferrals are in excess of the applicable limit is made on the basis of such other year.

If a plan provides for separate employer-provided limits on *separate portions of compensation* during the plan year (e.g., where a plan sets a deferral percentage limit for each payroll period), the determination of the amount of elective deferrals in excess of the employer-provided limit is still made on an annual basis, with the applicable limit for the year equal to the sum of the dollar limits on the separate portions of compensation.

If a plan limits elective deferrals for *separate portions of the plan year*, then, solely for purposes of determining the amount that is in excess of an employer-provided limit, the plan may provide, as an alternative rule, that the applicable limit for the plan year is the product of the employee's plan year compensation and the time-weighted average of the deferral percentage limits. For example, if a plan using this time-weighted average limits deferrals to 8% of compensation during the first half of the year and 10% of compensation during the second half of the year, the applicable limit would be 9% of each employee's plan year compensation.

The regulations include a *timing rule* for purposes of determining when elective deferrals in excess of an applicable limit are treated as catch-up contributions. This rule is necessary because the maximum amount of catch-up contributions is based on a participant's taxable year, but the determination of whether an elective deferral is in excess of an applicable limit is based on a taxable year, plan year, or limitation year (depending on the underlying limit). Under the timing rule, the determination as to whether elective deferrals in excess of an applicable limit can be treated as catch-up contributions is made as of the last day of the relevant year, except that if the limit is set on a taxable or calendar year basis, then the determination is made at the time the elective deferrals are made. For example, under a plan with a plan year ending on June 30, 2008, elective deferrals in excess of the employer-provided limit or the ADP limit for that plan year would be treated as catch-up contributions as of the last day of the plan year, up to the catch-up contribution limit for 2008. Amounts deferred after June 30, 2008 in excess of the statutory limit for the 2008 calendar year would also be treated as catch-up contributions at the time they are deferred, up to the catch-up contribution limit for 2008 reduced by elective deferrals treated as catch-up contributions as of June 30, 2008.

***Example 3:*** Employees Keith and John are highly compensated employees (HCE) earning $110,000 and are both eligible to make elective deferrals under their employer's §401(k) plan. The plan year is the calendar year. The plan provides that no HCE may make elective deferrals at a rate greater than 10%, except for catch-up contributions. In 2008, Keith and John are both 53 years old and both elect to defer 10% of salary plus a pro-rata portion of the $5,000 catch-up limit for 2008. Keith continues his election for the entire year, for a total 2008 elective contribution of $16,000 (($110,000 x 10%) + $5,000), while John resigns at the beginning of July after deferring $8,000 ($16,000 ÷ 2).

Once Keith's elective deferrals for 2008 exceed the statutory limit ($15,500), the rest of his elective deferrals are treated as catch-up contributions as they are made, up to the 2008 catch-up limit. Since the $500 in elective deferrals made in excess of the statutory limit ($16,000-$15,500) do not exceed the catch-up limit, the $500 is treated as a catch-up contribution. As of the last day of the plan year, Keith has exceeded the employer's limit of 10% ($11,000 for Keith) by an additional $4,500. Since the additional $4,500 in elective deferrals does not exceed the $5,000 catch-up limit for 2008, reduced by the $500 in elective deferrals previously treated as catch-up contributions ($5,000 - $500 = $4,500), it is also treated as a catch-up contribution, for a total of $5,000. In determining Keith's actual deferral ratio (ADR) for purposes of nondiscrimination testing (see Section 4.6-2), the $5,000 of catch-up contributions are subtracted from Keith's total elective deferrals for 2008, so his ADR is 10% ($11,000 ÷ $110,000). John's elective deferrals for the year ($8,000) do not exceed the statutory or plan limit for 2008, so none of his elective deferrals are treated as a catch-up contribution, and the entire amount must be used to determine his ADR.

*Treatment of catch-up contributions.* If an elective deferral is treated as a catch-up contribution, it is not subject to otherwise applicable limits under the plan, and the plan will not be treated as failing otherwise applicable nondiscrimination requirements because of the making of catch-up contributions. In other words, catch-up contributions are not taken into account in applying otherwise applicable limits to other contributions or benefits under the plan offering catch-up contributions or under any other plan of the employer. For example, catch-up contributions are subtracted from the participant's elective deferrals for the plan year prior to determining the participant's actual deferral ratio for purposes of ADP testing. This applies for both nonhighly compensated employees and highly compensated employees.

*Matching contributions.* An employer's plan can provide for matching catch-up contributions by using the same formula it uses for other elective deferrals. In doing so, the matching contributions must satisfy the actual contribution percentage test under §401(m)(2), taking into account all matching contributions.

*Universal availability.* If any plan of an employer provides for catch-up contributions, then all plans of the employer that provide elective deferrals must provide catch-up eligible participants with the same "effective opportunity" to make catch-up contributions. The universal availability requirement applies only with respect to catch-up eligible participants. However, it does not require plans that do not provide for elective deferrals to provide for catch-up contributions.

An "effective opportunity" to make catch-up contributions may be provided in several different ways. For example, a plan that limits elective deferrals on a payroll-by-payroll basis could provide participants with an effective opportunity to make catch-up contributions on a payroll-by-payroll basis (i.e., by allowing catch-up eligible participants to increase their deferrals above the otherwise applicable limit by a pro rata portion of the catch-up contribution limit for the year).

A plan will not fail to satisfy the universal availability requirement solely because an employer-provided limit does not apply to all employees or different employer-provided limits apply to different groups of employees. A plan may include different employer-provided limits for different groups of employees (e.g., an employer-provided limit for HCEs, but not for non-HCEs), so long as each limit meets the nondiscriminatory availability requirements. However, a plan is not permitted to include lower employer-provided limits for catch-up eligible participants.

The regulations clarify that employees covered by a collective bargaining agreement are disregarded for purposes of determining whether an employer's plan complies with the universal availability requirement. Also, a plan will not fail to satisfy the universal availability requirement because it restricts elective deferrals for catch-up eligible participants under a cash availability limit – a limit that restricts elective deferrals to amounts available after withholding from the employee's pay (e.g., after deduction of all applicable income and employment taxes). The regulations provide that a limit of 75% of compensation or higher will be treated as limiting employees to amounts available after other withholdings.

 **§457 PLAN EXCEPTION** The catch-up contribution provisions do not apply during a governmental §457(b) plan participant's last 3 years before retirement, when the normal elective deferral limit is increased, if the catch-up maximum is less than the increase in the normal elective deferral limit (see Section 4.6-4).

*Participants in multiple plans.* Many of the statutory limits that would otherwise limit the participant's elective deferrals are applied on an aggregated basis. For purposes of determining whether elective deferrals are in excess of a statutory limit, all elective deferrals in excess of the statutory limit are aggregated in the same manner as the underlying limit; the aggregate amount of elective deferrals treated as catch-up contributions because they exceed the statutory limit must not exceed the applicable dollar catch-up limit. In other words, the annual limit on catch-up contributions applies to all qualified retirement plans (§401(a), §401(k)), tax-sheltered annuity plans (§403(b)), simplified employee pension plans, and SIMPLE plans maintained by the same employer on an aggregated basis, as if all the plans were a single plan. The limit also applies to all eligible deferred compensation plans (§457(b)) of a state or local government employer on an aggregated basis.

For example, compliance with the §401(a)(30) statutory limit is determined based on elective deferrals under all employer-sponsored §401(k) and §403(b) plans. Therefore, all §401(k) plans and §403(b) contracts in the controlled group of the employer are aggregated for purposes of determining the total amount of elective deferrals in excess of the §401(a)(30) limit. The amount of elective deferrals treated as catch-up contributions by reason of exceeding the §401(a)(30) limit under the aggregated plans or contracts must not exceed the dollar amount of the catch-up limit for the taxable year.

Because employer-provided limits apply only to the plan containing the limit, and the ADP limit applies only to §401(k) plans, the regulations provide guidance on coordinating the amount in excess of these limits for employees participating in multiple plans offered by the same employer. A plan can permit a catch-up eligible participant to defer an amount that exceeds the employer-provided limit, regardless of whether the employee has already made catch-up contributions under another plan offered by the same employer. However, the deferrals in excess of the employer-provided limit can only be treated as catch-up contributions up to the catch-up limit for the year. Any deferrals that exceed the employer-provided limit and the catch-up limit may not be treated as catch-up contributions and must comply with all other applicable nondiscrimination rules, including being taken into account under the ADP test (see Section 4.6-2).

When the elective deferrals in excess of a statutory or employer-provided limit are determined on an aggregated basis, it must be determined under which plan the elective deferrals in excess of the limit were made. This may be determined in any manner that is not inconsistent with the manner in which such amounts were actually deferred under the plans. For example, if a catch-up eligible participant participates in a §401(k) plan only during the first six months of the year, and during the second six months of the year, while participating in a §403(b) plan, the participant's contributions reach and exceed the §401(a)(30) limit for the year, then all elective deferrals in excess of the §401(a)(30) limit for the year may be treated as made to the §403(b) plan.

*Example 4:* Employee Suzanne is 53 years old and a HCE earning $110,000 annually. Her employer sponsors two §401(k) plans, and Suzanne participates in Plan A from January - June and in Plan B from July - December. Plan A limits HCEs' elective deferrals to 6% of compensation, while the Plan B limit is 8%, and both plans allow catch-up contributions in excess of those percentages. Suzanne deferred $4,000 under each plan in 2008. The plan limit for Suzanne for 2008 is $7,700, the sum of the limits for each plan while she was a participant (($55,000 x 6%) + ($55,000 x 8%)). Therefore, Suzanne deferred $300 in excess of the plan limit ($4,000 + $4,000 - $7,700).

Because the amount of Suzanne's excess elective deferrals ($300) does not exceed the catch-up limit for 2008, the $300 is treated as a catch-up contribution. In determining Suzanne's ADR for nondiscrimination testing purposes, the $300 is subtracted from her elective deferrals, leading to an ADR of 7% ($7,700 ÷ $110,000) for both plans A and B. It is then determined that $300 of the excess elective deferrals were made under Plan A and none under Plan B, which is consistent with the manner in which the deferrals were actually made.

*Excludability of catch-up contributions.*[202] In determining the amount of elective deferrals included in gross income because they exceed the elective deferral limit, catch-up contributions are not treated as exceeding those limits. Under the final regulations, a catch-up eligible participant who participates in multiple plans of two or more employers may treat an elective deferral as a catch-up contribution (up to the maximum amount of catch-up contributions permitted for the taxable year) because it exceeds the participant's §402(g) limit for the taxable year. This allows a catch-up eligible participant who participates in plans of two or more employers an exclusion from gross income for elective deferrals that exceed the §402(g) limit, even though the deferrals do not exceed an applicable limit for either employer's plan. The total amount that an employee may exclude from income as catch-up contributions for a year cannot exceed the catch-up contribution limit for that year (and for that type of plan), without regard to whether the employee made catch-up contributions to plans maintained by more than one employer.

**Tax treatment of pension and profit sharing plans.** Pension and profit-sharing plans that meet certain requirements under IRC §401(a) regarding participation, vesting (i.e., a nonforfeitable right to benefits), contribution limits, benefit limits, and nondiscrimination in favor of highly compensated employees are known as "qualified" plans.[203] Employer contributions to qualified plans are excluded from wages and are not subject to federal income tax withholding and social security, Medicare, and FUTA taxes.[204] However, employee elective deferrals to qualified deferred compensation plans, which are considered "employer contributions," are subject to social security, Medicare, and FUTA taxes. (Nonqualified plans are discussed at Section 4.6-10.)

Employee after-tax contributions to a qualified plan generally must be included in the employee's income (treated as after-tax contributions) and are subject to federal income tax withholding and social security, Medicare and FUTA taxes. Even if the employee is required to participate in and contribute to the plan, the contributions are included in income if the employee is entitled to a refund of them upon separation from employment before retirement or death. If the employee's contributions are voluntary, they are taxable income no matter what the refund provisions are. (See Section 4.6-2 for an exception under cash or deferred arrangements.)

---

202.   IRS Reg. §1.402(g)-2.
203.   IRC §401(a); IRS Reg. §1.401-1; §1.401(a)-1.
204.   IRC §3121(a)(5)(A), (a)(5)(F); §3306(b)(5)(A), (b)(5)(F); §3401(a)(12)(A); IRS Reg. §31.3121(a)(5)-1(a); §31.3306(b)(5)-1(a); §31.3401(a)(12)-1(a).

**"PICKED-UP" CONTRIBUTIONS** Generally, amounts contributed to a qualified pension or profit-sharing plan that are designated as employee contributions will be treated as such. But where, under a state or local government plan, the employer "picks-up" the employee's contribution by paying it and then not charging the employee for it, the contribution is treated as an employer contribution for federal income tax withholding purposes. Where the picked-up contribution is treated as such because the payment comes from a salary reduction arrangement, the contribution is subject to social security and Medicare taxes.[205] To qualify for this treatment, the employer must take formal written action specifying its intention to pick up the contributions (no later than December 31, 2008) and must take the final action necessary to effectuate the contributions before the services are rendered that give rise to the contributions. The employees also must not be given the right to receive the contributed amounts instead of the employer contributing them to the plan.[206]

Payments from pensions and other retirement plans are taxable when received by the employee/retiree to the extent they can be attributed to employer contributions, investment gains, or pre-tax deferred amounts. The portion of the payments attributable to the employee's after-tax contributions is not taxable. In addition to regular income taxes, payments from a retirement plan made to an employee who has not reached age 59½ are subject to a 10% excise tax in most instances. Although retirement benefits paid from a qualified plan generally are included in income, they are not subject to social security, Medicare, and FUTA taxes. The federal income tax withholding requirements are discussed at Section 6.4-5, and the reporting requirements at Section 8.12-2.

**State tax treatment—residents only**. Pension plan payments may be subject to state income tax as well as federal income tax. One matter of controversy in this area has been state taxation of pension income received by nonresidents who at one time worked in the state. The APA, along with other organizations, recognized the nearly impossible recordkeeping and other administrative burdens such an approach would put on employers, and they worked to convince Congress to limit such taxation. These efforts proved fruitful when President Clinton signed H.R. 394, which prohibits states from imposing income tax on the "retirement income" of nonresidents.[207] "Retirement income" includes income from:

- a qualified plan under IRC §401(a);
- a simplified employee pension plan under IRC §408(k);
- an annuity plan under IRC §403(a) or (b);
- an individual retirement plan under IRC §7701(a)(37);
- an eligible deferred compensation plan as defined in IRC §457;
- a governmental plan as defined in IRC §414(d); or
- a trust under IRC §501(c)(18(D).

"Retirement income" also includes payments made under a nonqualified deferred compensation plan as defined in IRC §3121(v)(2) if:

- the income is part of a series of substantially equal periodic payments (made at least annually) made for the individual's life expectancy (or the lives of the individual and his or her beneficiary) or for a period of at least 10 years; or
- the income is received under a plan maintained for the sole purpose of providing retirement benefits in excess of the limits imposed by the Internal Revenue Code.

In 2006, this law was expanded to include amounts paid under a written plan that provides for retirement payments in recognition of prior service made to a retired partner.[208]

**Qualified annuity plans under §403(a).** An annuity plan meeting many of the same requirements as §401(a) pension and profit-sharing plans regarding vesting, participation, contribution and benefit lim-

---

205. IRC §414(h); §3121(v)(1)(B); §3306(r)(1)(B).
206. Rev. Rul. 2006-43, 2006-35 IRB 329.
207. P.L. 104-95.
208. P.L. 109-264.

its, and nondiscrimination is a "qualified annuity plan" under §403(a). Employer contributions to qualified annuity plans are not included in wages and are not subject to federal income tax withholding or social security, Medicare, and FUTA taxes.[209]

## 4.6-2 Cash or Deferred Arrangements (IRC §401(k))

An increasingly popular deferred compensation plan is the cash or deferred arrangement (CODA), which allows eligible employees to have their employer contribute part of their salary to a plan rather than receiving the salary in cash. The amount contributed is a pre-tax contribution that reduces the employee's taxable income. The contributions, as well as money earned from investing them, are not subject to federal (and in most cases state) income tax until they are withdrawn.

To qualify as a CODA, a plan must meet certain requirements under §401(k) of the Internal Revenue Code.[210] For that reason, CODAs are generally referred to as "§401(k) plans." The plan is usually made available to employees through a salary reduction agreement, under which the employee agrees to reduce his or her salary (thrift-type plan) or defer future raises or bonuses (bonus-type plan) and authorizes the employer to contribute this amount to the plan. Under the IRC, pre-tax contributions under a salary reduction agreement are known as employer contributions or employee elective deferrals. In addition to these elective deferrals, employers may contribute "matching" amounts (the match does not have to be an exact one) and employees may make after-tax contributions to a §401(k) plan.

 **STATE LAWS PREEMPTED** The Pension Protection Act of 2006 expanded the state law preemption provisions of the Employee Retirement Income Security Act (ERISA) to specifically preempt state laws that may prohibit or restrict the inclusion of an automatic contribution arrangement in a 401(k) plan.[211]

**Contribution limits.**[212] The Economic Growth and Tax Relief Reconciliation Act of 2001 (EGTRRA) contained many provisions that were designed to expand the opportunities for retirement savings, including annual increases in the amount of elective deferrals to defined contribution plans. For §401(k) plans, the final EGTRRA elective deferral amount was $15,000 in 2006, with the maximums adjusted for inflation to the next lowest multiple of $500 beginning in 2007. For 2008, the §401(k) plan elective deferral limit is $15,500.

Also, IRC §415 limits the total of all elective deferrals, employer matching contributions and forfeitures, and employee after-tax contributions in a year to the lesser of $46,000 in 2008 (indexed annually in $1,000 increments) or 100% of the employee's compensation for that year. The amount of compensation that can be taken into account when determining the maximum contributions to an employee's defined contribution plan account for plan years beginning in 2008 is $230,000.[213] This amount is indexed annually to the next lowest multiple of $5,000. Pre-tax elective deferrals to a §401(k), §403(b), §457, §125 or §132(f)(4) plan are included in an employee's compensation when determining the maximum contribution limit for the employee.

> *Example 1:* Employee Maria is 48 years old, earns $85,000 in 2008, and defers $7,000 to her employer's §401(k) plan, which the employer matches at $.50 to $1.00, for a matching contribution of $3,500 ($7,000 x $.50). Maria's elective deferral is well within the limit of $15,500 for 2008. For purposes of the §415 total contribution limit, her 2008 compensation is $85,000 so the total of her elective deferral and the employer's matching contribution must be no more than $46,000 (lesser of $46,000 or 100% of $85,000). The $10,500 contributed on her behalf ($7,000 elective deferral + $3,500 employer matching) meets the §415 requirement and would allow Maria to contribute up to $35,500 in after-tax dollars to the plan.

---

209. IRC §3121(a)(5)(B), (a)(5)(F); §3306(b)(5)(A), (b)(5)(F); §3401(a)(12)(B).
210. IRC §401(k); IRS Reg. §1.401(k)-1.
211. 29 USC §1144(e).
212. IRC §402(g); §415(c); IRS Reg. §1.402(g)-1; §1.415-6; §1.415-8.
213. IRC §401(a)(17).

**Example 2:** Employee Gloria is 45 years old and earns $240,000 in 2008. Her employer's §401(k) plan allows employees to elect to defer up to 6% of their salary into the plan. If Gloria elects to defer 6% of her salary into the plan in 2008, her employer will have to stop deferring Gloria's salary when her year-to-date compensation reaches the annual compensation limit of $230,000. At that point, Gloria will have contributed $13,800 to the plan and will not be able to defer salary up to the annual maximum of $15,500.

**"Catch-up" contributions.** Under EGTRRA, employees who are eligible to make elective salary deferrals to defined contribution plans and who would be at least 50 years old by the end of the plan year can defer an additional amount to the plan as a "catch-up" contribution (see Section 4.6-1 for details) beyond limits set by law or by the plan itself. The catch-up contribution maximum is the lesser of the "applicable dollar amount" or the employee's compensation for the year reduced by any other elective deferrals made during that year.[214] The applicable dollar amount for §401(k) plans is $5,000 for 2008 (adjusted for inflation to the next lowest multiple of $500).

**Example 1:** Employee Barbara, who is over 50, is a participant in a 401(k) plan. Barbara's compensation for 2008 is $30,000. The maximum statutory annual deferral limit is $15,500. Under the terms of the plan, the maximum permitted deferral is 10% ($3,000 in Barbara's case). Barbara can contribute up to $8,000 for the year ($3,000 under the normal operation of the plan, and an additional $5,000 as a catch-up contribution).

**Example 2:** Employee Esther, who is over 50, is a participant in a 401(k) plan. Esther's compensation for 2008 is $80,000. The maximum statutory annual deferral limit is $15,500. The plan incorporates the statutory annual deferral limit as the plan limit. Esther can contribute up to $20,500 for the year ($15,500 under the normal operation of the plan and an additional $5,000 as a catch-up contribution).

**Holding period for elective deferrals.** In 1996, the Labor Department shortened the maximum holding period for §401(k) plan contributions from 90 days to the 15th business day of the month following the month during which the amount deferred would have been paid to the employee. Employers that cannot meet the deadline can have an extra 10 business days, but they must provide reasons for the delay.[215]

**Nondiscrimination testing.**[216] In addition to meeting the general requirements of a qualified plan, a qualified §401(k) plan must not discriminate in favor of highly compensated employees in terms of the percentage of compensation actually deferred by participants. The definition of highly compensated employees includes any employee who:[217]

- was a 5% owner of the employer's stock or capital (if not a corporation) at any time during the current or preceding year; or
- received annual compensation greater than $105,000 (for 2008) during the preceding year (indexed annually to the next lowest multiple of $5,000).

If the employer wishes, it can limit the employees fitting under the second definition to those in the top-paid 20% of employees during the preceding year. Once an employer elects this option, it applies to all future years unless changed by the employer.[218]

Two of the special discrimination tests for §401(k) plans are based on the actual deferral percentage (ADP) of employees who are eligible to participate in the plan. Essentially, the tests require that the ADP of eligible highly compensated employees for the current plan year not exceed the ADP of eligible nonhighly compensated employees for the preceding plan year by more than a certain amount. For this test, employers include only those employees who were nonhighly compensated employees in the preceding plan year,

---

214.   IRC §414(v)(2).

215.   29 CFR §2510.3-102.

216.   IRC §401(k)(3), (5); IRS Reg. §1.401(k)-1(b).

217.   IRC §414(q); IRS Temp. Reg. §1.414(q)-1T.

218.   IRS Notice 97-45, 1997-33 IRB 7.

regardless of their status in the current year. This is done by averaging the ADPs for the two groups and then applying the tests.

 **OTHER CONTRIBUTIONS CAN BE INCLUDED** In addition to the actual elective deferrals for each employee, employer matching contributions and employee after-tax contributions may also be treated as elective deferrals for purposes of the ADP tests.

The first step is to determine each eligible employee's ADP for the applicable plan year by using the following formula:

$$\frac{\text{Employee's annual elective deferrals}}{\text{Employee's total annual compensation}} \times 100$$

 **CATCH-UP CONTRIBUTIONS AREN'T COUNTED** Any amount that an employee has elected to defer that is treated as a "catch-up" contribution must be subtracted from the employee's annual elective deferrals before calculating the employee's actual deferral percentage

Then the ADPs for each group are averaged by adding them together and dividing by the number of employees.

Remember that the employee's total annual compensation taken into account for purposes of the ADP test cannot exceed the "annual compensation limit" ($230,000 for plan years beginning in 2008).

 **SPECIAL OPTION FOR FIRST PLAN YEAR** During the first plan year of a §401(k) plan (except a successor plan), the ADP of the employer's nonhighly compensated employees is either 3% or the ADP as determined under the above formula for the current year. The choice is up to the employer.[219]

When this is done, the average ADP for eligible highly compensated employees may not be greater than:

1.  1.25 x the average ADP for eligible nonhighly compensated employees or

2.  the lesser of:

    a.  2 x the average ADP for eligible nonhighly compensated employees or

    b.  2% more than the average ADP for eligible nonhighly compensated employees.

If a §401(k) plan meets one of the ADP tests, it is deemed to have met the general nondiscrimination tests regarding contributions that apply to all qualified retirement plans under §401(a)(4). The employer can use the current plan year ADP for nonhighly compensated employees in applying these tests, but once it chooses to do so, any further change can only be made as provided by the IRS.[220]

Cash or deferred arrangements under §401(k) must also not discriminate in terms of eligibility for the plan. Such a plan qualifies if at least 70% of the nonhighly compensated employees are eligible to make elective deferrals to the plan or the percentage of nonhighly compensated employees who are eligible to make elective deferrals is at least 70% of the percentage of highly compensated employees who are eligible.[221]

**Contributions to more than one plan.** If a highly compensated employee defers income to more than one §401(k) plan of an employer, the employee's elective deferrals are totaled for purposes of applying the special ADP nondiscrimination test to each plan. But all the employer's plans are treated as one in determining the employee's ADP. Therefore, an employee's ADP for purposes of applying the ADP test to any

---

219.   IRC §401(k)(3)(E).
220.   IRS Notice 98-1, 1998-3 IRB 42.
221.   IRC §401(k)(3)(A)(i); §410(b)(1).

of the employer's plans is the total of all the employee's elective deferrals divided by the employee's total annual compensation.

**Employers have alternate ways to meet nondiscrimination tests.**[222] For plan years beginning after December 31, 1998, employers have alternate methods for meeting the ADP test which are based on matching or nonelective contributions made by employers. The employer meets the matching contribution requirement if, for nonhighly compensated employees, it matches 100% of each employee's elective deferral up to 3% of the employee's compensation and 50% of the employee's elective deferral over 3% and up to 5% of the employee's compensation. This is the basic matching formula.

The employer can also use an enhanced matching formula. Under an enhanced matching formula, the employer provides matching contributions on behalf of each nonhighly compensated employee under a formula that, at any rate of elective contributions, provides a total amount of matching contributions at least equal to the total amount of matching contributions that would have been provided under the basic matching formula. In addition, under an enhanced matching formula, the rate of matching contributions may not increase as an employee's rate of elective contributions increases. Also, under either formula, the employer must not match highly compensated employees' elective deferrals at a higher percentage than it does for nonhighly compensated employees.

> **Example**: Beginning January 1, 2008, Elweigh Manufacturing Co. maintains a §401(k) plan under which Elweigh provides a matching contribution equal to 100% of each employee's elective deferrals up to 4% of compensation. The plan's formula is an enhanced matching formula because each nonhighly compensated employee receives matching contributions at least equal to the total amount of matching contributions that would have been received under the basic matching formula, and the rate of matching contributions does not increase with the rate of the employee's elective deferrals.

The employer meets the nonelective contribution requirement if it is required to contribute an amount equal to at least 3% of each nonhighly compensated employee's compensation, regardless of whether the employee contributes to the plan. Employers using these safe-harbor tests are treated as using the current year testing method for that year (see footnote 220). Regardless of which test the employer chooses to use, it must notify employees in writing (in plain language) of their rights and obligations under the plan within a reasonable period of time before each year. The notice must describe the contribution formula the employer is using, any other contributions under the plan, the type and amount of compensation that can be deferred by the employees, how to make deferral elections, the period available for making deferral elections, and withdrawal and vesting provisions of the plan. The timing requirement for the notice is deemed to be met if it is provided to eligible employees from 30-90 days before each plan year. For newly established plans and for employees who first become eligible under an existing §401(k) plan, the notice must be provided no more than 90 days before the employee becomes eligible under the plan and no later than the employee's eligibility date.

Employers that allow employees under age 21 or with less than 1 year of service to participate in the plan have the option of disregarding those employees when applying the nondiscrimination tests, so long as they separately satisfy the minimum coverage rules discussed earlier.

The IRS has provided additional guidance on the alternative methods for meeting the nondiscrimination requirements. The guidance, which was issued in response to comments that suggested ways to make plan administration easier, relaxed the notice requirements for employers choosing the safe harbor alternatives and clarified other aspects of plan administration.[223] The changes and clarifications include:

- employers using the safe harbor methods may require that salary reductions be made using whole dollar amounts or whole percentages of pay;
- plan administrators can provide the §401(k) safe harbor notice electronically;

---

222. IRC §401(k)(12); IRS Reg. §1.401(k)-3; IRS Notice 98-52, 1998-2 CB 634.
223. IRS Notice 2000-3, 2000-4 IRB 413.

- sponsors of currently existing §401(k) plans can wait until December 1 each year to choose to adopt the §401(k) safe harbor 3% matching contribution method for that calendar year;
- §401(k) safe harbor plans can match elective or employee contributions on a payroll period, monthly or quarterly basis;
- §401(k) safe harbor plans are permitted to provide matching contributions for an employee's aggregate employee and elective contributions; and
- plan sponsors can opt out of the safe harbor prospectively during a plan year if they provide adequate notice to employees beforehand.

**Parallel tests for matching and after-tax contributions.**[224] IRC §401(m) contains tests similar to those under §401(k) that show whether there has been discrimination in favor of highly compensated employees in terms of employer matching contributions and employee after-tax contributions. These tests are based on the Actual Contribution Percentage (ACP) for each employee.

 **WATCH OUT** The nondiscrimination testing rules are intended to be applied by employers in such a way as to not manipulate the rules in a way that unfairly benefits highly compensated employees. Therefore, a plan will not meet the nondiscrimination requirements if the employer repeatedly changes its plan testing procedures or plan provisions with the effect of significantly increasing the permitted ADP for highly compensated employees.[225]

**Employers can make automatic salary reductions without an election.** After the IRS issued guidance that said employers could make automatic salary reductions and §401(k) plan contributions for employees who did not make an election to reduce their salary or take cash, the Pension Protection Act of 2006 solidified that position and added requirements regarding default election percentages, employer matching contributions, and notice of the right to make an election, among others.[226] In 2007, the IRS issued proposed regulations implementing the law's provisions that employers can rely on until final regulations are issued.[227]

An "automatic contribution arrangement" is a default election that applies in the absence of an affirmative election by an eligible employee. The employee is treated as having made an election to have a specified contribution made on his or her behalf under the plan.

**Qualified Automatic Contribution Arrangement (QACA).** IRC sections 401(k)(13) and 401(m)(12) provide a safe harbor with respect to nondiscrimination testing under the ADP and ACP tests for plans that provide for automatic contributions at a specified level and meet certain notice and other requirements. An arrangement that satisfies these requirements is referred to as a Qualified Automatic Contribution Arrangement (QACA). The proposed regulations provide that the plan provision implementing the QACA for an existing qualified plan must be adopted before the first day of the plan year and remain in effect for an entire 12-month plan year.

In addition, a plan may limit the amount of elective contributions that may be made by an eligible employee under a QACA, provided that each nonhighly compensated employee who is an eligible employee generally is permitted to make elective contributions in an amount that is at least sufficient to receive the maximum amount of matching contributions available under the plan for the plan year, and the employee is permitted to elect any lesser amount of elective contributions.

*Qualified percentages and the uniformity requirement.* In order to be a QACA, a plan must provide a specified schedule of automatic contributions (called qualified percentages) for each eligible employee, beginning with an initial minimum qualified percentage of 3% of compensation. This minimum qualified percentage begins when the employee first participates in the arrangement that is intended to be a QACA and ends on the last day of the following plan year. Thus, this initial period for a participant could last as long as two full plan years.

---

224. IRC §401(m)(2); IRS Reg. §1.401(m)-2.
225. IRS Reg. §1.401(k)-1(b)(3); §1.401(m)-1(b)(3).
226. P.L. 109-280, §902; IRC §401(k)(13); §401(m)(11)(B), (12); §414(w); Rev. Rul. 2000-8, 2000-7 IRB 617.
227. IRS Prop. Reg. §1.401(k)-1(e)(7); §1.401(k)-2(a)(5)(vi); §401(k)-3(a)(1)-(3), (e)(1), (h)(2), (j), (k); §1.401(m)-1(c)(2); §1.401(m)-2(a)(5)(iv); §1.401(m)-2(b)(2)(vi); §1.401(m)-3(a)(1)-(3), (f)(1); §1.414(w)-1.

After this initial period, the minimum qualified percentage increases by 1% for each of the next three plan years, and then is 6% for all plan years thereafter. Note that these are merely minimum qualified percentages and that a QACA can provide for higher percentages. However, the qualified percentage can never exceed 10% of compensation.

The qualified percentage must be applied uniformly to all eligible employees. The proposed regulations provide that a plan does not fail this uniformity requirement where the percentage varies because:

- of the number of years an eligible employee has participated in the automatic contribution arrangement intended to be a QACA;
- the rate of elective contributions in effect on the effective date of the default percentage under the QACA is not reduced; or
- the amount of elective contributions is limited so as not to exceed statutory limits on compensation, deferrals, or overall contributions.

In addition, an arrangement would not fail the uniformity requirement where an employee is not automatically enrolled during the six-month period following a hardship distribution when elective contributions must be suspended.

*Default election vs. affirmative election.* Under the proposed regulations, the default election would cease to apply to any eligible employee if the employee makes an affirmative election to not have any elective contributions made or to have elective contributions made in a specified percentage of compensation. Thus, an employee could make an affirmative election to contribute at a certain level and have that election apply for all subsequent plan years. Similarly, an employee could make an affirmative election to have no elective contributions made on his or her behalf.

*Safe harbor notice and the timing requirement.* Each eligible employee under a QACA must receive a safe harbor notice 30-90 days before each plan year. This would give the employee a reasonable period of time after receipt of the notice and before the first elective contribution is to be made to make an election with respect to contributions and investments.

The proposed regulations would also provide that in the case of an employee who does not receive notice within this period because he or she becomes eligible after the 90th day before the beginning of the plan year, the timing requirement is deemed to be satisfied if the notice is provided no more than 90 days before the employee becomes eligible (and no later than the date the employee becomes eligible).

In the case of a plan with immediate eligibility when an employee is hired, the timing rule would be satisfied if the employee is provided the notice on the first day of employment.

 **SAMPLE NOTICE** The IRS has posted on its website a "Sample Automatic Enrollment and Default Investment Notice" [www.irs.gov/pub/irs-tege/sample_notice.pdf]. Plan sponsors may use the notice to inform participants about their rights and obligations under EACAs and QACAs. The sample notice is for a hypothetical QACA that permits EACA withdrawals and has certain other characteristics. The sample notice also contains text that will satisfy the information requirement for participant notices under U.S. Department of Labor regulations on qualified default investment alternatives.

**Eligible Automatic Contribution Arrangement (EACA).** PPA 2006 also added IRC §414(w), which provides limited relief from distribution restrictions for an Eligible Automatic Contribution Arrangement (EACA) – a non-safe harbor arrangement.

*Withdrawal election.* An election to withdraw contributions that were made under an EACA must be made within 90 days of the "first elective contribution with respect to the employee under the arrangement." The proposed regulations would define the arrangement for this purpose as the EACA, and would provide that the 90-day window for making the withdrawal election begins on the date on which the compensation

that is subject to the election would otherwise have been included in gross income. In addition, the proposed regulations would provide that the effective date of the election must be no later than the last day of the payroll period that begins after the date of the election.

*Distributions.* The proposed regulations would provide that the distribution is generally the account balance attributable to the default elective contributions, adjusted for gains and losses. The distribution may be reduced by any generally applicable fees. However, the proposed regulations provide that the plan may not charge a different fee for this distribution than would apply to other distributions. Also, if the default elective contributions are not maintained in a separate account, the amount of the allocable gains and losses will be determined under rules similar to those applicable to the distribution of excess contributions.

The amount withdrawn is includible in gross income in the year in which it is distributed, except that amounts that are distributions of designated Roth contributions are not included in an employee's gross income a second time. The proposed regulations would require that this amount be reported on Form 1099-R, *Distributions From Pensions, Annuities, Retirement or Profit-Sharing Plans, IRAs, Insurance Contracts, etc.* And the proposed regulations would include these withdrawals in the list of distributions that are not eligible for rollover.

Any employer matching contribution with respect to the default elective contribution distributed must be forfeited. The proposed regulations would provide that the forfeited contribution must remain in the plan and be treated in the same manner under the plan terms as any other forfeiture under the plan.

*Default elective contributions.* An EACA must provide that the default elective contribution is a uniform percentage of compensation. The proposed regulations would provide that the permitted differences in contribution rates provided for a QACA also apply to an EACA.

*Notice requirements.* Notice must be provided to each employee to whom the EACA applies within a "reasonable period" before each plan year. The proposed regulations provide that if an employee becomes eligible in a given year, notice must be given within a "reasonable period" before the employee becomes eligible, and provide a deemed timing rule similar to the rule applicable to QACAs.

**Failure of an ADP test.** If a §401(k) plan fails the ADP test, all participants will be taxed on their elective deferrals unless the plan takes corrective action. This may include distributing certain elective deferrals (and any earnings on them) to highly compensated employees within a certain period of time (report them on Form 1099-R—see Section 8.12-2) or making contributions for nonhighly compensated employees to increase their average actual deferral percentage.

**Tax treatment of §401(k) plans.** Employee elective deferrals (including catch-up contributions) and employer matching contributions to qualified §401(k) plans up to the applicable contribution limits are not wages subject to federal income tax withholding. Federal income taxation is deferred until funds are actually received or distributed from the plan. However, employee elective deferrals are subject to social security, Medicare, and FUTA taxes. Employer matching contributions are not.[228] Employers should also check the states where they operate for any different treatment under state or local law regarding income tax withholding or unemployment and disability insurance (see Table 4.1 in Section 4.7).

**Reporting requirements.** Because employee elective deferrals and employer matching contributions to a §401(k) plan are not wages subject to federal income tax withholding, they are not included in Box 1 of the employee's Form W-2. The elective deferrals, however, must be included in Box 3 as social security wages and Box 5 as Medicare wages. Amounts withheld for social security and Medicare taxes must be shown in Boxes 4 and 6, respectively. The elective deferrals must also be included in Box 12, preceded by Code "D," and the employer must mark the check box in Box 13 labeled "Retirement plan." The Box 12 amount should include any catch-up contributions. (See Section 8.8-3 for details on Form W-2 reporting.)

---

228.   IRC §3121(v)(1)(A); §3306(r)(1)(A); §3401(a)(12); IRS Reg. §1.401(k)-1(a)(4)(iii); §31.3401(a)(12)-1.

**EXCESS DEFERRALS** Amounts deferred in excess of the maximum deferral amounts are included in the Box 12 total, but they are not included in Box 1. The employee must include the taxable excess amount on his or her personal income tax return.

For similar reasons, the employer does not include the elective deferrals or employer matching contributions on Line 2 of its quarterly Form 941 as taxable wages. But it does include the elective deferrals on Lines 5a and 5c as taxable social security and Medicare wages. (See Section 8.3 for details on Form 941 reporting.) The deferrals must also be included in Part 2, Line 3 of the employer's annual Form 940. (See Section 7.1-7 for details on Form 940 reporting).

 **EARLY DISTRIBUTION PENALTY** Employees who receive a distribution of the funds in their §401(k) plan account before they retire may be subject to an additional 10% excise tax on the taxable portion of the distribution. There are exceptions for employees who are: at least 59½ years old, disabled, reservists called to active duty for more than 179 days, separated from employment after reaching age 55 (age 50 for public safety employees), or receiving the distribution in periodic payments over their lifetimes.[229] (For the rules on rollovers of early distributions to avoid tax penalties, see Section 6.4-5).

**Generally not for public sector groups, but OK for nonprofits.** A §401(k) plan may generally not be part of a retirement plan maintained by a state or local government employer (except rural cooperative or Indian tribal government plans).[230] If a §401(k) plan operated by a state or local government employer was in place before the Tax Reform Act of 1986, it can remain available to employees. For plan years beginning after December 31, 1996, nonprofit organizations that are exempt from federal income tax under IRC §501 can offer a §401(k) plan to their employees.

**Veterans can make deferrals for years spent in military service.**[231] Under the Uniformed Services Employment and Reemployment Rights Act of 1994 (USERRA), veterans of U.S. military service have the right to make additional elective deferrals under their employer's §401(k) plan for the time they spent in military service. The employer must allow such deferrals to be made during the period beginning with the veteran's reemployment and lasting 3 times the period of military service, but no longer than 5 years. The employer must also match the employee's deferrals to the extent it would have been required to do so if the deferrals had been made during the period of military service.

Elective deferrals made for years spent in military service are not subject to the elective deferral or contribution limits for the year in which the deferrals are made and are not added to other contributions made for that year for purposes of determining whether those limits are exceeded. However, the deferrals are subject to the contribution limits for the year to which they relate, taking into account any deferrals that were made during the period of military service. Reemployed veterans will be treated as having received compensation during their period of military service equal to what they would have earned had they not been absent during the period of military service. If that amount is not certain, the veteran's compensation will be the average compensation the employee received from the employer during the 12 months before military service.

As far as nondiscrimination tests are concerned, employee elective deferrals and employer matching contributions are not taken into account either for the year in which they are made or for the year to which they relate. The elective deferrals must be reported either on Form W-2 in Box 12 preceded by code "D" and the year to which they relate, or on a separate statement showing the type of plan, the year to which the deferrals relate, and the amounts deferred. (For full details, see Section 8.8-3.)

**Small employers can offer a §401(k) option in a SIMPLE plan.** The Small Business Job Protection Act of 1996 added IRC §408(p), which allows employers with no more than 100 employees to establish Savings Incentive Match Plans for Employees of Small Employers (SIMPLE plans). A SIMPLE plan can be either an individual retirement arrangement for each employee or part of a §401(k) plan. For details, see Section 4.6-8.

---

229. IRC §72(t).
230. IRC §401(k)(4)(B); IRS Reg. §1.401(k)-1(e)(4).
231. IRC §414(u); 38 USC §4311-§4318.

**Deferrals can go into a Roth IRA.** Beginning in 2006, a cash or deferred arrangement may permit an employee who makes elective deferrals under a §401(k) plan (or a §403(b) annuity – see Section 4.6-3) to designate some or all of those contributions as contributions to a Roth IRA (individual retirement account).[232]

 **WHAT'S A ROTH IRA?** Roth IRAs are different from traditional IRAs in that contributions to a Roth IRA are not deductible from income, but distributions are not included in gross income if they meet certain qualifications (see Section 4.6-6).

*Defining designated Roth contributions.*[233] Under IRS' implementing regulations, designated Roth contributions are defined as elective contributions under a qualified cash or deferred arrangement that are:

- Designated irrevocably by the employee at the time of the cash or deferred election as designated Roth contributions;
- Included by the employer in the employee's income at the time the employee would have received the contribution amounts in cash if the employee had not made the cash or deferred election (i.e., by treating the contributions as wages subject to applicable withholding requirements); and
- Maintained by the plan in a separate account.

*One limit for both types of deferrals.* The total of an employee's pre-tax elective deferrals and designated Roth contributions may not exceed the annual maximum for pre-tax elective deferrals and catch-up contributions to a §401(k) plan – $20,500 for 2008.

*Rules governing designated Roth contributions.* Some aspects of designated Roth contributions must be reflected in plan terms. For example, contributions may be treated as designated Roth contributions only to the extent permitted under a plan. In addition, while a plan is permitted to allow an employee to elect the character of a distribution (i.e., whether the distribution will be made from the designated Roth contribution account or other accounts; see below), the extent to which this is permitted must be set forth in the plan. And the plan must provide that designated Roth contributions may be rolled over only to another plan maintaining a designated Roth contribution account or to a Roth IRA.

*Separate accounting.*[234] The regulations provide that contributions and withdrawals of designated Roth contributions must be credited and debited to a designated Roth contribution account maintained for the employee who made the designation, and the plan must maintain a record of the employee's investment (i.e., the designated Roth contributions that have not been distributed) with respect to the employee's designated Roth contribution account.

In addition, gains, losses, and other credits or charges must be separately allocated on a reasonable and consistent basis to the designated Roth contribution account and other accounts under the plan. The separate accounting requirement applies at the time the designated Roth contribution is contributed to the plan and continues to apply until the designated Roth contribution account is completely distributed.

*Elections.*[235] The rules regarding the frequency of elections to make pre-tax elective contributions apply to elections to make designated Roth contributions. A plan that provides for an automatic cash or deferred election if the employee does not make an affirmative election and that has both pre-tax elective contributions and designated Roth contributions must set forth the extent to which those default contributions are pre-tax elective contributions or designated Roth contributions. If the default contributions are designated Roth contributions, then an employee who has not made an affirmative election is deemed to have irrevocably designated the contributions as designated Roth contributions.

---

232.   IRC §402A; IRS Reg. §1.401(k)-1(f)(1) – (4).
233.   IRS Reg. §1.401(k)-1(f)(1).
234.   IRS Reg. §1.401(k)-1(f)(2).
235.   IRS Reg. §1.401(k)-1(f)(4).

*Direct rollovers.*[236] A direct rollover from a designated Roth account under a qualified cash or deferred arrangement may only be made to another designated Roth account or to a Roth IRA. In addition, a plan is permitted to treat the balance of a participant's designated Roth account and the participant's other accounts under the plan as accounts held under two separate plans. Therefore, if a participant's balance in the designated Roth account is less than $200, then the plan is not required to offer a direct rollover election with respect to that account.

*ADP testing.*[237] Designated Roth contributions are taken into account under the ADP test applicable to §401(k) plans in the same manner as pre-tax elective contributions. A highly compensated employee with elective contributions for a year that include both pre-tax elective contributions and designated Roth contributions may elect whether excess contributions are to be attributed to pre-tax elective contributions or designated Roth contributions.

A distribution of excess contributions is not includible in gross income to the extent it represents a distribution of designated Roth contributions. However, the income allocable to (i.e., interest earned on) a corrective distribution of excess contributions that are designated Roth contributions is includible in gross income in the same manner as income allocable to a corrective distribution of excess contributions that are pre-tax elective contributions.

*Taxation of distributions.*[238] The taxation of a distribution from a designated Roth account depends on whether or not the distribution is a qualified distribution. A qualified distribution from a designated Roth account is not included in the employee's gross income. A qualified distribution is a distribution that is made after a five-taxable-year period of participation and that is made:

- on or after the date the employee reaches age 59½,
- after the employee's death, or
- on account of the employee's disability.

The five-taxable-year period during which a distribution is not a qualified distribution begins on the first day of the employee's taxable year for which the employee first designated Roth contributions made to the plan and ends when five consecutive taxable years have been completed. However, if a direct rollover is made from a designated Roth account under another plan, the five-taxable-year period for the recipient plan begins on the first day of the employee's taxable year for which the employee first had designated Roth contributions made to the other plan, if earlier.

Certain contributions do not start the five-taxable-year period of participation:

- a year in which the only contributions consist of excess deferrals;
- excess contributions that are distributed to prevent an ADP test failure; and
- contributions returned to the employee under an EACA pursuant to IRC §414(w).

*Alternate payee or beneficiary.* In the case of distribution to an alternate payee or beneficiary, the age, death, or disability of the participant is used to determine whether the distribution is qualified. The only exception is in the case of a rollover by an alternate payee or surviving spouse to a designated Roth account under a plan of his or her own employer.

*Reemployed veteran.* Designated Roth contributions made by a reemployed veteran are treated as made in the taxable year with respect to which the contributions relate. Reemployed veterans may identify the year for which a contribution is made for other purposes (e.g., entitlement to a match), and the treatment of the five-year period of participation follows that identification. If an identification is not made, for purposes of determining the first year of the five years of participation, the contribution is treated as made in the veteran's first taxable year in which his/her military service begins or, if later, the first taxable year in which designated Roth contributions could be made under the plan.

---

236. IRS Reg. §1.401(k)-1(f)(3)(ii).
237. IRS Reg. §1.401(k)-1(f)(3)(i); §1.401(k)-2(b)(1)(ii), (b)(2)(vi)(C).
238. IRS Reg. §1.402A-1, Q&A 1–4.

*Reporting and recordkeeping.*[239] The plan administrator of a plan with a designated Roth account is responsible for keeping track of the five-taxable-year period for each employee and the amount of designated Roth contributions made on behalf of such employee. In addition, the plan administrator of a plan directly rolling over a distribution would be required to provide the plan administrator of the plan accepting the eligible rollover distribution with a statement indicating either:

- the first year of the five-taxable-year period for the employee and the portion of such distribution attributable to basis, or
- that the distribution is a qualified distribution.

If the distribution is not a direct rollover to a designated Roth account under another eligible plan, the plan administrator must provide to the employee, upon request, this same information, except that the statement need not indicate the first year of the five-taxable-year period.

The statement would have to be provided within 30 days following the direct rollover (or an employee request), and the plan administrator for the recipient plan is permitted to rely on these statements.

To the extent that a portion of a distribution is includible in income and is rolled over to a designated Roth account during the 60-day period by the distributee rather than by direct rollover, then the plan administrator of the recipient plan must notify the IRS of its acceptance of the rollover contribution. This reporting is only required to the extent provided in IRS forms and instructions, which will specify the address to which the notification must be sent and will require information such as the employee's name and social security number, the amount rolled over, and the year in which the rollover contribution was made.

*Distribution of excess elective deferrals.*[240] Even though designated Roth contributions are not excluded from income when contributed, they are treated as elective deferrals for purposes of §402(g). Thus, to the extent total elective deferrals for the year exceed the §402(g) limit for the year, the excess amount can be distributed by April 15th of the year following the year of the excess without adverse tax consequences.

However, if such excess deferrals are not distributed by April 15th of the year following the year of the excess, any distribution attributable to an excess deferral that is a designated Roth contribution is included in gross income and is not eligible for rollover.

If there are any excess deferrals that are designated Roth contributions that are not corrected prior to April 15th of the year following the excess, then the first amounts distributed from the designated Roth account are treated as distributions of excess deferrals and earnings until the full amount of those excess deferrals (and attributable earnings) are distributed.

# 4.6-3 Tax-Sheltered Annuities (IRC §403(b))

Public schools and tax-exempt charitable, religious, and educational organizations may purchase "tax-sheltered" annuities that meet the requirements of IRC §403(b) for their employees. These requirements include:

1. the annuity contract may not be purchased through a qualified plan under §401(a) or §403(a) or a §457(b) plan;

2. the employee's rights must be nonforfeitable unless the employee fails to pay premiums;

3. the plan (other than church plans) must meet certain nondiscrimination requirements (applicable to deferred compensation retirement plans generally) including universal availability;

---

239.   IRS Reg. §1.402A-2, Q&A 1–3.
240.   IRS Reg. §1.402(g)-1(a), (b)(5), (e)(2), (e)(5), (e)(8)(iv).

4.  the plan must offer all employees the chance to defer at least $200 in compensation annually if one employee is given the opportunity; and

5.  the elective deferral limits must be met if the plan provides for a salary reduction agreement.[241]

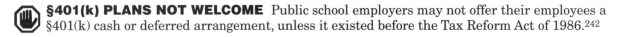 **§401(k) PLANS NOT WELCOME** Public school employers may not offer their employees a §401(k) cash or deferred arrangement, unless it existed before the Tax Reform Act of 1986.[242]

**Written plan requirement.**[243] Beginning in 2009, a §403(b) annuity contract must be issued pursuant to a written plan containing all the material terms and conditions of the plan related to eligibility, benefits, limitations, available contracts, and the time and form of plan distributions. The plan may incorporate by reference other documents, including the insurance policy or custodial account, which then become part of the plan. The plan may allocate to the employer or another person the responsibility for performing tunctions to administer the plan, including functions to comply with §403(b). Any such allocation must identify who is responsible for compliance.

The IRS has issued model plan language that may be used by public schools in adopting a written plan to comply with the final regulations.[244]

**Automatic salary reductions can qualify as elective deferrals.** See Section 4.6-2 for the rules allowing employers to make automatic salary reduction elections for employees who are eligible to make a salary reduction but do not elect between salary reduction and cash.

**Contribution limits.** There are two types of contribution limits that apply to annuities purchased under §403(b). A third, the maximum exclusion allowance, was repealed by the Economic Growth and Tax Relief Reconciliation Act of 2001, effective January 1, 2002.

*General defined contribution plan limitation.*[245] IRC §415 limits total employer and employee contributions to all defined contribution plans in which the employee participates to the lesser of 100% of the employee's annual compensation or $46,000 in 2008 (indexed annually to the next lowest multiple of $1,000). Pre-tax elective deferrals to a §401(k), §403(b), §457, §125 or §132(f)(4) plan are included in an employee's compensation when determining the maximum contribution limit for the employee. The amount of an employee's compensation that can be taken into account when determining the maximum contributions (other than elective deferrals) is $230,000 for plan years beginning in 2008 (indexed annually to the next lowest multiple of $5,000).

*Elective deferral limit.* The Economic Growth and Tax Relief Reconciliation Act of 2001 (EGTRRA) contained many provisions that were designed to expand the opportunities for retirement savings, including annual increases in the amount of elective deferrals to defined contribution plans. Where a §403(b) annuity plan provides for a salary reduction agreement, the final EGTRRA elective deferral amount was $15,000 in 2006, with the maximum adjusted for inflation to the next lowest multiple of $500 beginning in 2007. For 2008, the §403(b) plan elective deferral limit is $15,500.

However, the limit also includes any amounts deferred under a preexisting §401(k) plan, a simplified employee pension plan that provides for salary reductions (see Section 4.6-7), or a SIMPLE plan providing for salary reductions (see Section 4.6-8).[246]

---

241.  IRC §403(b); §501(c)(3); IRS Reg. §1.403(b)-3.
242.  IRC §401(k)(4)(B).
243.  IRS Reg. §1.403(b)-3(b)(3).
244.  Rev. Proc. 2007-71, 2007-51 IRB 1184.
245.  IRC §401(a)(17); §415(c), (g); IRS Reg. §1.403(b)-4; §1.415-8.
246.  IRC §402(g)(3); §403(b)(1)(E); IRS Reg. §1.403(b)-4(c)(1).

Employees participating in §403(b) plans can take advantage of a special provision in the law to exceed the maximum elective deferral amount. To use this provision, the employee must have at least 15 years of service with the employer. An eligible employee's 15-year deferral is limited to the least of the following:[247]

- $3,000 in additional contributions in any year;
- $15,000 reduced by any amounts contributed under this special provision in earlier years; or
- ($5,000 x the number of years of service) - total elective deferrals from previous years.

 **WATCH OUT**   Several times in recent years, IRS personnel have announced that the Service is increasing its §403(b) audit activity, having found that many plans are not properly monitoring when employees are exceeding the elective deferral limit, while others are not opening their plans to all eligible employees.

**"Catch-up" contributions.**   Under EGTRRA, employees who are eligible to make elective salary deferrals to defined contribution plans and who would be at least 50 years old by the end of the plan year can defer an additional amount to the plan as a "catch-up" contribution (see Section 4.6-1 for details) beyond limits set by law or by the plan itself. The catch-up contribution maximum is the lesser of the "applicable dollar amount" or the employee's compensation for the year reduced by any other elective deferrals made during that year.[248]  The applicable dollar amount for §403(b) plans is $5,000 in 2008 (adjusted for inflation annually to the next lowest multiple of $500).

*Example 1:*   Employee Barbara, who is over 50, is a participant in a 403(b) plan. Barbara's compensation for 2008 is $30,000. The maximum statutory annual deferral limit is $15,500. Under the terms of the plan, the maximum permitted deferral is 10% ($3,000 in Barbara's case). Barbara can contribute up to $8,000 for the year ($3,000 under the normal operation of the plan, and an additional $5,000 as a catch-up contribution).

*Example 2:*   Employee Esther, who is over 50, is a participant in a 403(b) plan. Esther's compensation for 2008 is $80,000. The maximum statutory annual deferral limit is $15,500. The plan incorporates the statutory annual deferral limit as the plan limit. Esther can contribute up to $20,500 for the year ($15,500 under the normal operation of the plan and an additional $5,000 as a catch-up contribution).

*Coordination of catch-up amounts.*[249]  Any catch-up amount contributed by an employee who is eligible for both an age-50 catch-up and a special §403(b) catch-up is treated first as an amount contributed as a special §403(b) catch-up and then as an age-50 catch-up.

**Universal availability of elective deferrals.**[250]  The universal availability rule generally requires that a plan offer all employees the chance to defer at least $200 in compensation annually if one employee is given the opportunity. An employee's right to make elective deferrals also includes the right to designate §403(b) elective deferrals as designated Roth contributions if any employee of the eligible employer may elect to have the organization make §403(b) elective deferrals as designated Roth contributions.

Certain classes of employees can be excluded for purposes of the universal availability rule:

- employees who are eligible to make elective deferrals under another §403(b) plan, a §401(k) plan, or a governmental §457(b) plan of the employer;
- nonresident alien employees;
- student employees not meeting minimum age and service requirements; or
- employees who work fewer than 20 hours a week and did not work more than 1,000 hours in the previous 12-month period (or a lower number set by the plan).

---

247.   IRC §402(g)(7); IRS Reg. §1.403(b)-4(c)(3).
248.   IRC §414(v)(2); IRS Reg. §1.414(v)-1; IRS Reg. §1.403(b)-4(c)(2).
249.   IRS Reg. §1.403(b)-4(c)(3)(iv).
250.   IRS Reg. §1.403(b)-5(b).

Exclusions for certain classes of employees for purposes of the universal availability rule, permitted under 1989 guidance, will no longer be permitted under the final regulations, beginning January 1, 2010:

- employees covered by a collective bargaining agreement;
- employees making a one-time election to participate in a governmental §457(b) plan instead of a §403(b) plan;
- professors providing services on a temporary basis to another public school for up to one year and for whom §403(b) contributions are being made at a rate no greater than the rate each such professor would receive under the §403(b) plan of the original public school; and
- employees affiliated with a religious order and who have taken a vow of poverty where the religious order provides for the support of such employees in their retirement.

Other rules may apply with respect to some of these individuals. For instance, individuals who work for an institution that is controlled by a church organization and whose compensation from the employer is not treated as wages for purposes of income tax withholding may be excluded from the §403(b) plan because they are not treated as employees of the entity maintaining the plan. Also, if an individual is performing services for a university as a visiting professor, but continues to receive compensation from his or her home university and elective deferrals are made on his or her behalf under the home university's §403(b) plan, that plan may treat the visiting professor as an eligible employee.

**Tax treatment of §403(b) plans.** As long as the annuity plan meets the qualifications of §403(b), employer contributions (including employee elective deferrals and catch-up contributions) to the plan to purchase annuity contracts are not wages subject to federal income tax withholding up to the contribution limits.[251] Distributions from the plan are taxable when the annuity payments are made to employees. Employee elective deferrals pursuant to a "salary reduction agreement," however, are subject to social security, Medicare and FUTA taxes. Other employer contributions are not.[252] Once again, employers must check the laws in the states where they operate for differences in state and local laws regarding income tax withholding and unemployment insurance contributions.

*Definition of 'salary reduction agreement.'*[253] The term "salary reduction agreement" includes a plan or arrangement whereby a payment will be made if the employee:

- elects to reduce his or her compensation pursuant to a cash or deferred election;
- elects to reduce his or her compensation pursuant to a one-time irrevocable election made at or before the time of initial eligibility to participate in such plan or arrangement; or
- agrees as a condition of employment to make a contribution that reduces his or her compensation.

**Reporting requirements.** Because employee elective deferrals and employer contributions to a §403(b) tax-sheltered annuity are not wages subject to federal income tax, they are not included in Box 1 of the employee's Form W-2. The elective deferrals, however, must be included in Box 3 as social security wages and Box 5 as Medicare wages. Amounts withheld for social security and Medicare taxes must be shown in Boxes 4 and 6, respectively. The elective deferrals must also be included in Box 12, preceded by Code "E," and the employer must mark the check box in Box 13 labeled "Retirement plan." The Box 12 amount should include any catch-up contributions. (See Section 8.8 for details on Form W-2 reporting.)

 **EXCESS DEFERRALS** Amounts deferred in excess of the maximum deferral amounts are included in the Box 12 total, but they are not included in Box 1. The employee must include the taxable excess amount on his or her personal income tax return.

For similar reasons, the employer does not include the elective deferrals or employer contributions on Line 2 of its quarterly Form 941 as taxable wages. But it does include the elective deferrals on Lines 5a and 5c as taxable social security and Medicare wages. (See Section 8.3 for details on Form 941 reporting.)

---

251.   IRC §403(b)(1).

252.   IRC §3121(a)(5)(D); §3306(b)(5)(D).

253.   IRS Reg. §31.3121(a)(5)-2.

The deferrals must also be included in Part 2, Line 3 of the employer's annual Form 940. (See Section 7.1-7 for details on Form 940 reporting).

**Deferrals can go to a Roth IRA.** Beginning in 2006, a §403(b) plan can permit employees who make elective deferrals to the plan to designate some or all of those contributions as contributions to a Roth IRA (individual retirement account). The "designated Roth contributions" are included in the employee's income and are subject to federal income, social security, Medicare, and FUTA taxes, but distributions of the contributions and the earnings on them are not taxable. For more information, see Section 4.6-2.

# 4.6-4 Deferred Compensation Plans for the Public Sector and Tax-Exempt Groups (IRC §457)

State and local government employers and tax-exempt organizations other than churches can set up deferred compensation retirement plans for their employees under IRC §457. Deferred compensation plans that meet the requirements of §457(b) are "eligible" plans, and employees may defer a portion of their salary into such a plan before taxes, up to certain limits. The §457 plan is treated in some ways as a nonqualified deferred compensation plan (see Section 4.6-10).

The requirements applicable to §457(b) plans include:[254]

*Eligibility.* Only individuals performing services for the employer are eligible for participation in the plan (including independent contractors).

*Nondiscrimination testing.* Unlike §401(k) plans, §457(b) plans can be provided in a discriminatory manner. The plan administrator need not calculate mathematical discrimination tests or apply coverage tests.

*Deferral limits.* The Economic Growth and Tax Relief Reconciliation Act of 2001 (EGTRRA) contained many provisions that were designed to expand the opportunities for retirement savings, including annual increases in the amount of elective deferrals to defined contribution plans. For §457(b) plans, the maximum amount that can be deferred in 2008 is the lesser of $15,500 (adjusted for inflation annually to the next lowest multiple of $500) or 100% of the employee's annual compensation. Pre-tax elective deferrals to a §401(k), §403(b), §457(b), §125, or §132(f)(4) plan are included in an employee's annual compensation when determining the maximum contribution limit for the employee.

*Special rule near retirement.* The plan may also provide that, for the last 3 years before a participant reaches the plan's normal retirement age, the maximum annual deferral limit is the lesser of twice the amount determined by the above method or the current year deferral limit plus the limits from previous years reduced by the participant's deferrals for those years.

*"Catch-up" contributions.* Under EGTRRA, employees who are eligible to make elective salary deferrals to defined contribution plans and who would be at least 50 years old by the end of the plan year can defer an additional amount to the plan as a "catch-up" contribution (see Section 4.6-1 for details) beyond limits set by law or by the plan itself. The catch-up contribution maximum is the lesser of the "applicable dollar amount" or the employee's compensation for the year reduced by any other elective deferrals made during that year.[255] The applicable dollar amount for governmental §457(b) plans in 2008 is $5,000 (adjusted for inflation annually to the next lowest multiple of $500).

> **Example 1:** Employee Barbara, who is 53, is a participant in a governmental §457(b) plan. Barbara's compensation for 2008 is $30,000. The maximum statutory annual deferral limit is $15,500. Under the terms of the plan, the maximum permitted deferral is 10% ($3,000 in Barbara's case). Barbara can contribute up to $8,000 for the year ($3,000 under the normal operation of the plan, and an additional $5,000 as a catch-up contribution).

---

254.   IRC §457(b) - (e), (g); IRS Reg. §1.457-1 to 10.
255.   IRC §414(v)(2); IRS Reg. §1.457-4(c)(2).

***Example 2:*** Employee Esther, who is 53, is a participant in a governmental §457(b) plan. Esther's compensation for 2008 is $80,000. The maximum statutory annual deferral limit is $15,500. The plan incorporates the statutory annual deferral limit as the plan limit. Esther can contribute up to $20,500 for the year ($15,500 under the normal operation of the plan and an additional $5,000 as a catch-up contribution).

 **BE CAREFUL** The catch-up contribution under §414(v) is not available to participants in a governmental §457(b) plan during their last 3 years before reaching the plan's normal retirement age, if the maximum deferral limit under the special rule would provide a higher maximum contribution. (Note: The maximum deferral limit under the special rule can be used only once unless the employee is covered by a §457(b) plan of another employer.)

Beginning in 2002, organizations that provide both §457(b) and deferred compensation plans under §401(k) or §403(b) no longer have to total all deferrals made by an employee when determining whether the §457 maximum deferral has been reached.

See Section 4.6-2 for rules under which employers can set up automatic salary reductions for employees who are eligible to do so but don't make an election between salary reductions and cash.

*Ownership of deferrals.* All the amounts deferred under a §457(b) plan maintained by a state or local government employer and the income earned on them must be placed in a tax-exempt trust (or custodial account or annuity contract) for the exclusive benefit of the employees and their beneficiaries. The amounts in the trust are not considered as having been paid to the employees merely because they are held in the trust, so the deferrals and the earnings on them are not included in the employee's income or subject to federal income tax withholding.

For tax-exempt employers, deferrals and earnings must remain assets of the employer subject to the employer's general creditors. Under these rules, funds earmarked for specific employees might be considered as having been constructively received by the employees and would have to be included in income.

Amounts deferred under a governmental §457(b) plan must be transferred to the trust within a reasonable time after payday, and the plan itself may provide for such transfers to take place within a specified period after the deferred amounts would have been paid to the employee (e.g., within 15 business days after the month during which the wages would have been paid to the employee).

*Distributions.*[256] Generally, no distributions to participants can be made before: the year the employee reaches age 70½, separation from employment (e.g., retirement), or the employee faces an unforeseeable emergency. However, a §457(b) plan may allow employees to elect to take an earlier distribution if the total amount payable is no more than $5,000 and no amount has been deferred for the employee during the 2-year period ending on the date of the distribution. Only one such distribution is allowed for a participant. The plan can also require that a distribution be taken in such situations or combine the two alternatives so that a cash-out is required for balances up to a certain amount and employees are permitted to take a distribution for balances above that amount but below $5,000. The plan can also set a lower maximum than $5,000 under either of these two alternatives. Plan distributions may also be made to satisfy a qualified domestic relations order even if the general rules governing distributions are not met.

**Tax treatment.** Elective employee deferrals and nonelective employer contributions to an eligible §457(b) plan are not included as wages and are not subject to federal income tax withholding, although they are subject to social security, Medicare, and FUTA taxes as soon as there is no substantial risk of forfeiture of the right to the benefit.[257] Excess deferrals, however, are subject to federal income tax withholding. If the plan is not eligible under §457(b), all deferrals and employer contributions are included in the participant's income in the first year in which there is no substantial risk of forfeiture of the right to the compensation.[258]

---

256.  IRS Reg. §1.457-6; §1.457-10(c).
257.  IRC §457(a); §3121(a)(5)(E); (v)(3); §3306(b)(5)(E); IRS Notice 2003-20, 2003-19 IRB 894.
258.  IRC §457(f); IRS Reg. §1.457-11.

Because of differences in the way some states and localities treat deferred compensation plans regarding income tax withholding and unemployment insurance, employers must be aware of the state and local rules wherever they operate.

After a change made by EGTRRA, distributions from a governmental §457(b) plan are no longer considered wages, but pension payments beginning in 2002, and federal income tax withholding is calculated as it is for other pension payments (see Section 6.4-5). The plan administrator is responsible for the withholding unless it directs the payor to withhold and provides the payor with all information necessary to compute the withholding tax liability. If the distributions are made under a §457(b) plan established by a tax-exempt organization, the employer or other person having control over the payment of the distributions is responsible for income tax withholding and reporting on the distributions.[259]

So long as amounts deferred under a §457(b) plan have been subjected to social security, Medicare, and FUTA taxes (if applicable) when deferred or when they were no longer subject to a substantial risk of forfeiture, distributions of those amounts and the earnings on them are not subject to those taxes when paid out.

**Reporting requirements.**[260] Because employee elective deferrals and employer nonelective contributions to a §457(b) plan (i.e., annual deferrals) are not wages subject to federal income tax withholding, they are not included in Box 1 of the employee's Form W-2. They must, however, be included in Box 3 as social security wages and Box 5 as Medicare wages. Amounts withheld for social security and Medicare taxes must be shown in Boxes 4 and 6, respectively. The elective and nonelective deferrals must also be included in Box 12, preceded by Code "G," but the employer should not mark the check box in Box 13 labeled "Retirement plan ." (See Section 8.8 for details on Form W-2 reporting, including how to report deferrals to a §457(b) plan.)

 **EXCESS DEFERRALS** Amounts deferred by the employee or contributed by the employer in excess of the maximum deferral amounts are included in the Box 12 total, but they are not included in Box 1. The employee must include the taxable excess amount on his or her personal income tax return.

For similar reasons, the employer does not include the employee elective deferrals or the employer nonelective contributions on Line 2 of its quarterly Form 941 as taxable wages. But it does include both on Lines 5a and 5c as taxable social security and Medicare wages. (See Section 8.3 for details on Form 941 reporting). The elective and nonelective deferrals must both be included in Part 2, Line 3 of the employer's annual Form 940. (See Section 7.1-7 for details on Form 940 reporting.)

Effective for distributions from governmental §457(b) plans made on or after January 1, 2002, such distributions are subject to the taxation and reporting rules that apply to pension payments. They are no longer taxed and reported as wages, after a change made by EGTRRA. Therefore, the amount of the distribution and any income tax withheld must be reported on Form 1099-R, *Distributions From Pensions, Annuities, Retirement or Profit-Sharing Plans, IRAs, Insurance Contracts, Etc.* (see Appendix page A-271). The entity making such distributions, usually the plan administrator, reports the total taxes it withheld on Form 945, *Annual Return of Withheld Federal Income Tax* (see Appendix page A-215), along with other nonpayroll income tax it withheld..

Alternatively, the IRS will permit the plan administrator (or payor) of §457(g) trusts, or custodial accounts or insurance contracts treated as such trusts, to use one of two alternatives:

- The plan administrator or payor may obtain and use an EIN solely for the purpose of reporting the total withholding from all such trusts, accounts, or contracts under its control on Form 945.

- The plan administrator or payor may obtain and use a separate EIN to report the withheld income tax for each such trust, account, or contract on Form 945.

---

259.   IRS Reg. §1.457-7; IRS Notice 2003-20, 2003-19 IRB 894.
260.   IRS Notice 2003-20, 2003-19 IRB 894.

The plan administrator or payor exercising any of these alternatives for depositing and reporting the tax withheld from §457(g) trust distributions must use the same name and EIN on Forms 1099-R as those under which the tax was deposited and the Form 945 filed.

Distributions paid to a participant under a tax-exempt entity's §457(b) plan are wages and are reported on Form W-2 in Box 1 and Box 11, with the amount withheld for federal income tax entered in Box 2. These amounts also must be reported on Form 941 on Lines 2 and 3, and on Form 940 on Part 2, Line 3. If deferred amounts were taken into account for purposes of social security and Medicare taxes when deferred or, if later, when the substantial risk of forfeiture lapsed, distributions attributable to those deferrals (including earnings on the deferrals) are not subject to social security or Medicare tax and do not have to be reported as social security or Medicare wages.

## 4.6-5 Employee-Funded Plans (IRC §501(c)(18)(D))

Pension plans created before June 25, 1959 that are funded solely by employee contributions receive tax-favored treatment if they meet certain qualifications. If the plan does not discriminate in favor of highly compensated employees (see Section 4.6-2) in terms of eligibility or benefits and meets certain contribution limits, employee deferrals under the plan may be excluded from income.[261]

*Deferral limits, tax treatment.* Deductible employee contributions to a §501(c)(18)(D) plan are limited to the lesser of $7,000 – the maximum contained in IRC §219(b)(3) – or 25% of the employee's compensation for the year, and are treated as employee pre-tax deferrals.

Employee pre-tax deferrals up to the appropriate limit are not subject to federal income tax withholding. The maximum deferral amount is also reduced by any pre-tax contributions to other CODAs maintained by the employer. The pre-tax deferrals are, however, subject to social security, Medicare, and FUTA taxes. Employers should check the laws in the states and localities where they operate for any differences in the treatment of their plans regarding state and local income tax withholding and unemployment insurance contributions.

**Reporting requirements.** Even though employee elective deferrals to a §501(c)(18)(D) plan are not wages subject to federal income tax withholding, they are included in Box 1 of the employee's Form W-2. The employee can then deduct these amounts on his or her personal income tax return. They must also be included in Box 3 as social security wages and Box 5 as Medicare wages. Amounts withheld for social security and Medicare taxes must be shown in Boxes 4 and 6, respectively. The elective deferrals must also be included in Box 12, preceded by Code "H," and the employer must mark the check box in Box 13 labeled "Retirement plan." (See Section 8.8 for details on Form W-2 reporting.)

For similar reasons, the employer does not include the elective deferrals on Line 2 of its quarterly Form 941 as taxable wages. But it does include the elective deferrals on Lines 5a and 5c as taxable social security and Medicare wages. (See Section 8.3 for details on Form 941 reporting.) The deferrals must also be included in Part 2, Line 3 of the employer's annual Form 940. (See Section 7.1-7 for details on Form 940 reporting).

## 4.6-6 Individual Retirement Accounts

Many employers offer their employees the opportunity to invest for their retirement through employer-sponsored individual retirement accounts (IRAs), either instead of or in addition to a qualified company plan. An employer-sponsored IRA must be in writing and created for the exclusive benefit of employees and their beneficiaries.

---

261. IRC §219(b)(3); §401(a)(30); §402(g); §501(c)(18)(D).

An employer-sponsored IRA must also limit employee contributions for a year to "the deductible amount" as shown in the following chart:[262]

| Calendar Year | Deductible Amount |
|---|---|
| 2002-2004 | $3,000 |
| 2005-2007 | $4,000 |
| 2008 | $5,000 |
| 2009 and beyond | Adjusted for inflation to next lowest multiple of $500 |

In addition, beginning in 2002, individuals who would be at least age 50 by the end of the year can deduct an additional "catch-up contribution" equal to the "applicable amount" shown in the following schedule:[263]

| Calendar Year | Applicable Amount |
|---|---|
| 2002-2005 | $500 |
| 2006 and beyond | $1,000 |

Under the Pension Protection Act of 2006, individuals who meet certain requirements can make an additional IRA catch-up contribution of up to $3,000 per year for 2007-2009, but they cannot choose both this catch-up contribution and the "age-50 and older" catch-up contribution.[264] To qualify, the individual must have been a participant in a §401(k) plan under which the employer matched at least 50% of the employees' elective deferrals with employer stock. In addition, before the year of the additional catch-up contribution, the employer must have been in bankruptcy and the employer or another person must have been indicted or convicted on a charge resulting from a business transaction related to the bankruptcy. Also, the individual must have been a participant in the §401(k) plan on the date 6 months before the bankruptcy case was filed.

The employee's contribution is deductible, but the deductible amount is reduced if the employee (or the employee's spouse) is an active participant in a qualified retirement plan offered by an employer, with the amount of the reduction based on the employee's adjusted gross income.[265] For married employees filing jointly when both are active participants in an employer's qualified retirement plan, the reduction begins at the "applicable dollar amount." For 2008, the applicable dollar amount is $85,000 (adjusted annually for inflation).

For other employees (except those who are married and file separately), the reduction begins at $53,000 in 2008 (adjusted annually for inflation).

For an employee who is married but filing a separate return, the applicable dollar amount is zero. If the employee and spouse are living apart for the whole year, however, they are not treated as married persons. The amount by which the deductible amount will be reduced is the amount that bears the same ratio to the deductible amount as the excess of the employee's adjusted gross income over the applicable dollar amount bears to $10,000 ($20,000 for joint filers beginning in 2007).

Where the employee's adjusted gross income is over $10,000 more than these amounts ($20,000 for joint filers beginning in 2007) and the employee or his or her spouse is an active participant in a qualified employer plan, no deduction is allowed.[266] For individuals who file jointly and are not active participants, but whose spouse is an active participant, the applicable dollar amount is $159,000 in 2008 (adjusted annually for inflation) and the deduction is eliminated when adjusted gross income hits $169,000. The employee may still contribute to the IRA, to a maximum of $2,000 per year for deductible and nondeductible contributions.

---

262. IRC §219(b)(5)(A); §408(a)(1); IRS Reg. §1.408-1.
263. IRC §219(b)(5)(B).
264. IRC §219(b)(5)(C).
265. IRC §408(g).
266. IRC §219(g)(1), (g)(2).

**Active participant defined.** The employee's status as an active participant in a qualified employer plan depends on whether the plan is a defined benefit or defined contribution plan. For an employee to be considered an active participant in a defined benefit plan, the employee must merely be eligible for the plan. If the plan is a defined contribution plan, the employee is an active participant if any contributions are made to the plan by the employer or the employee during the year.[267]

**Tax treatment.** Although employer contributions made on behalf of an employee to an IRA are included in the employee's income, they are not subject to federal income tax withholding up to the amount the employer reasonably believes the employee will be able to deduct on his or her personal income tax return. The income earned from contributions to the IRA is not subject to income tax until it is distributed. Employer contributions to an IRA are subject to social security, Medicare, and FUTA taxes.[268]

**Small employers can offer an IRA option in a SIMPLE plan.** The Small Business Job Protection Act of 1996 added IRC §408(p), which allows employers with no more than 100 employees to establish Savings Incentive Match Plans for Employees of Small Employers (SIMPLE plans). A SIMPLE plan can be either an individual retirement arrangement for each employee or part of a §401(k) plan. For details, see Section 4.6-8.

**Roth IRAs.** Roth IRAs were established by the Taxpayer Relief Act of 1997 as another retirement savings vehicle.[269] They are different from traditional IRAs in that contributions to a Roth IRA are not deductible from income, but distributions are not included in gross income if they meet certain qualifications. Individuals may put up to the maximum deductible amount for a traditional IRA in a Roth IRA in a year (there are no phase-outs because of active plan participant status), but that amount is reduced by any contributions by the individual to other IRAs for that year.

Also, the amount that can be contributed to a Roth IRA is phased out once the individual's adjusted gross income exceeds $159,000 for joint filers or $101,000 for single filers in 2008 (adjusted annually for inflation). Contributions are completely phased out at $169,000 for joint filers and $116,000 for single filers. Distributions are qualified (and not included in gross income) if they are made no sooner than 5 years after the year of the first contribution to the Roth IRA and they are made on or after age 59½ or death, made on account of disability, or used for first time homebuyer expenses.

In 1999, the IRS encouraged employers to help their employee save for retirement by facilitating direct deposit contributions to traditional and Roth IRAs through payroll deductions.[270] This followed encouragement from Congress for employers that do not sponsor retirement plans to "set up a payroll deduction system" to help employees save for retirement. Later in the year, the Department of Labor published an Interpretative Bulletin to encourage employers without retirement plans to establish payroll deduction programs for employees' IRAs.[271] The bulletin clarifies what the employer must do to provide an IRA payroll deduction program without inadvertently establishing an employee benefit plan that is governed by the Employee Retirement Income Security Act (ERISA). An IRA payroll deduction program will not be considered a "pension plan" when:

- no contributions are made by the employer;
- employees participate in the program on a voluntary basis;
- the employer's activities with respect to the IRAs are limited solely to permitting, without endorsement, the IRA sponsor to publicize its program to employees;
- contributions are collected through payroll deductions or dues checkoffs;
- the contributions are remitted to the IRA sponsor; and
- the employer does not receive any kind of consideration, other than reasonable compensation for services it actually renders in connection with the payroll deduction system.

---

267. IRC §219(g)(5), (g)(6); IRS Reg. §1.219-2; IRS Prop. Reg. §1.219-2.
268. IRS Reg. §31.3121(a); §31.3306(b); §31.3401(a)(12)-1(d).
269. IRC §408A.
270. IRS Ann. 99-2, 1999-2 IRB 44.
271. DOL Int. Bull. 99-1, 64 F.R. 32999, 6-18-99; 29 CFR §2510.3-2(d).

# 4.6-7 Simplified Employee Pensions (IRC §408(k))

For employers that do not have the means to sponsor or administer a qualified pension or profit-sharing plan because of the complexities and costs involved, the simplified employee pension (SEP) offers a meaningful alternative. A SEP is an IRA that meets requirements governing employee participation, nondiscrimination in favor of highly compensated employees, withdrawals, and written formulas to determine employer contributions.[272]

Employers must make contributions to the SEP on behalf of employees who have reached age 21, have worked for the employer for at least 3 of the last 5 years, and have earned at least $500 in 2008 (indexed annually to the next lowest multiple of $50). Employer contributions must be made on the basis of the same compensation-related formula (e.g., percentage of salary) for all employees up to the first $230,000 in compensation for 2008 (indexed annually to the next lowest multiple of $5,000). Employer contributions are limited to the lesser of 25% of the employee's compensation or $46,000 for 2008 (indexed annually to the next lowest multiple of $1,000).[273] Generally, the employer must contribute the same percentage of compensation for each employee to the SEP.

**Salary reduction agreement.**[274] Through the end of 1996, employers were permitted to set up a SEP that allows employees to have the employer contribute a portion of their salary to the plan on a pre-tax basis. The employee can elect to defer a certain amount of salary to the SEP. The Economic Growth and Tax Relief Reconciliation Act of 2001 (EGTRRA) contained many provisions that were designed to expand the opportunities for retirement savings, including annual increases in the amount of elective deferrals to defined contribution plans. For salary reduction SEP (§408(k)(6)) plans, the maximum amount that can be deferred is $15,500 in 2008 (adjusted for inflation annually to the next lowest multiple of $500).

*"Catch-up" contributions.* Under EGTRRA, employees who are eligible to make elective salary deferrals to defined contribution plans and who would be at least 50 years old by the end of the plan year can defer an additional amount to the plan as a "catch-up" contribution (see Section 4.6-1 for details) beyond limits set by law or by the plan itself. The catch-up contribution maximum is the lesser of the "applicable dollar amount" or the employee's compensation for the year reduced by any other elective deferrals made during that year.[275] The applicable dollar amount for salary reduction SEP §408(k)(6) plans is $5,000 in 2008 (adjusted for inflation annually to the next lowest multiple of $500).

> **Example 1:** Employee Barbara, who is 53, is a participant in a §408(k)(6) plan. Barbara's compensation for 2008 is $30,000. The maximum statutory annual deferral limit is $15,500. Under the terms of the plan, the maximum permitted deferral is 10% ($3,000 in Barbara's case). Barbara can contribute up to $8,000 for the year ($3,000 under the normal operation of the plan, and an additional $5,000 as a catch-up contribution).

> **Example 2:** Employee Esther, who is 53, is a participant in a §408(k)(6) plan. Esther's compensation for 2008 is $80,000. The maximum statutory annual deferral limit is $15,500. The plan incorporates the statutory annual deferral limit as the plan limit. Esther can contribute up to $20,500 for the year ($15,500 under the normal operation of the plan and an additional $5,000 as a catch-up contribution).

At least 50% of the employees eligible to participate in the salary-reduction SEP must defer income or no one can do it. Also, the salary reduction option is open only to employers with 25 or fewer employees, and it is not open to public sector employers or tax-exempt organizations. In addition, the SEP must meet the actual deferral percentage (ADP) test for nondiscrimination applicable to §401(k) cash or deferred arrangements (see Section 4.6-2).

Beginning in 1997, employers are no longer permitted to establish a salary reduction SEP. However, if the plan was established before January 1, 1997, the plan can continue to accept contributions and new

---

272.   IRC §408(k); IRS Prop. Reg. §1.408-7.
273.   IRC §402(h).
274.   IRC §408(k)(6).
275.   IRC §414(v)(2).

employees can participate in the plan under those rules. Small employers that wish to implement a salary reduction plan after 1996 can set up a Savings Incentive Match Plan (SIMPLE) for their employees (see Section 4.6-8).

 **OVERALL LIMIT** The total of all contributions to a SEP by the employer and through employee elective deferrals is limited to the lesser of 25% of the employee's annual compensation or $46,000 for 2008, indexed annually to the next lowest multiple of $1,000. The maximum amount of compensation taken into account is $230,000 for 2008, indexed annually to the next lowest multiple of $5,000.

**Tax treatment.** Employer contributions to a SEP up to the maximum contribution limit are not subject to federal income tax withholding or social security, Medicare, and FUTA taxes.[276] Excess employer contributions are included in the employee's gross wages. Amounts contributed by the employer on behalf of an employee through an employee elective deferral are excluded from wages up to the deferral limit. However, employee elective deferrals are subject to social security, Medicare, and FUTA taxes.[277]

**Reporting requirements.** Because employer contributions and employee elective deferrals to a §408(k) SEP are not wages subject to federal income tax, they are not included in Box 1 of the employee's Form W-2. The elective deferrals, however, must be included in Box 3 as social security wages and Box 5 as Medicare wages. Amounts withheld for social security and Medicare taxes must be shown in Boxes 4 and 6, respectively. The elective deferrals (including catch-up contributions) must also be included in Box 12, preceded by Code "F," and the employer must mark the check box in Box 13 labeled "Retirement plan." (See Section 8.8 for details on Form W-2 reporting.)

 **EXCESS DEFERRALS AND CONTRIBUTIONS** Amounts deferred in excess of the maximum deferral amounts are included in the Box 12 total, but they are not included in Box 1. The employee must include the taxable excess amount on his or her personal income tax return. Excess employer contributions must be included in Box 1.

For similar reasons, the employer does not include the elective deferrals or employer contributions up to the applicable limits on Line 2 of its quarterly Form 941 as taxable wages. But it does include the elective deferrals on Lines 5a and 5c as taxable social security and Medicare wages. (See Section 8.3 for details on Form 941 reporting.) The deferrals must also be included in Part 2, Line 3 of the employer's annual Form 940. (See Section 7.1-7 for details on Form 940 reporting).

## 4.6-8 Savings Incentive Match Plans for Employees of Small Employers (SIMPLE Plans)

The Small Business Job Protection Act of 1996 established a simplified tax-favored retirement plan for employees of small employers under IRC §408(p), known as a Savings Incentive Match Plan for Employees of Small Employers (SIMPLE Plan), which faces less burdensome nondiscrimination and administrative requirements than other employer-sponsored plans.[278] A SIMPLE plan can be either an individual retirement arrangement (IRA) for each employee (see Section 4.6-6) or part of a §401(k) cash or deferred arrangement (see Section 4.6-2).

SIMPLE plans can be offered by employers (including government and tax-exempt employers) that have no other qualified retirement plan and that had no more than 100 employees who received at least $5,000 of compensation from the employer during the preceding year, regardless of their eligibility for the plan during that year. An employer that establishes a SIMPLE plan for one or more years and becomes ineligible because its work force exceeded 100 during the preceding year will be considered eligible for the 2 years following the last year it was an eligible employer. Special rules govern the eligibility of employers that become ineligible because of an acquisition, disposition, or similar transaction.

---

276. IRC §3121(a)(5)(C), (a)(5)(F); §3306(b)(5)(C), (b)(5)(F); §3401(a)(12)(C); IRS Reg. §31.3401(a)(12)-1(d)(3).

277. IRC §402(g)(3)(B); §402(h); §3121(a)(5)(C); §3306(b)(5)(C); IRS Reg. §1.402(g)-1.

278. IRC §408(p); IRS Notice 98-4, 1998-2 IRB 26.

**Participation requirements**. Employers must allow all eligible employees to participate in the SIMPLE plan. Eligible employees are those employees who received at least $5,000 in compensation from the employer during any 2 prior years and who are reasonably expected to receive at least $5,000 in compensation during the current year. (The employer may have less restrictive eligibility requirements.) Employers have the option of excluding from the plan employees covered by a collective bargaining agreement if retirement benefits were the subject of bargaining, as well as nonresident aliens who do not receive earned income from the employer that is considered income from U.S. sources. "Compensation" includes wages subject to federal income tax withholding and employee elective deferrals into a retirement plan.

**Contribution limits and requirements**. The Economic Growth and Tax Relief Reconciliation Act of 2001 (EGTRRA) contained many provisions that were designed to expand the opportunities for retirement savings, including annual increases in the amount of elective deferrals to defined contribution plans. For SIMPLE plans, under either the IRA or §401(k) option, employees can elect to defer $10,500 in 2008 (adjusted for inflation annually to the next lowest multiple of $500), but the deferral amount must be expressed as a percentage of compensation:

Under EGTRRA, employees who are eligible to make elective salary deferrals to defined contribution plans and who would be at least 50 years old by the end of the plan year can defer an additional amount to the plan as a "catch-up" contribution (see Section 4.6-1 for details) beyond limits set by law or by the plan itself. The catch-up contribution maximum is the lesser of the "applicable dollar amount" or the employee's compensation for the year reduced by any other elective deferrals made during that year.[279] The applicable dollar amount for SIMPLE IRA or §401(k) plans is $2,500 for 2008 (adjusted for inflation annually to the next lowest multiple of $500).

Also, IRC §415 limits the total of all annual contributions by an employer and an employee to a defined contribution plan to the lesser of $46,000 in 2008 (indexed annually in $1,000 increments) or 100% of the employee's compensation for that year. The amount of compensation that can be taken into account when determining the maximum contributions to an employee's deferred compensation plan account for plan years beginning in 2008 is $230,000 (indexed annually to the next lowest multiple of $5,000). The compensation used for this calculation is the employee's income subject to federal income tax withholding plus any elective deferrals to the SIMPLE plan.

To qualify as a SIMPLE plan, the employer must match the employee's elective deferral dollar-for-dollar up to 3%. Alternatively, for any year the employer may make a nonelective contribution of 2% of the compensation of each eligible employee with at least $5,000 in compensation from the employer for that year, regardless of whether the employee defers any salary. The maximum amount of compensation taken into account for purposes of the nonelective contribution alternative is $230,000 for 2008, indexed annually to the next lowest multiple of $5,000. If the plan is an IRA, the employer can elect a matching contribution percentage of as low as 1% of each employee's compensation, but it cannot do so for more than 2 years during the 5-year period ending with the year of the employer's election of the lower percentage. For years before the employer established the SIMPLE plan, it is considered to have contributed 3% of employees' compensation.

**Vesting requirement**. All employee elective deferrals and employer matching and nonelective contributions to a SIMPLE plan must be fully vested and nonforfeitable when made.

**Nondiscrimination testing.** A SIMPLE §401(k) plan that meets the contribution and vesting requirements satisfies the special nondiscrimination tests for §401(k) plans in general (see Section 4.6-2).[280] No contributions other than employee elective deferrals and employer matching and nonelective contributions can be made to a SIMPLE plan.

---

279.   IRC §414(v)(2).
280.   IRC §401(k)11.

**Notification requirements.**[281] Employees must have 60 days before the beginning of the year—November 2 - December 31 (and before the first day they become eligible for the plan)—to participate in the SIMPLE plan or to modify their elective deferral amounts. Immediately before this 60-day period, the employer must notify the employees of their right to participate in the plan and give them a summary plan description. Violators are subject to a $50 fine for each day notice is not provided unless they can show reasonable cause for the failure to provide notice.

Employers that elect to use the 2% nonelective contribution or the lower percentage employer matching contribution to meet the employer contribution requirements discussed earlier must notify employees of their intention within a reasonable period of time before the employees' 60-day election period. Employers can meet this notice requirement by including it with the notice of election to participate in the plan immediately before the beginning of the election period.

Employees can cancel their participation in the SIMPLE plan at any time during the year. The plan may provide that employees who cancel their participation other than during the normal election period cannot resume participation until the beginning of the next calendar year.

**Holding period for elective deferrals.** While the general rule is that employees' elective deferrals under either a SIMPLE 401(k) plan or SIMPLE IRA must be paid over to the plan as soon as they can reasonably be segregated from the employer's general assets, the maximum holding period for each type of plan is different. For SIMPLE 401(k) plans, the maximum is the same as for other §401(k) plans, the 15th business day of the month following the month during which the amount deferred would have been paid to the employee. For SIMPLE IRAs, however, the maximum is the 30th day of the month following the month during which the amount deferred would have been paid to the employee.[282]

**Tax treatment.**[283] Employee elective deferrals to a SIMPLE IRA or §401(k) plan up to the applicable contribution limits are not wages subject to federal income tax withholding. However, they are subject to social security, Medicare, and FUTA taxes. Employer matching and nonelective contributions are not subject to federal income tax withholding or social security, Medicare, or FUTA taxes. Employers should check the states where they operate for any different treatment under state or local law regarding income tax withholding or unemployment and disability insurance (see Table 4.1 in Section 4.7 for the state treatment of §401(k) plan contributions). For SIMPLE IRAs, the employee's contributions are not subject to the general deduction limits applicable to other IRAs (see Section 4.6-6).

**Reporting requirements.** Because employee elective deferrals and employer matching or nonelective contributions to a SIMPLE plan are not wages subject to federal income tax withholding, they are not included in Box 1 of the employee's Form W-2. The elective deferrals, however, must be included in Box 3 as social security wages and Box 5 as Medicare wages. Amounts withheld for social security and Medicare taxes must be shown in Boxes 4 and 6, respectively. Elective deferrals under a SIMPLE §401(k) plan must also be included in Box 12, preceded by Code "D," elective deferrals under a SIMPLE IRA must also be included in Box 12, preceded by Code "S," (either Box 12 amount should include catch-up contributions) and the employer must mark the check box in Box 13 labeled "Retirement plan." (See Section 8.8 for details on Form W-2 reporting.)

 **EXCESS DEFERRALS** Amounts deferred in excess of the maximum deferral amount are included in the Box 12 total, but they are not included in Box 1. The employee must include the taxable excess amount on his or her personal income tax return.

For similar reasons, the employer does not include the elective deferrals or employer matching or nonelective contributions on Line 2 of its quarterly Form 941 as taxable wages. But it does include the elective deferrals on Lines 5a and 5c as taxable social security and Medicare wages. (See Section 8.3 for details on Form 941 reporting.) The deferrals must also be included in Part 2, Line 3 of the employer's annual Form 940. (See Section 7.1-7 for details on Form 940 reporting.)

---

281. IRC §408(l)(2)(C); §408(p)(2)(B)(ii); (C)(ii)(II); IRS Notice 98-4, 1998-2 IRB 26.
282. IRC §408(p)(5)(A)(i); 29 CFR §2510.3-102.
283. IRC §219(b)(4); §3121(a)(5)(H); §3306(b)(5)(H); §3401(a)(12)(D).

## 4.6-9 Employee Stock Ownership Plans

Another type of defined contribution plan that enjoys popularity because of its tax advantages is the employee stock ownership plan (ESOP). An ESOP is a stock bonus plan or combined stock bonus and money purchase plan designed to invest primarily in the employer's stock.[284] The plan must meet the general requirements under IRC §401(a) regarding participation, vesting, nondiscrimination, etc. (see Section 4.6-1).

An ESOP buys stock either with funds provided by employer contributions (nonleveraged ESOP) or with borrowed funds (leveraged ESOP). In a leveraged ESOP, the employer contributions to the plan are then used to repay the loan. Once the contributions have been made, the cash and stock are allocated to employees' individual accounts under a specific formula. The value of each account rises and falls based on the performance of the employer's stock.

**Tax treatment.** Employer contributions to a qualified ESOP are not wages and are not subject to federal income tax withholding or social security, Medicare, and FUTA taxes, but they may not exceed the lesser of 100% of the employee's annual compensation or $46,000 for 2008 (indexed annually to the next lowest multiple of $1,000).[285] Employers should check the laws of the states and municipalities where they operate to determine if there are differences in the treatment of ESOPs regarding state and local income tax withholding or unemployment compensation.

## 4.6-10 Nonqualified Deferred Compensation Plans

Generally, any employer plan designed to provide employees with compensation that will be deferred to a later date (usually after retirement) and that does not meet the requirements of IRC §401(a) is a nonqualified deferred compensation plan. Employers often use such plans to compensate certain high-level executives because they are not restricted by the nondiscrimination requirements that apply to qualified plans or the contribution and benefit limitations (e.g., the indexed annual contribution limit and the limit on annual compensation used to calculate benefits or contributions). A nonqualified plan may also base benefits on compensation that is not included in calculations for other employees, such as bonuses.

**Federal income tax treatment.** Before 2005, the rules governing the tax treatment of employer contributions (amounts deferred) to nonqualified deferred compensation plans and the earnings on those contributions were based solely on the doctrine of constructive receipt. Generally, this meant wages were taxable when they were set aside for and were accessible to the employee without significant restrictions (see Section 6.1 for more details).[286]

Nonqualified deferred compensation plans can be either funded or unfunded. Under the constructive receipt rules, if such a plan is unfunded, meaning there is nothing more than the employer's promise to make payments at some future time, the employer's contributions (amounts deferred) to the plan generally are not included in the employee's income and are not subject to federal income tax withholding until the payments are made (i.e., when the funds are actually received).

If the plan is funded and the employer makes contributions that are protected from its creditors or successors, the contributions and earnings based on them are wages subject to federal income tax withholding when the employee's interest is vested (i.e., no longer subject to be a substantial risk of forfeiture). Most nonqualified deferred compensation plans are unfunded, although they contain bookkeeping entries showing each employee's deferred amounts and interest earned.

**New, stricter rules took effect in 2005**.[287] In October 2004, President Bush signed into law the American Jobs Creation Act of 2004 (AJCA). The AJCA created IRC §409A, which places significant restric-

---

284. IRC §4975(e)(7).
285. IRC §415(c)(1)(A); §3121(a)(5)(A); §3306(b)(5)(A); §3401(a)(12)(A).
286. IRS Reg. §1.451-2.
287. Pub. Law 108-357.

tions on nonqualified deferred compensation plans by tightening the rules governing the inclusion of deferrals in gross income for federal income tax purposes (separate rules governing social security, Medicare, and FUTA taxation are not affected) and expanding the types of compensation plans and arrangements covered by the new rules.

The new requirements took effect for amounts deferred under a nonqualified deferred compensation plan after December 31, 2004, as well as to amounts deferred before that date if the plan under which they were deferred was materially modified after October 3, 2004. An amount will be treated as deferred on or before December 31, 2004 only if the employer has a binding legal obligation to pay an amount in a future year and the employee's right to the amount is earned and vested as of December 31, 2004.[288]

 **CONSTRUCTIVE RECEIPT STILL IMPORTANT** In guidance issued soon after the AJCA was enacted, the IRS made it clear that the new rules under §409A do not mean that the constructive receipt rules no longer apply (see the discussion above).

**Effective date for final guidance extended.**[289] Proposed regulations were issued by the IRS in 2005 dealing with many aspects of §409A other than the information reporting, withholding, and depositing requirements. Those proposed regulations were finalized in April 2007, with an effective date of January 1, 2008. However, the IRS extended the effective date to January 1, 2009. A plan adopted on or before December 31, 2008, will not be treated as violating §409A on or before that date if:

- the plan is operated through that date in reasonable, good faith compliance with the provisions of the statute and applicable guidance published with an effective date prior to January 1, 2008 (or, if an issue is not addressed, consistent with a reasonable, good faith interpretation of the statute and applicable guidance), and
- the plan is amended on or before that date to conform to the statute and the final regulations with respect to amounts subject to §409A.

Compliance with the proposed regulations, or the final regulations prior to January 1, 2009, is not required. However, before January 1, 2008, such compliance will constitute reasonable, good faith compliance with the statute. To the extent that provisions of the proposed regulations, the final regulations, or other guidance are inconsistent, then the plan may comply with any one of them. For periods after December 31, 2007, and before January 1, 2009, compliance with the final (but not the proposed) regulations will constitute reasonable, good faith compliance with the statute. To the extent that provisions of the final regulations or other guidance are inconsistent for periods after December 31, 2007, and before January 1, 2009, then the plan may comply with either of them.

A plan will not be operating in good faith compliance if discretion provided under the terms of the plan is exercised in a manner that causes the plan to fail to meet the requirements of §409A. However, an exercise of a right under the terms of the plan by a participant solely with respect to that participant's benefits under the plan, in a manner that causes the plan to fail to meet the requirements of §409A, will not be considered to result in the plan failing to be operated in good faith compliance with respect to other participants.

*Nonqualified deferred compensation plan defined.*[290] A nonqualified deferred compensation plan is defined as any plan that provides for the deferral of compensation other than:

- a qualified §401(a), §401(k), §403(a), §403(b); §457(b); SEP, SIMPLE, or §501(c)(18) retirement plan; or
- any bona fide vacation leave, sick leave, compensatory time, disability pay, or death benefit plan; or
- an Archer MSA, HSA, HRA, or other medical expense reimbursement plan that satisfies IRC §105 and §106.

---

288. AJCA, §885(d); IRS Notice 2005-1, 2005-2 IRB 274.
289. IRS Notice 2007-86, 2007-46 IRB 990.
290. IRC §409A(d); IRS Notice 2005-1, 2005-2 IRB 274, Q&A 4; IRS Reg. §1.409A-1(a), (b).

A plan provides for the deferral of compensation only if, under the terms of the plan and the facts and circumstances, the employee has a legally binding right during a taxable year to compensation that has not been actually or constructively received and included in gross income, and that, under the terms of the plan, is payable to (or on behalf of) him or her in a later year. The legally binding right may exist even though the right is subject to future conditions that constitute a substantial risk of forfeiture (e.g., a minimum period of service for the employer), so long as the compensation cannot be unilaterally reduced or eliminated.

An amount that is never subject to a substantial risk of forfeiture is considered to be no longer subject to a substantial risk of forfeiture on the date the employee has a legally binding right to the amount.

A deferral of compensation does not occur solely because compensation is paid after the last day of the employee's taxable year pursuant to the timing arrangement under which the employer normally compensates workers for services performed during a payroll period. For independent contractors, the payment must be made no later than 30 days after the contractor's taxable year ends to fit within this provision.

A deferral of income also does not occur if the terms of the plan require payment by, and an amount is actually or constructively received by the worker by, the later of:
- 2½ months from the end of the employee's first taxable year in which the amount is no longer subject to a substantial risk of forfeiture, or
- 2½ months from the end of the employer's first taxable year in which the amount is no longer subject to a substantial risk of forfeiture.

*Example 1:* An employer with a calendar year taxable year that on November 1, 2008 awards a bonus so that the employee is considered to have a binding legal right to the payment as of November 1, 2008, will not be considered to have provided for a deferral of compensation if, in accordance with the terms of the bonus plan, the amount is paid or made available to the employee on or before March 15, 2009.

*Example 2:* An employer with a September 1 to August 31 taxable year that on November 1, 2008 awards a bonus so that the employee is considered to have a legally binding right to the payment as of November 1, 2008, will not be considered to have provided for a deferral of compensation if, in accordance with the terms of the bonus plan, the amount is paid or made available to the employee on or before November 15, 2009.

*Safe harbor for independent contractors.*[291] IRS regulations provide that §409A generally does not apply to a deferral under an arrangement between a "service provider" (i.e., an independent contractor) and an unrelated employer if, during the contractor's taxable year that the contractor obtains a legally binding right to the deferred amount, the contractor is actively engaged in the trade or business of providing services (other than as an employee or corporate director) and provides significant services to two or more employers to which the contractor is not related and that are not related to one another.

The regulations contain a safe harbor under which an independent contractor is deemed to be providing significant services to two or more employers if the revenues generated from the services provided to any employer or group of related employers during the contractor's taxable year do not exceed 70% of the total revenues from the contractor's business.

The regulations clarify that if an independent contractor is eligible for this exclusion from §409A coverage, then the amount deferred under the qualifying arrangement (and earnings on the deferred amount) will not become subject to §409A in a later year if the contractor becomes an employee or otherwise subject to §409A.

There is also an additional safe harbor under which an independent contractor who has actually met the 70% threshold in the three immediately preceding years is deemed to meet the threshold for the current year, but only if at the time of the deferral the contractor does not know or have reason to anticipate that the contractor will fail to meet the current-year threshold.

---

291.    IRS Reg. §1.409A-1(h)(2).

*Separation (severance) pay arrangements.*[292] Separation pay arrangements upon an involuntary separation from service are not considered to be deferred compensation under §409A where:

- the entire amount of the payments does not exceed two times the employee's annual compensation for the year preceding the year in which the employee separates from service, or (if less) two times the limit on annual compensation that may be taken into account for qualified plan purposes under §401(a)(17) (i.e., $230,000 for 2008) for the calendar year in which the employee separates from service, and
- the arrangement requires that all payments be made by no later than the end of the second calendar year following the year in which the employee terminates service.

Separations due to participation in a "window program" are treated the same as arrangements with respect to involuntary separations from service. Under a window program, certain groups of employees are identified as being subject to a separation from service, and the employer provides an incentive to voluntarily separate from service and obtain a benefit.

*Separation from service.* An employee is treated as separating from service for purposes of §409A if the employee dies, retires, or otherwise terminates his/her employment with the employer.[293] Whether the employee has experienced a termination of employment is determined based on the facts and circumstances. The employment relationship will be treated as continuing intact while the individual is on military leave, sick leave, or other bona fide leave of absence if:

- the period of such leave does not exceed six months, or
- if longer, so long as the individual's right to reemployment with the employer is provided either by statute or contract.

*Note:* If the individual's right to reemployment is not provided either by statute or contract, then the employment relationship is deemed to terminate on the first day following the six-month period.

With respect to disability leave, the employment relationship will be treated as continuing for a period of up to 29 months, unless otherwise terminated by the employer or employee, regardless of whether the employee has a contractual right to reemployment.

Where an employee continues to perform some services, the general standard for determining that the individual has terminated employment is based on whether the facts and circumstances indicate that the employer and employee reasonably anticipated either:

- that no further services would be performed after a certain date, or
- that the level of bona fide services the employee would perform after such date would permanently decrease to no more than 20% of the average level of bona fide services performed over the immediately preceding 36-month period (or, if the employee has been providing services for less than 36 months, the full period in which the employee provided services to the employer).

Facts and circumstances to be considered include (but are not limited to) the following:

- whether the employee continues to be treated as an employee for other purposes (e.g., continuation of salary and participation in employee benefit programs),
- whether similarly situated "service providers" have been treated consistently, and
- whether the employee is eligible and realistically available to perform services for other employers in the same line of business.

An employee will be presumed to have separated from employment where the level of bona fide service performed changes to a level equal to 20% or less of the average level of services provided during the previous 36

---

292.    IRS Reg. §1.409A-1(b)(9); §1.409A-1(m).
293.    IRS Reg. §1.409A-1(h).

months. An employee will be presumed not to have separated from employment where the level of bona fide services performed is at least 50% of the average level of services provided during the previous 36 months. No presumption applies to a change to a level of services between 20% and 50% of the average level of services provided during the previous 36 months.

*Phased retirement.* The final regulations permit certain flexibility for a plan to define a separation from service as including a change to a reduced level of bona fide services, often referred to as a phased retirement.

A plan may treat another level of anticipated permanent reduction in the level of bona fide services as a separation from service, provided that:

- the level of permanent reduction must be set forth in the plan as a specific percentage, and
- the anticipated permanently reduced level of bona fide services must be greater than 20% but less than 50% of the average level of bona fide services provided in the immediately preceding 36 months.

*De minimis payments.*[294] The final regulations provide a limited payment exception to §409A for incidental benefits often provided on a separation from service, where the parties may not realize that the benefits are nonqualified deferred compensation. Under this exception, a payment or payments of an aggregate amount up to the amount of an elective deferral permitted to a qualified deferred compensation plan for the year of the separation from service (e.g., $15,500 for 2008) may be treated as not providing for a deferral of compensation.

The exclusion may apply only once with respect to amounts paid by an employer to an employee. So, for example, if an employer treats a right to payment of separation pay equal to the applicable limit in the first year following a separation from service as excluded, then the right to the amount is not treated as a deferral of compensation regardless of when the amount is actually paid. On the other hand, the employer may not treat any other right with respect to the same employee in the second year following separation from service as excluded under this exception.

*457 plans.*[295] Section 409A does not apply to eligible deferred compensation plans under §457(b). However, §409A applies to nonqualified deferred compensation plans to which §457(f) applies, separately and in addition to the requirements applicable to such plans under §457(f).

*Stock options.*[296] A non-discounted nonstatutory stock option that has no other feature for the deferral of compensation generally is not covered by §409A. However, a stock option granted with an exercise price below the fair market value of the underlying shares of stock on the date of grant generally is subject to §409A.

The final regulations clarify that consistency with respect to a valuation method is not required. Accordingly, an employer may use one valuation method to establish an exercise price and another valuation method to establish the payment or buyback amount. However, once an exercise price has been established, it may not be changed through the retroactive use of another method.

Similar rules apply to stock appreciation rights, where the right to compensation is based on the increase in value of employer stock between the date of grant and date of exercise of the right. To qualify for the exclusion, the compensation payable cannot be greater than the excess of the fair market value of the stock on the date of exercise over the price specified on the date of grant, and the exercise price may never be less than the grant price. Also, the stock appreciation right cannot include any feature for the deferral of compensation other than the deferral of income recognition until the right is exercised.

---

294. IRS Reg. §1.409A-1(b)(9)(v)(D).
295. IRS Reg. §1.409A-1(a)(4).
296. IRS Reg. §1.409A-1(b)(5).

The grant of an incentive stock option or an option under an employee stock purchase plan (even if discounted) does not constitute a deferral of compensation. However, if such an option is modified, extended, or renewed under circumstances that turn it into a nonstatutory stock option, the rules governing nonstatutory stock options must be applied.

*Reimbursement arrangements.*[297] Reimbursement arrangements related to a termination of services are not covered by §409A, to the extent that the arrangement covers only reimbursements and payments not otherwise deducted from income, for expenses incurred and reimbursed before the end of a limited period of time following the calendar year in which the termination occurs. The types of arrangements excluded include reimbursements for business expenses deductible under IRC §162 or §167, outplacement services, moving expenses, and medical expenses.

The "limited period of time" for expenses to be incurred or for in-kind benefits to be provided and third-party payments to be made is the end of the second calendar year following the calendar year in which the termination occurs. The limited period of time during which an employee can receive a reimbursement payment is the end of the third calendar year following the calendar year in which the termination occurs.

The final regulations clarify that for this purpose, reasonable moving expenses include reimbursement of an amount related to a loss incurred due to the sale of a primary residence, provided that the reimbursement does not exceed the loss actually incurred.

*Educational assistance.*[298] The regulations provide an exception from coverage under §409A for rights to educational benefits, where the benefits consist solely of educational assistance provided for the employee's benefit.

*Split-dollar life insurance arrangements.*[299] The requirements of §409A may apply to certain types of split-dollar life insurance arrangements. For example, policies structured under the endorsement method, where the employer is the owner of the policy but where the employee has a legally binding right to compensation includible in income in a taxable year after the year in which a substantial risk of forfeiture (if any) lapses, may provide a deferral of compensation.

However, split-dollar life insurance arrangements that provide only death benefits to or for the benefit of the employee may be excluded from coverage under §409A as a death benefit plan. Also, split-dollar life insurance arrangements treated as loan arrangements generally will not give rise to deferrals of compensation under §409A, provided that there is no agreement under which the employer will forgive the related indebtedness and no obligation on the part of the employer to continue to make premium payments without charging the employee a market interest rate on the funds advanced.

**Unfunded pension plans and §409A.**[300] Under the Pension Protection Act of 2006, employers face penalties if they set aside assets to fund nonqualified deferred compensation for their top five officers while their defined benefit plan is underfunded, while the employer is in bankruptcy, and during the 12-month period beginning 6 months before the employer's underfunded plan is terminated. Such assets are considered property transferred in connection with the performance of services under IRC §83 even if they are subject to the employer's general creditors, so they are included in the employee's income.

If the employer grosses up the amounts included in income, the taxes paid by the employer are subject to the 20% additional tax and interest on amounts that fail IRC §409A (see discussion following). Also, the employer cannot take a deduction for the taxes paid on the employee's behalf.

---

297.    IRS Prop. Reg. §1.409A-1(b)(9)(v).

298.    IRS Reg. §1.409A-1(b)(12).

299.    IRS Notice 2007-34, 2007-17 IRB 996.

300.    P.L. 109-280, §116a; IRC §409A(b)(3).

*Written plan requirement.*[301] Under §409A, a NQDC plan is established on the latest of the:

- date on which it is adopted;
- date on which it is effective; and
- date on which its material terms (amount and timing of payment) are set forth in writing in one or more documents.

To satisfy this requirement, the document or documents constituting the plan must specify, at the time an amount is deferred, the amount that the employee has a right to be paid (or, in the case of an amount determinable under an objective, nondiscretionary formula, the terms of such formula), the payment schedule or payment triggering events, and the conditions under which deferral elections may be made. Unwritten plans adopted and made effective before December 31, 2007, are treated as established as of the later of the adoption or effective date, provided that the material terms are set forth in writing by December 31, 2008.

*Deferrals are income if restrictions are not met.*[302] All amounts deferred under a nonqualified deferred compensation plan for a year are immediately included in the employee's income and are subject to federal income tax withholding if they are not subject to a substantial risk of forfeiture and the plan does not meet the new restrictions. This new rule also applies to earnings on the amounts deferred, as well as to amounts deferred in previous years (but only after 2004) that have not yet been included in gross income.

*Distribution restrictions.*[303] Distributions of deferred amounts meet the restrictions if they are not distributed earlier than:

- the employee's separation from service (if the employee works for more than one employer in a controlled group, the separation must be from all such employers)—6 months later if the employee is a "specified employee";
- the date the employee becomes disabled;
- the employee's death;
- a specified time (or under a fixed schedule) established at the time of deferral;
- a change in ownership or control of the employer; or
- an unforeseeable emergency, which is a severe financial hardship resulting from an illness or accident in the employee's family, a property loss due to casualty, or other circumstances arising from events outside the employee's control (only amounts needed to meet the emergency and pay applicable taxes can be distributed).

*Acceleration of payments not permitted.* Another restriction that nonqualified deferred compensation plans must meet is that the plan generally cannot provide for the acceleration of the time or schedule of any payment under the plan, unless provided for by regulations issued by the IRS.

A plan may not permit the acceleration of payments except:[304]

- to fulfill a domestic relations order;
- to comply with a certificate of divestiture;
- to pay income taxes due upon a vesting event under a §457 plan, provided that the amount of the accelerated payment is not more than the income tax withholding that would have been remitted by the employer if there had been a payment of wages equal to the income includible by the employee at the time of the vesting;
- where the payment accompanies the termination of the employee's interest in the plan, where the payment is no more than the applicable elective deferral amount under §402(g)—$15,500 in 2008;

---

301. IRS Reg. §1.409A-1(c)(3); IRS Notice 2007-78, 2007-41 IRB 780.
302. IRC §409A(a).
303. IRC §409A(a)(2); IRS Reg. §1.409A-3(a).
304. IRS Reg. §1-409A-3(j)

- to pay social security and Medicare taxes on compensation deferred under the plan or to pay federal income tax on this amount;
- to pay the amount included in income (reported on Form W-2 or 1099-MISC) as a result of the plan failing to meet the requirements of §409A;
- in canceling a deferral election after an unforeseeable emergency or hardship distribution, or because of a disability;
- pursuant to a plan termination or liquidation under certain circumstances;
- to pay state, local, or foreign tax obligations arising from participation in the plan that apply to an amount deferred under the plan before the amount is paid or made available to the participant;
- to pay debts owed by the employee to the employer that were incurred as part of the employment relationship; and
- as part of a settlement between the employee and the employer of a bona fide dispute over the employee's right to the deferred amount.

*Deferral election restrictions.*[305] Generally, the plan must provide that, for an initial decision to defer income, the election to defer compensation for services performed during a taxable year must be made not later than the close of the preceding taxable year. There are two exceptions to the general rule. The first is that employees who are newly eligible to participate in the plan may make a deferral election with respect to future compensation within 30 days after becoming eligible. The second involves deferral elections for performance-based compensation based on services performed over a period of at least 12 months (e.g., annual or multi-year bonuses). Such elections may be made no later than six months before the end of the period.

 **TEACHER EXEMPTION** The annualizing of pay by many educational institutions for teachers who teach 9 or 10 months in a school year got caught unintentionally under the deferral election requirements of §409A. Just before the 2007-2008 school year, however, the IRS suspended the election requirement for school years beginning before January 1, 2008.[306]

Subsequent elections to further delay plan distributions or to change the form of payment are also governed by certain restrictions. Such elections must not be effective for at least 12 months after the date of the election and must be made at least 12 months before the originally scheduled distribution date. Except in the case of the employee's disability, death, or unforeseeable emergency, an additional election must defer payment for at least an additional five years from the original distribution date.

*Bonuses.*[307] Generally, deferral elections must be made before the year during which services are performed to satisfy §409A. A deferral election with respect to bonus compensation based on services performed over a period of at least 12 months will be treated as meeting the requirements of §409A if the election is made at least six months before the end of the service period.

Bonus (i.e., performance-based) compensation is defined as compensation where the payment or amount of the compensation is contingent on satisfying organizational or individual performance criteria that are not substantially certain to be met at the time the criteria are established.

The criteria may be established up to 90 days after the beginning of the period of service to which the criteria relate. At the time of the deferral election, either the amount of the bonus must not be readily ascertainable or the right to the bonus must not be substantially certain.

Where a portion of a bonus would qualify as performance-based compensation if it were the sole amount available under the plan but another portion of the bonus does not qualify, the qualifying portion of the award will qualify if it is separately identifiable under the terms of the plan and each portion is determined independently of the other.

---

305. IRC §409A(a)(4)(B); IRS Reg. §1.409A-2.
306. IR 2001-142, 8-7-07.
307. IRS Reg. §1.409A-1(e); §1.409A-2(a)(8).

*Commissions.*[308] An employee can make a deferral election with respect to compensation in the form of sales commissions through December 31 of the calendar year preceding the year in which the customer makes the payment from which the commission is derived. The commission may be calculated as a portion of the purchase price of the product or service being sold (e.g., 10% of the purchase price) or by reference to the volume of sales (e.g., $100 per item sold).

This rule treats the services related to a commission payment as performed in the year in which the customer remits payment. Note, however, that the regulations permit the taxable year in which the sale occurs to be substituted for the year the customer remits payment (if the choice of year is applied consistently to all similarly situated employees).

Under the final regulations, for purposes of the initial deferral election rules, an employee's services with respect to investment commissions (earned due to the increase in value, or maintenance in overall value, of assets or accounts) are deemed to be performed over the 12 months immediately preceding the date when the overall value of the assets or accounts is determined for purposes of calculating the investment commission compensation.

*Restrictions on foreign trust arrangements.*[309] Amounts deferred under an "offshore" trust that is designed to pay deferred compensation are immediately taxable unless substantially all the services related to the deferrals are performed in the country where the trust assets are located. For each year the trust assets remain outside the U.S., earnings on the deferred amounts are also taxable when earned.

*Plans based on the employer's financial health.*[310] If a nonqualified deferred compensation plan provides that certain assets will be set aside to pay nonqualified deferred compensation in the event of a change in the employer's financial health, deferrals attributed to those assets are included in income if they are not subject to a substantial risk of forfeiture. For each year the plan assets remain restricted to paying benefits in the event of a change in the employer's financial health, earnings on the deferred amounts are also taxable when earned.

*Additional tax and interest penalties.*[311] If a nonqualified deferred compensation plan does not conform to the restrictions of §409A, all amounts deferred and other vested amounts (e.g., matching contributions), plus earnings on those amounts, are subject to federal income tax and an additional tax of 20% of the amount included in income. In addition, interest will be charged on underpaid taxes, calculated at the IRS underpayment rate plus 1%. The interest will be calculated from the year of the deferral or the year when the deferrals were no longer subject to a substantial risk of forfeiture.

*Federal income tax withholding.*[312] Any deferrals or earnings included in income because of the new rules in §409A are subject to federal income tax withholding. By imposing this obligation on employers, there is more incentive for employers to comply with the restrictions on nonqualified deferred compensation plans.

*Reporting requirements.*[313] All amounts deferred under one or more nonqualified deferred compensation plans in a calendar year totaling more than $600 must be reported by the employer on Form W-2, whether or not the amounts are included in income for that year. Such amounts must be reported in Box 12, with Code Y. For independent contractors, such amounts must be reported on Form 1099-MISC in Box 15a.

Amounts required to be included in income under a nonqualified deferred compensation plan must be reported on Form W-2 in Box 1 and also in Box 12, with Code Z. The amount reported in Box 12 using Code Z should include all amounts deferred under the plan for the taxable year and all preceding taxable years (plus earnings on those amounts) that are currently includible in gross income under §409A. For independent contractors, such amounts must be reported on Form 1099-MISC in Boxes 7 and 15b.

---

308.   IRS Reg. §1.409A-2(a)(12).
309.   IRC §409A(b)(1), (3).
310.   IRC §409A(b)(2), (3).
311.   IRC §409A(a)(1)(B); (b)(4)(A).
312.   IRC §3401(a), IRS Notice 2005-1, 2005-2 IRB 274, Q&A 31-32.
313.   IRC §6051(a)(13); §6041(g); IRS Notice 2005-1, 2005-2 IRB 274, Q&A 24-35; IRS Announcement 2005-5, 2005-3 IRB 353.

**Reporting and withholding requirements for 2007.**[314] Late in 2007, the IRS issued interim guidance clarifying the income tax withholding and Form W-2 and 1099-MISC reporting associated with nonqualified deferred compensation plans that applies to calendar year 2007 only.

*2005 — 2007 annual deferrals.* Notices 2006-100 and 2007-89 provide that for calendar years 2005 — 2007:

- An employer is not required to report amounts deferred during the calendar year (or earnings on those amounts) under a NQDC plan subject to §409A in Box 12 of Form W-2 using Code Y.
- A payer is not required to report amounts deferred during the year under a NQDC plan subject to §409A in Box 15a of Form 1099-MISC.

*Amounts includible in gross income.*[315] For 2007, an employer must treat amounts includible in gross income under §409A as wages for income tax withholding purposes. The amounts must be reported as wages paid on Line 2 of Form 941, *Employer's Quarterly Federal Tax Return*, and in Box 1 of Form W-2. An employer must also report such amounts as §409A income in Box 12 of Form W-2 using Code Z.

If the employee has received other regular wages from the employer during the year, amounts includible in gross income under §409A are supplemental wages for purposes of determining how much income tax to withhold (see Section 6.4-4). The amount required to be withheld is not increased on account of the additional income taxes imposed under §409A. Employees should thus be aware that estimated tax payments or increased withholding from regular wages may be required to avoid penalties.

For 2007, a payer must report amounts includible in gross income under §409A and not treated as wages as nonemployee compensation in Box 7 of Form 1099-MISC. A payer must also report such amounts as §409A income in Box 15b of Form 1099-MISC.

*Calculating amounts includible in income.* For purposes of Notice 2007-89, the amount includible in gross income because of a plan failure under §409A(a) and required to be reported by the employer or payer equals the portion of the total amount deferred under the plan that, as of December 31, 2007, is not subject to a substantial risk of forfeiture and has not been included in income in a previous year, plus any amounts of deferred compensation paid or made available to the employee or payee under the plan during 2007. An employer or payer may treat an amount as previously included in income if it was properly reported by the employer or payer on a 2005 or 2006 Form W-2, Form 1099-MISC, or Form W-2c or corrected Form 1099-MISC. Amounts previously reported and included in income should not be reported again.

Amounts includible in gross income under §409A(a) include only amounts deferred that are subject to §409A and not, for example, amounts deferred that were earned and vested prior to January 1, 2005, and that are not otherwise subject to §409A due to the application of the effective date provisions.

*Wage payment date of includible amounts.* Amounts includible in gross income under §409A(a) in 2007 that are either actually or constructively received by an employee during calendar year 2007 are considered wages paid when received by the employee for purposes of withholding, depositing, and reporting income tax. Amounts includible in gross income under §409A(a) in 2007 that are neither actually nor constructively received by the employee are treated as a payment of wages on December 31, 2007, for purposes of withholding, depositing, and reporting income tax.

For purposes of the employment tax deposit rules (see Section 8.2-1), if the income tax withholding liability for wages treated as paid on December 31, 2007, is paid to the IRS by the due date of the employer's fourth quarter 2007 Form 941, then failure-to-deposit penalties will not be imposed. If, as of December 31, 2007, the employer does not withhold income tax from the employee on such wages, or withholds less than the amount of income tax required to be withheld, the employee will receive credit for the withholding on a 2007 personal income tax return if the employer:

---

314.    IRS Notice 2007-89, 2007-46 IRB 998.
315.    IRS Notice 2007-89, 2007-46 IRB 998.

- withholds or gets from the employee the amount of the undercollection before February 1, 2008, and reports the wages on the employer's fourth quarter 2007 Form 941 and in Box 1 of the employee's Form W-2 for 2007; or
- pays the income tax withholding liability on behalf of the employee and reports the gross amount of wages and the employer-paid taxes on the employer's fourth quarter 2007 Form 941 and in Box 1 of the employee's Form W-2 for 2007.

*Calculating deferrals for 2007.* The interim guidance offers rules for determining the total amount deferred under a NQDC plan for purposes of calculating the amount required to be included in income under §409A(a) as of December 31, 2007. These rules are similar to the rules for calculating the amount to include in income under a NQDC plan for purposes of social security and Medicare taxation under IRC §3121(v)(2) (see the discussion following).

Account balance plans. For account balance plans, the amount deferred as of December 31, 2007, equals the amount that would be treated as an amount deferred on that date if the entire account balance (including all principal amounts, adjusted for income, gain, or loss credited to the employee's account) as of December 31, 2007, were treated as a principal amount credited to the employee's account on December 31, 2007. These same rules apply for purposes of determining the amount reported on Form 1099-MISC for 2007 with respect to a nonemployee.

Nonaccount balance plans. For nonaccount balance plans, where the amount deferred is reasonably ascertainable, the amount deferred as of December 31, 2007, equals the present value of all future payments to which the employee has obtained a legally binding right as of that date, calculated as if the employee had obtained all of such rights on December 31, 2007. An amount deferred is considered reasonably ascertainable on the first date on which the amount, form, and commencement date of the benefit payments attributable to the amount deferred are known, and the only actuarial assumptions needed to determine the amount are interest and mortality. These same rules apply for purposes of determining the amount reported on Form 1099-MISC for 2007 with respect to a nonemployee.

Stock rights. For a plan that is a stock right under Proposed Reg. §1.409A-1(1), the amount deferred as of December 31, 2007, equals the amount that the service provider would be required to include in income if the stock right were immediately exercisable and exercised on December 31, 2007. In general, this will mean with respect to a stock right outstanding as of December 31, 2007, that the amount deferred as of December 31, 2007, equals the fair market value of the underlying stock less the sum of the exercise price and any amount paid by the service provider for the stock right.

Other deferred amounts. For all deferred amounts not addressed by the account balance, nonaccount balance, and stock right plan rules, the amount deferred as of December 31, 2007, must be determined under a reasonable, good faith application of a reasonable, good faith method. This method must reflect reasonable, good faith assumptions with respect to any contingencies as to the timing or amount of any payment. Assumptions that result in the amount deferred being the lowest potential value of the future payment will be presumed not to be reasonable, good faith assumptions unless clear and convincing evidence demonstrates that the assumptions are reasonable.

 **WHAT ABOUT 2005 AND 2006?** The IRS issued interim guidance in late 2005 and 2006 to help employers deal with the reporting and taxation issues related to §409A because no regulations had been issued to help employers calculate deferrals and determine the proper amounts to withhold and report.

In December 2005, the IRS waived the deferral reporting requirements and suspended the income reporting requirements for 2005 because no guidance had been issued to aid employers or payers in determining the amounts deferred under a NQDC plan or the amounts constituting income under §409A.[316] But the notice did say that future guidance might require 2005 reporting of amounts includible in income under §409A.

---

316. IRS Notice 2005-94, 2005-52 IRB 1208.

Late in 2006, the IRS again issued interim guidance on the withholding and reporting requirements for amounts included in income under §409A for 2006. The requirements were the same as those issued the next year for 2007, with all the due dates exactly one year earlier.[317]

*2005 amounts includible in gross income.* Using the interim guidance for 2006, employers and payers are required to file an original or a corrected information return and furnish an original or a corrected Form W-2 or 1099-MISC for 2005 reporting any previously unreported amounts includible in gross income under §409A for 2005. If the employer or payer paid no wages or income to the employee or payee in 2005 other than amounts taxable under §409A, then an original Form W-2 or 1099-MISC must be filed for 2005.

The original or corrected information return and the original or corrected payee statement for 2005 must be filed and furnished by the deadlines applicable for filing an information return and furnishing a payee statement reporting amounts includible in income for 2006. Employers and payers that fail to comply with these reporting requirements for 2005 may be penalized.

An employer or payer will not be liable for income tax withholding or penalties for 2005 with respect to any previously unreported amounts of gross income includible under §409A that are reported on an original Form W-2 or 1099-MISC, or Form W-2c or a corrected Form 1099-MISC for 2005 in accordance with Notice 2006-100.

*Protection from future requirements for 2005 — 2007.* An employer or payer that complies with Notices 2006-100 and 2007-89 regarding computing amounts includible in gross income under §409A and withholding and reporting those amounts for 2005 — 2007 will not be liable for additional income tax withholding or penalties, or be required to file any subsequent forms as a result of future published guidance with respect to the computation of amounts includible in gross income under §409A.

If it is subsequently determined that the employer did not apply Notice 2006-100 or 2007-89 in determining amounts includible in gross income or wages for 2005 — 2007, any recalculation of these amounts may result in additional liability for income tax withholding for these years, plus any applicable penalties. In addition, the employer or payer will be required to file an original or corrected information return and furnish an original or corrected payee statement.

For purposes of determining any amount includible in income under §409A in a subsequent year, an amount will not be treated as previously included in income unless the amount has been reported appropriately on an information return and payee statement, or has been included in income by the service provider in a previous year.

**IRS issues guidance allowing §409A corrections.**[318] Late in 2007, the IRS issued guidance giving taxpayers the ability to correct certain operational failures of a nonqualified deferred compensation plan to comply with IRC §409A. The operational failures discussed must be unintentional and must be corrected in the same taxable year. They include failure to defer, excess deferral, incorrect payment, and incorrect exercise price of an otherwise excluded stock right. The guidance provides:

- methods for correcting certain operational failures in order to avoid income inclusion under §409A, and related information and reporting requirements;
- transition relief limiting the amount includible in income under §409A for certain operational failures occurring in an employee's taxable year beginning before January 1, 2010, that involve only limited amounts, and related information and reporting requirements; and
- an outline of, and request for comments on, a potential corrections program that would permit employers and employees to limit the amounts required to be included in income under §409A due to certain operational failures.

---

317.  IRS Notice 2006-100, 2006-51 IRB 1109.
318.  IRS Notice 2007-100, 2007-52 IRB 1243.

Note: For service recipients and service providers entitled to relief under this notice, Notices 2006-100 and 2007-89 relating to reporting and wage withholding are modified with respect to:

- the amount that is required to be included in income by a service provider under §409A, and
- the amount that is required to be reported by the service recipient as an amount includible in income under §409A on Form W-2 (Box 1 and Box 12, using Code Z) or Form 1099-MISC (Box 7 and Box 15b).

**Social security, Medicare, and FUTA taxes.** The treatment of employer contributions to a nonquali-fied deferred compensation plan is somewhat different in relation to social security, Medicare, and FUTA taxes. It does not matter whether the plan is funded or unfunded. Employer contributions and earnings are subject to social security, Medicare, and FUTA taxes on the later of:

- the date services are performed that form the basis for the contributions; or

- when there is no substantial risk of forfeiture of the employee's interest in the funds.[319]

As a practical matter, these contributions will most likely never be subject to social security or FUTA tax under this special timing rule since the executives earning the deferred compensation will almost always have exceeded the wage bases for those taxes before having the employer's contributions included as wages. They will be subject to Medicare tax, however, since it has no wage limit. (Because the contributions are subject to employment taxes at this earlier date, they are not subject to those taxes when the plan makes payments to the employee upon retirement.)

Early in 1999, the IRS issued final regulations designed to provide guidance as to when amounts deferred under or paid from a nonqualified deferred compensation plan are taken into account as wages for purposes of social security, Medicare, and FUTA taxes. Once an amount deferred is taken into account as wages, neither that amount nor the income attributable to it can be treated as social security, Medicare, or FUTA wages again.

*Nonqualified deferred compensation plan defined.*[320] For social security, Medicare, and FUTA tax pur-poses, a nonqualified deferred compensation plan is any plan or arrangement established by an employer for one or more of its employees that provides for the deferral of compensation (other than a qualified retirement plan). The plan must be in writing in order to be "established." Once its material terms are in writing, it will be established on the date when the plan is adopted or the date it takes effect, whichever is later. Unwritten plans that were adopted and took effect before March 25, 1996 are treated as established as of the date they were adopted or became effective, whichever was later, if they are put in writing by January 1, 2000.

There is a deferral of compensation only if an employee has a legally binding right to compensation that has not been actually or constructively received and that is payable in a later year. While an employee does not have a legally binding right to compensation if the employer can unilaterally reduce or eliminate it, the creation of a substantial risk of forfeiture (e.g., requiring employment for a set number of years before pay-ment) does not mean the compensation is subject to unilateral reduction or elimination. There is no deferral merely because compensation is paid after the last day of a calendar year under an employer's customary payroll arrangement.

> *Example*: Patrick's Pie Co. pays wages on a biweekly basis. The first week of the payroll period ending January 7, 2008 ends on December 31, 2007. The wages paid by Patrick's at the end of the payroll period on account of the services performed in the first week are not considered deferred compensation.

If there is a deferral of compensation that causes an amount to be deferred from one year to a date that is no more than a "brief" period of time after the end of that year, the employer has the option of treating the

---

319.    IRC §3121(v)(2); §3306(r)(2).
320.    IRS Reg. §31.3121(v)(2)-1(b).

amount deferred as if it were not subject to the special deferred compensation timing rules. The employer can choose this option only if it does so for all employees covered by the plan and all substantially similar nonqualified deferred compensation plans.

**Example**: We Sell It Co. establishes a plan that provides for bonuses for employees based on a formula that considers an employee's performance for the year. The bonus is calculated on March 1 of the following year and paid out on March 15. Even though there is deferred compensation under the bonus plan, the employer can choose to treat the bonuses as if they are not subject to the special timing rule.

Stock options (either when granted or exercised), stock appreciation rights, and certain other stock-related rights do not provide for deferral of compensation for social security, Medicare, or FUTA tax purposes. Also, certain welfare benefits, including vacation pay, sick leave, compensatory time, disability pay, severance pay, and death benefits, generally do not result from the deferral of compensation. Excess golden parachute payments (see Section 3.4-14) and window benefits provided in connection with an employee's termination, such as early retirement buy-outs or social security supplements, do not result from the deferral of compensation. Also, as a general rule, there is no deferral of compensation if the employee is terminated within 12 months of the establishment of the benefit or the plan providing the benefit and if the facts and circumstances indicate that the benefit or plan was established in contemplation of the employee's impending termination.

*Determining the amount deferred.*[321] The amount deferred must be the amount that is "taken into account" as wages for that period under the special timing rule. The manner in which the amount deferred for a period is determined depends on whether the nonqualified deferred compensation plan is an account balance plan or a nonaccount balance plan. A nonqualified deferred compensation plan is an account balance plan if:

- the principal amounts are credited to an individual account for an employee;
- the income (increase or decrease) attributable to the principal amounts is credited or debited to the individual account; and
- the benefits payable to the employee are based solely on the balance credited to the individual account.

The amount deferred for a period under an account balance plan equals the principal amount credited to the employee's account for the period, increased or decreased by any income attributable to the principal amount through the date that it must be taken into account. The plan remains an account balance plan even if it allows employees to receive their benefits in a form other than payment of the full account balance, so long as the amount payable is actuarially equivalent to payment of the account balance using reasonable actuarial assumptions. A nonaccount balance plan is any plan that is not an account balance plan. The amount deferred for a period under a nonaccount balance plan equals the present value of the additional future payments to which the employee has obtained a legally binding right during that period. To determine the present value, employers may use any reasonable actuarial assumptions and methods.

*When deferred amounts are "taken into account."*[322] An amount deferred is taken into account when it is included in computing the amount of wages subject to social security, Medicare, and FUTA taxes. But this is true only to the extent that any additional taxes, penalties, and interest that result from the inclusion are actually paid before the expiration of the applicable period of limitation for the year. The amount deferred for a year is combined with the employee's other wages for purposes of computing social security, Medicare, and FUTA taxes. Therefore, if the employee has other wages that equal or exceed the social security or FUTA wage base for that year, no portion of the amount deferred will actually result in additional social security or FUTA tax. This is also true for Medicare wages and taxes taken into account for years before 1994. Since there is no wage limit for Medicare tax for years after 1993, the entire amount deferred for such years (in addition to all other wages) is subject to the Medicare tax for the year and will not be considered taken into account unless the Medicare tax relating to the amount deferred is actually paid.

---

321. IRS Reg. §31.3121(v)(2)-1(c).
322. IRS Reg. §31.3121(v)(2)-1(d).

Amounts deferred under a nonaccount balance plan can be taken into account at a later date than that required under the general timing rule for nonqualified deferred compensation if all or a portion of the deferred amount is not "reasonably ascertainable" until that later date. An amount deferred is reasonably ascertainable when there are no actuarial or other assumptions needed to determine the amount deferred other than interest and mortality, even though the exact amount of the benefit may depend on future changes in the cost of living.

 **TIMING FLEXIBILITY PROVIDED** An employer may treat an amount deferred as taken into account on any date that is later than, but within the same calendar year, as the actual date on which the amount would otherwise have to be taken into account. For example, if services giving rise to an amount deferred are performed periodically during a year, the employer may treat the services as performed on December 31 of that year.

*Withholding rules.*[323] For purposes of withholding and depositing social security, Medicare, and FUTA taxes, an amount deferred is treated as wages paid by the employer and received by the employee at the time it is taken into account. If the employer is unable to calculate the amount deferred for a year by December 31, it has two alternative methods it can use.

Under the *estimated method*, an employer may treat a reasonably estimated amount as wages paid on the date on which the amount is taken into account. If the employer underestimates the amount deferred that should be taken into account and underdeposits social security, Medicare, or FUTA taxes, it can choose to treat the shortfall as wages either as of the date the amount was taken into account or any date up to 3 months afterwards. The shortfall does not include income credited to the amount deferred after the amount is taken into account. If the shortfall is treated as wages during the 3-month period after the amount is taken into account (the estimate date), the employer must take the shortfall into account as wages paid by the employer and received by the employee on that date, for purposes of social security and Medicare taxes. If the shortfall is treated as wages on the estimate date, the shortfall is treated as an error for purposes of withholding and depositing social security and Medicare taxes. The employer must report the shortfall as wages on Form 941 (and Form 941c, if applicable) and Form W-2 (or Form W-2c if the estimate date was in one year and the employer treated the shortfall as wages during the next year). Conversely, if the amount deferred is overestimated, the employer can claim a refund or credit.

Under the *lag method*, an employer may calculate the amount deferred on any date up to 3 months after the date the amount was required to be taken into account. The amount deferred will be treated as wages on the later date, and the amount deferred must be increased by income earned through the date on which the amount is taken into account.

*Effective date of the rules.*[324] The regulations apply to amounts deferred on or after January 1, 2000, amounts deferred before that date which cease to be subject to a substantial risk of forfeiture on or after January 1, 2000 or for which a resolution date occurs on or after January 1, 2000, and to benefits actually or constructively paid on or after January 1, 2000. For periods before January 1, 2000, an employer can rely on a reasonable, good faith interpretation of §3121(v)(2), taking into account any previous guidance issued by the IRS.

Because both the proposed and final rules provide that severance pay does not result from the deferral of compensation, the IRS ruled that an employer's switch to the opposite conclusion in 1999 after originally treating severance pay as taken into account when paid was not made in good faith.[325]

**Reporting requirements.**[326] Employer contributions (amounts deferred) to an unfunded nonqualified deferred compensation plan are not included in income and are not reported in Box 1 of the employee's Form W-2 as taxable wages. Amounts deferred to a funded, secured plan are income if the employee has no risk of

---

323.  IRS Reg. §31,3121(v)(2)-1(f).

324.  IRS Reg. §31.3121(v)(2)-1(g).

325.  ITA 199944032, 8-10-99.

326.  2008 Form W-2 Instructions; Publication 957, Reporting Back Pay and Special Wage Payments to the Social Security Administration

losing the benefits (e.g., no future service need be performed to require payment). Therefore, they must be reported in Box 1 as taxable compensation and generally in Box 11 as taxable income from a nonqualified plan.

Amounts deferred must be reported in Box 3 as social security wages and Box 5 as Medicare wages when they are taken into account (once there is no risk of forfeiture and the services on which the deferral is based have been performed). Accumulated deferrals from years prior to the expiration of the risk of forfeiture must be added to other social security and Medicare wages earned during the year. Such deferrals will also be reported in Box 11, *but only if they are for prior year services*.

Amounts distributed from a nonqualified deferred compensation plan that were not considered income when originally deferred must be reported in Box 1 and generally in Box 11. They need not be reported in Boxes 3 and 5 because they were reported as social security and Medicare wages when they vested. Box 11 should not be used to report both a distribution and a deferral for an employee during the same year.

Report to the SSA on Form SSA-131, *Employer Report of Special Wage Payments* (see page A-56), the total amount the employee earned during the tax year, which is normally the amount in Box 1 of Form W-2 less payments from a nonqualified plan, but including amounts deferred under the plan during the year.

However, do not file Form SSA-131 if contributions and distributions occur in the same year and the employee will not be age 62 or older by the end of that year.

Amounts deferred that must be included in Box 1 of Form W-2 must also be included on Line 2 of the employer's quarterly Form 941. Amounts deferred that are currently subject to social security and Medicare taxes must be reported on Lines 5a and 5c. (See Section 8.3 for details on Form 941 reporting.) These amounts must also be included in Part 2, Line 3 of the employer's Form 940. (See Section 7.1-7 for details on Form 940 reporting.)

**Right to nonqualified deferred compensation transferred as part of a divorce.**[327] In 2004, the IRS issued guidance on the income and employment tax consequences of the transfer of the right to nonqualified deferred compensation to a former spouse in connection with a divorce. In the IRS example used to illustrate the guidance, a husband is employed by a corporation that maintains 2 unfunded nonqualified deferred compensation plans under which the husband earns the right to receive payments upon termination of employment.

Under state law, unfunded deferred compensation rights earned by a spouse are martial property subject to equitable division between the spouses in the event of divorce. Under their divorce settlement, the husband transfers to his wife the right to receive deferred compensation payments under his employer's account balance plan and the right to receive a lump sum payment from the other plan when the husband terminates employment. Several years later, when the husband terminates employment, the wife receives lump sum payments from both deferred compensation plans.

The IRS ruled that the right to nonqualified deferred compensation deferred to the wife is property within the meaning of §1041, which means there is no income recognized when he transfers these rights to his wife. Furthermore, the husband is not required to include in gross income any income resulting from the payment of deferred compensation to her.

However, the wife must include the payments of deferred compensation in income in the year the payments are paid or made available to her. The same conclusions apply if the husband and wife live in a community property state and all or some of these income rights are community property subject to division between them as part of their divorce.

The IRS ruled that the transfer of interests in nonqualified deferred compensation from an employee spouse to a non-employee spouse in connection with divorce does not result in a payment of wages for social security, Medicare, and FUTA tax purposes. However, the nonqualified deferred compensation itself remains subject to social security, Medicare, and FUTA taxes to the same extent as if the rights to it had been retained by the employee spouse.

---

327. Rev. Rul. 2004-60, 2004-24 IRB 1051.

To the extent social security, Medicare, and FUTA taxation applies, the wages are the wages of the employee spouse; the employee portion of social security and Medicare taxes is deducted from the payments made to the non-employee spouse when the wages are taken into account for social security and Medicare tax purposes. For purposes of the social security and FUTA wage bases, the wages are credited to the employee spouse. The IRS also ruled that the income recognized by the non-employee spouse with respect to the amounts distributed from the nonqualified deferred compensation plans is subject to federal income tax withholding as wages.

Social security and Medicare wages and taxes withheld, if applicable, are reportable on Form W-2 in Boxes 3-6 with the name, address, and social security number of the employee spouse. However, no amount is included in Box 1 or Box 2 of the employee's Form W-2 with respect to these payments. Distributions from the nonqualified deferred compensation plans to the non-employee spouse are reportable as "other income" on Form 1099-MISC in Box 3 with the name, address, and social security number of the non-employee spouse. Federal income tax withholding with respect to these payments is included in Box 4. Income tax withholding on payments to the non-employee spouse is included on Form 945, filed by the employer. The social security and Medicare taxes are reported on the employer's Form 941, and the FUTA tax is reported on the employer's Form 940.

# 4.7 State Chart on Taxability of Cafeteria Plan and §401(k) Salary Reductions

As we have noted throughout this section, not all states treat salary reductions under a §125 cafeteria plan or a §401(k) cash or deferred arrangement in the same manner as the Internal Revenue Code. Table 4.1 shows how each state treats these salary reductions in relation to their inclusion in taxable income for state income and unemployment insurance tax purposes.

 **KEY TO TABLE** In the columns under the heading "Cafeteria Plan (§125) Deferrals," a "No" in the "Income Taxable" column means that salary deferrals to a cafeteria plan are not subject to state income tax. Although a "Yes" appears in this column for New Jersey, there is an exception for deferrals to premium only conversion plans (see Section 4.5-1). A "No" in the "U.I. Taxable" column indicates that the state follows the FUTA taxation rules—deferrals to a cafeteria plan are not taxable unless they are to a §401(k) plan.

In the columns under the heading "CODA (§401(k) Plan) Deferrals," a "Yes" in the "U.I. Taxable" column indicates that the salary deferral is taxable for U.I. purposes, but the state may or may not treat employer matching contributions the same way. Please check the states where you operate. An entry of N/A in any of the "Income Taxable" columns indicates that the state has no income tax on wages.

While these "yes" and "no" answers describe the general rule in a state, there may be limitations or variations, so employers should check the individual laws in the states where they operate to complete their research. [For more information on the state tax treatment of salary reduction amounts, see Table 3.6 of *APA's Guide to State Payroll Laws*.]

Table 4.1

| STATE TAXATION OF SALARY DEFERRALS TO CAFETERIA PLANS AND §401(k) PLANS | | | | |
|---|---|---|---|---|
| | Cafeteria Plan (§125) Deferrals | | CODA (§401(k) Plan) Deferrals | |
| **State** | **Income Taxable** | **U.I. Taxable** | **Income Taxable** | **U.I. Taxable** |
| Alabama | No | Yes | No | Yes |
| Alaska | N/A | No if used to purchase medical or life insurance or retirement benefits | N/A | No |
| Arizona | No | No | No | Yes |
| Arkansas | No | No | No | Yes |
| California | No | No | No | Yes |
| Colorado | No | No | No | Yes |
| Connecticut | No | Yes | No | Yes |
| Delaware | No | Yes | No | Yes |
| Dist. of Col. | No | Yes | No | Yes |
| Florida | N/A | No | N/A | Yes |
| Georgia | No | No | No | Yes |
| Hawaii | No | Yes | No | Yes |
| Idaho | No | No | No | Yes |
| Illinois | No | No if used to purchase medical or life insurance | No | Yes |
| Indiana | No | No | No | Yes |
| Iowa | No | Yes | | Yes |
| Kansas | No | No | No | Yes |
| Kentucky | No | Yes | No | Yes |
| Louisiana | No | No | No | Yes |
| Maine | No | No | No | Yes |
| Maryland | No | No | No | Yes |
| Massachusetts | No | Yes | No | Yes |
| Michigan | No | Yes | No | Yes |
| Minnesota | No | Yes | No | Yes |
| Mississippi | No | No | No | Yes |
| Missouri | No | No | No | Yes |
| Montana | No | Yes | No | Yes |
| Nebraska | No | No | No | Yes |
| Nevada | N/A | Yes | N/A | Yes |
| New Hampshire | N/A | Yes | N/A | Yes |
| New Jersey | Yes | Yes | No | Yes |
| New Mexico | No | No | No | Yes |

| STATE TAXATION OF SALARY DEFERRALS TO CAFETERIA PLANS AND §401(k) PLANS | | | | |
|---|---|---|---|---|
| | Cafeteria Plan (§125) Deferrals | | CODA (§401(k) Plan) Deferrals | |
| State | Income Taxable | U.I. Taxable | Income Taxable | U.I. Taxable |
| New York | No | Yes | No | Yes |
| North Carolina | No | No | No | Yes |
| North Dakota | No | Yes | No | Yes |
| Ohio | No | No | No | Yes |
| Oklahoma | No | No | No | Yes |
| Oregon | No | No if used to purchase medical or life insurance | No | Yes |
| Pennsylvania | No if used to purchase health or life insurance | Yes | Yes | Yes |
| Rhode Island | No | No | No | No |
| South Carolina | No | No | No | Yes |
| South Dakota | N/A | Yes | N/A | Yes |
| Tennessee | N/A | Yes | N/A | Yes |
| Texas | N/A | Yes | N/A | Yes |
| Utah | No | No | No | Yes |
| Vermont | No | Yes | No | Yes |
| Virginia | No | No | No | Yes |
| Washington | N/A | Yes | N/A | Yes |
| West Virginia | No | Yes | No | Yes |
| Wisconsin | No | No | No | Yes |
| Wyoming | N/A | No | N/A | Yes |

# 4.8 Review Questions and Exercises

## Review Questions

1. What major piece of social legislation guarantees employees the right to unpaid leave to care for a newborn child or a seriously ill family member?

2. Name the increasingly popular benefit offered by mid-size and large employers that gives employees a choice from a "menu" of cash compensation and nontaxable qualified benefits.

3. Can an employee of a public school who participates in a §403(b) tax-sheltered annuity also participate in a §401(k) plan?

4. Under the Family and Medical Leave Act, eligible employees are entitled to how many weeks of unpaid leave in a year to be with a newborn or newly adopted child, to take care of a seriously ill child, spouse, or parent, or to care for themselves if they are serious ill?

5.  What are three examples of changes in status that allow a cafeteria plan to permit an employee to change a cafeteria plan benefit election during the plan year?

6.  Name the three main nondiscrimination tests that cafeteria plans must satisfy to qualify for preferential tax treatment.

7.  Name the three major types of health care plans offered by employers to their employees.

8.  How does the Internal Revenue Code define "medical care" in terms of an employee's reimbursement for such medical care?

9.  What conditions must be satisfied for a self-insured health insurance plan to be nondiscriminatory in terms of eligibility and benefits?

10. What is the difference between sick pay and workers' compensation benefits?

11. In terms of third-party sick pay, what information should the employer provide the third party to aid the third party in properly meeting its withholding, depositing, and reporting responsibilities?

12. Employers are assigned "classification codes" based on their type of business for determining the employer's workers' compensation premium. Outline the classification code exemptions.

13. What are the advantages of pre-tax benefit contributions?

14. What information must the payroll department maintain for the proper administration of defined benefit plans?

15. What is a "defined contribution plan" and what are the characteristics of such a plan?

## True or False Questions

_____ 1.  If a self-insured health insurance plan is discriminatory, only those reimbursements and benefits that discriminate in favor of highly compensated employees are taxable and only to the highly compensated employees receiving the benefit.

_____ 2.  Where the employer's sick pay plan is self-insured, the employer must withhold federal income tax based on the employee's Form W-4 when payments are made to the employee.

_____ 3.  A pre-tax contribution will result in less take-home pay for the employee than an after-tax deduction.

_____ 4.  Pre-tax contributions by the employee are considered to be employer contributions when determining the taxable value of a benefit.

_____ 5.  Cafeteria plans that are the result of collective bargaining between an employer and a union are not exempt from the nondiscrimination tests applicable to cafeteria plans.

_____ 6.  Under a flexible spending arrangement, medical expenses are incurred when the medical care is provided, not when the employee is billed or pays for the care.

_____ 7.  The Family and Medical Leave Act of 1993 is administered and enforced by the Department of Labor's Wage and Hour Division.

_____ 8.   All pay received for overtime hours is excluded from an employer's total payroll when calculating workers' compensation premiums.

_____ 9.   Employers cannot require eligible employees to use any paid vacation, personal, sick, medical, or family leave as part of the 12-week guaranteed leave under the Family and Medical Leave Act.

_____ 10.  When an employee requests FMLA leave to care for a newborn or newly adopted child, he or she must give the employer 30 days' notice or as much as can be given under the circumstances.

_____ 11.  A cafeteria plan provides participants a choice among taxable (cash) and nontaxable (qualified) benefits.

_____ 12.  Employer contributions to an accident or health insurance plan that provides insurance for its employees and their spouses and dependents are considered wages and are subject to federal income withholding and social security, Medicare, and FUTA taxes.

_____ 13.  Any reimbursement for medical care expenses in excess of the amount actually spent or incurred by the employee is taxable income to the employee.

_____ 14.  Plastic surgery for cosmetic purposes is not "medical care" as defined by the Internal Revenue Code.

_____ 15.  Where an employer provides health insurance for its employees through a third-party insurance company, the plan may be tailored to favor highly compensated employees.

_____ 16.  Under the Family and Medical Leave Act, employees returning from leave are entitled to their previous job or one that is equivalent with no loss of pay or benefits that had accrued before the leave.

_____ 17.  The essential purpose of sick pay is to replace the wages of an employee who cannot work because of a non job-related illness or injury.

_____ 18.  The general rules for depositing withheld federal income, social security, and Medicare taxes do not apply to sick pay.

_____ 19.  The third-party administrator acting as the employer's agent may use the supplemental rate for federal income tax withholding from sick pay provided to employees.

_____ 20.  Payments received as workers' compensation benefits are not included in an employee's gross income and are not subject to social security, Medicare, or FUTA taxes.

_____ 21.  Health care flexible spending arrangements can only reimburse medical expenses incurred during the coverage period.

_____ 22.  If employees choose to take cash instead of purchasing benefits with their flex dollars under a cafeteria plan, the payments are wages subject to federal income tax withholding and social security, Medicare, and FUTA taxes.

_____ 23.  At the beginning of the year, Frances elects to buy medical and dental insurance as part of a package in her company's cafeteria plan. During the year Frances has the option to change to a different plan at any time.

_____ 24.  The amount contributed to a §401(k) plan through elective deferrals is a pre-tax contribution that reduces the employee's income subject to federal income tax withholding.

## Multiple Choice Questions

_____ 1.   At what age is an employee no longer subject to a 10% excise tax when the employee receives a distribution from his or her qualified retirement plan?

   a.   60
   b.   62
   c.   59½
   d.   58

_____ 2.   If an employer wants to offer a SIMPLE plan to its employees, how many employees must work for the company?

   a.   At least 100 employees
   b.   25 or more employees
   c.   No more than 100 employees
   d.   25 or fewer employees

_____ 3.   Which of the following developments is not a circumstance that would allow benefit changes during the plan year under a cafeteria plan?

   a.   A strike or lockout
   b.   The company institutes a 1% across-the-board salary reduction
   c.   A change in the participant's legal marital status
   d.   The employee terminates during the plan year

_____ 4.   The Family and Medical Leave Act applies to private sector employers with:

   a.   75 or more employees
   b.   150 or more employees
   c.   50 or more employees
   d.   50 or fewer employees

_____ 5.   For payments made to a disabled employee by a third party who is not an agent, the third party is not required to withhold federal income tax unless the employee requests that a certain amount be withheld by furnishing the third party with:

   a.   Form W-4
   b.   Form W-4S
   c.   Form W-4P
   d.   Form 1099-R

_____ 6.   An employee has been absent from work for nine months because of a non job-related illness and is not expected to return to work for another three months.  Which taxes must be withheld at this point from disability payments made to the employee by the employer?

   a.   Federal income tax
   b.   Social security and Medicare taxes
   c.   Social security, Medicare, and FUTA taxes
   d.   No withholding required

_____ 7.    An employee receives serious car injuries while away from work on February 15, 2008 and does not return to work until November 1, 2008.  Through what date must the employer withhold and pay social security, Medicare, and FUTA taxes on sick pay given to the employee by the employer?

      a.    July 15, 2008
      b.    August 15, 2008
      c.    August 31, 2008
      d.    September 1, 2008

_____ 8.    Which section of the Internal Revenue Code regulates cafeteria plans?

      a.    §125
      b.    §127
      c.    §128
      d.    §129

_____ 9.    An employer pays for 100% of the insurance for its employees as part of a sickness and disability benefits plan.  Assume an employee received $1,800 in disability pay from a third-party insurer during the first six calendar months of disability and $600 over the seventh and eighth months.  How much of the disability pay would be social security and Medicare taxable, and how much is FIT taxable?

      a.    $1,800 SS and Med. taxable, $1,800 FIT taxable
      b.    $1,800 SS and Med. taxable, $2,400 FIT taxable
      c.    $2,400 SS and Med. taxable, $2,400 FIT taxable
      d.    $2,400 SS and Med. taxable, $1,800 FIT taxable

_____ 10.   Under the employer's disability plan, the employer pays 80% of the cost of insurance and the employee pays the difference.  An employee received $3,000 in disability pay from a third-party insurer during the first six calendar months of disability, and $500 a month for each of the next three months.  How much of the disability pay is taxable for social security and Medicare, and how much is taxable for FIT?

      a.    $4,500 SS and Med. taxable, $4,500 FIT taxable
      b.    $3,000 SS and Med. taxable, $4,500 FIT taxable
      c.    $2,400 SS and Med. taxable, $4,500 FIT taxable
      d.    $2,400 SS and Med. taxable, $3,600 FIT taxable

_____ 11.   Which taxes are payments received as workers' compensation subject to?

      a.    Social security and Medicare taxes only
      b.    Federal income tax only
      c.    Social security, Medicare, and federal income taxes
      d.    Workers' compensation benefits are not taxable

_____ 12.   An agreement is made between the employer and the employees whereby the employer pays the employees all or part of their salary while they are receiving workers' compensation benefits, in return for which the employees turn over their workers' compensation benefits to the employer.  Under such an arrangement, any amount paid in excess of the employee's workers' compensation benefits is wages subject to:

      a.    Social security and Medicare taxes only
      b.    Federal income tax only
      c.    Social security, Medicare, and federal income taxes
      d.    Excess is not taxable

_____ 13.   Which of the following benefits is not a qualified benefit for a cafeteria plan?

    a.    Coverage under accident and health insurance plans (medical, dental, vision, sick pay, etc.)
    b.    Working condition fringes
    c.    Participating in a §401(k) plan cash or deferred arrangement
    d.    Group-term life insurance in excess of $50,000

_____ 14.   Under a dependent care assistance flexible spending arrangement, employees may be reimbursed up to what amount of dependent care expenses for each plan year?

    a.    $2,000
    b.    $3,000
    c.    $5,000
    d.    $10,000

_____ 15.   Mark contributes $75 per month to a flexible spending arrangement as part of a cafeteria plan to pay for medical and dental coverage for his family. At the end of the year (the plan has no grace period), Mark has $250 left in the account. What happens to the balance in the account?

    a.    The balance will be carried over to the following year
    b.    The balance is forfeited
    c.    It will be included in Mark's income
    d.    It can be transferred to a separate plan

_____ 16.   Tammy selects a dependent care package from her employer's cafeteria plan. The cost of the package is $200 per month. Tammy's employer pays $150 per month to her cafeteria plan and Tammy defers part of her salary to pay the difference. What taxes must the employer withhold?

    a.    FIT, social security, and Medicare taxes from the employer contribution
    b.    FIT, social security, and Medicare taxes from the employee contribution
    c.    FIT, social security, and Medicare taxes from both the employer and employee contributions
    d.    No taxes must be withheld from either the employer or employee contribution

_____ 17.   Johnny's employer contributes $150 per month to his stock bonus option plan as part of his benefits package. Johnny now wishes to take the $150 per month in cash. What will be the tax treatment of the benefit?

    a.    The $150 will be a tax-free benefit to Johnny
    b.    The $150 is subject to federal income tax withholding only
    c.    The $150 is subject to federal income tax withholding and social security, Medicare, and FUTA taxes
    d.    The $150 is subject to social security, Medicare, and FUTA taxes only

_____ 18.   At the start of the year, Donna elects to buy medical and dental insurance as part of her company's cafeteria plan. During the year Donna gets married and her husband has full medical and dental insurance which can be extended to cover his whole family. Donna wants to replace the medical and dental insurance with group-term life insurance. Which of the following statements is true?

      a.   If the amount is not spent by the end of the year it has to be forfeited
      b.   The replacement package becomes fully taxable
      c.   Once selected, benefits cannot be changed during the plan year
      d.   Since Donna has had a change in status and her new election is consistent with that change, this option is available to her

_____ 19.   Which department in a company generally administers defined benefit plans?

      a.   Benefits department
      b.   Human resources department
      c.   Payroll department
      d.   Accounting department

_____ 20.   For 2008, the maximum amount of salary that an employee may elect to defer to a §401(k) plan that does not allow catch-up contributions is:

      a.   $15,000
      b.   $14,000
      c.   $15,500
      d.   $13,000

_____ 21.   Which of the following statements is true concerning employee salary deferrals to a §401(k) plan?

      a.   They are subject to federal income tax withholding
      b.   They are subject to social security and Medicare tax withholding
      c.   They are subject to federal income, social security, and Medicare tax withholding
      d.   Employee contributions are not taxable

_____ 22.   The special discrimination tests for §401(k) plans are both based on the ADP of employees who are eligible to participate in the plan. What does ADP mean?

      a.   Automatic deferred pension
      b.   Actual deferred pension
      c.   Actual deferral percentage
      d.   Actual defined percentage

_____ 23.   Under §403(b), where an annuity plan includes a salary reduction agreement but does not allow catch-up contributions, assuming no other plan exists, what is the maximum amount employees can defer to the plan in 2008?

      a.   $15,000
      b.   $14,000
      c.   $15,500
      d.   Maximum exclusion allowance

_____ 24. Which taxes are elective deferrals to a §457(b) plan for public sector employees subject to if the employer is subject to social security and Medicare taxes?

    a.   Social security and Medicare taxes
    b.   Social security and Medicare taxes and federal income tax withholding
    c.   Social security, Medicare, and FUTA taxes
    d.   Social security, Medicare, and FUTA taxes and federal income tax withholding

## Problems

1. An employee who is injured away from work on July 24, 2008 receives $1,000 per month in disability payments from a third party for 10 calendar months beginning August 1, 2008. The employer has paid 60% of the disability insurance premiums, and the employee paid 40% through an after-tax payroll deduction.

    a.  Calculate the amount of the payments that are subject to social security and Medicare taxes.

    b.  Calculate the amount of the payments that are subject to federal income tax withholding.

2. An employee who is injured away from work on March 19, 2008 receives $900 per month in disability payments from a third party for 7 calendar months beginning April 1, 2008. The employer paid two-thirds of the disability premiums, and the employee paid the rest through an after-tax payroll deduction.

    a.  Calculate the amount of the payments that are subject to social security and Medicare taxes.

    b.  How much would be reported as federal wages on the employee's Form W-2, Box 1?

    c.  How much of the payments would be reported on the employee's Form W-2, Box 12, Code J?

3. Don earns $600 per week in 2008, claims single and zero withholding allowances on his Form W-4, and contributes $25 per week to his employer's cafeteria plan for medical and dental insurance. Using the wage-bracket method, Don's federal income tax withholding if the contribution is after-tax is $76.00. If the contribution is pre-tax, Don's FITW is $71.00. The social security rate is 6.2%, the Medicare tax rate is 1.45%, and the state tax rate is 10% of the amount withheld for federal income taxes.

    a.  If Don's contribution is pre-tax, calculate his net pay for the week.

    b.  If Don's contribution is after-tax, recalculate his net pay for the week.

4.  Match the following retirement plans with the section of the IRC that applies to each:

<table>
<tr><td></td><td>TITLE</td><td>MATCHING</td></tr>
<tr><td>a.</td><td>Simplified Employee Pensions</td><td>§501(c)(18)(D)</td></tr>
<tr><td>b.</td><td>Employee-Funded Plans</td><td>§457</td></tr>
<tr><td>c.</td><td>Deferred Compensation Plans for<br>Public Sector and Tax-Exempt Groups</td><td>§408(p)<br>§401(a)</td></tr>
<tr><td>d.</td><td>Tax-Sheltered Annuities</td><td>§408(k)</td></tr>
<tr><td>e.</td><td>Cash or Deferred Arrangements</td><td>§403(b)</td></tr>
<tr><td>f.</td><td>Qualified Pension and Profit<br>Sharing Plans</td><td>§401(k)</td></tr>
<tr><td>g.</td><td>SIMPLE Individual Retirement Accounts</td><td></td></tr>
</table>

5.  During 2008, Rachel Roberts has a salary of $50,000. She participates in a §401(k) plan that allows employees to elect to defer up to 15% of their annual compensation but does not allow catch-up contributions.

    a.  What is the maximum amount of her salary Rachel can defer to the §401(k) plan on a tax-deferred basis?

    b.  If Rachel's salary was $120,000, instead of $50,000, what is the maximum amount that she could defer to the §401(k) plan on a tax-deferred basis?

6.  During 2008, Sam Flashner, who is single and 33 years old, earned $27,500. Calculate the maximum IRA contribution that Sam is allowed.

7.  Sarah Simmons has an annual salary of $38,000. She is paid semimonthly, and she contributes $125 per month on a pre-tax basis to her employer's cafeteria plan and 5% of her salary on a pre-tax basis to a §401(k) plan. Assuming that Sarah has not reached the social security and FUTA taxable wage limits, calculate the following for the current pay period:

    a.  Federal income taxable wages

    b.  Social security taxable wages

    c.  Medicare taxable wages

    d.  FUTA taxable wages

8.  Timothy White is paid $3,760 per month. He contributes 7.5% of his salary before taxes to a §401(k) plan and 2% to an after-tax investment. The company matches his pre-tax contribution. He also participates in the company's cafeteria plan and contributes $75 per month before taxes. Assuming Timothy has not reached the social security and FUTA taxable wage limits, calculate the following for the current pay period:

    a.  Federal income taxable wages

    b.  Social security taxable wages

    c.  Medicare taxable wages

    d.  FUTA taxable wages

9. Compute the net pay for Susie Brown, who is paid weekly and claims married with 2 withholding allowances on her Form W-4 in 2008, based on the following information:

| | |
|---|---|
| Gross pay for the pay period | $650 |
| Pre-tax contributions to a qualified cafeteria plan | 6% |
| Federal income tax withheld (wage-bracket method) | $34 |
| Social security tax rate | 6.2% |
| Medicare tax rate | 1.45% |

10. Carol Conway is paid $900 in wages every Friday in 2008. Carol claims single and 1 withholding allowance on her Form W-4. She contributes 6% before taxes to a §401(k) plan, and $10 per week in pre-tax deductions to a qualified cafeteria plan. Using the wage-bracket method, the federal income tax withheld is $112.00. The social security rate is 6.20%, the Medicare rate is 1.45%, and there are no state taxes. Calculate Carol's net pay for the week.

# SECTION 5: PAYING THE EMPLOYEE

TABLE OF CONTENTS

# SECTION 5: PAYING THE EMPLOYEE

This section will discuss various aspects of paying employees that are not covered by either the Fair Labor Standards Act (see Section 2) or the Internal Revenue Code (see Sections 3 and 4). Among these everyday concerns for the payroll practitioner are:

- how often employees must be paid and how soon they must be paid after performing services for the employer;
- how soon employees must be paid after their employment is terminated;
- what methods can be used to pay employees (e.g., cash, check, direct deposit, paycards);
- what information regarding wages and deductions must be provided on payday;
- what employers must do with unclaimed paychecks;
- what to do with wages due an employee when the employee dies; and
- what happens when the calendar creates an extra pay period for the employer during the year.

Nearly all these areas are regulated by state law rather than federal law or in addition to federal law. Therefore, this section includes several state charts summarizing the law that applies in the states for each topic discussed. These charts describe the laws that were in effect in each state as of January 1, 2008. Before relying on the information in any of these charts, payroll practitioners should check APA's state and local payroll compliance newsletter, *PayState Update* (call 210-224-6406 for ordering information), their payroll loose-leaf service (see Section 13.4-1) or consult legal counsel for any later developments. Also, these charts outline the general requirements in each area covered. There may be different rules for special groups of employees (e.g., public sector employees).

## 5.1 Pay Frequency

As was mentioned in Section 2, the Federal Wage-Hour Law (Fair Labor Standards Act) does not regulate how often employees must be paid by their employer or how soon they must be paid after performing services (but see Section 2.1 for an exception to this general rule). These matters are left up to the individual states, and nearly all states regulate the timing of wage payments in some fashion.

Table 5.1 provides a quick look at state rules regarding frequency of payments and the amount of time that may lapse before wages must be paid after the pay period ends (i.e., lag time). The table contains requirements that are generally applicable, and each state may have exceptions and special provisions. (Remember that an employer may always pay its employees more frequently and sooner after the end of the pay period than state law requires.) [For more information on state pay frequency laws, see Table 2.1 of *APA's Guide to State Payroll Laws*.]

Table 5.1

| STATE-BY-STATE PAY FREQUENCY REQUIREMENTS | | |
|---|---|---|
| **State** | **Minimum Pay Frequency Required** | **Lag Time Before Pay** |
| Alabama | No general provision | No general provision |
| Alaska | Monthly; semimonthly if employee chooses | No provision |
| Arizona | Semimonthly; within 16 days of each other; FLSA-exempt employees can be paid monthly by out-of-state employer | 5 days after end of pay period (10 days if payroll system is out of state); 16 days for overtime or exception pay |
| Arkansas | Semimonthly; monthly for FLSA-exempt employees at larger companies earning at least $25,000 annually | No general provision |
| California | Semimonthly; monthly for FLSA-exempt employees | Wages earned 1st-15th of month, pay by 26th; 16th-31st, pay by 10th of next month; exempt employees by 26th of month for entire month (safe harbor: within 7 days after end of pay period) |
| Colorado | Monthly or every 30 days, whichever is longer | 10 days after end of pay period |
| Connecticut | Weekly; up to monthly if labor commissioner agrees | 8 days after end of pay period |
| Delaware | Monthly | 7 days after end of pay period |
| Dist. of Col. | Semimonthly; monthly for FLSA-exempt employees | 10 working days after end of pay period; union contract exception |
| Florida | No general provision | No general provision |
| Georgia | Semimonthly; even intervals; exemption for officials, superintendents, and department heads | No provision |
| Hawaii | Semimonthly; monthly if union contract or director of labor relations allows | 7 days after end of pay period; 15 if director of labor relations allows |
| Idaho | Monthly | 15 days after end of pay period |
| Illinois | Semimonthly; monthly for FLSA-exempt employees; union contract can provide different intervals | Semimonthly or biweekly—13 days; weekly—7 days; monthly—21 days; daily—1 day |
| Indiana | Semimonthly or biweekly; less frequently for FLSA-exempt employees | 10 business days after end of pay period |
| Iowa | Monthly, semimonthly, or biweekly | 12 days after end of pay period; excluding Sundays and holidays |
| Kansas | Monthly | 15 days after end of pay period |
| Kentucky | Semimonthly, less frequently for FLSA-exempt employees | 18 days after end of pay period |
| Louisiana | Semimonthly or biweekly for manufacturing, mining, or public service corporations | 10 days after end of pay period; 15 for public service corporations |
| Maine | Regular intervals of not more than 16 days; less frequently for FLSA-exempt employees and volunteer fire fighters | 8 days after end of pay period |
| Maryland | Semimonthly, biweekly; less frequently for FLSA-exempt employees | No provision |
| Massachusetts | Biweekly or weekly; semimonthly or biweekly for FLSA-exempts or salaried employees (monthly if they agree) | 6 days after end of pay period if workweek is 5 or 6 days; 7 days after end of pay period if workweek is 7 days or less than 5 days |

| STATE-BY-STATE PAY FREQUENCY REQUIREMENTS | | |
|---|---|---|
| **State** | **Minimum Pay Frequency Required** | **Lag Time Before Pay** |
| Michigan | Semimonthly; monthly OK if wages paid by 1st of next month; weekly or biweekly OK if paydays regularly scheduled | Wages earned from 1st-15th, pay by 1st of next month; 16th-end of month, pay by 15th of next month; 14 days after end of pay period for weekly or biweekly paydays |
| Minnesota | Every 31 days; semimonthly for public service corporations; 15-day intervals for laborers | Wages earned in first half of first 31-day period due on first payday; 15 days after end of pay period for public service corporations |
| Mississippi | Semimonthly, biweekly, or on 2nd and 4th Saturdays of month for manufacturers and public service corporations | 10 days after end of pay period; 15 days for public service corporations |
| Missouri | Semimonthly; every 15 days for manufacturers; monthly for FLSA-exempt employees | 16 days after end of pay period; 5 days for manufacturers |
| Montana | No general provision | 10 business days after end of pay period; next pay period if timesheets are late |
| Nebraska | On paydays designated by employer or agreed to by employer and employee | No general provision |
| Nevada | Semimonthly; FLSA-exempt employees paid by out-of-state employers can be paid monthly | Wages earned from 1st-15th, pay by end of month; 16th-end of month, pay by 15th of next month |
| New Hampshire | Weekly; biweekly, semimonthly, or monthly OK if commissioner agrees | 8 days after workweek when wages are earned |
| New Jersey | Semimonthly; monthly for exempt employees | 10 working days after end of pay period |
| New Mexico | Semimonthly, up to 16 days apart; monthly for FLSA-exempt employees | Wages earned from 1st-15th of month, pay by 25th; from 16th-end of month, pay by 10th of next month; 5 days extra for out-of-state payrolls |
| New York | Semimonthly; weekly for manual workers (semimonthly if commissioner of labor agrees); less frequently for FLSA-exempt employees paid over $600 a week | Manual workers—7 calendar days after end of pay period |
| North Carolina | Monthly, semimonthly, biweekly, weekly, or daily | No provision |
| North Dakota | Monthly or agreed-on paydays | No general provision |
| Ohio | Semimonthly; monthly if allowed by custom or contract and wages paid by first of next month | Wages earned 1st half of month, pay by 1st of next month; wages earned 2nd half of month, pay by 15th of next month |
| Oklahoma | Semimonthly; monthly for public sector, qualified nonprofit, and FLSA-exempt employees | 11 days after end of pay period |
| Oregon | Every 35 days | No provision |
| Pennsylvania | Regular paydays designated in advance | 15 days after end of pay period |
| Puerto Rico | Every 15 days | No provision |
| Rhode Island | Weekly; except salaried employees paid at biweekly, semimonthly, monthly, or annual rate | 9 days after end of pay period |
| South Carolina | As designated by employer | No provision |
| South Dakota | Monthly | No general provision |
| Tennessee | Semimonthly | Wages earned in 1st half of month, pay by 5th of next month; wages earned in 2nd half, pay by 20th of next month |

| STATE-BY-STATE PAY FREQUENCY REQUIREMENTS | | |
|---|---|---|
| **State** | **Minimum Pay Frequency Required** | **Lag Time Before Pay** |
| Texas | Semimonthly at equal intervals; monthly for FLSA-exempt employees | 1st and 15th are paydays if employer does not designate others |
| Utah | Semimonthly; monthly if employee hired for yearly salary | 10 days after end of pay period; wages paid monthly—7th of next month |
| Vermont | Weekly; biweekly or semimonthly if employer gives notice | 6 days after end of pay period; 13 under union contract |
| Virginia | Monthly—salaried employees and hourly employees earning 150% of state's average weekly wage, if they agree; semimonthly or biweekly—hourly employees | No provision |
| Washington | Monthly | 7 days after end of pay period; 10 days if paid more often than monthly |
| West Virginia | Biweekly | 5 days before payday |
| Wisconsin | Monthly; union contract may differ | 31 days after end of pay period |
| Wyoming | On regular paydays; semimonthly for railroads, mines, refineries, oil and gas production, factories, mills; monthly for state employees | Wages earned from 1st-15th, pay by 1st of next month; from 16th-end of month, pay by 15th of next month; by 8th day of next month for state employees |

## 5.2 Payment on Termination

Most states have a separate set of rules governing when employees must be paid when they separate from employment, either through discharge, layoff, or resignation. These requirements guarantee employees receive all the wages they have earned at or soon after their last day of employment. Table 5.2 summarizes the state requirements regarding payment of wages upon termination of employment.

The table contains generally applicable requirements, and employers should be alert for any provisions in the states where they operate that apply only to specific industries or groups of employees. Most states also have rules governing what must be included in an employee's final wage payment (e.g., fringe benefits owed, commissions, etc.), and a few even require severance pay where the employer shuts down, is acquired, or moves out of state. The table also notes any different requirements for temporarily laid-off, suspended, or striking employees. [For more information on state laws regulating payment of wages to terminated employees, see Table 2.4 of APA's Guide to State Payroll Laws.]

Table 5.2

| STATE-BY-STATE WAGE PAYMENT REQUIREMENTS UPON TERMINATION | | |
|---|---|---|
| **State** | **Involuntary Termination** | **Voluntary Resignation** |
| Alabama | No provision | No provision |
| Alaska | Within 3 working days | By next regular payday at least 3 days after employer gets notice of resignation |
| Arizona | Earlier of 3 working days or end of next regular pay period | Next regular payday or by mail if employee requests |
| Arkansas | Within 7 days | No provision |
| California | Immediately; within 72 hours for seasonal employees; by next payday for certain motion picture employees; within 24 hours for oil drilling employees | Within 72 hours; immediately if 72 hours' notice of quit is given; strikers and certain motion picture employees on next regular payday |

## STATE-BY-STATE WAGE PAYMENT REQUIREMENTS UPON TERMINATION

| State | Involuntary Termination | Voluntary Resignation |
|-------|-------------------------|------------------------|
| Colorado | Immediately or within 6 hours of payroll department becoming operational (by mail on request); next day if payroll is offsite | Next regular payday |
| Connecticut | Next business day; next regular payday if employee is suspended during labor dispute or laid off | Next regular payday |
| Delaware | Next regular payday; by mail on request | Next regular payday; by mail on request |
| Dist. of Col. | Next working day; within 4 days if responsible for employer's money; next regular payday if suspended due to labor dispute | Earlier of next regular payday or 7 days; 4 days if employee is responsible for employer's money |
| Florida | No provision | No provision |
| Georgia | No provision | No provision |
| Hawaii | Immediately; next working day if that is impossible; next regular payday if suspended due to labor dispute or temporarily laid off | Next regular payday (by mail on request); immediately if one pay period's notice is given |
| Idaho | Earlier of 10 days or next regular payday (not counting weekends and holidays); within 48 hours of employee's written request for payment | Earlier of 10 days or next regular payday (not counting weekends and holidays); within 48 hours of employee's written request for payment |
| Illinois | Immediately if possible; if not, by next regular payday; next regular payday if suspended due to labor dispute or temporarily laid off | Immediately if possible; if not, by next regular payday |
| Indiana | Next regular payday | Next regular payday |
| Iowa | Next regular payday; 30 days for commissions | Next regular payday; 30 days for commissions |
| Kansas | Next regular payday; by mail on request | Next regular payday; by mail on request |
| Kentucky | Later of next regular payday or 14 days | Later of next regular payday or 14 days |
| Louisiana | Next regular payday or 15 days after termination, whichever is earlier | Next regular payday or 15 days after quit, whichever is earlier |
| Maine | Earlier of next regular payday or 14 days after demand for payment | Earlier of next regular payday or 14 days after demand for payment |
| Maryland | Next regular payday | Next regular payday |
| Massachusetts | Immediately | Next regular payday; if there is none, the next Saturday |
| Michigan | Immediately, or as soon as amount due is determined | When amount due is determined |
| Minnesota | Immediately, or within 24 hours of demand | Next regular payday; if payday is less than 5 days after final workday, then by second payday, but no more than 20 days after discharge. |
| Mississippi | No provision | No provision |
| Missouri | Day of discharge; within 7 days if employee requests by mail | No provision |
| Montana | Immediately, unless employer's written policy extends the time period to the next regular payday or 15 days from date of termination, whichever is earlier | By next regular payday or 15 days from date of separation, whichever is earlier |
| Nebraska | Earlier of next regular payday or 2 weeks | Earlier of next regular payday or 2 weeks |

## STATE-BY-STATE WAGE PAYMENT REQUIREMENTS UPON TERMINATION

| State | Involuntary Termination | Voluntary Resignation |
|---|---|---|
| Nevada | Immediately | Earlier of next regular payday or 7 days |
| New Hampshire | Within 72 hours; next regular payday if suspended due to labor dispute or temporarily laid off | Next regular payday (by mail if employee requests); within 72 hours if 1 pay period's notice is given |
| New Jersey | Next regular payday (by mail at employee's request) | Next regular payday (by mail at employee's request) |
| New Mexico | Within 5 days; 10 days for wages paid by commission, task, or piece rates; next regular payday if suspended due to labor dispute | Next regular payday |
| New York | Next regular payday (by mail if employee requests) | Next regular payday (by mail if employee requests) |
| North Carolina | Next regular payday (by mail if employee requests) | Next regular payday (by mail if employee requests) |
| North Dakota | Next regular payday; or by certified mail at employee's address or as otherwise agreed | Next regular payday |
| Ohio | Next regular payday | Next regular payday |
| Oklahoma | Next regular payday (by certified mail if employee requests) | Next regular payday (by certified mail if employee requests) |
| Oregon | By the end of the first business day after discharge or termination | Earlier of next regular payday or 5 business days; immediately if 48 hours' notice is given |
| Pennsylvania | Next regular payday (by certified mail if employee requests) | Next regular payday (by certified mail if employee requests) |
| Puerto Rico | Next regular payday | No provision |
| Rhode Island | Next regular payday; within 24 hours if employer closes down, moves, or merges | Next regular payday |
| South Carolina | Within 48 hours or next regular payday (no more than 30 days) | Within 48 hours or next regular payday (no more than 30 days) |
| South Dakota | Next regular payday if all employer property is returned | Next regular payday if all employer property is returned |
| Tennessee | No later than 21 days or next regular payday | No later than 21 days or next regular payday |
| Texas | Within 6 days | Next regular payday |
| Utah | Within 24 hours | Next regular payday |
| Vermont | Within 72 hours | Next regular payday; if there is none, next Friday |
| Virginia | Next regular payday | Next regular payday |
| Washington | End of pay period | End of pay period |
| West Virginia | Within 72 hours; next regular payday if suspended due to labor dispute or temporarily laid off | Next regular payday (by mail if requested); immediately if 1 pay period's notice is given |
| Wisconsin | Next regular payday; within 24 hours if employer closes or moves | Next regular payday |
| Wyoming | Within 5 working days; next regular payday if suspended due to labor dispute or temporarily laid off | Within 5 working days |

## 5.3 Payment Methods

Another area in which the Federal Wage-Hour Law (FLSA) is generally silent is the actual methods or media used by employers to pay their employees. Individual states have assumed the task of making sure employees actually receive cash or its equivalent when they are paid for services performed. This section deals with the state requirements when employees are paid by cash or check (see Section 5.3-1), as well as the combined state and federal rules when the employer wishes to use direct deposit (electronic funds transfer) as a method of payment (see Section 5.3-2). This section also covers the newest method of paying employees – electronic paycards – which can provide the convenience of cash along with the advantages of electronic payments (see Section 5.3-3).

## 5.3-1 Cash or Check

All 50 states and the District of Columbia either expressly allow by law or regulation the payment of employees by cash or check or do not have a law or regulation regulating the method of payment (i.e., AL, and NE). While states differ to a degree in their regulation of the method of payment, they generally require that employees be able to cash their paychecks or other negotiable instruments provided by the employer for their face value without a charge or discount by a financial institution.

Most states require that the financial institution cashing employee paychecks be located in the state where the employees work, while some require that the financial institution be located conveniently for the employees (i.e., DE, IL, KS, MA, MN, NH, NJ, ND, OR, SD, WV). Employers should be aware of the requirements regarding employee paychecks for the states in which they operate. [For more information on state payment method requirements, see Table 2.2 of *APA's Guide to State Payroll Laws*.]

## 5.3-2 Direct Deposit (Electronic Funds Transfer)

An increasingly popular method of paying employees is direct deposit, a type of electronic funds transfer (EFT) allowing employers to deposit employees' pay directly into their designated bank accounts without having to handle a paycheck. Many employers and employees favor this method of payment. EFT first became widespread as a safe and secure method for distributing social security benefits. It eliminates many of the problems associated with employee paychecks, including:

- lost or stolen checks;
- unclaimed or uncashed checks;
- employee time off to cash checks;
- storage of cashed checks and related documents; and
- early preparation of vacation checks.

For employees, direct deposit provides instant access to their funds, eliminates the danger of losing a paycheck or having it stolen, and allows the accumulation of interest at the time of transfer. More than 70% of U.S. employees who have direct deposit available to them were paid through direct deposit in 2002 according to a survey by the American Payroll Association. In 2005, NACHA – The Electronic Payments Association estimated that more than 71% of the total U.S. workforce received their wages through direct deposit.[1]

**How the process works.** Direct deposit of payroll is the automatic deposit of an employee's pay into the employee's checking and/or savings account at a financial institution (bank, savings and loan, or credit union). For those employees being paid through direct deposit, the employer prepares an automated file of direct deposit records indicating where the employees' pay is to go. This file is then sent to a financial institution with the ability to process the file, known as the Originating Depository Financial Institution (ODFI).

The ODFI makes sure the file has been prepared correctly, checks for any exceptions and entries for employees' accounts maintained by the ODFI (known as "on us" accounts), and processes the file through the Automated Clearing House (ACH) network. The ACH network, operating under rules developed by NACHA,

---

1.  NACHA News Release, 5-8-06, "NACHA Reports Nearly 14 Billion ACH Payments in 2005".

processes electronic payments between the ODFI and the financial institutions designated by the employees to receive the payments and coordinates the financial settlement between the participating financial institutions.

To process the file through the ACH network, the ODFI delivers the file to the ACH Operator, which provides the actual data processing services for distribution of the financial transactions. The ACH Network is operated by the Federal Reserve Bank and the Electronic Payments Network. The ACH Operators provide delivery of files to the Receiving Depository Financial Institution (RDFI). They also settle funds between the ODFI and the RDFI, and deliver exception items to the ODFI from the RDFI.

The RDFIs designated by the employees accept the electronic payments, post them according to ACH rules, and settle with the ACH Operator for their value. They also post the direct deposits to their customers' (the employees') accounts and provide periodic statements to that effect. On payday, the employees receive an information statement containing the same data that would have been shown on the pay stub attached to their paycheck (date of payment, pay period dates, gross and net wages, hours worked, taxes, other deductions). Some employers now provide this information to their employees electronically, rather than on paper. [For more information on which states allow employers to provide pay statements electronically, see Table 2.3 of *APA's Guide to State Payroll Laws*.] The process is shown by the diagram in Table 5.3.

**Federal/state requirements.** Direct deposit is one area where the federal and state governments share regulatory responsibility. Title IX of the Consumer Credit Protection Act, the Electronic Fund Transfer Act, sets out the basic requirements for EFT, including direct deposits.[2] These requirements are further explained and implemented by Federal Reserve Board Regulation E.[3] Under the federal rules, an employer may not make it a condition of employment that an employee accept direct deposit at a *particular financial institution*.[4]

The regulations do say, however, that an employer can require an employee to accept direct deposit if it gives the employee a choice among financial institutions, or it can require an employee to choose between direct deposit at a particular financial institution or payment by check or cash.[5]

Table 5.3

## ACH FLOW

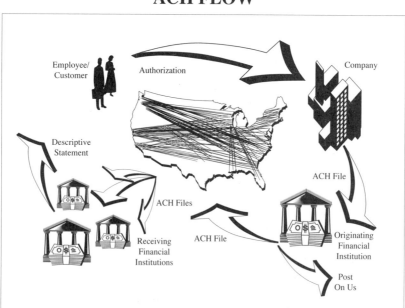

---

2.      P.L. 95-630; 15 U.S.C. §1693a-1693r.
3.      12 CFR Part 205.
4.      15 U.S.C. §1693(k); 12 CFR §205.10(e)(2).
5.      Supplement I to 12 CFR §205.10(e)(2).

Most states also have laws regulating direct deposit of employees' pay. Where those laws are more protective of employees (e.g., prohibiting compulsory direct deposit), they supersede the federal law and regulations (in much the same way that state laws prohibiting a tip credit against the minimum wage supersede the FLSA).[6] Table 5.4 summarizes these state laws (and official state opinions where such laws have not been passed) on direct deposit. It is a partial reprint from the APA's "The Guide to Successful Direct Deposit" (2008 Ed.).

**Employee authorization for direct deposit.** Before an employer can begin direct deposit for an employee, the employee must agree to allow the electronic transfer of funds from the employer to the employee with a direct deposit authorization. Under the ACH Operating Rules,[7] the authorization does not have to be in writing and the employer is not required to retain a written record of the authorization. This means that employers can secure the authorization through a phone call into the payroll department, the company e-mail network, or other electronic communication methods. It should be emphasized, however, that employers **should be very careful** before relying on verbal direct deposit authorizations. Many states require a written authorization before any type of direct deposit can occur, and the accuracy of the information required for the authorization can be verified much easier when in writing or provided electronically by employee self-service, rather than the telephone.

The following information must be provided as part of the employee's direct deposit authorization:

- the name and routing number of the financial institution designated by the employee to receive the direct deposit payments;
- the type of account into which the payments will be deposited; and
- the account number.

If a written direct deposit authorization form is used, the employee should be required to sign the completed form. Check to see if the state where the employee works requires the employee's spouse to sign the authorization if the account involved is a joint account.

Mistakes can occur with direct deposit as they can with any payroll function. In 1994, the ACH rules were changed to make it easier to correct errors such as duplicate payments, payments made to the wrong employee or to a terminated employee, or payments issued in the wrong amount. Under the rule, employers can simply generate a "single entry reversal" through the ACH network within 5 banking days from the date of the original entry. No debit authorizations are necessary from employees for single entry reversals made in the exact amount of the original payment and executed within the specified time frame for corrections. However, the rules do require that the employee be notified of the reversal no later than the settlement date of the reversing entry.

 **CHECK THE NUMBERS** To avoid problems later on in the direct deposit process, employers should check the accuracy of bank routing and employee account numbers on all authorization agreements by having employees submit deposit slips or canceled checks. Canceled checks are preferred, since deposit slips may have different bank numbers on them. A copy of an account statement can also be used. When the deposits are made to credit union accounts or accounts handled by investment companies, the employees should be told to contact the entity holding the account and obtain routing and account numbers for direct deposit through the ACH system.

**Prenotification.** Prenotification involves sending zero dollar amounts through the ACH network as a test before the first actual direct deposit for an employee. "Prenotes" are optional, but if one is used, it must be sent at least 6 banking days before any actual pay is sent through the network. This is another test of the accuracy of the information in the authorization agreement. If the entry cannot be processed by the ACH or RDFI, it will be sent back to the employer, which must work with the employee to rectify any incorrect information.

---

6.    12 CFR §205.12(b)(1).
7.    NACHA Rules, 1994, Art. 2, §2.1.2.

Where the entry is returned as incorrect, a new prenote must be sent before direct deposits can begin. New prenotes may also be sent when there is a change in the employee's account number, the RDFI's routing number, or the employer's identification number, with the same 6-day advance. It is essential for the employer to communicate with the employee regarding this process.

 **TO PRENOTE OR NOT TO PRENOTE** While prenotification is optional for employers beginning an employee on direct deposit, it might be a good idea to use this procedure. While avoiding a prenote may allow an employer to process an employee's direct deposit authorization more quickly, sending the prenote will help make sure that the information provided by the employee regarding his or her account numbers and financial institution is accurate.

**Direct deposit is not paperless.** Despite the advantages of direct deposit to both the employer and the employee and its elimination of many of the problems associated with paychecks, the system does not eliminate paper from the payroll system. Authorization agreements (when they are in paper form) still must be signed and checked for accuracy, and employees using direct deposit must be given information statements on payday showing the compensation they earned and the deductions taken for the pay period. A significant number of midsize and larger employers are now providing the pay stub information electronically rather than on paper as a way of moving further toward a paperless environment. State requirements for providing electronic pay statements must be carefully checked before such a move is undertaken.

**Costs and benefits must be weighed.** The cost savings an employer may realize from not handling paychecks must be balanced against the costs associated with a direct deposit system before the decision to implement direct deposit of payroll is made. The costs of direct deposit include the employer's loss of interest ("float") on payroll funds from the time a check is issued until the employee's bank clears it, the payroll service provider's charge for preparing the file for the ODFI, the ODFI's charges for its processing services, and bank service charges in those states where employees must be allowed to withdraw their wages in full.

 **FLOAT MAY NOT BE SO IMPORTANT** Under the Check Clearing in the 21st Century Act (Check 21), which took effect October 28, 2004, financial institutions do not have to transfer a paper check that has been presented for payment when it moves the check through the check clearing system.[8] It is now easier for them to create an electronic copy of the check for clearance, which will speed up the clearance process and reduce the available interest float.

Generally, the higher the number of employees who take part in a direct deposit program, the greater the savings for the employer. In order to convince employees to participate in direct deposit, employers should be prepared to conduct a campaign that will point out to employees the benefits of increased security and easier access to their funds and answer their questions regarding confidentiality and anxiety at not having an actual paycheck. For more information on preparing a cost/benefit analysis of a direct deposit program and on conducting a campaign to enlist employee participation, see the APA's *The Guide to Successful Direct Deposit* (2008 Ed.).

**Summary of state laws and rules.** Table 5.4 summarizes state labor code provisions, attorney general opinions, and statements from state officials regarding direct deposit. [For more information on state direct deposit requirements, see Table 2.7 of *APA's Guide to State Payroll Laws*.]

 **KEY TO TABLE** An "X" in the "Employee Must Authorize Program" column means the state does not allow compulsory direct deposit. This prohibition may be contained in the state's laws or it may have been expressed by the state's Attorney General or Labor Department where no law applies. An "X" in the "Employee Must Incur No Added Fees" column means that an employee participating in a direct deposit program in that state must not incur a charge for withdrawing his or her pay once it has been deposited. An "X" in the "Employee Must Choose Financial Institution" column means that an employee participating in a direct deposit program in that state must be allowed to choose the RDFI. An "E" in that column means the state follows federal Regulation E regarding the choice of financial institutions by participating employees.

---

8.    P.L. No. 108-100.

Table 5.4

| STATE-BY-STATE RULES ON DIRECT DEPOSIT | | | |
|---|---|---|---|
| **State** | **Employee Must Authorize Program** | **Employee Must Incur No Added Fees** | **Employee Must Choose Financial Institution** |
| Alabama | | | E |
| Alaska | X<br>Except for state employees, with some exceptions | | X |
| Arizona | X | X | X |
| Arkansas | Employee can opt out in writing and request a check; municipal employees must authorize | | E |
| California | X | | X |
| Colorado | X | X | X |
| Connecticut | X | X | X |
| Delaware | X | X | X |
| Dist. of Col. | X | X | E |
| Florida | X<br>Except for appointed state employees | | X |
| Georgia | X | | X |
| Hawaii | X<br>Except for state employees hired after 7-1-98 | X | X<br>State employees hired after 7-1-98 must choose a financial institution |
| Idaho | X | X | X |
| Illinois | X | X | X |
| Indiana | X | | X |
| Iowa | X<br>Except for new hires, unless a union contract forbids mandatory participation | X | X |
| Kansas | No, but employer must offer an alternative if employee doesn't designate a financial institution. | X | E |
| Kentucky | | X | E |
| Louisiana | | X | E |
| Maine | | X | E |
| Maryland | X | X | X |
| Massachusetts | | | X |

## STATE-BY-STATE RULES ON DIRECT DEPOSIT

| State | Employee Must Authorize Program | Employee Must Incur No Added Fees | Employee Must Choose Financial Institution |
|---|---|---|---|
| Michigan | X<br>Except for nonclassified state employees and elected officials | X | X |
| Minnesota | X<br>Except for state and munici-pal employees | X | X |
| Mississippi | | | E |
| Missouri | | | E |
| Montana | X | X | E |
| Nebraska | State employees only | | E |
| Nevada | X | X | X |
| New Hampshire | X | X | X |
| New Jersey | X | | E |
| New Mexico | X<br>Can be a condition of employment for new hires; mandatory for state employees | X<br>Except for new hires | X |
| New York | X | X | X |
| North Carolina | | | E |
| North Dakota | | X | X |
| Ohio | | | E |
| Oklahoma | | X | E |
| Oregon | X | X | X |
| Pennsylvania | X | | X |
| Rhode Island | X | | X |
| South Carolina | | X | E |
| South Dakota | | | E |
| Tennessee | | X | E |
| Texas | | X | X |
| Utah | X<br>Except for large employers with ⅔ of employees already on direct deposit | X | X |
| Vermont | X | X | X |
| Virginia | X<br>Can be a condition of employment for new hires | X<br>Except for new hires | X |

| STATE-BY-STATE RULES ON DIRECT DEPOSIT | | | |
| --- | --- | --- | --- |
| State | Employee Must Authorize Program | Employee Must Incur No Added Fees | Employee Must Choose Financial Institution |
| Washington | | X | E |
| West Virginia | X | | X |
| Wisconsin | | X<br>Unless direct deposit program is voluntary | E |
| Wyoming | X | | X |

## 5.3-3 Electronic Paycards

Despite the advantages of paying employees by direct deposit, for both employers and the employees themselves, there are some employees for whom direct deposit is not a viable option. Often, the principal stumbling block is the employee's lack of a banking relationship with a financial institution to which a direct deposit can be sent. As many as 10% of the employees in the U.S. are "unbanked" or "underbanked," and this percentage is considerably higher in certain industries, such as food service, hospitality, and agriculture.

Employers that want to take full advantage of the benefits of paying their employees through electronic funds transfer need a method other than direct deposit for their "unbanked" employees. One increasingly popular alternative is pre-paid electronic paycards, which are debit cards that the employer funds with the amount of the employee's net pay. The employee then accesses his or her pay by using the card to make purchases or withdraw cash.

**How paycards work.** In general, paycards work in a fashion similar to any other debit card. They are pre-funded, host-based cards that the employee can use to access his or her net pay at an ATM or a bank, or to make point-of-sale (POS) purchases. The employer funds the cards in the same way that it would fund direct deposit of payroll, subject to the NACHA rules.

**Choosing a paycard program.** Many variables need to be taken into account when an employer selects a paycard program. The programs offered by different paycard vendors can vary greatly in terms of features, benefits, and costs, and employers can have a tough time comparing programs because they have been available generally for less than 10 years.

**Branded vs. nonbranded paycards.** One of the most important variables to consider when selecting a paycard program is whether your employees will get "branded" or "nonbranded" cards. Branded cards have either a Visa®, MasterCard® or Discover Network® logo imprinted on them. They are accepted wherever Visa, MasterCard or Discover Card is accepted and require only the employee's signature for cardholder authorization. Branded cards also have a 4-digit personal identification number (PIN) the employee must use to withdraw funds from an ATM or check the card's balance. When the employee makes a POS purchase, the employee has the option of using the PIN or signing to provide cardholder authorization. Employees identify easily with such cards because they see them everywhere and recognize the brand names.

On the other hand, branded cards must be personalized, which means it can be 7-10 days before an employee can get one. If a branded paycard is lost or stolen, the employer must get it reissued and personalized again.

Nonbranded stored-value paycards have the logos of one or more major ATM or POS networks imprinted on them (e.g., STAR®, Pulse®, NYCE®, etc.) and can be used to make POS purchases, access account information, or withdraw funds from an ATM. Unlike branded cards, nonbranded cards require the use of a PIN for all transactions. Another major difference is that purchases and withdrawals with a nonbranded card

can only take place if the host computer has authorized them by acknowledging that there is enough in the account to fund the transaction (positive funds authorization). Purchases made with branded cards may be completed in some situations without positive funds authorization, most commonly when there is a floor amount set up so that purchases up to that amount do not need authorization, or where the authorization system is offline and transactions are automatically approved.

**Cardholder security is another factor to consider.** While all paycards come with information for employees on how to protect the card from loss or theft and keeping the PIN in a location separate from the card, a certain percentage of paycards will end up being lost or stolen. Lost or stolen branded cards are more susceptible to unauthorized use since only a signature is necessary to make purchases. Nonbranded cards risk unauthorized use only if the PIN is with the card when it is lost or stolen and can be identified as the PIN for the card. These risks, along with the cost of reimbursing employees, must also be taken into account in selecting a paycard program.

**Employee age, turnover can affect paycard selection.** If you employ minors under the age of 18, their inability to enter into contractual arrangements may affect your choice of a branded or nonbranded paycard program. An employee under 18 is only liable for their branded paycard use if the employer gets the written approval of the employee's parents before the card is issued. Employers with a high degree of turnover may also want to use a nonbranded card program, or have both branded and nonbranded cards and give branded cards to employees only after they have been working for the employer for a certain length of time (e.g., 6 months or 1 year).

**Paycards benefit employers and employees**. Regardless of the type of paycard program the employer chooses, there are several benefits for both the employer and its employees.

*Benefits for employers.*
- Reduced costs for manual checks, lost and stolen checks, stop payment orders, fraudulent cashing of duplicate checks, paycheck production and handling, and bank reconciliation fees;

- Enhanced efficiency by eliminating paper paychecks and using electronic pay statements;

- All employees are eligible for electronic funds transfer, whether or not they have a banking relationship;

- Increased employee productivity as less time is spent cashing paychecks.

- Reduction of escheat issues.

*Benefits for employees.*
- Reduced costs by eliminating check cashing fees;

- Increased independence by eliminating need to ask relatives or friends to cash checks or pay their bills;

- Employees cannot take on debt with stored-value payroll cards, which may improve their credit status;

- Increased safety by obtaining only the cash the employee needs rather than having to cash the entire paycheck;

- Easy to use;

- Employees are protected from loss because a lost or stolen card can be replaced with its full remaining value;

- ATM access means there are virtually no time or geographic limitations on funds access.

**Compliance issues.** Any employer that is considering implementing a paycard program will need to consider the legal and regulatory issues that affect paycards. Generally, the compliance issues are similar to those that apply to employee payments made by direct deposit, including laws and rules governing ACH transactions, employee privacy, and escheatment.

As with most new technology, the states have been slow to amend their wage payment laws to deal specifically with electronic paycards. A few have addressed the issue through regulations. Here are the latest developments as of the end of January 2008:

*Colorado* – The Division of Labor issued an advisory bulletin on paycards stating that employers may use paycards to pay employees' wages as long as employees have access to the entire amount of their net pay without charge, participation in the paycard program is completely voluntary, and employees have access to any checks they can write against the amount on the card within 10 days from the end of the pay period unless a different time period is mutually agreed to.

*Delaware* – The Department of Labor adopted regulations allowing the use of paycards for wage payments if employees have access to the full amount of their pay somewhere convenient to their work site without paying a fee.

*Iowa* – The Division of Labor said that if an employee voluntarily elects wage payment by electronic payroll debit card from among other options, such as direct deposit or payment by check, and is not charged a fee for accessing his or her wages, "no problems would arise."

*Kansas* – An employer may require employees to be paid by payroll debit card. Employees must be provided at least one free withdrawal each pay period of an amount up to and including the employee's total net pay. Employers are prohibited from charging any initiation, loading, or participation fees, but may charge for the cost required to replace lost, stolen, or damaged cards. The employer may make corrections, as provided by rules governing direct deposit, if an inadvertent overpayment occurs.

If an employer requires employees to be paid by payroll debit card, or by direct deposit with payroll debit cards as an alternative wage payment method, the employer must conduct one or more employee forums to educate employees regarding the use of direct deposit or payroll debit cards as offered by the employer, or must distribute to employees educational information on such topics at least 30 days prior to implementing the mandated electronic wage payment program.

*Maine* – Legislation was enacted allowing employers to pay wages through an automated teller machine (ATM) card or other means of electronic transfer so long as the employee can make one free withdrawal of the entire net pay or choose another method of payment that involves no additional cost to the employee.

*Maryland* – Legislation was enacted allowing employers to pay wages through a debit card or card account if the employee authorizes it and any fees are disclosed to the employee in writing in at least 12-point type.

*Michigan* – The wage payment law allows wages to be paid with paycards. Employees must consent in writing unless the employer had a mandatory paycard program before January 1, 2005. Employees cannot be required to pay any fees incurred by the employer in connection with the paycard program and must be able to get their wages in full on payday. There are also rules requiring disclosure of any fees charged by the card issuer or third parties and ownership of the funds on the card by the employee.

*Minnesota* – From 6-3-05 to 5-31-08, employers may pay wages by EFT to a payroll card account to which an employee has access through a payroll card if the employee is permitted one free withdrawal of the employee's total net pay. The employer may not charge the employee any fees associated with the account, and the employee can request one free transaction history each month. The employee must voluntarily agree to wage payment by payroll card and can switch to another payment method at any time.

# Section 5: Paying the Employee

*Missouri* – Effective 1-1-08, all state employees that are expected to be employed for longer than three months are required to participate in the state Payroll Direct Deposit program as a condition of employment. However, if an employee does not select a financial institution that will receive the direct deposit and he/she does not have or does not open a checking or savings account, the employee must be paid via a payroll card.

*Nevada* – The Labor Commissioner issued regulations that allow the use of paycards for wage payments if the employee can get immediate payment in full at a place that is easily accessible, at least one transaction is free, other fees are disclosed and the employee agrees to them in advance, and the employee voluntarily agrees to be paid with a paycard.

*New Hampshire* – An employer may pay wages to its employees via payroll cards if it provides employees at least one free means to withdraw the full amount of the balance on the card or in the payroll card account during each pay period at a financial institution or other location convenient to the place of employment. The employer may not pass any of its costs associated with the payroll cards/payroll card accounts on to the employees.

An employer that offers payroll cards must provide written disclosure in plain language of all the employees' wage payment options, the terms and conditions of the payroll card account option, and any fees that may be assessed. The payroll card must not have an expiration date, unless the employer agrees to provide a replacement card before the expiration date at no cost to the employee. An employer may initiate payment of wages by EFT to a payroll card account only after an employee has voluntarily consented in writing to that method of payment.

*North Carolina* – The Department of Labor's Wage and Hour Bureau said that paycards are an acceptable method of payment as long as the employee can withdraw all amounts due on payday and one-time use of the card by the employee on payday is at no cost to the employee.

*North Dakota* – Legislation was enacted to allow employers to pay wages through a stored value card at the election of the employee. The card must be issued by a federally insured bank or credit union and the value of the funds underlying the card must be insured by the Federal Deposit Insurance Corporation or National Credit Union Administration.

*Oklahoma* – Effective November 1, 2006, Oklahoma employers may require employees to receive wages via paycards, according to the General Counsel for the Oklahoma Department of Labor, but the employees cannot be charged the fees often associated with paycards, whether the fees are assessed by the employer or a third party with whom the employer has agreed to implement its payroll debit cards.

*Oregon* – Effective 1-1-08, an employer and an employee may agree that wages will be paid by payroll card provided the employee may: (1) make an initial withdrawal of the entire amount of net pay without cost to the employee; or (2) choose to use another means of payment of wages that involves no cost to the employee. The agreement must be made in the language that the employer principally uses to communicate with the employee. To revoke such an agreement, the employee (except for certain agricultural employees) must give the employer written notice of revocation. The agreement is revoked 30 days after the date the notice is received by the employer, unless the employer and employee agree otherwise.

*Vermont* – The Department of Labor and Industry said that Vermont law does not permit wages to be paid by debit card.

*Virginia* – The state has enacted legislation allowing employers to pay employees with a paycard if any applicable fees are disclosed. Also, the use of paycards cannot be mandated. However, employers may use paycards without the employee's consent if the employee hasn't designated a financial institution for direct deposit purposes and the employee works at a facility where the operation of amusement devices is authorized.

*West Virginia* – The Director of the Wage and Hour Section of the West Virginia Division of Labor stated that payroll debit cards are not allowed as a method of wage payment in West Virginia, in response to an inquiry from the American Payroll Association.

All states now allow employers to provide electronic pay statements, provided the employer meets requirements regarding access, printing, security, etc. [For more information on state rules governing electronic pay statements, see Table 2.3 of *APA's Guide to State Payroll Laws*]. [For more information on state rules governing electronic paycards, see Table 2.8 of *APA's Guide to State Payroll Laws*].

**Federal Reserve Board rules on regulating paycard accounts.**[9] In 2006, the Federal Reserve Board issued a final rule regarding the coverage of electronic paycard accounts under Regulation E, which implements the Electronic Fund Transfer Act. The final rule took effect July 1, 2007, but institutions could begin complying September 29, 2006.

*Definition of 'account'.*[10] Regulation E applies to any EFT that authorizes a financial institution to debit or credit a consumer's asset account. The final rule revises the definition of the term "account" to include a "payroll card account" directly or indirectly established by an employer on behalf of an employee to which EFTs of the employee's wages, salary, or other employee compensation are made on a recurring basis. A payroll card account is subject to the regulation whether the account is operated or managed by the employer, a third-party payroll processor, or a depository institution.

The definition generally includes a payroll card account that represents the means by which an employer regularly pays the employee's salary or other form of compensation, and would include, for example, card accounts for seasonal workers or employees who are paid on a commission basis. Moreover, the fact that an employee may only remain on the job for a short period of time, even just one pay cycle, does not negate coverage, so long as the employer intended to make recurring payments to the payroll card account.

 **POOLED ACCOUNTS ALSO COVERED**[11] Payroll card accounts also are covered whether the funds are held in individual employee accounts or in a pooled account with some form of "subaccounting" maintained by a depository institution (or by a third party) that enables a determination of the amounts of money owed to particular employees.

*Not included.*[12] The definition does not include "gift" cards issued by a merchant that can be used to purchase items in the merchant's store. Also not included in the definition of "account" are cards used only to make incentive-based salary-related payments (e.g., bonuses), or cards exclusively used to make non-salary-related payments (e.g., petty cash or travel per diems). Note, however, that to the extent bonus payments, payments to reimburse travel expenses, or any other payments are transferred to or from a payroll card account, such transfers would be considered EFTs covered by Regulation E.

If the employer only pays the employee by adding funds to an "account" accessible by a card in isolated or limited instances – e.g., in final-paycheck situations, or only in emergency situations when the customary, non-payroll-card method of payment does not work – but otherwise intends to regularly pay the employee by another method, such as by paper check or direct deposit, such a card "account" would not be covered under the definition.

 **HEALTH EXPENSE CARDS NOT COVERED**[13] Supplemental information to the final rule indicates that cards used solely for health-related expenses – such as cards linked to flexible spending accounts, health savings accounts, or health reimbursement arrangements – are not covered by Regulation E.

*Dual function card account.* Under a dual function card account, part of the account holds employer-funded "corporate expense funds," and the remaining segregated portion of the card holds employer-transmitted wages belonging to the employee. The final rule clarifies that the segregated corporate expense portion of the account accessible by the card is not a "payroll card account" because the funds are not primarily for personal, family, or household purposes. The remaining funds that consist of the employee's wages would qualify as funds held in a "payroll card account."

---

9.    12 CFR §205.2(b)(2); §205.18.
10.   12 CFR §205.2(b)(2); 71 F.R. 51440, 8-30-06.
11.   71 F.R. 51440, 8-30-06; 71 F.R. 1475, 1-10-06.
12.   Supplement I to Part 205, §205.2(b)(2).
13.   71 F.R. 51441, 8-30-06.

*Employers usually aren't 'financial institutions.'*[14] Regulation E applies to payroll card accounts in the same way that it applies to other types of accounts. In other words, under the final rule, employers and third-party service providers will only be covered by Regulation E as "financial institutions" if they hold the payroll card account or issue a payroll card and provide EFT services. Accordingly, the depository institution holding the funds will always be treated as a financial institution under the rule, but employers and service providers typically will not be covered.

To the extent that more than one party is a "financial institution" with respect to a particular payroll card account, such parties may enter into an agreement among themselves to ensure compliance with Regulation E. For example, disclosure obligations satisfied by one party, such as a service provider, for a payroll card account would satisfy any disclosure obligations for any other financial institution with respect to that payroll card account.

 **UNACTIVATED CARDS CAN BE PART OF OFFER** The final rule clarifies that an employer may include an *unactivated* payroll card with materials provided to employees about the terms and conditions of the payroll card account when the accounts are offered to employees, provided employees retain the option to receive compensation by means other than the payroll card account.

*Disclosures.*[15] The final rule requires financial institutions to include in the initial disclosures for payroll card accounts the means by which an employee can access information about his or her account, including the telephone number that the employee may call to obtain his or her account balance, and information on how the employee can electronically obtain a history of account transactions, such as the address of the Internet Web site.

Financial institutions must also include in their initial disclosures a summary of the employee's right to obtain a written history of account transactions upon request, including a telephone number to call to request a history. Additionally, financial institutions must provide an annual notice describing error-resolution rights. The final rule provides model forms that financial institutions can use to facilitate compliance with these requirements.

*Periodic statements.*[16] As an alternative to providing periodic statements, the final rule provides that financial institutions may instead:
- make available to the employee the account balance through a readily available telephone line;
- make available to the employee an electronic history (such as via an Internet Web site) of the employee's account transactions that covers at least 60 days preceding the date the employee electronically accesses the account; and
- provide promptly, upon the employee's oral or written request, a written history of the employee's account transactions that covers at least 60 days preceding the date of receipt of the employee's request.

The account history provided under these new procedures, whether it is provided electronically or in writing, must contain the same type of information that would be provided in a periodic statement, including information about fees, account balances, and an address and telephone number for inquiries. The final rule includes a model clause that financial institutions may use to inform employees about how to access their account information.

*Compulsory use.* In the preamble to an interim rule issued before the final rule, the FRB clarified that the compulsory use provisions of Regulation E (applicable to direct deposit) apply to payroll card accounts

---

14. Supplement I to Part 205, §205.18(a).
15. 12 CFR §205.18(c)(1), (2); Appendix to Part 205, Appendix A-7 – Model Clauses for Financial Institutions Offering Payroll Card Accounts.
16. 12 CFR §205.18(b); Supplement I to Part 205 §205.18(b).

because these accounts are established to receive EFTs of salary. But as long as an employer offered direct deposit to a financial institution as an alternative to a payroll card account for the receipt of wages, the compulsory use prohibition "should not be implicated."[17]

**Selecting a paycard vendor**. There are several issues that have to be resolved before you select a paycard vendor if you are considering paycards as a payment method. Before going forward, make sure paycards are a viable option for your organization by researching the compliance issues in the states where you operate and determining the size of the employee population that will potentially be using the cards.

Once the decision is made to go forward, here are some of the variables that need to be considered in selecting a paycard vendor:

*Type of card* – Decide whether the employer will use branded or nonbranded cards.

*Employer costs* – There are several types of employer costs associated with paycards, including setup fees (e.g., creating accounts, enrolling employees), payroll processing costs, and extra fees for one-time payments (e.g., off-cycle payments, termination payments).

*Employee costs* – There may be different costs for ATM and POS transactions depending on the vendor. Some of them may waive the fee for the first transaction each pay period, and there may be added fees for extra services, such as monthly statements or balance checks.

*Legal issues* – Make sure that any vendor you are considering can comply with the wage payment regulations in the states where the organization operates.

*System compatibility* – Make sure that the vendor's system is compatible with your employer's payroll system.

*Training* – Determine if the vendor offers training both for the payroll department on the software involved and for the employees who will be using the paycards.

**Paycard implementation issues.** Once the decision has been made to offer paycards as a payment method and a particular program has been selected, the employer has to go through much of the same processes that it does when first implementing a direct deposit program, including:

- Communicate the coming change to any levels of management that were not included as part of the selection process;

- Put together an implementation team with members from all affected departments – communications, human resources, payroll, operations, training, finance;

- Design and conduct a marketing campaign promoting paycards to employees by emphasizing the features and benefits they will realize (with help from your paycard vendor, if possible);

- Enroll employees in the program by getting the necessary information to set up their paycard accounts (e.g., name, address, phone number, SSN, Mother's maiden name);

- Make sure to have trained employees who can answer other employees' questions regarding the program once it is implemented.

---

17.    71 F.R. 1479, 1-10-06.

**GET MORE INFORMATION**  More detailed information regarding electronic paycards, the program selection and implementation process, and the costs and benefits involved, is contained in the 2008 edition of the APA's *The Guide to Successful Direct Deposit.*  For ordering information, call APA Membership Services at 210-224-6406 or go to www.americanpayroll.org.

## 5.4 Pay Statements Provided to Employees

It is up to each state to determine just what information must be included on an employee's pay stub or statement in the way of earnings, hours worked, tax withholdings, other deductions, pay period dates, etc. Table 5.5 summarizes the states' general pay statement information requirements, recognizing there may be exceptions for certain groups of employees or certain industries (e.g., statements showing hours worked or straight time vs. overtime pay may not be required for employees who are exempt from overtime pay requirements).  [For more information on state pay statement requirements, see Table 2.2 of *APA's Guide to State Payroll Laws.*]

Table 5.5

| STATE-BY-STATE RULES ON PAY STUB INFORMATION ||
|---|---|
| **State** | **Required Pay Stub Information** |
| Alabama | No provision |
| Alaska | Pay rate, gross and net earnings, pay period dates, federal tax deductions, employee SUI contributions, board and lodging costs, advances, other deductions |
| Arizona | Earnings and deductions if employee paid by direct deposit |
| Arkansas | No provision |
| California | Gross and net earnings, hours worked at each hourly rate for hourly workers, overtime hours worked during previous pay period if corrected in current pay period, piece rates and number of pieces, deductions, pay period dates, employee's name and company ID# or last 4 digits of social security number (may show full SSN before 1-1-08), employer's name and address |
| Colorado | Gross and net earnings, deductions, pay period dates, employee's name or social security number, employer's name and address |
| Connecticut | Gross and net earnings, straight time and overtime pay, hours worked, itemized deductions |
| Delaware | Wages due, pay period dates, itemized deductions, hours worked for hourly workers |
| Dist. of Col. | Payment date, gross and net earnings, deductions and additions, hours worked |
| Florida | Farm labor contractors with 10 or more employees: itemized deductions, semimonthly or at time of payment |
| Georgia | Labor pools and work-site employers: hours worked, pay rate, deductions |
| Hawaii | Total hours worked, gross and net earnings, amount and purpose of each deduction, payment date, pay period dates |
| Idaho | Itemized deductions |
| Illinois | Itemized deductions |
| Indiana | Hours worked, wages paid, itemized deductions |
| Iowa | Hours worked, earnings, and itemized deductions |
| Kansas | Itemized deductions (if requested) |
| Kentucky | Amount and purpose of deductions if employer has 10 or more employees |
| Louisiana | No provision |
| Maine | Pay period dates, hours worked, total earnings, itemized deductions |

| STATE-BY-STATE RULES ON PAY STUB INFORMATION | |
|---|---|
| **State** | **Required Pay Stub Information** |
| Maryland | Gross earnings, deductions; SSN prohibited |
| Massachusetts | Employer's and employee's name, payment date, hours worked, hourly pay rate, amount and nature of deductions, increases |
| Michigan | Hours worked, gross earnings, pay periods, itemized deductions |
| Minnesota | Employee's name, hours worked and hourly rate for nonexempt employees, gross and net earnings, list of deductions, pay period ending date |
| Mississippi | No provision |
| Missouri | Total deductions |
| Montana | Itemized deductions |
| Nebraska | No provision |
| Nevada | Itemized deductions |
| New Hampshire | Statement of deductions |
| New Jersey | Statement of total wages and deductions |
| New Mexico | Employer's name, gross wages and benefits, hours worked, itemized deductions |
| New York | Gross and net earnings, deductions, explanation of wage computation if requested |
| North Carolina | Itemized deductions |
| North Dakota | Hours worked, pay rate, required state and federal deductions, employee-authorized deductions |
| Ohio | No provision |
| Oklahoma | Itemized deductions |
| Oregon | Gross wages, itemized deductions, hours worked, pay rate, net pay, pay period dates, employer's name, address, and phone number; annual pay statement for previous year by March 10 if employee requests |
| Pennsylvania | No general provision |
| Puerto Rico | Employee's name, employer's name and address, type of craft or labor, dates of work and kind of work covered by payment, straight and overtime hours worked and amount paid for each, net pay, and an explanation of all additions and deductions; |
| Rhode Island | Hours worked (nonexempt employees), gross earnings, deductions (upon request of employee) |
| South Carolina | Gross pay, itemized deductions |
| South Dakota | No provision |
| Tennessee | No provision |
| Texas | Employee's name, pay rate, gross and net earnings, amount and purpose of deductions, hours worked or work done (if paid by piece rate) |
| Utah | Amount of each deduction |
| Vermont | Gross pay, hours worked, hourly rate, itemized deductions |
| Virginia | Gross earnings, amount and purpose of deductions (upon request) |
| Washington | Pay basis (hourly, daily, etc.), pay rate, gross earnings, deductions |
| West Virginia | Itemized deductions |
| Wisconsin | Amount of and reason for deductions |
| Wyoming | Itemized deductions |

# 5.5 Unclaimed Paychecks

It may seem highly unlikely, but the problem of what to do with paychecks that are unclaimed and uncashed by employees is one payroll departments frequently face. The problem most often arises where an employee is discharged or resigns and fails to pick up or claim any wages owed at the time. These unclaimed wages become a form of "abandoned property" the employer must pay over to the appropriate state agency (usually the treasury) if they remain unclaimed for a certain number of years. The state laws governing abandoned property are known as "escheat" laws, because the property "escheats" to the state.

Most states require employers to contact employees in an attempt to keep unclaimed wages from becoming abandoned property. They are also generally required to file annual reports with the state that include each employee's name, last known address, amount and payment date of the unclaimed wages, and the date of last contact with the employee. Table 5.6 shows the length of time before unclaimed wages become abandoned property in each state. [For more information on state escheat laws, see Table 2.6 of *APA's Guide to State Payroll Laws*.]

Table 5.6

| STATE-BY-STATE RULES ON UNCLAIMED WAGES | | | |
|---|---|---|---|
| **State** | **Unclaimed Wages Become Abandoned After ...** | **State** | **Unclaimed Wages Become Abandoned After ...** |
| Alabama | 1 year | Montana | 1 year |
| Alaska | 1 year | Nebraska | 1 year |
| Arizona | 1 year | Nevada | 1 year |
| Arkansas | 1 year | New Hampshire | 1 year |
| California | 1 year | New Jersey | 1 year |
| Colorado | 1 year | New Mexico | 1 year |
| Connecticut | 1 year | New York | 3 years |
| Delaware | 5 years | North Carolina | 2 years |
| Dist. of Col. | 1 year | North Dakota | 2 years |
| Florida | 1 year | Ohio | 1 year |
| Georgia | 1 year | Oklahoma | 1 year |
| Hawaii | 1 year | Oregon | 3 years |
| Idaho | 1 year | Pennsylvania | 2 years |
| Illinois | 5 years | Rhode Island | 1 year |
| Indiana | 1 year | South Carolina | 1 year |
| Iowa | 1 year | South Dakota | 1 year |
| Kansas | 1 year | Tennessee | 1 year |
| Kentucky | 3 years | Texas | 1 year |
| Louisiana | 1 year | Utah | 1 year |
| Maine | 1 year | Vermont | 1 year |

| STATE-BY-STATE RULES ON UNCLAIMED WAGES | | | |
|---|---|---|---|
| **State** | **Unclaimed Wages Become Abandoned After ...** | **State** | **Unclaimed Wages Become Abandoned After ...** |
| Maryland | 3 years | Virginia | 1 year |
| Massachusetts | 3 years | Washington | 1 year |
| Michigan | 1 year if more than $50 | West Virginia | 1 year |
| Minnesota | 1 year | Wisconsin | 1 year |
| Mississippi | 5 years | Wyoming | 1 year |
| Missouri | 5 years | | |

## 5.6 Wages Owed Deceased Employees

In an earlier section, we discussed the federal tax treatment of wages owed to an employee who dies after earning them (see Section 3.4-30). Most states also regulate wages owed to deceased employees, in terms of who the wages may be paid to, how much may be paid before administration of the deceased employee's estate, and what conditions must be met before payment can be made.

> *Example:* In California, a deceased employee's surviving spouse, conservator, or guardian may be paid up to $5,000 in wages owed the employee (including unused vacation). If the employer does not know the person claiming a right to the wages personally, that person must present an affidavit proving his or her identity and right to the wages. Once the employer accepts the affidavit, it is relieved of any liability concerning the wages should another person claim a right to them.

The law in California is somewhat typical of the requirements imposed by other states, although the amounts that can be paid vary greatly. Table 5.7 shows the amounts that employers can pay before the employee's estate is administered, who the wages can be paid to, and what conditions must be met to allow payment. Employers should check the law in the states in which they operate before attempting to pay wages to a deceased employee's surviving spouse or legal representative. [For more information on state laws governing payment of wages owed to deceased employees, see Table 2.5 of *APA's Guide to State Payroll Laws*.]

Table 5.7

| STATE REQUIREMENTS GOVERNING WAGES PAID TO DECEASED EMPLOYEES | | | |
|---|---|---|---|
| **State** | **Maximum Payable** | **To Whom** | **Conditions** |
| Alabama | All wages due | Surviving spouse or custodian of minor children | No will |
| Alaska | No provision | | |
| Arizona | $5,000 | Surviving spouse | Affidavit showing employee's death and status as surviving spouse; no appointment of, or pending application for, personal representative |
| Arkansas | No general provision | | |
| California | $5,000 | Surviving spouse or conservator | Affidavit of right and proof of identity |

| STATE REQUIREMENTS GOVERNING WAGES PAID TO DECEASED EMPLOYEES | | | |
|---|---|---|---|
| **State** | **Maximum Payable** | **To Whom** | **Conditions** |
| Colorado | All unpaid wages and compensation due | Surviving spouse or next legal heir; personal representative if already appointed | Affidavit showing claimant's relationship to deceased |
| Connecticut | $20,000 | Surviving spouse or next of kin; funeral director or physician if they have preferred claim | Application from surviving spouse or next of kin; affidavit of debt due from funeral director or physician |
| Delaware | $300 | Surviving children under 21, custodian, surviving spouse, children 21 and over, or deceased's parents (in that order) | Proper demand; no probate proceedings pending |
| Dist. of Columbia | No provision | | |
| Florida | All wages due, plus travel expenses up to $300 | Surviving spouse, children over 18, or deceased's parents (in that order) | None |
| Georgia | $2,500; all wages if state employee | Designated beneficiary, surviving spouse, or children's guardian (in that order) | None |
| Hawaii | $2,000 | Surviving spouse or adult child (in that order) within 30 days | Affidavit of relationship and receipt for payment |
| Idaho | No provision | | |
| Illinois | All unpaid wages due | Person owed for funeral expenses, spouse, or child | Small estate affidavit; estate not over $15,000 |
| Indiana | All unpaid wages due | Widow; if none, other distributee | Affidavit of right; estate not over $25,000; no pending application for personal representative |
| Iowa | No provision | | |
| Kansas | All unpaid wages due | Surviving spouse, children 18 or over, parents, siblings, or funeral director (in that order) | On demand; no actual notice of probate proceedings |
| Kentucky | All unpaid wages due | Spouse or guardian of minor children | No will; estate not over $15,000 |
| Louisiana | All unpaid wages due | Spouse or adult child (in that order) | Instrument indicating relationship to deceased |
| Maine | No provision | | |
| Maryland | No provision | | |
| Massachusetts | $100 | Surviving spouse, adult child or parent (in that order) | 30 days since death; no will |
| Michigan | All unpaid wages due | Employee's written designee; if none, surviving spouse, children, parents, or siblings (in that order) | None |
| Minnesota | $10,000 | Surviving spouse | Upon request; affidavit showing proof of relationship; no personal representative appointed |
| Mississippi | All unpaid wages due | Surviving spouse or next of kin | None |

| STATE REQUIREMENTS GOVERNING WAGES PAID TO DECEASED EMPLOYEES | | | |
|---|---|---|---|
| State | Maximum Payable | To Whom | Conditions |
| Missouri | No provision | | |
| Montana | No provision | | |
| Nebraska | No provision | | |
| Nevada | All unpaid wages due | Surviving spouse or distributee | Affidavit of right; 40 days after death; estate not over $20,000 |
| New Hampshire | $500 | Surviving spouse; adult children; parent; siblings; funeral expenses (in that order) | Affidavit showing proof of relationship |
| New Jersey | All unpaid wages due | Surviving spouse, children 18 or over, guardian of minor children, parents, siblings, or person paying funeral expenses (in that order) | Proper demand and proof of relationship; no notice of pending probate proceedings |
| New Mexico | All unpaid wages due | Surviving spouse | None |
| New York | $30,000 within 30 days of death; $15,000 from 31 days to 6 months; $5,000 if more than 6 months after death | Within 30 days of death—designated beneficiary or surviving spouse; after 30 days—surviving spouse, adult children, parent, sibling, niece or nephew, creditor, or person paying funeral expenses (in that order); after 6 months—distributee, creditor, or | Within 30 days of death—affidavit from spouse that wages do not exceed $30,000; after 30 days—affidavit showing date of death, relationship, that payments won't exceed $15,000, ($5,000 if after 6 months), names and addresses of persons receiving money funeral expenses |
| North Carolina | No provision | | |
| North Dakota | All unpaid wages due | Surviving spouse or next eligible heir (in that order) | Affidavit showing proof of relationship; no executor or administrator has been appointed |
| Ohio | $2,500 | Surviving spouse, adult children, or parent (in that order) | None |
| Oklahoma | $3,000 | Designated beneficiary, surviving spouse, children or guardians (in that order) | None |
| Oregon | $10,000 | Surviving spouse, children or guardians (in equal shares) | None |
| Pennsylvania | $3,500, including any benefits | Surviving spouse, child, parent, or sibling (in that order) | Payment even if administrator is appointed |
| Puerto Rico | No provision | | |
| Rhode Island | $150 | Surviving spouse, adult children, parents, siblings, or person paying funeral expenses (in that order) | Payment after 30 days after death; proof of relationship |
| South Carolina | No provision | | |
| South Dakota | No provision | | |
| Tennessee | $10,000 | Designated beneficiary; if none, then surviving spouse; children if deceased was female and head of household | None |

| STATE REQUIREMENTS GOVERNING WAGES PAID TO DECEASED EMPLOYEES | | | |
|---|---|---|---|
| **State** | **Maximum Payable** | **To Whom** | **Conditions** |
| Texas | No provision | | |
| Utah | All unpaid wages due | Successor | Affidavit stating estate does not exceed $25,000 at least 30 days since death, no petition for executor is pending, and entitlement to payment |
| Vermont | No provision | | |
| Virginia | $15,000 | Surviving spouse; if none, distributees | 60 days after death; no qualification of estate |
| Washington | $2,500; $10,000 for state government employees | Surviving spouse, children, or parents (in that order) | Proof of relationship; no executor or administrator has been appointed |
| West Virginia | $800; $1,000 after 120 days after death | Surviving spouse, adult children, parents, siblings, or person paying funeral expenses (in that order) | Proper demand and application |
| Wisconsin | All unpaid wages due | Surviving spouse, children or other dependent living with employee; within 5 days of death—surviving spouse, children, parents, or siblings (in that order) | Proper demand |
| Wyoming | No provision | | |

## 5.7 Extra Pay Periods Caused by the Calendar

Each year, some employers will find themselves faced with a dilemma caused by the calendar. Because a normal year has 365 days, one day of the week will occur 53 times in a year (52 weeks x 7 days/week = 364 days). In leap years, which have 366 days, two days of the week will occur 53 times. For employers who pay their employees on a weekly or biweekly basis, and whose paydays fall on the extra days of the week just mentioned, an extra pay period will occur—53 rather than 52 for weekly payers, 27 rather than 26 for biweekly payers (although it will occur less often for biweekly payers).

In 2008 which is a leap year, this problem arises for some weekly and biweekly payers with a Tuesday or Wednesday payday, because January 1 was a Tuesday and January 2 was a Wednesday (although biweekly payers whose first payday of the year was January 8 or 9 did not have the problem). The main problem these employers faced was whether to recompute weekly or biweekly paychecks for salaried employees who were earning a certain amount annually.

> *Example:* Irving, a salaried, exempt employee earning $52,000 per year, is paid weekly on Tuesday. His normal weekly gross wages are $1,000. If his employer pays him $1,000 per week every Tuesday in 2008, Irving would be paid $53,000 in 2008. To make sure Irving is paid $52,000 in 2008, his weekly pay is reduced to $981.13.

**Pay reductions may cause problems.** Employers are free to reduce salaried employees' pay for each pay period when faced with an extra pay period, so long as there is no contract guaranteeing a certain amount of pay each weekly or biweekly pay period and the employee's pay is not reduced below the minimum required by state or federal law. Hourly employees, however, must be paid their agreed-upon hourly wage for all hours worked, regardless of the extra pay period.

Even for salaried, exempt employees, many employers do not recompute their weekly or biweekly pay. Reasons for this include the probability of strained employer-employee relations if wages are reduced for each pay period, and the fact that even salaried employees are often promised a certain biweekly pay rather than guaranteed a yearly amount.

**Planning is a key.** The payroll department must be aware well in advance if a company is facing an extra payroll period in the upcoming calendar (or fiscal) year. If weekly or biweekly pay will not be recomputed, wage expenses may increase in such years, depending on the accounting method used for payroll, and they must be accounted for to upper management and the finance department.

Here are the days of the week that occur 53 times in the calendar years 2007-2012:

| | |
|---|---|
| 2007 | Monday |
| 2008 | Tuesday, Wednesday |
| 2009 | Thursday |
| 2010 | Friday |
| 2011 | Saturday |
| 2012 | Sunday, Monday |

# 5.8 Review Questions and Exercises

## Review Questions

1. What laws govern how often an employer must pay its employees?
   *State laws*

2. What are some of the advantages and disadvantages of direct deposit for an employer?.
   *Ad:*        *Dis: Paper, not mandatory, float time*

3. What laws cover unclaimed paychecks, and what is generally required of the employer?

4. Explain the process of prenotification under the Automated Clearing House System.

5. Many critics claim that direct deposit is not paperless. Explain why.

6. What are some of the problems that may arise when periodic pay is reduced as a result of an extra pay period caused by the calendar?

7. Name 5 states that do not allow compulsory direct deposit.

8. Name 5 states that prohibit employers from requiring employees to pay added fees to participate in a direct deposit program.

9. What are the steps involved in establishing an electronic funds transfer?

10. List the disadvantages of paying employees by paycheck as far as the employer is concerned.

## True or False Questions

     1. The Federal Wage-Hour Law (Fair Labor Standards Act) regulates how often employees must be paid by their employer or how soon they must be paid after performing services.

     2. Direct deposit is one area where the federal and state governments share regulatory responsibility.

_____ 3. The Fair Labor Standards Act regulates the payment of wages on termination of employment.

_____ 4. All states regulate the payment of wages owed to deceased employees.

_____ 5. A worker who is regularly paid on a weekly basis may receive 53 paychecks in a year.

_____ 6. Under an electronic funds transfer system (EFTS), the employees' wages are deposited directly into their personal accounts in one or more financial institutions.

_____ 7. A biweekly salary is paid twice a month, usually on the 15th and last day of the month.

_____ 8. On payday, the RDFI is responsible for crediting the employee's account when direct deposit is used as a method of payment.

_____ 9. Federal Reserve Board Regulation E establishes the basic rights, requirements and liabilities for the protection of employees being paid through EFT.

_____ 10. If 250 or more employees consent to direct deposit, then all employees must comply.

_____ 11. The Fair Labor Standards Act requires that employees be paid at least monthly.

_____ 12. A paycheck is classified as a negotiable instrument.

## Multiple Choice Questions

_____ 1. According to NACHA—The Electronic Payments Association, what was the portion of the U.S. workforce that had their pay directly deposited in 2005?

    a.   90%
    b.   25%
    c.   more than 71%
    d.   33%

_____ 2. The employer prepares an automated file of direct deposit records that indicates where its employees' pay is to be deposited. What is the name of the financial institution where this file is then sent?

    a.   Automated Clearing House
    b.   Originating Depository Financial Institution
    c.   NACHA
    d.   Receiving Depository Financial Institution

_____ 3. How many years must an employer keep the authorization agreement for direct deposit after revocation by the employee or the employee's separation from employment?

    a.   There is no retention requirement
    b.   At least one year
    c.   At least two years
    d.   At least three years

___ 4.   What are "escheat" laws?

    a.   Federal laws governing the treatment of unclaimed wages as abandoned property
    b.   State laws governing the treatment of unclaimed wages as abandoned property
    c.   State laws protecting employees from their employer
    d.   State laws outlining the frequency with which employees are paid

___ 5.   Which day of the week occurs 53 times in 2008?

    a.   Sunday
    b.   Saturday
    c.   Tuesday .
    d.   Friday

___ 6.   Once an employee has given authorization for EFT and the employer creates electronic pay transactions for deposit, where does the employer send them?

    a.   ACH
    b.   RDFI
    c.   ODFI
    d.   NACHA

C ___ 7.   Under the EFT system, what participating party receives the individual transactions and posts them to the customers'/employees' accounts?

    a.   ODFI
    b.   ACH
    c.   RDFI
    d.   NACHA

C ___ 8.   Which of the following laws and regulations does not regulate EFT?

    a.   Federal Reserve Board Regulation E
    b.   Title IX of the Consumer Credit Protection Act
    c.   Fair Labor Standards Act
    d.   Electronic Fund Transfer Act

a ___ 9.   Which of the following states follows federal Regulation E regarding the choice of financial institutions by participating employees?

    a.   Alabama
    b.   California
    c.   Florida
    d.   New York

B ___ 10.   Which of the following participants in the direct deposit process distributes EFT payments to the receiving financial institutions?

    a.   ODFI
    b.   ACH
    c.   RDFI
    d.   FRB

_C_ 11. Which of the following states requires that an employee participating in a direct deposit program not incur a charge for withdrawing his or her pay once it has been deposited?

    a.    Arkansas
    b.    Georgia
    c. ✓ Colorado
    d.    Florida

12. Which of the following features is a possible disadvantage of the direct deposit system to the employer?

    a.    Direct deposit
    b.    Loss of float ╱
    c.    Check printing cost
    d.    Check storage cost

# SECTION 6: WITHHOLDING TAXES

## TABLE OF CONTENTS

# SECTION 6: WITHHOLDING TAXES

Other than paying employees, the most important function of a company's payroll department is collecting various taxes required by federal, state, and local governments. Much of this is accomplished by withholding the required amounts from employees' wages and timely paying them over to the appropriate governmental unit. Approximately 70% of federal tax revenue comes from amounts withheld and/or paid by employers. Amounts withheld for social security and Medicare taxes are used to pay current benefits under those federal programs and to invest to provide for future benefit payments.

This section will explore the entire federal tax withholding process, from the determination of when wages are considered paid and the important role of social security numbers to how an employer determines how much federal income, social security, and Medicare tax to withhold and pay to the U.S. Treasury.

## 6.1 The Principle of Actual or Constructive Payment

Under federal regulations, employers must withhold federal income tax, social security tax, and Medicare tax when the employee is "actually or constructively paid," not when the wages are earned and become "payable."[1]

**When are wages actually or constructively paid to an employee?** It is easy enough to determine when an employee is paid if the employee is given cash or a check on payday that is dated that day and can be cashed at a local bank. This is actual payment. But what if the employee is not "actually paid" on payday? Under the principle of constructive payment, an employee is considered to have been paid wages when the wages have been made available to the employee without "substantial limitation or restriction."[2]

Therefore, the employee is not required to have actual possession of the wages for the principle of constructive payment to apply. It is enough that the wages are available to be drawn on or controlled by the employee. When the wages are made available to the employee in this manner, the employer must withhold required taxes.

*Example 1:* Employee George was out of town on July 11, 2008, a biweekly payday, because a business meeting with a client lasted longer than expected. His check was kept at the office until his return on Monday, July 14. Because his wages were made available on July 11, they were constructively paid to George on that day and his employer was responsible for withholding any applicable taxes at that time.

*Example 2:* Employee Lorraine is paid by direct deposit (see Section 5.3-2). Lorraine's savings account is credited with her net wage payment each Friday morning, which is payday. Even though Lorraine cannot get to the bank on Friday before closing and has to wait until Monday before withdrawing funds (she has no ATM card), she was constructively paid her wages on Friday when they were put in a separate account for her and were made available to her without restriction.

**Checks sent through the mail.** Employees who receive paychecks sent through the mail generally are not constructively paid when the checks are sent. The wages are not available to the employee until the check is delivered to the employee's home or other mail drop or unless the employer finds another way to provide a replacement check or cash to the employee before that time.

---

1.    IRS Reg. §1.451-2; §31.3121(a)-2; §31.3301-4; §31.3402(a)-1(b).
2.    IRS Reg. §31.3402(a)-1(b); Rev. Rul. 73-99, 1973-1 CB 412.

***Example 1:*** Employee Dave works in a remote office with four other employees whose checks are mailed from their employer's corporate headquarters on Tuesday for a Thursday payday. When bad weather threatens to delay postal delivery of the checks until the following Monday, the employer wires cash wages to the employees on Friday. Although the checks do not arrive until Monday, Dave and the other employees in his office are actually paid their wages on Friday, and taxes must be withheld at that time.

***Example 2:*** Joe's employer pays wages every other Friday, and employees who work from home, such as Joe, can either pick their checks up at the office or have them mailed to their homes. Even though Joe has his paychecks mailed to his home, where they generally arrive on the following Monday, Joe is constructively paid his wages on Friday, when they are made available to him.

**Postdating or backdating checks.** Regardless of the date that is printed on an employee's paycheck, the date it is actually or constructively provided to the employee is the date that triggers the employer's withholding and deposit obligations (see Section 8.2 for more on depositing withheld taxes). While the date on a paycheck may help prove the date of actual or constructive payment, it is not conclusive and may be challenged by other evidence.

**Why is the date of actual or constructive payment important?** In most situations, short delays that sometimes occur in making wages available to employees will not significantly affect the employer's or employee's withholding tax obligations. However, should these delays occur at the end of the calendar year there could be a significant difference in the amount of tax that should be withheld.

***Example:*** Employee Maureen is scheduled to receive her last paycheck of 2007 on Friday, December 28. Her biweekly wages are $4,000, and she has been paid $100,000, which exceeds the social security wage base for 2007 ($97,500). Because of system problems, Maureen's employer is unable to issue paychecks until January 2, 2008, although they are dated December 28, 2007. Maureen is not constructively paid her wages for withholding tax purposes until 2008, when her previous earnings for the year are zero.

Therefore, the entire $4,000 wage payment is subject to social security tax at the 2008 rate of 6.2% ($4,000 x .062 = $248), an amount her employer must match (see Section 6.7-3). If Maureen had received her paycheck on December 28, her wages would not have been subject to social security tax withholding or matching by the employer. The entire payment is also subject to Medicare tax regardless of when it is received since there is no Medicare wage base in 2007 or 2008.

# 6.2 Social Security Numbers

The original purpose of a social security number (SSN) was to establish an account for an individual so wages and self-employment income could be posted to the individual's account for the purpose of receiving social security retirement benefits. The SSN still serves that purpose, but it now serves many others as well, one of which is as an identification number used by the IRS in its dealings with the individual. Employers use their employees' SSNs to identify them when reports of wages paid and taxes withheld are made to the Social Security Administration and the IRS. Therefore, the employer must get each new employee's name and SSN (including resident and nonresident aliens), and enter them into its records exactly as shown on the social security card. If the employer does not provide the correct name and SSN on the employee's Form W-2, *Wage and Tax Statement* (see Section 8.8), it may be assessed a penalty by the IRS.

The SSN contains nine digits in the following format: 000-00-0000. Employers must ask each new employee for his or her social security number and should require the employee to produce his or her original social security card when the employee is hired to help make sure the employee's SSN is transcribed properly onto all forms. The employer may photocopy the card to further reduce the chance for error. Employees are required to show their social security card to their employer on the first day of work if they have it available. If it is not available, they must provide their name and number to the employer exactly as it is shown on their card, and show the card to the employer "promptly" thereafter. If an employee does not have a social security card but has a receipt from the SSA acknowledging that an application for a card has been filed, the employee must show the receipt to the employer. If

the employee has no social security card and no receipt acknowledging an application for one, the employee must provide the employer with a statement containing the information required on an application, apply for an SSN, and then show the new card to the employer.[3]

Employers are required to enter into their records each employee's name and SSN exactly as shown on the employee's social security card. If an employee does not produce a social security card on the first day of work, the employer must ask to see it. If the employee has an SSN but the card is not available, the employer must enter the employee's name and SSN as told by the employee into its records. If the employee provides a receipt acknowledging an application for an SSN, the employer must record the employee's name and address, the expiration date of the receipt, and the issuing SSA office. If the employee gives the employer a statement containing the information required to apply for an SSN, the employer must tell the employee that he or she is required to file an application with the SSA.[4]

The following are examples of invalid SSNs, meaning that SSA has never issued them:

- 111-11-1111; 333-33-3333; 123-45-6789
- SSNs having 000 or 666 as the first 3 digits
- SSNs greater than 773 as the first 3 digits
- SSNs having 00 as the fourth and fifth digits
- SSNs having 0000 as the sixth through ninth digits

For updated lists of the highest numbers being issued during any one month, go to the SSA's Internet website at www.socialsecurity.gov/employer/ssnv.htm.

Remember that requiring an employee to produce a social security card for examination or photocopying is illegal if made to substantiate the employee's right to work in the U.S. under the Immigration Reform and Control Act. The employee can produce any one of a number of documents, including a social security card, that prove his or her right to work (see Section 1.8). Once the documents are provided, the employer may photocopy them. *Make it clear that the request to see the employee's social security card is only for tax withholding and reporting purposes.*

 **WHERE TO GET AN SSN** Newly hired employees who do not have an SSN can get one by filling out and submitting Form SS-5, *Application for a Social Security Card* (see Appendix page A-46), to the Social Security Administration. The form can be obtained by calling, toll-free, 1-800-SSA-1213, or it can be downloaded from SSA's website at www.socialsecurity.gov. Employers should keep a stock of SS-5 forms on hand to give to employees who need an SSN. Because all children who are claimed as a dependent on a personal income tax return must have an SSN, fewer new employees will be hired without already having an SSN.

**Social security card improvements.** In 2007, the SSA made two improvements to the social security card that may make the tax withholding and wage reporting process go a little easier in the future.

- In April, the SSA added the "issued" (i.e., printed) date at the bottom of the front of the card on new and replacement cards.
- In September, the SSA began printing the individual's surname (i.e., last name) on a separate line on new and replacement cards, making it easier to determine the employee's first and last names.

**Requiring an SSN is not religious discrimination.** From time to time, an employee may claim that requiring the employee to provide a social security number is religious discrimination because the SSN represents the "mark of the beast" as described in the Bible. The federal courts have ruled that it's the IRS, not the employer, that imposes the SSN requirement, so requiring the SSN is not an employment requirement covered by the employment discrimination laws. The courts also said that employers need not accommodate religious

---

3.    IRS Reg. §31.6011(b)-2(b).
4.    IRS Reg. §31.6011(b)-2(c).

beliefs if the accommodation would involve violating the IRC and subjecting the employer to potential penalties, as this would be an undue hardship for the employer.[5]

# 6.2-1 Verifying Social Security Numbers

Other than asking to see the employee's original social security card, photocopying it, and making sure it is recorded properly on any forms filled out for the employee, the SSA has three SSN verification methods available to employers:

- Phone
- Paper list
- Internet

Employers must obtain each employee's name and social security number to be entered on the employee's Form W-2. If the Form W-2 does not contain the correct name and social security number, the employer may be penalized up to $50 for each incorrect W-2 (see Section 8.13-1).

**Telephone (up to 5 SSNs).** Employers can call SSA's toll free number for employers (800-772-6270) or the general SSA number (800-772-1213) weekdays from 7:00 am to 7:00 pm ET to verify up to 5 social security numbers.

**Paper (up to 50 SSNs).** Employers can submit a list of up to 50 employees to a local SSA office. The submission request should be on company letterhead. Some offices accept fax listings. Call your local office for the procedures to use.

**Employee Verification Service.** Another source available to identify mismatches between employees' names and social security numbers is through use of the Social Security Administration's "Employee Verification Service" (EVS). This system allows employers to submit a paper list of 50-300 employee names and SSNs for verification. Processing takes up to 30 days. At that point, it is up to the employer to contact each employee on the report whose information could not be verified, determine what is reflected on the employee's social security card, and update the employer's files with that information.

Before submitting the paper list, the employer must submit a registration form and a signed Privacy Act Statement to the SSA. The form and statement can be found on SSA's website. A paper list must be accompanied by a signed copy of the employer's privacy act statement. The service is free to employers so long as the purpose for the request is the preparation of employer reports. If you are using EVS to ensure that your employees' W-2 information is correct, you need to make sure that there is enough time for you to get the information into SSA, get the report of mismatches back, and get the employees' records corrected before year-end processing begins.

Once SSA has processed the registration form, the employer will receive a Requester Identification Code. This code should be shown on the paper submission and on any correspondence with SSA concerning a change in address, contact person, or telephone number. The code will not change from year to year. If you have any questions, call the EVS information line at 410-965-7140.

*Third-party EVS use.* EVS is also open to third-party service providers, who can participate in the service and offer it to their clients. The registration form and Privacy Act Statement for third-party providers are also found on SSA's website.

**SSN Verification Service.** In June 2005, the SSA made its Internet verification process – the Social Security Number Verification Service (SSNVS) – available to all employers after testing it as a pilot program for three years. SSNVS offers two options for name/SSN verification over the Internet:

---

5.    Seaworth v. Pearson, 203 F.3d 1056 (8 CA, 2000), cert. den., 121 S.Ct. 226 (2000); Baltgalvis v. Newport News Shipbuilding, Inc., 132 F. Supp 2d 414 (ED Va., 2001); Yisrael v. Per Scholas, Inc., No. 01 Civ. 8290 (DAB) (SD N.Y., 4-2-04)

- Verify up to 10 names and SSNs (per screen) online and receive immediate results. This method is generally used to verify newly hired employees.
- Upload batch files of up to 250,000 names and SSNs, and usually receive the results by the next government business day. This method suits employers that are verifying their entire data base or that hire a large number of workers at one time.

*Spreadsheet software program can be used.* Employers can use a spreadsheet software program to create an SSNVS file that is in the correct format. SSA offers the following formatting tips:

- If Excel is used, the file must not be in the ".xls" format.
- To create the file, one column must be at least 130 characters long. This column will hold all data for each record. To download the specifications for the record layout, go to www.ssa.gov/ employer/ssnvs_handbk.htm and click on "Submission File Format" (right hand column).
- To save an Excel file for processing:
  — Select Save As on the File Menu;
  — In the Save As dialog box, select the drop down box Save As type;
  — Select Formatted Text (space delimited) (*.prn); and
  — Type the filename and click Save
- Once you have saved your file, check it against the Submission File Format to ensure that the record length is 130 characters and that all fields are properly placed in their respective position. The Multiple Request Indicator field in positions 128-130 must be populated with "000" and may not be left blank.

*Registration is required.* SSNVS can be used by all employers and third-party service providers, but only to verify current or former employees and only for wage-reporting purposes. It cannot be used to verify job candidates' names and SSNs until they are hired. Here are the steps involved in using SSNVS:

- Register to use SSNVS at the Business Services Online portion of SSA's website – www.socialsecurity.gov/bso/bsowelcome.htm. Registration is required. Third-party providers only have to register once in their own company's name. Once you have completed the registration form and selected your own password, SSA will verify your identity against its records and display a user ID on the screen. You must select a new password every 365 days to keep the user ID from expiring.
- Request access and an activation code from the BSO home page. Log in and select Request Access and Activation Code. To access SSNVS you will need an activation code that will be mailed to your employer about 2 weeks after your request is confirmed.
- Your employer must give you the activation code before you can use SSNVS.
- Once you have the activation code, go to the BSO home page, select Login, and input your User ID, password, and activation code. At this point you will be able to use SSNVS, either by inputting information directly onto the screen (10 employees per screen) or submitting a file of up to 250,000 names/SSNs.

All the following information is required on phone verifications, but the date of birth and sex code, while desirable, are not required for paper and Internet verifications:

1. The employee's social security number
2. The employee's last name, first name, and middle initial
3. The employee's date of birth (MMDDCCYY)
4  The employee's sex code (M-Male; F-Female)

*Verification process.* Each SSN sent to the SSA through EVS or SSNVS will be returned (only the last 4 digits will be returned if the SSN matches SSA'a database) with one of the following verification codes:

- Blank = Verified
- 1 = SSN not in file (never issued to anyone)
- 2 = Name and DOB match, gender code does not match
- 3 = Name and gender code match; DOB does not match

- 4 = Name matches, DOB and gender code do not match
- 5 = Name does not match, DOB and gender code not checked
- 6 = SSN did not verify; other reason

*Death indicator.* The return file will also include a "death indicator" with one of the following codes:

- Y = SSA records indicate the person associated with that number is deceased
- N = SSA records indicate the person associated with that number is not deceased

*How to handle failed verifications.* The following steps should be taken when an employee's name/SSN combination fails to verify against SSA's data base:

- Compare the information that was submitted with the employer's employment records. If a typographical error was made, correct it and resend the corrected data to the SSA.
- If the employer's records match the information that was submitted, ask the employee to check his or her social security card and inform you of any difference between the information on the card and the employer's records. If an error is found in the employer's records, correct it and resend the corrected data to the SSA.
- If the employee's name and SSN match the employer's records, ask the employee to contact a local SSA office to determine and resolve the issue. Tell the employee to let you know of any changes made by the SSA, correct the employer's records, and resend the corrected data to the SSA.
- If the employee cannot provide a valid SSN, document your efforts to obtain the correct information and retain the documentation with your payroll records.
- If the employee no longer works for you, try to obtain the correct information from the employee and send it to the SSA on Form W-2c, *Corrected Wage and Tax Information.*
- If you are unable to contact the employee, document your efforts to do so.
- If you have already sent a Form W-2 with an incorrect name and/or SSN, then submit a Form W-2c to correct the mismatch. This can also be done through the BSO website.

**Restrictions on using SSNVS.** SSNVS is a useful system for verifying employees' names and SSNs for purposes of annual wage reporting, but it is not meant to be anything more than that. Here are some limitations on the use of SSNVS that employers need to keep in mind.

- Do not use SSNVS before hiring an employee. A firm job offer must be made before verification is appropriate.
- Do not use SSNVS as a basis in and of itself to take adverse action (e.g., termination, suspension) against an employee whose name and SSN cannot be verified. A mismatch does not imply that the employee (or the employer) intentionally provided incorrect information or that the employee is unauthorized to work in the U.S. Taking such adverse action could violate state or federal anti-discrimination law.
- If an employer wishes to verify employees' names and SSNs, it should apply its policy consistently rather than selectively.
- Third-party use of SSNVS is limited to organizations that contract with employers to handle wage reporting responsibilities or perform an administrative function directly related to annual wage reporting.
- SSNVS should not be used for non-wage reporting purposes, such as identity, credit checks, mortgage applications, etc.

**What to do when an employee changes his or her name.** When an employee presents a name change for inclusion in the payroll system, usually after a marriage or divorce, the employer should refuse to make the change until a new social security card with the employee's new name is presented for confirmation. If the employee has not obtained a new card, give him or her a Form SS-5 for completion and submission to the SSA. If the employer makes the name change in its payroll system before a new social security card is obtained, errors in posting earnings to the employee's social security account and in preparing the employee's Form W-2 could occur, leading to possibly lower social security benefits for the employee and penalties for the employer.

If an employee gets a new social security card to show his or her correct name and SSN after an adjustment to the employee's alien residence status, the employer should correct its records and show the new information on the employee's Form W-2. If Forms W-2 were filed for previous years showing the old name and SSN, the employer should file one Form W-2c to correct the name and SSN. Tell the employee to contact the local SSA office no earlier than 9 months after the Form W-2c is filed to make sure the records have been updated.

**Stricter security procedures delay SSN issuance for aliens.** Because of the heightened sensitivity to homeland security issues, SSA began a "Collateral Verification" program in 2002 under which it verifies the immigration documents presented by an alien against a USCIS database before assigning an SSN. SSA had always checked the USCIS database, but, because of an up-to-30-day delay in the updating of that database, if the person could not be found, but the presented documents looked valid, an SSN was issued. (SSNs for U.S. citizens are assigned after verification with a database of birth records.)

According to SSA, 55% of SSN applicants are verified immediately and receive their social security card within one week. About 15% take another 20 days to verify and get their SSN and card within 30 days. The remaining 30% of applicants are subject to a paper verification process involving SSA and USCIS. In all cases, SSA will send a letter to the SSN applicant documenting the application. Sometimes, once collateral verification has occurred and before a card has been issued, SSA will provide the SSN to the applicant over the phone once a security routine has been performed.

Other programs that may provide some short-term solutions include "Enumeration at Entry," whereby the U.S. State Department obtains the information necessary for an SSN by way of the Visa-issuance process and shares that with USCIS and SSA, and establishment of "Enumeration Centers," which can be staffed by SSA and USCIS employees who are expert at reviewing documents and can assign SSNs more quickly.

 **SSN IS NEEDED, EVEN IF THERE'S NO WITHHOLDING** Even if an employee is exempt from federal income tax withholding or social security and Medicare tax withholding (certain nonresident aliens), the employer must require an SSN from the employee to properly prepare and file information reports and statements (e.g., Form W-2).

## 6.2-2  SSA Sends Social Security Statements to Employees

**Social security benefits employers and employees.** To maximize the social security benefits employees will receive, it is important to credit employees' social security wages to their records for each year that they worked and paid social security taxes. Unfortunately, that does not always happen. Social Security Administration employees report that they cannot post more than $400 billion, accumulated since 1937, to any individual's account. That figure is growing by 3% each year!

Sometimes SSA cannot match the name and social security number on the employee's W-2 form to anyone on their data base. In order for the wages to post, the social security number and, generally, the first seven letters of the employee's last name must match. Because of mismatches, some employees may retire or become disabled and find that their benefits are less than they should be with some being ineligible for any benefits.

**SSA sends Social Security Statement to employees.** Beginning in October 1999, the SSA began sending its earnings verification statement – the Social Security Statement (SSS) – to all employees age 25 and over who are not already receiving social security benefits. The SSS replaced the Personal Earnings and Benefit Estimate Statement (PEBES), which employees had to request in order to receive it. The 4-page SSS allows employees to verify the accuracy of the information reported on their W-2 forms and posted on their earnings record. It also provides estimates of the monthly social security retirement, disability and survivors benefits that employees and their families could be eligible for currently and in the future.

The SSS is mailed annually about 3 months before the employee's birthday. Upon receipt, employees should verify that the name and social security number on the statement match the information on their social security card. To protect against identity theft, only the last 4 digits of the employee's SSN are shown on the statement. They should also determine whether the date of birth and earnings record are accurate. The statement tells employees what they should do if it contains incorrect information.

 **STATEMENTS CAN STILL BE REQUESTED** Employees may still request a Social Security Statement by filing Form SSA-7004, *Request for Earnings and Benefit Estimate Statement*. If they do so, they will not receive an automatically mailed statement during the same calendar year.

*SSS/Form W-2 relationship.* Because the Social Security Statement reflects information provided on an employee's Form W-2 (see the detailed discussion in Section 8.8), it is essential that employers submit timely and accurate Form W-2 information to the SSA. Discrepancies between information on the form and SSA's records prevent the proper crediting of wages to an individual's records. If the employer or the employee cannot be contacted to resolve the problem, the earnings will be put in the suspense file. In addition to affecting the employee's future social security benefits, uncredited earnings will also result in more questions for the payroll department when employees receive their statement.

*How employers can help.* For the inevitable questions that will come up, the SSA has offered some suggestions regarding when to refer the employee to the SSA and when it is appropriate for the payroll department to offer assistance.

The employer should have employees with a question contact the SSA when:

- their statement shows missing or incorrect earnings that occurred when the employee was: working for another employer; and/or working for more than one employer and more than one Form W-2 was submitted;

- the name and/or SSN on the statement is incorrect (i.e., does not match the employee's social security card or the employer's payroll records; or

- a state or local government employee receives a statement with missing or incorrect information pertaining to years before 1987.

The employer can offer assistance to the employee with a question if:

- it is determined that the misinformation on the statement is due to a filing error by the employer (e.g., an adjustment is made to the Form W-2 before it goes to the SSA but no copy of the corrected form is given to the employee); or

- the employee's name and/or SSN on their social security card does not match the information in the employer's payroll records.

The employer can encourage its employees to do their part in ensuring their wages are properly reported by:

- telling employees to promptly report name changes (e.g., after a marriage or divorce) by calling the SSA at 800-772-1213 and asking for Form SS-5, *Application for a Social Security Card*—telling the payroll department is not enough;

- validating the accuracy of the employee's name and number on the employer's payroll records before issuing a Form W-2; and

- being quick to respond to the SSA if contacted about name changes since it is likely that the SSA is attempting to resolve a name or SSN discrepancy reported on the Form W-2.

*Check records before submitting the W-2.* The SSA has also recommended that, before submitting Forms W-2 for its employees, employers should:

- review social security cards for each new hire and make sure the name and SSN on each are transcribed carefully and accurately;

- balance the sum of the 4 quarterly Form 941, *Employer's Quarterly Federal Tax Return,* wage totals with information reported on the W-2 forms;

- be careful when preparing Forms W-2 if the employer has both employees who are covered by social security and employees who are exempt from social security; and

- incorporate the SSA's standards and edits for paper and magnetic media Form W-2 filers into the payroll system, which will improve the integrity and quality of the wage reports.

*What to do when errors are detected.* If employee questions lead to the discovery that previously filed Forms W-2 have incorrect or missing social security earnings and/or taxes, a completed copy of Form W-2c, *Corrected Wage and Tax Statement,* should be filed with the SSA and given to the employee (see Section 8.9 for details). If a Form W-2 was not filed at all and should have been, an accurate original should be filed for the missing year.

 **E-FILING PROBLEMS** Electronic filers who have several employees with missing social security earnings should contact the SSA's Employer Service Liaison Officer for their region. (For a list of their phone numbers, see Section 8.14).

## 6.3 Employee Withholding Allowance Certificates

This section discusses the forms that employers, payers of pensions and annuities, and third-party payers of sick pay use to determine the proper amount of federal income tax to withhold from wages and other payments. These withholding allowance certificates provide the basis for calculations under the different withholding methods (see Section 6.4).

## 6.3-1 Form W-4

Every employer that pays wages is required to deduct and withhold federal income tax from those wages according to tables or procedures established by the Secretary of the Treasury, which has delegated that authority to the IRS.[6] The employer is also required to pay the full amount of income tax due on the wages to the Treasury, whether it deducts and withholds the full amount or not.[7]

Several methods can be used to calculate the correct amount of federal income tax to withhold from an employee's wages (see Section 6.4), but they all depend on information contained in Form W-4, *Employee's Withholding Allowance Certificate* (see page 6-12 for a sample filled-in Form W-4 and Appendix page A-91). A Form W-4 must be kept on file by the employer for each employee. If the employee does not provide an original, complete, valid, signed W-4, the employer must withhold as if the employee were single with zero withholding allowances.[8] Verbal or other written instructions are not enough to establish an employee's right to withholding allowances.

**When must a Form W-4 be submitted to the employer?** Newly hired employees should submit a completed and signed Form W-4 to their employer on or before the first day of work.[9] After that time, an employee must submit an amended W-4 within 10 days after a decrease in the number of withholding allowances to which the employee is entitled (e.g., the employee gets divorced). An employee who currently

---

6. IRC §3402(a)(1).
7. IRC §3403; IRS Reg. §31.3403-1.
8. IRS Reg. §31.3402(f)(2)-1(a).
9. IRC §3402(f)(2)(A); IRS Reg. §31.3402(f)(2)-1(a).

claims exempt from withholding must submit a new Form W-4 within 10 days after realizing that his or her claim of exemption is no longer valid because the employee will have income tax liability in the current year. Employees may file an amended W-4 form whenever the number of allowances they are entitled to increases or they feel they are entitled to claim exempt from withholding.[10]

**When is a Form W-4 effective?** A Form W-4 filed by a newly hired employee must be put into effect by the employer for the first payroll period ending after the form is filed.[11] An amended Form W-4 filed by a current employee because of a change in withholding allowances must be put into effect by the employer no later than the beginning of the first payroll period ending on or after the 30th day after the form is filed with the employer.[12] An employee's Form W-4 remains in effect until a new form is provided or the IRS tells the employer to withhold on a different basis.

> *Example:* Employee Harold submitted an amended Form W-4 on May 24 with one additional allowance reflecting the recent birth of his daughter. Harold is paid semimonthly on the 1st and 16th of each month, after payroll periods ending on the 11th and 26th. His employer must put his amended W-4 form into effect for the payroll period ending June 26 (and the July 1 payday), the first payroll period ending on or after June 23, 30 days after the amended W-4 was submitted.

The employer may put an amended Form W-4 into effect earlier than required.[13] However, if an employee submits an amended Form W-4 indicating changes in withholding allowances that will occur during the next calendar year (e.g., the employee's spouse or dependent died during the current year), the amended form may not be put into effect during the current year. By December 1 of each year, employers should ask their employees to file an amended Form W-4 for the next calendar year if they know the number of their allowances has changed or will change at the beginning of the year.[14]

**What does a Form W-4 tell the employer?** The Form W-4 is designed to tell the employer how many withholding allowances the employee is claiming, a number that will determine the amount to withhold from the employee's wages for federal income tax. The W-4 also indicates the employee's marital status and tells the employer if the employee is claiming totally exempt from withholding. It may also indicate that the employee wants an additional dollar amount withheld beyond the amount based on the withholding allowances claimed and whether the employee is a nonresident alien.

**What are withholding allowances?** For each withholding allowance claimed, the employee reduces the amount of wages subject to federal income tax withholding. Following is a list of the withholding allowances to which an employee is entitled.[15]

- One for the employee unless he or she can be claimed as a dependent by someone else.

- One for the employee's spouse unless the spouse is working and claiming an exemption for himself or herself.

- One for each dependent to be claimed on the employee's personal tax return (other than the employee's spouse).

- An additional allowance if the employee is single with one job (or has a second job paying less than $1,500 per year) or married with one job and the employee's spouse does not work (or earns less than $1,500 per year).

- An additional allowance if the employee's tax filing status is head of household.

---

10. IRC §3402(f)(2)(B); IRS Reg. §31.3402(f)(2)-1(b).
11. IRC §3402(f)(3)(A); IRS Reg. §31.3402(f)(3)-1(a).
12. IRC §3402(f)(3)(B)(i).
13. IRC §3402(f)(3)(B)(ii).
14. IRS Reg. §31.3402(f)(2)-1(c)(3).
15. IRC §3402(f)(1); IRS Reg. §31.3402(f)(1)-1.

- Additional allowances based on the employee's itemized deductions and income adjustments.

- An additional allowance if the employee has at least $1,500 in after-tax child care expenses for which a tax credit will be claimed.

- Additional allowances based on the employee's eligibility for the child tax credit.

**ONE ALLOWANCE FOR NONRESIDENTS** Nonresident aliens who are not residents of Canada, Mexico, or the Republic of Korea are allowed only one withholding allowance (see Section 14.2-3).[16]

**Dealing with a Form W-4 after a bankruptcy petition is filed.**[17] The employee/debtor is not required to file a new Form W-4 with the employer adjusting the employee's withholding allowances just because the employee has filed a Chapter 11 petition and the employee's post-petition wages are includible in the gross income of the bankruptcy estate. This is true even though the estate may be taxed at a higher tax rate than the employee and is entitled to only one personal exemption.

A new Form W-4 may be necessary, however, when the employee is no longer entitled to claim the same number of allowances claimed on the Form W-4 previously provided to the employer, such as for certain deductions or credits that now belong to the estate. Furthermore, even where not required, in some circumstances it may be prudent for the employee to file a new Form W-4 to increase the amount of income tax withheld from the employee's post-petition wages that will be allocated to the estate. Otherwise, estimated tax payments on behalf of the estate may be required in order to avoid an underpayment penalty.

*Example:* Employee Greg Gregson is married, his wife works outside the home and claims an allowance for herself on her Form W-4, and they have 3 children under age 12 living at home. They do not itemize their deductions, and their combined earnings for the year total $95,000. See below for Greg's filled-in 2008 Form W-4 which he submitted to his new employer.

------- Cut here and give Form W-4 to your employer. Keep the top part for your records. -------

| Form **W-4** Department of the Treasury Internal Revenue Service | **Employee's Withholding Allowance Certificate** ▶ Whether you are entitled to claim a certain number of allowances or exemption from withholding is subject to review by the IRS. Your employer may be required to send a copy of this form to the IRS. | OMB No. 1545-0074 2008 |
|---|---|---|

| **1** Type or print your first name and middle initial. Greg G. | Last name Gregson | **2** Your social security number 987 : 65 : 4321 |
|---|---|---|

| Home address (number and street or rural route) 111-22 Jurassic Drive | **3** ☐ Single ☑ Married ☐ Married, but withhold at higher Single rate. **Note.** If married, but legally separated, or spouse is a nonresident alien, check the "Single" box. |
|---|---|
| City or town, state, and ZIP code Anytown, VA 54321 | **4** If your last name differs from that shown on your social security card, check here. You must call 1-800-772-1213 for a replacement card. ▶ ☐ |

| **5** | Total number of allowances you are claiming (from line **H** above **or** from the applicable worksheet on page 2) | **5** | 7 |
|---|---|---|---|
| **6** | Additional amount, if any, you want withheld from each paycheck . . . . . . . . . . . . . . . | **6** | $ |
| **7** | I claim exemption from withholding for 2008, and I certify that I meet **both** of the following conditions for exemption. | | |
| | • Last year I had a right to a refund of **all** federal income tax withheld because I had **no** tax liability **and** | | |
| | • This year I expect a refund of **all** federal income tax withheld because I expect to have **no** tax liability. | | |
| | If you meet both conditions, write "Exempt" here . . . . . . . . . . . . . . . . ▶ | **7** | |

Under penalties of perjury, I declare that I have examined this certificate and to the best of my knowledge and belief, it is true, correct, and complete.

Employee's signature (Form is not valid unless you sign it.) ▶ *Greg g. Gregson*    Date ▶ *1/16/08*

| **8** Employer's name and address (Employer: Complete lines 8 and 10 only if sending to the IRS.) | **9** Office code (optional) | **10** Employer identification number (EIN) |
|---|---|---|

 **DON'T GIVE TAX ADVICE TO EMPLOYEES** If an employee asks a payroll practitioner how many allowances the employee can or should claim, the payroll practitioner should not advise the employee on this matter. Instead, the employee should be given a copy of IRS Publication 919, How Do I Adjust My Tax Withholding?, and the employee should determine the appropriate number of allowances to claim.

---

16.  IRC §3402(f)(6); IRS Reg. §31.3402(f)(6)-1.
17.  IRS Notice 2006-83, 2006-40 IRB 596.

**Some employees may claim exempt from withholding.** Employers do not have to withhold federal income tax from an employee's wages if the employee claims on the Form W-4 that he or she is exempt from withholding. In order to be exempt in 2007, the employee must complete **only** lines 1, 2, 3, 4 and 7 on the Form W-4 and certify that he or she:

- had a right to a refund of all federal income tax withheld in the prior year because the employee had no tax liability;

- expects to have no tax liability in the current year; and

- cannot be claimed as a dependent on someone else's income tax return if the employee's income will exceed $850 and will include more than $300 of nonwage income (e.g., dividends, interest) in 2008.[18]

> **WATCH OUT FOR STUDENTS CLAIMING EXEMPT** High school and college students are not automatically exempt from withholding, even though their prior year's withholding was totally refunded. They must meet all the tests for exemption other employees are required to meet, including the $900 limit on income (if this includes $300 in nonwage income) for dependents.

*Exemption must be claimed each year.* A claim of exemption from withholding is effective for one year, and a new Form W-4 attesting to the exempt status must be filed by February 15 of the following year or the employer must begin withholding from the next wage payment to the employee as if the employee were single with zero withholding allowances.[19] If, after filing a W-4 claiming exempt from withholding, the employee realizes he or she will incur tax liability for the current year, the employee has 10 days from that point to file an amended W-4 form.[20]

> **NONRESIDENT ALIENS TOO** A nonresident alien who claims exempt from withholding must file a new Form W-4 each year. (For other W-4 issues related to nonresident aliens, see Section 14.2-3).

*Spanish version of Form W-4 available.* Spanish-speaking employees may claim withholding allowances using Forma W-4(SP), *Certificado de Exencion de la Retencion del(la) Empleado(a)*, in place of Form W-4. Instructions, in Spanish, for completing Form W-4 or Forma W-4(SP) are available in Publication 579SP, Como Preparar la Declaracion de Impuesto Federal.

**When should an employer reject a W-4 Form?**[21] Although employers are not responsible for verifying the accuracy of the information on Forms W-4, an employer may not accept an invalid W-4 form from an employee. If one is presented, the employer must ask the employee to complete a new form. If the employee refuses to present a new, valid W-4 form, the employer must either keep withholding according to the most recent valid W-4 form on file for the employee or, if the employee is a new hire, withhold as if the employee were single with zero withholding allowances.

A W-4 form is invalid if it has been altered in any way or any unauthorized additions have been made to it. Alterations can include striking through any of the language on the form, such as the perjury statement, and unauthorized additions include any writing other than the entries requested. The only information that should be on the part of the form submitted to the employer is the employee's name, address, SSN, marital status, and total number of allowances claimed, any additional dollar amount to be withheld, whether the employee is claiming exempt from withholding, whether the employee's last name is different on his or her social security card, and the employee's signature under the perjury statement (along with the date signed). A Form W-4 is also invalid if the employee indicates to the employer in writing or verbally when the form is submitted that any information contained on the form is false.

---

18.  IRC §3402(n); IRS Reg. §31.3402(n)-1; Form W-4.
19.  IRS Reg. §31.3402(f)(4)-2(c).
20.  IRS Reg. §31.3402(f)(2)-1(b)(4); (f)(2)-1(c)(2).
21.  IRC §3402(f)(2)(A); IRS Reg. §31.3402(f)(2)-1(e); (f)(5)-1(b).

**CAUTION: FLAT DOLLAR AMOUNT OR PERCENTAGE INVALID** Employees cannot indicate on their W-4 form that they wish to have a flat dollar amount of tax or a percentage of earnings withheld rather than an amount based on the number of withholding allowances that can be claimed. A form altered to show the desire to have a specific dollar amount or a percentage of earnings withheld is invalid and must be rejected.[22] Line 6, which is used to indicate an *additional* amount to withhold, is not to be used for any other purpose, except that nonresident aliens are required to write "Nonresident Alien" or "NRA" above the dotted line (see Section 14.2-3).

 **DON'T TAKE TAX PAYMENTS FROM EMPLOYEES** Circular E warns employers not to take any withholding or estimated tax payments from employees in addition to withholding based on their Form W-4.

**Employees face penalties for false information.** Employees who claim more allowances on their Form W-4 than they are entitled to without a reasonable basis for the claim face a civil penalty of $500, in addition to any criminal penalties under the law.[23]

 **CHANGE IN PERJURY STATEMENT** Beginning with the 2005 Form W-4, the perjury statement (the "jurat") says that the employee has examined the form and that the entries on it are correct to the best of the employee's "knowledge and belief." Before 2005, the perjury statement was limited to the number of withholding allowances claimed or a claim of exempt status. The expanded perjury statement includes other elements on the form, such as the employee's name, address, marital status, and social security number.

**When must the employer submit Forms W-4 to the IRS?**[24] In most instances, employers must keep employees' W-4 forms in their records and are not required to send them to the IRS. However, the employer must submit a copy of the W-4 if:

- The IRS directs the employer to do so in a written notice to the employer; or
- The IRS directs the employer to do so in published guidance, such as a revenue procedure.

The notice may direct the employer to submit copies of Forms W-4:

- For one or more named employees;
- For all employees in a department or unit of the employer; or
- Where the W-4s meet certain criteria specified in the notice.

The notice will designate the IRS office where the copies of the Forms W-4 must be submitted. When sending Forms W-4 to the IRS, the employer must first complete Boxes 8 (Employer's name and address) and 10 (Employer Identification Number). As an alternative, the notice to the employer can require the employer to make copies of Forms W-4 available to IRS tax examiners for inspection.

 **CHANGE FROM EARLIER PROCEDURES** These Form W-4 submission procedures were first issued by the IRS in April 2005 and then finalized in July 2007. Previously, employers had to submit a copy of any W-4 on which an employee claimed more than 10 allowances or claimed exempt from withholding while earning more than an average of $200 per week. Some states continue to require employers to submit Form W-4 or a state equivalent to the state taxing authority if a certain number of allowances or an exemption from withholding is claimed. For more information, see Table 3.8 of APA's Guide to State Payroll Laws.

There is language immediately beneath the name of the form notifying employees that the number of allowances they claim or their claim of exempt status is subject to IRS review and that their employer may be required to send a copy of their Form W-4 to the IRS.

---

22.  IRS Reg. §31.3402(f)(5)-1; IRS Publication 15, Circular E, Employer's Tax Guide.
23.  IRC §6682; IRS Reg. §31.6682-1.
24.  IRS. Reg. §31.3402(f)(2)-1(g)(1)(i).

Even though a copy of the W-4 form has been submitted to the IRS, the employer must withhold based on that form unless and until the IRS notifies the employer the form is defective.[25]

Whether or not the employer submits a copy of an employee's Form W-4 to the IRS, the IRS may notify the employer in writing that the employee is not entitled to claim exempt from withholding or a total number of withholding allowances greater than the maximum number specified in the notice (commonly referred to as a "lock-in letter").[26] The letter will also specify the employee's marital status for purposes of calculating the required amount of withholding. The lock-in letter will specify the IRS office the employer can contact for further information.

A lock-in letter setting a maximum number of exemptions that an employee can claim may be issued by the IRS:

- *In cases where the employer has sent a copy of the employee's Form W-4 to the IRS,* after the IRS determines that the form contains a materially incorrect statement or the employee fails to respond adequately to a request for verification of the information on the form; or
- *In cases where the employer has not sent a copy of the employee's Form W-4 to the IRS,* after the IRS determines that the employee is not entitled to claim exempt from withholding or more than a specified number of withholding exemptions based on IRS records, such as the employee's personal income tax returns and Forms W-2.

The employer must withhold federal income tax from the employee's wages based on the maximum number of allowances specified in the lock-in letter.[27] The employer must put the lock-in letter into effect as of the date specified in the letter, which will be at least 45 calendar days after the date of the letter. The letters generally require employers to put the letter into effect with the first payroll after 60 days from the date of the letter. The purpose of this time period before implementation is to allow the employee to challenge the pending withholding adjustment with the IRS and for the IRS to make any adjustments in the letter that it finds are necessary.

Along with each lock-in letter, the IRS will send the employer a written notice for the employee that specifies the maximum number of withholding allowances permitted and the process by which the employee can submit information to the IRS to challenge that maximum.[28] The IRS will also mail a copy of the employee notice to the employee at his or her last known address.

If the employee is still employed by the employer, the employer must give the employee notice to the employee within 10 business days of receiving it from the IRS. The employer may use any reasonable business practice to furnish the copy of the notice to the employee – e.g., a paper copy of the notice or a copy transmitted using a secure electronic means of communication.

If the employee is no longer employed by the employer, it must send written notification of that fact to the IRS office designated in the employee notice.

The determination of whether an employee is employed by the employer is made as of the date of the notice, and is based on all the facts and circumstances, including whether the employer has treated the employment relationship as terminated for other purposes.[29] An employee who is not currently performing services is nevertheless employed for purposes of this rule if, on the date of the notice:

- the employer pays wages subject to income tax withholding to the employee with respect to prior employment on or after the date specified in the notice (e.g., severance pay),
- the employer reasonably expects the employee to resume performance of services for the employer within 12 months of the date of the notice, or

---

25.   IRS Reg. §31.3402(f)(2)-1(g)(1)(ii).
26.   IRS Reg. §34.3402(f)(2)-1(g)(2)(i).
27.   IRS Reg. §34.3402(f)(2)-1(g)(2)(v).
28.   IRS Reg. §34.3402(f)(2)-1(g)(2)(ii), (iii).
29.   IRS Reg. §31.3402(f)(2)-1(g)(2)(iii).

- the employee is on a bona fide leave of absence if the period of such leave does not exceed 12 months or if the individual retains a right to reemployment with the employer by contract or under an applicable statute, such as the Family and Medical Leave Act (see Section 4.2).

After the IRS has issued a lock-in letter and an employee notice, if the employee wants to claim complete exemption from withholding or more withholding allowances than the maximum specified by the IRS, the employee must submit a new Form W-4 and a written statement supporting the statements on the new form directly to the IRS.[30] The form and statement should not be submitted to the employer.

If an employer is required to provide a copy of the employee notice to an employee who is not currently employed but is expected to return to work within 12 months, and then returns to work more than 12 months after the date of the notice, the employer is not required to withhold based on the lock-in letter.[31] If an employee is terminated after the employer receives a lock-in letter for the employee, the employer must continue to withhold based on the lock-in letter for any wages paid to the employee after the termination date or if the employee returns to work within 12 months after the termination date.[32]

If the employee submits a new Form W-4 to the employer, the employer should disregard it until notified by the IRS to withhold based on that form. However, if the employee submits a Form W-4 resulting in more withholding than would result under the lock-in letter, then the employer should withhold based on that new Form W-4.

 **EXCLUSIONS FROM WITHHOLDING STILL APPLY** Receipt of an IRS lock-in letter does not impose a requirement to withhold income tax where one does not already exist. For example, an employer does not have to withhold income tax from payments made to an employee who is a U.S. citizen working in a foreign country if the employer reasonably believes that the payments are excluded from taxation under the foreign earned income exclusion (see Section 14.1-4). Issuance of a lock-in letter to an employer properly relying on this exclusion does not impose a withholding requirement on amounts covered by the exclusion. However, if withholding is required, such as on wages paid in excess of the amount excludable under §911, or if the exclusion ceases to apply, then the employer must withhold according to the lock-in letter.

**Substitute forms.** A substitute Form W-4 developed by the employer may be used if the employer also provides the tables, instructions, and worksheets contained in the Form W-4 in effect at that time. Employers must refuse to accept a substitute form developed by an employee, and any employee submitting such a form will be treated as having failed to furnish a Form W-4 to his or her employer.[33]

**Filing Form W-4 magnetically or electronically.** When directed by the IRS, employers may file Form W-4 information (whether submitted to the employer on paper or electronically) with the IRS magnetically (tape, cartridge, or diskette) or electronically. Before doing so, the employer must submit Form 4419, *Application for Filing Information Returns Electronically* (see Appendix page A-350), to request authorization. The specifications for filing Forms W-4 magnetically or electronically can be found in IRS Publication 1245, Specifications for Filing Form W-4, Employee's Withholding Allowance Certificate, Magnetically or Electronically. Additional information can be obtained by calling the Enterprise Computing Center-Martinsburg at 304-263-8700 or 866-455-7438 (toll-free). Form W-4 information must be filed using an eight-digit (YYYYMMDD) date field. Any Forms W-4 with supporting statements from the employee must be filed on paper.

**How long must the employer keep Forms W-4?** Employers must retain each employee's Form W-4, whether filed on paper or electronically, for at least four years after the date the last return was filed using the information on the Form W-4.[34]

---

30.   IRS Reg. §34.3402(f)(2)-1(g)(2)(x)(B).
31.   IRS Reg. §31.3402(f)(2)-1(g)(2)(vi).
32.   IRS Reg. §31.3402(f)(2)-1(g)(2)(ix).
33.   IRS Reg. §34.3402(f)(5)-1(a)(1).
34.   IRS Reg. §31.6001-1(e)(2); §31.6001-5(a)(13).

**Successor employers**. Where a successor employer acquires substantially all the property used in the trade or business of a predecessor employer (or a separate unit of the predecessor), and as part of the acquisition hires the predecessor's employees, there are two methods for dealing with the W-4 forms of those employees.[35] Under the standard procedure, the predecessor performs all the reporting duties for the employees it paid. Therefore, it must keep on file the Forms W-4 provided by its former employees, and the employees hired by the successor must provide their new employer with new Forms W-4.

Under the alternate procedure, the predecessor and successor agree that the predecessor will be relieved of certain reporting duties (e.g., providing Forms W-2) for its former employees who are hired by the successor. In that situation, the predecessor must transfer to the successor all current Forms W-4 for the transferred employees. The successor must keep the transferred employees' Forms W-4 on file and withhold according to the information provided on them. If the predecessor and successor both maintain compatible electronic Form W-4 systems (see the discussion following), the W-4s may be electronically transferred from the predecessor to the successor. The successor also has the option of acquiring and maintaining the predecessor's electronic W-4 system. If neither of these electronic transfer options is used, the transferred employees must provide new Forms W-4 to the successor employer, either electronically or on paper.

 **BE CAREFUL** If the alternate procedure applies, the successor employer is responsible for submitting to the IRS any Forms W-4 that fall under the requirements for submission and that were provided to the predecessor during the quarter of the W-4 transfer and the preceding quarter.

**Electronic Forms W-4**.[36] IRS regulations allow all Forms W-4 to be filed with employers electronically, so long as the employer's system meets the following requirements:

- The electronic system must ensure that the information received is the information sent by the employee.

- The system must document each time an employee accesses the system that results in the filing of a new or amended Form W-4.

- The access procedures must make it reasonably certain that the person filing the Form W-4 is the employee identified in the form.

- The electronically filed Form W-4 must provide the employer with the same information as the paper Form W-4 (the certificate only, not the worksheets); but the employee must be provided with all the worksheet information on the form so that an accurate calculation of allowances can be made.

- If the IRS sends a notice to an employer limiting the number of an employee's withholding allowances because the employee filed a defective Form W-4 (see the discussion earlier in this section), the electronic system, along with the rest of the employer's payroll system, must not allow an employee to file an electronic Form W-4 that does not comply with the notice.

- If the IRS requests it, the employer must provide a hard copy of the electronic Form W-4 and a statement that, to the best of the employer's knowledge, the electronic Form W-4 was filed by the named employee. The hard copy must contain the same information as a paper Form W-4, but it does not have to be a facsimile of the paper form.

- The electronically filed W-4 must be signed by the employee under penalties of perjury.

*Perjury statement and signature requirements*. The perjury statement in the electronic form must contain the same language that appears on the paper Form W-4. The system must tell the employee that he or she must make the declaration contained in the perjury statement and that the declaration is made by signing the Form W-4. The instructions and perjury statement must immediately follow the employee's income tax withholding selections (e.g., number of allowances, additional withholding amount) and immediately precede the employee's electronic signature.

---

35.    Rev. Proc. 2004-53, 2004-34 IRB 320.
36.    IRS Reg. §31.3402(f)(5)-1(c).

The employee's electronic signature must identify the employee filing the electronic Form W-4 and "authenticate" and "verify" the filing in the same way it does for a paper Form W-4. The signature must also be the final entry in the form. The regulations do not prescribe any particular form for the electronic signature, so long as it meets these requirements, which leaves the design of the signature (e.g., personal identification number, secured password) up to the employer.

**Employers can require electronic W-4 filing**. The regulations allow employers to adopt an electronic system under which all employees must file Forms W-4 electronically. However, in an explanation accompanying the regulations, the IRS said that it expects employers will make a paper option reasonably available upon request to any employee who has a "serious objection" to using the electronic system or whose access to or ability to use the system is limited (e.g., by a disability). The IRS also said the paper option would be satisfied if the employer tells employees how they can get a paper Form W-4 and where they should submit the completed form. The Service also warns employers that they must comply with other applicable laws governing employment, such as the Americans With Disabilities Act, and emphasizes that complying with the final regulations does not guarantee compliance with those other laws.

**Form W-4 used to report new hires for child support purposes**. See Section 1.9 for information on how employers use Form W-4 to report newly hired and rehired employees to aid in state and federal efforts to increase child support withholding and detect welfare and unemployment insurance fraud. More information than that provided by the employee is required to be placed on the Form W-4 before it is used to report new hires (employer's name, address, and EIN).

## 6.3-2 Form W-4P

In most instances, federal income tax must be withheld from pension and annuity payments made to retired employees. Unless directed otherwise, payers and plan administrators must withhold certain amounts, depending on whether the payments are periodic, nonperiodic, or eligible rollover distributions. Retirees can have input into the amount withheld if they file a Form W-4P, *Withholding Certificate for Pension or Annuity Payments* (see Appendix page A-93). By completing a Form W-4P, retirees can:

- elect not to have any income tax withheld (except for payments sent to U.S. citizens or resident aliens outside the U.S.);

- designate a certain number of withholding allowances to be used in calculating the amount withheld; or

- indicate an additional dollar amount to be withheld.

For details on the amount to withhold from pension and annuity payments, see Section 6.4-5. If a Form W-4P is not submitted, the employer must withhold on periodic pension payments as if the payee is married claiming 3 withholding allowances.

Forms W-4P may be filed electronically if the payer has a system for doing so. The requirements for the system are similar to those governing electronic Forms W-4.

## 6.3-3 Form W-4S

When an employee who is disabled by a non job-related illness or injury is being paid sick pay by a third-party insurer, no federal income tax will be withheld unless the employee requests it by submitting Form W-4S, *Request for Federal Income Tax Withholding From Sick Pay* (see Appendix page A-97) to the third party. The employee uses the form to tell the third party to withhold a flat dollar amount. The minimum amount that can be withheld is $20 per week, and after withholding, the employee must receive at least $10. If a payment is smaller or larger than a regular payment, the amount withheld must be changed in the same proportion as the payment.[37] Forms W-4S may be filed electronically if the payer has a system for doing so.

---

37.    IRC §3402(o); IRS Reg. §31.3402(o)-3; IRS Ann. 99-6, 1999-4 IRB 24.

The requirements for the system are similar to those governing electronic Forms W-4.

For more on third-party sick pay, see Section 4.3-2.

# 6.3-4  State Employee Withholding Allowance Certificates

More than 40 states have a state income tax and require withholding from wages to collect it. While many of those states allow employers to use the employee's federal Form W-4 to calculate state income tax withholding, others require that a state withholding allowance certificate be completed and submitted to the employer. Following is a table showing each state's requirements. States without an income tax are not included. [For more information on state employee withholding allowance certificates, see Table 3.8 of *APA's Guide to State Payroll Laws.*]

Table 6.1

| State | State Form | Federal W-4 OK? |
|---|---|---|
| Alabama | A-4, Employee's Withholding Exemption Certificate | No |
| Arizona | A-4, Employee's Arizona Withholding Percentage Election | No |
| Arkansas | AR4EC, Employee's Withholding Exemption Certificate | Yes(1) |
| California | DE 4, Employee's Withholding Allowance Certificate | Yes(1) |
| Colorado | No state form | Yes |
| Connecticut | CT-W4, Employee's Withholding Certificate | No |
| Delaware | No state form | Yes (2) |
| Dist. of Col. | D-4, Employee's Withholding Allowance Certificate | No |
| Georgia | G-4, Employee's Withholding Allowance Certificate | Yes (1) |
| Hawaii | HW-4, Employee's Withholding Allowance and Status Certificate | No |
| Idaho | No state form | Yes |
| Illinois | IL-W-4, Employee's Illinois Withholding Allowance Certificate | No |
| Indiana | WH-4, Employee's Withholding Exemption and County Status Certificate | No |
| Iowa | IA W4, Centralized Employee Registry Reporting Form/Employee Withholding Allowance Certificate | No |
| Kansas | K-4, Kansas Employee's Withholding Allowance Certificate | No, eff. 1-1-08 |
| Kentucky | K-4, Employee's Withholding Exemption Certificate | No |
| Louisiana | L-4 (R-1300), Employee Withholding Exemption Certificate | No |
| Maine | W-4ME, Employee's Maine Withholding Allowance Certificate | No(3) |
| Maryland | MW 507, Employee's Maryland Withholding Exemption Certificate | No |
| Massachusetts | M-4, Massachusetts Employee's Withholding Exemption Certificate | Yes(4) |
| Michigan | MI-W4, Employee's Michigan Withholding Exemption Certificate | No |
| Minnesota | No state form | Yes(5) |
| Mississippi | 89-350, Mississippi Employee's Withholding Exemption Certificate | No |
| Missouri | MO-W4, Employee's Withholding Allowance Certificate | No |
| Montana | No state form | Yes |

| State | State Form | Federal W-4 OK? |
|-------|-----------|-----------------|
| Nebraska | No state form | Yes |
| New Jersey | NJ-W4, Employee's Withholding Allowance Certificate | Yes(1) |
| New Mexico | No state form | Yes |
| New York | IT-2104, Employee's Withholding Allowance Certificate | Yes(1) |
| North Carolina | NC-4, Employee's Withholding Allowance Certificate | No |
| North Dakota | No state form | Yes |
| Ohio | IT-4, Employee's Withholding Exemption Certificate | No |
| Oklahoma | No state form | Yes |
| Oregon | No state form | Yes |
| Pennsylvania | No state form | No(6) |
| Rhode Island | No state form | Yes |
| South Carolina | No state form | Yes(7) |
| Utah | No state form | Yes |
| Vermont | W-4VT, Vermont Employee's Withholding Allowance Certificate | Yes |
| Virginia | VA-4, Employee's Virginia Income Tax Withholding Exemption Certificate | No |
| West Virginia | WV/IT-104, West Virginia Employee's Withholding Exemption Certificate | Yes(1) |
| Wisconsin | WT-4, Employee's Wisconsin Withholding Exemption Certificate/New Hire Reporting | Yes(1) |

Footnotes to Table 6.1

(1) State form should be filed if number of allowances and /or additional dollar amount to be withheld for state purposes will be different than on the federal Form W-4.

(2) If state and federal deductions and credits differ, employee should file federal Form W-4, or equivalent provided by the employer, and indicate on it "For State of Delaware Purposes."

(3) Maine designed Form W-4ME to be used to calculate employee withholding allowances for state income tax purposes in response to federal child tax credit legislation.

(4) If the same number of state and federal exemptions are claimed, complete federal Form W-4 only.

(5) If employees claim fewer Minnesota withholding allowances than federal allowances, have them complete a second W-4 form to list the Minnesota allowances claimed. Write "Minnesota Only" and "Federal Only" across the top of the respective forms.

(6) Pennsylvania does not permit any withholding exemptions. The tax rate is 3.07%.

(7) If an employee claims a different number of exemptions for state purposes, file a separate Form W-4 for state purposes and indicate on the form "For State Purposes." An employee is not allowed to claim a greater number of exemptions for state purposes than for federal purposes.

# 6.4  Methods of Withholding Federal Income Tax

The Internal Revenue Code allows employers to choose from several different methods for calculating the amount to withhold from an employee's wages for federal income tax. The most popular methods are the wage-bracket method and the percentage method. Employers with automated payroll systems or that use a service bureau (outside contractor) to process their payroll generally use the percentage method of withholding. Alternative withholding methods are also available for special needs and situations (e.g., supplemental wages, annualized wages, cumulative wages).

**Payroll period.** Whatever method is used, the basis for the calculation is the employer's "payroll period," or the frequency with which it pays its employees. Employers can have one (or several) of many payroll periods, including weekly, biweekly, semimonthly, monthly, quarterly, semiannual, annual, daily, or miscellaneous (see Section 5.1 for state laws controlling when employees must be paid). The withholding method chosen by the employer is then applied to wages earned during the payroll period to determine the amount to withhold.

**Rounding permitted.** When determining the amount to be withheld, employers may round off the withholding amount to the nearest dollar (not necessary under the wage-bracket method, where table amounts are expressed in whole dollars). Rounding is accomplished by increasing amounts of $.50 or more to the next whole dollar and by dropping amounts under $.50 (e.g., $1.52 is rounded to $2.00, while $1.48 is rounded to $1.00). If an employer uses rounding, it must do so consistently.[38]

# 6.4-1 Wage-Bracket Method

For non-computerized payrolls, and for manual checks cut by employers whose payrolls are automated, the easiest withholding method to use is the wage-bracket method.[39] Using this method, the amount to withhold is taken directly from wage-bracket tables issued by the IRS in Publication 15, *Circular E, Employer's Tax Guide* (see Appendix pages A-6 to A-25), which is published late each year for use during the upcoming year. There are two tables for each of the following payroll periods (one for single and one for married persons): weekly, biweekly, semimonthly, monthly, and daily or miscellaneous. The amounts in the tables are expressed in whole dollars.

**How to use the wage-bracket tables.** There are a few simple steps to take in calculating an employee's withholding using the wage-bracket tables.

1. Find the table that applies to the employee's payroll period and marital status (e.g., married persons—semimonthly payroll period).

2. Determine the employee's wages subject to federal income tax withholding by reducing the employee's gross wages by any pre-tax deductions.

3. Locate the wage bracket in the first two columns in which the employee's federal income taxable wage payment for the payroll period can be found (look on the second page of the table for wage amounts higher than those at the bottom of the first page).

4. Move across from the wage-bracket amount to the tax amount found in the column headed by the number of withholding allowances claimed by the employee on Line 5 of his or her Form W-4.

5. Add any extra dollar amount of withholding indicated by the employee on Line 6 of the Form W-4.

*Example:* Employee Patricia is married and receives $1,590 in wages subject to federal income tax withholding from her employer on a biweekly basis. Patricia claims 5 withholding allowances on her Form W-4. For wages paid in 2008, her employer goes to the married persons—biweekly payroll period table (reprinted below) and finds the appropriate wage bracket, $1,580 - $1,600. Under column 5, the proper amount to withhold from Patricia's wages is $61.

---

38.     IRC §3402(b)(4), (c)(5); IRS Reg. §31.3402(c)-1(e).
39.     IRC §3402(c); IRS Reg. §31.3402(c)-1; IRS Pub. 15, Circular E, Employer's Tax Guide.

## MARRIED Persons—BIWEEKLY Payroll Period
### (For Wages Paid in 2008)

| If the wages are— | | And the number of withholding allowances claimed is— | | | | | | | | | | |
|---|---|---|---|---|---|---|---|---|---|---|---|---|
| At least | But less than | 0 | 1 | 2 | 3 | 4 | 5 | 6 | 7 | 8 | 9 | 10 |
| | | The amount of income tax to be withheld is— | | | | | | | | | | |
| $1,380 | $1,400 | $132 | $112 | $92 | $72 | $54 | $41 | $27 | $14 | $1 | $0 | $0 |
| 1,400 | 1,420 | 135 | 115 | 95 | 75 | 56 | 43 | 29 | 16 | 3 | 0 | 0 |
| 1,420 | 1,440 | 138 | 118 | 98 | 78 | 58 | 45 | 31 | 18 | 5 | 0 | 0 |
| 1,440 | 1,460 | 141 | 121 | 101 | 81 | 61 | 47 | 33 | 20 | 7 | 0 | 0 |
| 1,460 | 1,480 | 144 | 124 | 104 | 84 | 64 | 49 | 35 | 22 | 9 | 0 | 0 |
| 1,480 | 1,500 | 147 | 127 | 107 | 87 | 67 | 51 | 37 | 24 | 11 | 0 | 0 |
| 1,500 | 1,520 | 150 | 130 | 110 | 90 | 70 | 53 | 39 | 26 | 13 | 0 | 0 |
| 1,520 | 1,540 | 153 | 133 | 113 | 93 | 73 | 55 | 41 | 28 | 15 | 1 | 0 |
| 1,540 | 1,560 | 156 | 136 | 116 | 96 | 76 | 57 | 43 | 30 | 17 | 3 | 0 |
| 1,560 | 1,580 | 159 | 139 | 119 | 99 | 79 | 59 | 45 | 32 | 19 | 5 | 0 |
| 1,580 | 1,600 | 162 | 142 | 122 | 102 | 82 | 61 | 47 | 34 | 21 | 7 | 0 |
| 1,600 | 1,620 | 165 | 145 | 125 | 105 | 85 | 64 | 49 | 36 | 23 | 9 | 0 |
| 1,620 | 1,640 | 168 | 148 | 128 | 108 | 88 | 67 | 51 | 38 | 25 | 11 | 0 |
| 1,640 | 1,660 | 171 | 151 | 131 | 111 | 91 | 70 | 53 | 40 | 27 | 13 | 0 |
| 1,660 | 1,680 | 174 | 154 | 134 | 114 | 94 | 73 | 55 | 42 | 29 | 15 | 2 |
| 1,680 | 1,700 | 177 | 157 | 137 | 117 | 97 | 76 | 57 | 44 | 31 | 17 | 4 |
| 1,700 | 1,720 | 180 | 160 | 140 | 120 | 100 | 79 | 59 | 46 | 33 | 19 | 6 |
| 1,720 | 1,740 | 183 | 163 | 143 | 123 | 103 | 82 | 62 | 48 | 35 | 21 | 8 |
| 1,740 | 1,760 | 186 | 166 | 146 | 126 | 106 | 85 | 65 | 50 | 37 | 23 | 10 |
| 1,760 | 1,780 | 189 | 169 | 149 | 129 | 109 | 88 | 68 | 52 | 39 | 25 | 12 |
| 1,780 | 1,800 | 192 | 172 | 152 | 132 | 112 | 91 | 71 | 54 | 41 | 27 | 14 |
| 1,800 | 1,820 | 195 | 175 | 155 | 135 | 115 | 94 | 74 | 56 | 43 | 29 | 16 |
| 1,820 | 1,840 | 198 | 178 | 158 | 138 | 118 | 97 | 77 | 58 | 45 | 31 | 18 |
| 1,840 | 1,860 | 201 | 181 | 161 | 141 | 121 | 100 | 80 | 60 | 47 | 33 | 20 |
| 1,860 | 1,880 | 204 | 184 | 164 | 144 | 124 | 103 | 83 | 63 | 49 | 35 | 22 |
| 1,880 | 1,900 | 207 | 187 | 167 | 147 | 127 | 106 | 86 | 66 | 51 | 37 | 24 |
| 1,900 | 1,920 | 210 | 190 | 170 | 150 | 130 | 109 | 89 | 69 | 53 | 39 | 26 |
| 1,920 | 1,940 | 213 | 193 | 173 | 153 | 133 | 112 | 92 | 72 | 55 | 41 | 28 |
| 1,940 | 1,960 | 216 | 196 | 176 | 156 | 136 | 115 | 95 | 75 | 57 | 43 | 30 |
| 1,960 | 1,980 | 219 | 199 | 179 | 159 | 139 | 118 | 98 | 78 | 59 | 45 | 32 |
| 1,980 | 2,000 | 222 | 202 | 182 | 162 | 142 | 121 | 101 | 81 | 61 | 47 | 34 |
| 2,000 | 2,020 | 225 | 205 | 185 | 165 | 145 | 124 | 104 | 84 | 64 | 49 | 36 |
| 2,020 | 2,040 | 228 | 208 | 188 | 168 | 148 | 127 | 107 | 87 | 67 | 51 | 38 |
| 2,040 | 2,060 | 231 | 211 | 191 | 171 | 151 | 130 | 110 | 90 | 70 | 53 | 40 |
| 2,060 | 2,080 | 234 | 214 | 194 | 174 | 154 | 133 | 113 | 93 | 73 | 55 | 42 |
| 2,080 | 2,100 | 237 | 217 | 197 | 177 | 157 | 136 | 116 | 96 | 76 | 57 | 44 |
| 2,100 | 2,120 | 240 | 220 | 200 | 180 | 160 | 139 | 119 | 99 | 79 | 59 | 46 |
| 2,120 | 2,140 | 243 | 223 | 203 | 183 | 163 | 142 | 122 | 102 | 82 | 62 | 48 |
| 2,140 | 2,160 | 246 | 226 | 206 | 186 | 166 | 145 | 125 | 105 | 85 | 65 | 50 |
| 2,160 | 2,180 | 249 | 229 | 209 | 189 | 169 | 148 | 128 | 108 | 88 | 68 | 52 |
| 2,180 | 2,200 | 252 | 232 | 212 | 192 | 172 | 151 | 131 | 111 | 91 | 71 | 54 |
| 2,200 | 2,220 | 255 | 235 | 215 | 195 | 175 | 154 | 134 | 114 | 94 | 74 | 56 |
| 2,220 | 2,240 | 258 | 238 | 218 | 198 | 178 | 157 | 137 | 117 | 97 | 77 | 58 |
| 2,240 | 2,260 | 261 | 241 | 221 | 201 | 181 | 160 | 140 | 120 | 100 | 80 | 60 |
| 2,260 | 2,280 | 264 | 244 | 224 | 204 | 184 | 163 | 143 | 123 | 103 | 83 | 63 |
| 2,280 | 2,300 | 267 | 247 | 227 | 207 | 187 | 166 | 146 | 126 | 106 | 86 | 66 |
| 2,300 | 2,320 | 270 | 250 | 230 | 210 | 190 | 169 | 149 | 129 | 109 | 89 | 69 |
| 2,320 | 2,340 | 273 | 253 | 233 | 213 | 193 | 172 | 152 | 132 | 112 | 92 | 72 |
| 2,340 | 2,360 | 276 | 256 | 236 | 216 | 196 | 175 | 155 | 135 | 115 | 95 | 75 |
| 2,360 | 2,380 | 279 | 259 | 239 | 219 | 199 | 178 | 158 | 138 | 118 | 98 | 78 |
| 2,380 | 2,400 | 282 | 262 | 242 | 222 | 202 | 181 | 161 | 141 | 121 | 101 | 81 |
| 2,400 | 2,420 | 285 | 265 | 245 | 225 | 205 | 184 | 164 | 144 | 124 | 104 | 84 |
| 2,420 | 2,440 | 288 | 268 | 248 | 228 | 208 | 187 | 167 | 147 | 127 | 107 | 87 |
| 2,440 | 2,460 | 291 | 271 | 251 | 231 | 211 | 190 | 170 | 150 | 130 | 110 | 90 |
| 2,460 | 2,480 | 294 | 274 | 254 | 234 | 214 | 193 | 173 | 153 | 133 | 113 | 93 |
| 2,480 | 2,500 | 297 | 277 | 257 | 237 | 217 | 196 | 176 | 156 | 136 | 116 | 96 |
| 2,500 | 2,520 | 300 | 280 | 260 | 240 | 220 | 199 | 179 | 159 | 139 | 119 | 99 |
| 2,520 | 2,540 | 303 | 283 | 263 | 243 | 223 | 202 | 182 | 162 | 142 | 122 | 102 |
| 2,540 | 2,560 | 306 | 286 | 266 | 246 | 226 | 205 | 185 | 165 | 145 | 125 | 105 |
| 2,560 | 2,580 | 309 | 289 | 269 | 249 | 229 | 208 | 188 | 168 | 148 | 128 | 108 |
| 2,580 | 2,600 | 312 | 292 | 272 | 252 | 232 | 211 | 191 | 171 | 151 | 131 | 111 |
| 2,600 | 2,620 | 315 | 295 | 275 | 255 | 235 | 214 | 194 | 174 | 154 | 134 | 114 |
| 2,620 | 2,640 | 318 | 298 | 278 | 258 | 238 | 217 | 197 | 177 | 157 | 137 | 117 |
| 2,640 | 2,660 | 321 | 301 | 281 | 261 | 241 | 220 | 200 | 180 | 160 | 140 | 120 |
| 2,660 | 2,680 | 324 | 304 | 284 | 264 | 244 | 223 | 203 | 183 | 163 | 143 | 123 |
| 2,680 | 2,700 | 327 | 307 | 287 | 267 | 247 | 226 | 206 | 186 | 166 | 146 | 126 |

**$2,700 and over**     Use Table 2(b) for a **MARRIED person** on page 38. Also see the instructions on page 36.

# Section 6: Withholding Taxes

**Using the daily or miscellaneous payroll period tables.** The wage-bracket tables for a daily or miscellaneous payroll period are used when wages are paid for a period other than a regular payroll period or without regard to a payroll period. The withholding amount is calculated as follows:

1. Determine the number of days in the period. When wages are paid for a period that is not a payroll period, the miscellaneous period equals the number of days in the period in relation to which wages are paid (including Saturdays, Sundays, and holidays). When wages are paid without regard to any period, the miscellaneous period dates back from the date of payment to the later of the last wage payment date, January 1, or the date of hire (including Saturdays, Sundays, and holidays).

2. Divide the current federal income taxable wage payment by the result in No. 1 to get a daily wage rate.

3. Use the daily or miscellaneous payroll period wage-bracket tables to calculate withholding on the daily wage rate.

4. Multiply the result in No. 3 (daily withholding rate) by the result in No. 1 (days since last wage payment) to get the amount to withhold from the current wage payment.

**Special situations.** While the application of the wage-bracket withholding method is relatively straightforward in most situations, there are several applications that may require further explanation.

*Wage payments above the maximum table amount.* Each wage-bracket table has a maximum wage payment amount beyond which the table cannot be used (e.g., for single persons—weekly payroll period, the maximum amount is $1,250). For wage payments equaling or exceeding the maximum amount, the percentage method of withholding must be used (see Section 6.4-2).

*Wage payments that equal a wage-bracket amount.* Where an employee's wage payment is equal to the higher amount in a wage bracket, the next highest wage bracket must be used to calculate the withholding. This is because the wage brackets include wage payments that equal or exceed the lower number but that are less than the higher number.

> ***Example:*** Employee George is single and in 2008 he is paid $880 in federal income taxable wages biweekly. In the single persons—biweekly payroll period table, there are wage brackets of $860 - $880 and $880 - $900. Because the lower wage bracket includes only those wage payments that are at least $860 but less than $880, George's withholding must be calculated using the $880 - $900 wage bracket for wage payments that are at least $880 but less than $900.

*Employees claiming more than 10 allowances.* Each wage-bracket table has columns for up to 10 withholding allowances. When an employee claims more than 10 allowances the employer has a choice of two methods for determining the amount to withhold.

1. Treat the employee as if he or she is claiming only 10 allowances, although this may result in overwithholding.

2. Follow these steps to take into account the extra withholding allowances:

   a. Multiply the number of withholding allowances exceeding 10 by the value of one allowance for the applicable payroll period (see Table 6.2).

   b. Subtract the result of this calculation from the employee's wage payment subject to federal income tax withholding.

   c. Use this amount and the column for 10 allowances to calculate the tax amount to withhold.

*Example:* Employee Sharleen is married, is paid $2,555 in federal taxable wages semimonthly in 2008, and claims 13 allowances. If the employer uses Method 1 to calculate her withholding, it will withhold $81 from her wages (use the withholding tables in Circular E at Appendix page A-17). If the employer uses Method 2, the withholding is calculated as follows:

> Excess allowances = 13 - 10 = 3
> Semimonthly allowance value from Table 6.2 = $145.83
> 3 x $145.83 = $437.49
> $2,555 - $437.49 = $2,117.51
> Withholding on $2,117.51 at 10 allowances = $32

The difference in the amount withheld under the two methods for all of 2008 (assuming Sharleen has no changes in salary, marital status, or number of allowances for the entire year) is $1,176 [($81 - $32) x 24 wage payments].

# 6.4-2 Percentage Method

Because of more numerous and complicated calculations, the percentage method of withholding is generally used by employers with automated payroll systems or by service bureaus that handle payroll processing for many different employers.[40] The percentage method is somewhat more flexible than the wage-bracket method and can be used for more different payroll periods, including quarterly, semiannual, and annual. The percentage method tables are also found in Circular E.

**How to use the percentage method tables.** There are several steps that must be taken in calculating the amount to withhold using the percentage method.

1. Find the number of withholding allowances claimed on Line 5 of the employee's Form W-4 in the left-hand column of the allowance table provided by APA (Table 6.2).

2. Move straight across to the column corresponding to the employee's payroll period to find the value of the withholding allowances claimed by the employee.

3. Determine the employee's wages subject to federal income tax withholding by reducing the employee's gross wages by any pre-tax deductions.

4. Subtract the value of the withholding allowances (result from No. 2) from the employee's federal income taxable wage payment.

5. Locate the percentage method withholding table for the employee's payroll period and marital status—(a) for single, (b) for married (see Appendix pages A-4 and A-5).

6. Use the formula detailed in the table to calculate the withholding tax.

7. Add any extra dollar amount of withholding from Line 6 of the employee's W-4 form.

---

40.    IRC §3402(b); IRS Reg. §31.3402(b)-1; IRS Pub. 15, Circular E, Employer's Tax Guide.

Table 6.2

| | WEEKLY | BIWEEKLY | SEMI-MONTHLY | MONTHLY | QUARTERLY | SEMI-ANNUALLY | ANNUALLY | DAILY OR MISC. |
|---|---|---|---|---|---|---|---|---|
| **ALLOWANCE TABLE FOR WAGES PAID IN 2008** | | | | | | | | |
| If the number of withholding allowances is: | | | | And wages are paid – | | | | |
| | | | The total amount of withholding allowances for the payroll period is: | | | | | |
| 0 | $ 0 | $ 0 | $ 0 | $ 0 | $ 0 | $ 0 | $ 0 | $ 0 |
| 1 | 67.31 | 134.62 | 145.83 | 291.67 | 875.00 | 1,750.00 | 3,500.00 | 13.46 |
| 2 | 134.62 | 269.24 | 291.66 | 583.34 | 1,750.00 | 3,500.00 | 7,000.00 | 26.92 |
| 3 | 201.93 | 403.86 | 437.49 | 875.01 | 2,625.00 | 5,250.00 | 10,500.00 | 40.38 |
| 4 | 269.24 | 538.48 | 583.32 | 1,166.68 | 3,500.00 | 7,000.00 | 14,000.00 | 53.84 |
| 5 | 336.55 | 673.10 | 729.15 | 1,458.35 | 4,375.00 | 8,750.00 | 17,500.00 | 67.30 |
| 6 | 403.86 | 807.72 | 874.98 | 1,750.02 | 5,250.00 | 10,500.00 | 21,000.00 | 80.76 |
| 7 | 471.17 | 942.34 | 1,020.81 | 2,041.69 | 6,125.00 | 12,250.00 | 24,500.00 | 94.22 |
| 8 | 538.48 | 1,076.96 | 1,166.64 | 2,333.36 | 7,000.00 | 14,000.00 | 28,000.00 | 107.68 |
| 9 | 605.79 | 1,211.58 | 1,312.47 | 2,625.03 | 7,875.00 | 15,750.00 | 31,500.00 | 121.14 |
| 10 | 673.10 | 1,346.20 | 1,458.30 | 2,916.70 | 8,750.00 | 17,500.00 | 35,000.00 | 134.60 |

***Example:*** In 2008, employee Harvey is paid federal income taxable wages of $2,300 biweekly and is married with 3 allowances claimed on his Form W-4. His withholding is calculated using the percentage method as follows:

| | |
|---|---|
| Taxable wages | $2,300.00 |
| Allowance value ($134.62 x 3) | - 403.86 |
| Wages subject to withholding | $1,896.14 |
| | |
| Percentage table formula | $1,896.14 |
| | - 906.00 |
| | $990.14 |
| | x .15 |
| | $ 148.52 |
| | + 59.80 |
| Tax to withhold | $ 208.32 |

**Daily or miscellaneous payroll periods.** Where an employee is paid without regard to a payroll period, or where there is no regular payroll period, the daily or miscellaneous payroll period percentage method tables must be used. For the procedure used to calculate the proper amount of withholding, see the discussion of the daily or miscellaneous wage-bracket withholding tables in Section 6.4-1.

## 6.4-3 Alternative Withholding Methods

Besides the wage-bracket and percentage methods of withholding, the IRS also authorizes several other withholding methods employers might find useful depending on their situation.

**Annualized wages.**[41] Under the annualized wages method, which is used in many automated payroll systems, withholding is calculated based on an annual payroll period and then divided among the actual payroll periods using the following steps:

1.  Multiply the employee's federal income taxable wages for a payroll period times the number of payroll periods in the calendar year.

---

41.    IRC §3402(h)(2); IRS Reg. §31.3402(h)(2)-1.

2. Determine the amount that would be required to be withheld from the result in step No. 1 based on an annual payroll period.

3. Divide the amount of withholding determined in step No. 2 by the number of payroll periods in the calendar year to reach the withholding amount for each payroll period.

**Example:** In 2008, employee Ingrid is paid $950 in federal income taxable wages semimonthly, and she is single with 2 withholding allowances claimed on her Form W-4. The amount to withhold for federal income tax for each semimonthly period would be figured as follows:

1. Annual taxable wages = $950 x 24 payroll periods = $22,800

2. Withholding using percentage method

| | |
|---|---|
| Taxable wages | $22,800.00 |
| Allowance value ($3,500 x 2) | - 7,000.00 |
| Wages subject to withholding | $15,800.00 |

Percentage method formula:

| | |
|---|---|
| Wages subject to withholding | $15,800.00 |
| | - 10,300.00 |
| | $ 5,500.00 |
| | x    .15 |
| Annual payroll period withholding tax | $ 825.00 |
| | + 765.00 |
| | $ 1,590.00 |

3. Withholding per payroll period = $1,590.00 ÷ 24 = $66.25

**Average estimated wages.**[42] Under the average estimated wages method, employers may withhold based on an employee's estimated wages during a quarter. However, the employer must make adjustments each quarter to bring the withholding on the estimated wages in line with the amount required to be withheld on wages actually paid. The steps in using this method are as follows:

1. Estimate the employee's total federal income taxable earnings for the quarter.

2. Divide the result in No. 1 by the number of payroll periods during the quarter to determine the estimated average wage.

3. Calculate the tax to be withheld from each estimated average wage payment as if that were the amount actually paid and withhold it from actual wage payments.

4. If the employee's wages should increase above the estimate during the quarter, an adjustment in withholding must be made with any wage payment made during the current quarter.

*Tipped employees.* Employers may find the average estimated wages method effective for tipped employees, when the tips and withholding on tips are estimated and necessary adjustments are made by withholding extra amounts from the employee's regular wages. The withholding adjustment may be made up to 30 days after the end of the quarter.

**Cumulative wages.**[43] The cumulative wages method is useful for adjusting withholding amounts for employees whose wage payments are inconsistently high and low. This method allows for lower withholding when payments are low and higher withholding when higher wage payments are received. For that reason, it is especially popular with employers of commissioned salespeople, whose commission payments may

---

42.    IRC §3402(h)(1); IRS Reg. §31.3402(h)(1)-1.
43.    IRC §3402(h)(3); IRS Reg. §31.3402(h)(3)-1.

vary greatly between periods of high and low selling activity. It is also valuable to employees who receive a bonus payment much larger than their regular wage payment.

In order to use this method, the employee must request it in writing and must have been paid at the same frequency since the beginning of the calendar year. The request remains in effect until revoked by the employee. The revocation must be put into effect by the employer no later than the first payroll period ending 30 days after the notice of revocation. Here are the steps that must be followed in using the cumulative wages method:

1. Add the employee's federal income taxable wages paid in the calendar year to date, including wages to be paid for the current payroll period.

2. Divide the result in No. 1 by the number of payroll periods that have occurred already in the calendar year, including the current payroll period. This provides an average wage payment for each payroll period.

3. Calculate the amount of withholding that would have applied to each average wage payment using the percentage method of withholding.

4. Multiply the result in No. 3 by the number of payroll periods in the calendar year to date, including the current one.

5. Subtract the amount previously withheld from the employee's wages in the calendar year from the result in No. 4. The remainder, if any, is the amount that must be withheld from the employee's current wage payment.

*Example:* In 2008, employee Sara is paid $3,000 in federal income taxable wages monthly and is single with 1 withholding allowance. She generally has $341.25 withheld from each paycheck under the percentage method. Sara receives a $5,000 bonus with her May paycheck, and $1,611.01 is withheld from her $8,000 combined pay. Alarmed at the size of the withholding, Sara asks her employer in writing to begin withholding under the cumulative wages method in June. Here is how the withholding for June would be calculated:

| | |
|---|---:|
| 1. Total taxable wages through June | $23,000.00 |
| 2. Average wage payment ($23,000 ÷ 6) | 3,833.33 |
| 3. Withholding on $3,833.33 (percentage method) | 537.42 |
| 4. $537.42 x 6 payroll periods | 3,224.52 |
| 5. Amount withheld through May [($341.25 x 4) + $1,611.01] | 2,976.01 |
| 6. June withholding amount ($3,224.52 - $2,976.01) | $ 248.51 |

Therefore, the amount withheld in June from Sara's pay is reduced by $92.74 using the cumulative wages method ($341.25 - $248.51).

**Part-year employment.**[44] Similar to the cumulative wages method, the part-year employment withholding method reduces withholding for employees who work only during part of the calendar year, usually on a seasonal basis or because they have been unemployed. The employee must request in writing that the method be used, and it applies only when the employee has a "term of continuous employment" lasting no more than 245 days. The request is good only for the calendar year during which it is made, and the method must be discontinued immediately if the employer finds the employee will work more than 245 days during the calendar year.

---

44. IRS Reg. §31.3402(h)(4)-1(c).

The steps used in calculating withholding under the part-year method are as follows:

1. Add the employee's wages subject to federal income tax withholding for the current payroll period and those previously paid during the current term of continuous employment.

2. Add the number of previous payroll periods in the current term of continuous employment to the number of payroll periods occurring between the employee's last employment (or the previous December 31, if later) and current employment (divide the number of days during that time by the number of calendar days in each payroll period).

3. Divide the result in No. 1 by the result in No. 2 to get the average wages per payroll period since the employee's last employment.

4. Calculate the withholding tax on each average wage payment.

5. Multiply the result in No. 4 by the result in No. 2 to get the total amount that should be withheld from the employee's wages through the current payroll period.

6. Subtract any federal income tax already withheld during the current term of continuous employment from the result in No. 5 to get the amount to be withheld from the employee's current wage payment.

***Example:*** In 2008 employee Tom works for a seasonal employer from February 5 through August 24, a period of less than 245 days (202 days) and did not work at all during January. Tom is paid $1,500 in federal income taxable wages in weekly payments, is single, and claims 1 withholding allowance on his Form W-4. His first pay period ends February 11. His withholding under the part-year employment method for that pay period would be calculated as follows:

| | |
|---|---|
| 1. Total wages so far | $1,500.00 |
| 2. Number of payroll periods this year so far | 6 |
| 3. Average wages per payroll period | $250.00 |
| 4. Withholding on average wage payment | $13.17 |
| 5. $13.17 x 6 payroll periods | $79.02 |
| 6. Amount to withhold ($79.02 - 0) | $79.02 |

**Other alternatives.**[45] The IRS allows employers to use methods of their own design for withholding federal income tax from their employees' wages so long as the amounts withheld are approximately equal to what would have been withheld under the percentage method of withholding. Deviations from the percentage method results are acceptable up to certain maximums, although a method that consistently underwithholds, even within the limits, will not be accepted.

## 6.4-4 Supplemental Wage Payments

In July 2006, the IRS issued final regulations defining supplemental wages and the methods for calculating the amount of federal income tax to withhold from them. The regulations, which took effect January 1, 2007, were necessitated when the American Jobs Creation Act of 2004 was enacted. The AJCA requires a higher rate of income tax withholding when the total supplemental wages paid to an employee exceed $1,000,000 in a calendar year.[46]

**Supplemental and regular wages defined.** Under the final regulations, an employee's pay may consist of regular and supplemental wages, and in general, all wages that are not regular wages are supplemental

---

45. IRC §3402(h)(4); IRS Reg. §31.3402(h)(4)-1(a).
46. P. L. 108-357, §904(b).

wages. Supplemental wages may be paid at the same time as regular wages for a payroll period or at any other time without regard for a payroll period.[47]

The regulations list several examples of supplemental wage payments:
- reported tips;
- overtime pay;
- bonuses;
- back pay;
- commissions;
- payments made under reimbursement or other expense allowance arrangements that are made under a nonaccountable plan;
- nonqualified deferred compensation payments included in wages;
- noncash fringe benefits;
- sick pay paid by a third party as an agent of the employer;
- amounts includible in gross income under IRC §409A;
- income recognized on the exercise of a nonstatutory stock option;
- wages imputed for health coverage of a non-dependent of an employee; and
- wages recognized on the lapse of restrictions on restricted property transferred from an employer to an employee.

Regular wages are amounts paid for a payroll period either at a regular hourly, daily, or similar periodic rate or in a predetermined fixed amount. Wages that vary from payroll period to payroll period based on factors other than the amount of time worked are supplemental wages.[48]

Amounts described under this definition of supplemental wages are supplemental wages regardless of whether the employee received any regular wages from the employer during the current or any prior calendar year.[49]

> **Example:** The only wages Jane has ever received from her employer are noncash fringe benefits and income recognized from her exercise of nonstatutory stock options. All of these payments are supplemental wage payments.

Amounts that are not wages subject to income tax withholding are neither regular wages nor supplemental wages.[50] One such amount specifically mentioned in the regulations is income from the disqualifying disposition of shares of stock acquired through the exercise of a statutory stock option (see Section 3.4-24). However, see the discussion below related to the employer's option to treat all Form W-2, Box 1 wages as supplemental wages.

 **SPECIAL OPTION FOR TIPS AND OVERTIME PAY**[51] Even though tips reported by employees and overtime pay meet the definition of supplemental wages, the regulations give employers the option of treating such payments as regular wages. The employer does not have to treat reported tips and overtime pay the same for each employee. Overtime pay is the amount required to be paid above the employee's normal pay rate by federal, state, or local law for working in excess of a normal workweek or workday (i.e., overtime premium pay).

**Withholding on supplemental wages of $1 million or less in a calendar year.** The final regulations continue to provide that, if an employee has not received cumulatively more than $1 million in supplemental wages during the calendar year, there are two withholding methods available to an employer with respect to a payment of supplemental wages.

---

47. IRS Reg. §31.3402(g)-1(a)(1)(i).
48. IRS Reg. §31.3402(g)-1(a)(1)(ii).
49. IRS Reg. §31.3402(g)-1(a)(1)(i); Cunningham v. Blue Care Network of Michigan, No. 07-11666, 2007 U.S. Dist. LEXIS 66214 (Ed Mich., 9-7-07).
50. IRS Reg. §31.3402(g)-1(a)(1)(iii).
51. IRS Reg. §31.3402(g)-1(a)(1)(iv), (v).

*Aggregate method.*[52] Under this method, the employer calculates the amount of withholding due by aggregating the amount of supplemental wages with the regular wages paid for the current payroll period or for the most recent payroll period of the year of payment, and treating the aggregate as if it were a single wage payment for the regular payroll period. If the supplemental wages are paid concurrently with wages for the current payroll period, then they must be aggregated with the wages paid for the current payroll period. The employer must use the aggregate method if the optional flat rate method (see below) cannot be used.

**Example 1:** Employee Ray wins a $1,000 prize in 2008 for a money-saving suggestion his employer has adopted. Ray's employer combines the prize with Ray's regular biweekly federal income taxable wage payment of $1,200 for the current payroll period, for a total of $2,200. Because the employer does not indicate the two types of payments, it must withhold as if Ray received a regular biweekly wage payment of $2,200. Ray is married and claims 3 withholding allowances on his Form W-4. Under the wage-bracket method, his employer must withhold $195 in federal income tax from Ray's combined wage payment.

**Example 2:** Employee Jack, who is single and claims 2 withholding allowances, is normally paid $1,400 in federal income taxable wages during 2008 on a biweekly basis. So far in 2008, Jack has received $14,000 in wages. Between paychecks, Jack receives a production bonus of $400. Using the aggregate method, the amount of federal income tax to withhold from the bonus payment is calculated this way:

| | |
|---|---|
| Total of latest wage payment and bonus ($1,400 + $400) | $1,800 |
| | |
| Withholding on total amount (wage-bracket method) | 225 |
| Withholding from latest wage payment ($1,400) | -141 |
| Withholding from supplemental wage payment | 84 |

*Optional flat rate method.*[53] Under this method, the employer disregards the amount of regular wages paid to an employee as well as the withholding allowances claimed or additional withholding amount requested by the employee on his/her Form W-4, and uses a flat percentage rate in calculating the amount of withholding. This method is available only if two conditions are met:

- The employer has withheld income tax from regular wages paid to the employee during the same year as the payment of supplemental wages or during the preceding calendar year.
- The supplemental wages are either: (a) not paid concurrently with regular wages or (b) separately stated on the payroll records of the employer (i.e., on the employee's pay stub).

Under the final regulations, the rate applicable to optional flat rate withholding is 25% for 2008 and will remain at 25% until income tax rates change.

**Example 3:** Employee Caroline, who is generally paid $1,400 in federal income taxable wages on the 1st and 15th of each month and has federal income tax withheld, receives a bonus of $2,500 on July 6. Her year-to-date wages is 2008 before receiving the bonus totaled $18,200. Her employer chooses to use the optional flat rate and withholds $625 from her bonus ($2,500 x .25). If the bonus is included with her regular wage payment on July 15 but her pay stub makes it clear that $1,400 is regular wages and $2,500 is the bonus, her employer may still withhold $625 from the bonus payment while withholding at the normal rate from the regular wage payment.

 **BE CAREFUL** If the conditions for using the optional flat rate method are met, then the decision as to which method to use is discretionary with the employer. If the conditions are not met, then the employer must use the aggregate method.

---

52.    IRS Reg. §31.3402(g)-1(a)(6).
53.    IRS Reg. §31.3402(g)-1(a)(7).

*What if the employee claims exempt from withholding?* If the employee has claimed exempt from federal income tax withholding on Form W-4, then the employer should not withhold on supplemental wages paid to the employee under either method if the total supplemental wages paid to the employee during the calendar year do not exceed $1,000,000.

**Employer must use higher flat rate on supplemental wages over $1 million.** Under the AJCA and the final regulations, if a supplemental wage payment, when taken together with all other supplemental wage payments paid by an employer to an employee during the calendar year, exceeds $1,000,000, then the employer must withhold federal income tax from the supplemental wages in excess of $1 million at a flat rate equal to the maximum rate of tax in effect that year.[54]

In 2008, the mandatory flat rate for supplemental wages in excess of $1,000,000 is 35%. The mandatory flat rate will remain at 35% until the maximum rate of income tax is increased. In applying this rate, the employer must disregard the employee's Form W-4, even if the employee claims to be exempt from withholding.

The final regulations include specific guidance for the treatment of certain compensation when determining whether the $1,000,000 threshold has been crossed:[55]

- *Compensation not subject to withholding.* Employers have the option of treating amounts includible in income as supplemental wages, even though the amounts are not subject to federal income tax withholding but are reported in Box 1 of Form W-2.

- *The payment that takes the total over $1,000,000.* If a supplemental wage payment results in the total supplemental wage payments to the employee from the employer during the calendar year exceeding $1,000,000, then the amount of that payment in excess of $1,000,000 is subject to mandatory flat rate withholding. However, under the final regulations the employer has the option of treating the entire amount of the payment that results in the employee receiving total supplemental wages of more than $1,000,000 as subject to mandatory flat rate withholding. Moreover, this treatment can apply on an employee-by-employee basis.

**Example 4:** Employee George, CFO of Big Co., had received $800,000 in supplemental wage payments before September 1, 2008. On September 2, George received a bonus of $300,000. Big Co. decided to withhold federal income tax using the optional flat rate method for the first $200,000 of the bonus payment. Big Co. withheld $50,000 ($200,000 x .25) from the first $200,000 and $35,000 from the remaining $100,000 using the mandatory flat withholding rate ($100,000 x .35), for a total of $85,000. If Big Co. decided to treat the entire bonus payment of $300,000 as a supplemental wage payment over $1,000,000, it would have withheld $105,000 from the bonus ($300,000 x .35).

- *Allocating salary deferral amounts.* Pretax deductions, including salary reduction deferrals, are not included when determining the total of an employee's supplemental wages. This does not mean, however, that pretax deferrals may not be deducted from supplemental wage payments, if that is what the employer's plan document requires. In determining the amount of supplemental wages paid, salary deferral amounts are allocated to the gross regular wage payments or to the gross supplemental wage payments from which they are actually deducted.

---

54.  IRS Reg. §31.3402(g)-1(a)(2); §31.3402(n)-1.
55.  IRS Reg. §31.3402(g)-1(a)(4).

**Example 5:** If an employee had a valid salary reduction agreement deferring 10% of all salary and bonuses, and the employee received wage payments based on $1,500,000 of gross salary and $1,000,000 of gross bonuses prior to reduction for the deferrals (and no other wages), the employer would allocate $150,000 to the gross regular wage payment and $100,000 to the gross supplemental wage payment. Thus, for purposes of the mandatory flat rate withholding, the employee has received $900,000 of supplemental wages.

 **WATCH OUT** In determining whether an employee's supplemental wage payments total more than $1,000,000 during a year, payments to the employee from all businesses under common control are treated as if they were paid by a single employer and must be aggregated.[56]

**Payments by agents of the employer.** The final regulations require that payments made by agents of the employer (i.e., third parties) to an employee on the employer's behalf must be considered in determining the applicability of mandatory flat rate withholding.[57]

*De minimis exception.*[58] An agent making total wage payments, including regular and supplemental wages, of less than $100,000 to an individual in any calendar year may disregard other supplemental wages from the common law employer or any other agent of the employer that would subject the employee to mandatory flat rate withholding. Similarly, an employer may disregard supplemental wage payments made by an agent to an employee in determining whether the employee has reached the $1,000,000 threshold if the agent has made total wage payments of less than $100,000 to the employee during the calendar year.

If an agent does reach the $100,000 threshold of wages paid to a single employee in a calendar year, then the employer, in determining the applicability of mandatory flat rate withholding, must take into account all supplemental wages paid by the agent in determining whether mandatory flat rate withholding applies to a wage payment made after the agent reaches the $100,000 threshold.

Similarly, with the payment that reaches the $100,000 threshold, the agent that has made $100,000 of wage payments to an employee during a calendar year is required to take into account all wages paid by the employer and any other agent of the employer that has reached the $100,000 threshold in determining the applicability of mandatory flat rate withholding.

Application of the de minimis rule is optional. An employer may take into account all supplemental wages paid by agents, regardless of how small the payments are from any particular agent, in determining whether the employee has received $1,000,000 of supplemental wages during the calendar year. Similarly, an agent is not required to apply the de minimis rule.

*Note:* The de minimis exception does not apply to the employer in situations where the employer has created an arrangement or arrangements with five or more agents if a principal effect of the arrangement or arrangements is to reduce applicable mandatory flat rate withholding with respect to an employee.

**State supplemental wage rates.** Table 6.3 provides the supplemental wage withholding rates for 2007 for those states that allow flat rate withholding from supplemental wages. (For more information on state supplemental wage withholding, see Table 3.7 of *APA's Guide to State Payroll Laws.*)

---

56.    IRS Reg. §31.3402(g)-1(a)(3)(i).
57.    IRS Reg. §31.3402(g)-1(a)(3)(ii).
58.    IRS Reg. §31.3402(g)-1(a)(4)(iii).

Table 6.3

| STATE SUPPLEMENTAL WAGE TAX RATES | | |
|---|---|---|
| | **State** | **Tax Rate** |
| Alabama | | 5.0% |
| Arkansas | | 7.0% |
| California | | 6.0%; 9.3% for stock options and bounses |
| Colorado | | 4.63% |
| Georgia | Annual wages:  under $8,000<br>$8,000 - $10,000<br>$10,000 - $12,000<br>$12,000 - $15,000<br>over $15,000 | 2.0%<br>3.0%<br>4.0%<br>5.0%<br>6.0% |
| Idaho | | 7.8% |
| Illinois | | 3.0% |
| Indiana | | 3.4% |
| Iowa | | 6.0% |
| Kansas | | 5.0% |
| Maine | | 5.0% |
| Michigan | | 4.35% |
| Minnesota | | 6.25% |
| Missouri | | 6.0% |
| Montana | | 6.0% |
| Nebraska | | 5.0% |
| New Mexico | | 4.9% |
| New York | | 7.35% |
| North Carolina | | 6.0% |
| North Dakota | | 3.92% |
| Ohio | | 3.5% |
| Oklahoma | | 5.5%; 5.25%, eff. 1-1-09 |
| Oregon | | 9.0% |
| Pennsylvania | | 3.07% |
| Rhode Island | | 7.0% |
| South Carolina | | 7.0% |
| Vermont | | 7.2%; 9.5% if the federal supplemental withholding rate of 35% is applied |
| Virginia | | 5.75% |

| STATE SUPPLEMENTAL WAGE TAX RATES | | |
|---|---|---|
| | State | Tax Rate |
| West Virginia  Annual wages: | under $10,000<br>$10,000 - $25,000<br>$25,000 - $40,000<br>$40,000 - $60,000<br>over $60,000 | 3.0%<br>4.0%<br>4.5%<br>6..0%<br>6.5% |
| Wisconsin   Annual wages: | under $7,970<br>$ 7,970 - $15,590<br>$15,590 - $115,140<br>over $115,140 | 4.6%<br>6.15%<br>6.5%<br>6.75% |

Connecticut, Delaware, District of Columbia, Hawaii, Kentucky, Mississippi, and New Jersey specify that supplemental wages be aggregated. Tax regulations in Arizona, Louisiana, Massachusetts, and Utah do not contain provisions for a special supplemental tax rate. Alaska, Florida, Nevada, New Hampshire, South Dakota, Tennessee, Texas, Washington, and Wyoming have no state income tax.

# 6.4-5  Withholding on Pensions and Annuities

Generally, distributions from an employer's retirement or deferred compensation plan (see Section 4.6-1) are subject to federal income tax withholding (e.g., pensions, annuities, governmental plans, profit-sharing plans, stock bonus plans, etc.). The method of withholding depends on the type of payment—periodic or nonperiodic. Whatever method is used, the amount of withholding cannot exceed the amount of money distributed plus the value of any property distributed. Also, no withholding is required if the distribution consists solely of the employer's securities and up to $200 in cash representing fractional shares.

**Periodic payments.**[59] Generally, payments from a retirement or deferred compensation plan are considered periodic if they are made over a period of more than one year (e.g., pension or annuity payments for the life of a retired employee). Employers and plan administrators must withhold federal income tax from periodic payments as if the payments were wages, using one of the allowable withholding methods. The payroll period to be used is the frequency of the payments (e.g., monthly, quarterly).

Payment recipients can use Form W-4P (see Section 6.3-2) to help determine their withholding. Through this form, the recipient can decline withholding altogether, specify marital status and the number of withholding allowances, or ask that an additional dollar amount be withheld. Payment recipients can ask that an additional amount be withheld only if they also enter a number of withholding allowances on the form. If no Form W-4P is filed, withholding must be calculated as if the recipient had claimed married with three withholding allowances. Recipients must be notified of their right to decline withholding no more than six months before the first payment, and annually thereafter they must be notified of their right to revoke or change their withholding election.

*Restrictions on right to refuse withholding.*[60] A recipient cannot elect to refuse withholding under the following circumstances:

- the recipient has the payments mailed to an address outside the U.S.;
- the recipient has not given the payer a resident address where the payments should be mailed; or
- the recipient has not given the payer his or her social security number, or the IRS has told the payer the SSN provided is inaccurate.

---

59.    IRC §3405(a); §3405(e)(10); IRS Reg. §35.3405-1B.
60.    IRC §3405(e)(13); IRS Notice 87-7, 1987-1 CB 420.

**Nonperiodic payments not eligible for rollover.**[61] All distributions that are not considered periodic payments are nonperiodic payments. All nonperiodic payments made after December 31, 1992 that are not eligible for rollover to another qualified plan, and are at least $200, are subject to withholding at the rate of 10%. Once again, however, the recipient of the payments may use a Form W-4P to elect no withholding. The recipient may also use Form W-4P to increase withholding by a specific dollar amount. The recipient's rights must be spelled out in a written notice provided before the first payment and annually thereafter. The right to decline withholding is subject to the same conditions that apply to recipients of periodic payments.

**Eligible rollover distributions.** Beginning January 1, 1993, the Unemployment Compensation Amendments of 1992 made significant changes in the tax treatment of certain nonperiodic payments from qualified deferred compensation plans. While the law expanded the types of payments and distributions that are eligible to be "rolled over" tax-free into another plan, it also requires mandatory withholding if the rollover is not accomplished before the money is actually distributed. The types of plans encompassed by the rules governing eligible rollover distributions were further expanded by the Economic Growth and Tax Relief Reconciliation Act of 2001 and the Pension Protection Act of 2006. Once made, the rollover election is irrevocable.

*What are eligible rollover distributions?*[62] Generally, all nonperiodic payments of all or any portion of the balance of a recipient's account in a qualified deferred compensation plan under IRC §401(a) (including a §401(k) plan), a §403(b) annuity, a governmental §457 plan, and an individual retirement arrangement (IRA) are eligible rollover distributions other than:

- substantially equal periodic payments made over the lifetime or life expectancy of the employee or his or her beneficiary, or made for a specified period of at least 10 years;

- any minimum distribution that is required under IRC §401(a)(9) regarding qualified plans;

- distributions not included in gross income, except for return of an employee's after-tax contributions for which separate accounting is maintained, and net unrealized appreciation of employer securities;

- returns of amounts deferred under a §401(k) or §403(b) plan that exceed the elective deferral limits;

- loans treated as deemed distributions;

- hardship distributions;

- dividends paid on employer securities; or

- distributions of the cost of current life insurance coverage.

 **WATCH OUT** Even though the types of plan distributions to which "eligible rollover distribution" status have been expanded, §401(k), §403(b), and §457 plans are not required to accept rollovers. In order for a §457 plan to accept rollovers from other types of retirement plans, it must agree to separately account for amounts rolled over from those other plans.[63]

*Withholding rules.*[64] Eligible rollover distributions are subject to mandatory federal income tax withholding of 20% unless the distribution is directly rolled over to another qualified plan, individual retirement account (includes a Roth IRA beginning in 2008), §403(b) annuity, or governmental §457 plan. Employees cannot elect to have no income tax withheld. If an employee chooses to receive part of an eligible rollover distribution and directly roll over the balance, withholding is required only on the portion received by the

---

61.   IRC §3405(b).
62.   IRC §402(c)(4); (f)(2)(A); §403(b)(8)(B); §457(e)(16); IRS Reg. §1.402(c)-2, Q&A 2 - 8; §1.403(b)-2, Q&A 2.
63.   IRC §402(c)(10).
64.   IRC §3405(c); IRS Reg. §1.401(a)(31)-1, Q&A 10; §31.3405(c)-1, Q&A 1, 2, 6, 14.

employee. Employers and plan administrators are not required (but are permitted) to allow an employee more than one direct rollover for each distribution.

 **SMALL DISTRIBUTIONS EXEMPT** No withholding is required if the total of all payments to an employee under one plan during the year total less than $200. If the first payment is less than $200 but the payer does not know whether all payments for the year will total less than $200, withholding from the first payment is not required. However, once the $200 threshold has been reached, the total of all payments made during the year to that point must be used to determine the amount to withhold from subsequent payments made during the year.

*How is a direct rollover accomplished?* [65] The IRS allows direct rollovers to be accomplished by any reasonable means of direct payment to the new plan, including:

- a wire transfer;
- mailing a check to the new plan;
- having the recipient deliver the check to the new plan.

When a wire transfer is used, the transfer must be directed only to the trustee or custodian of the plan. When a check is used, the check must be made out to ensure negotiability only by the trustee or custodian of the plan.

*Rollovers after distribution.* If an employee elects to receive a distribution, has 20% withheld by the payer, and then wishes to avoid taxation, earlier rules still apply allowing the employee to roll over the distribution within 60 days. The 80% of the distribution that is rolled over will not be taxable, but the 20% withheld is treated as an early distribution and is subject to federal income tax and, most likely, a 10% excise tax imposed on premature distributions. If the employee wants a fully tax-free rollover, he or she must make up from personal funds the 20% that was withheld and include it when rolling over the other 80%. The amount withheld can be claimed as a refund on the employee's personal income tax return. The 60-day requirement can be waived by the IRS in certain hardship situations, including cases of disaster, casualty, or other events beyond the reasonable control of the person subject to the requirement.[66]

*Payments of cash and property.* [67] When the eligible rollover distribution consists at least in part of property other than cash, the value of all property and cash must be considered when determining the amount to be withheld. If the amount of cash is insufficient to satisfy the withholding obligation, either the property must be sold and the remaining cash distributed to the recipient, or the recipient may agree to provide enough cash to the plan administrator to meet the obligation.

*Distribution of employer securities.* [68] If the distribution consists solely of employer securities and up to $200 in fractional shares, no withholding is required. If the distribution consists of employer securities, cash, and/or other property, the total value of the distribution is subject to withholding (other than net unrealized appreciation of the employer securities). However, the withholding obligation must be paid from the cash and other property, not the employer securities. In any event, the amount withheld cannot exceed the value of cash and other property received by the employee.

When employer securities are distributed, part of the distribution can include net unrealized appreciation on those securities (i.e., their increase in value since purchased and before distribution). This net unrealized appreciation is generally excluded from gross income at the time of distribution, and as such it is not included in the amount of an eligible rollover distribution that is subject to withholding.[69]

---

65.     IRS Reg. §1.401(a)(31)-1, Q&A 3, 4.
66.     IRC §402(c)(3).
67.     IRS Reg. §31.3405(c)-1, Q&A 9; §35.3405-1, Q&A F-1 - F-3.
68.     IRC §3405(e)(8); IRS Reg. §31.3405(c)-1, Q&A 11.
69.     IRS Reg. §31.3405(c)-1, Q&A 12; IRS Notice 93-3, 1993-1 CB 293.

*Who must withhold?*[70]  Generally, the plan administrator or payer of an annuity is responsible for the mandatory 20% withholding from eligible rollover distributions not directly rolled over to another plan.  The responsibility can be shifted from the plan administrator to the payer by providing certain information and directing the payer to withhold.  Once a direct rollover is elected by a recipient, the plan administrator is not liable for any taxes or penalties if the plan to which the distribution is rolled over is an ineligible plan.  But this is true only if the plan administrator reasonably relied on adequate information supplied by the recipient that was sufficient to accomplish the rollover.

A plan that accepts an invalid rollover contribution will be protected from disqualification if the plan administrator reasonably believes that the contribution is a valid rollover contribution and distributes the amount of the invalid rollover contribution (plus any earnings attributed to it) to the employee within a reasonable period of time after discovering that it is invalid.  The distributing plan does not have to have a favorable IRS determination letter for the receiving plan to reasonably conclude that the rollover is valid.[71]

*Offsets to satisfy plan loans.*[72]  Qualified deferred compensation plans and tax-sheltered annuities often allow employees to take loans from the plan secured by their account balances.  When employees with outstanding loans terminate employment, many plans offset any amount due against the employees' account balances.  The amount of the offset is generally an eligible rollover distribution if it would have been eligible had the money remained in the employee's account.

The IRS has provided special guidance for making a determination of the withholding obligation regarding plan loan offsets.

- Although the offset amount is an eligible rollover distribution, the plan does not have to allow a direct rollover of the offset amount, since it is needed to repay the loan.  The employee may use his or her own funds to roll over an amount equal to the offset amount within 60 days to avoid taxes on the offset amount.

- The offset amount must be included in valuing the total amount of the eligible rollover distribution that is subject to withholding.  However, the amount withheld cannot exceed the amount of cash and other property actually received by the employee, other than employer securities.

**Example 1:**  Employee Zach has an account balance of $15,000 in his employer's qualified deferred compensation plan and an outstanding loan from the plan of $5,000 secured by his account balance.  Zach has made no after-tax contributions to his plan account.  His employer does not allow direct rollovers with respect to plan loans.  After Zach resigns, he elects a direct rollover of his entire account balance.  His employer must pay $10,000 to Zach's designated retirement plan after offsetting the $5,000 still owed on the loan against the $15,000 in Zach's account.

The offset amount ($5,000) is an eligible rollover distribution, but no withholding is required because Zach received no cash or other property from which to withhold.  Zach may use his own funds to roll over $5,000 within 60 days and avoid taxes on the offset amount.  The result here is the same whether the employer treats the loan as being in default before the offset or the offset occurs automatically upon termination of employment.

**Example 2:**  Employee Zach is in the same situation as in Example 1, except he elects to receive the remainder of his account balance after the offset to repay the loan.  The amount of the eligible rollover distribution is $15,000 because the offset amount is used in calculating the amount of the distribution ($5,000 offset amount + $10,000 cash received by Zach).  Therefore, the amount to withhold is $3,000 ($15,000 x .20), and Zach actually receives $7,000 ($10,000 - $3,000).

---

70.    IRC §3405(d); IRS Reg. §31.3405-1, Q&A 4, 5, 7.
71.    IRS Reg. §1.401(a)(31)-1, Q&A 14.
72.    IRS Reg. §1.401(a)(31)-1, Q&A 16; §1.402(c)-2, Q&A 9; §31.3405(c)-1, Q&A 11; IRS Notice 93-3, 1993-1 CB 293.

*Notice requirements.*[73] Plan administrators must provide employees with a notice explaining the following information within a reasonable time before an eligible rollover distribution is to be made:

- the provisions allowing the employee to have the distribution directly rolled over to another eligible retirement plan;

- the provisions requiring that 20% of any portion of the distribution not directly rolled over be withheld for federal income tax;

- the provisions under which income tax may be avoided if the distribution is rolled over within 60 days of receipt by the employee;

- special provisions regarding net unrealized appreciation of employer securities;

- the treatment of distributions to foreign exempt trusts;

- the provisions under which distributions from the plan to which the distribution is rolled over may be subject to restrictions and tax consequences different than those applicable to distributions from the distributing plan;

- an election to receive or roll over one payment in a series of payments will apply to all future payments unless changed and

- that an automatic rollover to an IRA will be made if the employee receives a mandatory distribution over $1,000 and does not elect to receive the distribution or to roll it over directly to another eligible retirement plan.

Generally, the notice must be provided to the employee between 30 and 90 days before the distribution. The requirement of at least 30 days between receipt of the notice and the date of distribution can be waived if the employee elects either to receive or directly roll over the distribution within that time period. Once the election is made, the plan administrator may implement it. The plan administrator must notify the employee of his or her right to have at least 30 days to make the decision whether or not to elect a direct rollover. The notice can be included with the notice describing the rollover and withholding provisions, or it may be provided separately.

IRS regulations make it clear that notices may be provided in an electronic format and allow them to be provided earlier than 90 days before the distribution, so long as a summary is provided during the 30-90 day period. Also, plan participants must be told that they can get a paper notice rather than an electronic one at no charge.[74]

 **POSTING NOT GOOD ENOUGH** The written notice must be provided to individual employees during the applicable time period before the distribution is made. Posting one notice where all employees can see it does not satisfy the law's requirements.

*Depositing withheld taxes.* Amounts withheld under the mandatory withholding rules must be deposited in accordance with the general rules on depositing withheld taxes (see Section 8.2). There are three alternatives for plan administrators and payers.

- The plan administrator or payer may aggregate the withholding with all other amounts under its control and report the withholding on its Form 945 used to report nonpayroll withheld taxes.

- The plan administrator or payer may request a separate Employer Identification Number solely for the purpose of reporting withholding on all plan distributions.

---

73. IRC §402(f)(1); IRS Reg. §1.402(f)-1, Q&A 1-4; §1.403(b)-2, Q&A 3; IRS Notice 93-26, 1993-1 CB 308; IRS Notice 2000-11, 2000-6 IRB 572; IRS Notice 2002-3, 2002-2 IRB 289 (contains safe harbor notices updated for EGTRRA).

74. IRS Reg. §1.402(f)-1, Q&A 2, 5, 6; IRS Notice 99-1, 1999-2 IRB 8.

- The plan administrator or payer may use the EIN of each plan to report separately the withholding on distributions from each plan.

**Automatic rollovers of mandatory distributions.**[75] If a qualified plan provides for mandatory distributions of accrued benefits totaling no more than $5,000 to employees who are no longer covered under the plan, IRC §401(a)(31)(B) requires that, if the distributed amount is over $1,000 and is an eligible rollover distribution, the distribution must be rolled over to an IRA if the employee has received the required notice regarding rollovers and does not elect a direct rollover or to receive the distribution. The automatic rollover requirement applies to §401(k), §403(b), and §457(b) plans. In complying with the requirement, the plan administrator may set up an IRA on the employee's behalf.

## 6.5 Backup Withholding

Businesses regularly make payments to individuals and others who are not employees (e.g., partnerships, sole proprietors, trusts and estates). The Internal Revenue Code requires that the business report these payments to the IRS if they consist of interest or dividends, payments of wages due a deceased employee made to the employee's beneficiary or estate, compensation ($600 or more for the year) for services rendered by independent contractors, royalties, broker transaction payments, payments to health care providers and attorneys, or direct sales of $5,000 or more (for details on the reporting requirement, see Section 8.12-1).

**Requirement to withhold.**[76] Payers of reportable payments must withhold 28% for federal income tax ("backup" withholding) from such payments if:

- the payee fails to provide the payer with a Taxpayer Identification Number (TIN)—either a Social Security Number (SSN), IRS Individual Taxpayer Identification Number (ITIN), or Employer Identification Number (EIN)—or provides one that is obviously incorrect (e.g., wrong number of digits);

- the payer is notified by the IRS that the TIN provided by the payee is incorrect (through a "B" notice);

- the payer is notified by the IRS that a payee has underreported interest or dividend payments; or

- the payer does not receive from a payee receiving interest or dividend payments a certification that the payee is not subject to withholding.

 **ONLINE TIN MATCHING AVAILABLE** Payers can now verify up to 25 TINs online through IRS's Interactive TIN Matching System, and up to 100,000 TINs through the Bulk Tin Matching System. Results of the interactive match are returned almost immediately, while bulk match results are returned overnight. To register for this and other IRS e-services, go to https://la. www4.irs.gov/e-services/Registration/index.htm.

**When to withhold.**[77] As long as a TIN has not been provided by the payee, the payer must withhold from all payments made to the payee. If the payer receives a "B" notice from the IRS, withholding must begin no later than the first payment after 30 days from receipt of the notice and will last until another TIN is properly furnished. Once the payer receives the "B" notice, it has 15 days to send a copy of the "B" notice to the payee along with a Form W-9, *Request for Taxpayer Identification Number and Certification* (see Appendix, page A-116), which the payee is to complete, sign, and return.

If the Form W-9 is returned (after being properly completed) before 30 days have passed since the payer received the "B" notice, backup withholding is not required. If the Form W-9 is returned after withholding

---

75. IRC §401(a)(31)(B); IRS Notice 2005-5, 2005-3 IRB 337.
76. IRC §3406(a) - (d), (h)(1); IRS Reg. §31.3406(a)-1; §31.3406(b)(3)-1; §31.3406(d)-1(a); §31.3406(d)-5(a) - (h); §35a.9999-1, Q&A 26, 28; §35a.9999-2, Q&A 10, 11; §35a.9999-3, Q&A 3
77. IRC §3406(e), (h)(2); IRS Reg. §31.3406(d)-5(e) - (g); §31.3406(e)-1; §35a.9999-3, Q&A 41.

has begun, the payer has 30 days to stop withholding. If the payee provides 2 incorrect TINs in a 3-year period, the payer must backup withhold until the IRS or the SSA notifies the payer that a correct TIN has been supplied.

**Payment card transactions.**[78] In 2004, the IRS issued regulations and other guidance providing a limited exception to the backup withholding requirements for payment card transactions. Under the regulations, backup withholding does not apply to payment card transactions if the reportable payments are made through a Qualified Payment Card Agent and the payment is made to a qualified payee. A payee is qualified if the QPCA has validated the payee's TIN through the TIN Matching System or the payment is made within 6 months after the QPCA first obtained the payee's TIN.

**Withholding on government payments for services.**[79] Under the Tax Increase Prevention and Reconciliation Act of 2005, beginning in 2011, information reporting and withholding at the rate of 3% will be required on payments to individuals or business entities providing property or services to a government entity (including any agency, instrumentality, or political subdivision of federal or state government) with $100 million or more of annual expenditures that are subject to this withholding provision. The provision applies regardless of whether the government entity making the payment is the recipient of the property or services.

Payments subject to withholding under the provision include any payment made in connection with a government voucher or certificate program that functions as a payment for property or services. The provision does not apply to any payments made through a federal, state, or local government public assistance or public welfare program for which eligibility is determined by a needs or income test. However, payments under government programs to provide health care or other services that are not based on the needs or income of the recipients are subject to withholding, including programs where eligibility is based on the age of the beneficiary.

The provision does not apply to payments of wages to government employees (or other payments to employees with respect to their service as employees) or to any other payment with respect to which mandatory (e.g., U.S.-source income of foreign taxpayers) or voluntary (e.g., unemployment benefits) withholding applies under current law. The provision does not exclude payments that are potentially subject to backup withholding under §3406. If, however, payments are actually having backup withholding applied to them, then withholding under TIPRA does not apply.

See Sections 8.2-2 and 8.4 for the requirements regarding the depositing and reporting of backup withholding amounts.

## 6.6 Advance Earned Income Credit

Employees earning less than a certain amount in a year are entitled to the Earned Income Credit (EIC). The EIC is a tax credit that reduces any taxes owed.[80]

**How much is the credit?** For 2008, the credit for employees with one qualifying (dependent) child is 34% of the first $8,580 of earned income, for a maximum of $2,917 (40% of $12,060 for an employee with two or more qualifying children for a maximum of $4,824; 7.65% of $5,720 for an employee with no qualifying children for a maximum of $438). The credit begins to phase out in 2008 when a single employee's adjusted gross income (or earned income if that is higher) exceeds $15,740, at the rate of 15.98%, and is completely lost when adjusted gross income (or earned income if that is higher) reaches $33,995 (a phase-out rate of 21.06% and an income maximum of $38,646 for single employees with two or more qualifying children). For single employees with no qualifying children, the credit phases out at the rate of 7.65% once earned income reaches $7,160 and is completely lost when adjusted gross income (or earned income if that is higher) reaches $12,880 in 2008.

---

78. IRS Reg. §31.3406(g)-(1)(f); §31.3406(j)-1(a), (f); §301.6724-1(c)(6), (e)(1)(vi)(H), (f)(5)(vii); Rev. Proc. 2004-42, 2004-31 IRB 121; Rev. Proc. 2004-43, 2004-31 IRB 124.
79. IRC §3402(t).
80. IRC §32; IRS Reg. §1.32-2.

For employees who are married and file a joint tax return, the phase-out ranges are as follows in 2008: for employees with one qualifying child, the credit begins to phase out when the employee's earned income reaches $18,740 and is completely lost when earned income reaches $36,995; the phase-out range is $18,740 - $41,646 for employees with two or more qualifying children; and for employees with no qualifying children, the phase-out range is $10,160 - $15,880. The phase-out percentages are the same as those for single employees. These increased phase-out limits for married employees filing jointly are mandated by the Economic Growth and Tax Relief Reconciliation Act of 2001. The dollar amounts of the maximum credit, maximum earned income or adjusted gross income, and the point at which the credit begins phasing out, are adjusted annually for inflation. An employee's earned income includes wages, tips, and other employee compensation, but only if these amounts are included in the employee's gross income for the year.

**Special eligibility rules.** Employees with no qualifying children must meet other requirements besides the income maximum to qualify. Such employees must be at least 25 but less than 65 years old, live in the U.S. for at least half the year, and cannot be claimed as a dependent on someone else's tax return. Other recent changes in the eligibility rules include:

- Individuals who are nonresident aliens for any part of the taxable year are ineligible for the EIC unless they are married to a U.S. citizen or resident and elect to be treated as a resident alien for income tax purposes.[81]

- American military personnel stationed outside the U.S. while on extended active duty will be considered to live in the U.S. during that time.[82]

- Earned income does not include any amount received by an individual while an inmate in prison, including wages earned from work done in a work release program or while at a halfway house.[83]

- In 2008, an individual is ineligible for the EIC if the individual's total "disqualified" income for the year exceeds $2,950 (adjusted annually for inflation to the next lowest multiple of $50). Disqualified income includes taxable interest and dividends, tax-exempt interest, net income from rents and royalties not derived in the ordinary course of business, capital gain net income, and net passive income that is not self-employment income.[84]

- To be eligible to claim the EITC, the employee and his or her spouse must include their social security number(s) on their tax return. Failure to do so will be treated as a mathematical or clerical error, which will result in the IRS figuring the tax due without the credit and without first sending a notice of deficiency.

- Individuals who fraudulently claimed the EITC in an earlier year are ineligible to claim it for the next 10 years (2 years if the claim was made erroneously because of reckless disregard of rules or regulations).

- Earned income does not include workfare payments made under a public assistance program.

- Nontaxable combat pay should not be included in earned income for purposes of advance payments of the EIC, although employees may include it for 2007 when they figure the EIC on their personal income tax returns.

**Advance payments of EIC possible.**[85] Rather than receiving the entire EIC when they file their personal tax returns, eligible employees may receive advance payments of more than half of their EIC from their employers throughout the year. In 2008, employees with dependent children receiving less than $33,995 ($36,995 for married employees filing jointly) may elect to receive up to $1,750 of advance EIC payments spread out over their paychecks, which is 60% of the credit for one child. The maximum earned income amount applies to the total earned by both spouses if a joint tax return is filed. The remaining credit, as well as any credit due to childless workers, must be claimed on the employees' personal tax returns.

---

81.    IRC §32(c)(1)(E).
82.    IRC §32(c)(4).
83.    IRC §32(c)(2)(B)(iv).
84.    IRC §32(i).
85.    IRC §3507(a), (b)(2)(B); IRS Reg. §31.3507-1(a).

**Becoming eligible for advance payments.**[86] Employees who want to take advantage of advance EIC payments must file Form W-5, *Earned Income Credit Advance Payment Certificate* (see Appendix page A-99), which attests to their eligibility for the advance payments. Employers must put the form into effect for the first payroll period ending on or after the date the form is filed if it is the first W-5 form filed by the employee for the calendar year. Form W-5 is effective for the remainder of the calendar year. If a new form for the next calendar year is not filed before the first payroll processing of the next year, the employer must stop making advance EIC payments. Forms W-5 may be filed electronically with the employer. The employer's electronic system must meet requirements similar to those governing electronic Forms W-4 (see p. 6-16).

**How to handle invalid certificates.** Form W-5 is invalid if is incomplete, unsigned, or has an alteration or unauthorized addition. A certificate is also invalid if the employee has orally or in writing indicated that the form is false. Invalid certificates are considered void. Employers are not required to determine if a completed and signed Form W-5 is correct, but they should contact the IRS if they suspect the form has an incorrect statement.

**Changed circumstances.**[87] If an employee becomes ineligible for the EIC after filing Form W-5 because of a change in circumstances, the employee must revoke it in writing within 10 days of the change. If the employee's spouse files a Form W-5 with his or her employer while the employee has a W-5 in effect, the employee has 10 days to file an amended Form W-5 showing the spouse's filing. If the spouse's Form W-5 is no longer in effect for some reason, the employee may file an amended W-5 form noting the change. Amended Forms W-5 must be put into effect by the employer by the first payday after the first "status determination date" (Jan. 1, May 1, July 1, Oct. 1) occurring at least 30 days after the amended form is filed.

**What the employer must do.**[88] Wage-bracket and percentage method tables are provided by the IRS in Circular E for employers to determine the amounts of advance EIC payments they must provide to employees who have provided a completed Form W-5 (see the Appendix at pages A-26 to A-33). These tables are based on all compensation paid to an employee for services rendered that are subject to federal income tax withholding, on the employee's marital status, and on whether a married employee's spouse has a Form W-5 in effect. If the employee has claimed exempt from withholding on his or her Form W-4, earned income is the wages that would have been subject to withholding without the exemption.

**How to pay advance EIC.**[89] Advance EIC payments are not wages and do not change the amount of federal income, social security, and Medicare taxes that must be withheld from the employee's wages. The advance payments are made from the withheld taxes, and they are considered to have been withheld and paid over to the IRS on the day the wages were paid. After withholding taxes from an eligible employee's gross pay and determining net pay, the employer then adds the amount of the advance EIC payment to net pay.

> *Example:* In 2008, employee Mike is paid $900 in federal taxable wages every two weeks, is married with 2 dependent children, and claims 4 withholding allowances. Mike has a Form W-5 in effect and his spouse does not. He lives in a state that does not have an income tax. Mike's net pay is determined as follows (using the wage-bracket method for both federal income tax withholding and advance EIC payments):
>
> | | |
> |---|---:|
> | Taxable biweekly wages | $900.00 |
> | Federal income tax withheld | - 6.00 |
> | Social security tax withheld | - 55.80 |
> | Medicare tax withheld | - 13.05 |
> | Advance EIC payment | + 49.00 |
> | Net pay | $874.15 |

---

86.   IRC §3507(b), (e); IRS Reg. §31.3507-2; IRS Ann. 99-3, 1999-3 IRB 15.
87.   IRC §3507(e)(1)(B), (e)(3).
88.   IRC §3507(c); IRS Reg. §31.3507-1(b).
89.   IRC §3507(d); IRS Reg. §31.3507-1(c).

**STOP PAYMENTS IF WAGES EXCEED LIMIT** As soon as an employee's wage payments for 2008 reach $33,995 ($36,995 for married employees filing jointly) or advance EIC payments total $1,750, the employer must stop making advance EIC payments to the employee for the rest of the year.

**Allocating advance EIC payments to withheld taxes.**[90] As noted earlier, advance EIC payments are made from withheld federal income tax and employee and employer shares of social security and Medicare taxes. If the advance EIC payments total more than all these taxes' the employer has two choices:

1. Reduce each payment by the amount derived from the following formula:

$$\text{Amount to reduce} = \text{Payment amount} \times \frac{\text{Excess payments}}{\text{Total payments}}$$

2. Pay each employee the full payment amount and treat the excess over the available taxes as an advance payment of employment taxes.

**Required notices to employees.**[91] Employers are required to notify employees who have no federal income tax withheld from wages (for a reason other than they claimed exempt on Form W-4) of their possible eligibility for a tax refund because of the EIC. Employers are also encouraged to notify any employees whose wages for 2008 are less than $41,646 that they may be eligible to claim the earned income credit for 2008. Employers may provide notification by giving the employees:

- Copy B of Form W-2, *Wage and Tax Statement* (the copy filed with the employee's federal income tax return, see Appendix page A-62), which has the required EIC statement on the back (so long as the form is provided by the IRS or, if a substitute, has the required statement on Copy B);

- Notice 797, *Possible Federal Tax Refund Due to the Earned Income Credit*; or

- A written statement with the exact same wording as Notice 797.

*Time limits for providing notice.* If the employer timely provides its employees with substitute (privately printed) Forms W-2 that do not have the required notice on the back of the employee's copy, proper notice must be given within one week of the date the substitute Form W-2 is provided. If the employer does not provide Form W-2 on time, it must provide the proper notice to its employees by the date it was required to provide the W-2s (January 31). If Form W-2 is not required, the employer must provide proper notice to the employee by February 7.[92] Notices that are not furnished with the employee's Form W-2 must be hand delivered to the employee (not just posted for all employees to see) or sent to the employee by first class mail.

The IRS must also take steps to make employees who are receiving the EIC on their personal tax returns aware of the possibility that they may be eligible for advance payment of the credit.[93]

 **CALIFORNIA REQUIRES EITC NOTICE FOR ALL EMPLOYEES** Beginning in 2008, a California employer must notify all its employees in California that they may be eligible for the EIC within one week before or after, or at the same time, that the employer provides a Form W-2 to any employee. The employer must provide the notification by handing directly to the employee or mailing to the employee's last known address either: (1) instructions on how to obtain any notices available from the IRS for this purpose, including Notice 797 and Form W-5; or (2) a notice created by the employer, as long as it contains substantially the same language as the sample notice provided in the law. The employer will not satisfy the notification requirement by posting a notice on an employee bulletin board or sending it through office mail, although these methods are encouraged to help inform all employees of the EIC.

---

90. IRC §3507(d)(2), (d)(3); IRS Reg. §31.3507-1(c)(2), (c)(3).
91. IRS Reg. §31.6051-1(h); IRS Pub. 15, Circular E, Employer's Tax Guide.
92. IRS Reg. §31.6051-1(h); IRS Pub. 15, Circular E, Employer's Tax Guide.
93. IRC §3507(f).

**Penalties for not making advance EIC payments.**[94]  Generally, the failure to make an advance EIC payment is treated as a failure to withhold (see Section 6.9).  If an employer fails to make a required advance EIC payment, it will be liable for a penalty equal to the amount of the payment not made.  It does not matter whether the employee is eventually found to be ineligible for the EIC when he or she files a personal income tax return, so long as a Form W-5 was in effect requiring advance payments.

## 6.7 Social Security and Medicare Taxes

Employers and employees both pay taxes required by the Federal Insurance Contributions Act (FICA) to fund two federal government benefit programs:  Social Security and Medicare.  Social security is comprised of Old Age and Survivor's Insurance (OASI) and Disability Insurance (DI), and Medicare benefits are provided by the Health Insurance (HI) program.  The employee share of social security and Medicare taxes is withheld from wages and matched by the employer, which then pays both shares to the federal government.

The amount withheld for social security and Medicare taxes is calculated by applying a fixed tax rate to the employee's taxable wages.  For social security, the tax is applied only on wages up to the taxable wage base (or wage limit).  There is no Medicare wage limit (see Section 6.7-2).  (See Section 1 for information on which employees are subject to social security and Medicare taxes, and Sections 3 and 4 for how different wage and benefit payments are treated for social security and Medicare purposes.)  Once it is determined an employee's compensation is subject to social security and Medicare taxes, there are no withholding exemptions or allowances to consider, and the age of the employee does not matter.  Withholding must begin as soon as wages are actually or constructively paid (see Section 6.1).[95]

## 6.7-1 Social Security and Medicare Tax Rates

In 2008, the social security tax rate is 6.2% and the Medicare tax rate is 1.45%, for a total FICA tax rate of 7.65%.  The combined employee-employer FICA tax rate is 15.3%.  These rates have remained the same since 1990.

## 6.7-2 Social Security Wage Base

Social security tax is applied only up to a certain wage base.  Wages paid beyond that amount are not taxable.  For 2008, the social security wage base is $102,000.  Until 1994, Medicare tax also was applied only up to a certain wage base.  It was the same as the social security wage base through 1990, with a separate, and much higher, wage base established from 1991-1993.

The Omnibus Budget Reconciliation Act of 1993 eliminated the Medicare wage base, effective for wage payments made beginning January 1, 1994.  Because social security has a wage base and Medicare does not, separate accounting and reporting for each tax on forms sent to the IRS, SSA, and employees is necessary.

Below, Table 6.4 shows the social security and Medicare wage bases, tax rates, and maximum employee taxes for the period 1980-2008.

---

94.     IRC §3507(d)(4); IRS Reg. §31.3507-1(c)(4)
95.     IRS Reg. §31.3101-3; §31.3102-1; §31.3111-3.

Table 6.4

| SOCIAL SECURITY AND MEDICARE WAGE BASES AND TAX RATES | | | | | | |
|---|---|---|---|---|---|---|
| Year | Social Security Tax Rate | Social Security Wage Base | Social Security Maximum Tax | Medicare Tax Rate | Medicare Wage Base | Medicare Maximum Tax |
| 1980 | 6.13% | $25,900 | $1,587.67 | | | |
| 1981 | 6.65% | $29,700 | $1,975.05 | | | |
| 1982 | 6.70% | $32,400 | $2,170.80 | | | |
| 1983 | 6.70% | $35,700 | $2,391.90 | | | |
| 1984 | 6.70% | $37,800 | $2,532.60 | | | |
| 1985 | 7.05% | $39,600 | $2,791.80 | | | |
| 1986 | 7.15% | $42,000 | $3,003.00 | | | |
| 1987 | 7.15% | $43,800 | $3,131.70 | | | |
| 1988 | 7.51% | $45,800 | $3,439.58 | | | |
| 1989 | 7.51% | $48,000 | $3,604.80 | | | |
| 1990 | 7.65% | $51,300 | $3,924.45 | | | |
| 1991 | 6.20% | $53,400 | $3,310.80 | 1.45% | $125,000 | $1,812.50 |
| 1992 | 6.20% | $55,500 | $3,441.00 | 1.45% | $130,200 | $1,887.90 |
| 1993 | 6.20% | $57,600 | $3,571.20 | 1.45% | $135,000 | $1,957.50 |
| 1994 | 6.20% | $60,600 | $3,757.20 | 1.45% | | |
| 1995 | 6.20% | $61,200 | $3,794.40 | 1.45% | | |
| 1996 | 6.20% | $62,700 | $3,887.40 | 1.45% | | |
| 1997 | 6.20% | $65,400 | $4,054.80 | 1.45% | | |
| 1998 | 6.20% | $68,400 | $4,240.80 | 1.45% | | |
| 1999 | 6.20% | $72,600 | $4,501.20 | 1.45% | | |
| 2000 | 6.20% | $76,200 | $4,724.40 | 1.45% | | |
| 2001 | 6.20% | $80,400 | $4,984.80 | 1.45% | | |
| 2002 | 6.20% | $84,900 | $5,263.80 | 1.45% | | |
| 2003 | 6.20% | $87,000 | $5,394.00 | 1.45% | | |
| 2004 | 6.20% | $87,900 | $5,449.80 | 1.45% | | |
| 2005 | 6.20% | $90,000 | $5,580.00 | 1.45% | | |
| 2006 | 6.20% | $94,200 | $5,840.40 | 1.45% | | |
| 2007 | 6.20% | $97,500 | $6,045.00 | 1.45% | | |
| 2008 | 6.20% | $102,000 | $6,324.00 | 1.45% | | |

## 6.7-3  Calculating the Withholding Amounts

Using the applicable tax rates and wage bases, the employee share of social security tax in 2008 is 6.2% of the first $102,000 in wages, while the employee share of Medicare tax in 2008 is 1.45% of all Medicare taxable wages.  Therefore, the maximum amount that can be withheld in 2008 for social security tax is $6,324.00, while there is no maximum on Medicare tax withholding.  The employer must match from its own funds whatever amounts are withheld from its employees' wages.

***Example 1:*** Employee Alice is paid $1,050 weekly in 2008. Her social security and Medicare tax withholding from each paycheck during the year is calculated as follows:

Social security tax:

| | |
|---|---|
| Social security tax rate | 6.2% |
| Taxable wages per week | $1,050.00 |
| Social security tax withheld ($1,050 x .062) | $65.10 |

Medicare tax:

| | |
|---|---|
| Medicare tax rate | 1.45% |
| Taxable wages per week | $1,050.00 |
| Medicare tax withheld ($1,050 x .0145) | $15.23 |

The total employee share of social security and Medicare tax for Alice each week is $80.33 ($65.10 + $15.23). The employer must match this amount.

***Example 2:*** As of December 20, 2008, Employee Brad has received $101,400 in wages. On December 21, he is paid $1,500. Brad's social security and Medicare tax withholding from his December 21 paycheck is calculated as follows:

Social security tax:

| | |
|---|---|
| Brad's taxable wages through December 20 | $101,400.00 |
| Brad's taxable wages paid on December 21 | $1,500.00 |
| 2008 social security wage base | $102,000.00 |
| Social security tax rate | 6.2% |
| December 21 wages subject to social security | $600.00 |
| Social security tax withheld ($600 x .062) | $37.20 |

Medicare tax:

| | |
|---|---|
| Medicare tax rate | 1.45% |
| December 21 wages subject to Medicare | $1,500.00 |
| Medicare tax withheld ($1,500 x .0145) | $21.75 |

The total employee share of social security and Medicare tax for Brad on his December 21 paycheck is $58.95. The employer must match this amount.

 **ROUNDING RESTRICTED** When determining the amount of social security and Medicare taxes to withhold and match, employers may round fractions of cents to the nearest cent, but rounding to the nearest dollar is not permitted.[96]

**Employees working for more than one employer.**[97] If an employee works for more than one employer during the calendar year, each employer is liable for withholding and matching social security and Medicare taxes. The earnings from different employers cannot be combined for purposes of determining whether the social security wage base has been reached. An employee who has had more than the maximum amount of social security tax withheld can get a refund on his or her personal income tax return for that year, but the employer is not eligible for a refund.

*Wages paid by common law employers through statutory employer can't be combined.* Where a payroll services company paid production workers who worked for various movie and television production companies, a federal appeals court ruled that the production companies were the employees' common law employers and each had to be considered separately when determining the employees' social security wages.[98] Even though the payroll services company was the "statutory" employer that had control of the wage payments and was responsible for withholding social security tax from the production employees' wages, the determination of

---

96.    IRS Reg. §31.3102-1(c).
97.    IRS Reg. §31.3121(a)(1)-1(a)(3).
98.    Cencast Svcs., LP v. U.S., 2004 U.S. Claims LEXIS 257 (Ct. of Fed. Cl., 9-30-04).

what wages are subject to social security tax is based on the wages earned by the employees while working for their common law employers – the production companies.

**Successor employers.**[99] When determining what amount of social security tax to withhold from an employee's wages, a successor employer may credit toward the wage base wages earned by the employee for the predecessor employer during the calendar year. To be eligible for this exception to the general rule:

1. the successor must have acquired all or substantially all of the property used by the predecessor in its business (or in a separate unit of its business);

2. immediately before and after succession, the employee in question must have been employed by the predecessor and successor, respectively; and

3. the employee must have been paid wages by the predecessor during the calendar year of the acquisition.

*Employee leasing firms are not successors.* During the late 1990s, the IRS received several social security and Medicare tax refund requests from employee leasing firms operating as professional employer organizations (PEOs) for taxes withheld from employees during the first year of the leasing arrangement when they worked for both the client and the leasing firm. In 2000, the IRS issued an internal legal memorandum stating that separate wage bases apply to the compensation received by the leased employees for social security and FUTA tax purposes. The IRS said the PEOs are not successor employers because they do not acquire the client's business assets and the employees' continued use of the assets does not establish successor employer status.[100]

**Wages earned in one year but paid in the next.**[101] Remember from our discussion of constructive payment (see Section 6.1) that wages are subject to employment taxes when actually or constructively paid, not when earned. Therefore, wages earned in one year and paid in the next year are taxable for social security and Medicare tax purposes in the later year. Problems may arise when paychecks are mailed late in one year and received in the next. Constructive payment occurs when the check reaches the employee's mailbox, even though it may be dated earlier.

 **WATCH OUT FOR ELECTIVE DEFERRALS AND DEPENDENT CARE** There are two important exceptions to the general rule of constructive payment where social security and Medicare taxes are concerned. Elective deferrals to §401(k) plans and other deferred compensation plans, as well as compensation deferred under a nonqualified deferred compensation plan that is not subject to forfeiture, are subject to social security and Medicare taxes when deferred, not when the deferred amounts are paid to the employees. Dependent care assistance benefits are treated as received in the year when the benefit costs are incurred, rather than when they are paid, for purposes of determining how much of the benefits are taxable for social security or Medicare purposes.

## 6.7-4 Related Corporations and the "Common Paymaster" Option

Despite the general rule requiring each employer to withhold and pay social security and Medicare taxes for employees who work for more than one employer, related corporations can reduce that burden considerably.[102] Where two or more related corporations concurrently employ one or more employees and pay them through one of the corporations as a "common paymaster," the total social security and Medicare taxes that must be paid are determined as if the employees had one employer—the common paymaster—paying all their wages.

---

99.    IRS Reg. §31.3121(a)(1)-1(b).
100.   ILM 200017041, 3-3-00.
101.   IRS Reg. §31.3121(a)(1)-1(a)(2); Rev. Rul. 73-99, 1973-1 CB 412.
102.   IRC §3121(s); IRS Reg. §31.3121(s)-1.

**DOES NOT APPLY TO INCOME TAXES** Use of the common paymaster option has no application to the withholding of federal, state, or local income taxes.

**Related corporations.** To be considered related, corporations must meet one of the following tests at any time during a calendar quarter:

- they must be part of a "controlled group of corporations" under IRC §1563, which generally means one of the corporations must own at least 50% of the others' stock or the same five or fewer persons own at least 50% of the stock of each corporation;

- where a corporation does not issue stock, either 50% or more of the members of one corporation's board of directors are on the other corporation's board of directors or hold 50% or more of the voting power with respect to the other corporation;

- at least 50% of a corporation's officers are concurrently officers of the other corporation; or

- at least 30% of one corporation's employees are concurrently employed by the other corporation.

**Common paymaster.** The common paymaster is a member of a group of related corporations that pays wages to employees working for two or more of the corporations. It is responsible for all payroll records, as well as withholding, depositing, and reporting, for the employees it pays. The common paymaster may pay the employees by cash or with one check or with separate checks drawn on each employer's account (no other pay medium can be used). Compensation in the form of property provided by the related corporations to an employee must be separately taxed by each corporation.

 **NOT THE SAME AS COMMON PAY AGENT** Using a common paymaster for two or more related corporations is not the same as one or more employers designating another entity as their "common pay agent." For a discussion of the reporting rules governing common pay agents, see Section 8.8-3.

**Concurrent employment.** To be concurrently employed, an employee must be employed by two or more related corporations at the same time and performing services for each one separately, not just as a group. So long as the employer-employee relationship exists, the fact an employee is working for only one employer at any one time does not destroy concurrent employment status.

**Paying social security and Medicare taxes.** As discussed earlier, the employer share of the social security and Medicare taxes on the concurrently employed employees' wages is paid by the common paymaster. The common paymaster is liable for any taxes it fails to pay, but each related corporation is also jointly and severally liable for its portion of the taxes based on the percentage of compensation paid to each employee.

**WORKS FOR FUTA TOO** The common paymaster arrangement not only can be applied to social security and Medicare taxes, but to federal unemployment taxes as well (see Section 7). Its application to state unemployment taxes depends on the individual state involved.[103]

## 6.7-5 Self-Employment Tax

Self-employed individuals (e.g., independent contractors) must pay both the employer and the employee shares of social security and Medicare taxes, paying a combined rate of 12.4% for social security (up to the wage base) and 2.9% for Medicare (15.3% total). These obligations arise under the Self-Employment Contributions Act.[104]

The tax is determined and paid when the individual files his or her personal income tax return, and a deduction from gross income is allowed for a portion of the taxes to relieve the burden of paying both parts of the taxes.

---

103. IRC §3306(p); IRS Reg. §31.3306(p)-1.
104. IRC §1401; §1402.

# 6.7-6 What Wages Are Exempt From Social Security and Medicare Taxes

Details on whether certain payments to employees are wages for social security and Medicare tax purposes are found in Sections 3 and 4, where each payment is discussed separately. In general, all employee compensation is subject to social security and Medicare taxes unless specifically exempted under the Internal Revenue Code. Following is a list of several exempt payments:[105]

- sickness or injury payments made under a state workers' compensation law or under a law "in the nature of" a workers' compensation law;

- sick or disability benefits paid to or on behalf of an employee more than 6 calendar months after the last month the employee worked for the employer;

- payments made under a deferred compensation plan, except elective deferrals to the plan;

- payments made under a §125 flexible benefits plan (i.e., cafeteria plan) other than elective deferrals to a deferred compensation plan;

- noncash payments to an employee for work done outside the employer's trade or business or for domestic service in the employer's home;

- cash payments to an employee for domestic service totaling less than $1,600 for 2008 (indexed for inflation);

- cash payments to an employee for work done outside the employer's trade or business totaling less than $100 for the year;

- noncash payments to agricultural workers;

- cash payments to agricultural workers if the amount paid to the employee totals less than $150 for the year and the employer's total cash payments to all agricultural workers for the year total less than $2,500;

- cash payments totaling less than $100 for the year made to a homeworker who can be classified as a statutory employee (see Section 1.3-1);

- qualified moving expense reimbursements;

- cash tips totaling less than $20 in a month and noncash tips;

- death or disability retirement benefits paid under an employer plan;

- wages paid to an employee's beneficiary after the year of the employee's death;

- payments made by a tax-exempt organization to an employee totaling less than $100 for the year;

- reimbursement for or provision of excluded educational or dependent care assistance;

- the value of excludable meals and lodging provided by the employer;

- the value of excludable employee length-of-service and safety achievement awards, fellowships and scholarships, and nontaxable benefits under IRC §132; and

---

105. IRC §3121(a); IRS Reg. §31.3121(a)(1)-1 - (a)(18)-1.

- the value of the spread between the option price and the fair market value of stock acquired pursuant to an incentive stock option or an employee stock purchase plan.

## 6.7-7 What Types of Employment Are Exempt From Social Security and Medicare Taxes

In addition to the wage payments listed at Section 6.7-6, certain types of employment are also exempt from Social Security and Medicare taxes. Here is a list of some of them:[106]

- work done by temporary foreign agricultural workers;

- work performed by a child under age 18 for his or her parents (age 21 if the work is outside the course of the employer's trade or business or is domestic service);

- work on a foreign ship or aircraft outside the U.S. by non-U.S. citizens for a non-U.S. employer;

- work done by students who are enrolled and regularly attending classes at the school for which they are working and who are not "career employees" of the school (unless the school is a public educational institution that has opted for FICA coverage of student employees);

**IRS FINALIZES RULES ON STUDENT FICA EXEMPTION** In 2003, a federal district court in Minnesota rejected arguments from the IRS and ruled that the "student exemption" from social security and Medicare taxation applied to medical residents.[107] In 2004, however, the IRS issued final regulations clarifying the parameters of the student exemption that overturn the court's decision and apply social security and Medicare taxes to interns and medical residents.[108] Even after the regulations were finalized, the federal courts have continued to split over the issue.[109]

- work done for a foreign government or an international organization;

- work done by student nurses;

- work performed by nonresident aliens under an F, J, M, or Q visa (see Section 14.3 for an explanation of the types of visas);

- work performed by small fishing boat crews (normally less than 10 individuals) that receive a share of the catch (or the proceeds from the catch) and less than $100 cash compensation per trip for each crew member; and

- domestic service performed by an individual under age 18 if it is not his or her principal occupation.

## 6.8 State and Local Government Employees

Public sector employees (i.e., employees of state and local governments and their political subdivisions, such as cities, towns, villages, and school districts) have always been treated differently regarding their coverage under the social security and Medicare programs, most likely because of the prevalence of public employee retirement

---

106. IRC §3121(b); IRS Reg. §31.3121(b)(1)-1 - (b)(20)-1.
107. U.S. v. Mayo Foundation for Medical Education and Research, No. 01-1121, 2003 U.S. Dist. LEXIS 13603 (D Minn., 8-4-03).
108. §31.3121(b)(2)-1(d); §31.3121(b)(10)-2.
109. Mayo Foundation for Medical Education and Research v.U.S., 503 F. Supp. 2d 1164 (D Minn., 2007); U.S. v Mt. Sinai Medical Center of Fla., Inc., 486 F.3d 1248 (11 CA, 2007); The University of Chicago Hospitals v. U.S., No.1:05-cv-05120 (ND Ill., 9-8-06); Center for Family Medicine v. U.S., 456 F.Supp 2d 1115 (D S.D., 2006) – the issue must be determined on a case-by-case basis; U.S. v. Detroit Medical Center, No. 05-71722 (ED Mich., 12-1-06); Albany Medical Center v. U.S., No. 1:04-CV-1399 (ND N.Y., 1-10-07) – no FICA exemption for interns or residents.

systems. The trend throughout the late 1980s and early 1990s, however, has been to bring more of these employees, and their employers, under the umbrella of federal coverage and taxation.

Before 1986, a voluntary agreement between a state and the federal Department of Health and Human Services (§218 agreement) was required to cover the state's employees under the social security and Medicare programs. While agreements were in existence between all the states and HHS, it remained the state's option whether to choose coverage. Local governments were required to enter into agreements with the state government to also be covered under the §218 agreement.

**1986: Medicare coverage extended.**[110] All state and local government employees hired or rehired on or after April 1, 1986 are covered by Medicare and must pay the Medicare tax (which their employers must match) unless their state had already entered into a §218 agreement subjecting them to both social security and Medicare coverage. There are also several other exemptions from this mandatory coverage:

- employees hired to relieve unemployment;
- employees performing work that is excluded from social security and Medicare coverage (e.g., working for a foreign government or an international organization);
- employees hired to temporarily deal with natural disasters and emergencies;
- work performed in a public hospital, home, or similar institution by patients or inmates (although wages paid to inmates employed by a privately-owned penal institution are subject to social security and Medicare taxes);[111]
- election workers paid less than $1,400 per year in 2008 (adjusted annually for inflation);
- persons working solely for a fee;
- certain interns, student nurses, and other student employees at hospitals run by the District of Columbia.

**1991: Social security coverage expanded.**[112] Increasing concern for public sector employees who lacked adequate retirement benefits led to a further expansion of social security coverage for the public sector in 1991. As a result, all state and local government employees who are not members of a public employee retirement system or are not subject to a §218 agreement are subject to both social security and Medicare coverage and withholding for all work performed on or after July 2, 1991, regardless of when they were hired.

 **MEDICARE-ONLY COVERAGE DECREASES** Because of the expansion of social security coverage, most of the employees who had been subject only to Medicare coverage (i.e., hired between April 1, 1986 and July 1, 1991) became covered by both social security and Medicare as of July 2, 1991.

To avoid the requirement of social security coverage, the public employee retirement system must provide a minimum level of benefits similar to benefits provided by social security. Employees must actually participate in the system and accrue benefits or receive an allocation into their benefit account to be considered a member of the system. Employees are not members of a retirement system if they are not eligible to participate or their rights to benefits are subject to conditions other than vesting.

*What about part-timers and temporary employees?*[113] Unless they have a nonforfeitable right to the required "minimum level of benefits," part-time, seasonal, and temporary employees must have social security and Medicare taxes withheld from their wages. Part-time employees generally work less than 20 hours per week, while seasonal employees work full-time for less than five months in a year. Temporary employees must work under a contract that lasts no longer than two years, except in certain limited circumstances.

**Special rules for election workers**. Special exceptions and requirements have been enacted with regard to election workers, who generally work a few days a year for state and local governments or their instrumentalities (e.g., school district, fire district) at polling places.

---

110.  IRC §3121(u)(2).
111.  ILM 200526018, 1-30-04.
112.  IRC §3121(b)(7); IRS Reg. §31.3121(b)(7)-2; Rev. Proc. 91-40, 1991-2 CB 694.
113.  IRS Reg. §31.3121(b)(7)-2(d)(2).78 IRC §3401(a); IRS Reg. §31.3401(a)-2(b).

*Federal income tax withholding.* Amounts paid to election workers are not subject to federal income tax withholding. These amounts are considered to be "in the nature of fees paid to public officials," and such fees are not subject to federal income tax withholding.[114]

*Social security and Medicare taxes.* Election workers who receive less than $1,400 in 2008 (indexed annually for inflation) are not subject to social security and Medicare taxes on such payments.[115] However, if the election worker is paid more than $1,400 during 2008, the entire amount is subject to social security and Medicare taxes. There are special coverage rules for election workers who are covered under a Section 218 agreement, because a state and the Social Security Administration may specify the threshold for social security coverage.

*Reporting on Form W-2.* If an election worker receives less than $600 in a year and is not subject to social security coverage under a Section 218 agreement, no reporting is required on Form W-2. If the election worker earns $600 or more, the earnings must be reported in Box 1 of Form W-2. If the election worker earns $1,400 or more in 2008, all earnings must also be reported in Boxes 3 and 5 as social security and Medicare wages, respectively.[116]

> **Example 1:** The state of East Virginia pays Maria $200 in a year for services as an election worker and does not employ her in another position. There is no §218 agreement covering Maria, and she is not covered by the state's retirement plan. Maria's fee is not subject to social security, Medicare, or federal income tax withholding, and East Virginia does not have to issue her a Form W-2 reporting the amount of the fee.
>
> **Example 2:** The state of East Carolina pays Warren $200 in a year for services as an election worker and does not employ him in another position. There is a §218 agreement covering East Carolina's election workers if they are paid at least $100 in a year. Warren is not covered by the state's retirement plan. Warren's election worker fee is subject to social security and Medicare taxes, but not to federal income tax withholding, since his $200 fee exceeds the $100 §218 agreement threshold. East Carolina must report the fee paid and the social security and Medicare taxes withheld on Form W-2.
>
> **Example 3:** The state of East Virginia pays Joan $1,400 in 2008 for services as an election worker and does not employ her in another position. There is no §218 agreement covering East Virginia's election workers. Joan is not covered by the state's retirement plan. Joan's election worker fee is subject to social security and Medicare taxes, but not federal income tax withholding. East Virginia must report the fee paid and the social security and Medicare taxes withheld on Form W-2.
>
> **Example 4:** The state of East Virginia pays Yolanda $200 in a year for services as an election worker and also employers her in another position, in which she earned $300 in wages subject to federal income tax withholding. There is no §218 agreement covering East Virginia's election workers, and Yolanda is not covered by the state's retirement plan. Yolanda's election worker fee is not subject to social security and Medicare taxes or federal income tax withholding, although her $300 in wages is subject to federal income tax withholding. East Virginia must report on Form W-2 the $300 in wages and the income tax withheld. The $200 election worker fee does not have to be reported on Form W-2.
>
> **Example 5:** The state of East Virginia pays Zoe $200 in a year for services as an election worker and also employs her in another position, in which she earned $500 in wages subject to federal income tax withholding. There is no §218 agreement covering East Virginia's election workers and Zoe is not covered by the state's retirement plan. Zoe's election worker fee is not subject to social security and Medicare taxes or federal income tax withholding, although her $500 in wages is subject to federal income tax withholding. East Virginia must report on Form W-2 both the $200 and $500 payments and the amount of income tax withheld.

**New hires must be told about possible pension offsets.**[117] The Social Security Protection Act of 2004 requires state and local government employers to provide a statement to employees hired on or after January 1, 2005 in jobs not covered under social security. The statement explains how a pension from that job could reduce future social security benefits to which they may become entitled.

---

114. IRC §3401(a); IRS Reg. §31.3401(a)-2(b).
115. IRC §3121(b)(7)(F)(iv); §3121(u)(2)(B)(ii)(V).
116. IRC §6041(a); §6051(a); Rev. Rul. 2000-6, 2000-6 IRB 512.
117. Pub. Law 108-203.

Employers must give Form SSA-1945, *Statement Concerning Your Employment in a Job Not Covered by Social Security* (see Appendix page A-58), to the new employee before employment begins. The employee must sign the form, and the employer should submit a copy of the signed form to the pension paying agency. Form SSA-1945 explains to the new employee the potential effects of:

- the Windfall Elimination Provision, which reduces the amount of social security retirement or disability benefits for employees who receive a pension in a job not covered by social security; and
- the Government Pension Offset Provision, which reduces the amount of social security benefits received by such employees as a spouse or an ex-spouse.

**Federal employees also covered.**[118] Employees of the U.S. government who began work on or after January 1, 1984 must have social security tax withheld from their pay, while those hired before that date who were exempt from social security tax remain exempt so long as they are covered under the civil service retirement system. Federal employees generally are subject to Medicare coverage no matter when they were hired.

## 6.9 Penalties for Failure to Withhold

The Internal Revenue Code focuses most of its penalties for employers on the failure either to deposit the proper amount of taxes on time (see Section 8.2-3) or to file correct returns on time (see Section 8.7). Regarding withholding, the Code makes employers liable for payment of federal income tax deducted and withheld from employees' wages, while relieving employers of liability for the withheld amounts to anyone other than the federal government.[119]

Even though an employer fails to withhold federal income tax, if the employer can show the employee later paid the tax, the employer is no longer liable for the amount not withheld. However, this provision does not mean employers will not be faced with other penalties associated with the failure to withhold, such as late deposits or returns or the "responsible person" penalty (see Section 8.2-3).[120]

**Third-party liability.** There are special rules governing penalties for third parties who supply funds to an employer for the purpose of paying wages to that employer's employees, knowing that the employer cannot or will not deposit the required withholding taxes.[121] In such situations, the third party is liable for the amount of taxes not paid plus interest, up to a maximum of 25% of the funds supplied to pay wages.

The 25% limitation is an absolute maximum for both taxes and interest owed.[122] The time limit for the IRS to collect such taxes and interest is 10 years, although the parties may voluntarily agree to extend the time limit even further.

## 6.10 State and Local Income Tax Withholding

All but nine states (Alaska, Florida, Nevada, New Hampshire, South Dakota, Tennessee, Texas, Washington, and Wyoming) have state personal income taxes and require employers to deduct and withhold from employees' wages to satisfy those obligations. Many localities also have income taxes and require withholding. The individual withholding methods of these states and localities are beyond the scope of this book, although most jurisdictions have wage-bracket tables and some form of percentage method withholding similar to the federal withholding scheme. A directory of state income tax administrative agencies is found at Table 6.5.

[For more information concerning withholding and other aspects of state and local taxation, see Tables 3.1-3.10 of *APA's Guide to State Payroll Laws*.] For more information on local payroll taxes, see *APA's Guide to Local Payroll Taxes.*

---

118. IRC §3121(u)(1).
119. IRC §3403; IRS Reg. §31.3403-1; Schiaffino v. Genuardi's Family Markets, 250 F.3d 736 (3 CA, 2001); Heleen v. Radiation Safety and Control Services, Inc., No. 06-cv-24-SM, 2006 U.S. Dist. LEXIS 50113 (D N.H., 6-20-06).
120. IRC §3402(d); IRS Reg. §31.3402(d)-1.
121. IRC §3505; IRS Reg. §31.3505-1.
122. IRS Reg. §31.3505-1(b), (d).

Table 6.5
**Directory of State Income Tax Administrative Agencies**

**Alabama**
Department of Revenue
Income Tax Division
Withholding Tax Section
50 North Ripley St.
P.O. Box 327480
Montgomery, AL 36132-7480
(334) 242-1300
www.revenue.alabama.gov

**Arizona**
Department of Revenue
1600 W. Monroe St.
P.O. Box 29009
Phoenix, AZ 85038-9009
(602) 255-2060 (Phoenix)
(800) 843-7196
www.revenue.state.az.us/

**Arkansas**
Dept. of Finance and Administration
Withholding Tax Branch
P.O. Box 8055
Little Rock, AR 72203-8055
(501) 682-7290
www.arkansas.gov/dfa/income_tax/tax_wh_
forms.hrml

**California**
Employment Development Department
Taxpayer Assistance Center
P.O. Box 2068
Rancho Cordova, CA 95741
(888) 745-3886
www.edd.cahwnet.gov/taxind.htm

**Colorado**
Department of Revenue
State Capitol Annex
1375 Sherman St.
Denver, CO 80261-0009
(303) 238-7378
www.revenue.state.co.us/main/home.asp

**Connecticut**
Department of Revenue Services
25 Sigourney Street
Hartford, CT 06106
(860) 297-5962
(800) 382-9463 (in state)
www.ct.gov/drs/

**Delaware**
Department of Finance
Division of Revenue
Carvel State Office Building
820 N. French St.
Wilmington, DE 19801
(302) 577-8779
www.state.de.us/revenue/default.shtml

**District of Columbia**
Office of Tax and Revenue
Taxpayer Service Center
941 N. Capitol St., NE
Washington, DC 20002
(202) 727-4829
http://otr.cfo.dc.gov/otr/site/default.asp?otrnav_
gid=

**Georgia**
Department of Revenue
Withholding Tax Section
1800 Century Center Blvd., NE
Atlanta, GA 30345-3205
(404) 417-2311
www.etax.dor.ga.gov/withholding_tax_tsd.asp

**Hawaii**
Department of Taxation
P.O. Box 259
Honolulu, HI 96804-0259
(808) 587-4242
www.state.hi.us/tax/tax.html

**Idaho**
State Tax Commission
P.O. Box 36
Boise, ID 83722-0410
(208) 334-7660
http://tax.idaho.gov/index.html

**Illinois**
Department of Revenue
Willard Ice Building
101 W. Jefferson St.
Springfield, IL 62702
(217) 782-3336
(800) 732-8866 (in state)
www.revenue.state.il.us

### Directory of State Income Tax Administrative Agencies

**Indiana**
Department of Revenue
100 N. Senate Ave
Indianapolis, IN 46204-2253
(317) 233-4018
www.in.gov/dor

**Iowa**
Department of Revenue
Hoover State Office Bldg.
P.O. Box 10457
Des Moines, IA 50306-0457
(515) 281-3114
(800) 367-3388 (in state)
www.state.ia.us/tax

**Kansas**
Department of Revenue
Docking State Office Bldg., Rm 150
915 S.W. Harrison
Topeka, KS 66612
(785) 368-8222
www.ksrevenue.org

**Kentucky**
Department of Revenue
200 Fair Oaks Lane
Frankfort, KY 40620
(502) 564-4581
http://revenue.ky.gov/business/whtax.htm

**Louisiana**
Dept. of Revenue
P.O. Box 201
Baton Rouge, LA 70821-0201
(225) 219-7318
www.rev.state.la.us/

**Maine**
Maine Revenue Services
State Office Bldg.
P.O. Box 1061
Augusta, ME 04332-1061
(207) 626-8475
www.maine.gov/revenue

**Maryland**
Comptroller of Maryland
Revenue Administration Center
Taxpayer Service Station
Annapolis, MD 21411
(410) 260-7150
(800) 638-2937
www.comp.state.md.us/

**Massachusetts**
Department of Revenue
P.O. Box 7010
Boston, MA 02204
(617) 887-6367
(800) 392-6089 (in state)
www.dor.state.ma.us

**Michigan**
Department of Treasury
Sales, Use and Withholding Taxes Div.
Lansing, MI 48922
(517) 636-4730
www.michigan.gov/treasury

**Minnesota**
Department of Revenue
Mail Station 6501
St. Paul, MN 55146-6501
(651) 282-9999
(800) 657-3594
www.taxes.state.mn.us/

**Mississippi**
State Tax Commission
P.O. Box 1033
Jackson, MS 39215-1033
(601) 923-7088
www.mstc.state.ms.us/taxareas/
withhold/main.htm

**Missouri**
Department of Revenue
P.O. Box 3375
Jefferson City, MO 65105-3375
(573) 751-5752
www.dor.state.mo.us/.tax

**Montana**
Department of Revenue
P.O. Box 5835
Helena, MT 59604-5835
(406) 444-6900
www.mt.gov/revenue

## Directory of State Income Tax Administrative Agencies

**Nebraska**
Department of Revenue
301 Centennial Mall S.
P.O. Box 94818
Lincoln, NE 68509-4818
(402) 471-5729
(800) 742-7474
www.revenue.state.ne.us

**New Jersey**
Department of the Treasury
Division of Taxation
P.O. Box 281
Trenton, NJ 08695
(609) 292-6400
www.state.nj.us/treasury/taxation

**New Mexico**
Taxation and Revenue Department
1100 S. St. Francis Dr.
P.O. Box 630
Santa Fe, NM 87504-0630
(505) 827-0700
www.state.nm.us/tax

**New York**
Department of Taxation and Finance
W.A. Harriman Campus
Albany, NY 12227
(800) 972-1233
www.tax.state.ny.us

**North Carolina**
Department of Revenue
501 N. Wilmington St.
Raleigh, NC 27604
(877) 252-3052
www.dor.state.nc.us

**North Dakota**
Office of State Tax Commission
600 East Boulevard Ave.
Dept. 127
Bismarck, ND 58505-0599
(701) 328-3125
www.nd.gov/tax/

**Ohio**
Department of Taxation
800 Freeway Dr. N.
Columbus, OH 43229-0076
(888) 405-4039
http://tax.ohio.gov

**Oklahoma**
Oklahoma Tax Commission
P.O. Box 26860
Oklahoma City, OK 73126-0860
(405) 521-3279
www.oktax.state.ok.us

**Oregon**
Department of Revenue
955 Center St., N.E.
Salem, OR 97301-2555
(503) 945-8091
www.oregon.gov/DOR/

**Pennsylvania**
Department of Revenue
Bureau of Business Trust Fund Taxes
Department 280904
Harrisburg, PA 17128-0904
(717) 787-1064
www.revenue.state.pa.us

**Puerto Rico**
Department of the Treasury
P.O. Box 9024140
San Juan, PR 00902-4140
(787) 721-2020
www.hacienda.gobierno.pr/

**Rhode Island**
Department of Administration
Division of Taxation
One Capitol Hill
Providence, RI 02908
(401) 222-3911
www.tax.state.ri.us

**South Carolina**
Department of Revenue
P.O. Box 125
Columbia, SC 29214
(803) 898-5752
www.sctax.org

**Utah**
State Tax Commission
210 North 1950 West
Salt Lake City, UT 84134
(801) 297-2200
(800) 662-4335 (in state)
http://tax.utah.gov

**Directory of State Income Tax Administrative Agencies**

**Vermont**
Department of Taxes
P.O. Box 547
Montpelier, VT 05601-0547
(802) 828-2551
www.state.vt.us/tax/

**Virginia**
Division of Income Tax Withholding
P.O. Box 1115
Richmond, VA 23218-1115
(804) 367-8037
www.tax.virginia.gov/index.cfm

**West Virginia**
State Tax Department
1206 Quarrier St.
Charleston, WV 25301-3784
(304) 558-3333
www.state.wv.us/taxdiv

**Wisconsin**
Department of Revenue
P.O. Box 8902
Madison, WI 53708-8906
(608) 266-2776
www.dor.state.wi.us/

# 6.11 Review Questions and Exercises

## Review Questions

1. What is a Form W-4?

2. How long must the employer keep an employee's Form W-4 on file?

3. Explain the principle of constructive payment.

4. Why is the date of actual or constructive payment of wages important?

5. When must a newly hired employee's Form W-4 be put into effect?

6. What does a Form W-4 tell the employer?

7. What conditions must be satisfied for an employee to claim exempt from withholding?

8. Under what circumstances must an employer submit Forms W-4 to the IRS?

9. List six types of supplemental wage payments.

10. What method of withholding must be used if the employee claims exempt from withholding, has received $10,000 in regular and supplemental wages so far during the year, and is paid a bonus of $1,000 during a payroll period?

11. What are eligible rollover distributions?

12. What is backup withholding?

13. What requirements must an employee meet to be eligible for advance EIC payments in 2008?

14. When must the first Form W-5 filed by an employee for a calendar year be put into effect?

15. What methods may employers use to notify employees who have no income tax withheld and do not file exempt of their possible eligibility for a tax refund because of the EIC.

## True or False Questions

_____ 1.  An employer should refuse to change an employee's name until a new social security card with the employee's new name is presented.

_____ 2.  Under the principle of constructive payment, an employee is considered to have been paid wages that have been made available to the employee with "substantial limitation or restriction."

_____ 3.  Paychecks mailed to employees are not constructively paid when mailed unless the employees have the option of picking up their checks at the office on the day they are mailed.

_____ 4.  An amended Form W-4 filed by a current employee must be put into effect by the employer no later than the beginning of the first payroll period ending on or after the 30th day after the form is filed with the employer.

_____ 5.  If supplemental wages paid with regular wages are not clearly identified, the employer must withhold federal income tax as if the combined payment is a wage payment for that payroll period.

_____ 6.  Under the principle of constructive payment, an employee is considered to have been paid wages when they are earned and become payable.

_____ 7.  When an employee requests federal income tax withholding on sick pay, Form W-4S directs the third party to withhold a flat dollar amount.

_____ 8.  The backup withholding rate for 2008 is 25%.

_____ 9.  Before receiving advance EIC payments, an employee must file Form W-5 with his or her employer.

_____ 10.  Advance EIC payments are not wages and do not change the amount of federal income, social security, and Medicare taxes that must be withheld from the employee's wages.

_____ 11.  An employee's social security number is needed even if there is no withholding.

_____ 12.  If a new employee does not provide a Form W-4, the employer must withhold as if the employee were single with no allowances.

_____ 13.  Employees have the option on their Form W-4 to have a flat dollar amount of tax withheld from their pay.

_____ 14.  Pension recipients may claim a certain number of withholding allowances on Form W-4P to be used in calculating the amount to withhold.

_____ 15.  When determining the amount of federal income tax to withhold using the precentage method, employers may round off the withholding amount to the nearest dollar.

_____ 16.  When using the wage-bracket method of withholding, if the wage payments are above the maximum table amount, the employer has the option to use the flat supplemental wage rate.

_____ 17.  If an employee chooses to receive part of an eligible rollover distribution and to directly roll over the rest, federal income tax withholding is required only on the portion received by the employee.

_____ 18.  As soon as a single employee's wage payments for 2008 reach $33,995, the employer must stop making advance EIC payments to the employee for the rest of the year.

_____ 19.  Employers are required to notify employees who have no federal income tax withheld from wages and do not claim exempt of their possible eligibility for a tax refund because of the EIC.

_____ 20.  If an employee works for more then one employer, each employer is liable for withholding and matching social security and Medicare taxes.

## Multiple Choice Questions

_____ 1.  What program does the Social Security Administration provide to verify employees' social security numbers?

   a.   Immigration Reform and Control Act
   b.   Social Security Number Verification Service
   c.   New Hire Reporting
   d.   Online TIN Verification

_____ 2.  If the number of withholding allowances decreases for an employee, how long does the employee have to submit a new Form W-4?

   a.   10 days
   b.   30 days
   c.   15 days
   d.   1 year

_____ 3.  If a payer receives a "B" notice from the IRS, how long does the payer have to send a copy to the payee along with Form W-9, *Request for Taxpayer Identification Number and Certification?*

   a.   30 days
   b.   15 days
   c.   10 days
   d.   5 days

_____ 4.  What form must be filed by employees who want to receive advance EIC payments?

   a.   Form W-4
   b.   Form W-5
   c.   Form W-2
   d.   Form W-3

_____ 5.  An employee is supposed to receive his last paycheck of $1,500 for 2008 on Friday, December 26. Because of a system failure, paychecks are not available until Friday, January 2, 2009. Before December 26, the employee's 2008 earnings were $101,300. How much social security and Medicare taxes must be withheld?

   a.   Social security $93 and Medicare $21.75
   b.   Social security $93 and Medicare $0
   c.   Social security $0 and Medicare $21.75
   d.   Social security $43.40 and Medicare $10.15

_____ 6.  Which of the following forms must be completed to obtain a social security number?

   a.   Form SS-4
   b.   Form SS-5
   c.   Form SS-8
   d.   Form W-9

_____ 7.  Employees' paychecks are mailed from their corporate office on Monday for a Thursday payday. Because of a disaster in the area no mail will be delivered until Saturday, when the employees are not at work. So the employees can get paid during this week, the employer wires cash wages to the employees on Friday. The checks arrive at the office on Monday. When are the wages considered paid?

   a.   Thursday
   b.   Friday
   c.   Saturday
   d.   Monday

_____ 8.  Which form is completed by recipients of pension and annuity payments to determine the amount to withhold?

   a.   Form W-4
   b.   Form W-4S
   c.   Form W-4P
   d.   Form 1099-R

_____ 9.  Which of the following states allows employers to use the federal Form W-4 to calculate state income tax withholding?

   a.   Arizona
   b.   California
   c.   Michigan
   d.   North Carolina

_____ 10.  An employee claims single and one withholding allowance and is paid $550 every Friday in 2008. Using the wage-bracket tables, how much federal income tax must be withheld?

   a.   $48
   b.   $58
   c.   $57
   d.   $35

_____ 11.  What must an employer do after learning that a Form W-4 submitted by a current employee is invalid?

   a.   Not implement the Form W-4
   b.   Withhold as if the employee were single with zero allowances
   c.   Inform the IRS
   d.   Make the necessary corrections

_____ 12. A newly hired employee who is married with two children fails to complete Form W-4 by his first payday. What withholding status does the employer use when calculating the employee's withholding?

    a. Married, with 2 allowances
    b. Married, with 3 allowances
    c. Single, with 2 allowances
    d. Single, with 0 allowances

_____ 13. If a pension recipient fails to complete Form W-4P, what withholding status must be used by the payer to calculate withholding?

    a. Single, with 0 allowances
    b. Single, with 1 allowance
    c. Married, with 0 allowances
    d. Married, with 3 allowances

_____ 14. For 2008, single employees with dependent children may obtain advance EIC payments if their modified adjusted gross income is less than:

    a. $33,241
    b. $33,995
    c. $36,995
    d. $41,646

_____ 15. For 2008, how much can eligible employees receive in advance EIC payments?

    a. $1,750
    b. $1,712
    c. $1,648
    d. $2,917

_____ 16. A single employee with a dependent child is eligible for advance EIC payments. The employee is paid $450 each week in 2008. Using the wage-bracket method of determining advance EIC payments, how much is the employee's weekly advance EIC payment?

    a. $20
    b. $19
    c. $24
    d. $66

_____ 17. For 2008, what is the social security tax rate?

    a. 6.2% for the employee and 7.65% for the employer
    b. 6.2% for only the employer
    c. 6.2% for only the employee
    d. 6.2% for the employee and 6.2% for the employer

_____ 18. For 2008, what is the social security tax wage base?

    a. $90,000
    b. $102,000
    c. $94,200
    d. $97,500

_____ 19. An employee worked for three employers by August 20, 2008. The employee earned $26,000, $29,000, and $15,000 respectively from each employer. What is the total amount of social security and Medicare taxes that should have been withheld from the employee's wages?

    a.   $4,340.00
    b.   $2,627.00
    c.   $4,681.80
    d.   $5,355.00

_____ 20. A single employee with no dependents earns $43,000 in 2008 The employee claims 12 allowances on a Form W-4 for 2008. Which of the following is correct concerning the Form W-4?

    a.   The employee may claim 12 allowances
    b.   The employer will require the employee to verify the 12 allowances
    c.   The employer will disregard the Form W-4 and withhold as single with no allowances
    d.   The employer will notify the IRS of the claim by submitting a copy of the Form W-4

_____ 21. During 2008, a corporate officer is paid a semimonthly salary of $7,200 on the 15th and last day of the month. How much social security and Medicare taxes should be withheld from the officer's August 15 paycheck (i.e., 15th pay period)?

    a.   Social Security $0.00, and Medicare $104.40
    b.   Social Security $74.40, and Medicare $104.40
    c.   Social Security $74.40, and Medicare $17.40
    d.   Social Security $446.40, and Medicare $104.40

## Problems

(For the following problems, assume all wages are subject to federal income, social security, and Medicare taxes and are paid in 2008)

1. Calculate the amount of federal income tax to be withheld in each of the following situations using the percentage method.

    a.  Mark Hayes is single and claims one allowance. His income for the month is $1,800 and he is paid semimonthly.

                                                         $_____

    b.  Collin Jones is married and claims three allowances. Jones receives an annual salary of $42,500 and is paid on a monthly basis.

                                                         $_____

    c.  Sandra Stelone is single and claims two allowances. She receives an annual salary of $27,500 and is paid on a weekly basis.

                                                         $_____

2.  Calculate the amount of federal income tax to be withheld in each of the following situations using the percentage method.

    a.  David Smart is the managing director of Big Parts, Inc.  He is married and claims four allowances.  David receives an annual salary of $72,000.  He receives his paycheck quarterly.

        $_____

    b.  Jenny Smith is single and claims one allowance.  Her monthly salary is $2,650 and she is paid on a weekly basis.

        $_____

    c.  Craig Digger is married and claims three allowances.  He receives an annual salary of $53,000 and is paid biweekly.

        $_____

3.  Employee Jane is married and is paid $1,319 by her employer on a biweekly basis.  Jane claims 6 withholding allowances on her Form W-4.  How much is deducted for federal income tax each pay period?  (Use the wage-bracket method).

    $_____

4.  Penney Saver is paid by her employer on a biweekly basis.  Penney is married and claims 3 withholding allowances on her Form W-4.  She is paid $1,200 every two weeks.  Using the annualized method, calculate the amount of federal income tax to withhold for each period.

    $_____

5.  Tim Tanic is a salaried employee who is paid $6,000 on the last day of each month.  He is single and claims 2 allowances on his Form W-4.  Using the annualized method, calculate the amount of federal income tax to be withheld for each pay period.

    $_____

6.  Employee Bill receives a $2,000 bonus in addition to his regular wages and has received $50,000 in wages so far during the year.  Using the flat rate withholding method for supplemental wages, calculate Bill's federal income tax withholding on the bonus.

    $_____

7.  Helen Williams, a data processing clerk, is married and claims four withholding allowances.  Last week, in addition to her regular weekly wages of $550 she received a $1,000 bonus.  Her wages so far during the year totaled $10,000.  Using the flat rate for supplemental wages, calculate the federal income tax to be withheld from:

    a.  regular wages
            (using wage-bracket method)          $_____

    b.  supplemental wages                       $_____

    c.  total wages                              $_____

8. Mary Thomas, who is single and claims one withholding allowance, is normally paid $1,200 semimonthly and has received $9,600 in wages so far during the year. In between paychecks, Mary received an award of $750 for an advertisement she designed. Using the aggregate method and the wage-bracket tables, calculate the amount of federal income tax to withhold from Mary's supplemental wage payment.

$_____

9. Sarah is single and claims one withholding allowance. Last week she received $600 in regular weekly wages and a $100 production bonus listed separately on her pay stub. She had received $25,000 in wages before receiving the bonus. Using the wage-bracket tables, calculate Sarah's total withholding under:

   a. Flat rate method
   $_____

   b. Aggregate method
   $_____

10. John Frazier is paid $950 on the 15th and last day of the month, is married and claims 3 withholding allowances. John has a Form W-5 in effect for 2008 and his spouse does not. With a social security tax rate of 6.2%, a Medicare tax rate of 1.45%, and a state income tax rate of 3%, and using the wage-bracket method for both federal income tax withholding and advance EIC payments, calculate John's net pay for each pay period, assuming his wages remain the same throughout the year.

$_____

11. Ron Baker is employed by Jasper Tools Industries. He regularly earns $430 each week. Calculate the amount of social security and Medicare taxes to withhold from each paycheck.

   Social security
   $_____

   Medicare
   $_____

12. Sally is a salaried employee of the Wild West Rodeo Club. Her annual salary is $36,000 in 2008 and she is paid on a weekly basis. Calculate the amount of social security and Medicare taxes to withhold each week.

   Social security
   $_____

   Medicare
   $_____

13. Roy Wright is a salaried employee of the Alexander Masonry Company and is paid $2,200 every Friday. Before being paid on November 21, 2008 Roy had been paid 46 weeks salary to date. Calculate the amount of social security and Medicare taxes to withhold from Roy's pay on November 21, 2008.

   Social security
   $_____

   Medicare
   $_____

14. Joe Long earns $8,900 per month. Assuming his earnings remain the same each pay period, calculate the amount of social security and Medicare taxes to withhold from his December 2008 paycheck.

   Social security
   $_____

   Medicare
   $_____

# SECTION 7: UNEMPLOYMENT INSURANCE

## TABLE OF CONTENTS

# SECTION 7: UNEMPLOYMENT INSURANCE

To provide income for terminated employees while they are trying to secure another job, a joint federal-state system of unemployment insurance has evolved. These programs are funded by employer contributions on both the federal and state levels. Federal unemployment taxes are used to help fund the various unemployment insurance programs developed by the states. Each of the states also requires employers to contribute toward its unemployment insurance program in the form of state unemployment taxes.

## 7.1 Federal Unemployment Insurance

On the federal level, employer contributions in the form of unemployment taxes are required by the Federal Unemployment Tax Act (FUTA). The FUTA tax is paid only by employers and is calculated as a percentage of covered wages for each employee. FUTA taxes cannot be withheld from employees' wages. Several states require employee contributions (see Section 7.2-3), but most follow the federal method.

## 7.1-1 Who Must Pay FUTA Tax

Employers meeting one of the following criteria must pay federal unemployment tax:[1]

- nonfarm employers paying $1,500 or more in covered wages in any calendar quarter (1/1-3/31, 4/1-6/30, 7/1-9/30, 10/1-12/31) during the current or preceding calendar year;

- nonfarm employers employing at least one employee for at least part of one day in 20 different weeks (not necessarily consecutive) during the current or preceding calendar year;

- farm employers paying $20,000 or more in covered wages in any calendar quarter during the current or preceding calendar year;

- farm employers employing at least 10 employees for at least part of one day in 20 different weeks (not necessarily consecutive) during the current or preceding calendar year; or

- employers paying domestic employees $1,000 or more in any calendar quarter of the current or preceding calendar year for work performed in a private home, local college club, fraternity, or sorority.

**Some employers are not covered.** Despite meeting the above criteria, the following entities are not subject to FUTA tax:

- federal, state, and local government employers, including their political subdivisions, and Indian tribes;[2] and

- nonprofit religious, charitable, or educational organizations that are tax-exempt.[3]

---

1. IRC §3306(a); IRS Reg. §31.3306(a)-1(b).
2. IRC §3306(c)(6), (c)(7); IRS Reg. §31.3306(c)(6)-1, (c)(7)-1.
3. IRC §3306(c)(8); IRS Reg. §31.3306(c)(8)-1.

## 7.1-2  What Wages Are Exempt From FUTA

Details on whether certain payments to employees are wages for FUTA purposes are found in Sections 3 and 4, where each payment is discussed separately. In general, all employee compensation is subject to FUTA tax unless specifically exempted under the Internal Revenue Code. Following is a list of several exempt payments:[4]

- sick or disability benefits paid more than six calendar months after the last month the employee worked for the employer;

- sickness or injury payments made under a state workers' compensation law or a law in the nature of a workers' compensation law;

- payments made under a deferred compensation plan, except elective deferrals to the plan;

- payments made under a §125 flexible benefits plan (i.e., cafeteria plan), other than elective deferrals to a deferred compensation plan and payments made under an adoption assistance plan;

- noncash payments to an employee for work done outside the employer's trade or business;

- qualified moving expense reimbursements;

- death or disability retirement benefits;

- noncash payments to agricultural workers;

- reimbursement for or provision of excluded educational or dependent care assistance;

- the value of group-term life insurance coverage (including the amount over $50,000);

- the value of deductible meals and lodging provided by the employer;

- wages paid to a beneficiary after the year of an employee's death; and

- tips not reported by an employee to an employer (generally if less than $20 a month).

## 7.1-3  What Types of Employment Are Exempt From FUTA

In addition to the wage payments listed at Section 7.1-2, certain types of employment are also exempt from FUTA. Here is a list of some of them:[5]

- work performed for a federal, state, or local government employer, including political subdivisions;

- work on a foreign ship outside the U.S.;

- work done by full-time students for the school where they attend classes or for an organized camp;

- work done for a foreign government or an international organization (e.g., NATO, the United Nations);

---

4.  IRC §3306(b); IRS Reg. §31.3306(b)(2)-1 - (b)(10)-1.
5.  IRC §3306(c), (s); §3309(b); §3508; IRS Reg. §31.3306(c)(1)-1 - (c)(18)-1.

- work performed as student nurses or hospital interns;

- insurance agents who receive only commissions;

- newspaper deliverers under age 18 who deliver directly to customers;

- certain nonimmigrant aliens working under F, J, M or Q visas (see Section 14.3 for an explanation of the types of visas);

- work performed for a spouse or child;

- work performed by a child under age 21 for his or her parents;

- work performed by an inmate of a penal institution;

- worked performed by an election worker who is paid less than $1,400 in 2008 (adjusted annually for inflation);

- work performed by alien agricultural workers under an H-2A visa; and

- work performed by statutory nonemployees (direct sellers, newspaper deliverers, and real estate agents, see Section 1.3-2).

## 7.1-4 FUTA Tax Rate and Wage Base

Through 2008, employers pay FUTA tax on their employees' wages at the rate of 6.2%, which includes a permanent rate of 6.0% and a surtax of 0.2%. The FUTA surtax was scheduled to expire at the end of 2007, but it was extended for one year by the Energy Independence and Security Act of 2007.[6] The rate is applied to the first $7,000 of an employee's covered wages in a calendar year.

But most employers do not pay the full 6.2%. If they pay their state unemployment taxes in full and on time, employers can receive a credit against their FUTA tax rate of up to 5.4% (see Section 7.1-6 for more on calculating the credit). Employers receiving the full credit have an effective FUTA tax rate of 0.8% and pay $56 for each employee receiving at least $7,000 of covered wages ($7,000 x .008 = $56).

**Constructive payment rules apply.** As with federal income, social security, and Medicare taxes, FUTA tax applies only to wages when they are actually or constructively paid, not when earned (see Section 6.1). This can be important for wages earned at the end of one year, after an employee has surpassed the FUTA wage base, but paid in the next year. If the employee does not have access to the wages until the next year, the employer must pay FUTA tax based on those wages up to the $7,000 wage base.

**Employees working for more than one employer.** Similar to social security taxes, if an employee works for more than one employer, the wage limit must be applied to the wages paid by each employer (see Section 6.7-3).[7] The wages may not be aggregated by the employers in determining whether the wage limit was reached.

**Successor employers.** The rules allowing successor employers to consider the wages paid to an employee by a predecessor company when determining if the wage base for social security tax has been reached also apply to the FUTA tax wage base (see Section 6.7-3).[8] In addition, both the predecessor and the successor must be covered employers under FUTA for the exception to apply.

---

6.    Pub. L. 110-140; IRC §3301.
7.    IRC §3306(b)(1); IRS Reg. §31.3302(b)(1)-1(a)(3).
8.    IRC §3306(b)(1); IRS Reg. §31.3306(b)(1)-1(b).

**Common paymaster.** The rules allowing related corporations to combine wages paid to concurrently employed employees by a common paymaster when determining if the social security wage base has been met also apply to the FUTA tax wage base (see Section 6.7-4).[9]

# 7.1-5 Depositing and Paying FUTA Tax

Employers must determine their FUTA tax liability on a quarterly basis. In doing so, they can assume they will be entitled to the full 5.4% credit for state unemployment insurance contributions, at least for the first three calendar quarters of the year. Therefore, employers calculate their FUTA liability by multiplying their FUTA taxable wages for the quarter by 0.8%:[10]

taxable wages for quarter x .008 = quarterly FUTA liability

The amount of the employer's quarterly FUTA liability for the first three quarters of the year determines how the employer deposits the tax owed. In each of the first three quarters, if the employer owes more than $500, the full amount must be deposited (see Section 8.2 for more on depositing taxes) by the last day of the month following the end of the quarter. The deposit dates are:

First quarter ends March 31 ......................................Deposit due April 30
Second quarter ends June 30 .....................................Deposit due July 31
Third quarter ends September 30 .........................Deposit due October 31

 **DEPOSIT THRESHOLD INCREASED IN 2005** For quarterly tax deposit periods beginning on or after January 1, 2005, the quarterly FUTA tax deposit threshold increased from $100 to $500.

 **EXTRA DAY FOR WEEKENDS AND HOLIDAYS** If the FUTA tax deposit due date falls on a Saturday, Sunday, or federal or state legal holiday, the deposit is due on the next business day.

**Special rule for small amounts owed.** No deposit is necessary when the employer's FUTA liability for a calendar quarter is $500 or less. The liability is merely carried over and added to the employer's liability for the next quarter when that quarter's liability is calculated.

> *Example:* Arnie's Farmers Market had a FUTA taxable payroll of $20,000 for the first quarter of 2008, resulting in a FUTA tax liability of $160 ($20,000 x .008). Arnie's was not required to make a deposit of the FUTA tax owed by April 30, 2008 because the amount of the liability did not exceed $500.
>
> For the second quarter, Arnie's FUTA taxable payroll was $45,000, as more produce was sold, more employees were hired, and employees worked more hours. Arnie's second quarter FUTA tax liability was $360 ($45,000 x .008), but a deposit of $520 was necessary by July 31 because the total liability, including the first quarter liability of $160, determined the amount of FUTA tax owed.

**Final quarter liability.** Employers determine their fourth quarter FUTA liability when they complete Form 940, *Employer's Annual Federal Unemployment* (FUTA) *Tax Return* (see Appendix page A-146). In completing Form 940, the employer determines how much of the 5.4% state credit it is actually entitled to and how much its total FUTA balance for the year is. If the total balance due (after taking into account previous deposits and any undeposited amounts from prior quarters) is more than $500, the full amount owed must be deposited by January 31. If the balance due is $500 or less, payment can be attached to the employer's Form 940 when the form is filed (by January 31).[11]

---

9. IRC §3306(p); IRS Reg. §31.3306(p)-1.
10. IRC §6157; IRS Reg. §31.6302(c)-3.
11. IRC §7503; IRS Reg. §31.6071(a)-1; §301.7503-1.

*Example :* Continuing from the previous example, Arnie's third quarter 2008 FUTA taxable payroll was $30,000, resulting in a FUTA tax liability of $240 ($30,000 x .008). Therefore, Arnie's was not required to deposit the liability by October 31 and could carry it over to the fourth quarter. For the fourth quarter, Arnie's FUTA taxable payroll dipped to $10,000, since most of his employees had reached the FUTA wage base of $7,000. Arnie's FUTA tax liability for the quarter was $80 ($10,000 x .008), since it received the full 5.4% state tax credit.

When Arnie completed its 2008 Form 940, the total FUTA tax liability was calculated to be $840 ($160 + $360 +$240 + $80). Because the balance remaining to be paid was $320 ($840 - $520 already deposited), Arnie's could pay it with the Form 940 rather than depositing it.

## 7.1-6 Calculating the State Credits Against FUTA Tax Liability

As was mentioned earlier in this section, an employer's FUTA tax rate of 6.2% can be reduced by up to 5.4% through credits the employer can take based on the amount and timeliness of state unemployment taxes it pays.[12] There are two types of credit against FUTA liability. The "90%" or "normal" credit provides a reduction in FUTA liability for payments required and actually made under state unemployment compensation laws. The "additional" credit allows employers whose state unemployment tax rate is less than 5.4% because of a favorable unemployment history to receive credit for the difference between 5.4% and the percentage actually paid. An employer's total normal and additional credits against the FUTA tax rate of 6.2% cannot exceed 5.4%.[13]

**"90%" or "normal" credit.** The normal credit against FUTA tax liability equals the amount of an employer's required contributions paid timely into a certified state unemployment insurance fund. It is also called the 90% credit because the amount of the credit is limited to 90% of the basic 6.0% FUTA tax rate— 5.4%—(the other 0.2% is a surtax and is not used to determine the available credit). Several requirements must be met before state unemployment tax payments can be credited against FUTA liability. They include:

*Payment must be made by Form 940 due date.*[14] To receive the full normal credit, all state unemployment taxes owed must be paid by the filing date for Form 940, January 31 (or February 10, if the employer has timely deposited its full FUTA tax liability), even if the state payment deadline is later. If an extension for filing the form is granted (see Section 7.1-7), the employer can still receive full credit for state payments made by the extended filing date. For state unemployment taxes paid after the filing deadline, the credit is limited to 90% of the payments (full credit is allowed for whatever payments were made before the filing date). No credit is allowed for state payments made after the employer files its Form 940.

> *Example:* Ralph's Flower Mart, which has a state unemployment contribution rate of 5.4%, paid $1,500 of its $2,000 state 2007 unemployment tax liability by January 31, 2008 and the remainder when it filed its 2007 Form 940 a week later. Ralph's normal credit against FUTA liability for 2007 is $1,950 [($1,500 x 100%) + ($500 x 90%)].

 **CREDIT AVAILABLE FOR PAYMENT TO WRONG STATE** If an employer makes a timely payment of state unemployment taxes but sends the payment to the wrong state by mistake, it can still receive the full normal FUTA credit even though the payment to the correct state is made after Form 940 is due.[15]

*State must have "certified" unemployment insurance program.*[16] To qualify for the normal credit, the state law requiring payment of state unemployment taxes must be certified by the U.S. Department of Labor as complying with federal requirements regarding the joint federal/state unemployment insurance program.

---

12.   IRC §3302.
13.   IRC §3302(c); IRS Reg. §31.3302(c)-1.
14.   IRC §3302(a)(3); IRS Reg. §31.3302(a)-1(c)(2), (a)-1(c)(3).
15.   IRC §3302(a)(4); IRS Reg. §31.3302(a)-1(c)(4).
16.   IRC §3304.

The state must also make timely payments of all interest due on loans from the federal unemployment fund. Payments required of employers by an uncertified law cannot be credited against FUTA liability.

*Payments must be "required" by state law.*[17] Only those unemployment taxes that are required to be paid under state law can be credited against FUTA liability. Therefore, voluntary contributions allowed by some states to reduce an employer's unemployment tax rate cannot be part of the normal credit against FUTA liability. (They may, however, contribute to the "additional" credit an employer gets when paying a state tax rate of less than 5.4%.)

On the other hand, an employer that voluntarily chooses to participate in its state's unemployment insurance program without being required to do so receives the normal credit for timely payments it makes. The payments are considered to be required for purposes of determining the FUTA credit.

*Amounts owed must "actually" be paid.* Required state unemployment taxes must actually be paid into the state fund in order to be eligible for the normal credit against FUTA liability. Payments made by employers that are held in separate accounts while they challenge state tax rate assessments are not credited until the rate is finally set and the payments reach the state fund.

*State contributions must be paid by the employer.* Several states require employees as well as employers to make unemployment insurance contributions (Alaska, New Jersey, and Pennsylvania). Such employee contributions may not be taken as a credit against the employer's FUTA liability. But if the employer voluntarily pays the employees' share of state unemployment tax liability, it will receive normal credit for those payments.

 **NO CREDIT FOR STATE-EXEMPT EMPLOYERS** If an employer is exempt from coverage under state unemployment insurance laws in the states where it operates but is subject to FUTA, it must pay the full 6.2% FUTA tax rate. Depending on the law in individual states, however, the employer may voluntarily submit to state coverage and receive credit for payments made to the state.

**Additional credit.**[18] In order to allow employers with lower unemployment tax rates (based on their more stable employment history) to receive the same credit against FUTA tax liability as other employers, these lower rate employers are granted an additional credit equal to the difference between their tax rate and 5.4%. When added to the normal credit, the total credit cannot exceed 5.4%. The availability of the additional credit does not depend on the timeliness of the employer's state tax payments.

**Example 1:** Bill's Coffee House has a 2007 FUTA taxable payroll of $35,000 and a state unemployment tax rate of 4.7%. Regardless of the normal credit Bill's receives for its state tax payments, it will receive an additional credit of 0.7% or $245 [(5.4% - 4.7%) x $35,000].

**Example 2:** Assume the facts as stated in Example 1, and add that Bill's paid 80% of its state unemployment tax obligation by January 31, 2008 and the other 20% one week later but before filing its Form 940. Bill's net FUTA tax liability is calculated as follows:

| | |
|---|---|
| Total FUTA liability | = $35,000 x .062 = $2,170.00 |
| State tax liability | = $35,000 x .047 = $1,645.00 |
| Normal credit: | |
|     Amount paid timely | = $1,645 x .80 = $1,316.00 |
|     Amount paid late = $1,645 x .20 x .90 | = 296.10 |
|     Total normal credit | = $1,612.10 |
| Additional credit = [$35,000 x (5.4%-4.7%] | = 245.00 |
| Total credit | = $1,857.10 |
| Net FUTA liability = $2,170.00 - $1,857.10 | = $312.90 |

---

17.    Rev. Rul. 72-185, 1972-1 CB 327; Rev. Rul. 69-356, 1969-1 CB 270.

18.    IRC §3302(b); §3303; IRS Reg. §31.3302(b)-1.

**Successor employers.** Successor employers acquiring predecessor companies that are not employers under FUTA when the acquisition is made (e.g., they did not have employees for 20 weeks during the current or preceding year) receive a FUTA tax credit for state unemployment taxes paid by the predecessor that relate to employees who work for both the predecessor and the successor. The successor's credit equals the credit the predecessor would have been entitled to if it had been a covered employer during the year.[19]

**Credit reductions because of state loans.**[20] Under the joint federal/state unemployment insurance system, states with a high rate of unemployment and difficulty meeting their benefit obligations can borrow money from the federal unemployment insurance fund to pay benefits. If loans taken out during one year are not repaid by the end of the following calendar year, the FUTA credits for employers in those states are reduced, with the extra FUTA taxes paid being applied against each state's loan balance.

A state with an outstanding loan can avoid a credit reduction for its employers by repaying the loan by November 10 of the year the reduction is scheduled to take effect. If the loan is not repaid by that date, a credit reduction of 0.3% goes into effect, with employers in that state having their maximum credit reduced to 5.1% (5.4% - 0.3%) and their effective FUTA tax rate increased to 1.1% (0.8% + 0.3%). The more years a loan remains unpaid, the greater the credit reduction becomes, although there are limits for states that have made an effort to keep their balances in check.

*Post November 10 reprieve possible.* Even if a state has outstanding loans on November 10, it can avoid a credit reduction by meeting certain criteria regarding the amount it has paid back, whether it can meet upcoming payments without needing any further advances from the federal government, and the size of the net increase in the solvency of the state unemployment compensation system.[21]

**Figuring the reduction.**[22] Sometime after November 10 of each year, the credit reductions for that year are announced by the IRS and are included on Form 940 so employers in the affected states can figure the amount of their credit reduction.

For 2007, there were no credit reduction states, so the areas relating to credit reductions on the 2007 Form 940 have been shaded out.

# 7.1-7 Reporting FUTA Tax on Form 940

Employers covered by FUTA must report their liability annually on Form 940, *Employer's Annual Federal Unemployment (FUTA) Tax Return* (see Appendix page A-146).[23] As mentioned earlier, they may also pay their fourth quarter liability with Form 940 if the liability is $500 or less (see Section 7.1-3). The purpose of the form is to determine the employer's FUTA taxable wages for the calendar year and the FUTA tax liability on those wages after accounting for applicable state unemployment tax credits and FUTA tax deposits made during the year.

**Form 940-EZ eliminated beginning in 2006.** Through 2005, employers paying state unemployment taxes in only one state had the option of filing Form 940-EZ, a shortened version of Form 940, if they paid their state taxes by the Form 940 due date, all their FUTA taxable wages were also subject to state unemployment tax, and they did not pay wages in a credit reduction state. For 2006 and beyond, the IRS has eliminated Form 940-EZ as part of its project to revise Form 940 and make it easier for all employers to complete.

**What companies must file Form 940?** Each employer covered by the Federal Unemployment Tax Act must file a Form 940. When there has been a sale of the business entity, only the wages paid by that employer should be reported. If two companies merge or consolidate in a statutory merger, the entity that

---

19.　IRC §3302(e); IRS Reg. §31.3302(e)-1.
20.　IRC §3302(c)(2).
21.　IRC §3302(g).
22.　Form 940 Instructions.
23.　IRS Reg. §31.6011(a)-3.

results is the employer that must file the Form 940, since it is now considered the same employer as the absorbed corporation. It must report the wages paid by both corporations. The first return it files after the merger must have a statement attached with the following information: the fact of the merger; date of the merger; and the absorbed corporation's name, address, and employer identification number.[24] If the resulting entity files Schedule D (Form 941), *Report of Discrepancies Caused by Acquisitions, Statutory Mergers, or Consolidations*, that will satisfy the requirement for an accompanying statement (see Section 8.3-1).

*Successor employers.* Even though a successor employer may be allowed to include wages paid by a predecessor company to employees of both companies when determining whether the FUTA wage base has been met, generally each company must file its own Form 940 for wages it paid. There is an exception where the successor acquires a predecessor that was not an employer covered by FUTA (e.g., the sale takes place early in the year before the employer pays enough employees to be covered by FUTA). In that situation, the predecessor does not have to file a Form 940. (See Sections 7.1-4 and 7.1-6 for more on the FUTA obligations of successor employers.) The successor must file Form 940.

**IRS provides the form.**[25] By the end of the calendar year, employers that have filed Form 940 in the past will receive a new form from the IRS with a preprinted address label. The employer must also write its name and EIN in the boxes at the top of page 2 of the form. Employers that do not receive a Form 940 from the IRS should request the form so it can be received, completed, and returned on time. If an employer receives a Form 940 but has no FUTA tax liability because no wages were paid to employees, check Box c in the upper right corner of page 1, sign and date the form in Part 7, and return it to the IRS.

**Form must have employer's signature.**[26] Before returning the Form 940, the form must be signed in Part 7 by:

- the individual owning the business, if it is a sole proprietorship;

- the president, vice president, or other principal corporate officer, if the employer is a corporation (including a limited liability company treated as a corporation);

- an authorized member or partner of an unincorporated association or partnership (including a limited liability company treated like a partnership) having knowledge of the organization's affairs;

- the owner, if it is a single member limited liability company treated as a disregarded entity; or

- a fiduciary if the employer is a trust or estate.

Other individuals may sign the return as an agent of the employer if they have a valid power of attorney (see Section 8.3).

**When must Form 940 be filed?**[27] Generally, an employer must file Form 940 by January 31 of the year after the FUTA tax liability was incurred (e.g., Form 940 for 2007 FUTA liability must be filed by January 31, 2008). If January 31 is a Saturday, Sunday, federal holiday, or state holiday (in the state containing the IRS office where the return is to be filed), the form is due on the next business day (e.g., Form 940 for 2008 FUTA liability must be filed by February 2, 2009 because January 31, 2009 is a Saturday). Employers get an automatic extension to February 10 (February 11 in 2008 since February 10 is a Sunday) if they have deposited their FUTA tax liability in full and on time for all four quarters (although quarterly liabilities of $500 or less for the first three quarters may be carried over to the next quarter rather than deposited without affecting the right to the automatic extension). To get the extension, an employer whose fourth quarter liability is $500 or less must deposit the amount owed by January 31 rather than send in payment with Form 940.

---

24.     Rev. Rul. 62-60, 1962-1 CB 186; Rev. Proc. 2004-53, 2004-34 IRB 320.
25.     IRS Reg. §31.6011(a)-7(b); Form 940 Instructions.
26.     IRC §6061; IRS Reg. §31.6061-1.
27.     IRS Reg. §31.6071(a)-1(c); §301.7503-1.

Filers of Form 940 are allowed a special extension that is unavailable to filers of most other employment tax returns.[28] For good cause, the IRS will grant extensions of up to 90 days, so long as an application for the extension was filed by the due date of the form. The application may be in the form of a letter detailing the reasons for the extension request. Regardless of the filing extension, however, all FUTA tax payments must be made on time.

 **SOME PRIVATE DELIVERY SERVICES ARE AS GOOD AS MAIL** Before 1998, Form 940 was timely filed if it was postmarked by the U.S. Postal Service on or before the due date. If a method other than the U.S. mail was used to send the form, the date of receipt by the IRS determined the form's timeliness. These restrictions were relaxed somewhat in 1997 to allow the IRS to designate private delivery services that will qualify as comparable to the U.S. mail, so that a Form 940 will be timely filed if provided to the delivery service on or before the due date.[29] See Section 8.3-2 for details as to what private delivery services qualify for this treatment.

*Proof of delivery to IRS is not the same thing.*[30] While use of a designated private delivery service can serve as proof that Form 940 was timely sent to the IRS, it does not show that the document was delivered to IRS. If the IRS has no record that it ever received an employer's Form 940, the only way to prove delivery is to show that the employer used registered or certified mail through the U.S. Postal Service. The mail receipt establishes a presumption of delivery.

**Where must Form 940 be filed?**[31] After Form 940 has been completed and signed, it should be mailed, sent by private delivery service, or hand delivered to the IRS Service Center for the region where the employer has its principal place of business. The addresses of the IRS Service Centers are listed in the Form 940 instructions. If a FUTA tax payment is made with Form 940, different addresses listed in the instructions must be used.

*Changes in filing locations caused by IRS reorganization.* As part of the reorganization of the IRS mandated by the IRS Restructuring and Reform Act of 1998, nearly all employers file their 2007 Forms 940 in either the Cincinnati or Ogden Service Centers, which handle all receipt and processing of business returns (including employment tax returns). The only exceptions are returns sent with payments, which will go to addresses in Charlotte, NC or Atlanta. These changes are reflected on the address labels provided to employers with Form 940, as well as in the form's instructions.

See Section 8.14 for details on filing Form 940 electronically.

**How to amend incorrect Forms 940.**[32] Employers that make an error on Form 940 and need to file an amended return can do so by filing a new Form 940 for the same year as the year being amended with the correct numbers. Check Box a in the upper right corner of page 1 indicating an amended return is being filed. (For pre-2006 Forms 940 and 940-EZ, check the "Amended Return" box above Part I).

The employer should attach a statement explaining why the amended return is necessary (e.g., the 90% credit is being claimed for state contributions paid after the Form 940 due date). The amended return should be signed and sent to the same IRS address as the original Form 940 without payment. Employers filing an amended return after June 30 to claim contributions to a state unemployment fund paid after January 31 should attach a copy of the certification from the state. This will expedite the processing of the amended return. Employers that are claiming a refund of overpaid taxes must also attach Form 843, *Claim for Refund and Request for Abatement* (see Appendix page A-143), on which an explanation of the reason for the refund must be detailed.

---

28.  IRS Reg. §31.6081(a)-1(b).
29.  IRS Reg. §301.7502-1.
30.  IRS Reg. §301.7502-1(e)(1); IRS Prop. Reg. §301.7502-1(e)(1).
31.  IRC §6091; IRS Reg. §31.6091-1.
32.  Form 940 Instructions.

**Employers that go out of business.**[33] Employers that cease doing business and paying wages must file a Form 940 for the portion of the last calendar year they were in business and check Box d in the upper right hand corner of page 1 indicating no future returns will have to be filed. The form must also have a statement attached including the following information: the location where required records will be kept; who is responsible for keeping the records; and the name and address of the purchaser of the business or the fact that there was no purchaser or that the purchaser's name is unknown.

**Successor employers.**[34] Check Box b in the upper right hand corner of page 1 if the employer is a successor employer and:

- the employer is reporting wages paid before it acquired the business by a predecessor that was required to file a Form 940 because the predecessor was an employer for FUTA purposes; or
- the employer is claiming a special credit for state unemployment tax paid before the employer acquired the business by a predecessor who was not required to file a Form 940 because the predecessor was not an employer for FUTA tax purposes.

A successor employer is an employer that acquires substantially all the property used in a trade or business of another person (the predecessor) or used in a separate unit of a trade or business of a predecessor and, immediately after the acquisition, employs one or more people who were employed by the predecessor.

# 7.1-8 Form 940 Line-by-Line Instructions

**Combined Forms 940 and 940-EZ.** As mentioned in Section 7.1-7, the redesigned Form 940 replaces previous versions of both Form 940 and Form 940-EZ, beginning with the 2006 form. Employers that previously filed Form 940-EZ must use the redesigned Form 940.

*New worksheet and schedule.* An employer that had some (but not all) FUTA wages exempt from SUI tax or that paid any SUI tax after the Form 940 filing due date must complete a worksheet (in the form instructions) to calculate the adjustment. The worksheet should not be submitted with Form 940, but should be retained with the employer's records. An employer that had employees in a state where a credit reduction applies must complete Schedule A (Form 940), *Multi-State Employer and Credit Reduction Information*, and file it with Form 940.

**General instructions.** For the IRS to accurately scan and process Form 940, employers should follow the following guidelines:

- make sure the employer's business name and EIN are on every page of the form and any attachments;
- if a paper Form 940 is filed and a typewriter or computer is used to complete it, use a 12-point Courier font, if possible;
- enter dollars to the left of the preprinted decimal point and cents to the right;
- do not use dollar signs or decimal points;
- commas are optional; and
- if a line has a value of zero or does not apply, leave it blank.

**Line by Line Instructions.** Following are specific, line-by-line instructions for the 2007 Form 940, See Appendix page A-146 for a copy of Form 940 and page 7-16 for a filled-in sample Form 940.

*Employer identification number (EIN), name, trade name, and address.* If the employer is using a Form 940 with this information preprinted at the top, check to make sure the information is correct. If anything is incorrect, cross it out and type or print the correct information. If the employer is not using a preprinted Form 940, type or print the employer's EIN, name (legal name used when applying for the EIN), trade name (if there is one and it is different than the legal name), and address in the spaces provided at the top of page 1.

---

33.    IRS Reg. §31.6011(a)-6(a)(3), (a)-6(b); Form 940 Instructions.
34.    Form 940 instructions.

The employer's name and EIN also must be entered on the top of page 2. If the employer does not have an EIN by the time the first Form 940 is due, write "Applied For" and the date the employer applied in the space shown for the EIN on pages 1 and 2.

*Type of return.* In the upper right corner of page 1, check the appropriate box if any of them apply to the employer. If this is an amended return, check Box a. If the employer is a successor employer reporting wages or claiming state unemployment tax that a predecessor employer paid before the successor acquired the business, check Box b. If the employer made no payments to employees in 2007, check Box c. If this is a final return because the employer went out of business or stopped paying wages, check Box d.

*Part 1, Line 1a—State abbreviation.* If the employer pays state UI tax in only one state, enter the two-letter Postal Service abbreviation for that state on Line 1a.

*Part 1, Line 1b—Multi-state employer check box.* If the employer pays state UI tax in more than one state, check the box on Line 1b. The employer must also complete Part 1 of Schedule A (Form 940) and attach it to the Form 940.

*Part 1, Line 2—Credit reduction state check box.* If the employer pays wages in a state that is subject to a reduction of its state UI tax credit because it failed to pay back loans from the federal government, check the box on Line 2. The employer must also complete Part 2 of Schedule A (Form 940) and attach it to the Form 940.

*Part 2, Line 3—Total payments to all employees.* Enter here all payments actually or constructively paid to employees for their services during the calendar year, whether taxable for FUTA or not. Total payments include wages, salaries, commissions, bonuses, vacation pay, sick pay, the fair market value of property (e.g., food, lodging, noncash fringe benefits), reported tips, cafeteria plan benefits, adoption assistance benefits, payments to medical savings accounts, moving expense payments and reimbursements, employer contributions to deferred compensation plans (including elective deferrals), amounts deferred under a nonqualified deferred compensation plan, payments made by a predecessor to the employees of a business the employer acquired, and payments to nonemployees who are treated as employees by the state UI agency.

*Part 2, Line 4—Payments exempt from FUTA tax.* Enter here the total of payments made to employees that were entered on Line 3 but that are exempt from FUTA tax, either because the payments were not FUTA taxable wages or they were made for exempt services (see Sections 7.1-2 and 7.1-3).

If the employer enters an amount on Line 4, check the appropriate boxes on Lines 4a-4e to show the types of exempt payments that were made, as follows. Beginning in 2006, the employer no longer has to enter the individual amount of each type of exempt payment made to its employees.

- *Line 4a—Fringe benefits*—including the value of excludable meals and lodging, accident or health plan contributions, reimbursements (or payments to a third party) for qualified moving expenses, and cafeteria plan benefits
- *Line 4b—Group-term life insurance*
- *Line 4c—Retirement/Pension*—including employer contributions to a qualified plan, other than elective deferrals
- *Line 4d—Dependent care*—including payments that are excludable under Section 129
- *Line 4e—Other*—including certain payments for agricultural labor, payments to H-2A visa workers, payments made under a workers' compensation law, payments to certain statutory employees, payments to nonemployees who are treated as employees by the state UI agency, and payments for certain fishing activities

**WATCH OUT** Qualified moving expenses paid to a third party are not reported on Form W-2. However, according to the Form 940 instructions, these payments still must be included on Part 2, Line 3 of Form 940 in total payments to employees and then on Line 4 as an exempt payment. Therefore, payroll practitioners must get the necessary information regarding the payments from other departments in their company (e.g., accounts payable).

*Part 2, Line 5—Total of payments made to each employee in excess of $7,000.* Enter here all payments totaling over $7,000 for each employee during the year, since only the first $7,000 of covered wages are subject to FUTA tax. Do not include any exempt payments from Line 4.

<u>Successor employers.</u> If a successor employer acquired a business from a predecessor that was required to file Form 940, the successor can count the wages the predecessor paid to the employees who continue to work for the successor when the excess payments are determined. Include on Line 5 the payments made by the predecessor that were included on Line 3.

*Part 2, Line 6—Subtotal.* Enter here the total exempt payments (Line 4 + Line 5).

*Part 2, Line 7—Total taxable FUTA wages.* Enter here the total taxable wages (Line 3 - Line 6).

*Part 2, Line 8—FUTA tax before adjustments.* Enter here the FUTA tax liability before adjustments are applied. The amount is calculated by multiplying the total taxable wages from Part 2, Line 7 by .008.

 **A DIFFERENT APPROACH** Previous versions of Form 940 (through 2005) required the employer to first determine its FUTA tax at the maximum rate of 6.2% and then calculate and subtract its state UI tax credits to reach its actual FUTA tax liability for the year. Beginning with the 2006 version of the form, the employer first determines its FUTA tax at the minimum rate of .8% and then adds back any adjustments for late state UI payments, credit reduction states, or wages not subject to state UI tax to reach its actual FUTA tax liability for the year. For employers that do not have adjustments, this should make the Form 940 completion process easier (much the same as completing Form 940-EZ, which has been eliminated).

*Part 3, Line 9 – If all of the FUTA wages you paid were exempt from state unemployment tax.* If the employer did not have to pay any state unemployment tax because all the wages it paid were exempt (e.g., all the wages were paid to corporate officers or employees in exempt occupations), the employer must pay FUTA tax at the full 6.2% rate. If that is the case, the employer must multiply the total FUTA taxable wages from Line 7 X 5.4% (6.2% - .8% = 5.4%) and enter the result on Line 9, then go to Line 12.

*Part 3, Line 10 – If some of the FUTA wages you paid were exempt from state unemployment tax or you paid any state unemployment tax late.* If either of these situations applies, the employer must fill out the worksheet in the Form 940 instructions. For this purpose, state UI tax is paid late if it is paid after the due date for filing Form 940. As noted earlier, if state UI tax is paid late, the employer's credit for the payment of state UI tax is reduced. The worksheet takes the employer through the process of figuring the credit. After completing the worksheet, enter the amount from Line 7 of the worksheet on Line 10 of Form 940. The employer should keep the worksheet for its records, but should not file it with Form 940.

*Part 3, Line 11 – If credit reduction applies.* If the employer paid wages in a credit reduction state, enter the amount from Line 3 of Schedule A (Form 940) onto Line 11 of Form 940. Because there were no credit reduction states for 2007, Line 11 is shaded out on the 2007 Form 940.

*Part 4, Line 12 – Total FUTA tax after adjustments.* Add the amounts shown on Lines 8, 9, 10, and 11 and enter the result on Line 12.

*Part 4, Line 13—FUTA tax deposited for the year.* Enter here the total FUTA tax deposited for the year (including prior year overpayments) through January 31, 2008.

*Part 4, Line 14—Balance due.* Enter here the FUTA tax balance due (Line 12 - Line 13). If the amount is larger than $500, it must be deposited, not paid with the form. If the amount is under $1.00, it does not have to be paid.

*Part 4, Line 15—Overpayment.* Enter here any overpayment made to the U.S. Treasury when depositing FUTA taxes during the year (Line 13 - Line 12) and check the appropriate box for application of the overpayment to next year's return or a refund of the overpayment. If no box is checked, the overpayment will be refunded. If the amount is under $1.00, a refund will be sent or applied to next year's return only on written request.

*Part 5: Report your FUTA tax liability by quarter only if Line 12 is more than $500.* The employer must fill out Part 5 only if the amount on Line 12 is more than $500. If not, leave Part 5 blank.

*Part 5, Line 16—Report the amount of your FUTA tax liability for each quarter.* Enter the amount of your FUTA tax liability for each quarter on Lines 16a-16d. Do not enter the amount you deposited, which could be more or less than the quarterly liability amount because of the $500 deposit threshold for FUTA tax liability. The employer can determine its fourth quarter liability by adding the liability for the first three quarters and then subtracting the total from the amount on Line 12.

*Part 5, Line 17—Total tax liability for the year.* Add the amounts from Lines 16a-16d and enter the total on Line 17. The amount on Line 17 must equal the amount on Line 12.

*Part 6: May we speak with your third-party designee?* If the employer wants an employee, a paid tax preparer, or someone else to discuss Form 940 with the IRS, check the Yes box. Then enter the name of the third party designee in the space provided. The name must be that of a specific person, not a tax preparation firm. The designee must then choose a 5-digit Personal Identification Number (PIN) to be used when talking to the IRS about the form and enter it in the spaces provided.

By checking the Yes box, the employer is authorizing the IRS to talk with the designee about any questions it may have while the Form 940 is being processed. The authorization applies only to the Form 940 for the current year, and it automatically expires one year after the form's due date (regardless of extensions). If the employer or the designee wants to end the authorization before it expires, write to the IRS office where the form was filed. Use the "without a payment" address even if the form was filed with a payment.

By checking the Yes box, the employer is authorizing the third-party designee to:

- give the IRS any information that is missing from the form;
- ask the IRS for any information about processing the form; and
- respond to certain IRS notices that the employer has shared with the designee about math errors and processing the form (notices are not sent to the designee).

The employer is not authorizing the designee to:

- receive any refund check;
- bind the employer to anything, including any additional tax liability; or
- otherwise represent the employer before the IRS.

*Part 7: Sign here.* In Part 7, the employer must sign the form and print the name and title of the person signing the form. Then enter the date the form was signed and the daytime telephone number of the person signing the form. The person who must sign the form is determined by the type of entity filing the form. (See the discussion in Section 7.1-7.)

*Part 8: For paid preparers only (optional).* Part 8 can be filled out by a person who is being paid to complete Form 940, is not an employee of the employer filing the form, and is not filing the form as a reporting agent with a valid Form 8655, *Reporting Agent Authorization* (see Appendix page A-376). If completing this part, the preparer should sign and date where indicated and enter the identifying information requested in the spaces provided.

**Schedule A (Form 940) for 2007: Multi-State Employer and Credit Reduction Information.**
Schedule A (Form 940) must be filled out and attached to the employer's Form 940 if the employer was required to pay state unemployment taxes in more than one state or paid wages in a credit reduction state.

*Part 1, Line 1—Check the box for every state in which you were required to pay state unemployment taxes this year.* Employers that paid state UI taxes in more than one state must check the box next to the state Postal Service abbreviation for each state to which state UI taxes were paid.

*Part 2, Line 2—If you paid wages in any of these states.* If the employer paid wages to employees in any of the states listed on Lines 2a-2j, enter the total FUTA taxable wages paid in the first box for the line for the

appropriate state, then multiply that amount by the credit reduction number shown and enter the result in the box at the end of the line.

*Part 2, Line 3—Total credit reduction.* To calculate the total credit reduction, add the amounts from Lines 2b, 2d, 2f, 2h, and 2j and enter the total on Line 3. Then enter the amount from Line 3 onto Line 11 of Form 940.

There are no credit reduction states in 2007, so Lines 2 and 3 on the 2007 Schedule A are shaded out and should not be completed.

**Form 940-V, Form 940 Payment Voucher.** This voucher is to be completed only if you are sending any payment with the completed Form 940 (fourth quarter liability of $500 or less). Complete Boxes 1, 2, and 3 of the voucher, which require identifying information and the amount of the payment. Boxes 1 and 3 need not be completed if the employer's identifying information is preprinted there. Note that the addresses for sending Form 940 with a payment are different than those without a payment.

The check or money order should be made out to the "United States Treasury," and the employer's EIN, "Form 940" and "2007" should be written somewhere. Checks sent for payment that are made out to a state agency rather than the IRS will be returned to the employer. Detach Form 940-V along the dotted line. Do not staple the check or money order to the voucher.

 **PAYMENT CAN BE MADE BY EFTPS** An employer can pay the balance due using the Electronic Federal Tax Payment System. If the employer uses EFTPS, Form 940 should be returned to the address for forms sent without payment and Form 940-V does not have to be completed or filed.

*Credit card payments.* Businesses filing Form 940 with a balance due can pay the amount owed on the return by credit card over the phone or Internet. These payments can be made through either of two authorized third-party service providers that will obtain credit authorization during the transaction and provide a confirmation number as proof of payment. The service providers charge a convenience fee based on the amount of the payment.

Payments are processed through secure, commercial credit card networks and can be made 24 hours a day, 7 days a week. Payments are effective on the date the charge is authorized. *Note:* Federal tax deposits (FTDs) cannot be paid by credit card. Visit www.irs.gov (keyword: e-pay) for details on credit card payments, including a list of service providers and applicable convenience fees.

*Example:* A sample Form 940 for 2007 has been prepared for Briston Office Supply Co., which has 8 employees—5 in Michigan, 2 in Pennsylvania, and 1 in Minnesota. Briston paid all of its state unemployment taxes in Michigan and Pennsylvania and all but $200 of its Minnesota unemployment taxes by January 31, 2008. It paid the remainder of its Minnesota obligation on February 4, 2008, one day before filing its 2007 Form 940. All employees reached the state (MI—$9,000; MN—$24,000; PA—$8,000) and federal (FUTA—$7,000) unemployment tax wage bases. Other data needed for completing the Form 940 are as follows:

Employer's address: 423 Briston St., Newtown, MI 12345-0987

Employer's federal EIN: 45-6784567

| | |
|---|---|
| Payments to MI employees in 2007: | $150,450 |
| Payments to MN employees in 2007: | $35,200 |
| Payments to PA employees in 2007: | $80,000 |
| Total: | $265,650 |

| | |
|---|---|
| MI experience rate for all of 2007: | 7.5% |
| MN experience rate for all of 2007: | 4.75% |
| PA experience rate for all of 2007: | 4.9% |

Form **940 for 2007:** **Employer's Annual Federal Unemployment (FUTA) Tax Return**                850107

Department of the Treasury — Internal Revenue Service

OMB No. 1545-0028

| (EIN) Employer identification number | 4 5 — 6 7 8 4 5 6 7 |
|---|---|

**Name** (not your trade name)    Briston Office Supply Company

**Trade name** (if any)

**Address**    423 Briston Street
Number    Street    Suite or room number

Newtown    MI    12345-0987
City    State    ZIP code

**Type of Return**
(Check all that apply.)

- ☐ **a.** Amended
- ☐ **b.** Successor employer
- ☐ **c.** No payments to employees in 2007
- ☐ **d.** Final: Business closed or stopped paying wages

Read the separate instructions before you fill out this form. Please type or print within the boxes.

**Part 1: Tell us about your return. If any line does NOT apply, leave it blank.**

1  If you were required to pay your state unemployment tax in ...

    **1a One state only,** write the state abbreviation . . . . **1a** ☐ ☐

    **- OR -**

    **1b More than one state** (You are a multi-state employer) . . . . . . . . . **1b** ☑ Check here. Fill out Schedule A.

    Skip line 2 for 2007 and go to line 3.

2  If you paid wages in a state that is subject to **CREDIT REDUCTION** . . . . . . . . . **2** ☐ Check here. Fill out Schedule A (Form 940), Part 2.

**Part 2: Determine your FUTA tax before adjustments for 2007. If any line does NOT apply, leave it blank.**

3  Total payments to all employees . . . . . . . . . . . **3** | 265650 . 00

4  Payments exempt from FUTA tax . . . . . . . . **4** | 11500 . 00

    Check all that apply:  **4a** ☑ Fringe benefits    **4c** ☐ Retirement/Pension  **4e** ☐ Other
    **4b** ☑ Group term life insurance  **4d** ☐ Dependent care

5  Total of payments made to each employee in excess of $7,000 . . . . . . . **5** | 198150 . 00

6  **Subtotal** (line 4 + line 5 = line 6) . . . . . . . **6** | 209650 . 00

7  Total taxable FUTA wages (line 3 – line 6 = line 7) . . . . . . . . **7** | 56000 . 00

8  FUTA tax before adjustments (line 7 × .008 = line 8) . . . . . . . . **8** | 448 . 00

**Part 3: Determine your adjustments. If any line does NOT apply, leave it blank.**

9  If ALL of the taxable FUTA wages you paid were excluded from state unemployment tax, multiply line 7 by .054 (line 7 × .054 = line 9). Then go to line 12 . . . . . . . . . **9** | .

10  If SOME of the taxable FUTA wages you paid were excluded from state unemployment tax, OR you paid ANY state unemployment tax late (after the due date for filing Form 940), fill out the worksheet in the instructions. Enter the amount from line 7 of the worksheet onto line 10 . . **10** | .

    Skip line 11 for 2007 and go to line 12.

11  If credit reduction applies, enter the amount from line 3 of Schedule A (Form 940) . . . . . . **11** | .

**Part 4: Determine your FUTA tax and balance due or overpayment for 2007. If any line does NOT apply, leave it blank.**

12  Total FUTA tax after adjustments (lines 8 + 9 + 10 = line 12) . . . . . . **12** | 448 . 00

13  FUTA tax deposited for the year, including any payment applied from a prior year . . . . **13** | 448 . 00

14  **Balance due** (If line 12 is more than line 13, enter the difference on line 14.)
- If line 14 is more than $500, you must deposit your tax.
- If line 14 is $500 or less and you pay by check, make your check payable to the United States Treasury and write your EIN, *Form 940,* and *2007* on the check . . . . . . . **14** | .

15  **Overpayment** (If line 13 is more than line 12, enter the difference on line 15 and check a box below.) . . . . . . . . . . . . . . . . . . . **15** | .

Check one ☐ Apply to next return.
☐ Send a refund.

▶ You **MUST** fill out both pages of this form and **SIGN** it.

Next ➡

For Privacy Act and Paperwork Reduction Act Notice, see the back of Form 940-V, Payment Voucher.    Cat. No. 11234O    Form **940** (2007)

850207

| Name *(not your trade name)* | Employer identification number (EIN) |
|---|---|
| **Briston Office Supply Company** | **45-6784567** |

**Part 5: Report your FUTA tax liability by quarter only if line 12 is more than $500. If not, go to Part 6.**

16  Report the amount of your **FUTA** tax liability for each quarter; do NOT enter the amount you deposited. If you had no liability for a quarter, leave the line blank.

| | | |
|---|---|---|
| 16a  **1st quarter** (January 1 – March 31) . . . . . . . . .16a | 256 . 00 | |
| 16b  **2nd quarter** (April 1 – June 30) . . . . . . . . .16b | 77 . 00 | |
| 16c  **3rd quarter** (July 1 – September 30) . . . . . . . .16c | 69 . 00 | |
| 16d  **4th quarter** (October 1 – December 31) . . . . . . . .16d | 46 . 00 | |
| 17  **Total tax liability for the year** (lines 16a + 16b + 16c + 16d = line 17) 17 | 448 . 00 | Total must equal line 12. |

**Part 6: May we speak with your third-party designee?**

Do you want to allow an employee, a paid tax preparer, or another person to discuss this return with the IRS? See the instructions for details.

☐  **Yes.**  Designee's name

Select a 5-digit Personal Identification Number (PIN) to use when talking to IRS

☑  **No.**

**Part 7: Sign here. You MUST fill out both pages of this form and SIGN it.**

Under penalties of perjury, I declare that I have examined this return, including accompanying schedules and statements, and to the best of my knowledge and belief, it is true, correct, and complete, and that no part of any payment made to a state unemployment fund claimed as a credit was, or is to be, deducted from the payments made to employees.

✗ **Sign your name here**

*Barry Briston*

| Print your name here | **Barry Briston** |
|---|---|
| Print your title here | **President** |

Date  **2 / 4 / 2008**

Best daytime phone  ( ) –

**Part 8: For PAID preparers only (optional)**

If you were paid to prepare this return and are not an employee of the business that is filing this return, you may choose to fill out Part 8.

| Paid Preparer's name | | Preparer's SSN/PTIN | |
|---|---|---|---|
| Paid Preparer's signature | | Date | / / |

☐  Check if you are self-employed.

| Firm's name | | Firm's EIN | |
|---|---|---|---|
| Street address | | | |
| City | | State | ZIP code |

Form **940** (2007)

## Worksheet—Line 10

*Before you begin:* Use this worksheet to figure your credit if:

√    some of the wages you paid were excluded from state unemployment tax, OR
√    you paid any state unemployment tax late.

For this worksheet, **do not round your figures**.

Before you can properly fill out this worksheet, you must gather this information:

■ Taxable FUTA wages (from line 7 of Form 940)

■ Taxable state unemployment wages

■ The experience rates assigned to you by the states where you paid wages

■ The amount of state unemployment taxes you paid on time. (*On time* means that you paid the state unemployment taxes by the due date for filing the Form 940.) Include any state unemployment taxes you paid on nonemployees who were treated as employees by your state unemployment agency.

■ The amount of state unemployment taxes you paid late. (*Late* means after the due date for filing Form 940.)

1. **Maximum allowable credit** — Enter line 7 from Form 940 here:     56000 . 00    x    .054 = line 1     **1.**   3024 . 00

2. **Credit for timely state unemployment tax payments** — How much did you pay on time?     **2.**   5099 . 00

   • If line 2 is **equal to** or **more than** line 1, **STOP here.** (STOP) You have completed the worksheet. Leave line 10 of Form 940 blank.

   • If line 2 is **less than** line 1, continue this worksheet.

3. **Additional credit** — Were ALL of your assigned experience rates 5.4% or more?

   • **If yes**, enter zero on line 3. Then go to line 4 of this worksheet.

   • **If no**, fill out the computations below. List ONLY THOSE STATES for which your assigned experience rate for any part of the calendar year was less than 5.4%.

| State | Computation rate<br>The difference between 5.4% (.054) and your assigned experience rate (.054 − .XXX (assigned experience rate) = computation rate) | | Taxable state unemployment wages at assigned experience rate | | Additional Credit |
|---|---|---|---|---|---|
| 1. _____ | _____ . _____ | x | _____ . _____ | = | _____ . _____ |
| 2. _____ | _____ . _____ | x | _____ . _____ | = | _____ . _____ |
| 3. _____ | _____ . _____ | x | _____ . _____ | = | _____ . _____ |
| 4. _____ | _____ . _____ | x | _____ . _____ | = | _____ . _____ |
| 5. _____ | _____ . _____ | x | _____ . _____ | = | _____ . _____ |

If you need more lines, use another sheet and include those additional credits in the total.        **Total** _____ . _____

Enter the total on line 3     **3.** _____ . _____

4. **Subtotal** (Line 2 + line 3 = line 4)     **4.** _____ . _____

   • If line 4 is equal to or more than line 1, **STOP here.** (STOP) You have completed the worksheet. Leave line 10 of Form 940 blank.

   • If line 4 is less than line 1, continue this worksheet.

5. **Credit for paying state unemployment taxes late:**

   **5a.** What is your remaining allowable credit? (Line 1 − line 4 = line 5a)     **5a.** _____ . _____

   **5b.** How much state unemployment tax did you pay late?     **5b.** _____ . _____

   **5c.** Which is smaller, line 5a or line 5b? Enter the smaller number here.     **5c.** _____ . _____

   **5d.** Your allowable credit for paying state unemployment taxes late (line 5c x .90 = line 5d)     **5d.** _____ . _____

6. **Your FUTA credit** (line 4 + line 5d = line 6)     **6.** _____ . _____

   • If line 6 is equal to or more than line 1, **STOP here.** (STOP) You have completed the worksheet. Leave line 10 of Form 940 blank.

   • If line 6 is less than line 1, continue this worksheet.

7. **Your adjustment** (Line 1 − line 6 = line 7)     Enter line 7 on line 10 of Form 940.     **7.** _____ . _____

*Do not attach this worksheet to your Form 940. Keep it for your records.*

# Schedule A (Form 940) for 2007:

## Multi-State Employer and Credit Reduction Information

860307

OMB No. 1545-0028

Department of the Treasury — Internal Revenue Service

Employer identification number (EIN)   4 5 — 6 7 8 4 5 6 7

Name *(not your trade name)*   **Briston Office Supply Company**

### About this schedule:

- You must fill out Schedule A (Form 940) if you were required to pay your state unemployment tax in *more than one state* or if you paid wages in any state that is subject to *credit reduction.* FOR 2007, THERE ARE NO STATES SUBJECT TO CREDIT REDUCTION.
- File Schedule A (Form 940) as an attachment to your Form 940.

    For more information, read the Instructions for Schedule A (Form 940) on the back.

**Part 1: Fill out this part if you were required to pay state unemployment taxes in more than one state (including the District of Columbia, Puerto Rico, and the U.S. Virgin Islands). If any states do NOT apply to you, leave them blank.**

1   Check the box for every state in which you were required to pay state unemployment tax this year. For a list of state names and their abbreviations, see the Instructions for Schedule A (Form 940).

| | | | | | | | | | | |
|---|---|---|---|---|---|---|---|---|---|---|
| AK | CO | GA | IN | MD | MS | NH | OH | SC | VA | WY |
| AL | CT | HI | ☐ KS ✓ MI | MT | NJ | OK | SD | VT | PR |
| AR | DC | IA | ☐ KY ✓ MN | NC | NM | OR | TN | WA | VI |
| AZ | DE | ID | LA | MO | ND | NV | ✓ PA | TX | WI |
| CA | FL | IL | MA | ME | NE | NY | RI | UT | WV |

**Part 2: Fill out this part to tell us about wages you paid in any state (including the District of Columbia, Puerto Rico, and the U.S. Virgin Islands) that is subject to credit reduction. If any lines do NOT apply, leave them blank.**

2   If you paid wages in any of these states...

2a–b   **[Name of State]** Total taxable FUTA wages paid in [state] . . 2a                      × .00x = line 2b   2b

2c–d   **[Name of State]** Total taxable FUTA wages paid in [state] . . 2c                      × .00x = line 2d   2d

2e–f   **[Name of State]** Total taxable FUTA wages paid in [state] . . 2e                      × .00x = line 2f   2f

2g–h   **[Name of State]** Total taxable FUTA wages paid in [state] . . 2g                      × .00x = line 2h   2h

2i–j   **[Name of State]** Total taxable FUTA wages paid in [state] . . 2i                      × .00x = line 2j   2j

3   **Total credit reduction** (Lines 2b + 2d + 2f + 2h + 2j = line 3) . . . . . . . . . . .   3

Enter the amount from line 3 onto line 11 of Form 940.

**For Privacy Act and Paperwork Reduction Act Notice, see back of Form 940-V.**    Cat. No. 16997C    **Schedule A (Form 940) 2007**

*DO NOT COMPLETE FOR 2007*

# 7.1-9 Penalties for FUTA Noncompliance

In addition to paying the FUTA tax actually owed to the IRS, there are several penalties associated with late deposits, payments, and filing of returns. Following is a discussion of those penalties.

**Late filing of Form 940.**[35] Unless an employer has reasonable cause and is not guilty of willful neglect, late filing of Form 940 results in an "addition to tax," the amount of which depends on how late the return is filed. The amount is 5% of the amount of tax required to be shown on the return (reduced by any timely deposits and credits) for each month or fraction of a month the return is late, up to a maximum of 25% (15% per month up to a maximum of 75% of the tax required to be shown on the return if the late filing is fraudulent).

**Failure to pay FUTA tax.**[36] Unless there is reasonable cause and no willful neglect, late payment of tax owed as shown on the Form 940 results in an "addition to tax," the amount of which depends on how late the payment is made. The amounts are:

- 0.5% of any unpaid tax shown on the return (after accounting for credits) for each month or fraction of a month the payment is late, up to a maximum of 25%;

- an additional 0.5% per month of any unpaid tax not shown on the return but for which the IRS has issued a notice and demand, if the tax is not paid within 21 calendar days of the notice and demand (10 business days if the amount is at least $100,000), up to a maximum of 25%.

These additions to tax for failure to pay taxes are doubled to 1% per month or fraction of a month for amounts remaining unpaid after 10 days after the employer receives a notice of intent to levy from the IRS or 1 day after the day the employer receives a notice and demand for immediate payment from the IRS.[37]

**Failure to file and pay.**[38] In any month where an employer is subject to additions to tax both for a failure to file Form 940 and a failure to pay FUTA tax, the addition for failure to file is reduced by 0.5% of the unpaid tax.

**Reasonable cause.**[39] An employer that wishes to avoid the additional taxes for late filings or tax payments must make an affirmative statement under penalty of perjury setting forth all the facts supporting the claim of reasonable cause for its failure. If the facts show the employer "exercised ordinary business care and prudence," and still could not file the Form 940 on time, then reasonable cause exists and no addition to tax will be assessed. Reasonable cause also exists if the employer exercised ordinary business care and prudence and still was unable to pay the FUTA tax or would suffer undue hardship in doing so.

**Accuracy-related penalty.**[40] Employers can also be assessed an accuracy-related penalty for understating the amount of tax due on a return. The penalty applies if the amount of the understatement is due to negligence or disregard of rules or regulations. The amount of the penalty is 20% of the understated amount that can be traced to the employer's negligence. The accuracy-related penalty can be imposed in addition to a penalty for filing a late return, but not in addition to a fraud penalty.

**Failure to make timely FUTA deposits.**[41] Unless an employer has reasonable cause and is not guilty of willful neglect, late deposits of FUTA tax are subject to a penalty in addition to the tax owed that depends on the lateness of the deposit. The amounts are:

---

35.  IRC §6651(a)(1), (b)(1), (f); IRS Reg. §301.6651-1.
36.  IRC §6651(a)(2), (a)(3), (b)(2), (b)(3), (c)(2), (c)(3); IRS Reg. §301.6651-1; IRS Prop. Reg. §301.6651-1.
37.  IRC §6651(d).
38.  IRC §6651(c)(1).
39.  IRS Reg. §301.6651-1(c).
40.  IRC §6662; IRS Reg. §1.6662-1 - §1.6662-4; §1.6662-7.
41.  IRC §6656.

- 2% of the undeposited amount if it is paid within 5 days of the due date;

- 5% of the undeposited amount if it is paid within 6-15 days of the due date;

- 10% of the undeposited amount if it is paid more than 15 days after the due date; or

- 15% of the undeposited amount if it is not paid within 10 days after the employer receives its first IRS delinquency notice or on the same day a notice and demand for immediate payment is received.

 **WATCH OUT MANDATED EFT DEPOSITORS** The 10% penalty for depositing FUTA tax more than 15 days after the due date also applies to employers who are mandated to make federal tax deposits electronically through EFTPS but use a paper check and deposit coupon instead, even if the paper deposit is made timely (see Section 8.2-3 for details).

*Relief for certain small, new depositors.*[42] The IRS may waive the failure-to-deposit penalty for an employer's inadvertent failure to make a deposit of FUTA taxes if:

- the employer has a net worth of no more than $7 million ($2 million if the employer is an individual);
- the failure to deposit occurs during the first quarter the employer is required to deposit employment taxes; and
- the return for the tax (Form 940) is filed by the due date.

The failure-to-deposit penalty may also be abated for an employer of any size that sends its first payroll tax deposit to the IRS rather than depositing it with the appropriate government depository.[43] (See Section 8.2-3 for information on penalty and interest notice requirements that went into effect on July 1, 2003.)

## 7.2 State Unemployment Insurance

This section deals with the State Unemployment Insurance (SUI or SUTA) portion of the federal/state unemployment system. Although the Federal Unemployment Tax Act provides a framework for state funding and coverage requirements, states each have their own methods for determining tax rates, wage bases, and benefit eligibility and amounts. The basics of state unemployment insurance programs as they relate to the payroll process will be discussed here.

## 7.2-1 The Employment Relationship

Employers within a state are generally covered by the state's unemployment insurance program if they meet the requirements for coverage under FUTA (see Section 7.1-1), although some states provide even broader terms for coverage. But even if an employer is subject to a state's unemployment insurance law, it is covered only to the extent its workers are performing covered services as employees rather than as independent contractors. The different tests states use to determine whether an employer-employee relationship exists (e.g., common law, ABC) are discussed in Section 1.6-4, where Table 1.2 shows the test used by each state.

**Employees working in more than one state.** Where employees perform services all in one state, the employer pays unemployment taxes to that state. But all the aspects of unemployment insurance become more complex when employees work in more than one state. An incorrect determination of the state having

---

42.   IRC §6656(c); IRS Prop. Reg. §301.6656-3(a).
43.   IRC §6656(d); IRS Prop. Reg. §301.6656-3(b)

jurisdiction for unemployment insurance purposes can mean paying double taxes in some states while paying penalties and interest for failing to pay taxes in other states.

There are four factors employers can use in determining to which state an employee should be "allocated" for unemployment insurance purposes:

*Are services "localized?"* An employee's services are localized within a state if services performed outside the state are merely incidental to services performed inside the state (e.g., a temporary assignment to a company division in another state). If an employee's services are localized, the employer is subject to the unemployment insurance law of that state for the employee and the other allocation factors need not be considered.

*Does the employee have a "base of operations?"* Where an employee regularly works in more than one state (no localization), the employer should look to see if the employee has a base of operations in one of those states. A base of operations can be the place where an employee reports to work or returns from work, or a place where the employee has an office, receives instructions from the employer, receives mail and supplies, or keeps business records (e.g., a regional sales office where a sales representative with a multistate territory receives mail, keeps records, and gets instructions). If the employee has a single base of operations in a state where he or she works, that state's unemployment insurance law governs.

*Is there a "place of direction or control?"* If the employee's work is not localized and there's no base of operations, the next factor to analyze is whether there is a place of direction or control in one of the states where the employee performs services. A place of direction or control refers to an employer's facility from which it exercises or can exercise immediate control over the employee's services (e.g., a sales representative who works in several states without a base of operations but must check in with his sales manager, whose office is in one of the states where the salesperson works).

*What is the employee's "state of residence?"* In those relatively rare instances where none of the three previous factors can be applied, the state of the employee's residence has jurisdiction if the employee performs some work there (e.g., a computer manufacturer's troubleshooter who lives and works in one state, has a base of operations in another, and services customers in several other states).

**Reciprocal coverage arrangements.** In some instances, the employer can choose which state's unemployment insurance law will cover an employee's services. Nearly all the states participate in reciprocal coverage arrangements allowing employers to choose the state of coverage for certain multistate workers who move from state to state. Under such agreements, the employer can choose any state where the employee works, the state where the employee resides, or a state where the employer does business.

## 7.2-2  SUI Taxable Wages

Following the FUTA scheme, state unemployment contributions (taxes) are determined by applying a certain percentage to the taxable wages paid by the employer. FUTA requires that each state's taxable wage base must at least equal the FUTA taxable wage base of $7,000 per employee, and most states have wage bases that exceed the required amount. The states use varying formulas for determining the taxable wage base, with many tying theirs by law to the FUTA wage base and others using a percentage of the state's average annual wage.

The types of payments included as taxable wages by the states are generally those considered taxable wages for FUTA purposes (wages, salary, bonuses, commissions, noncash payments). But several states differ from the FUTA approach when it comes to sick or disability pay, cafeteria plan benefits, tips, and others. Employers must check the state laws and rules in the states where they have employees to determine whether the payments made to them are taxable wages. Check Table 4.1 for information on the SUI treatment of §401(k) plan and cafeteria plan contributions. Table 7.1 following includes the taxable wage bases in each state for 2008. [For more information on state unemployment insurance wage bases and tax rates, see Table 8.2 of *APA's Guide to State Payroll Laws.*]

Table 7.1

| STATE UNEMPLOYMENT TAXABLE WAGE BASES — 2008 | | | |
|---|---|---|---|
| State | 2008 Wage Base | State | 2008 Wage Base |
| Alabama | $ 8,000 | Montana | $23,800 |
| Alaska | 31,300 | Nebraska | 9,000 |
| Arizona | 7,000 | Nevada | 25,400 |
| Arkansas | 10,000 | New Hampshire | 8,000 |
| California | 7,000 | New Jersey | 27,700 |
| Colorado | 10,000 | New Mexico | 19,900 |
| Connecticut | 15,000 | New York | 8,500 |
| Delaware | 10,500 | North Carolina | 18,600 |
| Dist. of Col. | 9,000 | North Dakota | 22,100 |
| Florida | 7,000 | Ohio | 9,000 |
| Georgia | 8,500 | Oklahoma | 13,600 |
| Hawaii | 13,000 | Oregon | 30,200 |
| Idaho | 32,200 | Pennsylvania | 8,000 |
| Illinois | 12,000 | Puerto Rico | 7,000 |
| Indiana | 7,000 | Rhode Island | 14,000 |
| Iowa | 22,800 | South Carolina | 7,000 |
| Kansas | 8,000 | South Dakota | 9,000 |
| Kentucky | 8,000 | Tennessee | 7,000 |
| Louisiana | 7,000 | Texas | 9,000 |
| Maine | 12,000 | Utah | 26,700 |
| Maryland | 8,500 | Vermont | 8,000 |
| Massachusetts | 14,000 | Virginia | 8,000 |
| Michigan | 9,000 | Washington | 34,000 |
| Minnesota | 25,000 | West Virginia | 8,000 |
| Mississippi | 7,000 | Wisconsin | 10,500 |
| Missouri | 12,000 | Wyoming | 20,100 |

# 7.2-3 Contribution Rates and Experience Rating

The contribution rate is the rate an employer applies to its taxable payroll (total of taxable wages for each employee) to determine the amount of unemployment taxes it must pay. The rate is determined by the employer's "experience rating," which is based on the employer's unemployment benefit charges and average annual taxable payroll. The experience rating system is based on the insurance principle that premiums (contribution rates) are based on the risk involved (unemployment benefits charged to the employer). Therefore, experience rating generally rewards employers with low employee turnover by leading to a lower contribution rate. Employers with a great deal of turnover generally have a higher contribution rate.

The states use one of four methods to determine an employer's experience rate: reserve ratio, benefit ratio, benefit wage ratio, and payroll stabilization.

**Reserve ratio.** Under the reserve ratio method, which is used by a majority of states (see the chart on page 7-26), each employer is assigned an account, into which it pays unemployment taxes. The account is then reduced by the amount of unemployment benefits paid to the employer's former employees during the year. The reserve ratio is the balance (reserve) in the employer's account divided by the employer's average taxable payroll for a specific period of years (usually three), expressed as a percentage. Here is the formula:

$$\text{Reserve ratio} = \frac{\text{Unemployment taxes paid - Benefits charged}}{\text{Average taxable payroll}}$$

When an employer's reserve ratio has been calculated, the ratio determines the employer's unemployment tax rate according to tables issued by the state. The higher the ratio, the lower the tax rate.

**Example:** Since its inception in 1995, Lexington Hammers, Inc. has accumulated an unemployment tax account balance of $34,600. As of the state computation date of October 31, 2007, Lexington Hammers had an account balance of $32,400 after benefits charges of $2,200 for the previous year were subtracted. Lexington Hammers's average taxable payroll for the computation period was $800,000, and its reserve ratio was determined as follows:

$$\text{Reserve ratio} = \frac{\$34,600 - \$2,200}{\$800,000} = \frac{\$32,400}{\$800,000} = .041 = 4.1\%$$

The state's contribution rate for an employer with a reserve ratio of at least 3.9% but less than 4.2% in 2008 is 2.2%. Therefore, Lexington Hammers will pay 2.2% of its employees' taxable wages in 2008 into its state unemployment tax account. If its reserve ratio had been at least 4.2%, Lexington Hammers would have reduced its tax rate to 1.8%.

**Benefit ratio method.** The next most popular experience rating method, the benefit ratio method, considers the relationship between the unemployment benefits charged to the employer during a stated period and the employer's total taxable payroll for the same period (taxes paid are not part of the equation). The formula is as follows:

$$\text{Benefit ratio} = \frac{\text{Benefits charged}}{\text{Total taxable payroll}}$$

Once an employer's benefit ratio has been calculated, the employer's contribution rate for the upcoming year is determined by referencing tax rate tables issued by the state. The lower the benefit ratio, the lower the tax rate.

**Example:** As of state's June 30, 2007 computation date, Fairfield Flute Co. had a total of $4,800 in benefits charged against it over the past three years, with a total taxable payroll during that time of $400,000. Its benefit ratio was determined as follows:

$$\text{Benefit ratio} = \frac{\$4,800}{\$400,000} = 0.012 \ (1.2\%)$$

The stste's 2008 tax rate for employers with a benefit ratio of 1.2% is 2.3%. Therefore, Fairfield Flute will pay 2.3% of its employees' 2008 taxable wages in state unemployment taxes. A benefit ratio of 1.8% would have meant a tax rate of 2.6%.

**Benefit wage ratio method.** Two states (Delaware and Oklahoma) use the benefit wage ratio method, which focuses on the taxable wages used to determine the benefits payable to employees who were terminated during the applicable time period, rather than the benefits themselves. These wages are then compared to the employer's total taxable payroll during the same period by using the following formula:

Benefit wage ratio = Benefit wages paid
                           Total taxable payroll

Once an employer's benefit wage ratio has been calculated (expressed as a percentage), the employer's contribution rate for the upcoming year is determined by relating the benefit wage ratio to a state "experience factor" and then referring to tax rate tables issued by the state. The state experience factor is the benefit wages paid to all employees in the state for the stated period divided by the total payrolls of all employers. The lower the benefit wage ratio, the lower the tax rate.

*Example:* Dover Diapers, Inc. terminated 6 employees during the three-year period before the computation date of October 1, 2007, and they earned a total of $140,000 in base-period wages. During that time, Dover Diapers's total taxable payroll was $900,000. Its benefit wage ratio was calculated as follows:

Benefit wage ratio = $140,000 = .1556 = 15.56%
                      $900,000

The state's 2008 tax rate for employers with a benefit wage ratio that does not exceed 15.6% is 6.7% (including a variable supplemental assessment rate blended into the table rates). Therefore, Dover Diapers will pay 6.7% of its employees' 2008 taxable wages in state unemployment taxes. A benefit wage ratio of 13.7% would have meant a tax rate of 5.6%.

**Payroll stabilization.** Alaska is the only state that uses the payroll stabilization method to determine an employer's tax rate. Under this method, an employer's tax rate is determined by fluctuations in its payroll from quarter to quarter and year to year. Therefore, as more employees are terminated and the payroll decreases, the employer's tax rate increases. So long as the employer's payroll remains stable or increases, its tax rate will not be increased and may be decreased.

**State chart of experience rating methods.** Table 7.2 shows what method of experience rating each state uses in determining an employer's unemployment contribution rate. [For more information on state experience rating methods, see Table 8.2 of *APA's Guide to State Payroll Laws*.]

 **BE CAREFUL** In February 1999, the U.S. Department of Labor told state employment security agencies that they could not exclude from an employer's experience rating computations unemployment benefits paid to former employees who had previously received public assistance. Some states have considered such a policy to promote the hiring of public assistance recipients.

Table 7.2

| STATE EXPERIENCE RATING METHODS | | | |
|---|---|---|---|
| State | Method | State | Method |
| Alabama | Benefit ratio | Montana | Reserve ratio |
| Alaska | Payroll stabilization | Nebraska | Reserve ratio |
| Arizona | Reserve ratio | Nevada | Reserve ratio |
| Arkansas | Reserve ratio | New Hampshire | Reserve ratio |
| California | Reserve ratio | New Jersey | Reserve ratio |
| Colorado | Reserve ratio | New Mexico | Reserve ratio |
| Connecticut | Benefit ratio | New York | Reserve ratio |
| Delaware | Benefit wage ratio | North Carolina | Reserve ratio |
| Dist. of Col. | Reserve ratio | North Dakota | Reserve ratio |
| Florida | Benefit ratio | Ohio | Reserve ratio |
| Georgia | Reserve ratio | Oklahoma | Benefit wage ratio |
| Hawaii | Reserve ratio | Oregon | Benefit ratio |
| Idaho | Reserve ratio | Pennsylvania | Benefit/reserve ratio |
| Illinois | Benefit ratio | Puerto Rico | Reserve ratio |
| Indiana | Reserve ratio | Rhode Island | Reserve ratio |
| Iowa | Benefit ratio | South Carolina | Reserve ratio |
| Kansas | Reserve ratio | South Dakota | Reserve ratio |
| Kentucky | Reserve ratio | Tennessee | Reserve ratio |
| Louisiana | Reserve ratio | Texas | Benefit ratio |
| Maine | Reserve ratio | Utah | Benefit ratio |
| Maryland | Benefit ratio | Vermont | Benefit ratio |
| Massachusetts | Reserve ratio | Virginia | Benefit ratio |
| Michigan | Benefit ratio | Washington | Benefit ratio |
| Minnesota | Benefit ratio | West Virginia | Reserve ratio |
| Mississippi | Benefit ratio | Wisconsin | Reserve ratio |
| Missouri | Reserve ratio | Wyoming | Benefit ratio |

**Surcharges and assessments.** An employer's contribution rate is often made up of more than just its experience rate. When a state has more than ordinary benefit costs (e.g., payments on federal loans, extended benefits in times of high unemployment, added training expenses), it may pass those costs on in the form of a surtax or assessment on employers built into the contribution rate. The purpose of the surcharge may determine whether it can be included when an employer determines its state credits against FUTA tax liability (see Section 7.1-6).

**New employers.** Businesses that are just starting or are new to a particular state will generally not be allowed to qualify for an experience rate. They will be assigned a "new employer's rate" that will apply until they have been covered by the state's unemployment insurance laws for a few years. In many states, the assigned rate depends on the new employer's industry, with employers in industries having a history of high turnover being assigned higher rates (e.g., construction). New employers that are late in paying their unemployment taxes or are charged with more benefits than taxes they have paid (negative balance employers) may find themselves paying a higher rate than the new employer's rate they were assigned initially.

**Successor employers.** Generally, successor employers retain the tax rate they had immediately before the acquisition of the predecessor company occurred, if they were covered employers in the state at that time. If not, they most likely would assume the predecessor's tax rate for the rest of the year. The experience of both the predecessor and the successor would be used to determine the experience rate in following years.

**SUTA Dumping Prevention Act was designed to stop rate manipulation.**[44] The SUTA Dumping Prevention Act of 2004 requires states to enact laws aimed at stopping "businesses from wrongly manipulating their corporate structure to avoid paying their fair share of state unemployment taxes." State enactment of such laws is made a condition of eligibility for federal administrative grants.

*What is SUTA dumping?* SUTA dumping is an illegal practice of manipulating state UI rates to achieve a lower employer tax rate. In a typical SUTA dumping scheme, an existing business with a high (poor) experience rating forms a new company, transfers its employees to the new company, and then pays unemployment taxes under that company's lower new employer tax rate (thereby "dumping" the original company's high tax rate). Or, in what is known as a "shell transaction," a newly formed company purchases an existing business with a low experience rating. The low experience rating is then transferred to the newly formed company.

*State legislative action required.* The Act requires states to enact anti-SUTA dumping laws in order to be eligible for federal UI administrative grants. This provision applies to certifications for payments in rate years (as defined in state law) "beginning after the end of the 26-week period beginning on the first day of the first regularly scheduled session of the state legislature beginning on or after the date of the enactment [i.e., August 9, 2004] of this Act."

Nothing prohibits states from providing for earlier effective dates. Since all states have rate years beginning either January 1 or July 1, and almost all the states' first legislative sessions following August 9, 2004 began in the first three months of 2005, the amendments in most states are effective for rate years beginning on or after January 1, 2006, or on or after July 1, 2006, whichever is applicable in that particular state.

State UI laws must provide for the following:

- *Mandatory Transfers.* Unemployment experience must be transferred whenever there is substantially common ownership, management or control of two employers, and one of these employers transfers its trade or business (including its workforce), or a portion thereof, to the other employer. This requirement applies to both total and partial transfers of businesses.
- *Prohibited Transfers.* Unemployment experience may not be transferred, and a new employer rate (or the state's standard rate) will instead be assigned, when a person who is not an employer acquires the trade or business of an existing employer. This prohibition applies only if the state employment security agency finds that such person acquired the business solely or primarily for the purpose of obtaining a lower rate of contributions.
- *Penalties for SUTA Dumping.* "Meaningful" civil and criminal penalties must be imposed on persons "knowingly" violating or attempting to violate the two requirements discussed above. To be "meaningful" the penalty must have the effect of curtailing SUTA dumping. A monetary penalty must be of sufficient size that an employer will not be tempted to SUTA dump. A flat fine may not be a meaningful deterrent.

---

44.     Pub. Law 108-295; UIPL No. 30-04, 69 F.R. 58550, 9-30-04; UIPL No. 30-04, Change 1, 69 F.R. 65654, 11-15-04.

• *Procedures.* Procedures for identifying SUTA dumping must be established. The exact procedures do not need to be specified in state law, but state law must specifically provide for the establishment of such procedures.

**Nonprofit and public sector employers.** State and local government employers and certain nonprofit organizations are treated somewhat differently than other employers under state unemployment insurance laws. They provide two methods for such employers to satisfy their unemployment insurance liability. Under the *direct reimbursement* method, the employer reimburses the state for any unemployment benefits charged to it. If no or limited chargeable benefits are paid, the employer has no or limited unemployment insurance liability. Employers that choose this option must be confident they will not face a sudden financial emergency that could require terminating large numbers of employees.

Nonprofit and public sector employers can also choose to become experience-rated and pay state unemployment taxes according to the same method the state uses for other employers. (Nonprofit and public sector employers are not subject to FUTA tax.) The employer's choice will often be determined by its unemployment experience, as employers with low turnover generally find the direct reimbursement method less costly, while employers with a large amount of benefit charges usually opt for the standard payment method.

 **CHECK STATE LAWS CAREFULLY** Nonprofit and government employers must check their state laws very carefully before making their decision on how to finance their unemployment insurance liability. Each state imposes a deadline for selecting or terminating the direct reimbursement or payroll tax option (e.g., once the decision has been made it cannot be changed).

**Employee contributions.** Only three states (Alaska, New Jersey, and Pennsylvania) require employers to withhold unemployment contributions from their employees' wages, and the withholding rates are much lower than the contribution rates for employers in those states.

# 7.2-4 Voluntary Contributions

Employers in 27 states (nearly all using the reserve ratio method of experience rating) can make voluntary contributions to their unemployment tax accounts. These contributions increase the balances in those accounts, which in turn increase the employers' reserve ratios (or, in Michigan, decrease their benefit ratios) and decrease their unemployment tax rates. The goal of a voluntary contribution is to increase the reserve ratio to the next higher bracket on the state's unemployment tax rate table, which corresponds to the next lower tax bracket.

What the employer must determine before making the contribution is whether it will result in a tax savings. In other words, will the amount of the contribution be less than the taxes caused by the higher rate. If not, the contribution should not be made. Some states include the voluntary contribution amount on the employer's state unemployment contribution rate notice.

*Example:* In our reserve ratio example outlined earlier (see Section 7.2-2), Lexington Hammers had a reserve balance of $32,400 and an average taxable payroll of $800,000 on October 31, 2007, the state computation date. Without a voluntary contribution, Lexington Hammers's reserve ratio was 4.1%, producing a tax rate of 2.2%. The next reserve ratio bracket in the state table begins at 4.2% and carries a tax rate of 1.8%.

To reach that bracket, Lexington Hammers would have to contribute $1,200 ($800,000 x .042 = $33,600; $33,600 - $32,400 = $1,200). At 2.2%, and with a constant average payroll of $800,000, Lexington Hammers's 2008 unemployment taxes would be $17,600 ($800,000 x .022), while at 1.8% its 2007 taxes would be $14,400 ($800,000 x .018). The tax savings produced by the voluntary contribution would be $3,200 ($17,600 - $14,400). The net savings for Lexington Hammers, therefore, would be $2,000 ($3,200 - $1,200), making the voluntary contribution a profitable option.

**Not all employers are eligible.** States that offer the voluntary contribution option routinely impose restrictions on its use. Employers that may be barred from making such contributions include new employers, negative reserve balance employers, and employers that have not paid state taxes on time.

 **WATCH OUT** Employers that make voluntary contributions thinking they will get a reduced unemployment tax rate may be surprised if they have unpaid unemployment taxes or penalties on their account balance. The state may apply the voluntary contribution to these past due amounts first, thus reducing the voluntary contribution amount below the amount needed to reduce the employer's tax rate. When this occurs, the state may notify the employer and allow the employer to increase its voluntary contribution.

**State voluntary contribution chart.** Table 7.3 shows the states that allow voluntary contributions and how much time they give the employer to make the contribution. [For more information on voluntary unemployment contributions, see Table 8.3 of *APA's Guide to State Payroll Laws.*]

Table 7.3

| STATE DEADLINES FOR VOLUNTARY CONTRIBUTIONS | |
|---|---|
| **State** | **Deadline for Contribution** |
| Arizona | January 31 |
| Arkansas | March 31 |
| California | Last working day of March; not allowed if schedule E or F is in effect (schedule F+ is in effect in 2008) |
| Colorado | Before March 15 |
| Georgia | 30 days after rate notice is mailed; no later than 120 days after January 1 |
| Indiana | 30 days after rate notice is mailed; no later than 120 days after January 1 |
| Kansas | 30 days after rate notice is mailed; no later than 120 days after January 1 |
| Kentucky | 20 days after rate notice is mailed; no later than 120 days after January 1 |
| Louisiana | 30 days after rate notice is mailed, or 25 days after receipt if notice is delivered other than by mail (not allowed if a solvency tax, assessment for interest due on federal allowances, or temporary special assessment is in effect) |
| Maine | 30 days after rate notice is mailed; 10-day extension for good cause |
| Massachusetts | 30 days after rate notice is issued; no later than 120 days after January 1 |
| Michigan | 30 days after rate notice is mailed; no later than 120 days after January 1 |
| Minnesota | No later than 120 calendar days after January 1; must be made electronically |
| Missouri | January 15 |
| Nebraska | January 10 |
| New Jersey | 30 days after rate notice is mailed; 60-day extension for good cause; no later than 120 days after July 1 |
| New Mexico | March 1 |
| New York | March 31 |
| North Carolina | 30 days after rate notice is mailed |
| North Dakota | April 30 |
| Ohio | December 31 |

| STATE DEADLINES FOR VOLUNTARY CONTRIBUTIONS ||
|---|---|
| **State** | **Deadline for Contribution** |
| Pennsylvania | 30 days after rate notice is mailed; extension for good cause; no later than 120 days after January 1 |
| South Dakota | 15 days from date of rate notice |
| Texas | 60 days after rate notice is mailed; may be extended to 75 days, but no later than 120 days after January 1 |
| Washington | February 15; only for employers increasing by at least 12 rate classes |
| West Virginia | 30 days after rate notice is mailed |
| Wisconsin | November 30; 3-day extension if mailed by November 30 |

# 7.2-5  Joint or Combined Accounts

For employers having more than one affiliated subsidiary in a state, an attractive option for reducing unemployment contributions may be to join the subsidiaries for unemployment insurance purposes. By doing this, the companies have one joint unemployment tax account and one combined taxable payroll. If the companies have the right mixture of good and bad unemployment experience, combining accounts may save money for one or all of them.

> *Example:*  Joplin Bolts, Inc. (JBI) and St. Louis Scissors Corp. (SSC) are in the same state and are owned by the same holding company. Their average annual payrolls are $1,000,000 for JBI and $1,400,000 for SSC. JBI has a reserve unemployment tax account balance of $49,000, for a reserve ratio of 4.9% ($49,000 ÷ $1,000,000 = .049). This translates to a tax rate of 3.12%, using the state's 2008 contribution rate table (which includes a 30% surcharge), and a tax liability of $31,200 ($1,000,000 X .0312 = $31,200).
>
> SSC has a reserve balance of $61,400 and a reserve ratio of 4.4% ($61,400 ÷ $1,400,000 = .044), resulting in a tax rate of 3.25% and a tax liability of $45,500 ($1,400,000 x .0325 = $45,500). If JBI and SSC combine their accounts, their reserve account balance would be $110,400 ($49,000 + $61,400 = $110,400) and their reserve ratio would be 4.6% ($110,400 ÷ $2,400,000 = .046).
>
> Using the tax rate tables, their combined tax rate would be 3.12% and their combined tax liability would be $74,880 ($2,400,000 x .312 = $74,880), a savings of $1,820 over their total individual tax liabilities ($31,200 + $45,500 = $76,700) that would benefit SSC ($76,700 - $74,880 = $1,820).

**States attach strings.** Not all states offer the joint account option. Those that do place restrictions on eligibility, set deadlines for selecting the option, require accounts to remain joined for a stated period of time, and restrict the circumstances for withdrawing from the joint account. Therefore, employers should make sure a tax savings will result before exercising this option. Table 7.4 is a list of the states that offer the joint account option to both contributing and direct reimbursement (see page 7-31) employers. All other states allow the option only to direct reimbursement employers (certain nonprofit organizations and state and local government units). [For more information on state rules governing joint accounts, see Table 8.3 of *APA's Guide to State Payroll Laws.*]

Table 7.4

| STATES OFFERING JOINT ACCOUNT OPTION | | |
|---|---|---|
| Arizona | Hawaii | Ohio |
| Arkansas | Minnesota | South Carolina |
| California | Missouri | Washington |
| Connecticut | New Jersey | West Virginia |
| Delaware | New York | Wyoming |

## 7.2-6 The Unemployment Benefits Process

Because an employer's unemployment tax cost is directly tied to its unemployment experience (i.e., the number of employees it terminates and the amount of benefits they collect), understanding the unemployment benefits process (e.g., eligibility, benefit amounts, challenging claims) is important for anyone involved in payroll. This section describes that process and the way in which it affects payroll costs.

**Eligibility for benefits.** All states require claimants for unemployment benefits to meet certain standards to become and remain eligible for benefits. They include:

- earning a certain amount of wages in the "base period";
- being involuntarily unemployed for reasons other than misconduct connected with their work;
- filing a claim for benefits;
- registering for work with the state employment security office;
- being physically and mentally able to work;
- be looking for and available for work (other than during times of job training or jury duty);
- not being unemployed because of a labor dispute other than a lockout; and
- being truthful in applying for benefits.

*Parental leave benefits experiment ends.* In 2000, the Department of Labor (DOL) issued regulations that allowed state unemployment agencies to pay unemployment compensation to parents who take time off from work to be with newborn or newly-adopted children. The regulations allowed the state agencies to experiment with different methods for providing benefits under these circumstances. The compensation provided under these experimental programs was called Birth and Adoption Unemployment Compensation (BAA-UC).

However, in October 2003, the DOL repealed the BAA-UC regulations, noting that no state had yet passed a law implementing them and determining that the experiment was "poor policy" and a "misrepresentation of federal unemployment compensation law." The DOL also reversed its previous position and said that unemployment insurance was never meant to fund these types of claims where the claimant is not truly "able and available for work."[45]

*Able and available to work.* In 2007, the DOL issued a final rule to limit a state's payment of unemployment compensation (UC) only to individuals who are able and available to work, effective February 15, 2007.[46] A state that fails to comply with the rule will lose federal funding for the administration of its UC program. Employers in the state will not be eligible to receive credit against the federal unemployment tax. Although the DOL has consistently interpreted federal law to include an "able and available to work" requirement, the requirement had never been explicitly addressed in federal law or rules.

---

45.   68 F.R. 58540, 10-9-03.
46.   20 CFR §604.1 - 6.

A state may pay benefits only to an individual who is able and available to work for the week for which benefits are claimed. A state may consider an individual to be able to work during the week benefits are claimed if the individual is able to work for all or a portion of the week claimed, provided that any limitation on his or her ability to work is not considered a withdrawal from the labor market.

A state may consider an individual to be available for work during the week of unemployment claimed under any of the following circumstances:
- The individual is available for any work for all or a portion of the week claimed, provided that any limitation placed by the claimant on his or her availability is not considered a withdrawal from the labor market.
- The claimant limits his or her availability for suitable work as determined under state law, provided the state law definition of suitable work does not permit the claimant to limit his or her availability in such a way that the individual has withdrawn from the labor market.
- The individual is on temporary layoff and is available to work only for the employer that has temporarily laid off the individual.

The rule also applies the availability for work requirement to certain aspects of jury service, approved training, self-employed assistance, short-term compensation, and alien status.

**Benefit amounts.** The period for which a terminated employee is eligible to claim benefits is known as the "benefit year," and it begins when the employee files a claim for benefits. Generally, benefits can be collected for up to 26 weeks, unless extended because the claimant has a part-time job (although the total benefit entitlement is not increased) or the federal government has granted an emergency extension during periods of high unemployment. Once an employee has exhausted his or her benefits during a benefit year, the claim cannot be reopened, although a new claim can be filed in the next year.

The amount of a claimant's benefit entitlement depends on the wages earned by the terminated employee during the base period and the state's formula for calculating benefits. In most states, the base period is the first four calendar quarters out of the five preceding the quarter during which the employee first filed the claim for benefits.

> *Example:* Employee Sondra was laid off on February 14, 2008. She filed a claim for benefits one week later. Her base period for unemployment benefit purposes is October 1, 2006 - September 30, 2007.

In the mid-1990s, several employees challenged the standard base period formula, claiming that states should be required to use the immediately preceding four quarters as the base period if that would make the employee eligible for benefits or provide greater benefits to the employee. While these battles were being fought in state and federal courts, the Balanced Budget Act of 1997 was enacted, and it included a provision that guarantees states the discretion to administer base periods as they see fit.[47]

States use one of several methods to determine a claimant's weekly benefit amount and total benefit entitlement. Generally, the weekly benefit amount is either a fraction of the wages earned during the highest quarter of the base period or a percentage of the claimant's average weekly wage during a certain portion of the base period. Total unemployment benefits are generally limited to 26 times the weekly benefit amount or a fraction of total base period wages.

*Part-time employees get benefits.* Laid-off or terminated employees are not the only individuals who are eligible for unemployment benefits. Employees whose hours are reduced are also eligible, as long as they are not earning more than the weekly benefit amount. Generally, their weekly benefit amount is reduced by the amount of part-time wages earned. Some states also allow work-sharing plans where, instead of laying off employees, employers reduce their hours or days of work. The employees, in turn, get to keep their jobs and collect unemployment benefits for the time not worked.

---

47.    P.L. 105-33, §5401.

*Other payments can reduce benefits.* When an employee is terminated, certain payments provided by the employer can make the employee ineligible for unemployment benefits until the period covered by the payments has expired. Such payments include holiday pay, vacation pay, dismissal or severance pay, and payments in lieu of notice. Employers should check the individual states where they operate to determine the effect of such payments.

**Benefit charges to employers.** In the situation where the claimant's base period wages were all earned from one employer, that employer's unemployment tax account is charged with all the benefits received by the former employee. In situations where the claimant has been employed by more than one employer during the base period, states use one of several methods to allocate benefit charges:

- each employer is charged based on the percentage of base period wages it paid to the claimant (majority of states);
- the claimant's most recent employer receives the full charge;
- the employer who paid the claimant the most wages during the base period receives the full charge;
- the most recent base period employer of the claimant is charged first up to a maximum amount, then the next most recent, etc.

**Auditing benefit charge accounts.** All states issue periodic statements to employers that show all the benefits charged against the employer's account. Employers should not assume that these statements are correct, and they should be audited thoroughly. Some common errors to look for include:

- individuals who get benefits and wages in the same week;
- a charge to the account even though a protest against the claim remains unresolved;
- benefits received by a claimant during the disqualification period;
- two charges to the account for the same benefits;
- benefits paid beyond the maximum allowed by law; and
- incorrect account number.

**Challenging benefit claims.** While it may seem like a harsh step to take, employers can reduce their unemployment tax costs by making sure they challenge benefit claims for which they believe the former employee is ineligible. When faced with a claim for unemployment benefits, the employer should:

- be complete and truthful in listing the grounds for an employee's termination when responding to forms and notices from the unemployment benefits agency;

- document any and all evidence of misconduct that may be needed to challenge a claim for benefits;

- respond to notices and requests for information within the time frame allowed;

- detail any final payments made to terminated employees, since they may disqualify the employee, at least temporarily; and

- prod the unemployment agency to make sure the claimant is looking for work.

## 7.2-7 Reporting Requirements

Each state requires employers to submit quarterly contribution and wage reports containing some or all of the following information:

- total wages paid;
- taxable wages paid;
- nontaxable wages paid;

- number of employees each month;
- gross wages for each employee;
- taxable/nontaxable wages breakdown for each employee; and
- number of weeks worked by each employee.

Employers should check the states where they operate for the reporting requirements applicable in each.

**Magnetic media and electronic reporting.** Many of the states require employers to file their quarterly wage information on some type of magnetic media, either tape, cartridge, or diskette, or electronically over the Internet, while others allow such filing. In those states that require or permit magnetic media filing, some will accept only tape reporting, while others will accept either a tape or diskette. There is no consensus among the states regarding magnetic media and electronic reporting requirements, so employers must carefully research the requirements in the states where they operate. Most of the states that require magnetic media or electronic reporting, however, do use a threshold for triggering the requirement that is similar to the federal threshold for filing Forms W-2 electronically (250 or more W-2s—see Section 8.14).

 **STANDARDIZED DATA FORMAT INITIATIVE** In 1992, the Interstate Conference of Employment Security Agencies (now the National Association of State Workforce Agencies) began exploring the development of a uniform format for quarterly reporting of unemployment insurance wage records to ease the reporting burden on multi-state employers. A standardized data format was developed by September 1993, and ICESA encouraged the states to accept it as an alternative to unique state formats.

Table 7.5 is a chart showing whether magnetic media and/or electronic filing of wage information is mandatory or optional in each state, whether the state accepts diskettes, cartridges, and/or electronic reporting in addition to magnetic tape, whether the ICESA format for submission is accepted, and a telephone number to contact for more information in each state. There may be additional requirements not shown in Table 7.5, so employers must check the requirements in the states to which they report. [For more information on state magnetic media and electronic reporting requirements for quarterly contributions and wage reports, see Table 8.4 of *APA's Guide to State Payroll Laws*.]

Table 7.5

| STATE WAGE REPORTING MAGNETIC/ELECTRONIC REPORTING REQUIREMENTS | | | | | | |
|---|---|---|---|---|---|---|
| State | Magnetic/Electronic Reporting Required | Diskette Accepted | Cartridge Accepted | Electronic Reporting Accepted | NASWA/ ICESA Format Accepted | Phone Number for Information |
| Alabama | Yes, if at least 25 employees | Yes | No | Yes | Yes | 334-242-8450 |
| Alaska | Internet only, if at least 100 employees or $1 million in wages reported in current or preceding calendar year | No | No | Yes, required | No | 907-465-2757 |
| Arizona | Optional | Yes | Yes | Yes, for up to 999 employees | Yes | 602-771-3689 |
| Arkansas | Yes, if at least 250 employees | Yes | No | Yes | No | 501-682-1190 |

| STATE WAGE REPORTING MAGNETIC/ELECTRONIC REPORTING REQUIREMENTS | | | | | | |
|---|---|---|---|---|---|---|
| State | Magnetic/Electronic Reporting Required | Diskette Accepted | Cartridge Accepted | Electronic Reporting Accepted | NASWA/ ICESA Format Accepted | Phone Number for Information |
| California | Yes, if at least 250 employees | Yes | Yes | Yes | Yes | 916-654-6845 |
| Colorado | Optional | Yes | No | Yes, online filing for up to 100 employees; FTP for 80 or more employees | Yes | 303-318-9100 |
| Connecticut | Yes, if at least 250 employees | Yes | Yes | Yes | No | 860-263-6375 |
| Delaware | Optional | No | Yes | No | No | 302-761-8482 |
| Dist. of Col. | Yes, if at least 250 employees | Yes | Yes | No | Yes | 202-698-7550 |
| Florida | Electronic reporting required if at least 10 employees | No | No | Yes, required | No | 800-482-8293 |
| Georgia | Yes, if at least 100 employees | Yes | No | Yes | Yes | 404-232-3265 |
| Hawaii | Optional | Yes | Yes | Yes | Yes | 808-586-8913 |
| Idaho | Yes, if at least 300 employees | Yes | Yes | Yes | Yes | 208-332-3570 |
| Illinois | Yes, if at least 250 employees | Yes | Yes | Yes | Yes | 312-793-6298 |
| Indiana | Optional | Yes | Yes | No | Yes | 317-233-6689 |
| Iowa | Optional | Yes | No | Yes | Yes | 515-281-5339 |
| Kansas | Optional, electronically only | No | No | Yes | Yes | 785-368-8313 |
| Kentucky | Yes, if at least 250 employees | Yes | No | Yes | Yes | 502-564-2168 |
| Louisiana | Yes, if at least 250 employees | Yes | Yes | Yes | No | 225-342-2827 |
| Maine | Electronic, if at least 100 employees | No | No | Yes | No | 207-626-8475 |
| Maryland | Yes, if at least 100 employees | Yes | Yes | Yes | Yes | 410-767-4380 |

| STATE WAGE REPORTING MAGNETIC/ELECTRONIC REPORTING REQUIREMENTS | | | | | | |
|---|---|---|---|---|---|---|
| **State** | **Magnetic/Electronic Reporting Required** | **Diskette Accepted** | **Cartridge Accepted** | **Electronic Reporting Accepted** | **NASWA/ ICESA Format Accepted** | **Phone Number for Information** |
| Massachusetts | Electronic reporting required if quarterly wages are $50,000 or more; all employers beginning in 4th quarter 2008 | No | Yes | Yes | Yes | 617-887-5030 |
| Michigan | Optional | No | Yes | Yes | No | 800-638-3994 |
| Minnesota | Electronic reporting required for all employers | No | No | Yes, required | Yes | 651-296-6141 |
| Mississippi | Optional | Yes | Yes | No | Yes | 601-321-6215 |
| Missouri | Yes, if at least 250 employees | Yes | No | Yes | Yes | 573-751-3422 |
| Montana | Optional | Yes | Yes | Yes | Yes | 406-444-3834 |
| Nebraska | Electronic reporting required if annual payroll is $500,000 or more | No | Yes | Yes | No | 402-471-9898 |
| Nevada | Optional | Yes | Yes | Yes | No | 775-684-6385 |
| New Hampshire | Yes, if at least 250 employees | Yes | Yes | No | No | 603-224-3311 |
| New Jersey | Electronic reporting required if more than 4 employees | No | No | Yes | Yes | 609-984-7988 |
| New Mexico | Yes, if at least 250 employees | Yes | Yes | Yes | No | 505-841-8576 |
| New York | Yes, if at least 250 employees in 4 consecutive quarters | Yes | Yes | No | No | 518-457-7105 |
| North Carolina | Yes, if at least 100 employees | Yes | Yes | Yes | Yes | 919-733-9600 |
| North Dakota | Electronic reporting required if at least 100 employees | Yes | Yes | Yes | Yes | 701-328-2814 |
| Ohio | Optional | Yes | Yes | Yes | Yes | 614-752-9661 |
| Oklahoma | Optional | Yes | Yes | No | Yes | 405-557-7138 |
| Oregon | Optional | Yes | No | Yes | No | 503-947-1488 |

| STATE WAGE REPORTING MAGNETIC/ELECTRONIC REPORTING REQUIREMENTS | | | | | | |
|---|---|---|---|---|---|---|
| State | Magnetic/Electronic Reporting Required | Diskette Accepted | Cartridge Accepted | Electronic Reporting Accepted | NASWA/ ICESA Format Accepted | Phone Number for Information |
| Pennsylvania | Yes, if at least 250 employees | Yes | Yes | Yes | Yes | 717-783-5802 |
| Rhode Island | Yes, if at least 200 employees; service providers if at least 20 clients | Yes | Yes | Yes | No | 401-222-3521 |
| South Carolina | Yes, if at least 100 employees | Yes | Yes | Yes | Yes | 803-737-1071 |
| South Dakota | Optional | Yes | Yes | Yes | Yes | 605-626-2312 |
| Tennessee | Yes, if at least 250 employees | Yes | No | Yes | Yes | 615-741-3280 |
| Texas | Yes, if at least 10 employees | Yes | Yes | Yes | Yes | 512-463-2505 |
| Utah | Yes, if at least 250 employees; service providers if at least 100 clients | Yes | Yes | Yes | No | 801-526-9590 |
| Vermont | Optional | Yes | Yes | Yes | Yes | 802-828-4253 |
| Virginia | Yes, if at least 250 employees; electronic reporting required if at least 100 employees, eff. 1-1-09 | Yes | No | No | No | 804-786-4207 |
| Washington | Optional | Yes | Yes | Yes | Yes | 360-902-9636 |
| West Virginia | Optional | Yes | No | Yes | Yes | 304-558-2662 |
| Wisconsin | Yes, if at least 50 employees | Yes | Yes | Yes | No | 608-261-6700 |
| Wyoming | Optional | Yes | Yes | No | No | 307-235-3217 |

**NAME CHANGE FOR ICESA; NEW REPORTING SPECS?** In 2000, ICESA changed its name to the National Association of State Workforce Agencies (NASWA). In 2001, NASWA began reviewing the current quarterly wage report layout to determine whether it should implement major revisions to conform to the layout used by the Social Security Administration for Form W-2 electronic reporting (see Section 8.14).

**Multiple worksite reporting.** Employers with more than one worksite must not only file contribution and wage reports with each state, they must also file quarterly employment and wage reports with the state employment security agency that break down the information by industry and locality. This information, in turn, is used by the federal Bureau of Labor Statistics, which is responsible for compiling statistical information from state unemployment insurance data. The BLS uses the information to conduct surveys and provide analysis of different aspects of the U.S. employment situation.

For employers with one worksite, the necessary information can be taken from the employer's state unemployment contribution and wage reports. But for multiple worksite employers, the information must be broken down further before it can be used by the BLS. To facilitate the collection of this information and reduce the paperwork burden on multiple worksite employers, the BLS developed a standardized Multiple Worksite Report, BLS 3020 (MWR, see page 7-40).

The major difference between previous reporting methods and the MWR is that, rather than reporting by industry and locality, employers using the MWR report information on a worksite basis. Also, the standardization of the MWR reduces the burden on large employers with worksites in many different states that previously had to file different reports in each state.

**Mandatory vs. voluntary reporting.** All states are responsible for collecting employment data and providing it to the BLS, but not all of them require employers to file a report containing the information. For those that do, employers must now use the MWR in place of the old state form. To facilitate reporting, the standard MWR is customized to some degree for each state, with the name and address of the state employment security agency appearing on the front and back. The MWR also states whether reporting is mandatory or voluntary in that state. Table 7.6 is a list of the states where MWR reporting is mandatory. [For more information on who to contact about multiple worksite reporting in these states, see Table 10.1 of *APA's Guide to State Payroll Laws*.]

Table 7.6

| STATES WITH MANDATORY MWR | | |
|---|---|---|
| Alabama | Minnesota | Oklahoma |
| California | Montana | Oregon |
| Colorado | Nevada | Puerto Rico |
| Florida | New Hampshire | South Carolina |
| Georgia | New Jersey | Tennessee |
| Iowa | New York | Utah |
| Kansas | North Carolina | Vermont |
| Louisiana | North Dakota | Virginia |
| Maine | Ohio | West Virginia |

**Which employers must file the MWR?** In states where use of the MWR is mandatory, an employer must file an MWR if it:

- uses one unemployment insurance account number in that state for all its employees;
- has more than one worksite (or conducts multiple economic activities) in the state; and
- has a total of at least 10 employees at all its secondary worksites.

An employer's primary worksite in a state is the worksite having the most employees. Its secondary worksites are all its other worksites in that state.

*Example:* Pressman's Dry Cleaners has three establishments in New York, with 25 employees in Rochester, 7 in Buffalo, and 5 in Binghamton. Pressman's must file an MWR because the total number of employees in its secondary worksites is at least 10 (7 + 5 = 12).

**What information must be provided.** When an employer first completes an MWR, it must provide the name, address, and worksite description of all its primary and secondary worksites. Thereafter, the worksite information will be preprinted on the form when it is sent to the employer for completion, and only changes to the information will have to be noted. The other information that must be provided includes the number of employees at each worksite during each month of the quarter (those employed during the pay period that includes the 12th of the month) and the total quarterly wages paid to employees working at each worksite, as well as a contact name and phone number. Space is also provided for any comments the employer might want to add regarding significant changes from previous forms caused by strikes, layoffs, plant closings, new plants, etc.

**Filing the MWR magnetically or electronically.** The specifications for magnetic media and electronic MWR reporting are contained in a publication from the Bureau of Labor Statistics, *Electronic Data Reporting.* The specifications establish the accepted standard reporting format for MWR data. The magnetic media or electronic reports are filed centrally with BLS' Electronic Data Interchange (EDI) center rather than with individual states. The EDI Center then transmits needed data to the individual states.

State Agency Name
Division Name
Street or PO Box Address
City, State  Zip Code
In Cooperation with the U.S. Department of Labor

Page ___ of ___

**Multiple Worksite Report**

The information collected on this form by the Bureau of Labor Statistics and the State agencies cooperating in its statistical programs will be used for statistical and Unemployment Insurance program purposes, and other purposes in accordance with law.

*This report is authorized by law, 29 U.S.C. 2. Your voluntary cooperation is needed to make the results of this survey comprehensive, accurate, and timely.*

Form Approved
O.M.B. No. 1220-0134

See estimate of reporting hours in **Time of Completion** Statement on reverse side.

## SUPPLEMENT TO EMPLOYER'S QUARTERLY CONTRIBUTION REPORT

**A. EMPLOYER NAME AND MAILING ADDRESS**

**B. QUARTERLY REPORT INFORMATION**

U.I. NUMBER      :

QUARTER ENDING :

DUE DATE         :

**C. CONTACT PERSON**

NAME  :

TITLE  :

PHONE : (      )                                    Ext.

## D. WORKSITES

**SEE INSTRUCTIONS ON REVERSE SIDE.**

| (1) DO NOT USE | (2) NAME (division, subsidiary, etc.), STREET ADDRESS (physical location), CITY, STATE, AND ZIP CODE, WORKSITE DESCRIPTION (store number, plant name, etc.) | (3) NUMBER OF EMPLOYEES During the Pay Period Which Includes the 12th of the Month | | | (4) TOTAL QUARTERLY WAGES OF WORKSITE (Round to the nearest dollar) |
|---|---|---|---|---|---|
| | | | | | |
| | COMMENTS: | | | | |
| | | | | | |
| | COMMENTS: | | | | |
| | | | | | |
| | COMMENTS: | | | | |
| | | | | | |
| | COMMENTS: | | | | |
| | | | | | |
| | COMMENTS: | | | | |
| | | | | | |
| | COMMENTS: | | | | |
| | | | | | |
| | COMMENTS: | | | | |

**NOTE:** The totals must agree (except for rounding) with the Employer's Quarterly Contribution Report (Form Number).

**TOTALS**

BLS 3020

INCLUDE THE TOTALS FOR ALL WORKSITES ON THE LAST PAGE ONLY

## GENERAL INFORMATION

**PURPOSE OF THIS REPORT**

This Multiple Worksite Report is designed to collect information showing the distribution of the employment and wages of business establishments by industry and geographic area. These data will enable our agency to prepare accurate reports on the economic conditions of business activities by geographic area and industry within our State.

**TIME OF COMPLETION**

**Time of Completion** is estimated to vary from 10 minutes to 60 minutes per response, with an average of 22 minutes per response. This includes time for reviewing instructions, searching existing data sources, gathering and maintaining the data needed and completing and reviewing this information. If you have any comments regarding these estimates or any other aspect of this form, send them to the Bureau of Labor Statistics, Division of Occupational and Administrative Statistics, Room 4840, 2 Massachusetts Avenue N.E., Washington, D.C. 20212.

**FILING INSTRUCTIONS**

- The State Agency Name requires/requests that employers submit this report, in addition to the Employer's Quarterly Contribution Report (Form Number), if they operate the same business activity in more than one location or conduct different business activities from one or more locations within our State. Persons are not required to respond to the collection of information unless it displays a currently valid OMB number.

- The **DUE DATE** for filing this report is preprinted in **SECTION B** along with the **QUARTER ENDING** date.

## INSTRUCTIONS

**SECTION A**

The address (in Section A) for your firm has been preprinted from information that you have previously supplied to this agency. Please review it and make any necessary corrections.

**SECTION C**

Please enter your name, title, and phone number (including the area code) on the first page of the form in Section C. This information is needed in case any questions arise concerning this report.

**SECTION D**

| | |
|---|---|
| **COLUMN 2** | Please review the name (division, subsidiary, etc.), physical location address, and worksite description information (i.e., store number, plant name, or principal business activity that uniquely identifies each worksite) that has been preprinted for each of the worksites listed and correct where necessary. |
| **COLUMN 3** | For each month of the quarter, please enter the total number of full- and part-time employees at each worksite who worked during or received pay (subject to Unemployment Insurance wages) for the pay period which includes the 12th of the month. |
| **COLUMN 4** | Please enter total wages paid during the quarter for each worksite rounded to the nearest dollar. |
| **COMMENTS** | Please explain any large changes in employment or wages, such as store closure, strikes, layoffs, bonuses, seasonal changes, etc., in the comments section for that worksite. |
| **TOTALS** | THE TOTALS FOR COLUMNS 3 AND 4 MUST AGREE WITH THE CORRESPONDING TOTALS ON THE EMPLOYER'S QUARTERLY CONTRIBUTION REPORT (Form Number). |

**NEW OR OMITTED UNITS** (SINCE YOUR LAST QUARTERLY REPORT):

If any units of your company have been omitted because you have expanded operations to a new location or purchased units from another company, please complete columns 2-4 for each worksite.

In addition, for each unit, please provide in the comments section:

1. The name of the county in which each is located, if known.
2. A description of the business activity(s) that will be conducted at each worksite.

If units were purchased from another company, also provide:

1. The name of the company,
2. The effective date of the transaction, and ...
3. The Unemployment Insurance number of the seller, if known.

**SOLD OR INACTIVE UNITS** (SINCE YOUR LAST QUARTERLY REPORT):

Please indicate in the comments section any worksites that became inactive or were sold to another company.

In addition, for each unit sold, please provide in the comments section:

1. The name of the company,
2. The effective date of the transaction, and ...
3. The Unemployment Insurance number of the purchaser, if known.

**If more space is needed, please attach a separate sheet of paper using the same format.**

**PLEASE RETURN COMPLETED FORM(s) IN THE ENCLOSED RETURN ENVELOPE.**

**IF YOU HAVE ANY QUESTIONS CONCERNING THIS REPORT, PLEASE WRITE OR CALL:**

**State Agency Name**
**Division Name**
**Street or PO Box Address**
**City, State Zip Code**
**Telephone #(s)**

# 7.3 State Disability Insurance

Five states (California, Hawaii, New Jersey, New York, and Rhode Island) plus Puerto Rico provide benefits to employees who are temporarily disabled by a nonwork-related illness or injury through a tax-supported state fund. The funds operate in much the same way as state unemployment insurance systems and under many of the same rules regarding coverage, taxable wages, exemptions, benefit eligibility, etc.

 **PAID FAMILY LEAVE IN CALIFORNIA** In 2004, California began a Paid Family Leave (PFL) program that is paid for with employee contributions. The rate is included in the state disability insurance rate (see Table 7.7 below). Benefits are paid for PFL claims that began on or after July 1, 2004.

Employers may be required to pay a payroll tax similar to unemployment contributions, and must withhold and pay a percentage of their employees' wages. Employers that have employees in any one of these states should review the state laws carefully for their obligations regarding contributions, withholding, reporting, etc. Table 7.7 provides information on the taxable wage base and withholding and contribution amounts in states requiring withholding and/or employer contributions to a state disability insurance fund. [For more information on state disability insurance requirements, see Table 9.1 of *APA's Guide to State Payroll Laws*.]

Table 7.7

| STATE DISABILITY INSURANCE LAWS CHART | | | |
|---|---|---|---|
| **State** | **Employer Contributions** | **Employee Contributions** | **2007 Wage Base** |
| California | None required; may pay all or part of employees' amount | 0.8% of annual earnings up to wage base (includes paid family leave surcharge) | $86,698 (annual) |
| Hawaii | Half of plan costs plus additional needed to provide benefits | maximum of 0.5% of weekly earnings up to wage base ($4.21) | $842,56 (weekly) |
| New Jersey | 0.10%-0.75% of annual earnings up to wage base; 0.5% for new employers | 0.5% of annual earnings up to wage base | $27,700 (annual) |
| New York | Additional costs over employee amounts to provide benefits | 0.5% of weekly wages up to maximum of $.60 | $120.00 (weekly) |
| Puerto Rico | 0.3% of annual earnings up to wage base; may pay employee's share also | 0.3% of annual earnings up to wage base | $9,000 (annual) |
| Rhode Island | None required; may pay all or part of employee's share | 1.3% of annual earnings up to wage base | $54,400 (annual) |

# 7.4  Directory of State Employment Security Agencies

Table 7.8 is a directory of the state agencies that are responsible for administering unemployment and disability insurance programs.

Table 7.8

### Directory of State Unemployment Insurance Agencies

**Alabama**
Department of Industrial Relations
Unemployment Compensation Division
649 Monroe St.
Montgomery, AL 36131
(334) 242-8025
http://dir.alabama.gov/uc

**Alaska**
Department of Labor and Workforce
Development
Employment Security Tax Division
P.O. Box 115509
Juneau, AK 99811-5506
(907) 465-2757
(888) 448-3527
www.labor.state.ak.us/estax

**Arizona**
Department of Economic Security
Division of Employment and Rehabilitation
Services
Employment Administration
Unemployment Insurance Tax Section
P.O. Box 6123
Phoenix, AZ 85005-6123
(602) 364-2722
www.azdes.gov/esa/uitax/uithome.asp

**Arkansas**
Department of Workforce Services
#1 Pershing Circle
North Little Rock, AR 72114
(501) 682-3201
www.state.ar.us/esd/

**California**
Employment Development Department
P.O. Box 826880 - MIC 28
Sacramento, CA 94280-0001
(800) 300-5616
www.edd.ca.gov/employer.htm

**Colorado**
Department of Labor and Employment
Division of Employment and Training
Unemployment Insurance Tax Operations
633 17th Street, Suite 201
Denver, CO 80203
(303) 318-9100
(800) 480-8299
www.coworkforce.com/UIT

**Connecticut**
Department of Labor
Unemployment Insurance Tax Division
200 Folly Brook Blvd.
Wethersfield, CT 06109-1114
(860) 263-6550
www.ctdol.state.ct.us/uitax/txmenu.htm

**Delaware**
Department of Labor
Division of Unemployment Insurance
4425 N. Market St.
Wilmington, DE 19802
(302) 761-8482
www.delawareworks.com/unemployment/
welcome.shtml

**District of Columbia**
Department of Employment Services
Office of Unemployment Compensation
Tax Division
609 H Street NE, Suite 354
Washington, DC 20002
(202) 724-7000
http://does.dc.gov/does/
cwp/view,a,1232,q,537876.asp

**Florida**
Department of Revenue
Agency for Workforce Innovation
Unemployment Compensation Tax Division
107 E. Madison St.
Caldwell Bldg.
Tallahassee, FL 32399-4120
(850) 245-7105
www.floridajobs.org/unemployment/

## Directory of State Unemployment Insurance Agencies

**Georgia**
Department of Labor
Unemployment Insurance Division
148 International Blvd., N.E.
Atlanta, GA 30303-1751
(404) 232-3001
www.dol.state.ga.us/em/

**Hawaii**
Department of Labor and Industrial Relations
Unemployment Insurance Division
830 Punchbowl St., Room 325
Honolulu, HI 96813
(808) 586-8913/9070
http://hawaii.gov/labor/ui/index.shtml

**Idaho**
Department of Commerce and Labor
317 Main St.
Boise, ID 83735-0760
(208) 332-3570
http://labor.idaho.gov/

**Illinois**
Department of Employment Security
527 South Wells St.
Chicago, IL 60607
(312) 793-4880
www.ides.state.il.us/

**Indiana**
Department of Workforce Development
Indiana Government Center S.
10 N. Senate Ave.
Indianapolis, IN 46204
(888) 967-5663
www.in.gov/dwd/

**Iowa**
Iowa Workforce Development
Unemployment Insurance Services Division
Tax Section
1000 E. Grand Ave.
Des Moines, IA 50319-0209
(515) 281-5387
www.iowaworkforce.org/ui/uiemployers.htm

**Kansas**
Department of Labor
Division of Employment Security
401 S.W. Topeka Blvd.
Topeka, KS 66603
(785) 296-1796
www.dol.ks.gov/ui/html/enuidbr.html

**Kentucky**
Department for Workforce Investment
Office of Employment and Training
275 E. Main St., 2nd Fl. E.
Frankfort, KY 40621
(502) 564-2900
www.des.ky.gov/des/ui/ui.asp

**Louisiana**
Department of Labor
Office of Unemployment Insurance
Administration
1001 N. 23rd St.
P.O. Box 94094
Baton Rouge, LA 70804-9094
(225) 342-3035
www.laworks.net/unemploymentinsurance/
ui-wagetaxstatus.asp

**Maine**
Department of Labor
Bureau of Unemployment Insurance
Tax Division
19 Union St.
P.O. Box 259
Augusta, ME 04332-0259
(207) 287-3176
www.state.me.us/labor/uitax/uctax.html

**Maryland**
Department of Labor, Licensing and
Regulation
Division of Unemployment Insurance
1100 N. Eutaw St.
Baltimore, MD 21201
(800) 492-5524
www.dllr.state.md.us/employment/
unemployment.html

## Directory of State Unemployment Insurance Agencies

**Massachusetts**
Department of Labor and Workforce
Development
Division of Unemployment Assistance
Charles F. Hurley Bldg.
19 Staniford St.
Boston, MA 02114-2589
(617) 626-6535
www.detma.org/detui.htm

**Michigan**
Department of Labor and Economic Growth
Unemployment Insurance Agency
3024 W. Grand Blvd., Suite 11-500
Detroit, MI 48202
(800) 638-3994
www.michigan.gov/uia/

**Minnesota**
Department of Employment and Economic
Development
Unemployment Insurance Program
1st National Bank Bldg., Ste. E200
332 Minnesota St.
St. Paul, MN 55101-1351
(651) 284-3033
www.uimn.org

**Mississippi**
Department of Employment Security
1235 Echelon Pkwy.
P.O. Box 1699
Jackson, MS 39215-1699
(601) 321-6000
http://mdes.ms.gov/wps/portal/tax/index.
html#null

**Missouri**
Department of Labor and Industrial Relations
Division of Employment Security
421 E. Dunklin St., P.O. Box 59
Jefferson City, MO 65104-0059
(573) 751-3215
www.dolir.mo.gov/es/ui-tax/main.htm

**Montana**
Department of Labor and Industry
Unemployment Insurance Division
P.O. Box 8020
Helena, MT 59604-8020
(406) 444-3834
http://uid.dli.mt.gov/

**Nebraska**
Nebraska Workforce Development
Office of Unemployment Insurance
550 S. 16th St.
P.O. Box 94600
Lincoln, NE 68509
(402) 471-9835
www.dol.state.ne.us/nwd/center.cfm?
PRICAT=2&SUBCAT=2E

**Nevada**
Department of Employment, Training and
Rehabilitation
Unemployment Insurance Tax Services
500 E. Third St.
Carson City, NV 89713-0030
(775) 687-4545
https://uitax.nvdetr.org/crp_home

**New Hampshire**
New Hampshire Employment Security
32 S. Main St.
Concord, NH 03301
(603) 224-3311
www.nhworks.state.nh.us/ucpage.htm

**New Jersey**
Department of Labor and Workforce
Development
Division of Unemployment Insurance
P.O. Box 058
Trenton, NJ 08625-0058
(609) 292-7162
http://lwd.dol.state.nj.us/labor/ui/ui_index.html

**New Mexico**
Department of Workforce Solutions
Division of Workforce Transition Services
Unemployment Insurance Tax Bureau
P.O. Box 2281
Albuquerque, NM 87102
(505) 841-2000
www.dws.state.nm.us/dws_uitax.html

**New York**
Department of Labor and Workforce
Development
Division of Unemployment Insurance
W. Averell Harriman State Office Bldg.
Bldg. 12. Suite 2001
Albany, NY 12240
(518) 402-0208
www.labor.state.ny.us/ui/ui_index.shtm

## Directory of State Unemployment Insurance Agencies

**North Carolina**
Employment Security Commission
P.O. Box 25903
Raleigh, NC 27611-5903
(919) 707-1150
www.ncesc.com/business/ui/uimain.asp

**North Dakota**
Job Service North Dakota
P.O. Box 5507
Bismarck, ND 58506-5507
(701) 328-2814
www.jobsnd.com/insurance/employers.html

**Ohio**
Ohio Department of Job and Family Services
Office of Unemployment Compensation
P.O. Box 182404
Columbus, OH 43218-2404
(614) 466-2319
www.state.oh.us/adjfs/ouc/uctax/index.stm

**Oklahoma**
Employment Security Commission
Unemployment Insurance Division
P.O. Box 52003
Oklahoma City, OK 73152
(405) 557-0200
www.oesc.state.ok.us/ui/default.shtm

**Oregon**
Oregon Employment Department
Unemployment Insurance Tax Section
875 Union St., N.E.
Salem, OR 97311
(503) 947-1488
http://egov.oregon.gov/EMPLOY/UI/index.shtml

**Pennsylvania**
Department of Labor and Industry
Office of Unemployment Compensation Tax Services
7th Floor, Labor and Industry Bldg.
Seventh and Forster Streets
Harrisburg, PA 17121
(717) 787-7679
www.dli.state.pa.us/landi/cwp/view.asp?a=355&q=23510

**Puerto Rico**
Department of Labor and Human Resources
Bureau of Employment Security
Unemployment Security Division
Prudencio Rivera Martinez Bldg.
505 Munoz Rivera Ave.
Hato Rey, PR 00918
(787) 754–5261

**Rhode Island**
Department of Labor and Training
115 Pontiac Ave.
Cranston, RI 02920
(401) 243-9100
www.dlt.state.ri.us/

**South Carolina**
Employment Security Commission
1550 Gadsden St.
P.O. Box 995
Columbia, SC 29202
(803) 737-3070
www.sces.org/ui/index.htm

**South Dakota**
Department of Labor
Unemployment Insurance Division
700 Governors Dr.
Kneip Building-3rd Floor
Pierre, SD 57501-2291
www.state.sd.us/applications/LD01DOL/frameset.asp?navid=&filtertype=1

**Tennessee**
Department of Labor and Workforce Development
Employment Security Division
500 James Robertson Pkwy.
Davy Crockett Tower, 8th Floor
Nashville, TN 37245-1000
(615) 741-2486
www.state.tn.us/labor-wfd/ui/ui.htm

**Texas**
Texas Workforce Commission
101 E. 15th St., Suite 570
Austin, TX 78778-0001
(512) 463-2731
www.twc.state.tx.us/customers/bemp/bemp.html

**Directory of State Unemployment Insurance Agencies**

**Utah**
Department of Workforce Services
Division of Unemployment Insurance
P.O. Box 45249
Salt Lake City, UT 84145-0249
(801) 526-9235
http://jobs.utah.gov/employer/

**Vermont**
Department of Labor
Division of Unemployment Insurance
and Wages
5 Green Mountain Dr.
P.O. Box 488
Montpelier, VT 05601-0488
(802) 828-4344
www.labor.vermont.gov/sections/uiwages/

**Virginia**
Virginia Employment Commssion
P.O. Box 1358
Richmond, VA 23218-1358
(804) 786-4359
www.vec.virginia.gov/vecportal/unins/insur.cfm

**Washington**
Employment Security Department
Unemployment Insurance Division
P.O. Box 9046
Olympia, WA 98507-9046
(888) 836-1900
www.wa.gov/esd/ui/icapp/start.htm

**West Virginia**
Bureau of Employment Programs
Unemployment Compensation Division
P.O. Box 2761
Charleston, WV 25330-2761
(304) 558-2657
http://www.wvbep.org/bep/uc/

**Wisconsin**
Department of Workforce Development
Division of Unemployment Insurance
P.O. Box 7905
Madison, WI 53707-7905
(608) 266-3100
www.dwd.state.wi.us/ui/

**Wyoming**
Department of Employment
Unemployment Insurance Division
100 W. Midwest
P.O. Box 2760
Casper, WY 82602-2760
(307) 235-3264
http://wydoe.state.wy.us/doe.asp?ID=11

# 7.5 Review Questions and Exercises

## Review Questions

1. What is the "normal" credit an employer can take against FUTA tax liability?

2. Who can sign the employer's Form 940?

3. When is a Form 940 that has been mailed through the U.S. Postal Service considered filed?

4. What must an employer do in relation to filing Form 940 when it goes out of business?

5. What are the penalties for not paying FUTA tax timely?

6. What are the four factors that employers can use in determining which state an employee who is working in two or more states should be "allocated" to for unemployment insurance purposes?

7. What categories of employers are not subject to FUTA tax?

8. Name three types of employee compensation that are exempt from FUTA.

9. Name three types of employment that are exempt from FUTA.

10. How does an employer amend an incorrect Form 940?

11. What are the four methods that states use to determine an employer's experience rate?

12. States that offer the voluntary contribution option routinely impose restrictions on its use. What classifications of employers are often barred from making such contributions?

13. When faced with a claim for unemployment benefits, what should the employer do?

14. What standards (required by all the states) must be met by claimants to become and remain eligible for benefits?

## True or False Questions

_____ 1. An employer is not subject to FUTA tax if it is a tax-exempt nonprofit, religious, charitable, or educational organization.

_____ 2. FUTA tax applies only to wages when they are actually or constructively paid, not when earned.

_____ 3. An employer that voluntarily chooses to participate in its state's unemployment insurance program does not receive the normal credit for timely state payments it makes.

_____ 4. A successor employer retains the unemployment contribution rate it had immediately before the acquisition of the predecessor occurred if the successor was a covered employer in the state at that time.

_____ 5. Nonprofit and public sector employers must choose the direct reimbursement method to satisfy their state unemployment insurance liability.

_____ 6. The goal of a voluntary contribution is to increase the employer's reserve ratio to the next higher bracket on the state's unemployment rate table which corresponds to the next lower tax bracket.

_____ 7. Form 940 is considered to be timely filed if it is sent on or before the due date via the U.S. mail or a designated private delivery service.

_____ 8. States can set their own state taxable wage base for state unemployment insurance as long as it is at least equal to the FUTA wage base for that year.

_____ 9. Form 940 is filed each quarter by employers that are subject to FUTA tax.

_____ 10. Each state requires employers to contribute toward its unemployment insurance program in the form of state unemployment taxes.

_____ 11. If the employer's FUTA tax liability for the first quarter is $600, no deposit is required.

_____ 12. If the FUTA tax deposit due date falls on a Saturday, the deposit is due the Friday before.

_____ 13. If the employer's FUTA tax liability for the fourth quarter is $500 or less, payment can be sent in with the employer's Form 940 by the due date of the form.

_____ 14. The FUTA tax for 2008 is based on 6.2% of each employee's wages up to $102,000.

_____ 15. A credit against FUTA tax is available for state unemployment tax paid by the employer.

_____ 16. To qualify for the normal credit against FUTA tax liability, the state law requiring payment of state unemployment taxes must be certified by the U.S. Department of Labor as complying with federal requirements regarding the joint federal/state program.

_____ 17. If an employee changes jobs during the year, only the first employer pays FUTA taxes on behalf of the employee.

_____ 18. When employees perform services all in one state, the employer pays unemployment taxes to that state.

_____ 19. Employers that have a great deal of turnover generally have a lower experience rate.

_____ 20. When determining the reserve ratio, the higher the ratio, the lower the tax rate.

_____ 21. The period for which a terminated employee is eligible to claim benefits is known as the "taxable year."

_____ 22. In most states, the base period for claiming unemployment benefits is the first four calendar quarters out of the five preceding the quarter during which the employee first filed the claim for benefits.

_____ 23. Laid-off or terminated employees are the only individuals who are eligible for unemployment benefits.

## Multiple Choice Questions

_____ 1. What method is used by the majority of states to determine an employer's experience rate for its contribution to state unemployment insurance?

    a. Reserve ratio
    b. Benefit ratio
    c. Benefit wage ratio
    d. Payroll stabilization

_____ 2. What is the FUTA tax rate through 2008?

    a. 7.65%
    b. 1.45%
    c. 6.2%
    d. 5.4%

_____ 3. On what form must employers covered by FUTA report their liability?

    a. Form 945
    b. Form 940
    c. Form W-3
    d. Form 941

_____ 4.   All of the following methods areused to determine an employer's state unemployment insurance experience rate EXCEPT:

    a.   Age ratio
    b.   Reserve ratio
    c.   Benefit ratio
    d.   Benefit wage ratio

_____ 5.   What state uses the payroll stabilization method to determine an employer's state unemployment tax rate?

    a.   Minnesota
    b.   Michigan
    c.   Arkansas
    d.   Alaska

_____ 6.   Who pays FUTA tax?

    a.   Employees only
    b.   Employers only
    c.   Both employees and employers
    d.   Statutory nonemployees only

_____ 7.   How frequently are state unemployment reports filed?

    a.   Annually
    b.   Monthly
    c.   Quarterly
    d.   Semimonthly

_____ 8.   What is the FUTA wage base for 2008?

    a.   $7,000
    b.   $10,000
    c.   $102,000
    d.   $97,500

_____ 9.   An employer's wages subject to FUTA tax liability for the first three quarters of 2008 are $25,000, $26,000 and $18,000 respectively. How much FUTA tax must be deposited in the third quarter?

    a.   $52
    b.   $144
    c.   $552
    d.   $408

_____ 10.   What is the due date for depositing FUTA taxes for the third quarter?

    a.   September 30
    b.   October 31
    c.   November 30
    d.   December 31

_____ 11.   An employer's FUTA taxable wages for the first quarter of 2008 amount to $35,000. What is the employer's FUTA tax liability for the quarter?

     a.   $2,170
     b.   $280
     c.   $0
     d.   $56

_____ 12.   An employer paid $2,000 of its $3,000 2007 state unemployment tax liability by January 31, 2008 and the remainder when it filed its 2007 Form 940 a week later. What is the employer's normal credit against FUTA liability for 2007?

     a.   $900
     b.   $2,700
     c.   $2,900
     d.   $3,000

_____ 13.   What is the due date for Form 940?

     a.   December 31
     b.   January 15
     c.   January 31
     d.   February 15

_____ 14.   If an employer has made timely deposits of its full FUTA tax liability, what is the Form 940 due date?

     a.   January 10
     b.   January 15
     c.   January 31
     d.   February 10

_____ 15.   What is the prime factor that employers can use in determining to which state an employee should be "allocated" for unemployment insurance purposes?

     a.   Location of base of operations
     b.   Location of employee's residence
     c.   Place where the work is localized
     d.   Place of direction or control

_____ 16.   For how many weeks can unemployment benefits be collected without an extension?

     a.   26 weeks
     b.   38 weeks
     c.   40 weeks
     d.   52 weeks

_____ 17.   Cherise Pitts has two employees who are paid $17,000 and $5,000, respectively, during 2008. If Cherise timely pays 5.4% of their wages for state unemployment tax, what is the amount of her 2008 FUTA tax liability after the state tax credit is taken?
     a.   $0
     b.   $96
     c.   $112
     d.   $176

_____ 18.  In 2008, Wilson Corporation had three employees. Two of the employees worked full time and earned salaries of $25,000 each. The third employee worked only part time and earned $3,000. The employer timely paid state unemployment tax equal to 5.4% of each employee's wages up to the state's wage base. How much FUTA tax is due from Wilson Corporation for 2008, after the credit for state unemployment taxes is taken?

      a.   $0
      b.   $136
      c.   $168
      d.   $918

## Problems

1. Ruth's Shop had a FUTA taxable payroll of $14,000 for the first quarter of 2008. What is the FUTA tax liability for the first quarter? Was Ruth's Shop required to make a deposit of FUTA tax by April 30, 2008? Why?

2. The Boulder Company has a taxable payroll for 2007 for FUTA and state unemployment tax of $70,000. The SUTA tax rate in the state in which the Boulder Company does business is 3.2%, and Boulder paid its entire SUTA tax liability by January 31, 2008. Calculate:

   a. Net FUTA tax liability for 2007           $_____

   b. Net SUTA tax liability for 2007           $_____

   c. Total unemployment tax liability          $_____

3. Casey Company has five employees with earnings for 2007 as follows:

   | | |
   |---|---|
   | David Bates | $23,500 |
   | John Smith | $27,000 |
   | Doreen Saunders | $24,500 |
   | William Jones | $21,000 |
   | Sam Frazer | $21,000 |

   The state unemployment tax rate is 5.4% on the first $7,000 in wages paid to each employee, and Casey paid all its SUTA tax liability by January 31, 2008. Calculate the following amounts for Casey Company:

   a. FUTA tax before state tax credit        $_____

   b. SUTA tax                          $_____

   c. FUTA tax after state tax credit         $_____

## Section 7: Unemployment Insurance

4. Toni's Lumber paid the following wages during the first quarter of 2008:

| | |
|---|---|
| James Harker | $15,200 |
| Joe Kortsen | 17,500 |
| Betty Rice | 8,450 |
| Elliott Peterson | 6,000 |
| Sally Hanson | 11,200 |
| Pamela Barnhart | 14,450 |
| Allan Gunnel | 3,150 |
| Margaret Headley | 4,600 |
| Bill Jordan | 7,000 |
| Nellie Baxter | 5,400 |

Calculate Toni's first quarter FUTA tax liability     $_____

5. George Brown is a supervisor for Wind Power Alternatives in Los Angeles, CA. In March 2008, George was transferred by the company to its plant in Sacramento, CA. The company's contribution rate in the state of California is 4.9%, and the SUTA wage base is $7,000. During 2008, George's total earnings are $38,500, of which $6,000 was paid in Los Angeles and the remainder in Sacramento. Calculate:

   a. SUTA tax on wages paid in Los Angeles     $_____

   b. SUTA tax on wages paid in Sacramento     $_____

   c. Net FUTA tax on George's wages     $_____

6. On April 1, 2008 Martin Earnest left Phelps Tires in Philadelphia, PA to work for Bill's Auto in Pittsburgh, PA. Martin was paid $6,600 by Phelps and $32,000 by Bill's Auto during 2008. Assuming both employers are entitled to the full normal credit for timely paid state unemployment taxes, calculate:

   a. Net FUTA on wages from Phelps Tires     $_____

   b. Net FUTA on wages from Bill's Auto     $_____

7. In 2007 an employer charged its wages account with $72,680. Of this amount, $1,700 was not paid until the first payday in 2008. Further, the wages actually paid to employees in 2007 in excess of $7,000 each amounted to $26,230. The employer's state unemployment tax rate is 5.4%, the state unemployment wage base is $7,000, and all state unemployment taxes were paid by January 31, 2008. Calculate:

   a. Gross FUTA tax     $_____

   b. State tax credit against FUTA     $_____

   c. Net FUTA tax     $_____

8. The wages for the first quarter of 2008 for Western Fabrics of Colorado are as follows:

<u>Earnings Summary</u>

| Social Security Number | Employee Name | Total Earnings |
|---|---|---|
| 111-10-1234 | David Jones | $ 8,500 |
| 222-20-2345 | Sheryl Smith | 7,200 |
| 333-30-3456 | Johnny Foster | 7,600 |
| 444-40-4567 | Melissa Denney | 5,400 |
| 555-50-5678 | Jackie Stewart | 7,300 |
| 666-60-6789 | Kathy Jensen | 4,300 |
| 777-70-7890 | Paul Thornton | 2,600 |
| | Total Earnings | $42,900 |

Calculate the FUTA tax liability for the first quarter of 2008.

$_____

9. The following information is taken from the payroll records of Fine Arts of 31 West Street, Tulsa, OK 98243 for the four quarters of 2007.

<u>Fine Arts—Wages Paid in 2007</u>

| Employee | First Quarter | Second Quarter | Third Quarter | Fourth Quarter | Total |
|---|---|---|---|---|---|
| Samuel Diaz | $ 3,000 | $ 3,000 | $ 3,000 | $ 3,000 | $12,000 |
| Mary Evans | 3,200 | 3,400 | 3,400 | 3,400 | 13,400 |
| Paul Jackson | 4,000 | 4,000 | 5,300 | —— | 13,300 |
| Michael Flin | 3,600 | 3,600 | 4,000 | 4,000 | 15,200 |
| Maria Day | —— | 2,500 | 2,500 | 2,500 | 7,500 |
| Tom Solomon | —— | —— | 3,800 | 3,800 | 7,600 |
| Totals | $13,800 | $16,500 | $22,000 | $16,700 | $69,000 |

The employer paid $2,476.50 to the state unemployment fund during 2007.
The employer's federal ID number is 22-3412345
The employer's state reporting number is 86179.
The employer's phone number is (405) 918-1111.

Complete the Form 940 on pages 7-57 and 7-58 for Fine Arts for 2007.

# Section 7: Unemployment Insurance

10. Benson Products, Inc. has 20 employees on their payroll in 2008, and their wages are as follows:

    10 employees are each paid $1,800 per month,
    6 employees are each paid $2,000 per month, and
    4 employees are each paid $1,000 per month

    a.  Calculate the net FUTA tax for the first three quarters of 2008.

        First quarter                                    $_____

        Second quarter                                   $_____

        Third Quarter                                    $_____

    In December you learn that the 5.4% FUTA tax credit is reduced by 1.4% for employers in the state. The effective FUTA rate is now 2.2% (6.2% - 4.0%).

    b.  Calculate the tax liability for the fourth quarter by recalculating the tax liability at the new rate.

                                                         $_____

11. The Conrow Lumber Company has 20 employees, of which 15 are in California and 5 are in Arizona. All the wages paid by Conrow were taxable for FUTA and SUTA purposes. Conrow paid all its 2007 state unemployment taxes to both states by January 31, 2008. All employees reached the state SUTA wage base of $7,000 in both states, and also the federal FUTA wage base. Use the following information to complete the 2007 Form 940 on pages 7-59 and 7-60, and Schedule A (Form 940) on page 7-61:

    Employer's address: 1234 San Francisco Street, San Francisco, CA 56789-1234

    Employer's federal EIN:  86-2345678
    Employer's CA state reporting number:      1122334
    Employer's AZ state reporting number:      4455667

    Payments to CA employees in 2007:   $450,000
    Payments to AZ employees in 2007:   $150,000

    Conrow's CA state experience rate for all of 2007:   2.9%
    Conrow's AZ state experience rate for all of 2007:   2.7%

    The amount contributed to the state unemployment fund for both states is:
       California   $3,045
       Arizona      $ 945

    First quarter FUTA liability:        $896
    Second quarter FUTA liability:       $112
    Third quarter FUTA liability:        $ 56

12. MiloSuisse Textured Yarns has 50 employees in four states in 2007 (Arizona, California, Florida, and Mississippi). MiloSuisse paid all its state unemployment taxes to all four states by January 31, 2008. All employees reached the state unemployment wage base in the state where they worked and also the FUTA wage base. Use the following information to complete the 2007 Form 940 on pages 7-62 and 7-63, and Schedule A (Form 940) on page 7-64.

Employer's address: 1000 East State Street, Campton, Florida 13579-2468

Employer's federal EIN: 82-4020304

| | |
|---|---|
| Employer's Arizona reporting number: | 102030M |
| Employer's California reporting number: | 203040N |
| Employer's Florida reporting number: | 304050O |
| Employer's Mississippi reporting number: | 405060P |

| | |
|---|---|
| Payment to employees in Arizona in 2007: | $285,600 |
| Payment to employees in California in 2007: | $249,350 |
| Payment to employees in Florida in 2007: | $312,850 |
| Payment to employees in Mississippi in 2007: | $147,700 |
| Total | $995,500 |

Note: Of the total wages paid to all employees $20,000 was for group-term life insurance in excess of $50,000, and $36,000 went to cafeteria plans (not to pre-tax deferrals to a §401(k) plan).

The amount contributed to each state's unemployment fund for 2007 is:

| State | State Taxable Payroll | State Experience rate | contributions actually paid |
|---|---|---|---|
| Arizona | $100,200 | 2.8% | $2,805.60 |
| California | $110,400 | 3.4% | $3,753.60 |
| Florida | $125,000 | 2.9% | $3,625.00 |
| Mississippi | $ 64,600 | 3.5% | $2,261.00 |

| | |
|---|---|
| First quarter FUTA liability: | $1,350 |
| Second quarter FUTA liability: | $ 950 |
| Third quarter FUTA liability: | $ 350 |

**Form 940 for 2007:** **Employer's Annual Federal Unemployment (FUTA) Tax Return**          850107

Department of the Treasury — Internal Revenue Service                    OMB No. 1545-0028

**(EIN)**
Employer identification number    ☐☐ – ☐☐☐☐☐☐☐

Name *(not your trade name)* _____

Trade name *(if any)* _____

Address _____
Number    Street             Suite or room number

City                State        ZIP code

**Type of Return**
(Check all that apply.)

☐ **a.** Amended
☐ **b.** Successor employer
☐ **c.** No payments to employees in 2007
☐ **d.** Final: Business closed or stopped paying wages

Read the separate instructions before you fill out this form. Please type or print within the boxes.

**Part 1: Tell us about your return. If any line does NOT apply, leave it blank.**

1  If you were required to pay your state unemployment tax in ...

    **1a** **One state only,** write the state abbreviation . . . . **1a** ☐☐

    - OR -

    **1b** **More than one state** (You are a multi-state employer) . . . . . . . . . **1b** ☐ Check here. Fill out Schedule A.

            **Skip line 2 for 2007 and go to line 3.**

2  If you paid wages in a state that is subject to CREDIT REDUCTION . . . . . . . . . **2** ☐ Check here. Fill out Schedule A (Form 940), Part 2.

**Part 2: Determine your FUTA tax before adjustments for 2007. If any line does NOT apply, leave it blank.**

3  **Total payments to all employees** . . . . . . . . . **3** ☐

4  **Payments exempt from FUTA tax** . . . . . . . . **4** ☐

    Check all that apply: **4a** ☐ Fringe benefits    **4c** ☐ Retirement/Pension    **4e** ☐ Other
                      **4b** ☐ Group term life insurance    **4d** ☐ Dependent care

5  **Total of payments made to each employee in excess of $7,000** . . . . . . . . . . . **5** ☐

6  **Subtotal** (line 4 + line 5 = line 6) . . . . . . . . . **6** ☐

7  **Total taxable FUTA wages** (line 3 – line 6 = line 7) . . . . . . . . . . **7** ☐

8  **FUTA tax before adjustments** (line 7 × .008 = line 8) . . . . . . . . **8** ☐

**Part 3: Determine your adjustments. If any line does NOT apply, leave it blank.**

9  **If ALL of the taxable FUTA wages you paid were excluded from state unemployment tax,** multiply line 7 by .054 (line 7 × .054 = line 9). Then go to line 12 . . . . . . . . **9** ☐

10  **If SOME of the taxable FUTA wages you paid were excluded from state unemployment tax, OR you paid ANY state unemployment tax late** (after the due date for filing Form 940), fill out the worksheet in the instructions. Enter the amount from line 7 of the worksheet onto line 10 . . **10** ☐

                      **Skip line 11 for 2007 and go to line 12.**

11  **If credit reduction applies,** enter the amount from line 3 of Schedule A (Form 940) . . . . . **11** ☐

**Part 4: Determine your FUTA tax and balance due or overpayment for 2007. If any line does NOT apply, leave it blank.**

12  **Total FUTA tax after adjustments** (lines 8 + 9 + 10 = line 12) . . . . . . . . . . **12** ☐

13  **FUTA tax deposited for the year, including any payment applied from a prior year** . . . . **13** ☐

14  **Balance due** (If line 12 is more than line 13, enter the difference on line 14.)
    ● If line 14 is more than $500, you must deposit your tax.
    ● If line 14 is $500 or less and you pay by check, make your check payable to the United States Treasury and write your EIN, *Form 940,* and *2007* on the check . . . . . . . . . . **14** ☐

15  **Overpayment** (If line 13 is more than line 12, enter the difference on line 15 and check a box below.) . . . . . . . . . . . . . . . . . . . . **15** ☐

                             Check one ☐ Apply to next return.
                                    ☐ Send a refund.

▶ You **MUST** fill out both pages of this form and **SIGN** it.

Next ➡

For Privacy Act and Paperwork Reduction Act Notice, see the back of Form 940-V, Payment Voucher.    Cat. No. 11234O    Form **940** (2007)

_The Payroll Source_

7-58

850207

| Name *(not your trade name)* | Employer identification number (EIN) |

**Part 5: Report your FUTA tax liability by quarter only if line 12 is more than $500. If not, go to Part 6.**

16 Report the amount of your FUTA tax liability for each quarter; do NOT enter the amount you deposited. If you had no liability for a quarter, leave the line blank.

16a  1st quarter (January 1 – March 31) . . . . . . . . 16a ▢

16b  2nd quarter (April 1 – June 30) . . . . . . . . . . 16b ▢

16c  3rd quarter (July 1 – September 30) . . . . . . . 16c ▢

16d  4th quarter (October 1 – December 31) . . . . . . 16d ▢

17  Total tax liability for the year (lines 16a + 16b + 16c + 16d = line 17) 17 ▢  Total must equal line 12.

**Part 6: May we speak with your third-party designee?**

Do you want to allow an employee, a paid tax preparer, or another person to discuss this return with the IRS? See the instructions for details.

☐ Yes.  Designee's name ▢

Select a 5-digit Personal Identification Number (PIN) to use when talking to IRS ▢▢▢▢▢

☐ No.

**Part 7: Sign here. You MUST fill out both pages of this form and SIGN it.**

Under penalties of perjury, I declare that I have examined this return, including accompanying schedules and statements, and to the best of my knowledge and belief, it is true, correct, and complete, and that no part of any payment made to a state unemployment fund claimed as a credit was, or is to be, deducted from the payments made to employees.

✘ Sign your name here ▢   Print your name here ▢   Print your title here ▢

Date ▢   Best daytime phone ( ) –

**Part 8: For PAID preparers only (optional)**

If you were paid to prepare this return and are not an employee of the business that is filing this return, you may choose to fill out Part 8.

Paid Preparer's name ▢   Preparer's SSN/PTIN ▢

Paid Preparer's signature ▢   Date ▢

☐ Check if you are self-employed.

Firm's name ▢   Firm's EIN ▢

Street address ▢

City ▢   State ▢   ZIP code ▢

7-58

Form **940 for 2007:** **Employer's Annual Federal Unemployment (FUTA) Tax Return**

850107

Department of the Treasury — Internal Revenue Service

OMB No. 1545-0028

**(EIN)**
**Employer identification number** ☐☐ — ☐☐☐☐☐☐☐

**Name** *(not your trade name)*

**Trade name** *(if any)*

**Address**
Number    Street    Suite or room number
City    State    ZIP code

**Type of Return**
(Check all that apply.)

☐ **a.** Amended
☐ **b.** Successor employer
☐ **c.** No payments to employees in 2007
☐ **d.** Final: Business closed or stopped paying wages

Read the separate instructions before you fill out this form. Please type or print within the boxes.

**Part 1: Tell us about your return. If any line does NOT apply, leave it blank.**

1  If you were required to pay your state unemployment tax in ...

    **1a One state only,** write the state abbreviation . . . . **1a** ☐☐

    - OR -

    **1b More than one state** (You are a multi-state employer) . . . . . . . . **1b** ☐ Check here. Fill out Schedule A.

    **Skip line 2 for 2007 and go to line 3.**

2  If you paid wages in a state that is subject to **CREDIT REDUCTION** . . . . . **2** ☐ Check here. Fill out Schedule A (Form 940), Part 2.

**Part 2: Determine your FUTA tax before adjustments for 2007. If any line does NOT apply, leave it blank.**

3  **Total payments to all employees** . . . . . . . . . . . . . . **3** ☐

4  **Payments exempt from FUTA tax** . . . . . . **4** ☐

    Check all that apply: **4a** ☐ Fringe benefits  **4c** ☐ Retirement/Pension  **4e** ☐ Other
    **4b** ☐ Group term life insurance  **4d** ☐ Dependent care

5  **Total of payments made to each employee in excess of $7,000** . . . . . . . **5** ☐

6  **Subtotal** (line 4 + line 5 = line 6) . . . . . . . . . . **6** ☐

7  **Total taxable FUTA wages** (line 3 – line 6 = line 7) . . . . . . **7** ☐

8  **FUTA tax before adjustments** (line 7 $\times$ .008 = line 8) . . . . . . . . **8** ☐

**Part 3: Determine your adjustments. If any line does NOT apply, leave it blank.**

9  If ALL of the taxable FUTA wages you paid were excluded from state unemployment tax, multiply line 7 by .054 (line 7 $\times$ .054 = line 9). Then go to line 12 . . . . . . **9** ☐

10  If SOME of the taxable FUTA wages you paid were excluded from state unemployment tax, OR you paid ANY state unemployment tax late (after the due date for filing Form 940), fill out the worksheet in the instructions. Enter the amount from line 7 of the worksheet onto line 10 . **10** ☐

    **Skip line 11 for 2007 and go to line 12.**

11  If credit reduction applies, enter the amount from line 3 of Schedule A (Form 940) . . . . **11** ☐

**Part 4: Determine your FUTA tax and balance due or overpayment for 2007. If any line does NOT apply, leave it blank.**

12  **Total FUTA tax after adjustments** (lines 8 + 9 + 10 = line 12) . . . . . . . . **12** ☐

13  **FUTA tax deposited for the year, including any payment applied from a prior year** . . . . **13** ☐

14  **Balance due** (If line 12 is more than line 13, enter the difference on line 14.)
    ● If line 14 is more than $500, you must deposit your tax.
    ● If line 14 is $500 or less and you pay by check, make your check payable to the United States Treasury and write your EIN, *Form 940,* and *2007* on the check . . . . . . . . **14** ☐

15  **Overpayment** (If line 13 is more than line 12, enter the difference on line 15 and check a box below.) . . . . **15** ☐

    Check one ☐ Apply to next return.
    ☐ Send a refund.

    ▶ You **MUST** fill out both pages of this form and **SIGN** it.

Next ➡

**For Privacy Act and Paperwork Reduction Act Notice, see the back of Form 940-V, Payment Voucher.**    Cat. No. 11234O    Form **940** (2007)

850207

| Name *(not your trade name)* | Employer identification number (EIN) |
|---|---|

**Part 5: Report your FUTA tax liability by quarter only if line 12 is more than $500. If not, go to Part 6.**

16 Report the amount of your FUTA tax liability for each quarter; do NOT enter the amount you deposited. If you had no liability for a quarter, leave the line blank.

16a **1st quarter** (January 1 – March 31) . . . . . . . . 16a ⬜.

16b **2nd quarter** (April 1 – June 30) . . . . . . . . . 16b ⬜.

16c **3rd quarter** (July 1 – September 30) . . . . . . . 16c ⬜.

16d **4th quarter** (October 1 – December 31) . . . . . . 16d ⬜.

17 **Total tax liability for the year** (lines 16a + 16b + 16c + 16d = line 17) **17** ⬜. **Total must equal line 12.**

**Part 6: May we speak with your third-party designee?**

Do you want to allow an employee, a paid tax preparer, or another person to discuss this return with the IRS? See the instructions for details.

⬜ **Yes.** Designee's name _____

Select a 5-digit Personal Identification Number (PIN) to use when talking to IRS ⬜⬜⬜⬜⬜

⬜ **No.**

**Part 7: Sign here. You MUST fill out both pages of this form and SIGN it.**

Under penalties of perjury, I declare that I have examined this return, including accompanying schedules and statements, and to the best of my knowledge and belief, it is true, correct, and complete, and that no part of any payment made to a state unemployment fund claimed as a credit was, or is to be, deducted from the payments made to employees.

X **Sign your name here** _____

Print your name here _____
Print your title here _____

Date ___/___/___

Best daytime phone ( ) –

**Part 8: For PAID preparers only (optional)**

If you were paid to prepare this return and are not an employee of the business that is filing this return, you may choose to fill out Part 8.

Paid Preparer's name _____
Preparer's SSN/PTIN _____

Paid Preparer's signature _____
Date ___/___/___

⬜ Check if you are self-employed.

Firm's name _____ Firm's EIN _____

Street address _____

City _____ State _____ ZIP code _____

# Schedule A (Form 940) for 2007:

**860307**

OMB No. 1545-0028

## Multi-State Employer and Credit Reduction Information

Department of the Treasury — Internal Revenue Service

**Employer identification number (EIN)** ☐☐ – ☐☐☐☐☐☐☐

**Name** *(not your trade name)*

## About this schedule:

- You must fill out Schedule A (Form 940) if you were required to pay your state unemployment tax in *more than one state* or if you paid wages in any state that is subject to *credit reduction.* FOR 2007, THERE ARE NO STATES SUBJECT TO CREDIT REDUCTION.
- File Schedule A (Form 940) as an attachment to your Form 940.

For more information, read the Instructions for Schedule A (Form 940) on the back.

**Part 1:** Fill out this part if you were required to pay state unemployment taxes in more than one state (including the District of Columbia, Puerto Rico, and the U.S. Virgin Islands). If any states do **NOT** apply to you, leave them blank.

1  **Check the box for every state in which you were required to pay state unemployment tax this year.** For a list of state names and their abbreviations, see the Instructions for Schedule A (Form 940).

| | | | | | | | | | |
|---|---|---|---|---|---|---|---|---|---|
| ☐ AK | ☐ CO | ☐ GA | ☐ IN | ☐ MD | ☐ MS | ☐ NH | ☐ OH | ☐ SC | ☐ VA | ☐ WY |
| ☐ AL | ☐ CT | ☐ HI | ☐ KS | ☐ MI | ☐ MT | ☐ NJ | ☐ OK | ☐ SD | ☐ VT | ☐ PR |
| ☐ AR | ☐ DC | ☐ IA | ☐ KY | ☐ MN | ☐ NC | ☐ NM | ☐ OR | ☐ TN | ☐ WA | ☐ VI |
| ☐ AZ | ☐ DE | ☐ ID | ☐ LA | ☐ MO | ☐ ND | ☐ NV | ☐ PA | ☐ TX | ☐ WI | |
| ☐ CA | ☐ FL | ☐ IL | ☐ MA | ☐ ME | ☐ NE | ☐ NY | ☐ RI | ☐ UT | ☐ WV | |

**Part 2:** Fill out this part to tell us about wages you paid in any state (including the District of Columbia, Puerto Rico, and the U.S. Virgin Islands) that is subject to credit reduction. If any lines do **NOT** apply, leave them blank.

2  If you paid wages in any of these states...

2a–b **[Name of State]** Total taxable FUTA wages paid in [state] . . **2a** _____ × .00x = line 2b  **2b** _____

2c–d **[Name of State]** Total taxable FUTA wages paid in [state] . . **2c** _____ × .00x = line 2d  **2d** _____

2e–f **[Name of State]** Total taxable FUTA wages paid in [state] . . **2e** _____ × .00x = line 2f  **2f** _____

2g–h **[Name of State]** Total taxable FUTA wages paid in [state] . . **2g** _____ × .00x = line 2h  **2h** _____

2i–j **[Name of State]** Total taxable FUTA wages paid in [state] . . **2i** _____ × .00x = line 2j  **2j** _____

3  Total credit reduction (Lines 2b + 2d + 2f + 2h + 2j = line 3) . . . . . . . . . . **3** _____

Enter the amount from line 3 onto line 11 of Form 940.

**For Privacy Act and Paperwork Reduction Act Notice, see back of Form 940-V.**    Cat. No. 16997C    **Schedule A (Form 940) 2007**

Form **940 for 2007:** **Employer's Annual Federal Unemployment (FUTA) Tax Return**     850107
Department of the Treasury — Internal Revenue Service

OMB No. 1545-0028

**(EIN)**
Employer identification number ☐☐ – ☐☐☐☐☐☐☐

Name *(not your trade name)*

Trade name *(if any)*

Address

Number     Street     Suite or room number

City     State     ZIP code

**Type of Return**
(Check all that apply.)

☐ **a.** Amended
☐ **b.** Successor employer
☐ **c.** No payments to employees in 2007
☐ **d.** Final: Business closed or stopped paying wages

Read the separate instructions before you fill out this form. Please type or print within the boxes.

**Part 1: Tell us about your return. If any line does NOT apply, leave it blank.**

1  If you were required to pay your state unemployment tax in ...

   1a **One state only,** write the state abbreviation . . . . **1a** ☐☐
   - OR -
   1b **More than one state** (You are a multi-state employer) . . . . . **1b** ☐ Check here. Fill out Schedule A.
      Skip line 2 for 2007 and go to line 3.

2  If you paid wages in a state that is subject to **CREDIT REDUCTION** . . . . . . . . **2** ☐ Check here. Fill out Schedule A. (Form 940), Part 2.

**Part 2: Determine your FUTA tax before adjustments for 2007. If any line does NOT apply, leave it blank.**

3  Total payments to all employees . . . . . . . . . . . . **3** ☐

4  Payments exempt from FUTA tax . . . . . . . . . **4** ☐

   Check all that apply: **4a** ☐ Fringe benefits     **4c** ☐ Retirement/Pension     **4e** ☐ Other
   **4b** ☐ Group term life insurance     **4d** ☐ Dependent care

5  Total of payments made to each employee in excess of $7,000 . . . . . . . . . . . **5** ☐

6  **Subtotal** (line 4 + line 5 = line 6) . . . . . . . . . . **6** ☐

7  Total taxable FUTA wages (line 3 – line 6 = line 7) . . . . . . . . **7** ☐

8  FUTA tax before adjustments (line 7 × .008 = line 8) . . . . . . . . . **8** ☐

**Part 3: Determine your adjustments. If any line does NOT apply, leave it blank.**

9  If ALL of the taxable FUTA wages you paid were excluded from state unemployment tax, multiply line 7 by .054 (line 7 × .054 = line 9). Then go to line 12 . . . **9** ☐

10  If SOME of the taxable FUTA wages you paid were excluded from state unemployment tax, OR you paid ANY state unemployment tax late (after the due date for filing Form 940), fill out the worksheet in the instructions. Enter the amount from line 7 of the worksheet onto line 10 . **10** ☐

Skip line 11 for 2007 and go to line 12.

11  If credit reduction applies, enter the amount from line 3 of Schedule A (Form 940) . . . . . . **11** ☐

**Part 4: Determine your FUTA tax and balance due or overpayment for 2007. If any line does NOT apply, leave it blank.**

12  Total FUTA tax after adjustments (lines 8 + 9 + 10 = line 12) . . . . . . . . . **12** ☐

13  FUTA tax deposited for the year, including any payment applied from a prior year . . . . **13** ☐

14  Balance due (If line 12 is more than line 13, enter the difference on line 14.)
   • If line 14 is more than $500, you must deposit your tax.
   • If line 14 is $500 or less and you pay by check, make your check payable to the United States Treasury and write your EIN, *Form 940,* and *2007* on the check . . . . . . . . . . . **14** ☐

15  Overpayment (If line 13 is more than line 12, enter the difference on line 15 and check a box below.) . . . . . . . . . . . . . . . . . . . . . . . **15** ☐

Check one ☐ Apply to next return.
☐ Send a refund.

▶ You **MUST** fill out both pages of this form and **SIGN** it.

Next ➡

For Privacy Act and Paperwork Reduction Act Notice, see the back of Form 940-V, Payment Voucher.     Cat. No. 11234O     Form **940** (2007)

850207

| Name *(not your trade name)* | Employer identification number (EIN) |
|---|---|
| | |

### Part 5: Report your FUTA tax liability by quarter only if line 12 is more than $500. If not, go to Part 6.

16  Report the amount of your FUTA tax liability for each quarter; do NOT enter the amount you deposited. If you had no liability for a quarter, leave the line blank.

16a  **1st quarter** (January 1 – March 31) . . . . . . . . . 16a

16b  **2nd quarter** (April 1 – June 30) . . . . . . . . . 16b

16c  **3rd quarter** (July 1 – September 30) . . . . . . . 16c

16d  **4th quarter** (October 1 – December 31) . . . . . . 16d

17  Total tax liability for the year (lines 16a + 16b + 16c + 16d = line 17) **17**      Total must equal line 12.

### Part 6: May we speak with your third-party designee?

Do you want to allow an employee, a paid tax preparer, or another person to discuss this return with the IRS? See the instructions for details.

☐ **Yes.**  Designee's name

Select a 5-digit Personal Identification Number (PIN) to use when talking to IRS

☐ **No.**

### Part 7: Sign here. You MUST fill out both pages of this form and SIGN it.

Under penalties of perjury, I declare that I have examined this return, including accompanying schedules and statements, and to the best of my knowledge and belief, it is true, correct, and complete, and that no part of any payment made to a state unemployment fund claimed as a credit was, or is to be, deducted from the payments made to employees.

**X Sign your name here**

Print your name here

Print your title here

Date          /          /

Best daytime phone  (          )          –

### Part 8: For PAID preparers only (optional)

If you were paid to prepare this return and are not an employee of the business that is filing this return, you may choose to fill out Part 8.

Paid Preparer's name

Preparer's SSN/PTIN

Paid Preparer's signature

Date          /          /

☐ Check if you are self-employed.

Firm's name

Firm's EIN

Street address

City                    State

ZIP code

Page **2**

Form **940** (2007)

## Schedule A (Form 940) for 2007:

### Multi-State Employer and Credit Reduction Information

860307

OMB No. 1545-0028

Department of the Treasury — Internal Revenue Service

Employer identification number (EIN) ☐☐ – ☐☐☐☐☐☐☐

Name *(not your trade name)*

### About this schedule:

- You must fill out Schedule A (Form 940) if you were required to pay your state unemployment tax in **more than one state** or if you paid wages in any state that is subject to *credit reduction.* FOR 2007, THERE ARE NO STATES SUBJECT TO CREDIT REDUCTION.
- File Schedule A (Form 940) as an attachment to your Form 940.

   For more information, read the Instructions for Schedule A (Form 940) on the back.

**Part 1: Fill out this part if you were required to pay state unemployment taxes in more than one state (including the District of Columbia, Puerto Rico, and the U.S. Virgin Islands). If any states do NOT apply to you, leave them blank.**

1    Check the box for every state in which you were required to pay state unemployment tax this year. For a list of state names and their abbreviations, see the Instructions for Schedule A (Form 940).

| | | | | | | | | | |
|---|---|---|---|---|---|---|---|---|---|
| ☐ AK | ☐ CO | ☐ GA | ☐ IN | ☐ MD | ☐ MS | ☐ NH | ☐ OH | ☐ SC | ☐ VA | ☐ WY |
| ☐ AL | ☐ CT | ☐ HI | ☐ KS | ☐ MI | ☐ MT | ☐ NJ | ☐ OK | ☐ SD | ☐ VT | ☐ PR |
| ☐ AR | ☐ DC | ☐ IA | ☐ KY | ☐ MN | ☐ NC | ☐ NM | ☐ OR | ☐ TN | ☐ WA | ☐ VI |
| ☐ AZ | ☐ DE | ☐ ID | ☐ LA | ☐ MO | ☐ ND | ☐ NV | ☐ PA | ☐ TX | ☐ WI | |
| ☐ CA | ☐ FL | ☐ IL | ☐ MA | ☐ ME | ☐ NE | ☐ NY | ☐ RI | ☐ UT | ☐ WV | |

**Part 2: Fill out this part to tell us about wages you paid in any state (including the District of Columbia, Puerto Rico, and the U.S. Virgin Islands) that is subject to credit reduction. If any lines do NOT apply, leave them blank.**

2    If you paid wages in any of these states...

2a–b    [Name of State] Total taxable
         FUTA wages paid in [state] . . 2a ⬛          × .00x = line 2b   2b ⬛

2c–d    [Name of State] Total taxable
         FUTA wages paid in [state] . . 2c ⬛          × .00x = line 2d   2d ⬛

2e–f    [Name of State] Total taxable
         FUTA wages paid in [state] . . 2e ⬛          × .00x = line 2f   2f ⬛

2g–h    [Name of State] Total taxable
         FUTA wages paid in [state] . . 2g ⬛          × .00x = line 2h   2h ⬛

2i–j    [Name of State] Total taxable
         FUTA wages paid in [state] . . 2i ⬛          × .00x = line 2j   2j ⬛

3    Total credit reduction (Lines 2b + 2d + 2f + 2h + 2j = line 3) . . . . . . . . . . .   3 ⬛

*DO NOT COMPLETE FOR 2007*

Enter the amount from line 3 onto line 11 of Form 940.

**For Privacy Act and Paperwork Reduction Act Notice, see back of Form 940-V.**    Cat. No. 16997C    **Schedule A (Form 940) 2007**

# SECTION 8: DEPOSITING AND REPORTING WITHHELD TAXES

## TABLE OF CONTENTS

# SECTION 8: DEPOSITING AND REPORTING WITHHELD TAXES

Once an employer has withheld federal income, social security, and Medicare taxes from its employees' wages, the next step is paying the withheld amounts and any employer taxes that are due (employer share of social security and Medicare taxes and FUTA tax) to the federal government and reporting to both the government and employees the wages paid and taxes withheld. Withheld taxes are held in trust for the federal government and are governed by strict rules requiring their deposit by employers in financial institutions qualified to accept and process them. This section will explain the deposit rules, as well as provide specific guidance for completing and filing employers' tax and information returns.

## 8.1 Employer Identification Numbers

To ensure all payments (whether sent with the return or deposited earlier) are credited to the correct employer, each employer is assigned an Employer Identification Number (EIN). The EIN identifies an employer to the Internal Revenue Service and the Social Security Administration in much the same way a social security number identifies an employee. The EIN is a nine-digit number expressed in the following format: 00-0000000. It must be used whenever an employer is depositing taxes, filing a return, or communicating with the IRS or SSA.[1]

**How to get an EIN.** New employers that have not been assigned an EIN must apply for one. An employer can apply for an EIN online, by phone, or by completing Form SS-4, *Application for Employer Identification Number* (see Appendix page A-38) and faxing or mailing it to the IRS.[2]

*Application online.* Businesses can now obtain an EIN directly from the IRS website. Go to www.irs. gov/businesses/small/article/0,,id=102767,00.html. After an online application form is completed online, the system issues an EIN that may be used immediately. The online process eliminates the need to send paperwork to the IRS as well as the delay in issuing a number that may result from an incomplete application form, since an incomplete form cannot be submitted.

An accountant or tax preparer may use the website to request EINs on behalf of clients. The employer must sign a copy of Form SS-4 and a statement authorizing the representative to receive the EIN online. The representative must keep both documents on file. The website describes the elements required for an authorization statement, which a preparer may print out for the client to sign. When the EIN application process is complete, the taxpayer can view, print, and save the confirmation notice, as opposed to waiting for the IRS to mail it. Authorized third parties can also be provided with the EIN, but a third party cannot view, print, or save the confirmation notice. Instead, it is mailed to the taxpayer.

The online application process is not available to some EIN requesters, namely federal, state, or local government agencies, Indian tribal governments, real estate mortgage investment conduits, and employers with addresses outside the 50 states and the District of Columbia.

*Application by Tele-TIN.* Under the Tele-TIN program, an employer can get its EIN by telephone and use it immediately. The person calling on behalf of the employer should complete a Form SS-4 before calling so that all the relevant information will be readily available. Call the toll-free Tele-TIN number, 800-829-4933 (international applicants call 215-516-6999) from 7:00 am to 10:00 pm local time, Monday - Friday. The person making the call must be authorized to sign the form or be an authorized designee to receive the EIN. When the IRS representative provides the EIN, you should write it on the SS-4, sign and date it, and keep the form for your records.

---

1. IRC §6109; IRS Reg. §301.6109-1.
2. Form SS-4 Instructions; IRS Pub. 15, Circular E, Employer's Tax Guide.

If requested by the IRS representative, mail or fax the signed Form SS-4 (including any third-party designee authorization) within 24 hours to the IRS address provided by the IRS representative. Employer representatives can use Tele-TIN to apply for an EIN on behalf of the employer and request that the EIN be faxed to the employer on the same day. After an EIN is obtained by phone, the original Form SS-4 does not have to be faxed or mailed to the IRS unless the IRS representative requests it.

*Application by Fax-TIN.* Under the Fax-TIN program, an employer can receive its EIN by fax within 4 business days. Complete, sign, and fax Form SS-4 to the IRS using the Fax-TIN number for your state listed below. Fax-TIN numbers can only be used to apply for an EIN, and they are available 24 hours a day, 7 days a week. Make sure you provide your fax number so that IRS can fax the EIN back to you.

| State | Fax-TIN Number |
|---|---|
| CT, DE, DC, FL, GA, ME, MD, MA, NH, NJ, NY, NC, OH, PA, RI, SC, VT, VA, WV | 631-447-8960 |
| IL, IN, KY, MI | 859-669-5760 |
| AL, AK, AZ, AR, CA, CO, HI, ID, IA, KS, LA, MN, MS, MO, MT, NE, NV, NM, ND, OK, OR, PR, SD, TN, TX, UT, WA, WI, WY | 859-669-5760 |
| International | 215-516-1040 |

 **BE CAREFUL** Be sure that you do not call Tele-TIN after submitting Form SS-4 by fax for the same entity, because duplicate EINs may be issued.

*Application by mail.* Employers that want to apply for their EIN by mail should complete, sign, and submit Form SS-4 at least 4-5 weeks before the EIN is needed. The form must be mailed to the IRS service center for the employer's state, as shown in the table below. You will receive the EIN in about 4 weeks.

| State | Service Center Address |
|---|---|
| CT, DE, DC, FL, GA, ME, MD, MA, NH, NJ, NY, NC, OH, PA, RI, SC, VT, VA, WV | Attn: EIN Operation<br>Holtsville, NY 11742 |
| IL, IN, KY, MI | Attn: EIN Operation<br>Cincinnati, OH 45999 |
| AL, AK, AZ, AR, CA, CO, HI, ID, IA, KS, LA, MN, MS, MO, MT, NE, NV, NM, ND, OK, OR, PR, SD, TN, TX, UT, WA, WI, WY | Attn: EIN Operation<br>Philadelphia, PA 19255 |
| International | Attn: EIN Operation<br>Philadelphia, PA 19255 |

No matter which method is chosen to apply for an EIN, the application must be made no later than 7 days after the employer first pays wages.[3]

*Third party can receive EIN.* There is a section on Form SS-4 that allows the employer to authorize the individual named there to receive the employer's EIN and answer questions about the completion of the form. The employer must include the designee's name, address, phone number, and fax number. The designee's authority terminates at the time the EIN is assigned and released to the designee. The form must be signed by the employer for the authorization to be valid.

---

3.    IRS Reg. §31.6011(b)-1(a).

**Where there is no EIN.**  If an employer has not yet received its EIN before the due date of a deposit or return, the employer should write "Applied for" and the date of the application in the space provided for the EIN.  If the employer does not have an EIN by the time a tax deposit is due, the employer should send the payment with an explaination to the local IRS office or the service center where it files the return for the type of tax that is due.  The check or money order should be made payable to the United States Treasury and include the employer's name, address, type of tax, period covered, and date of application for an EIN (see Section 8.3-2 for more details on tax deposits).

**Use one EIN.**[4]  Regardless of the number of businesses the employer is operating or trade names it is using, only one Form SS-4 should be filed and one EIN used.  However, this general rule does not apply to separate but affiliated corporations, which each need an EIN.  If an employer has more than one EIN and is not sure which one to use, it should contact the IRS Service Center where the employer files its returns and provide the numbers assigned, the name and address to which each was assigned, and the address of the employer's main place of business.  The IRS will tell the employer which EIN to use.

**Mergers, consolidations, and reincorporations.**[5]  The proper EIN to use after a corporate merger or acquisition depends on its characterization under the Internal Revenue Code.  If the merger or reincorporation is a reorganization under the IRC, the surviving corporation should use its previously assigned EIN. However, a new EIN is necessary if a new corporation emerges from a consolidation that does not qualify as a reorganization.

*Example 1:*  After a statutory merger of Johnson Co. and Jordan, Inc., which each had their own EINs, only Jordan remains.  Johnson filed a final tax return, and Jordan must use its previously assigned EIN.

*Example 2:*  Alexander Corp. and Mathewson Corp., each with separate EINs, merge into a new company, Spahn Group, Inc.  With the merger, Alexander and Mathewson legally dissolve and file final tax returns.  Spahn Group must apply for a new EIN.

# 8.2  Depositing Withheld Income and Employment Taxes

The payment of withheld federal income, social security, and Medicare taxes, as well as the employer's share of social security and Medicare taxes and FUTA tax, is handled differently from the payment of other federal taxes.  Rather than paying the taxes when filing a return, employers generally must deposit the taxes in a federal depository (financial institution), unless the amounts are very small (e.g., a FUTA tax liability of less than $500 at the end of the year may be paid with the Form 940—see Section 7.1-5).  This section explains the rules governing the timing of tax deposits, the method of making them, and the penalties for making untimely or insufficient deposits.

# 8.2-1 Payroll Tax Deposit Rules

**Monthly or semiweekly depositor status.**  Employers  that file Form 941, *Employer's Quarterly Federal Tax Return* (see Section 8.3-1), are assigned one of two depositor status classifications under the deposit rules:  monthly or semiweekly.  The determination is based on the employer's total liability for federal income, social security, and Medicare taxes during a "lookback period" and generally lasts for an entire 12-month period.  The lookback period is the 12-month period running from July 1 of the second previous year through June 30 of the previous year.[6]

---

4.  IRS Pub. 15, Circular E, Employer's Tax Guide.
5.  Rev. Rul. 73-526, 1973-2 CB 404.
6.  IRS Reg. §31.6302-1(b)(4).

***Example:*** For calendar year 2008, the Form 941 lookback period is July 1, 2006 - June 30, 2007. For calendar year 2009, the lookback period is July 1, 2007 - June 30, 2008.

If an employer's four quarterly Forms 941 during the lookback period show a total federal income, social security, and Medicare tax liability of $50,000 or less, the employer is a monthly depositor for the upcoming year.[7] If the total liability exceeds $50,000, the employer is a semiweekly depositor. Although the depositor status determination generally lasts for an entire year, there are exceptions for employers with less than $1,000 of annual tax liability, less than $2,500 of quarterly tax liability, or more than $100,000 of accumulated tax liability discussed later in this section.

***Example***: Jessicart, Inc. reported its employment tax liability on quarterly Forms 941 as follows:

| 2008 Lookback Period | | 2009 Lookback Period | |
| --- | --- | --- | --- |
| 3rd quarter 2006 - | $12,000 | 3rd quarter 2007 - | $13,000 |
| 4th quarter 2006 - | $12,000 | 4th quarter 2007 - | $13,000 |
| 1st quarter 2007- | $12,000 | 1st quarter 2008 - | $13,000 |
| 2nd quarter 2007 - | $12,000 | 2nd quarter 2008 - | $13,000 |
| | $48,000 | | $52,000 |

Jessicart is a monthly depositor for 2008 because its total employment tax liability for the lookback period was less than $50,000. In 2009 however, Jessicart will be a semiweekly depositor because its total employment tax liability exceeded $50,000 for the lookback period.

For the determination, adjustments made on a Form 941 through Form 941c corrections are applied only to the lookback period during which the Form 941c was filed, not to the quarter which the Form 941 is correcting.[8] Therefore, adjustments to the last quarter of the lookback period (i.e., the second quarter of the previous year) made in the next lookback period are not considered as part of the initial lookback period when determining an employer's depositor status. No adjustment for purposes of status determination is made when Form 941c is filed with Form 843, *Claim for Refund and Request for Abatement* (see Section 8.6).

***Example:*** Barb's Bagels, Inc. filed quarterly 941 forms for the lookback period of July 1, 2006 - June 30, 2007 totaling $48,600 in federal income withholding and employment tax liability. For the quarter ending June 30, 2007, Barb's Form 941 showed an income withholding and employment tax liability of $15,200. During the third quarter of 2007, Barb's realized its second quarter Form 941 should have shown a tax liability of $17,200 (the liability was understated by $2,000) and attached a Form 941c to its third quarter 2007 Form 941. The $2,000 adjustment is not added to the tax liability for the 7-1-06 to 6-30-07 lookback period, so it does not affect Barb's status as a monthly depositor for 2008. The adjustment will be made and the $2,000 added to Barb's tax liability for the 7-1-07 to 6-30-08 lookback period. If the IRS determines the employer fraudulently understated its liability for the lookback period, severe penalties may be assessed.

*Different rules for very small employers.*[9] Beginning with calendar year 2006, employers with a total annual withheld federal income tax, social security tax, and Medicare tax liability of $1,000 or less file Form 944, *Employer's Annual Federal Tax Return* (see Section 8.5-5 and Appendix page A-203), rather than Form 941, and can deposit or pay their tax liability when they file Form 944. Employers that the IRS determines will qualify for the Employer's Annual Federal Tax Return Program (Form 944) will be notified by the IRS, and they are required to file Form 944 for that year, with some limited exceptions.

---

7.    IRS Reg. §31.6302-1(b)(2)(i),(b)(3).
8.    IRS Reg. §31.6302-1(b)(5).
9.    IRS Temp. Reg. §31.6011(a)-1T; §31.6011(a)-4T; §31.6302-1T(a)(4), (5).

An employer that has been notified of its qualification to file Form 944 may file Form 941 if:

- The employer notifies the IRS that it prefers to electronically file Form 941 quarterly instead of filing Form 944 annually, or that it anticipates its annual employment tax liability will exceed $1,000;
- The employer contacts the IRS according to the instructions in the notification it received of its Form 944 program eligibility; and
- IRS sends the employer a subsequent written notice that the employer's filing requirement has been changed to Form 941.

The lookback period for employers that are in the EAFTP for the current or preceding year is the second year preceding the current calendar year. Therefore, the lookback period for calendar year 2008 is calendar year 2006. Adjustments are handled the same way as those for Form 941, so that adjustments to the Form 944 lookback period that are made in the next lookback period are not considered as part of the initial lookback period when determining the employer's depositor status.

New employers that timely notify the IRS if they anticipate their estimated annual employment tax liability to be $1,000 or less will be notified of their qualification for EAFTP. If an employer in the EAFTP reports an annual employment tax liability of more than $1,000, the IRS will notify the employer that the employer's filing status has changed and that the employer will have to file Form 941 for succeeding tax years.

*Nonpayroll withholding treated separately.* In addition to withholding from wages, employers also must withhold federal income tax from several types of "nonpayroll" payments it makes, including:

- reportable payments subject to backup withholding (see Section 6.5);
- gambling winnings;
- retirement pay for service in the Armed Forces; and
- pensions, annuities, IRAs, and other deferred income (see Section 6.4-5).[10]

Withholding on these items is not reported quarterly on Form 941 (see Section 8.3), but annually on Form 945, *Annual Return of Withheld Federal Income Tax* (see Section 8.4). With regard to the depositor status of employers depositing federal income tax withheld from nonpayroll payments, employers are either monthly or semiweekly depositors for a year.[11]

An employer's depositor status for nonpayroll withheld taxes depends on the amount of tax liability it had for the nonpayroll tax liability lookback period—the second calendar year preceding the current calendar year. Employers are monthly depositors if the amount of nonpayroll withheld income tax liability accumulated in the lookback period is $50,000 or less, and semiweekly depositors if the amount of accumulated nonpayroll withheld taxes exceeds $50,000. Once an employer's nonpayroll withholding tax depositor status is determined, it must deposit the nonpayroll withheld taxes according to the same time frame and manner as deposits of payroll taxes (see discussion following).

> **Example**: For calendar year 2008, an employer's depositor status for nonpayroll withheld taxes depends on the amount of nonpayroll tax liability accumulated during calendar year 2006.

*New employers.*[12] New employers are classified as monthly depositors because they have no tax liability experience during the lookback period. They continue to deposit on that basis until they accumulate more than $50,000 in tax liability during a lookback period or trigger the one-day deposit rule (see discussion following). Their first lookback period will be measured from the date operations began until the next June 30. If a new employer anticipates having an annual employment tax liability of $1,000 or less, it can notify IRS, which will notify the employer as to whether it qualifies for the Employer's Annual Federal Tax Program (Form 944) and can deposit or pay its employment taxes when it files Form 944.

---

10.     IRS Reg. §31.6302-4(b).
11.     IRS Reg. §31.6302-4(c).
12.     IRS Reg. §31.6302-1(b)(4).

*Example:* Tad's Tackle Shop began operating on February 8, 2008. Tad's begins as a monthly depositor and will remain so until its tax liability for a lookback period exceeds $50,000. Tad's first lookback period runs from February 8, 2008 through June 30, 2008, and the total tax liability incurred during that period will determine Tad's depositor status for 2009.

*Successor employers.* A successor with the same EIN as its predecessor company has the same deposit requirements as the predecessor. A successor with a new EIN is a new employer and should deposit as a monthly depositor until that status changes.[13]

*Depositor status notices no longer sent annually by IRS.* Until 1997, the IRS sent each employer a notice in November advising it of its employment tax deposit status for the upcoming year. Now, however, this notice is mailed only to employers identified as having a change in their deposit schedule for the upcoming year.

*Different lookback period for railroad and farm employers.*[14] Agricultural employers and employers that pay taxes under the Railroad Retirement Tax Act file annual employment tax returns rather than quarterly returns. For this reason, they have a different lookback period than other employers. Their lookback period is the second calendar year preceding the year for which the depositor status determination is being made (e.g., calendar year 2006 is the lookback period determining depositor status for 2008). The $50,000 threshold separating monthly from semiweekly depositors is the same.

Agricultural employers are subject to further complications if they have both farm and nonfarm employees and file both Form 943 and Form 941. Their depositor status for Form 941 employees is determined separately, and with a different lookback period, from their depositor status regarding Form 943 employees.

*Example*: Silo Management Corp. employs both farm and nonfarm employees in 2008. Its status as a monthly or semiweekly depositor for its Form 941 tax liability in 2008 is determined by the lookback period running from July 1, 2006 to June 30, 2007. But its depositor status for Form 943 tax liability is determined by the lookback period of January 1, 2006 to December 31, 2006.

**Requirements for monthly depositors.**[15] Monthly depositors (i.e., employers with $50,000 or less in employment tax liability during the lookback period) must deposit their accumulated tax liability for each calendar month by the 15th of the following month.

*Example*: Keystone Key Corp. is a monthly depositor with a deposit liability of $23,000 at the end of April 2008. Keystone must deposit its employment tax liability by May 15, 2008. Even if Keystone's April liability is greater than $50,000, its depositor status does not change in 2008, although it will become a semiweekly depositor in 2009 (but see the discussion of the one-day deposit rule in this section).

**Requirements for semiweekly depositors.**[16] Semiweekly depositors (i.e., employers with more than $50,000 in employment tax liability during the lookback period) must deposit employment taxes for wages paid on Wednesday, Thursday, and Friday by the following Wednesday. Employment taxes for wages paid on Saturday, Sunday, Monday, and Tuesday must be deposited by the following Friday.

*Example*: Semiweekly depositor Nuts 'N Bolts, Inc. (NBI) pays wages on Friday, June 6, 2008 with an employment tax liability of $45,800. NBI has until Wednesday, June 11 to deposit the liability.

**One-day deposit rule.**[17] If an employer's accumulated employment tax liability reaches $100,000 on any day during a monthly or semiweekly deposit period, the taxes must be deposited by the close of the next

---

13. Letter from Ronald Barnes, Acting Assistant to IRS Commissioner, 2-24-93.
14. IRS Reg. §31.6302-1(g); §31.6302-2(c).
15. IRS Reg. §31.6302-1(c)(1).
16. IRS Reg. §31.6302-1(c)(2)(i).
17. IRS Reg. §31.6302-1(c)(3).

banking day. In determining whether the $100,000 threshold is met, monthly depositors consider only those taxes accumulated during the current calendar month, not any previous months. Semiweekly depositors take into account only those taxes accumulated during the current Wednesday-Friday or Saturday-Tuesday semiweekly period. Employers do not total their payroll and nonpayroll withheld tax liabilities to determine if the one-day deposit rule is triggered.[18]

> ***Example 1:*** Jerry's Jeans, a monthly depositor, pays wages on September 5, 12, 19, and 26, 2008 with a total payroll tax deposit liability of $104,500 ($20,000 of which is attributed to the September 26 payday). Jerry's must deposit this accumulated liability by September 29 and becomes a semiweekly depositor for the remainder of 2008 and all of 2009 (see below).

> ***Example 2:*** Midwest Movers, a monthly depositor, accumulated a payroll tax liability of $78,000 as of April 30, 2008. On May 7, 2008, it paid wages with $34,000 of employment tax liability. The one-day rule is not triggered since Midwest's monthly deposit obligation for April is fixed as of April 30 and it must deposit $78,000 by May 15, 2008. The $34,000 liability becomes part of Midwest's accumulated tax liability for May.

> ***Example 3:*** Eastbridge Clothiers, a semiweekly depositor, pays wages on Thursday, August 7, 2008 with an employment tax liability of $112,000. The entire amount must be deposited by Friday, August 8.

> ***Example 4:*** On Friday, August 8, 2008, Eastbridge Clothiers paid wages with an employment tax liability of $94,000, and on Monday, August 11, it paid bonuses with a tax liability of $25,000. Because the semiweekly period ended on Friday, August 8, the $94,000 must be deposited by Wednesday, August 13. That liability is not added to the $25,000 liability incurred on Monday, August 11 for purposes of applying the one-day rule. The $25,000 liability is a separate liability and must be deposited by Friday, August 15.

> ***Example 5:*** On Monday, August 11, 2008, Eastbridge Clothiers paid wages with an employment tax liability of $106,500, an obligation that must be deposited by Tuesday, August 12. On that Tuesday, Eastbridge accumulates $42,000 in employment tax liability. Despite the $106,500 deposit obligation incurred earlier in the same semiweekly period (Monday), the $42,000 obligation incurred on Tuesday is a separate obligation that must be deposited by Friday, August 15.

> ***Example 6:*** If the situation in Example 5 is reversed, and Eastbridge Clothiers accumulates employment taxes of $42,000 on Monday, August 11, 2008 and $106,500 on Tuesday, August 12, Eastbridge has a total deposit obligation of $148,500 that must be deposited by Wednesday, August 13.

*Impact of one-day rule on monthly depositors.*[19] If a monthly depositor accumulates at least $100,000 in tax liability on any day during a month, it not only must deposit the liability by the next day, but it also becomes a semiweekly depositor for the remainder of the current calendar year and the entire next calendar year. This rule also applies to monthly depositors of nonpayroll withheld tax as well. Remember, the two types of withheld taxes must be treated separately for purposes of determining an employer's depositor status and for determining whether the one-day deposit rule is triggered.

> ***Example:*** Chrissy's Hardware & Software, a rapidly expanding computer services firm, is a monthly depositor for 2008. But in September, Chrissy's adds two more outlets and accumulates an employment tax liability for the month of $103,200 with its September 25 payday. Chrissy's must deposit the entire amount by September 26, and Chrissy's becomes a semiweekly depositor for the rest of 2008 and all of 2009.

**Semiweekly periods bridging two quarters.**[20] A semiweekly deposit period (Saturday-Tuesday or Wednesday-Friday) may overlap the end of one quarterly (or annual) return period and the beginning of

---

18.    IRS Reg. §31.6302-4(d).
19.    IRS Reg. §31.6302-1(b)(2)(ii).
20.    IRS Reg. §31.6302-1(c)(2)(ii); IRS Pub. 15, Circular E, Employer's Tax Guide.

the next. In this situation, and if the employer pays wages on two days in different quarters during the semiweekly period, the employer will have two separate deposit obligations. For employers using the paper deposit method, two separate deposit coupons must be completed indicating the quarter during which the liability was incurred (see Section 8.2-2), although only one check for the total amount is necessary. For employers using EFTPS, two separate electronic deposits must be made.

*Example 1:* Carson Comics, Inc., a semiweekly depositor, pays wages on Monday, June 30, 2008 with an employment tax liability of $32,000. Quarterly bonuses are then paid on Tuesday, July 1, and an employment tax liability of $6,000 is incurred. Rather than a total deposit obligation of $38,000, Carson has two separate deposit obligations of $32,000 and $6,000 because the second quarter ended on Monday, June 30, during the semiweekly deposit period. Each obligation must be deposited separately by Monday, July 7, with each deposit indicating the proper quarter during which the liability was incurred.

*Example 2:* Assume the same facts as in Example 1, except that Carson's Monday, June 30 employment tax liability is $95,000. Even though the total deposit obligation for the semiweekly period would be $101,000 ($95,000 on Monday + $6,000 on Tuesday), the one-day deposit rule is not triggered. Each obligation must be treated separately because the second quarter ended and the third quarter began during the semiweekly period. Once again, the separate obligations must be deposited separately by Monday, July 7.

**Quarterly "de minimis" deposit rule.**[21] Employers with an accumulated tax liability of less than $2,500 for any quarter can deposit the liability according to their monthly or semiweekly depositor status or pay it with their Form 941 quarterly return. Depositors who are not sure whether they will remain under the $2,500 threshold for the entire quarter should make deposits according to their depositor status to avoid late payment penalties should their liability exceed $2,500.

**Annual Form 944 deposit or payment exception.**[22] Beginning in 2006, employers with an annual employment tax liability of $1,000 or less that are notified by the IRS of their qualification for the Employers' Annual Federal Tax Program can pay their liability with a timely filed Form 944, *Employer's Annual Federal Tax Return* (see Section 8.5-5). These employers are not required to deposit their employment tax liability under either the monthly or semiweekly deposit rules.

If an employer that is in the EAFTP exceeds $1,000 in employment tax liability during a calendar year, it no longer qualifies for the exception and must begin depositing according to the generally applicable deposit rules. The employer will file Form 944 for that year, but will file Form 941 for succeeding years. An employer that was in the EAFTP in the preceding year but is not eligible in the current calendar year because its annual employment tax liability for the preceding year exceeded the $1,000 threshold has until March 15 of the current year to deposit its January deposit obligation.[23]

*Example:* Steve's Stoneware Co. was a monthly depositor that was notified by the IRS to file Form 944 for 2008. Steve's reported a tax liability of $3,000 on its 2008 Form 944. Because Steve's tax liability for 2008 exceeded $1,000, Steve's cannot file Form 944 for 2009. Steve's is a monthly depositor for 2009, based on its tax liability during 2007, the lookback period.

Steve's accumulates $1,000 in employment tax liability for January 2009, which must be deposited by February 15. Steve's does not deposit the tax obligation by February 15 and accumulates another $2,000 in employment tax liability for that month, which must be deposited by March 15. Steve's deposits its entire employment tax liability of $3,000 on March 15. Because of the deposit extension allowed for preceding year EAFTP participants, Steve's will be considered to have timely deposited its January deposit obligation and will not be subject to a late deposit penalty.

---

21.    IRS Reg. §31.6302-1(f)(4).
22.    IRS Temp. Reg. §31.6302-1T(c)(5).
23.    IRS Temp. Reg. §31.6302-1T-(c)(6).

If an employer that is in the EAFTP exceeds $2,500 in employment tax liability during a calendar year, but its employment tax liability for a quarter does not exceed $2,500, the employer will be deemed to have deposited its employment taxes timely if it deposits all the employment taxes due for a quarter by the end of the month following the end of that quarter. Employment taxes accumulated during the fourth quarter can be either deposited by the following January 31 or paid with the employer's timely filed Form 944.[24] This rule gives employers in the EAFTP the benefit of using the same quarterly de minimis deposit rule as Form 941 filers if their annual employment tax liability exceeds $1,000 but does not exceed $2,500 for any quarter.

> *Example:* Molly's Pastries was a monthly depositor that was notified by the IRS to file Form 944 for 2008. Molly's accumulated employment tax liabilities of $1,000 for each of the first and second quarters of 2008, $1,500 for the third quarter, and $2,000 for the fourth quarter. Molly's deposited the full amount of the employment tax liability for each of the first three quarters of 2008 on April 30, July 31, and October 31, respectively, and paid its fourth quarter liability by attaching a check for $2,000 to its 2008 Form 944, which was mailed to the IRS on February 2, 2009. In doing so, Molly's will be deemed to have deposited all its 2008 employment taxes on time because it complied with the quarterly de minimis deposit rule.

**Saturday, Sunday, and holiday extension.** For all depositors, if the due date of the deposit is not a banking day (Saturday, Sunday, or a federal or state legal holiday), the deposit is due on the next banking day.[25] State holidays must be in the state in which deposits are normally paid. Under a separate rule, semiweekly depositors are guaranteed at least three banking days after the last day of the semiweekly period to make their deposit. Therefore, if any of the three weekdays following the semiweekly period is not a banking day, the employer has an additional day to make its deposit.[26]

> *Example 1:* Jack's Printing and Publishing Co. is a monthly depositor, and for May 2008 its employment tax liability is $4,500. Jack's normal due date for depositing these taxes is June 15, but since June 15, 2008 is a Sunday, the deposit is not due until Monday, June 16.

> *Example 2:* Norville Dry Cleaners, a semiweekly depositor, accumulates employment taxes of $12,000 on Wednesday, May 21, 2007. Because Monday, May 26 is a banking holiday (Memorial Day), Norville must deposit its employment taxes by Thursday, May 29, rather than Wednesday, May 28.

*IRS implements holiday change.* In 1996, the IRS issued regulations that change the definition of "legal holiday" by eliminating the list that had been in the regulations and substituting a reference to "legal holidays in the District of Columbia."[27] For more on this change, see Section 8.3-2.

**Shortfall rule.**[28] The IRS allows a "safe harbor" shortfall so employers are not penalized for depositing a small amount less than the entire amount of their deposit obligation. An employer satisfies its deposit obligation if the amount of the shortfall is no more than the greater of $100 or 2% of the entire amount due, so long as the original deposit is made timely and the shortfall is deposited by the appropriate "make-up date."

In other words, for deposits of up to $5,000, employers are in compliance if their deposit shortfall is no more than $100. For deposits of more than $5,000, the shortfall can be no more than 2% of the amount due. For monthly depositors, the amount of the shortfall must be deposited or remitted by the due date of the quarterly return (e.g., Form 941) for the quarter during which the employment tax liability was incurred. Circular E and the instructions for Form 941 make it clear this is the only situation in which an employer can pay more than $2,500 with its Form 941.

---

24.     IRS Temp. Reg. §31-6302-1T(f)(iii).
25.     IRC §7503; IRS Reg. §301.7503-1.
26.     IRS Reg. §31.6302-1(c)(2)(iii).
27.     IRS Reg. §301.7503-1(b).
28.     IRS Reg. §31.6302-1(f).

For semiweekly depositors, the shortfall must be deposited by the first Wednesday or Friday occurring on or after the 15th of the month after the month during which the original deposit was required to be made or, if earlier, by the due date of the quarterly employment tax return (e.g., Form 941). Semiweekly depositors cannot send in the shortfall payment with their Form 941. It must be deposited.

> ***Example 1:*** Mitchell Auto Body, a monthly depositor, accumulates $7,000 in employment taxes in March 2008. It must deposit at least $6,860 by April 15 and deposit or remit any shortfall by April 30, the due date of its first quarter Form 941.

> ***Example 2:*** Eastbridge Clothiers, a semiweekly depositor, deposits $12,000 on Wednesday, July 16, 2008. Several days later, Eastbridge finds a calculation error had been made and it actually should have deposited $12,200. Because the $200 shortfall is less than the greater of $100 or 2% of the total deposit obligation ($12,200 x .02 = $244), Eastbridge has complied with its deposit requirements if it deposits the shortfall by Friday, August 15.

> ***Example 3:*** On Friday, September 5, 2008, Eastbridge Clothiers deposits $14,000 and learns later the actual amount due was $14,500. Because the $500 shortfall is greater than the greater of $100 or 2% of the total deposit obligation ($14,500 x .02 = $290), Eastbridge did not comply with the safe-harbor rule and faces a failure-to-deposit penalty.

> ***Example 4:*** On Thursday, September 25, 2008, Eastbridge Clothiers pays wages with an employment tax liability of $60,000. On Wednesday, October 1, Eastbridge deposits $58,800, leaving a lawful shortfall of $1,200 ($60,000 x .02 = $1,200). Eastbridge must deposit the shortfall by October 31, the due date of its third quarter 2008 Form 941, since that date is earlier than November 19, the first Wednesday or Friday on or after the 15th of the month after the month the original deposit was due.

**Agricultural employers may deposit under two rules.**[29] For agricultural employers that have both farm and nonfarm employees, the deposit rules may be a bit more complex. As mentioned earlier in this section, agricultural employers file an annual employment tax return—Form 943, *Employer's Annual Tax Return for Agricultural Employees*, see Appendix page A-195—and have a different lookback period than other employers (calendar year). For this reason, agricultural employers that file both a Form 941 and a Form 943 may have a different depositor status (monthly or semiweekly) for each type of tax.

**Determining the timeliness of deposits.**[30] In general, payroll tax deposits are considered timely by the IRS if received by an authorized financial institution on or before the due date. Employers should be careful, since deposits received on the due date but after a bank stops posting business for the day will be considered late and may subject the depositor to a late deposit penalty.

 **SPECIAL RULE FOR MAILED DEPOSITS**[31] Deposits mailed through the U.S. Postal Service or private delivery services designated by the IRS are considered timely if postmarked or given to the private delivery service at least two days before the due date, even though they may be received after the due date. However, deposits of $20,000 or more made by semiweekly depositors must be received by the deposit due date. For details on which private delivery services have been "designated" by the IRS, see Section 8.3-2.

## 8.2-2 How to Deposit Payroll Taxes

IRS regulations require employers to make all timely deposits of withheld income and employment taxes with a financial institution authorized to accept federal tax deposits. After December 31, 2000, federal reserve banks no longer accept federal tax deposits. In 2008, the vast majority of payroll taxes (more than 90%) are paid electronically, through the Electronic Federal Tax Payment System (EFTPS). Only smaller

---

29.    IRS Reg. §31.6302-1(g)(1).
30.    IRS Reg. §31.6302-1(h)(5).
31.    IRC §7502(e); IRS Prop. Reg. §301.7502-2.

employers (those depositing less than $200,000 in federal taxes in the second preceding year) and new businesses can continue to use paper checks and deposit coupons. This section will detail the requirements governing each method of deposit.

**Electronic deposits are replacing FTD coupons.** A provision of the North American Free Trade Implementation Act (NAFTA) amended the Internal Revenue Code and requires the implementation of an Electronic Federal Tax Payment System (EFTPS) for the collection of federal depository taxes.[32] Congress determined that the electronic funds transfer (EFT) requirement would result in an increase in federal revenue by transferring money into Treasury's account faster than under the paper coupon deposit system, so it could earn more interest. Generally, EFT of tax deposits puts the deposited amounts in Treasury's account one day earlier than under the paper coupon deposit system.

 **EXCEPTIONS WHERE NO DEPOSIT IS REQUIRED** The EFT requirements do not apply to employers that are not required to make deposits under the current rules. This means that employers who have a total employment tax liability of less than $2,500 in a quarter can continue to pay their taxes with their Form 941. The same is true for monthly depositors who are paying a lawful deposit shortfall under the safe-harbor rules with their Form 941. Employers who are required to file Form 944 because they have an annual employment tax liability not exceeding $1,000 can pay their taxes with Form 944.

**EFTPS requirements.** Organizations that deposit more than $200,000 in total federal tax deposits (payroll and nonpayroll) in any year must use EFTPS to make all their federal tax deposits beginning with the first return period in the second succeeding calendar year. Employers that first exceeded the threshold in 2007 are required to deposit all their federal depository taxes electronically for return periods beginning on or after January 1, 2009. Once an employer is required to deposit electronically, it cannot go back to using paper coupons and checks if its deposits fall below $200,000 in a later year.

*Example*: Mike's Sporting Goods is a semiweekly depositor with a weekly payroll and total 2007 tax deposits of $245,000 (Mike's 2006 deposits totaled $150,000). Mike's is required to begin depositing its taxes electronically for return periods beginning on or after January 1, 2009. Mike's has a payday on Wednesday, December 31, 2008, which gives rise to an employment tax liability that must be reported on the fourth quarter 2008 Form 941 and deposited by Thursday, January 8, 2009. Mike's January 8 deposit can be made by check with a paper deposit coupon. Once Mike's incurs a payroll tax liability for its January 7, 2009 payroll, however, it will be required to make that deposit electronically, as well as all future deposits.

 **A FRESH START FOR SOME SMALL BUSINESSES** Employers that were required to deposit electronically in 1999 because they met a lower earlier threshold are not required to do so in future years unless they exceed the $200,000 threshold in a later calendar year.[33]

*Once triggered, EFTPS is a must for all depository taxes.* Once an employer becomes subject to the EFT requirement, it applies to all federal taxes the employer is required to deposit under IRC Section 6302. These taxes include corporate income, estimated income, and excise taxes, federal unemployment (FUTA) tax, tax withheld from nonresident aliens and foreign corporations, and estimated taxes paid by certain trusts.

**The Electronic Federal Tax Payment System.** Employers that are required to deposit employment and other federal depository taxes electronically must use the Electronic Federal Tax Payment System (EFTPS).[34]

---

32. IRC §6302(h).
33. Notice 99-20, 1999-1 C.B. 958.
34. Rev. Proc. 97-33, 1997-2 CB 371; 31 CFR §203.1 - §203.24.

*Treasury's Financial Agents.* For purposes of EFTPS, the Treasury has designated two Treasury Financial Agents (TFAs), Bank of America and Bank One. In addition to processing EFTPS enrollments, TFAs receive federal tax deposit information, originate ACH debit entries when instructed to do so, and provide customer service assistance to EFTPS users. Employers are assigned to a TFA based on the location of their principal financial institution, which will be electronically transmitting tax deposits for the employer.

*The EFTPS enrollment process.* Employers must enroll in EFTPS by completing and submitting Form 9779, *Business Enrollment Form for EFTPS* (see Appendix page A-400) or by enrolling online at www.eftps. gov. The enrollment verifies the employer's corporate name, EIN, and banking information, and notifies the IRS of the deposit method selected (EFTPS-Direct or EFTPS-Through a Financial Institution). Employers electing the EFTPS-Through a Financial Institution option must verify in advance whether their financial institution offers this service and whether the employer is eligible. A separate enrollment form must be completed for each EIN. The completed form should be sent to the address indicated in the form's instructions.

When the enrollment process is finished, within 15 business days EFTPS will send the employer Form 9787, *Business Confirmation/Update Form*, an EFTPS Payment Instruction Booklet with information on payment options and same day settlement procedures, and instructions on how to obtain an Internet password. A Personal Identification Number (PIN) will be mailed to the employer separate from the enrollment confirmation package. The enrollment process takes 2-10 weeks after EFTPS receives Form 9779, so employers should make sure they enroll at least 10 weeks before their first EFTPS deposit deadline.

 **BANKING SECURITY UPDATE** Beginning in December 2006, if the financial institution account information for a new enrollment in EFTPS matches the account information of an existing enrollment under a different EIN, the enrollment will not be processed. The taxpayer or tax professional will receive by mail an "EFTPS Authorized Account User Verification" form. The form must be notarized by the taxpayer's financial institution and returned to EFTPS in the provided pre-paid envelope to complete the enrollment.

*EFTPS express enrollment program for new business taxpayers.* The IRS has a program for new business taxpayers that offers them quicker access to EFTPS. The program affects all businesses receiving a new employer identification number (EIN).

Under the program, new business taxpayers with a federal tax obligation will be automatically pre-enrolled in EFTPS to make all their federal tax deposits. In addition to receiving their EIN, taxpayers will also receive a separate mailing containing an EFTPS personal identification number and instructions for activating their enrollment. New business taxpayers will activate their enrollment by calling an 800 number, entering their banking information, and completing an authorization for EFTPS to transfer funds from their account to Treasury's account for tax payments per their instructions.

 **WHAT ABOUT SERVICE PROVIDERS?** Procedures have been put in place to allow payroll service providers ("batch providers") to enroll their client companies in EFTPS (either on paper or electronically) and make payments on their behalf.[35] Mandated employers should contact their particular service provider to see if they have been enrolled. Service providers with questions about the enrollment process should call EFTPS customer service. Employers that have other federal tax deposits that are not made by the service provider must enroll in EFTPS separately to make those deposits. IRS suggests that employers enroll separately in any case so they have flexibility if they change service providers. EFTPS updated its "batch provider" software, with enhanced features and benefits, in 2006.

*Help available for employers.* Employers that want an additional enrollment form or that have questions about the enrollment process or any other aspect of EFTPS should call the EFTPS customer service helplines at (800) 555-4477 or the IRS e-help desk at (866) 255-0654.

---

35.     Rev. Proc. 98-32, 1998-1 CB 935.

*Involve other departments in your company.* Before enrolling in EFTPS, payroll practitioners should meet with their corporate tax department, cash managers, accounting staff, financial institutions, third-party processors, etc. This group should review current tax payment processes, analyze the EFTPS payment options, and go through the new electronic process step-by-step. Make sure everyone knows that separate enrollments are necessary for each type of tax.

*EFTPS payment options.*[36] The primary payment options available to employers are EFTPS-Direct (ACH Debit) and EFTPS-Through a Financial Institution (ACH Credit). Employers can choose either or both options on their enrollment form and can change their choice by contacting EFTPS. ACH is the Automated Clearing House, the financial network run by the Federal Reserve to transfer funds electronically (e.g., direct deposit of wages).

*EFTPS-Direct (ACH Debit).* EFTPS-Direct is an electronic payment method that allows the employer to access EFTPS directly to report its tax deposit information. On the date indicated by the employer, the employer instructs EFTPS to move the funds from the employer's account to the Treasury's account. At least one calendar day prior to the tax due date, before 8:00 pm Eastern Time, the employer must access EFTPS by Internet (EFTPS-OnLine), or telephone (EFTPS-Phone). The employer will be prompted for the necessary information to complete the tax deposit. Once the deposit information is processed and accepted, the employer will receive an EFT Acknowledgement Number verifying that the payment information was received by EFTPS, although it is not proof of payment.

Once the employer's tax payment instructions are accepted, EFTPS will originate an ACH debit transaction against the employer's designated account on the date indicated when the payment information was provided. The funds will then be transferred to the Treasury's account and the tax data will be reported to the IRS to update the employer's tax account records. The IRS will deem an ACH debit entry to have been made at the time the amount is withdrawn from the employer's financial institution and not returned or reversed. With EFTPS-Direct, both payment methods – EFTPS-OnLine and EFTPS-Phone – are interchangeable. Any method can be used for a deposit, so they can back each other up if one is not working.

Before making payments on the Internet using EFTPS-OnLine, the employer must obtain an Internet password using the instructions provided in the Confirmation Package. If you are already enrolled in EFTPS, you do not need to re-enroll to use EFTPS-OnLine, but you do need to obtain an Internet password. (*Note*: Every time you access EFTPS-OnLine, you will be required to input your EIN, PIN, and Internet password.) Call EFTPS Customer Service at 877-511-4899 to receive the EFTPS-OnLine Internet Password Voice Response System toll-free phone number. Call that number and when requested, enter your EIN, PIN, and the last eight digits of your Enrollment Trace Number (located in the upper right corner of the confirmation or PIN letter you received when you enrolled in EFTPS originally). Follow the instructions you receive, and the Voice Response System will give you a temporary Internet password. (*Note:* The first time you access EFTPS-OnLine, you will be asked to change your temporary Internet password.)

Employers using EFTPS-OnLine can access their payment history for up to 16 months, and they can search, print, or download their payment history by date, type of payment, amount, tax form, or EFT Acknowledgment Number. Other benefits of EFTPS-OnLine include the ability to schedule payments up to 120 days in advance, change bank accounts by phone without completing a new enrollment, select a PIN online when changing their bank account number and begin making payments from the new account immediately if they want to bypass verification by the bank, and access links to state electronic tax payment systems directly from the EFTPS website.

*EFTPS-Through a Financial Institution (ACH Credit).* An employer making a tax deposit by EFTPS-Through a Financial Institution instructs its financial institution to originate a federal tax deposit through the ACH system to Treasury's account. Before selecting this payment option on Form 9779, the employer must make sure that its financial institution offers this service, find out how much it costs, and whether the employer is eligible to use it.

---

36.  IRS Publication 966, EFTPS.

At least one day prior to the tax due date, the employer initiates the tax payment by notifying its financial institution. To ensure that the payment is initiated in time to properly credit the appropriate Treasury account on the deposit due date, the employer must take into account its financial institution's

*ACH processing deadline.* The financial institution will originate an ACH credit transaction to EFTPS, transferring the funds to the Treasury's account and the tax data to the IRS for updating the employer's tax account records.

Once the employer timely and accurately initiates a payment using EFTPS- Through a Financial Institution, the employer's financial institution is responsible for the timely origination of the ACH credit entry with the appropriate Treasury account number and the correct format. The employer will also receive an EFT Acknowledgement Number from EFTPS verifying that payment information was received by EFTPS. The employer's financial institution will not have access to EFTPS EFT Acknowledgement Numbers. An ACH credit entry that is not returned or reversed will be deemed made when the funds are paid into the Treasury's account. Employers using EFTPS-Through a Financial Institution can enroll in and use EFTPS-OnLine to make payment inquiries, but not to initiate or cancel a payment.

*What to do if something goes wrong.* A mandated EFTPS employer has several options if an attempt to make an EFTPS tax deposit is not completed successfully. If the employer cannot make a timely ACH debit or ACH credit entry, it can tell EFTPS or its financial institution to complete the transaction at the next time such an entry can be submitted and make a late deposit, although this option might subject the employer to a late deposit penalty. The employer can also switch from one payment option to the other or try the different EFTPS-Direct payment methods, if it has enrolled to use both options and a timely deposit can still be made using the other option. Another option for the employer is same day payment. The Electronic Tax Application (ETA) is a subsystem of EFTPS that receives, processes, and transmits federal tax deposits and related information for employers that make same day deposits through Fedwire value transfers, Fedwire non-value transactions, and Direct Access transactions. Before relying on same-day payments as a payment option, employers should make sure that their financial institution is capable of making such a payment. Information on making same-day payments is contained in the EFTPS Payment Instruction Booklet that is sent to employers after they enroll in EFTPS.

Same-day payments are deemed to be made on the date the payment is received by the Federal Reserve Bank (FRB). To make timely payments, employers must comply with their financial institution's deadline for initiating same-day payments for a particular day. The deadline for the FRB to receive payment is 2:00 p.m. FRB Head Office Local Zone Time, which is the local time of the FRB head office through which a financial institution sends a same day payment. Payments received after that time will not be accepted, and the employer must reoriginate the same-day payment or use another permissible method.[37] Upon request, an employer is entitled to receive a reference number from its financial institution to track the payment.

*Cancellations and reversals take longer.* If an employer wants to cancel a tax payment, it must cancel the payment instructions by 8:00 p.m. ET no later than two business days prior to the settlement date (e.g., a Monday payment must be canceled by 8:00 p.m. ET Thursday). If an employer selects the next business day as its settlement date, it will not be able to cancel the payment.

This means that only those payments due to settle at least two business days in the future can be canceled. In its EFTPS payment instructions, IRS explains that while ACH transmissions take just one day, reversals take two days. It also means that if a payment is initiated at 5:00 p.m., cancelled at 6:00 p.m., and a second payment is initiated at 7:00 p.m., both the 5:00 p.m. and 7:00 p.m. payments will go through, because payment initiations go through immediately.

*Holiday procedures.* If a deposit due date falls on a holiday, the employer must initiate payment one business day before the holiday so that it will be effective on the first business day after the holiday. For EFTPS purposes, holidays include the following (from the ACH holiday schedule):

---

37.    Rev. Proc. 98-32, 1998-1 CB 935, modifying Rev. Proc. 97-33, 1997-2 CB 371.

- New Year's Day – January 1
- Martin Luther King, Jr.'s Birthday – Third Monday in January
- Washington's Birthday – Third Monday in February
- Memorial Day – Last Monday in May
- Independence Day – July 4
- Labor Day – First Monday in September
- Columbus Day – Second Monday in October
- Veterans Day – November 11
- Thanksgiving Day – Fourth Thursday in November
- Christmas Day – December 25

If either January 1, July 4, November 11, or December 25 falls on a Sunday, the following Monday is a holiday. There is no provision for a Friday holiday should any of these holidays fall on a Saturday, or for state holidays that differ from these holidays, even though financial institutions may be closed on those days.

 **NO PAPER BACKUP FOR MANDATED TAXPAYERS** Employers that are required to deposit through EFTPS cannot use paper deposit coupons to make a deposit. Employers that volunteer to deposit electronically may use paper deposit coupons as a backup. For more on the penalties for failure to deposit electronically see Section 8.2-3.

*Proving a payment was made.* If an employer initiates an ACH debit or ACH credit entry, a statement from the employer's financial institution (or a third party obligated to prepare such statements for the financial institution) showing the following will be accepted as proof of payment:

- a transfer decreasing the employer's account balance;

- the amount and date of the transfer; and

- the U.S. Government as the payee.

For an ETA payment, a statement from the FRB that executed the transfer will be accepted as proof of payment if the statement:

- shows the amount and date of the transfer; and

- identifies the U.S. Government as the payee.

*Refunds and reversals.*[38] No refunds of overpayments will be made through EFTPS, and there is no expedited process for employment tax refunds. Employers should make refund requests using current tax refund procedures (Forms 843, *Claim for Refund and Request for Abatement*, and 941c, *Supporting Statement to Correct Information*). However, if an employer's error results in a "significant hardship," the employer can call the IRS for assistance at 800-829-1040 or file Form 911, *Application for Taxpayer Assistance Order*, with the Taxpayer Advocate. Reversals of an ACH credit or debit entry are governed by the ACH rules. Under those rules, an employer initiating a payment has 5 banking days to reverse that payment if an error has been made, such as a duplication of a transaction, payment to the wrong entity, or an incorrect dollar amount.

IRS personnel have suggested that a reversal should not be used in overpayment situations since the reversal cancels the entire payment and if a new payment for the correct amount is not initiated in time to meet the deposit due date, the employer may face a late deposit penalty unless it shows reasonable cause for the late deposit (see discussion following). The fact of the reversal, by itself, may not be enough to show reasonable cause. Employers are encouraged by the IRS to use the current paper method for requesting a refund in an overpayment situation.

---

38.    ILM 200152045, 11-15-01.

*Grounds for penalty abatement established.* One of the principal concerns of employers who are required to make electronic tax deposits has been how to establish reasonable cause for abating penalties assessed for failure to make timely deposits. Guidance in this area was provided by the IRS in Revenue Ruling 94-46, which analyzes two late deposit situations.[39]

> **Example 1:** Employer A was required to make an EFT tax deposit on January 5. Bank X (A's financial institution) required that EFT requests be made before 2:00 p.m. eastern time on the banking day before the day the EFT is to be completed. At 1:00 p.m. on January 4, A contacted X to initiate an EFT first quarter employment tax deposit of $30,000 on January 5 (by an ACH credit transaction). X issued an acknowledgement number or other certification of the request to A when the request was made. On January 5, A's account had at least $30,000.
>
> X initiated the EFT on January 6, withdrawing $30,000 from A's account and transferring it to Treasury's account. On May 18, A received a notice showing a failure to deposit penalty for the late deposit made January 6. A writes to the IRS requesting a waiver of the penalty and includes the acknowledgement number or other certification of the January 4 EFT initiation request. X's records also show that on January 4 A instructed it to make the EFT on January 5.

In discussing Example 1, the IRS noted that X's records, through the acknowledgement number or other certification provided by A to the IRS, verify that on January 4 at 1:00 p.m. eastern time, A instructed X to initiate an EFT of $30,000 to Treasury's account on January 5 for a first quarter employment tax deposit. The IRS found reasonable cause for A's failure to make a timely deposit on January 5 because it timely provided X with the following information:

- payment instructions;
- the correct amount of tax to be deposited;
- the correct type of tax to be deposited;
- the correct tax period for which the deposit was to be made;
- the correct date the funds were to be transferred from A's account to Treasury's account; and
- the number of A's bank account with sufficient funds to cover the EFT.

 **REASON FOR BANK'S FAILURE IRRELEVANT** The revenue ruling makes clear that once the employer has shown that all the necessary information was timely provided to the bank, the reason for the bank's failure to initiate the EFT on time does not matter. The failure to deposit penalty will be abated where the failure to timely deposit by EFT is due to the transmitting bank's action or inaction.

> **Example 2:** The facts are the same as in Example 1, except that X's records indicate that, on January 4, A instructed it to initiate the EFT on January 6. Also, A's books and records do not demonstrate that A instructed X to initiate the EFT on January 5.

In ruling on Situation 2, the IRS said that, based on X's records, A gave the incorrect date for X to initiate the EFT to Treasury's account. Therefore, A does not have reasonable cause for making the late deposit and is subject to a failure-to-deposit penalty. In order for A to establish reasonable cause in such a situation, A's contemporaneous books and records would need to demonstrate that A instructed X to transfer the funds on January 5.

 **BANK MAY BE PENALIZED** If an employer that makes a late electronic tax deposit can prove to the IRS that it delivered correct tax payment instructions to its financial institution in a timely manner, the IRS may assess a late fee on the financial institution equal to the amount of interest lost by Treasury due to the late payment. If the financial institution counters by claiming that the employer failed to meet its conditions for payment, the financial institution has the burden of proving the failure.

---

39. Rev. Rul. 94-46, 1994-2 CB 278.

*Recordkeeping diligence a must.* Employers can establish timely initiation of an electronic tax deposit by using the records of either their bank or the TFA (including an acknowledgment number) and/or the employer's own contemporaneous books and records. An employer's "contemporaneous books and records" may include, among others, a recording of telephone instructions or an electronic file saved when the instructions were given. Employers are well-advised to keep meticulous records of the instructions they give to financial institutions to initiate EFTPS tax deposits. They should also insist that the financial institution provide them with a record of the payment initiation from its files, as further proof that timely instructions and complete information were provided.

 **BANKS MAY CHARGE EFTPS FEES** The IRS does not charge fees for processing EFTPS payments. However, an employer's bank may charge such fees, depending on the individual arrangement between the employer and the bank. They may not charge fees for handling paper deposit coupons and checks, however.

*IRS announces federal-state EFTPS pilot.* Early in 2007, the IRS announced that Illinois taxpayers are the first in the nation to be able to pay state and federal withheld employment taxes at the same time through EFTPS. At the federal level, the pilot's goal is to encourage more taxpayers to enroll in and use EFTPS. At the state level, the pilot's goal is to improve the efficiency of the state tax collection system. Results of the pilot will be used to help determine whether to expand this service to other states and to add other state taxes for payment through EFTPS.

*No mag tape deposits.* The IRS no longer accepts magnetic tape deposits from reporting agents, who had previously been allowed to do so if they had at least 200 clients.[40]

**Paper deposits.** Employers who are not required to use EFTPS may use federal tax deposit coupons and pay by check, cash or money order. Along with the deposit, the employer must provide the authorized financial institution with a completed Form 8109, *Federal Tax Deposit Coupon* (see Appendix page A-366).[41] The coupon and deposit may also be mailed to: Financial Agent, Federal Tax Deposit Processing, P.O. Box 970030, St. Louis, MO 63197. The coupon contains blanks where the employer must indicate the type of tax being deposited (one type of tax per coupon) and the quarter during which the liability was incurred (not when the deposit is paid), as well as an area for entering the amount of the deposit.

*Example:* Eastbridge Clothiers, a semiweekly paper depositor, makes a deposit on Wednesday, September 10, 2008 of $14,247.50, representing its federal income, social security, and Medicare tax liability for the period of September 3-5. Here is how Eastbridge Clothiers would complete its federal tax deposit coupon when making the deposit.

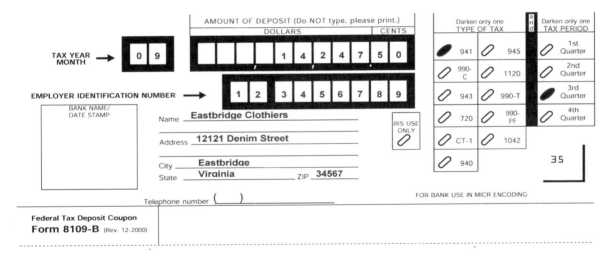

---

40.    Notice 99-42, 1999-35 IRB 325.
41.    IRS Reg. §31.6302-1(h)(3).

*Employers can request FTD coupons.* New employers are automatically enrolled in EFTPS (see Section 8.1 for information on obtaining an EIN). Employers that are allowed to use paper coupons to make federal tax deposits can order preprinted coupons with their name, address, and EIN by calling 800-829-4933. It will take 5-6 weeks for the coupons to be delivered.

*Making deposits before an EIN is assigned.*[42] New employers that have to make deposits after an EIN has been applied for but before it has been assigned must make the deposits with the local IRS office or the service center where they will file their returns, rather than a financial institution. The deposit must be accompanied by an explanation of the reason for making the deposit in this manner, and the check or money order must be made out to the U.S. Treasury and show the employer's name, address, kind of tax being deposited, calendar quarter covered, and date the EIN was applied for. The employer should not use Form 8109-B (see discussion following) in this situation.

*Making deposits when preprinted coupons are not available.*[43] In situations where an employer has been assigned an EIN but has not yet received its FTD coupon booklet (it takes 5 or 6 weeks), or where a new booklet has not been received, deposits can be made with an authorized financial institution if they are accompanied by Form 8109-B, which is an FTD coupon without any preprinted information. The employer must add its identifying information and fill out the payment information the same way as on the Form 8109. If using Form 8109-B, the employer must ensure that its EIN and name are correctly entered.

*Depositing nonpayroll withheld taxes.* As was mentioned earlier (see Section 8.2-1), employers must treat payroll and nonpayroll withheld taxes separately for deposit purposes. Each type of tax creates a separate deposit obligation, and the deposits must be made on separate FTD coupons.[44] Forms 8109 and 8109-B include a separate box in the "Type of Tax" section labeled "945" which is darkened when nonpayroll withheld taxes are deposited.

*Instruments of payment.*[45] Deposits made at an authorized financial institution (depository) may be made in cash, by postal money order, or a check drawn on and payable to the depository. A check drawn on another bank can only be used if the depository will accept that form of payment as immediate payment. After December 31, 2000, federal reserve banks no longer accept federal tax deposits. If the method of deposit (e.g., a personal check) is not considered an immediate credit item and takes time to "clear," the deposit will not be considered made until the item clears and funds are available. For deposits made on or near the due date, the clearing process could make them late and subject the employer to penalties.

**Depositing FUTA taxes.** FUTA taxes are deposited in the same manner as withheld income, social security, and Medicare taxes, although the due dates are different (see Section 7.1-5). The deposit must be accompanied by a completed FTD coupon and made at an authorized financial institution or through EFTPS.

**How to handle late payments.** When an employer receives a notice from the IRS that the employer has not paid the proper amount of withheld income and/or employment taxes and the IRS is demanding payment, the employer should not make a deposit of the delinquent taxes. The taxes should be paid directly to the employer's IRS service center, accompanied by a copy of the IRS's notice.

## 8.2-3 Penalties for Failure to Deposit on Time

Depositors that fail to deposit the entire amount of tax required by the due date (taking into consideration the safe-harbor rule) to an authorized financial institution or federal reserve bank without reasonable cause for the failure are subject to the following penalties:[46]

---

42.    IRS Reg. §31.6302-1(h)(4); Form SS-4 Instructions; IRS Pub. 15, Circular E, Employer's Tax Guide.
43.    IRS Pub. 15, Circular E, Employer's Tax Guide.
44.    IRS Reg. §31.6302-4(d).
45.    IRS Pub. 15, Circular E, Employer's Tax Guide.
46.    IRC §6656(a), (b).

- 2% of the undeposited amount if it is deposited within 5 days of the due date;

- 5% of the undeposited amount if it is deposited within 6-15 days of the due date;

- 10% of the undeposited amount if it is deposited more than 15 days after the due date (also applies to amounts paid to the IRS within 10 days after receipt of the first IRS delinquency notice and to deposits made with unauthorized financial institutions or directly to the IRS); or

- 15% of the undeposited amount if it is not paid within 10 days after the employer receives its first IRS delinquency notice or on the same day a notice and demand for payment is received.

*Special rule for electronic depositors.*[47] If an employer who is required to deposit employment taxes electronically uses a check and a paper deposit coupon instead, the employer is subject to the 10% failure-to-deposit penalty because it failed for more than 15 days to make the deposit in the correct manner, even though the paper deposit was made timely. If the same employer deposits electronically but is late in making the deposit, the penalty is determined by the lateness of the deposit as outlined above. If an employer who is making electronic deposits voluntarily makes a timely paper deposit instead, it is not subject to any failure-to-deposit penalty.

*Example 1*: Gigantic Corp. is required to make a federal tax deposit of $120,000 through EFTPS by August 14. Gigantic does not make the EFTPS deposit, but uses a deposit coupon instead to make the deposit on August 14 at an authorized depository. Because Gigantic did not make its deposit in the required manner, it is subject to the 10% failure-to-deposit penalty unless it can show reasonable cause for making the paper deposit.

*Example 2*: Rather than make the paper deposit on August 14, Gigantic Corp. waits until August 15 and makes the required deposit using EFTPS on that day. Unless it can show reasonable cause for the delay, Gigantic is subject to the 2% failure-to-deposit penalty for a deposit made in the correct manner that is one day late.

*Example 3*: Media Corp. is a voluntary user of EFTPS to make its federal tax deposits. It is required to make a federal tax deposit of $18,000 by August 14. Rather than using EFTPS, Media makes the full deposit on August 14 with a paper deposit coupon at an authorized depository. Media Corp. is not subject to a failure-to-deposit penalty.

**IRS ends penalty rebate offer for enrolling in EFTPS**. In 2004, the IRS announced an FTD-EFTPS penalty refund offer. This offer allows paper coupon users that were assessed an employment tax deposit penalty the opportunity to receive a one-time penalty refund. To qualify, an employer must use EFTPS for one year (four consecutive quarters), make all its Form 941 payments on time, and fully pay the penalty. In 2006, IRS said the rebate offer would only be available to eligible employers who receive a penalty notice for a quarter ending on or before December 31, 2006 and complete 4 quarters of EFTPS use by March 31, 2008.

*Employer can't shift deposit liability to payroll service provider or accountant.*[48] In advice to its field agents, the IRS said that employers that contracted with a payroll service provider to submit employment tax returns and make tax deposits were liable for penalties when the provider failed to submit the returns or make the deposits. It did not matter that the employers delegated their employment tax responsibilities to an agent. The contract between the employers and the service provider could not relieve them of their obligation to file the returns and pay the taxes and penalties. The IRS also said that any refunds of penalties due would be paid to the employers and not the service provider. Federal courts have taken the same position in cases involving employers that hired an outside accountant to keep records, file returns, and make payroll tax deposits.[49]

---

47.    Rev. Rul. 95-68, 1995-2 CB 272.
48.    FSA 1999-1207, 9-15-93.
49.    Dogwood Forest Rest Home, Inc. v. U.S., 181 F. Supp. 2d 554 (MD N.C., 2001); Pediatric Affiliates v. U.S., No. 06-1979 (3 CA, 4-16-07); Lanco Inns v. IRS, No. 01-CV-00510, 2006 U.S. Dist. LEXIS 44779 (ND N.Y., 6-30-06).

*Relief for certain small, new depositors.*[50]  The IRS may waive the failure-to-deposit penalty for an employer's inadvertent failure to make a deposit of withheld federal income, social security, and Medicare taxes if:

- the employer has a net worth of no more than $7 million ($2 million if the employer is an individual);
- the failure to deposit occurs during the first quarter the employer is required to deposit employment taxes or is the first deposit after the employer is required to change the frequency of its deposits; and
- the return for the tax (Form 941) is filed by the due date.

The failure-to-deposit penalty may also be abated for an employer of any size that sends its first payroll tax deposit to the IRS rather than depositing it with the appropriate government depository.

**Reasonable cause.**  An employer that wishes to avoid the penalty for failure to deposit payroll taxes on time must make an affirmative statement under penalty of perjury setting forth all the facts supporting the claim of reasonable cause for its failure.  The statement must be filed with the IRS district director or the director of the employer's IRS service center, who will make a determination whether there was reasonable cause for the failure to deposit.  If so, the penalty will be waived.[51]

*Can financial difficulty excuse failure to deposit?*  The federal courts are split on the issue of whether an employer's financial difficulty can ever be used to satisfy the reasonable cause standard.  In 2007, one federal appeals court considered an employer's claim that its financial distress excused its failure to deposit payroll taxes, but rejected the claim because the company did not show that it tried to reduce its other expenses in order to meet its deposit obligations.[52]  Other courts have agreed with the IRS' position and said that, because payroll taxes are held in trust for the federal government, an employer's financial situation can never be a basis for a finding of reasonable cause for a failure to deposit.[53]

**How the IRS applies employer tax deposits.**  Late in 2001, the IRS issued guidance on how it will credit employers' federal tax deposits for deposit periods beginning after December 31, 2001.[54]  The rules were required because of changes mandated by the IRS Restructuring and Reform Act of 1998.  Those changes require IRS to apply deposits to the most recent period within the tax period to which the deposit relates.[55]  Congress made these changes to reduce the chance that an employer would face a multiple failure-to-deposit penalty situation under the IRS's previous system of applying a deposit to satisfy any underdeposits from earlier in the same return period (the oldest first) before applying it to the current deposit obligation.

The rules apply to taxes reported on Forms 940 (*Employer's Annual Federal Unemployment (FUTA) Tax Return*), 941 (*Employer's Quarterly Federal Tax Return*), 943 (*Employer's Annual Tax Return for Agricultural Employees*), 945 (*Annual Return of Withheld Federal Income Tax*), and 1042 (*Annual Withholding Tax Return for U.S. Source Income of Foreign Persons*).

*Applying tax deposits.*  With limited exceptions, the Service will apply federal tax deposits to the most recently ended deposit period (or periods) within the specified tax period to which a deposit relates, and will apply any excess to deposit periods ending on or after the date of the deposit in period-ending-date order.  Applying this rule will, in some cases, prevent the cascading of penalties where an employer either fails to make deposits or makes late deposits.

*Penalty notices.*  Any employer that gets a penalty notice for a specified tax period may contact the IRS within 90 days of the penalty notice and designate the deposit period to which the deposit is to be applied.  The employer may either call the toll-free number shown on the penalty notice or write (including a revised schedule of deposits) to the Accounts Management Unit at the address shown on the penalty notice.  The

---

50. IRC §6656(c), (d); IRS Prop. Reg. §301.6656-3(a), (b).
51. IRS Reg. §301.6656-1(b).
52. Staff IT, Inc. v. U.S., 482 F.3d 792 (5 CA, 2007); cert. den., No. 07-221 (U.S. S.Ct., 10-1-07).
53. Brewery, Inc. v. U.S., 33 F.3d 589 (6 CA, 1994).
54. Rev. Proc. 2001-58, 2001-2 CB 579.
55. IRC §6656(e).

IRS will adjust the penalty amount to reflect the revised schedule of deposits and notify the employer of the adjustment in writing.

**Example 1:** For the second quarter of 2008, Horton Bros., a semiweekly employment tax depositor, accumulates the following employment tax deposit liabilities for its biweekly pay dates and makes the following deposits on the deposit due dates:

| Deposit Due Date | Required Deposit | Actual Deposit |
|---|---|---|
| 4/11/08 | $8,000 | $6,000 |
| 4/25/08 | $6,000 | $6,000 |
| 5/9/08 | $5,000 | $5,000 |
| 5/23/08 | $7,000 | $7,000 |
| 6/6/08 | $8,000 | $7,000 |
| 6/20/08 | $9,000 | $9,000 |

During July 2008, Horton completes its Form 941 for the second quarter and discovers the April 11 and June 6 underdeposits. On July 31, 2008, the due date for Form 941, Horton files its Form 941 and deposits $3,000. The IRS applies the deposits actually made to the most recently ended deposit periods. It then mails a notice to Horton dated October 21, 2008, advising that Horton is subject to a $300 failure-to-deposit penalty, calculated as follows:

| Deposit Due Date | Underdeposits | Days Late | Penalty Rate | Penalty Amount |
|---|---|---|---|---|
| 4/11/08 | $2,000 | 109 | 10% | $200 |
| 4/25/08 | 0 | 0 | N/A | 0 |
| 5/9/08 | 0 | 0 | N/A | 0 |
| 5/23/08 | 0 | 0 | N/A | 0 |
| 6/6/08 | $1,000 | 53 | 10% | $100 |
| 6/20/08 | 0 | 0 | N/A | 0 |
| TOTAL | | | | $300 |

Horton would have 90 days from October 21, 2008 in which to call the toll-free number on the notice, or write the Accounts Management Unit at the appropriate IRS Service Center, and designate the deposit period or periods within the specified tax period to which the deposits are to be applied. In this case, however, the manner in which the Service applied the deposits avoids cascading penalties and minimizes the failure-to-deposit penalty for the quarter.

**Example 2:** For the second quarter of 2008, TradeUn Ltd., a monthly employment tax depositor, pays its employees on the first of every month. Instead of waiting until the 15th day of the following month to make its deposits, TradeUn normally makes deposits on the 25th of each month for the deposit obligation incurred on the 1st of that month. TradeUn pays its employees on April 1, 2008, but for some reason fails to make the deposit on April 25. For May 2008, TradeUn pays its employees on May 1 and on May 25, unaware of the underdeposit for April, TradeUn makes a deposit to cover its May liability.

The IRS applies this deposit to the most recently ended deposit period, which in this case is April 2008, instead of the May 2008 liability as intended by TradeUn. This cycle of deposits continues until the end of the quarter. TradeUn can, however, minimize cascading penalties and reduce the penalty amount by timely contacting the appropriate Accounts Management Unit and designating May and June as the deposit periods to which the deposits are to be applied.

**Example 3:** For the second quarter of 2008, Grant Video Corp. (GVC), a semiweekly employment tax depositor, pays its employees every Friday. GVC accumulates $10,000 in employment tax deposit liability for each of its weekly pay dates. The table below shows the deposit period ending date and due date for GVC's deposits. It also shows the date of each deposit and the deposit period to which it is applied by the IRS. The table shows how the IRS applies GVC's deposits to the most recently ended deposit period for which a deposit has not been made.

Accordingly, the IRS applies GVC's deposit of April 23, 2008, and subsequent deposits through July 2, 2008, to deposit liabilities for periods which have ended, but for which the due dates have not occurred. Applying deposits in this manner, GVC's deposit liability for the period ending April 11, 2008, is not satisfied until GVC makes its deposit on June 25, 2008. Nonetheless, applying the deposits to the most recently ended deposit period avoids cascading penalties and minimizes the failure-to-deposit penalty for the quarter.

| Deposit Period Ending Date | Due Date of Deposit | Date of Deposit That IRS Applies To Deposit Period | Applicable Penalty |
|---|---|---|---|
| 04/04/08 | 04/09/08 | 04/09/08 | $ 0 |
| 04/11/08 | 04/16/08 | 06/25/08 | $ 1,000 |
| 04/18/08 | 04/23/08 | 04/21/08 | $ 0 |
| 04/25/08 | 04/30/08 | 04/28/08 | $ 0 |
| 05/02/08 | 05/07/08 | 05/05/08 | $ 0 |
| 05/09/08 | 05/14/08 | 05/12/08 | $ 0 |
| 05/16/08 | 05/21/08 | 05/19/08 | $ 0 |
| 05/23/08 | 05/29/08 | 05/27/08 | $ 0 |
| 05/30/08 | 06/04/08 | 06/02/08 | $ 0 |
| 06/06/08 | 06/11/08 | 06/09/08 | $ 0 |
| 06/13/08 | 06/18/08 | 06/16/08 | $ 0 |
| 06/20/08 | 06/25/08 | 06/23/08 | $ 0 |
| 06/27/08 | 07/02/08 | 07/02/08 | $ 0 |
| TOTAL PENALTY | | | $ 1,000 |

*Application to shortfall situation.* For purposes of applying deposits, a shortfall will be treated as a liability for a deposit period (the make-up period) ending immediately before the shortfall make-up date and after the end of any other deposit period ending before the shortfall make-up date. Thus, if a shortfall make-up date falls on the same date a deposit is due for another deposit period, the Service will apply a deposit made on the shortfall make-up date to the shortfall liability first. Any excess will then be applied to deposit periods other than the make-up period beginning with the most recently ended. If a deposit is made before the shortfall make-up date but after the end of a deposit period for which the deposit obligation has not been satisfied, the Service will apply the deposit to the liability for the deposit period first before applying any excess to the shortfall.

**Example 4:** For the third quarter of 2008, Trasher Waste Removal Services Co., a semiweekly employment tax depositor, pays its employees every Friday. Trasher accumulates a $10,000 employment tax deposit liability for each of its weekly pay dates. Trasher makes timely deposits of employment taxes in the amount of $9,800 on July, 9, 16, and 23. Under the shortfall make-up rules, Trasher must make a deposit of $600 by August 15. Trasher must also make a deposit of employment taxes for the deposit period August 6-8 on or before August 15.

*Deposit made on shortfall make-up date.* Trasher deposits $9,800 on July 30 and August 6 and $10,200 on August 15. The July 30 deposit is applied to the deposit period July 23-25, and the August 6 deposit is applied to the deposit period July 30-August 1. Because the August 15 deposit is made on the shortfall make-up date, the IRS first applies $600 to the shortfall liability for July; accordingly, Trasher owes no penalty with respect to the July deposits. The IRS applies the remaining $9,600 to the deposit period ending August 8, leaving an underdeposit of $400. As this amount is greater than 2% of the deposit liability ($10,000 x .02 = $200), Trasher will be subject to a failure-to-deposit penalty. The amount of the penalty will depend on when Trasher satisfies the underdeposit.

*Deposit made prior to shortfall make-up date.* Trasher makes the $10,200 deposit on August 14. Because the deposit is made prior to the shortfall make-up date, the IRS first applies $10,000 to the deposit liability for the deposit period ending August 8, fully satisfying this liability. The IRS applies the remaining $200 to satisfy the remainder of the deposit liability for the deposit period ending August 1. Trasher will not satisfy the shortfall make-up requirements with respect to the July deposits and will be subject to a failure-to-deposit penalty. The amount of the penalty will depend on when Trasher satisfies the underdeposits.

*Designation.* In either situation described in this example, Trasher may timely contact the Accounts Management Unit and designate the deposit periods (including the make-up period) to which the deposits are to be applied.

*One-day rule.* A deposit required by the $100,000 one-day deposit rule is treated as a liability for a deposit period ending on the day the depositor accumulates more than $100,000 in employment taxes.

**Example 5:** For the second quarter of 2008, Deliver-Eez, Inc., a semiweekly employment tax depositor, makes a timely deposit of employment taxes on April 9, 2008 for the deposit period April 2 to April 4. On Monday, April 7, Deliver-Eez accumulates $110,000 in employment taxes with respect to wages paid on that date. Deliver-Eez deposits those taxes by the end of the next business day, April 8. The deposit is treated as a liability for a deposit period ending on the day Deliver-Eez accumulated in excess of $100,000 in employment taxes. Accordingly, the Service applies Deliver-Eez's April 8 deposit to the one-day deposit liability for the deposit period ending April 7. Deliver-Eez's April 9 deposit is then applied to the liability for the deposit period ending April 4.

**Redesignating estimated tax payments as employment tax deposits.**[56] If an employer determines that its corporate income tax liability for the current tax year will be lower than the amount of estimated income tax payments the employer has already made, the employer can redesignate some of the estimated income tax it has paid as employment tax deposits. The employer can use the redesignated payments to satisfy deposit liabilities for federal income tax withholding and social security, Medicare, and FUTA taxes. Employers should call 866-562-2227 to make the redesignation. Employers should be careful to make sure that the redesignation does not result in an underpayment of the estimated income tax for the tax year, or a penalty may be assessed.

 **BE CAREFUL** The IRS has the ability to reallocate payroll tax deposits from one quarter to another and from one type of tax return to another (e.g., payroll taxes being allocated to a corporate tax deficiency). Before paying deposit penalties that have been assessed, the employer should examine its tax returns to determine if an allocation from one type of tax to another has been made.

**How to avoid an averaged failure-to-deposit penalty**. The IRS may assess an averaged failure-to-deposit penalty of 2%-10% on a monthly depositor that did not properly complete the monthly liability section of Form 941 when the employer's total adjusted tax liability shown on Form 941 exceeded $2,500 (see Section 8.3-3). The IRS may also assess an averaged FTD penalty of 2%-10% on a semiweekly depositor whose total adjusted tax liability shown on Form 941 exceeded $2,500 and that:

- completed the monthly liability section of Form 941 instead of Schedule B (Form 941),
- failed to attach a properly completed Schedule B (Form 941), or
- improperly completed Schedule B (Form 941) by, for example, entering tax deposits instead of tax liabilities in the numbered spaces (see Section 8.3-4).

*Computing the penalty.* The FTD penalty is computed by taking the employer's total adjusted tax liability shown on Form 941 and distributing it equally throughout the tax period. As a result, the employer's deposits and payments may not be counted as timely because the actual dates of the employer's tax liabilities cannot be accurately determined.

---

56.    IRS Announcement 2001-112, 2001-46 IRB 494.

*Avoiding the penalty.* An averaged FTD penalty can be avoided if the employer reviews its employment tax return prior to filing it. If the employer is a monthly depositor, tax liabilities (not deposits) should be reported in the monthly liability section of Form 941. If the employer is a semiweekly depositor, tax liabilities (not your deposits) should be reported on Schedule B (Form 941) on the lines that represent the dates employees were paid.

Employers should verify that their total liability shown on Form 941 or the bottom of Schedule B (Form 941) equals their total adjusted tax liability shown on Form 941.

**100% penalty for not withholding and paying taxes.**[57] Individuals who are responsible for collecting (withholding), accounting for, and paying over (depositing) income, social security and Medicare taxes and who willfully fail to do so are subject to an additional penalty equal to the total amount of the taxes involved. This is known as the "Trust Fund Recovery Penalty" or the "100% penalty." For many years, the IRS had used a broad definition of who was a "responsible person" when assessing the 100% penalty, including not just corporate officers or partners of a partnership, but accountants and others who had even less control over the employer's funds.

In 1993, however, the IRS revised its definition of responsible person to take into consideration the individual's duties and authority.[58] It will exclude non-owner employees who work under the direction of a manager, although they may have check-signing authority, and other employees who merely perform clerical tasks related to payroll and finance.

For the 100% penalty to be applied, the responsible person must have acted willfully in not withholding and paying over trust fund (withheld income and employment) taxes. But willfulness does not necessarily mean an intent to defraud the federal government. Paying other creditors rather than depositing payroll taxes is a willful failure to pay, even though the payments are made to keep the business from failing. Also, reasonable cause is not a defense to an assessment of the 100% penalty.

*Notice must be given before penalty is assessed.*[59] The 100% penalty cannot be imposed unless the IRS notifies the responsible person in writing by mail or in person at least 60 days before issuing a notice and demand for any such penalty.

*Liability for penalty may be shared.*[60] If the IRS determines that a responsible person is liable for the 100% penalty, it must disclose to that person (if a written request is made) the following information regarding the same failure to withhold and pay over payroll taxes:

- the names of any other responsible persons who it found liable for the same penalty;
- whether the IRS has attempted to collect the penalty from these other persons;
- the general nature of the collection activities; and
- how much has been collected.

In addition, a responsible person who has been found liable for and has paid a trust fund penalty can sue to recover from other responsible persons who have not paid their proportionate share of the penalty.

*Relief for volunteer association board members.*[61] The trust fund penalty does not apply to an unpaid, volunteer member of the board of trustees or directors of a tax-exempt organization if the member:

- is serving only in an honorary capacity;
- does not participate in the day-to-day or financial operations of the organization; and
- does not have actual knowledge of the underlying failure to collect and pay over taxes on which the penalty is imposed.

---

57.   IRC §6672(a); IRS Reg. §301.6672-1.
58.   IRS Revised Policy Statement P-5-60, 2-3-93.
59.   IRC §6672(b).
60.   IRC §6103(e)(9); §6672(d).
61.   IRC §6672(e).

*IRS has to get the word out.*[62] The IRS must take appropriate actions to ensure that employees are aware of their responsibilities regarding payroll tax withholding and depositing, including their possible liability for the 100% penalty. These actions include printing a warning on deposit coupon booklets and related tax returns, plus an information packet. The IRS is also required to develop materials explaining the conditions under which volunteer board members of tax-exempt organizations are subject to the trust fund penalty, and it will make the materials available to such organizations.

**Criminal penalty.**[63] In addition to the 100% penalty, responsible persons who willfully fail to collect and pay over taxes are guilty of a felony and can be fined up to $10,000 and/or imprisoned for up to 5 years.

**Penalty and interest notices must be detailed.** As part of the IRS Restructuring and Reform Act of 1998, IRS penalty and interest notices have to include some details as to how they were determined. All penalty notices issued after June 30, 2003, must include the name of the penalty, the IRC section under which it is imposed, and a computation of the penalty. The initial penalty assessment must also be personally approved in writing by the supervisor of the person making the assessment. Any notice that includes an interest component after June 30, 2003 must include the IRC section under which interest is imposed and a calculation of the interest. For penalty and interest notices issued after June 30, 2001, and before July 1, 2003, all the IRS has to do is include a phone number that the employer can call to request a copy of their tax assessment and payment history related to the penalty and/or the interest amounts.[64]

## 8.3 The Employer's Employment Tax Return—Form 941

The basic employment tax return filed by employers is Form 941, *Employer's Quarterly Federal Tax Return* (see Appendix page A-164).[65] The purpose of Form 941 is to provide the IRS with a report of each employer's total taxable wages paid and payroll tax liability, which can be matched against the employer's record of tax deposits and wage and tax information provided to employees on their W-2 forms.

## 8.3-1 Who Must File Form 941

Form 941 is a quarterly return which generally must be filed by all employers that withhold federal income tax from employee compensation and are subject to withholding and payment of social security and/or Medicare taxes. The following employers are exempt from filing Form 941:[66]

- seasonal employers that regularly do not pay wages in certain quarters (they must check the box on Line 17 on Form 941 for each quarter they file the form;

- businesses that withhold federal income tax from only nonpayroll items (e.g., backup withholding, pensions, annuities, gambling winnings) and do not withhold any taxes from employee compensation;

- employers that report only withheld taxes on domestic workers;

- employers that report only wages for employees in U.S. territories and possessions outside the continental U.S., plus Puerto Rico;

- agricultural employers, unless they also have employees who are not agricultural employees; and

- employers that have an annual employment tax liability of no more than $1,000.

---

62. Taxpayer Bill of Rights 2, P.L. 104-168, §904(b).
63. IRC §7202.
64. IRC §6631; §6751.
65. IRS Reg. §31.6011(a)-1(a); §31.6011(a)-4(a).
66. Form 941 Instructions.

**Note:** Many of the employers listed above must file other employment tax reporting forms. They are discussed in Section 8.5.

**Business reorganizations.**[67] If an employer sells or transfers its business, a separate Form 941 must be filed by both the previous and current owners for the quarter during which the sale took place. Each employer must report only the wages it paid and taxes it withheld. After a sale or transfer, the employer must attach a statement to the next Form 941 it files providing the new owner's name (or new name of the business); the form of the new business (i.e., sole proprietorship, partnership, or corporation); the type of change that took place (sale or transfer); the date of the change, and the name of the person keeping the payroll records and address where they will be kept.

 **SUCCESSOR EMPLOYERS** In certain situations, successor employers may be able to consider wages paid by a predecessor when determining whether an employee has reached the social security wage limit (see Section 6.7-3).

**Statutory merger or consolidation of two businesses.**[68] Where two companies merge or consolidate, the surviving corporation must file Form 941 for the quarter during which the change took place, reporting the wages paid and taxes withheld by both companies.

This reporting will result in discrepancies between the amounts shown on the surviving corporation's Forms W-2 and 941 for the year of the statutory merger or consolidation. The surviving corporation should file Schedule D (Form 941), *Report of Discrepancies Caused by Acquisitions, Statutory Mergers, or Consolidations* (see Appendix page A-179), to explain the discrepancies in the totals of social security wages, Medicare wages and tips, social security tips, federal income tax withheld, and advance earned income credit payments.

The surviving corporation's Schedule D should be filed after Forms W-2, *Wage and Tax Statement,* are prepared for the year of the acquisition and should be filed with the predecessor's first quarter Form 941 for the year after the year of the acquisition or with the surviving corporation's final Form 941 if the surviving corporation goes out of business after the merger or consolidation and the final Form 941 is due earlier.

Under Revenue Ruling 62-60, the surviving corporation is required to provide certain information to the IRS after a statutory merger or consolidation. A completed Schedule D from the surviving corporation will include notice that a statutory merger or consolidation has taken place, along with the date of the change and the name, trade name, address, telephone number, and EIN of the acquired corporation.

If wages and employment taxes withheld by the acquired corporation during the quarter of the merger or consolidation are to be included in the Forms W-2 prepared by the surviving corporation, there may be discrepancies between the acquired corporation's Forms W-2 and 941. If an acquired corporation files a final Form 941, it should also file a Schedule D with the final Form 941 to explain any discrepancies in the totals of social security wages, Medicare wages and tips, social security tips, federal income tax withheld, and advance earned income credit payments. The Schedule D will include notice that a statutory merger or consolidation has taken place, along with the date of the change and the name, trade name, address, telephone number, and EIN of the surviving corporation.

If either party files its Form 941 electronically, Schedule D (Form 941) can be filed on paper until the electronic filing specifications for Schedule D become available.

**Acquisition where successor hires predecessor's employees.**[69] There are options and other requirements that apply when a successor employer acquires substantially all the property used in a predecessor's business or in a separate unit of the predecessor's business and continues to employ some or all of the predecessor's employees after the acquisition. Under the standard procedure, the successor and predecessor will each file a Form 941 for the quarter of the acquisition, reporting only the wages paid and

---

67.    Form 941 Instructions.
68.    Rev. Proc. 2004-53, 2004-34 IRB 320; Rev. Rul. 62-60, 1962-1 CB 186.
69.    Rev. Proc. 2004-53, 2004-34 IRB 320.

taxes withheld by each. If the predecessor goes out of business as a result of the acquisition, it must file a final Form 941 for the quarter of the acquisition. If the standard procedure is used, Schedule D should not be filed.

Under the alternate procedure, the successor and predecessor agree that the predecessor will not have to report any wages paid to and taxes withheld from its employees who were hired by the successor on Form W-2. However, the predecessor is not relieved from reporting such wages and taxes on its Form 941. Therefore, there will be a discrepancy between the amounts reported on its Forms 941 and its Forms W-2 for the year.

The predecessor should complete a Schedule D (Form 941), *Report of Discrepancies Caused by Acquisitions, Statutory Mergers, or Consolidations* (see Appendix page A-179) to explain the discrepancies in the totals of social security wages, Medicare wages and tips, social security tips, federal income tax withheld, and advance earned income credit payments. Schedule D should also include the date of the acquisition and the name, trade name, address, telephone number, and EIN of the successor.

The predecessor's Schedule D should be filed after Forms W-2, *Wage and Tax Statement,* are prepared for the year of the acquisition and should be filed with the predecessor's first quarter Form 941 for the year after the year of the acquisition or with the predecessor's final Form 941 if that is due earlier.

> *Example:* A predecessor's business is acquired in the third quarter of 2008, and the predecessor continues to operate. The predecessor would file Schedule D with its Form 941 for the first quarter of 2009 (by April 30, 2009). If the predecessor goes out of business when the acquisition is completed, the predecessor would file Schedule D with its third quarter 2008 Form 941, which would be its final Form 941.

Under the alternate procedure, the successor will have similar discrepancies between its Forms 941 and W-2. The successor should also complete a Schedule D (Form 941) to explain the discrepancies in the totals of social security wages, Medicare wages and tips, social security tips, federal income tax withheld, and advance earned income credit payments. Schedule D should also include the date of the acquisition and the name, trade name, address, telephone number, and EIN of the predecessor.

The successor's Schedule D should also be filed after Forms W-2, *Wage and Tax Statement*, are prepared for the year of the acquisition and should be filed with the successor's first quarter Form 941 for the year after the year of the acquisition or with the successor's final Form 941 if the successor goes out of business after acquiring the predecessor and the final return is due earlier.

If either party files its Form 941 electronically, Schedule D (Form 941) can be filed electronically as well. When filing on paper, do not attach Schedule D (Form 941) to your Form 941. Instead, file Schedule D (Form 941) separately, using the following address:

> Stop 815G-Team 301
> Internal Revenue Service
> 201 Rivercenter Blvd.
> Covington, KY 41011

**Form 941 is scannable.** Form 941 has been created so that it can be scanned by IRS, resulting in easier, faster, and more accurate processing. However, the form is not printed in red "drop-out ink" such as that used on Copy A of paper Forms W-2. This means that substitute forms, such as those printed on plain paper using payroll software packages, will be acceptable.

Because scanning requires conformity, the IRS publishes specifications for producing substitutes for both Form 941 and Schedule B (Form 941).[70] Specifications for Schedule D (Form 941) substitute forms are not yet provided because the scanned forms are not yet available, but substitutes that follow the format for Form 941 will be acceptable. Forms should not be submitted to the IRS for specific approval. If an employer

---

70.    Rev. Proc. 2007-42, 2007-27 IRB 15.

is uncertain of any specification and wants it clarified, a letter can be submitted citing the specification and the employer's understanding of the specification to:

Internal Revenue Service
Attention: Substitute Forms Program
SE:W:CAR:MP:T:T:SP, IR-6406
1111 Constitution Ave., NW
Washington, DC 20224

Allow at least 30 days for the IRS to respond.

However, software developers and form producers should send a blank copy of their substitute Form 941 and Schedule B (Form 941) in PDF format to Dorene.Beard@irs.gov. Because the purpose of this submission is to assist the IRS in preparing to scan these forms, submitters will receive comments only if a significant problem is discovered through this process. Submitters are not expected to delay marketing their forms in order to receive feedback. *Note:* Submitters should not include "live" taxpayer data.

**Check the employer's business information.** If the Form 941 being used is preprinted with the employer's identifying information at the top, check to make sure that the information is correct. If any information is not correct, cross it out and enter the correct information. If an agent, attorney, or other tax preparer completes the form, check to make sure the employer's name and EIN match those on the preprinted form sent to the employer.

If a preprinted form is not being used, enter the employer's EIN, name, and address in the spaces provided. The employer's name and EIN must also be entered in the spaces provided at the top of page 2.

 **QUARTERLY CHECK BOX** Make sure you check the box at the top of Form 941 corresponding to the quarter for which the form is being filed – Box 1: January, February, March (First Quarter); Box 2: April, May, June (Second Quarter); Box 3: July, August, September (Third Quarter); Box 4: October, November, December (Fourth Quarter).

**Completing the form.** Please follow these guidelines when completing Form 941, which make it easier to process the form.

- use 12-point Courier font for all entries (if possible) if a typewriter or computer is being used to complete the form;
- omit dollar signs in dollar entries;
- enter dollars to the left of the pre-printed decimal points and cents to the right;
- the use of commas is optional;
- leave blank any data field with a value of zero;
- enter negative amounts using a minus sign; and
- enter the employer's name and EIN on all pages and attachments, but employers using the IRS-preaddressed form do not have to put their name and EIN on page 2.

**Form must have employer's signature.**[71] Before returning the completed Form 941, the form must be signed by:

- the individual owning the business, if the employer is a sole proprietorship;
- the president, vice president, or other principal corporate officer, if the employer is a corporation (including a limited liability company (LLC) treated as a corporation);
- an authorized member or partner of an unincorporated association or partnership (including an LLC treated as a partnership) having knowledge of the organization's affairs;
- the owner of a single member LLC treated as a disregarded entity; or
- a fiduciary if the employer is a trust or estate.

---

71.    IRS Reg. §31.6061-1; §1.6062-1; Form 941 Instructions.

*Forms signed by agents.*[72] It is very common for employers to contract with outside firms to handle their payroll processing, which includes preparing paychecks and completing and filing employment tax and information returns. Even though an employer's "agent" is not considered the employer, the agent can file employment tax returns on the employer's behalf once it obtains authorization to do so from the IRS. This can be accomplished by having the employer designate the agent on Form 2678, *Employer/Payer Appointment of Agent* (see Appendix page A-337). Once the employer completes the form and it is signed by a high-level company official, the agent must submit the form, along with a letter explaining the authorization request, to the director of the IRS service center where the agent will be filing the employment tax returns. The agent is authorized to act on the employer's behalf when the IRS mails its approval of the authorization request.

Employers that wish to have an attorney, accountant, other representative, or employee not listed above sign their employment tax returns must obtain a proper power of attorney beforehand by completing and filing Form 2848, *Power of Attorney and Declaration of Representative* (see Appendix page A-340). The employer must make certain to clearly explain the extent of the authority given the representative by the power of attorney.

**Third party can discuss form with IRS.** If an employer wants to allow an employee or some other firm or company to discuss the employer's Form 941 with the IRS, the employer must:

- check the "Yes" box in Part 4 of the form; and
- enter the name and 5-digit personal identification number of the third party (PIN is chosen by the third party).

By designating a third party, the employer is authorizing the designee to:

- provide the IRS with any information that is missing from the Form 941;
- call the IRS for any information about processing the form; and
- respond to the IRS concerning IRS notices that the employer has shared with the designee about math errors on the form and return preparation (IRS notices are not sent directly to the designee).

The third-party designee is not authorized to receive any refund check, bind the employer to anything, or otherwise represent the employer before the IRS. The designation automatically expires one year from the due date of the Form 941 and it can be revoked beforehand by either the employer or the designee in a written statement submitted to the IRS office where the Form 941 was filed at the "without a payment" address.

**Alternative signature methods.**[73] In 1996, the IRS issued regulations making it clear that it has the authority to prescribe any method of signing any return or statement required under the Internal Revenue Code. In 1998, Congress required the IRS to develop procedures for the acceptance of electronic signatures as part of the IRS Restructuring and Reform Act. See Section 8.14 for details on electronic filing of Form 941.

*Facsimile signatures allowed.*[74] In 2005, the IRS issued a revenue procedure expanding the authority of corporate officers or duly authorized agents to sign employment tax forms by facsimile, including alternative methods such as computer software programs, rubber stamps, or mechanical devices. The new guidance applies to all forms in the 94X series, including Forms 941, 940, 943, 944, and 945, plus Forms 1042, *Annual Withholding Tax Return for U.S. Source Income of Foreign Persons* (see Section 14.2-6), and 8027, *Employer's Annual Information Return of Tip Income and Allocated Tips* (see Section 3.4-27).

The person filing the form must retain a letter, signed by the officer or agent authorized to sign the return, declaring under penalties of perjury that the facsimile signature appearing on the form is the signature adopted by the officer or agent and that the facsimile signature was affixed to the form by the officer or agent at his or her direction.

---

72.   IRS Reg. §31.6011(a)-7(a).
73.   IRS Reg. §301.6061-1(b).
74.   Rev. Proc. 2005-39, 2005-28 IRB 82.

The letter must list each return by name and identifying number. The letter should not be sent to the IRS unless specifically requested by the Service, and it should be maintained for at least four years after the due date of the tax to which the return relates or the date the tax is paid, whichever is later.

 **HELP FOR SERVICE PROVIDERS** The IRS has advised APA that, as a practical matter, this procedure is primarily a convenience for payroll service providers. For example, a service provider appointed as an agent to sign returns on behalf of several employers could prepare a single letter (listing the enclosed returns) for all the returns it is filing in a single batch.

**New employers.**[75] Employers that have yet to be assigned an EIN should type the words "Applied for" and the date of the application in the space provided for the EIN.

**Employers going out of business.**[76] An employer that will no longer be in business or will not be paying wages subject to federal income withholding, social security, and Medicare taxes should do the following:

- check the box on Line 16 when completing its last Form 941 indicating it will not file any returns in the future and enter the last date on which wages were paid;
- attach a statement showing the address where the employer's records will be kept, the name of the person keeping the records, and, if the business has been sold or transferred, the name and address of the new owner and the date of the sale or transfer.

If the employer is no longer in business as the result of a statutory merger or consolidation, or if it qualifies as a predecessor or successor after an acquisition, the employer should generally file Schedule D (Form 941), *Report of Discrepancies Caused by Acquisitions, Statutory Mergers, or Consolidations*. See the discussion of Schedule D earlier in this section.

**Payments made with Form 941.** Employers are generally required to deposit withheld income and employment taxes in an authorized financial institution within a certain time period after paying wages (see Section 8.2-1). But if an employer's total tax liability for a quarter is less than $2,500, the employer can either deposit the amount or pay it with Form 941. Monthly depositors may pay any lawful deposit shortfalls (see Section 8.2-1) for the quarter with Form 941, even if the amount exceeds $2,500.[77]

Payments can be made by including Form 941-V, *Form 941 Payment Voucher* (see Appendix page A-166) with the employer's Form 941. The following information must be included on the voucher:

- Employer identification number (EIN), but if an EIN has not yet been assigned, write "Applied for" and the date of the application in the space provided;
- Darken the oval for the quarter for which the tax payment is made (only one);
- Employer's name and address; and
- Amount paid.

Employers paying tax due with Form 941 cannot take advantage of the 10-day filing extension granted to employers that have deposited their entire tax liability on time throughout the quarter (see Section 8.3-2).

*Credit card payments.* Beginning January 1, 2006, businesses filing Form 941 with a lawful balance due can pay the amount owed on the return by credit card over the phone or Internet. These payments can be made through either of two authorized third-party service providers that will obtain credit authorization during the transaction and provide a confirmation number as proof of payment. The service providers charge a convenience fee based on the amount of the payment.

---

75. Form 941 Instructions.
76. IRS Reg. §31.6011(a)-6; Form 941 Instructions.
77. Form 941 Instructions; IRS Pub. 15, Circular E, Employer's Tax Guide.

Payments are processed through secure, commercial credit card networks and can be made 24 hours a day, 7 days a week. Payments are effective on the date the charge is authorized. *Note:* Federal tax deposits (FTDs) cannot be paid by credit card. Visit www.irs.gov (keyword: e-pay) for details on credit card payments, including a list of service providers and applicable convenience fees.

*Paying with EFTPS.* Payments can also be made using the Electronic Federal Tax Payment System. If an employer pays a balance due through EFTPS, Form 941 should be sent to the address for forms filed without a payment and Form 941-V should not be filed.

## 8.3-2  When and Where to File Form 941

In general, employers must file Form 941 by the last day of the first month following the end of each calendar quarter.[78] However, if the employer has made timely deposits of all its payroll tax liability for the quarter, an automatic extension of the filing period to the 10th day of the next month is granted. The IRS will not grant any further extensions. (See Section 8.2-1 for a discussion of the rules governing the timeliness of payroll tax deposits). Employers that go out of business must file their final Form 941 by the due date for the quarter during which they ceased paying wages. Table 8.1 summarizes the Form 941 filing schedule.

Table 8.1

| FORM 941 FILING DEADLINES | | | |
| --- | --- | --- | --- |
| Quarter | Quarter Ends | 941 Due Date | Automatic Extension |
| Jan. - Mar. | March 31 | April 30 | May 10 |
| Apr. - June | June 30 | July 31 | August 10 |
| July - Sept. | September 30 | October 31 | November 10 |
| Oct. - Dec. | December 31 | January 31 | February 10 |

**Saturdays, Sundays and holidays.** If the Form 941 due date falls on a Saturday, Sunday, or legal holiday, the due date becomes the next business day. Legal holidays include federal holidays, as well as state legal holidays if the IRS service center where the employer files its Form 941 is located in that state.[79] For employers taking advantage of the automatic extension, if the 10th day of the next month falls on a Saturday, Sunday, or legal holiday, the filing period is further extended until the next business day. Table 8.2 lists the federal holidays for 2008 and 2009 and the days they will be observed.

*IRS implements holiday change.* In 1996, the IRS issued regulations that changed the definition of "legal holiday" by eliminating the list that had been in the regulations and substituting a reference to "legal holidays in the District of Columbia."

---

78.   IRS Reg. §31.6071(a)-1(a)(1).
79.   IRC §7503; IRS Reg. §301.7503-1(b); IRS Pub. 509, Tax Calendars.

Table 8.2

| FEDERAL HOLIDAYS 2008-2009 | | |
|---|---|---|
| **Holiday** | **Day Observed—2008** | **Day Observed—2009** |
| New Year's Day | Tuesday, Jan. 1 | Thursday, Jan. 1 |
| Martin Luther King Jr.'s Day | Monday, Jan. 21 | Monday, Jan. 19 |
| Presidents Day | Monday, Feb. 18 | Monday, Feb. 16 |
| Emancipation Day | Wednesday, Apr. 16 | Thursday, Apr. 16 |
| Memorial Day | Monday, May 26 | Monday, May 25 |
| Independence Day | Friday, July 4 | Friday, July 3 |
| Labor Day | Monday, Sept. 1 | Monday, Sept. 7 |
| Columbus Day | Monday, Oct. 13 | Monday, Oct. 12 |
| Veterans Day | Tuesday, Nov. 11 | Wednesday, Nov. 11 |
| Thanksgiving Day | Thursday, Nov. 27 | Thursday, Nov. 26 |
| Christmas Day | Thursday, Dec. 25 | Friday, Dec. 25 |

**When are mailed forms considered filed?**[80]  If an employer mails its 941 forms rather than delivering them, they are considered filed on the date of the postmark put on the envelope by the U.S. Postal Service, so long as the full amount of postage has been prepaid.  Therefore, they may be timely filed even though they are received by the IRS after the due date.  Registered mail is considered postmarked as of the registration date.  Certified mail is considered postmarked as of the date the sender's receipt is postmarked by the postal employee.  In order to prove the postmark date, employers should use certified or registered mail and get a postmark date stamped on the mailing certificate by a postal employee.  This will serve as proof of mailing in case the envelope arrives late at the IRS.

Until 1997, this "postmark rule" applied only to the U.S. mail, not to private delivery services (PDS).  Forms sent by a PDS had to be received by the IRS on or before the due date to be considered timely.  This rule was changed by the Taxpayer Bill of Rights 2 to include forms and documents delivered by "designated private delivery services," with the IRS making the determination as to whether a PDS qualifies to be "designated."[81]

The current list of designated PDSs includes:

- *DHL Worldwide Express* (DHL) — DHL "Same Day" Service, DHL Next Day 10:30 am, DHL Next Day 12:00 pm, DHL Next Day 3:00 pm, and DHL 2nd Day Service;
- Federal Express (FedEx) — FedEx Priority Overnight, FedEx Standard Overnight, FedEx 2Day, FedEx International Priority, and FedEx International First; and
- *United Parcel Service* (UPS) — UPS Next Day Air, UPS Next Day Air Saver, UPS 2nd Day Air, UPS 2nd Day Air A.M., UPS Worldwide Express Plus, and UPS Worldwide Express.[82]

PDSs are required to either (1) record electronically to its data base the date on which an item was accepted for delivery (DHL, UPS); or (2) mark on the cover of the item the date on which it was given to the PDS for delivery (FedEx).  The date that is recorded or marked is treated as the postmark date for the "timely mailing, timely filing" rule.  For items delivered by DHL or UPS after the due date, the postmark date is

---

80.    IRC §7502; IRS Reg. §301.7502-1.
81.    IRC §7502(f); Rev. Proc. 97-19, 1997-1 CB 644.
82.    IRS Notice 2004-83, 2004-52 IRB 1030.

presumed to be the day that precedes the delivery date by the amount of time for a normal delivery by the type of service used (e.g., if an item is delivered by UPS 2nd Day Air five days after the due date, the postmark would be presumed to be three days after the due date). The employer can overcome this presumption by showing that the date recorded in the electronic data base is on or before the due date.

For items delivered by FedEx after the due date, if the item has a label generated and applied by a FedEx employee, the date marked on the label is treated as the postmark date, even if the item also has a label generated and applied by the employer. If an item has only a label generated by an employer, the date marked on the label is treated as the postmark date if the item is received within the normal delivery time for the type of service used. If an item is not delivered within the normal delivery time, the employer must establish that the item was given to or picked up by a FedEx employee on or before the due date and what the cause was for the delayed delivery.

**Proof of mailing may not prove delivery.**[83]  Other than direct proof of actual delivery, the only way to prove that federal tax documents were delivered to the IRS is to prove the use of registered or certified mail through the U.S. Postal Service. A registered or certified mail receipt establishes both proof of mailing and a presumption that a document has been delivered to the IRS if the Service has no record of ever having received the document. While proof that a designated PDS was used can prove that a document was timely mailed to the IRS, it does not establish a presumption of delivery to the IRS. In 2004, the IRS asked for comments from the public on whether delivery by a PDS should be considered equivalent to delivery by registered or certified mail.

**Where must Form 941 be filed?**  Employers should file their Forms 941 with the IRS office assigned to their region. The addresses are supplied in the instructions for Form 941 (see Appendix page A-168). If the employer is sending in a payment of taxes due with its Form 941, the form and the payment voucher should be sent to the separate payment address for the employer's region listed in the Form 941 instructions.

*Changes in filing locations caused by IRS reorganization.*  As part of the reorganization of the IRS mandated by the IRS Restructuring and Reform Act of 1998, all employers file their Forms 941 in either the Cincinnati or Ogden Service Centers, which will handle all receipt and processing of business returns (including employment tax returns). Employers are assigned to a service center based on their location, but all tax exempt organizations, Indian tribal governmental entities, and federal, state, and local governmental entities file in the Ogden Service Center. The only exceptions are returns sent with payments, which will go to addresses in Atlanta or Charlotte, N.C. In 2007, a change to the Form 941 instructions added "U.S. Department of the Treasury" as the first line of the "Without a payment" addresses. These changes are reflected on the address labels provided to employers with Form 941, as well as in the form's instructions.

**Color-coded mailing labels provided**.  When employers receive their Forms 941 from the IRS each quarter, they will get two color-coded preaddressed labels with the forms. Employers that are not making a payment with their return should use the yellow label to send their return to the IRS. Employers that owe tax should use the white label to send their return, payment, and voucher to the separate address for payments.

## 8.3-3  Form 941—Line-by-Line Instructions

Following are specific, line-by-line instructions for the 2008 Form 941. (A sample, filled-in Form 941 appears on pages 8-41—8-42).

***Part 1: Answer these questions for this quarter***

**Line 1 – Number of employees who received wages, tips, or other compensation this quarter.**
Enter here the number of employees paid during the pay period that included March 12 (First Quarter), June 12 (Second Quarter), September 12 (Third Quarter), or December 12 (Fourth Quarter) for the quarter indicated at the top of the form. This line should be completed for each Form 941. Do not include household

---

83.    IRS Reg. §301.7502-1(e).

employees, pensioners, farm employees, employees who received no pay during the quarter, or active members of the U.S. Armed Forces.

**Line 2—Total wages, tips, and other compensation.** Enter here the total wages paid, tips reported, taxable fringe benefits, sick pay paid by third parties transferring reporting liability to the employer, and other compensation paid to employees. This includes amounts reportable in Box 1 of the employees' Forms W-2 that are not subject to withholding, but not amounts that are not included in gross income (e.g., nontaxable and nonreportable fringe benefits, pre-tax contributions to employee benefit plans such as §401(k) and §125 plans, qualified moving expense reimbursements). Do not include supplemental unemployment compensation benefits even if income tax was withheld. Include third-party sick pay that was paid to employees if you get timely notice of the amount paid and taxes withheld from the third party.

**Line 3—Total income tax withheld from wages, tips, and other compensation.** Enter here the federal income tax withheld by the employer from wages paid, tips reported, taxable fringe benefits, and supplemental unemployment compensation benefits, plus any excise tax withheld on golden parachute payments.

**Line 4 – If no wages, tips, and other compensation are subject to social security or Medicare tax.** Check the box on Line 4 if no wages, tips, and other compensation reported on Line 2 are subject to social security and Medicare taxes. Leave the box blank if it does not apply.

**Line 5a—Taxable social security wages.** Enter in Column 1 the total amount of employees' wages subject to social security tax (up to $102,000 per employee for 2008), including taxable fringe benefits, sick pay, and elective deferrals to §401(k) plans. Do not include tips on this line. Multiply the total taxable wages from Line 5a, column 1 by 12.4% and enter the result in Column 2.

**Line 5b—Taxable social security tips.** Enter in Column 1 the total amount of employees' reported tips subject to social security tax (up to $102,000 in wages and tips for each employee for 2008). Report the tips even if the social security tax could not be collected from the employee because wages were insufficient. The total for an employee reported on Lines 5a and 5b in column 1 should not exceed $102,000 for 2008. Do not report allocated tips on Form 941. Multiply the total taxable tips from Line 5b, column 1 by 12.4% and enter the result in Column 2.

**Line 5c—Taxable Medicare wages and tips.** Enter in Column 1 the total amount of employees' wages subject to Medicare tax (no wage limit), including taxable fringe benefits, sick pay, and elective deferrals to §401(k) plans. Also include reported tips, even if the Medicare tax could not be collected from the employee because wages were insufficient. Multiply the total taxable wages and tips by 2.9% and enter the result in Column 2.

**Line 5d—Total social security and Medicare taxes.** Enter here the total social security and Medicare taxes (Column 2 Line 5a + Line 5b + Line 5c).

**Line 6 – Total taxes before adjustments.** Enter here the total income tax withheld and social security and Medicare taxes before adjustments (Lines 3 + 5d).

**Line 7 – Tax adjustments.** Several types of adjustments of income, social security, and Medicare taxes are reported on Lines 7a-7g. *Current period adjustments* are taken on Lines 7a-7c. *Prior period adjustments* are taken on Lines 7d-7g.

**Line 7a – Current quarter's fractions of cents.** Enter here the difference between the total social security and Medicare taxes on Line 5d and the amount actually withheld from employees' wages that is due to rounding to the nearest penny.

**Line 7b – Current quarter's sick pay.** Enter here the employee's share of social security and Medicare taxes on third-party sick pay that were withheld by the third-party payer.

**Line 7c – Current quarter's adjustments for tips and group-term life insurance.** Enter here adjustments for the uncollected employee share of social security and Medicare taxes on reported tips and on group-term life insurance coverage in excess of $50,000 provided to former employees.

**Line 7d – Current year's income tax withholding.** Enter here adjustments needed because of errors made in calculating federal income tax withholding for prior quarters of the same calendar year. Adjustments for errors made in earlier years may not be made unless the error to be corrected is an administrative one (e.g., a mathematical or transposition error made in reporting the actual amount withheld), because employees use the amount shown on Form W-2 when they file their income tax return. Adjustments for administrative errors made in earlier years should be reported here.

**Line 7e – Prior quarters' social security and Medicare taxes.** Enter adjustments for prior periods' social security and Medicare taxes. If reporting both an overpayment and an underpayment, enter only the net difference. Also enter here any social security and Medicare tax adjustments in amounts reported on Line 7g of prior period Forms 941.

**Line 7f – Special additions to federal income tax.** This line is to be used only if the IRS has sent the employer a notice instructing it to enter information here.

**Line 7g – Special additions to social security and Medicare.** This line is to be used only if the IRS has sent the employer a notice instructing it to enter information here.

**Line 7h – Total adjustments**. Combine all the adjustments reported on Lines 7a-7g and enter the result here.

*Prior period adjustments* that are taken on Lines 7d-7g must be accompanied by an explanation of the adjustment on Form 941c, *Statement to Correct Information* (see Section 8.6) or an equivalent statement. Do not file Form 941c separately, since it is not an amended return but an explanation of adjustments. Prior period adjustments must also be included on Line 15 (monthly depositors) or Schedule B (semiweekly depositors) and should be placed in the entry area corresponding with the date when the error was found. If an adjustment is entered correcting an error in an employee's social security or Medicare wages or taxes withheld for a prior year, the employer must also file Forms W-2c and W-3c (see Section 8.10).

**Line 8 – Total taxes after adjustments.** Enter here the total taxes, including adjustments, by combining the amounts on Lines 6 and 7h.

**Line 9 – Advance earned income credit payments made to employees.** Enter here the advance payments of earned income credit made to employees during the quarter (see Section 6.6). If the amount of AEIC payments is more than total taxes (Line 8) for the quarter, the employer can claim a credit applied to the Form 941 for the next quarter. The employer should attach a statement to Form 941 identifying the amount of the excess payments and the pay periods in which it was paid.

**Line 10 – Total taxes after adjustment for advance EIC.** Enter here the amount of net federal income, social security, and Medicare taxes (Line 8 – Line 9). This amount must equal the total amount on Line 15 (monthly depositors) or in the "Total liability for the quarter" area of Schedule B (Form 941).

**Line 11 – Total deposits for this quarter.** Enter here the total federal income, social security, and Medicare taxes deposited for the quarter, including any deposits that had to be made to cover prior period liabilities resulting from adjustments shown on Line 7h. Also include any overpayments from a prior period that are applied to this return.

**Line 12—Balance due.** Enter here the balance of any taxes due to the IRS (Line 10 - Line 11). There should be a balance due only if the employer's total taxes for the quarter (Line 10) are less than $2,500 or if the employer is a monthly depositor sending in a shortfall payment with the return. If the balance due is less than $1.00, it does not have to be paid.

**Line 13—Overpayment.** Enter here any overpayment made when depositing payroll taxes during the quarter (Line 11 - Line 10) and check the appropriate box for application of the overpayment to the next quarter's return or a refund of the overpayment. If no box is checked, the overpayment will be applied to the next quarter's return. The IRS may apply an overpayment to any past due tax account under the employer's EIN. If the overpayment is less than $1.00 it will be refunded or applied to the next quarter only if the employer requests it in writing. Do not make an entry on both Lines 12 and 13.

***Part 2: Tell us about your deposit schedule and tax liability for this quarter.***

**Line 14 – State abbreviation.** Enter here the postal abbreviation for the state where payroll tax deposits are made by FTD coupon and paper check or initiated for EFTPS transfers. IRS uses the state shown to determine banking days for purposes of deposit due dates. Official holidays for the state shown are not counted as banking days.

If deposits are made in two or more states, enter "MU." When an employer deposits in multiple states, the IRS cannot determine whether any portion of its deposits was affected by a state holiday and may assess a late deposit penalty for deposits made in one of the states where the employer made deposits. If an employer receives a penalty notice and one or more of its deposit due dates was extended because of a state bank holiday, respond to the notice by referring to the state holiday and the applicable deposit amount.

**Line 15 – Tax liability.** If the amount on Line 10 is less than $2,500, check the appropriate box. If this box is checked, the employer can pay its tax liability with Form 941 with a check or through EFTPS or a credit card.

If the employer is a monthly schedule depositor, check the appropriate box and enter the tax liability for each month in the quarter in the Month 1, Month 2, and Month 3 boxes respectively. Then enter the total tax liability for the quarter in the "Total Liability for Quarter" box. This amount must equal the amount in Line 10.

If a monthly schedule depositor is reporting adjustments on Line 15 and the net tax liability for any month is negative because of the adjustment, the employer should not enter a negative amount for that month. Instead, the employer should enter -0- for the month and subtract that negative amount from the tax liability for the next month.

If the employer was a semiweekly schedule depositor for any part of the quarter being reported, check the appropriate box. Semiweekly schedule depositors must complete Schedule B (Form 941), *Report of Tax Liability for Semiweekly Schedule Depositors* and submit it with Form 941.

 **WATCH OUT** Make sure to report the employer's tax liability on the correct form, and do not report deposits rather than liabilities. If liabilities are not properly reported or a semiweekly depositor reports liabilities on Line 15 rather than on Schedule B, the IRS may assess an averaged failure-to-deposit penalty (see page 8-25).

If unused negative adjustments are carried over to the next quarter, do not show them on Line 7h for the current quarter, because the Line 15 total must equal Line 10. Instead, report them on the next quarter's Form 941 on Line 7h and adjust the liability reported on Line 15.

***Part 3: Tell us about your business***

**Line 16 – If your business has closed or you storred paying wages.** If the employer's business has closed and this is a final Form 941, the employer should mark the box on Line 16 and enter the final date wages were paid.

**Line 17 – If you are a seasonal employer.** Seasonal employers do not have to file a Form 941 for quarters when they do not pay wages. For quarters when they do pay wages, seasonal employers should mark the box on Line 17.

### Part 4: May we speak with your third-party designee?

If the employer wants to allow a third party to discuss the employer's Form 941 with the IRS, the "Yes" box should be checked and the third party's name, phone number, and 5-digit PIN should be entered in the appropriate boxes. If the employer does not want to designate a third party to discuss the Form 941 with the IRS, the "No" box should be checked.

### Part 5: Sign here

The individual who is authorized to sign Form 941 should sign in the appropriate box and print his or her name, title, and phone number and the date signed. By signing, the individual attests under penalties of perjury that the information on the form and any attachments are true to the best of that person's knowledge and belief.

### Part 6: For paid preparers only (optional)

This section should be completed only by someone who was paid to prepare the Form 941 is not employed by the employer filing the form. The preparer should sign in the appropriate box and provide the other requested identifying information. The preparer should also give a copy of the signed form to the employer in addition to the original that will be filed with the IRS. If the preparer is a reporting agent that has a valid Form 8655, *Reporting Agent Authorization* (see Appendix page A-376), on file with the IRS for the employer, this section does not have to be completed.

## 8.3-4 Schedule B (Form 941)

Semiweekly depositors at any time during a quarter must file an attachment to Form 941—Schedule B, *Report of Tax Liability for Semiweekly Schedule Depositors* (see Appendix page A-176 and page 8-43 for a sample, filled-in form). This includes monthly depositors that accumulate at least $100,000 in employment tax liability during a month. Schedule B records an employer's payroll tax liability, not deposits made. The form contains three sections. Months 1, 2, and 3 correspond to each month of the quarter and are divided into 31 blocks where employers should enter the tax liability incurred on each day of the quarter.

Each of these sections also includes a box (Total liability for Month 1, 2, and 3) where the total liability for the month is entered. The total payroll tax liability for the quarter should be entered in the box "Total liability for the quarter." This total must match the total from Line 10 (Total taxes) of Form 941.

At the top of the form, the employer should enter its name and EIN and check the appropriate box to indicate the quarter for which this Schedule B is being filed.

It is important to note that Schedule B is used to show an employer's federal employment tax liabilities, not deposits made by the employer. The IRS gets deposit information from FTD coupons or EFTPS and matches it against Schedule B to determine if the employer has deposited its federal employment tax liabilities on time. If a semiweekly depositor does not properly complete and file Schedule B with its Form 941, it may be assessed an averaged failure-to-deposit penalty (see page 8-25).

**Prior period adjustments.** On Schedule B, the employer must take into account adjustments to correct errors on prior period returns that are reported on a current Form 941. These adjustments are reported on lines 7d-7g of the 2008 Form 941 (lines 4 and 9 of pre-2005 Forms 941). If the adjustment corrects an underreported liability in a prior quarter, include the adjustment amount in the total liability reported for the entry space that corresponds to the date the employer discovered the error. If the adjustment corrects an overreported liability, use the adjustment amount to offset subsequent liabilities until it is used up.

**Example:** The following information is used to complete a Form 941 and Schedule B for the third quarter of 2008 for Eastbridge Clothiers, a semiweekly depositor that pays wages biweekly on Fridays (see following pages):

Name:       Eastbridge Clothiers
Address:    12121 Denim St., Eastbridge, VA 34567
EIN:        12-3456789

| | |
|---|---:|
| No. of employees on Sept. 12: | 1,500 |
| Total wages and other compensation: | $1,500,000.00 |
| Social security wages: | 1,350,000.00 |
| Medicare wages: | 1,500,000.00 |
| Federal income tax withheld: | 225,000.00 |
| Social security tax withheld: | 83,700.00 |
| Medicare tax withheld: | 21,750.00 |
| | |
| July 3 tax liability/deposit: | $63,000.00 |
| July 18 tax liability/deposit: | 63,000.00 |
| August 1 tax liability/deposit: | 63,000.00 |
| August 15 tax liability/deposit: | 63,000.00 |
| August 29 tax liability/deposit: | 63,000.00 |
| September 12 tax liability/deposit: | 62,000.00 |
| September 26 tax liability/deposit: | 58,900.00 |

Form **941 for 2008:** Employer's QUARTERLY Federal Tax Return

950108

(Rev. January 2008)

Department of the Treasury — Internal Revenue Service

OMB No. 1545-0029

**(EIN)**
Employer identification number: 1 2 — 3 4 5 6 7 8 9

**Name** *(not your trade name)* Eastbridge Clothiers

**Trade name** *(if any)*

**Address** 12121 Denim Street

Number   Street   Suite or room number

Eastbridge   VA   34567

City   State   ZIP code

**Report for this Quarter of 2008**
(Check one.)

- [ ] **1:** January, February, March
- [ ] **2:** April, May, June
- [✓] **3:** July, August, September
- [ ] **4:** October, November, December

Read the separate instructions before you fill out this form. Please type or print within the boxes.

### Part 1: Answer these questions for this quarter.

| | |
|---|---|
| 1 Number of employees who received wages, tips, or other compensation for the pay period including: *Mar. 12* (Quarter 1), *June 12* (Quarter 2), *Sept. 12* (Quarter 3), *Dec. 12* (Quarter 4)   **1** | 1500 |
| 2 Wages, tips, and other compensation   **2** | 1500000 . 00 |
| 3 Total income tax withheld from wages, tips, and other compensation   **3** | 225000 . 00 |

4 If no wages, tips, and other compensation are subject to social security or Medicare tax . . [ ] Check and go to line 6.

5 Taxable social security and Medicare wages and tips:

| | Column 1 | | Column 2 |
|---|---|---|---|
| 5a Taxable social security wages | 1350000 . 00 | × .124 = | 167400 . 00 |
| 5b Taxable social security tips | . | × .124 = | . |
| 5c Taxable Medicare wages & tips | 1500000 . 00 | × .029 = | 43500 . 00 |

| | |
|---|---|
| 5d Total social security and Medicare taxes (*Column 2,* lines 5a + 5b + 5c = line 5d) . . **5d** | 210900 . 00 |
| 6 Total taxes before adjustments (lines 3 + 5d = line 6) . . . . . . . . . . . . . **6** | 435900 . 00 |

7 **TAX ADJUSTMENTS** (read the instructions for line 7 before completing lines 7a through 7g):

| | |
|---|---|
| 7a Current quarter's fractions of cents . . . . . | . |
| 7b Current quarter's sick pay . . . . . . . . . | . |
| 7c Current quarter's adjustments for tips and group-term life insurance | . |
| 7d Current year's income tax withholding (attach Form 941c) . . | . |
| 7e Prior quarters' social security and Medicare taxes (attach Form 941c) | . |
| 7f Special additions to federal income tax (attach Form 941c) . . . | . |
| 7g Special additions to social security and Medicare (attach Form 941c) | . |

| | |
|---|---|
| 7h **TOTAL ADJUSTMENTS** (combine all amounts: lines 7a through 7g) . . . . . . **7h** | . |
| 8 Total taxes after adjustments (combine lines 6 and 7h) . . . . . . . . **8** | 435900 . 00 |
| 9 Advance earned income credit (EIC) payments made to employees . . . . . . . **9** | . |
| 10 Total taxes after adjustment for advance EIC (line 8 – line 9 = line 10) . . . . **10** | 435900 . 00 |
| 11 Total deposits for this quarter, including overpayment applied from a prior quarter . . . **11** | 435900 . 00 |
| 12 Balance due (If line 10 is more than line 11, write the difference here.) . . . . . . . **12** For information on how to pay, see the instructions. | . |
| 13 Overpayment (If line 11 is more than line 10, write the difference here.) [____] . Check one [ ] Apply to next return. [ ] Send a refund. | |

▶ You **MUST** fill out both pages of this form and **SIGN** it.

Next ➡

For Privacy Act and Paperwork Reduction Act Notice, see the back of the Payment Voucher.   Cat. No. 17001Z   Form **941** (Rev. 1-2008)

950208

| Name *(not your trade name)* | Employer identification number (EIN) |
|---|---|
| Eastbridge Clothiers | 12-3456789 |

## Part 2: Tell us about your deposit schedule and tax liability for this quarter.

If you are unsure about whether you are a monthly schedule depositor or a semiweekly schedule depositor, see *Pub. 15 (Circular E)*, section 11.

14 **V** **A** Write the state abbreviation for the state where you made your deposits OR write **"MU"** if you made your deposits in *multiple* states.

15 Check one: ☐ **Line 10 is less than $2,500.** Go to Part 3.

☐ **You were a monthly schedule depositor for the entire quarter. Fill out your tax liability for each month.** Then go to Part 3.

Tax liability: Month 1 ☐ .

Month 2 ☐ .

Month 3 ☐ .

Total liability for quarter ☐ . Total must equal line 10.

☑ **You were a semiweekly schedule depositor for any part of this quarter. Fill out** *Schedule B (Form 941): Report of Tax Liability for Semiweekly Schedule Depositors,* **and attach it to this form.**

## Part 3: Tell us about your business. If a question does NOT apply to your business, leave it blank.

16 If your business has closed or you stopped paying wages . . . . . . . . . . . . . . ☐ Check here, and

enter the final date you paid wages ☐ / / .

17 If you are a seasonal employer and you do not have to file a return for every quarter of the year . . ☐ Check here.

## Part 4: May we speak with your third-party designee?

Do you want to allow an employee, a paid tax preparer, or another person to discuss this return with the IRS? See the instructions for details.

☐ **Yes.** Designee's name and phone number ☐ ( ) –

Select a 5-digit Personal Identification Number (PIN) to use when talking to IRS. ☐ ☐ ☐ ☐ ☐

☑ **No.**

## Part 5: Sign here. You MUST fill out both pages of this form and SIGN it.

Under penalties of perjury, I declare that I have examined this return, including accompanying schedules and statements, and to the best of my knowledge and belief, it is true, correct, and complete.

X **Sign your name here** *Daniel Hatter*

Print your name here **Daniel Hatter**

Print your title here **President**

Date 10 / 31 / 2008

Best daytime phone ( ) –

## Part 6: For paid preparers only (optional)

| Paid Preparer's Signature | |
|---|---|
| Firm's name (or yours if self-employed) | |
| Address | |
| | EIN |
| | ZIP code |
| Date / / Phone ( ) – | SSN/PTIN |

☐ Check if you are self-employed.

Page **2**

Form **941** (Rev. 1-2008)

# Schedule B (Form 941):

## Report of Tax Liability for Semiweekly Schedule Depositors

(Rev. January 2006)     Department of the Treasury — Internal Revenue Service

990306

OMB No. 1545-0029

**(EIN)**
Employer identification number   1  2  —  3  4  5  6  7  8  9

**Name** *(not your trade name)*   Eastbridge Clothiers

**Calendar year**   2  0  0  8     *(Also check quarter)*

**Report for this Quarter ...**
(Check one.)

☐ **1:** January, February, March

☐ **2:** April, May, June

☑ **3:** July, August, September

☐ **4:** October, November, December

Use this schedule to show your **TAX LIABILITY** for the quarter; **DO NOT** use it to show your deposits. You must fill out this form and attach it to Form 941 (or Form 941-SS) if you are a semiweekly schedule depositor or became one because your accumulated tax liability on any day was $100,000 or more. Write your daily tax liability on the numbered space that corresponds to the date wages were paid. See Section 11 in *Pub. 15 (Circular E), Employer's Tax Guide,* for details.

**Month 1**

| # | | # | | # | | # | | |
|---|---|---|---|---|---|---|---|---|
| 1 | . | 9 | . | 17 | . | 25 | . | **Tax liability for Month 1** |
| 2 | . | 10 | 63000 . 00 | 18 | . | 26 | . | |
| 3 | 63000 . 00 | 11 | . | 19 | . | 27 | . | 126000 . 00 |
| 4 | . | 12 | . | 20 | . | 28 | . | |
| 5 | . | 13 | . | 21 | . | 29 | . | |
| 6 | . | 14 | . | 22 | . | 30 | . | |
| 7 | . | 15 | . | 23 | . | 31 | . | |
| 8 | . | 16 | . | 24 | . | | | |

**Month 2**

| # | | # | | # | | # | | |
|---|---|---|---|---|---|---|---|---|
| 1 | 63000 . 00 | 9 | . | 17 | . | 25 | . | **Tax liability for Month 2** |
| 2 | . | 10 | . | 18 | . | 26 | . | |
| 3 | . | 11 | . | 19 | . | 27 | . | 189000 . 00 |
| 4 | . | 12 | . | 20 | . | 28 | . | |
| 5 | . | 13 | . | 21 | . | 29 | 63000 . 00 | |
| 6 | . | 14 | . | 22 | . | 30 | . | |
| 7 | . | 15 | 63000 . 00 | 23 | . | 31 | . | |
| 8 | . | 16 | . | 24 | . | | | |

**Month 3**

| # | | # | | # | | # | | |
|---|---|---|---|---|---|---|---|---|
| 1 | . | 9 | . | 17 | . | 25 | . | **Tax liability for Month 3** |
| 2 | . | 10 | . | 18 | . | 26 | 58900 . 00 | |
| 3 | . | 11 | . | 19 | . | 27 | . | 120900 . 00 |
| 4 | . | 12 | 62000 . 00 | 20 | . | 28 | . | |
| 5 | . | 13 | . | 21 | . | 29 | . | |
| 6 | . | 14 | . | 22 | . | 30 | . | |
| 7 | . | 15 | . | 23 | . | 31 | . | |
| 8 | . | 16 | . | 24 | . | | | |

Fill in your total liability for the quarter (Month 1 + Month 2 + Month 3) = Total tax liability for the quarter ►
**Total must equal line 10 on Form 941** (or line 8 on Form 941-SS).

**Total liability for the quarter**

435900 . 00

**For Paperwork Reduction Act Notice, see separate instructions.**     Cat. No. 11967Q     **Schedule B (Form 941)** Rev. 1-2006

## 8.3-5  IRS Offers Advice on Avoiding Form 941 Errors

The IRS has offered employers advice to help them avoid the most common errors made when completing Form 941.[84]  This list is adapted for the 2008 Form 941.

- Report separately the taxable social security wages and the social security tax on Line 5a in Columns 1 and 2, the taxable social security tips and the social security tax on Line 5b in Columns 1 and 2, and the taxable Medicare wages and tips and the Medicare tax on Line 5c in Columns 1 and 2.
- Use the most recent preprinted Form 941 sent to you by the IRS.  If the return is prepared by a third-party preparer, make certain the employer's name is printed exactly as it appears on the preprinted IRS form.
- Verify that Line 10 is the sum of Lines 6 and 7h, minus line 9.
- Verify the calculation of the social security tax on Line 5a (12.4% x social security wages) and the Medicare tax on Line 5c (2.9% x Medicare wages and tips).
- Never submit a form with an entry on both lines 12 and 13; an employer cannot have both a balance due and an overpayment.
- Use caution before making entries on Lines 7f or 7g; these lines are not normally used unless an IRS employee directs an employer to enter special information.
- Enter the "Total taxes after adjustments" figure on Line 8, not Line 7h.
- If submitting a non-taxable return, send in both pages of Form 941; sending in just one page will result in the document being rejected as an incomplete return.
- Check totals on Forms 941 and W-3 or the electronic file being sent to SSA to make sure they match.
- Always sign the return and print the signing individual's name and title in the space provided.

## 8.4  Annual Reporting of Nonpayroll Withholding—Form 945

The IRS removed all nonpayroll items from Form 941, hoping to reduce the complexity of the form and ease the reconciliation among Forms 941, W-2, and W-3.  Accordingly, the Service has developed Form 945, *Annual Return of Withheld Federal Income Tax* (see Appendix page A-215).  On Form 945, businesses report amounts withheld throughout the year from nonpayroll items such as pensions, annuities, gambling winnings, etc., as well as backup withholding.  Total deposits of these nonpayroll withheld taxes will also be reported on Form 945, and any amount withheld that has not yet been deposited when the form is completed must be paid with the form.

The last section of Form 945 is a monthly summary of tax liability.  Businesses should enter their nonpayroll withholding tax liability for each month on Lines A-L, with the total being entered on Line M.  This area should be filled out only by monthly depositors of nonpayroll withholding tax with at least $2,500 in nonpayroll withheld taxes.  Semiweekly depositors (and monthly depositors that accumulate at least $100,000 in nonpayroll withheld tax liability during a month) must use Form 945-A, *Annual Record of Federal Tax Liability* (see Appendix page A-221).  Form 945-A is completed in the same way as Schedule B of Form 941, requiring an entry for each day nonpayroll withholding tax liability was incurred during the year, as well as monthly and yearly totals.

*Third party can be designated to work with IRS.*  The employer can allow the IRS to discuss its Form 945 with a designated third party by completing the "Third-party Designee" area above the signature line of the form.  The third-party designee may be an employee or an outside tax preparation firm.  Enter the third party's name and any 5 digits the designee chooses as its personal identification number (PIN).

---

84.    IRS Notice 941, Avoid Common Errors in Preparing Form 941.

By designating a third party, the employer is:

- authorizing the IRS to call the designee to answer any questions relating to the information reported on the Form 945;
- authorizing the designee to exchange information concerning the Form 945; and
- authorizing the designee to request and receive written information related to the Form 945 including copies of specific notices, correspondence, and account transcripts.

The third-party designee is not authorized to receive any refund check, bind the employer to anything, or otherwise represent the employer before the IRS. The designation automatically expires one year from the due date of the Form 945, but it can be revoked beforehand by either the employer or the designee in a written statement submitted to the IRS service center where the Form 945 was filed.

 **SEPARATE DEPOSITOR STATUS** Employers must be aware that their depositor status for Form 941 taxes may be different from their Form 945 depositor status. See Section 8.2-1 for an explanation of depositor status determinations for employers withholding nonpayroll taxes.

**When and where to file Forms 945 and 945-A.**[85] The 2007 Forms 945 and 945-A are due January 31, 2008 with an extension to February 11 for employers that have timely deposited all their nonpayroll withheld taxes for the year. These forms for 2008 are due February 2, 2009. Employers that are required to file Form 945 for one year must file Form 945 for subsequent years only if the employer has nonpayroll withheld income taxes for that year. An employer should not file a final return if it is reasonably foreseeable that it will withhold nonpayroll taxes in a future year.

Form 945 (and Form 945-A, if applicable) should be filed at the IRS location listed in the Form 945 instructions. If the return is being filed with a payment and Form 945-V, *Form 945 Payment Voucher*, it must be returned to a different address, which is also listed in the form's instructions.

**Color-coded mailing labels provided**. When employers receive their Forms 945 from the IRS each year, they will get two color-coded preaddressed labels with the forms. Employers that are not making a payment with their return should use the yellow label to send their return to the IRS. Employers that owe tax should use the white label to send their return, payment, and voucher to the separate address for payments.

## 8.5 Other Federal Employment Tax Returns

In addition to Forms 941 and 945, there are other reporting forms certain employers may be required to use depending on the type of business the employer is engaged in, the type of tax reported, the amount of taxes reported, where the employer's business is located, and whether the employer has failed to withhold, deposit, or report timely.

## 8.5-1 Monthly Reporting for Delinquent Employers—Form 941-M

Employers that fail to withhold or deposit taxes or file returns on time may be required by the IRS to report employment taxes monthly rather than quarterly, using Form 941-M, *Employer's Monthly Federal Tax Return* (see Appendix page A-189). The IRS will notify an employer of its monthly reporting requirement by sending Form 2481, *Notice to Make Special Deposits of Taxes*.

**When does the monthly filing start and end?**[86] The employer must file its first Form 941-M for the month during which it receives notification from the IRS. However, if the notification is received after the end of the first month of a quarter, the prior months of the quarter must also be included on the first report.

---

85. IRS Reg. §31.6011(a)-4(b); §31.6071(a)-1; Form 945 Instructions.
86. IRS Reg. §31.6011(a)-5.

The employer must continue to file Form 941-M for each month thereafter until the IRS notifies the employer monthly reporting is no longer required. The last monthly filing should be for the last month of the quarter during which the discontinue notice is received.

**When and where to file Form 941-M.**[87] An employer required to file Form 941-M must do so by the 15th of the month after the month for which the report is made. The form should be sent using the pre-addressed envelope provided by the IRS.

**Tax deposit schedule may be affected.**[88] In addition to monthly reporting, another headache for delinquent employers receiving a Form 2481 notice from the IRS is a shorter time period for making deposits. All deposits must be made no more than 2 banking days after the payment of wages causing the deposit liability and must be made into a special deposit account providing a trust fund for the U.S. government.

## 8.5-2 Employers Operating Outside the Continental U.S.—Forms 941-PR and 941-SS

Employers that have employees in Puerto Rico must file Form 941-PR, *Employer's Quarterly Federal Tax Return*, while employers operating in American Samoa, Guam, the Northern Mariana Islands, and the Virgin Islands must file Form 941-SS, *Employer's Quarterly Federal Tax Return*. Each of these forms is used to report an employer's liability for social security and Medicare taxes, but not federal income tax withholding. These employers must also file Form 941 to report federal income tax withholding liability.

## 8.5-3 Employers of Domestic Employees

Individuals who hire domestic employees must report and pay both the employer and employee share of social security and Medicare taxes on wages it pays these employees on their personal tax return, Form 1040, on Schedule H. The threshold for requiring the withholding and paying of social security and Medicare taxes is $1,600 per year for 2008 (indexed annually to the next lowest multiple of $100).[89]

The employer must also withhold, report, and pay federal income tax if the employee requests it. Household employers are required to make payments of withheld taxes throughout the year.

 **TEENAGE BABYSITTER EXEMPTION** Household employment by workers under the age of 18 is exempt from social security and Medicare taxes, regardless of how much they earn, unless such employment is the worker's principal occupation.

**Employers that also have Form 941 liability.** Sole proprietors who file Form 941 for business employees may report the wages of their household employees on Form 941 as well, if the household employees meet the $1,600 per year wage threshold (for 2008). If an employer reports both types of wages on its Forms 941, the tax liability for wages paid to household employees must be included when the employer's total liability during the lookback period is determined for purposes of fixing the employer's depositor status.

## 8.5-4 Annual Reporting by Agricultural Employers—Form 943

Employers of farmworkers that must withhold federal income tax and withhold and pay social security and Medicare taxes on farmworkers' wages are required to report the wages paid and taxes withheld on Form 943, *Employer's Annual Federal Tax Return for Agricultural Employees* (see Appendix page A-195).[90]

---

87.  IRS Reg. §31.6071(a)-1(a)(2).
88.  IRC §7512; IRS Reg. §301.7512-1.
89.  IRC §3121(a)(7)(B); §3121(b)(21); §3121(x); §3510; IRS Notice 95-18, 1995-18 IRB 13.
90.  IRS Reg. §31.6011(a)-1(a)(2)(ii); Form 943 Instructions.

Form 943 serves the same purpose as Form 941 for nonagricultural employers, only it is filed annually rather than quarterly. Employers that employ both agricultural and nonagricultural employees must file both Forms 941 and 943 for each type of worker, respectively.

The last section of Form 943 is a monthly summary of tax liability. Agricultural employers who are monthly depositors should enter their withholding and employment tax liability for each month on Lines A-L, with the total being entered on Line M. Semiweekly depositors (and monthly depositors that accumulate at least $100,000 in payroll tax liability during a month) must use Form 943-A, *Agricultural Employer's Record of Federal Tax Liability* (see Appendix page A-201). Form 943-A is completed in the same way as Schedule B of Form 941, requiring an entry for each day payroll tax liability was incurred during the year, as well as monthly and yearly totals.

**When and where must Form 943 be filed?** In general, Form 943 must be filed by the last day of the first month (January 31) after the year being reported on the form. However, employers that have deposited all their taxes on time are entitled to an automatic 10-day extension. The form should be filed with the IRS service center listed in the Form 943 instructions.

**Special deposit rules for agricultural employers.** Because of their unique annual reporting requirement, agricultural employers are subject to a different lookback period than the period that applies to other employers for determining their depositor status. The lookback period for agricultural employers is the second calendar year preceding the current calendar year (see Section 8.2-1). Also, they may have two separate deposit requirements if they pay wages to nonagricultural employees as well as farmworkers.

## 8.5-5  Annual Reporting by Small Employers—Form 944

Starting with tax year 2006, in an effort to reduce the administrative burden on small employers, employers that are notified by the IRS of their qualification to participate in the Employers' Annual Federal Tax Program (Form 944) (EAFTP) will file new Form 944, *Employer's Annual Federal Tax Return,* instead of Form 941.

**Annual tax liability of $1,000 or less triggers eligibility.**[91] Employers whose filing history shows that they owe $1,000 or less in employment taxes per year will be notified in writing by the IRS that they qualify for the EAFTP. New employers that timely notify the IRS that they anticipate their estimated annual employment tax liability to be $1,000 or less will be notified of their eligibility for the EAFTP. Employers that are notified of their qualification for the EAFTP generally must file Form 944 and can pay their employment tax liability when they file the form (see Section 8.2-2).

If an employer participating in the EAFTP reports an annual tax liability of more than $1,000 on Form 944, the IRS will notify the employer that its filing status has changed and will have to begin filing Form 941 quarterly in succeeding years. The employer's filing status will not change during the year that its employment tax liability exceeds $1,000. Such employers will also have to comply with the general rules on depositing employment taxes (see Section 8.2-2).

**Exceptions to Form 944 filing requirement.** Even though an employer has been notified of its qualification for the EAFTP, an employer may still file Form 941 instead if:

- The employer anticipates that its annual employment tax liability will exceed $1,000 or the employer prefers to file Form 941 electronically;
- The employer asks the IRS to file Form 941, in compliance with instructions for doing so in the notification of EAFTP eligibility; and
- The IRS sends a subsequent written notice to the employer stating that its filing requirement has been changed to Form 941.[92]

---

91.    IRS Reg. §31.6071(a)-1(a)(1); IRS Temp. Reg. §31.6011(a)-1T(a)(5)(i), (ii); §31.6011(a)-4T(a)(5)(i), (ii).
92.    IRS Temp. Reg. §31.6011(a)-1T(a)(5)(iii); §31.6011(a)-4T(a)(5)(iii).

**Differences from Form 941 are minimal.** Form 944 is nearly identical to Form 941. The differences are as follows:

- There is no question about the number of employees on the payroll on any specified (quarterly) date.
- If the total employment tax for the year is $2,500 or more, each month's liability must be indicated in Part 2.
- There is no check box for seasonal employers.

**When and where must Form 944 be filed?** Form 944 must be filed by the last day of the first month (January 31) after the year being reported on the form. However, employers that have deposited all their taxes on time are entitled to an automatic 10-day extension. The form should be filed with the IRS service center for the employer's region listed in the Form 944 instructions.

# 8.6 Making Adjustments, Correcting Returns, and Obtaining Refunds and Credits—Forms 941c and 843

When errors are made in withholding or reporting federal income, social security, and Medicare taxes, employers must follow procedures set forth in IRS regulations to correct the errors and pay the proper amount of taxes. The method of correction depends on the type of tax involved, whether the employer withheld or reported too little or too much, and when the error was made and discovered. Form 941 is used as the standard reporting form in the discussion of these correction methods. Similar rules apply to other forms used by employers to report withholding of income and employment taxes.

**Federal income, social security or Medicare tax undercollected—discovered before Form 941 is filed.**[93] If an employer withholds too little or does not withhold at all from its employees' wages for federal income, social security, or Medicare tax, and discovers the error before filing its Form 941 for the quarter, it must report and pay the proper withholding amount on the Form 941.

**Social security or Medicare tax undercollected or underpaid—discovered after Form 941 is filed.**[94] If an employer underwithholds or pays less than its full share of social security or Medicare tax, and discovers the error after filing its Form 941 for the quarter during which the error occurred, the employer can make an "adjustment" that will avoid the accumulation of interest on the underpayment. The adjustment is made by reporting the underpayment on the employer's timely filed Form 941 for the quarter during which the error is discovered and paying the underpayment to the IRS at that time (whether or not the money is eventually collected from the employee). If the adjustment is reported but timely payment is not made, interest on the underpayment accrues from the day after the due date of the return. If the adjustment is not reported on the employer's Form 941 for the quarter when the error is discovered, it must be reported on the employer's next Form 941, with interest accruing from the due date of the earlier Form 941.

**Federal income tax underwithheld—discovered after Form 941 is filed.**[95] If an employer underwithholds federal income tax from its employees' wages and discovers the error after filing its Form 941 for the quarter during which the error occurred, the employer can avoid paying interest on the undercollection if it reports the undercollection as an adjustment on its timely filed Form 941 for the quarter during which the error is detected. If the adjustment is not reported on the employer's Form 941 for the quarter when the error is discovered, it should be reported on the employer's next Form 941, with interest accruing from the due date of the earlier Form 941. In any event, the undercollection must be reported by the due date of the employer's Form 941 for the fourth calendar quarter of the year during which the error occurred.

---

93.    IRS Reg. §31.6205-1(b)(1), (c)(1).
94.    IRS Reg. §31.6205-1(b)(3); ILM 1997-28, 8-20-97.
95.    IRS Reg. §31.6205-1(c)(3).

**LIMIT ON INTEREST-FREE ADJUSTMENTS**[96]  Interest-free adjustments of underwithheld income tax or undercollected or underpaid social security or Medicare tax are not available after receipt from the IRS of a notice and demand for payment based on an assessment, or a Notice of Determination in a worker classification dispute under IRC §7436. Before it receives a Notice of Determination, the employer may stop the accrual of interest by depositing a cash bond in the amount of the proposed tax liability.

 **RECOVERING UNDERCOLLECTIONS FROM EMPLOYEES**[97]  If an employer withholds too little from an employee's wages for federal income, social security, or Medicare tax, the undercollected amount may be deducted from any compensation given to the employee, whether it is wages or not (underwithheld income tax must be withheld during the same calendar year the error occurred). If this is not done, the employer and employee can work out another way to handle payment to the employer. Each employee must be treated separately, so an overcollection of taxes from one employee cannot be used to offset an undercollection from another.

**Federal income, social security or Medicare tax overcollected—discovered before Form 941 is filed.**[98]  If an employer withholds too much from its employees' wages for federal income, social security or Medicare tax, and discovers the error before filing Form 941 for the quarter during which the error was made, it does not have to report the overwithheld amount if it repays the overwithheld amount by the due date of the Form 941 and keeps in its records a receipt from the employee showing the date and amount of payment.

In addition, if only overwithheld federal income tax must be repaid to the employee, the repayment must occur before the end of the calendar year during which the error was made. Therefore, overwithholdings during the fourth quarter of the year must be discovered and repaid by December 31 of that year, even though Form 941 for that quarter is not due until January 31 of the following year.

Overwithheld amounts not repaid by the due date of Form 941 must be reported and paid to the IRS with Form 941. The employer must also include a statement explaining the overcollection that includes the name and social security number of the employee involved and the amount of the overcollection that was not repaid.

**Social security or Medicare tax overcollected—discovered after Form 941 is filed.**[99]  If an employer withholds too much from its employees' wages for social security or Medicare tax, and discovers the error after filing Form 941 for the quarter during which the error was made, the employer must repay the overwithheld amount or reimburse the employees by withholding less from their future wages. The repayment or reimbursement must be made by the end of the quarter following the quarter during which the overcollection was discovered. If repayment is made in a year after the year the error was made, the employee will be issued a Form W-2c.

If the employer repays the employee, the employer must keep as part of its records a receipt from the employee showing the date of the repayment and the amount repaid (e.g., a canceled check). If the repayment takes place after the year during which the error occurred, the employer must also keep as part of its records a statement provided by the employee saying the employee has not and will not seek a refund or credit for the overcollected amount from the IRS, or any refund or credit already sought has been rejected.

**Federal income tax overcollected—discovered after Form 941 is filed.**[100]  If an employer overwithholds federal income tax from its employees' wages and discovers the error after filing Form 941 for the quarter during which the error was made, the employer also can either repay or reimburse the employee for the overwithheld amount. However, the employer must repay the overwithheld amount before the end of the calendar year during which the error was made, as well as keep the employee's written statement as to the date and amount repaid. Employers that reimburse employees for overwithheld amounts by reducing future withheld taxes can do so only during the same calendar year that the error occurred.

---

96.    IRS Reg. §31.6205-1(a)(6).
97.    IRS Reg. §31.6205-1(b)(3), (c)(4).
98.    IRS Reg. §31.6413(a)-1(a).
99.    IRS Reg. §31.6413(a)-1(b)(1).
100.   IRS Reg. §31.6413(a)-1(b)(2).

**Making adjustments on Form 941.**[101] If an employer has properly repaid overwithheld amounts to employees, it can claim a credit against taxes due by making an adjustment on Form 941. For federal income tax repayments, the adjustment can be made on any Form 941 filed for the same calendar year the error occurred and was discovered. For social security or Medicare tax repayments, the adjustment must be made no later than the due date for the Form 941 filed for the quarter after the quarter during which the error was discovered. The adjustment is made on either Line 7d or Line 7e of Form 941 depending on the tax involved.

There is one situation where an employer can make an adjustment for incorrect federal income tax withholding in an earlier year. That is where the error is purely administrative and does not change the amount actually withheld from the employee's wages. This can occur if the correct amount is withheld from wages but incorrectly reported on Form 941 because of a mathematical or transposition error.

**Explaining the adjustment on Form 941c.**[102] Once an adjustment is made on Form 941 for under-withheld or overwithheld taxes, the employer must also complete and attach Form 941c, *Statement to Correct Information* (see Appendix page A-185), or a statement that includes similar information. This procedure also applies to adjustments made on Forms 943, 944, and 945. (Form 941c should not be filed by itself.) The purpose of Form 941c is to explain the nature of the adjustment and show the erroneous and corrected amounts of tax withheld. If a written statement is attached instead of Form 941c, it must include:

- the circumstances of the error;

- the ending date of the quarter in which the error was made;

- the amount of the error;

- the date the error was discovered;

- how the employer and employees handled the underwithholding or overwithholding of federal income tax;

- whether any social security or Medicare overwithholding was repaid or the employee gave written consent to any refund or credit claimed by the employer; and

- if the social security or Medicare tax overwithholding occurred in an earlier year, a statement that the employee has stated in writing that no claim of credit or refund has been or will be made regarding the overwithholding.

**Employer refunds and credits.** In those situations where an employer withholds the correct amount of federal income, social security, and Medicare taxes from employees' wages but erroneously overpays that amount, the employer can choose between claiming a credit or a refund of the amount overpaid. This option is not available where the overpayment is due to the employer's overwithholding of taxes.

 **TIME LIMITATION ON CLAIM**[103] Any claim an employer makes for a credit or refund of over-paid social security, Medicare, or FUTA taxes must be filed within three years of the date the return was filed containing the overpayment or within two years of the date of the overpayment, whichever is later. Forms 941 filed for any quarter within a calendar year are considered filed as of April 15 of the following year, and taxes paid with such forms are considered paid as of the same date.

A credit for such a tax overpayment is taken as a deduction on Form 941, which must be accompanied by Form 941c or a similar statement explaining the reason for the credit.[104] A refund of a tax overpayment

---

101.  IRS Reg. §31.6402(a)-2; §31.6413(a)-2; Form 941 Instructions.
102.  IRS Reg. §31.6402(a)-2(a)(2); §31.6413(a)-2(b); Form 941 Instructions.
103.  IRC §6511(a); §6513(c); IRS Reg. §301.6511(a)-1; §301.6513-1(c).
104.  IRS Reg. §31.6402(a)-2(a).

(including overpaid FUTA taxes) is claimed on Form 843, *Claim for Refund and Request for Abatement (see Appendix page* A-143), which provides space for the employer to explain the reason for the refund.[105]

If the credit or refund involves overpayment of the employee share of social security or Medicare tax, the employer must include a statement that the employee has consented in writing to the credit or refund or a statement that the tax has been repaid to the employee. The actual written consent or receipt (e.g., a canceled check) showing the date and amount of payment must be kept by the employer in its records. If the social security or Medicare tax was collected in a prior calendar year, the employer must also include a statement that it has obtained the employee's written acknowledgement that no claim for a credit or refund of the tax has been or will be filed by the employee. The employer must keep the employee's written acknowledgement in its records.[106]

The IRS has concluded that a check endorsement stipulation attached to the refund check sent to the employee does not meet this requirement.[107] The stipulation included the required language stating that the employee had not and would not seek a refund or credit for the overpaid amounts, that the employee was not self-employed during the years at issue, that the employee had not received a social security tax refund because he worked for more than one employer and his wages exceeded the wage base for the year, and that the employee acknowledged the stipulation under penalties of perjury. However, the IRS said the employer would have only a signature on a cancelled check and that "a strong possibility exists that the employee [would endorse] the check without reading the statement." The IRS said it is imperative that the certifications and the signature appear "in close proximity" in one document.

The IRS also rejected an endorsement stipulation placed directly on the back of the check. The IRS noted that the endorsement stipulation on the back of the check – abbreviated because of space limitations – would not contain all of the required language or a written declaration that it was executed under penalties of perjury.

*No expedited refund process available.*[108] There is no expedited process for refunding excess deposits of withheld employment taxes. The employer must wait until the quarter is over and then file a Form 941c along with Form 941 (seeking a credit) or 843 (seeking a refund) unless:

- a return or reversal can be made under the ACH rules for deposits made using EFTPS, or

- the error results in a significant hardship, in which case the employer should contact the IRS for relief at 800-829-1040 or file Form 911, *Application for Taxpayer Assistance Order*, with the Taxpayer Advocate.

## 8.7 Penalties for Late Reporting and Paying Tax

When an employer is late filing its employment tax returns (Forms 941, 943, etc.), not only must the tax that is actually owed with the return be paid, but there are additional penalties imposed by the IRS. Following is a discussion of those penalties. (See Section 8.2-3 for a discussion of the penalties for making late or improper deposits of withheld taxes.)

**Late filing of employment tax returns.**[109] Unless an employer has reasonable cause and is not guilty of willful neglect, late filing of Form 941 or other employment tax returns results in an "addition to tax," the amount of which depends on how late the return is filed. The amount is 5% of the amount of tax required to be shown on the return (reduced by any timely deposits and credits) for each month or fraction of a month that the return is late, up to a maximum of 25% (15% per month up to a maximum of 75% of the unpaid tax if the late filing is fraudulent).

---

105.   IRS Reg. §301.6402-2(c).
106.   IRS Reg. §31.6402(a)-2(a)(2).
107.   FSA 200044001, 3-3-00.
108.   ILM 200152045, 11-15-01.
109.   IRC §6651; ILM 200543058, 9-28-05.

**Failure to pay employment taxes.** Unless there is reasonable cause and no willful neglect, late payment of tax owed as shown on an employment tax return (e.g., Form 941, 943, 944) results in an "addition to tax," the amount of which depends on how late the payment is made. The amounts are:

- 0.5% of any unpaid tax shown on the return (after accounting for credits) for each month or fraction of a month that the payment is late (based on the due date of the return without regard to extensions of time for filing), up to a maximum of 25%;

- an additional 0.5% per month of any unpaid tax that is not shown on the return but for which the IRS has issued a notice and demand, if the tax is not paid within 21 calendar days of the notice and demand (10 business days if the amount is at least $100,000) up to a maximum of 25% (beginning at the end of the 21-day or 10-day period).

These penalties increase to 1% of the unpaid tax for each month beginning:

- 10 days after the day the employer is notified by the IRS that it intends to levy on (attach) the employer's assets; or

- on the day after the day the employer is notified by the IRS that it demands immediate payment and will immediately levy on the employer's assets because it feels the tax may be otherwise uncollectible.

In addition, if any portion of a tax underpayment is due to the employer's negligence or disregard of IRS regulations, the employer will be assessed a penalty of 20% of the amount not paid that is attributable to the negligence or disregard.[110] If any portion of the tax is not paid because of fraud, a penalty of 75% of the underpayment due to fraud will be assessed.[111] (Both penalties cannot be assessed on the same underpayment.)

**Failure to file and pay.**[112] In any month where an employer is subject to additions to tax both for a failure to file an employment tax return and a failure to pay tax, the addition for failure to file is reduced by 0.5% of the unpaid tax.

**Reasonable cause.**[113] An employer wishing to avoid the additional taxes for late filings or tax payments must make an affirmative statement under penalty of perjury setting forth all the facts supporting the claim of reasonable cause for its failure. If the facts show that the employer "exercised ordinary business care and prudence," and still could not file the employment tax return on time, then reasonable cause exists and no addition to tax will be assessed. Reasonable cause also exists if the employer exercised ordinary business care and prudence and still was unable to pay the taxes owed or would suffer undue hardship in doing so. The date for determining whether reasonable cause excused the failure to pay employment taxes not shown on the return is the end of the 21-day or 10-day period after the IRS issues a notice and demand for payment.

**Interest.**[114] Any withheld federal income, social security, or Medicare tax that remains unpaid by the last date allowed for payment (determined without regard to any extension of the time for payment) accumulates interest from that date until the date paid at the federal short term rate plus 3%. Interest on additions to tax that are assessed for failure to file Form 941 on time accumulates from the due date of the return (including any extensions) to the date of payment of the addition to tax. If the IRS makes a notice and demand for payment of the addition to tax, and the employer makes the payment within 21 calendar days of the notice and demand (10 business days if the amount is at least $100,000), interest stops accumulating on the date the notice and demand for payment is made.

---

110.   IRC §6662; IRS Reg. §1.6662-2; §1.6662-3.
111.   IRC §6663.
112.   IRC §6651(c).
113.   IRS Reg. §301.6651-1(c); ILM 200543058, 9-28-05.
114.   IRC §6601; IRS Reg. §301.6601-1; IRS Prop. Reg. §301.6601-1.

Interest on penalties assessed for late deposits or payment of withheld federal income, social security, or Medicare tax accumulates only if the penalty is not paid within 21 calendar days from the date of an IRS notice and demand for payment of the penalty (10 business days if the amount of the penalty is at least $100,000), and the interest is imposed only from the date of the notice and demand to the date of payment.

**Criminal penalties.** Additions to tax, civil penalties, and interest are not the only penalties employers face when employment taxes are not paid and returns are not filed. Certain actions can also bring criminal fines and imprisonment. They include:

- for the willful failure to file a return, pay tax, or keep records, a fine of up to $25,000 ($100,000 for corporations) and/or imprisonment for up to one year;[115]

- for the willful delivery to the IRS of a tax return known to be fraudulent, a fine of up to $10,000 ($50,000 for corporations) and/or imprisonment for up to one year;[116]

- for the willful attempt to evade the payment of any tax, a fine of up to $100,000 ($500,000 for corporations) and/or imprisonment for up to five years;[117]

- for signing any return, statement, or other document under the penalty of perjury without believing it to be true, a fine of up to $100,000 ($500,000 for corporations) and/or imprisonment for up to three years.[118]

**Penalty and interest notices have to be detailed**. As part of the IRS Restructuring and Reform Act of 1998, IRS penalty and interest notices have to include some details as to how they were determined. All penalty notices issued after June 30, 2003, must include the name of the penalty, the IRC section under which it is imposed, and a computation of the penalty. The initial penalty assessment must also be personally approved in writing by the supervisor of the person making the assessment. Any notice that includes an interest component after June 30, 2003 must include the IRC section under which interest is imposed and a calculation of the interest. For penalty and interest notices issued after June 30, 2001, and before July 1, 2003, all the IRS has to do is include a phone number that the employer can call to request a copy of their tax assessment and payment history related to the penalty and/or the interest amounts.[119]

# 8.8 Information Reporting for Employees—Form W-2

Once an employer has paid wages to and withheld taxes from its employees during a calendar year, it must then report to the employees the amounts paid and withheld so the employees can complete their personal income tax returns and pay any amount owed to the IRS. These amounts must also be reported to the Social Security Administration so employees' earnings and benefit accounts can be properly credited. The SSA also shares employees' earnings and tax information with the IRS.

The employer accomplishes this with Form W-2, *Wage and Tax Statement* (see Appendix page A-60).[120] Different parts of this six-part form are sent to the employee, the Social Security Administration, and state and local taxing agencies, with one part kept by the employer for its records. This section will explain the rules governing the completion, reporting deadlines, production, and other aspects of Form W-2.

---

115. IRC §7203.
116. IRC §7207.
117. IRC §7201.
118. IRC §7206(1).
119. IRC §6631; §6751.
120. IRC §6051; IRS Reg. §31.6051-1(a).

# 8.8-1 Employers Must Provide W-2s

The first issue that must be determined is whether a Form W-2 must be provided at all. This question is answered by the Internal Revenue Code, which requires a Form W-2 to be provided by any employer engaged in a trade or business that pays compensation to an employee for work performed, even if the employee is not paid in cash (there is no minimum amount that triggers reporting).[121] A Form W-2 is also required if the employer withheld federal income tax from the employee or would have done so if the employee had claimed no more than one withholding allowance. A separate IRC section also requires Form W-2 reporting for all wages, as defined for federal income tax withholding purposes, and for all noncash compensation provided to an employee that is not subject to withholding, if the total of the wages and the noncash compensation is at least $600 in a calendar year.[122]

**Furnishing W-2s after a merger or consolidation.**[123] When there has been a merger or consolidation of two employers and one surviving corporation, the survivor is considered to be the same employer as the acquired company. Therefore, it must provide Forms W-2 to all the employees who worked for the absorbed company and the survivor during the calendar year of the merger or consolidation which contain the wages paid by both companies. This reporting requirement will generally lead to differences between the amounts reported on the companies' Forms 941 and W-2. Each company should explain such discrepancies between their Forms 941 and W-2 by filing Schedule D (Form 941), *Report of Discrepancies Caused by Acquisitions, Statutory Mergers, or Consolidations* (see Appendix page A-179). For more information on Schedule D, see Section 8.3-1.

**Successorship options.**[124] Where one company acquires another's business property (either the entire property or a separate business unit) and retains employees who worked for the acquired company, there are two options the companies can use in determining which is responsible for providing W-2 forms to their employees and the government. They include:

*Standard procedure.* In most instances, the predecessor makes a final payment of wages to its employees and reports the wages and taxes withheld on Form W-2 (see Section 8.8-2 for details on when the predecessor must file the Forms W-2). The successor reports only the wages and taxes it pays and withholds. Employee Withholding Allowance Certificates (W-4 forms) used by the predecessor must be kept in its files for four years after the final wage payment, and new Forms W-4 must be provided to the successor. The same retention rules apply to Forms W-5, *Earned Income Credit Advance Payment Certificate* (see Appendix page A-99).

*Alternate procedure.* In the alternative, the successor and predecessor can agree that, for employees continuing their employment with the successor, the successor will provide Forms W-2 that include wages paid and taxes withheld by both parties during the year of the acquisition. Therefore, the predecessor must provide W-2 forms only for employees who did not work for the successor after the acquisition.

Use of this procedure will mean both the predecessor and the successor will have different wage and tax amount totals for their Forms 941 than for their Forms W-2. Each company should explain the discrepancies between their Forms 941 and W-2 by filing Schedule D (Form 941), *Report of Discrepancies Caused by Acquisitions, Statutory Mergers, or Consolidations* (see Appendix page A-179). For more information on Schedule D, see Section 8.3-1.

The predecessor must transfer to the successor all current Forms W-4 that were provided to the predecessor by the employees who are working for the successor, along with any IRS "lock-in" letters for such employees. The successor must use those Forms W-4 to determine the proper amount of federal income tax withholding until the employee submits a revised form. If Forms W-4 were submitted to the predecessor during the quarter of the acquisition or the preceding quarter that must be provided to the IRS (see Section 6.3-1), the successor assumes that responsibility for the acquired employees.

---

121. IRC §6051(a).
122. IRC §6041(a); IRS Reg. §1.6041-2(a)(1).
123. Rev. Rul. 62-60, 1962-1 CB 186; Rev. Proc. 2004-53, 2004-34 IRB 320.
124. Rev. Proc. 2004-53, 2004-34 IRB 320.

If the predecessor and successor maintain compatible automated Form W-4 systems, the predecessor may transfer the Forms W-4 of the acquired employees electronically. Another option is for the successor to acquire the predecessor's system. If these options do not apply, the acquired employees must provide the successor with a new Form W-4, either electronically or on paper according to the successor's system. The predecessor must transfer to the successor all current Forms W-5 that were provided by the acquired employees. The rules governing the transfer of electronic Forms W-5 are the same as those for the electronic Form W-4

**Bankruptcy filing by employee does not change W-2 requirement.** The Bankruptcy Abuse Prevention and Consumer Protection Act of 2005 added Section 1115 to the Bankruptcy Code. Under this section, the bankruptcy estate, rather than the debtor, generally must include in its gross income the debtor's gross earnings (i.e., wages and other compensation) from his or her performance of services after the commencement of the case ("post-petition services").[125]

This rule is subject to an exception where a Chapter 11 case is converted to a Chapter 7 or a Chapter 13 case. In the case of such a conversion, earnings from post-conversion services are taxed to the debtor rather than the bankruptcy estate.

As a result of the enactment of Section 1115, post-petition wages earned by a debtor are generally treated for income tax purposes as gross income of the estate, rather than the debtor. The reporting and withholding obligations of a debtor's employer, however, have not changed. With respect to the wages of a Chapter 11 debtor, the employer should continue to reflect such wages and the taxes withheld on a Form W-2 issued to the debtor under the debtor's name and social security number.[126]

**Reporting payments to election workers**. If an election worker receives less than $600 in a year, no reporting is required on Form W-2 unless social security and Medicare taxes were withheld under a Section 218 agreement (see Section 6.8). If the election worker earns $600 or more, the earnings must be reported in Box 1 of Form W-2. If the election worker earns $1,400 or more in 2008 (adjusted annually for inflation to the next lowest multiple of $100), all earnings must also be reported in Boxes 3 and 5 as social security and Medicare wages, respectively.

**Special problems in providing Forms W-2.** Despite employers' best efforts, the delivery of Forms W-2 to their employees does not always run smoothly, and there are several problems that occur routinely.

*Undeliverable Forms W-2.*[127] Where an employer has been unable, after a reasonable effort, to deliver the employee's copies of Form W-2, it must keep those copies for four years. The copies can be discarded if a revised W-2 form is sent to a new address. Mailing the Form W-2 to an employee's last known address is considered a reasonable effort to make delivery.

*Reissued Forms W-2.*[128] If an employee loses a Form W-2 or it is destroyed, the employer can issue a new copy to the employee and should write "Reissued Statement" on it unless the form is provided to the employee electronically. The employer should not send Copy A of the form to the SSA, however, since that information had already been sent when the first set of forms were produced.

 **CONSIDER CHARGING FOR THOSE EXTRA W-2s** While employers cannot charge employees for providing them with an original or a corrected Form W-2, they can charge employees for providing them with additional copies of a form that has been lost or destroyed.[129] There are no penalties under the IRC for refusing to provide an additional copy of Form W-2, although refusing to do so may cause unwanted customer service problems within an organization.

---

125.   P.L. 109-8, §321; 11 USC §1115(a)(2).
126.   Notice 2006-83, 2006-40 IRB 596.
127.   IRS Reg. §31.6001-1(e)(2); §31.6051-1(a)(3).
128.   Form W-2 Instructions.
129.   Form W-2 instructions.

*Corrected Forms W-2.*[130] When an error is made on an employee's Form W-2, the method of correction depends on when the correction is made. If Copy A of the form has not yet been sent to the SSA, the employer merely has to provide the employee with corrected copies of the Form W-2 with "CORRECTED" written on them, check the "Void" box on the original Copy A, and send the new Copy A, with nothing extra written on it, to the SSA. If the "Void" Form W-2 is on a page with a correct W-2, send the entire page to SSA. The "Void" form will not be processed. If Copy A has already been filed with the SSA, the employer must use the current edition of Form W-2c, *Corrected Wage and Tax Statement* (see Appendix page A-84), to correct the error. See Section 8.10 for more details on Form W-2c.

If the printer skips a line when the employer prints its Forms W-2 and this results in information falling out of the designated boxes, the forms must be reprinted. If the information is not properly displayed, the W-2 forms cannot be processed by the SSA.

*Employee address corrections.* If an employer files Form W-2, Copy A with the SSA showing an incorrect employee address but all other information on the form is correct, a Form W-2c should not be filed with the SSA merely to correct the address. If the address was incorrect on the employee's copies of the Form W-2, the employer must do one of the following:

- Issue a new Form W-2 with correct information, and indicate "Reissued Statement" on the new copies unless they are sent electronically. Do not send Copy A to the SSA.

- Issue a Form W-2c to the employee showing the correct address in Box f. Do not send Copy A to the SSA.

- Mail the Form W-2 with the incorrect address to the employee in an envelope showing the correct address, or otherwise deliver it to the employee.

*Multiple Forms W-2.* Throughout the years, the IRS has issued several rulings that outline the circumstances under which it is acceptable or not acceptable to issue multiple Forms W-2 to an employee reporting different types of payments. Employers that wish to issue multiple W-2 forms should examine the list closely.

Issuing multiple Forms W-2 is acceptable when:[131]

- employers with facilities in several states and a decentralized payroll system that makes payments from each location have a longstanding practice of providing multiple W-2 forms to employees working in more than one location;

- employers have used separate payrolls and provided multiple W-2 forms in prior years for special types of compensation, such as executive bonuses and taxable group-term life insurance;

- employers have payroll systems that have difficulty combining nontaxable, reportable "other compensation" along with wages and tips;

- employers filing on paper must report more than four items in Box 12 of Form W-2 (only the extra items in Box 12 will be included on the second W-2 form);

- employers include 100% of the value of an employee's use of a company-provided vehicle in the employee's income; and

- employers encounter last-minute third-party sick pay adjustments that would increase wages reported on previously issued Forms W-2 (if there are 250 or more separate W-2 forms, they must be filed electronically).

---

130.    IRS Reg. §31.6051-1(c); Form W-2 instructions.
131.    Rev. Rul. 70-158, 1970-1 CB 267; Rev Rul 70-579, 1970-2 CB 288; Form W-2 Instructions.

# 8.8-2  When and Where to Furnish Form W-2

As mentioned earlier, Form W-2 consists of as many as six parts, each of which must be completed and provided to certain parties at a specified time.

**Copy A.** Copy A of Form W-2, or electronic media containing Copy A if the employer is required to file in this manner, is an information return and must be sent to the Social Security Administration (not the employee or the IRS).[132]  For employers filing Copy A on paper, the due date is the last day of February after the year to which the form applies (e.g., March 2, 2009 for calendar year 2008 Copy A because February 28 is a Saturday).  For employers filing Copy A information electronically, the due date is March 31 after the year to which the form applies (e.g., March 31, 2009 for calendar year 2008).  The due date for electronically filed Form W-2 information was extended by the IRS Restructuring and Reform Act of 1998.[133]  See section 8.9 for details on annual reconciliation Form W-3, which must be sent with an employer's Forms W-2 (only those who file on paper).

**Where to file.**  All paper filers must send paper Copies A, as well as Form W-3, to the same location:

> Social Security Administration
> Data Operations Center
> Wilkes-Barre, PA 18769-0001

However, employers who send the forms by certified mail must use a ZIP code of 18769-0002.  Employers who use a carrier other than the U.S. Postal Service (i.e., a private delivery service) send Copies A and Form W-3 to:

> Social Security Administration
> Data Operations Center
> Attn: W-2 Process
> 1150 East Mountain Drive
> Wilkes-Barre, PA 18702-7997.

**Copies B, C, and 2.**  These are the employee's copies of Form W-2 (known as information statements) and must be sent to the employee by January 31 of the year after the year to which the form relates (e.g., by February 2, 2009, for 2008 Forms W-2 because January 31 is a Saturday).[134]  Copy B is filed by the employee with the employee's federal income tax return, Copy 2 must be filed with the employee's state or local income tax return, and Copy C is for the employee's records.  While several states allow Copy 2 to be provided to the employee after January 31 (February 15 for Nebraska, New Jersey, New York, and West Virginia), compliance with the federal requirement will keep the employer in compliance with any state requirements.

*Employees who terminate before year-end.*  If an employee leaves employment (voluntarily or involuntarily) before the end of a calendar year, there are two possibilities:

1.  the employer can wait until the next January 31 to send Form W-2 to the ex-employee, or

2.  if the employee asks for a Form W-2 in writing before the end of the year, the employer must send it within 30 days of the request.

Several states have shorter periods for providing Copy 2 to an employee who has been terminated. Arizona requires that Copy 2 be provided within 15 days of separation from employment. The following states require that Copy 2 be provided immediately upon termination or final payment of wages: Arkansas, California, District of Columbia, Virginia, West Virginia, and Wisconsin.

---

132.  IRS Reg. §31.6071(a)-1(a)(3)(ii).
133.  IRC §6071(b); IRS Reg. §31.6071(a)-1(a)(3)(i).
134.  IRC §6051(a).

**Employers can provide employees' copies of Form W-2 electronically.** Employers can provide employees their copies of Form W-2 by giving the forms to the employees in person, mailing the forms to their homes, or making them available electronically on a company intranet, an Internet website, or as an e-mail attachment. Employers that want to provide Forms W-2 to their employees electronically must comply with various requirements governing consent, disclosure, format, posting, notice, and retention, as specified in regulations issued by the IRS.[135]

*Consent.* An employee must have affirmatively consented to receive the Form W-2 electronically and must not have withdrawn that consent before the form is furnished. The consent must be made electronically in a manner that reasonably demonstrates that the employee can access the W-2 in the electronic format in which it will be provided. As an alternative, the consent may be made in a different manner (e.g., in an e-mail or a paper document) if it is confirmed electronically in the manner in which an electronic consent is provided.

The consent requirement is not met if the employee withdraws the consent and the withdrawal takes effect before the Form W-2 is provided to the employee. The employer may provide that a withdrawal of consent takes effect either on the date it is received by the employer or on a later date. The employer can also provide that a request for a paper Form W-2 will be treated as a withdrawal of consent.

If a change in the employer's computer hardware or software needed to access the Form W-2 creates a material risk that the employee will not be able to access the Form W-2, the employer must, before changing the hardware or software, notify the employee. The notice must describe the revised hardware and software required to access the Form W-2 and inform the employee that a new consent to receive the Form W-2 in the revised electronic format must be provided to the employer. After implementing the hardware or software changes, the employer must obtain a new consent or confirmation of consent from the employee to receive the Form W-2 electronically.

*Example 1:* Matt's Marketing, Inc. sends employee Eddie an e-mail stating that Eddie may consent to receive Form W-2 electronically on a website rather than on paper. The e-mail contains an attachment instructing Eddie how to consent to receive Form W-2 electronically. The e-mail attachment uses the same electronic format that Matt's Marketing will use for its electronically furnished Forms W-2. Eddie opens the attachment, reads the instructions, and submits the consent in the manner provided in the instructions. Eddie has consented to receive his Form W-2 electronically in a manner consistent with the regulations.

*Example 2:* Pete's Produce Co. sends employee Diane a letter stating that Diane may consent to receive Form W-2 electronically on a website rather than on paper. The letter contains instructions explaining how to consent to receive Form W-2 electronically by accessing the website, downloading the consent document, completing the consent document, and e-mailing the completed consent document back to Pete's Produce. The consent document on the website uses the same electronic format that Pete's Produce will use for the electronic Form W-2. Diane reads the instructions and submits the consent in the manner provided in the instructions. Diane has consented to receive her Form W-2 electronically in a manner consistent with the regulations.

*Example 3:* Home Supplies, Inc. posts a notice on its website stating that employee Juan may receive Form W-2 electronically rather than on paper. The website contains instructions on how Juan may access a secure Web page and consent to receive his Form W-2 electronically. By accessing the secure Web page and giving consent, Juan has consented to receive his Form W-2 in a manner consistent with the regulations.

*Paper Forms W-2 provided after consent is withdrawn.* If an employee withdraws consent to receive Form W-2 electronically and the withdrawal takes effect before the Form W-2 is provided electronically, a paper Form W-2 must be provided to the employee. A paper Form W-2 provided after the January 31 due date will be considered timely if it is provided within 30 days after the employer receives the withdrawal of consent.

---

135. IRS Reg. §31.6051-1(j)(1)-(7); IRS Publication 15-A, Employer's Supplemental Tax Guide.

**ALL W-2s CAN BE PUT ON WEBSITE**  Employers can store all their Forms W-2 on their website, even for those employees who do not consent to receive their Form W-2 that way. The employees who do not give consent must also be sent paper Forms W-2.

*Required disclosures.*  Prior to or at the time an employee consents to receive Form W-2 electronically, the employer must provide a clear and conspicuous statement to the employee containing the following disclosures:

- that the Form W-2 will be furnished on paper if the employee does not consent to receive it electronically;
- the scope and duration of the consent, such as whether it applies to all Forms W-2 until consent is withdrawn or just to the Form W-2 furnished on the next January 31;
- any procedures for obtaining a paper copy of Form W-2 after providing consent to receive it electronically and whether a request for a paper Form W-2 will be treated as a withdrawl of consent;
- that the employee may withdraw consent at any time on 30 days' notice by writing (electronically or on paper) to the contact person or department named in the disclosure statement and that the employer will confirm the withdrawal of consent in writing (electronically or on paper);
- the date on which a withdrawal of consent takes effect;
- the conditions under which the employer will stop providing electronic Forms W-2 to the employee (e.g., the employee's termination);
- the procedures for updating the information needed by the employer to contact the employee, and any changes in the employer's contact information;
- a description of the hardware and software required to access, print, and retain the Form W-2, and the date the Form W-2 will no longer be available on the website; and
- that the Form W-2 may be required to be printed and attached to a federal, state, or local income tax return.

*Format.*  The electronic version of a Form W-2 furnished to an employee must contain all required information and comply with applicable revenue procedures on substitute statements (see Section 8.8-4).

*Posting.*  The employer must post the Forms W-2 on a website accessible to employees or attach the form to an e-mail that is sent to employees on or before January 31 of the year following the calendar year to which the W-2s relate.

*Notice.*  The employer must notify an employee that the Form W-2 is posted on a website on or before January 31 of the year following the calendar year to which the form relates. The notice may be delivered by mail, e-mail, or in person, and must provide instructions to the employee on how to access and print the W-2. The notice must include the following statement in capital letters: "IMPORTANT TAX RETURN DOCUMENT AVAILABLE." If the notice is provided by e-mail, this language must be on the subject line of the e-mail.

If an e-mail notice is returned as undeliverable, and the correct e-mail address cannot be obtained, then the employer must provide the notice by mail or in person within 30 days after the e-mail notice is returned. If the employer has to correct an electronic Form W-2 with a Form W-2c, the Form W-2c must be provided electronically as well. If the employer posts Forms W-2c on a website, the employer must notify the employees of that posting by mail, e-mail, or in person within 30 days after it is made. The Form W-2c or the notice of posting must be furnished by mail or in person if an e-mail notice of the website posting of the Form W-2 or W-2c was returned as undeliverable and the employee has not provided a new e-mail address..

*Retention.*  The employer must maintain access to the Forms W-2 on the website through October 15 of the year following the calendar year to which they relate (or the next business day if October 15 is a Saturday, Sunday, or holiday). In addition, the employer must maintain access to Forms W-2c that are posted on the website through October 15 of the year following the calendar year to which the forms relate or for 90 days after that posting, whichever is later.

**W-2s MAY BE PROVIDED AS E-MAIL ATTACHMENTS**  Even though the regulations speak only of making electronic Forms W-2 available on a website (either on a company intranet or the Internet), IRS personnel have indicated that the absence of language specifically allowing Forms W-2 to be provided as e-mail attachments does not mean that the forms cannot be provided in that manner.

**Employers going out of business face accelerated W-2 due dates**. Employers that cease paying wages face accelerated deadlines for providing Forms W-2 to the SSA and their employees.  Such employers are required to file their final Form 941 by the end of the month following the end of the quarter during which they went out of business (see Section 8.3-2).  They have to provide Copies B, C, and 2 of Form W-2 to their employees by the same date.  Copy A of these Forms W-2, along with the transmittal document for paper filers (Form W-3) must be sent to the SSA by the end of the second month following the end of the quarter during which the employer went out of business.[136]  For information on automatic extensions of these deadlines for electronic filers, see the discussion following.

> *Example*: Acme Co. ceases operations and pays final wages on September 20, 2008.  Acme's final Form 941 is due to the IRS on October 31, 2008, the last day of the month following the end of the third quarter (September 30, 2008).  Acme must also provide Copies B, C, and 2 of Form W-2 to its former employees by October 31, 2008.  It must provide Copy A of the Forms W-2, along with Form W-3, if applicable, to the SSA by December 1, 2008.

*Different rules for monthly filers*.  Employers that are required to file monthly tax returns on Form 941-M, *Employer's Monthly Federal Tax Return* (see Section 8.5-1), must file their final return by the 15th of the calendar month following the end of the month during which they cease paying wages.  Such employers must provide W-2 forms to their employees by the end of the month during which the final Form 941-M is due.  The employer must provide Forms W-2 and Form W-3 or an electronic file to the SSA by the end of the second calendar month after the end of the month for which the final return is made.

*What about terminated employees?*  The accelerated due dates do not affect the right of terminated employees to receive a Form W-2 by the later of 30 days after the employee requests one in writing or 30 days after the last payment of wages.  IRS regulations provide that terminated employees who worked for an employer that ceased operations will receive their W-2 forms no later than the end of the month during which the employer's final form 941 or 941-M is due.

*Successorship and merger situations*.  When a successor employer acquires substantially all or a separate unit of a business and employs the predecessor's employees, the "standard procedure" for wage reporting is that each employer reports the wages it paid employees on Form W-2 (see Section 8.8-1).  When this procedure is used, the predecessor employer is covered by the accelerated Form W-2 deadlines if it ceases paying wages.  If the "alternate procedure" is used, whereby the successor assumes the Form W-2 filing responsibility for all the predecessor's employees that the successor continues to employ, and the predecessor ceases paying wages, the predecessor is covered by the accelerated Form W-2 deadlines, but only for the employees who are not hired by the successor.  The successor is not covered by the accelerated deadlines unless it ceases paying wages later in the year.  Where a final Form 941 is not filed because a merger does not involve the cessation of business operations but only a change in corporate or business form, the expedited filing requirements do not apply.

*Not applicable to domestic, farm, or very small employers*.  The expedited filing requirements do not apply to employers filing Form 944 or to employers with respect to their domestic employees working in the employer's private home, or to their agricultural employees, since such filings are made on an annual basis (see Sections 8.5-3 — 8.5-5).

*Employers with employees in U.S. possessions*.  The accelerated due dates do apply to employers with employees in U.S. possessions and territories.  Such employers file variations of Forms 941, W-2, and W-3, and are subject to the filing requirements for those forms (see Section 8.5-2).

---

136.    IRS Reg. §31.6051-1(d)(1)(ii); §31.6071(a)-1(a)(3)(ii).

**Copy 1.** Copy 1 must be sent to the applicable state and/or local tax agencies, according to deadlines set forth by each state, along with a state annual reconciliation return, the equivalent of Form W-3 (see Section 8.9). Employers must be careful, since the federal deadline for sending Copy A and Form W-3 to the SSA (last day of February) is later than several state deadlines. Also, some states do not require the filing of Form W-2 or an annual reconciliation.

The following states require that Copy 1 and an annual reconciliation return be sent to the state by January 31: California (annual reconciliation return only), District of Columbia, Idaho, Kentucky, Mississippi (Copy 1 by Feb. 28 if on magnetic media), Pennsylvania, and Wisconsin. Nebraska requires that Copy 1 be provided by March 15. The deadline for electronically filed returns is March 31 in Colorado (no annual reconciliation required), Idaho, Iowa and Utah (the last day of February or February 28 for all others).

**Copy D.** The employer retains Copy D for its own records.

**Filing extensions.**[137] If an employer needs an extension of the date for filing Copy A on paper or electronically with the SSA, it should complete and file Form 8809, *Application for Extension of Time to File Information Returns* (see Appendix page A-393) before the original due date. If the request for extension involves more than 10 employers, the IRS encourages filers to submit the request on magnetic media (tape, cartridge, or diskette) or electronically. Magnetic media or electronic filing is required if the request involves more than 50 employers. See IRS Publication 1220, *Specifications for Filing Forms 1098, 1099, 5498 and W-2G Electronically or Magnetically*, for more information. The first 30-day extension is automatic, and the employer does not have to sign the Form 8809 or explain the reason for requesting the extension. The employer can request a second 30-day extension by sending another Form 8809 to the IRS during the first extension period with a signature and an explanation of the reason for the request.

Employers can also request an extension of the due date for providing Forms W-2 to employees by sending a letter to: IRS-Enterprise Computing Center—Martinsburg, Information Reporting Program, Attn: Extension of Time Coordinator, 240 Murall Drive, Kearneysville, WV 25430 on or before the date the forms must be provided to employees. The letter must include:

- employer's name, address, and EIN;
- a statement that the request is being made for an extension to provide Forms W-2 to employees;
- brief statement of the reasons for the request; and
- the employer's signature or that of an authorized agent.

*Automatic extension of the accelerated deadlines for electronic filers going out of business.*[138] Employers that go out of business during the year face an accelerated deadline for providing Forms W-2 to their employees and filing them with the SSA (see the discussion earlier). But if such an employer is required to file its Forms W-2 electronically (see Section 8.14) or voluntarily filed them electronically during the previous year, the deadline for providing Forms W-2 to its employees is extended to the later of the expedited due date or October 31. The deadline for filing Forms W-2 with the SSA is extended to the later of the expedited due date or November 30. These extensions do not apply to the furnishing of a Form W-2 within 30 days to a terminated employee who requests it in writing.

**Saturdays, Sundays, and holidays.**[139] Where the due date for filing or providing Form W-2 copies falls on a Saturday, Sunday, or legal holiday, the due date is extended until the next business day.

# 8.8-3 Box-by-Box Instructions for Form W-2

Certain information must always be included on Form W-2, including:

- the employer's name, address, and EIN;

---

137. IRS Reg. §1.6081-8; §31.6051-1(d)(2); §31.6081(a)-1(a)(2)(i); Forms W-2, W-3, and 8809 Instructions.
138. Rev. Proc. 96-57, 1996-2 CB 389.
139. IRC §7503; IRS Reg. §301.7503-1.

- the employee's name, address, and SSN;
- the total amount of wages, tips, and other reportable compensation; and
- withheld federal income, social security, and Medicare taxes.

**General completion information**. All entries on Form W-2 should be typed in black ink in 12-point Courier font, if possible, since handwritten entries and other color inks hinder data entry processing, and should not be in script type, inverted font, italics, or dual case alpha characters. Entries in the boxes should not cross any of the vertical or horizontal lines that separate the boxes. Employers should not erase, white out, or strike over an entry. For information on how to present dollar entries, see Section 8.8-5. Paper Copies A of Form W-2 should be filed either alphabetically by employees' last names or numerically by employees' SSNs to help the SSA locate specific forms.

Employers should not staple or tape Form W-3 to the related Forms W-2 or the Forms W-2 to each other. The forms are machine-read, and staple holes or tears interfere with machine reading. Do not fold Forms W-2 and W-3. They should be sent in a flat mailing. Large numbers of Forms W-2 can be sent in separate packages. The employer's name and EIN must be shown on each package. Number them in order (1 of 4, 2 of 4, etc.) and put Form W-3 in package 1. Show the number of packages at the bottom of Form W-3 below the title. If the forms are mailed, they must be sent first class.

**Box-by-box 2008 Form W-2 instructions**. Here are instructions for completing each box of the 2008 Form W-2, which contain several minor changes from the 2007 version. See page 8-70 for a sample, filled-in 2008 Form W-2.

**Void.** This box should be checked only if the form is incorrect and is being corrected before Copy A has been filed with the SSA. The voided Copy A should not be sent to the SSA (unless it is on a page with a correct W-2), or with corrected employee copies being sent to the employee. Do not include any amounts shown on Void Forms W-2 in the totals on Form W-3.

**Box a—Employee's social security number.** Enter here the number shown on the employee's social security card. If the employee does not have an SSN, advise the employee to apply for one and enter "Applied for" in Box d if paper Forms W-2 are being filed with the SSA. If filing electronically, enter zeroes in the record layout. The employer may also enter zeroes on the paper copies of Form W-2 given to the employee. A Form W-2 or W-2c with the correct SSN must be filed when the employee receives a social security card and shows it to the employer, depending on whether Copy A has already been filed with the SSA.

 **REPORTING AN INCORRECT SSN** According to the SSA, if an employer learns that the SSN provided by an employee is incorrect but does not have any other SSN for the employee when it completes the employee's Form W-2, the employer should document any actions it has taken to try to obtain a correct SSN and report on Form W-2 the SSN provided by the employee.

**Box b—Employer identification number.** Enter here the employer identification number (EIN) assigned by the IRS and used on the employer's quarterly or annual employment tax returns (e.g., Forms 941, 943 or 944). Enter "Applied for" if the number has not yet been received.

**Box c—Employer's name, address, and ZIP code.** Enter here the employer's name, address, and ZIP code as they are shown on the quarterly or annual employment tax returns (e.g., Forms 941, 943 or 944).

*Rules for agents filing for employer.* Common pay agents that have filed an approved Form 2678, *Employer/Payer Appointment of Agent* (see Appendix page A-337), are governed by special Form W-2 reporting rules. Generally the agent should enter its name as the employer in Box c and file one Form W-2 for each employee. However, if the agent:

- is acting as an agent for 2 or more employers or is an employer itself and is acting as an agent for another employer; and
- pays social security wages in excess of the social security wage base ($102,000 in 2008) to an employee,

the agent must file separate Forms W-2 showing the wages paid by each employer to the employee. On each Form W-2, the agent should put its EIN in Box b. The employer's EIN should be shown in Box h of Form W-3 if the Forms W-2 relate to only one employer (other than the agent); if not, leave the box blank (see Section 8.9-2). In Box c of each Form W-2, the agent should enter the following:

> name of agent
> agent for (name of employer)
> address of agent

 **BE CAREFUL** These reporting procedures for agents do not apply in the common paymaster situation (see Section 6.7-4).

**Box d—Control number.** This is not a required field and is for the employer to use in identifying individual Forms W-2. Be careful that any entry here does not cross over into the form identification box.

**Box e—Employee's name.** Enter here the employee's name as shown on the employee's social security card—first name and middle initial (without a period) to the left of the vertical line, and last name to the right of the vertical line (use first initial instead of first name if the employee's name won't fit and ignore the vertical line). If the employee's name has changed, use the name on the original card until a new card is shown. On copy A of Forms W-2 filed with SSA, do not show titles or academic degrees at the beginning or end of the employee's name (e.g., Mr., Ms., Dr., MD or PhD). Also, do not put Jr., Sr. or a numerical suffix (e.g., III, IV) in the "Suff." box after the last name, unless it appears on the social security card. Although the suffix box ("Suff.") was added to the Form W-2 in 2006, the SSA still prefers that a suffix not be entered on Copy A. Electronic filers may enter a suffix in the optional suffix field in the record layout, and may place the suffix on paper copies of Forms W-2 provided to employees.

*Compound surnames can be tricky.* As compound surnames become more prevalent throughout the workforce, employers must take care in entering them on an employee's Form W-2. Parts of compound surnames may be connected with a hyphen, or separated with a blank space. Do not join the separate parts into a single name. Here are some examples:

- Susan B. Smith-Johnson should be entered in Box e as: Susan B Smith-Johnson, or Susan B Smith Johnson.
- Maria Elena Rodriguez de Perez should be entered in Box e as: Maria E Rodriguez-de-Perez, or Maria E Rodriguez de Perez.
- Juan Garcia y Vega (no middle name) should be entered in Box e as: Juan Garcia-y-Vega, or Juan Garcia y Vega.

Single-letter prefixes such as O or D must not be separated from the rest of the surname by a blank, but should be connected by an apostrophe or joined to the rest of the surname.

Third-party payers of sick pay filing third-party sick pay recap Forms W-2 must enter "Third-Party Sick Pay Recap" in place of the employee's name in Box e and should not enter the employee's SSN in Box d.

**Box f—Employee's address and ZIP code.** Enter here (can be close enough to the employee's name to allow mailing in a window envelope or as a self-mailer) the employee's last known address. If part of the address is missing (street address, state name, and/or ZIP code), make sure the W-2 form can be located quickly by creating an exception report, in case the form cannot be delivered. This box is combined with Box e on all copies except Copy A. For a foreign address, give the information in the following order: city, province or state, postal code, and the name of the country (no abbreviation for the country name).

**Box 1—Wages, tips, other compensation.** Report all wages, tips, and other reportable compensation actually or constructively paid (see Section 6.1) to the employee during the calendar year, even though they may have been earned during the previous year. Such amounts include:

- total wages, bonuses (including signing bonuses), prizes, and awards, but not elective deferrals unless made under a §501(c)(18)(D) plan;

- total noncash payments (including reportable fringe benefits);

- total reported tips (not allocated tips);

- taxable employee business expense reimbursements (see Section 3.3-5);

- cost of accident and health insurance premiums paid on behalf of 2% shareholder-employees by an S corporation;

- distributions from a nonqualified deferred compensation plan or a nongovernmental §457 plan;

- amounts included in income under a nonqualified deferred compensation plan because of §409A;

- the value of group-term life insurance in excess of $50,000;

- employee contributions to an Archer MSA or health savings account;

- employer contributions to an Archer MSA or health savings account to the extent they are includible in the employee's income;

- employer contributions for long-term care services to the extent the coverage is provided through a flexible spending arrangement;

- employee taxes paid by the employer;

- employer payments or reimbursements for nonqualified moving expenses;

- taxable benefits (cash) paid under a cafeteria plan;

- designated Roth contributions made to a §401(k) or §403(b) plan;

- cost of current insurance protection under a compensatory split dollar life insurance arrangement; and

- other reportable compensation from which no federal income tax was withheld (e.g., certain scholarships and fellowship grants, payments to statutory employees).

**Box 2—Federal income tax withheld.** Enter here the total federal income tax withheld from the employee's wages, including that withheld from third-party sick pay (unless the third party has reporting responsibilities). Also include the 20% excise tax withheld on excess golden parachute payments.

**Box 3—Social security wages**. Enter here the total wages paid subject to employee social security tax, but not including tips and allocated tips. This includes employee business expense reimbursements reported in Box 1 and elective deferrals to plans described in Box 12, Codes D, E, F, G and S (even though not included in Box 1). It also includes the value of group-term life insurance coverage over $50,000 that is taxable to former employees (see Section 3.3-1). Amounts deferred under a nonqualified deferred compensation plan and elective and nonelective deferrals to §457 plans must be included here if they are no longer subject to forfeiture and the services giving rise to them have been performed (see Section 4.6-10). Also include employee and nonexcludable employer contributions to an Archer MSA, employee contributions to a SIMPLE retirement account, designated Roth contributions, and adoption benefits. The total of Boxes 3 and 7 should not exceed $102,000 for 2008 (maximum social security wage base).

**Box 4—Social security tax withheld.** Enter here the total employee social security tax withheld (not the employer's share) or paid by the employer for the employee. Do not subtract any advance EIC payments. For 2008 the amount should not exceed $6,324.00.

**Box 5—Medicare wages and tips.** Enter here the total wages paid and reported tips subject to employee Medicare tax. This includes the same types of wages and tips subject to social security tax. However, there is no limit on the amount of wages and tips subject to Medicare tax.

**Box 6—Medicare tax withheld.** Enter here the total employee Medicare tax withheld or paid by the employer for the employee. Do not subtract any advance EIC payments. If the employer is a government (public sector) employer with employees paying only the Medicare tax (not social security), enter the Medicare tax in this box.

**Box 7—Social security tips.** Enter here the amount of tips reported by the employee to the employer during the year even if employee funds were insufficient to collect the social security tax on the tips. The total of Boxes 3 and 7 should not exceed $102,000 for 2008.

**Box 8—Allocated tips.** Large food or beverage establishments should enter here the amount of tips allocated to the employee (see Section 3.4-27). The amount should not be included in Box 1, 3, 5, or 7.

**Box 9—Advance EIC payment.** Enter here the amount paid to the employee as advance earned income credit.

**Box 10—Dependent care benefits.** Enter here the total amount of dependent care assistance benefits provided by the employer under IRC §129 (see Section 3.4-8). The amounts reported indicate amounts that were paid or incurred by the employer for the employee, including the fair market value of employer-provided or employer-sponsored day care facilities and employee pre-tax contributions under a §125 plan. An employer that has provided a grace period under its cafeteria plan for dependent care assistance may report the annual salary reduction amount elected by the employee. Any amount reported in Box 10 which exceeds $5,000 must also be entered in Boxes 1, 3, and 5.

**Box 11—Nonqualified plans**. The instructions for Box 11 have undergone significant changes recently, since there has been much confusion over the years regarding what the information is used for and who uses it. According to the Form W-2 instructions, the purpose of Box 11 is to help the SSA determine if any portion of the amounts reported in Box 1, 3, or 5 was earned in a year earlier than the year being reported. SSA uses this information to verify that they have properly applied the social security earnings test and paid the correct amount of benefits, since employees who are collecting social security benefits before they reach full retirement age face a reduction in benefits if they earn more than a certain amount in a year.

Generally, enter here the amount of distributions to an employee from a nonqualified deferred compensation plan or nongovernmental §457 plan. Put that amount in Box 1 as well. If no distributions were made to the employee, show the amount of any deferrals under a nonqualified deferrred compensation or any §457 plan (plus earnings) that became subject to social security and Medicare taxes during the year (but were for prior year services) because they were no longer subject to a substantial risk of forfeiture. The deferral amount should also be put in Boxes 3 and 5. If the deferrals that are included in Boxes 3 and 5 relate to current year services (services performed in the year to which the Form W-2 relates), *do not report them in Box 11.*

Also, if the employee received distributions and had taxable prior year deferrals during the year, *do not complete Box 11.* These amounts are subject to special reporting rules outlined in IRS Publication 957, Reporting Back Pay and Special Wage Payments to the Social Security Administration, and must be reported on Form SSA-131, *Employer Report of Special Wage Payments* (see Appendix page A-56). See Section 8.15 for more information.

Government employers should enter in Box 11 amounts deferred to ineligible §457(f) plans (see Section 4.6-4) when the substantial risk of forfeiture ends. These amounts should also be entered in Boxes 1, 3, and

5. Amounts deferred under eligible §457(b) plans should be entered in Boxes 3, 5, and 11 for the year when the substantial risk of forfeiture ends, and on Form 1099-R for the year when plan distributions are made. Distributions from nonqualified deferred compensation plans or §457 plans paid to beneficiaries of deceased employees should be reported on Form 1099-R (see Section 8.12-2). Military retirement plan payments should also be reported on Form 1099-R.

**Box 12—See instructions for Box 12.**  Enter here only items described in the following explanation, with the alphabetical code to the left of the vertical line in Boxes 12 a-d and the amount to the right of the vertical line. Use capital letters for the codes. Paper Forms W-2, Copy A must contain no more than four items in Box 12, although electronic filers can include more. For paper filers, another Form W-2 can be used to report the additional items, but do not include any entries in Boxes 1-11. As with other Form W-2 entries, do not use dollar signs or commas in Box 12 amounts, only decimal points (see Section 8.8-5).

*Code A—Uncollected social security or RRTA tax on tips.*  Enter here the amount of social security or Railroad Retirement Tax Act (RRTA) tax on an employee's tips that could not be collected because of insufficient employee funds (regular wages and amounts contributed by the employee for withholding purposes). This amount should not be included in Box 4. The Code A amount + Box 4 should = (Boxes 3 + 7) x 6.2%.

*Code B—Uncollected Medicare tax on tips.*  Enter here the amount of Medicare or RRTA Medicare tax on an employee's tips that could not be collected because of insufficient employee funds (regular wages and amounts contributed by the employee for withholding purposes). This amount should not be included in Box 6. The Code B amount + Box 6 should = Box 5 x 1.45%.

*Code C—Taxable cost of group-term life insurance coverage over $50,000.*  Enter here the taxable cost of employer-provided group-term life insurance coverage over $50,000, minus the employee's after-tax contributions. Also include this amount in Boxes 1, 3 and 5.

*Code D—Elective deferrals to an employee section 401(k) cash or deferral arrangement (plan).*  Enter here the employee's total elective deferrals to a §401(k) cash or deferred arrangement and amounts deferred to a SIMPLE retirement account that is part of such an arrangement, even if they exceed the annual elective deferral limit (not employer nonelective or matching contributions or employee after-tax contributions). Include any catch-up contributions. Do not report any excess deferral in Box 1.

> **Example:**  Marianna, a 48-year-old employee at Irving Electronics, elected to defer $15,300 to Irving Electronics' §401(k) plan for 2008 and made a $1,000 designated Roth contribution. She also made a voluntary after-tax contribution of $600. Irving Electronics made a qualified non-elective contribution of $1,000 to the plan on Marianna's behalf, plus a nonelective profit-sharing employer contribution of $2,000.
>
> Marianna's total elective deferral of $15,300 is reported in Box 12 with Code D and the designated Roth contribution is reported in Box 12 with Code AA, even though the 2008 limit for elective deferrals and designated Roth contributions is $15,500 (see Section 4.6-2). The return of the excess is not reported on Form W-2, but on Form 1099-R. The $600 voluntary contribution may be reported in Box 14, but not Box 12. The employer's nonelective contributions also may be reported in Box 14, but do not have to be reported on Form W-2.

*Code E—Elected deferrals under a section 403(b) salary reduction agreement.*  Enter here the employee's total elective deferrals to a §403(b) salary reduction agreement to purchase an annuity contract, even if they exceed the annual elective deferral limit (not employer nonelective or matching contributions or employee after-tax contributions). Include any catch-up contributions. Do not report any excess deferral in Box 1.

*Code F—Elected deferrals under a section 408(k)(6) salary reduction SEP.*  Enter here the employee's total elective deferrals to a §408(k)(6) salary reduction Simplified Employee Pension plan, even if they exceed the annual elective deferral limit (not employer nonelective or matching contributions or employee after-tax contributions). Include any catch-up contributions. Do not report any excess deferral in Box 1.

*Code G—Elected deferrals and employee contributions (including nonelective deferrals) to any governmental or nongovernmental section 457(b) tax-exempt organization plan.*  Enter here the total elective and nonelective contributions made to a §457(b) deferred compensation plan for government employees or tax-exempt organizations, even if they exceed the annual elective deferral limit. Include any catch-up contributions. Do not report amounts contributed to an ineligible §457(f) plan or amounts deferred under a §457(b) plan that are subject to a substantial risk of forfeiture.

*Code H—Elected deferrals a section 501(c)(18)(D) tax exempt organization plan.* Enter here the total elective deferrals to a §501(c)(18)(D) tax-exempt organization plan (not employer nonelective or matching contributions or employee after-tax contributions). Include any catch-up contributions. Also include this amount in Box 1.

 **CATCH-UP CONTRIBUTIONS**[140] In 2008, employees who are 50 years old or older can defer an extra $5,000 into an eligible retirement plan (i.e., 401(k), 403(b), 408(k) SEP, 408(p) SIMPLE, 457, or 501(c)(18)(D) plan) above the statutory or plan limit as a "catch-up" contribution. Any catch-up contribution amount should be added to the employee's elective deferral under such plans for purposes of reporting the amount in Box 12.

*Code I.* Not used at this time.

*Code J—Nontaxable sick pay.* Enter here the amount of third-party sick pay that is not included in income because of the employee's after-tax contributions to the sick pay plan.

*Code K—20% excise tax on excess golden parachute payments.* Enter here the 20% excise tax on excess golden parachute payments (see Section 3.4-14) made to key corporate employees after a merger or acquisition. If the excess payments are considered wages, also enter the 20% tax in Box 2 as federal income tax withheld.

*Code L—Substantiated employee business expense reimbursements.* Enter here the amount of employee business expense treated as substantiated (nontaxable) only if the employer reimburses its employees for expenses under a per diem or mileage allowance that exceeds the government-approved rates. The taxable portion must be included in Boxes 1, 3, and 5.

*Code M—Uncollected social security or RRTA tax on cost of group-term life insurance coverage over $50,000.* Enter here the amount of uncollected social security or RRTA tax on the value of excess group-term life insurance coverage for former employees. (Box 3 + Box 7) x .062 = Code M + Box 4.

*Code N—Uncollected Medicare tax on cost of group-term life insurance coverage over $50,000.* Enter here the amount of uncollected Medicare or RRTA Medicare tax on the value of excess group-term life insurance coverage for former employees. Box 5 x .0145 = Code N + Box 6.

*Code P—Excludable moving expense reimbursements paid directly to employee.* Enter here the amount of moving expense reimbursements paid to employees (not payments made to third parties on behalf of employees) that were not included in the employees' income because they were paid for qualified moving expenses (see Section 3.3-2). Payments to third parties for qualified moving expenses are no longer reported by the employer on Form W-2.

*Code Q – Nontaxable combat pay.* Military employers should enter here any nontaxable combat pay provided to members of the U.S. armed services, National Guard, and Reserves.

*Code R—Employer contributions to an Archer MSA.* Enter here the amount of employer contributions to an Archer MSA. Amounts that are not excludable from the employee's gross income must also be included in Box 1. To the extent that it was not reasonable at the time of payment to believe that the employer contributions would be excludable from the employee's gross income, the employer's contributions must also be included in Boxes 3 and 5.

---

140.    IRS Announcement 2001-93, 2001-44 IRB 416; Form W-2 Instructions.

*Code S—Employee salary reduction contributions under a section 408(p) SIMPLE.* Enter here the amount of employee salary reduction contributions to a SIMPLE retirement account, but not if the retirement account is part of a §401(k) cash or deferred arrangement (such amounts are reported with Code D). Do not report this amount in Box 1, even if there is an excess deferral, but the amount must be reported in Boxes 3 and 5.

*Code T—Adoption benefit.* Enter here the total amount paid or expenses incurred by the employer for qualified adoption expenses provided to an employee under an adoption assistance program. Also include benefits paid or reimbursed from the pre-tax contributions made by the employee to a §125 adoption plan account. But do not include adoption benefits forfeited from a cafeteria plan. Do not include this amount in Box 1, but it must be included in Boxes 3 and 5.

*Code V—Income from the exercise of nonstatutory stock options.* Enter here the spread (i.e., the fair market value minus the exercise price) from your employees' (or former employees') exercise of nonstatutory stock options. Also include this amount in Boxes 1, 3, and 5. This requirement does not apply to the exercise of a statutory stock option (i.e., incentive stock option or employee stock purchase plan) or to the sale of stock acquired from the exercise of a statutory stock option.

*Code W—Employer contributions to a Health Savings Account.* Enter here the amount of employer contributions to a health savings account (HSA), including amounts the employee contributes through a §125 cafeteria plan. Amounts that are not excludable from the employee's gross income must also be included in Box 1. To the extent that it was not reasonable at the time of payment to believe that the employer contributions would be excludable from the employee's gross income, the employer's contributions must also be included in Boxes 3 and 5.

*Code Y – Deferrals under a section 409A nonqualified deferred compensation plan.* Enter here any amounts deferred to a nonqualified deferred compensation plan as defined in IRC §409A (see Section 4.6-10). Earnings on current and prior year deferrals also must be reported here.

*Code Z – Income under section 409A on a nonqualified deferred compensation plan.* Enter here amounts that must be included in income because of a section 409A nonqualified deferred compensation plan (see Section 4.6-10). These amounts must also be reported in Box 1. This income is also subject to an additional 20% tax, plus interest, that is reported on the employee's personal income tax return.

*Code AA – Designated Roth contributions to a section 401(k) plan.* Enter here designated Roth contributions to a §401(k) plan (see Section 4.6-2). This amount must also be reported in Boxes 1, 3, and 5. Do not use this code to report elective deferrals to the plan, which are reported under Code D.

*Code BB – Designated Roth contributions under a section 403(b) salary reduction agreement.* Enter here designated Roth contributions to a §403(b) plan (see Section 4.6-3). This amount must also be reported in Boxes 1, 3, and 5. Do not use this code to report elective deferrals to the plan, which are reported under Code E.

**Reporting "makeup" deferrals for veterans.** If any elective deferrals (or nonelective contributions to a §457 plan) are makeup amounts under the Uniformed Services Employment and Reemployment Rights Act of 1994 (USERRA, see Section 4.6-2), the prior year amounts must be reported separately. The employer has two options. The prior year elective deferrals can be reported on Form W-2 in Box 12 preceded by the appropriate code and the year to which they relate (e.g., D 01 2250.00 for a §401(k) plan deferral), or on a separate statement showing the type of plan, the year to which the deferrals relate, and the amounts deferred. If reported on Form W-2, the code and the year should be placed to the left of the vertical line.

**Box 13.** Check the following boxes if they apply.

*Statutory employee.* Check this box if the employee is a statutory employee whose wages are subject to social security and Medicare taxes, but not federal income tax withholding (see Section 1.3-1).

*Retirement plan.* Check this box if the employee was an "active participant" in an employer's retirement plan, including §401(a) qualified plans (including a §401(k) plan); §403(a) and §403(b) annuity plans; government employer plans other than §457 plans; §408(k) Simplified Employee Pension plans; §408(p) SIMPLE retirement accounts; and §501(c)(18) tax-exempt trusts. Also check this box if the employee actively participates in a collectively bargained union retirement plan. Do not check for contributions made to a nonqualified deferred compensation plan or a §457 plan.

An active participant is defined differently depending on the type of plan.[141] For defined benefit plans, all employees who are eligible to participate, even if they have chosen not to, are active participants in the plan. For defined contribution plans, employees who receive allocations to their accounts in a plan year ending during the calendar year are active participants in the plan. Employers should be careful because allocations are not always made in the same year as contributions, especially employer matching contributions.

*Third-party sick pay.* Check this box only if you are a third-party sick pay payer filing a Form W-2 for an insured's employee or an employer reporting sick pay payments made by a third party to an employee.

**Box 14—Other.** If the employer treats 100% of the lease value of a company-provided car as income to the employee and reports it in Box 1, the employer must also report this amount in Box 14 or in a separate statement to the employee. This box also serves as an optional field where the employer may report other information such as:

- state disability insurance tax withheld
- union dues
- uniform payments
- health insurance premiums
- nontaxable income
- educational assistance payments

The employer may also enter the following retirement plan contributions:

- nonelective employer contributions made on behalf of an employee;
- voluntary after-tax contributions deducted from an employee's pay (but not designated Roth contributions);
- required employee contributions; and
- employer matching contributions.

The employer should label each item reported in Box 14.

**Boxes 15 through 20—State and local income tax information.** Report state and local tax information in these boxes. It may be required by state and local agencies if the same W-2 form copies are used for the employer's state and local returns. They are not required for any federal amounts. Enter the two-letter postal abbreviation for the name of the state to the left of the vertical line in Box 15 and the employer's state ID number to the right of the vertical line. There are enough boxes to report amounts for two states and two localities, with one state and/or locality above and one below the broken line. If only one state and/or locality is reported, place the amounts above the broken line. If information for more than two states or localities must be reported, use a separate Form W-2.

---

141.　IRS Notice 87-16, 1987-1 CB 446; Notice 98-49, 1998-2 CB 365; IRS Pub. 590, Individual Retirement Arrangements.

**Example:** Sam Tailor is an employee of Eastbridge Clothiers whose wage and tax information for all of calendar year 2008 is listed below. A completed Copy A of Sam's 2008 Form W-2 follows.

| | |
|---|---|
| Wages, tips, etc. | $36,500.00 |
| Federal income tax withheld | 8,030.00 |
| Social security wages | 37,230.00 |
| Social security tax withheld | 2,308.26 |
| Medicare wages | 37,230.00 |
| Medicare tax withheld | 539.84 |
| §401(k) plan elective deferral | 730.00 |

| 22222 | Void ☐ | a Employee's social security number 333-44-5555 | For Official Use Only ▶ OMB No. 1545-0008 | |
|---|---|---|---|---|

| b Employer identification number (EIN) 12-3456789 | | 1 Wages, tips, other compensation 36500.00 | 2 Federal income tax withheld 8030.00 |
|---|---|---|---|
| c Employer's name, address, and ZIP code Eastbridge Clothiers 12121 Denim Street Eastbridge, VA 34567 | | 3 Social security wages 37230.00 | 4 Social security tax withheld 2308.26 |
| | | 5 Medicare wages and tips 37230.00 | 6 Medicare tax withheld 539.84 |
| | | 7 Social security tips | 8 Allocated tips |
| d Control number | | 9 Advance EIC payment | 10 Dependent care benefits |
| e Employee's first name and initial Samuel T | Last name Tailor / Suff. | 11 Nonqualified plans | 12a See instructions for box 12 Code D 730.00 |
| 1234 Thread Street Eastbridge, VA 34567 | | 13 Statutory employee ☐ Retirement plan ✔ Third-party sick pay ☐ | 12b |
| | | 14 Other | 12c |
| | | | 12d |
| f Employee's address and ZIP code | | | |

| 15 State VA | Employer's state ID number 123456 | 16 State wages, tips, etc. 36500.00 | 17 State income tax 2190.00 | 18 Local wages, tips, etc. | 19 Local income tax | 20 Locality name |
|---|---|---|---|---|---|---|
| | | | | | | |

Form **W-2** **Wage and Tax Statement** **2008** Department of the Treasury—Internal Revenue Service

**Copy A For Social Security Administration** — Send this entire page with Form W-3 to the Social Security Administration; photocopies are **not** acceptable.

**For Privacy Act and Paperwork Reduction Act Notice, see back of Copy D.**

Cat. No. 10134D

**Do Not Cut, Fold, or Staple Forms on This Page — Do Not Cut, Fold, or Staple Forms on This Page**

# 8.8-4 Substitute Forms W-2

Employers may use W-2 forms generated by the IRS or they may use "substitute" forms, also known as privately printed forms. Substitute forms must be printed according to specifications set forth by the IRS.[142] Two sets of specifications govern substitutes of Copy A filed by employers who file on paper rather than electronically. These specifications set forth the size, paper type, ink, etc. that must be used, as well as requiring the substitute to be "an exact replica of the IRS printed form ... with respect to layout and contents." One set of specifications is for "red-ink" substitute forms, which are exact replicas of the official IRS-printed forms regarding layout and content because they are read by SSA's scanner equipment. The second set of specifications is for "laser-printed" black and white forms.

Substitute forms provided to employees as information statements (Copies B, C, and 2), whether by paper or electronic filers (who do not file a paper Copy A with the SSA), must meet the following requirements:

- All substitutes must be a form with boxes, box letters and numbers, and box titles matching the IRS printed form where applicable.

- The electronic tax logo on the official IRS form employee copies is not required on the substitute form copies. Employers are encouraged to delete the form identifying number (22222) and the word "Void" (plus the checkbox that goes with it) from the employee copies of Forms W-2 to avoid any confusion by employees.

- Certain "core information" must appear with the same box numbers and titles as shown on the IRS printed form, either in the upper right corner of the form (horizontal format), or across the top (vertical format). Because Copy A can be printed only in horizontal format, electronic filers are the only filers that use the vertical format for employee copies of Form W-2. This core information includes:

    Box 1 - Wages, tips, other compensation
    Box 2 - Federal income tax withheld
    Box 3 - Social security wages
    Box 4 - Social security tax withheld
    Box 5 - Medicare wages and tips
    Box 6 - Medicare tax withheld

- Boxes 1-6 (as well as Boxes 15-20 when they are used), must be at least $1\frac{1}{8}$ inches wide and $\frac{1}{4}$ inch deep. Boxes 1 and 2 on Copy B are required to be outlined in a bold 2-point rule or otherwise highlighted to distinguish them. The top margin of the form is $\frac{3}{8}$ inch.

- If an employer is required to withhold state income tax, the following boxes become core information and must be located at the bottom of the substitute form (if there is no state income tax reporting, these boxes need not be included):

    Box 15 - State and Employer's state I.D. number
    Box 16 - State wages, tips, etc.
    Box 17 - State income tax

- If an employer is required to withhold local income tax, the following boxes become core information and must be located at the bottom of the substitute form (if there is no local income tax reporting, these boxes need not be included):

    Box 18 - Local wages, tips, etc.
    Box 19 - Local income tax
    Box 20 - Locality name

---

142.    Rev. Proc. 2007-43, 2007-27 IRB 26; IRS Publication 1141, General Rules and Specifications for Private Printing of Substitute Forms W-2 and W-3.

- The maximum allowable dimensions for employee copies of Form W-2 are 6½ inches (depth) by 8½ inches (width). The minimum allowable dimensions are 2.67 inches (depth) by 4.25 inches (width).

- All identifying information for the employer and the employee must appear on the substitute form in boxes similar to those on the IRS printed form, but they can be placed in any area of the form other than where the core information must appear, and the lettering system (a-c, e-f) need not be used. Box d (control number) is not required.

- The form number (W-2), form title (Wage and Tax Statement), and tax year (2008) must be clearly printed on all copies of the substitute form. The tax year must be printed in non-reflective black ink, and the use of 24 pt. OCR-A font is recommended for the employee's copies. The IRS recommends (but does not require) that this information be printed in the lower left of the form, with the description of the form copy (e.g., Copy B, to be filed with the employee's federal tax return) placed below the Form W-2 designation.

- The catalog number shown on the IRS version of Form W-2—10134D—should not be printed on substitute forms. However, the OMB number must be printed as either OMB No. 1545-0008 (preferred) or OMB# 15450008.

- The reference to the Department of the Treasury—Internal Revenue Service must be included on all copies of substitute Forms W-2. The IRS recommends (but does not require) that it be located on the bottom right of the form.

- Boxes 7-14 need not be included on the substitute form unless the employer is required to report information in those boxes. If any of the boxes are used, however, they should have the same number and title as on the IRS printed form. They may be placed on the form according to the employer's wishes. If Box 9 (Advance earned income credit payment) is used it must be enclosed in a 2-point rule or highlighted in some other manner. If Box 8 (Allocated tips) is used, the IRS recommends, but does not require, that this box also be outlined in a bold 2-point rule or otherwise highlighted.

- Boxes 12 and 14 may be given specific headings showing what is entered there (e.g., "§401(k)" plan if the only entry is elective deferrals to a §401(k) plan). These boxes may be larger than other boxes, and Box 12 can contain more than the four items allowed on the IRS printed form. Each entry in Box 12 should have the same code as the one assigned by the IRS.

- All substitute form copies must be printed on white paper.

- Employees must be given at least two copies (Copies B and C) of the substitute form (plus at least one copy of Copy 2 if they are filing state or local tax returns). If the copies are not labeled as to their disposition (e.g., filed with federal return, employee's copy, filed with state return) the employer must provide details in writing.

- Instructions similar to those found on the reverse of Copies B, C and 2 of the IRS printed form must be provided by the employer on the substitute form. The exact language regarding earned income credit eligibility must be used or the employer must provide Notice 797, Possible Federal Tax Refund Due to the Earned Income Credit, to employees.

Generally, employers wishing to use substitute forms should not send a sample to the IRS or SSA for approval prior to use. But questions about a particular specification and whether an employer's interpretation of it is correct may be submitted. If the question pertains to the red-ink Form W-2 (Copy A) or Form W-3, an e-mail can be sent to taxforms@irs.gov, or a letter should be sent to:

Internal Revenue Service
ATTN: Substitute Forms Program
SE: W: CAR: MP: T: T: S: SP, Room 6406
1111 Constitution Avenue, N.W.
Washington, DC 20224

The employer should also include an example of the form using the employer's interpretation of the specification. Allow at least 30 days for the IRS or SSA to respond.

**Laser printed forms can be used.** The SSA will accept black and white laser printed Forms W-2 and W-3 that meet certain specifications in IRS Pub. 1141 and that are approved in advance by the SSA. You can contact the SSA at laser.forms@socialsecurity.gov to obtain a template and further instructions on submitting sample forms. Send samples of your laser printed forms to:

Social Security Administration
Data Operations Center
ATTN: Laser Forms Approval
Room 235
1150 E. Mountain Drive
Wilkes-Barre, PA 18702-7997.

# 8.8-5 Miscellaneous Form W-2 Issues

Following is an explanation of several other issues surrounding the completion of Form W-2 that employers must be familiar with.

**Hyphenation.**[143] When submitting paper Forms W-2 to the SSA, the employer's EIN and the employee's SSN must include hyphens. The EIN should appear as 00-0000000, and the SSN should appear as 000-00-0000.

**Dollar amounts.**[144] Dollar amounts should be entered without commas or dollar signs, but with decimal points, and the cents portion must be shown. Always show cents, with .00 used for even dollar amounts.

*Example:* If an employee's Box 1 wages, tips, and other compensation total $127,354.25, the employer should enter that amount in Box 1 as 127354.25.

**Electronic reporting.** Employers filing 250 or more Forms W-2 for a calendar year are required to file them electronically. See Section 8.14 for more on electronic reporting.

# 8.9 Providing Wage and Tax Information to the SSA—Form W-3

Once an employer has provided its employees with their parts of the Form W-2 (Copies B, C, and 2), it must send Copy A of each form to the SSA. If filing paper W-2 forms (Copy A), the employer must send them along with Form W-3, *Transmittal of Wage and Tax Statements* (see Appendix page A-67). All the W-2 forms (Copy A) and the Form W-3 constitute an information return. Form W-3 contains totals of the amounts reported on the employer's W-2 forms, acting as a "reconciliation" of those forms.

 **FORM W-3 NOT FOR ELECTRONIC FILERS** Form W-3 is used only by employers that file paper Copies A of Form W-2 with the SSA. Employers that file electronically do not file a transmittal document.

---

143.    IRS Announcement 92-11, 1992-4 IRB 34.
144.    Form W-2 Instructions.

**Mergers and acquisitions.** Where there has been a corporate merger or consolidation during the year, only the surviving company should file a Form W-3, since it is also responsible for filing Forms W-2 for employees of the acquired corporation (see Section 8.8-1).

**Successors.** When one employer has acquired another during the year, the successor and the predecessor should file a Form W-3 only for the W-2 forms for which they are responsible (see Section 8.8-1).

**Substitute forms.** Substitute or privately printed forms may be used instead of the IRS printed Form W-3, but they must comply with specifications similar to those governing Copy A of Form W-2 (see Section 8.8-4).

## 8.9-1  When and Where to File Form W-3

The due date for filing Form W-3 is the same as the due date for filing paper Copy A of Form W-2 with the SSA—the last day of February.[145]  Therefore, Form W-3, along with Copy A of the W-2 forms, must be sent (postmarked by the U.S. Postal Service or accepted for delivery by a designated private delivery service) by the last day of February.  If the last day of February is a Saturday, Sunday, or legal holiday (see Section 8.3-2 for the definition of a legal holiday), the due date is extended until the next business day.[146]

All paper filers must send Form W-3, along with paper copies of Form W-2, Copy A to the same location:

> Social Security Administration
> Data Operations Center
> Wilkes-Barre, PA 18769-0001

However, employers who send the forms by certified mail must use a zip code of 18769-0002.  Employers who use a carrier other than the U.S. Postal Service (i.e., a private delivery service) should send Copies A of Form W-2 and Form W-3 to:

> Social Security Administration
> Data Operations Center
> Attn:  W-2 Process
> 1150 East Mountain Drive
> Wilkes-Barre, PA 18702-7997

To take advantage of the deadline extension offered when Forms W-2 and W-3 are mailed, employers must use first class U.S. mail or a designated private delivery service (see Section 8.3-2).

**Filing extensions.**[147]  An automatic extension (up to 30 days) of the time to file Form W-3 is available, as with Forms W-2, by completing and sending to the IRS Form 8809, *Request for Extension of Time to File Information Returns* (see Appendix page A-393) by the due date of the form.  The form does not have to be signed and no reason for requesting the extension needs to be provided.  If the request for extension involves more than 10 employers, the IRS encourages filers to submit the request on magnetic media (tape, cartridge, or diskette) or electronically.  Magnetic media or electronic filing is required if the request involves more than 50 employers.  See IRS Publication 1220, Specifications for Filing Forms 1098, 1099, 5498, and W-2G Magnetically or Electronically, for more information.  During the extension period, one further 30-day extension may be granted if another Form 8809 is filed that includes the employer's signature and an explanation of the reason for the extension.

**Form W-3 may be filed by someone other than the employer.** A payroll service bureau or paying agent may send Form W-3 on the employer's behalf and sign the form for the employer if the following conditions are met:

---

145.   IRS Reg. §31.6071(a)-1(a)(3)(ii).
146.   IRC §7503; IRS Reg. §301.7503-1.
147.   IRS Reg. §1.6081-8; Forms W-3 and 8809 Instructions.

- the service bureau or agent is authorized to sign by a written or oral agency agreement valid under state law; and

- the service bureau or agent writes "For (name of payer)" next to the signature.

The employer's EIN should be the same as it appears on its employment tax returns (e.g., Forms 941, 943 or 944).

## 8.9-2 Box-by-Box Instructions for Form W-3

Here are instructions for completing each box of the 2008 Form W-3, which contain several minor changes from the 2007 version. The general completion instructions are the same as for Form W-2 (see Section 8.8-3).

**Box a—Control number.** This is an optional box for the employer to use for numbering the transmittal.

**Box b—Kind of payer.** This box has separate check boxes for different types of employers. Only one box should be checked on a Form W-3, unless the second marked checkbox is "Third-party sick pay." If more than one box applies to an employer, the employer must file a separate Form W-3 with the Forms W-2 for each type.

*941.* Check this box if the employer files Form 941, *Employer's Quarterly Federal Tax Return.*

*Military.* Check this box if the employer is sending Forms W-2 for members of the uniformed armed services.

*943.* Check this box if the employer files Form 943, *Employer's Annual Tax Return for Agricultural Employees.* Make sure another Form W-3 is filed if the employer has nonagricultural employees as well.

*944.* Check this box if the employer files Form 944, *Employer's Annual Federal Tax Return.*

*CT-1.* Check this box if the employer is a railroad employer sending Forms W-2 for employees covered by the Railroad Retirement Tax Act, but do not show employee RRTA wages and tax in Boxes 3, 4, 5, 6, and 7. Employers covered by RRTA having employees that pay social security and Medicare taxes must file a separate Form W-3 with their Forms W-2 and check the "941" box on that form.

*Hshld. emp.* Mark this box if the employer is a household employer sending Forms W-2 for household employees, and the employees' taxes were not included on Form 941.

*Medicare government employee.* Check this box if the employer is a government agency sending Forms W-2 for employees who are subject to the Medicare tax, but not social security tax. Make sure another Form W-3 is filed for employees paying both social security and Medicare taxes, and check the "941" box on that form.

*Third-party sick pay.* Check this box and another box such as the "941" box if you are a third-party sick pay payer (or an employer reporting sick pay payments made by a third party) that files Forms W-2 with the "Third-party sick pay" checkbox in Box 13 marked. Mark both check boxes that apply and file a single Form W-3 for the regular and "Third-party sick pay" Forms W-2.

**Box c—Total number of Forms W-2.** Enter here the total number of Forms W-2, Copy A being transmitted with this Form W-3, minus any voided statements.

**Box d—Establishment number.** The employer can use this box to identify separate establishments in its business. A separate Form W-3 can be used for each establishment.

**Box e—Employer identification number.** Enter here the employer identification number (EIN) assigned by the IRS and used on the employer's quarterly or annual employment tax returns (e.g., Forms 941, 943 or 944). Enter "Applied for" if the number has not yet been received.

**Box f—Employer's name.** Enter here the employer's name as shown on the employer's quarterly or annual employment tax returns (e.g., Forms 941, 943 or 944).

**Box g—Employer's address and ZIP code.** Enter here the employer's address and ZIP code as shown on the employer's quarterly or annual employment tax returns (e.g., Forms 941, 943 or 944).

**Box h—Other EIN used this year.** Enter here an EIN used earlier in the year by the employer on Form 941, 943 or 944 (including a prior owner's EIN) that differs from the one in Box e. If more than one was used, attach a letter indicating them. When an agent who has filed an approved Form 2678, *Employer/Payer Appointment of Agent* (see Appendix page A-337), files an employer's Forms W-2 and W-3, the agent's EIN, name, and address should be in Boxes e, f, and g, respectively, while the employer's EIN should be placed in Box h.

**Boxes 1-11.** Enter in each box the total amounts from the Forms W-2, Copy A being sent with the Form W-3, disregarding the voided forms.

**Box 12—Deferred compensation.** Enter here the total amounts from the Forms W-2, Box 12, Codes D-H, S, Y, AA and BB as one lump sum without any codes.

**Box 13—For third-party sick pay use only**. Third-party payers of sick pay (or employers using the optional rule for Form W-2, see Section 4.3-2) filing third-party sick pay recap Forms W-2 and W-3 must enter "Third-Party Sick Pay Recap" in this box.

**Box 14—Income tax withheld by payer of third-party sick pay.** Employers enter here any amounts employees have had withheld from third-party payments of sick pay, but only if the third party properly transferred Form W-2 and 941 reporting liability to the employer. This amount is also included in Box 2. When the Box 14 amount is subtracted from the Box 2 amount, the result should be the same as the federal income tax withheld as reported on all Forms 941 filed for the year. For detailed instructions regarding the Form W-2/W-3 reporting responsibilities for employers and payers of third-party sick pay, see Section 4.3-2.

**Box 15—State/Employer's state ID number.** Enter to the left of the vertical line the two-letter postal abbreviation for the name of the state having information reported on Forms W-2. Enter the employer's state ID number to the right of the vertical line. If the Forms W-2 being submitted with the Form W-3 contain information from more than one state, enter an "X" to the left of the vertical line, and do not enter any state ID number.

**Boxes 16-19—State and local wage and tax information.** Enter here the total of state and/or local wages and income tax in their corresponding boxes on the Forms W-2 included with the Form W-3. If the Forms W-2 include amounts from more than one state or locality, report them as one sum in the appropriate box on Form W-3.

**Contact information boxes.** Below Boxes 15 and 18 there are four boxes for the following employer information: contact person; telephone number; fax number; and e-mail address.

## 8.10 Correcting Information Statements—Forms W-2c and W-3c

When errors have been made on a previously filed Form W-2, the employer must correct them by filing Form W-2c, *Corrected Wage and Tax Statement* (see Appendix page A-84). Form W-2c must be accompanied by Form W-3c, *Transmittal of Corrected Wage and Tax Statements* (see Appendix page A-86), when it is sent to the SSA.

Form W-2c consists of six parts, the same as Form W-2, with different parts being given to the employee, the SSA, and the state or local tax agency, if applicable. Copy A of Form W-2c must be sent to the SSA along with Form W-3c, which totals the information from all the W-2c forms being submitted.

**Special situations.**[148] Even if the employer is submitting only one Form W-2c to the SSA, it must also send in the Form W-3c transmittal. Even if the only corrections being submitted are to employees' names and/or SSNs, Form W-3c must be filed and the employees should be advised to correct the corresponding information on their original Form W-2.

The employer should complete Form W-2c through Box i, as appropriate. Make sure to report the employee's previously reported incorrect SSN in Box h and/or incorrect name in box i. Do not complete Boxes 1-20.

If the only correction that needs to be made to an employee's Form W-2 is to the employee's address, a Form W-2c does not have to be completed and filed. If the address was incorrect on the employee's copies of the Form W-2, the employer must do one of the following:

- Issue a new Form W-2 with correct information, and indicate "Reissued Statement" on the new copies unless they are sent electronically. Do not send Copy A to the SSA.

- Issue a Form W-2c to the employee showing the correct address in Box b. Do not send Copy A to the SSA.

- Mail the Form W-2 with the incorrect address to the employee in an envelope showing the correct address, or otherwise deliver it to the employee.

If the only data being corrected on a Form W-2c are state and/or local data, Copy A should not be sent to the SSA. Only the employee and state or local tax agency copies must be sent.

If an employee is given a new social security card following an adjustment to the employee's resident status that shows a different name or social security number, the employer needs to file a Form W-2c for the most current year only. It is no longer necessary to file Forms W-2c for all prior years.

**Electronic filing requirement.** The IRS requires employers with 250 or more Forms W-2c during a calendar year to file them electronically with the SSA.[149] The requirement applies only to Forms W-2c filed to correct Forms W-2 for the immediate prior year. (See section 8.14 for more information on this new requirement and for details on the Electronic Filing Specifications for Form W-2c (EFW2C)).

**Correcting more than one W-2 for an employee in a year.** If an employee received more than one Form W-2 under the same employer identification number and correction is needed, the employer can either:

- consider all the Forms W-2 for the employee when determining what to enter on Form W-2c; or
- file a Form W-2c to correct one of the multiple Forms W-2 issued to the employee.

**Undeliverable Forms W-2c.** Forms W-2c that cannot be delivered to employees after a reasonable effort to do so must be kept by the employer for four years.[150]

**Box-by-box instructions for Form W-2c.** Following are specific box-by-box instructions for completing Form W-2c (last revised January 2006).

**Box a—Tax year/Form corrected.** If Form W-2 is being corrected, enter all 4 digits of the year of the form being corrected. If Form W-2c, W-2AS, W-2GU, W-2CM, or W-2VI is being corrected, enter all 4 digits of the year of the form being corrected, plus "c," "AS," "GU," "CM," or "VI" to designate the form being corrected (e.g, "2007' and "GU" to correct a 2007 Form W-2GU).

---

148. Forms W-2c and W-3c Instructions.
149. Rev. Proc. 2002-51, 2002-29 IRB 175; IRS Pub. 1223, General Rules and Specifications for Substitute Forms W-2c and W-3c; Rev. Proc. 2006-19, 2006-13 IRB 677.
150. IRS Reg. §31.6001-1(e)(2); Forms W-2c and W-3c Instructions.

**Box b—Employee's correct SSN.** Enter the employee's correct social security number even if it was correct on the original Form W-2.

**Box c—Corrected SSN and/or name.** If the employee's name and /or SSN is being corrected, check this box, enter the employee's correct SSN and name in Boxes b and e, and enter the employee's SSN and/or name as incorrectly shown on the original Form W-2 in Boxes h and/or i.

**Box d—Employer's federal EIN.** Show the correct federal employer identification number for the employer.

**Boxes e and f—Employee's name, address, and ZIP code.** Enter the employee's correct first name and middle initial (without a period) above the dotted line and to the left of the first vertical line. Enter the employee's last name above the dotted line and to the right of the first vertical line. The employer can enter Jr., Sr., or a numerical suffix (e.g., III or IV) to the right of the second vertical line. Enter the employee's correct address and ZIP code below the dotted line.

**Box g—Employer's name, address, and Zip code.** Enter the employer's name, address, and ZIP code.

**Box h—Employee's incorrect SSN.** Enter the employee's SSN as it was entered on Form W-2 only if it was originally entered incorrectly.

**Box i—Employee's name (as incorrectly shown on previous form).** Enter the employee's name as it was entered on Form W-2 only if it was originally entered incorrectly.

**Boxes 1-20—Form W-2 amounts.** Complete only those items being corrected. For those items, enter in the "Previously reported" column the information or amount on the original Form W-2. Enter in the "Correct information" column the correct information or amount. Use Box 2—Federal income tax withheld—only to correct an administrative error (if the amount entered in Box 2 of the incorrect Form W-2 was not the amount that was actually withheld). If a government employer is correcting only social security wages and/or tips for a Medicare Qualified Government Employee (MQGE) for 1991 and later years, the employer must also complete Box 5—Medicare wages and tips. Enter the total Medicare wages and tips, including MQGE-only wages, even if there is no change to the total Medicare wages and tips previously reported.

If a single Form W-2c does not have enough blank boxes for corrections, use additional Forms W-2c. If the only changes to Form W-2c are to state and/or local information, don't send Copy A of Form W-2c to the SSA. Just send Form W-2c to the appropriate state or local taxing authority, and give copies to the employee.

**Box 13—Checkboxes.** Mark the checkboxes in Box 13 under "Previously reported" as they were incorrectly marked on the original Form W-2. Under "Correct information," mark them as they should have been marked (e.g., a box where a mark was entered incorrectly on the original W-2 should be marked under "Previously reported" but left blank under "Correct information" on Form W-2c).

 **WHAT TO DO WHEN BOX NUMBERS CHANGE** According to IRS personnel, if an employer has to file a Form W-2c to correct amounts reported on a Form W-2 issued before 2001, the employer should use the latest version of Form W-2c, even though the box numbers on the original Form W-2 and the Form W-2c are not the same. For example, if an employer is correcting amounts from Box 13 of a 2000 Form W-2, it should put the incorrect and correct amounts in Box 12 of the current Form W-2c. If the data is put in the corresponding fields on the current Form W-2c, the SSA will be able to process it.

**General instructions for Form W-3c.** As mentioned earlier, Form W-3c must be sent with any Forms W-2c being sent to the SSA (even a single Form W-2c), even if the only corrections are to employees' names and/or SSNs. The purpose of Form W-3c is to summarize the information on the individual Forms W-2c. If the only correction is to the employer's EIN or a previously filed Form W-3, Form W-3c can be sent to the SSA by itself. If the EIN is the only information being corrected, the employer should complete only Boxes a, b, e, f, and h, enter its contact information, and sign the form. A separate Form W-3c must be sent for each type of Form W-2 being corrected, each tax year, and each kind of payer except for third-party sick pay.

**Specific instructions.** Complete the applicable identifying information in Boxes a-g (use a 4-digit year in Box a). Boxes h-j should be completed only if the employer is correcting its EIN, establishment number, or state ID number. If the previous Form W-3 was marked incorrectly for "Type of payer," report the prior, incorrect payer type in the "Explain decreases here" area. Mark the checkbox in Box c for "Third-party sick pay" if the employer is a third-party sick pay payer (or an employer reporting sick pay payments made by a third party) correcting Forms W-2 and the "Third-party sick pay" checkbox in Box 13 of Form W-2c under "Correct information" is marked. When applicable, this checkbox and a second checkbox on Form W-3c (e.g., 941/941-SS) must be marked.

**Boxes 1-12—Previously reported and corrected amounts.** Enter the totals of each box and each column from Forms W-2c. For Box 12, enter only the total of codes D-H, S, Y, AA, and BB. Zero amounts must be shown as -0- in any boxes being corrected.

**Box 14—Income tax withheld by 3rd party sick pay payer.** Use these boxes to correct amounts of income tax withheld by a third-party sick pay payer that were incorrectly reported on Form W-3. Enter the incorrect amount in the left-hand box and the correct amount in the right-hand box.

**Boxes 16-19—State and local information.** If the only changes to the original forms are to the state and/or local information, do not send either Copy A of Form W-2c or Form W-3c to the SSA. Just send the forms to the appropriate state or local taxing authority.

**Explain decreases here.** Explain any decreases to amounts "Previously reported." Also, report here any previous, incorrect entry in Box c, "Kind of payer." If the corrections necessitate an adjustment on an employment tax return (e.g., Form 941 or 943), check the "Yes" box below the explanation and on the next line enter the date the return was filed.

**Signature.** Sign and date the form. Also enter the title, phone number, name of a person to contact, fax number, and e-mail address.

**Form W-3c may be filed by someone other than the employer.** A payroll service provider or paying agent may send Form W-3c on the employer's behalf and sign the form for the employer if the following conditions are met:

- the service provider or agent is authorized to sign by a written or oral agency agreement that is valid under state law; and

- the service provider or agent writes "For (name of payer)" next to the signature.

**Forms W-2c and W-3c are scannable.** Forms W-2c and W-3c have been reformatted and are printed in red dropout ink to allow scanning of paper forms by machine. Privately printed substitutes for copy A of Form W-2c and Form W-3c must be printed on 8.5 X 11-inch paper using their revised formats and nonreflective black ink. See IRS Publication 1223 for detailed specifications for printing substitute Forms W-2c and W-3c.[151]

**Helpful hints in preparing Forms W-2c and W-3c.** The SSA offers the following suggestions for filing accurate correction reports:

- employers using the U.S. Postal Service should send completed Forms W-2c and W-3c to: SSA, Data Operations Center, P.O. Box 3333, Wilkes-Barre, PA 18767-3333; employers using other carriers (e.g, designated private delivery services) should send completed forms to: SSA, Data Operations Center, Attn: W-2c Process, 1150 East Mountain Drive, Wilkes-Barre, PA 18702-7997 (forms sent to other SSA addresses will be returned to the employer);

---

151. Rev. Proc 2006-19, 2006-13 IRB 677.

- use only standard or approved substitute forms as specified in Publication 1223, *Specifications for Private Printing of Forms W-2c and W-3c;*[152]

- even if the only corrections are to the employee's name or SSN, file both a Form W-2c and a Form W-3c and tell the employee to contact SSA and obtain an application for a social security card— Form SS-5;

- do not use Form W-2c to correct Form W-2G, *Certain Gambling Winnings*;

- do not "zero-fill" (e.g., 0.00) any line items on Form W-2c that are not being corrected—leave them blank;

- make sure the employer's EIN is correct on all forms;

- do not staple or tape Forms W-2c to Form W-3c;

- determine whether the erroneous information reported on the original Form W-2 or W-3 was also reported incorrectly on the employer's Form 941;

- file a separate Form W-3c for each tax year and each type of form;

- on paper Forms W-2c and W-3c, all entries should be typed in 12-point Courier font, if possible, in dark black ink; and

- large numbers of forms can be shipped in separate packages, with the employer's name and EIN on each, number the packages (1 of 4, 2 of 4, etc.), put Form W-3c in package 1, and show the number of packages at the bottom of Form W-3c below the title.

**APA OFFERS FILL-IN FORMS**  Fill-in versions of Forms W-2c and W-3c – approved by the SSA – are available on the American Payroll Association website at www.americanpayroll.org/news/formW2c.html.  Employers may complete these forms on their computer, print them out, distribute the employees' copies, and file Copy A with the SSA.

# 8.11  The Reconciliation Process for Employers

With so many different aspects to the tax collection, payment, and reporting process—withholding and depositing taxes, preparing and filing employment tax returns, providing information statements, and preparing and filing information returns—employers must have a way to keep track of each step and its relationship to the others.  Balancing is not only for the sake of having accurate and consistent records.  If the amounts withheld, deposited, paid, and reported do not balance or agree, an employer will find that the government agencies involved—the IRS, SSA, and state and local taxing authorities—will soon be knocking at the door demanding an explanation and assessing noncompliance penalties.

To help prevent "out-of-balance" conditions and reduce their confrontations with federal and state tax agencies, employers must periodically "reconcile" their wage and tax information.  They should make sure the amounts withheld, deposited, paid, and reported agree with each other, and if they do not, find out why and make corrections.  Performing reconciliations regularly throughout the year allows employers to correct discrepancies with time to spare before the process of preparing and filing quarterly and year-end tax and information returns begins, thus saving the payroll department from quarterly and year-end disasters.

---

152.   Rev. Proc. 2006-19, 2006-13 IRB 677.

**Pay period, tax deposit, and quarterly reconciliations.** With each pay period and tax deposit, the employer must ensure values produced by the automated payroll system agree with amounts taken from prior reconciliations and updated by amounts taken from the current payroll register and the tax deposit ledger. Then, before the last tax deposit for each of the first three quarters of the year, the employer must determine whether its deposits for the quarter equal the tax liability that will be reported on the quarterly Form 941. If not, the difference should be added to or subtracted from the last deposit of the quarter. This requires reconciliation before the due date of the last deposit for each quarter.

**Annual or year-end reconciliation.** This is probably the most important time for reconciliation of payroll wage and tax information. If an employer's totals from its four quarterly Forms 941 do not agree with the totals from its Forms W-2 (as shown on Form W-3 for certain amounts, the IRS and/or the SSA will inquire as to why and expect corrections to be made. These amounts include:

- social security wages;
- social security tips;
- Medicare wages and tips; and
- advance earned income credit.

Adjustments on Forms 941 and/or corrections to Forms W-2 and W-3 will also have to be made if any of the following situations occurs:

- Forms 941 are adjusted after the employer's Forms W-2 and W-3 for the calendar year have been filed;
- end-of-year bonuses are not included in the last form 941 for the year;
- adjusted amounts for a prior year are reported on a current year Form 941 and incorrectly included in the current year Form W-3 totals;
- taxable fringe benefits for November and December are treated as received in the following year under the special accounting rule, but are incorrectly shown as current year payments; or
- amounts reported on previous Forms 941 as wages were actually payments to an independent contractor.

The year-end reconciliation process should actually begin just after the end of the prior year-end process. At that time, a payroll reconciliation form similar to Table 8.3 should be prepared.

 **BE CAREFUL** Line 2 of Form 941 (Wages and tips, plus other compensation) cannot be corrected or adjusted on subsequent Forms 941 if a mistake was made on the original, since the only adjustments allowed are to federal income tax withheld and social security and Medicare taxes withheld and paid. This means that such mistakes will cause the Line 2 totals to disagree with the total wages reported on Forms W-2. Although the IRS does not ask employers to reconcile these amounts, employers should document any errors nonetheless to avoid confusion during year-end processing.

Table 8.3

| RECONCILIATION FORM | | | | |
|---|---|---|---|---|
| 941/W-2/W-3 Items | QTR 1 | QTR 2 | QTR 3 | YTD |
| Federal Wages | | | | |
| Federal Income Tax W/H | | | | |
| Social Security Wages | | | | |
| Social Security Tax W/H | | | | |
| Social Security Tips | | | | |
| Medicare Wages and Tips | | | | |
| Medicare Tax Withheld | | | | |
| Advance EIC Payments | | | | |

At the end of each quarter, ask for a preliminary "W-2 Audit" showing total wages paid and taxes withheld, as determined by the payroll system. These totals must be compared against the numbers on the payroll reconciliation form. By verifying wage and tax information regularly during the year, there is ample time to reconcile any errors before year-end and before W-2 forms need to be processed.

 **NEGATIVE WAGE AND TAX REPORT** When requesting the "W-2 Audit," also request an exception report showing any employees with negative wages or taxes at the federal, state, or local level. If there are any, this will serve as a warning that an error has been made that must be resolved before year-end. Also, any negative amount reported on a Form W-2 will cause the employee record to be dropped.

**Annual reconciliation worksheet.** An annual payroll reconciliation worksheet should be prepared at the end of the fourth quarter (see Table 8.4) so the numbers can be compared to the totals on the transmittal of the employer's Forms W-2 on Form W-3, or on the electronic file. Differences must be reconciled before returns are filed to avoid problems with the IRS and SSA.

Table 8.4

| ANNUAL RECONCILIATION WORKSHEET | | | | |
|---|---|---|---|---|
| 941/W-2/W-3 Items | YTD @ QTR 3 | QTR 4 | YTD | W-3/6559 TOTALS |
| Federal Wages | | | | |
| Federal Income Tax W/H | | | | |
| Social Security Wages | | | | |
| Social Security Tax W/H | | | | |
| Social Security Tips | | | | |
| Medicare Wages and Tips | | | | |
| Medicare Tax W/H | | | | |
| Advance EIC Payments | | | | |

The annual reconciliation worksheet provides a permanent record for the employer which assists the verification that all reported wage and tax information was in balance. This permanent record is necessary because the IRS and/or the SSA may not detect and pursue discrepancies until the next calendar year or later. When and if they do contact the employer, they may require the employer to produce a reconciliation or corrections. Therefore, the worksheet should become part of the year-end file and retained accordingly.

**IRS and SSA combine to detect and correct discrepancies.** As pointed out earlier in this section, employment tax returns (e.g., Forms 941, 943 or 944) are sent to the IRS, while Forms W-2 and W-3 are sent to the SSA. To make sure that employers' Form 941 totals agree with their Form W-2/W-3 totals, the IRS provides the SSA with information it receives from employers, including any 941c forms explaining adjustments made on the Forms 941, and SSA provides the IRS with Form W-2 data.

The SSA then compares the Forms 941 and the W-3 forms for the following amounts:

- social security wages;
- social security tips;
- Medicare wages and tips; and
- advance earned income credit.

If discrepancies are found, letters are sent to the employer notifying it of the discrepancy and requesting a response. The SSA sends the notice if the employer's Form 941 totals are greater than those on the Form W-2/W-3. If the opposite is true, the IRS sends the notice. The outcome of the correspondence (i.e., whether or not the employer responded to the notices and did or did not reconcile its account) is then forwarded to the IRS for action regarding possible penalties and other assessments.

Employers that receive a reconciliation letter should review it and compare it with their records. If the employer finds an error in its records, it should make the corrections instructed by the letter. The employer must make sure to complete the questionnaires accompanying the letter to insure that any corrections made are associated with the employer's previously submitted reports. Failure to respond to the letter may result in the assessment of additional taxes or the reduction of benefits payable to employees when they retire or become disabled.

# 8.12 Information Returns for Nonemployee Payments—1099 Series

In addition to the reporting requirements for wage payments and other compensation paid to employees, employers also must report certain payments they make to nonemployees, such as fees paid to independent contractors, payments from pension plans, and payments to estates and beneficiaries. While these payments and the consequent reporting may not originate with the payroll department in most companies, payroll professionals should be aware of them.

Most reportable payments must be reported on a form in the 1099 series. Similar to Form W-2, an annual 1099 information statement must be sent to the nonemployee payee detailing the payments and any withholding, while a copy is sent to the IRS (not the SSA) along with a transmittal form (Form 1096). The 1099 forms help the IRS determine whether individuals are reporting all their taxable nonwage income on their personal income tax returns. This discussion focuses on two of the 1099 forms that payroll practitioners may encounter most often, the 1099-MISC and the 1099-R. For information on two new forms in the series, Forms 1099-LTC, *Long-Term Care and Accelerated Death Benefits,* and Form 1099-SA, *Distributions From an HSA, Archer MSA, or Medicare Advantage MSA,* see Section 4.1-2 and 4.1-3, respectively.

# 8.12-1  Miscellaneous Payments Made by Businesses—Form 1099-MISC

Businesses (whether individuals, partnerships, or corporations) making certain payments to nonemployees in the course of their business must report those specific payments to the nonemployee and the IRS on Form 1099-MISC *Statement for Recipients of Miscellaneous Income* (see Appendix page A-261).[153]  All nonprofit organizations engaged in a trade or business must comply with this reporting requirement.

**Phone number must be placed on form.**[154]  Payers are required to include not only their name and address on Form 1099-MISC, but also the phone number of an information contact who can answer payees' questions about the form.

**Reportable payments.**[155]  Following is a list of some of the types of nonemployee payments that must be reported on Form 1099-MISC:

*Service payments to individuals.*  Payments totaling at least $600 in a calendar year made to noncorporate entities (e.g., individuals, partnerships) for services rendered to the business must be reported in Box 7 of Form 1099-MISC.  Nonemployee compensation may be in the form of fees, commissions, or prizes and awards (only those received for services rendered).  Service payments made to corporations are not reportable, except for payments to corporate health care providers and gross proceeds paid to incorporated law firms.

*Payments to health care providers.*  Payments made by businesses to health care service suppliers or providers must be reported in Box 6 if they total $600 or more in a year, whether the payee is an individual or a corporation.

There is an exception to this reporting requirement for payments to a health care provider made under a flexible spending arrangement or a health reimbursement arrangement that are considered employer health coverage (see Section 4.1-2.).

*Royalty payments.*  Royalty payments must be reported in Box 2 if they total at least $10 during the year.

*Payments to attorneys.*  Payments of gross proceeds to an attorney or law firm that are not reportable as attorneys' fees in Box 7 or on Form W-2 must be reported in Box 14 of Form 1099-MISC.  Under the final rules, which are effective for payments made on or after January 1, 2007, reporting is required for payments totaling $600 or more in a year whether or not:

- the payment is to an individual, partnership, or corporation;
- the attorney keeps some of the payment as compensation for legal services rendered; or
- some portions of the payment must be reported to another party on another information return (e.g., W-2).[156]

The final rules also require the payer to ask the attorney for the attorney's TIN at or before the time a reportable payment is made.  The attorney is required to provide the TIN, but does not have to certify that it is correct.  If the attorney does not provide the TIN, the payment is subject to backup withholding (see Section 6.5).  Other parts of the final rules are aimed at special situations that may arise in situations involving gross proceeds payments:

- if a check is delivered to a person who is not a payee on the check or to a payee who is not an attorney, the payment must be reported to the first-listed payee attorney on the check;

---

153.   IRC §6041; §6041A.
154.   IRC §6041A(e)(1).
155.   IRC §6041(a); §6041A(a); IRS Reg. §1.6041-1(a); §1.6041-3; IRS Prop. Reg. §1.6041A-1(a).
156.   IRS Reg. §1.6041-3; §1-6045-5; Form 1099-MISC instructions.

- if there is more than one attorney listed as payees on the check, reporting is required with respect to the attorney who received the payment;
- an attorney who receives a reportable payment of gross proceeds must file information returns for payments the attorney makes to any other attorneys;
- reporting is not required with respect to payments made to a nonresident alien individual or entity that does not engage in a trade or business in the U.S. and that does not perform any labor or personal services in the U.S.
- a payment to an attorney, in the case of a payment by check, means a check on which the attorney is named as a sole, joint, or alternative payee, including where the check is written to the attorney's client trust fund;
- payments of compensation or profits paid or distributed to its partners by a partnership engaged in providing legal services are not reported as gross proceeds;
- payments of dividends or corporate earnings and profits paid to its shareholders by a corporation engaged in providing legal services are not reported as gross proceeds; and
- payments made to an attorney in the attorney's capacity as a bankruptcy trustee are not reported as gross proceeds.

*Deferrals under a section 409A nonqualified deferred compensation plan.* Enter in Box 15a amounts of at least $600 deferred by a nonemployee to a nonqualified deferred compensation plan as defined in IRC §409A (see Section 4.6-10). Earnings on current and prior year deferrals also must be reported here.

*Income under section 409A on a nonqualified deferred compensation plan.* Enter in Boxes 7 and 15b amounts that must be included in a nonemployee's income because a nonqualified deferred compensation plan failed to comply with §409A (see Section 4.6-10). This income is also subject to an additional 20% tax, plus interest.

*Payments after bankruptcy case begins.*[157] Payments to independent contractors for services after the contractor has filed a bankruptcy petition should be reported to the bankruptcy estate on Form 1099-MISC under the estate's EIN, not to the contractor under the contractor's TIN.

*Government payments for services.*[158] Under the Tax Increase Prevention and Reconciliation Act of 2005, beginning in 2011, information reporting and withholding at the rate of 3% will be required on payments to individuals or business entities providing property or services to a government entity (including any agency, instrumentality, or political subdivision of federal or state government) with $100 million or more of annual expenditures that are subject to this withholding provision. The provision applies regardless of whether the government entity making the payment is the recipient of the property or services. No guidance as to how such payments will be reported were issued by the end of 2007.

*Other payments.* Prizes and awards of at least $600 must be reported in Box 3 if they are not given for services rendered, although certain charitable, scientific, artistic, and educational awards need not be reported if they are designated for transfer to a charitable organization or government subdivision. Also reported in Box 3 are other payments that do not meet the requirements of another box, including payments made after an employee's death to the deceased employee's estate or beneficiary, payments of at least $600 to jurors, and payments to former employees serving in the military (see Section 3.4-19).[159]

**Backup withholding.** Amounts withheld from nonemployee compensation because the payee failed to provide a valid taxpayer identification number (backup withholding) must be reported in Box 4 of Form 1099-MISC. For details on when backup withholding must be undertaken, see Section 6.5.

**Filing Form 1099-MISC.**[160] Copies B and 2 of Form 1099-MISC must be sent to the nonemployee who received the payments by January 31 of the year after the year during which the payments were made (e.g., February 2, 2009 for 2008 Forms 1099-MISC). An extension of time for providing statements to payees may

---

157. P.L. 109-8, §321; 11 USC §1115(a)(2); Notice 2006-83, 2006-40 IRB 596.
158. IRC §3402(t).
159. ILM 199932004, 3-11-99; Form 1099-MISC instructions.
160. IRC §6071(b); IRS Prop. Reg. §1.6041A-1(e), (f).

be requested by sending a letter to: IRS-Enterprise Computing Center-Martinsburg, Information Reporting Program, Attn: Extension of Time Coordinator, 240 Murall Dr., Kearneysville, WV 25430. The request must be postmarked by the due date for the statements. The letter must show the reason for the requested extension. Extensions are limited to 30 days.

*Electronic delivery to payees.* Businesses can deliver the Forms 1099-MISC electronically to any payee who consents in a manner similar to the one permitted with respect to Form W-2 (see Section 8.8-2).

For paper filers, Copy A must be filed with the IRS by February 28 after the year of payment (or by the next business day if February 28 is a Saturday, Sunday, or legal holiday; e.g., March 2, 2009 for 2008 Forms 1099-MISC). For employers filing Copy A information electronically, the due date is March 31 after the year to which the form applies (e.g., March 31, 2009 for calendar year 2008 Copy A). An automatic extension of the time for filing Copy A with the IRS (up to 30 days) is available to the employer by filing Form 8809, *Application for Extension of Time to File Information Returns* (see Appendix page A-393), by the due date, but there is no need to sign the form or explain the reason for the extension. A further 30-day extension is also possible if another Form 8809 is filed during the extension period with the employer's signature and an explanation of the reason for the request.

The employer must send its paper Copies A of Form 1099-MISC with a transmittal form—Form 1096, *Annual Summary and Transmittal of U.S. Information Returns* (see Appendix page A-255). Form 1096 serves the same purpose as Form W-3 does for an employer's Forms W-2. It summarizes the information appearing on the employer's 1099 forms. A new Form 1096 must be filed for each type of Form 1099 being filed. All forms must be sent to the appropriate IRS service center listed on the 1099 series instructions, depending on where the employer is located.

**Substitute forms.**[161] As with Forms W-2, employers can use substitute or privately printed Forms 1099-MISC, so long as they conform to the specifications set forth by the IRS.

**Electronic reporting.** Businesses that must file 250 or more Forms 1099-MISC are required to file them electronically, unless a waiver has been obtained. For more information on the electronic reporting requirements for information returns, see Section 8.14. Electronic filing is accomplished through the IRS's Filing Information Returns Electronically (FIRE) system (see IRS Pub. 1220, Specifications for Filing Forms 1098, 1099, 5498, and W-2G Electronically or Magnetically, and Pub. 3609, Filing Information Returns Electronically).[162]

 **NO MORE MAG MEDIA** Beginning with 2008 Forms 1099-MISC filed in 2009, the IRS will no longer accept magnetic media filings. Employers filing 250 or more Forms 1099-MISC must file them electronically with the IRS. Other employers can file either on paper or electronically.

## 8.12-2 Pension and Retirement Plan Distributions—Form 1099-R

Payers who make distributions of retirement income must report those payments and any amount withheld for federal income tax on Form 1099-R, *Distributions From Pensions, Annuities, Retirement or Profit-Sharing Plans, IRAs, Insurance Contracts, etc.* (see Appendix page A-271).[163]

**Reportable payments.** Distributions from all types of retirement plans (including governmental §457(b) plans), as well as payments of matured annuity, endowment, and life insurance contracts, must be reported on Form 1099-R. Both periodic and lump-sum distributions must be reported. Also report death benefits paid by employers that are not paid as part of a pension, profit-sharing, or retirement plan.

---

161. Rev. Proc. 2007-50, 2007-31 IRB 244; IRS Pub. 1179, General Rules and Specifications for Substitute Forms 1096, 1098, 1099, 5498, and W-2G (and 1042-S).
162. Rev. Proc. 2007-51, 2007-30 IRB 143.
163. IRC §6047.

**Taxable and nontaxable amounts reported separately.**[164] Payers must report not only the entire amount distributed during the year, but also the separate taxable and nontaxable amounts distributed. The gross distribution is entered in Box 1, the taxable amount in Box 2a, and the nontaxable amount in Box 5.

**Distributions under $10 need not be reported.**[165] An amendment contained in the Small Business Job Protection Act of 1996 altered the reporting requirements for Form 1099-R by stating that no form need be filed if the total distribution to the payee during the year is less than $10.

**Phone number of payer encouraged, but not required.** The requirement that the payer's phone number be included with its name and address, which applies to Forms 1099-MISC (see Section 8.12-1), does not apply to Forms 1099-R.

 **DETERMINING TAXABLE AND NONTAXABLE AMOUNTS** All employer contributions to a qualified retirement plan, as well as employee pre-tax contributions (e.g., elective deferrals to a §401(k) plan), plus the earnings on all plan contributions, are included in the taxable amount of a distribution. The nontaxable amount is the portion of the distribution attributable to employee after-tax contributions, which were already taxed as wages before the contribution was made.

There are two situations where the taxable and nontaxable amounts do not have to be reported separately. If the payer cannot, after a reasonable effort, determine the taxable amount, it should check Box 2b and leave Boxes 2a and 5 blank unless the distribution is from a traditional IRA, SEP, or SIMPLE plan (the amount will be in Boxes 1 and 2a). If the first payment from the plan was made before January 1, 1993, the employer has the option of separating taxable and nontaxable distribution amounts.

**Designated Roth contributions.** Beginning with Forms 1099-R filed for 2006, trustees must report the year when the employee began making designated Roth contributions from a §401(k) or §403(b) plan in the box, "1st year of design. Roth contrib." Designated Roth account distributions must be reported on Form 1099-R, with distribution code B in Box 7. The employee's basis in the distributions (designated Roth contributions) is reported in Box 5.

**Reporting direct rollovers.**[166] Payers making a direct rollover of a plan distribution must report the amount distributed on Form 1099-R as it would any other distribution. However, the payer must also add a distribution code in Box 7 identifying the distribution as a direct rollover. For distributions directly rolled over to an Individual Retirement Account or an eligible retirement plan, payers should enter Code G in Box 7. If the rollover is to an IRA of the spouse of a deceased plan participant, Codes 4 and G should be entered in Box 7.

If the direct rollover distribution includes deductible voluntary employee contributions (DECs), only one Form 1099-R is needed to report the direct rollover of the entire distribution. But if DECs are actually distributed, they must be reported on a separate Form 1099-R.

 **MAKE SURE PAYEE IS NAMED ON FORM** Payers completing Form 1099-R must be careful when reporting a direct rollover. They must use the name and taxpayer identification number of the payee, not those of the trustee of the IRA or employer plan to which the funds were rolled over.

**Filing Form 1099-R.**[167] Copies B, C, and 2 of Form 1099-R must be sent to the payee by January 31 of the year after the year during which the distributions were made (e.g., February 2, 2009 for 2008 Forms 1099-R). An extension of time for providing statements to payees may be requested by sending a letter to: IRS Enterprise Computing Center-Martinsburg, Information Reporting Program, Attn: Extension of Time Coordinator, 240 Murall Dr., Kearneysville, WV 25430. The request must be postmarked by the due date for the statements. The letter must show the reason for the requested extension. Extensions are limited to 30 days.

---

164. Rev. Proc. 92-86, 1992-2 CB 495; Form 1099-R Instructions.
165. IRC §6047(d)(1).
166. IRS Announcement 93-20, 1993-6 IRB 65.
167. IRC §6071(b); IRS Reg. §1.6047-1(a); Form 1099-R Instructions.

*Electronic delivery to payees.* Employers can deliver Forms 1099-R electronically to any payee who consents in a manner similar to the one permitted with respect to Form W-2 (see Section 8.8-2).

For paper filers, Copy A must be filed with the IRS by February 28 after the year of payment (e.g., March 2, 2009 for 2008 Forms 1099-R). For employers filing Copy A information electronically, the due date is March 31 after the year to which the form applies (e.g., March 31, 2009 for calendar year 2008 Copy A). An automatic extension of the time for filing Copy A with the IRS (up to 30 days) is available to the employer by filing Form 8809, *Application for Extension of Time to File Information Returns* (see Appendix page A-393), by the due date, but there is no need to sign the form or explain the reason for the extension. A further 30-day extension is also possible if another Form 8809 is filed during the extension period with the employer's signature and an explanation of the reason for the request.

The employer must send its paper Copies A of Form 1099-R with a transmittal form—Form 1096, *Annual Summary and Transmittal of U.S. Information Returns* (see Appendix page A-255). A new Form 1096 must be filed for each type of Form 1099 being filed. All forms must be sent to the appropriate IRS service center listed on the 1099 series instructions, depending on where the employer is located.

**Substitute forms.** As with Forms W-2, employers can use substitute or privately printed Forms 1099-R, so long as they conform to the specifications set forth by the IRS (see section 8.12-1).

**Electronic reporting.** Businesses that must file 250 or more Forms 1099-R are required to file them electronically, unless a waiver has been obtained. For details on the electronic reporting requirements for information returns, see Section 8.14. Electronic filing is accomplished through the IRS's Filing Information Returns Electronically (FIRE) system (see IRS Pub. 1220, Specifications for Filing Forms 1098, 1099, 5498, and W-2G Electronically or Magnetically, and Pub. 3609, Filing Information Returns Electronically).[168]

 **NO MORE MAG MEDIA** Beginning with 2008 Forms 1099-R filed in 2009, the IRS will no longer accept magnetic media filings. Employers filing 250 or more Forms 1099-R must file them electronically with the IRS. Other employers can file either on paper or electronically.

# 8.13 Penalties for Incorrect or Late Information Returns and Statements

Because some copies of information statements and returns must be sent to the IRS or the SSA (Copy A of Form W-2, Form W-3, Form 1096), while others are sent to employees or other payees (Copies B, C, and 2 of Form W-2, Copies B and 2 of Form 1099-MISC), there are distinct penalties imposed for failure to file in each situation.

## 8.13-1 Failure to File Information Returns

Penalties are assessed against employers or payers that file information returns with the IRS or SSA (Forms W-2, W-3, 1096, or 1099 series) after the due date ("failure to file timely") or with incorrect or incomplete information ("failure to file correct information") without reasonable cause. For the purpose of assessing these penalties, any filing extension that had been granted must be taken into account when determining the due date of a return. The severity of the penalty generally depends on how late the return is filed or how late the correct or complete information is provided to the IRS or SSA.

**General rules.** The general penalties are as follows:[169]

- $15 per return if the failure to file or provide correct information is corrected within 30 days after the due date, with a maximum penalty of $75,000 a year ($25,000 for small businesses);

---

168.    Rev. Proc. 2007-51, 2007-30 IRB 143.
169.    IRC §6721(a), (b), (d); IRS Reg. §301.6721-1(a), (b), (e).

- $30 per return if the failure to file or provide correct information is corrected more than 30 days after the due date but before August 1 of the same year the return is due, with a maximum penalty of $150,000 a year ($50,000 for small businesses); and

- $50 per return if the failure to file or provide correct information is not corrected by August 1, with a maximum penalty of $250,000 ($100,000 for small businesses).

*Example:* Sneakers, Inc. files 400 Forms 1099-MISC with correct information within 30 days after the due date and 2,000 correct W-2s more than 30 days after the due date but before August 1. Sneakers faces a penalty of $66,000 consisting of $6,000 for the Forms 1099-MISC (400 x $15) and $60,000 for the Forms W-2 (2,000 x $30).

 **HIGHER PENALTY APPLIES**[170] If a return is both late and provides incorrect or incomplete information, and a correction of one failure is made during one time period and the other failure is corrected during a later time period, the higher penalty is imposed.

*Example:* A return filed 45 days late with incorrect information that is not corrected until after August 1 is subject to the maximum penalty of $50.

**Small business maximums are lower.**[171] The lower maximum penalties noted above for small businesses apply to businesses with average annual gross receipts of up to $5 million for the three most recent tax years.

**Willful failures bring higher penalties.**[172] Where an employer "intentionally disregards" the information return filing requirements and willfully fails to file on time or to include all the correct information, the penalty for each return is the greater of $100 or 10% of the correct amount of tax required to be shown on the return. There is no maximum penalty for a willful violation.

An employer cannot be assessed a penalty both for a failure to file a return (or for filing incorrect information) and for intentionally disregarding the information return filing requirements when the assessments involve the same violation. Where the IRS assessed a failure-to-file penalty and then determines that there was intentional disregard of the filing requirements, it will most likely abate the initial penalty and make a new assessment for the more serious violation.[173]

**Payers can be sued for filing fraudulent returns.**[174] In addition to facing penalties from the IRS, businesses that file fraudulent information returns can be sued by the payee named on the return for damages of at least $5,000 or the actual damages suffered by the payee, including costs of pursuing the action and attorneys' fees, if that is greater. The payee must file a copy of the complaint in the suit with the IRS at the same time it is filed with the court.

**Small number of incorrect or incomplete returns corrected at no cost.**[175] Employers are not penalized for timely filed returns with incorrect or incomplete information corrected before August 1, up to the greater of 10 returns or 0.5% of the total number of information returns the employer must file during the year. If more than this "de minimis" number of returns are corrected, the rule is applied so the employer will receive the lowest penalty. The de minimis exception does not apply to reduce the penalty for filing returns late, although once the return is filed, if any errors on it are corrected by August 1, the exception may be applicable.

---

170.    IRS Reg. §301.6721-1(b)(4).
171.    IRC §6721(d); IRS Reg. §301.6721-1(e).
172.    IRC §6721(e); IRS Reg. §301.6721-1(f).
173.    ILM 200127043, 4-25-01.
174.    IRC §7434.
175.    IRC §6721(c); IRS Reg. §301.6721-1(d).

*Example 1:* Silicon Valley Corp. files all of its information returns—5,000 Forms W-2—on time with the SSA, 60 of which contain incorrect information. Corrections are made on May 1. No penalty is imposed for 25 of the failures to provide correct information (i.e., the greater of 10 or .005 x 5,000 = 25) even though the total number of failures exceeds the de minimis amount. The penalty for the other 35 incorrect W-2 forms is $30 per return, or $1,050 (35 x $30), since the corrections were made after 30 days but before August 1.

*Example 2:* The next year, SVC expands in size and files 10,000 Forms W-2 on time, again with 60 having incorrect information corrected on May 1. But SVC also files 2,000 Forms 1099-MISC on September 6. The total of 12,000 information returns is used to determine the application of the de minimis exception. Therefore, no penalty is imposed for the 60 W-2 forms corrected on May 1 (i.e., the greater of 10 or .005 x 12,000 = 60). The penalty for the 2,000 returns filed on September 6 is $100,000 (2,000 x $50 maximum penalty).

**Insignificant errors are not penalized.**[176] No penalty will be assessed against an employer for "inconsequential" errors or omissions on an information return. Errors are inconsequential when they do not prevent the IRS from processing the return or applying it to its intended use (e.g., misspelling the word "Avenue" in an employee's address, misspelling the employee's first name). There are certain errors or omissions, however, that are never inconsequential, including those relating to:

- a taxpayer identification number (SSN or EIN);
- an employee's or payee's last name; and
- any monetary amount.

Other errors or omissions may or may not be inconsequential depending on whether they prevent the return from being delivered properly or processed and applied as intended.

**No penalty for errors due to reasonable cause.**[177] Penalties will be waived for an employer if it can prove there was a reasonable cause for the failure to file or to include complete or correct information on a return. The employer can prove reasonable cause by showing there were "mitigating factors" leading to the failures. Such factors include:

- it is the first time the employer had to file the type of information return involved or had to file electronically; or

- the employer has had a history of complying with information return reporting requirements, including lowering its error rate from year to year.

An employer can also show reasonable cause by proving that the filing failures were caused by events beyond the employer's control, which may include:

- the unavailability of business records needed to prepare the required returns because of a fire or other casualty or a new law or regulatory change close to the reporting due date;

- the inability to afford the computer hardware necessary for first time electronic filing (only if the employer tried to contract out the filing and filed the returns on paper);

- reasonable reliance on erroneous written information from the IRS;

- the failures were committed by an agent who had reasonable cause for making them; or

- the failure of an employee to provide correct information needed to prepare the required return.

---

176.    IRS Reg. §301.6721-1(c).
177.    IRC §6724; IRS Reg. §301.6724-1.

Even if such factors are present, however, the employer will still be penalized if it failed to act in a "responsible manner" both before and after the failure to file timely and/or correctly.

**IRS may assess penalties for Form W-2 name/SSN mismatches.** At the American Payroll Association's annual Congress in May 2002, the IRS announced that it would begin assessing a $50 penalty against employers for each 2002 Form W-2 that contains a mismatch between the employee's name and social security number, with the first proposed assessment notices going out in June 2004. At the 2003 APA Congress, IRS officials indicated that the Service was pulling back from its penalty stance while it studied which employers provided the most or the highest percentage of incorrect employee name/SSN combinations.

In the summer of 2004, the IRS sent a letter to APA confirming that "in lieu of a systemic penalty program the IRS intends to continue focusing its efforts on those employers with the most egregious mismatch rates." The letter acknowledged that a widespread penalty program would not be an effective use of the IRS's resources without additional funding, especially in an area that is "generally compliant."

*IRS issues guidance on abating possible penalties.* Late in 2004, the IRS updated Publication 1586, Reasonable Cause Regulations and Requirements for Missing and Incorrect Name/TINs, to include information on Form W-2 name/SSN mismatch penalties and how an employer can show reasonable cause to have such penalties abated. Generally, this means that an employer must demonstrate that it acted in a responsible manner and took steps to avoid the failure.

Where an employer is seeking a waiver of a penalty based on the failure of an employer to provide a correct social security number (SSN), special requirements apply for establishing that the employer acted in a responsible manner.

*SSN is missing.* If an employer receives a penalty notice because an employee's SSN was missing from the Form W-2, the employer must show that it made an initial solicitation of the employee's SSN at the time the employee began work – in person, by mail, or by telephone. The employer can show that it made the initial solicitation if it has a Form W-4 on file for the employee that was submitted when the employee began work. The employer must also have made an annual solicitation for the employee's SSN during the same calendar year (or by January 31 of the following year if the employee began work in December). If the employer still does not receive an SSN from the employee, the employer must have made a second annual solicitation by December 31 of the year following the year in which the employee began work. The annual solicitations may be made by mail or telephone.

*SSN is incorrect.* If an employer receives a penalty notice because an employee's SSN is incorrect on Form W-2, the employer must show that it made an initial solicitation of the employee's SSN at the time the employee began work – in person, by mail, or by telephone – and that it used the SSN provided by the employee. No additional solicitations are necessary unless the IRS sends a penalty notice to the employer notifying it that the employee's SSN is incorrect. Following receipt of such an IRS penalty notice, the employer is required to make an annual solicitation for the correct SSN. If another IRS penalty notice is received in a later year, a second annual solicitation is required. The solicitation for the SSN must be made by December 31 of the year in which the penalty notice was received (January 31 of the next year if the penalty notice was received in December), and may be made by mail, telephone, electronically, or in person. (Note: A solicitation is not required if no reportable payments will be made to the employee in that year.)

*The end of the inquiry.* An employer may rely on the SSN that an employee provides in response to a solicitation, and the employer must use that SSN in filing a Form W-2 for that employee. If the employer receives an IRS notice of an incorrect SSN after having made two annual solicitations and reporting the SSN provided by the employee, the employer is not required to make further solicitations. The employer's initial and two annual solicitations will demonstrate that it has acted in a responsible manner before and after the failure and will establish reasonable cause.

**SOLICITATION IS KEY** In establishing reasonable cause for abating a mismatch penalty, it is the solicitation of the correct SSN that is important, not the employee's reply. Form W-4 may be used for any required annual solicitation of an employee's SSN.

*The role of SSNVS.* Employers may use the SSA's Social Security Number Verification Service (SSNVS) to verify employees' names and SSNs, but they are not required to do so. SSNVS is an optional way for employers to identify potential discrepancies and correct SSNs before receiving penalty notices.

It is important to note that the database used by SSA to match names and SSNs may not be identical to the IRS database. Mismatches reported under SSNVS are not considered IRS notices and do not trigger any solicitation requirements under IRS rules for reasonable cause waivers. A mismatch determined by SSNVS will not necessarily result in an IRS penalty notice and annual solicitation requirements.

*Recordkeeping.* After making an initial or annual solicitation, the employer should retain the employee's response or note the employee's response in its records. The employer should also note that a solicitation was made, especially if no response was received from the employee. Since Form W-4 may be used for solicitation, an employer that retains an employee's Form W-4 in its records will be able to document the solicitation.

 **WHAT ABOUT SSA NO-MATCH LETTERS?** The IRS receives its mismatch information from the SSA, which sends W-2/W-3 data to the IRS after it finishes its processing for earnings allocation purposes. The SSA also sends out "no-match" letters to employers that submit a wage report containing more than 10 Forms W-2 that the SSA cannot process, if the mismatched forms represent more than 0.5% of the Forms W-2 in the report. These no-match letters are not IRS notices and do not trigger annual solicitation requirements to demonstrate reasonable cause for incorrect SSNs. See Section 1.8 for requirements imposed on employers by the Department of Homeland Security when they receive a no-match letter.

*No 'single/zero' withholding after mismatch is found.* If an employee fails to provide a complete Form W-4 when he or she begins employment, the employee is considered single with zero withholding allowances for federal income tax purposes (see Section 6.3-1). However, IRS regulations do not impose single/zero withholding if the SSN reported on a complete Form W-4 eventually proves to be incorrect.

**Penalty notification and assessment procedure.** The IRS sends out Notice 972CG, *Notice of Proposed Civil Penalty* (see Appendix page A-224), to employers for information returns that:

- were filed late;
- were not filed on magnetic media or electronically (if required); or
- had missing and/or incorrect taxpayer identification numbers (SSNs or EINs).[178]

Included with Notice 972CG is a listing of missing and incorrect name and TIN combinations, as well as a copy of Publication 1586.

Notice 972CG is a proposal, not an assessment. Employers have 45 days to respond to the notice. Interest does not begin to accrue until an actual penalty is assessed, not while it is still a proposal. Employers receiving the notice must submit a written explanation to show why the proposed penalties should not be assessed. If the IRS accepts the explanation, it will send the employer a letter explaining that no further action is necessary.

If the employer's explanation provides an acceptable reason for part of the proposed penalty, the assessment will be for the difference. If the explanation is not accepted, the IRS will assess the full amount of the penalty. The IRS will also assess the penalty if the employer does not reply to the notice. After submitting an explanation, the employer will receive a balance due notice and an explanation of IRS's decision, along with details on how to appeal the decision.

---

178.    IRS Announcement 94-93, 1994-29 IRB 40; IRS Announcement 94-141, 1994-50 IRB 22.

**Penalty and interest notices have to be detailed**. As part of the IRS Restructuring and Reform Act of 1998, IRS penalty and interest notices have to include some details as to how they were determined. All penalty notices issued after June 30, 2003, must include the name of the penalty, the IRC section under which it is imposed, and a computation of the penalty. The initial penalty assessment must also be personally approved in writing by the supervisor of the person making the assessment. Any notice that includes an interest component after June 30, 2003 must include the IRC section under which interest is imposed and a calculation of the interest. For penalty and interest notices issued after June 30, 2001, and before July 1, 2003, all the IRS has to do is include a phone number that the employer can call to request a copy of their tax assessment and payment history related to the penalty and/or the interest amounts.[179]

## 8.13-2 Failure to Provide Information Statements to Employees

If an employer fails to provide an employee or other payee with a required information statement (e.g., Copy B of Form W-2 or 1099-MISC) on time and/or with incorrect or incomplete information, a penalty of $50 per statement may be imposed, up to a maximum of $100,000. The penalty is $50 no matter how long after the due date a correct statement is provided to the employee or payee. Only one penalty is assessed per statement, even if both a "failure to furnish timely" and a "failure to include correct information" have occurred.[180]

**No lower maximums for small businesses.** Unlike the penalties imposed for not timely filing correct information returns, there is no reduction in the $100,000 maximum penalty for small businesses that fail to timely furnish correct employee or payee statements.

**Willful failures bring higher penalties.**[181] Where an employer "intentionally disregards" the requirement to provide employees with timely and correct information statements, the penalty for each statement is the greater of $100 or 10% of the monetary amounts required to be shown on the statement. There is no maximum penalty for a willful violation.

**No "de minimis" exception.** There is no exception allowing employers to correct errors on a small number of information statements without penalty.

**No penalty for inconsequential errors.**[182] No penalty will be assessed against an employer for "inconsequential" errors or omissions on an information statement. Errors are inconsequential when they would not reasonably be expected to prevent the employee or payee from receiving the information on time and using it to file a personal tax return. However, errors relating to the following are never inconsequential:

- any monetary amount;
- significant errors in the employee's or payee's address;
- use of an appropriate substitute or privately printed form; or
- the manner of furnishing the statement.

**No penalty for errors due to reasonable cause.**[183] Employers that can show there was a reasonable cause for their failure to furnish timely and correct information will not be penalized. For details as to what must be shown to prove reasonable cause, see Section 8.13-1.

**Fraud brings criminal and civil penalties.**[184] If an employer willfully provides a false or fraudulent Form W-2 to an employee or willfully fails to provide a Form W-2 in the proper manner and on time, the employer faces a criminal fine of up to $1,000 and/or one year in jail. The employer also faces a civil penalty of $50 for each violation. (For other criminal penalties an employer can face, see Section 8.7).

---

179. IRC §6631; §6751.
180. IRC §6722(a), (b); IRS Reg. §301.6722-1(a).
181. IRC §6721(c); IRS Reg. §301.6722-1(c).
182. IRS Reg. §301.6722-1(b).
183. IRC §6724; IRS Reg. §301.6724-1.
184. IRC §6674; §7204; IRS Reg. §31.6674-1.

For the requirements on what information IRS must include with penalty and interest notices, see Section 8.13-1.

# 8.14 Electronic Reporting Requirements

**Form W-2 requirements.** Employers that file 250 or more Forms W-2 (Copy A) must file them electronically.[185] For forms in the 1099 series, as well as Form 8027, *Employer's Annual Information Return of Tip Income and Allocated Tips* (see Appendix page A-358) and Form 1042-S, *Foreign Person's U.S. Source Income Subject to Withholding* (see Appendix page A-234), employers meeting the 250-form threshold are also required to file electronically. Several nonpayroll-related information returns are also subject to electronic reporting requirements. Employers filing less than 250 of these forms may voluntarily file electronically.

It is important for employers to note that the 250-return threshold does not mean the employer must have 250 employees at the time W-2 forms must be filed to trigger the magnetic media or electronic reporting requirement. An employer with fewer than 250 employees that had high turnover during the year may well have to file at least 250 W-2 forms and, if so, it must file them electronically. Also, the 250-form threshold applies to each type of form separately, not in total.

**Exceptions based on hardship.**[186] Employers that can prove filing information returns electronically would be significantly more expensive than filing paper forms can get a hardship waiver of the reporting requirement. The employer must apply for the waiver to the IRS (not the SSA, even for W-2 forms) by completing and sending in Form 8508, *Request for Waiver From Filing Information Returns Electronically/Magnetically* (see Appendix page A-374), at least 45 days before the due date of the return. The waiver is good for one year only and must be applied for each year if the employer feels it is necessary for future years.

Form 8508 should be sent to the following address:

> Internal Revenue Service
> Enterprise Computing Center-Martinsburg
> Information Reporting Program
> 240 Murall Drive
> Kearneysville, WV 25430

**No more magnetic media for W-2s.** Beginning with 2006 Forms W-2 filed in 2007, the SSA no longer accepts Form W-2 data reported on magnetic media. Electronic filing is the only option for employers filing 250 or more Forms W-2. The SSA also does not accept CD-ROM, DLX cartridges, 4490 cartridges, or electronic filing by VAN or OWRS via dial-up networking.

**Filing extensions.** An employer may get an automatic extension of the time to file information returns on magnetic media or electronically for up to 30 days by completing and filing Form 8809, *Application for Extension of Time to File Information Returns* (see Appendix page A-393). The form must be sent no later than the due date of the return, and it does not have to be signed or include a reason for the extension. A second 30-day extension can be applied for with another Form 8809 that is signed by the employer and includes an explanation of the reason for the extension. Form 8809 should be sent to the same address as Form 8508 shown above. If the request for extension involves more than 10 employers, the IRS encourages filers to submit the request on magnetic tape cartridge, or electronically through the Filing Information Returns Electronically (FIRE) system. Magnetic media or electronic filing is required if the request involves more than 50 employers.

**Electronic filing requirement for Forms W-2c.** Beginning in 2007, the IRS requires employers that file 250 or more Forms W-2c during a calendar year to file them electronically with the SSA.[187] The requirement applies only to Forms W-2c filed to correct Forms W-2 for the immediate prior year.

---

185. IRS Reg. §301.6011-2; IRS Temp. Reg. §301.6011-2T; SSA Pub. EFW2, May 2007.
186. IRS Reg. §301.6011-2(c)(4); IRS Temp. Reg. §301.6011-2T(c)(2).
187. SSA Pub. 42-014, Specifications for Filing Forms W-2c Electronically (EFW2C).

*Example 1:* Tiki's Taco Shops, Inc. filed 300 2007 Forms W-2 and 350 2008 Forms W-2. During 2009, Tiki's has to correct all 300 of the 2007 Forms W-2 and 200 of the 2008 Forms W-2. None of these 500 Forms W-2c has to be filed electronically, since less than 250 of the W-2s filed for the previous year (2008) are being corrected.

*Example 2:* The facts are the same as in Example 1, except that Tiki's has to correct 300 of the 2008 Forms W-2. The 300 Forms W-2c filed to correct the 2008 Forms W-2 must be filed electronically, while the 300 Forms W-2c filed to correct the 2007 Forms W-2 can be filed on paper or electronically.

For guidance on filing Forms W-2c electronically, employers should call one of the SSA's Employer Service Liaison Officers (see Table 8.5). The specifications for filing are contained in EFW2C (Specifications for Filing Forms W-2c Electronically).

**Requirements extended to U.S. possessions**.[188] IRS regulations and the SSA require employers filing wage and tax statements for employees in Puerto Rico (Form 499R-2/W-2PR), the U.S. Virgin Islands (Form W-2VI), Guam (Form W-2GU), and American Samoa (Form W-2AS) to file such statements electronically if they file 250 or more during the calendar year.

**Transmittal form no longer needed.** For pre-2005 Forms W-2, employers that filed Copy A on magnetic tapes or cartridges were required to send along with each magnetic media report Form 6559, *Transmitter Report and Summary of Magnetic Media*. Form 6559 served the same purpose as Form W-3, summarizing the wage and tax information on the Forms W-2. If information was being sent for more than two employers, the transmitter (agent or service bureau) had to use Form 6559-A, *Continuation Sheet for Form 6559*, for the information related to the other employers.

As noted earlier in this section, beginning with 2006 Forms W-2 employers can no longer file their W-2 information with the SSA on magnetic media. Therefore, Forms 6559 and 6559-A are no longer required to be used as transmittal forms, since electronic filing does not require a transmittal form.

**SSA Employer Service Liaison Officers.** Table 8.5 is a directory listing the telephone numbers of the SSA Employer Service Liaison Officers (formerly Regional Magnetic Media Coordinators) and the states making up each region that they serve.

---

188.    IRS Reg. §301.6011-2.

Table 8.5

| DIRECTORY OF SSA Employer Service Liaison Officers | | | |
|---|---|---|---|
| **Calls From** | **Telephone** | **Calls From** | **Telephone** |
| Alabama, Florida, Georgia, Kentucky, Mississippi, North Carolina, South Carolina, Tennessee | Kirk Jockell (404) 562-1315 (Atlanta) Kirk.jockell@ssa.gov | Connecticut, Maine, Massachusetts, New Hampshire, Rhode Island, Vermont | Regina Bachini (617) 565-2895 (Boston) Regina.bachini@ssa.gov |
| Alaska, Idaho, Oregon, Washington | Tim Beard (206) 615-2125 (Seattle) Tim.beard@ssa.gov | New Jersey, New York Puerto Rico, Virgin Islands | Tyrone Benefield (212) 264-1117 (New York) Tyrone.s.benefield@ssa.gov |
| American Samoa, Arizona, California, Guam, Hawaii, Nevada Northern Marianna Islands | Bill Brees (510) 970-8247 (San Francisco) Bill.brees@ssa.gov | Delaware, District of Columbia, Maryland, Pennsylvania, Virginia, West Virginia | Frank O'Brien (215) 597-4632 (Philadelphia) Frank.obrien@ssa.gov |
| Arkansas, Louisiana, New Mexico, Oklahoma, Texas | Debbie Forsythe (281) 449-2955 (Dallas) Debbie.forsythe@ssa.gov | Illinois, Indiana, Michigan, Minnesota, Ohio, Wisconsin | Paul Dieterle and Pat Hayes (312) 575-4244 (Chicago) Paul.dieterle@ssa.gov |
| Colorado, Montana, North Dakota, South Dakota, Utah, Wyoming | Carolyn Sykes (303) 844-2364 (Denver) Carolyn.sykes@ssa.gov | Iowa, Kansas, Missouri, Nebraska | Kelli Chappelow (816) 936-5649 (Kansas City) kelli.chappelow@ssa.gov |

**Penalties for noncompliance.** If an employer fails to file Forms W-2 electronically despite being required to do so, the failure is considered a failure to file a return, even if paper Forms W-2 have been submitted.[189] As with other failures to file a return, the amount of the penalty per return depends on how long it takes the employer to correct the failure. (See Section 8.13-1 for more on penalties for failure to file information returns.) The failure-to-file penalty will be assessed only for those returns in excess of the 250-return threshold.

*Example:* An employer submits 800 paper Forms W-2 on time and with the correct information. Even though it was required to submit all 800 forms electronically, the employer will be assessed a failure-to-file penalty on only 551 of the forms (800 - 249).

For electronic Forms W-2 that are filed late, the penalty amount is based on when the SSA receives processable information. SSA notifies the IRS of the receipt dates for all late-filed electronic reports. If the SSA returns a timely-filed report as unprocessable, the employer has 45 days to correct and return the report to the SSA. If a processable file is returned within this period, no late filing penalty will be assessed.

**Electronic wage reporting over the Internet.** Employers that are required to file electronically must file their Forms W-2 over the Internet through SSA's Business Services Online (BSO). BSO is available at www.socialsecurity.gov/employer and can be used to file Forms W-2 from the third week of December through the end of the filing season (March 31). Resubmittal reports can be filed year round. Once the W-2 file has been transferred to SSA, the employer will get an on-screen Acknowledgement of Receipt for its

---

189.    IRS Reg. §301.6011-2(f).

records. It contains a control number (Wage File Identifier-WFID) that the employer can use to check the processing status of the transmission.

Employers that are filing electronically for the first time must register first at SSA's Business Services Online (BSO) website, www.socialsecurity.gov./bso/bsowelcome.htm. At the end of the registration process, which can also be done by voice phone at 800-772-6270, the employee registering for the employer will be given a User ID by SSA. The employee will select a password which it must change once every 365 days. If the employee provides an e-mail address while registering, the SSA will send an e-mail notice when it's time to change the password. This User ID and password, along with the employer's EIN, will be needed to upload W-2 files and obtain transmission status reports. Users need Internet access and a web browser with 128-bit encryption and cookies enabled. SSA encourages the use of file compression, and PKZIP and WinZip are the only compression software SSA currently supports. Test files are encouraged, especially for first time electronic filers, and they should be submitted during the month of December. Registration should also be done during December.

The SSA continues to enhance BSO and allows employees to request access to several BSO services, including:

- *Report wages to the SSA.* This service allows an employee to send Forms W-2 and W-2c to the SSA by uploading a formatted file or by keying them in an online form. The capability to view submission processing status is available. Notices to resubmit a wage file can be acknowledged online. A one-time, 15-day extension of the 45-day deadline for resubmitting wage data can be requested.
- *View file/wage report status, errors, and error notices.* This service allows the user to view the processing status, errors, and error notices for wage files and/or wage reports submitted for the employee's employer.
- *Acknowledge resubmission notice.* Employers can acknowledge a notice from the SSA asking that the employer's data be resubmitted.
- *View name and SSN errors.* This service allows an employee to view the processing status, errors (including name and SSN mismatches), and error notices for wage files and/or wage reports submitted for the employee's employer.

For more detailed information on the registration process and BSO in general, download SSA's BSO Handbook at www.socialsecurity.gov/employer/bsohbnew.htm.

Once an employee has requested the BSO services that are needed, the SSA will send an activation code to either the employee or the employer, depending on the service requested. (No activation code is required to report wages to the SSA.) Some applications within the BSO group of services require a higher level of security, so the employer must approve the use of some of them, including SSNVS. Once the activation code is entered, the BSO service selected can be used immediately. The following table shows the type of user, the type of access, and the activation code destination.

It is important to make sure that employees no longer authorized to use BSO do not have an active User ID. There are two ways to deactivate a User ID:

- Go to the BSO website and log in to remove access to BSO. Remember that:
  - You can remove only those services to which you have access; and
  - If you remove access to any service(s) in error, you will need to re-request access on the Request Access to BSO Services page.
- Call 800-772-6270 (toll-free) between 7 a.m. and 7 p.m. ET, Monday - Friday. Remember that:
  - You should deactivate a User ID if an employee leaves the company (the User ID belongs to the company, not the employee);
  - You should deactivate a User ID if an employee no longer requires a service(s) in BSO; and
  - You may deactivate some or all access to BSO.

| If you are a: | And you selected access to: | Then your activation code will be mailed to: |
|---|---|---|
| Regular user (non self-employed or foreign registrant) | Report Wages to the SSA | No activation code is required. You may begin to use the service immediately. |
| Regular user (non self-employed or foreign registrant) | View File/Wage Report Status, Errors, and Error Notices | The address you provided during registration |
| Regular user (non self-employed or foreign registrant) | View Name and Social Security Number Errors | The address SSA has on file for your employer. |
| Self-employed registrant | Report Wages to the SSA | No activation code is required. You may begin to use the service immediately. |
| Self-employed registrant | View File/Wage Report Status, Errors, and Error Notices | The address you provided during registration |
| Foreign registrant | Any BSO service | The address SSA has on file for your employer. |

In addition to BSO, federal and state agencies connected to SSA's National Computer Center by a dedicated telecommunication line can use that system to file W-2 information via Electronic Data Transfer (EDT). The system uses Sterling Commerce's Connect: Direct software. For more information on this filing option, call SSA at 800-772-6270, 7:00 a.m. - 7:00 p.m., ET, Monday-Friday,.

 **HELP IS AVAILABLE** Employers with questions about BSO can call 888-772-2970 from 8:30 a.m. - 4:00 p.m. Eastern Time, Monday - Friday, fax 410-597-0237, or e-mail bso.support@ssa.gov. Information is also available at SSA's website—http://www.socialsecurity.gov/bso/bsowelcome. htm.

**Employers can fill in and submit W-2s/W-3s and W-2cs/W-3cs online.** Employers can complete up to 20 Forms W-2 online and submit them to SSA using BSO. SSA hopes that this program will encourage small filers to file electronically by not requiring them to incur programming costs. Employers wishing to use W-2 Online must register with SSA and obtain a User ID and password. Employers can save and print their employees' copies of Forms W-2 as well. Employers can submit up to 20 Forms W-2 per Form W-3 per session, with no limit on the number of sessions.

Employers can also file online Forms W-2c to correct previously submitted prior year Forms W-2. This includes Forms W-2 submitted on paper, Internet, or W-2 online. With W-2c Online, employers can create, print, save, and submit up to 5 Forms W-2c in each report (with one Form W-3c). Employers can submit up to 5 Forms W-2c per Form W-3 per session, with no limit on the number of sessions.

The ability to save W-3 Online or W-3c Online reports applies to entering the data and then saving the data before submitting the file. In this context, the process of saving reports works as follows:

- Enter up to 20 Forms W-2;
- Save the work, but do not submit the file for processing by SSA; and
- Return anytime before the March 31 e-file deadline, open the file, make any necessary corrections, and submit the file.

After a W-2 Online file has been submitted, SSA makes an Adobe Acrobat® .pdf backup/reference file of the employee and employer paper copies available for 30 days. Submitters can download the .pdf file within the 30 days if they wish to keep that in addition to the Copy D on paper.

W-2c Online does not contain any test features, so the employer should not submit any data that is not intended to be processed by the SSA. Also, W-2c Online can only be used to correct the prior year's Forms

W-2 (e.g., online W-2cs can be filed in 2008 only to correct 2007 Forms W-2). Some items cannot be corrected on an online W-2c, including a previous W-2c, corrections limited to state and/or local wage and tax data, corrections of wages earned in U.S. territories, corrections of U.S. military wages, third-party sick pay recap Forms W-2 and W-3c, and correction of an EIN or employment type.

**Electronic filing specs.** Beginning with 2007 Forms W-2 filed in 2008, the Form W-2 electronic filing specifications can be found in SSA Publication 42-007, Specifications for Filing Forms W-2 Electronically (EFW2), and the Form W-2c specifications can be found in SSA Publication 42-014, Specifications for Filing Forms W-2c Electronically (EFW2C). These publications replace the Magnetic Media and Electronic Filing Specifications (MMREF-1 and MMREF-2, respectively). These publications are generally available on SSA's website in May.

The EFW2 has one record length (512 characters) for all records and for all media, does not require intermediate totals, has fields to accept electronic signature and User ID information (eliminating the need to file paper), and incorporates requirements for domestic and U.S. territorial wage information. Additional features include electronic acknowledgment of receipt, online status information, and testing of files before submission. The EFW2C has the same advantages, with a single record length of 1024 characters so original and corrected data can be included. Employers using EFW2 and EFW2C can also download AccuWage and AccuW2c software, which can be used to test wage reports for proper formatting before submittal to SSA.

**WHAT ABOUT THE STATES?** All the states that accept or require electronic filing of Form W-2 information (see Table 8.7) accept EFW2-formatted files for Forms W-2.

*SSA provides vendor list for employers.* The SSA publishes an annual list of vendors that prepare electronic files of Forms W-2 and W-3 for submission to the agency. Inclusion on the list does not imply SSA approval or endorsement. The vendor list contains the names of:

- service providers that can file annual wage report information electronically; and

- vendors that provide software packages for employers or third-party providers who wish to produce annual wage reports electronically for transmission to the SSA.

**Electronic filing requirements for Forms 1099.**[190] Employers filing 250 or more of any single type of Form 1099 must file them electronically. Before doing so for the first time, however, they must apply for approval to file electronically by completing and filing Form 4419, *Application for Filing Returns Electronically* (see Appendix page A-350). Form 4419 should be submitted to the IRS at least 30 days before the due date of the return. Once approval is received, the employer does not have to reapply each year unless electronic filing is discontinued for a year or the employer is submitting its own files electronically for the first time and a service provider had submitted them in the past. Only one form is needed even if the employer is required to file more than one type of form electronically. Form 4419 can also be faxed to 304-264-5602.

Employers and payers file Forms 1099 electronically with IRS through the Filing Information Returns Electronically (FIRE) system at http://fire.irs.gov. For details, see IRS Pub. 1220, Specifications for Filing Forms 1098, 1099, 5498, and W-2G Electronically or Magnetically.

**Electronic filing requirements for Form 8027.**[191] Large food or beverage establishments (more than 10 employees) where tipping is customary must file Form 8027, *Employer's Annual Information Return of Tip Income and Allocated Tips* (see Section 3.4-27 and Appendix page A-358), to determine if tips have been underreported and must be allocated. A separate Form 8027 must be filed for each establishment owned by the restaurant, and if 250 or more must be filed, they must be filed electronically.

---

190. IRS Reg. §301.6011-2; Rev. Proc. 2007-51, 2007-30 IRB 143; IRS Pub. 1220, Specifications for Filing Forms 1098, 1099, 5498, and W-2G Electronically or Magnetically.
191. IRS Reg. §301.6011-2; Rev. Proc. 2006-29, 2006-27 IRB 13; IRS Pub. 1239, Specifications for Filing Form 8027, Employer's Annual Information Return of Tip Income and Allocated Tips, Magnetically/Electronically.

Before filing Form 8027 electronically for the first time, the employer must apply for approval to do so by completing and filing Form 4419 (see earlier discussion on 1099 series electronic filing requirements) at least 30 days before the filing deadline for the return.

**Information Reporting Program help for employers.** The IRS Enterprise Computing Center-Martinsburg Customer Service Section is available to help employers with their information reporting questions dealing with magnetic/electronic filing and tax law issues, other than Form W-2/W-3 electronic filing issues. Hours of operation are 8:30 a.m. - 4:30 p.m. Eastern Time, Monday - Friday. The customer service center can be reached several different ways:

By phone:  304-263-8700
     866-455-7438 (toll-free)
     304-267-3367 (TDD)
By e-mail:  mccirp@irs.gov

**Magnetic media discontinued for Forms 940 and 941.**[192] In August 2003, the IRS announced that it would stop processing magnetic tape for Forms 940 and 941 in February 2004. The last forms IRS accepted on magnetic tape from employer agents filing more than 100 forms were the 2003 Form 940 and the fourth quarter 2003 Form 941. The IRS said it was making this move as part of its initiatives to encourage electronic filing of business tax returns.

**Employment tax e-file system for Forms 940, 941, 944, and 941c.**[193] The Employment Tax e-file System offers an electronic filing method for Form 940 and 941 filers. It also allows electronic return originators (EROs) to offer their clients electronic employment tax filing.

*Features of the system:*
- *Filing options.* The Employment Tax e-file System accepts Forms 940, 940PR, 941, 941PR, 941SS, 941c, Schedule B, and Schedule D.
- *Flexible filing.* Forms 940 and 941 can be filed in a single transmission file.
- *Explicit error conditions.* The error conditions pinpoint the location of the error in the transmission, and provide complete information for each error identified.
- *Instant acknowledgments.* Transmissions are processed upon receipt and acknowledgments returned in near real-time.
- *Integrated payment option.* Eligible filers may submit a required payment along with their return, subject to limitations imposed by federal tax deposit rules.
- *Completely electronic signature process.* Taxpayers and reporting agents can sign their returns with their own IRS-issued personal identification number (PIN).

*Who can participate?*
- *Authorized IRS e-file providers / electronic return originators.* EROs get approval to file by filing an IRS e-file Application.
- *Reporting agents.* An accounting service, franchiser, bank, or other person authorized to prepare and electronically file Forms 940 and 941 for a taxpayer can sign all of the electronic returns they file with a single PIN signature.
- *Third-party transmitters.* A firm, organization, or individual that receives electronic return data from taxpayers, EROs, and reporting agents may reformat the data (if necessary), batch it with returns from other filers, and transmit it to the IRS.
- *Software developers.* Companies that develop software for their own use or for commercial sale for the purpose of electronically filing employment tax returns must have the software and must pass an assurance testing process before being approved for e-filing.

---

192. 68 FR 41290, 8-1-03.
193. Rev. Proc. 2005-60, 2005-35 IRB 449; IRS Pub. 3823, Employment Tax e-file System Implementation and User Guide; IRS Pub. 3112, IRS e-file Application and Participation; IRS Pub. 3715, Technical Specifications Guide for the Electronic Filing of Form 940, Employer's Federal Unemployment (FUTA) Tax Return.

# Section 8: Depositing and Reporting Withheld Taxes

- *Online filing providers.* An online filing provider allows taxpayers to prepare returns themselves by entering return data directly into commercially available software, software downloaded from an Internet site and prepared offline, or through an online Internet site.

*How to participate.* Reporting agents, transmitters, EROs, and software developers wishing to file employment tax forms for themselves or their clients must first submit an IRS e-file application, Application to Participate in the IRS e-file Program. The application can be filed online after registering for e-services on the IRS website.

Applications must be received by the following dates preceding the quarter ending dates:

| Application Due Date | Quarter Ending Date |
|---|---|
| December 15 (prior year) | March 31 |
| March 15 | June 30 |
| June 15 | September 30 |
| September 15 | December 31 |

All applicants will be notified of their acceptance or rejection into the Employment Tax e-file System within 45 days of the receipt of their application. Accepted applicants will also receive the identification items shown in Table 8.6 below. Reporting agents will also receive a Validated Agent's List within the same 45 days, and failure to use the names and EINs provided on the list may delay processing.

Table 8.6

| Identification Item | ERO | Reporting Agent | Transmitter | Software Developer |
|---|---|---|---|---|
| Electronic Tramsmitter Identification Number (ETIN) | | | X | X |
| Password | | | X | X |
| Electronic Filing Identification Number (EFIN) | X | X | X | X |
| Personal Identification Number (PIN) | | X | | |

*PIN registration.* All returns filed through the Employment Tax e-file System must be signed electronically with a Personal Identification Number (PIN). If a return is prepared by any participant other than a reporting agent, the taxpayer must sign the return. Reporting agents are issued a 5-digit PIN during the e-file application process. Employers that need a PIN must complete an online registration process. They can register through an approved IRS e-file provider that offers this service and the provider will transmit the registration to the IRS. The employer should get its PIN by mail within 7-10 days after the registration has been processed. Only one PIN can be issued per EIN.

The employer's PIN is valid for filing as soon as it is received. If the employer decides to use the services of another e-file provider after receiving its PIN, the employer does not have to register again. The PIN is not linked to the provider that transmitted the original registration.

*Reporting agent authorization.*[194] Reporting agents must submit, for each employer for which they file electronically, Form 8655, *Reporting Agent Authorization* (see Appendix page A-376), or another document that clearly contains the same information. Form 8655 may be signed and submitted electronically. Form 8655

---

194. Rev. Proc. 2007-38, 2007-25 IRB 1442; IRS Pub. 1474, Technical Specifications Guide for Reporting Agent Authorization for Magnetic Tape/Electronic Filers.

authorizes the reporting agent to file any of the listed forms electronically on the employer's behalf and to receive copies of notices, correspondence, and transcripts or other information with respect to the returns filed by the agent. Form 8655 can also be used to allow an agent to sign and file paper Forms 940, 941, 943, 944, 945, and 1042, or to make federal tax deposits and payments for taxes reported on Forms 940, 941, 943, 944, 945, and 1042.

*Submitting a test file.* All prospective electronic filers must transmit an initial test electronic transmission of Form 941 by the following test file due dates:

| Initial Test File Due Date | For Quarter Ending |
|---|---|
| April 10 | March 31 |
| July 10 | June 30 |
| October 10 | September 30 |
| January 10 | December 31 |

After evaluating the test file, the IRS will notify the applicant in writing of its approval or denial of electronic filing privileges. If the application is denied, the filer has 15 days to submit a new test file or contact the e-file Help Desk at 866-255-0654 to make other arrangements. Otherwise, the prospective filer can submit a new application for a later quarter.

*Electronic filing information.* The due dates for filing paper Forms 941 also apply to electronically filed 941 forms. An electronically filed Form 941 is not considered filed until it has been acknowledged as accepted for processing by the IRS.

Electronic transmissions that cause processing interruptions may be rejected and reporting agents will be asked to resubmit their transmissions. Once the reporting agents acknowledges the rejection, the reporting agent should correct the error and retransmit the return on the same calendar day. If the reporting agent chooses not to retransmit or the return still is not accepted, the reporting agent must file a paper Form 941 by the later of the due date of the return or 5 calendar days after the rejection or the notice that the return cannot be retransmitted. The reporting agent must also include an explanation as to why the form is late.

A transmitter must transmit the electronic file to the IRS by the later of 3 days after it receives the return or the due date of the return without regard to filing extensions. If a processing interruption occurs, and the transmitter cannot promptly correct the reason for the rejection, the transmitter has 24 hours after it receives the rejection to take reasonable steps to inform the online filer that the return has not been filed. The transmitter must provide the online filer with the reject codes and their sequence numbers.

If the online filer chooses not to correct the electronic return or cannot provide a file that the IRS can accept, the online filer must file a paper return by the later of the due date of the return or 5 calendar days of the rejection or notice that the return cannot be transmitted, along with an explanation as to why the form is late.

Within 2 days of the transmission, a transmitter must retrieve the acknowledgement file in which the IRS says whether it accepts or rejects the returns, match the file to the original transmission file, and send the online filer either an acceptance notice or a rejection notice. If the transmitter does not receive an acknowledgement of acceptance within 2 work days of the transmission or gets an acknowledgement for a return it did not transmit, the transmitter should immediately contact the IRS e-Help Desk at 866-255-0654.

A software developer must promptly correct any software errors that may cause, or have caused, an electronic return to be rejected, promptly distribute any such software corrections, and ensure any software package that will be used to transmit returns from multiple reporting agents has the capability of combining these returns into one IRS transmission file.

*Paper forms as a backup.* An electronic filer that is a reporting agent may use an Employment Tax e-file System authorization to file a paper Form 941 under the program only under the following circumstances:

- the late receipt of tax information from an employer that would otherwise make the return late;

- the amendment of returns filed under the Employment Tax e-file Program;
- the rejection of an electronic transmission that would make the return late;
- an authorization by the IRS for a filer participating in the program to file forms on paper instead of electronically; or
- the suspension of a reporting agent from the Employment Tax e-file Program.

**IRS discontinues EDI format for electronically filed forms.**[195] Effective October 28, 2006, the IRS discontinued acceptance of electronically filed Forms 940 and 941 in the EDI (electronic data interchange) and proprietary formats. Decline in the use of these formats, coupled with increasing costs to maintain them, were cited as the reasons for the decision. The IRS will continue to support the XML (extensible markup language) file format for electronically filed Forms 940 and 941.

**Form 941 filing by telephone discontinued.**[196] The 941 TeleFile system was discontinued by the IRS as of August 16, 2005, after a steady decline in use as other electronic filing alternatives became available.

**State magnetic media/electronic reporting requirements.** The following chart (Table 8.7) provides information regarding individual state requirements governing the reporting of Form W-2 wage and tax information. [For more information on State Magnetic Media requirements, see Table 4.2 of *APA's Guide to State Payroll Laws*.]

Table 8.7

| STATE W-2 MAGNETIC MEDIA/ELECTRONIC REPORTING REQUIREMENTS | | | | | |
|---|---|---|---|---|---|
| **State** | **Magnetic/ Electronic Filing Required** | **Diskette Accepted** | **Tape/Cartridge Accepted** | **Transmittal Required** | **Phone Number for Information** |
| Alabama | Yes, if at least 250 (electronic filing only) | No | No | No | 334-242-1300 |
| Alaska | Not applicable—no income tax | | | | |
| Arizona | Optional | Yes | Yes | No | 602-255-2060 |
| Arkansas | Yes, if at least 250 employees | Yes | No | No | 501-682-2212 |
| California | Not applicable—W-2s are not required | | | | |
| Colorado | Yes, if Fed requires | Yes, or CD, until 2-28-09 | No | No | 303-205-8792 |
| Connecticut | Yes, if at least 25 state W-2s and Fed requires (electronic filing only) | No | No | No | 860-297-5962 |
| Delaware | Yes, if Fed requires (electronic filing only) | No | No | No | 302-577-8200 |
| District of Columbia | Yes, if at least 50 | Yes | Cartridge only | Yes | 202-442-6313 |

---

195. 71 FR 12235, 3-9-06.
196. IRS Announcement 2005-26, 2005-17 IRB 969.

## STATE W-2 MAGNETIC MEDIA/ELECTRONIC REPORTING REQUIREMENTS

| State | Magnetic/ Electronic Filing Required | Diskette Accepted | Tape/Cartridge Accepted | Transmittal Required | Phone Number for Information |
|---|---|---|---|---|---|
| Florida | Not applicable—no income tax | | | | |
| Georgia | Yes, if at least 250 | Yes | Cartridge only | Yes | 404-417-2311 |
| Hawaii | Magnetic media reporting of W-2s not allowed | | | | |
| Idaho | Yes, if at least 50 Idaho employees and Fed requires (electronic filing only) | No | No | No | 208-332-6632 |
| Illinois | No, unless at least 250 W-2s and state requests W-2s to be filed | Yes | Yes | No | 217-782-3336 |
| Indiana | Optional | Yes | Cartridge only | Yes | 317-233-5656 |
| Iowa | Not applicable—W-2s are not required | | | | |
| Kansas | Yes, if at least 51; electronic filing only | No | No | No | 785-368-8222 |
| Kentucky | Yes, if at least 100 | Yes | No | Yes | 502-564-7287 |
| Louisiana | Yes, if at least 250 | Yes | No | No | 225-219-0102 |
| Maine | Yes, if at least 100 employees | Yes (or CD) | No | Yes | 207-626-8475 |
| Maryland | Yes, if at least 100 | Yes | No | No | 410-767-1300 |
| Massachusetts | Yes, if at least 50 | No | Yes | Yes | 617-887-6367 |
| Michigan | Yes, if at least 250 | Yes | Cartridge only | Yes | 517-636-4456 |
| Minnesota | Yes, if Fed requires (electronic filing only) | No | No | No | 651-282-9999 |
| Mississippi | Yes, if at least 100 employees or Fed requires | Yes | No | Yes | 601-923-7088 |
| Missouri | Yes, if at least 250 | Yes | Yes | Yes | 573-751-7200 |
| Montana | Optional | No | No | No | 406-444-6900 |
| Nebraska | Optional; Yes, if at least 250, eff. In 2009 | Yes | No | Yes | 402-471-5698 |

| STATE W-2 MAGNETIC MEDIA/ELECTRONIC REPORTING REQUIREMENTS | | | | | |
|---|---|---|---|---|---|
| State | Magnetic/ Electronic Filing Required | Diskette Accepted | Tape/Cartridge Accepted | Transmittal Required | Phone Number for Information |
| Nevada | Not applicable—no income tax | | | | |
| New Hampshire | Not applicable—no income tax | | | | |
| New Jersey | Optional | No | No | Yes | 609-633-1132 |
| New Mexico | Optional | Yes | Yes | No | 505-827-1746 |
| New York | Not applicable—W-2s are not required to be sent | | | | |
| North Carolina | Yes, if at least 250 | Yes | No | Yes | 877-252-3052 |
| North Dakota | Yes, if Fed requires; if employer uses payroll service provider | Yes | No | No | 701-328-3275 |
| Ohio | Optional | No | Cartridge only | Yes | 614-752-1972 |
| Oklahoma | Not applicable—W-2s not required | | | | |
| Oregon | Not applicable—W-2s not required unless state requests | | | | |
| Pennsylvania | Yes, if at least 250 | No | Cartridge only | Yes | 717-787-7635 |
| Rhode Island | Yes, if at least 25 employees in R.I. and Fed requires | Yes | Yes | Yes | 401-574-8829 |
| South Carolina | Yes, if more than 25 employees in S.C. and Fed requires | Yes | Yes | Yes | 803-898-1450 |
| South Dakota | Not applicable—no income tax | | | | |
| Tennessee | Not applicable—no income tax | | | | |
| Texas | Not applicable—no income tax | | | | |
| Utah | Yes, if Fed requires (electronic filing only) | No | No | No | 801-297-7626 |
| Vermont | Magnetic media reporting of W-2s not allowed | | | | |
| Virginia | Yes, if at least 250 | Yes | Cartridge only | Yes | 804-367-8037 |
| Washington | Not applicable—no income tax | | | | |

| STATE W-2 MAGNETIC MEDIA/ELECTRONIC REPORTING REQUIREMENTS | | | | | |
|---|---|---|---|---|---|
| State | Magnetic/ Electronic Filing Required | Diskette Accepted | Tape/Cartridge Accepted | Transmittal Required | Phone Number for Information |
| West Virginia | Yes, if at least 250; electronic filing only | No | No | No | 304-558-3333 |
| Wisconsin | Yes, if at least 250 | No | Cartridge only | No | 608-267-3327 |
| Wyoming | Not applicable—no income tax | | | | |

# 8.15 Reporting "Special Wage Payments" to the SSA

"Special wage payments" refer to payments made by an employer to an employee or a former employee that the employee earned in a prior year. Special wage payments can have a significant impact on a retired employee (who is currently receiving social security benefits) unless the SSA is notified about such payments. The retiree's benefits can be reduced when the SSA applies the annual earnings test.

**Beneficiary's earnings limited**. Social security benefits are meant to replace, in part, earnings lost due to retirement. Therefore, the amount of benefits which a beneficiary under age 65 may receive each year depends on the amount of the beneficiary's earned income, with benefits being reduced when earned income exceeds a certain limit. However, wages or payments received in one year but earned in a previous year are not counted under the "annual earnings test." The 2008 annual earnings limits are $13,560 for retirees age 62-full retirement age and $36,120 for retirees in the year they reach full retirement age, but only until the month they reach full retirement age. Once retirees reach full retirement age, there is no earnings limit.

**Examples of special wage payments**. Special wage payments include, but are not limited to, the following:

- bonuses
- accumulated vacation or sick pay
- severance pay
- back pay
- standby pay
- sales commissions
- stock options
- payments on account of retirement, or deferred compensation reported on a Form W-2 for one year but earned in a prior year.

**Reporting requirements**. Guidance for reporting special wage payments can be found in IRS Publication 957, Reporting Back Pay and Special Wage Payments to the Social Security Administration. Employers must report special wage payments for federal income, social security, and Medicare tax purposes in the year the payments are received on Form W-2 (but see Section 4.6-10 for exceptions for certain payments and deferrals under a nonqualified deferred compensation plan). In addition to Form W-2 reporting, the employer must report to SSA special wage payments made during the year to retired employees and employees who are still working while collecting social security benefits. Reports should not be made for employees who are under age 62. These reports should be submitted in time to reach SSA by April 1. There are several reporting methods that can be used:

*Magnetic media*. Special wage payments may be reported on magnetic tape or 3480 cartridges (not on diskettes). The specifications for the report and the transmittal are included in Publication 957. Tapes or cartridges should be mailed to:

Social Security Administration
Tape Operations Section
Attn: Outside Agency
National Computer Center
6201 Security Boulevard
Baltimore, MD 21235

*Paper listing*. A paper listing can be used to report special wage payments made to several employees. The format for submission is in Publication 957. Paper listings should be mailed to the employer's local SSA office.

 **WATCH OUT** Magnetic media and paper listings should not be used to report payments from nonqualified deferred compensation plans (or Section 457 plans) if deferrals to and payments from the plans occurred during the tax year. Report such payments on Form SSA-131 (see discussion following).

*Form SSA-131*. Employers can use Form SSA-131, *Employer Report of Special Wage Payments* (see Appendix page A-56), to report special wage payments to one employee. The form should be used to report nonqualified deferred compensation and §457 plan deferrals and payments that could not be reported in Box 11 of Form W-2, but only if the employee also received special wage payments during the tax year. The employer can submit Form SSA-131 to its local SSA office, or the employee can submit it to the SSA office handling his or her claim for benefits. The form must be submitted before SSA can exclude the special wage payments for purposes of the earnings test. Use a separate form for each employee.

Report on Form SSA-131 the total amount the employee earned during the tax year. Generally, the amount earned is the amount reported in Box 1 of Form W-2 minus payments from a nonqualified deferred compensation or §457 plan, but including any amounts deferred under the plan during the tax year.

# 8.16 Review Questions and Exercises

## Review Questions

1. What are the general deposit requirements for monthly, semiweekly and one-day depositors?

2. Define the shortfall rule for semiweekly depositors.

3. What are the rules regarding the timeliness of mailed payroll tax deposits?

4. What is Form 8109 and what is it used for?

5. What is the 100% penalty?

6. What must be done with an undeliverable Form W-2c?

7. What is the purpose of Form 941-M?

8. What steps must be taken to obtain an EIN by phone?

9. What is the lookback period for determining an employer's Form 941 payroll tax depositor status?

10. Ken's Bike Shop began operating on March 5, 2008. What is Ken's Form 941 lookback period for 2009?

11. Employer Mark starts business on July 7, 2008. As a new employer, Mark is classified as a monthly depositor. On Friday, July 11, Mark pays wages and accumulates a tax liability of $55,000. On Friday, July 18, Mark again accumulates taxes of $55,000 after his second payday. How much is Mark's deposit obligation? When must it be paid?

12. Outline the penalties for failing to make payroll tax deposits on time.

13. What are the requirements for filing Form 941 by employers that are going out of business?

14. On Form 941, how does the employer treat fractional cents that cause differences in calculating the employer's and employees' social security and Medicare taxes?

15. What is Schedule B used for?

16. What form is used to record nonpayroll withheld taxes?

17. What is the penalty for late filing of employment tax returns?

18. What is the purpose of backup withholding?

19. Which amounts on Forms 941, W-2, and W-3 does the SSA compare to make sure employers are taxing and reporting wages correctly?

20. What are the penalties for failure to file information returns on time and with correct information?

## True or False Questions

_____ 1. Employers that deposited more than $50,000 in withheld income and employment taxes in 2006 face a 10% penalty if they do not make their tax deposits through EFTPS for liabilities incurred on or after January 1, 2008.

_____ 2. New employers deposit their payroll tax liability as a semiweekly depositor.

_____ 3. The shortfall rule allows an employer to deposit 95% of its payroll tax liability without a penalty.

_____ 4. New employers that must make a deposit before being assigned an EIN must make their deposit with the IRS service center where they will file their returns.

_____ 5. Employers are entitled to a 10-day filing extension for Form 941 if they have deposited all payroll taxes when due throughout the quarter.

_____ 6. An EIN is obtained from the Social Security Administration using Form SS-4.

_____ 7. If a semiweekly period overlaps quarters and you have two paydays—one in each quarter—you can choose which quarter to include the wages for purposes of making payroll tax deposits.

_____ 8. A new EIN is necessary if a new corporation emerges from a consolidation that does not qualify as a reorganization.

_____ 9. The Form 941 payroll tax deposit lookback period for calendar year 2008 is January 1, 2007 - June 30, 2007.

_____ 10. An employer has accumulated payroll taxes on Form 941 of $42,000 during the 2008 look-back period. The employer is a semiweekly depositor for 2008.

_____ 11. If an employer accumulates taxes of $100,000 or more on any one day during a deposit period, it must deposit the liability by the next banking day.

_____ 12. Payroll tax deposits that are mailed through the U.S. Postal Service are considered timely if postmarked at least one day before the due date.

_____ 13. Government employers that withhold federal income tax and only the Medicare portion of FICA taxes must report these taxes on Form 941.

_____ 14. If an employer sells or transfers its business, a separate Form 941 must be filed by both the previous and current owners for the quarter in which the sale took place.

_____ 15. If a monthly depositor has a total tax liability for a quarter of less then $2,500, the employer must pay it with Form 941.

_____ 16. Copy A of all paper W-2 Forms and Form W-3 must be filed with the SSA by the last day of February of the year following the calendar year for which wages are reported.

_____ 17. When receiving undercollected taxes from employees, any overcollection of taxes from one employee may be used to offset an undercollection from another.

_____ 18. Where there has been a merger or consolidation of two employers and one survives, the surviving corporation is considered to be the same employer as the acquired company and therefore must provide Forms W-2 to all the employees of the acquired company.

_____ 19. Allocated tips should be included in Box 1 of Form W-2.

_____ 20. Employers wishing to use substitute W-2 forms should send a sample to the IRS or SSA for approval prior to use.

_____ 21. Dollar amounts should be entered on Form W-2 without commas or dollar signs.

_____ 22. Form W-3 is used only by employers that file paper Copies A of Form W-2 with the SSA.

_____ 23. Nonprofit organizations engaged in a trade or business are exempt from the 1099 reporting requirements.

_____ 24. All paper Forms 1099 must be sent to the SSA with the appropriate transmittal form by February 28 of the year following the year in which payments were made.

_____ 25. Businesses that must file 250 or more Forms 1099-MISC are required to file them electronically.

## Multiple Choice Questions

_____ 1. When depositing withheld income and employment taxes, what form must be used by a paper depositor?

    a. Form 941c
    b. Form SS-4
    c. Form 8109
    d. Form 945

_____ 2.  When an employer has been unable, after a reasonable effort, to deliver an employee's copies of Form W-2, how long must it keep those copies?

    a.    Five years
    b.    Three years
    c.    Two years
    d.    Four years

_____ 3.  Where does the employer send Form 1099-MISC?

    a.    IRS
    b.    SSA
    c.    INS
    d.    Wage and Hour Division

_____ 4.  Distributions from retirement plans and payments of matured annuity, endowment, and life insurance contracts must be reported on what form?

    a.    Form W-2P
    b.    Form W-2
    c.    Form W-3
    d.    Form 1099-R

_____ 5.  If a monthly depositor accumulates $100,000 in tax liability on any day during a month, how does this affect the employer's depositor status?

    a.    Remains monthly
    b.    Becomes semiweekly for the rest of the year
    c.    Becomes semiweekly for the rest of the current year and all of next year
    d.    Becomes a one-day depositor for the rest of the year

_____ 6.  What is the Form 941 tax deposit lookback period for calendar year 2008?

    a.    July 1, 2005 - June 30, 2006
    b.    Jan. 1, 2006 - Dec. 31, 2006
    c.    July 1, 2006 - June 30, 2007
    d.    Jan. 1, 2007 - Dec. 31, 2007

_____ 7.  When must a semiweekly depositor with a Friday payday deposit its employment tax liability?

    a.    The following Tuesday
    b.    The following Wednesday
    c.    The following Thursday
    d.    The following Friday

_____ 8.  What are the due dates for Form W-2?

    a.    To employees and SSA by Jan. 31
    b.    To employees by Jan. 31 and to SSA by the last day of February (March 31 if filed electronically)
    c.    To employees and IRS by Feb. 28
    d.    To employees by Jan. 31 and to IRS by Feb. 28

_____ 9. What form is completed by new employers when requesting an EIN?

    a.   Form SS-4
    b.   Form SS-5
    c.   Form SS-8
    d.   Form W-9

_____ 10. What form is used to report backup withholding?

    a.   Form 941
    b.   Form 942
    c.   Form 943
    d.   From 945

_____ 11. How frequently are new employers that anticipate having an annual tax liability of more than $1,000 required to make withheld federal income and employment tax deposits?

    a.   Semiweekly
    b.   Monthly
    c.   The next banking day
    d.   Quarterly

_____ 12. On May 31, a monthly depositor's payroll tax liability is $15,000. When is the deposit due?

    a.   June 7
    b.   June 1
    c.   June 15
    d.   June 30

_____ 13. XYZ Corporation, a semiweekly depositor, has a payroll tax liability of $65,000 on the first Thursday in December 2008. When must the liability be deposited?

    a.   The following Wednesday
    b.   The following Friday
    c.   The 15th of the following month
    d.   With the quarterly Form 941

_____ 14. Northwestern Shipping Corp. accumulates payroll tax liability on the Friday before Labor Day of $131,640. When is the deposit due?

    a.   The Friday before Labor Day
    b.   The following Tuesday
    c.   The following Wednesday
    d.   The following Friday

_____ 15. Adjustments for fractional cents are reported on what line of Form 941?

    a.   8
    b.   7a
    c.   4
    d.   9

_____ 16. If an employer overwithholds federal income tax from its employees' wages and discovers the error after filing Form 941 for the quarter during which the error was made, which option is not available to the employer?

     a. The employer may reimburse the employee for the overwithheld amount
     b. The employer may reduce future withheld taxes during the same calendar year that the error occurred
     c. The employer may apply the overwithheld amount to the next calendar quarter in the same year that the error occurred
     d. The employer may apply the overwithheld amount to the following year to reduce the amount withheld in the new year

_____ 17. What form must be attached to Form 941 to explain adjustments taken on Form 941?

     a. Form 941-M
     b. Form 941c
     c. Form 843
     d. An amended Form 941

_____ 18. What form is used to request a refund of overpaid taxes?

     a. Form 941
     b. Form 941c
     c. Form 940
     d. Form 843

_____ 19. To satisfy federal, state, and local taxing agency requirements, which copies of the Form W-2 must the employee receive by January 31?

     a. Copies A, B, & C
     b. Copies B, C, & 1
     c. Copies B, C, & 2
     d. Copies B, 1, & 2

_____ 20. When an employee leaves employment before the end of the calendar year and requests Form W-2 in writing, how long does the employer have to send it?

     a. 10 days from the request
     b. 15 days from the request
     c. 20 days from the request
     d. 30 days from the request

_____ 21. On Form W-2, what box is used to report wages, tips, and other compensation?

     a. Box 1
     b. Box 10
     c. Box 12
     d. Box 14

_____ 22. Employer-provided dependent care assistance must be reported in Boxes 1, 3, and 5 of Form W-2 when the assistance exceeds what amount?

     a. $2,000
     b. $3,000
     c. $5,000
     d. $7,500

_____ 23.  What code is entered in Box 12 of Form W-2 when the value of group-term life insurance over $50,000 is reported?

    a.    Code C
    b.    Code D
    c.    Code E
    d.    Code F

_____ 24.  What is the threshold amount for requiring reporting of service payments to individuals who are not employees on Form 1099-MISC?

    a.    $10
    b.    $400
    c.    $600
    d.    $550

_____ 25.  What is the transmittal form that accompanies each Form 1099 series if the forms are filed on paper?

    a.    Form W-3
    b.    Form 1096
    c.    Form 8109
    d.    Form 1099-R

## Problems

1.  In Box 12 of Form W-2, match the following codes with the item to which they relate.  Code A, B, C, D, E, F, G, H, J, K, L, M, N, P, Q, R, S, T, V, W, Y, Z, AA, BB

_____ Sick pay not included as income
_____ Value of group-term life insurance over $50,000
_____ Section 403(b) elective deferrals
_____ Nontaxable combat pay
_____ Section 401(k) elective deferrals
_____ Section 457(b) elective deferrals
_____ Health savings account contributions
_____ Adoption benefits
_____ Designated Roth contributions to a Section 401(k) plan
_____ Excludable moving expense reimbursements paid to employee
_____ Section 408(k)(6) elective deferrals
_____ Section 501(c)(18)(D) elective deferrals
_____ Deferrals under a Section 409A nonqualified deferred compensation plan
_____ Uncollected Medicare tax on tips
_____ Medical savings account contributions
_____ Uncollected social security tax on tips
_____ Nonstatutory stock options
_____ Designated Roth contributions to a Section 403(b) plan
_____ Nontaxable part of employee business expense reimbursements
_____ Tax on excess golden parachute payments
_____ Income under Section 409A on a nonqualified deferred compensation plan
_____ Uncollected social security tax on value of group-term life insurance coverage over $50,000
_____ Uncollected Medicare tax on value of group-term life insurance coverage over $50,000
_____ SIMPLE retirement account contributions

2. Allied Steel Products is a monthly depositor with 18 employees on its payroll during the fourth quarter of 2008. The total wages paid during the quarter were $83,254.90, with federal income tax withheld of $8,991.49. The total tax liability and deposits for the quarter are:

   October $9,654.87, November $5,866.35, December $6,208.27

   All wages are subject to social security and Medicare taxes. Complete the blank Form 941 on pages 8-117—8-118, assuming there are no adjustments necessary.

3. Value Carpet Center has a payroll of $36,000 during the third quarter of 2008. Taxable social security wages amount to $34,000. All wages are subject to Medicare tax. Income tax withheld amounted to $5,800 and the company paid $1,200 in advance earned income credit. The monthly tax liabilities and deposits are as follows:

   | | |
   |---|---|
   | July | $3,500 |
   | August | 3,500 |
   | September | 2,860 |

   Complete the blank Form 941 on page 8-119—8-120, assuming no adjustments are necessary.

4. The following information is taken from the payroll of Bimms & Ferrow, Inc. for the third quarter of 2008. The company is a semiweekly depositor and pays wages semimonthly on the 15th and last day of each month.

   | | |
   |---|---|
   | Name: | Bimms & Ferrow, Inc. |
   | Address: | 3456, Mid West Street, Kansas City, KS 25783 |
   | EIN: | 43-1234567 |

   | | |
   |---|---|
   | Total wages and other compensation | $2,400,000 |
   | Social security wages | 2,000,000 |
   | Medicare wages | 2,400,000 |
   | Federal income tax withheld | 360,000 |
   | July 15 tax liability/deposit: | $114,200 |
   | July 31 tax liability/deposit: | 114,200 |
   | August 15 tax liability/deposit: | 113,600 |
   | August 31 tax liability/deposit: | 112,800 |
   | September 15 tax liability/deposit: | 111,900 |
   | September 30 tax liability/deposit: | 110,900 |

   Complete Form 941 and Schedule B on pages 8-121—8-123, assuming no adjustments are necessary.

5. From the following information obtained from the employees' earnings records of the Sanchez Corporation, prepare a 2008 Form W-2 (pages 8-124 and 8-125) for each individual and Form W-3 (page 8-126) to transmit the W-2 forms to the SSA.

   Company information:

   Address: 640 San Francisco St., Suite 6, Sacramento, CA 35123
   Federal ID Number: 12-3456789
   State ID Number: 985-4321

Personnel and Payroll Information:

Employee No.1
David V. Sandoval
4213 Central Ave.
Sacramento, CA 35814
SSN 486-11-3245

| | |
|---|---:|
| Wages, tips, etc. | $39,500.00 |
| Federal income tax withheld | 5,925.00 |
| Social security wages | 42,500.00 |
| Social security tax withheld | 2,635.00 |
| Medicare wages | 42,500.00 |
| Medicare tax withheld | 616.25 |
| State income tax withheld | 1,777.50 |
| §401(k) plan elective deferral | 3,000.00 |
| Dependent care assistance | 1,000.00 |

Employee No.2
William T. Foster
123 University Heights
Sacramento, CA 35111
SSN 234-56-7890

| | |
|---|---:|
| Wages, tips, etc. | $28,481.50 |
| Federal income tax withheld | 4,272.23 |
| Social security wages | 30,481.50 |
| Social security tax withheld | 1,889.85 |
| Medicare wages | 30,481.50 |
| Medicare tax withheld | 441.98 |
| State income tax withheld | 1,281.67 |
| §401(k) plan elective deferral | 2,000.00 |
| Group-term life over $50,000 | 481.50 |

Employee No.3
Helen G. Roseville
7000 Mt. Pleasant Rd.
Sacramento, CA 35900
SSN 987-65-4321

| | |
|---|---:|
| Wages, tips, etc. | $31,800.00 |
| Federal income tax withheld | 4,770.00 |
| Social security wages | 34,200.00 |
| Social security tax withheld | 2,120.40 |
| Medicare wages | 34,200.00 |
| Medicare tax withheld | 495.90 |
| State income tax withheld | 1,431.00 |
| §401(k) plan elective deferral | 2,400.00 |
| Personal use of company vehicle | 1,800.00 |
| Educational assistance payments | 2,500.00 |

Employee No.4
Beryl Horstmann
1212 Forest Ridge Dr.
Sacramento, CA 35196
SSN 246-80-1357

| | |
|---|---:|
| Wages, tips, etc. | $18,000.00 |
| Federal income tax withheld | 2,700.00 |
| Social security wages | 19,000.00 |
| Social security tax withheld | 1,178.00 |
| Medicare wages | 19,000.00 |
| Medicare tax withheld | 275.50 |
| State income tax withheld | 540.00 |
| §401(k) plan elective deferral | 1,000.00 |
| Educational assistance payments | 800.00 |
| Advance EIC payments | 624.00 |

6. World Wide Express electronically files all of its information returns—2,600 Forms W-2—on time with the SSA, 40 of which contain incorrect information. Corrections were made on May 30.

   a. How many returns are subject to penalty?                    _____

   b. What is the penalty?                                   $_____

7. Blare Textiles electronically files all of its information returns—1,400 Forms W-2—on time with the SSA, 30 of which contain incorrect information. Corrections were made on May 10.

   a. How many returns are subject to penalty?                    _____

   b. What is the penalty?                                   $_____

8. Better Build PC electronically filed all of its information returns—500 Forms W-2—on time with the SSA, but it did not file its 50 Forms 1099-MISC with the IRS until August 10.

   What is the penalty for late filing?                      $_____

9. An employer is required to file information returns electronically, but instead mailed 380 paper Forms W-2 on time with the correct information.

   How many returns are subject to the failure-to-file penalty?       _____

Form **941 for 2008:** **Employer's QUARTERLY Federal Tax Return**

(Rev. January 2008)

Department of the Treasury — Internal Revenue Service

950108

OMB No. 1545-0029

**(EIN)**
**Employer identification number** ☐☐ — ☐☐☐☐☐☐☐

**Name** (not your trade name)

**Trade name** (if any)

**Address**

Number          Street                                        Suite or room number

City                                        State          ZIP code

**Report for this Quarter of 2008**
(Check one.)

☐ **1:** January, February, March

☐ **2:** April, May, June

☐ **3:** July, August, September

☐ **4:** October, November, December

Read the separate instructions before you fill out this form. Please type or print within the boxes.

**Part 1: Answer these questions for this quarter.**

**1** Number of employees who received wages, tips, or other compensation for the pay period including: *Mar. 12* (Quarter 1), *June 12* (Quarter 2), *Sept. 12* (Quarter 3), *Dec. 12* (Quarter 4)    **1** ☐

**2** Wages, tips, and other compensation . . . . . . . . . . . . .    **2** ☐

**3** Total income tax withheld from wages, tips, and other compensation . . . . . .    **3** ☐

**4** If no wages, tips, and other compensation are subject to social security or Medicare tax . .    ☐ Check and go to line 6.

**5** Taxable social security and Medicare wages and tips:

|  | Column 1 |  | Column 2 |
|---|---|---|---|
| **5a** Taxable social security wages | ☐ | × .124 = | ☐ |
| **5b** Taxable social security tips | ☐ | × .124 = | ☐ |
| **5c** Taxable Medicare wages & tips | ☐ | × .029 = | ☐ |

**5d** Total social security and Medicare taxes (*Column 2,* lines 5a + 5b + 5c = line 5d) . .    **5d** ☐

**6** Total taxes before adjustments (lines 3 + 5d = line 6) . . . . . . . . . . .    **6** ☐

**7** TAX ADJUSTMENTS (read the instructions for line 7 before completing lines 7a through 7g):

**7a** Current quarter's fractions of cents . . . . . . . . . . .    ☐

**7b** Current quarter's sick pay . . . . . . . . . . . . . .    ☐

**7c** Current quarter's adjustments for tips and group-term life insurance    ☐

**7d** Current year's income tax withholding (attach Form 941c) . .    ☐

**7e** Prior quarters' social security and Medicare taxes (attach Form 941c)    ☐

**7f** Special additions to federal income tax (attach Form 941c) . .    ☐

**7g** Special additions to social security and Medicare (attach Form 941c)    ☐

**7h** TOTAL ADJUSTMENTS (combine all amounts: lines 7a through 7g) . . . . . .    **7h** ☐

**8** Total taxes after adjustments (combine lines 6 and 7h) . . . . . . . . .    **8** ☐

**9** Advance earned income credit (EIC) payments made to employees . . . . . .    **9** ☐

**10** Total taxes after adjustment for advance EIC (line 8 – line 9 = line 10) . . . . . .    **10** ☐

**11** Total deposits for this quarter, including overpayment applied from a prior quarter . . .    **11** ☐

**12** Balance due (If line 10 is more than line 11, write the difference here.) . . . . . .    **12** ☐
For information on how to pay, see the instructions.

**13** Overpayment (If line 11 is more than line 10, write the difference here.)    ☐    Check one ☐ Apply to next return.
☐ Send a refund.

▶ You **MUST** fill out both pages of this form and **SIGN** it.    Next ➡

**For Privacy Act and Paperwork Reduction Act Notice, see the back of the Payment Voucher.**    Cat. No. 17001Z    Form **941** (Rev. 1-2008)

950208

| Name *(not your trade name)* | Employer identification number (EIN) |
|---|---|

---

**Part 2: Tell us about your deposit schedule and tax liability for this quarter.**

If you are unsure about whether you are a monthly schedule depositor or a semiweekly schedule depositor, see *Pub. 15 (Circular E)*, section 11.

14 ☐☐ Write the state abbreviation for the state where you made your deposits OR write "MU" if you made your deposits in *multiple* states.

15 Check one: ☐ **Line 10 is less than $2,500.** Go to Part 3.

☐ **You were a monthly schedule depositor for the entire quarter. Fill out your tax liability for each month.** Then go to Part 3.

Tax liability: Month 1 [     . ]

Month 2 [     . ]

Month 3 [     . ]

Total liability for quarter [     . ] **Total must equal line 10.**

☐ **You were a semiweekly schedule depositor for any part of this quarter.** Fill out *Schedule B (Form 941): Report of Tax Liability for Semiweekly Schedule Depositors,* and attach it to this form.

---

**Part 3: Tell us about your business. If a question does NOT apply to your business, leave it blank.**

16 If your business has closed or you stopped paying wages . . . . . . . . . . . . . . . . ☐ Check here, and

enter the final date you paid wages [ / / ] .

17 If you are a seasonal employer and you do not have to file a return for every quarter of the year . . ☐ Check here.

---

**Part 4: May we speak with your third-party designee?**

**Do you want to allow an employee, a paid tax preparer, or another person to discuss this return with the IRS?** See the instructions for details.

☐ **Yes.** Designee's name and phone number [   ] (   ) –

Select a 5-digit Personal Identification Number (PIN) to use when talking to IRS. ☐☐☐☐☐

☐ **No.**

---

**Part 5: Sign here. You MUST fill out both pages of this form and SIGN it.**

Under penalties of perjury, I declare that I have examined this return, including accompanying schedules and statements, and to the best of my knowledge and belief, it is true, correct, and complete.

X **Sign your name here** [   ]

Print your name here [   ]

Print your title here [   ]

Date [ / / ]

Best daytime phone (   ) –

---

**Part 6: For paid preparers only (optional)**

| Paid Preparer's Signature | [   ] | | |
|---|---|---|---|
| Firm's name (or yours if self-employed) | [   ] | | |
| Address | [   ] | EIN | [   ] |
| | [   ] | ZIP code | [   ] |
| Date [ / / ] | Phone (   ) – | SSN/PTIN | [   ] |

☐ Check if you are self-employed.

---

Page **2**

Form **941** (Rev. 1-2008)

**Form 941 for 2008:** **Employer's QUARTERLY Federal Tax Return**

(Rev. January 2008)    Department of the Treasury — Internal Revenue Service

950108

OMB No. 1545-0029

**(EIN)**
**Employer identification number** ☐☐ – ☐☐☐☐☐☐☐

**Name** *(not your trade name)*

**Trade name** *(if any)*

**Address**
Number    Street    Suite or room number

City    State    ZIP code

**Report for this Quarter of 2008**
(Check one.)

☐ **1:** January, February, March

☐ **2:** April, May, June

☐ **3:** July, August, September

☐ **4:** October, November, December

Read the separate instructions before you fill out this form. Please type or print within the boxes.

**Part 1: Answer these questions for this quarter.**

**1** Number of employees who received wages, tips, or other compensation for the pay period including: *Mar. 12* (Quarter 1), *June 12* (Quarter 2), *Sept. 12* (Quarter 3), *Dec. 12* (Quarter 4)    **1**

**2** Wages, tips, and other compensation . . . . . . . . .    **2**

**3** Total income tax withheld from wages, tips, and other compensation . . . . . . .    **3**

**4** If no wages, tips, and other compensation are subject to social security or Medicare tax . .    ☐ Check and go to line 6.

**5** Taxable social security and Medicare wages and tips:

|  | Column 1 | | Column 2 |
|---|---|---|---|
| **5a** Taxable social security wages | | × .124 = | |
| **5b** Taxable social security tips | | × .124 = | |
| **5c** Taxable Medicare wages & tips | | × .029 = | |

**5d** Total social security and Medicare taxes (*Column 2,* lines 5a + 5b + 5c = line 5d) . .    **5d**

**6** Total taxes before adjustments (lines 3 + 5d = line 6) . . . . . . . . .    **6**

**7** TAX ADJUSTMENTS (read the instructions for line 7 before completing lines 7a through 7g):

**7a** Current quarter's fractions of cents . . . . . . . .

**7b** Current quarter's sick pay . . . . . . . . .

**7c** Current quarter's adjustments for tips and group-term life insurance

**7d** Current year's income tax withholding (attach Form 941c) . . .

**7e** Prior quarters' social security and Medicare taxes (attach Form 941c)

**7f** Special additions to federal income tax (attach Form 941c) . . .

**7g** Special additions to social security and Medicare (attach Form 941c)

**7h** TOTAL ADJUSTMENTS (combine all amounts: lines 7a through 7g) . . . . . . .    **7h**

**8** Total taxes after adjustments (combine lines 6 and 7h) . . . . . . . .    **8**

**9** Advance earned income credit (EIC) payments made to employees . . . . . . .    **9**

**10** Total taxes after adjustment for advance EIC (line 8 – line 9 = line 10) . . . . . . .    **10**

**11** Total deposits for this quarter, including overpayment applied from a prior quarter . . .    **11**

**12** Balance due (If line 10 is more than line 11, write the difference here.) . . . . . . .    **12**
For information on how to pay, see the instructions.

**13** Overpayment (If line 11 is more than line 10, write the difference here.)    Check one    ☐ Apply to next return.
☐ Send a refund.

▶ You **MUST** fill out both pages of this form and **SIGN** it.    Next ➡

For Privacy Act and Paperwork Reduction Act Notice, see the back of the Payment Voucher.    Cat. No. 17001Z    Form **941** (Rev. 1-2008)

950208

| Name *(not your trade name)* | Employer identification number (EIN) |
|---|---|

**Part 2: Tell us about your deposit schedule and tax liability for this quarter.**

If you are unsure about whether you are a monthly schedule depositor or a semiweekly schedule depositor, see *Pub. 15 (Circular E)*, section 11.

14 ☐☐ Write the state abbreviation for the state where you made your deposits OR write "MU" if you made your deposits in *multiple* states.

15 Check one: ☐ Line 10 is less than $2,500. Go to Part 3.

☐ You were a monthly schedule depositor for the entire quarter. Fill out your tax liability for each month. Then go to Part 3.

Tax liability: Month 1 ☐ .

Month 2 ☐ .

Month 3 ☐ .

Total liability for quarter ☐ . Total must equal line 10.

☐ You were a semiweekly schedule depositor for any part of this quarter. Fill out *Schedule B (Form 941): Report of Tax Liability for Semiweekly Schedule Depositors,* and attach it to this form.

**Part 3: Tell us about your business. If a question does NOT apply to your business, leave it blank.**

16 If your business has closed or you stopped paying wages . . . . . . . . . . . . . . . . ☐ Check here, and

enter the final date you paid wages ☐ / / .

17 If you are a seasonal employer and you do not have to file a return for every quarter of the year . . ☐ Check here.

**Part 4: May we speak with your third-party designee?**

Do you want to allow an employee, a paid tax preparer, or another person to discuss this return with the IRS? See the instructions for details.

☐ Yes. Designee's name and phone number ☐ ( ) –

Select a 5-digit Personal Identification Number (PIN) to use when talking to IRS. ☐☐☐☐☐

☐ No.

**Part 5: Sign here. You MUST fill out both pages of this form and SIGN it.**

Under penalties of perjury, I declare that I have examined this return, including accompanying schedules and statements, and to the best of my knowledge and belief, it is true, correct, and complete.

X Sign your name here ☐ 

Print your name here ☐

Print your title here ☐

Date ☐ / /    Best daytime phone ( ) –

**Part 6: For paid preparers only (optional)**

| Paid Preparer's Signature | |
|---|---|
| Firm's name (or yours if self-employed) | |
| Address | EIN |
| | ZIP code |
| Date / / Phone ( ) – | SSN/PTIN |

☐ Check if you are self-employed.

Form **941** (Rev. 1-2008)

Form **941 for 2008:** **Employer's QUARTERLY Federal Tax Return**
(Rev. January 2008)      Department of the Treasury — Internal Revenue Service

950108

OMB No. 1545-0029

**(EIN)**
**Employer identification number** ☐☐ — ☐☐☐☐☐☐☐

**Name** *(not your trade name)* _____

**Trade name** *(if any)* _____

**Address** _____
Number     Street          Suite or room number

_____
City     State     ZIP code

**Report for this Quarter of 2008**
(Check one.)

☐ **1:** January, February, March

☐ **2:** April, May, June

☐ **3:** July, August, September

☐ **4:** October, November, December

Read the separate instructions before you fill out this form. Please type or print within the boxes.

**Part 1: Answer these questions for this quarter.**

**1** Number of employees who received wages, tips, or other compensation for the pay period including: *Mar. 12* (Quarter 1), *June 12* (Quarter 2), *Sept. 12* (Quarter 3), *Dec. 12* (Quarter 4)   **1** ☐

**2** Wages, tips, and other compensation . . . . . . . . . . . **2** ☐

**3** Total income tax withheld from wages, tips, and other compensation . . . . . . . **3** ☐

**4** If no wages, tips, and other compensation are subject to social security or Medicare tax . . ☐ Check and go to line 6.

**5** Taxable social security and Medicare wages and tips:

|  | Column 1 | | Column 2 |
|---|---|---|---|
| **5a** Taxable social security wages | ☐ | × .124 = | ☐ |
| **5b** Taxable social security tips | ☐ | × .124 = | ☐ |
| **5c** Taxable Medicare wages & tips | ☐ | × .029 = | ☐ |

**5d** Total social security and Medicare taxes (*Column 2,* lines 5a + 5b + 5c = line 5d) . . **5d** ☐

**6** Total taxes before adjustments (lines 3 + 5d = line 6) . . . . . . . . **6** ☐

**7** TAX ADJUSTMENTS (read the instructions for line 7 before completing lines 7a through 7g):

**7a** Current quarter's fractions of cents . . . . . . . . . . ☐

**7b** Current quarter's sick pay . . . . . . . . . . . ☐

**7c** Current quarter's adjustments for tips and group-term life insurance ☐

**7d** Current year's income tax withholding (attach Form 941c) . . . ☐

**7e** Prior quarters' social security and Medicare taxes (attach Form 941c) ☐

**7f** Special additions to federal income tax (attach Form 941c) . . . ☐

**7g** Special additions to social security and Medicare (attach Form 941c) ☐

**7h** TOTAL ADJUSTMENTS (combine all amounts: lines 7a through 7g) . . . **7h** ☐

**8** Total taxes after adjustments (combine lines 6 and 7h) . . . . . . . **8** ☐

**9** Advance earned income credit (EIC) payments made to employees . . . . . **9** ☐

**10** Total taxes after adjustment for advance EIC (line 8 – line 9 = line 10) . . . . . **10** ☐

**11** Total deposits for this quarter, including overpayment applied from a prior quarter . . . **11** ☐

**12** Balance due (If line 10 is more than line 11, write the difference here.) . . . . . **12** ☐
For information on how to pay, see the instructions.

**13** Overpayment (If line 11 is more than line 10, write the difference here.) ☐   Check one ☐ Apply to next return.   ☐ Send a refund.

▶ You **MUST** fill out both pages of this form and **SIGN** it.      Next ➡

   Cat. No. 17001Z    Form **941** (Rev. 1-2008)

950208

| Name *(not your trade name)* | Employer identification number (EIN) |
|---|---|
| | |

## Part 2: Tell us about your deposit schedule and tax liability for this quarter.

If you are unsure about whether you are a monthly schedule depositor or a semiweekly schedule depositor, see *Pub. 15 (Circular E)*, section 11.

14 ☐ ☐ Write the state abbreviation for the state where you made your deposits OR write "MU" if you made your deposits in *multiple* states.

15 Check one: ☐ Line 10 is less than $2,500. Go to Part 3.

☐ You were a monthly schedule depositor for the entire quarter. Fill out your tax liability for each month. Then go to Part 3.

Tax liability: Month 1 [                 . ]

Month 2 [                 . ]

Month 3 [                 . ]

Total liability for quarter [                 . ] Total must equal line 10.

☐ You were a semiweekly schedule depositor for any part of this quarter. Fill out *Schedule B (Form 941): Report of Tax Liability for Semiweekly Schedule Depositors*, and attach it to this form.

## Part 3: Tell us about your business. If a question does NOT apply to your business, leave it blank.

16 If your business has closed or you stopped paying wages . . . . . . . . . . . . . . . . ☐ Check here, and

enter the final date you paid wages [   /   /   ] .

17 If you are a seasonal employer and you do not have to file a return for every quarter of the year . . ☐ Check here.

## Part 4: May we speak with your third-party designee?

Do you want to allow an employee, a paid tax preparer, or another person to discuss this return with the IRS? See the instructions for details.

☐ Yes. Designee's name and phone number [                 ] ( ) –

Select a 5-digit Personal Identification Number (PIN) to use when talking to IRS. ☐ ☐ ☐ ☐ ☐

☐ No.

## Part 5: Sign here. You MUST fill out both pages of this form and SIGN it.

Under penalties of perjury, I declare that I have examined this return, including accompanying schedules and statements, and to the best of my knowledge and belief, it is true, correct, and complete.

X **Sign your name here** [                 ]

Print your name here [                 ]

Print your title here [                 ]

Date [   /   /   ]

Best daytime phone ( ) –

## Part 6: For paid preparers only (optional)

| Paid Preparer's Signature | | | |
|---|---|---|---|
| Firm's name (or yours if self-employed) | | | |
| Address | | EIN | |
| | | ZIP code | |
| Date [   /   /   ] | Phone ( ) – | SSN/PTIN | |

☐ Check if you are self-employed.

# Schedule B (Form 941):

**Report of Tax Liability for Semiweekly Schedule Depositors**

(Rev. January 2006)          Department of the Treasury — Internal Revenue Service

990306

OMB No. 1545-0029

**(EIN)**
Employer identification number

☐ ☐ – ☐ ☐ ☐ ☐ ☐ ☐ ☐

**Name** *(not your trade name)*

**Calendar year** ☐ ☐ ☐ ☐          (Also check quarter)

**Report for this Quarter ...**
(Check one.)

☐ **1:** January, February, March

☐ **2:** April, May, June

☐ **3:** July, August, September

☐ **4:** October, November, December

Use this schedule to show your **TAX LIABILITY** for the quarter; **DO NOT** use it to show your deposits. You must fill out this form and attach it to Form 941 (or Form 941-SS) if you are a semiweekly schedule depositor or became one because your accumulated tax liability on any day was $100,000 or more. Write your daily tax liability on the numbered space that corresponds to the date wages were paid. See Section 11 in *Pub. 15 (Circular E), Employer's Tax Guide,* for details.

**Month 1**

| 1 | 9 | 17 | 25 | **Tax liability for Month 1** |
| 2 | 10 | 18 | 26 | |
| 3 | 11 | 19 | 27 | |
| 4 | 12 | 20 | 28 | |
| 5 | 13 | 21 | 29 | |
| 6 | 14 | 22 | 30 | |
| 7 | 15 | 23 | 31 | |
| 8 | 16 | 24 | | |

**Month 2**

| 1 | 9 | 17 | 25 | **Tax liability for Month 2** |
| 2 | 10 | 18 | 26 | |
| 3 | 11 | 19 | 27 | |
| 4 | 12 | 20 | 28 | |
| 5 | 13 | 21 | 29 | |
| 6 | 14 | 22 | 30 | |
| 7 | 15 | 23 | 31 | |
| 8 | 16 | 24 | | |

**Month 3**

| 1 | 9 | 17 | 25 | **Tax liability for Month 3** |
| 2 | 10 | 18 | 26 | |
| 3 | 11 | 19 | 27 | |
| 4 | 12 | 20 | 28 | |
| 5 | 13 | 21 | 29 | |
| 6 | 14 | 22 | 30 | |
| 7 | 15 | 23 | 31 | |
| 8 | 16 | 24 | | |

Fill in your total liability for the quarter (Month 1 + Month 2 + Month 3) = Total tax liability for the quarter ▶

**Total must equal line 10 on Form 941** (or line 8 on Form 941-SS).

**Total liability for the quarter**

**For Paperwork Reduction Act Notice, see separate instructions.**          Cat. No. 11967Q          Schedule B (Form 941) Rev. 1-2006

| 22222 | Void ☐ | **a** Employee's social security number | For Official Use Only ▶ OMB No. 1545-0008 | |
|---|---|---|---|---|

| **b** Employer identification number (EIN) | | **1** Wages, tips, other compensation | **2** Federal income tax withheld |
|---|---|---|---|
| **c** Employer's name, address, and ZIP code | | **3** Social security wages | **4** Social security tax withheld |
| | | **5** Medicare wages and tips | **6** Medicare tax withheld |
| | | **7** Social security tips | **8** Allocated tips |
| **d** Control number | | **9** Advance EIC payment | **10** Dependent care benefits |
| **e** Employee's first name and initial | Last name | Suff. | **11** Nonqualified plans | **12a** See instructions for box 12 |
| | | **13** Statutory employee ☐ Retirement plan ☐ Third-party sick pay ☐ | **12b** |
| | | **14** Other | **12c** |
| | | | **12d** |
| **f** Employee's address and ZIP code | | | |

| **15** State | Employer's state ID number | **16** State wages, tips, etc. | **17** State income tax | **18** Local wages, tips, etc. | **19** Local income tax | **20** Locality name |
|---|---|---|---|---|---|---|

Form **W-2** **Wage and Tax Statement** **2008**

Department of the Treasury—Internal Revenue Service

**Copy A For Social Security Administration** — Send this entire page with Form W-3 to the Social Security Administration; photocopies are **not** acceptable.

**For Privacy Act and Paperwork Reduction Act Notice, see back of Copy D.**

Cat. No. 10134D

**Do Not Cut, Fold, or Staple Forms on This Page — Do Not Cut, Fold, or Staple Forms on This Page**

| 22222 | Void ☐ | **a** Employee's social security number | For Official Use Only ▶ OMB No. 1545-0008 | |
|---|---|---|---|---|

| **b** Employer identification number (EIN) | | **1** Wages, tips, other compensation | **2** Federal income tax withheld |
|---|---|---|---|
| **c** Employer's name, address, and ZIP code | | **3** Social security wages | **4** Social security tax withheld |
| | | **5** Medicare wages and tips | **6** Medicare tax withheld |
| | | **7** Social security tips | **8** Allocated tips |
| **d** Control number | | **9** Advance EIC payment | **10** Dependent care benefits |
| **e** Employee's first name and initial | Last name | Suff. | **11** Nonqualified plans | **12a** See instructions for box 12 |
| | | **13** Statutory employee ☐ Retirement plan ☐ Third-party sick pay ☐ | **12b** |
| | | **14** Other | **12c** |
| | | | **12d** |
| **f** Employee's address and ZIP code | | | |

| **15** State | Employer's state ID number | **16** State wages, tips, etc. | **17** State income tax | **18** Local wages, tips, etc. | **19** Local income tax | **20** Locality name |
|---|---|---|---|---|---|---|

Form **W-2** **Wage and Tax Statement** **2008**

Department of the Treasury—Internal Revenue Service

**Copy A For Social Security Administration** — Send this entire page with Form W-3 to the Social Security Administration; photocopies are **not** acceptable.

**For Privacy Act and Paperwork Reduction Act Notice, see back of Copy D.**

Cat. No. 10134D

**Do Not Cut, Fold, or Staple Forms on This Page — Do Not Cut, Fold, or Staple Forms on This Page**

| 22222 | Void ☐ | a Employee's social security number | For Official Use Only ▶ OMB No. 1545-0008 | | |
|---|---|---|---|---|---|
| b Employer identification number (EIN) | | | | 1 Wages, tips, other compensation | 2 Federal income tax withheld |
| c Employer's name, address, and ZIP code | | | | 3 Social security wages | 4 Social security tax withheld |
| | | | | 5 Medicare wages and tips | 6 Medicare tax withheld |
| | | | | 7 Social security tips | 8 Allocated tips |
| d Control number | | | | 9 Advance EIC payment | 10 Dependent care benefits |
| e Employee's first name and initial | Last name | | Suff. | 11 Nonqualified plans | 12a See instructions for box 12 |
| | | | | 13 Statutory employee ☐  Retirement plan ☐  Third-party sick pay ☐ | 12b |
| | | | | 14 Other | 12c |
| | | | | | 12d |
| f Employee's address and ZIP code | | | | | |

| 15 State | Employer's state ID number | 16 State wages, tips, etc. | 17 State income tax | 18 Local wages, tips, etc. | 19 Local income tax | 20 Locality name |
|---|---|---|---|---|---|---|
| | | | | | | |

Form **W-2** **Wage and Tax Statement**    **2008**

Department of the Treasury—Internal Revenue Service

**Copy A For Social Security Administration** — Send this entire page with Form W-3 to the Social Security Administration; photocopies are **not** acceptable.

**For Privacy Act and Paperwork Reduction Act Notice, see back of Copy D.**

Cat. No. 10134D

**Do Not Cut, Fold, or Staple Forms on This Page — Do Not Cut, Fold, or Staple Forms on This Page**

| 22222 | Void ☐ | a Employee's social security number | For Official Use Only ▶ OMB No. 1545-0008 | | |
|---|---|---|---|---|---|
| b Employer identification number (EIN) | | | | 1 Wages, tips, other compensation | 2 Federal income tax withheld |
| c Employer's name, address, and ZIP code | | | | 3 Social security wages | 4 Social security tax withheld |
| | | | | 5 Medicare wages and tips | 6 Medicare tax withheld |
| | | | | 7 Social security tips | 8 Allocated tips |
| d Control number | | | | 9 Advance EIC payment | 10 Dependent care benefits |
| e Employee's first name and initial | Last name | | Suff. | 11 Nonqualified plans | 12a See instructions for box 12 |
| | | | | 13 Statutory employee ☐  Retirement plan ☐  Third-party sick pay ☐ | 12b |
| | | | | 14 Other | 12c |
| | | | | | 12d |
| f Employee's address and ZIP code | | | | | |

| 15 State | Employer's state ID number | 16 State wages, tips, etc. | 17 State income tax | 18 Local wages, tips, etc. | 19 Local income tax | 20 Locality name |
|---|---|---|---|---|---|---|
| | | | | | | |

Form **W-2** **Wage and Tax Statement**    **2008**

Department of the Treasury—Internal Revenue Service

**Copy A For Social Security Administration** — Send this entire page with Form W-3 to the Social Security Administration; photocopies are **not** acceptable.

**For Privacy Act and Paperwork Reduction Act Notice, see back of Copy D.**

Cat. No. 10134D

**Do Not Cut, Fold, or Staple Forms on This Page — Do Not Cut, Fold, or Staple Forms on This Page**

DO NOT STAPLE

| 33333 | a  Control number | For Official Use Only ▶ OMB No. 1545-0008 | | |
|---|---|---|---|---|

| b Kind of Payer ▶ | 941 ☐   Military ☐   943 ☐   944 ☐ <br> CT-1 ☐   Hshld. emp. ☐   Medicare govt. emp. ☐   Third-party sick pay ☐ | 1  Wages, tips, other compensation | 2  Federal income tax withheld |
|---|---|---|---|

| | | 3  Social security wages | 4  Social security tax withheld |
|---|---|---|---|

| c  Total number of Forms W-2 | d  Establishment number | 5  Medicare wages and tips | 6  Medicare tax withheld |
|---|---|---|---|

| e  Employer identification number (EIN) | 7  Social security tips | 8  Allocated tips |
|---|---|---|

| f  Employer's name | 9  Advance EIC payments | 10  Dependent care benefits |
|---|---|---|

| | 11  Nonqualified plans | 12  Deferred compensation |
|---|---|---|

| | 13  For third-party sick pay use only |
|---|---|

| | 14  Income tax withheld by payer of third-party sick pay |
|---|---|

| g  Employer's address and ZIP code | |
|---|---|
| h  Other EIN used this year | |

| 15  State    Employer's state ID number | 16  State wages, tips, etc. | 17  State income tax |
|---|---|---|

| | 18  Local wages, tips, etc. | 19  Local income tax |
|---|---|---|

| Contact person | Telephone number <br> (    ) | For Official Use Only |
|---|---|---|

| Email address | Fax number <br> (    ) | |
|---|---|---|

Under penalties of perjury, I declare that I have examined this return and accompanying documents, and, to the best of my knowledge and belief, they are true, correct, and complete.

Signature ▶                    Title ▶                    Date ▶

Form **W-3** Transmittal of Wage and Tax Statements    **2008**    Department of the Treasury
Internal Revenue Service

**Send this entire page with the entire Copy A page of Form(s) W-2 to the Social Security Administration.**

**Do not** send any payment (cash, checks, money orders, etc.) with Forms W-2 and W-3.

## Reminder

**Separate instructions.** See the 2008 Instructions for Forms W-2 and W-3 for information on completing this form.

## Purpose of Form

A Form W-3 Transmittal is completed only when paper Copy A of Form(s) W-2, Wage and Tax Statement, are being filed. Do not file Form W-3 alone. Do not file Form W-3 for Form(s) W-2 that were submitted electronically to the Social Security Administration (see below). All paper forms **must** comply with IRS standards and be machine readable. Photocopies and hand-printed forms are **not** acceptable. Use a Form W-3 even if only one paper Form W-2 is being filed. Make sure both the Form W-3 and Form(s) W-2 show the correct tax year and Employer Identification Number (EIN). Make a copy of this form and keep it with Copy D (For Employer) of Form(s) W-2 for your records.

## Electronic Filing

The Social Security Administration strongly suggests employers report Form W-3 and W-2 Copy A electronically instead of on paper. SSA provides two e-file options:

● Free fill-in Forms W-2 for employers who file 20 or fewer Form(s) W-2.

● Upload a file for employers who use payroll/tax software to print Form(s) W-2, if the vendor software creates a file that can be uploaded to SSA.

   For more information, go to *www.socialsecurity.gov/employer* and select "First Time Filers" or "Returning Filers" under "BEFORE YOU FILE."

## When To File

Mail any paper Forms W-2 under cover of this Form W-3 Transmittal by February 28, 2009. Electronic fill-in forms or uploads are filed through SSA's Business Services Online (BSO) Internet site and will be on time if submitted by March 31, 2009.

## Where To File Paper Forms

Send this entire page with the entire Copy A page of Form(s) W-2 to:

**Social Security Administration
Data Operations Center
Wilkes-Barre, PA 18769-0001**

**Note.** If you use "Certified Mail" to file, change the ZIP code to "18769-0002." If you use an IRS-approved private delivery service, add "ATTN: W-2 Process, 1150 E. Mountain Dr." to the address and change the ZIP code to "18702-7997." See Publication 15 (Circular E), Employer's Tax Guide, for a list of IRS-approved private delivery services.

**For Privacy Act and Paperwork Reduction Act Notice, see the back of Copy D of Form W-2.**
Cat. No. 10159Y

# SECTION 9: OTHER DEDUCTIONS FROM PAY

## TABLE OF CONTENTS

# SECTION 9: OTHER DEDUCTIONS FROM PAY

Adding to the complexity of the payroll department's responsibilities, employees' paychecks are often subject to deductions other than those for federal, state, or local taxes and for the purchase of various employee benefits. The payroll department staff may be required to make deductions from an employee's wages for child support, medical support, unpaid taxes, or a court order to repay a debt. Also, employees may request that some of their wages be deducted to pay a credit union loan, pay union dues, buy U.S. savings bonds, pay home or automobile insurance premiums, or pay for goods purchased on time through a wage assignment. These additional deductions and the employer's obligations relating to them will be discussed in this section.

## 9.1 Involuntary Deductions

Involuntary deductions are those over which an employer or employee has no control. The employer is required by law to deduct a certain amount of the employee's pay and send (remit) it to a person or government agency to satisfy the employee's debt. Failure to deduct and remit will generally subject the employer to a penalty equal to the amount required to be deducted, plus possible fines and interest.

A familiar problem for employers is determining deduction amounts when several orders for involuntary deductions are received against an employee's wages. If there is not enough pay left in the employee's wages, after any exempt amounts have been taken into consideration, to pay all the orders, the employer must decide which order should be deducted first (i.e., determining the priority of the orders). As each type of involuntary deduction is discussed in this section, its priority in relation to other deductions will also be explained.

## 9.1-1 Tax Levies

Employees who fail to timely pay their taxes may become subject to a federal or state tax "levy" after other collection efforts have been exhausted. The levy requires their employer to deduct the amount owed (plus penalties and interest) from their wages and remit it to the proper government agency. The employer is faced with the task of determining:

- the amount of the employee's wages that is subject to the levy; and

- whether there are other claims on the employee's wages that take priority over the levy.

**Federal tax levies.** A federal tax levy is accomplished by "garnishing" or "attaching" an employee's wages to the extent that they are not exempt from levy.[1] The employee's employer receives notice of the levy when the IRS sends Form 668-W, *Notice of Levy on Wages, Salary, and Other Income* (see Appendix page A-130). Form 668-W consists of six parts. Part 1 is the employer's copy, informing the employer of the amount of the levy and the employer's obligation to withhold and remit the levy amount.

Parts 2-5 must be given to the employee. Part 2 is the employee's copy of the levy notice. Parts 3-5 require the employee to provide information to the employer and the IRS regarding his or her tax filing status and any dependents who can be claimed as personal exemptions (except children covered by a child support order against the employee that takes priority over the levy). Parts 3 and 4 must be returned to the employer within three days of the date the employer receives the form. The employer then sends Part 3 to the IRS (after completing the reverse side) and keeps Part 4. Part 5 is the employee's copy of the tax filing status and exemption information. Part 6 is retained by the IRS.

---

1.    IRC §6331.

## Section 9: Other Deductions From Pay

**Priority vs. other attachment orders.** Tax levies must be satisfied before all other garnishment or attachment orders, except for child support withholding orders (see Section 9.1-2) in effect before the date of the levy. See Section 9.1-4 for the effect of a bankruptcy order on a federal, state, or local tax levy. Where more than one jurisdiction has levied on an employee's wages for past due taxes and there are insufficient nonexempt funds to satisfy all of them, the one received first by the employer must be satisfied before any others, unless the IRS instructs otherwise.

**Figuring the amount to deduct and remit.** All amounts paid to an employee are subject to levy unless specifically exempt under the Internal Revenue Code or IRS regulations (see the list following). Federal tax levies are not governed by the exemption rules that apply to garnishments or child support withholding orders under the Consumer Credit Protection Act (see Sections 9.1-2 and 9.1-3). Following is a list of the payments that are exempt from a federal tax levy:[2]

- unemployment compensation benefits;
- workers' compensation benefits;
- annuity and pension payments under the Railroad Retirement Tax Act and to certain armed services personnel;
- certain armed service-connected disability payments;
- certain public assistance payments (welfare and supplemental social security benefits); and
- amounts ordered withheld under a previously issued court order for child support.

*Some payments are no longer exempt.*[3] Under the Taxpayer Relief Act of 1997, the IRS can attach a continuing levy on up to 15% of certain payments that had been totally exempt from levy, including: federal payments not based on income or assets of the payee, unemployment compensation benefits, workers' compensation benefits, annuity and pension payments under the Railroad Retirement Tax Act, federal employee wage and salary payments up to the exempt amount (see the discussion below), supplemental social security benefits, and state or local public assistance payments. In 2000, the IRS began implementing a new Federal Payment Levy Program in conjunction with the existing tax levy program. In the first phase, the program was used to reduce federal retirement benefits and payments to government vendors who owe federal taxes. In 2001, federal employees' salaries were added to the program. The program has since been expanded to include some social security benefits and other federal payments, and determinations whether to institute a continuous levy will be made on a case-by-case basis.

In addition, each employee is entitled to an amount exempt from levy equal to the employee's standard deduction (based on Form 1040 tax filing status) and personal exemptions—including one for the employee—divided by the number of pay periods in the year (e.g., 52 for employees paid weekly, 26 biweekly).[4] Employees paid on a daily basis have their standard deduction and personal exemption amounts divided by 260, the number of workdays in a year (52 weeks x 5 workdays per week). Employees who are paid on a one-time basis or on a recurrent, but irregular basis (not the employer's regular payroll period) are entitled to the weekly exempt amount for each week to which the payment is attributable.

The value of the employee's standard deduction and personal exemptions is determined for the year the levy is received. The employee is also entitled to additional exempt amounts if the employee and/or the employee's spouse is at least 65 years old and/or blind. If the employee does not submit a verified, written statement regarding the employee's tax filing status and personal exemptions (Parts 3 and 4 of Form 668-W serve this purpose), the employer must figure the exempt amount as if the employee's filing status is married filing separately with one personal exemption.[5] Employers cannot rely on the employee's Form W-4 to determine the filing status and number of exemptions. The IRS issues tables for figuring the exempt amount each year as IRS Publication 1494 (see pages 9-4 and 9-5 for the 2007 and 2008 tables.). They are enclosed with each notice of levy.

---

2.    IRC §6334(a); IRS Reg. §301.6334-1.
3.    IRC §6331(h); IRS Notice 98-62, 1998-51 IRB 1.
4.    IRC §6334(d); IRS Reg. §301.6334-3; §301.6334-4.
5.    IRS Reg. §301.6334-4.

## 1. Tables for Figuring Amount Exempt from Levy on Wages, Salary, and Other Income—Forms 668-W(c), and 668-W(c)(DO))

Publication 1494, shown below, provides tables that show the amount of an individual's income that is exempt from a notice of levy used to collect delinquent tax in 2007. (Amounts are for each pay period.)

**2007**

### Filing Status: Single

| Pay Period | \multicolumn{7}{Number of Exemptions Claimed on Statement} | | | | | | |
|---|---|---|---|---|---|---|---|
| | 1 | 2 | 3 | 4 | 5 | 6 | More than 6 |
| Daily | 33.65 | 46.73 | 59.81 | 72.88 | 85.96 | 99.04 | 20.58 plus 13.08 for each exemption |
| Weekly | 168.27 | 233.65 | 299.04 | 364.42 | 429.81 | 495.19 | 102.89 plus 65.39 for each exemption |
| Biweekly | 336.54 | 467.31 | 598.08 | 728.85 | 859.62 | 990.38 | 205.77 plus 130.77 for each exemption |
| Semimonthly | 364.58 | 506.25 | 647.92 | 789.58 | 931.25 | 1072.92 | 222.92 plus 141.67 for each exemption |
| Monthly | 729.17 | 1012.50 | 1295.83 | 1579.17 | 1862.50 | 2145.83 | 445.83 plus 283.33 for each exemption |

### Filing Status: Married Filing Joint Return (and Qualifying Widow(er)s)

| Pay Period | Number of Exemptions Claimed on Statement | | | | | | |
|---|---|---|---|---|---|---|---|
| | 1 | 2 | 3 | 4 | 5 | 6 | More than 6 |
| Daily | 54.23 | 67.31 | 80.38 | 93.46 | 106.54 | 119.62 | 41.15 plus 13.08 for each exemption |
| Weekly | 271.15 | 336.54 | 401.92 | 467.31 | 532.69 | 598.08 | 205.77 plus 65.39 for each exemption |
| Biweekly | 542.31 | 673.08 | 803.85 | 934.62 | 1065.38 | 1196.15 | 411.54 plus 130.77 for each exemption |
| Semimonthly | 587.50 | 729.17 | 870.83 | 1012.50 | 1154.17 | 1295.83 | 445.83 plus 141.67 for each exemption |
| Monthly | 1175.00 | 1458.33 | 1741.67 | 2025.00 | 2308.33 | 2591.67 | 891.67 plus 283.33 for each exemption |

### Filing Status: Unmarried Head of Household

| Pay Period | Number of Exemptions Claimed on Statement | | | | | | |
|---|---|---|---|---|---|---|---|
| | 1 | 2 | 3 | 4 | 5 | 6 | More than 6 |
| Daily | 43.27 | 56.35 | 69.42 | 82.50 | 95.58 | 108.65 | 30.19 plus 13.08 for each exemption |
| Weekly | 216.35 | 281.73 | 347.12 | 412.50 | 477.88 | 543.27 | 150.96 plus 65.39 for each exemption |
| Biweekly | 432.69 | 563.46 | 694.23 | 825.00 | 955.77 | 1086.54 | 301.92 plus 130.77 for each exemption |
| Semimonthly | 468.75 | 610.42 | 752.08 | 893.75 | 1035.42 | 1177.08 | 327.08 plus 141.67 for each exemption |
| Monthly | 937.50 | 1220.83 | 1504.17 | 1787.50 | 2070.83 | 2354.17 | 654.17 plus 283.33 for each exemption |

### Filing Status: Married Filing Separate Return

| Pay Period | Number of Exemptions Claimed on Statement | | | | | | |
|---|---|---|---|---|---|---|---|
| | 1 | 2 | 3 | 4 | 5 | 6 | More than 6 |
| Daily | 33.65 | 46.73 | 59.81 | 72.88 | 85.96 | 99.04 | 20.58 plus 13.08 for each exemption |
| Weekly | 168.27 | 233.65 | 299.04 | 364.42 | 429.81 | 495.19 | 102.89 plus 65.39 for each exemption |
| Biweekly | 336.54 | 467.31 | 598.08 | 728.85 | 859.62 | 990.38 | 205.77 plus 130.77 for each exemption |
| Semimonthly | 364.58 | 506.25 | 647.92 | 789.58 | 931.25 | 1072.92 | 222.92 plus 141.67 for each exemption |
| Monthly | 729.17 | 1012.50 | 1295.83 | 1579.17 | 1862.50 | 2145.83 | 445.83 plus 283.33 for each exemption |

## 2. Table for Figuring Additional Exempt Amount for Taxpayers at Least 65 Years Old and / or Blind

| Filing Status | * | Additional Exempt Amount | | | | |
|---|---|---|---|---|---|---|
| | | Daily | Weekly | Biweekly | Semimonthly | Monthly |
| Single or Head of Household | 1 | 5.00 | 25.00 | 50.00 | 54.17 | 108.33 |
| | 2 | 10.00 | 50.00 | 100.00 | 108.33 | 216.67 |
| Any other Filing Status | 1 | 4.04 | 20.19 | 40.38 | 43.75 | 87.50 |
| | 2 | 8.08 | 40.38 | 80.77 | 87.50 | 175.00 |
| | 3 | 12.12 | 60.58 | 121.15 | 131.25 | 262.50 |
| | 4 | 16.15 | 80.77 | 161.54 | 175.00 | 350.00 |

* ADDITIONAL STANDARD DEDUCTION claimed on Parts 3, 4, and 5 of levy.

### Examples

These tables show the amount exempt from a levy on wages, salary, and other income. For example:

1. A single taxpayer who is paid weekly and claims three exemptions (including one for the taxpayer) has $299.04 exempt from levy.

2. If the taxpayer in number 1 is over 65 and writes 1 in the ADDITIONAL STANDARD DEDUCTION space on Parts 3, 4, and 5 of the levy, $324.04 is exempt from this levy ($299.04 plus $25.00).

3. A taxpayer who is married, files jointly, is paid biweekly, and claims two exemptions (including one for the taxpayer) has $673.08 exempt from levy.

4. If the taxpayer in number 3 is over 65 and has a spouse who is blind, this taxpayer should write 2 in the ADDITIONAL STANDARD DEDUCTION space on Parts 3, 4, and 5 of the levy. Then, $753.85 is exempt from this levy ($673.08 plus $80.77).

Publication **1494** (2007)   www.irs.gov   Catalog Number 11439T   Department of the Treasury — Internal Revenue Service

**1. Tables for Figuring Amount Exempt from Levy on Wages, Salary, and Other Income—(Forms 668-W(c), 668-W(c)(DO) and 668-W(ICS))**

Publication 1494, shown below, provides tables that show the amount of an individual's income that is exempt from a notice of levy used to collect delinquent tax in 2008. (Amounts are for each pay period.)

**2008**

### Filing Status: Single

| Pay Period | 1 | 2 | 3 | 4 | 5 | 6 | More than 6 |
|---|---|---|---|---|---|---|---|
| Daily | 34.42 | 47.88 | 61.35 | 74.81 | 88.27 | 101.73 | 20.96 plus 13.46 for each exemption |
| Weekly | 172.12 | 239.42 | 306.73 | 374.04 | 441.35 | 508.65 | 104.81 plus 67.31 for each exemption |
| Biweekly | 344.23 | 478.85 | 613.46 | 748.08 | 882.69 | 1017.31 | 209.62 plus 134.62 for each exemption |
| Semimonthly | 372.92 | 518.75 | 664.58 | 810.42 | 956.25 | 1102.08 | 227.08 plus 145.83 for each exemption |
| Monthly | 745.83 | 1037.50 | 1329.17 | 1620.83 | 1912.50 | 2204.17 | 454.17 plus 291.67 for each exemption |

*Number of Exemptions Claimed on Statement*

### Filing Status: Married Filing Joint Return (*and Qualifying Widow(er)s*)

| Pay Period | 1 | 2 | 3 | 4 | 5 | 6 | More than 6 |
|---|---|---|---|---|---|---|---|
| Daily | 55.38 | 68.85 | 82.31 | 95.77 | 109.23 | 122.69 | 41.92 plus 13.46 for each exemption |
| Weekly | 276.92 | 344.23 | 411.54 | 478.85 | 546.15 | 613.46 | 209.62 plus 67.31 for each exemption |
| Biweekly | 553.85 | 688.46 | 823.08 | 957.69 | 1092.31 | 1226.92 | 419.23 plus 134.62 for each exemption |
| Semimonthly | 600.00 | 745.83 | 891.67 | 1037.50 | 1183.33 | 1329.17 | 454.17 plus 145.83 for each exemption |
| Monthly | 1200.00 | 1491.67 | 1783.33 | 2075.00 | 2366.67 | 2658.33 | 908.33 plus 291.67 for each exemption |

*Number of Exemptions Claimed on Statement*

### Filing Status: Unmarried Head of Household

| Pay Period | 1 | 2 | 3 | 4 | 5 | 6 | More than 6 |
|---|---|---|---|---|---|---|---|
| Daily | 44.23 | 57.69 | 71.15 | 84.62 | 98.08 | 111.54 | 30.77 plus 13.46 for each exemption |
| Weekly | 221.15 | 288.46 | 355.77 | 423.08 | 490.38 | 557.69 | 153.85 plus 67.31 for each exemption |
| Biweekly | 442.31 | 576.92 | 711.54 | 846.15 | 980.77 | 1115.38 | 307.69 plus 134.62 for each exemption |
| Semimonthly | 479.17 | 625.00 | 770.83 | 916.67 | 1062.50 | 1208.33 | 333.33 plus 145.83 for each exemption |
| Monthly | 958.33 | 1250.00 | 1541.67 | 1833.33 | 2125.00 | 2416.67 | 666.67 plus 291.67 for each exemption |

*Number of Exemptions Claimed on Statement*

### Filing Status: Married Filing Separate Return

| Pay Period | 1 | 2 | 3 | 4 | 5 | 6 | More than 6 |
|---|---|---|---|---|---|---|---|
| Daily | 34.42 | 47.88 | 61.35 | 74.81 | 88.27 | 101.73 | 20.96 plus 13.46 for each exemption |
| Weekly | 172.12 | 239.42 | 306.73 | 374.04 | 441.35 | 508.65 | 104.81 plus 67.31 for each exemption |
| Biweekly | 344.23 | 478.85 | 613.46 | 748.08 | 882.69 | 1017.31 | 209.62 plus 134.62 for each exemption |
| Semimonthly | 372.92 | 518.75 | 664.58 | 810.42 | 956.25 | 1102.08 | 227.08 plus 145.83 for each exemption |
| Monthly | 745.83 | 1037.50 | 1329.17 | 1620.83 | 1912.50 | 2204.17 | 454.17 plus 291.67 for each exemption |

*Number of Exemptions Claimed on Statement*

**2. Table for Figuring Additional Exempt Amount for Taxpayers at Least 65 Years Old and / or Blind**

| Filing Status | * | Daily | Weekly | Biweekly | Semimonthly | Monthly |
|---|---|---|---|---|---|---|
| Single or Head of Household | 1 | 5.19 | 25.96 | 51.92 | 56.25 | 112.50 |
| | 2 | 10.38 | 51.92 | 103.84 | 112.50 | 225.00 |
| Any other Filing Status | 1 | 4.04 | 20.19 | 40.38 | 43.75 | 87.50 |
| | 2 | 8.08 | 40.38 | 80.77 | 87.50 | 175.00 |
| | 3 | 12.12 | 60.58 | 121.15 | 131.25 | 262.50 |
| | 4 | 16.15 | 80.77 | 161.54 | 175.00 | 350.00 |

*Additional Exempt Amount*

\* ADDITIONAL STANDARD DEDUCTION claimed on Parts 3, 4, and 5 of levy.

### Examples

These tables show the amount exempt from a levy on wages, salary, and other income. For example:

1. A single taxpayer who is paid weekly and claims three exemptions (including one for the taxpayer) has $306.73 exempt from levy.

2. If the taxpayer in number 1 is over 65 and writes 1 in the ADDITIONAL STANDARD DEDUCTION space on Parts 3, 4, and 5 of the levy, $336.69 is exempt from this levy ($306.76 plus $25.96).

3. A taxpayer who is married, files jointly, is paid biweekly, and claims two exemptions (including one for the taxpayer) has $688.46 exempt from levy.

4. If the taxpayer in number 3 is over 65 and has a spouse who is blind, this taxpayer should write 2 in the ADDITIONAL STANDARD DEDUCTION space on Parts 3, 4, and 5 of the levy. Then, $769.13 is exempt from this levy ($688.46 plus $80.77).

**Reset**

Publication **1494** (2008)    www.irs.gov    Catalog Number 11439T    Department of the Treasury — Internal Revenue Service

**BE CAREFUL OF LEVIES SPANNING MORE THAN ONE YEAR**[6] Where the total amount of a federal tax levy cannot be collected during a calendar year, the employer faces the issue of which year's table to use in figuring the exempt amount during the new year. If the employee does not complete a new Part 3 of Form 668-W, the employer must continue to use the table for the year during which the levy notice was received. The employee may complete a new Part 3 even if the employee's tax filing status or number of exemptions has not changed, in order to take advantage of higher exempt amounts contained in the new year's tables.

**Exempt amount subtracted from "take-home" pay.**[7] The amount of an employee's wages that is ultimately subject to the federal tax levy is the amount remaining after the exempt amount has been subtracted from the employee's "take-home pay." The definition of take-home pay is a controversial matter that continues to confuse many employers. The confusion relates to just what deductions may be taken from an employee's gross pay in determining take-home pay.

A 1994 IRS letter ruling clarified that the following items may be subtracted from an employee's gross wages when calculating take-home pay:[8]

- federal, state, and local taxes, even if the amounts increase while the levy is in effect due to salary or tax rate increases or changes in the employee's Form W-4;

- involuntary and voluntary deductions in effect before the employer received the levy, including child support withholding orders and other garnishments, elective deferrals (e.g., §401(k) plan salary reductions), health and life insurance premiums, charitable donations, etc.;

- increases in preexisting deductions beyond the employee's control, including those caused by increases in the employee's pay, such as elective deferrals of a certain percentage of salary, and those caused by increases in the cost of benefits, such as health or life insurance premiums (but not including voluntary decisions to increase the deferral percentage or to change the type of coverage provided); and

- deductions instituted after the levy is received and made as a condition of employment, such as a required deduction for union dues in a union shop environment.

**Direct deposit is not a deduction.** One issue that has proved troublesome to many employers in calculating an employee's take-home pay is how to treat net pay amounts authorized by the employee to be direct deposited in one or more of the employee's bank accounts. The IRS ruling clarified that the method of paying an employee's take home pay is irrelevant. Direct deposit is not considered a payroll deduction, but merely a method of payment, according to the Service, and amounts designated for direct deposit are subject to levy.

 **GOT A QUESTION? ASK THE IRS** In clarifying these take-home pay issues, the IRS did say there may be instances where it will disallow deductions which normally would be allowed. If that's the case, the IRS will notify the employer as to how to proceed. If employers have any questions about how to handle a federal tax levy, they should contact the IRS at the number listed on the Form 668-W.

**New voluntary deductions come from exempt amount.** Once an employee's take-home pay has been determined, all but the exempt amount is subject to the levy. Any payroll deductions initiated by the employee after the levy has been received by the employer must be deducted from the exempt amount when determining the employee's net pay, unless they are required as a condition of employment.

---

6.  IRS Reg. §301.6334-3(e).
7.  Form 668-W, Part 1 Instructions; IRS Policy Statement P-5-29.
8.  LTR 9511043, 12-21-94.

***Example:*** Employee Arthur receives $1,600 every two weeks from his employer, Biolife of East Virginia (BEV). On August 1, 2007, BEV received a Form 668-W stating that a federal tax levy was being issued against Arthur's wages for $25,000. Arthur claimed married filing jointly with 3 personal exemptions (including himself) on Part 3 of the form and gave it to the payroll department. As of August 1, Arthur had the following deductions:

| | |
|---|---|
| Federal income tax: | $107.00 |
| Social security tax: | 99.20 |
| Medicare tax: | 23.20 |
| State income tax: | 40.00 |
| §401(k) plan (3% of salary): | 48.00 |
| Health insurance (after-tax): | + 45.00 |
| Total: | $362.40 |

Arthur's take-home pay is $1,237.60 ($1,600 - $362.40). The exempt amount of Arthur's take-home pay (taken from the 2007 table) is $803.85. Therefore, the amount subject to levy is $433.75 ($1,237.60 - $803.85).

On April 1, 2008, Arthur gives BEV a new Form 668-W, Part 3 claiming married filing jointly with 4 exemptions, and his deductions have changed to the following amounts:

| | |
|---|---|
| Federal income tax: | $ 85.00 |
| Social security tax: | 99.20 |
| Medicare tax: | 23.20 |
| State income tax: | 40.00 |
| §401(k) plan (5% of salary): | 80.00 |
| Health insurance (after-tax): | + 55.00 |
| Total: | $382.40 |

Arthur's §401(k) deduction changed from $48.00 to $80.00 when he changed his elective deferral percentage from 3% to 5%. His health insurance deduction increased from $45.00 to $55.00 when the premiums were raised, although he was receiving the same coverage as before the increase. In calculating Arthur's take-home pay, BEV cannot subtract from gross wages the $32.00 increase in the §401(k) deduction because it was the result of a voluntary increase in the elective deferral percentage after the levy was in effect. The $10.00 increase in the health insurance deduction may be subtracted because it was the result of an increase in the cost of coverage, not a change in coverage chosen by Arthur.

Therefore, Arthur's take-home pay as of April 1, 2008 was $1,249.60 ($1,600 - $382.40 + $32.00). The exempt amount of Arthur's take-home pay (taken from the 2008 table) is $957.69. The amount subject to levy is $291.91 ($1,249.60 - $957.69). Arthur's net pay is $925.69 ($957.69 - $32.00) after subtracting the elective deferral increase from the exempt amount.

**Employee has two jobs; only one employer receives levy notice.**[9] Where an employee receives wages from more than one employer and only one receives a notice of levy, the employer must determine the exempt amount in the usual way unless the IRS notifies the employer that the exempt amount should be reduced because the other wages are not subject to levy.

***Example 1:*** Employee Charles is receiving $600 weekly from Eastside Publishing and $200 weekly from the Downtown Pub when he becomes a delinquent taxpayer in 2008. The amount of his take-home pay from Eastside that is exempt from levy is $172.12 (Charles reported single with 1 exemption). If the IRS notifies Eastside when the Form 668-W is sent that Charles is receiving wages from another employer that are not being levied on and exceed his exempt amount, Eastside can rely on the notification and treat all of Charles's take-home pay as subject to levy. If no such notice is sent, Eastside must treat $172.12 of Charles's take-home pay as exempt from levy.

---

9.     IRS Reg. §301.6334-2(c).

***Example 2:*** If Charles is receiving $100 weekly from the Downtown Pub that is not being levied on and Eastside receives notification of that fact from the IRS with Form 668-W, it must reduce Charles's exempt amount by $100. The resulting exempt amount would be $72.12 ($172.12 - $100.00). If no such notice is sent, Eastside must treat $172.12 of Charles's take-home pay as exempt from levy.

**When and where to make payments of withheld amounts.**[10] Form 668-W instructs employers to remit amounts withheld for levy on the same day wages are paid to the employee. The first payment to the IRS should accompany Part 3 of the form, after both the employer and the employee complete the information requested. Payments should be sent to the IRS at the address shown on the front of Part 1 (the employer's copy). Withholding and remittance must begin with the first payment of wages to the employee after the employer receives Form 668-W, regardless of when the wages were earned. The check made payable to the IRS should have the employee's name and social security number on its face.

**When to stop withholding.**[11] According to Form 668-W, the employer must continue to withhold and make levy payments until it receives Form 668-D, *Release of Levy / Release of Property from Levy* (see Appendix page A-124). This means the employer may not stop withholding when the payments match the total due the IRS stated on the front of Part 1 of Form 668-W. Withholding must continue because interest and possible penalties continue to accumulate on the amount remaining due after each levy payment is made.

Form 668-D will contain the final amount due and release the employee's wages from levy after that amount is paid. When the total face amount due has been withheld and paid, the employer or the employee should contact the IRS if a Form 668-D has not been received.

**Procedure when employment ends.** If the employee named on Form 668-W is no longer employed by the employer when the form is received, the employer must note that on the reverse side of Part 3 and return it to the IRS, along with the employee's last known address. If employment terminates while the levy is in effect, the employer should notify the IRS office where payments have been sent of the termination and the name and address of the employee's new employer, if known. The employer must deduct and remit any nonexempt amounts contained in severance or dismissal pay provided the employee.

**Employer not liable to employee for amounts withheld.**[12] If an employer honors a notice of levy (Form 668-W) from the IRS and withholds and pays over nonexempt amounts as instructed, the employer is not liable to the employee for the amount of wages paid to the IRS.

**Penalties for failing to withhold and remit.**[13] Employers failing to withhold and pay over amounts not exempt from levy after receiving Form 668-W are liable for the full amount required to be withheld, plus interest from the wage payment date. Any amount paid by the employer as a penalty will be credited against the taxes owed by the employee. In addition, the employer is liable for a penalty equal to 50% of the amount recoverable by the IRS after the failure to withhold and remit. This penalty is not applicable where there is a genuine dispute as to the amount to be withheld and paid over or the legal sufficiency of the levy. An employer had no defense against a penalty for failure to withhold and remit under a levy where the employee who was the subject of the levy was the employer's controller and she never informed anyone about it after the order to withhold was received in the mail.[14]

**Voluntary deduction agreement may prevent levy.** An employee who owes federal taxes may be able to avoid the imposition of a federal tax levy through a "Payroll Deduction Agreement." Under such an agreement, the employee and the IRS agree that a certain amount of federal taxes is owed and that the employee's employer will deduct an amount from the employee's wages each pay period and pay it over to the IRS until full payment is made. The agreement is carried out by having the employee fill out Form 2159, *Payroll Deduction Agreement* (see Appendix page A-312), with certain identifying information and the

---

10.  IRC §6331(e); IRS Reg. §301.6331-1(b)(1).
11.  IRC §6343; IRS Reg. §301.6343-1; §301.6343-2.
12.  IRC §6332(e); IRS Reg. §301.6332-1(c).
13.  IRC §6332(d); IRS Reg. §301.6332-1(b).
14.  U.S. v. Park Forest Care Center, Inc., 2001 U.S. Dist. LEXIS 16330, No. 99-S- 2461 (D Colo., 9-13-01).

amount to be deducted each pay period. **If the employer agrees to participate**, it will sign the agreement and begin deducting and remitting to the IRS.

In the agreement, the IRS reserves the right to levy against the employee's income and property if the conditions of the agreement are not met and to cancel the agreement if it feels that collection of the taxes owed is in jeopardy. There has been some confusion in the employer community as to whether the employee can have the deductions discontinued once they have begun, since the agreement was entered into voluntarily. While there has been no specific, written guidance on this question from the IRS, IRS personnel did tell the APA that the employer may discontinue withholding at the request of the employee. At that point, it would be up to the IRS to decide how it will collect the remainder of the taxes owed.

## 9.1-2 Child Support Withholding Orders

In response to a great uproar during the 1980s over the fact that a high percentage of noncustodial parents were not paying court- or agency-ordered child support, the U.S. Congress required the states to pass increasingly strict laws that now make wage withholding to pay child support the rule rather than the exception. In fact, since January 1, 1994, all initial orders for child support require wage withholding unless both parents or the court and one parent agree to a different method of payment.[15] Even if such an agreement is reached, wage withholding will become automatic once the noncustodial parent owing the child support is one month late in paying support.[16]

Under the Personal Responsibility and Work Opportunity Reconciliation Act of 1996, state laws must provide that all child support orders issued or modified before October 1, 1996 that were not subject to withholding on that date, will become subject to income withholding immediately once child support payments are overdue, without the need for a court or administrative hearing. State laws must also allow state child support agencies to transmit withholding orders by electronic means and without advance notice to the parent owing support. Subsequent notice of the withholding order must be provided, along with information regarding procedures for contesting the withholding order.[17] Beginning October 1, 2007, states must adjust child support orders of families receiving public assistance every 3 years.[18]

This means payroll departments have seen a dramatic increase in the number of child support withholding orders that must be implemented. To deal with the increased volume, payroll practitioners must be aware of the requirements that govern child support withholding orders.

**Child support enforcement framework.** Enforcement of child support orders is a joint federal/state responsibility, with federal laws providing standards state laws must meet or exceed in order to qualify for federal funding of state child support enforcement programs. These state standards are contained in Part D of Title IV of the Social Security Act.[19] Title IV-D and the Consumer Credit Protection Act (CCPA) provide the legal framework around which state child support withholding laws are constructed. At the federal level, the Office of Child Support Enforcement (OCSE) is responsible for implementation, while each of the states has its own Child Support Enforcement (CSE) agency.

The federal requirements, along with any allowable state variations, are explained in the following paragraphs:

*Maximum amount to withhold.*[20] Under the CCPA, the maximum amount that can be withheld from an employee's wages for spousal or child support is:

---

15. 42 USC §666(a)(8)(B)(i).
16. 42 USC §666(b)(3)(B).
17. 42 USC §666(a)(1)(B), (b)(4), (b)(11).
18. 42 USC §666(a)(10)(A)(i); Deficit Reduction Act of 2005, P.L. 109-171, §7302.
19. 42 USC §651-669.
20. CCPA §303(b); 15 USC §1673(b); 29 CFR §870.11(b).

- 50% of the employee's "disposable earnings" if the employee is supporting another spouse and/or children; and
- 60% if the employee is not supporting another spouse and/or children.

These amounts increase to 55% and 65%, respectively, if the employee is at least 12 weeks late (i.e., in arrears) in making support payments. If arrearages are being paid, the total of the current support and the arrearages cannot exceed the applicable maximum amount.[21] State child support withholding laws may impose lower limits on the amount that may be withheld, but may not exceed the limits imposed by the CCPA.

*Calculating disposable earnings.* Disposable earnings are determined by subtracting all deductions required by law from an employee's gross earnings (wages, commissions, bonuses, sick pay, and periodic pension payments). Deductions required by law include withholding for federal, state, or local income tax, social security or Medicare tax, state unemployment or disability tax, and mandated payments for state employee retirement systems. Voluntary deductions, such as health and life insurance premiums, union dues, and retirement plan contributions, are not subtracted from earnings to calculate disposable earnings. (State law needs to be checked, as some states require health insurance premiums to be deducted when determining disposable earnings.) Wages already subject to withholding for tax levies, bankruptcy orders, other child support withholding orders, or wage garnishments are not considered deductions required by law. Therefore, they should not be subtracted from gross earnings when determining the maximum amount subject to child support withholding. However, if the tax levy or other order has priority over the current child support withholding order, the amount required to be deducted under the order having priority must be taken into account when determining whether the CCPA maximum has been reached.[22]

 **WHAT ABOUT ONE-TIME PAYMENTS?** The CCPA definition of "earnings" subject to the limits on child support withholding includes all "compensation paid or payable for personal services," no matter what it is called. Interpreting this definition, the Michigan supreme court ruled that annual profit-sharing payments, recognition awards, and union contract signing bonuses were earnings under this definition and the CCPA limits were properly applied.[23] State child support agencies suggest that employers inform the agencies as far in advance as possible before one-time payments are made so they can let the employers know what portion of any such payments is subject to a child support withholding order. OCSE provides some help in this area for employers by including lump sum contact information, an address for lump sum correspondence for the states, and information regarding the state treatment of lump sum payments on its website at www.acf.hhs.gov/programs/cse/newhire/employer/contacts/ls_matrix.pdf and adding specific lump sum compliance information to its online *Intergovernmental Referral Guide*.

**Example:** Ralph's employer receives a child support withholding order while Ralph's wages are already subject to a federal tax levy under which the employer is currently withholding 45% of Ralph's disposable earnings every two weeks ($1,200). For the purposes of this example, assume that the amount of Ralph's disposable earnings and take-home pay are the same. Ralph is not supporting another spouse or family other than those mentioned in the child support order and is not more than 12 weeks in arrears in making child support payments. Ralph's disposable earnings remain $1,200 after the child support withholding order is received, but his employer may deduct only 15% of Ralph's disposable earnings to satisfy the child support withholding order (60% maximum under the CCPA).

 **WHAT ABOUT TIPS?** According to OCSE, tips received by an employee in cash or on a debit/credit card receipt are not part of the employee's earnings under the CCPA. However, amounts paid to the employee by the employer from service charges added to a customer's bill are earnings subject to child support withholding. OCSE adopted the position of the U.S. Department of Labor, which is responsible for interpreting the CCPA (see Section 9.1-3).

---

21. 42 USC §666(b)(1).
22. 29 CFR §870.11(b)(2).
23. Genesee County Friend of the Court v. General Motors Corp., 464 Mich. 44 (Mich. S.Ct., 2001), reversing 1999 Mich. App. LEXIS 290 (Mich. Ct.App., 1999).

***Example:*** Gary's employer receives a child support withholding order demanding that $700 of Gary's disposable earnings be withheld each pay period and sent to the state child support enforcement agency if he is paid biweekly ($350 if he is paid weekly). The state where Gary lives and works follows the federal law in determining the maximum that may be withheld for child support. Gary is not late in paying support, and is not supporting another wife or child. Gary's disposable earnings and the amount withheld for child support are determined as follows:

|  | Net Pay Before Child Support | Disposable Earnings |
|---|---|---|
| Gross biweekly earnings: | $1,600.00 | $1,600.00 |
| Federal income tax: | - 300.00 | - 300.00 |
| State income tax: | - 48.00 | - 48.00 |
| Social security tax: | - 99.20 | - 99.20 |
| Medicare tax: | - 23.20 | - 23.20 |
| Health insurance premium: | - 50.00 | |
| §401(k) plan contribution: | - 80.00 | |
| U.S. savings bonds: | - 10.00 | |
| | $ 989.60 | $1,129.60 |

Child support withholding maximum: $1,129.60 x 60% = $677.76

Since the child support withholding maximum is less than the $700 demanded in the withholding notice, only $677.76 can be withheld from Gary's pay for child support. His final net pay is $311.84 ($989.60 - $677.76). The remainder ($23.24) will be owed in arrears.

*Priority of withholding orders.*[24] Orders to withhold wages for child support take priority over all other garnishments or attachments issued against the employee's wages except for tax levies received by the employer before the child support withholding order. Under recent amendments to the federal Bankruptcy Code, debts due for child support are nondischargeable debts and withholding is not affected by the filing or granting of a bankruptcy petition. Employers must continue to withhold despite the employee's bankruptcy.[25] (See Section 9.1-4.)

*When order takes effect.* The employer must put the wage withholding order into effect no later than the first pay period beginning after 14 working days following the mailing of the notice to withhold to the employer. States may require that the order take effect sooner. The employer must continue to withhold until notified otherwise in writing by the court or agency involved.[26]

*Uniform order to withhold.* In 2007, the Office of Child Support Enforcement approved a revised version of the standard child support withholding order, *Income Withholding for Support* (see pages 9-15 — 9-17 and A-402) that employers should be seeing in all of their withholding situations, whether initiated by a state child support enforcement agency, a court, or a private entity. The form serves as an order to withhold when issued by a state or tribal IV-D agency, a court, or an attorney authorized by state law to issue withholding orders.[27] If the form is issued by any other individual or entity, it must be accompanied by a copy of the underlying withholding order before the employer is required to begin withholding. If the form is served by an attorney authorized by state or tribal law to issue withholding orders, the attorney must include a copy of the state or tribal law containing such authorization.

*Changes in 2007 withholding order.* The revised *Income Withholding for Support* issued in November 2007 contained several changes to the previous version of the standard withholding order:

---

24. 42 USC §666(b)(7); 45 CFR §303.100(e)(1)(vii).
25. 11 USC §507(a)(1); §523(15), (18); 11 USC §362(b)(2); OCSE IM-05-05, 5-4-05.
26. 45 CFR §303.100(e)(1)(iv).
27. Income Withholding for Support - Instructions

Identity of the sender. The new form provides a clearer indication of the entity submitting the IWO (i.e., Child Support Enforcement (CSE) agency, court, private entity, etc.) at the beginning of the document. Note that Private individual/entity includes tribes that are not operating under a CSE program.

Employer/Income Withholder's Name. This field has been changed from *Employer/Withholder's Name* to include other withholders of income.

Blank box for barcodes. There is now a blank space at the right side of the form to accommodate court stamps or barcodes.

Lump sum. A *One-Time Order/Notice – Lump Sum Payment checkbox* has been added to allow the issuer of the IWO to indicate that a lump sum should be attached to satisfy an arrearage. In addition, a line has been added to allow the issuer to indicate the amount of the lump sum and that the request is for a one-time only payment. The form also includes specific instructions to the employer to continue payments for ongoing IWOs. The employer is directed to contact the issuer if it has any questions. OCSE explains that the IWO should be prepared for the attachment of regular payments or the attachment of a lump sum payment, not both. Issuers should check the appropriate box.

Case identifier. This field has replaced the *Case Number* used on the previous form.

Order identifier. This field has been added so that a state can identify a specific order. It is to be used at the state's discretion and may be used for, e.g., the court number, docket number, or other issuer's identifier. (Use of this identifier is optional.)

Child's name. The fields for the child's name and date of birth have been moved to the front of the form. This allows the employer to easily identify who the IWO is for and to avoid implementing duplicate orders.

Remittance identifier. This field has been added in the *Remittance Information* section. The previous IWO required that states use the Case Identifier. However, some states use a social security number, participant identification number, or other identifier, which may now appropriately be entered in this field.

EFT/EDI. Under *Remittance Information,* the state's routing transit number and bank account number (for sending payments electronically) have been removed and the employer is directed to contact the applicable state EFT/EDI office at OCSE's website.

Document tracking identifier. This field has been added to the footer on page one for use by states participating in OCSE's electronic IWO (eIWO) application. This field is optional for other users of the form.

Withholding limits. This section has been revised to provide a clearer explanation of the Consumer Credit Protection Act, as well as better guidance on tribal orders and withholding in cases with arrears of more than 12 weeks.

Contact information. Fields have been added to provide contact information for the employer and employee/obligor (i.e., phone/fax, e-mail/website address) for questions regarding the order. A correspondence address has been added for the employer to send correspondence or a termination notification.

Identifying information. Fields have been added at the top of the last page – for employee/obligor's name, case identifier, order identifier, and employer's name – so that the employer can return this page to report the termination of employment of the employee.

Notification of termination of employment. In this section, checkboxes have been added to allow the employer to indicate that:
- This person has never worked for this employer.
- This person no longer works for this employer.

Fields have also been added for *Last known phone number, Date final payment made to SDU or Tribal CSE agency,* and *Final payment amount.*

OMB expiration date. This date, together with an explanation of its purpose, has been added (as a footnote) to the second page of the form. The footnote reads as follows: "OMB Expiration Date – 10/31/2010. The OMB Expiration Date has no bearing on the termination date or validity of the income withholding order; it identifies the version of the form currently in use."

*Time to remit payment.*[28] The employer must send payment of the withheld wages to the party noted on the withholding notice within 7 business days of the date wages are paid to the employee. State law may set a shorter time limit for making payment. Timeliness is determined by the postmark if the payment is mailed, or if the payment is transmitted electronically, by the date the transmission is proven to have been initiated by the employer.

*Where payment is to be made.*[29] By October 1, 1998 (October 1, 1999 in states that currently process such payments through local courts), all states were required to establish a "state disbursement unit" for the collection and disbursement of child support payments in all Title IV-D cases and all other cases (e.g., court-issued child support orders) in which a child support order is issued on or after January 1, 1994. Once the state disbursement unit is established, employers in the state will send wages withheld for child support to the unit for payment to the custodial parent. Disbursements from the state disbursement unit must be made within 2 business days of their receipt from an employer if there is enough information to identify the payee.

All the states except South Carolnia had SDUs operating by the end of 2007. South Carolina's SDU was still under development at this time.

*Combining payments from several employees.*[30] The employer may send one check or electronic payment each pay period to cover all child support withholdings for the period if they are all to be sent to the same withholding agency and the employer separately itemizes the amount withheld from each employee and notes the date each amount was withheld. State restrictions on combining payments may be more severe. Some states also allow or require the use of electronic funds transfer to make payments.

*No discharge because of withholding.*[31] The employer is prohibited from discharging, disciplining, or otherwise discriminating against an employee because the employee's wages are subject to withholding for child support. Violators can be fined an amount set by state law.

*Administrative fees for employers.*[32] Employers may charge the employee an administrative fee for processing the wage withholding order each pay period. The maximum amount is set by state law, and the fee must be withheld from the employee's other wages, not the child support payment. However, the total of the child support payment and the administrative fee cannot exceed the maximum for child support withholding set by the CCPA (or a lower maximum set by state law). According to the federal Office of Child Support Enforcement, an employer can withhold its administrative fee even if the amount ordered to be withheld for child support equals or exceeds the maximum allowed by law. The amount of the support that would have been withheld but for the fee becomes part of the arrearages owed by the noncustodial parent.

> **Example**: Tim's employer receives a child support withholding order requiring that $300 be withheld from Tim's weekly pay, but the maximum amount that can be withheld from Tim's pay under federal and state law is $275, so Tim will be $25 in arrears each week. Also, the state where Tim works allows employers to withhold a $5 administrative fee each time child support is withheld. If Tim's employer wants to collect the administrative fee, it will withhold $270 for current child support, take the $5 fee from Tim's remaining wages, and increase Tim's weekly arrearages to $30.

---

28.  42 USC §666(b)(6)(A)(i); 45 CFR §303.100(e)(1)(ii), (ix)
29.  42 USC §654B.
30.  42 USC §666(b)(6)(B); 45 CFR §303.100(e)(1)(viii).
31.  42 USC §666(b)(6)(D); 45 CFR §303.100(e)(1)(v).
32.  42 USC §666(b)(6)(A)(i); 45 CFR §303.100(e)(1)(iii).

*Notification after employee leaves employment.*[33] If an employee whose wages are subject to a child support withholding order separates from employment for any reason, the employer has a certain amount of time set by state law to notify the child support enforcement agency of the employee's last known address and, if known, the name and address of the employee's new employer. (Federal regulations require such notification "promptly.") If the employee has been injured or is ill and cannot work, the employer should notify the court or agency that sent the withholding notice and provide the employee's name and the name and address of the entity paying workers' compensation or disability benefits. If none of the benefits are being paid by the employer, the employer is not responsible for withholding.

*Penalty for not withholding.*[34] If the employer fails to withhold the amount required by the withholding order (up to the legal maximum), it is liable for the full amount not withheld and any fine set by state law. The employer need not alter its pay periods to comply with the law. It can contact the agency administering the order to arrange a revision of the amount to withhold that fits the employer's pay cycle.

**Enforcement of withholding orders from other states**. One of the most troublesome issues for employers is handling child support withholding orders issued by a court or agency in a state other than the state where the employee works. In 1993, an interstate commission adopted a model law addressing these issues—the Uniform Interstate Family Support Act (UIFSA). Under UIFSA §501, an employer must put into effect a child support withholding order that it receives directly from another state's child support enforcement agency so long as the order appears "regular on its face." Registration of the order with the child support enforcement agency in the employee's work state is not necessary under UIFSA.

Under UIFSA, employers must follow *the rules as stated on the order* that specify:

- the duration and amount of periodic payments of current child support, stated as a specific amount;

- the person or agency designated to receive payments and the address to which the payments are to be forwarded;

- medical support, whether in the form of periodic cash payments, stated as a specific amount, or ordering the noncustodial parent to provide health insurance coverage for the child under a policy available through the parent's employer;

- the amount of periodic payment of fees and costs for a support enforcement agency, the issuing court, and/or the custodial parent's attorney, stated as specific amounts; and

- the amount of periodic payments of arrears and interest on arrears, stated as specific amounts.

Employers must follow *the rules of the employee's work state* when determining:

- the employer's administrative fee for processing an income withholding order;

- the maximum amount permitted to be withheld from the noncustodial parent's income;

- the time periods within which the employer must implement the withholding order and forward the amount withheld; and

- the priorities for withholding and allocating income withheld for multiple withholding orders.

---

33.    45 CFR §303.100(e)(1)(x).
34.    42 USC §666(b)(6)(C); 45 CFR §303.100(e)(1)(vi).

## INCOME WITHHOLDING FOR SUPPORT

☐ **ORIGINAL INCOME WITHHOLDING ORDER/NOTICE FOR SUPPORT (IWO)** ☐ **AMENDED IWO**
☐ **ONE-TIME ORDER/NOTICE - LUMP SUM PAYMENT**
☐ **TERMINATION of IWO**

Date: _____

☐ Child Support Enforcement (CSE) Agency  ☐Court  ☐ Attorney  ☐ Private Individual/Entity  (Check One)

**NOTE:** If you receive this document from someone other than a State or Tribal Child Support Enforcement agency or a court, a copy of the underlying order that contains a provision authorizing income withholding must be attached.  Or if under State law an attorney in that State, or if under Tribal law a Tribal legal representative, may issue an income withholding order, the attorney or Tribal legal representative must include a copy of the State or Tribal law authorizing the attorney or Tribal legal representative to issue an income withholding order.

State/Tribe/Territory  _____     Case Identifier _____
City/County/Dist./Tribe _____     Order Identifier _____
Private Individual/Entity_____

_____          RE:
Employer/Income Withholder's Name                Employee/Obligor's Name (Last, First, MI)

Employer/Income Withholder's Address             Employee/Obligor's Social Security Number (if known)

                                                 Custodial Party/Obligee's Name (Last, First, MI)

Employer/Income Withholder's Federal EIN

Child's Name (Last, First, MI)              Child's Birth Date

*ORDER INFORMATION*: This document is based on the support or withholding order from _____.
You are required by law to deduct these amounts from the employee/obligor's income until further notice.
$_____ Per _____ current child support
$_____ Per _____ past-due child support  -  Arrears greater than 12 weeks? ☐ Yes ☐No
$_____ Per _____ current cash medical support
$_____ Per _____ past-due cash medical support
$_____ Per _____ current spousal support
$_____ Per _____ past-due spousal support
$_____ Per _____ other (must specify) _____.
for a total of $_____ per _____ to be forwarded to the payee below.

*AMOUNTS TO WITHHOLD:* You do not have to vary your pay cycle to be in compliance with the *Order Information*.  If your pay cycle does not match the ordered payment cycle, withhold one of the following amounts:

$_____ per weekly pay period              $ _____ per semimonthly pay period (twice a month)
$_____ per biweekly pay period (every two weeks)   $ _____ per monthly pay period

$_____ **ONE-TIME LUMP SUM PAYMENT  Do not stop any existing IWO unless you receive a termination order.**

*REMITTANCE INFORMATION*:  If the employee/obligor's principal place of employment is _____
_____, you must begin withholding no later than the first pay period that occurs _____ days after the date of _____.
Send payment within _____ working days of the pay date. If you cannot withhold the full amount of support for any or all orders for this employee/obligor, withhold up to _____% of disposable income for all orders. If the employee/obligor's principal place of employment is not _____, see the ADDITIONAL INFORMATION FOR EMPLOYERS AND OTHER INCOME WITHHOLDERS for limitations on withholding, applicable time requirements and any allowable employer's fees.

Document Tracking Identifier_____     OMB 0970-0154

For EFT/EDI instructions, contact the EFT/EDI office at the website listed below. **If paying by check, make check payable to:** _____. **Include this *Remittance Identifier* with**

**payment**: _____. Send check to: _____

**FIPS code (If necessary)**: _____

Signature (if required by State or Tribal law): _____
Print Name: _____
Title of Issuing Official: _____

☐ If checked, you are required to provide a copy of this form to the employee/obligor. If the employee/obligor works in a State or for a Tribe that is different from the State or Tribe that issued this order, a copy must be provided to the employee/obligor even if the box is not checked.

---

## ADDITIONAL INFORMATION FOR EMPLOYERS AND OTHER INCOME WITHHOLDERS

State-specific information may be viewed on the OCSE Employer Services website located at:
http://www.acf.hhs.gov/programs/cse/newhire/employer/contacts/contacts.htm

**Priority:** Withholding for support has priority over any other legal process under State law (or Tribal law if applicable) against the same income. If a Federal tax levy is in effect, please notify the contact person listed below.

**Combining Payments:** You may combine withheld amounts from more than one employee/obligor's income in a single payment to each agency/party requesting withholding. You must, however, separately identify the portion of the single payment that is attributable to each employee/obligor.

**Reporting the Pay Date:** You must report the pay date when sending the payment. The pay date is the date on which the amount was withheld from the employee/obligor's wages. You must comply with the law of the State (or Tribal law if applicable) of the employee/obligor's principal place of employment with respect to the time periods within which you must implement the withholding and forward the support payments.

**Employee/Obligor with Multiple Support Withholdings:** If there is more than one Order/Notice against this employee/obligor and you are unable to fully honor all support Orders/Notices due to federal, State, or Tribal withholding limits, you must follow the State or Tribal law/procedure of the employee/obligor's principal place of employment. You must honor all Orders/Notices to the greatest extent possible, giving priority to current support before payment of any past-due support.

**Lump Sum Payments:** You may be required to report and withhold from lump sum payments such as bonuses, commissions, or severance pay. Contact the agency or person listed below to determine if you are required to withhold or if you have any questions about lump sum payments.

**Liability:** If you have any doubts about the validity of the Order/Notice, contact the agency or person listed below. If you fail to withhold income as the Order/Notice directs, you are liable for both the accumulated amount you should have withheld from the employee/obligor's income and any other penalties set by State or Tribal law/procedure.

---

**Anti-discrimination:** You are subject to a fine determined under State or Tribal law for discharging an employee/obligor from employment, refusing to employ, or taking disciplinary action against an employee/obligor because of a child support withholding. _____

---

**Withholding Limits:** You may not withhold more than the lesser of: 1) the amounts allowed by the Federal Consumer Credit Protection Act (CCPA) (15 U.S.C. 1673(b)); or 2) the amounts allowed by the State or Tribe of the employee/obligor's principal place of employment. Disposable income is the net income left after making mandatory deductions such as: State, Federal, local taxes, Social Security taxes, statutory pension contributions and Medicare taxes. The Federal limit is 50% of the disposable income if the obligor is supporting another family and 60% of the disposable income if the obligor is not supporting another family. However, that 50% limit is increased to 55% and that 60% limit is increased to 65% if the arrears are greater than 12 weeks. If permitted by the State, you may deduct a fee for administrative costs. The support amount and the fee may not exceed the limit indicated in this section.

OMB Expiration Date – 10/31/2010. The OMB Expiration Date has no bearing on the termination date or validity of the income withholding order; it identifies the version of the form currently in use.

## Section 9: Other Deductions From Pay

Employee/Obligor's Name: _____ Case Identifier: _____
Order Identifier: _____ Employer's Name: _____

**Arrears greater than 12 weeks?** If the *Order Information* does not indicate whether the arrears are greater than 12 weeks, then the employer should calculate the CCPA limit using the lower percentage.

For Tribal orders, you may not withhold more than the amounts allowed under the law of the issuing Tribe. For Tribal employers who receive a State order, you may not withhold more than the lesser of the limit set by the law of the jurisdiction in which the employer is located or the maximum amount permitted under section 303(d) of the CCPA (15 U.S.C. 1673 (b)).

Depending upon applicable State law, you may need to take into consideration the amounts paid for health care premiums in determining disposable income and applying appropriate withholding limits.

**Additional Information:**
_____
_____
_____

**NOTIFICATION OF TERMINATION OF EMPLOYMENT:** You must promptly notify the Child Support Enforcement agency and/or the person listed below by returning this form to the correspondence address if:

☐ This person has never worked for this employer.

☐ This person no longer works for this employer.

Please provide the following information for the terminated employee:

Termination date: _____ Last known phone number: _____

Last known home address: _____
_____
_____

Date final payment made to the State Disbursement Unit or Tribal CSE agency: _____

Final payment amount: _____ New employer's name: _____
_____

New employer's address:
_____
_____

**CONTACT INFORMATION**
**To employer:** If the employer/income withholder has any questions, contact _____
_____ by phone at _____, by fax at _____, by email or website at:
_____

Send termination notice and other correspondence to:
_____
_____

**To employee/obligor:** If the employee/obligor has questions, contact _____
_____ by phone at _____, by fax_____, by email or website at
_____

IMPORTANT: The person completing this form is advised that the information may be shared with the employee/obligor.

*State laws adopt UIFSA.* Under the Personal Responsibility and Work Opportunity Reconciliation Act of 1996, all states were required to adopt UIFSA by January 1, 1998, including any amendments to UIFSA that had been officially adopted by August 22, 1996.[35] All the states adopted UIFSA by mid-1998. The PRWORA also specifically addressed several out-of-state order issues by requiring state laws to mandate that employers follow the income withholding law of the noncustodial parent's work state in determining:

- the employer's administrative fee;
- the maximum amount permitted to be withheld for child support;
- the time period for implementing the withholding order and remitting withheld amounts;
- the priorities for withholding and allocating income withheld for multiple withholding orders; and
- any withholding terms or conditions not specified in the order.[36]

State laws must also provide that employers who comply with an out-of-state income withholding order that is "regular on its face" are not liable to any person or agency for withholding or making payments in compliance with the order.

**Electronic data processing and payments.** In December 1992, the Bankers EDI Council approved the final Child Support Application Banking Convention for nationwide use. Federal law requires the states to develop automated data processing systems that can manage the state's child support program, including a state case registry, and receive amounts withheld for child support and accompanying accounting information by electronic means beginning October 1, 1997, although the system did not have to meet all the requirements imposed by the Personal Responsibility and Work Opportunity Reconciliation Act of 1996 until October 1, 2000.[37] In May 2000, OCSE announced that states would have to accept electronic payments in both the CCD+ and CTX 820 Remittance formats. All states except South Carolina can receive electronic child support withholding payments. For a current list of EFT/EDI state contacts, go to OCSE's web site at www.acf.hhs.gov/programs/cse/newhire/employer/contacts/eftedi_statecontacts.htm#SC. As of the end of 2007, California, Florida, Illinois, Indiana, Massachusetts, Oregon, Pennsylvania, and Virginia require most employers to remit child support payments electronically.

*How the process works.* Several steps must take place to implement electronic payment of child support withholding orders. Each participant in the process—employers, financial institutions, and CSE agencies—has a role to play.

What employers must do:

- State CSE agencies provide employers the agency's bank account and transit routing numbers. A nationally standardized, one-page instruction sheet provides required information from the court or agency withholding order to simplify the withholding process.

- Employers will have to modify their systems to set up a payroll deduction with the ACH file information, loading the CSE agency's bank account and other information for each employee subject to a withholding order.

- Systems changes may be required to send an additional batch behind the payroll ACH file providing for the storage and transmission of the necessary child support withholding files.

- Other solutions besides modifying the existing payroll system include:
  — purchasing software to facilitate the transmission of the deductions with the addenda record;
  — outsourcing the process to a third-party garnishment processing provider;
  — using a Web-based payment system to transmit payment and case information to a third party that combines payments with those from other employers and sends them to the SDUs;
  — using no-fee Web-based applications or software made available by a number of states.

35.  42 USC §666(f).
36.  42 USC §666(b)(6)(A)(i).
37.  42 U.S.C. §654(24).

- Once the employer's system is capable of transmitting withheld child support, the employer should contact each SDU to which payments will be made. Even though the states have to follow the Banking Convention there may be differences in how certain fields are filled, and it is important to know what those are before beginning to make the payments.

- The ACH file for payroll and child support withholding must be sent to the employer's originating depository financial institution (ODFI).

What the ODFI must do:

- The ODFI processes the ACH file as usual, passing the payroll and child support transactions onto the Federal Reserve or other ACH operator.

What the receiving depository financial institution must do:

- The RDFI receives the child support transactions and deposits the funds to the child support agency's account.

- It also passes on deposit addendum record information to the CSE agency or court in report format, either electronically or on hard copy.

What the CSE agency or court must do:

- The CSE agency or court must post the individual deposit transactions to the appropriate accounts according to the addendum record information received from the RDFI.

- It then passes the funds along to the custodial parent with a check, by direct deposit to the parent's account, or by loading a debit card.

*Benefits of electronic payments.* Each participant in the electronic payment system also stands to benefit in several ways from its participation.

Benefits to employers:

- reduce (and eventually eliminate) manual effort required to pass child support withholding information from the payroll system to accounts payable for processing checks to CSE agencies and/or courts;

- reduce the cost of processing per item, plus the cost savings from less manual effort, because of the lower cost of ACH processing vs. check processing, reduced account reconciliation charges, reduced postage costs, etc.;

- reduce the time and effort spent replacing lost checks and tracing mispostings.

Benefits to financial institutions:

- opportunity for additional business with the offering of a new service to child support agencies and courts;

- conversion of prior check processing to more efficient ACH processing at no added cost.

Benefits to CSE agency and custodial parents:

- ability to move to a more efficient electronic method of posting payments to accounts and to increase accuracy and cost effectiveness of posting payments;

- faster receipt of child support payments by custodial parents, which reduces complaints and time spent researching lost payments;

- added security and convenience of direct deposit of child support payments into custodial parents' accounts.

**Payments over the Internet.** By 2007, several states had made free or low-cost Web-based payments available. The payments are ACH debit transactions designed mainly for small or mid-sized businesses without the ability to invest in setting up ACH credit transactions. Web-based payments are available in Arkansas, California, Florida, Illinois, Indiana, Iowa, Louisiana, Maryland, Massachusetts, Michigan, Missouri, Montana, Nebraska, New Hampshire, New Mexico, New York, North Carolina, North Dakota, Ohio, Oklahoma, Oregon, Pennsylvania, Tennessee, Texas, Virginia, Washington, and West Virginia, and the list is expected to expand in 2008. A couple of states also offer pay-by-phone payment capability.

**Electronic Income Withholding Orders.** In August 2004, an electronic income withholding order workgroup was formed as part of an initiative to develop an electronic format for the income withholding order (e-IWO). The workgroup consists of OCSE, APA, several state CSE agencies, a payroll processor, and several large employers.

The workgroup developed workflows and record layouts that enable:

- states to send income withholding orders electronically to employers; and
- employers to accept the electronic form and provide other information regarding the noncustodial parent (e.g., the employee is no longer employed by the employer or has not been an employee of the employer).

The e-IWO formats were tested in a pilot program in Colorado, Indiana, North Carolina, Oregon, and Texas by several large employers. The program was evaluated in 2006. The program also tested various transport systems to find the most cost-effective ways for employers and state CSE agencies. Outreach efforts to introduce and educate states and employers about the e-IWO process began in 2006.

*The e-IWO process.* The e-IWO process involves the electronic sharing of information between a state child support enforcement agency and an employer. This information may be characterized as follows:

- New/original or amended order information (child support enforcement agency to employer);
- File and receipt acknowledgement (employer to child support enforcement agency);
- Termination of noncustodial parent employment (employer to child support enforcement agency);
- Termination of order information (child support enforcement agency to employer); and
- Lump sum payments (child support enforcement agency to employer).

Through a secure, agreed-upon method, the child support enforcement agency and the employer exchange data files based on a defined, standard file layout. The formats that have been tested for states and employers to submit are flat file and XML. Through these various methods, states and employers have the ability to select the technology that best meets their needs. So far, Texas is the only state that has offered the e-IWO option to employers in general.

*User's guide issued by OCSE.* In June 2006, OCSE issued the Electronic Income Withholding (e-IWO) User's Guide. The guide is designed to provide states and employers (public and private) with the necessary information and recommendations to implement the e-IWO process. The guide provides:

- background on income withholding for child support;
- an overview of an e-IWO;
- the e-IWO process;
- the e-IWO for state IV-D agencies, federal agencies, and employers.
- appendices containing e-IWO record layouts and requirements;

- draft business rules for the original, amended, termination, and lump sum conditions found near the top of the Order/Notice form (the lump sum is on the back of the form) for income withholding;
- the standard income withholding order form (*Income Withholding for Support*);
- communication options for employers to electronically transmit the "Read Receipt" and "Acknowledgement" records to a state, tribe, or territory;
- a report evaluating the e-IWO pilot project; and
- contact information.

Employers can download the 101-page publication from OCSE's Web site at www.acf.hhs.gov/programs/cse/newhire/employer/publication/eiwo_userguide.pdf. For further information on the e-IWO project or to find out how to participate, contact Bill Stuart at 518-399-9241 or William.K.Stuart@lmco.com.

**International child support enforcement.**[38] The Secretary of State has the authority (with the agreement of the Secretary of HHS) to declare child support enforcement reciprocity with foreign countries that have certain procedures for establishing and enforcing child support orders issued in favor of U.S. residents. These procedures must include: procedures for U.S. residents—at no cost—to establish paternity, establish and enforce child support orders, and distribute child support payments; and designation of an agency of the foreign country as a central authority that would facilitate support enforcement and ensure compliance with standards.

In October 2004, the Department of State published an updated list of the countries that are currently "designated foreign reciprocating countries":

| Country | Effective Date |
|---|---|
| Australia | May 21, 2001 |
| Canadian Provinces: | |
|     Alberta | September 4, 2002 |
|     British Columbia | December 15, 1999 |
|     Manitoba | July 11, 2000 |
|     New Brunswick | February 1, 2004 |
|     Northwest Territories | February 7, 2004 |
|     Nunavut | January 20, 2004 |
|     Newfoundland/Labrador | August 7, 2002 |
|     Nova Scotia | December 18, 1998 |
|     Ontario | August 7, 2002 |
| Czech Republic | May 3, 2000 |
| Ireland | September 10, 1997 |
| Netherlands | May 1, 2002 |
| Norway | June 10, 2002 |
| Poland | June 14, 1999 |
| Portugal | March 17, 2001 |
| Slovak Republic | February 1, 1998 |
| Switzerland | September 30, 2004 |

The Secretary of HHS is responsible for facilitating support enforcement in cases involving residents of the U.S. and foreign reciprocating countries, including developing uniform forms and procedures, using the Federal Parent Locator Service to provide information on the location of the noncustodial parent, and providing other necessary oversight and assistance activities. On the state level, states can enter into their own reciprocal agreements with foreign countries if no federal agreement exists. Also, state child support enforcement plans must provide that requests for services by a foreign reciprocating country will be treated the same as requests from another state and that no costs will be assessed against the foreign country, although they may be assessed against the parent owing support.

---

38.    42 USC §659A.

**Complying with more than one withholding order.** If an employer receives more than one child support withholding order for an employee, state law governs how they must be handled. If the orders are from different states, the law in the state where the employee works applies. These considerations generally come into play when the total withholding amount required under all orders exceeds the maximum allowed under the applicable state law.

States handle this problem in one of several ways. The first method is to allocate the available wages to each order depending on its percentage in relation to the total amount required to be withheld. Another method is to allocate the available wages equally toward each order until each order is individually complied with or the maximum amount of allowable withholding is reached. The final method (currently used only in Montana) is to give the orders priority depending on when they were received by the employer. This means the order received first must be satisfied in full (if possible) before the next oldest order is satisfied, until the maximum amount has been withheld. Current support must be calculated prior to amounts past due (arrearages). When medical support has also been ordered, nearly all states require its satisfaction after current child support obligations.

*Example 1:* Executive Sweets Candy Co., an Indiana employer, receives one child support withholding order for employee George on September 8, 2008 demanding $450 per pay period and another on November 17, 2008 demanding $300. Executive Sweets determines the maximum amount that can be withheld from George's pay under Indiana law is $600. Indiana requires a pro rated allocation when the total to be withheld exceeds the maximum amount allowed. Once the second child support withholding order is received, the amount to be withheld for each order is determined as follows:

For the first order:

| | |
|---|---|
| Total amount from both orders | $750 |
| % applicable to first order | $450 ÷ $750 = 60% |
| Amount to withhold | $600 x .60 = $360 |

For the second order:

| | |
|---|---|
| % applicable to second order | $300 ÷ $750 = 40% |
| Amount to withhold | $600 x .40 = $240 |

*Example 2:* Assume the same facts as in Example 1, except that Executive Sweets is in Texas, which requires available wages to be allocated equally until the maximum amount allowed is reached. Once the second child support withholding order is received, the employer can withhold $300 for each order, which reaches the maximum of $600.

*Example 3:* Assume the same facts as in Example 1, except that Executive Sweets is in Montana, which is the only first come-first served state. After November 17, when the second withholding order is received, the full $450 must be withheld to satisfy the first order received, leaving a payment of $150 to be made on the second order ($600 maximum - $450 for the first order).

**Handling employee complaints.** It is not unusual for the payroll department to be confronted by an employee whose wages have been withheld to pay child support and who claims either that the amount withheld was wrong or that the employee received no notice before withholding began. In either situation, the employer is obligated to continue withholding according to a valid withholding order unless it receives notification in writing from the agency or court issuing the order that a change is necessary. The employee should be told to contact the agency or court issuing the order if a mistake has allegedly been made.

The same holds true if the employee begins supporting a new spouse and/or children, thus lowering the maximum amount of disposable earnings subject to withholding. It is up to the employee to bring this change to the attention of the court or agency that issued the withholding order, which can then issue a revised order with a lower maximum to the employer.

**Employee attempts to avoid withholding.** Because a reduced amount of disposable earnings lowers the maximum amount of wages subject to child support withholding, some employees may seek to increase the amount of federal and state income tax withheld from their wages. If an employee does this by decreasing the number of withholding allowances claimed, the employer should not question the employee's choice, and it is not obligated to bring it to the attention of the agency issuing the child support order. The employee will generally not succeed in evading the child support obligation, since the IRS will withhold child support arrearages from any tax refund due the employee.

**Handling child support for employees serving in the military.** According to OCSE, the employer should notify the state child support agency either by calling, writing, or faxing when it is notified by an employee/reservist subject to a child support withholding order that he or she is being mobilized. Be sure to include the date of activation. Child support agencies around the country have been asked to give the highest priority to reviewing cases involving military personnel who are being activated, and to redirect income withholding notices from the civilian employers involved to the appropriate office of the Department of Defense (Defense Finance and Accounting Service) so that the child support payments would not be interrupted.

As reservists return home, the Department of Defense will notify the child support agencies when an individual transfers from military status to civilian status. Once an employee returns to work, the employer should reactivate the income withholding order it has on file. Some states may send a letter or issue a new income withholding order, but most of them will expect the employer just to reinstitute existing orders. If an employer has any questions, it should contact the state agency involved.

**Employers must withhold from independent contractors.** Payments to be made to independent contractors who perform services for a business constitute property that is subject to a child support withholding order.

**Collecting arrearages.** Current support obligations must be paid before any past due amounts. The total current support and arrearages may never exceed the applicable state or federal maximum withholding amount. Where more than one order has been received for an employee, generally current amounts due on each must be paid before any past due amounts.

**Federal, state, and local employees.**[39] Employees of the U.S. government are subject to child and spousal support withholding orders on the same basis as private sector employees, although they may not be subject to other types of garnishment (see Section 9.1-3). If a federal government employee becomes the subject of more than one child or spousal support withholding order, the allocation to each payee is determined by the law of the state where the employee works. Any other valid garnishment orders must be satisfied on a first-come, first-served basis out of the employee's available wages, with the order received earliest being satisfied in full before any others. Federal employees' wages are also subject to an administrative offset by the Financial Management Service for amounts owed for past child and spousal support that have been referred by the state issuing the original order.[40] The states have laws making the wages of state and local government employees subject to garnishment for child support.

 **OCSE OFFERS ONLINE HELP FOR EMPLOYERS** OCSE's "Employer Services" website includes information, helpful tips, calculation examples, publications, and other resources. Available topics include new hire reporting, medical support, and state-by-state information. Access the Employer Services Web site at www.acf.hhs.gov/programs/cse/newhire/employer/home.htm.

**Medical child support orders.** As the movement toward wage withholding to enforce child support orders gained momentum, the next step was to use the same procedures to provide medical insurance for children owed support. All the states have passed laws allowing courts to require medical child support as part of a child support order and requiring employers to enroll children and withhold premiums from the employee's pay to the same extent as other employees with similar coverage. New child support orders issued by a state child support agency must include a medical support provision.

---

39.    42 USC §659.
40.    Pub. L. 104-134; 62 FR 36205, 7-7-97.

For child support orders issued after February 8, 2006, state CSE agencies must look to either parent or both parents, not just the noncustodial parent, to provide health insurance for their children.[41]

All employer-sponsored group health plans are required to comply with state laws regulating medical child support and to honor "qualified medical child support orders."[42] However, the plans cannot be forced to offer any new or different benefits. "Qualified medical child support orders" are judgments or orders issued by a court or an administrative agency, including those approving settlement agreements, that recognize the right of a child to be covered under the same group health plan for which the noncustodial parent is eligible. They also must specify:

- the name and address of the noncustodial parent;
- the name and address of any children to be covered by the order;
- a description of the coverage each child must be provided, or the way in which it will be determined;
- the length of time coverage must be provided; and
- each plan governed by the order.

States must also enact specific laws to make sure both insurers and employers comply with medical child support orders.[43] Under these requirements, each state's laws must:

- prohibit insurers from denying medical insurance under a parent's coverage to a child because the child was born out of wedlock, is not a dependent on the parent's income tax return, or does not live with the parent or in the insurer's service area;

- where a qualified medical child support order exists, require insurers and employers to allow the parent to enroll the child without restrictions (e.g., at times other than open enrollment) and to enroll the child themselves if the parent does not do it;

- where a qualified medical child support order exists, require employers to withhold the employee's share of health insurance premiums (if required by the employer's plan) and pay it to the insurer;

- require insurers to make it easier for custodial parents to submit and collect on claims where the noncustodial parent's insurer carries the child's coverage; and

- permit state medicaid agencies to garnish an employee's wages so the state can be reimbursed for payments made to the employee on behalf of a child who is eligible for medicaid.

The Child Support Performance and Incentive Act of 1998 required the Secretaries of Labor and Health and Human Services to develop a National Medical Support Notice (NMSN) for use by state agencies in enforcing the health care coverage provisions in a child support order.[44] The NMSN is considered a "qualified medical support notice." The Notice must include a "separate and easily identifiable employer withholding notice" that tells the employer:

- which provisions of state law require the employer to withhold employee contributions toward health care coverage under the child support order;
- how long the withholding requirement is effective;
- the applicability of the CCPA withholding limits;
- the applicability of state law prioritization provisions if the total amount for regular support and medical support exceeds the withholding limits; and
- the name and telephone number of a contact at the state agency regarding the Notice.

---

41.   42 USC §666(a)(19)(A); P.L. 109-171, §7307(a)(1).
42.   OBRA '93 §4301; ERISA §609.
43.   OBRA '93 §13623; SSA §1908.
44.   Pub. L. 105-200, §401(b); 42 USC §666(a)(19); ERISA §609(a)(5); 45 CFR §303.32.

In December 2000, regulations including a final National Medical Support Notice were issued.[45] The notice consists of two parts — one for the employer and one that employers send to their plan administrator. The Notice must be used by state agencies to enforce medical support orders issued under Title IV-D. A copy of the Notice appears on pages 9-26—9-27. By the end of 2004, all the states had begun using the NMSN. State laws must include provisions:

- requiring employers to transfer the Notice to the employer's health plan within 20 business days after the date of the Notice;
- requiring the state agency to send the Notice along with a child support withholding order if the employee is a newly hired employee; and
- requiring employers to notify the state agency if an employee covered by a Notice terminates employment.

Once an order is deemed by the plan administrator to be a "qualified medical child support order," the administrator has 40 business days from the date of the Notice to tell the state agency whether coverage is available for the child and, if so, whether the child is already covered under the plan or what the custodial parent has to do to initiate coverage. The plan administrator must also provide the custodial parent with a description of the coverage and any forms necessary to begin coverage of the child, and will notify the employer when the enrollment process has been completed.

**Employer's responsibilities.** Once an employer receives an NMSN for an employee, it should do the following:

- *Step 1* – Determine whether any of the categories on the Employer Response portion of the notice apply. If any apply, complete the Employer Response form and send it to the CSE agency that issued the NMSN within 20 business days.
- *Step 2* – If none of the categories on the Employer Response form apply and the child is eligible for coverage but not already enrolled in the employee's health insurance plan, send Part B of the NMSN to the plan administrator. If the child is already enrolled, contact the issuing agency to provide coverage information.
- *Step 3* – The plan administrator will notify the employer when enrollment is complete. The employer must then make the appropriate payroll deductions for the employee's premium payments under the plan.
- *Step 4* – If the employer determines that the full premium amount cannot be deducted because the total support deductions exceed the amount allowed under the CCPA, the law in the employee's work state determines the priority for payment. After making this determination, if the full health care premium cannot be paid, notify the issuing agency by checking category 4 on the Employer Response form and sending the complete form to the issuing agency.
- *Step 5* – If enrollment in the health plan cannot be completed until after a waiting period of more than 90 days or other contingency, notify the plan administrator when the employee is eligible for enrollment. The employer should also notify the issuing agency of the time frame for enrollment.

---

45.     65 F.R. 82127, 65 F.R. 82153, 12-27-00.

APPENDIX
## NATIONAL MEDICAL SUPPORT NOTICE
## PART A
## NOTICE TO WITHHOLD FOR HEALTH CARE COVERAGE

This Notice is issued under section 466(a)(19) of the Social Security Act, section 609(a)(5)(C) of the Employee Retirement Income Security Act of 1974 (ERISA), and for State and local government and church plans, sections 401(e) and (f) of the Child Support Performance and Incentive Act of 1998.

| | |
|---|---|
| Issuing Agency: _____ <br> Issuing Agency Address: _____ <br> _____ <br> Date of Notice: _____ <br> Case Number: _____ <br> Telephone Number: _____ <br> FAX Number: _____ | Court or Administrative Authority: _____ <br> Date of Support Order: _____ <br> Support Order Number: _____ |

_____ )
Employer/Withholder's Federal EIN Number

RE* _____
Employee's Name (Last, First, MI)

_____ )
Employer/Withholder's Name

_____
Employee's Social Security Number

_____ )
Employer/Withholder's Address

_____
Employee's Mailing Address

_____ )
Custodial Parent's Name (Last, First, MI)

_____ )
Custodial Parent's Mailing Address

_____
Substituted Official/Agency Name and Address

_____ )
Child(ren)'s Mailing Address (if different from Custodial Parent's)

_____ )
_____ )
_____ )
Name, Mailing Address, and Telephone
Number of a Representative of the Child(ren)

| Child(ren)'s Name(s) | DOB | SSN | Child(ren)'s Name(s) | DOB | SSN |
|---|---|---|---|---|---|
| _____ | ___ | ___ | _____ | ___ | ___ |
| _____ | ___ | ___ | _____ | ___ | ___ |
| _____ | ___ | ___ | _____ | ___ | ___ |

The order requires the child(ren) to be enrolled in [ ] any health coverages available; or [] only the following coverage(s): __Medical; __Dental; __Vision; __Prescription drug; __Mental health; __Other (specify):_____

## EMPLOYER RESPONSE

If either 1, 2, or 3 below applies, check the appropriate box and return this Part A to the Issuing Agency within 20 business days after the date of the Notice, or sooner if reasonable. NO OTHER ACTION IS NECESSARY. If neither 1, 2, nor 3 applies, forward Part B to the appropriate plan administrator(s) within 20 business days after the date of the Notice, or sooner if reasonable. Check number 4 and return this Part A to the Issuing Agency if the Plan Administrator informs you that the child(ren) is/are enrolled in an option under the plan for which you have determined that the employee contribution exceeds the amount that may be withheld from the employee's income due to State or Federal withholding limitations and/or prioritization.

☐ 1.  Employer does not maintain or contribute to plans providing dependent or family health care coverage.

☐ 2.  The employee is among a class of employees (for example, part-time or non-union) that are not eligible for family health coverage under any group health plan maintained by the employer or to which the employer contributes.

☐ 3.  Health care coverage is not available because employee is no longer employed by the employer:

Date of termination: _____

Last known address: _____

Last known telephone number: _____

New employer (if known): _____

New employer address: _____

New employer telephone number: _____

☐ 4. State or Federal withholding limitations and/or prioritization prevent the withholding from the employee's income of the amount required to obtain coverage under the terms of the plan.

Employer  Representative:

Name: _____    Telephone Number: _____

Title: _____    Date: _____

EIN (if not provided by Issuing Agency on Notice to Withhold for Health Care Coverage):_____

*Federal employees face medical support orders.* On October 30, 2000, President Clinton signed into law the Federal Employees Health Benefits Children's Equity Act. This law enables the federal government to enroll an employee and his or her family in the Federal Employees Health Benefits program when a state court orders the employee to provide health insurance for the employee's child and the employee is not already enrolled in the program and cannot provide proof of coverage in another program.[46]

 **PROVIDING MEDICAL INFORMATION IS OK** The NMSN requests the release of private health care information, and OCSE says that it is not a violation of the Health Insurance Portability and Accountability Act (HIPAA) for an employer or health plan to provide the requested information. That is because the NMSN is considered a written administrative request from a law enforcement official, which is lawful under HIPAA's Privacy Rule (see Section 10.9).

**State child support withholding laws.** Following is Table 9.1 summarizing state requirements in several areas where the states have some latitude under the federal guidelines to create their own withholding rules, including when to begin withholding, when to remit payment, when to notify the withholding agency as to an employee's termination, and maximum administrative fees. [For more information on state child support withholding requirements, see Tables 6.1 – 6.4 of *APA's Guide to State Payroll Laws.*]

- If a (1) appears in the "When to Start Withholding" column, it means the state has the same requirement regarding the beginning of withholding as the federal law—14 working days after the withholding order is mailed to the employer.

- If a (2) appears in the "When to Send Payment" column, it means the state has the same remittance time limit as the federal law—7 business days after payday or has no specific provision and is therefore governed by the federal rule.

- If a (3) appears in the "When to Send Termination Notice" column, it means the state follows the federal requirement or has no specific provision and is therefore governed by the federal requirement that the termination notice be sent "promptly."

- If a (4) appears in the "Withholding Limits" column, it means the state has the same limits as those in the federal Consumer Credit Protection Act—50% of the employee's disposable earnings if the employee is supporting another spouse and/or children (55% if the employee is 12 weeks in arrears) and 60% if the employee is not supporting another spouse and/or children (65% if the employee is 12 weeks in arrears).

Table 9.1

| STATE LAWS ON CHILD SUPPORT WITHHOLDING | | | | | |
|---|---|---|---|---|---|
| State | When to Start Withholding | When to Send Payment | When to Send Termination Notice | Maximum Administrative Fee | Withholding Limits |
| Alabama | immediately upon receipt | (2) | (3) | $2 per month | (4) |
| Alaska | immediately upon receipt | (2) | (3) | $5 per payment | (4) |
| Arizona | 14 days after receipt | 2 business days after payday | 10 days after termination | greater of $1 per pay | 50% of period or $4 per month |
| Arkansas | (1) | payday | immediately | $2.50 per pay period | (4) |

| STATE LAWS ON CHILD SUPPORT WITHHOLDING | | | | | |
|---|---|---|---|---|---|
| State | When to Start Withholding | When to Send Payment | When to Send Termination Notice | Maximum Administrative Fee | Withholding Limits |
| California | 10 days after service | (2) | when next payment is due | $1.50 per payment | 50% of disposable earnings |
| Colorado | (1) | (2) | 10 days after termination | $5 per month | (4) |
| Connecticut | first pay period after 14 days from service | (2) | (3) | no provision | (4); 85% of first $145 exempt |
| Delaware | 7 days after first payday after receipt | payday | (3) | no provision | (4) |
| Dist. of Col. | (1) | payday | 10 days after termination | $2 per payment | (4) |
| Florida | first pay period after 14 days from service | 2 business days after payday | (3) | $5 for first payment, $2 for all others | (4) |
| Georgia | (1) | 2 days after payday | (3) | $25 for first payment, $3 for all others; $1.50 per payment to state | (4) |
| Hawaii | first pay period within 7 days from mailing | 5 days after payday | immediately | $2 per payment | (4) |
| Idaho | immediately upon receipt | (2) | (3) | $5 per payment | 50% of disposable earnings |
| Illinois | (1) | (2) | (3) | $5 per month | (4) |
| Indiana | (1) | payday | 10 days after termination | $2 per payment; $55 annually to state | (4) |
| Iowa | 10 days after receipt | (2) | (3) | $2 per payment | (4) |
| Kansas | next payday after 14 days after service | (2) | (3) | lesser of $5 per pay period or $10 per month | (4) |
| Kentucky | order specifies date to begin | date noted in order | (3) | $1 per payment | 50% of disposable earnings |
| Louisiana | pay period after receipt of notice to withhold | (2) | 10 days after termination | $5 per pay period | 50% of disposable earnings |
| Maine | immediately upon receipt | (2) | 15 days after termination | $2 per transaction | (4) |

## STATE LAWS ON CHILD SUPPORT WITHHOLDING

| State | When to Start Withholding | When to Send Payment | When to Send Termination Notice | Maximum Administrative Fee | Withholding Limits |
|---|---|---|---|---|---|
| Maryland | pay period after receipt | 7 business days after payday | 10 days after termination | $2 per payment | (4) |
| Massachusetts | next payday more than 3 days after notice | 3 days after payday | 3 days after payday | $1 per payment | (4) |
| Michigan | 7 days after service | 3 days after payday | (3) | no provision | (4) |
| Minnesota | first pay period after 14 days from service | (2) | 10 days after termination | $1 per payment | (4) |
| Mississippi | first pay period after 14 days from service | (2) | (3) | $2 per payment; up to $15 per month to Dept. of Human Services. | (4) |
| Missouri | 2 weeks after mailing | (2) | (3) | $6 per month | (4) |
| Montana | first pay period after service | (2) | (3) | $5 per month | (4) |
| Nebraska | first pay period after receipt of notice | (2) | 30 days after termination | $2.50 per month | (4) |
| Nevada | (1) | (2) | (3) | $3 per payment; $2 per payment to state treasurer | (4) |
| New Hampshire | (1) | payday | 15 days after termination | $1 per payment | (4) |
| New Jersey | first pay period ending after postmark date | payday | (3) | $1 per payment | (4) |
| New Mexico | next payday after service | (2) | (3) | $1 per payment | 50% of disposable earnings |
| New York | first pay period after 14 days from service | (2) | (3) | no provision | (4) |
| North Carolina | first pay period after 14 days from service | (2) | (3) | $2 per payment | 40% of disposable earnings for 1 order; 50% if more than 1 |
| North Dakota | first pay period after service | (2) | 7 days after termination | $3 per month | 50% of disposable earnings |

## STATE LAWS ON CHILD SUPPORT WITHHOLDING

| State | When to Start Withholding | When to Send Payment | When to Send Termination Notice | Maximum Administrative Fee | Withholding Limits |
|---|---|---|---|---|---|
| Ohio | (1) | (2) | 10 days after termination | greater of $2 or 1% of payment | (4) |
| Oklahoma | next payday after receipt | (2) | 10 days after termination | $5 per payment; up to $10 per month | (4) |
| Oregon | first pay period after 5 days after date of order; 2nd pay period if payment already prepared when order is received | (2) | next payday | $5 per month | 50% of disposable earnings |
| Pennsylvania | first pay period after 14 days from service | (2) | (3) | 2% of payment | (4) |
| Rhode Island | 1 week after service | (2) | 10 days after termination | $2 per payment | (4) |
| South Carolina | next pay period after service | 7 days after payday | 20 days after termination | $3 per payment | (4) |
| South Dakota | next payday after service | (2) | 5 days after termination | $3 per month | 50% of income |
| Tennessee | 14 days after mailing | (2) | promptly | lesser of $5 per month or 5% of payment | 50% of gross minus taxes and child's health insurance premium |
| Texas | first pay period after receipt | payday | 7 days after termination | $10 per month | 50% of disposable earings |
| Utah | first pay period after 5 working days from service | (2) | 5 days after termination | one-time $25 fee | (4) |
| Vermont | 10 days after receipt or next payday | (2) | 10 days after termination | $5 per month | (4) |
| Virginia | next payday after service | payday; 4 days after payday if EFT is used | (3) | $5 per payment | (4) |
| Washington | immediately upon receipt | (2); 5 days after payday in non-IV D cases | (3) | $10 for first payment, $1 for all others | 50% of disposable earnings |

| STATE LAWS ON CHILD SUPPORT WITHHOLDING | | | | | |
|---|---|---|---|---|---|
| State | When to Start Withholding | When to Send Payment | When to Send Termination Notice | Maximum Administrative Fee | Withholding Limits |
| West Virginia | (1) | payday | (3) | $1 per payment | 40% of disposable earnings if supporting another spouse or child; 50% if not; amounts go to 45% and 55% if employee is 12 weeks in arrears |
| Wisconsin | 1 week after receipt | 5 days after pay-day | 10 days after ter-mination | $3 per payment | (4) |
| Wyoming | first pay period after service | 7 days after pay-day | 30 days after ter-mination | $5 per payment | (4) |

**State child support enforcement agencies.** Following is a directory of the child support enforcement agencies in each state, as well as the regional offices of the federal Office of Child Support Enforcement, showing the agencies' names, addresses, and telephone numbers.

## STATE CHILD SUPPORT ENFORCEMENT AGENCIES

**Alabama**
Alabama Department of Human Resources
Child Support Enforcement Division
P.O. Box 304000
Montgomery, AL 36130-4000
(334) 242-9300
www.dhr.state.al.us/Index.asp

**Alaska**
Department of Revenue
Child Support Services Division
550 West Seventh Ave., Ste. 310
Anchorage, AK 99501-6699
(907) 269-6900 (800) 478-3300
www.csed.state.ak.us/

**Arizona**
Department of Economic Security
Division of Child Support Enforcement
P.O. Box 40458
Phoenix, AZ 85067-9917
(602) 252-4045 (800) 882-4151
www.de.state.az.us/dcse/

**Arkansas**
Department of Finance and Administration
Office of Child Support Enforcement
400 E. Capitol
P.O. Box 8133
Little Rock, AR 72203
(501) 682-6039 (800) 216-0224
www.state.ar.us/dfa/child_support/ocse_index.html

**California**
Department of Child Support Services
P.O. Box 419064
Rancho Cordova, CA 95741-9064
(916) 464-5000 (866) 249-0773
www.childsup.cahwnet.gov/

**Colorado**
Department of Human Services
Division of Child Support Enforcement
1575 Sherman St., 5th Fl.
Denver, CO 80203-1714
(303) 866-4300
www.childsupport.state.co.us/do/home/index

**Connecticut**
Department of Social Services
Child Support Resource Center
25 Sigourney Street
Hartford, CT 06106-5033
(800) 842-1508
www.ct.gov/dss/cwp/view.asp?a=2353%cz%ad&q=30518

**Delaware**
Health and Social Services
Division of Child Support Enforcement
P. O. Box 904
84A Christiana Road
New Castle, DE 19720
(302) 577-7171
www.dhss.delaware.gov/dhss/dcse/index.html

**District of Columbia**
Office of the Attorney General
Child Support Enforcement Division
441 4th St., NW, Ste. 550N
Washington, DC 20001
(202) 442-9900
http://csed.dc.gov/

**Florida**
Department of Revenue
Child Support Enforcement Program
P.O. Box 8030
Tallahassee, FL 32314-8030
(800) 622-5437
http://dor.myflorida.com/dor/childsupport/

**Georgia**
Department of Human Resources
Office of Child Support Enforcement
2 Peachtree St., N.W.
Atlanta, GA 30303-3142
(404) 463-8800 (800) 227-7993
www.ocss.dhr.georgia.gov

**Hawaii**
Dept. of Attorney General
Child Support Enforcement Agency
601 Kamokila Blvd., Ste. 251
Kapolei, HI 96707
(808) 692-8265 (888) 317-9081
www.hawaii.gov/ag/csea

## STATE CHILD SUPPORT ENFORCEMENT AGENCIES

**Idaho**
Department of Health and Welfare
Bureau of Child Support Services
P.O. Box 83720
Boise, ID 83720-0036
(208) 334-2479 (800) 356-9868
www.idahochild.org

**Illinois**
Department of Public Aid
Child Support Enforcement Division
509 S. 6th St.
Springfield, IL 62701
(800) 447-4278 (800) 526-5812
www.ilchildsupport.com

**Indiana**
Family and Social Services Administration
Division of Child Services
Child Support Bureau
402 W. Washington St., Room W360
Indianapolis, IN 46204
(317) 232-4877 (800) 840-8757
www.in.gov/dcs/support/index.html

**Iowa**
Department of Human Services
Child Support Recovery Unit
501 Sycamore St.
P.O. Box 7200
Waterloo, IA 50704-7200
(888) 229-9223
https://childsupport.dhs.state.ia.us/welcome.asp

**Kansas**
Department of Social and Rehabilitation Services
Child Support Enforcement Program
P.O. Box 497
Topeka, KS 66601
(785) 296-4687
www.srskansas.org/cse/iwo

**Kentucky**
Cabinet for Health and Family Services
Department for Community Based Services
Dvision of Child Support
P.O. Box 2150
Frankfort, KY 40602-2150
(800) 248-1163
(502) 564-2285
http://chfs.ky.gov/dcbs/dcs/

**Louisiana**
Department of Social Services
Office of Family Support
Support Enforcement Services
530 Lakeland Avenue
Baton Rouge, LA 70804
(225) 342-5760
www.dss.state.la.us/departments/ofs/Support_Enforcement_Services.html

**Maine**
Department of Health and Human Services
Office of Integrated Access and Support
Division of Support Enforcement and Recovery
11 State House Station
Whitten Rd.
Augusta, ME 04333
(207) 624-7829
www.maine.gov/dhhs/oias/dser/index.html

**Maryland**
Department of Human Resources
Child Support Enforcement Program
311 W. Saratoga St.
Baltimore, MD 21201
(410) 962-1110 (800) 728-9987
www.dhr.state.md.us/csea/index.htm

**Massachusetts**
Department of Revenue
Division of Child Support Enforcement
P. O. Box 7057
Boston, MA 02204
(800) 332-2733
www.cse.state.ma.us

**Michigan**
Department of Human Services
Office of Child Support
P.O. Box 30037
Lansing, MI 48909
(866) 540-0008 (800) 817-0805
www.michigan.gov/dhs

**Minnesota**
Department of Human Services
Child Support Enforcement Division
P.O. Box 64946
St. Paul, MN 55164-0946
(651) 431-4400 (800) 657-3954
www.dhs.state.mn.us/ecs/childsupport/Default.htm

## STATE CHILD SUPPORT ENFORCEMENT AGENCIES

**Mississippi**
Department of Human Services
Child Support Enforcement Division
750 N. State Street
Jackson, MS 39205
(866) 388-2836
www.mdhs.state.ms.us/cse.html

**Missouri**
Department of Social Services
Child Support Enforcement Program
P.O. Box 2320
Jefferson City, MO 65102-2320
(800) 859-7999
www.dss.mo.gov/cse

**Montana**
Department of Public Health and Human Services
Child Support Enforcement Division
P. O. Box 202943
Helena, MT 59620-2943
(406) 444-9855 (800) 346-3437
www.dphhs.mt.gov/csed/index.shtml

**Nebraska**
Department of Health and Human Services
Child Support Enforcement Program
P.O. Box 94728
Lincoln, NE 68509-4728
(402) 441-8715 (877) 631-9973
www.hhs.state.ne.us/cse/cseindex.htm

**Nevada**
Department of Health and Human Services
Division of Welfare and Supporting Services
Child Support Enforcement Unit
1470 East College Parkway
Carson City, NV 89706
(775) 684-0500
www.welfare.state.nv.us/child.htm

**New Hampshire**
Department of Health and Human Services
Division of Child Support Services
129 Pleasant St.
Concord, NH 03301-3857
(603) 271-4745 (800) 852-3345 x4745
www.dhhs.state.nh.us/DHHS/DCSS/default.htm

**New Jersey**
Department of Human Services
Division of Family Development
Office of Child Support
P.O. Box 716
Trenton, NJ 08625-0716
(877) 655-4371
www.njchildsupport.org

**New Mexico**
Human Services Department
Child Support Enforcement Division
P.O. Box 25110
Santa Fe, NM 87504
(800) 288-7207
www.state.nm.us/hsd/csed.html

**New York**
Department of Family Assistance
Office of Temporary and Disability Assistance
Division of Child Support Enforcement
40 N. Pearl St.
Albany, NY 12243
(866) 227-7035 (800) 846-0773
https://newyorkchildsupport.com/home.html

**North Carolina**
Department of Health and Human Services
Division of Social Services
Office of Child Support Enforcement
P.O. Box 20800
Raleigh, NC 27619-0800
(919) 255-3800 (800) 992-9457
www.dhhs.state.nc.us/dss/

**North Dakota**
Department of Human Services
Child Support Enforcement Division
1600 E. Century Ave., Suite 7
P.O. Box 7190
Bismarck, ND 58507-7190
(701) 328-6575
www.nd.gov/dhs/services/childsupport

**Ohio**
Department of Job and Family Services
Office of Child Support
P.O. Box 182709
Columbus, OH 43218-2709
(614) 752-6561 (800) 686-1556
http://jfs.ohio.gov/ocs/

## STATE CHILD SUPPORT ENFORCEMENT AGENCIES

**Oklahoma**
Department of Human Services
Child Support Enforcement Division
P.O. Box 53552
Oklahoma City, OK 73152
(800) 522-2922
www.okdhs.org/childsupport/

**Oregon**
Department of Justice
Division of Child Support
(Department of Human Services oversees program)
1495 Edgewater St., NW, Suite 170
Salem, OR 97304
(503) 986-6297
http://dcs.state.or.us/

**Pennsylvania**
Department of Public Welfare
Child Support Program
P.O. Box 8018
Harrisburg, PA 17105-8018
(717) 783-9659 (877) 676-9580
www.humanservices.state.pa.us/csws

**Puerto Rico**
Department of Social Services
Child Support Enforcement Program
P.O. Box 3349
San Juan, PR 00902-9938
(787) 767-1500

**Rhode Island**
Department of Administration
Division of Taxation and Child Support Enforcement
77 Dorrance St.
Providence, RI 02903
(401) 222-3845 (800) 370-0411
www.childsupportliens.com/

**South Carolina**
Department of Social Services
Child Support Enforcement
P.O. Box 1469
Columbia, SC 29202-1469
(803) 898-9210 (800) 768-5858
www.state.sc.us/dss/csed/

**South Dakota**
Department of Social Services
Division of Child Support
700 Governors Dr.
Pierre, SD 57501
(605) 773-3641 (800) 286-9145
http://dss.sd.gov/childsupport/

**Tennessee**
Department of Human Services
Child Support Services
400 Deadrick St.
Nashville, TN 37248-0070
(615) 313-4700 (800) 838-6911
www.tennessee.gov/humanserv/cs/cs_main.htm

**Texas**
Office of the Attorney General
Child Support Division
P.O. Box 12548
Austin, TX 78711-2548
(512) 460-6000
(800) 252-8014
www.oag.state.tx.us/cs/cs/index.shtml

**Utah**
Department of Human Services
Office of Recovery Services
Child Support Services
P. O. Box 45033
Salt Lake City, UT 84145-0033
(801) 536-8500 (800) 662-8526
www.ors.state.ut.us/child_support_services.htm

**Vermont**
Agency of Human Services
Office of Child Support
103 S. Main St.
Waterbury, VT 05671-1901
(800) 786-3214
www.ocs.state.vt.us/

**Virginia**
Department of Social Services
Division of Child Support Enforcement
7 N. Eighth St., 1st Fl.
Richmond, VA 23219
(804) 726-7000 (800) 257-9986
www.dss.virginia.gov/family/dcse.htm

## STATE CHILD SUPPORT ENFORCEMENT AGENCIES

**Washington**
Department of Social and Health Services
Division of Child Support
P.O. Box 11520
Tacoma, WA 98411-5520
(360) 664-5200 (800) 457-6202
www1.dshs.wa.gov/dcs/index.shtml

**West Virginia**
Department of Health and Human Resources
Bureau for Child Support Enforcement
350 Capitol St., Room 147
Charleston, WV 25301
(304) 558-3780 (800) 249-3778
www.wvdhhr.org/bcse

**Wisconsin**
Department of Workforce Development
Division of Workforce Solutions
Bureau of Child Support
P.O. Box 7935
Madison, WI 53707-7935
(608) 266-9909
www.dwd.state.wi.us/bcs/

**Wyoming**
Department of Family Services
Child Support Enforcement Program
122 West 25th Street
Herschler Bldg. 1301 1st floor
East Cheyenne, WY 82002-0490
(307) 777-6948
http://dfsweb.state.wy.us/csehome/cs.htm

## FEDERAL OFFICES OF CHILD SUPPORT ENFORCEMENT

**Region 1**
(Serving: CT, ME, MA, NH, RI, VT)
OCSE Regional Representative
John F. Kennedy Federal Bldg.
20th Fl., Rm. 2303
Boston, MA 02203
(617) 565-2455

**Region 2**
(Serving: NY, NJ, PR, VI)
OCSE Regional Representative
Federal Bldg., Rm. 4114
26 Federal Plaza
New York, NY 10278
(212) 264-2890

**Region 3**
(Serving: DE, DC, MD, PA, VA, WV)
OCSE Regional Representative
Public Ledger Bldg., Ste. 864
150 S. Independence Mall W.
Philadelphia, PA 19106
(215) 861-4000

**Region 4**
(Serving: AL, FL, GA, KY, MS, NC, SC, TN)
OCSE Regional Representative
101 Marietta Tower, Ste. 821
Atlanta, GA 30323
(404) 331-2180

**Region 5**
(Serving: IL, IN, MI, MN, OH, WI)
OCSE Regional Representative
233 N. Michigan Ave., Ste. 400
Chicago, IL 60601-5519
(312) 353-4237

**Region 6**
(Serving: AR, LA, NM, OK, TX)
OCSE Regional Representative
1301 Young St., Rm. 914
Dallas, TX 75202-5433
(214) 767-9648

**Region 7**
(Serving: IA, KS, MO, NE)
OCSE Regional Representative
Federal Bldg., Rm. 276
601 E. 12th St.
Kansas City, MO 64106
(816) 426-3981

**Region 8**
(Serving: CO, MT, ND, SD, UT, WY)
OCSE Regional Representative
Federal Office Bldg., Rm. 926
1961 Stout St.
Denver, CO 80294
(303) 844-3100

**Region 9**
(Serving: AZ, CA, HI, NV, GU)
OCSE Regional Representative
50 United Nations Plaza
Mail Stop 351
San Francisco, CA 94102
(415) 556-5176

**Region 10**
(Serving: AK, ID, OR, WA)
OCSE Regional Representative
2201 Sixth Ave., Ste. 600
Seattle, WA 98121-1827
(206) 615-2547

## 9.1-3 Creditor Garnishments

Child support withholding orders are just one type of "garnishment" of an employee's wages. When an employee (debtor or obligor) has a debt that remains unpaid, a wage garnishment is one legal means by which the person who is owed the money (creditor or obligee) can obtain payment. This method requires that the employee's employer withhold the unpaid amount from the employee's wages. In some states, a wage garnishment is known as a "wage attachment" or "income execution."

The employer can be required to withhold a portion of the employee's wages for a wage garnishment only if the creditor first brings a court proceeding where proof of the debt is offered and the employee has a chance to respond. As was noted in Section 9.1-2, garnishments for child support withholding are treated somewhat differently since they may be ordered by a state child support enforcement agency rather than a court.

**Federal law limits garnishment amount and employee terminations.** In a more limited sense than child support wage withholding (see Section 9.1-2), creditor garnishments are also governed by a joint federal/state scheme. The federal Consumer Credit Protection Act (Title III) places restrictions on states in their regulation of creditor garnishments, both:

- on the amount that may be garnished; and

- on the freedom to discharge an employee because the employee's wages have been garnished.[47]

*Limit on amount that can be garnished.* The CCPA states that the maximum amount of an employee's "disposable earnings" that can be garnished to repay a debt is the lesser of:

- 25% of the employee's disposable earnings for the week; or

- the amount by which the employee's disposable earnings for the week exceed 30 times the federal minimum hourly wage then in effect.[48]

 **STATE LAWS MAY STILL APPLY** The garnishment limits in the CCPA preempt state laws to the extent the state laws allow greater amounts to be garnished. But state law will apply if the maximum amount subject to garnishment is lower than the federal maximum or if the state does not allow creditor garnishments at all.[49]

Disposable earnings are determined by subtracting all deductions required by law from an employee's gross earnings (wages, commissions, bonuses, sick pay, and periodic pension payments).[50] Deductions required by law include withholding for federal, state, or local income tax, social security or Medicare tax, state unemployment or disability tax, and mandated payments for state employee retirement systems (but not amounts designated for direct deposit into an employee's bank account). Voluntary deductions, such as health and life insurance premiums, union dues, and retirement plan contributions, are generally not subtracted from earnings to calculate disposable earnings. In some states, health insurance contributions may be included in the calculation of disposable pay, especially if the contributions are mandated under a child support order.

 **TIPS MAY OR MAY NOT BE EARNINGS** According to the U.S. Department of Labor, tips given directly to employees by customers are not considered earnings for the purpose of determining disposable earnings for creditor garnishments, whereas service charges added to the bill that are later given to the employee by the employer are earnings.[51] Employers must check the state laws in the states where they operate.

---

47. CCPA §301 - §307; 15 USC §1671 - §1677; 29 CFR Part 870.
48. CCPA §303(a); 15 USC §1673(a); 29 CFR §870.10(a).
49. CCPA §307(1); 15 USC §1677(1).
50. CCPA §302; 15 USC §1672.
51. W-H Op. Ltr., WH-95, 12-15-70.

If the employee is paid less frequently than weekly, the amount exempt from garnishment increases accordingly based on a multiple of the weekly amount, as shown in Table 9.2.[52]

Table 9.2

| AMOUNT SUBJECT TO GARNISHMENT, EFFECTIVE JULY 24, 2007 – JULY 23, 2008 | | | |
|---|---|---|---|
| **Weekly** | **Biweekly** | **Semimonthly** | **Monthly** |
| Disposable earnings are $175.50 or less: NONE | Disposable earnings are $351.00 or less: NONE | Disposable earnings are $380.25 or less: NONE | Disposable earnings are $760.50 or less: NONE |
| Disposable earnings are more than $175.50 but less than $234.00: AMOUNT ABOVE $175.50 | Disposable earnings are more than $351.00 but less than $468.00: AMOUNT ABOVE $351.00 | Disposable earnings are more than $380.25 but less than $507.00: AMOUNT ABOVE $380.25 | Disposable earnings are more than $760.50 but less than $1,014.00: AMOUNT ABOVE $760.50 |
| Disposable earnings are $234.00 or more: MAXIMUM 25% | Disposable earnings are $468.00 or more: MAXIMUM 25% | Disposable earnings are $507.00 or more: MAXIMUM 25% | Disposable earnings are $1,014.00 or more: MAXIMUM 25% |

| AMOUNT SUBJECT TO GARNISHMENT, EFFECTIVE JULY 24, 2008 – JULY 23, 2009 | | | |
|---|---|---|---|
| **Weekly** | **Biweekly** | **Semimonthly** | **Monthly** |
| Disposable earnings are $196.50 or less: NONE | Disposable earnings are $393.00 or less: NONE | Disposable earnings are $425.75 or less: NONE | Disposable earnings are $851.50 or less: NONE |
| Disposable earnings are more than $196.50 but less than $262.00: AMOUNT ABOVE $196.50 | Disposable earnings are more than $393.00 but less than $524.00: AMOUNT ABOVE $393.00 | Disposable earnings are more than $425.75 but less than $567.67: AMOUNT ABOVE $425.75 | Disposable earnings are more than $851.50 but less than $1,135.33: AMOUNT ABOVE $851.50 |
| Disposable earnings are $262.00 or more: MAXIMUM 25% | Disposable earnings are $524.00 or more: MAXIMUM 25% | Disposable earnings are $567.67 or more: MAXIMUM 25% | Disposable earnings are $1,135.33 or more: MAXIMUM 25% |

| AMOUNT SUBJECT TO GARNISHMENT, EFFECTIVE JULY 24, 2009 | | | |
|---|---|---|---|
| **Weekly** | **Biweekly** | **Semimonthly** | **Monthly** |
| Disposable earnings are $217.50 or less: NONE | Disposable earnings are $435.00 or less: NONE | Disposable earnings are $471.25 or less: NONE | Disposable earnings are $942.50 or less: NONE |
| Disposable earnings are more than $217.50 but less than $290.00: AMOUNT ABOVE $217.50 | Disposable earnings are more than $435.00 but less than $580.00: AMOUNT ABOVE $435.00 | Disposable earnings are more than $471.25 but less than $628.33: AMOUNT ABOVE $471.25 | Disposable earnings are more than $942.50 but less than $1,256.67: AMOUNT ABOVE $942.50 |
| Disposable earnings are $290.00 or more: MAXIMUM 25% | Disposable earnings are $580.00 or more: MAXIMUM 25% | Disposable earnings are $628.33 or more: MAXIMUM 25% | Disposable earnings are $1,256.67 or more: MAXIMUM 25% |

---

52.    CCPA §303(a); 15 USC §1673(a); 29 CFR §870.10(c).

***Example 1:*** Employee Michelle's disposable earnings for a week are $250, when her employer receives a garnishment order on February 10, 2008 requiring that $300 be withheld. The maximum amount of Michelle's disposable earnings that can be garnished is determined as follows:

$250 x 25% = $62.50
$250 - $175.50 = $74.50

Because $62.50 is less than $74.50, only $62.50 may be deducted to satisfy the garnishment order.

***Example 2:*** Employee Josephine's disposable earnings for a semimonthly period are $400, when her employer receives a garnishment order on February 12, 2008 requiring that $150 be withheld. The maximum amount of Josephine's disposable earnings that can be garnished is determined as follows:

$400 x 25% = $100.00
$400 - $380.25 (from chart) = $19.75

Because $19.75 is less than $100.00, only $19.75 may be deducted to satisfy the garnishment order.

***Example 3:*** Employee James is a sales representative who receives a $500 weekly draw against commissions, with disposable earnings of $400. For one month, James's commissions totaled $2,500 after deductions required by law, for a balance due James of $500. Each payment to James as a draw and the balance due is separately subject to the CCPA's restrictions. Therefore, 25% of the disposable earnings from each draw ($100.00) is subject to garnishment, as is 25% of the balance of $500 ($125).

 **WATCH OUT FOR MINIMUM WAGE CHANGES** Because the amount subject to garnishment under the CCPA is keyed to the federal minimum hourly wage when the employee's wages are payable (not when the garnishment order is issued), any change in the minimum wage will change the amount that can be garnished. Table 9.2 shows the effect of the minimum hourly wage increases taking effect on July 24, 2007 (to $5.85), July 24, 2008 (to $6.55), and July 24, 2009 (to $7.25).

*Limit applies to multiple garnishments.*[53] The federal garnishment maximum applies no matter how many garnishments are received for an employee. If the maximum is already being withheld when a second garnishment is received, nothing may be withheld for the second garnishment. If more than the maximum is withheld and the employee receives less than the required minimum wage because of the excess withholding, the employer may be subject to penalties for violating the Fair Labor Standards Act.

*Exception for other types of garnishments.*[54] The general limit on garnishments under the CCPA does not apply to certain types of garnishments. An exception in the law itself allows for higher maximums for child support withholding orders (see Section 9.1-2). Also, the limit does not apply to tax levies, which are governed by the Internal Revenue Code (see Section 9.1-1), or to bankruptcy orders (see Section 9.1-4). Special provisions are also applicable to garnishments for delinquent student loans (see Section 9.1-5) and other federal agency debt collections (see Section 9.1-6).

In determining an employee's disposable earnings, wages already subject to withholding for child support, tax levies, or bankruptcy orders are not considered deductions required by law. Therefore, they should not be subtracted from gross earnings when determining the maximum amount subject to garnishment. However, if the child support withholding order, tax levy, or bankruptcy order has priority over the creditor garnishment and constitutes at least 25% of the employee's disposable wages, no amount can be withheld for the creditor garnishment.[55]

---

53.    29 CFR §870.11(b)(2).
54.    CCPA §303(b); 15 USC §1673(b); 29 CFR §870.11(a), (b)(1).
55.    29 CFR §870.11(b)(2); Voss Products, Inc. v. Carlton, 147 F. Supp. 2d 892 (ED Tenn., 2001).

***Example 1:*** Employee Ralph's disposable earnings for a biweekly pay period are $1,000 when his employer receives a child support withholding order from a state child support enforcement agency demanding that $400 be withheld from each paycheck to satisfy the order. After withholding the $400, Ralph's disposable earnings remain $1,000 under the CCPA. But if Ralph's employer later receives a garnishment order for $500 while the child support withholding order is still in effect, nothing may be withheld for the garnishment because 40% of Ralph's disposable earnings are already being withheld ($400 ÷ $1,000).

***Example 2:*** Assume the same facts as in Example 1, except that the child support withholding order is for $200 per biweekly pay period. With disposable earnings of $1,000 per pay period, that means that 20% of Ralph's disposable earnings are being withheld for child support ($200 ÷ $1,000). That leaves 5% available to satisfy the garnishment order (25% (maximum) - 20%). Therefore, Ralph's employer must withhold $50 for the garnishment order (5% x $1,000).

*No discharge for one garnishment.*[56] Employers are prohibited by the CCPA from terminating an employee because the employee's "earnings have been subjected to garnishment for any one indebtedness." Employers that violate this provision can be fined up to $1,000 and/or imprisoned for up to 1 year. This prohibition applies to all garnishments, including tax levies, bankruptcy orders, and child support withholding orders. (Other federal laws provide even greater protection for employees whose wages are withheld to pay child support, see Section 9.1-2).

Most of the controversy over this provision has arisen as the Department of Labor and the courts have struggled to define the term "one indebtedness." Generally, an employee is subject to a garnishment for one indebtedness in the following situations:

- several garnishment proceedings are brought against an employee for one debt (e.g., an employee obtains a release of one garnishment, but the debt remains unpaid and another garnishment order is obtained);[57]

- several debts are grouped into one garnishment proceeding by the creditors;[58]

- a second garnishment cannot be carried out because the maximum amount is already being withheld for the first garnishment;[59]

- an employer receives several garnishment orders for an employee, but the employee succeeds in obtaining releases from all but one before withholding can begin;[60]

- an employee's second garnishment is received more than one year after the first;[61]

- an employee's second garnishment is received after the employee has begun a new job with a new employer.[62]

 **WATCH FOR EMPLOYEE-FRIENDLY STATE LAWS** While the CCPA provides a minimum standard of employee protection, it does not preempt state laws that provide greater protection for employees by increasing the number of garnishments that can serve as the basis for termination or by prohibiting all terminations because of garnishment.[63] Some states also protect employees from discipline by employers that is short of discharge (e.g., suspension without pay, demotion).

---

56.  CCPA §304; 15 USC §1674.
57.  W-H Op. Ltr., WH-42, 6-12-70; WH-57, 7-21-70.
58.  W-H Op. Ltr., WH-38, 6-5-70.
59.  Brennan v. Kroger Co., 76 LC 33,232, (7 CA 1975).
60.  Donovan v. Southern California Gas Co., 715 F.2d 1405 (9 CA 1983).
61.  W-H Op. Ltr. WH-116, 1-19-71.
62.  W-H Op. Ltr. WH-15, 6-12-69; WH-38, 6-5-70.
63.  CCPA §307(2); 15 USC §1677(2)

**Federal, state, and local employees.**[64] Generally, public sector employees' wages are exempt from garnishment unless specifically provided otherwise by state law. On the federal level, U.S. government employees are subject to garnishment for child support or alimony, as well as overdue taxes. Employees of the U.S. Postal Service are not protected by the immunity for federal employees since the USPS is an independent agency. On the state and local level, all states have passed laws subjecting state and local government employees to garnishment, although some have limited their exposure to child and spousal support withholding orders only. [For more information on state creditor garnishment rules, see Table 7.1 of *APA's Guide to State Payroll Laws*.]

**Areas of state regulation.** In areas other than the maximum amount subject to garnishment and employee termination because of garnishment, the states have a great deal of latitude in determining the procedures governing creditor garnishments of employees' wages. These areas include:

- the priority of multiple garnishments;

- whether the employer must continue to withhold if the full amount stated in the garnishment order exceeds the maximum that can be withheld from the first payment of wages;

- time limits for remitting withheld amounts;

- whether the employer can charge an administrative fee for processing the garnishment;

- the procedure to follow when an out-of-state garnishment order is received; and

- penalties for failure to withhold and remit according to the garnishment order.

*Out-of-state garnishment orders.* The U.S. Constitution provides that full faith and credit must be given in each state to the public acts, records, and judicial proceedings of every other state.[65] Therefore, if a creditor obtains a garnishment order against a debtor from a court in one state it can generally get that order enforced in another state to which the debtor has moved. However, an employer served with an out-of-state creditor garnishment for one of its employees is not required to obey the order unless:

- The order has been registered with a court in the state where the employee works; or
- The employer does business in the state that issued the original garnishment order.

While an employer would have to obey an out-of-state garnishment order under either of these circumstances, the law of the employee's work state would generally be applied to determine the limits on the garnishment, deadlines for withholding and remitting payment, administrative fees, etc.

**Employer's responsibilities.** When an employer receives a garnishment order from a court or government agency, it is bound to comply with the order to withhold and remit the amount demanded, up to the maximum allowed by law. While preparing to comply, the employer should do the following:

- check to make sure the underlying claim is valid and the amount stated on the order is correct by contacting the agency or court issuing the order;

- tell the employee about the garnishment order to make sure the employee has received a notice that garnishment would be taking place and has had the chance to object;

- tell the employee about any exemptions that might apply under state or federal law;

- tell the employee how the garnishment will affect his or her wages and net pay;

- determine whether the amount demanded in the garnishment exceeds the maximum allowed by federal or state law;

---

64. 42 USC §659(a); Franchise Tax Board of the State of California v. U.S. Postal Service, 467 U.S. 512 (1984).
65. U.S. Const., Art. IV, §1; 28 USC §1738.

- if the employee is already subject to one or more garnishment orders, determine their order of priority and how the available disposable earnings must be allocated; and

- contact legal counsel to review the garnishment order and answer any outstanding questions regarding validity, disposable earnings determinations, complying with out-of-state orders, priorities and allocation, etc.

## 9.1-4 Bankruptcy Orders

Bankruptcy is governed by the federal Bankruptcy Code. Once an employee voluntarily declares bankruptcy or is found to be bankrupt by a court, the satisfaction of the employee's creditors is handled by the "bankruptcy trustee" appointed by the court. Until the employer is notified by the bankruptcy court or the trustee to do otherwise, the employer should continue to withhold. Once the employee's employer receives a bankruptcy order from the trustee under a court-approved plan requiring a certain amount of the employee's wages to be paid to the trustee to satisfy the employee's creditors, the employer must stop withholding on any other garnishments against the employee except for child support withholding orders.

**General rules.** Bankruptcy orders issued under Chapter XIII of the Bankruptcy Act take priority over any other claim against the employee's wages, including federal and state tax levies received before the bankruptcy order, other than child support withholding orders. The reasoning behind ceasing other withholding for garnishments once a bankruptcy order is received is that the debts underlying those garnishments will be paid by the trustee out of the money withheld under the bankruptcy order.

If an employer continues to withhold and remit in satisfaction of other withholding orders, creditors may receive double payments and the employer may open itself to a lawsuit brought by the employee for the withheld wages. The only time an employer should continue to withhold for other garnishments is if the trustee specifically provides instructions to do so. If the creditor is not listed in the bankruptcy order, verify with the trustee before stopping the garnishment.

 **DO NOT DISCHARGE THE EMPLOYEE** Federal bankruptcy law prohibits employers from terminating employees because they become the subject of a bankruptcy proceeding.

**Special rules for child support orders.** The Bankruptcy Abuse Prevention and Consumer Protection Act of 2005 contained several amendments to the Bankruptcy Code that directly affect the way employers handle child support withholding orders before and after a bankruptcy petition is filed and/or granted.[66] The most important thing to note is that employers now have to obey a child support withholding order regardless of whether a bankruptcy petition is filed by the noncustodial parent employee either before or after the withholding order.

*No stay of child support withholding.* In general, the filing of a bankruptcy petition automatically puts on hold (i.e., stays) any court proceedings or judgments against the debtor. However, certain proceedings are exempt from the automatic stay provision, and the list of the exemptions was expanded by the 2005 amendments to include the commencement or continuation of actions or proceedings pertaining to:

- child custody or visitation;
- the dissolution of a marriage;
- domestic violence;
- withholding of income that is property of the debtor or the estate for payment of domestic support obligations;
- withholding, suspension, or restriction of a driver's license, or a professional, occupational, or recreational license under state law;
- reporting of overdue support owed by a parent to consumer reporting agencies;

---

66.    Pub. L. No. 109-8.

- interception of specified tax refunds; and
- enforcement of medical obligations under Title IV of the Social Security Act.[67]

A "domestic support obligation" is a debt (including interest) that accrues before, on, or after the date of an order for relief in a bankruptcy case that is owed to or recoverable by:

- a spouse, former spouse, or child of the debtor, or such child's parent, legal guardian, or responsible relative; or
- a governmental unit.[68]

To qualify as a domestic support obligation, the debt must be in the nature of alimony, maintenance, or support (including assistance provided by a governmental unit). The debt must be established pursuant to:

- a separation agreement, divorce decree, or property settlement agreement;
- an order of a court of record; or
- a determination made in accordance with applicable non-bankruptcy law by a governmental unit.

*Domestic support obligations have top priority for payment.* The Bankruptcy Code gives "first priority in payment" to allowed unsecured claims for domestic support obligations, without regard to whether a claim is filed by the claimant or by a governmental unit on behalf of the claimant.[69]

Note, however, that where a trustee administers assets that may be available to pay domestic support obligations, specified administrative expenses of the trustee must be paid before these claims.

*Postpetition domestic support payments.* If a debtor is required by judicial or administrative order or statute to pay a domestic support obligation, then the debtor must pay all amounts payable under such order or statute that become payable "postpetition" (i.e., after the debtor filed his/her bankruptcy petition) in order to obtain court approval of a discharge of the debtor's debts. On the other hand, failure to pay a domestic support obligation that first becomes payable postpetition is cause for dismissal of the debtor's case.

*Amounts owed for child support cannot be discharged by bankruptcy.* The Bankruptcy Code provides that a domestic support obligation is nondischargeable, meaning that a person filing for bankruptcy cannot get the court to void such a debt. In addition, other obligations to a spouse, former spouse, or child of the debtor incurred in connection with a divorce, separation, or related action are also nondischargeable, regardless of the debtor's inability to pay such debts.[70]

*Bankruptcy trustee's duties.*[71] A bankruptcy trustee may not void a bona fide payment of a debt for a domestic support obligation as a preferential transfer. In addition, the bankruptcy trustee must provide written notices as follows:

- to the domestic support claimant of the right to use the services of a state child support enforcement agency in the state where the claimant resides for assistance in collecting child support during and after the bankruptcy case (including the agency's address and telephone number as well as an explanation of the claimant's right to payment under the Bankruptcy Code);
- to the agency of such claim (including the name, address, and telephone number of the child support claimant); and
- at the time the debtor is granted a discharge, to both the child support claimant and the agency that the debtor was granted a discharge (including the debtor's last known address, the last known name and address of the debtor's employer, and the name of each creditor holding a debt that was either nondischargeable or that was reaffirmed by the debtor).

---

67.    11 USC §362(b)(2).
68.    11 USC §101(14A).
69.    11 USC §507(a)(1).
70.    11 USC §523(a)(5).
71.    11 USC §704(a)(10), (c); §1106(a)(8), (c); §1202(b)(6), (c); §1302(b)(6), (d).

**Retirement plan loans.** Before the 2005 amendments, the automatic stay provisions of the Bankruptcy Code prevented the collection of loans taken by employees from their retirement plans. An employee could repay such a debt only by getting an order from the bankruptcy court allowing him/her to do so. In reality, most bankruptcy courts did not often enter such orders because a loan repayment to a retirement plan was considered a payment from the employee to himself or herself rather than to other creditors. Therefore, the loan was discharged because of the bankruptcy filing and the amount of the loan that had not yet been repaid became taxable to the employee.

The amended Bankruptcy Code exempts from the automatic stay the withholding of income from an employee's wages under a prior agreement authorizing such withholding solely to repay a loan from a pension, profit-sharing, stock bonus, or other employer-sponsored plan established under IRC §§401, 403, 408A, 414, 457, or 501(c).[72] Retirement plan loans also cannot be discharged pursuant to a bankruptcy filing.

## 9.1-5 Student Loan Collections

Because of the high percentage of students who were failing to repay loans for education granted under the Federal Family Education Loan Program (formerly the Guaranteed Student Loan Program), in 1991 Congress amended the Higher Education Act to allow for garnishment of employees' wages to repay delinquent loans. Student loan garnishments are subject to the following restrictions:

**Maximum amount subject to garnishment.**[73] No more than the lesser of 15% of an employee's disposable earnings or the excess of the employee's disposable earnings over 30 times the federal hourly minimum wage then in effect may be garnished to satisfy a delinquent student loan unless the employee consents in writing to a higher percentage.

Even though the Higher Education Act limits garnishments to 15% of an employee's wages, this limit applies to each individual holder of a student loan. Where an employee faces multiple student loan garnishments, the maximum amount that can be garnished in total is the CCPA limit of 25% of disposable earnings or the excess of the employee's weekly disposable earnings above 30 times the federal minimum hourly wage, whichever is less.[74]

**Protection from discharge.**[75] Employees may not be discharged or otherwise discriminated against because of a garnishment order to repay a student loan.

**Notice before garnishment.**[76] Employees must receive at least 30 days' notice before withholding begins and must be given a chance to work out a repayment schedule with the agency guaranteeing the loan to avoid garnishment.

**No guidance on priorities.** The 1991 amendments provide no guidance as to the priority of a student loan garnishment if the employee's wages are also subject to garnishments for other debts. However, the Department of Education has allowed child support withholding orders to take priority.

**Grace period after reemployment.**[77] Employees who lose their jobs and become reemployed within 12 months after termination are given 12 months from their date of reemployment before a student loan garnishment order can be put into effect.

**Normal pay period OK.**[78] Employers do not have to change their normal pay period or payday to comply with a student loan garnishment order.

---

72.     11 USC §362(b)(19); §522(b)(2)(C); §523(a)(18), (n).
73.     20 USC §1095a(a)(1), (d); 34 CFR §682.410(b)(10)(i)(A).
74.     Halperin v. Regional Adjustment Bureau, Inc., 206 F.3d 1063 (11 CA, 2000).
75.     20 USC §1095a(a)(8); 34 CFR §682.410(b)(10)(i)(O).
76.     20 USC §1095a(a)(2), (a)(4), (b); 34 CFR §682.410(b)(10)(i)(B)-(D).
77.     20 USC §1095a(a)(7); 34 CFR §682.410(b)(10)(i)(G).
78.     20 USC §1095a(a)(6).

**Penalties for noncompliance.**[79] If an employer fails to comply with a lawful student loan garnishment order, it is liable for the amount not withheld from wages, as well as punitive damages, court costs, and attorneys' fees. Employers that unlawfully terminate employees because of a student loan garnishment may be ordered to reinstate the employee with backpay and to pay punitive damages and attorneys' fees.

## 9.1-6 Federal Agency Debt Collections

Because student loans aren't the only type of federal government debts that have been subject to a high percentage of nonpayment, Congress enacted the Debt Collection Improvement Act of 1996. Part of this law allows federal government agencies that administer a program under which they provide money to individuals to garnish the wages of individuals who fail to repay their debt according to their agreement with the agency. These garnishments can only be applied to nontax debts, since tax debts are collected through tax levies issued by the IRS (see Section 9.1-1). This law preempts state laws governing garnishments.

**Maximum amount subject to garnishment.**[80] The amount of a federal agency loan garnishment is limited by the Consumer Credit Protection Act as well as the Debt Collection Improvement Act. The amount to be garnished is the lesser of:

- the amount indicated on the garnishment order up to 15% of the employee's disposable pay, or

- the amount by which the employee's disposable pay exceeds 30 times the federal minimum hourly wage then in effect.

*Example:* Tim's employer receives a federal agency loan garnishment order in February 2008, and his disposable pay at that time is $190.00 per week. 30 times the federal minimum wage is $175.50. Therefore, the maximum amount that may be garnished weekly is the lesser of $28.50 (15% x $190.00) or $14.50 ($190.00 - $175.50).

Where an employee owes multiple debts to one federal agency, the agency may issue multiple withholding orders for the debts, so long as the total amount garnished does not exceed the limit for one garnishment.

Under rules issued by the Financial Management Service to implement federal agency wage garnishments, employers are required to certify information about the employee's employment status and disposable pay (defined as amounts required to be deducted by law and to pay for health insurance) on a form accompanying the withholding order and to pay over amounts withheld "promptly" after payday.[81] The employer must begin withholding within the "reasonable period of time" indicated in the withholding order (generally within 2 pay cycles following receipt of the order). The employer must continue withholding until notified to stop by the agency.[82]

**Protection from discharge.**[83] Employees may not be discharged, disciplined, or otherwise discriminated against because of a garnishment order to repay a federal agency loan.

**Notice before garnishment.**[84] Employees must receive notice of a federal agency garnishment before withholding is to begin and must be given a chance to contest the garnishment or work out a voluntary repayment schedule with the agency before the withholding order is sent to the employer. The employee can also demand a hearing to determine the existence and amount of the debt.

---

79. 20 USC §1095a(a)(6), (a)(8); 34 CFR §682.410(b)(10)(i)(F).
80. 31 USC §3720D(b); Reg. 31 CFR §285.11(i)(2), (3)(iii).
81. Reg. 31 CFR §285.11(c); (h); (i)(5).
82. Reg. 31 CFR §285.11(i)(8).
83. 31 USC §3720D(e); Reg. 31 CFR §285.11(m).
84. 1 USC §3720D(b)(5); Reg. 31 CFR §285.11(e), (f).

**Priority of multiple withholding orders.**[85] Unless otherwise provided by federal law, federal agency wage garnishments have priority over other types of withholding orders served on the employer after the federal agency wage garnishment, except for family support orders. If an employee's pay is already subject to another type of withholding order when the employer receives a federal agency wage garnishment, or if a family support withholding order is served on the employer at any time, the amount subject to the federal agency wage garnishment is the lesser of:

- the amount of the order up to 15% of the employee's disposable pay or the amount of the employee's disposable pay in excess of 30 times the federal minimum wage then in effect, or
- 25% of the employee's disposable pay minus the amounts withheld under the withholding orders with priority.

Wage assignments by an employee that would interfere with or prevent the collection of the debt owed to the agency through a federal agency wage garnishment are void unless the employee makes the assignment under a family support judgment or order.[86]

Similar rules have been issued by the Department of Education, Social Security Administration, and General Services Administration to recover non-tax debts and benefit overpayments.[87]

**Grace period after reemployment.**[88] Employees who lose their jobs involuntarily are given 12 months from their date of reemployment before a federal agency loan garnishment order can be put into effect. The employee must notify the agency of his or her involuntary termination of employment.

**Normal pay period OK.**[89] Employers do not have to change their normal pay period or payday to comply with a federal agency loan garnishment order.

**Penalties for noncompliance.**[90] If an employer fails to comply with a lawful federal agency loan garnishment order, it is liable for the amount not withheld from wages, as well as punitive damages, court costs, and attorneys' fees. The agency can sue the employer for amounts not withheld. Employers that unlawfully terminate or otherwise discriminate against employees because of a federal agency loan garnishment may be ordered to reinstate the employee with back pay and to pay punitive damages and attorneys' fees.

# 9.1-7 Federal Wage-Hour Law Restrictions on Deductions

The Consumer Credit Protection Act and the Debt Collection Improvement Act are not the only federal laws regulating the types and amounts of deductions that may be made from an employee's wages. The Fair Labor Standards Act, also known as the Federal Wage-Hour Law (see Section 2 for a full explanation of the law), places its own restrictions on such deductions when they bring an employee's wages below the minimum wage and overtime pay guaranteed by the Act.

**Board, lodging, and other facilities.**[91] Where an employee voluntarily accepts meals, lodging, or other facilities provided by an employer primarily for the employee's benefit, the reasonable cost of the facilities may be deducted from wages paid to the employee, even if the deduction results in the employee receiving less than the required minimum wage or overtime pay. Goods and services connected with employment, such as tools, required uniforms, and company-provided security, are not facilities, and deductions for providing them may be taken only if they do not bring the employee's wages below the minimum.

---

85.     Reg. 31 CFR §285.11(i)(3).
86.     Reg. 31 CFR §285.11(i)(7).
87.     68 FR 8148, 2-19-03; 68 FR 74177, 12-23-03; 68 FR 68760, 12-10-03.
88.     31 USC §3720D(b)(6); Reg. 31 CFR §285.11(j).
89.     31 USC §3720D(f)(3); Reg. 31 CFR §285.11(i)(b).
90.     31 USC §3720D(e), (f); Reg. 31 CFR §285.11(o).
91.     FLSA §3(m); 29 USC §203(m); W-H Reg. 29 CFR §531.36.

If the employer makes a profit from providing the facilities, deductions for providing them are unlawful only if the profit reduces the employee's wages (including the reasonable cost of the facilities) below the minimum. If the deductions do not reduce the employee's wages below the minimum, none of the tests described here have to be considered.

*Example 1:* Employee Sheila earns $8.25 per hour for a 40-hour workweek in May 2008 and receives facilities from her employer with a reasonable cost of $25. If Sheila's employer deducts $25 from her wages of $330 ($8.25 x 40 = $330), the FLSA tests for facilities need not be met because her reduced gross wages would be $305, which exceeds the minimum requirement for a 40-hour workweek ($5.85 x 40 = $234).

*Example 2:* Employee Sherman earns $6.10 per hour for a 40-hour workweek in May 2008 but is paid only $204 after his employer deducted $40 for facilities furnished to him during the week [(40 x $6.10) - $40 = $204]. If the reasonable cost of the facilities is at least $30, Sherman's employer has complied with the FLSA's minimum wage requirement ($204 + $30 = $234; 40 hours x $5.85 minimum hourly wage = $234). If the employer made a profit from furnishing the facilities or deducted for the cost of items that cannot be considered facilities, the total of such deductions may not exceed $10 in this situation ($244 earned - $10 = $234 required minimum).

*Example 3:* Assume the same facts as in Example 2, except that Sherman works 44 hours in the workweek. According to the Wage and Hour Administrator, the same deductions are allowed as would have been allowed during a 40-hour workweek.[92]

**Buying and maintaining uniforms.**[93] If an employee is required to wear a uniform while at work that cannot be used as ordinary streetwear and the employer picks up the cost of the uniform and/or its maintenance, the employer cannot deduct any amount of such cost that brings the employee's wages below the minimum required by the FLSA.

**Loans to employees.** Employers can deduct amounts equal to the principal of loans made to employees from their wages, even if the deduction reduces the employee's wages below the required minimum under the FLSA. Deductions for interest on the loan or administrative costs associated with the loan are allowed only if they do not bring the employee's wages below the required minimum.[94]

**Salary advances and overpayments.** Deductions to recover salary advances or overpayments due to bookkeeping errors may be taken by the employer even if they reduce the employee's current wage below the required minimum, but employers should consider spreading out the recovery of amounts overpaid or advanced to reduce the economic hardship on the employee.[95]

**Docking pay for missed worktime.**[96] "Docking" or reducing an employee's pay because the employee misses work due to lateness can cause special problems where the employee earns an amount that is close to the minimum wage and is penalized beyond an amount that equals the time actually lost. If the employee is docked the same amount of pay as time lost, there is no FLSA violation. However, if the employee is docked an additional amount as a penalty, the employer acts unlawfully if the additional reduction brings the employee's wages below the minimum required for the hours actually worked.

*Example 1:* Employee Alex earns $5.85 an hour for a 40-hour workweek in June 2008. In one week, he was late a total of 1½ hours and was docked $8.77. He received total wages for the week of $225.23. There was no FLSA violation because he was paid the minimum wage for the hours actually worked ($5.85 x 38.5 = $225.23).

---

92.  W-H Reg. 29 CFR §531.37.
93.  W-H Op. Ltr. WH-274, 6-7-74.
94.  W-H Op. Ltr., 3-20-98.
95.  W-H Op. Ltr., 3-20-98.
96.  W-H Reg. 29 CFR §778.307.

***Example 2:*** Assume the same facts as in Example 1 except Alex was docked an additional 1½ hours' pay as a penalty for his lateness, for a total deduction of $17.55 ($5.85 x 3). Alex received total wages for the week of $216.45. Since this was less than the required minimum for the hours actually worked ($225.23), the employer violated the FLSA.

Where an employee works more than 40 hours in a workweek and is entitled to overtime pay for the extra hours, any reduction in pay for time lost due to lateness cannot reduce the amount of overtime due the employee for the extra hours actually worked. The employee's pay can be docked only at the regular rate of pay, which must be figured before any deductions are made.

***Example:*** Employee Peggy's regular rate of pay is $6.10 an hour, and in a workweek in June 2008 where she was scheduled to work 52 hours, she missed 2 hours due to lateness. Peggy's employer pays her for only 48 hours, docking her 2 hours' pay for each hour of work missed. Her total wages for the week are $317.20 [($6.10 x 48) + ($3.05 x 8)]. Peggy's employer violated the FLSA because she was not paid for the full 10 overtime hours she worked. The employer should first have determined her wages for the hours she actually worked [($6.10 x 50) + ($3.05 x 10) = $335.50] and then docked her 2 hours' pay at her regular rate for a total of $323.30 [$335.50 - ($6.10 x 2)].

**Deductions for taxes.**[97] Amounts withheld from an employee's pay for federal, state, and local income taxes, as well as the employee's share of social security and Medicare taxes, are considered wages paid to the employee. The fact the employee may receive net pay below the FLSA-required minimum does not make these deductions unlawful. However, the employer may not deduct any amount from an employee's wages to pay for the employer's share of any tax, including social security, Medicare, federal unemployment, and state unemployment and disability taxes.

**Garnishments and wage assignments.**[98] Employers can deduct amounts from an employee's wages to satisfy garnishment orders from a court or government agency or to satisfy a voluntary "assignment" of wages by an employee to some third party (see Section 9.2-1), even if the deduction reduces the employee's wages below the minimum required by the FLSA. The payment of the deducted amounts to the third party is considered the same as payment to the employee, so long as the employer derives no profit or other benefit from making the deduction. Also, any amount deducted in excess of the limits on garnishment contained in the CCPA (see Sections 9.1-2 and 9.1-3) is not considered wages paid to the employee and may not reduce the employee's wages below the required minimum.

**Union dues.** If required by a union contract, an employer can deduct union dues from an employee's wages and pay that amount to the union even if the deduction reduces the employee's wages below the FLSA minimum. But if the deduction (or "check-off") is unlawful under a law other than the FLSA (e.g., a federal or state labor relations law), it cannot reduce the employee's wages below the minimum wage or overtime required by the FLSA.

**Cash shortages, bad checks.** Generally, employers may not deduct amounts from a nonexempt employee's wages to make up for cash shortages, bounced checks, or customers who fail to pay their bills if the deductions would reduce the employee's wages below the minimum wage or overtime required under the FLSA.[99] There is an exception to this general rule where the employee has stolen the amount involved, but only if the employee's guilt has been decided by a court, either after a trial or upon a plea of guilty.[100] For the rules that apply to FLSA-exempt employees, see section 2.4-1.

**Employer insurance bonds.**[101] An employer that bonds an employee by buying insurance to protect against fraud or negligence attributed to the employee may not require the employee to pay for the bond before starting work. The cost of the bond may be spread out and deducted from the employee's subsequent wages, but only to the extent that the deductions do not reduce the employee's wages below the FLSA minimum.

---

97. W-H Reg. 29 CFR §531.38.
98. W-H Reg. 29 CFR §531.39; 29 CFR §531.40.
99. Hodgson v. Frisch's Dixie, Inc., 469 F.2d 82 (6 CA 1972); Mayhue's Super Liquor Store, Inc. v. Hodgson, 464 F.2d 1196 (5 CA 1972), cert. den. 409 U.S. 1108 (1973).
100. W-H Op. Ltr. 239, 10-1-73.
101. See footnote 98.

## 9.2 Voluntary Deductions

In addition to deductions for withholding taxes, garnishments, tax levies, employee loans, etc., that are involuntarily deducted from an employee's pay, an employee can also voluntarily agree to wage deductions that must be implemented by the payroll department. These deductions may include wage assignments to repay a debt, charitable deductions, wages withheld to purchase U.S. savings bonds, credit union loan repayments, etc.

## 9.2-1 Wage Assignments

A wage assignment is a voluntary agreement by an employee (assignor) to have a portion of the employee's wages assigned to a third party (assignee). Generally, employees assign wages to secure a debt. The assignment gives the creditor an opportunity to recover the unpaid amount if the employee fails to repay the debt. A wage assignment also allows both the third party and the employee to avoid the time and expense connected with court-run garnishment proceedings.

Wholesale or retail outlets that allow customers to pay for merchandise in installments will sometimes ask the customer to enter into a wage assignment agreement as a manner of guaranteeing payment. Assignments are also used to secure loans from financial institutions. Sometimes an assignment will be used to pay the debt directly, rather than waiting for the employee to default. And in some cases, noncustodial parents may be allowed to voluntarily assign a portion of their wages to pay child support rather than having to submit to a child support withholding order.

**Garnishment limits do not apply.** Voluntary wage assignments are not covered by the Consumer Credit Protection Act, which sets the maximum amounts that can be deducted from an employee's pay to satisfy creditor garnishments and child support withholding orders. But if the debt secured by the assignment remains unpaid and becomes the subject of a court-ordered garnishment, the resulting garnishment is governed by the CCPA.

**State law governs wage assignments.** While wage assignments are not subject to federal law restrictions, the states regulate them to varying degrees. Where they do not, wage assignments are governed by the general law of contracts as developed by state courts. Following is a discussion of some of the facets of wage assignments that are generally regulated by the states.

*Validity of wage assignments.* Some states do not allow voluntary wage assignments of any kind. Most of the others allow employees to agree to an assignment of wages that have already been earned, although not yet paid, while many states prohibit the assignment of future wages (i.e., wages not yet earned). This also is one area where the federal government has become involved. Federal Trade Commission regulations prohibit loan companies and retail installment sellers from securing payment with a wage assignment unless:

- the assignment can be revoked at any time by the employee;

- the assignment is a payroll deduction plan starting at the time of the transaction; and

- the assignment applies only to wages already earned when the assignment is made.[102]

Several states have passed laws incorporating similar restrictions on assignments arising out of consumer credit transactions or prohibiting such assignments altogether.

*Maximum amount that can be assigned.* Those states that allow assignment of future wages often restrict the amount of an employee's wages that can be assigned in the form of a maximum percentage or a dollar amount. They also may put a limit on how long into the future an assignment can be enforced.

---

102.    16 CFR §444.2(a)(3).

*Priorities.* Where more than one wage assignment is presented to the employer, generally the one received first must be given priority if the full amount for both cannot be withheld. In those states that require wage assignments to be registered with a local court or municipal clerk, priority must be given to the assignment filed earlier. In such a state, an employer that has been withholding to satisfy an assignment that has not been properly registered may have to give priority to a subsequent assignment for which the proper procedures have been followed.

*Small loan restrictions.* Many states have special laws regarding wage assignments to secure "small loans" provided by finance companies. These laws usually limit the amount of the loan that can be secured by a wage assignment and attach several procedural requirements, including:

- the assignment must be in writing;
- the assignment must be signed by the employee and his or her spouse;
- the amount borrowed must be given to the employee when the assignment is signed; and
- the employer must receive a copy of the loan agreement, the assignment, and the state laws regulating the assignment.

*Notice requirements.* In several states, creditors holding a wage assignment cannot collect from the employer without providing notice to the employer and/or the employee either before or at the time the wage assignment is presented to the employer. In states where an assignment is not binding on the employer unless the employee has received notice of its pending execution, the employer should check with the employee once an assignment is received to make sure the notice requirement has been met. If the employee claims that no notice was given, the employer should contact the creditor for a copy of the notice and proof that it was served on the employee.

*Federal, state, and local employees.* As with garnishments, wage assignments cannot be enforced against a public sector employer unless a law allows public employees to assign their wages. Some states have enacted laws that treat government employees the same as private sector employees where wage assignments are concerned, while others place more restrictions on the public sector.

 **CHECK YOUR STATE LAWS** Because of the different treatment of wage assignments provided by the states, employers must be sure to check their own state's laws when faced with a wage assignment. Notifying legal counsel might also be a good idea, at least where there are any questions regarding the validity of a wage assignment or its priority if the employee involved has any other proceedings against his or her wages. For more information on states' treatment of wage assignments, see Table 7.2 of *APA's Guide to State Payroll Laws*.

## 9.2-2 Union Dues

In addition to mandatory deductions for union dues required by a collective bargaining agreement (see Section 9.1-6), in some situations employees have the option of paying union dues on their own or having them deducted from their wages by their employer. This voluntary check-off procedure is authorized by federal labor law (Labor Management Relations Act), so long as the amount withheld is for union dues, initiation fees, and assessments only.[103]

The federal law also requires the employer to get a written, signed authorization from each employee allowing wages to be deducted. Once signed, the authorization cannot be revoked for one year or until the union contract expires. To be irrevocable beyond that point, the employee would have to sign another authorization.

---

103. LMRA §302(c)(4).

## 9.2-3 Credit Union Deductions

Many employees save money with or borrow money from a "credit union," an organization formed by employees (often in conjunction with their collective bargaining representative) that serves as a savings and loan company. When it is time to repay a credit union loan or place funds in a savings account, the employee may wish to have a portion of his or her wages deducted by the employer and paid over to the credit union. Employers often encourage the formation and use of credit unions by agreeing to the payroll deductions. Before deducting any wages, however, employers should get written, signed authorizations from employees that detail the amount to be withheld, the duration of the withholding, and the party to whom the withheld wages will be paid.

## 9.2-4 U.S. Savings Bonds

Another type of voluntary payroll deduction allows employees to purchase Series EE U.S. Savings Bonds in denominations beginning at $100. The purchase price of the bond is one-half of the bond's denomination or "face value." Therefore, the purchase price of a $500 bond is $250.

**Interest accumulation.** Interest begins to accumulate in the month during which payments for the bond are received by the party issuing the bond. If the employee cashes in (redeems) the bond less than five years after the month of issue, the value of the bond is the purchase price plus interest earned at a set rate that is somewhat lower than the guaranteed minimum rate. After five years, the bond earns interest at the guaranteed minimum rate or at a market-based rate that is computed every six months (May and November).

If the employee redeems the bond after five years but before it reaches maturity, its value will be computed as the original purchase price plus interest earned at the higher of the two rates. If the employee redeems the bond at maturity (12 years), the employee receives the greater of the face value of the bond or the value of the bond based on the market-based interest rate.

**Tax advantages for the employee.** The main tax advantage to the employee of Series EE bonds purchased through payroll deductions is that the interest earned is free from federal income tax until the bond is redeemed. The interest may be totally tax-free if the bond is used to finance the college education of the employee's children. The interest is also not taxable at the state or local level. Remember, however, the deductions themselves are after-tax deductions, so the money taken from the employee's wages has already been subject to federal and state income and employment taxes.

**Authorization procedures.** Employees who wish to participate in a savings bond payroll deduction program can do so by completing and signing an enrollment card that details the amount to withhold nd the type of bond to be purchased. Enrollment cards are supplied by the employer, and they can be obtained from any regional office of the U.S. Treasury Department.

**Employer responsibilities.** Other than providing enrollment cards and making the deductions and payments, employers also must make sure the proper amounts have been deducted and remitted by reconciling the deductions and the bonds purchased. And they must return any excess amounts deducted to the employees or use them toward the purchase of more bonds. When employees leave the job, they must receive any amounts that have been deducted but have not yet been used to purchase a bond.

*Example:* Employee Sharon has $25 deducted from her biweekly paycheck toward the purchase of $500 savings bonds. When she resigned from her job, $125 had been deducted toward the purchase of her next bond. Sharon's employer must give her a refund of the $125 since it was not enough to purchase the bond, which cost $250.

**Administration of the program.** Employers can choose how involved they wish to get in the administration of the payroll deduction program. They can become "issuing agents" who draft the bonds and give them to employees as they are purchased, or they can provide enrollment data and payment for the bonds to a third-party administrator, federal reserve bank, or other depository institution that issues the bonds.

When acting as an issuing agent, the employer is paid an administrative fee based on the number of bonds issued. It must also keep accurate records of the employees who own the bonds, including their addresses, as well as the serial numbers, denominations, and issue dates of the bonds and the original employee enrollment cards.

In 1998, the Treasury Department issued proposed rules that would allow service bureaus operating payroll savings plans on behalf of employers to issue savings bonds (and to collect "issuing agent" fees if they inscribe the bonds). The service bureau would first have to obtain the approval of the Commissioner of the Bureau of the Public Debt after applying through a Federal Reserve Bank.[104] In 1999, the Treasury Department began offering its new Series I Savings Bonds through payroll deductions as well.

## 9.2-5 Charitable Contributions

Many employers work with local and national charities to provide their employees with the opportunity to make voluntary donations to those charities through payroll deductions. The payroll department makes the deductions and processes their remittance to the appropriate charitable organizations.

This process has become more complicated by IRS requirements for appropriate substantiation when individuals deduct the amount of their charitable contributions from their income on their personal income tax returns. In 1994, the Omnibus Budget Reconciliation Act of 1993 created IRC §170(f)(8), which prohibits taxpayers from deducting charitable contributions of $250 or more without substantiation of the gift and any substantial goods or services received in return.[105] The required substantiation is a "contemporaneous written acknowledgement" (before the taxpayer files his or her personal tax return for the year of the contribution) from the charitable organization that includes the following information:

- the amount of cash and a description of any noncash property contributed,
- whether the charitable organization provided any goods or services in return for the contribution, and
- a description and good faith estimate of the value of these goods or services.

**Payroll problems recognized.** In issuing regulations to deal with the new law, the IRS recognized that, in a payroll deduction situation, the charitable organization will generally not know the names of the contributing employees or the amounts they contributed during a given year, since employers do not pay over the withheld amounts in separate checks for each employee, but in one lump sum. This makes it difficult for charities to provide, and for employees to obtain, the acknowledgement required to substantiate the contributions.

**Employer and charity share reporting burden.**[106] To make it feasible for employees to obtain the required acknowledgement, the regulations allow them to substantiate contributions by a combination of two documents:

- a pay stub, Form W-2, or other document provided by the employer that shows the amount withheld for payment to a charitable organization, and
- a pledge card or other document prepared by the charitable organization or another party (e.g., the employer) at the direction of the charitable organization that includes a statement that no goods or services are provided in return for employee contributions made by payroll deduction.

**$250 threshold applies separately to each deduction.** The regulations also address the issue of how to apply the $250 threshold triggering the acknowledgement requirement when contributions are made by payroll deduction. The amount withheld from each wage payment to an employee is treated as a separate contribution. Thus, these substantiation requirements do not apply unless the employer withholds at least $250 from a single paycheck for purposes of paying it to a charitable organization.

---

104. 63 F.R. 23695, 4-30-98.
105. IRC §170(f)(8); IRS Reg. §1.170A-13(f)(1)-(18).
106. IRS Reg. §1.170A-13(f)(11).

**Substantiation requirement applies to all payroll deduction contributions in 2007.** In 2006, the Pension Protection Act of 2006 created IRC §170(f)(17), which disallows deductions for charitable contributions of money unless they are substantiated by a bank record or a written communication from the charitable organization showing the name of the organization and the date and amount of the contribution.[107] This requirement is effective for contributions made in taxable years beginning after August 17, 2006, so it became effective for nearly all employees for the taxable year beginning January 1, 2007.

**Same payroll problems lead to new guidance.** Recognizing once again that these new requirements would cause problems in the area of charitable contributions by payroll deduction because employers do not provide individual donor (employee) information to the charitable organizations to which they send the deducted contributions, IRS issued guidance as to how employers should handle the substantiation issue.[108]

For contributions of any amount made by payroll deduction, a "written communication from the donee organization" as required under §170(f)(17) includes:

- a pay stub, Form W-2, or other document provided by the employer that shows the amount withheld during a taxable year from the employee by the employer for the purpose of payment to a donee organization, together with
- a pledge card or other document prepared by or at the direction of the donee organization that shows the name of the donee organization.

**Slightly different rules depending on the contribution amount.** Both §170(f)(8) and §170(f)(17) must be complied with where they apply. What this means for employers is that beginning in 2007 they should provide documentation of all charitable contributions made by their employees, either on the employees' pay stubs or Forms W-2, or in a separate statement, not just individual contributions of $250 or more.

To comply with §170(f)(17), they should also provide employees that had any amounts deducted for charitable contributions with a pledge card or other document prepared by the charitable organization (or by the employer if the charitable organization requests it) that contains the name of the charitable organization. To substantiate a contribution of $250 or more made by payroll deduction for purposes of §170(f)(8), the pledge card or other document must also include a statement to the effect that the organization does not provide goods or services in exchange for contributions made by payroll deduction. Including such a statement on all pledge cards and other documents showing the name of the charitable organization would ensure the employees have the substantiation they need under both Code sections.

> *Example:* Employee Rena has $50 withheld from each monthly paycheck in 2008 and sent to the United Way by her employer, Bona Fido, Inc., a dog obedience school. Even though Rena has not had any single deductions of $250 or more from her pay in 2008 for her United Way contributions, her employer should report the amount to her on her pay stub or Form W-2 since she needs it to substantiate her charitable deduction when she files her 2008 tax return. The employer should also give her a copy of her pledge card or other document on which she authorized the deduction, which she will also need to substantiate her charitable deduction. (The employer probably has to note the deduction on Rena's pay stub anyway under state law requiring deductions to be listed on employees' pay statements–see Section 5.4.)

**Employees get tax-free grants from charity created by employer.**[109] An employer set up a public charitable foundation to make grants and loans to employees and their dependents who demonstrate a need for the money. The foundation was funded by after-tax voluntary payroll deductions from employees, and each employee received a statement showing their deductions at the end of the year. The IRS ruled that the employees' deductions qualified as charitable contributions they could deduct on their personal income tax returns. It also ruled that grants or loans to employees from the charity are not subject to federal income, social security, Medicare, or FUTA tax because they were gifts from the charity under IRC §102(c).

---

107.    P.L. 109-280, §1217; IRC §170(f)(17).
108.    Notice 2006-110, 2006-51 IRB 1127.
109.    LTR 200307084, 11-14-02.

## 9.3 Review Questions and Exercises

### Review Questions

1. How does Form 668-W define an employee's take-home pay that is subject to a federal tax levy?

2. What is the penalty for failing to withhold and remit payment as prescribed under an IRS notice of levy?

3. What is the CCPA and how does it affect child support withholding?

4. When is group health insurance deducted from an employee's gross wages in determining disposable pay?

5. Does an employer have to withhold child support from payments to independent contractors?

6. How does the federal garnishment limit apply to multiple garnishments?

7. What is the amount that will be garnished from an employee's pay to satisfy a delinquent federal agency loan?

8. Your state sets 50% of "disposable earnings" as the maximum for child support withholding. Your employee is not supporting another spouse and/or children, so the CCPA's maximum is 60%. What percentage do you use?

9. Name three voluntary deductions that are not subtracted from earnings to calculate disposable pay.

10. What are medical child support orders?

11. What changes were enacted by OBRA '93 to make sure that both insurers and employers in each state comply in carrying out medical child support orders?

### True or False Questions

_____ 1. You receive an IRS levy on an employee. You must receive Parts 3 and 4 filled out and signed by the employee before executing the levy.

_____ 2. Creditor garnishments are always allowed up to 25% of disposable earnings.

_____ 3. The amount of an employee's wages that is subject to a federal tax levy is the amount remaining after the exempt amount has been subtracted from the employee's "gross pay."

_____ 4. If an employee receives wages from more than one employer and only one receives a notice of levy, the employer must determine the exempt amount in the usual way unless the IRS notifies the employer that the exempt amount should be reduced because the other wages are not subject to levy.

_____ 5. Withholding for a federal tax levy must continue until a release is received from the IRS because interest continues to accumulate on the amount that remains due after each levy payment is made.

_____ 6. Employers failing to withhold and pay over amounts not exempt from levy after receiving Form 668-W are not liable for the full amount required to be withheld.

_____ 7.   Orders to withhold wages for child support take priority over all other garnishments or attachments issued against the employee's wages except for tax levies received by the employer before the child support withholding order.

_____ 8.   Disposable pay is the same as take-home pay.

_____ 9.   An employer may be required to deduct a creditor garnishment from an employee's wages by order of the creditor.

_____ 10.  Involuntary deductions are those over which an employer and employee have no control.

_____ 11.  For levies carrying over to the next calendar year, if an employee does not complete a new Part 3 of Form 668-W, the employer must use the exempt amount table for the year during which the most recent Part 3 statement of exemptions was filed.

_____ 12.  Enforcement of child support orders is a joint federal and state responsibility.

_____ 13.  State child support withholding laws may impose lower limits on the amount that may be withheld than federal law.

_____ 14.  State law may allow employers to charge the employee an administrative fee for processing a wage garnishment order each pay period.

_____ 15.  If an employer fails to withhold child support for the amount required by the notice to withhold, it is liable for the full amount not withheld, up to the state and federal maximums.

_____ 16.  If an employer receives more than one child support withholding order for an employee, state law governs how they must be handled.

_____ 17.  An employer should not withhold child support from payments made to independent contractors.

_____ 18.  Government employees are subject to a different set of child support withholding order requirements than those applicable to private sector employees.

_____ 19.  An employer can terminate an employee because of inconvenience caused in administering a creditor garnishment order.

_____ 20.  Public sector employees' wages are exempt from creditor garnishment unless provided otherwise by state law.

## Multiple Choice Questions

_____ 1.   What form does an employer receive from the IRS to levy on an employee's salary?

   a.   Form 668-D
   b.   Form 916
   c.   Form 668-W
   d.   Form 2159

_____ 2.  What is the threshold for requiring employers to report to employees their charitable contributions made through payroll deductions during a calendar year so the employee may claim the contribution on a personal income tax return?

    a.  more than $3,000 in total deductions for the year
    b.  any amount deducted during the year
    c.  more than $250 deducted from a single paycheck
    d.  more than $600 in total deductions for the year

_____ 3.  What law governs the maximum amount that can be withheld from an employee's wages for spousal or child support?

    a.  Family Support Act of 1988
    b.  Omnibus Budget Reconciliation Act of 1993
    c.  Child Support Enforcement Amendments of 1984
    d.  Consumer Credit Protection Act

_____ 4.  An employee subject to a student loan garnishment loses her job and gets another one six months later.  How long is it before the garnishment can be reinstated?

    a.  6 months from her date of reemployment
    b.  12 months from her date of reemployment
    c.  9 months from her date of reemployment
    d.  No grace period is allowed

_____ 5.  If all the following withholding orders are received at the same time, which must the employer deduct first?

    a.  Creditor garnishment
    b.  Student loan garnishment
    c.  Federal tax levy
    d.  State tax levy

_____ 6.  How many parts does Form 668-W, *Notice of Levy on Wages, Salary and Other Income*, contain?

    a.  Three parts
    b.  Four parts
    c.  Five parts
    d.  Six parts

_____ 7.  Under the CCPA, what is the maximum amount that can be withheld from an employee's wages for spouse or child support when the employee is not supporting another family and is 15 weeks in arrears for the support owed?

    a.  65% of gross pay
    b.  60% of disposable pay
    c.  65% of disposable pay
    d.  55% of disposable pay

_____ 8.  When determining the amount to send to the IRS to satisfy a tax levy, the exempt amount is deducted from what amount?

    a.  Gross pay
    b.  Disposable pay
    c.  Take-home pay
    d.  Federal income tax withheld

# Section 9: Other Deductions From Pay

_____ 9. When an employer receives Form 668-W from the IRS, when must the employer begin to withhold and remit?

    a. With the first payment of wages after receipt of Form 668-W
    b. Within 14 days after receipt of Form 668-W
    c. Within 30 days after receipt of Form 668-W
    d. Within 30 days after receipt of Form 668-W or the first date of payment of wages, whichever is later

_____ 10. When does an employer stop withholding for a federal tax levy?

    a. When Form 668-W is received
    b. When Form 668-D is received
    c. When Form 668-S is received
    d. When the IRS collection officer calls

_____ 11. Under the CCPA, what is the maximum amount that can be withheld from an employee's wages for spouse or child support when the employee is supporting another family and is not in arrears for the support owed?

    a. 50% of gross pay
    b. 50% of take-home pay
    c. 50% of disposable pay
    d. 55% of disposable pay

_____ 12. Which of the following deductions is not a voluntary deduction?

    a. Child support
    b. Charitable contributions
    c. §401(k) plan contributions
    d. Life insurance premiums

_____ 13. When an employer receives a federal tax levy for an employee who is paid on a one-time basis or a recurring but irregular basis, how is the exempt amount from levy determined?

    a. the employee is entitled to the weekly exempt amount for the entire time to which the payment is attributable
    b. the employee is entitled to the weekly exempt amount for each week to which the payment is attributable
    c. the employee is entitled to the daily exempt amount for each day to which the payment is attributable
    d. the employee is entitled to the monthly exempt amount for the entire time to which the payment is attributable

_____ 14. Which of the following laws restricts states in their regulation of creditor garnishments?

    a. Fair Labor Standards Act
    b. Omnibus Budget Reconciliation Act of 1993
    c. Family Support Act of 1988
    d. Consumer Credit Protection Act

_____ 15. Under federal law what is the maximum amount of an employee's "disposable earnings" that can be garnished to repay a debt to a creditor?

    a.    25%
    b.    27%
    c.    50%
    d.    65%

## Problems

1. You implement a child support withholding order. Your employee complains that it is the wrong amount. You verify that you are withholding the amount stated in the order correctly. What should you do?

2. John Frazier's gross pay is $500 per week. On June 1, 2008, his employer receives a Form 668-W stating that a tax levy was being issued against John's wages for $8,000. John claims single with 1 personal exemption on Part 3 of the form. As of June 1, John had the following deductions:

| | |
|---|---|
| Federal income tax: | $75.00 |
| State income tax: | 15.00 |
| Social security tax: | 31.00 |
| Medicare tax: | 7.25 |
| §401(k) plan: | 20.00 |
| Total | $ 148.25 |

How much of John's wages per pay period are subject to the tax levy?

$_____

3. Matthew Winters is married and files jointly, claiming 4 exemptions on Part 3 of Form 668-W for a tax levy being issued against his semimonthly wages of $2,000. Matthew's employer receives the notice on September 15, 2008. Prior to this period, Matthew's deductions for each pay period consisted of:

| | |
|---|---|
| Federal income tax: | $360.00 |
| State income tax: | 156.80 |
| Social security tax: | 124.00 |
| Medicare tax: | 29.00 |
| §401(k) plan: | 80.00 |
| Health ins. (after-tax) | 100.00 |
| Total | $ 849.80 |

What amount of Matthew's wages per pay period is subject to the tax levy?

$_____

4.  a.  David Christensen receives a salary of $3,500 each month. On September 1, 2008, David's employer receives a Form 668-W stating that a federal tax levy was being issued against David's wages for $10,500. David claims married filing jointly with 2 exemptions on Part 3 of the form. As of September 1, 2008, David had the following deductions:

| | |
|---|---|
| Federal income tax: | $525.00 |
| State income tax: | 206.00 |
| Local income tax: | 122.50 |
| Social security tax: | 217.00 |
| Medicare tax: | 50.75 |
| §401(k) plan (2% of salary): | 70.00 |
| Health insurance (after tax): | 50.00 |
| Total: | $1,241.25 |

What amount of David's wages per pay period is subject to the tax levy?

$_____

b.  On November 1, 2008, David gave his employer a new Form 668-W, Part 3 claiming married with 3 exemptions. He also increases his elective deferral in the §401(k) plan to 4% of his salary. His health insurance deduction increases from $50 to $70 because of a premium increase. As a result, his deductions have changed to the following amounts:

| | |
|---|---|
| Federal income tax: | $500.00 |
| State income tax: | 206.00 |
| Local income tax: | 122.50 |
| Social security tax: | 217.00 |
| Medicare tax: | 50.75 |
| §401(k) plan (4% of salary): | 140.00 |
| Health insurance (after tax): | 70.00 |
| Total: | $1,306.25 |

What amount of David's wages is now subject to tax levy as a result of the changes?

$_____

c.  What is David's net pay as a result of these changes?

$_____

5.  Mindy earns $8.50 per hour and is paid weekly. Last pay period she worked 40 hours. Her deductions include:

| | |
|---|---|
| Federal income tax: | $33.00 |
| State income tax: | 3.30 |
| Social security tax: | 21.08 |
| Medicare tax: | 4.93 |
| U.S. Savings Bonds: | 15.00 |

What is Mindy's disposable pay.

$_____

6. Barry earns $7.50 per hour for a regular 40-hour week. Last week Barry worked 48 hours. His regular deductions include:

| | |
|---|---|
| Federal income tax: | $58.50 |
| State income tax: | 11.70 |
| Social security tax: | 24.18 |
| Medicare tax: | 5.66 |
| Child support: | 25.00 |

   What is Barry's disposable pay?                                    $ _____

7. Terry earns $10.00 per hour for a 40-hour week and is paid biweekly. During the last pay period, Terry worked 43 hours in the first week and 39 hours in the second week. His regular deductions include:

| | |
|---|---|
| Federal income tax: | $125.25 |
| State income tax: | 25.05 |
| Social security tax: | 51.77 |
| Medicare tax: | 12.11 |
| Creditor garnishment: | 50.00 |
| Life insurance premium: | 10.00 |
| Union dues: | 5.00 |

   What is Terry's disposable pay?                                    $ _____

8. Employee Jane's disposable earnings for the week are $320. Her employer receives a garnishment order requiring that $250 be withheld on February 1, 2008.

   What is the amount of Jane's disposable earnings that can be garnished under federal law?

   $ _____

9. Employee Don is paid $2,600 on the 15th and last day of each month. His regular deductions include:

| | |
|---|---|
| Federal income tax: | $390.00 |
| State income tax: | 195.00 |
| Social security tax: | 161.20 |
| Medicare tax: | 37.70 |
| Child support: | 100.00 |
| Tax levy: | 50.00 |
| Life insurance premium: | 30.00 |
| United Way contribution: | 25.00 |
| Health insurance (after-tax): | 30.00 |
| Savings: | 50.00 |

   On February 1, 2008, Don's employer receives a creditor garnishment order requiring $500 to be withheld. Calculate the maximum amount of Don's disposable earnings that can be withheld for this garnishment under federal law.

   $ _____

# SECTION 10: RECORDKEEPING AND RECORD RETENTION

## TABLE OF CONTENTS

# SECTION 10: RECORDKEEPING AND RECORD RETENTION

Compliance with the various federal, state, and local laws affecting payroll is impossible without keeping accurate records for each employee. While different laws may require the gathering and processing of different types of records and retention by the employer for varying lengths of time, the failure to maintain the proper records can be quite costly in terms of noncompliance penalties as well as penalties for violating the recordkeeping requirements themselves. This section explains the recordkeeping and record retention requirements of the different payroll laws, as well as procedures for making sure those records are available when needed and are destroyed when no longer needed.

## 10.1 Federal Wage-Hour Law (FLSA)

The basic federal payroll recordkeeping requirements (other than those dealing with federal income or employment taxes) are contained in regulations issued by the Wage and Hour Division of the Department of Labor under the Fair Labor Standards Act.[1] The FLSA requires certain records to be kept by all covered employers for all employees (although certain records related to overtime pay requirements need not be kept for exempt "white collar" employees) and retained for either two or three years.

Records that must be kept for each employee for at least three years after their last date of entry include:[2]

- name, as it appears on the employee's social security card;
- home address, including apartment number, if any, and Zip code;
- date of birth, if under age 19;
- sex and occupation (for use in determining Equal Pay Act compliance);
- the beginning of the employee's workweek (time and day);
- regular rate of pay for overtime weeks, the basis for determining the rate, and any payments excluded from the regular rate;
- hours worked each workday and workweek;
- straight-time earnings (including the straight-time pay portion of overtime earnings);
- overtime premium earnings;
- additions to and deductions from wages for each pay period (e.g., bonuses, withheld taxes, benefits contributions, garnishments);
- total wages paid for each pay period; and
- date of payment and the pay period covered.

Records that must be kept for at least three years from the last date they were in effect include:[3]

- collective bargaining agreements;
- certificates authorizing the employment of industrial homeworkers, minors, learners, students, apprentices, and handicapped workers; and
- records showing total sales volume and goods purchased.

Records that must be kept for at least two years from their last date of entry include:[4]

- basic employment and earning records supporting the data for each employee's hours of work, basis for determining wages, and wages paid (e.g., time or production cards);

---

1. FLSA §11(c); 29 USC §211(c).
2. 29 CFR §516.2; 29 CFR §516.5.
3. 29 CFR §516.5.
4. 29 CFR §516.6.

- order, shipping, and billing records showing customer orders, shipping and delivery records, and customer billings; and
- records substantiating additions to or deductions from employees' wages, including purchase orders, operating cost records, wage assignments, and garnishments.

 **SIGNATURE ON TIME CARD NOT REQUIRED** There is no requirement in the FLSA or the regulations that employees (or their supervisors) sign their time cards or other evidence of hours worked. Most companies, however, do require the employee and/or the supervisor to sign time records where they are kept on paper as part of their overall policies to ensure accurate reporting and recordkeeping.

Records that must be kept for at least two years from their last effective date include:[5]

- wage rate tables and piece rate schedules; and
- work time schedules establishing the hours and days of employment.

**Records for white collar employees.**[6] For employees who are exempt from the minimum wage and overtime provisions of the FLSA because they are bona fide executive, administrative, or professional employees (including computer-related professionals paid on a salary basis) or outside sales employees (see Section 2.4-1), employers need not keep records related to such employees' regular rate of pay, hours worked, straight-time earnings and overtime pay, and deductions from wages. However, employers must include in their records the basis on which wages are paid so each employee's total earnings for each pay period can be calculated. Similar rules govern other employees who are exempt from the FLSA's overtime pay requirements.

**Hospital employees.**[7] In addition to other required records, hospitals and residential care facilities whose employees have a work period of 14 consecutive days (rather than 7 for other employees) must keep records of the time and day on which the 14-day period begins, hours worked each day and each 14-day period, and straight-time and overtime premium earnings paid in each 14-day period. They also must keep a copy of the written agreement between the hospital and the employee allowing use of the 14-day work period or a memorandum summarizing its terms if the agreement is oral (see Section 2.6-1).

**Tipped employees.**[8] Employers using the tip credit to pay a certain portion of a tipped employee's minimum wage (see Section 2.5-1) must keep, in addition to other required records, the following:

- some notation on the records showing the employee's wages are determined partly by tips;
- the amount reported by the employee to the employer as tips (weekly or monthly), which may be taken from IRS Form 4070, *Employee's Report of Tips to Employer* (see Section 3.4-27 and Appendix page A-348);
- the amount of the tip credit taken by the employer;
- hours worked and straight-time earnings for time worked other than as a tipped employee; and
- hours worked and straight-time earnings for time worked as a tipped employee.

**Industrial homeworkers.**[9] In addition to other required records, employers using industrial homeworkers (employees who produce goods for the employer in their homes) must keep the following records:

- for each batch of work, the date the work was given out or started, the amount of work given out, the date the work was turned in, the amount of work turned in, the articles worked on and the work done, piece rates paid, hours worked, and wages paid;

---

5.     29 CFR §516.6(a)(2).
6.     29 CFR §516.3.
7.     29 CFR §516.23.
8.     29 CFR §516.28.
9.     29 CFR §516.31.

- the name and address of any agent, distributor, or contractor of the employer that gives work to homeworkers; and
- the name and address of each homeworker.

**Employees receiving remedial education.**[10] Where employees are exempt from overtime pay requirements for time spent receiving remedial education (see Section 2.7-6), the employer must keep, in addition to other required records, records of the hours spent by each employee receiving such remedial education and the wages paid for those hours.

**Employees receiving subminimum wages under a DOL certificate.**[11] The FLSA allows employers to obtain a certificate from DOL's Wage and Hour Division to pay learners, student-learners, messengers and apprentices less than the generally applicable minimum hourly wage if certain conditions are met. In addition to the records required to be kept for all nonexempt employees, the employer must keep certain additional records for 3 years after the last employment under a subminimum wage program, including a copy of its application and the certificate from DOL. Each worker employed under a subminimum wage certificate must be identified as such on the employer's payroll records, with each employee's occupation and rate of pay being shown.

When a learner is hired, the employer must obtain a statement signed by the employee showing the learner's experience (or lack thereof) in the employer's industry during the prior 3 years, including any vocational training. The employer must also keep all records pertaining to the filing or cancellation of job orders placed with the local state or territorial Public Employment Service Office for occupations to be performed by learners. Employers also must keep copies of any apprenticeship program and apprenticeship agreement under which an apprentice is employed. For student-learners, notations should be made in the employer's records when additional hours are worked because school is not in session.

**Form of records and availability for inspection.**[12] There is no requirement in either the FLSA or its regulations that employers keep records in any particular form. It is only necessary that they be accurate, complete, and able to be understood. Employers may store their records on microfilm or microfiche, but they must have viewing equipment available and provide transcriptions when asked to do so. Records may also be created and stored electronically.

The records required by the FLSA must be available for inspection by the Wage and Hour Division and kept "safe and accessible" by the employer either at the worksite or at a central location where its records are customarily maintained. If the records are maintained at a central location, they must be made available within 72 hours of a notice of inspection from the Division.

**Penalties for recordkeeping violations.**[13] Willful violations of the recordkeeping requirements can bring a criminal penalty of up to $10,000 and/or imprisonment for up to 6 months, although a jail sentence can be imposed only for second and subsequent convictions.

 **POOR RECORDKEEPING HAS OTHER COSTS** In addition to the statutory penalties for recordkeeping violations, employers can suffer other severe financial losses as well. If an employee (or a group of employees) files suit claiming an employer failed to pay the required minimum wage and/or overtime pay and the employer has incomplete records, the court will most likely accept the employee's evidence of hours worked and wages received. (See also Section 2.7-3 on recordkeeping related to employees' travel time.)

**Government contractors.** Recordkeeping requirements similar to those in the FLSA exist under laws regulating federal government contractors (see Section 2.10).[14] Separate logs of occupational injuries and illnesses must be kept and preserved for 5 years under the Walsh-Healey Public Contracts Act.[15]

---

10. 29 CFR §516.34.
11. 29 CFR §520.203; §520.412; §520.508.
12. 29 CFR §516.1(a); 29 CFR §516.7.
13. FLSA §15(a)(5); §16(a); 29 USC §215(a)(5); §216(a).
14. 41 CFR §50-201.501 (Walsh-Healey Public Contracts Act); 29 CFR §3.4(b) (Copeland Anti-Kickback Act); 29 CFR §4.6(g)(1); 29 CFR §4.185 (McNamara-O'Hara Service Contract Act).
15. 41 CFR §50-201.502; 29 CFR §1904.2 - §1904.6.

# 10.2 Internal Revenue Code

The Internal Revenue Code requires all employers that must withhold and pay over federal income, social security, and Medicare taxes to maintain the following records for each employee:[16]

- the employee's name, address, occupation, and social security number;
- the total amount and date of each payment of compensation made to the employee (including reported tips and the fair market value of noncash payments) and any amount withheld for taxes or otherwise;
- the amount of compensation subject to withholding for federal income, social security, and Medicare taxes, and the amount withheld for each tax (also the date withheld if withholding occurred on a different day than payment);
- the pay period covered by each payment of compensation;
- the reason why the total compensation and the taxable amount for each tax is different, if that is the case;
- the employee's Form W-4, *Employee's Withholding Allowance Certificate* (see Section 6.3-1) and Form W-5, *Earned Income Credit Advance Payment Certificate* (see Section 6.6);
- beginning and ending dates of the employee's employment;
- statements provided by the employee reporting tips received;
- information regarding wage continuation payments made to the employee by an employer or third party under an accident or health plan, including the beginning and ending dates of the period of absence from work and the amount and weekly rate of each payment (including payments made by third parties), as well as copies of Forms W-4S, *Request for Federal Income Tax Withholding From Sick Pay*;
- fringe benefits provided to the employee and any required substantiation;
- requests from an employee to use the cumulative method of wage withholding;
- adjustments or settlements of taxes;
- copies of returns filed (on paper or electronically), including Forms 941, 943, 944, 945, W-3, and Copy D of Form W-2 (also Forms W-2 sent to employees and returned as undeliverable);
- amounts and dates of tax deposits made;
- the employer's EIN;
- amounts and date of annuity and pension payments, along with copies of Forms W-4P, *Withholding Certificate for Pension or Annuity Payments* (see Section 6.3-2).

**Retention period.**[17] These records must be kept by the employer for at least four years after the due date of the tax (or the date the tax is actually paid, if later) for the return period to which the records relate. Information related to taxes paid by employees must be retained by the employer for at least four years after the due date of the employee's personal tax return (generally the following April 15). If an employer files a claim for refund, credit, or abatement of withheld income and employment taxes, records related to the claim must be retained for at least four years after the filing date of the claim.

**Records of allocated tips.**[18] Employers must keep records substantiating any information returns and employer statements to employees regarding tip allocations for at least three years after the due date of the return or statement to which they relate.

**Benefit plans.** Employers with a health insurance, cafeteria, educational assistance, adoption assistance, or dependent care assistance plan providing benefits that are excluded from income must keep whatever records are needed to determine whether the plan meets the requirements for excluding the benefit amounts from income.[19]

**FUTA tax records.**[20] Employers subject to the Federal Unemployment Tax Act (FUTA) must keep records to substantiate the following for at least four years after the due date of Form 940, *Employer's Annual Federal Unemployment (FUTA) Tax Return*, or the date the required FUTA tax was paid, whichever is later:

---

16.    IRS Reg. §31.6001-2; §31.6001-5; IRS Pub. 15, Circular E, Employer's Tax Guide.
17.    IRS Reg. §31.6001-1(e)(2).
18.    IRS Reg. §31.6053-3(l).
19.    IRC §6039D(b).
20.    IRS Reg. §31.6001-4(a).

- the total amount of employee compensation paid during the calendar year;
- the amount of compensation subject to FUTA tax;
- state unemployment contributions made, with separate totals for amounts withheld and not withheld from employees' wages;
- all information shown on Form 940; and
- the reason why total compensation and the taxable amount are different, if that is the case.

**Records processed by computer.** The IRS has set up specific procedures for preserving records contained in an automatic data processing (ADP) system, which is any system that processes records other than manually, including microcomputer systems, mainframes, electronic storage systems, Data Base Management Systems (DBMS) and all systems using Electronic Data Interchange (EDI) technology.[21] Employers are not relieved of their recordkeeping responsibilities because they use a service provider to process their payroll (see Section 12).

The IRS procedures apply to all employers with at least $10 million in assets, as well as to smaller businesses where the following conditions exist:

- information is available only in machine-sensible records, not in hardcopy format;
- computations based on the machine-sensible records cannot be checked or redone without a computer; or
- the IRS has notified the employer that its machine-sensible records must be preserved.

*General requirements.* The procedures themselves are generally aimed at achieving one goal—making it easy for the IRS to determine the employer's correct tax liability. To that end, they require that all detail and source documents be readily identifiable. All machine-sensible records that the employer is required to retain must be made available to the Service upon request and must be capable of being processed. The IRS requires that machine-sensible records be kept so long as their contents may become material to the administration of the tax laws as they relate to the employer, which is at least until the expiration of the statute of limitations for assessment, including any extensions. The records meet the requirement of allowing the Service to determine the employer's correct tax liability if they reconcile with the employer's books and returns. This reconciliation can be established through an audit trail showing the relationship between the total of the amounts in the employer's records by account and account totals in the employer's books and returns.

*Documentation.* The employer must keep and make available to the IRS documentation of the business processes that:

- create the retained records;
- modify and maintain its records;
- support and verify entries made on the employer's return and determine the correct tax liability; and
- show the authenticity and integrity of the taxpayer's records.

The documentation the employer must maintain must be sufficiently detailed to identify:

- the functions being performed as they related to the flow of data through the system;
- the internal controls used to ensure accurate and reliable processing;
- the internal controls used to prevent the unauthorized addition, alteration, or deletion of retained records; and
- the charts of accounts and detailed account descriptions.

For each file that is retained, the employer must maintain and make available to the IRS upon request documentation of:

---

21.     Rev. Proc. 98-25, 1998-1 CB 689; Rev. Rul. 71-20, 1971-1 CB 392.

- record formats or layouts;
- field definitions (including the meaning of all codes used to represent information);
- file descriptions
- evidence that periodic checks of the retained records were performed to meet certain records management standards, which will allow the employer to mitigate penalties for data losses; and
- evidence that the retained records reconcile to the employer's books and tax returns.

*DBMS.* An employer has the option to create files solely for the use of the IRS. An employer that chooses to do this and uses a DBMS can meet these recordkeeping requirements by creating and retaining a sequential file that contains the transaction-level detail from the DBMS and that meets the other requirements. An employer that creates such a file must document the process that created the file in order to establish the relationship between the created file and the original DBMS records.

*EDI.* An employer that uses EDI technology must retain machine-sensible records that, in combination with any other records (e.g., the underlying contracts, price lists, and price changes), contain all of the detailed information required by section 6001 of the Code. The extent of the detail in the retained electronic and other records, if any, must be equivalent to the level of detail contained in an acceptable paper record. The employer may capture this information at any level within the accounting system provided the audit trail, authenticity, and integrity of the retained records can be established.

*Resources for examination.* At the time of an audit, the employer must provide the IRS with the resources (e.g., hardware, software, terminal access, computer time, personnel, etc.) needed to process the employer's machine-sensible books and records. The employer's system must not be subject to any agreement that would limit or restrict the Service's access to and use of the system on the employer's premises (or wherever the system is maintained), including personnel, hardware, software, files, indexes, and software documentation. The District Director has the discretion, at the employer's request, to:

- identify which of the employer's resources are not necessary to process books and records;
- allow the employer to convert its records to a different medium;
- allow the employer to meet the Service's processing needs during off- peak hours; and
- allow the employer to provide the IRS with third-party equipment.

*Maintenance of machine-sensible records.* While the Revenue Procedure makes it clear that the implementation of records management practices is a business decision within the employer's discretion, it does recommend such records management practices as labeling of records, providing a secure storage environment, creating back-up copies, selecting an offsite storage location, and testing to confirm records integrity. The Revenue Procedure also notes the National Archives and Record Administration's Standards for the Creation, Use, Preservation and Disposition of Electronic Records as an example of a records management resource for employers.

The NARA standard requires an annual sampling of magnetic computer tape reels to identify lost data and to identify and correct the reasons for the loss. In libraries with 1,800 or fewer storage units (e.g., magnetic tape reels), a 20% random sample or a sample size of 50 units, whichever is larger, should be read. In libraries with more than 1,800 units, a sample of 384 units should be read. While this sampling standard is specifically for magnetic computer tape, the IRS recommends that all retained machine-sensible records be sampled and tested as described in the standard.

*Notification of data loss.* Employers must notify their District Director if any machine-sensible records are lost, stolen, destroyed, damaged, or otherwise no longer capable of being processed, or are found to be incomplete or materially inaccurate. The notice must identify the affected records and include a plan demonstrating how the employer proposes to replace or restore the records so they will be capable of being processed, how long it will take to do that, and how the recordkeeping requirements will continue to be met with regard to the affected records. An employer that suffers a partial loss of data from one storage unit will not be subject to penalties if the employer can show that its data maintenance practices conform with the NARA sampling standard.

*Records evaluation and testing.* The District Director may conduct a records evaluation whenever it deems it appropriate to review the employer's record retention practices, and must inform the employer of the results of the evaluation. The District Director may also periodically initiate tests to establish the authenticity, readability, completeness, and integrity of an employer's machine-sensible records, including a review of integrated systems such as EDI or an electronic storage system and the employer's internal controls and security procedures. The employer will be told the results of the tests.

*Record Retention Limitation Agreement.* An employer may limit the records it has to retain by asking to enter into a Record Retention Limitation Agreement with its District Director. The employer's request must identify the records it proposes not to maintain and explain why they will not become material to the administration of the tax law. It's up to the District Director whether to enter into an RRLA. In an RRLA, the District Director may waive any of the specific requirements in Rev. Proc. 98-25, and the employer remains subject to all requirements that are not waived. Subsequently added systems are not subject to the RRLA, and the same is true for later-acquired subsidiaries that are not already subject to their own RRLA.

*Penalties for noncompliance.* The District Director may issue a Notice of Inadequate Records if the employer fails to comply with the requirements regarding machine-sensible records. The employer may also be subject to other applicable penalties, including the accuracy-related civil penalty and willful failure criminal penalty.

**Electronic storage systems**. The IRS allows taxpayers to use electronic storage systems to maintain books and records, provided they comply with certain requirements.[22] An electronic storage system is a system used to prepare, record, transfer, index, store, preserve, retrieve, and reproduce books and records, by either electronically imaging hardcopy documents or transferring computerized books and records to an electronic storage media.

*Requirements of the system.* An electronic storage system must create an accurate and complete transfer of the hardcopy documents or the computerized books and records to an electronic storage media, and must index, store, preserve, retrieve, and reproduce the electronically stored books and records. The system must include:

- reasonable controls to ensure the integrity, accuracy, and reliability of the system;
- reasonable controls to prevent and detect the unauthorized creation of, addition to, alteration of, deletion of, or deterioration of electronically stored books and records;
- an inspection and quality assurance program that provides regular evaluations of the system;
- a retrieval system that includes an indexing system; and
- the ability to reproduce a legible and readable hardcopy.

Written procedures that describe in detail the complete electronic storage system must be maintained and should be available to the IRS on request. The system must provide support for the employer's books and records and must be cross-referenced. All books and records produced by the system must exhibit a high degree of legibility and readability when displayed on a video display terminal or on paper.

Electronic books and records must be retained until no longer material to the administration of the tax laws. At the time of an IRS audit, the employer must be able to retrieve and reproduce electronically stored books and records (including hardcopies if requested) and provide the IRS with the resources necessary for promptly locating, retrieving, reading, and reproducing on paper any electronically stored books and records. An IRS district director may periodically test an employer's electronic storage system, which may include evaluation and use of equipment and software and the employer's procedures.

*Destruction of hardcopy documents.* Hardcopy documents and original computerized records can be destroyed after the taxpayer has completed its own testing of the system which establishes compliance with IRS requirements and instituted procedures to ensure continued compliance.

---

22.    Rev. Proc. 97-22, 1997-1 CB 652.

*Penalties for noncompliance.* The district director may issue a Notice of Inadequate Records if the employer's electronic storage system fails to meet the requirements of the revenue procedure. In addition, failure to meet the requirements may also subject the employer to applicable penalties including the accuracy-related civil penalty and the willful failure criminal penalty. These penalties may not apply if the employer maintains its original books and records separate from the electronic storage system or maintains books and records in compliance with the computerized records requirements discussed earlier. Employers who use a service bureau or time-sharing service with an electronic storage system for their books and records are not relieved of the responsibilities outlined in the revenue procedure.

**Penalties for faulty recordkeeping.** The willful failure to comply with the recordkeeping requirements under the IRC is a misdemeanor punishable by a fine of up to $25,000 ($100,000 for corporations) and/or imprisonment for up to 1 year, plus the costs of prosecution.

 **PROBLEMS CAN BE COMPOUNDED** A penalty for failure to properly keep records may be the least of an employer's problems, since an audit that uncovers poor recordkeeping will also most likely lead to penalties for underwithheld and underpaid taxes, late filing of statements and returns, and other violations. These can add up to considerably more than the cost of a recordkeeping violation.

## 10.3 Federal Anti-Discrimination Laws

Various federal laws that prohibit discrimination by employers in hiring, firing, disciplining, compensating, or making other decisions involving employees also have their own recordkeeping requirements payroll practitioners should be aware of, even though such records may be the responsibility of their companies' human resource departments. With the increasing popularity of integrated data bases and shared responsibilities, the responsibility for gathering and maintaining such records may well fall to the payroll department.

## 10.3-1 Civil Rights Act of 1964 (Title VII)

Title VII of the Civil Rights Act of 1964 prohibits employers from discriminating against employees on the basis of race, color, religion, sex, or national origin.[23] There are no general recordkeeping requirements under the law or regulations issued by the Equal Employment Opportunity Commission. However, in order to accurately complete reports required each year by the EEOC, employers must make and keep employment records regarding hiring, promotion, demotion, transfer, layoff or termination, rates of pay, and selection for training or apprenticeship.[24]

The records must be kept for at least one year from the date they were made or the date of the personnel action to which they relate, whichever is later. If a charge of discrimination has been filed with the EEOC, or the EEOC or U.S. Attorney General has sued on the individual's behalf, any relevant records must be preserved until the final disposition of the charge or suit. State and local government employers must keep such records for two years or until the disposition of any charge or suit (three years for records used to complete EEOC report forms).[25]

**Rules apply to ADA also.** The recordkeeping requirements under Title VII are also applicable to employers covered by the Americans with Disabilities Act of 1990, which is administered and enforced by the EEOC.[26]

---

23. 42 USC §2000e-1 - §2000e-17.
24. 29 CFR §1602.12 - §1602.14.
25. 29 CFR §1602.30 - §1602.31; §1602.39 - §1602.40; §1602.48 - §1602.49.
26. 29 CFR §1602.14.

## 10.3-2  Age Discrimination in Employment Act of 1967 (ADEA)

The Age Discrimination in Employment Act of 1967 prohibits employers from making hiring, termination, or other personnel decisions based on the age of individuals who are at least 40 years of age.[27]  The ADEA contains several recordkeeping and retention provisions.

**Records retained for three years.**[28]  The following records must be made by the employer for each employee and preserved for at least three years:  name, address, date of birth, occupation, pay rate, and compensation earned each week.

**Records retained for one year.**[29]  If an employer makes or obtains the following records, it must keep them for at least one year from the date of the personnel action to which they relate:  job applications, resumes, or other responses to advertised job openings; records related to the failure to hire an individual or to the promotion, demotion, transfer, selection for training, layoff, recall, or discharge of an employee; job orders submitted to employment agencies or unions; employer-administered tests or physical exams used in making personnel decisions; and job advertisements.  Copies of an employer's benefit plans or seniority systems must be kept for at least one year after they are no longer in effect.  If the employer is charged with age bias under the ADEA, the records that relate to the challenged personnel action must be preserved until the final disposition of the charge.

 **NO DUPLICATION REQUIRED**  If the records required by the ADEA are already kept by the employer for other purposes or can be extracted from information recorded in another form, no duplication of records is needed for the purposes of the ADEA.[30]

**Availability for inspection.**  As with other employer records, records required by the ADEA must be kept at the employee's worksite or a central recordkeeping location.  They also must be made available for inspection by the EEOC.  The employer has up to 72 hours to provide the records if they are kept at a central recordkeeping location.[31]

## 10.3-3  Government Contractor Regulations

Federal government contractors and subcontractors are subject to more comprehensive recordkeeping requirements than other employers.  They must retain information on applicants and employees that will allow the Department of Labor's Office of Federal Contract Compliance Programs to determine whether affirmative action goals for the hiring and promotion of minorities, veterans, and the disabled have been met.

## 10.3-4  Immigration Reform and Control Act (IRCA)

Employers must retain the completed Form I-9, *Employment Eligibility Verification* (see Section 1.8 and Appendix page A-34), for at least three years after the date of hire or one year after the date of termination, whichever is later.

> ***Example 1:***  Employee Kristen was hired by Whittler's Wood Products Corp. on January 24, 2003.  She remained employed by Whittler's until she resigned and left the company on August 20, 2008.  Whittler's must keep Kristen's Form I-9 until at least August 20, 2009, one year after her last day of employment.

---

27.    29 USC §621 - §634.
28.    29 CFR §1627.3(a).
29.    29 CFR §1627.3(b).
30.    29 CFR §1627.2.
31.    29 CFR §1627.6; §1627.7.

*Example 2:* Assume the same facts as in Example 1, except that Kristen leaves Whittler's on June 23, 2004. In this situation, Whittler's must keep Kristen's I-9 form until at least January 24, 2006, 3 years after her date of hire.

The form must be made available for inspection by the Department of Labor within three days of a request. The forms may be made available on microfilm or microfiche if they are clear and readable and viewing and printing equipment is made available to the inspector.[32] The forms may also be stored electronically[33] (for details on electronic creation and storage of Forms I-9, see Section 1.8). To facilitate Form I-9 inspections, employers should consider an electronic storage system that includes an indexing system and the ability to reproduce legible and readable hard copies of electronically stored Forms I-9. The employer should also keep any copies it has made of documents provided by employees to support their right to work in the U.S., although there is no requirement to do so.

# 10.3-5 Family and Medical Leave Act (FMLA)

The Family and Medical Leave Act of 1993 generally requires employers with 50 or more employees to grant employees up to 12 weeks of unpaid leave to care for a newborn or newly adopted child or for themselves or a parent, child, or spouse who has a serious illness (see Section 4.2).[34] Employers are required to make, keep, and retain records relating to their FMLA obligations in accordance with the recordkeeping requirements under the Fair Labor Standards Act (see Section 10.1).[35]

Records required to be kept under the FMLA for each employee include the following:[36]

- basic payroll and identifying employee data, including name, address, occupation, rate or basis of pay and terms of compensation, daily and weekly hours worked per pay period, additions to and deductions from wages, and total compensation paid;
- dates of FMLA leave taken by employee (leave must be designated as FMLA leave in the records);
- hours of the FMLA leave, if it is taken in increments of less than one workday;
- copies of written notices of intention to take FMLA leave provided by the employee;
- copies of all general and specific notices given to employees as required under the FMLA;
- any documents (written and electronic) describing employee benefits or employer policies and practices regarding the taking of paid and unpaid leave;
- premium payments for employee benefits; and
- records of any dispute between the employer and employee over the designation of leave as FMLA leave.

**Exception for exempt employees.**[37] For employees who are exempt from FLSA recordkeeping regulations regarding minimum wage or overtime compliance (e.g., white collar employees), the employer does not have to keep a record of hours worked if:

- FMLA leave eligibility is presumed for any exempt employee who has worked for the employer for at least 12 months; and
- the employer and employee agree in writing to the employee's normal work schedule if intermittent FMLA leave is to be taken.

**Medical records to be confidential.**[38] Any documents relating to medical certifications, recertifications, or medical histories of an employee or a member of the employee's family that are created for purposes

---

32.   IRCA Reg. 8 CFR §274a2(b)(2).
33.   Pub. Law No. 108-390.
34.   29 U.S.C. §2602 - §2654.
35.   29 U.S.C. §2616(b).
36.   FMLA Reg. 29 CFR §825.500(c).
37.   FMLA Reg. 29 CFR §825.110(c); §825.500(f).
38.   FMLA Reg. 29 CFR §825.500(g).

of the FMLA must be kept in files separate from general personnel files and treated as confidential medical records. These rules do not apply in the following situations:

- an employee's supervisor may be informed regarding necessary restrictions on the work an employee can perform and any accommodations that are needed;
- first aid and safety personnel may be told whether an employee's physical or medical condition might require emergency treatment; and
- relevant information must be provided on request to federal government officials investigating FMLA compliance.

**Covered employers with no eligible employees.**[39] Employers that are covered by the FMLA but have no employees who are eligible for FMLA leave (e.g., the employer has more than 50 employees total but does not have 50 or more of them working within 75 miles of each other) need only keep the basic payroll and identifying employee data discussed earlier.

**Limit on record inspections.**[40] The FMLA prohibits the Department of Labor from requiring an employer to submit books or records for inspection more than once during any 12-month period unless the DOL is investigating a complaint or has reasonable cause to believe an FMLA violation exists. Employers need not submit any FMLA records to the DOL without a specific request from a Department official.

**Record format is flexible.**[41] As under the Federal Wage-Hour Law, an employer's FMLA records need not be kept in any particular order or form. Also, employers are not required to "revise their computerized payroll or personnel records systems to comply" with the recordkeeping requirements. The records must be kept for at least three years. The records may be kept on microfilm or on an automatic data processing system if adequate projection or viewing equipment and clear reproductions are available. Records kept in computer form must be made available for transcription or copying.

# 10.4 State Unemployment Insurance Laws

In addition to the federal recordkeeping requirements, each state's unemployment insurance law requires that certain payroll and employment records be made and preserved by employers for each employee for a certain number of years. The records also must be available for inspection and copying by the state employment security agency. While the exact records required in each state differ to some extent, the following records are generally required:

- name
- social security number
- dates of hire, separation, rehire, reinstatement after temporary layoff
- amounts of compensation paid (cash and noncash) in each payroll period
- payroll period beginning and ending dates
- paydays
- date and reason for termination of employment
- time lost during a payroll period because the employee was unavailable for work

There is little consistency among the state unemployment insurance laws regarding the time period for preserving required records. Table 10.1 shows the minimum retention period for each state. Employers in states where the retention period is less than that required under FUTA (4 years) should nevertheless retain the required records for at least 4 years. Also, in many states the retention period begins at the end of the current calendar year. [For more information on state unemployment insurance recordkeeping requirements, see Table 8.5 of *APA's Guide to State Payroll Laws*.]

---

39.    FMLA Reg. 29 CFR §825.500(d).
40.    29 U.S.C. §2616(c); FMLA Reg. 29 CFR §825.500(a).
41.    FMLA Reg. 29 CFR §825.500(b).

Table 10.1

| STATE UNEMPLOYMENT INSURANCE RECORD RETENTION REQUIREMENTS | | | |
|---|---|---|---|
| **State** | **Minimum Retention Period (in Years)** | **State** | **Minimum Retention Period (in Years)** |
| Alabama | 5 | Montana | 5 |
| Alaska | 5 | Nebraska | 4 |
| Arizona | 4 | Nevada | 4 |
| Arkansas | 5 | New Hampshire | 6 |
| California | 4 | New Jersey | 5 |
| Colorado | 5 | New Mexico | 4 |
| Connecticut | 4 | New York | 3 |
| Delaware | 4 | North Carolina | 6 |
| Dist. of Col. | 5 | North Dakota | 5 |
| Florida | 5 | Ohio | 5 |
| Georgia | 4 | Oklahoma | 4 |
| Hawaii | 5 | Oregon | 3 |
| Idaho | 3 | Pennsylvania | 4 |
| Illinois | 5 | Puerto Rico | 5 |
| Indiana | 5 | Rhode Island | 4 |
| Iowa | 5 | South Carolina | 5 |
| Kansas | 5 | South Dakota | 4 |
| Kentucky | 6 | Tennessee | 7 |
| Louisiana | 5 | Texas | 4 |
| Maine | 4 | Utah | 3 |
| Maryland | 5 | Vermont | 6 |
| Massachusetts | 4 | Virginia | 4 |
| Michigan | 6 | Washington | 4 |
| Minnesota | 8 | West Virginia | 4 |
| Mississippi | 5 | Wisconsin | 6 |
| Missouri | 3 | Wyoming | 4 |

**Microfilm and electronic storage may be used.** The state unemployment insurance laws do not require that records be kept in any particular form. They all allow employers the option of preserving records on microfilm, so long as full-size printed copies can be made, and nearly all allow records to be kept on magnetic tape or electronically.

# 10.5 State Wage-Hour Laws

Most state wage-hour laws have recordkeeping requirements similar to those under the Fair Labor Standards Act (see Section 10.1). In general, the state wage-hour laws require that the following information be preserved for each nonexempt employee:

- name
- address
- position
- hours worked each day and week
- amount of compensation paid each pay period
- rate of pay
- age (if the employee is a minor)

The minimum retention period for these records differs from state to state (with 3 years being the most popular), while some states have no recordkeeping requirements at all. Table 10.2 shows the minimum retention periods for each state. (The entry "No provision" indicates the state either has no law requiring the maintenance of wage-hour records or has no specific retention period for the records it requires.) [For more information on state wage-hour recordkeeping requirements, see Table 1.5 of *APA's Guide to State Payroll Laws*.]

Table 10.2

| STATE WAGE-HOUR RECORD RETENTION REQUIREMENTS | | | |
|---|---|---|---|
| State | Minimum Retention Period (in Years) | State | Minimum Retention Period (in Years) |
| Alabama | No general provision | Montana | No provision |
| Alaska | 3 | Nebraska | No provision |
| Arizona | 4 | Nevada | 2 |
| Arkansas | 3 | New Hampshire | No specific period |
| California | 2 | New Jersey | 6 |
| Colorado | 2 | New Mexico | 1 |
| Connecticut | 3 | New York | 6 |
| Delaware | 3 | North Carolina | No provision |
| Dist. of Col. | 3 | North Dakota | No provision |
| Florida | No general provision | Ohio | 3 |
| Georgia | No provision | Oklahoma | No provision |
| Hawaii | No general provision | Oregon | 2 |
| Idaho | 3 | Pennsylvania | 3 |
| Illinois | 3 | Puerto Rico | No provision |
| Indiana | No provision | Rhode Island | 3 |
| Iowa | No general provision | South Carolina | 3 |
| Kansas | 3 | South Dakota | Reasonable period |
| Kentucky | 1 | Tennessee | No provision |
| Louisiana | 1 | Texas | No provision |
| Maine | 3 | Utah | 3 |
| Maryland | 3 | Vermont | 2 |
| Massachusetts | 2 | Virginia | No general provision |
| Michigan | 3 | Washington | 3 |
| Minnesota | 3 | West Virginia | 2 |
| Mississippi | No provision | Wisconsin | 3 |
| Missouri | 3 | Wyoming | 2 |

**Child support withholding, creditor garnishments, etc.** The federal and state laws that govern child support withholding orders, creditor garnishments, and other wage attachments generally do not contain specific recordkeeping and retention requirements. However, employers should preserve any records gathered or made in relation to such matters (e.g., court or agency orders, the employer's answers to requests for information) for at least three years after the last withholding from the employee's wages. This will satisfy federal and state wage-hour law record retention requirements.

If the employer becomes involved in a legal action over the withholding order other than the issuance of the order itself (e.g., a suit by the employee demanding return of the withheld wages), the employer should preserve all related records until the final disposition of the action, including any possible appeals. If the order to withhold comes from the IRS in the form of a federal tax levy, the employer should keep any related records (e.g., Forms 668-W, 668-D—see Section 9.1-1) for at least four years from the last withholding or until any related legal action is concluded.

# 10.6  Unclaimed Wages

Wages not claimed by employees (e.g., uncashed paychecks) must eventually be turned over to state treasuries under each state's abandoned property (escheat) laws. The time periods determining when such unclaimed wages are considered abandoned were discussed in Section 5.5. When wages are abandoned, employers must make a report to the state and remit the abandoned amounts. They must also generally keep a record of the employee's name and last known address for a specific period of time after the wages become reportable. Table 10.3 contains the minimum retention period for such data (not the wages themselves) under each state's escheat law. [For more information on state unclaimed wages recordkeeping requirements, see Table 2.6 of *APA's Guide to State Payroll Laws*.]

Table 10.3

| STATE ABANDONED WAGES RECORD RETENTION CHART | | | |
|---|---|---|---|
| State | Minimum Retention Period (in Years) | State | Minimum Retention Period (in Years) |
| Alabama | No provision | Montana | 10 |
| Alaska | 7 | Nebraska | 7 |
| Arizona | 5 | Nevada | 7 |
| Arkansas | 10 | New Hampshire | 10 |
| California | 7 | New Jersey | 5 |
| Colorado | 5 | New Mexico | 10 |
| Connecticut | 10 | New York | 5 (after Dec. 31 of year report is filed) |
| Delaware | No provision | North Carolina | 10 |
| Dist. of Col. | 10 | North Dakota | 10 |
| Florida | 5 | Ohio | 5 |
| Georgia | 10 | Oklahoma | 10 |
| Hawaii | 5 | Oregon | 3 |
| Idaho | 7 | Pennsylvania | No provision |
| Illinois | 5 | Rhode Island | 7 |
| Indiana | 10 | South Carolina | 10 |

| STATE ABANDONED WAGES RECORD RETENTION CHART | | | |
|---|---|---|---|
| State | Minimum Retention Period (in Years) | State | Minimum Retention Period (in Years) |
| Iowa | 4 | South Dakota | 10 |
| Kansas | 10 | Tennessee | 10 |
| Kentucky | 5 | Texas | 10 |
| Louisiana | 10 | Utah | 5 |
| Maine | 10 | Vermont | No provision |
| Maryland | 10 | Virginia | 5 |
| Massachusetts | 5 | Washington | 6 |
| Michigan | 10 | West Virginia | 10 |
| Minnesota | No provision | Wisconsin | 5 |
| Mississippi | No provision | Wyoming | 5 |
| Missouri | 5 | | |

## 10.7  Direct Deposit Considerations

Before an employer can begin direct deposit of an employee's wages into the employee's checking and/or savings accounts, it must receive a direct deposit authorization from the employee (see Section 5.3-2). Until 1994, NACHA—the Electronic Payments Association required that the authorization be retained by the employer for at least two years after the employee discontinues direct deposit. In 1994, this requirement was eliminated when the rules were changed to allow nonwritten authorizations.

## 10.8  Record Retention Procedures

Knowing and understanding what records must be accumulated and preserved under the various federal and state payroll-related laws is just the first step in the recordkeeping and retention process. The sheer volume of material that must be created and retained makes it imperative that employers have a coordinated system of data entry, retention, retrieval, and destruction.

## 10.8-1  Employee Master File

To comply with the varying federal and state recordkeeping requirements, employers should create a master file of employee data that meets the most stringent of those requirements. In general, if federal requirements are met, state requirements will be met as well. Table 10.4 suggests the types of data that should be included in the master file for each employee.

Table 10.4

| EMPLOYEE MASTER FILE DATA | |
|---|---|
| **Employee Data**<br>• Name (match with social security card)<br>• Address (with Zip code and apartment number)<br>• Sex<br>• Date of birth<br>• Work location | • Social security number<br>• Company-assigned employee number (if not SSN)<br>• Occupation/classification<br>• State where employee works |
| **Employment/Wage-Hour Data**<br>• Hire date/time<br>• Termination date<br>• Payment date<br>• Exempt/nonexempt status (FLSA)<br>• Hourly rate of pay<br>• Additions to and deductions from pay<br>• Shift differential or bonus | • Frequency of payment/pay period<br>• Hours worked per day<br>• Hours worked per week<br>• Workweek<br>• Straight time hours/pay<br>• Overtime hours/pay |
| **Tax and Payroll Data**<br>• Allowances claimed (federal/state/local)<br>• Additional withholding requested | • Filing status<br>• Exempt from withholding |
| **For Payroll Period and Calendar Year**<br>• Total wages subject to federal/ state/local income taxes<br>• Total social security tax withheld<br>• Total Medicare tax withheld<br>• Total wages subject to Medicare tax<br>• Total compensation | • Total federal/state/local income taxes withheld<br>• Total wages subject to social security tax<br>• Total state unemployment and/or disability taxes withheld<br>• Taxes paid by employer but not deducted from wages |

 **NOT ALL DATA WILL BE NEEDED** Not every piece of information listed here will apply to all employees. For example, if an employee is exempt from the minimum wage and overtime pay requirements of the Fair Labor Standards Act, it is generally not necessary to record the employee's hours of work or hourly rate of pay. Also, if the employee works in a state where there is no state disability tax withheld, that entry need not be in the employee's file.

**Updating the file.** While there are no legal requirements as to how often employee information in a master file must be updated, it should be as up-to-date as possible. Current records provide employers with the best protection during audits or federal and state agency investigations.

**Combining files.** More and more, companies are placing all employee data into one master file that includes payroll, human resources, and benefits information. This allows greater access to necessary information, but also requires more reliable controls and security measures to protect the data and employees' privacy (see Section 12.5).

## 10.8-2 Documents Needed From New Employees

In addition to gathering information from new employees and setting them up in the master file, employers must also obtain certain documents from new employees and keep them on file for various lengths of time. They include:

- *Form W-4, Employee's Withholding Allowance Certificate*—must be retained for at least four years after the last date the information on it is used to prepare an employer's tax return.

- *State withholding allowance certificate*—if the state does not accept the federal Form W-4 or if the number of state withholding allowances is different than that on the Form W-4.

- *Local withholding allowance certificates or certificates of residence or nonresidence*—if required by the local jurisdiction where the work is performed or the employee resides.

- *Form I-9, Employment Eligibility Verification*—up to the payroll department if completing and retaining the form is not the responsibility of the human resource department; must be retained for three years after hire or one year after termination, whichever is longer.

## 10.8-3 Record Retention and Storage Methods

Because of the large volume of records, reports, etc., an employer must gather and retain (e.g., payroll records, tax returns, information statements), a space-saving method of storage is a necessity, especially for material retained beyond the legally required minimum. Many businesses retain records for much longer than the required minimum, often for as long as the company is in business.

One common example is employment tax returns (Form 941). Internal Revenue Service regulations require that a copy of such returns be kept for 4 years after the tax is due or paid, whichever is later.[42] On the other hand, the IRS has 3 years from the date the return is deemed to have been filed (the later of the actual filing date or the following April 15) to assess any taxes that remain due or any additions to tax or penalties.[43] It then has 10 years to collect those assessments, by levy or otherwise.[44] And the employer has 3 years after filing the return or 2 years after paying the tax (including any later assessments) to file a claim for refund.[45] Therefore, in some instances employer tax returns and the information used to support them (e.g., payroll registers, payroll tax deposits) may be needed up to 15 years later.

**Paper storage.** The various federal and state laws generally do not require that records be kept in any particular form and sometimes specifically allow record retention on microfilm or microfiche or electronically. Employers may wish to retain copies of paper records and returns for the legally required retention period because they are easier to read and copy should they be needed for a Department of Labor investigation or IRS audit.

If an employer is going to retain a large volume of paper records, it should consider storing them off premises, which would save space at the employer's facility. They also must be labeled accurately as to their content and whether they support any other documents (e.g., accounting ledgers, tax returns) so they can be retrieved and copied within the required time (usually 72 hours) for government investigators or auditors.

**Micromedia storage (microfilm or microfiche).** As mentioned earlier, payroll and employment records can be stored on microfilm or microfiche, which provides several advantages over paper storage, including reduced space needed for storage, reduced storage costs, less chance of losing individual documents, increased confidentiality, and increased durability. But there are also drawbacks to micromedia storage. The main problem is one of quality control—the camera may not photograph 100% of every document, the image may be partially unreadable, and verification of the image after it develops can be a time-consuming process.

When storing records on micromedia, employers must be sure to have viewing, printing, and copying equipment available during government records inspections. Special equipment is necessary because these photographic images cannot be directly interpreted by computer systems.

---

42.    IRS Reg. §31.6001-1(e)(2).
43.    IRC §6501(a), (b)(2); IRS Reg. §301.6501(a)-1; §301.6501(b)-1(b).
44.    IRC §6502(a); IRS Reg. §301.6502-1(a).
45.    IRC §6511(a); IRS Reg. §301.6511(a)-1(a).

**Media imaging.** Because of the quality control and computer linkup problems associated with micromedia record storage, many companies have turned to more advanced forms of media imaging. These provide
better quality and allow easier access to stored documents. Two of the more popular methods are optical
character recognition (OCR) capture and image capture. OCR uses scanning technology that converts the
shape of an image to a computer-readable code. Image capture allows a window of information on a document to be captured and stored on some form of magnetic media (e.g., CD-ROM) or electronically. This
method provides compact storage and the ability to print excellent quality documents on a laser printer.

**Electronic vaulting.** Employers often back up and store records at a secure site away from their premises so they are not affected if there is some type of disaster at the employer's premises. But how long would
it take the employer to make use of those records if its systems cannot be accessed? Protecting the data is
not enough. The ability to process and use the data quickly must also be maintained, and one way to do this
is through electronic vaulting.

Electronic vaulting involves the duplication – through shadowing or mirroring – of the employer's data
and processing applications by uploading changes through the Internet at a remote site either at the same
time as or shortly after the employer's system is updated. For more information on electronic vaulting as
part of a comprehensive business continuity plan, see Section 12.6.

**Retrieval and destruction of records.** Whatever method an employer uses to create and preserve its
employment and payroll records, it should have a policy governing record retention, retrieval, and destruction. The written policy should clearly state how long records are to be retained (and how the containers
should be labeled), how they can be retrieved (especially important if records are stored off site), and when
and how they should be disposed of. Such a policy, if it is consistently enforced, will allow the employer to
know what documents are being preserved and which have been disposed of at any given time. This knowledge can be especially important in the event of a disaster, so the employer can easily determine which
records were destroyed and what needs to be replaced.

Many employers that use some form of magnetic or electronic media to store their records (e.g., microfiche, diskette, CD-ROM) may figure that they do not need a record disposal policy because their records
take up much less space than records preserved on paper. But a consistently applied policy of retention and
disposal can be good protection in the event of a lawsuit, where the selective destruction of records might be
taken as proof that only documents damaging to the employer were destroyed.

**Method of record destruction must be "reasonable."** The Federal Trade Commission (FTC) issued
final regulations in 2004 on the proper disposal of consumer report information and records.[46] The regulations implement a requirement imposed by the Fair and Accurate Credit Transactions Act of 2003 (FACT
Act) that persons who possess or maintain, for a business purpose, "consumer information" derived from
"consumer reports" must "properly dispose" of it.[47]

Properly disposing of such information means taking "reasonable measures" (a flexible standard) to protect against unauthorized access to or use of the information in connection with its disposal. The regulations apply to any business, regardless of industry, that obtains a consumer report, or information derived
from a consumer report, for employment screening purposes.

*Consumer report and consumer information.* A consumer report is defined as "any written, oral, or other
communication of any information by a consumer reporting agency bearing on a person's credit worthiness,
credit standing, credit capacity, character, general reputation, personal characteristics, or mode of living
which is used or expected to be used or collected in whole or in part for the purpose of serving as a factor in
establishing the consumer's eligibility for ... employment purposes."

Consumer information is defined as any record about an individual, whether in paper, electronic, or other
form, that is a consumer report or is derived from a consumer report. Information that does not identify particular individuals is not covered by the definition.

---

46.   16 CFR §§682.1 – 682.5.
47.   P.L. No. 108-159.

*Reasonable measures for disposal.* Disposal of consumer information is defined to include discarding or abandoning the information, as well as selling, donating, or transferring any medium, including computer equipment, on which it is stored. The FTC explains that "reasonable measures" to protect against unauthorized access to or use of consumer information in connection with its disposal "are very likely to require" elements such as the establishment of policies and procedures governing disposal, as well as appropriate employee training. Note that both service providers and record owners are responsible for properly disposing of consumer information they possess or maintain.

Certain basic steps are likely to be appropriate for many employers. For example, shredding or burning paper records containing consumer information will generally be appropriate. If a business has stored consumer information on electronic media (e.g., computer discs or hard drives), disposal of such media could be accomplished by simply smashing the material with a hammer. In some cases, appropriate disposal of electronic media might also be accomplished by overwriting or "wiping" the data prior to disposal. Whether "wiping," as opposed to destruction, of electronic media is reasonable, as well as the adequacy of particular utilities to accomplish that "wiping," depends on the circumstances.

# 10.9   Health Insurance Portability and Accountability Act

The Health Insurance Portability and Accountability Act of 1996 (HIPAA) was principally designed to help employees and their families maintain health insurance coverage when the employees change or lose jobs. HIPAA's scope is much broader, however, and it includes provisions dealing with how employers, hospitals, physicians, and insurers handle confidential patient information.[48]

These provisions include a requirement that the Secretary of Health and Human Services (HHS) publish standards for the electronic exchange, privacy, and security of health information (i.e., Administrative Simplification Provisions). HIPAA also required the Secretary of HHS to issue privacy regulations governing individually identifiable health information if Congress failed to do so within 3 years after HIPAA became law. When Congress failed to act, HHS issued proposed rules (Standards for Privacy of Individually Identifiable Health Information, i.e., the Privacy Rule) that were finalized in 2000, amended in 2002, and became generally applicable on April 14, 2003 (April 14, 2004 for "small health plans").[49]

The Privacy Rule and the Administrative Simplification Provisions apply to health plans, health care clearinghouses, and to any health care provider who transmits health information in electronic form in connection with transactions for which the Secretary of HHS has adopted standards under HIPAA (the "covered entities").

**Individually identifiable health information.**[50] The Privacy Rule protects all "individually identifiable health information" created or received by a covered entity or its business associate, in any form of media, whether electronic, paper, or oral. This information is also known as "protected health information." Individually identifiable health information is information, including demographic data, relating to:

- the individual's past, present, or future physical or mental health or condition;
- the provision of health care to the individual; or
- the past, present, or future payment for the provision of health care to the individual;

and that identifies the individual or for which there is a reasonable basis to believe it can be used to identify the individual. Individually identifiable health information includes many common identifiers (e.g., name, address, birth date, SSN).

The Office for Civil Rights within HHS is responsible for implementing and enforcing the Privacy Rule.

---

48.     P. L. 104-191.
49.     45 CFR §160.101 - §160.312; §164.102 - §164.534.
50.     42 USC §1320d(6); 45 CFR §160.103; 164.501.

## *Section 10: Recordkeeping and Record Retention*

Any employer that provides health care coverage to its employees, either through a fully insured or self-insured health plan, must comply with the Privacy Rule.[51] Under HIPAA, an employer must obtain an employee's authorization when conducting routine transactions with its insurance companies, including inquiries dealing with pre-employment and fitness-for-duty medical examinations.

Protected health information does not include employment records that a covered entity maintains in its capacity as an employer nor does it include education and certain other records subject to, or defined in, the Family Educational Rights and Privacy Act.[52]

**De-identified health information.** De-identified health information neither identifies nor provides a reasonable basis to identify an individual. There are no restrictions on the use or disclosure of de-identified health information.[53]

The Privacy Rule provides two ways to de-identify information:
- a formal determination by a qualified statistician; or
- the removal of specified identifiers of the individual and of the individual's relatives, household members, and employers, and is adequate only if the covered entity has no actual knowledge that the remaining information could be used to identify the individual.

**Disclosure of protected information.**[54] A covered entity may not use or disclose protected health information, except either:
- as the Privacy Rule permits or requires; or
- as the individual who is the subject of the information (or the individual's personal representative) authorizes in writing.

**Mandatory disclosures.**[55] A covered entity must disclose protected health information in only two situations:
- to individuals (or their personal representatives) specifically when they request access to, or an accounting of disclosures of, their protected health information; and
- to HHS when it is undertaking a compliance investigation or review or enforcement action.

**Permitted disclosures.**[56] A covered entity is permitted, but not required, to use and disclose protected health information, without an individual's authorization, for the following purposes or situations:
- to the individual (unless required for access or accounting of disclosures);
- if required by law, for a judicial or administrative proceeding, or for law enforcement purposes;
- treatment, payment, and health care operations;
- disclosures with an opportunity to agree or object (e.g., emergency situations);
- disclosures incidental to an otherwise permitted use and disclosure;
- public interest and benefit activities; and
- providing limited data for the purposes of research, public health, or health care operations.

**Providing medical information is OK in a National Medical Support Notice.** The National Medical Support Notice (NMSN) requests the release of private health care information, and Office of Child Support Enforcement says that it is not a violation of HIPAA for an employer or health plan to provide the requested information. That is because the NMSN is considered a written administrative request from a law enforcement official (see page 9-28).

**Authorization for disclosure.**[57] A covered entity must obtain an individual's written authorization for any use or disclosure of protected health information that is not for treatment, payment, or health care

---

51.  45 CFR §160.103.
52.  45 CFR §164.501(d)(2).
53.  45 CFR §164.502(d); 164.504.
54.  45 CFR §164.502(a)(1); 164.506; 164.508.
55.  45 CFR §164.502(a)(2); 164.524; 164.528.
56.  45 CFR §164.502(a)(1)(iii); 164.510; 164.512(a) – (j).
57.  45 CFR §164.508.

operations or otherwise permitted or required by the Privacy Rule. A covered entity may not condition treatment, payment, enrollment, or benefits eligibility on an individual granting an authorization, except in limited circumstances.

An authorization must be written and specific. It may allow use and disclosure of protected health information by the covered entity seeking the authorization, or by a third party. Examples of disclosures requiring authorization include disclosures to a life insurer for coverage purposes, disclosures to an employer of the results of a pre-employment physical or lab test, or disclosures to a pharmaceutical firm for their own marketing purposes.

Authorizations must be in plain language and contain specific information about the information to be disclosed or used, the persons disclosing and receiving the information, expiration of the authorization, right to revoke in writing, and other data.

**Authorization needed for marketing.**[58] A covered entity must obtain an authorization to use or disclose protected health information for marketing, except for face-to-face marketing communications between a covered entity and an individual, and for a covered entity's provision of promotional gifts of nominal value. An authorization for marketing that involves the covered entity's receipt of direct or indirect remuneration from a third party must reveal that fact. No authorization is needed, however, to make a communication that falls within one of the exceptions to the marketing definition, described below.

Marketing is any communication about a product or service that encourages recipients to purchase or use the product or service.[59] Marketing is also an arrangement between a covered entity and any other entity whereby the covered entity discloses protected health information, in exchange for direct or indirect remuneration, for the other entity to communicate about its own products or services encouraging the use or purchase of those products or services.

The following activities are excluded from the definition of marketing:
- communications to describe health-related products or services, or payment for them, provided by or included in a benefit plan of the covered entity making the communication;
- communications about participating providers in a provider or health plan network, replacement of, or enhancements to, a health plan, and health-related products or services available only to a health plan's enrollees that add value to, but are not part of, the benefits plan;
- communications for treatment of the individual; and
- communications for case management or care coordination for the individual, or to direct or recommend alternative treatments, therapies, health care providers, or care settings to the individual.

**'Minimum necessary' use and disclosure.**[60] The Privacy Rule requires the "minimum necessary" use and disclosure of protected information. This means that a covered entity must make reasonable efforts to use, disclose, and request only the minimum amount of protected health information needed to accomplish the intended purpose of the use, disclosure, or request.

When the minimum necessary standard applies to a use or disclosure, a covered entity may not use, disclose, or request an entire medical record for a particular purpose, unless it can specifically justify the whole record as the amount reasonably needed for the purpose. The minimum necessary requirement does not apply to:[61]

- disclosure to, or a request by, a health care provider for treatment;
- disclosure to an individual who is the subject of the information, or the individual's personal representative;

58.     45 CFR §164.514(e).
59.     45 CFR §164.501.
60.     45 CFR §164.514(d).
61.     45 CFR §164.502(b).

- use or disclosure made pursuant to an authorization;
- disclosure to HHS for complaint investigation, compliance review or enforcement;
- use or disclosure that is required by law; or
- use or disclosure required for compliance with the HIPAA Transactions Rule or other HIPAA Administrative Simplification Rules.

**Uses of protected health information inside a covered entity.**[62] For internal uses, a covered entity must develop and implement policies and procedures that restrict access and uses of protected health information based on the specific roles of the members of their workforce. These policies and procedures must identify the persons, or classes of persons, in the workforce who need access to protected health information to carry out their duties, the categories of protected health information to which access is needed, and any conditions under which they need the information to do their jobs.

**Routine or recurring requests for disclosure.** Covered entities must establish and implement policies and procedures (which may be standard protocols) for routine, recurring disclosures, or requests for disclosures, that limit the protected health information disclosed to that which is the minimum amount reasonably necessary to achieve the purpose of the disclosure. Individual review of each disclosure is not required. For non-routine, non-recurring disclosures, or requests for disclosures that they make, covered entities must develop criteria designed to limit disclosures to the information reasonably necessary to accomplish the purpose of the disclosure and review each of these requests individually in accordance with the established criteria.

**Disclosure to another covered entity.**[63] If another covered entity makes a request for protected health information, a covered entity may rely, if reasonable under the circumstances, on the request as complying with this minimum necessary standard. Similarly, a covered entity may rely upon requests as being for the minimum necessary protected health information when they are from:
- a public official who represents that the information requested is the minimum necessary for the stated purpose;
- a professional (such as an attorney or accountant) who is the covered entity's employee or business associate seeking the information to provide services to the covered entity and who represents that the information requested is the minimum necessary for the stated purpose; or
- a researcher who provides the documentation or representation required by the Privacy Rule for research.

**Group health plan disclosures to plan sponsors.**[64] A group health plan and the health insurer or HMO offered by the plan may disclose the following protected health information to the "plan sponsor" (i.e., the employer, union, or other employee organization that sponsors and maintains the group health plan):
- enrollment or disenrollment information with respect to the group health plan or a health insurer or HMO offered by the plan.
- if requested by the plan sponsor, summary health information for the plan sponsor to use to obtain premium bids for providing health insurance coverage through the group health plan, or to modify, amend, or terminate the group health plan. "Summary health information" is information that summarizes claims history, claims expenses, or types of claims experience of the individuals for whom the plan sponsor has provided health benefits through the group health plan, and that is stripped of all individual identifiers other than the five digit zip code (though it need not qualify as de-identified protected health information).
- protected health information of the group health plan's enrollees for the plan sponsor to perform plan administration functions. The plan must receive certification from the plan sponsor that the group health plan document has been amended to impose restrictions on the plan sponsor's use and disclosure of the protected health information. These restrictions must include the representation that the plan sponsor will not use or disclose the protected health information for any employment-related action or decision or in connection with any other benefit plan.

---

62.    45 CFR §164.514(d)(2).
63.    45 CFR §164.514(d)(3)(iii).
64.    45 CFR §164.504(a), (f).

**Administrative requirements.**[65] The Privacy Rule may require employers to take a closer look at how they handle workers' medical records. It sets out a number of administrative areas that covered entities are required to address. These areas are applicable to both large and small covered entities and are flexible, so that each covered entity can analyze its needs and implement an appropriate solution. What is appropriate for a particular covered entity will depend on the nature of the covered entity's business, as well as the covered entity's size and resources. These administrative areas are outlined below.

*Privacy policies and procedures.* A covered entity must develop and implement written privacy policies and procedures consistent with the Privacy Rule.

*Privacy administrator.* A covered entity must designate a privacy official responsible for developing and implementing its privacy policies and procedures, and a contact person or contact office responsible for receiving complaints and providing individuals with information on the covered entity's privacy practices.

*Workforce training and management.* Workforce members include employees, volunteers, trainees, and may also include other persons whose conduct is under the direct control of the entity (whether or not they are paid by the entity). A covered entity must train all workforce members on its privacy policies and procedures, as necessary and appropriate for them to carry out their functions. A covered entity must have and apply appropriate sanctions against workforce members who violate its privacy policies and procedures or the Privacy Rule.

*Mitigation of wrongful disclosures.* A covered entity must mitigate, to the extent practicable, any harmful effect it learns was caused by use or disclosure of protected health information by its workforce or its business associates in violation of its privacy policies and procedures or the Privacy Rule.

*Protection of data.* A covered entity must maintain reasonable and appropriate administrative, technical, and physical safeguards to prevent intentional or unintentional use or disclosure of protected health information in violation of the Privacy Rule and to limit its incidental use and disclosure pursuant to otherwise permitted or required use or disclosure. For example, such safeguards might include shredding documents containing protected health information before discarding them, securing medical records with a lock and key or pass code, and limiting access to the keys or pass codes.

*Complaint procedures.* A covered entity must have procedures for individuals to complain about its compliance with its privacy policies and procedures and the Privacy Rule. The covered entity must explain those procedures in its privacy practices notice. Among other things, the covered entity must identify the contact to whom individuals can submit complaints at the covered entity and advise that complaints also can be submitted to the Secretary of HHS.

*Retaliation and waivers prohibited.* A covered entity may not retaliate against a person for exercising rights provided by the Privacy Rule, for assisting in an investigation by HHS or another appropriate authority, or for opposing an act or practice that the person believes in good faith violates the Privacy Rule. A covered entity may not require an individual to waive any right under the Privacy Rule as a condition of obtaining treatment, payment, or enrollment or benefits eligibility.

*Recordkeeping and retention requirements.* A covered entity must maintain, until six years after the later of the date of their creation or last effective date, its privacy policies and procedures, its privacy practices notices, disposition of complaints, and other actions, activities, and designations that the Privacy Rule requires to be documented.

A fully-insured group health plan that has no more than enrollment data and summary health information is only required to comply with the:
- ban on retaliatory acts and waiver of individual rights, and
- documentation requirements with respect to plan documents if such documents are amended to provide for the disclosure of protected health information to the plan sponsor by a health insurance issuer or HMO that services the group health plan.

---

65.     45 CFR §164.530.

**Effect on state laws.**[66] State laws that are contrary to the Privacy Rule are preempted, which means that the Privacy Rule will apply, instead of the state law provisions. A state law is contrary to the Privacy Rule if it would be impossible for a covered entity to comply with both the state and federal requirements, or if the state law is an obstacle to accomplishing the full purposes and objectives of the Administrative Simplification Provisions of HIPAA. However, a state law is not preempted if it relates to the privacy of health information and is more protective of such information than the Privacy Rule.

**Enforcement and penalties.** The Privacy Rule provides processes for persons to file complaints with HHS, describes the responsibilities of covered entities to provide records and compliance reports and to cooperate with, and permit access to, information for investigations and compliance reviews. There are significant civil and criminal penalties for noncompliance.

*Civil money penalties.*[67] HHS may impose civil money penalties on a covered entity of $100 per failure to comply with a Privacy Rule requirement. The penalty may not exceed $25,000 per year for multiple violations of the identical Privacy Rule requirement. HHS may not impose a civil money penalty under specific circumstances, such as when a violation is due to reasonable cause and did not involve willful neglect and the covered entity corrected the violation within 30 days of when it knew or should have known of the violation.

*Criminal penalties.*[68] A person who knowingly obtains or discloses individually identifiable health information in violation of HIPAA faces a fine of $50,000 and up to one year of imprisonment. The criminal penalties increase to $100,000 and up to five years imprisonment if the wrongful conduct involves false pretenses, and to $250,000 and up to 10 years imprisonment if the wrongful conduct involves the intent to sell, transfer, or use individually identifiable health information for commercial advantage, personal gain, or malicious harm. Criminal sanctions are enforced by the Department of Justice.

 **COULD AN EMPLOYER BE SUED?** Some attorneys familiar with HIPAA and the Privacy Rule have speculated that the Privacy Rule might be used as a reasonable standard of conduct to which covered entities must adhere. Violation of that standard, they believe, could support a common law invasion of privacy action for data breaches.

# 10.10  Review Questions and Exercises

## Review Questions

1.  What records must an employer keep under the FLSA for an employee who is receiving remedial education?

2.  What are the criminal penalties for FLSA recordkeeping violations?

3.  What is the general retention period under the Internal Revenue Code for copies of employer tax returns and information returns?

4.  If the Department of Labor requests a Form I-9 for inspection, how long does the employer have to produce it?

5.  Under the FLSA, name four types of employment data records that must be kept for each covered employee for at least three years after the last date of entry.

---

66.     42 USC §1320d-7; 45 CFR §160.201 – 160.205.
67.     42 USC §1320d-5.
68.     42 USC §1320d-6.

6. What records must be kept under the FLSA for at least two years from their last date of entry?

7. What additional records must be kept under the FLSA by employers of hospital employees?

8. What additional records must be kept under the FLSA by employers of tipped employees?

9. What is the goal of the IRS in establishing procedures for employer records processed by computers?

10. What are the retention requirements for Form I-9?

11. What are the advantages of storing payroll and employment records on microfilm or microfiche?

12. What is the main disadvantage of storing payroll and employment records on micromedia?

13. What procedure should be followed for the retrieval and destruction of records?

## True or False Questions

_____ 1. Payroll records retained in compliance with IRS recordkeeping requirements must be kept in paper form.

_____ 2. After an employer forwards abandoned (uncashed) paychecks to the appropriate state agency, state law may require that the employer keep a record of the employee's name and last known address for a specified period of time.

_____ 3. Records required by the FLSA must be made available for inspection by the Wage and Hour Division within 48 hours of a notice of inspection.

_____ 4. Employers that withhold and pay federal income, social security, and Medicare taxes must maintain records according to the Internal Revenue Code.

_____ 5. Employers that use a payroll service provider are relieved of their recordkeeping responsibilities.

_____ 6. The trend today is for a company to maintain one employee master file that includes payroll, human resources, and benefits information.

_____ 7. Even though "white collar" workers may be exempt from the FLSA's overtime pay requirements, records of their hours worked must still be kept by the employer.

_____ 8. The FLSA does not require employers to keep records in any particular form.

_____ 9. Employers that store payroll records on microfilm or microfiche must have viewing equipment available when an inspection is requested.

_____ 10. Records required to be kept under the FLSA must be stored at the employer's worksite for inspection.

_____ 11. If an employer has incomplete records and an employee files a lawsuit for unpaid overtime, the court will most likely accept the employee's evidence of hours worked and wages received.

_____ 12.   Form W-4 must be retained by the employer for three years.

_____ 13.   The IRS requires that machine-readable records be kept at least until the expiration of the statute of limitations for the tax year to which they relate.

_____ 14.   The minimum retention period for state unemployment insurance records differs from state to state.

_____ 15.   Federal and state laws generally require that a copy of records be retained in paper form for audit purposes.

## Multiple Choice Questions

_____ 1.   Under the FLSA, all of the following records are required to be kept for at least three years from the last date they were in effect except for?

   a.   Records showing additions to or deductions from employees' wages
   b.   Collective bargaining agreements
   c.   Certificates authorizing the employment of minors
   d.   Records showing total sales volume and goods purchased

_____ 2.   Under the FLSA, which of the following records must be kept for more than two years from the last date they were in effect?

   a.   Wage rate tables
   b.   Piece rate tables
   c.   Work time schedules establishing the hours and days of employment
   d.   Collective bargaining agreements

_____ 3.   Which of the following forms is used by the employee to report tips to the employer?

   a.   Form 8019
   b.   Form 4070
   c.   Form 8027
   d.   Form 1099-MISC

_____ 4.   If the records required by the FLSA are maintained at a central location, how soon after a Department of Labor request must the employer make them available?

   a.   24 hours
   b.   48 hours
   c.   72 hours
   d.   10 days

_____ 5.   Under the Walsh-Healey Public Contracts Act, how long must a separate log of occupational injuries and illnesses be kept?

   a.   2 years
   b.   3 years
   c.   4 years
   d.   5 years

_____ 6.  How long are FUTA tax records normally required to be retained?

      a.  3 years
      b.  4 years
      c.  5 years
      d.  Indefinitely

_____ 7.  How long does the ADEA require that records of an employee's name, address, date of birth, occupation, pay rate, and compensation earned be kept?

      a.  2 years
      b.  3 years
      c.  4 years
      d.  5 years

_____ 8.  What law requires Form I-9 to be retained?

      a.  Immigration Reform and Control Act of 1986
      b.  Civil Rights Act of 1964
      c.  Age Discrimination in Employment Act 1967
      d.  Americans with Disabilities Act of 1990

_____ 9.  Which of the following laws governs unclaimed wages?

      a.  Federal wage-hour laws
      b.  State escheat laws
      c.  Equal employment opportunity laws
      d.  Labor relations laws

_____ 10.  How long must an employer maintain records it is required to keep under the Family and Medical Leave Act?

      a.  4 years
      b.  6 years
      c.  3 years
      d.  1 year

# SECTION 11: PAYROLL ACCOUNTING

## TABLE OF CONTENTS

# SECTION 11: PAYROLL ACCOUNTING

While accounting may not be the payroll department's prime responsibility, it nevertheless is an important interface and payroll practitioners must be comfortable with basic accounting principles and understand the effect of payroll data on a company's financial accounts. The accuracy and timeliness of data gathered by the payroll department regarding wages paid, taxes withheld, and other deductions play an important role in allowing the finance department to prepare complete financial statements for the organization that will stand up to the scrutiny of stockholders, auditors, or an IRS revenue agent.

Within a company's overall system of financial recordkeeping, there are several areas that make use of data provided by the payroll department. They include:

- *General accounting* uses payroll data to record transactions in the company's books of account and to prepare financial statements both for internal and external purposes.

- *Cost accounting* uses payroll data to determine the cost of producing a product or providing a service and to show ways of controlling these costs (e.g., wage data used to determine the cost of labor).

- *Budgeting* involves projecting the costs and revenues associated with various business activities and trying to keep the costs—including payroll costs—within target limits.

This section will provide an explanation of basic accounting principles and how they apply to the payroll function. Because payroll accounting also includes the responsibility for safeguarding the records and assets being accounted for, this section will also discuss methods of internal and external control that protect the integrity of the payroll process.

## 11.1 Accounting Principles

Accounting is a way of keeping track of an organization's financial transactions by identifying and classifying those transactions. This information is then used to prepare the company's financial statements, which describe the company's cash flow, profits, losses, assets, liabilities, and net worth. They are used by management, stockholders, auditors, etc. to gauge the company's financial health and prospects for the future.

Accounting standards are not set by law but by private organizations. Since 1974, the Financial Accounting Standards Board (FASB) has set the standards for recording financial transactions. (The Government Accounting Standards Board performs the same function in the public sector.) Before 1974, a variety of organizations issued a set of concepts and principles that have come to be known as Generally Accepted Accounting Principles (GAAP). They include:

**Business entity concept.** Every organization that operates separately is treated as a business under the business entity concept. The purpose of accounting is to report each entity's financial position on a balance sheet and its profitability on an income statement. The employees, owners, and managers of a business entity must keep their personal transactions separate from those of the business entity.

**Continuing concern concept.** This concept assumes a business entity will continue to operate indefinitely as a business. If the business is for sale, it would not be a continuing concern and its assets would be valued at their fair market value. Continuing concerns value their assets at their cost since they are not for sale.

**Time period concept.** Each organization must determine its own accounting period based on the type of business it is engaged in. For its yearly accounting period, an organization can choose either the calendar year or another 12-month period (fiscal year, e.g., 6-1-07 to 5-31-08). In most organizations, the end of the fiscal year coincides with the least business activity for the year.

**Cost principle.** Because organizations are assumed to continue as going concerns, all goods and services purchased (assets) are recorded at the cost of acquiring them. The cost is measured by the cash spent or the cash equivalent of goods or services provided in return for those purchased. Once valued, an asset remains at that value for its life minus any depreciation in accordance with the continuing concern concept and the objectivity principle (see discussion following).

**Objectivity principle.** Transactions must be recorded objectively to ensure personal opinions and emotions are not part of the recorded transaction. This principle ensures accounting information will be useful for lenders and investors. Generally, valuing an asset at cost meets this principle since it requires a deal between a buyer and a seller with different goals in completing the transaction.

**Matching principle.** Expenses and revenue are recorded in the accounting period in which the expense is incurred or the revenue is earned. Under the matching principle, transactions may have to be recorded before any money actually changes hands, but after the essence of the transaction has been completed. The matching principle allows a comparison between different organizations' financial statements.

**Realization principle.** The realization principle governs the recording of revenue. Revenue is the income received for goods and services provided by the organization. Revenue is recognized (or realized) and reported when earned, which is during the accounting period when the goods have been transferred or the services provided. The amount recognized is the cash received or the fair market value of goods and services received.

**Consistency principle.** Transactions must be recorded in a consistent manner based on the particular accounting method, principle, or period. Users of accounting information require that transactions be recorded consistently so they can make sound financial decisions regarding the organization, especially when comparing previous accounting periods to the current period.

# 11.1-1 Account Classifications

All of a company's transactions are recorded and classified into various accounts using a "double entry" system that is based on two equations.

The first equation is:

> Assets - Liabilities = Equity

This equation provides the basis for the financial statement called a Balance Sheet, which shows the company's financial position at a particular point in time.

> The second equation is actually made up of two:

> Revenue - Expenses = Net Income

> Net Income - Income Distributed + Contributed Capital = Equity

This equation is the basis for two financial statements, the Income Statement and the Statement of Retained Earnings.

11-3

In order for each equation to remain in balance (i.e., amounts on one side equal amounts on the other side), a "double entry" for each transaction is required. One account is increased, while another is decreased.

**Types of accounts.** There are generally five types of accounts used by businesses to classify transactions: assets, liabilities, expenses, revenue, and equity. Asset, liability, and expense accounts generally are the only ones affected by entries from the payroll department.

*Asset accounts.* Assets are anything that provides an economic benefit or value to the company over a period of time. Asset accounts are divided into three types: Current; Property, Plant, and Equipment; and Deferred. The classification of an asset depends on when and if it can be converted into cash or a cash equivalent that can be used by the company (i.e., the liquidity of the asset). Following is a list of some of a typical company's assets:

| **Current** | **Tangible or Property, Plant and Equipment** | **Intangible or Deferred** |
|---|---|---|
| Cash | Land and improvements | Trademarks |
| Notes receivable | Buildings | Patents |
| Accounts receivable | Computers and software | Leases |
| Inventory | Furniture | Goodwill |
| Prepaid expenses | Automobiles | Copyrights |

*Expense accounts.* Expense accounts show the company's costs for goods and services consumed during the accounting period. The items generally are provided by other organizations, but they also include the labor supplied by the company's employees. Examples of typical company expenses include:

- Wages paid to employees
- Employer-paid benefit costs
- Maintenance for computers
- Office supply costs
- Employer share of payroll taxes

*Liability accounts.* Liabilities are company debts that must be paid in the future. They represent a claim against the company's assets. Liabilities are divided into two categories: Current and Long-Term. If the company must pay the liability during the accounting period (e.g., fiscal year), it is a current liability. If the liability can be paid after the current accounting period ends, it is a long-term liability. Some transactions that represent liabilities include:

- Income and employment taxes withheld but not yet deposited
- Contributions owed to a company benefit plan
- Accounts payable
- Wages payable
- Union dues deducted from pay but not yet paid to the union

*Revenue accounts.* Revenue accounts identify amounts received for goods sold and services rendered during the accounting period. The income can be in the form of cash, the expectation of receiving cash, or services.

*Equity accounts.* Equity represents the owner's investment in the company (i.e., its net worth). Generally, equity accounts are divided into two components: Contributed Capital and Retained Earnings. Contributed capital is the amount the company's owners—proprietors, partners, or shareholders—have contributed to the organization. Retained earnings is the amount by which revenue has exceeded expenses, reduced by any amount returned to the owners.

# 11.1-2 Account Balances

As noted earlier, the double entry system of accounting was developed to allow the basic accounting equations to remain in balance. This does not mean that each separate account will balance, but that all the company's accounts, when considered as a whole, will balance at any point during an accounting period. Each type of account has what is called a "normal" balance on either one side or the other of the equation. (Each entry must be in balance, therefore all entries are always in balance.)

**Debits, credits, and "T-accounts."** To understand basic accounting procedures, payroll practitioners should be familiar with the manual method for recording transactions, even though the overwhelming majority of accounting systems are computerized today and interface with the payroll system. Knowing the basics will make it easier to trace a transaction even in a computerized system.

Transactions are recorded by placing either "debit entries" (dr) or "credit entries" (cr) on either side of a symbolic diagram of an account. While many people assume that a debit is a minus to an account and a credit is a plus, in accounting terms a debit entry goes on the left side of an account while a credit entry goes on the right side of the account. Whether the entry increases or decreases the account depends on the type of account and its normal balance.

When entries are recorded in an account, they are placed in what is known as a "T-account" because it forms the letter T.

Using the left and right side format makes the determination of the account's balance much easier. The entries on each side are totaled and then the smaller is subtracted from the larger to calculate the balance in the account. An account with a larger debit total than credit total has a debit balance, while an account with a larger credit total than a debit total has a credit balance. Table 11.1 provides the normal balance of each type of account.

Table 11.1

| CHART OF NORMAL ACCOUNT BALANCES | |
|---|---|
| **Type of Account** | **Normal Account Balance** |
| Asset | Debit |
| Liability | Credit |
| Equity | Credit |
| Revenue | Credit |
| Expense | Debit |
| Income Distributed | Debit |
| Contributed Capital | Credit |

**Posting entries.** Whether a transaction is posted (i.e., recorded) as a debit or credit in a T-account depends on the type of account. In an asset account (e.g., the payroll checking account), which has a normal debit balance, any entry increasing the asset appears on the debit side, while any entry decreasing the asset is posted on the credit side. Therefore, depositing money in the checking account would generate a debit entry, while writing a check on the account is a credit. Liability account entries are the opposite. Taking out a loan would increase liabilities and generate a credit entry, while paying back the loan is a debit. These concepts are shown in Table 11.2.

Table 11.2

**Any Asset or Expense Account**

| Debit | Credit |
|---|---|
| increases | decreases |

**Any Liability or Revenue Account**

| Debit | Credit |
|---|---|
| decreases | increases |

**Unit of measurement.** All transactions involving U.S. businesses are recorded on their books in a common unit of measurement—the U.S. dollar. Financial reports would not be useful to individuals needing to use them if some information was reported in dollars and some in another currency. Businesses in other countries use their own nation's base currency (e.g., the European Union's euro, or the Japanese yen) as a common unit of measurement. Dollars are also used rather than any type of nonmonetary unit of measurement (e.g., a count of items).

**Chart of accounts.** In most companies, a "chart of accounts" lists each account by name and number, with a number being used to identify each account. Generally, the numbering scheme will contain logic providing for easy identification of the broad type of account involved (e.g., asset or liability), as well as its more specific character. In large organizations, the account number can contain 15-20 digits, with specific digits designating company divisions, departments, and locations as well as the type of account. Following is an example of a very basic numbering scheme for a chart of accounts.

Generally, the first digit in the account number will identify the basic type of account.

    1 -    Asset accounts
    2 -    Liability accounts
    3 -    Equity accounts
    4 -    Revenue accounts
    5 -    Expense accounts

The second digit provides a somewhat more specific definition of the account.

    11 -    Current assets
    12 -    Long-term investments
    13 -    Plant, property, and equipment
    14 -    Intangible assets

A third digit can identify the individual account.

    111 -    Cash
    112 -    Accounts receivable
    113 -    Inventory
    114 -    Prepaid expenses

*Example:* Account No. 112 would be identified as the company's current asset account called Accounts Receivable.

# 11.2 Journal Entries

The journal is a record of the transactions of a company during the accounting period. For each transaction, the journal shows both the debits and credits to be entered in specific accounts and a description of the transaction. In many circumstances, these single transactions are entered into subsidiary journals and then combined before being entered into the journal.

*Example:*

|  |  | Debit | Credit |
|---|---|---|---|
| 6/15/08 | Payroll bank account | $50,000 | |
| | Corporate bank account | | $50,000 |

Description of above: Transfer cash for payroll expense

|  |  | Debit | Credit |
|---|---|---|---|
| 6/18/08 | Computer software expense | $1,000 | |
| | Cash | | $1,000 |

Description of above: Cash purchase of computer software

Recording journal entries in the journal is also called journalizing into the book of original entry.

**Compound entries.** A journal entry that has more than one debit or credit is called a compound entry. Most payroll journals typify this type of entry.

**Subsidiary ledgers.** With the computerization of most companies' accounting systems, journals are frequently replaced by subsidiary ledgers, from which summarized entries are posted directly to the general ledger (see discussion following). Entries documenting payroll expenses and liabilities may be contained in a subsidiary ledger known as the Payroll Register. Other subsidiary ledgers containing entries for several accounts might include Accounts Payable, Accounts Receivable, and Fixed Assets.

**General ledger.** After entries have been recorded in the journal/subsidiary ledger, they are posted to the General Ledger (i.e., the book of final entry). The general ledger is a record of a company's transactions by account to which journal entries are periodically transferred (e.g., daily, weekly, or monthly, depending on the volume of transactions). The general ledger keeps a running total of all the entries and period-to-date balance for all the company's accounts. Entries are not posted to the general ledger without first being entered into a journal/subsidiary ledger to ensure both debit and credit entries have been made.

*Example:* On August 2, 2008, the opening balance in Barry's Bagels' payroll checking account is $2,000. Later that day, a payment of $500 is made, decreasing or crediting the account, and a $1,000 deposit is made, increasing or debiting the account. After posting these two journal entries, the balance in the payroll checking account in the general ledger would be $2,500 (debit).

The general ledger is used to prepare an organization's financial statements—the balance sheet, income statement, statement of retained earnings, and statement of cash flow. The balance sheet provides a look at the company's financial condition at a specific point in time by listing its assets, liabilities, and equity. The income (or profit and loss) statement shows the company's net income or loss for an accounting period, which is the difference between revenue and expenses for the period. The statement of retained earnings shows the amount of income remaining and available for investment after any distributions to stockholders or other owners. The statement of cash flow shows the sources and uses of cash during the accounting period.

Rather than listing each account individually and providing voluminous detail, the financial statements combine general ledger accounts into logical classifications that can be more easily understood and compared. For example, the liability section of the balance sheet may include a line for Accounts Payable, which includes all amounts owed to company suppliers of goods and services.

# 11.3 Recording Payroll Transactions

Payroll transactions—paying wages, deducting from wages, remitting withheld taxes, child support, and insurance premiums, etc.—are generally recorded initially in the Payroll Register. Generally, the payroll register lists each employee along with the wages paid and each amount deducted for each payroll period, and may well contain the quarter-to-date and year-to-date totals. Relevant or current information is then posted to the journal in the form of journal entries for: Payroll Expenses; Payroll Deductions; Payroll Cash Distribution; and Employer Tax Liabilities.

**Payroll expenses.** Payroll expenses may be recorded in one of two ways: functionally or by type of pay. If payroll expenses are recorded functionally, entries must be based on the processes supported by the expenses (e.g., manufacturing, sales, administration). This means the payroll would have to be distributed into different labor distribution expense accounts and a separate Labor Distribution Subsidiary Ledger would have to be kept. Its total would have to agree with the gross pay total in the payroll register. Recording payroll expenses by type of pay breaks down employees' wages into regular and overtime pay.

Journals can be developed to record payroll expenses under either method. The payroll expense journal will debit an expense account for the labor costs (salary expense) and credit a liability account (accrued salaries/wages). Entries to the payroll expense journal are recorded in the accounting period (e.g., fiscal month) containing the day the pay period ends, not the day employees get their paychecks. Therefore, if a pay period runs from June 14 through June 27, but paychecks are not issued until July 2, the payroll expenses are recorded as a journal entry in June, despite the July payday.

> **Example 1:** Downtown Shoe Repair Co. has a biweekly gross payroll of $6,000 with the following deductions:
>
> | | |
> |---|---|
> | Federal income tax | $1,200 |
> | State income tax | $ 300 |
> | Social security tax | $ 372 |
> | Medicare tax | $ 87 |
> | Health insurance premiums | $ 200 |
>
> DSR also must pay the following employment taxes based on its biweekly payroll:
>
> | | |
> |---|---|
> | Social security tax | $372 |
> | Medicare tax | $ 87 |
> | Federal unemployment tax | $ 48 |
> | State unemployment tax | $324 |
>
> The payroll expenses for DSR's biweekly payroll would be recorded in the payroll expense journal as follows:
>
> | Account/Description | Debit | Credit | Type of Account |
> |---|---|---|---|
> | Salary expense | $6,000 | | Expense |
> | Salaries/wages payable | | $6,000 | Liability |

**Payroll deductions.** Amounts deducted from employees' wages that must be paid to a third party (e.g., IRS, state revenue agency) become a liability to the employer. The date the employer makes the deductions from the employees' wages is the date the liability is incurred.

For easy reconciliation and balancing, each type of liability incurred by making a deduction from wages is recorded into the payroll deduction journal under a separate account. Examples of liability accounts include:

- Federal Income Tax Withheld
- Social Security Tax Withheld

- Medicare Tax Withheld
- State Income Tax Withheld
- State Disability Insurance Tax Withheld
- Union Dues Withheld
- Medical Insurance Premiums Withheld
- Child Support Orders Withheld
- Federal Tax Levies Withheld
- State Tax levies Withheld
- Garnishments Withheld

Entries made to the payroll deduction journal credit the liability account set up for each type of deduction and debit the liability account Salaries/Wages Payable. These entries are recorded in the accounting period in which the employees are paid, because the liability for the deduction is incurred on payday. Therefore, if a pay period runs from June 14 to June 27, but paychecks are not issued until July 2, the payroll deductions are recorded as journal entries in July.

*Example 2:* Using the facts from Example 1, DSR's biweekly payroll deductions would be recorded in the payroll deduction journal as follows:

| Account/Description | Debit | Credit | Type of Account |
|---|---|---|---|
| Salaries/wages payable | $2,159 | | Liability |
| Federal income tax withheld | | $1,200 | Liability |
| State income tax withheld | | 300 | Liability |
| Social security tax withheld | | 372 | Liability |
| Medicare tax withheld | | 87 | Liability |
| Health insurance premiums | | 200 | Liability |

**Payroll cash distribution/net pay.** When the employees are paid, entries must be made into the payroll cash distribution journal debiting the accrued salaries/wages liability account and crediting the payroll checking (cash) account. Entries made to the payroll cash distribution journal are recorded in the accounting period in which the employees are paid, since that is when the liability for paying the wages is discharged. Therefore, if a pay period runs from June 14 to June 27, but paychecks are not issued until July 2, the payroll cash distributions are recorded as journal entries in July.

*Example 3:* Using the same facts as in Example 1, the payroll cash distribution for DSR's biweekly payroll would be recorded in the payroll cash distribution journal as follows:

| Account/Description | Debit | Credit | Type of Account |
|---|---|---|---|
| Salaries/wages payable | $3,841 | | Liability |
| Payroll checking account (cash) | | $3,841 | Asset |

**Employer tax liabilities.** Employers must also pay their share of social security and Medicare taxes and federal and state unemployment taxes. These liabilities are based on the amount of wages paid to the employees that are subject to each type of tax. Therefore, the payroll register must contain the amount of wages on which each tax is imposed.

Because employer taxes are not deducted from employees' wages, the employer incurs additional expenses based on its liability for each type of tax, which are recorded into the employer tax liabilities journal. Entries made into the journal will debit an expense account for the amount of the expense and credit a liability account. Entries made to the employer tax liabilities journal are recorded in the accounting period in which the employees are paid, since that is when the liability is incurred. Therefore, if a pay period runs from June 14 to June 27, but paychecks are not issued until July 2, the employer's tax liabilities are recorded as journal entries in July.

***Example 4:*** Using the facts from Example 1, DSR's tax liabilities for its biweekly payroll would be recorded in the employer tax liabilities journal as follows:

| Account/Description | Debit | Credit | Type of Account |
|---|---|---|---|
| Payroll tax expense | $831 | | Expense |
| Social security tax payable | | $372 | Liability |
| Medicare tax payable | | 87 | Liability |
| Federal unemployment tax payable | | 48 | Liability |
| State unemployment tax payable | | 324 | Liability |

 **PAYMENTS TO THIRD PARTIES** When amounts deducted from employees' wages and the employer's share of payroll taxes are paid over to the appropriate third party, entries must be made into the payroll cash distribution journal showing the discharge of those liabilities. These entries would debit each liability account involved and credit the proper checking (cash) account.

**Posting a manual check into the different accounts.** The following example shows how the entire posting process works when a manual check is issued to an employee outside the regular check run.

***Example 5:*** Employee Ernest was hired by DSR after the current payroll was processed, so he did not receive a paycheck in the regular run. In order to pay him on payday, the payroll manager issued Ernest a manual check. Ernest's gross biweekly pay is $1,000. The deductions from his pay include:

| | |
|---|---|
| Federal income tax | $120.00 |
| State income tax | $ 50.00 |
| Social security tax | $ 62.00 |
| Medicare tax | $ 14.50 |
| Health insurance premium | $ 60.00 |

DSR also owes $62.00 for social security tax and $14.50 for Medicare tax, plus FUTA tax of $8.00 and state unemployment tax of $24.00.

Here is how Ernest's salary expenses would be recorded in the payroll expense journal:

| Account/Description | Debit | Credit | Type of Account |
|---|---|---|---|
| Salary expense | $1,000.00 | | Expense |
| Salaries/wages payable | | $1,000.00 | Liability |

Ernest's payroll deductions would be posted in the payroll deduction journal as follows:

| Account/Description | Debit | Credit | Type of Account |
|---|---|---|---|
| Salaries/wages payable | $306.50 | | Liability |
| Federal income tax withheld | | $120.00 | Liability |
| State income tax withheld | | 50.00 | Liability |
| Social security tax withheld | | 62.00 | Liability |
| Medicare tax withheld | | 14.50 | Liability |
| Health insurance premiums | | 60.00 | Liability |

When Ernest is paid, the actual check would be entered in the payroll cash distribution journal as follows:

| Account/Description | Debit | Credit | Type of Account |
|---|---|---|---|
| Salaries/wages payable | $693.50 | | Liability |
| Payroll checking account (cash) | | $693.50 | Asset |

DSR must also record the employer's tax expenses in the employer tax liabilities journal:

| Account/Description | Debit | Credit | Type of Account |
|---|---|---|---|
| Payroll tax expense | $108.50 | | Expense |
| Social security tax payable | | $62.00 | Liability |
| Medicare tax payable | | 14.50 | Liability |
| FUTA tax payable | | 8.00 | Liability |
| State unemployment tax payable | | 24.00 | Liability |

Ernest's deductions and DSR's tax expenses will be combined with the amounts from the regular payroll run to make the payments. All of the amounts related to Ernest's check should be recorded in the payroll system for tax deposit, quarter-to-date and year-to-date accumulation, and Form W-2 purposes.

## 11.4 Accounting Periods

For most individuals, their tax year or accounting year is the same as the calendar year—January 1 to December 31. But there is nothing in the Internal Revenue Code requiring either individuals or businesses to choose the calendar year as their accounting year. While some companies do end their accounting year on December 31, many have chosen an accounting year ending on another day when business is somewhat slack. Any 12-month accounting period adopted by a business that ends on a day other than December 31 is called a fiscal year.[1]

An accounting period is any length of time covered by an income statement, which could be a month, a quarter, a half-year, or a year. Regardless of the accounting periods or fiscal year a company uses, payroll taxes are always reported on a calendar year basis. Therefore, the payroll department may have two year-end reconciliation processes, one at fiscal year-end and one at calendar year-end.

Many of a company's transactions will overlap several accounting periods or fiscal years, such as when equipment expected to last several years is purchased. When this occurs, the company's accountants must allocate a portion of the asset to expense each accounting period. Accountants use a variety of techniques to make the allocation. If this allocation is not done, recording the transaction will not provide a true picture of the company's financial condition.

## 11.5 Accruals and Reversals

For those few small companies that use the cash accounting method to record transactions, with journal entries made only when cash or its equivalent actually changes hands, the accounting procedures described so far will serve to accurately present their financial condition. Most organizations, however, use the accrual method of accounting, under which revenue is recognized when earned and expenses are recognized when incurred. Either method is acceptable to the IRS, depending on certain circumstances.[2] Only accrual accounting is acceptable under Generally Accepted Accounting Principles.

Unfortunately, paydays, the last day of pay periods, and the last day of accounting periods (e.g., fiscal months or years) generally do not all occur on the same day. For this reason, companies must accrue or

---

1.    IRC §441; IRS Temp. Reg. §1.441-1T.
2.    IRC §446(c); IRS Reg. §1.446-1.

account for payroll expenses through the end of each accounting period. This accrual is designed to satisfy the Matching Principle (see Section 11.1), under which any revenue, expenses, and liabilities must be matched to the accounting period in which they were earned or incurred.[3] This makes it easier for managers, auditors, and others to determine a company's financial condition and compare it to previous years and other similar organizations.

**Estimated accruals necessitate reversals.** Payroll accrual entries made at the end of an accounting period estimate the payroll expenses and liabilities incurred between the last payroll period ending date and the end of the accounting period. They are generally based on estimates of daily payroll expenses and liabilities. Because they are estimates, they must be reversed during the next accounting period when the actual expenses and liabilities are recorded.

*Example:* Splendid Suburbia, Inc., a manufacturer of lawn and patio furniture, has a biweekly payroll period and a fiscal year that ends on March 31. The last payroll period ending date during the fiscal year is March 21, with the wages for that payroll period paid on March 27. Expenses and liabilities incurred for this payroll period will be recorded on those dates. In order to accurately state its liabilities and expenses linked to wages earned from March 22 through March 31, SSI must make accrual and reversing entries for those wages. Otherwise, its expenses and liabilities would be understated for the fiscal year ending March 31 and overstated for the fiscal year beginning April 1.

SSI's estimated daily payroll is $3,000, and none of its employees have reached the social security, FUTA, or state unemployment wage base. The state unemployment tax rate is 5.4%. The March 31 accrual entries would be recorded as follows:

| Account/Description | Debit | Credit |
|---|---|---|
| Accrued Payroll Expenses | $30,000 | |
| Accrued Payroll Liability | | $30,000 |

This entry records the estimated salaries due from March 22 through March 31. The entry will be reversed in the next fiscal period.

| Account/Description | Debit | Credit |
|---|---|---|
| Accrued Payroll Tax Expense | $4,155 | |
| Accrued Social Security Tax Payable | | $1,860 |
| Accrued Medicare Tax Payable | | 435 |
| Accrued FUTA Tax Payable | | 240 |
| Accrued SUI Tax Payable | | 1,620 |

This entry records the estimated tax expenses on wages from March 22 through March 31. The entry will be reversed in the next fiscal period.

---

3.    IRS Reg. §1.461-1(a)(2).

Based on the March 31 accrual entries, the following reversing entries will be made on April 1.

| Account/Description | Debit | Credit |
|---|---|---|
| Accrued Payroll Expenses | | $30,000 |
| Accrued Payroll Liability | $30,000 | |

This entry reverses estimated salaries from March 22 through March 31 recorded in the previous fiscal period.

| Account/Description | Debit | Credit |
|---|---|---|
| Accrued Payroll Tax Expense | | $4,155 |
| Accrued Social Security Tax Payable | $1,860 | |
| Accrued Medicare Tax Payable | 435 | |
| Accrued FUTA Tax Payable | 240 | |
| Accrued SUI Tax Payable | 1,620 | |

This entry reverses estimated tax expense on salaries from March 22 through March 31 recorded in the previous fiscal period.

**Vacations.** An organization's vacation policy will determine the entries needed to accurately record vacation expenses and liabilities. If employees accrue vacation leave (e.g., 1 day per month worked) which can be used at some later date, the employer incurs a liability at the time of the leave accrual. When the employee uses vacation time, the liability is reduced by the payment to the employee. The entries made to the general ledger would be as follows:

| Account/Description | Debit | Credit |
|---|---|---|
| Accrued Vacation Expense | $3,500 | |
| Vacation Liability Payable | | $3,500 |

This entry records the employees' accrual of vacation leave for the month.

| Account/Description | Debit | Credit |
|---|---|---|
| Accrued Vacation Expense | | $2,000 |
| Vacation Liability Payable | $2,000 | |

The actual vacation expense and cash entries are made when the salary expenses are posted from the payroll register.

**Bonuses.** In the same vein as vacation leave, nondiscretionary bonuses must be recorded when earned by the employees, even though they may not be paid until some later time. Therefore, when the employee has met all the criteria for receiving the bonus, the employer incurs a liability. That liability will be reduced by the amount of the bonus when it is paid to the employee. Generally, the entries to the general ledger would be as follows:

| Account/Description | Debit | Credit |
|---|---|---|
| Accrued Bonus Expense | $5,000 | |
| Bonus Liability Payable | | $5,000 |

This entry records the accrual of the bonus earned by the employee during the month.

| Account/Description | Debit | Credit |
|---|---|---|
| Accrued Bonus Expense | | $5,000 |
| Bonus Liability Payable | $5,000 | |

The actual bonus expense and cash entries are made when the salary expenses are posted from the payroll register.

# 11.6 Balancing and Reconciling Payroll Accounts

The double entry method of accounting provides a ready-made way to check the accuracy of the recording of payroll transactions. The recorded debits and credits for each transaction, each journal, and the general ledger should balance. This means the total of the debits should equal the total of the credits after each transaction and at the end of the accounting period. Balancing should be done at several points along the way, and certainly before and after journal entries are posted to the general ledger.

In order to ensure that employee paychecks are correct and that the correct amount of taxes is withheld, deposited, and reported on time, periodic verification of general ledger entries is a necessity, along with reconciliation (i.e., finding the reason for any differences and explaining them) of any discrepancies. This is done by comparing general ledger accounts to the records for taxes withheld and paid.

*Example:* Following is the general ledger account for the month of April for Splendid Suburbia, Inc.'s social security tax withheld.

**Account No. 213-114-67**
**Social Security Tax Withheld**

|  | Debit | Credit |
|---|---|---|
| Beginning balance on 4-1 |  | 2,000 |
| Accounts payable check #1034 | 2,000 |  |
| Social security tax withheld |  | 1,820 |
| Social security tax withheld |  | 1,760 |
| Accounts payable check #1251 | 1,820 |  |
| Ending balance as of 4-30 |  | 1,760 |

It is easy to see that not all the social security tax withheld by SSI during April was paid during that month. The difference must be reconciled. The following steps should be taken.

*Check against the payroll register.* Check to see the amount of social security tax withheld posted to the general ledger account agrees with the amount from the totals on the payroll register for the month. If so, move on to the next step. If not, the difference must be researched and correcting entries made or an appropriate check issued.

*Verify checks issued by accounts payable.* Make sure that all checks written by accounts payable have been posted to the correct account.

*Verify the end-of-the-month balance.* Check to see that the balance agrees with payroll department records. It is quite possible that taxes withheld during April did not have to be paid by the end of the month. If an accounts payable check has been posted to the general ledger account in May for the withheld social security tax, the account is reconciled, as shown here:

**Account No. 213-114-67**
**Social Security Tax Withheld**

|  | Debit | Credit |
|---|---|---|
| Beginning balance on 5-1 |  | 1,760 |
| Accounts payable check #1337 (dated 5-1) | 1,760 |  |
| Reconciliation balance |  | 0 |

# 11.6-1 Periodic Balancing and Reconciliation

Certain verification procedures should be carried out to check the accuracy of payroll records at each significant stage of the payroll process—paying wages, depositing taxes, and reporting wages and withheld taxes.

*Every payroll period.* Making sure that the payroll register—the basic payroll data record—is accurate each payroll period will save bigger headaches later when payrolls and errors have multiplied and errors become harder to detect.

 **FIX IT NOW FOR LESS** As with any flaw in a business process or procedure, the earlier it is detected, the easier and cheaper it is to fix.

Before finalizing the payroll register for each payroll period, the register should be checked even in computerized environments to make sure of the following:

- gross wages less deductions equals the net amount payable to employees;

- the total amount of withheld social security and Medicare taxes equals the current rate for each multiplied by the total taxable wages for the payroll period (other withheld taxes should also be checked for historical reasonableness); and

- there are no missing paychecks.

*Before filing Forms 941 and 940.* In preparing to file quarterly Form 941, *Employer's Quarterly Federal Tax Return* (see Appendix page A-164) and annual Form 940, *Employer's Annual Federal Unemployment (FUTA) Tax Return* (see Appendix page A-146), employers should verify the following:

- social security and Medicare tax deposits for the quarter equal the current tax rates for each multiplied by the taxable wages for each;

- the total tax deposits for the quarter equal the number in the liability section of Form 941 (Line 15 of Form 941 or the "total liability for the quarter" box on Schedule B, whichever applies); and

 **BE CAREFUL** Monthly depositors (see Section 8.2-1) may pay any lawful deposit shortfalls with their quarterly Forms 941. Therefore, their total tax deposits for the quarter would not equal their total quarterly liability if they take advantage of the 98% safe harbor. In such cases, a reconciliation must be undertaken to make sure the quarterly deposits plus the shortfall amount equal the total quarterly liability.

- the total payments to all employees on Line 3 of Form 940 can be reconciled with the total on Line 2 of the four quarterly Forms 941 filed for the year (they do not need to be equal, but a record of the reconciled items should be retained).

*Before sending employees their W-2 forms.* Verify that the total amounts of withheld taxes and social security and Medicare taxable wages reported on the quarterly Forms 941 equal the total of all the Forms W-2 being sent to employees. The total wages reported on Line 2 of the Forms 941 need not equal the total wages, tips, and other compensation reported in Box 1 of the W-2 forms. This is not used by the IRS as a reconcilable item, only as a statistical item. However, an internal reconciliation should be completed to explain any differences. (For more on payroll reconciliations, see Section 8.11.)

# 11.6-2 Payroll Bank Account Reconciliation

Most companies have a special bank account just for payroll. Money will be transferred from the employer's general bank account immediately before payday to the payroll bank account to cover employees' paychecks. If the account is not at -0- after the employees cash their checks, a reconciliation must be completed to research and explain any difference. In most instances, the difference can be attributed to either checks that are not cashed by employees, deposits that have not yet been credited to the account, or bank charges that reduce the account but are not reflected in the employer's general ledger.

Internal and external auditors will advise employers that employees who issue or control checks on an account should not be responsible for the reconciliation of that account. An employee outside the payroll department should be responsible for the payroll bank account reconciliation.

Following are the steps that should be taken in reconciling the payroll bank account when it has a balance that is not -0-.

*Step 1.* Add any deposits and interest and subtract any miscellaneous bank charges that show up on the bank statement but not on the general ledger.

*Step 2.* Compare the bank statement with the ledger, checking off each check withdrawal or deposit on the ledger that is listed on the statement.

*Step 3.* Total all uncleared checks.

*Step 4.* Subtract the uncleared checks from the ending balance on the bank statement.

*Step 5.* Compare the ending balance from the ledger to the revised ending balance on the bank statement.

*Step 6.* Check again to make sure that all cleared checks have been recorded, no encoding errors have been made by the bank, and all deposits, interest, and miscellaneous charges have been accounted for if the account remains out of balance.

 **DIRECT DEPOSIT HELPS** The payroll bank account reconciliation process is made much easier when employees are paid by direct deposit or electronic paycards. Uncleared checks are no longer worrisome since employees using direct deposit or paycards have their wages clear the payroll bank account on payday.

**Check-cashing problems.** For those employers with problems caused by paychecks that are not cashed before bank statements are issued, here are some options. Checks that have not been cashed within a reasonable time should be tracked, and if there are more than a few or the same employees are involved each time, an investigation may be necessary. If so, it might be a good idea to involve human resources in the process when dealing with the employees involved. Large employers may also want to set up a second payroll bank account and alternate using them each month to allow employees more time to cash checks before bank statements need to be reconciled. If these problems are not solved, uncashed or unclaimed paychecks can become unclaimed wages subject to state escheat laws (see Section 5.5).

 **WARN LATE CHECK-CASHERS** It might be a good idea for employers to warn any employees who are chronically late in cashing their paychecks that many banks will not cash them after a certain period of time (e.g., 6 months), and that they should consider getting paid by direct deposit or electronic paycard.

## 11.7 Financial Statements and Audits

Most organizations publish annual financial statements after they have been audited by independent certified public accountants (not employees of the company's finance department). These statements generally include:

- Balance sheet at the end of the most recent fiscal year and the preceding fiscal year;

- Statement of revenue and expenses (income statement), possibly including changes in retained earnings, at the end of the most recent fiscal year and the preceding fiscal year;

- Statement of cash flows;

- Notes to financial statements; and

- Report of the independent accountants (auditors).

 **PAYROLL'S IMPACT** Other than the auditors' report, all the financial statements are significantly impacted by information and records gathered and recorded by the payroll department. Poor payroll processing and reporting practices can lead to financial statements that materially misrepresent a company's financial condition.

## 11.7-1 Balance Sheet

On a typical balance sheet, assets are listed first, followed by liabilities and net worth (shareholders' equity). Each major portion of the balance sheet is further divided into smaller segments—the types of assets and liabilities.

**Current assets.** The first type of asset listed on the balance sheet is current assets—those that will be converted into cash within one year. They are listed in order of liquidity, or how long it will take to turn them into cash. Cash is listed first, and then other assets based on the length of time before they are converted into cash. Payroll's impact on current assets is the payment of employees' wages and the remittance of deductions from those wages, both of which generate entries crediting, or reducing, the cash account. In organizations that produce inventory for sale, the account for that inventory may have entries for salary expenses since the cost of goods sold should include the employees' wages.

**Plant, property, and equipment.** These assets are expected to be held for more than 1 year. Payroll will have input into this balance sheet item if the organization builds its own plant, property, and equipment. The labor that goes into constructing the plant facilities will be capitalized, with the amount being the portion of the employees' wages, benefits, and taxes identified as a cost of producing the asset. Until the construction is completed, the capitalized wages, benefits, and taxes would be part of the construction in progress account.

**Deferred assets.** These assets generally include intangible assets such as goodwill or the value of a patent. While the payroll impact on deferred assets may be minimal, if the organization has a funded nonqualified deferred compensation plan (see Section 4.6-10), the funds will be recognized as a corporate asset (required reporting for government-sponsored funded §457(b) plans).

**Current liabilities.** These liabilities must be paid within the next year. Most payroll journal entries affect accounts classified as current liabilities, since most payroll liabilities must be paid within a few days or weeks (e.g., withheld taxes, child support and garnishment deductions, union dues, etc.). Accrued vacation or personal leave that must be taken by the employees during the current year would also be recorded as a current liability.

**Long-term liabilities.** If a company's accrued leave policy allows leave time to be carried over from one year to the next, the liability for leaves may be split between current and long-term liability. The amount of the split depends on the carryover history of the company. The continuation of health benefits for a company's retirees requires another allocation between current and long-term liability.

**Shareholders' equity (net worth).** The shareholders' equity represents the owners' share of the business after all debts have been paid. Balance sheet items might include: common stock—listed at a nominal (par) value that has no relationship to its actual market value; retained earnings—income reinvested in the business rather than distributed to the owners; and contributed (paid-in) capital—additions to equity that do not come from revenue, but are receipts on stock issues or donations.

## 11.7-2 Income Statement

The income statement summarizes the organization's revenues and expenses, determining the organization's earnings for the current and preceding fiscal years. All companies whose shares are traded on a stock exchange (publicly held companies) and which sell bonds must prepare annual income statements, and most prepare them more often, usually at least quarterly.

**Gross margin on sales.** Gross margin on sales is measured as the net sales (gross sales less returns and discounts) minus the cost of goods sold (supplies, raw materials, labor), not including the cost of overhead, taxes, or revenue generated other than by sales (e.g., interest income).

**Operating income (operating profit).** The company's operating income takes into consideration overhead costs, such as depreciation and selling and administrative expenses, but not the organization's income tax or nonoperating revenue/expenses (e.g., interest income/expenses). This item provides a good look at how profitable a firm's business operations are in terms of goods and services produced and sold.

**Nonoperating revenue.** This item includes income earned other than from the sale of goods or services produced by the company, such as interest on a checking/savings account or bonds or capital gains from investments or sales of assets.

**Nonoperating expenses.** This item includes interest expenses, such as interest paid on loans or bonds, and income taxes.

**Net earnings (net income/loss).** This is the "bottom line" of the income statement. It shows how much profit or loss the company has after paying its taxes.

**Earnings per share.** This item shows the amount of net earnings divided by the average number of outstanding shares of stock during the accounting period.

 **PAYROLL IMPACT** Payroll journal entries generally find their way into the following areas of the (1) income statement: operating expenses; and nonoperating revenue; and (2) balance sheet: current assets; and current liabilities.

## 11.7-3 Notes to Financial Statements

A company's annual report will generally include notes explaining various elements of the financial statements and how they were constructed, as well as a summary of the company's accounting policies. This summary deals only with accounting policies that have a major impact on the financial statements. Those accounting policies that have changed significantly since the previous year, such as a change in accrual or vesting policies under the employer's benefits plans, are discussed in detail, explaining the impact of the change.

The notes usually contain a discussion of the company's retirement or deferred compensation plans if they have a significant impact on the financial statements. A note describing such a plan would include the IRC section under which the plan is organized (e.g., §401(k)), whether it is a defined benefit or defined contribution plan, which employees are eligible, how it is funded and current status of funding vested and nonvested liabilities, vesting requirements, and how claims are paid.

## 11.7-4 Auditing Financial Statements

Financial statements are audited by independent certified public accountants who determine whether the statements adequately depict the company's financial condition. They also determine whether the notes to financial statements adequately summarize the company's accounting policies regarding any future benefit plan liabilities. Their independence from the company helps guard against any possible conflict of interest while examining the company's books and accounting practices.

Another matter independent auditors consider in forming an opinion as to a company's financial outlook is whether the organization has internal controls in place to adequately safeguard its assets and record transactions properly. This may involve a determination of whether the company follows generally accepted accounting principles (see Section 11.1) and the extent and soundness of internal controls (see Section 11.8).

**Auditors and the payroll department.** As part of the external auditor's tasks, reviewing the payroll department is generally an important consideration. They must determine whether the information gathered and recorded by payroll is accurate and whether the policies and procedures being used are fiscally sound and secure.

To determine the accuracy of payroll data, auditors will often conduct a "compliance test" on a sample of cancelled paychecks and the information supporting the net pay on each one. The auditors will review time cards, Forms W-4, payroll registers, deduction authorizations, and journal and general ledger entries to determine that calculations and resulting journal entries are correct. Other tests may be used to determine whether taxes were properly withheld and deposited.

The auditors will also want to review the payroll department's procedures regarding the processing of paychecks and the input of payroll data. They are looking to see that one person is not responsible for the entire check processing procedure, that blank checks are stored securely, and that data input is verified and approved by someone other than the person who input the data. See Section 11.8 for more on the segregation of duties as a matter of internal control of payroll processing. The auditors may also want to observe the actual payroll distribution process to determine whether checks for absent employees are returned to payroll until the employee returns to work and whether there is adequate protection against "phantom employees."

## 11.8 Internal Controls

Internal controls are a system of checks and balances applied within an organization to ensure the accuracy of its financial records and the security of its assets. As a byproduct of this process, internal controls also encourage employees to comply with company policies and procedures and help gauge the efficiency of the organization's operation. A company's internal auditors periodically review the internal controls and make recommendations on how they can be improved. The basic components of a solid system of internal controls are as follows:

**Segregation of job duties.** The principle of segregation of job duties means that critical job processes are not totally the responsibility of one person or department. Segregation of job duties greatly reduces the opportunities for fraud or embezzlement of company funds. Many payroll practitioners will never face an embezzlement problem, but the failure to segregate job duties makes the company vulnerable to theft and is a "red flag" for outside auditors and potential shareholders that a serious security problem exists.

The urge not to segregate duties is often the greatest in small companies where the payroll department may consist of only one individual. But this urge should not be heeded as some critical duties can be given to employees outside the department. Here are some examples:

- the accounting department completes all payroll bank account reconciliations;
- department heads are asked to check employee lists against the list of employees who received paychecks;
- store paychecks outside the payroll department, but keep the key in the payroll department.

**Rotation of job duties.** It is only natural for employees who have been working at one job for several years to devise shortcuts for completing that job. While these shortcuts may make the employees more efficient in getting their work done, they also are often designed to avoid having to deal with the company's internal control procedures (e.g., the employee responsible for payroll distribution lets individual departments keep paychecks for absent employees until they return rather than requiring that the checks be sent to a central location—perhaps human resources or finance—for safekeeping).

To prevent this avoidance of a company's internal controls, it is a good idea to rotate employees into different jobs periodically during the payroll processing cycle—after proper training, of course. If this is done, the payroll manager or controller may uncover practices designed to circumvent internal controls and can correct them. Once again, the small payroll department presents a somewhat different set of problems. Rotation is often nearly impossible. However, requiring payroll personnel to take a vacation during a payroll processing cycle can have the same effect as job rotation.

Failure to rotate job duties can have other negative consequences as well. Having only one person who is capable of putting together the data needed to make timely federal and/or state tax deposits is unwise, since that employee's absence from work at a crucial time could result in stiff late payment penalties and interest. Other payroll department staffers, including managers, should be able to gather and process this critical information.

**Payroll distribution.** In nearly all companies, payroll is distributed in the form of paychecks or direct deposit. Paycheck distribution is generally governed by company policies which specifically set forth who may receive a paycheck. In most instances, companies should require that paychecks be delivered only to the employee whose name is on the check. Most companies allow for exceptions in emergencies where the employee is unable to receive the paycheck but has provided written authorization for another person to receive it.

Security of paychecks is an important matter, and company policies in this area are often an indicator of how secure other company assets are. Paychecks should never be left in unlocked desks or file cabinets. Paychecks that cannot be delivered to employees should be returned to a department other than payroll and secured until the employee can receive the check. Security may not need to be quite as strict for direct deposit statements, which are not negotiable, although there are employee privacy issues to consider.

**Phantom employees.** While the problem of "phantom" employees may not be a major one in most companies, those with many remote locations can fall victim to schemes creating nonexistent employees with false names, social security numbers, etc. One method of preventing the processing of paychecks for phantom employees is the "physical payout" (or payoff). During a physical payout, paychecks and direct deposit statements are distributed at each location by payroll department or internal audit employees. In order to receive a paycheck, each employee must produce a type of photo identification. Physical payouts should be conducted without advance notice to employees.

**Negative pay deductions.** If too much money has been deducted from an employee's pay by mistake, one method of refunding the amount of the extra deduction is by use of a negative deduction. Because this is an easy way for unscrupulous payroll department personnel to improperly boost their own or other employees' pay, any negative deductions should receive intense scrutiny from the payroll manager. Another method of preventing abuse of negative deductions is to make sure the person responsible for making the deductions is not the same person who reconciles payroll withholding amounts to the general ledger each month.

**Payroll bank account.** The balancing and reconciliation of the payroll bank account with the general ledger should be segregated from the payroll department.

**Blank checks.** The payroll department's largest source of potential exposure is the storage of blank checks. Blank check stock should be secured away from the payroll department and away from the method for affixing signatures to the checks. Furthermore, checks should never be signed until the documentation supporting them has been reviewed for accuracy and approved.

**Time reporting.** Overreporting of hours worked and incorrect classification of paid time can lead to large losses for a business. Therefore, it is essential that internal control procedures ensure accurate time reporting. Where time cards or time sheets are used to record time worked, they should be reviewed and approved by department supervisors or managers before they are sent to payroll for processing. An employee's supervisor should know how many hours were worked.

The payroll department should also review the time cards and time sheets for the proper supervisory approvals, as well as accuracy of calculations and compliance with company policies. The original source data should also be compared with the payroll register to verify the data were entered properly.

Many companies are moving toward automated time and attendance reporting, with employees swiping a card through a reader whenever they enter or leave their work area or entering their arrival and departure times into a computer or on the phone (see Section 12.7). Automation greatly increases the employer's control over the time reporting function and eliminates some of the approval steps, freeing managers for other tasks. A combination of manual and automated systems can be used by employers with combined hourly and salaried staffs that do not wish to apply the automated system to the exempt employees. They can also use "exception reporting" for exempt employees, who will only record their time off rather than all their time worked.

**Computer system edits.** The proper edits or alerts in an employer's computerized payroll system can make sure any unusual situations are brought to the payroll manager's attention. These situations may include: new employees; employees terminating from the company; unreasonable worktime reported; negative net pay; and negative deductions (see Section 12.5-1).

**Using an internal auditor.** The job of a company's internal auditor is to review the efficiency of the organization's internal control procedures and recommend changes where needed. It is up to the company's managers to ensure compliance with the internal controls. The internal auditor also is charged with recognizing areas where improvement is needed and recommending enhancements to the existing internal controls.

In payroll, the internal auditor makes sure systems and procedural changes have the approval of upper management. The internal auditor is also interested in the security of the data gathered and recorded by payroll and the assets it uses. Auditors also determine if the existing internal controls reduce the company's exposure to employee fraud and theft. Following are some specific ways in which the internal auditor can help the payroll department.

- In large companies, the internal auditor assists in identifying the procedures for segregating and rotating job duties within and outside the payroll department. In smaller companies, an auditor can help persuade the payroll manager of the need to move some duties to other departments if segregation within the department is impossible.

- The internal auditor can check sporadically to make sure that undelivered paychecks are sent to another department for safekeeping until the employees can receive them, rather than remaining in the employees' departments or being sent back to payroll.

- The internal auditor and his or her staff can conduct a physical payout to detect phantom employees.

- The internal auditor should be involved from the beginning when a company is deciding on the acquisition of a new payroll system so proper edits are installed to note unusual situations.

**Sarbanes-Oxley Act impacts payroll departments.** In 2002, the Public Company Accounting Reform and Investor Protection Act, also known as the Sarbanes-Oxley Act (SOX), was enacted in response to the corporate finance scandals at Enron, WorldCom, Adelphia, and other public companies.[4] SOX sets up the framework for the establishment of the Public Company Accounting Oversight Board and imposes requirements on publicly held companies that were designed to restore investor and public confidence in corporate financial management.

 **SOX EXPANSION LIKELY** While the Sarbanes-Oxley Act applies only to companies whose stock is publicly traded and whose finances are governed by the Securities Exchange Act of 1934, several states are considering their own versions of SOX that may apply more broadly to smaller companies and non-profit organizations.

In general, SOX requires public companies to have a framework for identifying, documenting, and evaluating their internal controls over financial reporting, and it provides a logical way to analyze a company's control system. SOX also prohibits a public accounting firm from providing both external auditing and most non-auditing services to the same client, and it requires audit partners to rotate every five years.

*Certification of financial reports.*[5] Under SOX, a public company's chief executive officer and chief financial officer must certify for each annual or quarterly report filed under the Securities Exchange Act that:

- the signing officers have reviewed the report;
- as far as the officer knows, the report does not contain any statement of a material fact that is not true or omit any material fact;
- as far as the officer knows, the financial statements and other financial information in the report fairly present the financial condition and operational results of the company;
- the signing officers are responsible for designing and maintaining the company's internal controls so that material information is available;
- the signing officers have evaluated the effectiveness of the internal controls within 90 days of filing the report and presented their conclusions in the report based on those evaluations;
- the signing officers have disclosed to the company's external auditors and the board of directors' audit committee all significant problems in the design and operation of the company's internal controls and any fraud involving management or other employees who have an important role in the internal controls; and
- the signing officers have indicated whether there have been any significant changes in the company's internal controls or in other factors that could affect the internal controls after they were evaluated, including any corrective actions taken with regard to significant deficiencies or material weaknesses.

*Complaint procedures must be established.*[6] A public company's audit committee must set up procedures for the receipt, retention, and treatment of complaints received by the company regarding accounting, internal controls, or auditing matters, including anonymous complaints from employees about questionable financial practices. It is unlawful for a company to discharge, harass, threaten, or otherwise discriminate against an employee who lawfully provides information or assists in an investigation regarding questionable financial conduct. Employees have the right to sue their employer for any such retaliation, and retaliation can also result in criminal penalties.

*No loans to officers or directors.*[7] Public companies may not make personal loans to any director or executive officer, with some limited exceptions for credit cards, consumer credit, and home improvement loans.

---

4.    Pub. Law No. 107-204.
5.    SOX §302.
6.    SOX §301; 806; 1107.
7.    SOX §402.

## *Section 11: Payroll Accounting*

*Internal control assessments and reports.*[8] The company's annual report must contain an internal control report that contains a statement of management's responsibility for designing and maintaining adequate internal controls and management's assessment of the effectiveness of the internal controls over financial reporting. The company's external auditors must attest to and report on management's assessment, certifying the underlying controls and processes used to determine financial results.

*Impact on payroll.* So why should payroll managers and others involved in the payroll process be concerned with SOX? Because of the importance of internal controls over financial reporting to SOX compliance, payroll is directly involved in making sure that a public company's officers and board have reliable information and efficient processes. Payroll information impacts a company's balance sheet and its income statement. Therefore, inadequate internal controls over the payroll process could result in material misrepresentations of the company's financial posture, which has to be certified by the CEO and CFO.

*Payroll's role in SOX compliance.* Following are some of the things that need to occur in the payroll department to make sure that adequate internal controls are in place to help the company's SOX compliance efforts:

- develop process and workflow maps that show each function;
- create written documentation for each step in the payroll process and update documentation where it already exists;
- audit recordkeeping and retention procedures to make sure that records are organized and can be retrieved easily;
- identify gaps and risks that can lead to a lack of control and security (e.g., inadequate separation of duties);
- communicate the gaps and risks to management;
- prepare an action plan to address the gaps and risks through adequate internal controls;
- develop a way to measure progress in addressing the gaps and risks, and
- document the design, evaluation, and testing of the internal controls, which will form the basis for management certification of the internal controls and attestation by the outside auditor.

 **WATCH OUT** Many auditors, both internal and external, have little experience with payroll audits. In order to avoid a conflict of interest during such audits, payroll managers should avoid having to train the auditors in the specifics of a payroll audit and should insist that auditors coming to the payroll department receive adequate training before they get there.

*What about third-party payroll vendors?* More than half of all payroll departments outsource all or part of their payroll process, whether it's payroll processing itself or tax filing, garnishments, or paycards. As is true with other types of compliance, outsourcing of all or part of the payroll process does not relieve a public company of its responsibility under SOX to have adequate internal controls. It is up to the payroll manager to ensure that the company's payroll service providers have adequate controls over the parts of the payroll process they deliver.

One way to do this is to guarantee that your company has a right to audit the service provider's processes when the contract between the company and the service provider is signed. An easier way to do this is to require what is known as a SAS (Statement on Auditing Standards) 70 report from the service provider. A SAS 70 report shows that the service provider has had its control objectives and activities examined by an independent auditing firm in a SAS 70 examination. There are two types of SAS 70 reports.

Type I. In a Type I report, the independent auditor expresses an opinion on whether the service provider's description of its control procedures presents fairly the relevant aspects of the service provider's controls as of a specific date and whether the controls were suitably designed to achieve specified control objectives.

---

8.    SOX §404.

<u>Type II.</u> In a Type II report, the auditor will express an opinion on the same items that are contained in a Type I report and whether the controls that were tested were operating effectively enough to provide reasonable assurance that the control objectives were achieved during the period specified, which must be at least six months. In most cases, a Type II report is preferable.

After the employer receives the service provider's SAS 70 report, it should review the report thoroughly to determine whether the report actually relates to the processes that the vendor is performing for the employer. It is the employer that is ultimately responsible for certifying the adequacy of its internal controls, even when the system containing those controls is supplied by an outside third party.

If the employer finds that the SAS 70 is too broad or generic and does not properly relate to the specific services the vendor is providing, the employer can request another report that is more specific, although it may be significantly more costly, or it can ask its outside auditors to produce the compliance documentation and perform the testing of the internal controls at the third party's premises.

# 11.9 Controlling Check Fraud

The negotiating of fraudulent checks has always been a serious problem for the American financial system and American employers, but it has become even more prevalent in recent years, as technological advances have made it easier to reproduce or overcome most security features. This section will look at different levels of check security features and the benefits and drawbacks of each. Much of the material in this section has been adapted with permission from a seminar presentation by William Chandler, Vice President of Relyco, Inc., at the American Payroll Association's Sixteenth Annual Congress, April 19-23, 1998.

**Group 1 security.** Group 1 security features are manufactured into the check paper. They are difficult and expensive to reproduce because the equipment is costly and a large volume of checks must be produced to make them cost effective.

- *Mould Made and Fourdriner Watermarks* — These are considered "true" watermarks, as opposed to printed watermarks. They actually alter the structure of the paper, causing a picture or pattern to appear only when the paper is held up to a light source. They do not reproduce on copiers, and if they are reproduced through printing as phantoms, they can be seen without holding them up to a light source.

- *Overt Fibers and Planchettes* — Overt fibers and planchettes are found in many national currencies. They are readily visible to the naked eye, but they can also be reproduced fairly well on modern color copiers.

- *Covert Fibers* — Covert fibers are invisible to the naked eye, but glow when held under an ultraviolet (black) light. While they both may appear on a good color copy, they will not glow in ultraviolet light.

- *Chemical Reactants* — Chemical reactants are "safety papers" that produce visible chemical reactions when contacted by a variety of chemical solvents and eradicators. Chlorine bleach produces a multi-language "VOID"; solvents produce a variety of chemical stains that are readily visible to the naked eye.

- *Toner Bond Enhancers* — Toner bond enhancers include a variety of trademarked paper products that are chemically treated to form a stronger bond between the MICR toner and paper, thus deterring manual alteration of the information on a check. They can be an expensive add-on option, and may not be worth the additional cost since they may reduce toner adherence.

**Group 2 security.** Group 2 security features are printed onto the paper either when the paper is converted from raw material to check stock or when the check MICR or OCR lines, payee, and amount information is completed. Each feature combines the creative use of design and ink to defeat some type of tampering, and when used in combination, they can significantly hinder fraudulent copying of and tampering with a check.

- *Screened Printing* — Under magnification, screened printing appears as discreet dots on an original document, while on color copies it appears as a series of broken lines.

- *Microprinting* — Microprinting is extremely difficult to reproduce accurately because of the size of the type, and copies do not have a fine enough resolution to reproduce legible text.

- *Simulated Watermarks* — Simulated watermarks use "white" links to produce a pattern on the check that is only visible when held at an angle to a light source. Because it is white, technology to copy the simulated watermark has not yet been developed.

- *Warning Bands and Security Icons* — These features alert the teller and/or check recipient to the presence of certain security features that should be verified before processing the check. They can be printed anywhere on the document and identify any feature. They are usually used in combination with other Group 1 and 2 security features and can offer a strong check fraud deterrent.

- *"VOID" Features* — "VOID" features can deter simple check copying, since using varying dot sizes causes copiers to enhance the printed "VOID" so that it renders the copied check nonnegotiable. However, many modern copiers can defeat this feature by adjusting the copier's settings. But if it is used together with other security features, the "VOID" can be quite effective.

- *Prismatic Printing* — By printing two or more colors that change in density and blend together on the check form, prismatic printing makes it difficult for a color copier to accurately reproduce the true colors of the check.

- *Anti-Splice Lines* — Anti-splice lines are printed on the back of the check and consist of repetitive parallel lines that serve to deter the cutting and pasting of numbers from one location to another on the face of the check.

- *Aniline Dye* — These printed dyes penetrate the paper and bleed to the back side. They cannot be accurately copied, and they cannot be removed without destroying the paper.

- *Holograms and Foils* — Holograms and foils are stamped onto the paper rather than printed, resulting in a metallic or "3D" image that can only be reproduced at great cost.

- *Thermochromic Ink* — This special ink is temperature sensitive and its color will fade to white when exposed to body temperature or other heat source. Color copies will not have these color fading properties. They should be used with a notice to check for their presence.

- *Nonnegotiable Backer* — Remittance advice information does not always cover the full stub portion of a check. By printing NONNEGOTIABLE on the back of the stub, excess paper cannot be used to reproduce a duplicate check on the original paper. This is particularly important when using a safety paper with built-in security features.

- *Security Lock Icons and Descriptions* — Printing a security "lock icon" on the face of a check alerts the recipient to look for specific features in order to confirm check authenticity. A list of the features can then be printed on the back of the check for them to reference.

**Group 3 security**. Group 3 security is also called "Positive Pay"—bank sponsored electronic data checking. While it is the most effective security measure, it is also currently the most costly and labor intensive. It requires the actual one-to-one comparison of the check information with company and bank records of the document as it was created. There also must be extensive data sharing between the bank and check originator.

Positive Pay requires verification of check number and check value before the check is processed. In this way, fraud to the check originator is limited to insiders who know in advance what the actual value of a specific number check should be. Currently, this feature is used only in corporate banking where sophisticated data processing and reporting systems are available. It may never be practical for personal check verification because of the data sharing requirements.

**Training bank personnel in detection is a problem**. Bank tellers must process hundreds of checks in short periods of time, and they are generally untrained in the identification of fraudulent checks beyond checking the payee's identification. Nonexistent or poor training defeats the effectiveness of most Group 1 and 2 security features for the receiving bank. Proper training could keep many fraudulent checks out of the banking system and save all parties a considerable amount of money.

# 11.10 Check 21 and Its Impact on Payroll

On October 28, 2004, the Check Clearing for 21st Century Act, also known as "Check 21," went into effect.[9] The law was designed to promote innovation in the U.S. payments system while updating and eliminating some of the legal barriers governing how banks process paper checks.

**Substitute checks used in clearing process.** Check 21 permits the use of a new category of negotiable instrument called a substitute check. A substitute check is a paper reproduction of an original check that contains an image of the front and back of the original check. The copy is suitable for automated processing in the same manner as the original check and meets other technical requirements.

Check 21 allows financial institutions to truncate original checks (i.e., remove them from the check clearing process), electronically process check information, and deliver substitute checks to banks that wish to continue receiving paper checks. The substitute checks are treated as legal equivalents of the original checks written by an individual or entity.

For a substitute check to qualify under Check 21 as the legal equivalent of an original check, it must be a paper reproduction of the original check that:

- contains an image of the front and back of the original check;
- displays a Magnetic Ink Character Recognition (MICR) line containing all the information appearing on the MICR line of the original check or, to the extent that generally applicable industry standards for substitute checks allow, only some of that information;
- conforms in paper stock, dimension, and otherwise with generally applicable industry standards for substitute checks; and
- is suitable for automated processing in the same manner as the original check.

The substitute check must also include a legend that states, "This is a legal copy of your check. You can use it the same way you would use the original check." This legend serves as a warranty that the substitute check is a legal equivalent of the original check for all purposes. When a financial institution elects to transfer, present, or return a substitute check (or a paper or electronic representation of a substitute check), it is agreeing that the substitute check contains an accurate image of the front and back of the original check and a legend stating that it is the legal equivalent of the original check. The financial institution is also agreeing that no depositary bank, drawer, or endorser will be asked to pay a check that it has already paid.

---

9.     Pub. Law 108-100.

**Regulatory changes.** In order to implement Check 21, the Federal Reserve Board had to modify its Regulation CC, the Availability of Funds and Collection of Checks. The amended regulations include provisions that:

- set forth the requirements of Check 21 that apply to banks;
- provided revised model disclosures and model notices relating to substitute checks; and
- established bank endorsement and identification requirements for substitute checks.

**The impact on payroll.** One of the first impacts of Check 21 that payroll departments felt was the loss of check "float" – the interest gain on checks that have been issued but not yet cleared through the check clearing system. As financial institutions have expanded their internal check image processing systems and begun to process electronic images of checks rather than original paper checks, bank customers, including employers, have noticed that checks are clearing much faster than they did in the past.

This trend will have a significant impact on mid-size and larger employers that have mastered the art of managing their float patterns in the past. With this in mind, payroll departments should discuss the potential implications of Check 21 with their organization's finance or treasury departments to ensure greater attention to fund management of payroll accounts. This is especially true when an employer is making special payments (e.g., bonuses, off-cycle checks) or if it has a low direct deposit participation rate and a high percentage of paper paychecks.

Another issue that may surface is how an employer can prove it made a tax payment if there is no original cancelled check to show to the IRS. In answer to this question, the Federal Reserve Board has stated, "Substitute checks that meet the legal equivalence requirements of the Check 21 Act can, by the terms of the Act, be used wherever an original check is required." It should also be noted that employers using EFTPS to make electronic tax payments have alternative methods of proving tax payments that do not involve substitute checks.

# 11.10 Review Questions and Exercises

## Review Questions

1. Who would be interested in the financial records of a business?

2. What are subsidiary ledgers?

3. What is the chart of accounts?

4. Name the five types of accounts that are generally used by businesses to classify transactions.

5. Payroll expenses may be recorded in one of two ways, functionally or by type of pay. Explain.

6. Within a payroll system there are checks and balances to ensure the accuracy of a company's financial records and the security of its assets. What are they called?

7. Explain accrual accounting as it applies to payroll.

8. What are reversals, and how do they affect accounting?

9. What reconciliation steps should be taken before filing quarterly and year-end returns?

10. What are earnings per share?

11. What is the purpose of an external audit?

12. What is the role of an internal auditor?

13. What is a balance sheet?

14. What effect does revenue have on owner's equity?

15. What effect do expenses have on owner's equity?

16. What is the purpose of the journal?

## True or False Questions

_____ 1. Under generally accepted accounting principles, the realization principle governs the recording of revenue.

_____ 2. After entries have been recorded in the journal, they are posted to the General Ledger.

_____ 3. Regardless of the accounting periods or fiscal year that a company uses, payroll taxes do not have to be reported on a calendar year basis.

_____ 4. The income statement summarizes an organization's revenues, expenses, and earnings for the current year only.

_____ 5. The balance sheet is a financial statement that shows the financial position of a business on a certain date.

_____ 6. Accounts payable are assets.

_____ 7. In a business, the assets must always be equal to the liabilities minus the owner's equity.

_____ 8. The property owned by a business is known as its liabilities.

_____ 9. Revenue can be obtained in the form of cash or accounts receivable.

_____ 10. Payments of expenses decrease assets and decrease owner's equity.

_____ 11. Amounts charged for the sale of services or goods are referred to as revenue.

_____ 12. After all amounts on the balance sheet have been recorded in accounts, the total debits must equal the total credits.

_____ 13. Entering an amount on the left side of an account is called debiting the account.

_____ 14. A separate account is kept for each asset, liability, and owner's equity item that a business has.

_____ 15. The revenue earned during the accounting period appears on the balance sheet.

_____ 16. Any accounting period of 12 consecutive months can serve as a company's fiscal year.

_____ 17. The purpose of a journal entry is to provide all the essential information about a business transaction.

_____ 18. A journal entry containing more than one debit or more than one credit is called a compound entry.

_____ 19. General ledger accounts are arranged in the order they appear on the chart of accounts.

_____ 20. At the end of each pay period, many businesses enter the hours worked, gross earnings, deductions, and net pay of their employees in a payroll register.

_____ 21. The general ledger is classified as a record of original entry.

_____ 22. The payroll expense journal will debit salaries/wages payable and credit an expense account for the labor cost.

_____ 23. Payroll expenses are accrued when the payroll period ending date and the accounting period ending date do not coincide.

_____ 24. Paychecks that cannot be delivered should be returned to the payroll department.

_____ 25. One method of reducing phantom employees is the physical payout.

_____ 26. Blank checks should never be stored in the same place as the check signing machine.

## Multiple Choice Questions

_____ 1. When revenue and expenses are recorded in the same accounting period, which accounting concept is being applied?

   a. Business entity
   b. Matching
   c. Realization
   d. Continuing concern

_____ 2. When the same accounting concepts are applied in the same way in each accounting period, which accounting concept is being applied?

   a. Objectivity
   b. Continuing concern
   c. Consistency
   d. Business entity

_____ 3. When each transaction is described by a business document that proves the transaction did occur, which accounting concept is being applied?

   a. Objectivity
   b. Cost
   c. Matching
   d. Business entity

_____ 4. In the modern audit process how does testing occur?

   a. Checking every transaction
   b. Checking those transactions indicated by the company
   c. Checking similar transactions to the last audit
   d. Sampling

_____ 5.	How are marketable securities classified?

a.	Current assets
b.	Tangible assets
c.	Intangible assets
d.	Current liabilities

_____ 6.	Where are business transactions first recorded?

a.	Journal
b.	General ledger
c.	Trial balance
d.	Balance sheet

_____ 7.	If a pay period ends August 22, employees are paid August 29, and the payroll tax deposit is due September 15, when should the payroll expenses be recorded?

a.	August 22
b.	August 23
c.	August 29
d.	September 15

_____ 8.	Which of the following accounts describes the legal obligation of a business to pay its debts?

a.	Asset
b.	Liability
c.	Owner's equity
d.	Expenses

_____ 9.	FUTA and SUTA taxes payable are what types of accounts?

a.	Owner's equity
b.	Assets
c.	Liabilities
d.	Net worth

_____ 10.	When a company purchases a computer on credit for $2,500, which of the following journal entries is made?

a.	Debit assets and debit liabilities
b.	Debit assets and credit liabilities
c.	Credit assets and debit liabilities
d.	Credit assets and credit owner's equity

_____ 11.	What financial statement shows the net income or net loss of a business?

a.	Income statement
b.	Balance sheet
c.	Statement of owner's equity
d.	Statement of cash flow

_____ 12.　What is the difference between the debits and credits to an account called?

     a.　Single-entry
     b.　Double-entry
     c.　Cross-footing
     d.　Balance

_____ 13.　What effect do revenues have on accounts?

     a.　Increasing expenses
     b.　Decreasing liabilities
     c.　Decreasing owner's equity
     d.　Increasing owner's equity

_____ 14.　In what account is the payment of salaries and wages recorded?

     a.　Asset
     b.　Liability
     c.　Expense
     d.　Revenue

_____ 15.　What is a common name for a journal?

     a.　Record of final entry
     b.　Record of secondary entry
     c.　Record of original entry
     d.　Record of cross-reference

_____ 16.　What is the process of transferring entries from the journal to the general ledger called?

     a.　Journalizing
     b.　Posting
     c.　Footing
     d.　Balancing

_____ 17.　What document records payroll data for each payroll period?

     a.　Earnings record
     b.　Payroll register
     c.　Payroll ledger
     d.　Accounts receivable ledger

_____ 18.　What account is credited for child support withheld?

     a.　Child support expense
     b.　Child support payable
     c.　Accounts payable
     d.　Payroll taxes expense

_____ 19.　Which account has an entry when the deposit of state income tax withheld is made?

     a.　Employees' income tax payable
     b.　Payroll tax expenses
     c.　State tax expense
     d.　State income tax payable

_____ 20. What journal entry is made to record the deposit of federal income tax?

    a. Debit payroll taxes expense, credit federal income tax payable
    b. Debit cash, credit federal income tax payable
    c. Credit payroll taxes expense, debit cash
    d. Debit federal income tax payable, credit cash

_____ 21. Which of the following is not a payroll department internal control?

    a. Segregation of duties
    b. Physical payouts
    c. Computer edits
    d. Balancing accounts

## Problems

1. Classify each item that follows as an asset, liability, or owner's equity.

    a. Cash_____
    b. Loan payable to a bank_____
    c. Delivery equipment_____
    d. Account payable to a creditor_____
    e. Office furniture_____
    f. Owner's financial interest_____
    g. Petty cash_____
    h. Mortgage payable to a bank _____
    i. FUTA taxes payable_____

2. Some of the ledger accounts of the Morris Word Processing Service, owned and operated by Paul Morris, are listed below. In the columns at the right, indicate by a check mark (✓) whether these accounts are shown on the income statement or the balance sheet.

| Accounts | Income Statement | Balance Sheet |
|---|---|---|
| a. Accounts payable | _____ | _____ |
| b. Accounts receivable | _____ | _____ |
| c. Advertising expense | _____ | _____ |
| d. Cash | _____ | _____ |
| e. Salaries payable | _____ | _____ |
| f. Duplicating equipment | _____ | _____ |
| g. Paul Morris, capital | _____ | _____ |
| h. Miscellaneous expense | _____ | _____ |
| i. Office furniture | _____ | _____ |
| j. Rent expense | _____ | _____ |

# Section 11: Payroll Accounting

3. Enter the normal balance (debit or credit) for each of the following accounts.

    a. Accounts receivable          _____
    b. Social security tax payable   _____
    c. Sales                         _____
    d. Sales tax payable             _____
    e. Accounts payable              _____
    f. Wage garnishments payable     _____
    g. Payroll taxes expense         _____
    h. Professional fees payable     _____
    i. Freight expense               _____
    j. Life insurance premiums payable _____

4. The payroll records of Redwood Lumber for the week ended January 4, 2008 are as follows:

| | |
|---|---|
| Gross earnings | $50,000.00 |
| Social security tax withheld | 3,100.00 |
| Medicare tax withheld | 725.00 |
| Federal income tax withheld | 7,500.00 |
| State income tax withheld | 750.00 |
| City income tax withheld | 375.00 |
| Life insurance premium withheld | 200.00 |
| Health insurance premium withheld | 120.00 |
| Credit union contributions withheld | 100.00 |
| Savings Bond deductions | 350.00 |

   Record the weekly payroll information for January 4, 2008 in the journal.

5. Solar Products' payroll was $40,000 on January 18, 2008. The applicable tax rates are as follows: Social security, 6.2%; Medicare, 1.45%; FUTA, 0.8%; and SUTA, 2.7%. Show the journal entry that would be made to record the employer's payroll taxes, assuming no employee has reached any applicable wage limit.

6. Employer Gail Winters and her employees are subject to social security, Medicare, FUTA and SUTA taxes. During the payroll period ending January 18, 2008, her employees earned wages of $30,000, all of which is taxable. The federal income tax withheld amounted to $4,500. The employer pays FUTA tax of $240 and SUTA tax of $810.

    a. Journalize the payroll for the payroll period ending January 18, 2008.

    b. Journalize and record the employer's payroll taxes on January 18, 2008.

    c. Journalize and record the payment of wages to the employees on January 25, 2008.

7. Anderson Distributors pays its employees on a weekly basis. The totals for the payroll for the week ended January 4, 2008 are as follows:

| | |
|---|---|
| Regular wages | $12,400.00 |
| Overtime pay | 1,800.00 |
| Commissions paid | 2,200.00 |
| Social security tax withheld | 1,016.80 |
| Medicare tax withheld | 237.80 |
| Federal income tax withheld | 2,460.00 |
| State income tax withheld | 246.00 |
| Life insurance premiums withheld | 30.00 |
| Health insurance premiums withheld | 22.00 |

Use 0.8% to calculate the employer's FUTA tax and 2.7% to calculate the employer's SUTA tax.

Show the journal entries that should be made to record the payroll.

8. a. Assume that the gross weekly payroll is $100,000 for Emerson Hardware Distributors and the accounting month ends on Thursday, during the weekly payroll period. Since the weekly payroll period has not ended as of the end of the accounting month, the company needs to accrue for four days (Mon. - Thurs.), which is 80% of the weekly payroll. Use 0.8% for FUTA tax and 3% for SUTA tax.

Make the entries to record the accrued payroll for Emerson Hardware Distributors for Monday, August 18, to Thursday, August 21, 2008.

b. Based on the August 21 accrual, record the reversal entries to be made on August 22, 2008, when the employees are paid.

9. At the start of 2008, employees of New Frontiers accrue vacation amounting to $4,000 for the month. During the third week in January, an employee uses vacation time amounting to $900.

a. Make the entry to record the employees' accrual of vacation leave for the month of January.

b. Make the entry to record the employees' actual use of vacation leave.

# SECTION 12:  PAYROLL SYSTEMS AND TECHNOLOGY

## TABLE OF CONTENTS

# SECTION 12: PAYROLL SYSTEMS AND TECHNOLOGY

When payroll practitioners speak of a "payroll system," they no longer mean a manual payroll operation run with an adding machine for determining wages paid and taxes withheld and a typewriter for producing paychecks. In even the smallest businesses, a payroll system today is an automated, computerized system. The computers may belong to a service provider that handles the company's payroll, to the company itself, or to a separate entity that allows several businesses to share its computer resources over the Internet.

But computers themselves are not the only components of a payroll system. The system also includes programs and applications that tell the computer what information to process and how to process the information and the employees who operate the system. This section will provide an explanation of what a payroll system can do, how it can work with other computer systems used by the employer, the steps to follow in selecting an appropriate payroll system, and the kinds of controls and security needed to guarantee the system's integrity.

## 12.1 Objectives of a Computerized Payroll System

Most businesses recognize that, in order to succeed in a highly competitive world, they must meet the needs of their customers. Their payroll systems must meet that same goal, even though the customers they must satisfy are a different, and often more demanding, group. The payroll department's customers include:

- the employees it pays;
- other departments in the company;
- the company's upper management; and
- the federal, state, and local government agencies to whom withheld income and employment taxes, child support payments, etc., are paid and reported.

In the payroll world, customer satisfaction means compliance: with federal, state, and local government taxation and reporting requirements; with company policies on paying employees, recordkeeping, and accounting; and with upper management's business and cost-saving objectives. Specifically, a successful payroll system must:

- *Provide for compliance with federal, state, and local withholding, depositing, and reporting requirements*—income and employment taxes must be withheld from wage payments, timely and properly deposited in an appropriate financial institution for each type of tax withheld (along with the employer's share of payroll taxes), and properly reported to the agency administering each tax.

- *Issue timely and accurate paychecks, direct deposits and other disbursements*—accurately paying employees on payday is a paramount objective of the payroll system, so it must accurately withhold for: all federal, state, and local taxes; tax levies, garnishments, and child support payments; and fringe benefit deductions and wage deferrals. It must also correctly calculate any additional pay due the employee in the form of bonuses, commissions, overtime premiums, etc.

- *Maintain adequate records of all data and transactions*—information used to calculate each payroll, deposit taxes, and prepare reports must be maintained by the system in a way that allows for easy storage and retrieval should they be needed.

- *Prepare internal reports*—company policies generally will require the preparation of internal reports detailing payroll information so upper management can accurately determine labor costs and other expenses.

- *Guarantee the security of the system*—access must be limited and privacy of records assured to make sure the company's assets are secure and that audits will provide an accurate picture of the company's financial condition.

## 12.2 Interfacing and Integration

Payroll systems do not exist in a vacuum in their respective companies. The data used and produced by the system are often required by other company systems to meet their information needs. This requirement is especially acute where payroll and human resources are concerned, since these two departments, along with benefits, control nearly all employee-related data. In many companies, this has led to integration of the payroll and human resources systems (and sometimes benefits as well) into one shared database. In others, the two departments transfer data from one system to the other and to other company systems as well through interfaces.

## 12.2-1 Interfacing—Working With Other Systems and Departments

The place where two systems meet is called the interface. When two systems are interfaced, they can talk to each other and be understood, sharing data needed by both. Direct interfacing between payroll and many other company systems is critical to the success of not only the payroll system but the other systems as well.

If information needed by more than one system can be used by each system after being entered only once, the cost of entering the data, the need for verification, and the chances for data entry errors are greatly reduced. The following internal and external systems generally require a direct interface with the payroll system and benefit the most from a fully automated linkage.

**Human resources.** While many companies in recent years have developed a shared database for payroll and human resources information, those that have not yet done so or have chosen not to do so must find a way to move information between the two systems and update that information. Interfaces will be needed to check the data that are duplicated between the files (e.g., names, addresses, social security numbers, salary, exempt/nonexempt status) as well as to update the information in each file.

**Benefits.** Once again, if the payroll and benefits systems do not share an integrated database, an interface must be designed so that data regarding benefits deductions and eligibility, pension accruals and contributions, group-term life insurance benefits, etc., can be transferred to the payroll system, cross-checked, and updated. Data must also be passed from the payroll system to the benefits system, including year-to-date wages, year-to-date benefit plan contributions, etc.

**Labor cost data collection.** For accounting and cost allocation purposes, many companies require close tracking of labor so that costs can be assigned to the products produced or services provided. Therefore, the payroll system may be required to provide such labor distribution cost information and to interface with the data collection systems that will process the information.

**Payroll bank accounts.** The paycheck bank reconciliation process (see Section 11.6-2) may require communication between the payroll system and the file generated with issued paychecks.

**Direct deposit/EFT.** As part of a company's direct deposit program, which electronically posts employees' pay in their bank accounts, the payroll system will have to produce a file that is formatted according to requirements of the automated clearing house with which it deals. This allows transfer of wage amounts from the employer's originating depository financial institution, through the ACH, and finally to the receiving depository financial institution (the employee's bank or credit union). See Section 5.3-2 for more on direct deposit. A similar file would need to be produced if the employer pays some of its employees with payroll debit cards. See Section 5.3-3 for more on paycards.

**Time and attendance.** Automated time and attendance systems that provide for electronically recording each employee's entry and exit from the work area and transfer of the information to the payroll system eliminate a great deal of data entry costs and errors (see Section 12.7). This system may work together with the employer's labor cost data collection system.

**Accounts payable.** Some very important information needs to be passed between an employer's accounts payable system and its payroll system for proper tax withholding, depositing, and reporting to be accomplished. This information includes relocation expense payments and reimbursements, travel and expense reimbursements, child support and garnishment payments, cash awards and prizes, and others. An automated interface between the two systems greatly increases the chances that this information will be processed timely and accurately.

**General ledger/cost accounting.** As was noted in Section 11, there is a very strong relationship between payroll and accounting. Payroll journal entries, prepared from the payroll register or other subsidiary ledgers, should be provided by some method of interface to the general ledger/accounting systems. This greatly reduces the possibility of errors and the labor costs associated with manual preparation and transfer of such entries.

**Outside benefit plan administrators.** Payroll system information (e.g., benefit eligibility, elections, deductions, etc.) is often needed by outside administrators of the employer's benefit plans to ensure proper processing of claims, credit for benefit accruals, and payment of benefits. Automated interfaces would once again make this process run smoother and cheaper.

**Social Security Administration.** As noted in Section 8.14, employers may be required to submit individual employee wage and tax information to the Social Security Administration in an electronic format. As specified in SSA's Specifications for Filing Forms W-2 Electronically (EFW2), employers interface wage and tax data annually. Beginning with 2006 Form W-2 data, SSA receives the interface only over the Internet through its Business Services Online (BSO). Using SSA's AccuWage software allows employers to ensure that the data provided are accurate and will be processed. All states that allow or require magnetic or electronic filing accept the EFW2 format for annual tax and wage reporting.

**State unemployment insurance.** As noted in Section 7.2, employers are required to submit individual employee wage information to each state's unemployment insurance agency. Depending on the state's capabilities and requirements, employers may submit the data in a magnetic or electronic format. Many states use a standardized format (see Table 7.5) for the data submitted quarterly.

**Tax deposits.** Many states currently require employers to deposit taxes electronically, and more than 90% of withheld federal income and employment taxes are deposited using the Electronic Federal Tax Payment System (see Section 8.2-2 for details). Each state may use different methods, but generally the ACH system discussed in Section 5.3-2 is the basis for the deposits. When using electronic means to deposit taxes, employers must use the same caution as when making deposits with checks to ensure accuracy and timeliness requirements are met.

**State disbursement units.** The states are required to have centralized state disbursement units that can accept electronic payments of withheld child support, and some states require that payments be made electronically (see Section 9.1-2). Employers must make sure that their payroll and accounts payable systems can handle the transfer of information necessary to make these electronic payments through the ACH network.

# 12.2-2 Integration of Payroll and Human Resource Systems

In recent years, an increasing number of companies have implemented Integrated Human Resource Management Systems (IHRMS) that provide a shared database for human resources, payroll, and benefits information. The change from separate systems that interfaced with one another to an integrated database is quite a change for these organizations and can seem foreboding and overwhelming. But an integrated system eliminates double data entry, makes better use of available staff, eliminates timing issues, and greatly reduces data discrepancies.

**Reasons for integration.** Each company may have its own specific reasons for deciding to implement an integrated payroll/human resources system. Some of the more common reasons include:

- Streamlining the payroll, human resources, and benefits functions, which make up the highest percentage of costs in most organizations.

- The lack of complete data in any single separate database, which means the information needed to make intelligent business decisions is often unavailable, provided in different versions, or contains different data because of the timing of the interface.

- Significant improvements in existing systems are often impossible because a lot of time and energy is spent supporting necessary interfaces among the existing systems and databases.

- Providing a secure database that serves as the foundation for the implementation of an employee and/or manager self-service application (see Section 12.8-1).

**Procedures for implementation.** If an organization is considering an IHRMS as an option for a new computer system, the implementation procedures detailed in the following sections would have to be applied to the human resources function as well as the payroll function. The current human resources and payroll systems would have to be analyzed, current and future requirements carefully stated, and goals detailed to provide a basis for determining whether integration is both desirable and feasible. If an IHRMS is part of a larger system acquisition, such as an Enterprise Resource Planning (ERP) System that also includes accounting, inventory, etc., the managers who are responsible for the payroll and human resources functions need to make sure that they are included on the project team or are able to provide input on the needs and goals of a new system in their areas.

## 12.3  Hardware and Software Alternatives—Pros and Cons

There are several choices open to the payroll manager or project team looking to acquire a new computerized payroll system. They must decide what type of computer equipment (hardware) will drive the system, as well as what kinds of programs (software) will be needed to produce the desired results—accurate and timely paychecks and compliance with government requirements and company policies. Generally, there are four alternatives:

- service provider,
- in-house computer with custom-designed software,
- in-house computer with vendor-supplied software, and
- a combination of these elements.

## 12.3-1  Service Providers—Outsourcing the Payroll

Payroll service providers (or outsourcing companies) can be seen as the computerized equivalent of freelance accountants, who previously handled the payroll and accounting for small firms that could not afford to hire a full-time accountant or payroll professional. A service provider is an independent company that processes its clients' payrolls for a fee. It takes the raw data provided by the employer (hours worked, salaries, etc.) and processes it so that paychecks and direct deposits can be created and reports can be generated (including tax deposits and filings in many instances).

The hardware and software used to process the payroll belong to the service provider, with programs being designed to meet many of the employer's needs. Frequent and open communication between the client and the service provider is necessary to determine just what data must be provided to the service provider to achieve the processing results desired by the employer. The data provided to the service provider may be sent electronically or on paper (requiring the service provider to key the data), with paychecks, direct deposit advices, written reports, and computer files being sent to the employer in return.

As would be expected, the cost of using a service provider depends largely on the volume of data to be processed (i.e., the number of paychecks, direct deposits, and reports produced) and the amount of programming needed to produce the desired results. Historically, service providers have been more attractive to smaller companies having little or no computer sophistication of their own. In recent years, however, many larger companies have found service providers to be a less costly alternative to in-house processing, especially as service providers have become more user-friendly and willing to meet the specific needs of larger, more diversified companies.

Employers may also use service providers to process only a part of the overall payroll process, such as tax filing, garnishments, or payroll debit cards, and they may use different outsourcing companies for each function. The decision to do so will depend on the in-house resources and expertise available to the employer, as well as on the cost of outsourcing vs. in-house processing.

**Advantages of service provider payroll processing.** Following are some of the advantages of having a payroll processed by an independent service provider's hardware and software.

- *Low fixed costs.* The employer pays only a fee for the service provider's processing. No initial investment in or maintenance of hardware or software is necessary, except for the possible purchase of personal computers for compiling and broadband services for transmitting data electronically.

- *No extra room or employees.* Because the processing is done on the service provider's computers, the employer does not need extra room or a special climate-controlled facility for new computers of its own (any personal computers can fit within existing space) or new employees to run and maintain new hardware and software.

- *New services can be added.* As the user/employer expands, its increased processing needs can generally be met quickly by paying more for added services.

- *Reduction in processing delays.* Because most service providers have backup systems in more than one place, employers' payrolls can be processed even when hardware or software problems (e.g., weather, computer viruses, etc.) occur if the employer can provide the data to the service provider.

- *Reasonable processing costs.* Employers pay only for the actual time and labor used in processing the payroll.

- *Fewer research problems.* Service providers assume responsibility for updating their software with the latest tax law changes, tax rates, reporting requirements, and other information.

- *Networking possibilities.* Payroll practitioners using service providers can join "user groups" to network with other clients and learn from each other's problems encountered with the software and solutions they have found.

- *Training and support.* The service center and customer service representative assigned to the employer can provide valuable training and support services.

**Disadvantages of the service provider approach.** Despite the possible cost savings in using a service provider for payroll processing, there are some significant disadvantages as well.

- *Lack of control over security.* Because the employer's data is stored off premises, the employer must rely on the service provider to provide adequate security and privacy guarantees. Also, where information is transferred by nonelectronic means (e.g., mail, messenger), there is a greater risk of loss or theft.

- *Responsibility for filing and depositing errors.* Even though many service providers accept responsibility for any mistakes they make, it is the employer who is ultimately responsible for penalties and assessments under the Internal Revenue Code.

- *Little time for changes.* Because employers must submit payroll data to the service provider by a scheduled time before payday (as much as a week), late changes are difficult to process.

- *Unique needs create problems.* The service provider may not have the programming personnel needed to meet a user's changing individual needs quickly.

- *Possibly high variable costs.* A user's payroll processing costs may vary widely and are at the discretion of the service provider.

- *No control over breakdowns.* The employer has no control over the service provider's reliability, no matter how much checking has been done before contracting with the vendor.

**The ASP alternative.** Another possible outsourcing solution is an application service provider (ASP). The main difference between a service provider and an ASP is the party that is actually processing the payroll. While a service provider collects information from the employer, enters it into their payroll application, and cuts checks, among other duties, an ASP provides the employer's payroll department with an application to perform the payroll functions.

The payroll application is most often installed on the ASP's servers and accessed securely by the employer through the Internet. In this way, the employer can use its existing PC workstations to access the application without the need for new servers. Just as with a service provider, the employer can usually count on a scheduled and reasonable fixed cost when using an ASP. The cost is generally based on a fee for processing each employee's payment. There is little initial investment, and in most situations there is no need to hire new employees to operate the system. Some of the same disadvantages affecting service providers in general also apply to ASPs, and they will have to be considered in making a decision to outsource.

**Business Process Outsourcing.** Among larger employers and outsourcing companies, the latest trend is toward Business Process Outsourcing (BPO), which is the outsourcing of end-to-end business processes and functions, including their required support services, such as payroll and benefits administration. In this type of environment, the BPO company takes over an entire business process from the client, such as payroll, human resources, and benefits administration, and runs it.

## 12.3-2 In-House Payroll Systems

As the name suggests, an in-house computerized payroll system is located on company premises, whether the hardware is owned or leased by the employer. Naturally, this gives the employer greater control over the hardware system and the ability to design its own security for the system. Also, the system is operated by the employer's own employees—programmers, systems analysts, data-entry personnel, operators, etc.

**Hardware options.** The actual hardware used by the employer depends on the size of the company and whether different areas of the company will have their own computer systems. *Mainframe computers* are the largest and most powerful computers used for business, and in most companies where they are used they comprise the entire computer system. Each department is linked to the mainframe and has to share its storage capacity and processing capabilities with other departments. The payroll department (or a combination of payroll, benefits, and human resources) would have its own mainframe only in extremely large organizations. One of the reasons is the expense of a mainframe, which can be justified only by using most of its processing capacity.

*Minicomputers*, which are smaller and less costly than mainframes, may serve the same purpose as a mainframe in small and mid-size companies, with each department sharing access to the system. They can also run a diverse variety of software that can be tailored to the payroll department's needs.

*Microcomputers*, or *personal computers* (PCs), have gained great popularity in recent years as their power, speed, and capacity have increased. They are also extremely flexible, with a great number of vendors offering many different types of software and add-on products that can be shuffled to produce the right combination for each employer.

**Microcomputer networks.** More options are available today because of technology allowing a group of PCs to communicate with each other in a network. A network connects computers and applications. This is quite important in a payroll department that is using an in-house computer system. The network consists of two basic elements, the physical connection and the software that supports the application in its interactions between the PCs and the server.

In a *Local Area Network* (LAN) environment, all computers are physically attached to each other and data are transmitted at high speeds over short distances, with the main computer or file server (a minicomputer or workstation) managing the LAN. In a *Wide Area Network* (WAN) environment, information can be transmitted over long distances using telephone lines and the Internet.

Printers, modems, and other peripheral equipment are accessible to each PC so each employee need not have his or her own equipment. Also, each employee with a network PC has access to the departmental software and equipment at all times unless he or she has been locked out for security reasons. LANs eliminate the inefficiency of making employees wait to use one centrally located computer or share portable storage devices (e.g., diskettes, CDs, or flash drives), as well as the need for each PC to have its own software programs.

**Client/server technology—another option.** Client/server is a method of network computing in which the application programs are distributed by running on a personal computer. The data reside on a "server," which can be a mainframe, minicomputer, or workstation PC. The payroll application itself resides on the PCs in the payroll department and is maintained by the server. A client/server system provides a great deal of flexibility in processing.

Client/server applications are generally composed of some or all of the following elements:

- the hardware
- the graphical user interface
- the file management system
- the network operating system
- the communications protocol

There are several system configurations that meet the definition of client/server. Here are two examples:

1. A simple configuration would be a PC as a server networked in a LAN to a number of other PCs as clients.

2. A larger configuration might be a minicomputer as a server linked in a LAN environment to PC clients.

Client/server networks can grow by building on the configuration. Telecommunications capabilities may be added to make a WAN that allows distant users access to the network. A workstation may be added as a server for the PCs with the minicomputer connected to it.

**Data processing options**. There are two alternatives when it comes to methods of processing payroll data on an in-house system.

- *Real-time processing*. As data are entered into a real-time payroll system, the system does calculations, updates records, and returns results to the user for immediate availability. This allows the user to communicate with the data while the program is being run.

- *Batch processing*. In a batch processing system, data are collected and coded in groups for processing. Then the group (or job) is given to a company's computer center, where it is batched with similar jobs, and returned to the user when processing is complete. Generally, the user cannot have access to the data as they are being run, unless the batch is run in the background.

While batch processing is generally less expensive than real-time processing, it may not provide the immediate results that are required from a modern payroll system.

**Advantages of an in-house mainframe or minicomputer system.** Following is a list of the advantages of having a computer system on the premises.

- *Control of the system.* The employer controls the entire computer system—hardware, software, and personnel—and with it data collection, storage, and processing.

- *Convenient access.* The computer is located on the employer's premises.

- *Downtime can be reduced.* Since the employer is responsible for maintaining the computer, it can keep downtime to a minimum with proper maintenance, which may save more than the cost of maintenance in the long run.

- *System security.* The employer can control data access by installing appropriate restrictions on which employees have access to the data.

- *Scheduling flexibility.* The employer can determine the schedule for processing the payroll and can allow extra access time when special needs arise.

- *Interactive applications.* Many newer systems allow payroll personnel to ask questions of the computer through the keyboard.

**Disadvantages of in-house mainframe or minicomputer systems.** Although they are convenient and allow an employer a greater degree of control than other computer systems, in-house systems can bring added costs and other disadvantages as well.

- *Sufficient secure space needed.* Not only will the employer need the room to house the computer, but it may need a special climate-controlled, fire proof area secure from theft or tampering.

- *High fixed costs.* Computer hardware and software are expensive, as are maintenance and upgrades. Sufficient allowances must be made for possible increases in capacity needed in the future.

- *Additional staffing.* Employers using minicomputers or mainframes need special personnel to operate and/or maintain the system.

- *Working below capacity.* Computer systems must be used efficiently (i.e., at full or near-full capacity) to generate any cost savings, which may be a problem during slow business periods or times of layoff.

- *System obsolescence.* With new computer technologies seemingly being introduced every week, even recently purchased computers or software can become obsolete fairly quickly.

- *Disaster recovery a must for sound business practice.* Because of the dangers of having a computer system with the associated data all in one place should a disaster hit (e.g., fire, blackout, electrical storm), sound business practice requires the employer to have a payroll disaster recovery plan that has been tested and is ready to use (see Section 12.6). (This should actually be a part of any computerized payroll system.)

- *Wrong computer chosen.* Despite all the investigation and research done before purchasing a computer, it may prove to be inadequate or have too much capacity for the employer's needs.

**REDUCE THE RISK OF MAKING THE WRONG CHOICE** Before deciding to purchase an in-house computer system, employers may want to lease the computer or contract with a service provider to see what types of hardware and software are used to process the employer's payroll. This can give the employer an idea of what to buy.

**Advantages of in-house microcomputer (PC) networks.** While most of the same advantages provided by having an in-house mainframe or minicomputer would apply in the PC network situation (e.g., control, convenience, scheduling, reliability, and security), there would be other benefits as well:

- *Data sharing.* A network of microcomputers provides a cost-effective method of sharing resources and data among payroll department employees and beyond, depending on how large the network is. Sharing information and resources improves the efficiency and productivity of the payroll department

- *Improved communications.* The ability to share information throughout the network will enhance communications both within the payroll area and throughout the company, which makes payroll better able to meet its customer service objectives.

**Disadvantages of in-house microcomputer networks.** Despite the obvious efficiencies and productivity gains to be realized from an in-house PC network that can produce payroll as well as enhance communications, there are some drawbacks that must be considered and resolved:

- *Initial installation costs.* Besides the computers themselves, cabling to connect all the PCs in the network will have to be installed. Also, outside vendors may have to be used for the network installation and any future major expansions, depending on its size and the availability of in-house expertise.

- *Network manager needed.* Starting a PC network in payroll may require the company to establish a network management function.

- *Need to keep system up to date.* To prevent the network from becoming obsolete, upgrades will be needed from time to time that could prove to be costly.

**Software considerations for an in-house system.** Computers only process information as they are told to do by the programs they run. For that reason, an in-house computer system is only as good as the software that is run on it. The software can come from three sources: it can be off the shelf, vendor-supplied, or developed and customized by the employer's own programmers. Off-the-shelf software is just what it says, a ready-to-use software program that is installed on the payroll system's existing hardware. Vendor-supplied software is a packaged set of programs that is designed, updated, and maintained by the software vendor and is installed on the employer's in-house hardware. Customized software is designed and written by the employer's own programmers, with the employer's staff retaining responsibility for maintaining and updating it.

**Advantages of off-the-shelf software.** Buying a mass-produced, ready-to-use software package can provide attractive benefits to those employers with relatively simple payrolls.

- *Use it right away*. Once the software is purchased, it can be used immediately, taking into consideration the time to learn how to use the program.

- *Low cost*. Off-the-shelf software is generally less expensive than vendor-supplied programs.

- *Ease of use*. With some initial training, off-the-shelf software is generally easy to use, which is a necessity for a program that is sold to a wide market.

- *Wide variety of programs*. Today, there are many manufacturers offering basic payroll software, which also helps keep the cost down.

- *Yearly updates*. Most off-the-shelf software programs are updated yearly by their manufacturers to reflect compliance changes.

**Disadvantages of off-the-shelf software**. Even though off-the-shelf software can be easy to use and cost less than other methods, there are significant limitations that may make it less than desirable for many employers.

- *PC-based only*. Off-the-shelf software is generally available only to run on microcomputer-based systems, rather than mainframes or minicomputers.

- *No modifications*. It is very difficult and usually impossible for an employer to modify an off-the-shelf software program for its own unique needs.

- *Small employers only*. Because of its limitations, off-the-shelf software is generally useful only to small employers with simple payrolls.

**Advantages of vendor-supplied software packages.** Letting someone else handle the programming can have its advantages, as shown by the following list.

- *Speedy implementation*. Because the programs are already written, they can often be used right away unless modifications are needed. Most employers should expect to make at least some modifications to adapt the programs to their specific needs.

- *Significant cost savings*. Packaged software programs are generally lower in cost than customized software because there are little or no design or code-writing costs. The initial fee generally includes the cost of installation and possibly some training. The major saving is in maintenance, since a maintenance fee is paid to keep the system updated and it may be much less than the cost of having in-house maintenance personnel.

- *Vendor does the updating*. The employer does not have to worry about keeping its software updated with the latest tax rates (especially important for multistate employers) and tax law changes. The vendor assumes the responsibility and costs are usually covered by a yearly fee. The employer must have the resources to implement changes provided by the vendor.

- *Ease of use*. Because vendors want to sell their packages to as broad an audience as possible, they are designed to be easy to use and come with full documentation for each procedure.

- *User group networking*. Payroll practitioners using vendor-supplied software can join "user groups" to network with other clients and learn from problems each has encountered and solutions they have found.

- *Reduced reliance on in-house systems personnel*. With the proper software package, payroll personnel can make their own changes to adapt to changing forms of compensation and deductions and report requirements without waiting for programmers to find the time to make the changes in a customized system.

12-11

- *Better documentation.* Vendor-supplied software packages generally provide more comprehensive and accurate documentation for users than a package that has been customized to meet specific employer needs.

**Disadvantages of purchased software packages.** While vendor-supplied software may provide cost savings and help avoid time-consuming programming and general tax research, it also may have its disadvantages.

- *Specific needs may not be met.* Because of their general design, vendor-supplied software packages generally will never meet 100% of an employer's needs. Most packages will need at least some small modifications, which means increased programming costs.

- *Possibly slow changes.* Needed changes may not be made by the vendor as quickly as is necessary for accurate withholding and reporting.

- *Extensive training needed.* In order to operate the software package independent of the vendor, payroll department personnel may need training sponsored by the vendor and/or must spend time studying the manuals and other documentation provided by the vendor.

- *Lengthy processing.* Some software packages take a longer time to run than others, thus tying up the employer's computers when they could be used by someone else more efficiently.

- *Improper fit.* The software package may be too costly for a small employer's payroll or may require more capacity than the employer's computer can deliver.

**Advantages of customized software.** While costly, in-house designed software can have advantages in increased control and flexibility, as shown by the following.

- *Special needs met.* A system designed by the employer is designed and written to meet the employer's specific needs and desires, as well as to fit the employer's existing hardware.

- *Employer has control.* The combination of an in-house computer and customized software gives the employer ultimate control of the entire payroll system—hardware, software, and employees.

- *Increased flexibility.* Changes can be made when needed because the employer controls the personnel who make the changes and the payroll processing schedule, as long as resources are available to make the changes.

- *Reduced training needs.* Employees who are included in the development of the system software need little further training, although employee turnover will always mean needed training for newly hired employees.

**Disadvantages of customized software.** Programming costs may be the major disadvantage of in-house developed software programs, but there are others as well employers must be aware of.

- *Additional time and staff needed.* Designing software, writing code for it, and maintaining it take a great deal of time and may require hiring qualified programmers who are familiar with the employer's needs and the existing hardware.

- *Update responsibility.* The employer is responsible for making all the tax law changes and tax rate and table updates to the software on time to avoid the possibility of late penalties and assessments. This means resources must be made available to maintain the system.

- *Limits on expansion.* As the employer's needs grow and change, the original software program may not be able to adapt. Proper planning for growth is essential during development.

- *Employees leave the company.* The original programmer or systems analyst may leave the company before someone else is trained to maintain or upgrade the software.

- *Poor documentation.* Company programmers and analysts may not be proficient in writing detailed documentation or diligent in updating it as the software is upgraded. They also may not have the time needed to produce the documentation.

## 12.4  Selecting a Computerized Payroll System

The process of selecting a computerized payroll system, or changing from your current computerized system, is one that involves many different decisions affecting the entire company. Not only must the basic decision be made as to what type of system to use—service provider or in-house—a variety of questions leading up to that decision must be answered first.

The company must decide:

- whether the system will be integrated for all employee-related information and what interfaces with other departments will be necessary;
- what functions the system must perform;
- who will need access to the system;
- how the data will be processed; and
- how much money can be spent.

These questions can be answered only after receiving input from all involved users of payroll information in the company as to their needs and desires. This section will deal with the steps an employer must work through to answer these questions and then select and implement a computerized payroll system.

## 12.4-1  Build a Project Team

Selecting and implementing a computerized payroll system is not a job for only one person or even one department. Because of the effect the selection decision will have on the company, the initial step is to put together a project team or task force representing all the potential end users of the system. That means any department that will interface with the payroll system, share its database, or otherwise use the information stored there must be represented on the project team. These departments generally include, among others:

- payroll
- human resources
- benefits
- accounting
- tax
- budget/finance
- data processing/MIS
- management

When selecting the members of the project team, be sure to look for those employees from other departments who have knowledge of their departments' needs regarding payroll and human resources as well as computer systems in general. Also, make sure they can commit the time necessary to work on the system selection project, their managers support their participation, and they will be employees who will use the new system on a daily basis.

 **DON'T FORGET ANYONE**  In order to make sure no area has been forgotten in selecting the project team, prepare a flowchart of the entire payroll process and determine the areas that are affected.

# 12.4-2 Analyze What the System Needs to Do

The project team's first, and maybe most important, job is to complete a thorough "needs and wants analysis." Like the selection process itself, a needs analysis must be undertaken in several stages.

**Document the current system and its problems.** At this stage, the team must break down the current payroll system and document each component systematically. This is known as a Current Situation Analysis (CSA).

- Document the flow of work into the system—I-9, W-4 and W-5 forms, state withholding allowance certificates, child support withholding orders, tax levies, deduction authorization forms (e.g., §401(k) plan, union dues), direct deposit authorization forms, time cards or time sheets, and other input documents.

- Document the flow out of the system—paychecks, check stubs, direct deposit statements, payroll registers, reports to federal, state, and local governments, internal reports, master file printouts, employee salary histories, etc.

- Document the procedures for maintenance of the system—who is called, response time, and average downtime.

- Identify who receives information from the payroll system, how often they get it, and whether they are using the information.

- Have the end users identify and prioritize complaints, problems, and restrictions of the current system and analyze their cause (e.g., too few fields for earnings and deductions, improper labor distribution, inadequate interfacing, untimely tax rate updates, inadequate controls or security).

- Identify any actual or potential compliance problems with the current system.

- Document any manual processes currently used by payroll or other departments that might be eliminated by automation.

- Identify all costs of the current system—tax updates, corporate policy changes, computer time, paper, system shutdowns, etc.

**Define the objectives you need to meet regarding the new system.** There are several questions you have to answer at this stage in relation to the scope of the project, the time frame that must be met, and the available resources.

- *Scope.* What do you want to accomplish with the new system?

- *Time.* How much time is needed to select and implement a new system? Is there a required date by when the new system must be functional?

- *Resources.* Who will be involved in the process? What is the planning budget and the budget for the new system? What is the budget for training and support once the new system is operational?

**Define the requirements a new payroll system must meet.** Once the current payroll system and its strengths and weaknesses have been analyzed and documented, the next step in a needs and wants analysis is to list the requirements a new system must meet and would be nice to have to qualify for selection.

- What earnings and deductions calculations must be performed, and what information is needed to make those calculations?

- What internal and government reports must the system generate?

- How much more or less information should be included on documents output from the system, and should they be sent to more or fewer individuals?

- What integration or interfaces are required in the new system?

- What training will have to be provided?

- What will be the company's future system needs, based on estimates of growth, resources, decentralization, mergers, etc. and their effect on payroll processing?

- What type of support will be needed from the system manufacturer or software vendor?

- Should the system be integrated for all employee information used by payroll, human resources, and benefits?

In determining what a new payroll system should do, it is important for the team to keep in mind any restraints that might restrict their selection, such as inadequate budgeted funds or the limitations of current hardware that will not be replaced. Team members must prioritize their needs and desires and be ready to decide which ones a new system absolutely must meet and which ones are desirable but not "must-haves."

# 12.4-3 Prepare a Request for Proposal

After the needs analysis has been completed and the team has a good idea of what its new system should contain and how it should perform, the next step is to prepare a "request for proposal" (RFP) or a "request for quotation" (RFQ). The RFP is a document that asks for bids from potential vendors of hardware or software, as well as service providers. It should provide a detailed explanation of what the employer wants from its system so a vendor can determine whether its hardware or software can meet those needs or whether it can customize its software to the employer's satisfaction. If the team is moving toward the purchase of an in-house system, the RFP can be used to help design the system, and responses from vendors can be compared for costs and services.

 **WHERE TO FIND VENDORS** Before the team can distribute a request for proposal, it must locate prospective vendors. There are several methods available to accomplish this task. One way is to use the American Payroll Association's online member directory, which shows what hardware, software, and/or service provider different companies are using, as well as the online vendor directory, both of which can be accessed at www.payroll.org. Another way is to attend payroll, human resources, or benefits trade shows where vendors exhibit their products such as the APA's Annual Congress Exhibit Hall. Finally, there are many hardware and software catalogs and magazines that can serve as a valuable resource.

The RFP should be sufficiently detailed in defining both the technical and functional requirements of the new system. It also must require each vendor to use a predetermined form so their proposals can easily be compared. The RFP may ask for short (Yes/No) answers in the form of a checklist the vendor must fill in, as well as provide space for explanatory answers if the vendor feels that more information will help the employer evaluate its proposal or if a detailed answer is required by the employer. The RFP should include the following information about the employer:

- purpose in issuing the proposal;
- why a new system is needed and what has been done so far;
- specific payroll information—size, frequency, union vs. nonunion, salaried and hourly;
- number of fields required for earnings and deductions;
- functional requirements of a new system now and in the future;
- whether human resources and benefits will be integrated with the payroll system and what interfaces will be required;

- whether the vendor should include the cost of training in the bid, taking into account the time needed, travel if required, and number of employees to be trained;
- level of support expected;
- contract terms and conditions (after review by the legal department); and
- instructions to the vendor on how to submit the proposal.

## 12.4-4 Select a System

Once the proposals or bids have been received, the hardware, software, or services offered by the vendors and service providers must be analyzed and evaluated to see if they meet the employer's needs before one or a combination is selected. The steps to be taken by the project team in this part of the selection process are as follows:

- Ask to see a demonstration of the vendor's products or services at the vendor's premises and at companies currently under contract with the vendor. Make as many site visits to current users as is feasible, and include companies not referred by the vendor, since that will provide a truer picture of the products' strengths and weaknesses. Make sure employees who will be end users of the vendor's products are included so they can talk to their counterparts in the other company rather than just to management.

- Try to schedule site demonstrations at companies with a similar environment to the employer in terms of industry type, size, hardware, etc. The closer the match, the more accurate the comparison will be. If site visits are not practicable, check the vendor's references by phone and try to call other companies not referred by the vendor.

- If the vendor claims a product can "take care of" a certain situation or problem, ask for a demonstration of how it can be done and how long it takes.

- Make sure all necessary government reports, tax deposits, advance earned income credit payments, etc., can be accomplished by the vendor's software and that W-2 forms are prepared in compliance with SSA requirements and meet the SSA's edit criteria.

- If the team is considering vendor-supplied software for an already existing in-house computer, ask the vendor to demonstrate the software on the employer's hardware, which may provide a more realistic response time than a demonstration on the vendor's mainframe.

- Make sure the proposal details the service and training support that the vendor will provide before and after the product is installed or the service is purchased, as well as the cost involved.

- Make sure all costs have been included in the proposal, including those that will be incurred after the new system is implemented (e.g., training, annual maintenance).

- Make sure the vendor's products are flexible enough to handle anticipated and unanticipated changes in earnings, deductions, pay frequencies, required reports, information storage, and fiscal year vs. calendar year.

- Make sure all internal and external interfaces required can be provided by the software or service provider and find out the cost.

- Make sure information will be processed in the way that is most beneficial to the employer (batch, online, or realtime).

- If the employer uses direct deposit, make sure any demonstration shows that the vendor's products can handle all facets of direct deposit, including multiple accounts for employees and electronic pay statements.

- Require a flexible, "user-friendly" report writer. Ad hoc reports frequently may be required without technical assistance.

- Make sure that all documentation/user manuals are easy to use and are kept up to date and distributed as needed.

- Make sure the vendor demonstrates the security features of its products and that they will be satisfactory to the employer's internal and external auditors.

- Make sure there is a well-established user group.

**ABOVE ALL, BE THOROUGH** Impress on all members of the project team that a thorough analysis of the vendors' proposals and products, keeping in mind the employer's needs and desires, is paramount in selecting the right computer system. The more questions that are asked, the more information the team has to make its selection. If a vendor balks at answering some of the questions, that may be a good indication its products are not right for the job. Listen closely to current users, especially when they have difficulty answering questions.

**Mistakes to avoid.** Following is a list of mistakes that are commonly made during the system selection process that can end up scuttling an entire project or costing a company a good deal more than anticipated once a system is installed.

- Failing to provide project team members time to do the job right by requiring them to perform their current duties while on the team.
- Failing to include representatives of all potential user departments on the project team;
- Failing to prioritize needs and desires, especially when cost considerations make it impossible for all of them to be met; requirements may need to be weighted to ensure the most important ones are met;
- Not considering future company needs and plans regarding expansion, downsizing, decentralization, etc.;
- Making decisions without sufficient input;
- Failing to consider all the costs associated with a new system (e.g., training, maintenance, upgrades);
- Seeing software demonstrated on different hardware than what you will be using;
- Seeing demonstrations or making reference calls only with companies referred by the vendor or service provider;
- Failing to negotiate performance guarantees;
- Failing to thoroughly check for signs of obsolescence, which is especially important with the fast pace of technological advances; and
- Failing to check the vendor's financial background and outlook for the future.

**KEEP A SCORECARD** As you meet to review each vendor's bid and demonstrations, keep a graphic record of their ability to meet the requirements set up by the project team. A matrix with the requirements listed along the side and the vendors along the top can be used as a type of checklist to see which vendors best fill the different requirements.

**Verify feasibility before making a final recommendation.** The importance of the selection decision, in terms of the time and money invested and the long-term financial implications, demands that before a final recommendation is made as to hardware, software, or a service provider, all information that goes into making the decision be checked and rechecked.

- Make sure the vendor's promises are proven by demonstrations and the results are verified with current customers.

- Check the references again to make sure that, during and after implementation, the necessary training, maintenance, and other avenues of support (e.g., user groups) are actually available and reliable.

- Go through any available documentation and user manuals one more time and have potential end users judge its usefulness and readability.

- Go over the estimates of the employer's future needs and verify that the vendor's products are flexible and expandable enough to meet them and go beyond.

- Check future budget projections to guard against budget-busting costs from the system after its purchase (e.g., annual maintenance fees).

- Verify the financial soundness of the vendor, although this may be difficult if the vendor is privately owned.

Once these verifications have taken place and the project team is sure of the direction in which to go and what computer system, software, or service provider will do the job, a recommendation to management for approval of the expenditure is the next step. The recommendation should summarize the documentation of the current system and its problems, as well as the needs a new system must meet, what options were reviewed, and the reasons why the vendor's products are being recommended to meet them.

## 12.4-5 Implement the System

After the system has been selected and the purchase approved, the next step in the process is implementation. It, too, is made up of many small steps. One consideration should be kept in mind at all times when planning a system implementation. Be patient and allow ample time to test the system and correct errors before actual processing begins.

 **IF YOU ARE UNDER THE GUN** and are pressured into a shorter implementation timetable than would normally be prudent, make sure the bare basics of the system are implemented first. The extras that will make the payroll department's job easier can be added later, when time and other resources are available.

**Preparing for implementation.** Before the system can actually be tested, there are several planning steps the project team must take.

- Clearly define the goals and requirements the new system must meet, with a level of specification that may not have been needed up to this point in the selection process.

- Make sure team members have the time to devote to the implementation part of the project. Department managers must arrange temporary reassignments where necessary. This is a continuing commitment that should be made initially before the project begins.

- For many system implementations, outside consultants will be hired to work with the project team. They may work for the software provider or be independents with knowledge of the particular system. These advisors should help facilitate the implementation process rather than lead it. If they are programmers or analysts, they need to train the appropriate employees who will be expected to maintain and support the new system after the implementation, when the consultants leave.

- Allow sufficient time for completion of the entire implementation and for each task involved, taking into consideration possible unforeseen problems and delays. Every member of the team must feel the schedules are realistic and must accept the responsibility for complying with them. Management and the project team must buy into the idea that the goal is a successful system implementation, not a quick implementation.

- The project team manager must have the support and cooperation of upper management and the other team members at this crucial stage of the process. Lack of support could derail the entire project.

**Training team members and the payroll staff.** Training is one of the most important facets of the implementation. The project team members must be well-trained and understand the new system's functions and capabilities. With such knowledge, implementation will go much more smoothly. They, in turn, can train the end users of the system—the payroll staff, as well as employees of other departments (e.g., human resources, benefits, accounting). This is where the team's research into the vendor's training programs should pay big dividends.

**Conducting a 'gap analysis.'** The next step in the implementation is the "gap analysis." During this phase, the functionalities of the old and new systems are compared to determine if there are any gaps in the functionality of the new system. This can be accomplished by having team members give current system users a preview of the new system by modeling each process performed by the current system in the new system. Once gaps have been identified, the team will have to find a way to get the same results from the new system, hopefully without having to modify it. Modifications can increase costs, delay final implementation, and make future upgrades more difficult.

**Converting old data and adding new data.** It might seem easy to take data from the old system and convert it to the new system, but that is not always the case. The location of the data must be identified in the old system, as must the location of the file for the data in the new system, before the conversion can take place. This process is known as "data mapping." Also, if the data will appear in a different form in the new system, this must be taken into account in a conversion program design.

A workbook should be developed identifying all requirements to convert each data element. Test the conversion with a small, representative piece of the data before attempting to convert all the data. After the conversion has taken place, but while the data are still in both systems, the converted data must be verified by comparing the data in each system.

Besides converting data from the old system, there may be new data that must be manually entered into the new system and/or new functions carried out on the data that must be performed manually. Any such manual entry of data must be closely scrutinized and verified to avoid errors.

**Testing the new system.** When the team is ready to test the new system, a piecemeal approach may best serve to avoid problems in the future. At first, individual processes of the software can be "unit tested" for each type of deduction, report, etc., the system will be expected to handle. Testing in this fashion makes it easier to spot problems and find solutions. Do not attempt to test with all the converted data. Use a representative sample of the data.

Once the individual "units" of the system have been tested, it is time to "system test" it as a whole. This testing should include not only the production of accurate paycheck data and reports, but whether the system can manage the necessary interfaces, meet all the printing requirements, produce accurate payroll registers, etc. The system must be able to handle these combined activities with a representative sample of data before moving to the next stage. Once a sample has been tested in this fashion, "acceptance" testing can be accomplished using a large volume of data simulating actual productions.

 **MAKE SURE THE SYSTEM CAN SPOT ERRORS** When testing the new system, either in part or in whole, ask it to perform functions or make calculations that make no sense. In this way, the logic built into the system is tested.

**Parallel testing.** The final test before going "live" with a new system is called parallel testing. In a parallel test, the same data are processed by both the old and new systems (or the old system and the selected service provider). The data can be taken from a representative department in the company that would require the system to perform all the functions it would typically be called on to perform, or it can include company-wide data. Parallels can also be run for different pay cycles and for pay periods at different times during the quarter or year. The project team may want to build from a smaller parallel test to a larger one.

The parallel tests should be run after the actual payroll has been processed by the old system and should include the entire process of producing a payroll, from compiling time records to completing reports. After each test, the results must be compared to determine if the new system is producing accurate results. The results may differ somewhat from those produced by the old system, because the new system is expected to do more and be even more accurate. Parallel testing may identify unknown problems with the old system that must be solved to determine where the problem is located.

 **DON'T LET STRESS HOLD UP THE PROJECT** By the time a system has been selected and implementation is at hand, team members and payroll department employees may be feeling the stress of long hours and the inevitable frustration of "debugging" the new system. Good communication and motivation skills are essential for managers at this point, because nothing will prevent a smooth switchover to a new system faster than employee resistance to change. Frequent team meetings to discuss the status of implementation and resolve outstanding issues improve communications.

**System conversion.** By this time, all the data conversion procedures have been tested, as has the system itself, and the team is ready to take the new system live. First, however, more planning is necessary to make sure not only the payroll department, but all other departments that will interface with the system, are prepared. Work flow to and from the new system must be documented and agreed on, since fewer and/or different people may be sending paperwork to or receiving paperwork from the payroll department when the new system is up and running. Communication at this point to all departments is very important.

It is also very important for the project team to develop contingency plans for what must be done should something go wrong either during the conversion or the first pay cycle. As with any other process, going "live" is never exactly the same as testing a new way of doing things, and problems must be anticipated.

# 12.4-6 Evaluate the System's Performance

Once the new system has been used to produce an actual payroll, the results must be examined very carefully for accuracy and completeness. If problems are detected, this is the time to take care of them. If things are running smoothly, the extras that were not built into the system because of time constraints can be given attention.

Even after a successful initial implementation of a new system there are problems that must be watched for, including:

- new internal report requirements or old requirements that were missed that the system was not designed to meet;
- unexpected legislation on the federal, state, or local level with payroll implications (e.g., state new hire reporting requirements);
- radical changes in company benefit plans requiring new types of deductions and reports;
- a new union is elected or an existing union negotiates contract changes that affect payroll; or
- system expansion is necessary but difficult because of a lack of flexibility.

Periodic reviews of the system should be undertaken to identify problems and prioritize their resolution.

# 12.5 Controls and Security for the Computerized Payroll System

Once the new payroll system is operational and has begun processing payrolls, the project team's final responsibility is to develop and institute procedures to make sure errors are kept to a minimum and the system and the data stored there are secure. Even the best, most feature-packed automated system can shut down or produce incorrect results if there are insufficient controls or security precautions. This section explains some of the means for keeping the payroll system on track and free from internal or external disasters.

# 12.5-1 Putting Controls Into the Process

While the goal of all payroll departments is 100% accuracy, no payroll system is perfect. Problems can develop with any one component of the system—hardware, software, security, policies, or employees—resulting in errors, compliance problems, and costly penalties. But the project team can make sure certain control procedures are built into the system to detect errors and make certain employees are properly trained in spotting potential problems.

**System edits.** A system edit is a warning or alert built into the system that checks for errors and either corrects the error or notifies the operator that something may be wrong. System edits generally check for inputs or outputs outside accepted ranges (e.g., negative net pay for an employee). Following is a list of commonly used system edits:

- A report that alerts the computer operator to a payment being generated for an employee who has been terminated or is about to leave the company (e.g., has given notice of resignation);

- A report that alerts the operator to new hires, so their pay and hours worked can be verified;

- An error message when the system fails to generate a payment for an active employee;

- An error message when the system calculates negative net pay for an employee;

- An error message when the system calculates negative deductions for an employee;

- A report for the operator when gross earnings exceed a certain amount;

- A report for the operator when an employee's overtime hours exceed a certain amount, or for all overtime hours if there are not supposed to be any employees working overtime; and

- A report for the operator when the employee's pay rate changes.

**Periodic data auditing and sampling.** While system edits will detect many of the problems and mistakes that occur once a system is implemented, data falling within the acceptable edit parameters may still not be valid. Periodic audits of a sample of the data can identify such data invalidity problems. It is up to the employer to determine the sampling parameters to ensure validity.

**Batch controls.** Data entered into the payroll system must be controlled to ensure that the data that should be entered actually have been entered. Batching the data into groups of similar data, developing totals of the data to be entered, and then comparing the totals of the data entered into the system to the previously developed totals is one method of batch controls. This ensures that the amounts that are anticipated to be entered into the system have been entered. However, it does not ensure that the data have been correctly entered into the system.

**Correction procedures.** If system-generated totals from the entered data do not agree with the batch control totals or other controls, procedures must be in place to determine the error, how it was caused, and how it should be corrected. Ideally, control totals will have interim (i.e., component) totals that correspond to interim totals that the system generates. Once the incorrect data entries have been identified, they must be corrected. This will require developing batch controls for the data correction entries.

**Balancing and reconciliation.** Accounting control procedures (see Section 11.6) involving balancing and reconciliation also serve as controls of the payroll system. They make sure all accounts are in balance and different wage and tax totals that should be equal are reconciled if they are not. These procedures include:

- Pre-tax deposit reconciliation of payroll tax liability accounts to verify the company's unpaid tax liability;

- Balancing liability accounts for payroll deductions to the payroll registers to ensure accuracy;

- Monthly reconciliation of the payroll bank account, including follow-up on all outstanding and stale-dated checks; and

- Quarterly reconciliation of tax withholding amounts on Form 941.

- Annual reconciliation of wages and tax withholding amounts on Forms W-2.

# 12.5-2 System Documentation

One of the easiest ways for a company to lose control over its entire payroll system is to rely on verbal communication of policies and procedures. Documentation is a very important part of a company's overall control mechanism. The documentation should be simple and complete enough to allow an employee to perform functions described in the documentation with little or no other assistance.

**What to include**. The first thing that must be included is a confidentiality statement that emphasizes to employees the confidential nature of the manual itself as well as the employee data they will be working with when they use the system. This applies whether the system is a payroll or human resource system, or an integrated system. Introductions to both the manual and the system itself are also important at this stage. The introduction to the manual should briefly explain what the contents are and how to use it, while the system introduction should contain a high-level overview of the system, how it relates to other company systems (e.g., general ledger, time and attendance, pension), key words used in the system, and how the files and employee data base in the system are structured.

Helpful information on getting around in the system is also necessary, with step-by-step instructions on accessing the system from the point that the computer is turned on, what online help is available and where to find it, what special function keys have been included (e.g., the F2 key moves you to the next panel of information), and what inquiry screens will appear and what they will say.

The "guts" of the manual will be the actual payroll or human resource processing sections. They should include a processing calendar that lets all users know when different events need to occur to make the process work. In documenting your payroll process, the following functional topics (at a minimum) should be explained in detail, with samples of step-by-step procedures included:

- schedules
- time entry
- adjustment and corrections entry
- check calculations
- payroll history
- production cycle
- taxes
- employee data base management
- reports

Other important information that hasn't yet been included can be brought together in an appendix that contains more detailed information on where to get help, what to do about online edits and messages, the security of the system, a glossary of terms, and tables of codes for earnings, jobs, tax entities, accounts, departments, etc.

**What to leave out**. While the goal of system documentation is to be as inclusive as possible, a system manual should not include company policies or technical material. Company policies on vacation accrual, sick pay, leaves of absence, etc., should be left out of the system documentation because they are usually contained in an employee handbook or policies and procedures manual and they may well differ from site to site, especially if you are processing payroll for a group of different but related entities. Employees who are using the system need very little, if any, technical information.

**How to package the documentation**. While it may seem unimportant at first glance, presenting your documentation in an attractive package can make a big difference in whether it actually gets taken off the shelf and used. Use a loose leaf binder for easier updating and create a cover that is pleasing to the eye, using company logos and colors where available. Durable, colored dividers for each section should also be used since they make it easier to find information.

Once a complete manual has been printed and assembled, you must distribute printed copies where they will be needed. Before distribution, you should number each manual and create a list showing the number and where it is being distributed. It is also a good idea to assign each manual to a job (e.g., director of payroll, payroll administrator) rather than to an employee because the manual belongs to the company, not the employee.

**How to keep the manual up to date**. System documentation will quickly become useless unless it is kept up to date with recent changes to the system or the procedures that must be followed. An electronic copy of the documentation should be kept on the company's local area network (if there is one), with another copy put on diskettes as a backup. It is also wise to keep a paper copy of each section in a file folder and so written notations can be made as changes are made, which can then be keyed in to the master. Once the changes have been made, print out the changed pages—with the current date at the bottom—and distribute them to all those who already have the documentation. It also may be a good idea to reissue the entire manual periodically, but no more often than once a year, because of the possibility that pages will rip from the binders, updates will be lost or not filed, or binders will be damaged.

**Documentation promotes control**. If the system and its procedures are documented and everyone in the payroll department has access to the documentation, there is no good reason why tasks cannot be performed in the same manner by each employee. Without written procedures, shortcuts become the rule and employees will not learn all there is to know about a job. Also, documentation makes it much easier for a payroll manager to rotate job assignments (an essential security measure), schedule reassignments when employees will be on vacation, and deal with unexpected absences because of illness, injury, or personal matters.

Documented procedures also make training of new, rotated, or newly assigned employees much easier and allow individuals to train at their own pace. In addition to serving as a training manual, the documentation also provides a quick reference for employees and gives internal and external auditors an accurate idea of what should be taking place in the payroll department.

# 12.5-3 Providing Security for the System

When most people think of security, they think of armed bank guards or the uniformed security guard in the lobby of their workplace. In actuality, because a great deal of a company's funds are controlled by the payroll department, security of the payroll system should be a top priority when a new system is designed or purchased. Theft and embezzlement are a constant concern for payroll departments. But these are not the only security problems. A computerized payroll system presents other concerns as well, including physical and climate-related problems.

**Personnel concerns.** While no payroll manager likes to think his or her employees are capable of theft or embezzlement of company funds, security measures must be taken to prevent it from happening. Such measures are certain to be reviewed by internal and external auditors who are trying to determine if a company adequately safeguards its assets. The manager should tell employees the security precautions are not an indication of distrust on the part of management, but a necessary measure to protect the company against what could be devastating losses.

Many of the personnel-related security measures to follow are discussed in detail in Section 11.8—Internal Controls. They include:

- *Segregation of job duties*—critical job processes should not be handled from start to finish by one employee.

- *Rotation of job assignments*—helps ensure that standard procedures for different jobs will be followed and employee absences can be tolerated.

- *Paychecks go only to employees*—when distributed by payroll or department heads, paychecks should not be given to someone other than the employee whose name is on the check except in emergencies where written authorization has been obtained.

- *Conduct "physical payouts"*—requiring employees to show identification to receive their paychecks, to discourage the creation of "phantom employees."

- *In small payroll departments*—where segregation and rotation are impractical, some payroll tasks should go to other departments, such as accounting.

- *Background checks*—employers should conduct credit and criminal history background checks on all employees being considered for positions where they will be responsible for highly confidential personal and financial information.

**System security.** The project team must seriously consider the following security measures when an automated system is designed or purchased:

- *Limit system access*—only those employees who must use the system should have access, and passwords should be changed frequently, especially after an employee leaves the department; determine if only certain employees can input new data or update specific data elements. Where employees from other departments must have access to the payroll system or the integrated payroll/human resources/benefits system (e.g., electronic changes to W-4 information or benefit elections), the system must allow access only for those limited purposes.

- *Secure files*—make sure only those employees with authorization have access to payroll department files.

- *Develop audit trails*—the system must produce a record of who entered and exited the system and what they did while having access.

- *Protect against computer "viruses"*—make sure anti-virus programs are installed in all computers, that they do not conflict with the software installed there, that they are updated on an ongoing basis, all disks brought in from outside are tested for viruses before being used, and downloading of material and progroams from the Internet is sharply restricted.

- *Back up data regularly and store off site*—to protect against data loss should the system hardware or software fail or if power is lost (should be done at a minimum after each payroll is processed).

**Physical plant issues.** As part of any computer security program, the hardware must be protected against fire, temperature extremes, and other physical stressors that can damage the equipment. While they may look solid, computers can be very sensitive. Such precautions include:

- *Climate-controlled rooms*—these are necessary for mainframes or minicomputers stored in one central area, so variations in temperature and humidity can be controlled.

- *Keep terminals from overheating*—too much heat can cause personal computer malfunctions, so vents should be unobstructed and internal fans should be checked periodically.

- *Do not store in cold area*—computers that have been stored or transported in rooms or vehicles exposed to cold temperatures should not be turned on soon after being brought into a warm room because condensation will cause water to penetrate the components.

- *Protect against power surges*—lightning or power "spikes" can harm personal computers, so surge protectors or other power filters should be connected to all terminals; similar devices for telephone lines can protect modems and fax machines.

- *Keep dirt out of components*—dust and dirt shorten the life span of personal computers, so use dust covers and adopt policies that forbid smoking, drinking, or eating near computers; also keep them away from construction zones and work areas that produce dust and dirt.

- *Keep the humidity down*—because moisture can corrode circuit boards and other computer components, keep offices ventilated and dry.

- *Check for adequate power*—regular checks of the electrical system should be made as systems expand to make sure that adequate power is supplied to handle them.

# 12.6 Disaster Recovery

Something no one in the payroll department wants to think about is what might happen in the event of a natural or man-made disaster. But with the news in recent years of fires, floods, hurricanes, earthquakes, bioterrorism, and explosions, a project team charged with choosing a new payroll system must plan for the unthinkable—that the new system (or the existing one) will be rendered inoperable for a period of time, but employees still must be paid and taxes withheld and deposited on time.

 **LIMITED HELP FROM THE IRS** In recent years, the IRS has made some allowances to help those employers who are adversely affected by natural disasters. Employers in states battered by hurricanes, floods, earthquakes, etc., have been given extra time to file required returns and deposit withheld taxes. The IRS now has the authority to postpone taxpayer deadlines and tax liabilities for up to one year for all taxpayers (including business entities) determined to be affected by a Presidentially declared disaster.[1]

As part of the security measures for a new payroll system, or for the existing payroll process if need be, the project team needs to develop a business continuity plan that includes the following disaster recovery procedures:

**Find and secure interim office space.** A search should be conducted to locate interim office space (e.g., hotel meeting rooms, company warehouses) in case the employer's facility is rendered uninhabitable. Once appropriate space has been found, make an agreement with the owner giving the employer the right of first access in the event of a disaster. Agreements for more than one suitable space may be desirable for even greater protection. Some organizations have developed office space for such contingencies and entered into contracts to have all necessary equipment delivered within a specified period of time.

**Arrange office equipment rental.** Whether the employer's offices are uninhabitable or the payroll department's equipment is rendered unusable, arrangements for the rental and installation of temporary office equipment (e.g., computers, fax machines, phone lines) must be made.

**Find suitable temporary housing for employees.** Having employees who can be at an interim office while the employer is recovering from a disaster is very important, so temporary living space must be arranged for them in advance. Alternate transportation may also be planned in advance to get employees to and from the interim office.

**Keep backup files off premises.** A procedure for keeping backup payroll and employee information files off the employer's premises should be a part of any disaster recovery plan. This assures access to files if they cannot be recovered from the employer's facility immediately after a disaster.

---

1.     IRC §7508A; IRS Reg. §301.7508A-1

**Keep employee safety uppermost in any plans.** The safety, well-being, and whereabouts of employees should be the first things determined immediately after a disaster strikes. Managers should be prepared to assist employees and their families with their immediate needs. All managers should have a list of their employees' home and emergency phone numbers, as well as general emergency numbers, available at all times.

**Communicate the plan.** Make sure any disaster contingency plans are documented and provided to all employees so everyone is thinking along the same lines should disaster strike. Indecision can cost employees their lives and employers their business.

**Electronic vaulting can ensure a quicker recovery.** Payroll is a business function that needs to be up and running quickly when disaster strikes, and one way to better ensure a quick recovery is electronic vaulting. With electronic vaulting, an employer's operating systems, applications software, and data are duplicated at a disaster recovery site and updated frequently so the employer has the least down time possible.

Because of the expense of duplicating an employer's business processes and information and keeping them up to date, electronic vaulting has generally been limited to very comprehensive, high-end disaster recovery solutions for large companies. But because of the importance of a quick recovery and advances in technology and telecommunications, electronic vaulting has become a more viable solution for a wider range of organizations.

Duplicating the employer's information can be accomplished in two ways – shadowing or mirroring. Using either method, information is transmitted over high-speed fiber optic circuits to a remote recovery site so that it is stored in two places and becomes immediately available if processing is interrupted at the employer's site. While the terms are almost the same, shadowing involves updates that can lag from the time data was originally entered, while mirroring means that the two storage units are exactly the same at all times.

# 12.7 Automated Time and Attendance

Labor costs are usually one of the largest expenses an organization faces, and research has shown that as much as 1% - 3% of this cost is wasted on errors, processing costs, faulty time recording, and noncompliance penalties. Time and attendance automation can help control these costs.

While some organizations have "homegrown" systems that manage a portion of the time and attendance process, many still enter time from cards or timesheets manually into their payroll system. Many people ask, "Doesn't my payroll system automate time and attendance?" The answer is, "Usually not to the extent automated by time and attendance systems."

Time and attendance systems automate the process from zero-to-gross, or time collection up to gross payroll amounts. Payroll systems, on the other hand, automate the process from the gross amount to the net amount on the check. With some payroll and time and attendance systems, there are overlapping functions, but a well thought-out approach will use the right system for the right function and the result will be cost-effective payroll processing.

Think about all the pay policies, state and federal regulations, and union agreements that factor into the payroll process. Each has its own set of requirements and formulas that may depend on the circumstances of the job or the employee. A time and attendance system enforces all those policies, regulations, and agreements, so that employees are paid accurately, fairly, and on time.

Time and attendance systems also distribute the work of the payroll process to employees, managers, and operations people, so payroll professionals do not have to spend a significant amount of time just reminding people to turn in timesheets and then manually calculating gross pay based on complex pay rules.

**Time and attendance automation benefits.** There are several tangible benefits to time and attendance automation. Here are some of the most significant:

- *Less time spent on processing.* Time and attendance systems automatically alert employees and managers when timesheets are due. If these alerts go unanswered, the system will escalate the urgency of the requests and also notify management. Once time information has been gathered, time and attendance systems automatically apply pay policies and calculate gross pay. Finally, the gross pay amount, accrual balances, and other relevant information are automatically fed into the payroll system. Many companies slash manual processing time from days to just hours with an automated system.

- *Fewer errors introduced during processing.* Imagine the entire payroll process as a chain with many links. Some of those links may be automated and consistent, while others may still be done manually. Each manual link in the chain is left open to errors and inconsistently applied rules. By eliminating manual links in the process, organizations are able to significantly decrease or eliminate errors.

- *Decreased costs.* The use of manual time clocks and/or written timesheets may be inefficient and costly. Time cards can be punched incorrectly and timesheets can contain illegible handwriting. These issues become more acute when work schedules become more flexible. This means more work for those employees and the payroll professionals that process their time and, as they say, time is money.

**FLSA, FMLA and SOX compliance.** In today's environment, compliance with legislative and regulatory requirements is essential. Penalties are steep if an employer improperly tracks time or fails to comply with time and labor regulations. Some of the requirements you may be subject to include:

- Family and Medical Leave Act (FMLA) eligibility and tracking
- Fair Labor Standards Act (FLSA) compliance for overtime, including average rate calculations
- Sarbanes-Oxley Act
- State overtime laws
- For global installations, the regulations in other regions or countries

A 2007 survey by WorkForce Software has determined that many organizations are not well prepared to manage FLSA, FMLA, and Sarbanes-Oxley compliance.[2]

While 75% of the surveyed organizations rated their pay rules as 'moderately complex' to 'very complex,' only 34% have a time and attendance system to manage the process, and 68% have no system to manage FLSA compliance. Furthermore, 91% of the organizations surveyed ranked their ability to manage compliance as 'good' to 'excellent,' yet U.S. Department of Labor (DOL) statistics show that 48% of companies audited have failed to comply with federal labor laws. Clearly, there is a discrepancy between expectations and the facts.

Noncompliance can be costly for employers, resulting in DOL penalties, state wage and hour agency penalties, employee lawsuits, etc. In fiscal year 2007, the DOL recovered more than $180.6 million in back wages for FLSA violations for more than 311,000 employees, and employers paid another $3.9 million in FLSA civil penalties.[3]

Results show that organizations that use time and attendance systems are in a better position to manage compliance than organizations that handle the job manually. The survey found that 42% of organizations with time and attendance software reported excellent compliance compared to only 32% that did not use a time and attendance system. In addition, only 12% of organizations without time and attendance software rated their compliance ability as excellent, while 37% of organizations with a time and attendance system rated compliance as excellent.

---

2. Workforce Software Payroll Best Practices Survey – April 2007.
3. DOL WHD 2007 Statistics Fact Sheet, 12-27-07.

Organizations with 'moderately' to 'very complex' pay rules get a major return on investment (ROI) when using time and attendance software. Time and attendance software can automate pre-defined pay rules for the company to meet federal and state regulations. The system records accurate timekeeping, gathers pre-defined criteria, supports union rules and contracts, supports retroactive pay, keeps an audit trail, and more, to support employers.

Other key findings for compliance from the Workforce Software survey are as follows:

- 46% of organizations using web-based time and attendance systems report excellent compliance compared with only 36% that do not use web-based software.

- Organizations that use time and attendance software to track FMLA leave requests and usage are 6% more likely to report excellent compliance than those who do not track FMLA requests.

Because of the number of permutations, these and other wage and hour regulations are very complex and difficult to administer. A time and attendance solution should provide the means to manage them all. Moreover, the solution should be flexible enough to adapt to unknown future regulatory changes.

**Selecting a time and attendance system.** At the heart of an enterprise time and attendance system is a "rules engine" that applies appropriate rules in a consistent and repeatable manner. The rules govern the process flow and determine who should be made aware of certain events, and what is expected of that person once they have been alerted.

A time and attendance system should integrate with your human resources, payroll, and cost accounting systems. A flexible system should provide multiple methods of integration, including database-to-database, file-to-file, and via system calls. The system should be able to accommodate these integration methods without the need for source-level programming.

**Configuration versus customization.** Software vendors bring up the point that their systems can be modified by configuration instead of customization, but what does that mean? When you think of configuration, think sheet music. A single orchestra can play hundreds of songs without changing musicians because the music can be configured via the sheet music. Applications that are easily configured are built with a wide range of behaviors that are dictated by the "configuration options" or sheet music for the application.

Using this same analogy, customization is like building different-sized drums to get different tones. A drum's size or shape can be changed to modify the tone that the drum gives off when struck, but it can only produce that tone.

After being customized, applications can only perform a fixed set of functions. Once customized, the application cannot easily be updated by the next version of that application sold by the vendor, because any changes made by the customer will be lost as the new application overwrites the changes previously made. Configured applications, on the other hand, are easily updated because the changes were made to the "sheet music," not the instruments.

Examples of functionality that should be managed through configuration (data only) changes are:

- California meal rules
- Piece rate calculations
- Attendance bonuses
- Multiple assignments
- Retroactive adjustments

**Other time and attendance attributes.**

- *Web-based:* Most enterprise applications are web-based because they can be distributed and maintained more easily across the organization. Web-based applications can run in any web browser on any desktop.

- *Alert notifications:* Automated business processes are great, but sometimes employees and managers need to be told about exceptions to the process. For example, an organization may want the manager to know when one of her employees has arrived late to work more than three times in a given period. A time and attendance system should be able to notify the manager in a number of different ways, including e-mail, pager, via the application dashboard, or by phone.

- *Secure:* Any enterprise application, time and attendance included, should be secure against unwanted changes to the data, or to the wrong person viewing it. The time and attendance application should prevent any changes to time punch information and protect an individual employee's time or other personal information from being viewed by anyone other than the employee or the employee's manager.

- *Employee and manager self-service:* Employee self-service portals provide a way to empower employees to gain online access to critical information and to enter time and attendance transactions. Employee-based information including timesheets, accruals, reports, time-off requests, and pay previews should be available online to employees and displayed in a graphical, user-friendly format. Employees can utilize a self-service portal to create time-off requests that, if approved, are automatically posted to the appropriate (current or future) timesheet. An employee can access his or her information through a kiosk, a company PC, or a home PC. This feature takes the responsibility for dealing with requests from managers and HR/Payroll.

  Managers should be able to use the web-based interface to easily manage the timesheets and schedules of the employees for whom they are responsible. With it, they can approve timesheets for all employees at once, a subset of the group, or for just one employee.

  Managers can also drill down to individual timesheets to see errors and make corrections. They can reject timesheets with optional e-mail messages. Employees must then correct any existing errors and resubmit the timesheet for approval. Multiple levels of approval should be supported in the system such that approval at one level automatically routes the timesheets to the next level with optional e-mail notification.

- *No PC software:* To minimize costs, a web-based time and attendance application should be accessible through any supported web browser with no installation or desktop upgrades necessary. It should support several data collection methods, including: online timesheets, browser-based time clock, wall mounted badge readers, biometric devices, touch screen terminals, magnetic stripe readers, barcode scanners, wireless devices, and touch tone interactive voice response (IVR).

# 12.8 The New Wave — Self-Service and the Internet

Other than the seemingly continual advances in business technology over the last decade, there are other forces driving payroll departments to make the most efficient use of these new tools. The uncertain economy of 2001-2007, along with the continuing wave of mergers and acquisitions and the increasingly competitive global economy, have all required payroll departments to make do with fewer staff and to reduce costs wherever possible. To do this, payroll professionals have looked to technology for the answers.

# 12.8-1 Employee and Manager Self-Service

In many organizations, paper-based systems are still being used to manage payroll and human resources processes, including the most time-consuming administrative tasks such as benefits enrollments and changes, address changes, forms distribution, and communicating policy changes. The mandate for payroll and HR is to reduce the costs that result from performing these manual tasks, thus freeing up personnel in these areas for more value-added work, while providing better quality service to their customers — the organization's employees.

One way to meet this mandate has gained increasing popularity over the last few years — employee self-service. Simply, an employee self-service application gives an employee access to his or her personnel data and allows the employee to review, print out, and/or update certain portions of that data. The most common applications so far include data updates and benefits enrollments and changes, but now that the benefits of employee self-service have manifested themselves (e.g., reduced administrative tasks for payroll and HR, greater accuracy of data), new uses are being added all the time, including:

- electronic paystubs providing employees with current and historical payroll data;
- electronic W-2s and W-2c's;
- completion of Form W-4 and equivalent state forms;
- completion and storage of Form I-9;
- updating voluntary deduction information;
- updating direct deposit information;
- helping employees model changes such as calculation of net pay if they were to make changes to withholding allowances, 401(k) contributions, etc.;
- reporting hours worked and leave time taken;
- reporting travel and entertainment expenses;
- providing retirement estimates;
- retirement plan administration; and
- access to company information and policies.

Organizations that are using employee self-service applications have found that they are getting more accurate and more timely information at a small fraction of the cost of doing it through paper systems. These benefits are realized because the information is being provided directly from the source rather than being translated from handwritten forms and then entered into a system. While there are some data changes that should not be allowed to be made by employees (e.g., changes in title and salary), employee self-service has proved to be a hit for all parties involved.

There are several ways in which employee self-service applications can be delivered and used by employees, many of whom do not have ready access to a personal computer.

*Kiosks.* Employee self-service kiosks are specialized workstations located for easy employee access, where employees can inquire and modify their payroll and HR data. They generally have user-friendly touch screen capabilities that enable employees without computer experience to easily access, retrieve, and modify data. As changes are made by employees, they automatically update the employee's data in all the related systems or are stored in a hold file for processing. Kiosks are most often used for benefits enrollment, name, address and dependent changes, time entry and leave balance inquiries. While kiosks provide easy access for employees working in a particular location, they cannot be used by remote or mobile employees.

*Interactive Voice Response.* With an Interactive Voice Response (IVR) system, employees make changes by touch-tone phone to their payroll and HR data. Changes can be made from the office, at home, or in a car, wherever there's a phone. Employees can also review information, including benefits accruals, pay history, benefits enrollment status and vacation accruals. Employees make their choices through a series of menus, the IVR server translates the changes, and the employees have an opportunity to review what they have chosen before their information is updated in the employer's systems. Employees are also often able to automatically retrieve documents by fax. While IVR offers flexibility and empowerment for employees, it does not provide a method to make "text" changes, which limits the types of data that can be changed.

*Internet and Intranets.* The increasing prevalence of employee self-service is due to the explosion of the Internet and company intranets as a way of delivering and collecting information. Internet technology creates a "virtual office" that can be shared across divisions, departments and locations, while allowing remote and mobile employees to keep up on corporate activities and changes as they occur. This is increasingly important in an age when more and more employees work from home or other locations that are not on the employer's premises.

Whether a company relies on the Internet or a company intranet, the principle is the same — access via PC enables employees from different locations to access, share, retrieve, and update information. Using the Internet hastens the move to paperless payroll and HR administration while at the same time increasing communication to employees. It also encourages employees to look for information on their own time. They can complete forms online and submit them to HR after reviewing company policies and procedures, as well as update their own information in real-time.

The benefits don't stop there, however. Once employees are comfortable with employee self-service, they will spend less time completing forms and making inquiries to the payroll and HR departments. Then they can spend more time on their primary responsibilities, and the payroll and HR professionals can focus their attention on strategic functions rather than administrative tasks.

**Manager self-service**. Under the same data ownership principles that drive employee self-service, several organizations are implementing manager self-service applications to enhance their productivity and value to their employer. Self-service applications allow managers to see data when they want to see it and how they want to see it, cutting down the time they need to review information and make decisions.

In the payroll/HR arena, managers may be notified of upcoming employee performance appraisals and merit increase decisions, with the ability to review historical information on-line. They may also have access to comprehensive compensation information, including salary administration, job descriptions, compensation programs, and market survey data. Line managers may also be able to initiate promotions, salary increases, and transfers which then can be routed to approving managers via workflow management systems. The costs involved in maintaining a secure website, the software, and PC access for employees must be considered when implementing employee and manager self-service.

**Self-service through an outsourcing company – the ASP/SaaS model.** An increasingly popular model for implementing employee self-service is the Application Service Provider (ASP) model – also called Software as a Service (SaaS) or On-Demand Software. Under this type of arrangement, the employer is not required to maintain an expensive in-house system to support self-service. The ASP itself hosts each application (e.g., payroll, human resources, benefits) at its location. Through an Internet connection, the employee gains access to the provider's software as if it resided on his or her own computer. The flexibility of the Internet makes this a very appealing alternative in organizations where employees have easy Internet access.

# 12.8-2  Implementing Internet Technology

Before companies can begin offering employee self-service over the Internet or a corporate intranet, they have to go through many of the same processes that are used in selecting a new payroll/HRMS system (see Section 12.4). Every organization is different and their use of the Internet unique, but there are certain steps that should be taken, once the decision has been made that the investment in new technology and processes is a sound one.

**Build a project management team**. A project management team should be formed, with multiple levels of employees representing a broad array of departments, including: information systems, marketing, payroll, human resources, benefits, and others. The project team must decide who will manage the content and functions of the site.

**Select hardware and software**. Significant evaluations and decisions need to be made when establishing a corporate Internet website or intranet.

- *Client software* — which web browser or browsers to use (e.g., Mozilla Firefox, Microsoft Internet Explorer, etc.);
- *Server software* — which web server to use;
- *Type of TCP/IP (Transmission Control Protocol/Internet Protocol) connection* — enables data to be transferred from one computer to another; and
- How to coordinate the use of the Internet with the payroll/HRMS database.

**Encourage use of the technology**. Nothing can kill a new technology project easier than lack of use by the intended end users. By including all levels of the company from the beginning, training and acceptance of the Internet will happen a lot easier. To make sure that the technically inexperienced are not left out, the approach should be simplistic and user-friendly: an easy-to-navigate site that is geared to the employee with the least computer skills. Even if this is done, training of employees is still necessary as a way of encouraging use.

**Address security concerns**. Security is an absolutely essential concern and should be a primary focus of any employee self-service system that allows access to sensitive payroll and HR data. If proper measures are taken, the benefits of the technology will outweigh any remaining minor concerns.

**Develop codes of conduct**. The project committee must develop appropriate policies on Internet codes of conduct. The codes should identify what the company considers acceptable and unacceptable uses of the Internet or intranet, as well as who is responsible for messages communicated there. The policies should also address copyright issues as well as the repercussions from noncompliance.

# 12.8-3   Web-Enabled Applications

With all the movement toward the Internet and corporate intranets as a way of sharing information company-wide, the term that describes the methods of gaining access to company information and initiating the processing of changes to that information is "Web-enabled applications."

**Web-enablement defined**. A Web-enabled application is one that uses the Internet as another means of accessing an organization's data and the HRMS application logic itself. One example is an application that enables employees to see their paystub information from your payroll/HR application through the Internet. Web-enabled applications promote employee self-service by allowing internal users to access and act on the information they need when and where it is convenient for them. They should be designed to work in conjunction with other self-service tools, such as kiosks and IVR.

**How Web-enablement works**. The two most important elements of Web-enabled applications are accessing the data and accessing the application logic behind the data, which allows data changes to be validated and processed. Access to the application logic is important to keep employers from having to rewrite the logic specifically for the Web-enabled application. One example is employee address changes. If an employer wants to Web-enable its employee address change application, and its current system validates the state based on the zip code entered, the employer has to determine how to access the current application logic or rewrite the logic to do the validation within the Web application.

**Elements needed for Web-enablement**. In order to develop Web-enabled applications, the following elements are required:

- Internet infrastructure to allow large numbers of users to gain secure access easily — including Web server, software, modems, firewall security, technical support and maintenance;
- Web-enabling tools — which combine a Java Rapid Application Development programming environment with an application server to manage session management, security and database connectivity;
- Core technology expertise — including Java, JavaScript, VB Script, Active X controls and HTML;
- HRMS application expertise — including functional, technical, and architectural expertise and an understanding of application interfaces that enable access to the application logic;
- Design and media skills — to ensure that the applications are easy-to-follow and use, functional and visually appealing; and
- Workflow strategy — to ensure that Web-enablement fits with existing and planned tools, and to enable those who do not have regular PC access to take advantage of IVR, kiosks, fax-back and other tools to meet their needs.

# 12.9  Review Questions and Exercises

## Review Questions

1.  Name four other systems that often interface with payroll within a company.

2.  Name three commonly used system edits in payroll systems.

3.  Who are the payroll department's customers?

4.  List three major reasons why payroll, human resources, and benefits would benefit from an integrated system.

5.  When selecting a new system, who should be included on the project team?

6.  What are the objectives of an automated payroll system?

7.  What is the main disadvantage of using a service provider?

8.  List the advantages of using an in-house computerized payroll system.

9.  What are the disadvantages of vendor-supplied software?

10. What are the advantages of using customized software?

11. As part of a "needs and wants analysis" in choosing a new payroll system, a Current Situation Analysis is essential. What does this entail?

12. What should be included in a request for proposal (RFP)?

13. What are three common mistakes made during system selection which could seriously damage the project at a later phase?

14. What are four environmental concerns (i.e., physical plant issues) commonly addressed in protecting system hardware?

## True or False Questions

_____ 1.  A service provider is an independent company that processes its clients' payrolls for a fee.

_____ 2.  Before you can select a new system, you must document in detail what your current system can and cannot do.

_____ 3.  The place where two systems meet is called the interface.

_____ 4.  Local Area Networks (LANs) eliminate the inefficiency of making employees wait to use one centrally located computer or share mobile storage devices.

_____ 5.  Documentation of the payroll system and its procedures is not a very important part of a company's overall control mechanisms.

_____ 6.  A disadvantage of using a service provider is that it may not have the programming personnel needed to timely meet a user's changing individual needs.

_____ 7.  Off-the-shelf payroll software is often quite inexpensive.

_____ 8.   An advantage of off-the-shelf software is that it is easy to modify to an employer's needs.

_____ 9.   An in-house computer system is only as good as the software that is run on it.

_____ 10.  Customized software is designed and written by the employer's own programmers, and is maintained and updated by the service provider.

_____ 11.  The initial step in selecting a new payroll system is to prepare a request for proposal.

_____ 12.  If a vendor balks at answering some of the questions about a proposal, that may be a good indication that its products are not right for the job.

_____ 13.  The final test before going live with a new system is called project testing.

_____ 14.  An RFP can be used to design an in-house payroll system.

_____ 15.  A system edit is a warning or alert built into the system that checks for errors.

## Multiple Choice Questions

_____ 1.   What is the main objective of any payroll system?

   a.   Prepare internal reports
   b.   Provide for compliance with federal, state, and local withholding, depositing, and reporting requirements
   c.   Accurately paying employees in a restricted time frame on payday
   d.   Maintain adequate records of all data and transactions

_____ 2.   All of the following features are disadvantages of using a service provider for processing your payroll EXCEPT:

   a.   Lack of control over security
   b.   Low fixed costs
   c.   Little time for changes
   d.   Responsibility for filing errors

_____ 3.   What is the final test before going "live" with a new system?

   a.   Parallel test
   b.   Spot test
   c.   Stress test
   d.   Conversion test

_____ 4.   What is a warning or alert called that is built into the system that checks for errors and either corrects the error or notifies the operator that something may be wrong?

   a.   Monitor edit
   b.   System edit
   c.   Control edit
   d.   Procedure edit

_____ 5. What system is designed to eliminate the time taken to punch in and out and to write and sign information on time cards, as well as the errors that such procedures can cause?

   a. Software system
   b. Automated time and attendance system
   c. In-house system
   d. Time-sharing system

_____ 6. Which of the following systems is least likely to interface with payroll?

   a. Human Resources
   b. Marketing
   c. Benefits
   d. Accounting

_____ 7. All of the following features are advantages of an in-house payroll system EXCEPT:

   a. Convenient access
   b. Low fixed costs
   c. Customized software
   d. Interactive applications

_____ 8. All of the following features are disadvantages of an in-house computer system EXCEPT:

   a. High fixed costs
   b. System obsolescence
   c. Sufficient secure space needed
   d. Scheduling flexibility

_____ 9. All of the following features are disadvantages of vendor-supplied software EXCEPT:

   a. Little reliance on in-house systems personnel
   b. Lengthy processing
   c. Extensive training needed
   d. Possible slow changes

_____ 10. All of the following features are advantages of customized software EXCEPT:

   a. Special needs are met
   b. Increased flexibility
   c. Additional time and staff needed
   d. Reduced training needs

_____ 11. All of the following behaviors are common mistakes to avoid when selecting a new system EXCEPT:

   a. Making decisions without sufficient input
   b. Failing to consider all the costs associated
   c. Not considering future company needs regarding expansion and downsizing
   d. Including personnel from all related departments on the project team

_____ 12. After the new system has been selected and approved, what is the next step in the selection process?

    a. Specify scope
    b. Implementation
    c. Review
    d. Define requirements

_____ 13. Auditors are often concerned with whether RFPs for new computer systems are well formulated. Which of the following items should typically be included in a request for proposal?

    a. The hardware configuration
    b. An emphasis on software rather than hardware
    c. Detailed specifications of the current workload
    d. An emphasis on the tasks to be performed rather than specific hardware capabilities

_____ 14. An employer has decided to change from an old to a new automated payroll system. In implementing the new system, both the old and the new system are maintained during the testing period. What is this changeover technique called?

    a. Debugging
    b. Pilot testing
    c. Parallel testing
    d. Back-up system conversion

_____ 15. What method of internal control requires employees to show identification to get paid, thus discouraging the creation of phantom employees?

    a. Physical payouts
    b. Segregation of duties
    c. Job rotation
    d. System edits

# SECTION 13: MANAGING A PAYROLL DEPARTMENT

TABLE OF CONTENTS

# SECTION 13: MANAGING A PAYROLL DEPARTMENT

Most newly promoted payroll managers achieve their new position not because they have shown great management skills in the past, but because they are technically proficient in the processing of payroll. As is the case in many departments, promotions to management are based on the skill with which the employee has handled previous assignments. Once promoted, they are expected to hire, train, and supervise other employees, make policy and procedure decisions that guarantee compliance, and plan budgets, often with little or no training in how to manage these tasks.

After a review of some basic management concepts, this section will outline the management skills most necessary to successfully oversee a payroll department. Along the way, we will provide some idea of what your job as a payroll manager entails and how you can apply these skills to the particular issues and opportunities presented by payroll management.

## 13.1 Basic Management Theory

The tasks that make up the bulk of the manager's/supervisor's job are vastly different from those the manager performed before becoming a manager. Generally, the production work of payroll processing is done by other employees of the department. Payroll managers in mid-size and large organizations are responsible for planning, staffing, training, evaluating, counseling, delegating, recognizing, reporting, etc. How they should approach these tasks has been the subject of dozens of books on management theory and the best way to get the most out of employees.

Following are a couple of the most commonly recognized management theories, as they have been described in recent years.

**Situational leadership.** In examining different management styles, Paul Hersey, Ken Blanchard, and Dewey Johnson noted that the way managers handled their staffs often depended on the way they dealt with two factors: tasks and relationships.[1]

- *Task behavior (guidance).* High task managers emphasize control over their employees—control over the lines of communication, work procedures, and patterns of organization.

- *Relationship behavior (support).* High relationship managers place few restrictions on communication with their staff and often seek their support and friendship. They also push employees to accept responsibility and reach their full potential.

Hersey and Blanchard concluded that the different combinations of these factors led to four different management styles (shown in Table 13.1):

- *Low task / high relationship*—little control sought by the manager; good deal of mutual trust and support.

- *High task / high relationship*—manager controls the job and procedures; also relies on personal communication with employees to coach them in performing the job.

- *Low task / low relationship*—most jobs delegated to staff; little personal contact desired by manager.

---

1.   Paul Hersey, Kenneth Blanchard, Dewey Johnson, *Management of Organizational Behavior: Leading Human Resources* (8th Edition), Prentice Hall, Englewood Cliffs, NJ, 2000.

- *High task/low relationship*—manager seeks to control staff and direct performance; but with little feedback or dialogue with employees.

Table 13.1

| Supporting | Coaching |
|---|---|
| Low Task<br>High Relationship | High Task<br>High Relationship |
| Delegating | Directing |
| Low Task<br>Low Relationship | High Task<br>Low Relationship |

What situational leadership proponents emphasize is successful managers use not just the management style that comes naturally to them, but whatever style fits the demands of the particular job or function and the employee or group of employees seeking to accomplish it. In the payroll department, this might mean exercising a high degree of control over the work done and procedures followed by a new payroll clerk or a newly promoted first line payroll supervisor, while providing frequent feedback. An experienced payroll tax researcher or computer programmer, however, might need little in the way of control over the work they perform.

**Principle-centered leadership**. The theory of principle-centered leadership was developed by Stephen Covey.[2] It deals with four fundamental dimensions which grow out of leadership centered on principles such as integrity, justice, and the Golden Rule. These four interdependent dimensions (outlined below) become the internal sources of an organization's strength.

*Security* is the collective sense of strength and self-esteem felt by the professionals who work in an organization. In payroll, we can assess our strength by asking a series of questions.

- How well do we do our jobs?
- Do we provide accurate information?
- Is our final product accurate?
- Do we serve our customers well?

A principle-centered approach focuses on the strengths of our contribution rather than the weaknesses of the individuals we are serving.

*Guidance* is the direction on which we base our decisions and actions. In payroll, guidance can be a combination of influences from management and the customer (employees, government, management). An example where these influences may conflict is the paycheck, since employees want it as soon as possible, while management may want to delay it as long as possible. The payroll department must provide a compromise that works for both parties. If the payroll department's guidance grows from a center that emphasizes integrity, honesty, and fairness, the end result will be equitable.

*Wisdom* is the ability to maintain balance and perspective among the diverse internal and external forces that influence the organization's reality. In the payroll department, wisdom can be viewed through the ability of the manager to constantly acquire, sort, filter, and provide information, maintaining a high level of competence and effectiveness in the department.

---

2. Stephen R. Covey, *Principle-Centered Leadership*, Simon & Schuster, New York, NY, 1990.

*Power* is the energy to decide, to act, and to change. In the payroll department, power can be seen as the capacity to accomplish the task at hand regardless of external conditions. A payroll team develops power by accepting the responsibility to act according to basic human principles. This sort of power allows teamwork in choosing and achieving peak quality service and in evaluating performance and setting goals for ongoing improvement.

Principle-centered leadership can be summed up in a simple statement: Treat people the way you want to be treated. Actions to take toward establishing principle-centered leadership in an organization include involving all employees in developing personal, team, departmental, and organizational mission statements and in identifying and setting goals and the actions necessary to achieve them.

**Empowerment.** Employee empowerment has become one of the most often repeated phrases in management texts and seminars. The purpose of empowering employees is to give them the tools to accomplish an objective and allow them the space to develop the methods of attaining those objectives. While empowerment is practiced in many different ways, the key objective is for the employee to take ownership of the process, leading to a motivated, effective, and responsible employee who derives satisfaction from being allowed to develop their own methods to accomplish an objective.

The empowerment process involves five steps, which can be applied to a typical payroll situation, such as the preparation of manual checks for employees who did not receive a scheduled pay raise in the current payroll. A payroll department employee could be empowered to handle the situation by applying the five steps to empowerment as follows:

- *Step 1: Establish the desired results.* The expected results are that the employees will have their pay corrected with a manual check, their future paychecks will be adjusted properly, and they will receive quality customer service.

- *Step 2: Provide guidelines.* The manual checks must comply with all applicable federal, state, and local requirements, as well as company policies.

- *Step 3: Identify resources available to accomplish the task.* The following information is provided: tax tables, company policies on manual checks, wage and hour guidelines, and contacts who can handle questions.

- *Step 4: Hold people accountable.* The employee will be evaluated based on the satisfaction level of employees receiving the manual checks and the degree of compliance with the guidelines that have been provided.

- *Step 5: Identify consequences.* If the employee fails to complete the task timely and accurately, the company will be exposed to possible financial penalties, the reputation of the payroll department in the organization will suffer, and the failure will be noted on the employee's performance record.

**No one way is the right way, but...** Each of the management theories described here has its proponents and its detractors, and each will be more or less popular over time. However, it seems that the current and future demands of the American workplace will make it necessary for all managers, not just payroll managers, to tailor their management style to fit different situations—different jobs and different employees.

Workforce diversity is here now and is here to stay. It is common knowledge that the work force is getting older, contains more women, is accommodating an increasing percentage of physically and mentally challenged workers, and has workers from more diverse backgrounds than ever before. Each one of these workers brings a different set of job and life experiences to the workplace that affect the way they do a job. The ability to manage them successfully requires that managers be flexible and use the management style for each situation that will get the most out of the employee and the most for the organization.

## 13.2  Management Skills

Despite the subjectivity involved in determining what makes a good manager, there are certain fundamental skills that must be mastered and that make up the duties and responsibilities of most managerial positions. They include: strategic planning/organizing; staffing; giving directions; controlling progress; and reporting to upper management. Each of these fundamental skills, as well as their components, will be discussed in this section. Keep in mind, as you read this section, that all these skills are used in various combinations and are dependent on each other; none of them exists in a vacuum.

Something else to keep in mind as you read is the recent emphasis in management studies on "quality" as a management objective. Providing quality products and service for customers sounds almost too obvious to mention as a management goal. But many companies lost their way (and their healthy bottom line) when they strayed too far from that notion. The payroll department in an organization has several customer groups, including the employees it pays, the taxing authorities to which it pays and reports taxes, other company departments, and company management. Providing a quality product to these customers means providing a perfect paycheck, accurate and timely depositing and reporting of taxes, accurate reporting to management, and cost savings for the company at large.

## 13.2-1  Strategic Planning and Organizing

The fundamental starting point for any task, big or small, is the formulation of a strategic plan for completing the task and organizing the employees and other resources so they can work toward that goal. The same holds true for the payroll department itself. There must be a plan for the department to achieve its goal of satisfying employees, government, and upper management.

The process of planning and organizing consists of several key activities, including:

**Defining goals and objectives.** The goals or objectives must be defined at the beginning of the planning phase of a task. They are not the same as the task. For example, the overall task (or mission) might be the elimination of errors on employee paychecks. One goal that might be set in planning to attain that mission could be a 75% reduction in benefit plan deduction errors. Setting such a goal will keep employees' minds on the payroll department's mission of providing quality service to their employee/customers. It is also a specific goal against which progress can be measured more easily.

**Defining the time frame.** The next step is to determine the time frame for achieving the goal that has been set. Without a specific time frame, goals have a tendency to never be achieved. The manager must take into account all the other factors that go into planning and organizing a task—the goals, available resources, cost constraints, etc.—in determining a realistic time frame for achievement. Attempting to achieve a goal in an unreasonable period of time will defeat the department's overall mission of quality customer service and lead to overstressed and disgruntled employees.

**Defining the subtasks.** Achieving any goal requires breaking up the overall project into subtasks for the employees involved, each with its own time frame for completion. Timely completion of the subtasks should lead to attainment of the objective.

> *Example:* When the payroll manager at Ralph's Rest Home was planning and organizing the selection of a new automated payroll system, one of the first tasks for her and the project team was to perform a needs and wants analysis (see Section 12.4-2). As part of this task, the payroll manager broke it down into subtasks, including: documenting the paper flow into and out of the current system; documenting system maintenance procedures; identifying current interfaces with the system; and identifying and prioritizing complaints regarding the system. Each subtask then was assigned to certain members of the team, and they were given a completion date both sides were comfortable with.

**Analyzing available resources.** Another important planning/organizing activity is an analysis of the resources available to achieve the stated goal. The payroll manager has several resources available within the company at his or her disposal. They include:

- employees of payroll and other departments;
- company equipment (e.g., computer hardware and software);
- company funds;
- ideas from inside and outside the organization; and
- information.

**Evaluating costs.** Before implementing a plan, the payroll manager must know what it will cost to achieve the stated goals. Budget constraints may well determine the goals and time frames that are set for achievement.

> *Example:* When Rena, payroll manager at Park Ridge, Inc., is trying to reduce benefit deduction errors on employee paychecks, she concludes the optimal solution is integration of the payroll and benefits databases, rather than separate data entry into each one. Upon further investigation, however, she learns this would mean an entirely new automated system costing much more than is available in the payroll department budget. Less costly alternatives, such as an electronic transfer of the data from one database to another after a single entry, should be explored.

## 13.2-2 Staffing

In this context, staffing is a very broad term, taking in those management skills that make up the supervisory portion of a manager's duties. The main skills include hiring, training, delegating, and coaching employees, and the failure to master any one of them can sabotage the best laid plans of any manager and wreak havoc with the stated quality goals of the payroll department.

**Hiring the right employees.** One of the most important decisions a payroll manager can make is whether to hire a particular person. The stakes are high, since employees who perform well as enthusiastic team members can lead to an efficient, cost-effective payroll department, while hiring the wrong individuals can lead to dissension, inefficiency, and costly turnover. As with any important task, hiring consists of more than one activity.

*Prehiring analysis.* The hiring process actually begins with the decision to fill an open position or create a new one, and an analysis of the tasks which the job to be filled is to accomplish.

 **TIME TO REORGANIZE?** This might be a good time to rethink the structure of the payroll department, cross-train employees, and match needed skills with employees' abilities before making a final determination as to what the scope of the open job will be.

*Job description.* Once the scope of the position to be filled has been determined, a detailed job description must be created or updated from previous versions. A job description not only aids in the hiring process, but guides managers in the future in delegating to the employee, deciding what training is necessary, and completing performance reviews and appraisals. The more specific the job description, the more help it will be.

The job description should list the duties and responsibilities of the position, as well as the technical and performance skills (communication, writing, customer service) needed to be successful in the position. Some of the questions the payroll manager can use in developing job descriptions include:

- What are the educational requirements necessary to perform the job?

- What knowledge/skills must the applicant have before being offered the job?

- What training opportunities can be provided to the new employee?

- What is the level of supervision required in this job?

- How much communication and interaction with other employees and entities outside the employer will be necessary?

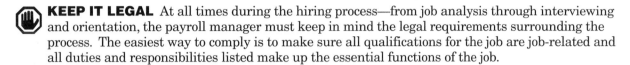 **KEEP IT LEGAL** At all times during the hiring process—from job analysis through interviewing and orientation, the payroll manager must keep in mind the legal requirements surrounding the process. The easiest way to comply is to make sure all qualifications for the job are job-related and all duties and responsibilities listed make up the essential functions of the job.

*Example:* Following is a sample job description for a job as a mid-level payroll department employee.

1. Summary of Job Description

   Process nonexempt or exempt payroll associated with new hires, rehires, promotions, raises, tax information, benefit deductions, awards, leaves of absence, relocation reimbursements and bonuses, garnishments, child support withholding, etc. Will interface with all employees within the company and provide quality customer service to employees.

2. Key Responsibilities

   - Responsible for controlling timely and accurate payroll input through internal system and external payroll service provider.

   - Ensures that only authorized salary information is used, proper accounts are affected, and accruals are accurate.

   - Maintains *confidentiality* of employee information.

3. Minimum Education/Job-Related Experience or Equivalent

   High School Diploma plus one year accounting experience.

4. Specialized Skills Required

   - Accounting experience in an accounting position or previous payroll experience.

   - Proficiency on 10-key calculator, personal computer skills, including Microsoft Word and Excel.

   - Strong Internet research skills.

   - Accuracy, time management, organization, and communication skills.

   - Ability to work with interruptions.

   - Familiarization with customer service environment.

   - Working knowledge of accounting principles, auditing concepts, and controls.

   - Strong human relations and interpersonal skills.

   - Ability to use judgment and initiative.

5. Specific Responsibilities

- Working knowledge of payroll system acquired from on-the-job training sufficient to process nonexempt (400 employees) and exempt (600 employees) payroll on one processing schedule.

- Working knowledge of all payroll policies and procedures relative to their specific payroll or correct pay calculation (i.e., when does overtime or double time apply, pre-tax deductions, social security and disability insurance wage maximums, calculating manual checks).

- Working knowledge of other internal systems, if applicable, which involves auditing of time cards for correct pay calculations.

- Working knowledge (as related to payroll) of month-end procedure, including preparation of salary expense sheet, payroll expense sheet, cash account reconciliation, adjustment vouchers, cash forecasts, and reversal of double accruals.

6. Contacts With Others

Internal: Human Resources, Internal Audit, Accounting, Tax, Benefits, all employees.

External: Service providers, government agencies.

7. Problem Solving

- Participating in problem solving or projects which affect their functional areas.

- Ability to trace reconciling problems back to the source and decide on appropriate correcting entries.

*Recruiting.* Once the job analysis and job description have been completed, recruiting to fill the position can begin. Payroll managers have several options open to them. In most companies, open positions are first posted for current employees, allowing them to express an interest in transferring to payroll. Allowing such moves can improve employee morale and lower turnover by providing career development opportunities. Also, applicants from inside the organization have readily verifiable job histories and qualifications. A possible negative result is that a transfer creates another opening that must be filled.

When recruiting from outside the company, the human resources department may use a professional recruiting agency. Since human resources does the initial recruiting, the payroll manager will not be involved with advertising and screening resumes, but the cost must be taken into consideration. In many larger companies, the payroll manager can rely on the human resources department to act as an outside recruiter. However, the payroll manager must inform the screener of all specific requirements, so those individuals not meeting the requirements can be eliminated from consideration.

*Interviewing.* Once you have screened the applicants' resumes and job applications and chosen the most likely candidates, the interview process is next. Whether the interviews are handled by individuals or in a group, make sure all interviewers are familiar with the job description and the qualities being sought in a successful candidate. What the interviewers should be looking for is evidence of the technical and performance skills identified in the job description.

Develop a list of questions to be asked of all candidates to ensure no preference is shown to any candidate. Ask questions that require the candidate to evaluate his or her skills (e.g., what types of work do you have the most difficulty with).

One of the best ways to get at the needed information is to ask open-ended questions rather than questions that call for one-word answers. This forces the applicant to explain past behavior and allows the interviewer to see beyond the resume and assess the validity of the applicant's skills. When the interviewing process is over, make sure the best applicant is picked based on the objective criteria set out in the job description. If no one meets the criteria, begin the selection process again or change the criteria.

 **USE APA'S KAC TO ASSESS PAYROLL KNOWLEDGE, SKILLS** One of the best ways to make sure that job candidates have the knowledge, skills, and abilities they need is to have them undergo a self-assessment through APA's Knowledge Assessment Calculator (KAC). The individual doing the hiring can see the results of the KAC immediately after the candidate takes the 50-question assessment. KACs are available at 3 different skill levels, and they cover all areas of the payroll body of knowledge. For more information, go to www.payrollkac.com or call APA at 210-226-4600.

**Delegating tasks and responsibility.** If payroll managers are unsuccessful at delegating responsibility and authority, they will end up doing what they did before they became managers and still be responsible for their managerial duties as well. This will inevitably lead to burned-out managers and unfulfilled employees. Therefore, payroll managers must learn the strengths and weaknesses of their employees and assign tasks, responsibility, and authority matching each employee's skills and abilities.

*Assigning responsibility.* The payroll manager must decide which employee will be assigned the responsibility for each task or portion of a task in the department. When assigned a task, the employee must be informed of resources available, constraints (e.g., time, budget), and deadline requirements.

*Assigning authority.* Next, the payroll manager must decide what level of authority goes along with each assigned responsibility. The types of authority that may be assigned include: budgetary, allocating resources, hiring and firing, etc. It is important for all managers to remember employees cannot be given the responsibility for completing a task unless they have the resources and authority needed to get the job done. Asking a payroll department supervisor to oversee the processing of a special payroll involving a high number of new hires without giving the employee the authority to hire temporary help will almost certainly guarantee a late payroll, irate employees, and a disgruntled supervisor.

*Hold on to the accountability.* While it may often seem like an attractive thing to do, managers cannot delegate their accountability for a project or a process. The payroll manager is always accountable for an error-filled payroll, regardless of who was responsible for the task that produced the errors. When problems occur, the manager must take responsibility and not seek to blame the employee to whom the task has been delegated.

*Strike a balance.* Most managers, during their initial phase after being promoted, either delegate too little because they are afraid to relinquish control or delegate too much to employees who cannot handle it. As they gain experience, the important thing is to strike a balance by learning the knowledge, skills, and abilities of their employees and matching them to tasks at hand. This is an ongoing process as employees grow and develop and tasks change, and managers must pay sufficient attention to avoid potentially costly problems.

**Training.** Even though the payroll manager may have selected employees with excellent technical and performance skills to staff the payroll department, they may not be ready or able to perform all the duties and responsibilities of their jobs without training. A newly hired employee with several years of payroll and accounting experience will still need to be trained in the company's accounting procedures, and a payroll clerk coming from another company that used one service provider will need training to work with a different service provider or software used by the new employer.

While training will not solve all problems employees are having on the job, it may solve some the payroll manager erroneously attributed to a "bad attitude." If an employee receives training and still does not improve performance, it may be that a different type of training is the answer rather than disciplinary action.

***Example:*** After acquiring Eastbridge Clothiers Co., Bayside Mills, Inc. decided to completely reconfigure its chart of accounts (see Section 11.1-2). When Sondra Sam, Bayside's payroll manager, learned of the upcoming change, she passed out copies of the new chart to her payroll staff. After the next payroll was processed and accounting entries made, the Chief Financial Officer complained to Sondra that more than 30% of the entries had been incorrectly coded. After speaking to her employees, Sondra arranged for an accounting manager to demonstrate to her staff the new coding procedures in a group training session, which led to an error rate of less than 5% with the next payroll.

**Training can improve skills and knowledge, not attitude.** It is important for the payroll manager to keep in mind just what training can and cannot do. While training can improve performance, it is not a cure-all for every performance problem. Proper training can improve an employee's knowledge and skills, improvements which they can then use to bring their job performance up to standard or to prepare them for a new job or promotion. What training will not do is improve an employee's poor attitude or work ethic, problems that can possibly be resolved by disciplinary action or counseling.

**Link training to payroll's mission.** As noted earlier, the overall task or mission of the payroll department is to provide quality service to its customers—the employees, government agencies, other internal company departments, and upper management. This mission must be kept in mind when devising training for payroll department employees. Training must be aimed at improving the skills and knowledge needed to achieve the department's mission.

**Types of training opportunities.** There are many different options open to the payroll manager when employees need training, ranging from formal classroom sessions to informal talks with individual employees.

*Classroom training.* Employees can be enrolled in courses offered by educational institutions, software vendors, or service providers to improve the skills or knowledge needed to perform their current job or to expand on those skills or knowledge for future opportunities. There are also a myriad of other formal training opportunities, such as workshops, seminars, and conferences offering sessions on various payroll-related topics, such as those offered by the American Payroll Association.

 **LEARNING BY COMPUTER** Payroll skills can also be taught using Web-based training offered by the American Payroll Association. The APA offers training over the Internet through its PayTrain® and *Fundamentals of Payroll* courses, which allow the user to choose a self-directed or instructor-assisted course of study. These programs can be as flexible as the needs of the individual being trained, and they allow training to take place when time is available, without disrupting the payroll department's schedule.

*Giving feedback.* Providing feedback to an employee and letting them know immediately how they are progressing is an important training tool. It tells employees whether they are on the right track or not and gives them the chance to bring up concerns before they become problems. Be sincere with feedback you provide, whether it is positive or negative.

*Coaching.* Somewhat more formal than providing feedback, coaching involves helping the employee by observing and offering suggestions for improvement.

***Example:*** Many payroll managers will often sit with new payroll clerks as they begin entering payroll information and will offer immediate feedback and support.

*Demonstrations.* Training often includes an actual demonstration of how a duty or problem should be handled. This was true in the earlier example of the payroll manager who arranged for a company accounting manager to demonstrate the new chart of accounts for employees.

*Setting goals.* One way to train employees in new behaviors and methods so that the lessons are applied and old bad habits are not repeated is to have employees develop their own goals and training plan. In this scenario, the employee and the manager sit down together, discuss the employee's plans for professional growth and development, and agree on steps to achieve those goals.

**APA TOOL FOR ASSESSING TRAINING NEEDS**  The American Payroll Association has developed an online tool for employees and their managers to use to assess the employees' training needs and determine the appropriate APA training offerings that meet those needs.  The Knowledge Assessment Calculator® offers testing at 3 levels of payroll expertise, with immediate scoring and recommendations for appropriate APA training.  Go to www.payrollKAC.com for more information.

# 13.2-3  Directing Employees

A major responsibility for any manager is directing employees in their work activities, whether as individuals or as teams.  This is where the payroll manager's communication skills become most important, because getting each employee to work toward attainment of the department's overall goal of quality service can be quite challenging.  Each employee comes to the job with an already-acquired value system and personal motivation to a greater or lesser degree.  Because these qualities are "givens" that the manager must work with, the manager's ability to communicate—by listening, providing feedback, coaching, and leading—can be the determining factor in whether the department's goals are met.

**Providing feedback.**  Managers provide feedback to employees all the time whether they know it or not.  A smile, a look away, a "well done" when a job is finished, all provide an employee with some idea of whether an employee's performance is up to par.  Whether the feedback is effective in producing the results desired by the manager is another matter entirely, however.  Effective feedback contains two elements that lead to behavior modification where necessary or to continued improved behavior.

- Information as to the performance that was expected and whether the employee has performed up to expectations, and

- A reward to reinforce and encourage continued positive behavior or a punishment to encourage modified behavior.

***Example:***  Linda, the payroll manager, has assigned Terry to respond to employee inquiries on payday regarding their paychecks.  After observing Terry on several paydays and noting a reduced number of follow-up complaints from employees, Linda says to Terry, "Thank you for handling our 'dissatisfied customers' so professionally.  I think they were especially pleased when you gave them a stated time frame for the department to handle their problems.  Since you have been handling these calls, I have not received any further complaints about rudeness on the phone or a failure to follow-up."  These comments provided Terry with information about what he did and how it produced desired results, as well as the knowledge that Linda was pleased with his performance.

 **KEEP THE MISSION IN MIND**  When providing feedback, the same as for other management activities, the payroll manager must remember to focus on the payroll department's mission of providing quality service.  The feedback should be designed to produce behavior that will further this mission.

While information and reinforcement are essential for providing effective feedback, there are several other guidelines that managers need to be aware of.

*If the behavior does not matter, ignore it.*  When providing feedback to employees, focus on business and the accomplishment of business-related objectives.  While an employee's behavior may be personally annoying to you or other staff members, ignore it unless it adversely affects the business of the department.

*Do not personalize, focus on the behavior.*  One of the two basic elements of effective feedback is providing information about what is expected from the employee and what has been accomplished.  The information should deal with what the employee did or did not do and should be specific rather than general to avoid irrelevant arguments and confrontations.  When providing feedback, avoid using "You" as much as possible, focusing on what "I" observed and how the behavior affected "me" or a third party.

***Example:*** Do not accuse an employee of having a "lousy attitude" when the behavior that needs to be changed is regularly arriving late to work. Tell the employee how often he or she was late and what an adverse effect this had on the workloads of other employees in the department.

*Keep feedback current.* In order for either positive or negative feedback to be useful, it must be given as soon as possible after the behavior has occurred. If this is not done, the employee will often not make the connection between the feedback and the behavior, so the desired modification will not occur.

*Base feedback on observations, not hearsay.* Relying on the words of other employees to provide feedback can lead to mistakes and a loss of credibility and trust. Base your feedback only on what you have observed of the employee's behavior.

*Be specific, don't generalize.* Phrases such as "great job," "you're terrific," or "I'm concerned about your work" do not give an employee enough information to know what behaviors are being encouraged or discouraged. Always be specific when providing feedback. And remember to be consistently specific whether giving praise or criticism.

> ***Example:*** Employees like nothing less than to hear, "You handled the meeting well, but you should not have interrupted the personnel manager and there were not enough handouts for everyone." The first part of the feedback tells the employee little about what he or she did right and should be encouraged to continue, while the second part mentions each wrong behavior.

*Praise, don't punish.* Even in situations where negative feedback must be given, positive reinforcement of an employee's strengths should be emphasized since employees generally respond much better when criticism is balanced by praise. Provide examples of how improvement can be made, rather than just telling the employee how bad his or her performance has been. Also, negative feedback should generally be given in private rather than embarrassing the employee in public.

**Listening, an underutilized ability.** In recent years, research has shown most people are not good listeners and we generally retain less than 25% of what we hear eight hours after we hear it. But listening is a very important skill for managers, since the failure to understand an employee makes it almost impossible to successfully direct that employee's work activities. Listening is a skill that can be learned and improved upon, but it takes constant dedication and requires the manager's full attention.

Following is a list of some of the common barriers to listening in an office setting that prevent one person from hearing and understanding what someone else is saying:

- distractions from phone calls, people walking by the office, other interruptions;
- tuning out by thinking about something else or faking attention;
- reacting emotionally rather than rationally;
- failing to pay attention to the speaker's body language;
- not meaning what you say or saying what you mean when speaking; and
- anticipating what you will say next without really listening.

There are some obvious counter measures for several of these barriers, including:

- having someone hold your calls until the meeting with the employee is finished;
- keeping your office door closed to discourage interruptions;
- making it clear that you are not to be disturbed except for emergencies;
- focusing on what the speaker is saying rather than how you will respond;
- making sure you look at the speaker while he or she is talking.

But none of these actions will ensure that the listener—the payroll manager in this situation—will actually listen to and understand what is being said. One of the most popular and effective methods for improving listening skills is to practice "reflective listening," a simple device whereby the listener repeats what she thinks she heard and asks the speaker for verification. This makes clear what was said and helps avoid potential misunderstandings. It also forces the listener to focus on what was said rather than any distractions that might be present.

Table 13.2 contains some common "bridging statements" that can be used to verify and clarify a speaker's statements and emotions before misunderstandings take place.

Table 13.2

---

*Clarifying to get additional facts:*
   "Could we go over that again?"
   "I didn't follow what you said. Would you clarify your last statement?"
   "What does that imply?"

*Paraphrasing or repeating to clear up misunderstandings:*
   "As I understand, you think ... Is that right?"
   "Correct me if I'm wrong, but you seem to be saying ... Did I hear you right?"
   "From your point of view, you think ... Did I hear you correctly?"
   "In other words, your opinion is ... Right?"

*Reflecting feelings:*
   "You appear to be feeling ...Am I mistaken?"
   "You seem to be ... Are you?"
   "Maybe you feel ... Do you?"

*Summarizing main ideas:*
   "What you've said so far is ... Is that right?"
   "To sum up, we've concluded that ... Did I miss anything?"
   "Your main points are ... Anything else?"

---

**Coaching.** Much the same as coaches do with players on a sports team, payroll managers use their communication skills (feedback and listening) to coach their players (i.e., employees). Coaching helps improve the knowledge and skills employees need to perform their jobs. Coaching involves a one-on-one session between the payroll manager and the employee, generally used for new employees or when there has been a change in the employee's workplace environment. These situations include:

- orientation and training of new employees;
- teaching of new job skills or knowledge;
- explaining departmental policies and procedures;
- explaining the corporate culture and political realities of the company;
- one-on-one follow-up to make sure training session material has been understood;
- performance appraisals;
- when the payroll manager is new to the department;
- when an employee initiates the coaching by seeking performance improvements; and
- when an employee receives a new work assignment.

**Counseling.** Whereas coaching deals with performance improvements that can be gained by increasing technical knowledge and performance skills, counseling is used by managers who want to help an employee resolve a personal or attitude problem that is adversely affecting job performance. Similar to coaching, counseling requires the manager to use effective feedback and listening skills, with listening being especially important. Situations where counseling may be appropriate include:

- after a corporate reorganization, merger, or acquisition;
- after corporate layoffs, downsizing, or rightsizing, the remaining employees may need counseling;
- when budget problems reduce or freeze salary increases, even for the best employees;
- when promotional and career development opportunities are limited;

- when there is conflict between employees in the department;
- when an employee feels he or she is being treated unfairly;
- when an employee is not pleased with a new work assignment or feels unsure about his or her ability to handle it;
- when an employee has personal problems off the job that are interfering with job performance (but see caution following); and
- when an employee is feeling overworked, overstressed, and burned out.

 **COMPANY COUNSELING MAY BE A BETTER ALTERNATIVE** As part of their benefit plans, many midsize and large companies make professional counseling programs available to their employees. Rather than try to take the place of a professional counselor, the payroll manager should make the employee aware of such programs if the employee admits that a severe personal problem is harming his or her work performance.

**Leadership.** Coaching and counseling are accomplished on a one-to-one basis between a manager and an employee. In contrast, leadership must be provided by the manager to groups of employees or the entire department. Some of the qualities that can help make a payroll manager a strong leader include:

- *Having a vision.* A strong payroll manager must have a clear vision of where the manager and the department should be headed, what their mission is, and how that vision and mission blend in with those of the overall organization. With a vision of quality service, everyday work, which can seem mundane and ordinary at times, becomes more purposeful and exciting. A leader must also communicate that vision, be prepared for those who challenge it, and then accquire the resources to achieve the vision.

- *Building team support.* Without the support of the department's employees, the manager's goals and vision will be unreachable. The payroll manager can build team support by creating an atmosphere where employees are treated fairly, their ideas are given thoughtful consideration, and their needs are deemed important and worth meeting.

- *Seeking partners.* Payroll managers cannot exist apart from the rest of the company. To be leaders, they must network and seek the advice and support of managers from other departments.

- *Accepting accountability.* Leaders accept accountability for things that happen by owning the outcome. They admit when a mistake was made or a problem is found in the payroll process and take ownership of it until the problem is solved. Leaders also make good on their commitments and acknowledge the contributions of other staff members rather than taking undue credit for themselves.

- *Making decisions and taking action.* Good leaders are decisive and then take action to put their decisions into practice. Deciding what's wrong with a practice or procedure in payroll will not solve anything unless action is taken to put a solution in place.

- *Leading by example.* To be a leader, the payroll manager must take the initiative and be the first one to step forward when a difficult problem needs solving or a crisis looms. Leading by example also means acting with integrity by following your principles even when the consequences may not be pleasant.

# 13.2-4 Controlling Performance

Once a goal has been set and work has taken place to meet that goal, the next step for the payroll manager is to measure the progress that has been made and take corrective actions if the progress is less than expected. This entire process is one of controlling performance to meet the stated objectives and mission. There are several steps to controlling performance.

- *Setting standards.* In order to measure performance and progress toward meeting a goal, the standards set for meeting the goal must be specific and measurable. While a payroll department's overall mission may be to "provide quality service to employees, the government, and upper management," the attainment of such a goal can never be absolutely determined. However, the goal of reducing time card transposition errors by 75% over the next eight pay periods can be measured and used as a standard.

- *Monitoring actual progress.* Once the standard has been set, the payroll manager must monitor what is actually happening. Using the example above, the manager should track the progress made in reducing time card errors after each pay period, as well as any subtasks designed to accomplish the overall objective.

- *Comparing progress with standards.* The manager must now measure the progress being made against the objective set at the beginning of the project.

- *Taking corrective actions.* If progress toward the standard is not sufficient, the payroll manager should not wait until the end of the project period to make adjustments. Midstream adjustments can be made after analyzing what is causing the lack of progress. Generally, the overall goals should not be changed at this stage.

**Controlling to improve employees' performance.** If progress is not on pace to meet the objective, the payroll manager must exercise control over the employees performing the work to bring things back on track. Even though employees have been trained and given the opportunity to improve their technical and performance skills, that does not mean they will be motivated to strive to meet the department's goals.

Motivating employees is not easy, but the most successful strategy generally is to concentrate on rewarding the employee's positive behavior and providing positive feedback. This does not mean payroll managers should ignore manifestations of a negative attitude or indications an employee is not a "team player." But rewarding positive behavior rather than taking notice only of negative behavior will generally get better results. Employees who exhibit negative behaviors must be told how those behaviors affect the manager and other employees.

Applying the principles of situational leadership to motivating employees, managers must realize employees respond differently to different motivators. It is up to the payroll manager to be aware of what motivators might best spur each employee to a better performance. These motivators can include:

*Money.* Money is the most obvious motivator, and most all employees are motivated by it to at least some degree. But remember that many employees are motivated more by recognition, leadership, additional responsibility, or other motivators than by money. When providing a salary increase to an employee, make sure to let the employee know what specific positive behavior led to the increase (e.g., fewer accounting entry errors, performance on project team to select new payroll system).

 **HAVE ALTERNATIVES AVAILABLE** When salary increases are reduced or frozen because of company budget constraints or business downturns, managers must use motivators other than money to reward positive behavior. This can be troublesome for employees who are motivated primarily by money and for managers who traditionally reward employees in this manner. Some possibilities include recognition plaques, preferred parking, increased time off, etc.

*Achievement.* Some employees, often the best performers, are driven by a personal need to succeed and be the best. It may seem that external motivation of such employees is not necessary, but that is not true. The following actions can help keep these employees focused and motivated to do even better:

- Delegating responsibility and authority for important tasks to them;
- Public or private recognition of their accomplishments;
- Giving them new and challenging assignments; and
- Letting them work with less supervision and guidance.

*Leadership.* Other employees place importance on leading others, influencing the group, giving direction, and having control. You can reward employees who have demonstrated the potential for leadership by:

- Publicly recognizing their leadership talents;
- Promoting them to supervisory positions;
- Making them leaders of project teams or task forces; and
- Taking them into your confidence and seeking their input.

*Affiliation.* Some employees place a good deal of emphasis on the social aspects of the workplace—being liked by other employees and accepted into the group. The payroll manager can help meet their needs by:

- Being friendly with them and including them in lunchtime or after-work activities;
- Assigning them to project teams and task forces;
- Providing them with networking opportunities by sending them to payroll-related conferences, seminars, and workshops; and
- Encouraging them to join and participate in professional organizations.

*Recognition.* Other employees are motivated by receiving recognition of their efforts as evidence of their importance and prestige in the department. For those employees, possible motivators include:

- Giving them public credit for their accomplishments;
- Giving them an important-sounding title, within company limits;
- Giving them awards or plaques recognizing their efforts; and
- Initiating departmental contests and competitions that give them a chance to win.

**Controlling the process to improve performance.** In Sections 11 and 12, procedures to control payroll processes were discussed. This is an area that may be easier for the payroll manager to control. The following actions are among those that can be taken:

- System review, evaluation, and updating;
- System edits;
- Account balancing and reconciliation;
- Documentation of policies and procedures;
- Internal controls, such as job segregation, job rotation, file security, physical payouts, etc. (see Section 11.8); and
- External audits.

# 13.2-5 Reporting

Feedback and listening are not the only communication skills a payroll manager needs to master. The manager must be able to communicate to his or her immediate supervisor, other department heads, and upper management in written reports detailing payroll developments that will affect the organization. The types of reports that might be required include:

- New legislative and/or regulatory developments, such as new tax rates or wage bases, new rules governing employee business expenses, or changes in the way states treat employee benefits;

- Monthly labor costs—pay rates, regular and overtime hours worked, compensation, paid time off, etc.;

- Annual wages, taxes, and benefits;

- Variance between compensation paid and budgeted; and

- Reports required from all department heads detailing ongoing projects, overtime pay, salary costs, future plans, budgets, etc.

Whatever type of report the payroll manager is expected to provide, there are several important points to keep in mind:

- The report must include only the information the person using it needs to make a decision. This means data that might obscure the vital information should be left out or summarized. The sheer volume of numbers presented will not impress the reader of the report.

- The report must be provided in time for decisions based on it to be made. Do not be late with reports that bear on future budgetary decisions, especially those affecting the payroll department.

- Write clearly and be brief wherever possible. Big words and long, convoluted sentences do not impress upper level managers who have more than enough reports to read already.

- Leave out the payroll jargon. A perfectly good report with valid statistical information can be ruined if the payroll manager is the only one who can understand it.

**Reporting tools.** The number of requests made by executive management to the Payroll Department is increasing at a rate equal to, or exceeding, the advances in the technology being developed to provide information. Because employee salaries and benefits comprise a significant expense for any business, the need for information about changes in the business (event-based management) and the speed of turn-around are critical to making the right business decisions today and to setting a clear strategic vision for the future.

Recently developed reporting technology accesses data from a variety of data base sources and presents that data using an Executive Dashboard. The Executive Dashboard typically presents data using easy-to-comprehend charts and graphs showing current state, trend analysis, and future projections. In addition, the Executive Dashboard can be customized by the user to provide charts and graphs specific to the needs of the user. Dashboards can be either private, available only to the user, or made public on a shared server or intranet site. Executives, aware of the significant impact of payroll dollars, will increasingly depend on accurate, complete, and instantaneous data analysis.

# 13.3 Specific Management Issues

Up till now, this section has concentrated on the basic management skills a payroll manager must master to achieve success. The discussion now will move to some more specific skills that can help the payroll manager keep his or her department on track to fulfilling its overall mission of providing quality service to its customers.

# 13.3-1 Conducting and Attending Meetings

In recent years, meetings have come to be seen as a necessary evil in the business environment, as horror stories abound of day-long meetings with little or nothing accomplished. While this is sometimes true, meetings are an important vehicle for managers to make their ideas known and to show their leadership ability. Efficiently run meetings can also make very efficient use of the time spent and actually save time if issues are resolved.

Here are some guidelines for conducting meetings in your organization.

**Plan according to the type of meeting.** The manager who will conduct the meeting must first decide what type of meeting it will be by deciding on the objectives that need to be met.

- Will the meeting be informational only? Is the purpose of the meeting to inform employees of changes in policies or procedures?

- Is the meeting being held so the manager can get opinions or information from employees as input for making a decision?

- Will a decision be made at the meeting by those attending? Should they be given the chance to present their views to other attendees at the meeting?

- Is the meeting being held to exchange new ideas (brainstorming)?

Once the objective of the meeting has been determined, make sure that a meeting is absolutely necessary. If not, the amount of planning and preparation needed to hold a meeting is not worth the time it will take. Possible alternatives to a meeting include a memo or conference call.

 **BE CAREFUL** Negative information (e.g., salary freezes, layoffs, etc.) should not be provided by the payroll manager in a memo to the staff. Personal or group meetings should be held.

In planning the meeting, other considerations include the location (as central as possible for the attendees), sufficiency of chairs and lighting, and a minimum of interruptions.

**Meeting preparation.** When preparing for a meeting, put together an agenda and consider how long the meeting will be. Decide which items will be considered first, keeping in mind that saving important matters for the end of a long meeting is not a good idea. The agenda should be distributed to attendees far enough in advance of the meeting for them to prepare any required materials. It should outline the items to be discussed and the goals of the meeting. An agenda may not be practical or necessary before holding an informational meeting.

**Keep the meeting on track.** One reason many meetings go on longer than necessary is that the individual calling the meeting does not control it. The manager should start the meeting on time and briefly go over the agenda so everyone is clear on the meeting purpose. Move the meeting along so all important topics are addressed, and end the meeting on time with a summary of what was accomplished.

**Promote participation.** Meetings are generally much more productive when the individual running the meeting does not do all the talking (except for informational meetings). Ask open-ended questions to increase attendees' participation, and do not wait until near the scheduled ending time to ask for other opinions or questions.

**Keep a written record.** If you cannot run the meeting and keep notes at the same time, ask another attendee to do so. In this way, misunderstandings are kept to a minimum.

## 13.3-2 Keep Written Policies and Procedures

Proper documentation is one of the best ways to ensure uniformity, simplify training, and provide a reference tool for new employees. Time and money spent on documentation will pay off in higher quality service to employees, government agencies, and upper management. Making sure this is accomplished is the responsibility of the payroll manager. Items that should be documented include:

- company policies on overtime, benefits, vacations, sick leave, termination, recordkeeping, etc.;
- procedures for handling payroll, tax deposits, quarterly returns, liabilities, direct deposit, account reconciliations, etc.;
- all aspects of and tasks involved in the payroll process, from beginning to end;
- disaster recovery plans;
- payroll computer system user manuals;
- payroll department job descriptions; and
- file descriptions.

See also Section 12.5-2 on providing system documentation.

# 13.3-3 Crisis Management

While most payroll managers do not like to think about it, crisis management is one of the most important leadership tests they will have. The ability to prevent and control a crisis so that damage to the department and the company is minimal can sometimes make or break a manager's career. When things are going smoothly, no one may notice the manager, but when a crisis presents itself, how that manager handles it will be noticed by everyone, especially upper management.

In payroll, a crisis can take one of many forms. It can be the sudden resignation of a long-time employee who holds the payroll processing procedures in his or her head, a delayed payroll system conversion that runs into year-end, the surprise purchase of a new subsidiary, or an electrical storm that grounds the payroll system. Whatever form it takes, a crisis is any event that has a direct impact on the department's and organization's ability to accomplish its objectives.

**Preventing a crisis—be proactive.** Some business traumas are preventable and some are not. Here are some of the precautionary measures a payroll manager can take to minimize the chances that a crisis will occur:

- Make sure the tools are available to do the job, which might include amassing a crisis prevention team from the different departments that interface with payroll (plus the payroll service provider, if applicable);

- Plan and schedule for the "worst case scenario" when analyzing the potential crisis situations and their impact and probabilities;

- Make sure there is a "back-up" for all your systems—consider whether manual checks are a legitimate alternative during a crisis;

- Maintain an open communication network so potential problems can get an airing before they occur;

- Cross train payroll personnel so they can handle each other's duties, and make sure you know who the other employees are in the company with payroll experience;

- Conduct a regular review of all department policies, procedures, and documentation;

- Deal promptly and effectively with issues that adversely affect employee attitudes and morale—do not let the "grape vine" or rumor mill determine the information your employees receive;

- Conduct a regular and comprehensive review of all payroll department output; and

- Keep your priorities flexible so the department can adapt to current situations.

**Managing or controlling a crisis.** Even though the payroll manager has taken all reasonable precautions to prevent them, an unanticipated crisis will inevitably occur. The next step is to manage the department and organization through the crisis so that damage to the department's mission of quality service is minimized. Following are some of the steps the payroll manager should consider:

- Keep his or her own behavior under control and present a calm, cool exterior to the employees, so they can react in the same manner;

- Identify and isolate the crisis and the people who will deal with it—create a crisis center where they can work undisturbed but can communicate with others, such as a conference room;

- Tackle the problem at hand and do not worry about what went wrong in creating the crisis—there is no time for that now;

- Analyze the situation for multiple solutions and rank them from an overall business perspective;

- Keep the lines of communication open to your staff and others who provide input to or need output from payroll;

- Determine the appropriate course of action and initiate decisive action, using the information and personnel available—there is no time for an in-depth analysis;

- Notify all who need to know of the chosen course of action and their responsibilities in carrying it out;

- Document and carefully monitor the progress of the plan to resolve the crisis, determining whether it is practical and effective and allowing for adjustments where necessary;

- Document the results of the crisis and the action taken to deal with it, since the crisis may occur again; and

- When the crisis is over, express your appreciation to all concerned for their team effort in helping the department and the company cope.

**After the crisis—lessons to be learned.** Once the crisis is over, there are several things the payroll manager can do to ensure the lessons it taught are not forgotten:

- Conduct a meeting of the team to discuss the crisis and determine which of the problems that occurred during the crisis are preventable;

- Initiate a plan to prevent those problems that can be prevented from reoccurring;

- List the successful results of the crisis management operation and include them in a "Crisis File" for future reference;

- List all the issues that were not satisfactorily resolved and formulate procedures to resolve them; and

- Express your appreciation to your staff once again for their hard work during the crisis.

**Extracting positives from the crisis.** Other than the immediate post-crisis steps the payroll manager should take, there are several other ways to take something positive away from a crisis situation, including:

- Meeting with your boss to discuss the crisis and the outcome, new controls and procedures to help prevent future crises, the performance of the payroll department staff, and any changes in working conditions or tools that might be needed;

- Sharing your experiences by networking with other payroll professionals and finding out how they solved similar problems;

- Assessing your staff after their performance under stress, taking notice of those who displayed outstanding skills;

- Assessing your own performance during the crisis and working toward improving your weaker skills;

- Following through to make sure all new procedures have been implemented and tested; and

- Using the opportunity of the crisis to build on the team spirit of the payroll department staff.

# 13.3-4 Time Management

At 5:00 (or 6:00, or whenever the payroll manager gets to go home), one complaint heard from most payroll managers is "Where did this day go?" Time is one commodity that cannot be bought or sold or saved for another day, so it must be used wisely and efficiently. Also, managers must find time to do the things they were hired or promoted to do—plan, organize, develop, evaluate, measure, etc. Managers who are constantly moving from crisis to crisis, or who fail to delegate properly, have no time to focus on the payroll department's overall mission of quality service or their own personal goals and objectives.

Demands on a manager's time are categorized as either important or not important and urgent or not urgent. Important demands contribute to the overall payroll department mission and include proactive activities such as planning and crisis prevention. Time spent on urgent demands is reactive time, or time spent "putting out fires" in the department.

**Prioritizing is up to the manager.** The four combinations of these time categories tell the manager what his or her priorities should be (shown in Table 13.3):

1. Urgent and important—crisis management, immediate attention needed;

2. Not urgent but important—planning and prevention activities;

3. Urgent but not important—pressing activities that may be easy to accomplish;

4. Not urgent and not important—easily accomplished, time wasting activities.

Table 13.3

| Urgent<br>and<br>Important | Not Urgent<br>but<br>Important |
|---|---|
| Urgent<br>but<br>Not Important | Not Urgent<br>and<br>Not Important |

The payroll manager's goal should be to prioritize duties and responsibilities so enough time is spent in the "not urgent but important" quadrant, which includes the activities of planning and prevention—the "real" management activities.

**Scheduling and delegating—keys to time management.** Managing to put most of your working time in the "not urgent but important" category is not an easy task for a payroll manager, considering the many interruptions and distractions that seem to fill up each day. But there are ways to help become proactive rather than reactive and to find time where there did not seem to be any.

The first way to help organize your priorities is to begin scheduling your activities. At the beginning of each week, be sure to schedule several "not urgent but important" activities and allow sufficient time for their completion. Focus on activities that will bring the greatest results ("high-leverage" activities). As you make your schedule, keep in mind the goals of both the department and yourself. The physical tool or planner you use to schedule your time is unimportant, so long as it is easy to use, allows for flexibility as demands change, has room for notes, and is portable.

Another way to help gain time for yourself to manage is through effective delegation of tasks to others in the department. As mentioned earlier, many payroll managers, especially newly promoted ones, are often reluctant to delegate for fear of losing control and because they enjoy the duties they had before being promoted (see Section 13.2-2). But delegation is critical to proper time management. It allows for time to be spent on "high-leverage" activities.

To delegate effectively, the payroll manager must encourage ownership of the task or project delegated by conferring responsibility and authority on the employee. The manager should specify the results expected from the project (quality and quantity), as well as available resources, budget, and schedule. But let the employee determine the methods for completing the project (within certain guidelines), possibly with suggestions from the manager. While delegation may take some time, it will save much more for the manager if done effectively. It also allows employees to manage themselves more and be supervised less, freeing up even more time for the manager.

While the entire scope of time management and the ways to properly deal with it are beyond the scope of this book, these ideas should help the payroll manager cope better with the sometimes extraordinary demands on his or her time and allow some time for planning how to meet the department's overall quality service mission.

**Controlling your e-mail.** The nearly universal use of e-mail as a communication tool in the business world has made it possible to improve productivity through the instantaneous delivery of information. But e-mail has also become a time-wasting burden because those who use it often expect an immediate answer. Employees are tempted to turn their e-mail on when they arrive at work in the morning and leave it on all day, until they leave the office. With each "ping" of the computer announcing the arrival of a new e-mail message, the temptation is there to stop whatever work you are doing and check the message, fearing that something "important" that needs an immediate response will otherwise be missed.

These interruptions often negate whatever productivity advantages e-mail provides because an employee who stops work to check and/or answer e-mail messages takes some time to readjust when they finish the e-mail and return to the task they were performing. One way to avoid these problems might be to let others in the organization know that you will check e-mail only at certain times of the day so that immediate answers are not expected and you are not subjected to phone calls asking why you did not answer your e-mail messages. Another option is to not check e-mail when you first get to work, because that can lead to a long session of handling easy but unimportant and time-consuming tasks that knocks you off your schedule before you get started.

# 13.3-5 Team Building

In recent years, management training courses and theorists have placed a great deal of emphasis on the importance of employee cooperation and teamwork. Some of the reasons generally given for this upsurge in popularity are that successful teams can increase productivity, use resources more effectively, reduce costs while improving quality, and make better use of innovation to solve problems because of the increased commitment and involvement of the team members.

Getting employees to believe in teamwork and to be successful team members, however, is not an easy task for the payroll manager. Some employees may feel such "rah rah" tactics are merely a corny way to manipulate them, while others will insist they work best alone. To succeed, a policy of establishing teamwork as a way of doing business must have the support of top management, as any other innovative project must have. It also must have high priority and wide visibility throughout the company.

**Characteristics of a successful team.** The complete process of building a successful team is beyond the scope of this book, but following are the characteristics that define effective teams and team players:

- the team has clear and specific goals and objectives;
- team meetings have a relaxed atmosphere where members can offer help and share experiences;
- each member has a role in reaching the team's goals;
- team members listen without judging and with interest in what others are saying;
- there is civilized disagreement among team members, who criticize constructively;
- decisions are reached by a consensus of support, not unanimity, with even disagreeing members pledging to support the final decision;
- there is open communication and trust among members;
- each member has a clear assignment;
- all members are responsible for the team's success or failure;
- the team builds networks with employees outside the team and asks for their feedback;
- the team contains a diversity of employee styles—contributors, collaborators, communicators, and challengers; and
- the team performs a formal or informal self-assessment.

**Four stages of team development.** There are generally four stages of team development. Understanding which stage of development a team is in allows the team leader to determine the team's needs and initiate appropriate actions to move forward. The four stages of team development are forming, storming, norming, and performing (adapted from Tuckman's Team Development Model). There are also several general statements that can be made about the stages of team development.

- Each of these stages builds on the previous one.
- Each stage prepares the way to the performing stage.
- Skipping any stage affects performing negatively.
- With every new challenge, the process repeats itself.

Table 13.4 – Stages of Team Development

| Stage 1: Forming | Stage 2: Storming | Stage 3: Norming | Stage 4: Performing |
|---|---|---|---|
| • Start-up stage<br>• Individuals aren't clear on what they are supposed to do<br>• The mission is not owned by the group<br>• Purpose and expectations are unclear<br>• No trust yet<br>• High learning<br>• No group history; unfamiliar with team members<br>• Norms of the team are not established<br>• People check one another out<br>• People aren't committed to team | • Responsibilities and roles are articulated<br>• Agendas are displayed<br>• Problem-solving doesn't work well<br>• Some want to modify the team's mission<br>• Trying new ideas<br>• Splinter groups form<br>• Some set boundaries<br>• Anxiety abounds<br>• Some push for position and power<br>• Competition is high<br>• Cliques drive team<br>• Little team spirit<br>• Many personal attacks as members express concerns and frustrations<br>• Level of participation is at its highest for some and its lowest for others | • Success occurs<br>• Team has resources for doing the job<br>• Appreciation, trust, and openness developing<br>• Members accept one another<br>• Purpose well-defined<br>• Feedback is high, well-received, and objective<br>• Confidence is high<br>• Leader reinforces team behavior<br>• Develop norms for conflict resolution, decision making, and completing tasks<br>• Hidden agendas become open<br>• Team is creative<br>• Increased individual motivation<br>• Achieves commitment from all members on direction and goals | • Members feel very motivated<br>• Individuals defer to team's needs<br>• No surprises<br>• Little waste; very efficient operations<br>• Members have objective outlooks<br>• Group has structure, purpose, and roles<br>• Individuals take pleasure in success of team - big wins<br>• "WE" vs. "I"<br>• High pride and trust<br>• High openness and support<br>• High empathy<br>• Superior team performance<br>• OK to risk confrontation<br>• Achieves recognition |

Table 13.5 – Reaching the Next Stage of Team Development

| Action Steps Forming to Storming | Action Steps Storming to Norming | Action Steps Norming to Performing |
|---|---|---|
| • Set a mission<br>• Set goals and objectives<br>• Establish roles<br>• Recognize need to move out of Forming stage<br>• Identify the team, its tools and resources<br>• Leader must be directive<br>• Figure ways to build trust<br>• Define a reward structure<br>• Take risks<br>• Bring group together periodically to work on common tasks<br>• Assert power<br>• Make firm commitment to be on team | • Team leader should actively support and reinforce team behavior, facilitate group for wins, create positive climate<br>• Leader must ask for and expect results<br>• Recognize, publicize team wins<br>• Agree on individuals' roles and responsibilities<br>• Buy into objectives and activities<br>• Listen to each other<br>• Set and take team time together<br>• Everyone works actively to set a supporting environment<br>• Have the vision - We can succeed<br>• Request and accept feedback<br>• Build trust by honoring commitments<br>• Keep up and the team wins | • Maintain traditions<br>• Praise and flatter each other<br>• Self-evaluate without fuss<br>• Recognize and reinforce synergy team behavior<br>• Share leadership role in team based on who does what best<br>• Share rewards for successes<br>• Communicate all the time<br>• Share responsibility<br>• Delegate freely within team<br>• Commit time to the team<br>• Keep reaching for new, higher goals<br>• Be selective of new team members; train to maintain the team spirit |

**Managing different employee styles.** The above list mentioned that successful teams include a diversity of employee styles. These styles must be managed and "fused" by the team leader (payroll manager) to get the most out of each team member.

*Contributors.* These employees are task and result oriented and value professionalism and efficiency. They are generally willing to share their expertise and information and are organized and dependable.

*Collaborators.* Cooperation among team members and commitment to a clearly defined team goal are most important to the collaborators on the team. They are flexible and open and believe in broad participation by team members.

*Communicators.* Excellent communication skills, such as listening, patience, humor, and tact, are the hallmark of these employees, who are often the "peacekeepers" during team meetings. They also maintain a positive approach, even when tension and friction threaten to envelop the team and bring it down.

*Challengers.* These "devil's advocates" question the team's goals and methods and are more than willing to disagree with other team members. They are open about problems and are likely to look for innovative ways to solve them.

Here are some ways in which the payroll manager can best use the strengths of these different employee styles to reach the team's goals:

- get to know the team members outside the meeting room;
- clearly define the team's purpose;
- clarify each member's role;
- develop an action plan;
- encourage questions, disagreement, and innovation;
- share the spotlight with team members;
- emphasize the importance of participation;
- celebrate the team's successes and make sure others know about them; and
- critically assess the team's effectiveness.

# 13.3-6 Performance Evaluations

Performance evaluations are a formal way of giving feedback. They provide a formal, written record of how employees are performing relative to preset goals that are designed to help the department and company meet their overall business objectives. The basic purpose of performance evaluations is to improve the employee's performance in relation to the goals that have been set. But there are other reasons why companies conduct performance evaluations, as well:

- to weed out the good performers from the bad;
- to provide documentation for salary increase decisions;
- to determine which employees are promotable;
- to support a decision whether a poor performer needs more training or must be disciplined;
- to encourage employees' personal growth and development; and
- to provide documentation for employment decisions that may later be legally challenged by the employee.

**Effective performance evaluations.** While there are many different types of performance evaluation systems and formats, there are several elements that are generally found when a company has a successful system:

- objective job-related goals and performance criteria based on some form of observable behavior or results and communicated clearly and in writing to the employee after being discussed with the manager;

- managers conducting the evaluations are trained in delivering feedback in general and in the employer's evaluation system in particular;

- there are written guidelines for administering the evaluation system;

- employees who disagree with the evaluation are allowed to challenge it and receive an explanation of how it was determined; and

- the evaluation system does not place unreasonable technical and time constraints on managers.

**Ineffective performance evaluations.** Even a well-designed performance evaluation system with objective standards and written guidelines can produce unintended negative results. When this occurs, the problem generally lies with the manager who conducted the evaluation. Three common mistakes that managers commit include:

*Guilt over negative evaluations.* Many managers feel uncomfortable in situations where they determine an employee's pay raise or job status, and they feel guilty about giving negative feedback. Therefore, they tend to give most or all of their employees average to better than average evaluations, even the fair or poor performers. Such an approach will not help the employee improve his or her performance because it removes the incentive to do so. Also, less-than-honest evaluations can come back to haunt the company if an adverse employment decision is made later on and the reason given is poor performance, resulting in a lawsuit and a decision that has little support.

*No accountability for the manager.* Quite often, managers are judged merely by how well their department produces goods or provides services. If they are not also held accountable for how they evaluate their employees, they will have little incentive to do it well. Managers should be appraised on their ability to coach employees to higher performance levels, and conducting effective performance evaluations should be part of their written job description.

*Improper application of standards.* Even if they do not feel guilty about criticizing an employee's performance, some managers fail to properly apply the objective standards that have been set up to rate an employee's performance. They make subjective conclusions in very broad terms that help no one—the employee or the company. Managers should be required to back up their conclusions with objective supporting evidence, as well as specific suggestions for improving performance during the next evaluation period.

**EVALUATION IS AN ONGOING PROCESS** While most performance evaluation systems provide for a formal evaluation on an annual basis, managers should be constantly monitoring their employees' performance to see if it is on track for meeting the goals and objectives set out during the previous evaluation. Perhaps several informal evaluations should be carried out during the year to review each employee's progress.

# 13.3-7 Promoting Quality Customer Service in Payroll

Since the mid-1980s, the emphasis in American business, at least in those companies that want to compete successfully, has been on providing quality products and services to customers that distinguish the company from its competition. This realization that satisfying the customer should be the primary focus of any business operation also holds true for the payroll function within organizations.

The primary customer for the payroll department is the company's employees, and the product it produces for them is their paycheck or direct deposit of their wages. In most industries, providing a quality product can mean allowing a certain percentage of defects, which can be expected even in a well-designed and operated process. In payroll, however, providing a quality product means being accurate and timely 100% of the time. Employees and other payroll department customers inside and outside the organization (accounting, upper management, IRS, SSA) expect and demand that the information they receive be totally accurate and on time.

**What is customer service in payroll?** Customer service in the payroll department goes beyond providing accurate and timely payment information to employees. The other products produced by the payroll department include financial information for the accounting function, reports to upper management on labor cost distribution, employment tax costs, etc., employment tax deposits and wage and tax reporting to the IRS and SSA, and payments to child support withholding agencies, among others.

Because of the personal nature of employee compensation and the detailed financial aspects of payroll products, customer service in payroll also means adding value to those products by being proactive in preventing problems that will cause inaccuracies or delays and being responsive to customer needs. In striving to provide quality customer service in the payroll department, there are several basic principles that should serve as goals and objectives.

*Reliability.* The payroll department must be able to provide what its mission promises—dependable, accurate and timely payments and payment information to employees and other parties inside and outside the organization. This is absolutely essential for a successful payroll operation. Employees need to receive their paychecks and/or direct deposit on the scheduled payday and they must be accurate. Other payroll products as well must be provided accurately and on time on a consistent basis, or the company may face stiff penalties for late tax deposits and payments or inaccurate or late reporting.

*Responsiveness.* Members of the payroll department must be willing and able to respond promptly to the needs and questions of their customers. With many different deadlines and duties all calling for attention, the ability to respond to customer needs in time to meet those deadlines is an important skill for any payroll manager to instill in herself and her staff.

*Assurance.* When customers, especially employees, call the payroll department with a question or a concern, they need to be assured that they will receive an accurate and courteous response. Payroll department employees must be able to convey to employees their competence by projecting confidence in the responses they are providing. If the payroll staffer is uncertain of an answer, it is better to ask for time to research the issue rather than provide incorrect or incomplete information, although a definite time for providing an answer should be given and adhered to.

*Empathy.* Because of the personal nature and importance of employee financial information, employees must be treated with respect and caring by the payroll department, no matter how basic their questions may be. They need to receive individual attention and they need to know that their information will be kept confidential.

_Tangibles_. The tangible piece of payroll customer service involves the physical facilities and equipment, as well as the appearance of the department and its employees. The payroll department should be able to be reached easily by phone, e-mail, etc. If the payroll department offices are frequented by employees, they should not be in a state of disarray, with files and paper piled on every desk. Such an environment will never inspire confidence in employees that their needs will be handled promptly or confidentially and will quickly lower their expectations regarding the payroll department.

**How to instill quality customer service values in your department**. Good customer service does not just happen because the payroll manager decides that it will. Employees must be trained in what the desired outcomes are when employees or other parties have a question or concern about payments or information they are receiving from payroll. Here are a couple of ways for payroll department employees to learn what is expected of them in providing quality customer service.

_Role plays_. Interactive role plays are a very effective way of demonstrating what good customer service can provide, since they encourage payroll department employees to put themselves in the shoes of the customer. During training sessions, payroll department employees can use their own experiences to provide examples of the types of customer service they are asked to provide and how a positive outcome can be reached. The role playing also allows the other payroll staffers to give feedback on how the situation was handled and whether they would have handled it differently.

_Case studies_. If role playing is not feasible in the payroll department's training environment, written or videotaped examples of actual customer service scenarios can also be an effective training tool. The department's employees can evaluate the performance of those involved in the case studies and make recommendations for improvement based on their experiences.

# 13.3-8 Providing Customer Service in a Shared Services Environment

Employees in an organization generally interact with several service-oriented functional departments, among them Payroll, Human Resources, Benefits, Compensation, and Accounts Payable. Each separate interaction may involve the completion of a form, one or more phone calls, data entry into multiple databases, multiple reviews and approvals, and/or long waits before a request is acted on.

As a result, employees become dissatisfied, error rates increase, morale and productivity suffer, and transactional costs increase. Therefore, it should come as no surprise that many American businesses have been looking for a way to improve these processes and their services to employees, while at the same time reducing the cost of providing those services to remain competitive. One way to do this is by consolidating these services into a "shared services" environment.

**What is "shared services?"** In its simplest form, shared services is the consolidation of related functions and integration of the processes involved with them throughout an entire organization. In the payroll context, shared services most often means the melding of employee service functions and integration of the processes they use so that employees have to make only one phone call or complete one e-mail to finish a transaction or get a problem resolved. It may mean the establishment of a "call center" where employees can make one call to someone who has been cross-trained on the different functions and can provide a real-time solution, or the creation of an Intranet web page where employees can ensure that status changes they need to make are entered properly and timely.

**Advantages shared by employees and management**. A successful shared services environment can provide employees with better quality customer service from better-trained personnel using fully integrated and streamlined processes and technologies. For management, shared services offers the opportunity for reduced costs through consistent application of company policies and procedures, a closer link between customers/employees and processes, reduced error rates, increased efficiencies, economies of scale, and a renewed focus on their dual mission of employee service and cost containment.

**Considerations in establishing a shared services environment**. Following is a list of issues that must be taken into account in establishing a typical shared services environment. Keep in mind that differences in company size, complexity of benefits and services offered, number of work sites, etc., will have a profound effect on implementation.

*Determine the need for change*. Get a handle on your current cost of providing employee services. Are high transactional costs, maintenance of redundant data bases and systems, and bloated department staffing reducing your ability to compete? Survey employees and find out what they think of your existing procedures for providing employee services.

*Define your goals*. Make sure you know what your goals are for the shared services environment (e.g., operational excellence, low-cost provider of services, superior service).

*Analyze your current processes from end-to-end*. Determine if re-engineering of processes is necessary as part of establishing a shared services environment. Plan to eliminate redundancies and multiple handoffs.

*Prepare to deal with corporate culture issues*. Resistance to change can cripple a shared services implementation. Fostering cooperation and teamwork may be difficult. Employees in traditionally separate departments may well feel threatened if they anticipate having to compete for their jobs in a restructured department that will need fewer total employees. Emphasize the opportunities for growth in a new environment and provide cross-training and innovative compensation programs.

*Focus on the process rather than the function*. You have to shift the focus from the traditional emphasis on functional departments to one that emphasizes process management and the implementation of best practices.

*Conduct a cost/benefit analysis and a feasibility study*. You must be able to measure any increased initial costs of implementation and how quickly anticipated cost savings would be realized. Determine the budgetary and personnel resources available for implementation.

*Determine the functions to be included*. In a typical shared services environment, administrative and some corporate functions are aligned, including Human Resources, Payroll, Benefits, Compensation, Relocation, Accounts Payable, Travel and Expense Reimbursement, and Industrial Relations. Other functions that may be included are Information Technology Services, Record Retention, Facilities Management, Fleet Services, Mailroom/Distribution, Supply Chain Services, and Legal Services.

*Determine structural issues*. You must make structural decisions involving the chain of command, dissolving the traditional department structure, whether the shared services center will become a separate business unit, and how the organization chart will be set up.

*Determine service delivery methods*. There are several ways of operating a shared services environment that can stand alone or be used in combinations, including interactive voice response (IVR), a call center with cross-trained generalists and internal issue experts, and online interactive systems. The IVR and online systems can also be used to provide employee and manager self-service options for changing and approving employee data, if that is part of the overall strategy (see Section 12.8-1).

# 13.4 Research Needs

One of the most important aspects of a payroll manager's responsibilities is keeping on top of current developments in the payroll field. While the payroll manager does not "process the payroll" in the manner he or she did as a nonmanagerial employee, the manager is treated as the payroll expert by other company departments and upper management.

As such, the payroll manager is expected not only to stay abreast of the latest tax law amendments and regulatory changes, but to understand what they will mean to the payroll department and the company as a whole. The payroll manager must also be aware of other employment-related laws that might affect payroll, and be well-versed in the company's union contracts and all company policies and procedures dealing with payroll.

**GOOD ADVICE FOR ALL PAYROLL PRACTITIONERS** While the material in this section is designed for payroll managers who sometimes fall out of touch with payroll developments, it is also applicable to any payroll practitioner who wants to keep up with the latest developments in the field.

# 13.4-1 Tracking Tax Laws and Regulations

The basic federal payroll tax requirements that form the backbone of most companies' payroll compliance systems are contained in the Internal Revenue Code and the Internal Revenue Service Regulations. The IRC contains the tax laws passed by Congress and signed by the president (e.g., income, employment, estate, and excise taxes). The IRS regulations are interpretations of the law developed by the IRS and approved by the U.S. Treasury Department that are designed to help taxpayers comply with the laws.

**The IRC and IRS regulations.** The Internal Revenue Code comprises Title 26 of the United States Code, a compilation of all federal laws. Therefore, IRC §217 (moving expense deductions) is also known as 26 USC §217. IRS regulations can be found in Title 26 of the Code of Federal Regulations, which contains all federal agency regulations interpreting federal laws. Before their inclusion in the U.S. Code, laws are referred to by their Public Law number. For example, Pub. L. 108-357 (American Jobs Creation Act of 2004) was the 357th law enacted during the 108th session of Congress. IRS regulations interpreting the law dealing with moving expense deductions can be referred to as IRS Reg. §1.217 or 26 CFR §1.217 (see also the discussion of Treasury Decisions and the Federal Register later in this section).

 **REGULATION PREFIXES** All regulations relating to income taxes contain the prefix "1" before the section number, which corresponds to the IRC section number of the law being interpreted. A different prefix is attached to the section number if another type of tax is involved. For employment tax regulations, the prefix is "31." Therefore, the regulations interpreting IRC §3121 (what are wages for social security and Medicare tax purposes) can be found at IRS Reg. §31.3121 or 26 CFR §31.3121.

*Proposed, temporary, and final regulations.* In general, IRS regulations fall into one of three categories: proposed, temporary, or final. Proposed regulations are issued with the purpose of eliciting public comment for IRS consideration. After the comment period has ended, the IRS will usually hold one or more public hearings on the proposal and then will consider all the written and oral comments. During the comment period, and while the comments are being considered, the IRS may also issue temporary regulations on the same subject matter if quick guidance is needed. Proposed regulations follow the same numbering scheme as final regulations, although they are generally preceded by the prefix "IRS Prop. Reg."

Temporary regulations can be relied on by IRS personnel and payroll practitioners until final regulations are issued. They are identified by a "T" following the regulation number (e.g., Reg. §1.125-1T). After considering all the comments on the proposed regulations, the IRS will issue final regulations containing whatever changes it feels are necessary from the original proposal. Once the final regulations are issued and take effect, the temporary regulations are no longer effective. The final regulations are issued as Treasury Decisions, which are expressed as "T.D." followed by a number (e.g., T.D. 8451). They also appear in the Federal Register (see discussion later in this section).

In certain situations, other steps may be added to the regulatory process. Before proposed regulations are issued, the IRS may issue an "Advance Notice of Proposed Rulemaking," which merely states the IRS is considering issuing regulations on a particular topic and provides questions for the public to comment on regarding that topic. And, before final regulations are issued, the IRS may issue "interim" final regulations, which have the same effect as final regulations but give the public another chance to comment.

 **APA OFFERS RESEARCH HELP** The American Payroll Association helps make your payroll research easier with *Federal Payroll Tax Laws and Regulations*, which includes the full text of all payroll-related sections of the IRC and IRS Regulations in one easy-to-use volume. This book is updated annually so that the latest amendments are at your fingertips. It is also included on APA's *Research Ready CD*, along with *The Payroll Source*® and other research materials. Call 210-224-6406 or visit www.americanpayroll.org to order.

**Other IRS guidance.** Regulations are not the only form of IRS guidance. There are several other forms of periodic and "as needed" guidance, including:

*Revenue Procedures (Rev. Proc.).* IRS Revenue Procedures are official statements from the Service on how to carry out tax compliance. They appear, for example, as Rev. Proc. 2008-18, with 2008 referring to the year the Rev. Proc. was issued and 18 referring to the number of the Rev. Proc.

*Revenue Rulings (Rev. Rul.).* An IRS Revenue Ruling is a decision by the Service on how a section of the IRC is to be applied to a certain given set of facts. Revenue Rulings appear, for example, as Rev. Rul. 2008-63, with 2008 referring to the year the Rev. Rul. was issued and 63 referring to the number of the Rev. Rul.

*Private Letter Rulings (PLR).* A Private Letter Ruling is an IRS decision on how the tax laws apply to a set of facts involving a single taxpayer. The taxpayer must request the ruling, and it applies only to that taxpayer—it cannot be relied on by other taxpayers to justify their actions. All information that can specifically identify the taxpayer is removed from the PLR. Those rulings may also take the form of a technical advice memorandum.

*Internal Legal Opinions.* In recent years, the IRS has begun releasing more of its internal documents explaining its legal positions on various issues, in response to requests and demands by news organizations under the Freedom of Information Act. These documents include Service Center Advice (SCA), Field Service Advice (FSA), and Internal Legal Memoranda (ILM).

*Publications (Pubs.).* IRS Publications explain taxpayer obligations regarding a particular aspect of the tax laws. For example, IRS Pub. 15, Circular E, Employer's Tax Guide, explains an employer's obligations to withhold, deposit, and report withheld income and employment taxes.

*Announcements, Notices, and News Releases.* IRS Announcements, Notices, and News Releases are issued on an as-needed basis. They are issued as a means of informing and reminding taxpayers of their tax obligations, new IRS programs, new rate schedules, etc. IRS Announcements appear, for example, as Announcement 2008-137, with 2008 referring to the year of the Announcement and 137 referring to the number of the Announcement. The same numbering system applies to IRS Notices. IRS News Releases appear, for example, as IR-2008-102, with IR referring to Internal Revenue, 2008 to the year of the News Release, and 102 to the number of the News Release.

**Federal government resources.** Much of the information contained in the guidance mentioned here is compiled in several publications and other resources provided by the federal government. Federal government publications are generally easier to obtain than the original documents themselves, although they may include information unrelated to payroll.

*Congressional Record.* The Congressional Record is printed for each day at least one house of the U.S. Congress is in session. It contains all actions taken by the House of Representatives and the Senate, including bill introductions, votes on bills and amendments, actions taken by committees and subcommittees, remarks from members, and Public Law numbers assigned to bills signed by the president.

*Federal Register (F.R.).* The Federal Register is printed daily except for Saturdays, Sundays, and federal holidays. It contains proposed, temporary, and final regulations issued by federal government agencies (including the IRS), as well as meeting announcements and other information the agencies are required to provide to the public. Citations to the Federal Register appear, for example, as 73 F.R. 7243, 3-10-08, with 73 referring to the Volume number, 7243 to the page number, and 3-10-08 to the date of the particular Federal Register issue.

*Internal Revenue Bulletin (IRB).* Unlike the other federal government publications, the Internal Revenue Bulletin contains only federal tax-related information. Issued weekly, each IRB contains recently issued Revenue Rulings, Revenue Procedures, IRS Regulations (Treasury Decisions), Announcements, Notices, and News Releases. Citations to the IRB appear, for example, as 2008-5 IRB 125, with 2008 referring to the year, 5 to the IRB number, and 125 to the page at which the information appears. IRB pages are numbered consecutively from issue to issue from January through June and July through December within a given year.

*Cumulative Bulletin (CB).* Cumulative Bulletins are annual hard cover compilations of information contained in the IRBs. There are anywhere from 1-3 CBs issued each year, depending on the amount of information to be included. Citations to the CB appear, for example, as 2008-2 CB 486, with 2008-2 CB referring to the second Cumulative Bulletin of 2008 and 486 referring to the page on which the information appears.

*SSA/IRS Reporter.* The *SSA/IRS Reporter* is a quarterly newsletter mailed to employers with their Form 941 that brings employers the latest news on changing wage and tax reporting requirements. It is put together by technical writers at both agencies and is an important tool for making employers aware of new developments, how to cut down on reporting and filing errors, and other information resources provided by the agencies. Employers are encouraged to reprint articles from the *Reporter* in their in-house publications. Space is also allocated to other federal agencies, from time to time, such as U.S. Citizenship and Immigration Services and the Office of Child Support Enforcement. Since 2003, each issue of the *Reporter* has also included an article from the APA on an important payroll reporting or tax filing issue.

*IRS on the Internet.* The IRS's home page on the World Wide Web can be accessed at www.irs.gov. Written in a simple user-friendly format, the website offers everything from tax forms and publications to complex tax information for both individuals and businesses. There are separate sections of the site for individuals, businesses, charities and non-profits, tax professionals, government entities, and retirement plans, plus web pages devoted to tax scams and fraud, understanding taxes, and many more.

*IRS forms and assistance.* Answers to specific federal tax and reporting questions can be obtained by calling, toll-free, 800-829-1040. IRS forms and publications can be obtained, free of charge, by calling, toll-free, 800-829-3676 (800-TAX-FORM). They can also be downloaded from the IRS website.

*Customer Service Section for information reporters.* Questions about W-2 forms (paper only) and other IRS information reports can be answered at the call site installed at the IRS's Enterprise Computing Center - Martinsburg. The Customer Service Section (CSS) can be reached from 8:30 a.m. to 4:30 p.m. EST at 866-455-7438 (toll-free) or 304-263-8700 (not a toll-free call). The CSS can also be reached via e-mail at mccirp@irs.gov. IRS's electronic services are supported by its e-Help desk at 866-255-0654.

*SSA website.* The Social Security Administration website at www.socialsecurity.gov/employer1.htm contains general information on wage reporting as well as specific technical information on Forms W-2, W-3, etc. Employers filing wage information electronically can access the software specifications that assure accurate reporting. Registration to file electronically or to verify employees' SSNs can be accomplished at the Business Services Online portion of the site. Other SSA publications are also available for downloading. Other information that can be accessed includes: a list of the highest social security numbers that have been issued, issues of the *SSA/IRS Reporter* (see discussion earlier); and information on the SSN Verification Service.

See Section 13.4-3 for a list of these and other payroll-related websites.

**State government resources.** Each state has its own tax laws and regulations contained in publications that are similar in many respects to the U.S. Code and the Federal Register. These publications generally contain all of a state's laws and a periodic account of all regulatory action. Many state revenue agencies also publish employer tax guides that explain the employer's withholding, depositing, and reporting obligations under state law. Many state tax, child support and employment agencies also have their own websites on the Internet. They can be accessed through the APA's website at www.americanpayroll.org/weblink/statelocal/.

**Nongovernment resources.** In addition to the laws, regulations, and other guidance published by the federal and state governments, various private publishers offer printed and electronic information to help payroll practitioners better understand their obligations.

*IRC and IRS Regulations.* Because it can be cumbersome and time-consuming to research payroll tax information in publications that contain nontax information, several major tax publishers offer the full text of the Internal Revenue Code and the IRS regulations in paperback form, on CD-ROM, or over the Internet. They may also offer IRS Revenue Rulings, Revenue Procedures, and Private Letter Rulings in print or electronically. All these materials contain information regarding all types of federal taxes, not just those related to payroll.

The American Payroll Association offers its own paperback collection of the full text of Internal Revenue Code sections and IRS Regulations that affect payroll operations. *Federal Payroll Tax Laws and Regulations* further limits the amount of information that payroll practitioners have to sift through to find the legal and regulatory support for the conclusions they have drawn, a significant saving of time and labor, by eliminating information that has nothing to do with payroll. This book is also found on APA's *Research Ready CD*, which also includes *The Payroll Source®, Federal Payroll Non-Tax Laws and Regulations*, and *APA's Guide to State Payroll Laws*.

*Loose-leaf payroll services.* A loose-leaf service is a publication that offers a text explanation of a subject that is updated with new pages to replace the old, as well as a periodic newsletter detailing current developments. Payroll loose-leaf services provide an explanation of federal, state, and local payroll-related laws, regulations, and requirements, plus forms, tax tables, and other vital information that is generally updated biweekly. Each publisher generally has a research library that will help answer subscribers' questions about the service. Such services, which are also available online, are invaluable to time-pressed payroll practitioners for conducting state and local tax research because of the many taxing jurisdictions involved. The major payroll loose-leaf services include:

- *Payroll Guide*, published by Research Institute of America Group, Alexandria, Va.;
- *Payroll Administration Guide* and *Payroll Library*, published by the Bureau of National Affairs, Inc., Washington, D.C.; and
- *Payroll Management Guide*, published by CCH, Inc., Chicago, Ill.

*Newsletters.* Payroll newsletters provide current information on payroll-related developments and are published periodically. Aside from the newsletters that accompany the payroll loose-leaf services, there are several others available that stand by themselves, including the American Payroll Association's compliance newsletter for APA members, *Payroll Currently,* and *PayState Update* (for ordering information, call 210-224-6406).

*General interest publications.* Do not overlook general interest publications when doing your reading to keep current on payroll developments. The daily newspaper, business publications, news magazines, and other publications may have one or more articles on recent payroll, accounting, or management developments that can help you. Make at least some time to read each day, if possible.

## 13.4-2 Employment Laws and Regulations

Tax laws and regulations on the federal and state level are not the only legal requirements payroll managers and practitioners need to comply with and be aware of. Wage-hour, garnishment, child support, immigration, anti-discrimination, family leave, and escheat laws and regulations are only some of the other employment-related requirements that affect the payroll department. Research in these areas through government publications generally follows the same path as payroll tax research, although the code titles and sections are different.

Following is a list of these employment-related laws and their corresponding titles and beginning section numbers in the U.S. Code:

| | |
|---|---|
| Fair Labor Standards Act | 29 USC §201 |
| Portal-to-Portal Act | 29 USC §251 |
| Walsh-Healey (Public Contracts) Act | 41 USC §35 |
| Davis-Bacon Act | 40 USC §276a |
| Service Contract Act | 41 USC §351 |

| | |
|---|---|
| Immigration Reform and Control Act | 8 USC §1324a |
| Americans With Disabilities Act | 42 USC §12101 |
| Civil Rights Act of 1964 (Title VII) | 42 USC §2000e |
| Age Discrimination in Employment Act | 29 USC §621 |
| Consumer Credit Protection Act | 15 USC §1671 |
| Family and Medical Leave Act | 29 USC §2601 |
| Social Security Act | 42 USC §401 |

Regulations interpreting these laws appear at corresponding titles in the Code of Federal Regulations, although the section numbers do not match those in the U.S. Code, as they do for tax laws and regulations.

The American Payroll Association publishes a paperback collection of U.S. Code sections and regulations that are important to payroll practitioners but are not tax-related. *Federal Payroll Non-Tax Laws and Regulations* includes the full text of all the non-tax federal laws and regulations that affect payroll operations, which are often harder for payroll practitioners to research than tax-related issues. The topics covered include federal wage and hour requirements, garnishment and child support, family and medical leave, direct deposit, and more. This book makes a perfect compliment to *The Payroll Source®* and *Federal Payroll Tax Laws and Regulations*.

 **ALL TOGETHER ON CD** The APA offers all three of these indispensable publications, plus *APA's Guide to State Payroll Laws,* together on the *Research Ready CD*. To make your research easier, direct links are provided from cited laws and regulations in *The Payroll Source* to the full text of the laws and regulations in the other volumes. Call 210-224-6406 or visit www.americanpayroll.org for more information on these and other APA publications.

Private sector publishers also offer loose-leaf services and newsletters dealing with these employment issues, although many of them are also covered in the payroll services.

## 13.4-3  Payroll-related Websites

With the increasing availability of payroll-related information on the Internet, it is critical for payroll professionals to be familiar with the most important and useful sites on the World Wide Web. The following list includes many of them.

American Payroll Association
     www.americanpayroll.org
     www.nationalpayrollweek.com

Internal Revenue Service
     IRS home page: www.irs.gov
     IRS forms and publications: www.irs.gov/formspubs/index.html
     IRS employer information: www.irs.gov/businesses/index.html

Social Security Administration
     SSA home page: www.socialsecurity.gov
     SSA wage reporting guide for employers: www.socialsecurity.gov/employer1.htm
     SSA forms: www.socialsecurity.gov/employer/pub.htm

U. S. Citizenship and Immigration Services
     USCIS home page: www.uscis.gov/portal/site/uscis

U. S. Immigration and Customs Enforcement
     ICE home page: www.ice.gov/

Department of Labor
DOL home page: www.dol.gov
Employment law assistance: www.dol.gov/elaws/

Federal Laws and Regulations
U.S. Code: www.access.gpo.gov/uscode/index.html
Code of Federal Regulations: www.access.gpo.gov/ecfr/
Federal Register: www.gpoaccess.gov/fr/index.html
Congressional Record: http://thomas.loc.gov

State Payroll Resources
Federation of Tax Administrators (FTA): www.taxadmin.org
FTA – State tax agency links: www.taxadmin.org/fta/link/default.html
FTA – State tax forms links: www.taxadmin.org/fta/link/forms.html
Links to state unemployment information: www.icesa.org/links.cfm

Office of Child Support Enforcement
OCSE home page: www.acf.dhhs.gov/programs/cse/index.html
OCSE information for employers:
www.acf.dhhs.gov/programs/cse/newhire/employer/home.htm
OCSE state links: www.acf.dhhs.gov/programs/cse/extinf.htm

Direct Deposit and Electronic Payments
NACHA (The Electronic Payments Association): www.nacha.org
Direct Deposit and Direct Payment Coalition: www.directdeposit.org

## 13.4-4  Company Policies and Procedures

In Section 12.5-2, we mentioned how important it was to have documented policies and procedures in the payroll department to make sure short cuts were not being taken to avoid security measures, and in Section 13.2-2, we emphasized that such documentation made it much easier to train employees in the correct way of doing things. Once these procedures are documented, it is important for the payroll manager to make any changes necessitated by amendments to overall company policies and procedures or those used by other departments interfacing with payroll (e.g., accounting, human resources).

Because of this responsibility, it is also important for the payroll manager to keep up to date on the latest changes in company-wide or other departmental changes in policies and procedures. The payroll manager should develop a functioning network of colleagues throughout the company to be kept abreast of coming changes. And when it comes time to select a new company-wide computer system, the payroll manager should push for an integrated system that includes all policies and procedures, as well as their updates and changes, or at least for interfaces with appropriate departments that would provide the same information.

## 13.4-5  Union Contracts

Despite the continuing decrease in the percentage of U.S. workers who are represented by labor unions—a 25-year slide to 12.0% in 2006—payroll managers in organizations that have employees working under a union contract have certain obligations to fulfill regarding those contracts.[3]

 **PUBLIC SECTOR NOT AFFECTED** The dropoff in union representation has mainly taken place in the private sector, where only 7.4% of workers were represented by a union in 2006. In the public sector, union representation stood at 36.2%.

---

3.    USDL 07-0113, 1-25-07.

Union contract obligations can affect several areas of payroll processing, including:

*Dues checkoffs.* After the employee has provided signed authorization to have union dues deducted and paid over to the union, the payroll department must administer the deduction and remittance.

*Fringe benefit contributions.* The contract may require the employer to contribute to union benefit funds (pension, health, etc.) based on the number of hours worked by employees or the wages they earn. Payroll must track the necessary information and provide reports as required.

*Upcoming layoffs.* Contract provisions generally require less senior employees to be laid off in the event of corporate downsizing. Adequate notice of layoffs is necessary for payroll to prepare termination paychecks in time to comply with the contract and state law requirements.

*Wage increases.* When union contracts are settled and signed after the previous contract has expired, they often include retroactive pay provisions that must be carefully examined and administered.

*Probationary employees.* The payroll department must track new hires who are on probation before becoming permanent employees.

*Overtime and other premium pay.* The overtime and premium pay rates for hours worked outside the normal workweek may be higher in a union contract than 1½ times the employee's regular rate of pay.

Because of these and other union contract provisions impacting payroll—such as shift differentials, call-in pay, equipment allowances—payroll managers must:

- keep a current copy of all union contracts applicable to company employees on file;
- read each contract thoroughly to spot payroll-related provisions;
- establish and document procedures to establish and identify union employees on the payroll database;
- establish payment schedules and reconciliation procedures for payments made to the unions; and
- establish a schedule and procedures for compiling reports required by the organization and the union.

# 13.5 Review Questions and Exercises

## Review Questions

1. In situational leadership, the way managers handle their staff depends on the way they deal with what two factors?

2. What are the fundamental skills that must be mastered in most managerial positions?

3. The planning and organizing process consists of defining three key activities. What are these activities?

4. List the five questions the payroll manager must answer when developing a job description.

5. What types of questions work best in an interview?

6. Why must payroll managers learn the strengths and weaknesses of their employees before delegating tasks to them?

7. What are the four communication skills the manager must possess in directing employees?

8. Name three qualities that can help make a payroll manager a strong leader.

9. How is achievement a motivator for some employees?

10. List four rewards you can give employees who have demonstrated the potential for leadership.

11. What are the three important characteristics of a payroll management report?

12. Once a crisis is over, what are some of the things the payroll manager can do to ensure the lessons it taught are not forgotten?

13. What are the four combinations of time categories which tell a manager what his or her priorities should be?

14. What are some of the characteristics of a successful team?

15. Name the three most common mistakes that managers commit when conducting employee performance appraisals.

16. Other than IRS regulations, what other sources of guidance are available for the interpretation of tax laws?

17. List those areas affected by union contract obligations which can affect areas of payroll processing.

18. What steps must be taken to conduct a successful meeting, once the type of meeting has been determined?

19. What are the four stages of team development?

## True or False Questions

_____ 1. Most newly promoted payroll managers achieve their position because they have shown great management skills in the past.

_____ 2. The goal of a shared services environment is to have employees' payroll and benefits questions answered with one phone call.

_____ 3. The current demands of the American workplace make it necessary for managers to tailor their management workstyle to fit different jobs and different employees.

_____ 4. There must be a plan for the payroll department to achieve its mission of satisfying employees, government, and upper management.

_____ 5. Timely completion of the subtasks won't lead to attainment of the objectives.

_____ 6. Before implementing a plan, the payroll manager must know what it will cost to achieve the stated goals.

_____ 7. Legal requirements governing the hiring process are for the lawyers to worry about—not payroll managers.

_____ 8. Problem solving includes the ability to trace reconciling problems back to the source and decide on appropriate corrections.

_____ 9. The payroll manager can let each employee decide what responsibility or task or portion of a task he or she will take.

_____ 10. If an employee receives training and still does not improve, disciplinary action is the next step to take.

_____ 11. Training is a cure-all for every performance problem.

_____ 12. Training must be aimed at improving the skills and knowledge needed to achieve the department's mission.

_____ 13. A reward to reinforce and encourage continued positive behavior or a punishment to encourage modified behavior is an element of effective feedback.

_____ 14. Telling an employee how often he or she was late and what an adverse effect this had on the workloads of other employees will achieve better results than accusing an employee of having a "lousy attitude."

_____ 15. If positive or negative feedback is to be useful, it must be given as soon as possible after the behavior has occurred.

_____ 16. Always be specific when giving feedback, whether it is positive or negative.

_____ 17. Reflective listening is a technique where the listener repeats what they think they heard and asks the speaker for verification.

_____ 18. If the employee admits that a severe personal problem is harming his or her work performance, the payroll manager should try to take the place of a professional counselor.

_____ 19. For payroll managers, crisis management is probably the least important leadership test they will have.

_____ 20. A regular review of all department policies, procedures, and documentation is vital in crisis prevention.

_____ 21. Managers who are constantly moving from crisis to crisis are seen to be productive and efficient.

_____ 22. Building a team network must have high priority and wide visibility throughout the company.

_____ 23. Performance evaluations are considered to be an informal way of giving feedback.

_____ 24. One of the most important aspects of a payroll manager's responsibilities is keeping on top of current developments in the payroll field.

_____ 25. The final stage of team development is norming.

## Multiple Choice Questions

_____ 1.    Each of the following conditions is a fundamental dimension that grows out of principle-centered leadership EXCEPT:

    a.    Security
    b.    Wisdom
    c.    Tenacity
    d.    Guidance

_____ 2.    What do situational leadership proponents emphasize?

    a.    Using a style that comes naturally
    b.    Whatever style fits the demands of the particular job
    c.    Payroll department edicts
    d.    Company edicts

_____ 3.    What must occur for the payroll department to achieve its goal?

    a.    There must be a plan
    b.    Planning will not help
    c.    Read the daily astrology page
    d.    Roaming around solves all goal achievement needs

_____ 4.    All of the following resources are available within the company EXCEPT:

    a.    Employees in the payroll department
    b.    Other departments
    c.    The local bank's funds
    d.    Company funds

_____ 5.    Where does the hiring process begin?

    a.    Decision not to fill a position
    b.    Decision not to create a position
    c.    Decision not to analyze a job
    d.    Decision to terminate the incumbent

_____ 6.    Which of the following requirements would not appear in a mid-level payroll job description?

    a.    Maximum age
    b.    Minimum education
    c.    Specialized skills
    d.    Key responsibilities

_____ 7.    Where should negative feedback be given?

    a.    Where everyone can benefit from hearing it
    b.    Negative feedback should never be given
    c.    Directly to the human resources department
    d.    In private to the worker

_____ 8.   All of the following aspects of a job may be delegated EXCEPT:

    a.   Authority
    b.   Responsibility
    c.   Accountability
    d.   Job tasks

_____ 9.   What is the most successful strategy for motivating employees?

    a.   Taking notice of negative behavior only
    b.   Not providing positive feedback
    c.   Realizing an employee is not a "team player"
    d.   Rewarding an employee's positive behavior

_____ 10.  Each of the following behaviors is an example of affiliation other than:

    a.   Not including employees in lunch and after-work activities
    b.   Putting employees on project teams and task forces
    c.   Encouraging employees to join and participate in professional organizations
    d.   Providing employees with networking opportunities

_____ 11.  Each of the following actions is considered a good guideline when conducting meetings EXCEPT:

    a.   Plan
    b.   Prepare
    c.   Start with a meal
    d.   Control the time

_____ 12.  The statement "the only people who can manage time are those who use it well," defines an application of what skill?

    a.   Planning
    b.   Organizing
    c.   Good meeting skills
    d.   Time management

_____ 13.  A manager building a successful team must deal with employees who have different personal styles. Each of the following styles is represented on a team other than:

    a.   Contributors
    b.   Controllers
    c.   Collaborators
    d.   Communicators

_____ 14.  Each of the following objectives is considered to be a valid reason why companies conduct performance evaluations EXCEPT:

    a.   To provide documentation for salary increase decisions
    b.   To determine which employees are promotable
    c.   To fire employees who conflict with other employees
    d.   To encourage employees' personal growth and development

_____ 15. When the IRS publishes regulations they are coded "T.D." What does T.D. stand for?

    a. Tax Data
    b. Tax Development
    c. Technical Decision
    d. Treasury Decision

_____ 16. The Employer's Tax Guide, Circular E is found in which IRS Publication?

    a. IRS Pub. 12
    b. IRS Pub. 15
    c. IRS Pub. 18
    d. IRS Pub. 37

_____ 17. What is an IRS decision on how the tax laws apply to a set of facts involving a single tax-payer called?

    a. Private Letter Ruling
    b. News Release
    c. Revenue Ruling
    d. Revenue Procedure

_____ 18. Managers are involved in all of the following processes as part of their managerial responsibilities other than:

    a. Planning
    b. Organizing
    c. Directing
    d. Completing tasks

_____ 19. Which of the following individuals is performing as a manager?

    a. A door-to-door salesperson
    b. A person repairing a machine
    c. An individual checking the quality of work performed by others
    d. An individual deciding which of two assigned tasks to do next

# SECTION 14: PAYROLL FOR U.S. EMPLOYEES ABROAD AND ALIENS IN THE U.S.

## TABLE OF CONTENTS

# SECTION 14: PAYROLL FOR U.S. EMPLOYEES ABROAD AND ALIENS IN THE U.S.

In recent years, there has been much written in the business and general press about the "global economy" and its impact on the way U.S. companies conduct business. An increasing number of U.S. companies are buying, selling, and manufacturing goods in foreign countries. As they become more involved in business on a global scale, U.S. businesses are also sending more of their employees abroad on foreign assignments and bringing more employees from foreign countries to work in the U.S.

This increase in foreign assignments for U.S. employees and in U.S. assignments for aliens has also had a profound impact on the payroll departments in these companies. The rules governing wage and tax withholding and reporting for such employees are more complex and require a high degree of coordination among payroll, human resources, and benefits. This section provides an explanation of the rules regarding the payroll ramifications of U.S. employees working abroad (expatriates) and aliens working in the U.S., including provisions designed to help these employees avoid double taxation of their income.

## 14.1 U.S. Citizens and Resident Aliens Working Abroad

In general, wages earned by U.S. citizens and resident aliens working in a foreign country are subject to federal income tax withholding unless the wages can be excluded from the employee's gross income under the foreign earned income exclusion or foreign housing exclusion. Withholding may also be reduced for employees who are eligible for a tax credit for foreign tax payments, by increasing the number of allowances taken on their Form W-4. Finally, wages earned abroad may be exempt from withholding if the employer is required to withhold foreign taxes under the law of the foreign country.

Employees working for U.S. companies abroad are generally also subject to social security and Medicare taxes, although coverage is optional if the employer is a foreign affiliate of a U.S. company. Such employees' wages are also subject to FUTA tax.

## 14.1-1 Federal Income Tax Withholding

In general, U.S. employers must withhold federal income tax from the wages of their employees working abroad unless those wages fit under one of several exemptions.

 **EXEMPTIONS FOR CITIZENS ONLY**[1] The withholding exemptions explained in the following paragraphs generally apply only to employees who are U.S. citizens. Resident aliens working outside the U.S. are not eligible for the exemptions, and all taxable amounts paid to them by U.S. employers are subject to federal income tax withholding (see Section 14.1-4 for an exception to this general rule involving U.S. tax treaties).

**Foreign earned income or housing cost exclusion.**[2] Federal income tax is not withheld from an employee's wages to the extent that the employer reasonably believes that the wages will be excluded from the employee's income under the foreign earned income or housing cost exclusion (see Section 14.1-4). Employees who believe they will qualify for either exclusion must give their employer a signed statement to that effect. This exemption does not apply to federal government employees.

---

1.    IRC §3401(a)(8).
2.    IRC §3401(a)(8)(A)(i); IRS Reg. §31.3401(a)(8)(A)-1(a).

They can prepare their own statement or use Form 673, *Statement for Claiming Exemption From Withholding on Foreign Earned Income Eligible for the Exclusion(s) Provided by Section 911* (see Appendix page A-141). The completed form tells the employer whether the employee qualifies for the exclusions under the bona fide residence or physical presence test, how long the employee intends to remain in the foreign country during the year, and what the employee's estimated housing expenses for the year will be. This information helps the employer calculate how much of the employee's wages will be exempt from federal income tax withholding.

**Wages subject to foreign income tax withholding.**[3] The employer is not required to withhold federal income tax from an expatriate employee's wages if the employer is required by foreign law to withhold foreign income tax from those wages. The same is true for U.S. possessions. A mere agreement to withhold between the employer and the employee is not enough to support the exemption—the withholding must be required by foreign law. A signed statement attesting to the foreign withholding requirement should be kept on file by the employer. This exemption does not apply to federal government employees.

**Wages for work in U.S. possessions other than Puerto Rico.**[4] If an employer reasonably believes at least 80% of the wages it pays an employee during the year will be for work done in a U.S. possession other than Puerto Rico, it does not have to withhold federal income tax from the employee's wages. Such possessions include Guam, American Samoa, and other U.S. islands.

**Wages for work in Puerto Rico.**[5] If an employer reasonably believes an employee will be a bona fide resident of Puerto Rico for the entire year, wages paid to the employee are not subject to federal income tax withholding.

*Who is a resident of a possession?*[6] An employee is generally considered a bona fide resident of a U.S. possession if the employee:

- is physically present in the possession for 183 days during the year;
- does not have a tax home outside the possession during the year; and
- does not have a closer connection to the U.S. or a foreign country than to the possession.

Employees also will be considered to have met the "presence test" test if:

- they were physically present in the possession at least 549 days during the three-year period consisting of the current year and the two immediately preceding years, provided that they were also present in the possession for at least 60 days during each year of the period;
- they spend no more than 90 days in the U.S. during the year;
- they spend more time in the possession than in the U.S. and do not have more than $3,000 in U.S. earned income; or
- they have no significant connection to the U.S.

**Extra withholding allowances for the foreign tax credit.** Aside from the withholding exemptions mentioned here, employees who expect to take a credit or deduction for foreign taxes paid on income that is not subject to the foreign earned income or housing cost exclusion can take extra withholding allowances on their Form *W-4, Employee's Withholding Allowance Certificate* (see Appendix page A-91), thus reducing their withholding.

**Filing and reporting rules must be followed.** Where the U.S. employer is paying its employees working abroad and they have income that is subject to federal income, social security, Medicare, and federal unemployment taxes, the employer must follow the regular deposit, payment, and return rules. This means that Forms 941, 940, W-2, etc., must be filed by their regular deadlines reporting the wages paid and taxes withheld and deposited (see Sections 7 and 8).

---

3.     IRC §3401(a)(8)(A)(ii); IRS Reg. §31.3401(a)(8)(A)-1(b).
4.     IRC §3401(a)(8)(B); IRS Reg. §31.3401(a)(8)(B)-1.
5.     IRC §3401(a)(8)(C); IRS Reg. §31.3401(a)(8)(C)-1.
6.     IRC §937(a); IRS Reg. §1.937-1(c)-(e).

# 14.1-2  Social Security and Medicare Taxes

In general, wages paid to U.S. citizens and resident aliens working abroad for a U.S. employer are subject to social security and Medicare tax withholding, which the employer must match (see Section 6.7-1).[7]  The foreign earned income and housing cost exclusions (see Section 14.1-4) do not apply to exempt an employee or employer from social security or Medicare tax.  Employees who work abroad for a foreign affiliate of a U.S. employer are not subject to social security and Medicare coverage and taxes unless the employer elects coverage.[8]  Expatriate employees may also be subject to foreign social security tax.

**Totalization agreements.**[9]  To alleviate the burden of double social security taxation and to integrate coverage of employees, the U.S. government has entered into binational social security agreements, also known as "totalization" agreements, with several European countries, Australia, Chile, Japan, South Korea, and Canada.  Under a totalization agreement, expatriate employees working "temporarily" in the foreign country (generally up to 5 years) are subject to U.S. social security and Medicare taxes only, to the same extent their compensation would be subject to those taxes had they remained in the U.S.  Wages earned by employees working "permanently" in the foreign country are subject only to the foreign country's social security taxes.

*Establishing U.S. social security coverage.*  To establish that an employee's wages are subject to U.S. social security and Medicare taxes but are exempt from foreign social security tax, the employer must get a certificate of U.S. coverage for the country where the employee will be assigned by sending a letter to: U.S. Social Security Administration, Office of International Programs, P.O. Box 17741, Baltimore, MD 21235-7741 (or fax to 410-966-1861).  The letter should contain:

- the employee's name and U.S. social security number;
- the employee's date and place of birth;
- the country of the employee's citizenship;
- the country of the employee's permanent place of residence;
- the name and address of the employee's employer in the U.S. and in the foreign country;
- the employee's (and any accompanying dependents') health insurance coverage (France and Japan only);
- the date and place the employee was hired; and
- the beginning and expected ending date of the employee's foreign assignment.

 **ALSO AVAILABLE ONLINE**  The employer can also complete an online application for a certificate of coverage at the SSA's website, www.socialsecurity.gov/international/CoC_link.html.  Employers using this service will get their certificate up to several weeks faster than by mail or fax.

*Establishing foreign social security coverage.*  If an employee will be permanently working in the foreign country and will be exempt from U.S. social security and Medicare taxes under a totalization agreement, the employer must get a certificate of coverage from an authorized social security official or agency of the foreign country.  The certificate should be kept by the employer and not sent to the IRS.  The certificate should contain:

- the employee's name, address, and foreign social security number;
- the name and address of the employee's employer in the U.S. and in the foreign country;
- the fact that the employee's wages are covered by the totalization agreement and are subject to the foreign country's social security system; and
- the beginning and expected ending date (if any) of the employee's foreign assignment.

---

7.    IRC §3121(b).
8.    IRC §3121(l).
9.    Social Security Act §233, 42 USC §433; IRS Pub. 54, Tax Guide for U.S. Citizens and Resident Aliens Abroad.

If the authorities in the foreign country will not provide such a statement, the employee or the employer should get a statement from the SSA's Office of International Programs, at the address listed earlier, to the effect that the employee's wages are not covered by the U.S. social security system. This statement should be kept by the employer since it establishes the exemption of the employee's wages from social security tax.

*Countries under totalization agreements.* The U.S. now has totalization agreements with 21 countries—Australia, Austria, Belgium, Canada, Chile, Finland, France, Germany, Greece, Ireland, Italy, Japan, Luxembourg, the Netherlands, Norway, Portugal, South Korea, Spain, Sweden, Switzerland, and the United Kingdom. In 2004, the U.S. signed a totalization agreement with Mexico, but the agreement was still awaiting approval by the U.S. Congress and Mexico's legislature in early 2008. In 2007, totalization agreements were signed with the Czech Republic and Denmark, and they are awaiting approval of the governments of the countries and the U.S. Congress.

Under all but 1 of these agreements, a "temporary" assignment can last no more than 5 years. The agreement with Italy allows temporary assignments to run for an indefinite period of time.

*Online resources for employers.* The SSA website at www.socialsecurity.gov/international provides employers with new online resources. Click on "International Agreements" for links to:

- <u>General overview</u>. Look here to learn how the totalization agreements program helps people who work in the U.S. and abroad.
- <u>Description and text of each agreement</u>. Look here for online versions of SSA pamphlets describing each of the U.S. agreements, as well as the complete text of each.
- <u>Certificates of coverage</u>. Look here to learn how to request the documentation needed to avoid social security taxes in a foreign country under a totalization agreement and to access the SSA's online Certificate of Coverage service, which allows employers to request certificates via the Internet.
- <u>Status table</u>. Look here for a table showing the signing date, effective date, and legal citation for all agreements in force and the status of pending agreements.

**Foreign affiliate coverage elections.**[10] As mentioned earlier, a foreign affiliate of a U.S. employer can elect social security coverage for U.S. citizens and resident aliens working there. Otherwise they are not covered. To elect coverage, the U.S. employer enters into an agreement with the IRS by completing and filing Form 2032, *Contract Coverage Under Title II of the Social Security Act* (see Appendix page A-310). The election applies to all U.S. citizens and resident aliens employed (and hired later) by the foreign affiliate outside the U.S., to the extent their wages and work would be subject to social security tax in the U.S.

A foreign affiliate is a foreign business entity in which a U.S. company has at least a 10% interest. The U.S. employer is responsible for paying both the employer and employee shares of the U.S. social security and Medicare taxes. The employer is not obligated to withhold or cause the foreign affiliate to withhold the employee share of the taxes from the employee's wages, although the employee can agree to such withholding with the U.S. employer.

Once the agreement has been entered into through Form 2032, the IRS will assign the U.S. employer a separate employer identification number for reporting the wages and taxes covered by the agreement, as well as provide a supply of Forms 941. The wages and taxes covered by the agreement must be reported on a different Form 941 than the one the employer uses to report wages and taxes for its other employees, and the employer should write "3121(l) Agreement" at the top of the form, as well as any attachments. The Form 941 is due on the last day of the month after the end of the return period, and the taxes may be paid with the return rather than deposited in a financial institution.

 **AGREEMENT IS PERMANENT**[11] Contract coverage agreements may not be terminated on or after June 15, 1989, but are ended only when the foreign affiliate ceases being a foreign affiliate.

---

10.     IRC §3121(l); IRS Reg. §36.3121(l)(1)-1 - (l)(10)-4.
11.     IRC §3121(l)(2), (l)(3).

## 14.1-3 Federal Unemployment Tax

In general, employment by U.S. citizens working abroad for a U.S. employer is covered by the Federal Unemployment Tax Act (FUTA) if the work performed would be covered in the U.S.[12] FUTA tax does not apply to resident aliens working abroad or to American employees of foreign affiliates (no coverage election is available).

There is a coverage exception for Canada and the Virgin Islands eliminating dual coverage. U.S. citizens working for a U.S. employer in those jurisdictions are covered by local unemployment compensation laws. The employer must pay the full 6.2% FUTA for employees if the state having jurisdiction does not require employer unemployment insurance tax payments. If no state payments are made, no credit against FUTA liability can be taken.

## 14.1-4 Foreign Earned Income and Housing Cost Exclusions

Under IRC §911, U.S. citizens and resident alien employees working outside the U.S. (i.e., expatriates) who qualify for the foreign earned income exclusion can choose to exclude the first $87,600 of foreign earned income in 2008 from their gross income.[13] These employees may also exclude certain housing cost amounts from their gross income. An employer need not withhold federal income tax from any wages paid to a qualifying employee it reasonably believes will be excluded from income under the §911 exclusions.[14]

The maximum exclusion amount is adjusted for inflation to the next lowest multiple of $100.

To qualify for the foreign earned income or housing cost exclusion, the employee must have foreign earned income, the employee's "tax home" must be in a foreign country, and the employee must meet either a bona fide residence or physical presence test that proves the employee is not living in the U.S. during the year in question.

 **WHAT'S A FOREIGN COUNTRY?** For purposes of the §911 exclusions, a foreign country is any territory under the soverignty of a government other than the U.S. Therefore, all territories and possessions of the U.S. are not foreign countries, including Puerto Rico, Guam, the Virgin Islands, the Northern Mariana Islands, American Samoa, and others.[15] Antarctica is also not a foreign country because of a treaty signed by the U.S. and other countries that leaves open all questions of sovereignty over Antarctica, making it a "sovereignless region," according to the U.S. Tax Court.[16]

**Foreign tax home.** The employee's tax home must be in a foreign country for the entire period of residence or physical presence in that country during the year.[17] In general, an employee's tax home is the location of his or her regular or principal place of business or employment. If there is no regular or principal place of business, the employee's tax home is where the employee regularly lives (i.e., has an abode). An employee cannot have a foreign tax home if he or she regularly lives in the U.S. But the expatriate employee is not considered to regularly live in the U.S. merely because the employee temporarily spends time in the U.S. (e.g., vacations) or maintains a house or apartment there that is occupied by the employee's spouse and/ or dependents.[18]

---

12.    IRC §3306(c).
13.    IRC §911(a), (b).
14.    IRC §3401(a)(8)(A)(i).
15.    IRS Reg. §1.911-2(h); IRS Pub. 54, Tax Guide for U.S. Citizens and Resident Aliens Abroad.
16.    Arnett v. Commissioner, No. 8866-03 (U.S. Tax Ct., 1-25-06); aff'd No. 06-1934 (7CA, 1-16-07).
17.    IRS Reg. §1.911-2(a).
18.    IRC §911(d)(3); IRS Reg. §1.911-2(b).

*Example:* An auditor works one month in each of six foreign countries during a year auditing her employer's foreign affiliates and spends the month in between each assignment back in the U.S. with her husband and children in their family residence. The employee has her abode in the U.S. during the year and cannot have a foreign tax home during that same year.

One factor determining whether an employee's tax home is in the U.S. or a foreign country is whether the employee is on a temporary or indefinite assignment. IRS regulations defining the term "tax home" give the term "temporary assignment" the same meaning it has under the rules governing travel expenses away from "home" (see Section 3.3-5).

Under those rules, temporary assignments are those lasting up to one year.[19] The IRS has adopted a "realistic expectation" test that focuses on whether employment in a single location is realistically expected to last for more or less than one year, rather than on the actual length of employment at a temporary location:[20]

- if employment away from home in a single location is realistically expected to last (and does in fact last) for one year or less, the employment will be treated as temporary in the absence of facts and circumstances indicating otherwise;

- if employment away from home is expected to last for more than one year or there is no realistic expectation that the employment will last for one year or less, the employment will be treated as indefinite, regardless of whether it actually exceeds one year; and

- if employment away from home is realistically expected not to exceed one year, the employment will be treated as temporary (in the absence of facts and circumstances indicating otherwise) until the date that the taxpayer's realistic expectation changes.

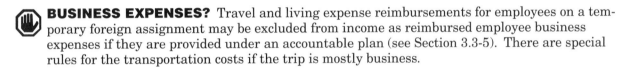 **BUSINESS EXPENSES?** Travel and living expense reimbursements for employees on a temporary foreign assignment may be excluded from income as reimbursed employee business expenses if they are provided under an accountable plan (see Section 3.3-5). There are special rules for the transportation costs if the trip is mostly business.

**Bona fide residence test.**[21] Employees wishing to qualify for the §911 exclusions can do so by proving they have been bona fide residents of a foreign country for an uninterrupted period that includes at least one full taxable year (January 1 through December 31 for calendar year taxpayers). Whether an employee is a bona fide resident of a foreign country depends on several factors:

- whether the employee brings his or her family and they intend to make the foreign country their home for the duration of the assignment;

- purchase of a home or signing a long-term lease in the foreign country;

- involvement in the culture and social life of the foreign country;

- the terms of the employment agreement regarding the foreign assignment; and

- the type of visa or residence permit secured by the employee.

*Example 1:* Employee Geri arrives with her family in Tokyo on October 1, 2007. The assignment is indefinite, and Geri and her family establish residence immediately, intending to live in Tokyo until she is transferred elsewhere. If Geri remains on assignment in Tokyo and maintains her residence there through December 31, 2008, she becomes a bona fide resident and is eligible for the foreign earned income and housing cost exclusions.

---

19.   IRC §162(a); IRS Reg. §1.911-2(b); IRS Pub. 54, Tax Guide for U.S. Citizens and Resident Aliens Abroad.
20.   Rev. Rul. 93-86, 1993-2 CB 71.
21.   IRC §911(d)(1)(A); IRS Reg. §1.911-2(c).

**Example 2:** Assume the same facts as in Example 1, except that Geri is unexpectedly transferred back to the U.S. on November 12, 2008. Geri does not qualify as a bona fide resident of a foreign country because her Tokyo residence was interrupted before a full tax year was spent there. However, she may still qualify for the exclusions under the physical presence test discussed later in this section.

The facts supporting the employee's claim of bona fide residence in a foreign country are reported by the employee to the IRS on Form 2555, *Foreign Earned Income* (see Appendix page A-318). Form 2555 should be submitted by the employee with the personal tax return on which the foreign earned income exclusion is claimed. The IRS makes the determination of the employee's qualification for the exclusion.

*Intent to return, temporary visits OK.* An employee can be a bona fide resident of a foreign country even though he or she intends to return to the U.S. at the end of the foreign assignment. The place the employee intends to return to is the employee's "domicile," which is not necessarily the same as the employee's residence.[22] Employees can also move from one foreign country to another or make temporary visits to the U.S. while on foreign assignment for vacation or business without losing the exclusions.[23]

**Example:** Employee Geri, from our earlier examples, goes to the U.S. with her family in May 2008 for a 3-week vacation and then returns to Tokyo, where she stays on assignment until April 10, 2009. The temporary visit to the U.S. does not prevent Geri from qualifying as a bona fide resident of Japan as of December 31, 2008, the end of one full tax year as a resident there.

*Statement of nonresidency kills exclusion.* An employee who makes a statement to the tax authorities in a foreign country claiming to be a nonresident of that country, and is not taxed as a resident of that country, does not qualify under the bona fide residence test. If the statement has been submitted but no decision as to the employee's status as a resident of the foreign country has yet been made, the employee still does not qualify as a bona fide resident of that country.[24]

 **ABSENTEE BALLOT DOES NOT DISQUALIFY** Sending in an absentee ballot to vote in a U.S. election does not disqualify an expatriate employee from being a bona fide resident of the country where he or she is living. But giving inconsistent information to local election officials about the terms of the foreign assignment can be evidence in determining bona fide resident status.[25]

*Citizens and some resident aliens can qualify.* Employees can qualify for the foreign earned income and housing cost exclusions under the bona fide residence test if they are citizens of the U.S. They can also qualify if they are resident aliens who are citizens or nationals of a country with which the U.S. has an income tax treaty with a clause prohibiting the U.S. from imposing more burdensome restrictions on citizens of the foreign country than on U.S. citizens.[26]

*Treaties may prevent qualification.* Employees that are covered under special agreements or treaties between the U.S. and a foreign country exempting them from foreign income taxes may not be allowed to qualify for the foreign earned income exclusion as bona fide residents of that country. This "special status" generally applies to employees of the U.S. armed forces and sometimes their civilian contractors.

*Qualifying for part of a year.* Once an employee has established bona fide residence in a foreign country for a full tax year, the employee qualifies as a bona fide resident for the entire period, from the first day of residence to the last. Therefore, the employee can qualify as a bona fide resident for part of a year.

**Example:** Employee Geri, from our earlier examples, resides in Tokyo with her family while on indefinite assignment from October 1, 2007 to April 12, 2009. Since Geri was a bona fide resident for all of 2008, she qualifies as a bona fide resident from October 1, 2007 to April 12, 2009.

---

22. IRS Reg. §1.871-2(b); §1.911-2(c).
23. IRS Reg. §1.911-2(c).
24. IRC §911(d)(5); IRS Reg. §1.911-2(c).
25. IRS Pub. 54, Tax Guide for U.S. Citizens and Resident Aliens Abroad.
26. Rev. Rul. 91-58, 1991-2 CB 340.

*Assignment from one foreign post to another.* If an employer gives an employee another foreign assignment after finishing one, the employee may or may not have a break in foreign residence between assignments that could disqualify the employee from attaining bona fide resident status.

> *Example 1*: Employee Geri, from our earlier examples, resides in Tokyo with her family while on indefinite assignment from October 1, 2007 to November 30, 2008. On December 1, 2008, Geri and her family are returned to the U.S. by her employer (along with their household possessions) to wait for another foreign assignment. Geri's foreign residence ended on November 30, 2008 and did not begin again until she was assigned to another indefinite assignment in a foreign country and physically entered that country. Since Geri was not a bona fide resident of Japan for the entire tax year of 2007 or 2008, she did not qualify under the bona fide residence test in either year, although she may qualify under the physical presence test explained later.

> *Example 2*: Assume the same facts as in Example 1, except that when Geri finishes her assignment in Tokyo she is given a new assignment in Singapore. On December 1, 2008, Geri returned to the U.S. with her family for a vacation. On January 2, 2009, they arrived in Singapore for Geri's new assignment. Because Geri did not interrupt her bona fide residence abroad, she qualified on December 31, 2008 as a bona fide resident of a foreign country from the beginning of her residency in Tokyo.

**Physical presence test.** Another way that expatriate employees (both U.S. citizens and resident aliens) can qualify for the foreign earned income exclusion is by meeting the physical presence test. This test is met if the expatriate employee is physically present in a foreign country (or countries) for 330 full days during any consecutive 12-month period. The 330 qualifying days do not have to be consecutive, and all periods spent in foreign countries (whether for employment or personal reasons) during the 12-month period are totaled to determine whether the test has been met.[27]

*Purpose of stay is unimportant.* Qualifying under the physical presence test does not depend on the employee's purpose in staying in a foreign country. No intention as to residence or other factors need be considered.

*"Full day" means just that.*[28] A full day is a continuous period of 24 hours beginning at midnight and ending with the following midnight. Things to remember when determining what constitutes a full day in a foreign country include:

- If an employee leaves the U.S. for a foreign country, time spent over international waters does not count as time spent in a foreign country.

> *Example:* Employee Aaron flies to Spain, leaving the U.S. on August 23. He arrives in Spain at 7:00 a.m. on August 24. His first full day in Spain is August 25.

- If an employee leaves the U.S. for a foreign country and passes over a foreign country before midnight on the day the employee left, the first full day in a foreign country is the day after leaving the U.S.

> *Example:* Employee Joan flies to France, leaving the U.S. during the afternoon of November 21. Her plane passes over Spain at 10:00 p.m. on November 21, and Joan arrives in France at 1:00 a.m. on November 22. Joan's first full day in a foreign country is November 22.

- If an employee leaves one foreign country to travel to another, no full days are lost unless the travel is not within a foreign country (e.g., on international waters) and takes 24 hours or more.

---

27.    IRC §911(d)(1)(B); IRS Reg. §1.911-2(d).
28.    IRS Reg. §1.911-2(d)(2).

**Example 1:** Employee Charles leaves Japan by air on January 14 at 10:00 p.m. and arrives in Australia on January 15 at 7:00 a.m. Because the trip over international waters took less than 24 hours, Charles does not lose any full days.

**Example 2:** Later in the year, Charles makes the same trip by ship and leaves Japan on June 27 at 8:00 a.m., arriving in Australia at 10:00 a.m. on June 29. Because the trip on international waters took more than 24 hours, Charles loses June 27-29 as full days.

- If an employee traveling from one foreign country to another is physically present in the U.S. for less than 24 hours during that time, the time spent in the U.S. is treated as time spent not in a foreign country (i.e., the same as time spent over international waters).

*Flexibility in determining 12-month period.*[29] It is up to the employee to determine the consecutive 12-month period used for meeting the physical presence test. The period can begin with any day of any calendar month. It ends the day before the same calendar day, 12 months later. Other matters to keep in mind when determining the 12-month period include:

- Any consecutive 12-month period can be used, so long as the 330 full days in a foreign country fall within the period.

- The 12-month period does not have to begin with the first full day in a foreign country or end with the last full day or the day the employee leaves the foreign country. It can begin before or after any of those days, so as to give the employee the greatest income exclusion.

**Example:** Employee Janet takes several short foreign assignments over a period of 18 months, from July 15, 2007 to January 18, 2009. Because of long vacations in the U.S. in August and September 2007 and November and December 2008, Janet must choose a 12-month period beginning and ending during the middle part of her foreign assignments in order to meet the 330-day requirement.

- When an employee has been in a foreign country for longer than 12 months, overlapping 12-month periods can be chosen to benefit the employee.

**Example:** Employee Steven is on a foreign assignment in London, England from March 10, 2007 (first full day) until January 14, 2009 (last full day), and he spends July 2007 and August 2008 on vacation in the U.S. Steven can take advantage of the overlapping 12-month periods to meet the physical presence test for the entire London assignment as follows: one 12-month period can begin March 10, 2007 and end March 9, 2008; the second period can begin January 15, 2008 and end January 14, 2009.

**Time requirements waived for some countries.**[30] The minimum time requirements for both the bona fide residence and physical presence tests do not apply where the employee is forced to leave a foreign country because of war, civil unrest, or similar adverse conditions. However, the employee must show one of the tests would have been met had the adverse conditions not existed, and that he or she had a foreign tax home and was a bona fide resident of or physically present in the foreign country before being forced to leave.

The determination of whether such adverse conditions exist is up to the IRS. Also, only days actually spent in the foreign country are counted as qualifying days for purposes of determining the amount of the employee's foreign earned income or housing cost exclusion. A list of designated countries and the periods for which the waiver applies is published annually by the IRS.

29.	IRS Reg. §1.911-2(d)(1); IRS Pub. 54, Tax Guide for U.S. Citizens and Resident Aliens Abroad.
30.	IRC §911(d)(4); IRS Reg. §1.911-2(f).

If an employee left one of the countries on the list on or after the date listed for that country, the employee can qualify for the bona fide residence or physical presence test for 2006 without meeting the minimum time requirement. The employee must be a bona fide resident of or be physically present in the country on or before the beginning date of the waiver. (An updated list had not been released at press time.) The list is as follows:[31]

| Country | Date of Departure on or After |
|---------|------------------------------|
| East Timor | May 23, 2006 |
| Lebanon | July 27, 2006 |
| Nepal | April 26, 2006 |

**U.S. travel restrictions cannot be violated.**[32] Employees who are in a foreign country in defiance of U.S. law restricting travel to that country are not bona fide residents of or physically present in a foreign country while in violation of the law. Such restrictions apply to Cuba in 2007, except for individuals working at the U.S. Naval Base in Guantanamo Bay.

**Foreign earned income exclusion.** Under §911, up to $87,600 of foreign earned income may be excluded from a qualifying employee's gross income in 2008 ($85,700 in 2007). There are several definitions and restrictions that must be applied in determining the amount of the exclusion.

*Foreign earned income.*[33] Foreign earned income is income earned by an employee from sources within a foreign country while the employee has a foreign tax home and qualifies for the exclusion under the bona fide residence or physical presence test. Earned income includes all compensation, such as wages, salaries, commissions, tips, bonuses, tax reimbursements, cost of living allowances, educational reimbursements, professional fees, etc., paid for personal services rendered, including noncash payments.

Foreign earned income does not include: pension or annuity payments (including social security benefits); payments from the federal government to its employees; amounts already excluded as meals and lodging furnished for the employer's convenience; employer contributions to a nonexempt employee trust or a nonqualified annuity contract; or amounts received more than one year after the close of the taxable year in which they were earned.

*Determining the source of earned income.* The source of earned income is determined by where the employee performed the services that produced the income. Foreign earned income is income earned for working in a foreign country. Where or how the employee is paid has no bearing on the source of the income.

If an employee cannot determine how much earned income is for work done in the U.S., or the income is paid for work done partly in the U.S. and partly in a foreign country, the amount of U.S. source earned income must be determined using the method that most correctly shows the proper source. In most cases, the determination can be made on a time basis with the following formula:

$$\frac{\text{Number of days worked in the U.S.}}{\text{Total number of days worked}} \quad X \quad \text{Total income} \quad = \quad \text{U.S. source income}$$

> **Example:** Employee Jack, a U.S. citizen, is a bona fide resident of Canada who earns $77,000 a year in salary 2008. He also receives a $6,000 cost of living allowance and a $6,000 education allowance that are not limited to being earned while working outside the U.S. Jack's total income is $89,000, and he works a 5-day week, for a total of 240 workdays after subtracting vacation time. Jack worked 30 days in the U.S. during the year. His U.S. source income is determined as follows:

---

31.   Rev. Proc. 2007-28, 2007-16 IRB 974.
32.   IRS Pub. 54, Tax Guide for U.S. Citizens and Resident Aliens Abroad; Notice 2006-84, 2006-41 IRB 677.
33.   IRC §911(b), (d)(2); IRS Reg. §1.911-3(a), (b), (c); IRS Pub. 54, Tax Guide for U.S. Citizens and Resident Aliens Abroad.

$$\frac{\text{30 days worked in U.S.}}{\text{240 total days worked}} \quad \text{X} \quad \$89,000 \quad = \quad \text{U.S. source income}$$

$$\frac{30}{240} \quad \text{X} \quad \$89,000 \quad = \quad \text{U.S. source income}$$

$$.125 \quad \text{X} \quad \$89,000 \quad = \quad \$11,125$$

Jack's foreign earned income = $89,000 - $11,125 = $77,875

*Limit on excludable amount.*[34] Qualified employees cannot exclude more than the lesser of $80,000 of foreign earned income or the excess of foreign earned income over the foreign housing cost exclusion (discussed later).

*Attributing income to the year earned.*[35] Foreign earned income must be attributed to the year the services were performed giving rise to the income. This means bonuses, tax equalization payments, or tax reimbursements received by an employee in a year after they were earned must be considered income in the year they were earned, not in the year paid. Make sure any bonuses for work performed both in a foreign country and the U.S. are allocated to each and only the portion allocated to work performed in the foreign country is included in foreign earned income.

> **Example 1:** Employee Bill is working in Switzerland and, because of certain sales quotas he met during 2008, he receives a bonus of 10% of his 2008 salary in February 2009. The bonus is considered foreign earned income in 2008 for purposes of applying the exclusion limitation.

> **Example 2:** Assume the same facts as in Example 1, except that Bill earned $5,000 of his 2008 salary for work performed in the U.S. and $45,000 for work done in Switzerland. When Bill receives his 10% bonus in February 2009 ($5,000), $500 must be allocated to U.S. source income and $4,500 to foreign earned income in 2008.

Furthermore, the income can be excluded in the year it is received only to the extent it would have been eligible for the exclusion in the year in which it was earned. In essence, this rule allows for the unused exclusion from the year in which the income was earned to be carried forward to the year in which the income is received.

 **ELIGIBILITY ENDS AFTER ONE YEAR** Income received after the end of the tax year following the tax year in which the services were performed giving rise to the income is not eligible for the foreign earned income exclusion.

*Example:* Employee Sara qualifies as a bona fide resident of a foreign country with a foreign tax home for all of 2007 and 2008. In 2007, Sara received $76,700 for services performed in the foreign country and claimed no foreign housing cost exclusion. Sara can exclude the entire $76,700 earned and received in 2007 on her 2007 personal tax return. In 2008, Sara receives a $10,000 tax equalization payment based on work done in 2007 plus $85,000 for work done in the foreign country in 2008.

In 2008, Sara can exclude $9,000 of the $10,000 received for services performed in 2007 by filing an amended personal tax return for 2007. The remaining $1,000 must be included in income in 2007 because it could not have been excluded in 2007 had it been received in that year ($85,700 - $76,700 = $9,000). In 2008, Sara can exclude the entire $85,000 received in 2008 for work done during that year.

---

34.  IRS Reg. §1.911-3(d)(2).
35.  IRS Reg. §1.911-3(e).

*Year-end payroll exception.*[36] An exception to the general attribution rules exists for wages earned during the last payroll period of one year and paid during the next year. Such wages are attributable entirely to the year of payment if:

- the payment is based on the employer's normal payroll period for the particular employee;
- the payroll period includes the last day of the year;
- the payroll period is no longer than 16 days; and
- payday is the same number of days after the payroll period as other paydays during the year.

*Moving expense reimbursements.*[37] Foreign earned income may include employer reimbursements for job-related moving expenses connected with an employee's move to, from, or between foreign countries. The following amounts must be included as earned income:

- reimbursements of, or payments for, nondeductible moving expenses;
- reimbursement amounts that exceed the deductible expenses and that are not returned to the employer;
- reimbursements made under a nonaccountable plan, whether or not they are for deductible expenses; and
- reimbursements of moving expenses the employee deducted in an earlier year (for details on the general rules regarding moving expenses, see Section 3.3-2).

The next step is determining when the reimbursement is considered earned. If the employee moves from the U.S. to a foreign country, the reimbursement is considered pay for future services. If the employee has at least 120 qualifying days under the bona fide residence or physical presence test during the year of the move, all of the amounts reimbursed are attributed to the year of the move. If the number of qualifying days is less than 120, the amounts reimbursed must be allocated to the year of the move and the year after the move in proportion to the number of qualifying days in each year. If the move is between foreign countries, and the employee qualifies for at least 120 days during the year of the move under the bona fide residence or physical presence test, any reimbursements considered earned income are attributed to the year of the move.

If the employee's move is from a foreign country to the U.S., any moving expense reimbursement that must be included in income is generally considered U.S. source income. However, if the employer has agreed in writing to reimburse the employee for the move regardless of whether the employee continues to work for the employer, any earned income is considered compensation for past services performed in the foreign country. In this situation, the includible reimbursement is attributed to the year of the move under the 120-day rule explained earlier. If the 120-day requirement is not met, the includible reimbursement must be allocated to the year of the move and the year before the move in proportion to the number of qualifying days in each year.

 **WHAT ABOUT STORAGE EXPENSES?** If an employee is reimbursed for storage expenses, the reimbursement is for services performed during the period of time for which the storage expenses are incurred. Whether the reimbursement is earned income or not depends on the status of the reimbursement under the general rules governing moving expense reimbursements.

**Foreign housing cost exclusion.**[38] In addition to the foreign earned income exclusion, employees who have a foreign tax home and qualify under the bona fide residence or physical presence test can take an exclusion for a limited amount of reasonable foreign housing expenses exceeding a base housing amount.

*Reasonable housing expenses.*[39] Housing expenses eligible for the exclusion include the reasonable expenses paid during the time the employee qualified for the exclusion by or on behalf of the employee and the employee's spouse or dependents living with the employee. Housing expenses include rent, utilities, insurance, occupancy taxes, fees paid for securing a lease, furniture rental, household repairs, and automobile parking costs.

---

36.     IRS Reg. §1.911-3(e)(3).
37.     IRS Reg. §1.911-3(e)(5); IRS Pub. 54, Tax Guide for U.S. Citizens and Resident Aliens Abroad.
38.     IRC §911(c); IRS Reg. §1.911-4.
39.     IRC §911(c)(3); IRS Reg. §1.911-4(b).

Reasonable housing expenses do not include:

- lavish or extravagant expenses under the circumstances;
- telephone and cable television charges;
- deductible interest and taxes;
- capital expenditures, such as a house (including mortgage payments), home improvements, or furniture; or
- the cost of domestic labor (e.g., maids or gardeners).

*Base housing amount.*[40] The base housing amount is 16% of the maximum foreign earned income exclusion, figured on a daily basis, multiplied by the number of days during the year the employee met the bona fide residence or physical presence test. The maximum foreign earned income exclusion is determined on January 1 of the year in which the employee's tax year begins.

*Housing cost exclusion limitation.*[41] The reasonable housing expenses that are used to calculate the housing cost exclusion are limited to 30% of the maximum foreign earned income exclusion, figured on a daily basis, multiplied by the number of days during the year the employee met the bona fide residence or physical presence test. The maximum foreign earned income exclusion is determined on January 1 of the year in which the employee's tax year begins.

The following chart shows the maximum foreign earned income exclusion, housing cost exclusion limitation, base housing amount, and maximum foreign housing cost exclusion for 2007 and 2008. These numbers will change each year with the maximum foreign earned income exclusion, which is adjusted for inflation annually.

|  | Maximum Foreign Earned Income Exclusion | Housing Cost Exclusion Limitation | Base Housing Amount | Maximum Foreign Housing Cost Exclusion |
|---|---|---|---|---|
| 2007 | $85,700 | $25,710 | $13,712 | $11,998 |
| 2008 | $87,600 | $26,280 | $14,016 | $12,264 |

The Treasury Secretary, through the IRS, can adjust the housing cost exclusion limitation for specific locations with significantly higher housing costs. For 2007, IRS issued a list of adjusted housing cost exclusion limitations in IRS Notice 2007-77.[42] The IRS will adjust the list each year and announce the adjustments in either a notice, changes to the instructions for Form 2555, *Foreign Earned Income* (see Appendix page A-318), or a revised table on the IRS website at www.irs.gov.

**Example 1:** Employee John qualifies for the foreign housing cost exclusion under the physical presence test for all of 2008, spending $24,500 on reasonable housing expenses. On January 1, 2008, the maximum foreign earned income exclusion was $87,600. John's foreign housing cost exclusion for 2008 is calculated as follows:

foreign housing cost exclusion = reasonable housing expenses - base housing amount

base housing amount = maximum foreign earned income exclusion x 16%

base housing amount = $87,600 x .16 = $14,016

foreign housing cost exclusion = $24,500 - $14,016 = $10,484

---

40.   IRC §911(c)(1)(B); IRS Reg. §1.911-4(c).
41.   IRC §911(c)(2).
42.   IRS Notice 2007-77, 2007-40 IRB 735.

***Example 2:*** Assume the same facts as in Example 1, except that John's reasonable housing expenses were $31,500, and John spent the entire year in a foreign locality that was not on the list of the IRS's foreign high cost localities. Since John's reasonable housing expenses exceeded the housing cost exclusion limitation of $26,280, John's reasonable housing expenses are limited to $26,280. John's foreign housing cost exclusion for 2008 is calculated as follows:

foreign housing cost exclusion = reasonable housing expenses – base housing amount

base housing amount = $87,600 x .16 = $14,016

foreign housing cost exclusion = $26,280 - $14,016 = $12,264

***Example 3:*** Assume the same facts as in Example 1, except that John qualifies under the physical presence test for 340 days during 2008 rather than the full calendar year and his reasonable housing expenses are $22,800. The first step in determining John's foreign housing cost exclusion is to calculate a daily base housing amount for 2008:

daily base housing amount = $\dfrac{\text{annual base housing amount}}{\text{number of days in the year}}$

daily base housing amount = $14,016 ÷ 366 = $38.30

John's base housing amount and foreign housing cost exclusion for 2008 are calculated as follows:

2008 base housing amount = daily base housing amount x number of qualifying days

2008 base housing amount = $38.30 x 340 = $13,022

2008 housing cost exclusion = reasonable housing expenses - base housing amount

2008 housing cost exclusion = $22,800 - $13,022 = $9,778

*Housing cost exclusion limitation.*[43] A qualified employee who has elected the housing cost exclusion can only exclude either the full amount of the housing costs less the base amount, or foreign earned income, whichever is less.

*Applying the exclusion limits.*[44] Remember that the employee's foreign earned income exclusion is limited to the lesser of $87,600 for 2008 (prorated daily for each qualifying day if the employee is not a bona fide resident or physically present for the full year) or the excess of the employee's total foreign earned income over the elected housing cost exclusion.

***Example:*** Employee Alice earned $89,000 in 2008, all of which qualified as foreign earned income, and Alice was physically present in a foreign country for all of 2008. Her foreign housing expenses totaled $24,000, resulting in a maximum foreign housing cost exclusion of $9,984 ($24,000 - $14,016 base housing amount). Since the housing exclusion is claimed first to help determine the allowable foreign earned income exclusion, only $79,016 is available for the foreign earned income exclusion in 2008 (the lesser of $87,600 or $89,000 - $9,984). Therefore, she will have an unused 2008 foreign earned income exclusion of $8,584 ($87,600 maximum - $79,016 actual) available for use against future income related to 2008, so long as it is received by December 31, 2009.

---

43. IRS Reg. §1.911-4(d).
44. IRC §911(d)(7); IRS Reg. §1.911-3(d)(2), (d)(3).

*Tax rates on income not excluded.*[45]  If an employee takes the foreign earned income and/or the foreign housing cost exclusion, amounts earned in excess of the exclusions is taxed by applying the tax rates that would have been applied had the individual not elected the exclusion(s).

*Qualified second foreign household.*[46]  Housing expenses may also include the costs of maintaining a second foreign household for the expatriate employee's spouse and dependents.  If the family does not live with the employee because living conditions at the employee's residence are dangerous, unhealthy, or otherwise adverse, reasonable housing expenses may include costs incurred at both households.  The expenses for both households can be combined for purposes of computing the housing cost exclusion.  Examples of adverse conditions qualifying the second foreign household for the exclusion include war or civil unrest in the area or the fact the employee lives on the employer's premises in a remote location, such as a construction site, for the employer's benefit.

**Two-earner families.**[47]  The foreign earned income exclusion is available to each spouse to the extent each spouse actually has foreign earned income and otherwise qualifies for the exclusion.  Community property laws are disregarded, so each spouse is eligible for the exclusion based only on his or her earned income.  Also, a couple may not use one spouse's unused exclusion against the foreign earned income of the other spouse to increase that other spouse's exclusion.  If the spouses live together, the housing cost exclusion may be apportioned between them as they wish.  If they live apart, there are special rules that must be followed.

**Disallowance of double benefits.**[48]  If an employee elects to take the foreign earned income or housing cost exclusion, the employee cannot claim any credit or take any deduction that can be allocated to the excluded income.  To be disallowed, the deduction must be directly related to the excluded income.  Before 1994, this rule primarily affected employees in the area of moving expenses.  Now, however, qualified moving expense reimbursements (see Section 3.3-2) are excluded from gross income altogether, so they would not qualify as foreign earned income.  And nonqualified moving expenses are not deductible.  Therefore, reimbursements for nonqualified moving expenses may qualify as foreign earned income and no deduction would be allowed for the expenses regardless of the disallowance rule.

**Exclusion elections and revocations.**[49]  The foreign earned income and housing cost exclusions are not automatic—they must be elected by the employee on the employee's personal tax return.  They may be elected separately or together by completing the appropriate section of Form 2555, *Foreign Earned Income* (see Appendix page A-318), and filing it with the employee's personal tax return.  If the employee is electing only the foreign earned income exclusion, has earned income of only salaries and wages of $87,600 or less in 2008, files a return for a full calendar year, and does not have business or moving expenses, the employee can use Form 2555-EZ, *Foreign Earned Income Exclusion* (see Appendix page A-332).  The election remains in effect for that year and all subsequent years until revoked.  Once revoked, the same election cannot be made again until the sixth year following the year for which the revocation was effective, unless the IRS gives its consent through a letter ruling.

**Earned income tax credit restrictions**.  U.S. citizens or resident aliens who claim the foreign income or housing cost exclusion are not eligible for the earned income tax credit.[50]

**Employer-provided meals and lodging.**[51]  In general, employees working in the U.S. as well as abroad can exclude the value of meals and lodging provided by the employer if the meals and lodging are provided for the convenience of the employer on the employer's premises and the employee accepts the lodging as a condition of employment.  A less restrictive test is applied to expatriate employees living in an employer-provided "foreign camp" at a remote site.

45.  IRC §911(f).
46.  IRS Reg. §1.911-4(b)(5).
47.  IRS Reg. §1.911-5.
48.  IRC §911(d)(6); IRS Reg. §1.911-6.
49.  IRC §911(e); IRS Reg. §1.911-7.
50.  IRC §32(c)(1)(D).
51.  IRC §119(c); IRS Reg. §1.119-1(c)(2), (d).

**NO "DOUBLE DIPPING"** Employees that take an exclusion for employer-provided lodging cannot also elect the foreign housing cost exclusion for the value of the lodging.

**Foreign tax credit or deduction.**[52] As another method of avoiding double taxation of foreign source income, expatriate employees may take a credit against U.S. tax for qualifying foreign income taxes. This credit is generally limited to the U.S. tax on the employee's foreign source income, and cannot exceed the foreign taxes actually paid. In the alternative, the employee can take a deduction from income for the foreign taxes on the employee's personal income tax return. Generally, the credit option will provide larger tax savings, since it is a dollar-for-dollar reduction in tax liability.

Foreign income taxes cannot be credited against U.S. tax to the extent the foreign taxes were paid on foreign earned income excluded under the foreign earned income or housing cost exclusion. Therefore, an employee whose entire income is excluded cannot take a federal tax credit or deduction. If less than the employee's entire income is excluded, an allocation of the foreign taxes paid to the foreign income excluded must be made.

The foreign tax credit is claimed by completing Form 1116, *Computation of Foreign Tax Credit*, and including it with the employee's Form 1040. The foreign tax deduction is claimed on Schedule A of Form 1040.

 **TAX TREATY RELIEF** Relief from double taxation is also provided by tax treaties the U.S. has with other nations. For more on tax treaties, see Section 14.1-5.

# 14.1-5 U.S. Income Tax Treaties

The U.S. has entered into more than 55 income tax treaties with foreign countries. The treaties are designed to clarify each country's taxing jurisdiction and to avoid double taxation of income. These treaties can be relied on by U.S. citizens and resident aliens working abroad to gain significant reductions in foreign income taxes.

**Possible treaty benefits.** Generally, reductions in U.S. taxes are not possible because of "tax saving" clauses in the treaties that allow the U.S. to tax its citizens and residents as if there was no treaty. One benefit for resident aliens working abroad is that the nondiscrimination clauses in most treaties (prohibiting discriminatory treatment of citizens or residents of either country) allow them to qualify for the foreign earned income and housing cost exclusions under the bona fide residence test as well as the physical presence test.

Some other common tax treaty benefits include:

- *Personal service income.* An employee's wages for personal services performed in the treaty country are partially or totally exempt from taxation by the foreign country if the employee is in the foreign country for a limited number of days (e.g., no more than 183) and meets certain other requirements.

- *Professors and teachers.* Wages received by a U.S. teacher or professor in a treaty country are exempt from foreign taxes under most treaties for temporary periods of up to 2 or 3 years.

- *Students, trainees, and apprentices.* Amounts received by U.S. residents for study, research or business and technical training are generally exempt from the treaty country's income tax. Grants and allowances from governmental and nonprofit organizations may also be exempt so long as they are not payments for work performed.

- *Tax credit provisions.* To avoid double taxation, tax treaties provide for credits and deductions to reduce taxes imposed by the foreign country.

---

52.    IRC §901(a), (b); IRS Reg. §1.901-1; IRS Pub. 514, Foreign Tax Credit for Individuals.

- *Tax saving clauses.* Tax saving clauses provide that treaties do not affect U.S. taxation of its own citizens and residents. Therefore, most of the treaties' benefits related to a treaty country's taxes are available only to U.S. citizens who are not residents of the treaty country and U.S. resident aliens who are not citizens of the treaty country.

To claim a treaty benefit for services performed in a foreign country, the employee will have to produce proof of U.S. residency in the form of a letter from the IRS – Form 6166, *Certification of U.S. Residency*. Employees can obtain the letter by completing and submitting Form 8802, *Application for United States Residency Certification* (see Appendix page A-378). Once the employee receives the certificate of residency, it should be included with the application materials required by the country where the employee is seeking a reduced tax rate. The IRS anticipates that it should take no more than 30 days to process the Form 8802 and issue the certification.

The IRS began charging a user fee of $35 to process Forms 8802 in November 2006. The fee covers a single Form 8802 requesting up to 20 Forms 6166 for a single taxpayer identification number. The fee increases if more than 20 Forms 6166 are requested.

 **LEARNING ABOUT THE TREATIES** IRS Publication 54, Tax Guide for U.S. Citizens and Resident Aliens Abroad, contains general tax treaty information, as well as a table of tax treaties listing the countries with which the U.S. has tax treaties and official material offering further explanation. The individual treaties are published in the Internal Revenue Bulletin and the Cumulative Bulletin (see Section 13.4-1), and some have been implemented through IRS regulations. More detailed explanations can also be found in IRS Publication 901, U.S. Tax Treaties, and IRS Publication 597, Information on the U.S.—Canada Income Tax Treaty. Detailed summaries of the individual tax treaties between the U.S. and other countries can be found in the *Guide to Global Payroll Management*, published by the American Payroll Association. This volume also contains digests of the payroll withholding laws of more than 50 foreign countries. For information on how to order this and other APA publications, call 210-224-6406 or visit www.american-payroll.org.

**Relationship with the IRC.** In general, tax treaties are given priority over conflicting provisions of the Internal Revenue Code if they both apply to a certain taxpayer. One exception is when the IRC provision specifically mentions that it supersedes a treaty.

# 14.1-6 Employer Tax Reimbursement Policies

Most U.S. companies sending U.S. citizens and resident alien employees abroad have compensation policies designed to ensure these employees receive total compensation that will provide for a standard of living comparable to what they would have had if they were still living and working in the U.S. Such compensation policies take into account additional costs of living abroad, including income taxes.

Income and social security taxes are often higher in foreign countries than in the U.S., even more so because they tax the extra compensation provided to U.S. employees to offset the higher cost of living in the foreign country. In general, most compensation and tax reimbursement policies are designed to ensure the employee will not have to pay combined taxes on income in the two countries exceeding the taxes that would have been paid if the employee had remained in the U.S.

**General compensation components.** To make sure their overseas employees do not suffer in comparison to their U.S. counterparts, most companies offer one or more of the following additions to an expatriate employee's basic compensation package:

- a housing allowance that helps the employee afford housing comparable to what he or she occupied in the U.S. and/or to maintain a home in the U.S. while working abroad;

- relocation expense reimbursements to cover the cost of moving to the foreign country;

- an education allowance to send the employee's children to a private or boarding school;

- a vacation allowance for trips to the U.S. while on foreign assignment;

- deferred compensation payments linked to profit-sharing or performance-related incentives;

- a hardship allowance for employees working and living in undesirable conditions;

- an automobile allowance to help the employee buy or lease a car in the foreign country;

- a cost-of-living allowance to make up for the higher cost of living in the particular foreign country; and

- a foreign service premium or bonus to encourage employees to take foreign assignments.

**Tax protection plans.** The idea behind tax protection is that the employee will be reimbursed by the employer to the extent the employee's combined income and social security taxes in the U.S. and the foreign country exceed the amount the employee would have paid if living and working in the U.S. If the employee's combined actual taxes are lower because the foreign taxes are low or nonexistent (e.g., Saudi Arabia) or the employee qualifies for exclusions from U.S. tax, the employee gets a tax benefit he or she can retain.

In practice, if the employee needs tax protection, the employee pays the foreign taxes that equal its U.S. tax liability while the employer pays any excess foreign taxes owed as well as the employee's U.S. tax liability. This leaves the employee in the same financial position as if he or she had remained in the U.S.

U.S. companies with large expatriate work forces that move employees from one country to another fairly often may run into problems with a tax protection plan. An expatriate employee may be reluctant to move from a foreign country with low taxes to a high tax country because of the lost tax benefit, even though the employee would be paying no more in the new country than he or she would pay in the U.S. Also, the laws in the foreign country may change to provide for increased taxes while the expatriates are on assignment there, possibly causing economic difficulties and morale problems even though they are theoretically no worse off than if they had been working in the U.S.

**Tax equalization plans.** The solid trend among U.S. companies has been away from tax protection and toward tax equalization. Tax equalization plans are designed to make taxes a neutral factor when determining an expatriate employee's compensation package. The idea is that all expatriates should continue to incur a tax burden equal to what they would incur if they were living and working in the U.S., regardless of the actual foreign tax liability. Under this method, the employee gets no tax benefit, while the employer can take advantage of the employee's assignment to a low tax country.

The employer's savings from having employees assigned to low tax countries can be used to offset its extra costs for employees in high tax countries. Also, the foreign taxes can be reduced by reducing the expatriate employee's taxable salary by the amount that he or she would pay if the employee were living in the U.S. Regular salary deductions also make it easier for the employee to manage his or her cash flow because the employee's taxes are satisfied by these payments of "hypothetical taxes" (see discussion following) and because the employee does not have to be concerned about complex foreign country tax rules and procedures.

**Hypothetical taxes.** Whether an employer uses tax protection or tax equalization to reimburse an employee for higher foreign taxes, the employer must determine the tax that the employee would have paid if the employee had remained in the U.S. This is known as the hypothetical or stay-at-home tax. Small employers with few expatriates may determine the tax based on the individual circumstances of the employees, including individual compensation incentives and income tax deductions taken in previous years.

Larger employers with more ambitious expatriate assignments would find such an individualized plan very cumbersome to administrate. Instead, they often compute the hypothetical tax based on base salary and normal incentive compensation, using a formula that includes a standard allowance for deductions to be used in calculating the hypothetical tax. The deduction allowance is intended to cover all types of normal deductions, such as home mortgage interest, charitable contributions, state and local taxes, etc., without referring to the employee's actual deductions.

*Other family income.* The employer must decide whether to include income from sources other than the employee's earnings when computing the hypothetical tax. These may include investment income, stock options, or income earned by an employee's spouse or children. Failure to include it may not leave the employee in a tax neutral position.

 **WHAT ABOUT STATE TAXES?** Employers must determine whether they are going to include hypothetical state and local taxes when determining their employees' hypothetical taxes. Companies whose headquarters are in a state with significant state and local income taxes often include them in the hypothetical tax calculation because employees working in the home office would have to pay them. But using the taxes in the headquarters state for the hypothetical tax calculation would seem unfair to employees who worked for the employer in a different, lower taxed state before being sent abroad.

# 14.1-7 Expatriate State Tax Issues

Generally, state income taxes are imposed on all state residents based on their total income, with the tax base being federal adjusted gross income or taxable income (with some modifications). Nonresidents are taxed only on their income from state sources. Therefore, the tax burden on expatriate employees will necessarily be less in most situations if they can show that they are no longer state residents while on foreign assignment.

The determination of residency is based on various tests depending on the state, but often depends on whether the expatriate remains a domiciliary of the state. "Domicile" is a legal concept similar to residence, but it is distinct and turns on an individual's attachments to the state.

**Determining domicile.** An employee's domicile is the place where the employer has his or her "true, fixed, and permanent home" to which the employee intends to return after being absent. Employees can have only one domicile at a time, and they retain it until another is established. An employee can be a domiciliary of a state without being a resident of that state, and the opposite is also true.

The following factors generally indicate an employee's domicile:

- where the employee votes;
- where the employee maintains a residence;
- where the employee's immediate family lives and where children attend school;
- whether the employee owns a new abode or has a short-term lease;
- where the employee returns after vacations or other leaves from work;
- the state issuing the employee's driver's license; and
- where bank accounts and business associations are maintained.

**Determining residence.** An employee's residence, on the other hand, is the place where the employee lives for more than a "temporary or transitory" purpose. The employee's intent is irrelevant. Physical presence and tangible connections determine residency. It is possible for employees to be residents of more than one state at a time.

Some of the factors generally indicating residency include:

- physical presence;
- where family members live and children attend school;
- where the employee works, has business interests, and owns property; and
- where bank accounts and business interests are maintained.

**Determining residence for tax purposes.** Nearly all states treat a domiciliary as a resident of the state for tax purposes. Many also treat nondomiciliaries as residents depending on how long they are in the state during a year and whether they have a "permanent place of abode" in the state. To somewhat ease the state tax burden on expatriates who are on long-term foreign assignments, a number of states treat domiciliaries as nonresidents for tax purposes if they are absent from the state for a certain period of time, even though they may intend to return.

*Example 1:* New York state domiciliaries are taxed as nonresidents if: (1) they maintain a permanent place of abode outside the state, do not have one inside the state, and are not in New York for more than 30 days during the taxable year; or (2) they are in a foreign country or countries for 450 out of 548 consecutive days (approximately 15 out of 18 months), they are not in New York for more than 90 days during the 548-day period, and they do not maintain a permanent place of abode in the state where their dependents stay for more than 90 days during the period.

*Example 2:* California domiciliaries are taxed as nonresidents if they are not in the state for more than 45 days in any consecutive 18-month period and are working on a contractual foreign assignment.

**Planning problems.** The use of domicile as the criterion for determining an expatriate's tax residence and the various definitions of residency continue to cause U.S. employers problems when they try to design comprehensive expatriate compensation plans. Further complications arise because not all states allow for the foreign earned income and housing cost exclusions found in IRC §911 (e.g., New Jersey and Pennsylvania do not).

Also, many states do not allow an employee to take a credit against state taxes owed for foreign taxes paid. Some states allow such a credit for Canadian provincial income taxes paid on income earned in Canada (e.g., Connecticut, Michigan, Minnesota, New York, Vermont). Others allow a deduction from income to be taken if it was also taken on the employee's federal tax return.

# 14.2 Resident and Nonresident Aliens Working in the U.S.

The taxation and reporting of income earned by foreign citizens (aliens) working in the U.S. depend on whether the employee is a resident or nonresident alien. In general, resident aliens are taxed on their worldwide income and their employers treat them the same way they treat U.S. citizens. Nonresident aliens, however, are taxed only on their income from U.S. sources, with some exceptions.

In the year in which an alien arrives in or departs from the U.S., the alien can be both a resident and a nonresident alien and be taxed as one or the other for part of the year. Special tax rules apply to certain employees of foreign governments and international organizations, students, and teachers, as well as residents of certain U.S. possessions and foreign countries. This section will explain the rules for determining resident/nonresident alien status and the taxation of each.

## 14.2-1 Determining Resident/Nonresident Alien Status

Generally, foreign citizens working in the U.S. are considered nonresident aliens unless they qualify as residents. The determination of residency made under the Internal Revenue Code applies only to the alien's status for U.S. income tax purposes, not immigration or other federal and state taxes. Under the Code, an alien qualifies as a resident if he or she meets either one of two tests—the lawful permanent resident test or the substantial presence test.

**Lawful permanent resident test.**[53] Under the "green card" or lawful permanent resident test, aliens who are lawful permanent residents of the U.S. are considered residents for income tax purposes. Because

---

53.    IRC §7701(b)(1)(A)(i); (b)(6); IRS Reg. §301.7701(b)-1(b); SCA 199950009, 9-13-99.

the lawful permanent resident test is based on the alien's legal right to be in the U.S., not on the alien's physical presence in the U.S., a green card holder is treated as a U.S. resident until that status is revoked or abandoned. This holds true for "commuter" green card holders from Canada or Mexico who work in the U.S., even though they reside in Canada or Mexico. Also, resident aliens are taxed on their worldwide income in much the same way as U.S. citizens (see Section 14.1).

 **PERMANENT RESIDENT STATUS APPLIES FOR FULL YEAR** If an alien is a lawful permanent resident of the U.S. for any part of a calendar year, the alien is a resident alien for the entire calendar year.

**Substantial presence test.**[54] Focusing on an alien's physical presence to determine residence, the substantial presence test states that an alien is considered a U.S. resident for income tax purposes if:

- the alien is present in the U.S. for at least 31 days during the current calendar year; and

- the total number of days of U.S. presence during the current calendar year, plus one-third of the U.S. days during the first preceding calendar year, plus one-sixth of the U.S. days during the second preceding calendar year, is at least 183 days (no rounding allowed—fractions must be used).

*Example 1:* Francois, a French business executive employed by a U.S. company, is present in the U.S. for 132 days during the current year, 110 days during the first preceding year, and 86 days in the second preceding year. To determine his status for the current year, Francois counts all 132 days in the U.S. in the current year, plus 1/3 of the 110 U.S. days in the first preceding year (36 2/3 days), and 1/6 of the U.S. days in the second preceding year (14 1/3 days). The total of 132 + 36 2/3 + 14 1/3 = 183 days. Francois meets the substantial presence test and is a resident alien for the current year.

*Example 2:* Maria, a Brazilian employee for a U.S. company, is present in the U.S. for 20 days in the current calendar year and for the entire 2 preceding calendar years. Because Maria was in the U.S. for less than 31 days in the current calendar year, she does not qualify as a resident alien under the substantial presence test for that year.

The substantial presence test has nothing to do with the alien's intent in staying in the U.S. or whether the alien has an immigrant or nonimmigrant visa.

 **WHAT IS PRESENCE?**[55] For the purpose of applying the substantial presence test, an alien is present in the U.S. on any day in which he or she is physically present in the U.S. for any part of that day. For example, if an alien employee arrived in the U.S. at 9:00 p.m. on September 13, 2008, his or her days of physical presence in the U.S. in 2008 would be 110 (18—Sept., 31—Oct., 30—Nov., 31—Dec.).

*Some days do not count.*[56] The following days spent by an alien in the U.S. do not count when determining residency under the substantial presence test:

- days spent in the full-time employ of an international organization or with diplomatic status;[57]
- days spent in the U.S. as a teacher or trainee under a "J" or "Q" visa (see Section 14.3), unless the teacher or trainee has been exempt from the substantial presence test as a teacher or trainee for any part of 2 of the 6 preceding calendar years (any part of 4 of the preceding 6 calendar years if the teacher or trainee is being paid by a foreign employer);[58]

---

54.   IRC §7701(b)(1)(A)(ii), (b)(3); IRS Reg. §301.7701(b)-1(c).
55.   IRC §7701(b)(7)(A); IRS Reg. §301.7701(b)-1(c)(2).
56.   IRC §7701(b)(3)(D)(i); IRS Reg. §301.7701(b)-3(a).
57.   IRC §7701(b)(5)(A)(i), (b)(5)(B); IRS Reg. §301.7701(b)-3(b)(1)(i); (b)(2).
58.   IRC §7701(b)(5)(A)(ii), (b)(5)(C), (b)(5)(E)(i); IRS Reg. §301.7701(b)-3(b)(1)(ii), (b)(3), (b)(7)(i), (b)(7)(ii).

- days spent in the U.S. as a student under an "F," "J," "M," or "Q" visa (see Section 14.3), unless the student has been exempt from the substantial presence test for any part of more than 5 calendar years and the student has not convincingly demonstrated that he or she does not intend to live permanently in the U.S. and has not complied with all student visa requirements;[59]
- days spent in the U.S. because of a medical condition that arose in the U.S.;[60]
- days spent by a professional athlete in the U.S. to compete in a charitable sporting event;[61]
- days on which residents of Mexico or Canada regularly commute to the U.S. to work and then return home;[62] and
- days spent in transit between two points in foreign countries during which the alien spends less than 24 hours in the U.S.[63]

*Closer connection exception.*[64] Aliens that qualify under the substantial presence test may still be deemed to be nonresident aliens if they can show that they have a closer connection to a foreign tax home than to the U.S. An alien meets the closer connection exception if the alien:

- is present in the U.S. for fewer than 183 days during the calendar year;
- has a tax home in a foreign country during the current year (e.g., permanent residence, family, personal property, bank accounts, driver's license, etc., are there); and
- has not applied for lawful permanent resident status.

**First-year resident election.**[65] Some aliens who fail to meet the substantial presence or green card test can elect resident status for the year in which they arrive in the U.S. To be eligible for the election, they must meet certain tests regarding their length of stay in the election year and their ability to meet the substantial presence test during the next calendar year.

**Dual residency status.**[66] An employee may be a resident alien and a nonresident alien in the same year, a situation normally occurring in the year of arrival in and departure from the U.S. Employers must treat such individuals appropriately according to their status for each part of the year. Aliens who qualify as residents under the green card test are considered to be residents from the first day of the calendar year during which they qualify. Their resident status ends when they are officially no longer lawful permanent residents. Aliens who qualify as residents under the substantial presence test are generally considered to be residents from the first day through the last day they are physically present in the U.S.

**Tax treaty impact.**[67] The Internal Revenue Code rules for determining U.S. residency do not supersede income tax treaties between the U.S. and foreign countries. Therefore, if an alien employee meets one of the U.S. residency tests and is also considered a resident of a foreign country under certain "tie-breaker" provisions of an income tax treaty, the alien is treated as a nonresident for U.S. tax matters covered by the treaty.

**Claiming resident status**. An alien can claim resident status by giving the employer a written statement stating that he or she is a resident of the U.S. or by completing and submitting to the employer Form W-9, *Request for Taxpayer Identification Number and Certification* (see Appendix page A-116). The employer should keep such documentation on file rather than sending it to the IRS. If an alien does not claim resident status in writing or on Form W-9, the employer may treat the employee as a nonresident alien.

---

59. IRC §7701(b)(5)(A)(iii), (b)(5)(D), (b)(5)(E)((ii); IRS Reg. §301.7701(b)-3(b)(1)(iii), (b)(4), (b)(7)(iii).
60. IRC §7701(b)(3)(D)(ii); IRS Reg. §301.7701(b)-3(c).
61. IRC §7701(b)(5)(A)(iv); IRS Reg. §301.7701(b)-3(b)(1)(iv), (b)(5).
62. IRC §7701(b)(7)(B); IRS Reg. §301.7701(b)-3(e).
63. IRC §7701(b)(7)(C); IRS Reg. §301.7701(b)-3(d).
64. IRC §7701(b)(3)(B), (b)(3)(C); IRS Reg. §301.7701(b)-2.
65. IRC §7701(b)(4); IRS Reg. §301.7701(b)-4(c)(3).
66. IRC §7701(b)(2); IRS Reg. §301.7701(b)-4.
67. IRS Reg. §301.7701(b)-7.

## 14.2-2  Federal Income Tax Withholding and Employment Taxes for Resident Aliens

In general, wages paid to U.S. resident aliens are subject to federal and state income withholding and employment taxes to the same extent that wages paid to U.S. citizens are.[68] This means that employers must withhold and deposit federal income, social security, and Medicare taxes, as well as state and local income taxes (also state disability and unemployment taxes where required). They also must pay the employer share of social security, Medicare, and federal unemployment taxes.

To accomplish this, employers must obtain each resident alien employee's social security number and have the employee complete a Form W-4, *Employee's Withholding Allowance Certificate* (see Appendix page A-91). (See Section 14.2-3 for information on aliens who cannot obtain a social security number.) Under the Immigration Reform and Control Act (see Section 1.8), the employer must retain a completed Form I-9, *Employment Eligibility Verification* (see Appendix page A-34), attesting to the resident alien's identity and authorization to work in the U.S. Wages paid to and taxes withheld from resident alien employees must be deposited and reported by the employer the same way it does for all other employees, on Forms 941 and W-2.

 **RESIDENT ALIENS WORKING ABROAD**  Resident aliens working abroad for a U.S. employer are generally treated the same as U.S. citizens and are entitled to the same income exclusions (see Section 14.1-4). However, they are not entitled to qualify for the exclusions under the bona fide residence test unless they are working in a treaty country that has a nondiscrimination clause in its income tax treaty with the U.S.

**Business expense rules apply to nonresident aliens.**  In 1998, the IRS clarified that the accountable plan rules (see Section 3.3-5) and the working condition fringe benefit rules (see Section 3.1-2) apply to nonresident aliens as well as U.S. citizens and resident aliens. The rules apply to independent contractors as well as employees.

## 14.2-3  Federal Income Tax Withholding for Nonresident Aliens

Nonresident aliens are subject to the same federal income tax withholding requirements as other employees for all of their income that is from U.S. sources.[69] To accomplish this, employers must obtain each nonresident alien employee's social security number and have the employee complete a Form W-4, *Employee's Withholding Allowance Certificate* (see discussion following). Under the Immigration Reform and Control Act (see Section 1.8), the employer must retain a completed Form I-9, *Employment Eligibility Verification* (see Appendix page A-34), attesting to the nonresident alien's identity and authorization to work in the U.S. Wages paid to and taxes withheld from nonresident alien employees must be deposited and reported by the employer the same way it does for all other employees, on Forms 941 and W-2.

**TINs for aliens who can't get an SSN.**  The IRS issues Individual Taxpayer Identification Numbers (ITINs) to aliens who are not eligible for a social security number but who still must file a tax or information return.[70] However, aliens who are authorized to work in the U.S. as an employee should be able to obtain an SSN, and employers should request an SSN from all employees for tax reporting and withholding purposes. The ITIN is for tax purposes only and cannot be used as proof of identity or authorization to work under IRCA.

ITINs take the same form as an SSN—000-00-0000—but they all begin with the number 9, and no SSN begins with that number. Aliens apply for an ITIN by completing and submitting Form W-7, *Application for IRS Individual Taxpayer Identification Number* (see Appendix page A-102). They also must submit documentation to establish their identity and alien status (two different documents unless a passport is submitted). Examples of such documentation include a passport, driver's license, birth certificate, identity card, or immigration documentation. The instructions to Form W-7 require originals or copies certified either by

---

68.  IRS Reg. §1.871-1.
69.  IRC §861(a)(3); §864(b); §871(b)(2); IRS Reg. §1.861-4; §1.864-2; §1.871-1.
70.  IRS Reg. §301.6109-1.

the issuing agency or someone else who is legally qualified to certify them. The IRS will accept documents notarized by notary publics (including foreign notaries as outlined by the Hague Convention), so long as the notary sees the original document and the copy.

To help eliminate the nontax use of ITINs, the IRS revised Form W-7 and the accompanying instructions in December 2003.[71] In general, an alien who must obtain an ITIN is required to attach the alien's original, completed tax return for which the ITIN is needed to the Form W-7. There are several exceptions to this requirement for aliens who need an ITIN for tax-related purposes but do not have to file a tax return (e.g., foreign scholars, professors, and researchers claiming a treaty benefit or getting a scholarship or fellowship but who can't get an SSN). The IRS has also changed the appearance of the ITIN from a card to an authorization letter to avoid any possible similarities with a social security card.

IRS regulations provide that an application for an ITIN must be made far enough in advance of the taxpayer's first required use of the ITIN to permit its issuance in time for the taxpayer to comply with the required use (e.g., the timely filing of a tax return). Taxpayers who comply with the IRS's new ITIN application process will be deemed to have satisfied this requirement.

The original, completed tax return and the Form W-7, along with the supporting documentation proving identity and foreign status, must be filed with the IRS at the address below, regardless of where the alien might otherwise be required to file the tax return. They can also be brought to any IRS Taxpayer Assistance Center in the U.S. and most IRS offices abroad. The tax return will be processed in the same manner as if it were filed at the address specified in the tax return instructions. No separate filing of the tax return (e.g., a copy) with any other IRS office is requested or required. Aliens are responsible for filing the original, completed tax return, with the Form W-7, by the due date applicable to the tax return for which the ITIN is needed. The address for filing Forms W-7 is:

> Internal Revenue Service
> ITIN Operation
> P.O. Box 149342
> Austin, TX 78714-9342

*Acceptance agents.*[72] Authorized "acceptance agents" can submit application forms and supporting documentation on behalf of an alien seeking an ITIN. Acceptance agents can also accept even broader responsibility by becoming a "certifying acceptance agent." Certifying acceptance agents review the supporting documentation submitted by the alien along with Form W-7 and certify to the IRS that they have reviewed the documents and found them to be authentic, complete, and accurate.

Certain financial institutions, colleges or universities, federal agencies, professional tax return preparers, and others authorized by IRS regulations or procedures are eligible to become acceptance agents once they have been approved and enter into in an agreement with the IRS. Written requests to become an acceptance agent should be sent to:

> Internal Revenue Service
> Mail Stop 983
> Andover, MA 05501

Other than requesting approval as an acceptance agent, an applicant's written request must also include the following information:

- name, address, employer identification number, and electronic filing identification number (if available);
- description of the types of persons the applicant expects to help obtain an ITIN;
- description of the applicant (e.g., bank, university, etc.) and the state or country under whose laws it is organized;

---

71. IR-2003-140, 12-17-03; IRS Notice 2004-1, 2004-2 IRB 268.
72. Rev. Proc. 2006-10; 2006-2 IRB 293.

- a list of the offices or branches that will be covered by the agreement, and their addresses;
- the business relationship the applicant has with the individuals it expects to assist in obtaining ITINs;
- the name and phone number of someone the IRS can contact regarding the application; and
- if the applicant is a tax preparer, whether the applicant wants to be included on a published list of acceptence agents.

Generally, applicants must pass a suitability background check before being admitted to the acceptance agent program. Applicants will be subject to an IRS review of their tax filing history, and the individual who has the authority to sign the acceptance agreement will be subject to a credit history check and an FBI background check, unless the individual is authorized to practice before the IRS and provides evidence of current professional status.

If the applicant is approved, the IRS will provide instructions regarding the procedures for entering into an acceptance agent agreement. The agreement will vary somewhat from party to party, but will generally contain procedures for:

- providing and maintaining a supply of Forms W-7 and sending a Form W-7 to any client or customer that the acceptance agent knows has been issued a temporary tax identification number by the IRS;
- assisting in completing the Form W-7 (e.g., by making sure all items are completed and that the ITIN applicant understands what information is required);
- IRS communication with the acceptance agent;
- promptly submitting completed Forms W-7;
- collecting and reviewing required supporting documentation;
- assisting individuals with notification procedures in the event of a change in alien status (e.g., from nonresident to resident);
- IRS verification of compliance with the acceptance agent agreement; and
- expiration and termination of the acceptance agent agreement.

Acceptance agent agreements expire on December 31 of the fourth full calendar year after the year in which the agreement became effective (i.e., agreements entered into in 2007 expire on December 31, 2011). To avoid a lapse in acceptance agent status, an agent that wishes to retain that status should file a new application with the IRS at least six months before the expiration date.

Either the acceptance agent or IRS may terminate the agreement by delivering written notice of termination to the other party. If the IRS gives notice of termination, the acceptance agent has 30 days to file an explanation of how it will correct any violations of the agreement and how it will modify its procedures to avoid violations in the future. The IRS will respond to the agent within 30 days of receiving the explanation.

Certifying acceptance agents can submit a Form W-7 on behalf of an ITIN applicant without including supporting documentation because they are certifying that they have reviewed and verified the applicant's identity and alien status and have kept a record of the supporting documentation. They must also provide a copy of the documentation to the IRS upon written request.

**SSN assignments delayed by homeland security efforts.** In 2002, employers began to see a significant delay in the time it took for nonresident alien employees to obtain a social security number. That is because the Social Security Administration started its Collateral Verification program, under which it verifies the immigration documents presented by a nonresident alien against a USCIS database before assigning an SSN.

**Special instructions for Form W-4.**[73] Just like any other employee, a nonresident alien should give the employer a valid, completed Form W-4 so the employer can determine how much federal income tax to withhold. But there are special instructions that must be followed (rather than those appearing on the Form

---

73.    IRS Pub. 515, Withholding of Tax on Nonresident Aliens and Foreign Entities; IRS Pub. 15, Employer's Tax Guide.

W-4) because of certain restrictions nonresident aliens face regarding their filing status, number of allow-ances, and inability to claim the standard deduction on their personal tax returns. These rules underwent significant changes, effective January 1, 2006, which the IRS hopes will lead to more accurate withholding.

- Nonresident aliens must request withholding as if they are single, regardless of their actual marital status.

- Nonresident aliens can claim only one withholding allowance on Line 5 unless they are residents of Canada, Mexico, South Korea, or are U.S. nationals. Students and business apprentices from India may also claim additional allowances under certain circumstances.

- Nonresident aliens must write "Nonresident Alien" or "NRA" above the dotted line in Line 6.

- Nonresident aliens cannot claim "Exempt" withholding status on Line 7.

Other rules regarding the validity and timing of a nonresident alien employee's Form W-4 are explained in the general discussion of W-4 forms at Section 6.3-1.

*New withholding calculation rules.*[74] Beginning with wages paid on or after January 1, 2006, employers are required to calculate income tax withholding on wages of nonresident alien employees (except for students and business apprentices from India) using a new procedure. Under this procedure, the employer adds an amount to the wages of the nonresident alien employee solely for purposes of calculating the income tax withholding for each payroll period; the specific amount depends on the payroll period. The added amount is not income or wages to the employee, does not affect federal income, social security, Medicare, or FUTA tax liability for the employer or the employee, and should not be reported as income or wages on the employee's Form W-2, *Wage and Tax Statement*.

Employers determine the income tax to be withheld by applying the withholding tables to the sum of the wages paid for the payroll period plus the additional amount. Adding this amount will offset the assumed standard deduction that is incorporated into the tables without requiring income tax to be withheld from wages that will fall below the personal exemption amount when annualized.

The amount required to be added to the wages of a nonresident alien for purposes of calculating federal income tax withholding is the highest wage amount to which a zero withholding rate applies as shown in the Table for the Percentage Method of Withholding for a single person (including a head of household) for each payroll period (see Appendix page A-4). For 2008, these amounts are as follows:

| Payroll Period | Add Additional |
|---|---|
| Weekly | $51.00 |
| Biweekly | $102.00 |
| Semimonthly | $110.00 |
| Monthly | $221.00 |
| Quarterly | $663.00 |
| Semiannually | $1,325.00 |
| Annually | $2,650.00 |
| Daily or Miscellaneous | $10.20 |

If the employer uses the percentage method, after adding the additional amount, the employer should then subtract an amount for withholding allowances shown on Form W-4 for the payroll period and apply the percentage method withholding tables to the remainder. If the employer uses the wage-bracket method, the employer should not subtract an amount for withholding allowance(s) after adding the additional amount because withholding allowances are reflected in the wage-bracket withholding tables.

---

74. Notice 2005-76, 2005-46 IRB 947.

**Example:** Jorge, a nonresident alien employee who earns $250 each month in 2008, completes Form W-4, claiming single status, one withholding allowance, and writing "nonresident alien" above the dotted line on Line 6. Because the employee is paid monthly, the employer adds $221 to the wages solely for purposes of calculating the amount of withholding. This $221 is not entered on the employee's Form W-2. Using the wage-bracket withholding method, nothing is withheld from Jorge's wages. If the employee's wages are the same for every month in the year, the employee will have $3,000 of gross income from U.S. sources. After subtracting $3,500 for the personal exemption amount, the employee will have no taxable income and no income tax liability.

*Implementing the new withholding requirements.* Employers hiring new nonresident alien employees who will receive remuneration for services performed in the U.S. for the first time on or after January 1, 2006, should instruct the new employees to complete Form W-4 in accordance with the new procedures. An employer that already has one or more nonresident alien employees with Forms W-4 on file requesting additional withholding pursuant to the previous rules should advise these employees to file new Forms W-4 in compliance with the new rules. Employers maintaining electronic Form W-4 systems should make an appropriate modification in their systems to allow employees to identify themselves as nonresident aliens. Also, employers using substitute forms should make an appropriate modification to their forms.

*Effective date and transition relief.* The new Form W-4 and withholding calculation rules went into effect with respect to wages paid to nonresident alien employees on or after January 1, 2006. However, with respect to wages paid prior to January 1, 2007, the IRS will not assert that an employer is liable for under-payments of income tax withholding and related interest and penalties resulting solely from the failure to apply the new withholding procedure, provided the employer has made a good faith effort to implement the new withholding requirements as soon as possible. Note that this transitional relief does not affect the liability of employees for federal income tax.

In a second release, the IRS has also announced that it is eliminating the Form 1040NR, *U.S. Nonresident Alien Income Tax Return* filing requirement for a nonresident alien individual who earns less than the amount of one personal exemption in U.S. wages "effectively connected" to a U.S. trade or business and who is required to file a U.S. tax return because of those wages, effective for tax years beginning on or after January 1, 2006.[75]

 **SOCIAL SECURITY CARDS NOT REQUIRED FOR IRCA** Employers must be aware that they cannot require nonresident aliens to produce their social security cards as proof of authorization to work in the U.S. under IRCA. The employees can produce any document allowed under regulations issued by U. S. Citizenship and Immigration Services. However, employers can ask employees to produce their social security cards to make sure that the social security number is recorded accurately for wage and tax reporting purposes. The employer should also make a copy of the employee's social security card when it is produced.

**U.S. source income.**[76] Nonresident aliens in the U.S. are subject to federal income tax withholding on their "U.S. source income." For nonresident alien employees and their employers, the important factor is where the employee performs services. In most situations, compensation paid to an employee for work performed in the U.S. is U.S. source income subject to federal income tax withholding. It makes no difference where the employer is located, where the employment agreement (if applicable) was signed, or where or when the wages are paid. Compensation paid to a nonresident alien for services performed outside the U.S. is not U.S. source income and is not subject to federal income tax withholding.

*Wages for work performed partly inside and partly outside the U.S.*[77] If a nonresident alien is paid wages for work performed partly inside and partly outside the U.S., the general rule is that the amount to be included in income from U.S. sources is determined on the basis that most correctly reflects the proper source of the income under the facts and circumstances of the particular case. If the nonresident alien is an

---

75. Notice 2005-77, 2005-46 IRB 951.
76. IRC §861(a)(3); §864(b); IRS Reg. §1.861-4(a).
77. IRS Reg. §1.861-4(b).

employee, the wages and fringe benefits should generally be allocated to U.S. source income on a time basis according to the following formula:

U.S. source income = Wages paid x $\frac{\text{Number of days working in U.S.}}{\text{Total number of workdays}}$

**Example:** Pierre, a player for a U.S. professional hockey team, is a citizen and resident of Canada. During 2008, Pierre received $550,000 for 238 days of playing and training, of which 174 days were spent in the U.S. and 64 were spent in Canada. Pierre's U.S. source income is calculated as follows:

U.S. source income = $550,000 x $\frac{174}{238}$

U.S. source income = $402,101

Although the time basis is generally determined by comparing the number of days worked within the U.S. to the total number of days worked by an employee, the regulations permit use of a unit of time that is less than a day where appropriate (e.g., in the case of an airline flight crew member).

*Geographic method for sourcing income.* There is an exception to the time basis rule for certain employee fringe benefits, which should be sourced on a geographic basis (e.g., at the employee's principal place of work). The fringe benefits to which this exception applies are:

- Housing – based on the employee's principal place of work – limited to rent, utilities (not phone charges), real and personal property insurance, occupancy taxes not otherwise deductible, non-refundable fees paid for securing a leasehold, rental of furniture and accessories, household repairs, residential parking, fair value of rental housing provided by the employer;
- Education – based on the employee's principal place of work – limited to tuition and expenses, room and board, and uniforms, for education at an elementary or secondary school;
- Local transportation – based on the employee's principal place of work – for the employee and the employee's family, limited to actual expenses incurred and fair rental value of a vehicle provided by the employer that is used primarily for local transportation, but not the cost of a vehicle bought by the employee;
- Tax reimbursement – based on the location of the jurisdiction that imposed the tax for which the employee is reimbursed;
- Hazardous or hardship duty pay – based on the location for which the hazardous or hardship duty pay is provided, and the pay is limited to what the U.S. government would pay its officers and employees at that location; and
- Moving expense reimbursements – generally based on the location of the employee's new principal place of work, unless the employee shows that using the employee's former principal place of work would be more appropriate under the circumstances.

*Note:* the amount of the fringe benefit must be both reasonable and adequately substantiated.

*Alternative methods for sourcing income.* Under the regulations, a different approach may be used to determine the source of compensation received by an employee in appropriate circumstances. For example, where an employee's compensation is tied to the performance of specific actions rather than earned over a specific time period, an alternative basis for determining the source of the compensation might be more appropriate.

In order to use an alternative basis for sourcing compensation, an employee must provide the IRS with information related to the alternative basis as required by applicable federal tax forms (to be issued). According to the IRS, it is expected that the forms and accompanying instructions will require individuals with $250,000 or more in compensation for the tax year to respond to questions on the form and attach to their income tax returns a written statement that describes:

- the specific compensation income, or the specific fringe benefit, for which an alternative method is used;
- for each such item, the alternative method of allocation of source used;
- for each such item, a computation showing how the alternative allocation was computed; and
- a comparison of the dollar amount of the compensation sourced inside and outside the U.S. under both the employee's alternative basis and the time or geographic basis.

Note that the IRS also has the flexibility to use an alternative basis for sourcing an employee's compensation if the IRS method would determine the source of the employee's income in a more reasonable manner than the method used by the employee.

 **WATCH OUT** In 2007, the IRS proposed an exception to the "time basis" method for determining the source of a nonresident alien employee's income for services performed both inside and outside the U.S. The proposed regulations would establish an "event basis" rule for sourcing the income of an artist or athlete who is compensated for labor or personal services provided at a specific event.[78] Check APA's biweekly membership payroll compliance newsletter, *Payroll Currently,* for updates. (Call 210-224-6406 or go to www.americanpayroll.org for information on how to join APA.)

*Multi-year compensation arrangements.* The source of compensation arrangements that relate to services performed over more than one year (e.g., stock option plans, transfers of restricted property, and other deferred compensation arrangements) is determined on a time basis over the period to which the compensation is attributable. Determination of the applicable period is based on the facts and circumstances of the particular case.

*Non-employees.* For individuals who are not employees, the source of compensation is determined based on the facts and circumstances of the particular case.

*Wages received in a different year than when earned.* Compensation received by a nonresident alien employee before or after the year it is earned is considered U.S. source income if it would have been U.S. source income if paid in the year earned. Therefore, a bonus paid in 2008 for work done in the U.S. in 2007 is taxable, U.S. source income when received by the employee.

**Independent contractors.** Payments to nonresident aliens who are independent contractors are subject to withholding at a flat 30% rate, unless they are exempt or the rate is reduced by a tax treaty provision.[79]

**Exceptions to the withholding rules.** There are several exceptions to the general withholding rules governing nonresident aliens, as well as special rules for residents of certain countries and U.S. possessions. Some of these are explained below.

*"Commercial travelers."*[80] Withholding is not required on small amounts of wages paid to nonresident aliens who are in the U.S. for a short period of time. The specific conditions that must be satisfied for this "commercial traveler" exception to apply are as follows:

- The nonresident alien employee is in the U.S. for no more than a total of 90 days during the taxable year;

- Compensation received for work performed in the U.S. totals no more than $3,000 during the taxable year; and

- The nonresident alien is employed by: a U.S. employer in a foreign country or a U.S. possession or by a foreign employer not engaged in a trade or business in the U.S.

---

78.   IRS Prop. Reg. §1.861-4(b)(2)(ii)(G).
79.   IRC §1441(a); IRS Reg. §1.1441-1.
80.   IRC §861(a)(3); §864(b)(1); IRS Reg. §1.861-4(a)(1); §1.864-2(b).

If the nonresident alien does not qualify for the commercial traveler exception, the employer must withhold federal income tax from the wages paid for services performed in the U.S. This may require an allocation where wages are paid for work performed inside and outside the U.S.

*Residents of Canada or Mexico.*[81] Compensation paid to residents of Canada or Mexico who frequently enter and leave the U.S. is not subject to federal income tax withholding if the residents are performing duties in transportation services or in building, operating, or maintaining an international project, such as a dam, bridge, or waterway crossing between the U.S. and Canada or Mexico. Qualified employees must submit a written, signed, and dated statement to the employer indicating the employee is not a U.S. citizen or resident, is a resident of Canada or Mexico, and expects to perform exempt duties during the tax year.

Residents of Canada or Mexico who work solely in the U.S. and commute to work from home or do not work in an exempt industry are subject to federal income tax withholding. However, they are not restricted to one withholding allowance on their Forms W-4.[82] They are governed by the same rules regarding withholding allowances as U.S. citizens and resident aliens.

*Residents of Puerto Rico.*[83] Compensation paid to nonresident aliens who are residents of Puerto Rico, for work performed in Puerto Rico, is not subject to federal income tax withholding (see Section 14.1-1). Also exempt are wages paid to such nonresident aliens who perform work outside the U.S. and Puerto Rico, but to qualify for this exemption the employee must submit a written, signed, and dated statement to the employer indicating the employee is not a U.S. citizen or resident and is a resident of Puerto Rico who does not expect to be a resident of Puerto Rico for that entire year.

A similar exemption is available to nonresident aliens who are residents of Puerto Rico for work performed outside the U.S. for the U.S. government or one of its agencies, but only if the employee does not expect to be a resident of Puerto Rico for the entire taxable year. To qualify for this exemption the employee must submit a written, signed, and dated statement to the employer indicating the employee is not a U.S. citizen or resident and is a resident of Puerto Rico who does not expect to be a resident of Puerto Rico for that entire year.

*Residents of South Korea.*[84] Nonresident aliens who are residents of South Korea may claim withholding allowances on their Forms W-4 for themselves, their spouses, and any dependent children living with them in the U.S. for at least part of the year. The allowances for an employee's spouse and children must be allocated based on the ratio of the employee's U.S. source income to his or her total income for the year.

**Earned income tax credit restrictions.** Earned Income Tax Credit (see Section 6.6) eligibility is denied to individuals who are nonresident aliens for any portion of a taxable year beginning after December 31, 1994.[85] There is an exception, however, for nonresident aliens who are married to a U.S. citizen or resident and who elect to be treated as a resident alien for income tax purposes under IRC §6013(g) or (h).

**Tax treaty exemptions.**[86] The U.S. has income tax treaties with more than 55 countries that exempt or reduce the amount of withholding from wages earned by nonresident aliens in the U.S. if certain conditions are met. Some treaties have different exemptions or reductions for income earned by independent contractors (independent personal services) and by employees (dependent personal services). An example of a treaty that treats both types of personal services similarly is the treaty between the U.S. and Australia. Under that treaty, nonresident aliens are exempt from taxation in the U.S. if they are in the U.S. for no more than 183 days during the taxable year, their compensation is paid by an Australian company, and the Australian company cannot deduct the compensation in determining its U.S. income.

---

81.   IRS Reg. §1.1441-4(b)(1)(iii); §31.3401(a)(6)-1(c).
82.   IRC §873(b)(3); IRS Reg. §1.873-1(c)(3); §31.3402(f)(6)-1.
83.   IRS Reg. §31.3401(a)(6)-1(d).
84.   Korea-U.S. Income Tax Treaty, 1979-2 CB 435.
85.   IRC §32(c)(1)(E).
86.   IRS Pub. 515, Withholding of Tax on Nonresident Aliens and Foreign Entities.

Some other common tax treaty benefits include:

*Professors and teachers.* Wages received by a nonresident alien teacher or professor in the U.S. are exempt from U.S. taxes under most treaties for temporary periods of up to 2 or 3 years.

*Students, trainees, and apprentices.* Amounts received by nonresident aliens for study, research or business and technical training are generally exempt from U.S. income tax. Grants and allowances from governmental and nonprofit organizations may also be exempt so long as they are not payments for work performed.

*Foreign government employees.* Each treaty has provisions exempting income earned by certain nonresident alien employees of foreign governments.

*Artists, athletes, and entertainers.* Most tax treaties allow entertainers and athletes to enter into "central withholding agreements" with the IRS that may provide for withholding below the IRC-required rate, but high enough to cover the entertainers' or athletes' anticipated U.S. income tax liability. The nonresident aliens must request such an agreement by submitting to the IRS information concerning the time period and events to be performed in the U.S., estimated gross income from the performances, and the agents who will be responsible for withholding from their income. Requests for a central withholding agreement should be sent at least 90 days before it is needed to: Central Withholding Agreement Program, IRS, SE:S:C:CP:IIC MS 0175, 1220 SW 3rd Ave., Portland, OR 97204. Some athletes and entertainers may be exempt from U.S. income tax under a tax treaty if their compensation and presence in the U.S. are within stated limits.

 **LEARNING ABOUT THE TREATIES** IRS Publication 515, Withholding of Tax on Nonresident Aliens and Foreign Corporations, contains general tax treaty information, as well as a table of tax treaties providing information about tax exemptions for nonresident aliens. The individual treaties are published in the Internal Revenue Bulletin and the Cumulative Bulletin (see Section 13.4-1), and some have been implemented through IRS regulations. More detailed explanations can also be found in IRS Publication 901, U.S. Tax Treaties, and IRS Publication 597, Information on the U.S.—Canada Income Tax Treaty.

Detailed summaries of the individual tax treaties between the U.S. and other countries can be found in the *Guide to Global Payroll Management*, published by the American Payroll Association. This volume also contains digests of the payroll withholding laws of more than 50 foreign countries. For information on how to order this and other APA publications, call 210-224-6406 or visit www.americanpayroll.org.

**Procedure for claiming exemptions.**[87] A nonresident alien employee or independent contractor who claims an exemption from tax under a provision of an income tax treaty must file Form 8233, *Exemption From Withholding on Compensation for Independent (and Certain Dependent) Personal Services of a Nonresident Alien Individual* (see Appendix page A-368), with the employer or payer of the compensation for services. The form must be mailed by the employer or payer for approval within 5 days of receipt to the IRS at this address: Internal Revenue Service, International Section, P.O. Box 920, Bensalem, PA 19020-8518.

A copy of Form 8233 must be given to the nonresident alien employee or independent contractor, and the employer or payer should keep one copy.

**Resident aliens may also claim treaty benefits.** Generally, only a nonresident alien may use the terms of a tax treaty to reduce or eliminate U.S. tax on certain types of income specified in the treaty. However, most tax treaties contain a provision known as a "saving clause." Exceptions specified in the saving clause may permit an exemption from tax to continue for certain types of income even after the recipient has become a U.S. resident alien for tax purposes.

---

87. IRS Reg. §1.1441-4(b)(2); §31.3401(a)(6)-1(f); Rev. Proc. 2005-44, 2005-29 IRB 110.

In order to claim the benefit, the resident alien must submit Form W-9, *Request for Taxpayer Identification Number and Certification* (see Appendix page A-116), along with an attachment that includes the following information:

- the treaty country (generally the same treaty under which you claimed exemption from tax as a nonresident alien);
- the treaty article addressing the income;
- the treaty article containing the saving clause and its exceptions;
- the type and amount of income that qualifies for the exemption from tax; and
- sufficient facts to justify the exemption from tax under the terms of the treaty article.

**Foreign students receiving scholarships or fellowships.** Scholarships and fellowships granted to nonresident alien students to cover tuition and related expenses (e.g., fees, books, supplies, and required equipment) are exempt from federal income tax withholding and reporting if the students are degree candidates and are temporarily in the U.S. as nonimmigrants under "F", "J", "M", or "Q" visas (see Section 14.3).[88] Payments that do not qualify for the exemption because they are unrelated to tuition (e.g., food, lodging, etc.) are subject to withholding at a rate of 14%.[89]

 **PAYMENTS FOR TEACHING MAY BE TAXED**[90] If a nonresident alien student receiving a scholarship or fellowship is required to perform teaching, research, or other work as a condition of receiving the scholarship, the student is receiving gross income unless all candidates for the same degree are required to do the same work. The income is determined by reference to payments made for similar work to individuals who are not receiving a scholarship or fellowship and is subject to withholding at regular rates.

If the nonresident alien student receiving scholarship or fellowship money is not a degree candidate, the payments are included in income and are subject to federal income tax withholding.[91] The withholding rate is 14% if the grantor is:

- a tax-exempt organization under IRC §501(c)(3);
- a federal, state, or local government agency;
- a foreign government;
- an international organization; or
- a binational or multinational educational and cultural foundation or commission created under the Mutual Educational and Cultural Exchange Act of 1961.

Otherwise, the withholding rate is 30%.[92]

*Special rule for nonresidents studying abroad.* Before determining whether the exclusion for scholarship or fellowship money applies, an initial determination must be made as to whether the money is U.S. source income. If not, the grant money is not included in income regardless of the scholarship exclusion. Scholarships and fellowships awarded by a U.S. citizen, company, or governmental agency constitute U.S. source income and are subject to federal income tax withholding unless the activities will be conducted by a nonresident alien outside the U.S. Such amounts are income from sources outside the U.S.[93]

Scholarships and fellowships awarded by a foreign government, corporation, or resident, or an international organization are considered income from sources outside the U.S., and therefore are not taxable when awarded to nonresident aliens.[94]

---

88.      IRC §117(a), (b).
89.      IRC §1441(b)(1); IRS Reg. §1.1441-2(c)(1).
90.      IRC §117(c).
91.      IRC §117(a).
92.      IRC §1441(b)(2).
93.      IRS Reg. §1.863-1(d)(2)(i); (iii).
94.      IRS Reg. §1.863-1(d)(ii).

*Form W-4 option.*[95] When nonresident alien students receive taxable income from scholarships or fellowships (other than for teaching or other services), the basic withholding rate is 14%. However, the IRS allows such students to reduce that rate by filing a Form W-4 with the payer. While the student is limited to claiming single filing status with one personal exemption as a nonresident alien (unless the student is from Canada, Mexico, or Korea or is a U.S. national), the student may be eligible to claim other allowances based on deductions that can be taken related to the U.S. source income (e.g., travel expenses). A new Form W-4 must be filed each year, along with a statement that the student filed a U.S. tax return for the previous year or will file one for the current year.

*Wages paid by a foreign employer.* Wages paid by a foreign employer to a nonresident alien while the alien is temporarily in the U.S. on an "F", "J", "M," or "Q" visa (see Section 14.3) are exempt from federal income tax. A foreign employer can be a foreign individual, partnership, or corporation or an office of a U.S. entity maintained in a foreign country or U.S. possession.

To qualify for the exclusion the nonresident alien must file a statement with the employer claiming the exemption. The statement must:

- be provided in duplicate;
- contain the alien's name, address, and taxpayer identification number;
- certify that the alien is not a citizen or resident of the U.S. and that the income to be paid is exempt from federal income tax (as well as why it is exempt);
- be dated;
- identify the tax year and the income to which it applies; and
- signed by the alien including a written declaration that it is made under the penalty of perjury.

**Treaty benefits.**[96] Many income tax treaties provide exemptions from U.S. tax for nonresident alien students, teachers, and researchers. To claim the exemption and avoid federal income tax withholding, on wages, the alien must file Form 8233 in duplicate with the payer. One copy must be sent by the payer to the IRS at the address mentioned earlier. Any nonresident alien who claims that part or all of a scholarship or fellowship is exempt from income tax because of a treaty must file Form W-8BEN, *Certificate of Foreign Status of Beneficial Owner for United States Tax Withholding* (see Appendix page A-108) with the payer. If the nonresident alien is claiming treaty benefits in regard to both compensation and a scholarship or fellowship, he or she should file Form 8233 for both.

# 14.2-4 Social Security and Medicare Taxes for Nonresident Aliens

With several important exceptions, social security and Medicare taxes generally apply to all wages paid for work performed in the U.S., regardless of the citizenship or residency status of the employee or the employer.[97] This is true for nonresident aliens even though the particular employee may be exempt from federal income tax under the IRC. Following are several exceptions to this general rule.

**Nonresident alien students.** Amounts earned by nonresident aliens who are temporarily in the U.S. as students, scholars, or exchange visitors under an "F," "J," "M," or "Q" visa (see Section 14.3) are not subject to social security or Medicare tax if the work they perform is carried out to further the purpose for which they entered the U.S.[98] The exemption does not extend to the spouse or children of such nonresident aliens, who may be admitted to the U.S. under a derivative visa.

Scholarships and fellowships granted to nonresident alien students are exempt from social security and Medicare taxes to the same extent they are exempt from federal income tax withholding.[99]

---

95.  IRS Reg.§1.1441-4(c)(2);  Rev. Proc. 88-24, 1988-1 CB 800.
96.  IRS Reg. §1.1441-4(b)(2).
97.  IRC §3121(b).
98.  IRC §3121(b)(19); IRS Reg. §31.3121(b)(19)-1.
99.  IRC §3121(a)(20).

**Agricultural workers.**[100] Foreign agricultural workers who are admitted to the U.S. temporarily are not subject to social security or Medicare tax.

**Work performed on foreign ships or planes.**[101] Wages earned for work performed on ships or planes that are not American are not subject to social security or Medicare tax if the work is performed outside the U.S. and the employee is not a U.S. citizen or the employer is not a U.S. company.

**Work performed for a foreign government.** Nonresident aliens working for a foreign government are exempt from social security or Medicare tax, whether or not the foreign government grants an equivalent exemption to U.S. citizens working for the U.S. government.[102] If the nonresident alien is working for an instrumentality of the foreign government, there is no exemption from social security or Medicare tax unless the foreign government grants an equivalent exemption to U.S. citizens working for the U.S. government or its instrumentalities.[103]

**International organizations.** Nonresident aliens working for an international organization (e.g., NATO) in the U.S. are not subject to social security or Medicare tax.[104]

**Totalization agreements.**[105] To alleviate the burden of double social security taxation and to integrate coverage of employees, the U.S. government has entered into binational social security agreements, also known as "totalization" agreements, with several European countries, Australia, Chile, Japan, Republic of Korea, and Canada. Under a totalization agreement, nonresident aliens working "temporarily" (less than five years) in the U.S. would be subject to social security tax in their country of residence only. Wages earned by nonresident alien employees working "permanently" in the U.S. would be subject only to U.S. social security and Medicare taxes (see Section 14.1-2).

Nonresident aliens claiming to be exempt from U.S. social security tax must give their employer proof of their coverage under their home country's social security system. Generally, this comes in the form of a "certificate of coverage" issued by the home country's social security agency that must be retained by the employer and shows the beginning and ending date of the exemption. If the home country will not provide it, the employee must get a special certificate showing the exemption from the SSA's Office of International Programs.

## 14.2-5 Federal Unemployment Tax for Nonresident Aliens

In general, federal unemployment (FUTA) tax applies to all wages paid for work performed in the U.S., regardless of the citizenship or residency status of the employee or the employer.[106] This is true for nonresident aliens even though the particular employee may be exempt from federal income tax under the IRC. The exemptions from FUTA for wages received and work performed by nonresident aliens in the U.S. are generally the same as those under social security and Medicare taxes (see Section 14.2-4), although there are no international agreements, such as totalization agreements, exempting temporary employment by a nonresident alien in the U.S.[107]

**Agricultural workers.** Wages earned by nonresident alien agricultural workers temporarily admitted to the U.S. under "H" visas are exempt from FUTA.[108]

---

100. IRC §3121(b)(1).
101. IRC §3121(b)(4).
102. IRC §3121(b)(11); IRS Reg. §31.3121(b)(11)-1.
103. IRC §3121(b)(12); IRS Reg. §31.3121(b)(12)-1.
104. IRC §3121(b)(15); IRS Reg. §31.3121(b)(15)-1.
105. Social Security Act §233, 42 USC §433; IRS Pub. 54, Tax Guide for U.S. Citizens and Resident Aliens Abroad.
106. IRC §3306(c); IRS Reg. §31.3306(c)-2.
107. IRC §3306(c)(4), (c)(11), (c)(12), (c)(16), (c)(19); IRS Reg. §31.3306(c)(4)-1; (c)(11)-1; (c)(12)-1; (c)(16)-1; (c)(18)-1.
108. IRC §3306(c)(1)(B).

## 14.2-6 Depositing and Reporting Obligations

Businesses paying compensation to nonresident aliens face different depositing and reporting obligations depending on whether the compensation is paid to an employee or a nonemployee and what type of compensation is paid.

**Wages paid to employees.** If an employer pays wages to a nonresident alien employee, the amounts withheld for federal income, social security, and Medicare taxes, as well as the employer share of social security and Medicare taxes, must be deposited according to the general rules (see Section 8.2). The wages paid and taxes withheld and deposited must be reported on Form 941, *Employer's Quarterly Federal Tax Return* (see Section 8.3), along with amounts related to the employer's other employees. Annually, each employee must be sent a Form W-2, *Wage and Tax Statement* (see Section 8.8), reporting the individual employee's wages and withheld taxes.

**Other compensation.**[109] Compensation paid to independent contractors for services, plus other non-wage income (e.g., scholarship money that is not excluded), may also be subject to withholding, but the depositing and reporting rules are not the same.

*Deposit requirements.*[110] Amounts withheld from nonwage income paid to nonresident aliens must be deposited in an authorized financial institution using Form 8109, *Federal Tax Deposit Coupon* (see Appendix page A-366), with the oval next to "1042" darkened or through the Electronic Federal Tax Payment System. (See Section 8.2-2 for electronic tax deposit requirements.) The deposits must be made according to the following schedule:

- If the "withholding agent" has a tax liability of $2,000 or more at the end of any quarter-monthly period (ending on the 7th, 15th, 22nd, and last day of the month), the withheld amount must be deposited within 3 banking days after the period ends. There is a 90% safe-harbor rule, and the payer complies if the shortfall is made up by the first deposit required after the 15th of the following month. However, any shortfall of at least $200 in December must be deposited by January 31 of the following year.

- If the tax liability is at least $200 but less than $2,000 at the end of any month, the deposit is due by the 15th of the next month. If a deposit is made under the quarter-monthly rule during a month other than December, any balance of less than $2,000 can be carried over to the next month. If a quarter-monthly deposit is made in December, any balance of less than $2,000 should be paid to the IRS with Form 1042 by its due date of March 15 (see discussion following).

- If the tax liability at the end of any month other than December is less than $200, the liability can be carried over to the next month.

- If the tax liability at the end of the calendar year is under $200, the amount can be paid with Form 1042 or deposited by its due date (see discussion following).

*Reporting requirements.* Amounts paid and taxes withheld from nonwage compensation must be reported by the payer annually on Form 1042, *Annual Withholding Tax Return for U.S. Source Income of Foreign Persons*, (see Appendix page A-230). All such income must be included on Form 1042 even if no taxes were withheld because of an IRC or tax treaty exemption. The form must be filed by March 15 of the year following the year to which it relates. It should be sent to: Ogden Service Center, P.O. Box 409101, Ogden, UT 84409.

For all income received by a nonresident alien that does not have to be reported on a Form W-2, the payer must send each alien, as well as the IRS, Form 1042-S, *Foreign Person's U.S. Source Income Subject to Withholding* (see Appendix page A-234). The due date for sending Form 1042-S to the IRS is also March 15, and paper forms should be sent with Form 1042-T, *Annual Summary and Transmittal of Forms 1042-S* (see Appendix page A-254) to the IRS's Ogden Service Center. Copy A of the Form 1042-S goes to the IRS, while

---

109.   IRS Pub. 515, Withholding of Tax on Nonresident Aliens and Foreign Entities.
110.   IRS Reg. §1.6302-2.

Copies B and C must be sent to the payee. All nonwage income must be reported on the Form 1042-S, even if no income tax was withheld because of a tax treaty or other exemption. Substitute forms can be used with prior IRS approval or if they meet the specifications set out in IRS Publication 1179.[111]

 **BE CAREFUL** The IRS warns employers to take extra care in entering the country name and code for the nonresident alien's latest country of legal residence on Form 1042-S.

*Electronic filing of Forms 1042-S.* If a withholding agent has 250 or more Forms 1042-S to file, it must do so electronically. Beginning with 2008 Forms 1042-S filed in 2009, the IRS will no longer accept magnetic media filings. (See Section 8.14 for generally applicable electronic reporting procedures.) A completed Form 4419, *Application for Filing Information Returns Electronically* (see Appendix page A-350), should be filed with the IRS's Enterprise Computing Center-Martinsburg at least 30 days before the due date of the return, since electronic filing will not be accepted without IRS approval. Employers required to file electronically must file over the Internet through the IRS' FIRE system at http://fire.irs.gov. A paper Form 1042 must be completed and filed with the IRS even if Forms 1042-S are filed electronically, but Form 1042-T should not be sent with an electronic filing. If you have questions, call IRS/ECC-MTB at 304-263-8700 or 866-455-7438 (toll-free), from 8:30 am - 4:30 pm Eastern time or send an e-mail to mccirp@irs.gov.[112]

 **SATURDAYS, SUNDAYS, AND HOLIDAYS** If any due date for depositing or reporting taxes or wages related to nonresident aliens falls on a Saturday, Sunday, or legal holiday, the due date is extended until the next business day.

Extensions of the deadline for filing Form 1042-S on paper or electronically can be requested by filing Form 8809, *Application for Extension of Time to File Information Returns*, by March 15. Payers can get an automatic extension for 30 days. A second 30-day extension may be obtained if a second Form 8809 is filed before the end of the initial extension and the payer signs the form and provides the reason for needing the extension. Form 8809 can also be filed on magnetic media or electronically, and a transmitter seeking an extension for more than 50 withholding agents must do so. An approved extension of time to file Form 1042-S electronically does not extend the time for providing a paper copy to the payee. Such extensions can be obtained only by sending a letter specifying the reason for the request to the IRS Enterprise Computing Center-Martinsburg by the due date, and they generally last a maximum of only 15 days. Extensions of the deadline for filing Form 1042 can be requested by filing Form 7004, *Application for Automatic 6-Month Extension of Time to File Certain Business Income Tax, Information, and Other Returns* (see Appendix page A-354) with the Ogden Service Center or electronically.

Magnetically filed extension of time requests should be sent to:

IRS-Enterprise Computing Center-Martinsburg
Information Reporting Program
Attn: Extension of Time Coordinator
240 Murall Drive
Kearneysville, WV 25430

For information on obtaining a hardship waiver of the Form 1042-S electronic reporting requirement, see Section 8.14.

*Penalties for late filing and deposits.* The penalty for late filing of Form 1042 is usually 5% of the tax that should have been shown on the return for each month or part of a month the return is late, up to 25% of the unpaid tax. The penalty for filing a late and/or incorrect Form 1042-S depends on when a correct form is filed. The penalty for each form is:

* $15 if the correct form is filed within 30 days, up to a maximum of $75,000 ($25,000 for a small business);

---

111. Rev. Proc. 2007-50, 2007-31 IRB 244.
112. Rev. Proc. 2006-34, 2006-38 IRB 460; IRS Pub. 1187, Specifications for Filing Forms 1042-S, Foreign Person's U.S. Source Income Subject to Withholding, Electronically or Magnetically.

- $30 if the correct form is filed by August 1, up to a maximum of $150,000 ($50,000 for a small business);
- $50 if the correct form is filed after August 1 or no correct form is filed, up to a maximum of $250,000 ($100,000 for a small business).

The penalty for failing to provide a complete and correct Form 1042-S to each nonresident alien is $50 per statement up to $100,000. If the requirement is intentionally disregarded, the penalty becomes the greater of $100 per statement or 10% of the total amounts to be reported on all statements.

If a deposit is late or only part of the deposit is paid, a penalty is assessed on the amount of the underpayment unless the payer can show the failure to deposit in full and on time was due to reasonable cause and not willful neglect. The penalty is:

- 2% of the underpayment if the deposit is made within 5 days of the due date;
- 5% of the underpayment if the deposit is made within 6-15 days of the due date;
- 10% of the underpayment if the deposit is made more than 15 days after the due date; or
- 15% of the underpayment if the deposit is not made within 10 days after the IRS issues the first notice demanding payment.

 **HELP IS AVAILABLE** Employers that need assistance with the reporting of nonresident alien withholding, magnetic media filing, and processing requirements should contact: Enterprise Computing Center-Martinsburg, Information Reporting Program; telephone (304) 263-8700 or (866) 455-7438 (toll-free); fax (304) 264-5602.

## 14.2-7 State Tax Issues for Nonresident Aliens

Compensation paid to nonresident aliens will generally be subject to state and local income taxes if the work was performed within the state, although most states require a minimum stay within the state below which taxes are not assessed. Also, because a state's definition of residency may be different than that under the Internal Revenue Code (see Section 14.1-7), an employee might be a nonresident alien for federal income tax purposes and a state resident for state tax purposes. For this reason, employers must pay particular attention to state residency tests when bringing in foreign nationals.

*Example 1:* In New Jersey, a resident is anyone who is domiciled in the state or who spends more than 183 days in the state during the year and has a permanent place of abode in the state.

*Example 2:* In Illinois, a resident is anyone who resides in Illinois for other than a temporary or transitory purpose, or who is domiciled in Illinois and leaves the state only for a temporary or transitory purpose.

*Example 3:* In Kentucky, a resident is anyone who is domiciled in the state or who spends 183 days in the state during the year and has a permanent place of abode in Kentucky.

## 14.3 Types of Visas

There are basically two types of visas for foreign nationals seeking admission to the U.S.—immigrant visas and nonimmigrant visas. Immigrant visas are sought by individuals who wish to become lawful permanent residents of the U.S., while nonimmigrant visas are sought by those who are in the country for a more temporary reason. This section will provide a brief explanation of most of the different types of visas an employer should be familiar with.

**Immigrant visas ("Green Cards").** Immigrant visas, or "green cards" are issued to foreign nationals entering the U.S. as lawful permanent residents or who become lawful permanent residents. An immigrant visa is an I-551 Permanent Resident Card, formerly called the Alien Registration Receipt Card or Resident

Alien Card. Forms I-551 with these earlier names are valid until their expiration date. When presented by a newly hired employee, it proves both identity and authorization to work under the Immigration Reform and Control Act.

 **WATCH OUT** Old green cards (Form I-151) are no longer valid proof of immigrant status, identity, and employment eligibility. Lawful permanent resident aliens should have Form I-551, which has the bearer's photograph, signature, and fingerprint, plus other security features.

**Nonimmigrant visas.** Nonimmigrant or temporary visas are issued to foreign nationals who wish to enter the U.S. for a specific purpose and will not be in the country indefinitely. They may, however, qualify as resident aliens under the substantial presence test (see Section 14.2-1), so employers should not assume they are nonresident aliens for tax purposes. Following is a partial listing of nonimmigrant visas in alphabetical order.

_B-1, Visitors for business._ This visa is used by students, workers, or foreign press representatives being paid by a foreign employer. The visa lasts one year, with six month extensions possible.

_D-1, Foreign crewmen._ This visa is for foreign crewmen on an aircraft or sea vessel. They can work only on the aircraft or vessel on which they arrived or on an aircraft or vessel owned by the same transportation company.

_E-1, Treaty traders._ This visa is used by traders (and their spouses and children) in the U.S. only to carry on trade between the U.S. and the visa holder's home country if that country has a commercial treaty relationship with the U.S. The visa is for 1 year, with 2-year extensions. The traders can work only for their sponsoring employers, while their spouses are authorized for employment without restrictions, and their dependents generally may not work in the U.S. at all.

_E-2, Investors._ This visa is open to foreign investors (and their spouses and children) who are in the U.S. to direct a business in which they have invested or will invest a substantial amount of money. The visa is for 1 year, with 2-year extensions. The investors can work only for their sponsoring employers, while their spouses are authorized for employment without restrictions, and their dependents generally may not work in the U.S. at all.

_E-3, Specialty occupations._ This visa is for residents of Australia coming to the U.S. to work in specialty occupations, and their spouses and dependents. The definition of "specialty occupation" is similar to that for H-1B visas (see below). The visa is limited to 10,500 individuals annually, not counting spouses and children.

_F-1, Students._ This visa is used by full-time students at an approved U.S. educational institution. The students can work in work-study programs that further their academic program, with the earnings being exempt from social security, Medicare, and FUTA taxes. Under a pilot program, holders of F-1 visas can take part-time jobs off-campus under certain conditions designed to ensure that they are not being hired at low wages and taking jobs from American workers. The students must have at least nine months in school and cannot work more than 20 hours in the off-campus job while school is in session. Where labor shortages are proven or the student faces economic hardship, part-time jobs up to 20 hours a week may be secured outside the pilot program if the student has at least one year at school.

Midway through 1998, the INS (predecessor to USCIS) announced that nonresident alien students from Indonesia, Malaysia, South Korea, Thailand, and the Philippines may work more than 20 hours per week without losing their F-1 visa status. The rules were relaxed because of the severe economic problems in these countries. The USCIS also allowed the students to reduce their work loads to 6 credit hours per semester for undergraduate study and 3 credit hours per semester for graduate study.

_H-1B, Specialty workers._ This visa is open to college-educated or experienced professionals in specialty occupations and fashion models and lasts for one year with one-year extensions available. An H-1B visa can be given where the occupation requires highly specialized knowledge and at least a bachelor's degree (valid for no more than 3 years). For researchers for the Department of Defense (H-1B2), the visa is valid up to 5 years; up to 6 years for fashion models (H-1B3). H-1B1 visas are treated the same as H-1B visas, but are issued only to nationals of Chile and Singapore. H-1C visas are available to registered nurses for 3 years, with one 2-year extension. H-1C and H-1B visa holders can work only for the sponsoring employer. Spouses and dependents are admitted under the H-4 classification and are not authorized for employment.

*J-1, Exchange visitors.* This visa is available to students, trainees, and teachers who are in the U.S. to participate in an exchange program. The visa lasts for 1-5 years and exempts the holder from social security, Medicare, and FUTA taxes. The spouse and children of the visa holder may not work without USCIS authorization.

*L-1 (A and B), Intracompany transfers.* These visas are sought when a company wants to temporarily transfer executives or professionals whose jobs require specialized knowledge to a U.S. branch or affiliate. The visa lasts 3 years, with extensions available to 7 years for managers and executives, 5 years for workers in a specialized field of knowledge.

*M-1, Nonacademic or vocational students.* M-1 visa holders can take temporary jobs for practical training related to their course of study. The visa is available for 1 year or the period of time it takes to complete the course of study, plus 30 days to depart.

*O-1 and O-2, Extraordinary ability.* Employers wishing to bring aliens of extraordinary ability in the arts, sciences, education, or athletics to the U.S. can seek this visa. Aliens accompanying the visa holder as part of the visa holder's support staff can get an O-2 visa. The visa is valid for the period stated on the petition, plus 10 days before and after. One-year extensions are available.

*P-1, etc., Entertainers, athletes.* Athletes, artists, or entertainers with this visa can work only for the employer that sought the visa. The visa is valid for 5 years for individual athletes, 1 year for members of a team or artists or entertainers. Aliens accompanying the visa holder as part of the visa holder's support staff can enter the U.S. under the same status.

*Q, Cultural exchange visitors.* Nonimmigrants entering the U.S. as part of a cultural exchange program can work for the employer seeking the visa if the program provides training and employment and shares the history and culture of the alien's country. The visa is valid for the duration of the program, but extensions are available.

*R-1, Religious occupations.* These visas can be obtained by aliens in religious occupations, but they can be employed only by the religious organization that sponsored them. The total stay may not exceed 5 years.

*TN, NAFTA professionals.* This visa is for Canadian and Mexican professionals working under the North America Free Trade Agreement. The visa is valid for 1 year, with 1-year extensions, and the visa holder can work only for the sponsoring employer. The spouse and children of the visa holder can enter the U.S. with a TD visa but cannot work in the U.S.

## 14.4 Review Questions and Answers

### Review Questions

1. Name two things that reasonable housing expenses do not include.

2. How does the IRS define a "tax home"?

3. What factors determine whether an expatriate employee is a bona fide resident of a foreign country?

4. How do U.S. citizens and resident aliens qualify for the foreign earned income exclusion under the physical presence test?

5. What types of income constitute "foreign earned income"?

6. What are totalization agreements?

7. What are some common income tax treaty benefits?

8. What is an education allowance?

9. What are tax protection plans?

10. What are tax equalization plans?

11. What factors determine an employee's domicile?

12. What factors determine an employee's residence?

13. How do employers determine if employees are resident or nonresident aliens?

14. What factors determine an alien's status under the substantial presence test?

15. What special conditions must be satisfied for "commercial travelers" to be exempt from federal income tax withholding?

### True or False Questions

_____ 1. Wages earned abroad by a U.S. citizen or resident alien may be exempt from federal income tax withholding if the employer is required to withhold foreign taxes under the law of the foreign country.

_____ 2. U.S. citizens and resident alien employees working outside the U.S. can exclude up to $80,000 of foreign earned income from their gross income in 2008.

_____ 3. U.S. citizens and resident alien employees working for companies outside the U.S. may exclude certain housing costs from their gross income.

_____ 4. For purposes of the foreign earned income exclusion, Guam is considered to be a foreign country.

_____ 5. An employee cannot have a foreign tax home if he or she regularly lives in the U.S.

_____ 6.   Employees on foreign assignments expected to last more than one year are on indefinite assignment and maintain a foreign tax home.

_____ 7.   Travel and living expense reimbursements for employees on a temporary foreign assignment must be included in income.

_____ 8.   An employee can be a bona fide resident of a foreign country even though he or she intends to return to the U.S. at the end of the foreign assignment.

_____ 9.   Foreign earned income is considered to be income in the year it was earned, not in the year in which it is paid.

_____ 10.  Expenses incurred for a move from the U.S. to a foreign country are not included in foreign earned income.

_____ 11.  Under a totalization agreement, expatriate employees working temporarily in a foreign country are subject only to U.S. social security tax, not the social security taxes of the foreign country.

_____ 12.  Expatriates are U.S. citizens or resident aliens working abroad.

_____ 13.  The foreign earned income exclusion is only available to one spouse even if both have foreign earned income.

_____ 14.  For state income tax purposes, nonresidents are taxed only on their income from state sources.

_____ 15.  The determination of residency made under the Internal Revenue Code applies to an alien's status for U.S. income tax purposes.

_____ 16.  Lawful permanent residents of the U.S. are considered residents for income tax purposes.

_____ 17.  The substantial presence test has nothing to do with the alien's intent to stay in the U.S.

_____ 18.  Under IRCA, nonresident aliens are required to produce their social security cards as proof of authorization to work in the U.S.

_____ 19.  Nonresident aliens exempt from federal income tax are also exempt from social security and Medicare taxes.

_____ 20.  Employers are required to pay FUTA tax on wages paid to nonresident aliens working in the U.S.

_____ 21.  If a withholding agent has 250 or more Forms 1042-S to file, it must do so electronically.

_____ 22.  Immigrant visas are sought by individuals who wish to become lawful permanent residents of the U.S.

## Multiple Choice Questions

_____ 1.  What is the maximum amount that can be exlcuded from gross income under the foreign earned income exclusion for 2008?

    a.  $80,000
    b.  $85,700
    c.  $87,600
    d.  Cannot exclude income earned abroad

_____ 2.  Which of the following entities is a foreign country for purposes of qualifying for the §911 exclusions?

    a.  Puerto Rico
    b.  Mexico
    c.  Guam
    d.  Virgin Islands

_____ 3.  What is the maximum that a temporary foreign assignment can realistically be expected to last?

    a.  3 months
    b.  6 months
    c.  9 months
    d.  12 months

_____ 4.  Which of the following facts does not indicate the intent to meet the bona fide residence test?

    a.  Purchase of a home or signing a long-term lease in a foreign country
    b.  A temporary assignment of up to three months
    c.  Involvement in the cultural and social life of a foreign country
    d.  The type of visa or residence permit secured by the employee

_____ 5.  What form is filed to claim bona fide resident status?

    a.  Form 1042
    b.  Form 2442
    c.  Form 2555
    d.  Form 1116

_____ 6.  What is the place the employee intends to return to after a foreign assignment?

    a.  Tax home
    b.  Vacation home
    c.  Residence
    d.  Domicile

_____ 7.  How many days must an individual be present in a foreign country over a 12-month period to qualify for the foreign earned income exclusion under the physical presence test?

    a.  365 days
    b.  330 days
    c.  120 days
    d.  90 days

_____ 8.   Which of the following payments is not foreign earned income?

      a.   Professional fees
      b.   Social security benefits
      c.   Tax reimbursements
      d.   Cost of living allowances

_____ 9.   Which of the following costs is not a reasonable housing expense?

      a.   Occupancy taxes
      b.   Fees paid for securing a house
      c.   Furniture rental
      d.   Cost of domestic labor

_____ 10.   What percentage of the maximum foreign earned income exclusion is used to determine the base housing amount?

      a.   14%
      b.   16%
      c.   18%
      d.   30%

_____ 11.   Employee Sam qualifies for the foreign housing cost exclusion under the physical presence test for all of 2008, spending $21,250 on reasonable housing expenses. On January 1, 2008, the maximum foreign earned income exclusion was $87,600. What is Sam's foreign housing cost exclusion for 2008?

      a.   $7,234
      b.   $21,250
      c.   $14,016
      d.   $87,600

_____ 12.   During 2008, Matt qualified for the foreign housing cost exclusion under the physical presence test for 335 days, spending $15,000 on reasonable housing expenses. The maximum foreign earned income exclusion on January 1, 2008 was $87,600  What was Matt's base housing amount for 2008?

      a.   $14,016
      b.   $1,149
      c.   $12,831
      d.   $2,169

_____ 13.   With which of the following countries does the U.S. not have a totalization agreement?

      a.   Belgium
      b.   Finland
      c.   New Zealand
      d.   Sweden

_____ 14.   What is the term for the income tax an employee would have paid if the employee had remained in the U.S. rather than taking a foreign assignment?

      a.   Hypothetical tax
      b.   Excise tax
      c.   Equalization tax
      d.   Gift tax

_____ 15. What income earned by resident aliens is subject to federal income tax?

     a.    U.S. income
     b.    Foreign income
     c.    World-wide income
     d.    Unearned income

_____ 16. Employee Ben, an alien, is present in the U.S. for 155 days during the current year, 123 days during the first preceding year, and 144 days in the second preceding year. How many days is Ben present in the U.S. during the current year under the substantial presence test?

     a.    150 days
     b.    220 days
     c.    223 days
     d.    365 days

_____ 17. Foreign students receiving scholarships or fellowships are not exempt from federal income tax withholding when holding what visa?

     a.    F-1
     b.    J-1
     c.    M-1
     d.    B-1

_____ 18. Which of the following visas is an immigrant visa?

     a.    B-1
     b.    F-1
     c.    H-1
     d.    I-551

_____ 19. What visa is available to students or teachers on an exchange program?

     a.    J-1
     b.    L-1
     c.    O-1
     d.    P-1

_____ 20. Employers wishing to bring aliens of extraordinary ability in the arts, sciences, education, or athletics to the U.S. seek what visa?

     a.    B-1
     b.    H-1
     c.    O-1
     d.    Q-1

# SECTION 15: PREPARING FOR THE CPP EXAM

TABLE OF CONTENTS

# SECTION 15: PREPARING FOR THE CPP EXAM

In recent years, the pressures of economic and legislative developments on the payroll function have broadened the scope of payroll beyond its basic purpose of paying employees. Today's professional uses the latest electronic processing technologies for executing the payroll and interfaces with other functions in the organization. During the same time, payroll has come under a wide array of mandates, from the federal income tax withholding that affects nearly all employees to salary deferrals into retirement plans, new hire reporting, Sarbanes-Oxley Act compliance, and child support withholding. Among all the internal operations of contemporary U.S. business, none are subject to as many governmental regulations and requirements as payroll.

## 15.1 History and Purpose of Certification

Originally a technical skill, payroll has developed into today's professional discipline. Payroll professionals are knowledgeable in all aspects of payroll, stay abreast of changes in processing technologies and, through independent research, remain current with the legislative and regulatory environment applicable to their business. A payroll professional must be proficient in all aspects of taxation and tax reporting, information technology, human resources (including benefits), and accounting as each of these relate to the payroll environment. Today's payroll professional functions as an integral member of the management team, involved in many issues which affect today's corporate operations. Since 1985, the American Payroll Association (APA) has offered the Certified Payroll Professional (CPP) certification to recognize those who have achieved a professional skill level.

**Certification criteria**. Certification is the recognition of one's professional skills by one's peers. The Certified Payroll Professional designation is awarded by APA to those who:

1. meet the eligibility requirements for admission to the examination,
2. successfully complete the examination, and
3. subscribe to the APA Code of Ethics.

Certification is granted for a five-year period, at which time recertification is required to maintain the designation.

**CPP Committee oversees program**. APA's Certification Program is administered by APA's Certification Board, which is made up of the Certified Payroll Professional (CPP) Committee and the Fundamental Payroll Certification (FPC) Committee. (See Section 15.16 for more on the FPC designation). The CPP Committee consists of six Certified Payroll Professionals serving staggered two-year terms. APA has contracted with Pearson VUE to administer the exam so that it meets accepted testing standards.

The goals of the APA CPP Committee's certification program are:

* to promote the standard for payroll professionals that is accepted by the business community and the public at large;

* to encourage professional growth and individual study by the payroll professional;

* to provide the standard of requisite knowledge for the payroll professional;

* to measure by means of the CPP examination the attainment and application of that standard; and

- to recognize formally those colleagues who continue to meet the requirements of the APA CPP Committee.

Members of the APA's Certification Advisory Group assist the CPP Committee by writing questions for possible inclusion in APA's bank of payroll test questions. The questions are reviewed by editors at Pearson VUE to ensure compliance with accepted question-writing techniques. The edited questions are then reviewed and revised, if necessary, by the CPP Committee and Pearson VUE for accuracy and relevancy to the activities of experienced payroll professionals. Approved questions are then included in the bank of questions from which exam questions are selected to create new examination forms for each exam.

 **NEW METHODS OF TESTING, RECERTIFICATION** As part of its ongoing effort to boost the professionalism and recognition of payroll practitioners, the American Payroll Association has made some significant changes over the years in the methods and processes it uses to certify and recertify payroll professionals. Candidates for CPP Examination now take the test electronically and can choose the day on which they take the test, within a given testing period.

Also, for Certified Payroll Professionals who seek to recertify through continuing education, the process for doing so has been streamlined to make recertification less of an administrative burden. Other changes have been made to ensure the continuing integrity of the recertification process. Be sure to read the following sections closely, and look for more detailed information in the CPP Examination Handbook and in recertification information sent to each CPP by the APA.

## 15.2 Examination Eligibility Requirements

APA's CPP Committee has expanded the CPP examination eligibility criteria to include "related experience" in the practice of payroll, which is now defined to include the areas of Payroll Systems and Payroll Taxation. Also, based on the level of payroll-related experience and management-level work, payroll professionals may qualify to sit for the exam by obtaining additional education.

APA's CPP Committee requires that payroll professionals fulfill one of the following criteria before they can become eligible to take the CPP exam:

*Criteria 1.* The payroll professional has been practicing payroll a total of at least three years out of the five years preceding the date of the examination. The practice of payroll is defined as direct or related involvement in at least one of the following:

- Payroll Production, Payroll Reporting, Payroll Accounting, Payroll Systems, or Payroll Taxation
- Payroll Administration
- Payroll Education/Consulting

*Criteria 2.* Prior to sitting for the examination, the payroll professional has been employed in the practice of payroll as defined in Criteria 1 for at least the last 24 months, and has completed within the last 24 months all of the following courses offered by the APA:

- Payroll Practice Essentials (3-day course),
- Comprehensive Payroll and Tax Compliance (3-day course offered through the end of 2006) – or Intermediate Payroll Concepts (2-day course) and Advanced Payroll Concepts (2-day course),
- Strategic Payroll Practices (2-day course)

OR

- Payroll 101: The Standard Foundation of Payroll Administration and
- Payroll 201: The Payroll Administration Course

*Criteria 3.* Before sitting for the examination, the payroll professional has been employed in the practice of payroll as defined in Criteria 1 for at least the last 18 months, has obtained the Fundamental Payroll Certification, and has completed within the last 18 months all of the following courses offered by APA:

- Comprehensive Payroll and Tax Compliance (3-day course offered through the end of 2006) – or Intermediate Payroll Concepts (2-day course) and Advanced Payroll Concepts (2-day course), and
- Strategic Payroll Practices (2-day course)

OR

- Payroll 201: The Payroll Administration Course

Eligibility criteria should not be considered as the only criteria for preparation for the CPP exam. Candidates for the CPP exam, qualifying through any of the criteria, should be aware that a number of study aids are available as added preparation. No one source should be considered the only basis for preparation. Successful candidates indicate that they pursued a three-month course of study and review based on the CPP Exam Content Outline.

Payroll professionals who are currently certified and are recertifying through examination or continuing education are exempt from the eligibility requirements. The CPP Committee reserves the right to review qualifications and determine applicant eligibility. Requests for additional information about what qualifies as payroll practice should be directed to the APA, 660 N. Main Avenue, Suite 100, San Antonio, TX 78205-1217, (210) 226-4600.

**Supervisor verification required**. You will be required to submit documentation of your eligibility at the Pearson VUE Assessment Center when you arrive to take the exam. Your immediate supervisor must verify your experience by signing the "Verification of Application" section of your examination application. If you are not currently engaged in payroll practice, your experience must be verified by the signature of a prior payroll supervisor. Additionally, your coursework must be verified if you are qualifying to take the examination under Criterion 2 or 3. Please refer to the CPP Examination Handbook for more information.

By submitting an application, the applicant authorizes the APA's CPP Committee to contact the supervisor signing the "Verification of Application" section to substantiate the applicant's eligibility. The Committee reserves the right to audit applications after each examination to verify applicant eligibility.

**Testing dates and registration**. For the Fall 2008 exam, testing will occur from September 13 through October 11 at more than 100 Pearson VUE test centers. Registration to reserve a seat at the testing center must be done online or by phone no fewer than 3 business days before taking the exam. Testing centers, however, have a finite number of seats. Early registration is encouraged to assure that a seat on the desired date will be available. For the Spring 2009 exam, testing will occur from March 28 through April 25, 2009.

# 15.3 Examination Fees

The fee for the Fall 2008 and Spring 2009 exams is $355.00.

Candidates are generally required to pay their examination fee by credit card, debit card, or electronic check when they register, and they may not pay at the testing center. (See the CPP Examination Handbook for details.)

Candidates who do not have or do not wish to use a credit card, debit card, or electronic check may choose to pre-pay their examination fees. These candidates should first call Pearson VUE's Customer Care Center to obtain a candidate ID number, and then send to Pearson VUE a Pre-Payment Request Form, along with a company check or money order (made payable to Pearson VUE) for the amount of the examination fee.

Pearson VUE will process mailed requests within 10 business days and will notify candidates by mail when processing is complete. Candidates may then make a reservation. Payment cannot be made by any method at the test center.

Candidates are individually liable for the full amount of the examination fee. Once an appointment for an examination has been initiated, the candidate is responsible for paying the full fee. If the candidate cannot test for any reason, or decides not to test, the appointment must either be changed or canceled according to Pearson VUE policy. To change or cancel your reservation without having to pay the examination fee, you must notify Pearson VUE by phone or online at least 4 business days before your scheduled examination. If you contact Pearson VUE less than 4 business days before your scheduled examination, you will be charged the full examination fee.

Candidates are responsible for knowing all regulations regarding fees and examination scheduling as presented in the CPP Examination Handbook. **There are no exceptions.** Examination fees are non-refundable and non-transferable other than under the conditions explained above. For more details, see the CPP Examination Handbook.

In Fall 2008 and Spring 2009, Certification Exams will be offered from September 13 through October 11, 2008, and from March 28 through April 25, 2009.

# 15.4 Making an Examination Reservation

**Online reservations**. Making your reservation online is faster and more convenient than other methods, and provides an immediate confirmation of your examination date. Online reservations must be made at least 3 business days before the desired exam date. To make an online reservation, go to www.Pearsonvue.com.

After you have submitted your reservation, you will receive an e-mail confirmation from Pearson VUE of the examination date, time, and location. Print out the confirmation and save it for your records.

**Phone reservations.** To make a reservation for the examination, call Pearson VUE's Customer Care Center at 800-470-8757 (toll-free), Monday through Friday from 8:00 a.m. to 11:00 p.m., Eastern Time, from 8:00 a.m. to 5:00 p.m. on Saturday, or on Sunday from 10:00 a.m. to 4:00 p.m. A Customer Care Representative will help you select the optimal test date and test location for your schedule, provide specific instructions and directions, provide you with a confirmation number, and answer any questions you may have about testing.

You must have the following information available when you call to make an examination reservation:

- your credit card, debit card, or electronic check information;
- your full name, street address, e-mail address, social security number, daytime telephone number, and date of birth; and
- the examination date and location of the Pearson VUE test center where you want to take the exam.

Depending on the availability of the assessment center, you may make a reservation for the examination up to three (3) business days before your desired test date. For example, if you call Pearson VUE's Customer Care Center on a Tuesday to make an examination reservation, you may test as early as the following Friday. For testing purposes, Saturday is considered a business day. Exams are generally not given on Sunday or Monday, but there are exceptions, so please check with Pearson VUE when making your reservation. This schedule is illustrated in the following chart.

| If you call for an exam reservation on: | You may test on or after the following: |
|---|---|
| Monday | Thursday |
| Tuesday | Friday |
| Wednesday | Saturday |
| Friday | Monday |
| Saturday | Tuesday |
| Sunday | Wednesday |

Exam reservations are made on a first-come first-served basis. You should schedule early to ensure a reservation within the 4-week testing period. Reservations can be made beginning 60 days before the testing period begins. Seating is extremely limited during the last 2 weeks of each exam period, so you should make your reservation early if you want to take the exam during that time frame.

If you make your reservation at least 7 days before the desired examination date, Pearson VUE will mail you a confirmation notice within 48 hours of your call. Otherwise, Pearson VUE will send the confirmation via e-mail.

**Fax reservations.** As an alternative, you may register for the examination by fax. Do this by completing the Fax Reservation Form found in the CPP Examination Handbook and faxing it to Pearson VUE at 888-204-6291 at any time of the day. The form must be faxed at least 4 business days before the desired examination date. A confirmation of this fax reservation will be transmitted within 1 day of receiving this form. Examination reservations may not be canceled or changed by fax.

You may not take the examination more than once during any testing period. For example, if you take the exam during the Fall 2008 testing period (9/13/08 - 10/11/08) and do not pass, you may not take the exam again until the Spring 2009 testing period (3/28/09 - 4/25/09).

**Changing or canceling a reservation.** You can change or cancel an exam reservation by phone or online (not by fax), but you must do so at least 4 business days before the scheduled exam date. If you change or cancel a reservation without proper notice, you will forfeit the examination fee. If you provide proper notice of a cancellation, you will receive a full refund of the exam fee.

To change or cancel an exam reservation by phone, call Customer Care at 800-470-8757. To change or cancel a reservation online, log in at the Pearson VUE website, which will show you a list of your reservations and enable you to change or cancel each one as you wish. You will receive an e-mail notification of your change or cancellation from Pearson VUE. The change or cancellation notice schedule is illustrated in the following chart.

| If the exam is on: | Candidates must cancel by the previous: |
|---|---|
| Monday | Wednesday |
| Tuesday | Thursday |
| Wednesday | Saturday |
| Thursday | Sunday |
| Friday | Monday |
| Saturday | Tuesday |

**Special testing arrangements**. In the event that an examination is offered at a test center only on Saturdays and you cannot take the examination for religious reasons, you may request a non-Saturday examination administration. Such a request must be put in writing on official stationery by your religious advisor and faxed to (610) 617-9397 or mailed to Pearson VUE. Special accommodations are also available to candidates with disabilities. For details on how to arrange for a non-Saturday exam administration or special accommodations due to a disability, see the CPP Examination Handbook.

# 15.5  What to Take With You to the Examination

Take the following items with you to the test center on examination day:

- Two forms of identification, including one form of government-issued identification containing a photograph and name exactly as that used by the candidate when registering (e.g., driver's license, state ID, military ID, passport) and another form of identification with your name shown exactly as it is on your candidate registration (e.g., credit card. social security card); candidates will not be admitted without proper identification.

- The confirmation number you were given when you made your examination reservation.

- Proof of name change if your name has changed since you made your reservation. (Bring identification showing the name under which you registered and your current name.)

- The completed *Application for Certification by Examination for Payroll Professionals*, with the "Verification of Application" section signed by your supervisor or former supervisor. The form is provided in the CPP Examination Handbook.

**If you do not present all of the above items on examination day, you will be denied admission to the test and will be considered absent. However, you will owe the full examination fee.**

# 15.6  Testing Center Rules

Each exam center will be administered by staff of Pearson VUE. After all candidates have been admitted, the administrator will discuss the rules for the testing site. Pay careful attention to the instructions and ask questions to ensure no misunderstandings exist concerning the rules of the site. Before your examination begins, you will be required to review a tutorial that highlights all of the features and functions of the computerized testing system. You will also be able to request assistance regarding computer features and functions during the examination.

The following are general guidelines which are followed for all testing centers.

- Be on time. You should report to the testing center no later than 30 minutes before the scheduled time for the examination. The exact reporting time, date, and location of the examination will be given to you when you make your reservation. Allow sufficient time to find parking and the testing room. When you arrive, the Pearson VUE registrar will take your picture. It will be displayed on your score report. You must be on time. The administration will begin when the first question is displayed on the screen. *Candidates who arrive after their scheduled exam time will not be admitted and will owe the full examination fee.* You will have 4 hours to complete the examination, after which the unit will automatically turn off.

- If you are unable to attend a scheduled examination, you may be excused for one of the following reasons: your illness or that of an immediate family member, death in the immediate family, disabling traffic accident, court appearance or jury duty, military duty, or weather emergency. Absences for other reasons will not be excused and you will forfeit the exam fee. You must submit written verification and supporting documentation for excused absences to Pearson VUE within 14 days of the scheduled exam date.

- Dress appropriately. While every attempt is made to provide a comfortable testing temperature, heating or cooling may sometimes not function properly. You may want to take a coat or sweater to your center. Except in extreme cases, test administrations are not canceled because of heating or cooling problems at a center.

- You must take your confirmation number to your testing center. You will be admitted only at the testing center and on the date you made a reservation to take the exam.

- You must have two forms of identification. One must be a government-issued ID containing a photograph and the candidate's name exactly the same as the name used when registering. Government-issued photo ID's include a driver's license with photo, state-issued non-driver ID with photo, military photo ID, or a passport. The other form of ID must also include the same name the candidate used when registering (credit card, social security card, work ID). Candidates will not be admitted without proper identification.

- Earplugs are available at each test site for candidates' use. Request them if you need them before the exam begins.

- You may not bring a writing tool to the exam. Pearson VUE will provide you with one. You may write the calculations for test questions on the scratch paper that will be provided at the testing center. All scratch paper will be collected at the end of the exam by the administrator. You may not use your own scratch paper.

- A printed exam supplement is required to take the exam and should be provided by the proctor before the exam begins. *If you do not receive one, ask for one before beginning the exam*

- You are encouraged to use a calculator during the examination; however, it is not required. All exam questions can be answered without a calculator. Only silent, non-printing, battery or solar-powered calculators will be allowed. PROGRAMMABLE CALCULATORS WITH ALPHABETIC KEY PADS FROM A - Z ARE NOT ACCEPTABLE AND WILL BE CONFISCATED DURING THE EXAM. Sharing of calculators by examinees will not be allowed. Please note that a malfunction of your calculator during the examination will not entitle you to either additional testing time or reason to challenge your examination results. Battery-operated calculators are preferable, since lighting at the test centers may not be bright enough to activate solar calculators.

- You may not take books, papers, or other reference materials into the testing room.

- No food or beverages may be taken into the testing room.

- No smoking will be allowed in the testing room.

- You may not take valuables or personal belongings such as a purse, paper, personal digital assistant (PDA), Blackberry, cellular phone or other electronic device (other than a calculator) into the examination.

- You may not ask questions *about the test* after the examination begins. You may ask the proctor for scratch paper or to explain to you how the computer works.

- Visitors, pets, and children are not allowed in the testing room.

- No rest periods are scheduled during the examination. You will be permitted to take rest breaks on an individual basis based on the proctor's rules. No additional time will be given to examinees who take rest breaks. Any examinee who must leave the testing room will have to first receive permission from the proctor and will be escorted while outside the testing room. No test materials or notes may be taken from the room. Talking during a rest break will result in your being denied re-admittance to the testing room. Any examinee denied readmittance to the testing room for talking will forfeit all fees paid and will not have his or her examination scored.

- Any candidate who gives or receives assistance during the examination will be required to turn in all test materials immediately and to leave the room. The candidate's exam will not be scored, no fees will be refunded, and to retest the candidate will have to re-apply to take the examination, including payment of all applicable fees. Pearson VUE reserves the right to cancel any test score if there is a nonstandard test administration or an incident that involves a breach of security or cheating.

- It is of utmost importance that all candidates listen carefully to all instructions given by the proctor and follow the directions completely.

## 15.7 Format of the Examination

The examination will be administered electronically. You will have four hours to complete the examination. The certification examination consists of 190 multiple-choice questions, including 25 pre-test questions placed randomly.

The questions are designed to test your payroll knowledge and ability to apply that knowledge to the payroll environment. An exam supplement booklet containing tables and forms required to correctly answer the questions will be provided by Pearson VUE at the test center. Each question has four answer choices listed, only one of which is correct. The answer to each question can be derived independently of the answer to any other question.

The pre-test items are not counted in the scoring of the examination. They are distributed among the other scorable items and will be used for statistical purposes. The items are similar to the scorable items on the exam and candidates will not know which items are scorable and which are not. Candidates should answer all examination questions.

## 15.8 Electronic Testing

Your examination will be administered on a computerized testing station. Your photo and identifying information will be displayed at your test station to ensure that you are at the correct location. The computer will enable you to easily select an answer, change the answer, skip questions, mark questions for review, check your exam status, and keep track of your remaining time. In addition, the computer has a "Request Assistance" button that electronically connects you to the test center manager's station. If you select the "Request Assistance" button, the test center manager will immediately be alerted to your need for help.

The test center administration station monitors all individual test stations electronically. The assessment center manager can oversee the administration of all examinations, respond to requests for help, and ensure the security and privacy of each testing situation.

Before your examination begins, you will be required to go through a tutorial that consists of a series of HELP screens that will teach you how to use all of the features and functions of the computer. The time you spend in the initial tutorial section will not reduce the amount of time you have to work on your examination. You will also be able to access these HELP screens during the test. However, the timing of the examination will not be stopped when you use the HELP screens once the examination has begun.

Once you have viewed all 190 questions on the exam, the computer will display a screen stating "review" or "continue." By selecting "continue," you will end your test and will not be able to go back to any questions you may have skipped or marked for review. So be certain that when you select "continue," you are ready to end your test and submit your exam to be scored.

# 15.9 Possible Study Aids

A number of study aids are available. None should be considered the only method available for study. When you study, you should use a number of texts to ensure a wide diversity of information. The following list is not to be considered a complete list of all materials available for your use in studying.

APA's *The Payroll Source*®

APA's PayTrain®

APA's *Payroll Practice Essentials*

APA's *Intermediate Payroll Concepts*

APA's *Advanced Payroll Concepts*

APA's *Strategic Payroll Practices*

APA's *Payroll 101: The Standard Foundation of Payroll Administration*

APA's *Payroll 201: The Payroll Administration Course*

APA's *Basic Guide to Payroll*

APA's *The Guide to Successful Direct Deposit*

APA's *Guide to Global Payroll Management*

*Payroll Accounting* by Bernard Bieg

BNA's *Payroll Administration Guide*

CCH's *Payroll Management Guide*

RIA's *Payroll Guide*

IDG's *Customer Service for Dummies*

Internal Revenue Service Publications:
    Circular E, Employer's Tax Guide (#15)
    Employer's Supplemental Tax Guide (#15-A)
    Employer's Tax Guide to Fringe Benefits (#15-B)
    Exemptions, Standard Deductions and Filing Information (#501)
    Scholarships and Fellowships (#520)
    Moving Expenses (#521)
    Taxable and Nontaxable Income (#525)
    Reporting Tip Income (#531)
    Business Expenses (#535)
    Earned Income Credit (#596)

**Study plans.** A successful study plan will be one that allows sufficient time for all materials to be covered. Waiting until the last minute to study is a sure course for failure. The successful candidate will have begun their course of study several months before the exam date, using a variety of sources and techniques.

**CHAPTER STUDY GROUPS AVAILABLE** A number of local chapters of the American Payroll Association have study programs. Group study has shown to be a successful method of preparation for the CPP exam. In addition, having familiar faces from the study group at the exam will reduce your nervousness. To find out more about a chapter study group in your area, call APA at 210-226-4600 and ask for the Chapter Relations department.

When preparing for the Management and Systems portions of the exam, what your company does may not be applicable. Both Management and Systems questions must be part of the common body of payroll knowledge. In order to be part of the common body of knowledge, the practice must be widely known and observed, as judged by the CPP Committee. Be careful to study a variety of widely respected sources, since limiting the sources studied limits your exposure to the common body of knowledge.

Successful completion of the Fall 2008 or Spring 2009 exam requires demonstration of the knowledge of payroll practice and applicable regulations which were in effect as of January 1, 2008. For the Fall 2008 and Spring 2009 examinations, tables and forms required to answer questions will be those which were in effect as of January 1, 2008 and will be provided with the exam. The 2008 Form W-2 will be applicable for the Fall 2008 and Spring 2009 exams.

# 15.10 Content of the Certification Examination

Each certification examination is weighted in approximately the following manner (these statistics include the pre-test questions):

| | |
|---|---|
| Core Payroll Concepts | 27.5%, approximately 52 questions |
| Compliance | 23.0%, approximately 44 questions |
| Principles of Paycheck Calculations | 20.0%, approximately 38 questions |
| Payroll Process and Systems | 8.5%, approximately 16 questions |
| Accounting | 6.0%, approximately 11 questions |
| Management and Administration | 15.0%, approximately 29 questions |

To successfully complete the exam, you do not need to pass all six parts.

**Exam content outline**. Each question on the exam falls within a specific portion of the exam's content outline. You should begin your study with a review of the content outline to identify areas of weakness. In developing your study plan, concentrate on those areas of weakness. However, do not neglect the areas with which you are familiar in your study plan. You should be aware of areas in which the methods used by your organization differ from federal law. For example, always using an employee's highest pay rate for overtime calculations rather than using the employee's weighted average pay rate. The complete content outline of the examination follows:

I.   Core Payroll Concepts
   A.   Worker status
   B.   Fair Labor Standards Act
   C.   Employment taxes
   D.   Employee benefits
   E.   Employee/employer forms
   F.   Professional responsibility
   G.   Methods and timing of pay
   H.   Customer service

II. Compliance
    A. Escheatment
    B. Regulatory
    C. Reporting
    D. Record retention
    E. Penalties

III. Principles of Paycheck Calculations
    A. Compensation/benefits
    B. Involuntary deductions
    C. Voluntary deductions (pre- and post-tax)
    D. Employer taxes and contributions
    E. Net, disposable, take-home pay

IV. Payroll Process and Systems
    A. Maintain master file components
    B. Concepts and functionalities
    C. Disaster recovery plan
    D. Selection
    E. Implementation/upgrades
    F. Maintenance/updates

V. Accounting
    A. General ledger account classification
    B. General ledger account balance
    C. Payroll journal entry
    D. Account reconciliation

VI. Management and Administration
    A. Policies and procedures (e.g., overtime, benefits, leave)
    B. Auditing
    C. Staffing, employee development, and core competencies
    D. Management skills and practices
    E. Communication

# 15.11 Test Taking Hints

The most difficult aspect of the Certified Payroll Professional exam is that it will probably be an unknown—something new—a testing experience that you have not experienced before. Most individuals taking the exam for the first time have not taken an exam for many years. Because the exam is an unknown, the key to success is being relaxed. Reducing anxiety will allow you to be relaxed.

The following are tips on reducing anxiety and being relaxed during the exam.

- Know the location of the testing center. If possible locate it before the day of the exam.

- Allow sufficient time to arrive at the testing center 30 minutes before your appointment. Plan for unexpected delays on the way to the testing center. You may encounter bad weather, road construction, or road closures.

- Know where you will be able to park near the testing center.

- Get a good night's sleep the night before the exam. Last minute cramming will only increase your anxiety. Generally, last minute study only introduces confusion and is not productive.

- Plan your study schedule to leave the night before the exam free from study requirements.

- Wear comfortable clothing to the exam. Business attire is not required when taking the exam. Tight clothing is not comfortable and will restrict your ability to be relaxed.

- Practice with your calculator before the exam. Use it at work and during your study. The calculator should be battery powered, so be sure that fresh batteries have been placed in the calculator.

- Be aware of the time remaining. Wear a watch and track the time remaining. You will be surprised how quickly it goes by.

- Do not spend excess time on any one question. Easy questions are worth the same number of points as difficult questions, so if a question stumps you, mark it for review and go to the next question. After completing the remaining questions, come back to the question that stumped you. But remember that selecting "continue" after you have gone through all the questions will end your test and it will be scored.

- Each question requiring calculation will have incorrect answers that can be derived by using an incorrect method. If time is available, you may want to check your calculations. Write the steps you have taken in deriving the calculations on the scratch paper provided by the testing center for your review.

- Read each exam question carefully. Be careful of questions which use the words BEST, NOT, ALWAYS, NEVER, EXCEPT.

- Before beginning the first question of the exam, be sure you are comfortable with using the computerized testing program. Ask questions of the Pearson VUE personnel at the testing center before you look at the first test question.

- Verify all answers to gross-up questions.

There are no penalties for answering questions incorrectly. Passing or failing the exam is based on the number of questions correctly answered. Questions not answered cannot be counted as correct answers and give no credit toward passing. If you have difficulty with a question, mark it for review to ensure that you have time to answer all questions.

## 15.12  How Your Examination Is Scored

Your answers to the exam and the correct answers are stored on computer files from which your score and statistical reports are generated. Pearson VUE understands the importance of your test results, so it uses many quality control procedures to ensure the accuracy and confidentiality of your answers, the correct answers, and your score. As you answer questions, your answer will be compared to the correct answer and the result will be stored. If you change an answer, it will revise the previously stored result. Pearson VUE's computerized testing station will produce your raw and scaled scores when you complete the exam. A scaled score of at least 300 is required to pass the exam.

## 15.12-1  Your Score Report

Your individual score report will be given to you when you complete the exam. It will provide your total test scaled score and indicate whether you passed or failed the examination. Passing or failing is based on your total test scaled score. A scaled score of at least 300 is needed to pass.

Your score report will also provide your individual section raw scores. For each section of your examination, the number of questions answered correctly is reported. Each question answered correctly counts as one point in the raw score. You may use your section scores as an indication of individual areas of strength and weakness.

To order a duplicate score report, send a Duplicate Score Request (found in the CPP Examination Handbook) along with a money order for $15 per score report to Pearson VUE.

A candidate can request that Pearson VUE hand-score his or her examination by sending a written request that contains:

- the examination date;
- the candidate's name and social security number (at the time of the examination);
- the candidate's confirmation number;
- the candidate's mailing address; and
- the hand-scoring fee of $15 per hand-score in the form of a money order made payable to Pearson Vue (no checks or cash).

The hand-scoring request should be sent to:

Pearson VUE – APA Handscores
P.O. Box 13785
Philadelphia, PA 19101-3785

## 15.12-2  How the Passing Score Was Set

The passing score for this examination was recommended by a panel of payroll professionals who used a method called *item mapping*. The *item mapping* process incorporates actual performance of the test questions by graphically presenting the difficulty of questions in the test bank. This graphic presentation, or item map, displays questions along a scale based on their difficulty. The panel then judges the performance of a minimally qualified candidate with regard to the test questions displayed on the item map. The cut score study concludes when the panel reaches agreement on which questions have a high likelihood of being answered correctly and which have a low probability of being answered correctly by a minimally qualified candidate. Using this process, the panel recommended the passing score to the CPP Committee, which set the passing score. The passing score represents the minimum level of knowledge that must be demonstrated to pass the examination.

## 15.12-3  Raw Scores and Scaled Scores

A raw score on this examination is the number of questions answered correctly. When all examinees take exactly the same examination, their raw scores can be used to compare their performances. However, when there are different forms of an examination (different forms of an examination measure the same knowledge, but use different questions), some exams will be easier or more difficult than other exams. Because of this variation in difficulty, raw scores do not reliably relate the performances of examinees who take different exams.

To make it possible to compare the performances of examinees taking different forms of an examination, a statistical procedure called equating is used to compensate for any variations in difficulty between exams. After equating, the passing raw score for each exam is converted to 300 on a common scale for all exams. Since all exams are equated and all scores are converted to the same scale, all examinees who receive the same scaled score have demonstrated equivalent ability, regardless of which exam they took.

Since two different forms of the CPP Examination are administered during each examination period, equating and scaled scores are used. This ensures that each examinee who achieves the passing scaled score of 300 on his or her examination has demonstrated equivalent minimal competency regardless of the examination form taken.

## 15.12-4  Examination Results

Your scores are strictly confidential. Unless you request an official transcript, they will be reported only to you, the APA, and the CPP Committee.

If you have questions concerning your test results, you should direct them via e-mail, fax, or in writing to APA's Certification Department. However, because of the need to maintain test security, test questions and answers cannot be made available for review. Neither the APA nor Pearson VUE will provide a list of questions you answered incorrectly or correctly. The only information available regarding your performance on the test is provided on your score report.

## 15.13  Attainment of Certification

Payroll professionals who pass the certification examination and accept the APA Code of Ethics (see Section 15.17) will receive a certificate and will be entitled to use the letters "CPP" (Certified Payroll Professional) after their names for 5 full calendar years. To retain the right to use the CPP designation after the initial 5-year period, a Certified Payroll Professional must recertify either by retaking the exam or through continuing education (see Section 15.14). A CPP who has previously achieved the Fundamental Payroll Certification (FPC) will drop the FPC designation and recertify only the CPP.

## 15.14  Recertification

The CPP designation is valid for five full calendar years following the year in which certification is originally or previously obtained. CPPs awarded in 2003, for example, will expire on December 31, 2008. The certifications of individuals certified or recertified during 2008 will expire on December 31, 2013.

Current CPPs may recertify for an additional five years by retaking and passing the certification examination during the fifth year or by meeting the continuing education requirements.

The APA will mail all CPPs advance notice and a recertification invoice with their applicable recertification deadline by November 1 of the year in which they are scheduled to recertify. CPPs who do not receive this notice and invoice by November 7 should contact APA's Certification Department at (210) 226-4600, ext. 2238. It is the responsibility of each CPP to contact APA Membership Services to report name or mailing address changes before the recertification deadline. Whether a CPP receives notice of the recertification deadline from APA or not, the CPP is responsible for recertifying by the deadline. CPPs are responsible for maintaining a record of qualifying educational programs attended during their recertification period.

## 15.14-1  Recertification by Exam

CPPs choosing to recertify by examination must pass the certification exam during the fifth year of their original or previous certification. The eligibility requirements for taking the CPP exam do not apply to candidates for recertification. If a CPP's certification has expired, however, the recertification policies do not apply, and the former CPP must meet all eligibility requirements and retake the examination. The certification status of all applicants seeking to take the examination for recertification will be verified by Pearson VUE and APA.

## 15.14-2  Recertification by Continuing Education

The second option for recertification is to accumulate at least 120 hours of qualifying payroll-related continuing education during the five-year period before certification expires. CPP continuing education is tracked as Recertification Credit Hours (RCHs). RCHs are defined as the number of actual educational clock hours spent as a participant or instructor in direct participation in a structured educational format.

Recertification Credit Hours can be earned by participating in any of the seminars or programs administered by the American Payroll Association. The APA awards RCHs and Continuing Education Units (CEUs) for all its programs and seminars, and 1 CEU is defined as 10 RCHs. A CPP may also attend qualifying APA local chapter educational activities, various seminars or educational events sponsored by organizations other than the APA or its affiliates, or college/university courses.

RCHs qualify as payroll-related in one of two ways. First, if the educational subject is covered in the Content Outline for the CPP exam. Or second, if the subject fits in any one of five categories:

1. Payroll management
2. Accounting
3. Payroll systems/human resource systems
4. Taxation training or taxation updates
5. Human resources/personnel training

**New RCH approval process.** Beginning September 1, 2006, in order for a candidate for recertification to earn RCHs for participating in educational events other than those offered by the APA's national office, the educational event must be offered by a provider that has been approved by the APA to offer RCHs and must be an event that has been approved by the APA for a certain number of RCHs. The APA instituted this approval process to ensure the continuing integrity of its recertification program by making sure that RCHs are awarded only for educational programs providing payroll-related content.

For more information on the recertification process and/or to locate a list of approved RCH providers, visit the APA website at www.americanpayroll.org/certi.html. You can also call APA's Certification Department at (210) 226-4600, ext. 2238 or e-mail certification@americanpayroll.org if you have a question about whether a particular educational event has been approved for RCHs.

Soon after you receive your CPP certification, the APA will send you detailed information on the recertification process, including how to earn and record recertification credit hours, what to submit to the APA as evidence of recertification, and recertification audits.

Whether a CPP elects to accumulate Recertification Credit Hours or to re-take the examination every five years, the APA is confident that the CPP designation will continue to mirror the high standards of the payroll professional.

## 15.15 Benefits of Being a CPP

Upon successful completion of the CPP Certification Examination, CPPs may be eligible to receive undergraduate college credits as recommended by the American Council on Education's Credit-by-Examination Program. CPPs wishing to determine their eligibility may contact the admissions office of their college or university and request a review of their CPP examination scores. An official transcript mailed directly to the college or university by Pearson VUE may be required. For more information regarding the credit recommendations, please contact the APA's certification department at (210) 226-4600, ext. 2238.

## 15.16 Basic Level Certification Available

The American Payroll Association also offers a second certification program for payroll practitioners— Fundamental Payroll Certification (FPC). The APA recognized a need, particularly among larger companies and organizations and payroll service providers, for a certification program to acknowledge the level of knowledge attained by less-experienced payroll practitioners, those with a narrow field of responsibility, and those working to serve the payroll industry. For more information, see the FPC Examination Handbook that is mailed to all APA members. It can also be ordered by calling 210-226-4600. It is available for download at www.americanpayroll.org/certi.html.

## 15.17 American Payroll Association Code of Ethics

1. To be mindful of the personal aspect of the payroll relationship between employer and employee, and to ensure that harmony is maintained through constant concern for the Payroll Professional's fellow employees.

2. To strive for perfect accuracy and timeliness of all payroll activities.

3. To keep abreast of the state of the payroll art with regard to developments in payroll technologies.

4. To be current with legislative developments and actions on the part of regulatory bodies, insofar as they affect payroll.

5. To maintain the absolute confidentiality of the payroll, within the procedures of the employer.

6. To refrain from using Association activities for one's personal self-interest or financial gain.

7. To take as one's commitment the enhancement of one's professional abilities through the resources of the American Payroll Association.

8. To support one's fellow Payroll Professionals, both within and outside one's organization.

## 15.18 Practice Test Number 1

 **CAUTION:** All of the practice test questions have been written using accepted question writing techniques. However, none of the questions has been edited by the administrators of the CPP exam or reviewed by APA's CPP Committee for appropriateness to be included on the CPP exam.

Assume all questions relate to 2008, unless otherwise indicated.

1. How, if at all, are payments made to employees during absence from work due to illness under their employer's sick pay/disability plan treated for social security and Medicare taxation?
   The Payroll Source Section 4.3-2
   Certification Examination Content Outline Section IIIA

   a. Social Security and Medicare taxable for the first 6 calendar months
   b. Not subject to Social Security and Medicare tax
   c. Social Security and Medicare taxable after the first 3 months
   d. Social Security and Medicare taxable the entire time

2. Under the FLSA, all of the following payments are included in the regular rate of pay EXCEPT:
   The Payroll Source Section 2.6-3
   Certification Examination Content Outline Section IB

   a. Remuneration paid employees
   b. Salaries, commissions, bonuses
   c. Holiday pay
   d. Room and board provided by employer

3.  To qualify as an executive exempt from the minimum wage and overtime requirements of the FLSA, what must the worker's responsibilities include?
    The Payroll Source Section 2.4-1
    Certification Examination Content Outline Section IB

    a.  Manage 2 or more full-time equivalent employees
    b.  Receive a salary of at least $1,000 per week
    c.  Have no ability to hire and fire
    d.  Nonexempt duties performed exceed 30% of time worked

4.  When must an employee file a new Form W-4 to continue exempt status in the following tax year?
    The Payroll Source Section 6.3-1
    Certification Examination Content Outline Section IIB

    a.  When the employee earns more than $300.00 in unearned income
    b.  December 31
    c.  February 15
    d.  When the employee earns more than $455.00 a week

5.  What is the minimum an employee must be paid under the FLSA when the employee is paid $8.00 per hour for the first 30 hours of work and $10.00 per hour for the next 20 hours of work in a workweek?
    The Payroll Source Section 2.6-4
    Certification Examination Content Outline Section IIIA

    a.  $440.00
    b.  $480.00
    c.  $484.00
    d.  $490.00

6.  What form may employees receiving $20.00 or more in tips per month use to report the tips to their employer?
    The Payroll Source Section 3.4-27
    Certification Examination Content Outline Section IIC

    a.  Form 4782
    b.  Form 4070
    c.  Form 3903
    d.  Form 8109

7.  All of the following areas are regulated by the Fair Labor Standards Act EXCEPT:
    The Payroll Source Section 2.1
    Certification Examination Content Outline Section IB

    a.  Child labor
    b.  Overtime compensation
    c.  Holiday payments
    d.  Minimum wage

8.  In order to use the optional flat rate for determining the federal income tax to withhold from a supplemental wage payment, how must supplemental wage payments made at the same time as a regular wage payment be treated?
    The Payroll Source Section 6.4-4
    Certification Examination Content Outline Section IIIA

    a.  The supplemental wages must be identified separately.
    b.  The supplemental wages must be combined with the wage payment when calculating taxes.
    c.  The supplemental wages must be combined with the wages paid for the last preceding payroll period or with the wages to be paid for the current payroll period.
    d.  Supplemental payments can never be paid with regular wage payments.

9.  What are disposable earnings?
    The Payroll Source Section 9.1-2
    Certification Examination Content Outline Section IIIE

    a.  Contributions deducted from the employees' pay, which are a liability for the employer
    b.  Contributions of employees to a disability benefit fund
    c.  Earnings remaining after withholding for income taxes and other amounts required by law
    d.  Earnings remaining after a federal tax levy is deducted

10. What must an employee be paid under the FLSA if the employee is paid $10.00 per hour, works 40 hours in a workweek, and is paid 8 hours for a holiday in accordance with company policy?
    The Payroll Source Section 2.6-4
    Certification Examination Content Outline Sections IB; IIIA

    a.  $400.00
    b.  $480.00
    c.  $500.00
    d.  $520.00

11. An employer pays an employee a bonus of $2,000.00, and chooses to pay the employment taxes on the bonus. The employee lives and works in a state which has no income tax and has year-to-date wages of $55,000. What amount is included in the employee's wages?
    The Payroll Source Section 3.4-11
    Certification Examination Content Outline Section IIIA

    a.  $3,060.44
    b.  $2,969.56
    c.  $2,000.00
    d.  $1,347.00

12. If an employee is subject to a federal tax levy, what deductions from the employee's pay are allowed when determining the amount due the IRS?
    The Payroll Source Section 9.1-1
    Certification Examination Content Outline Section IIIB

    a.  All mandatory taxes only
    b.  All mandatory taxes, dependent health insurance, and child support deductions only
    c.  All mandatory taxes and all wage attachments currently in place only
    d.  All mandatory taxes and all voluntary and involuntary deductions currently in place only

13. What kind of account is Accrued Salaries Payable?
    The Payroll Source Section 11.1-1
    Certification Examination Content Outline Section VA

    a. Asset
    b. Expense
    c. Liability
    d. Revenue

14. What phase of in-house system design follows the Development Phase?
    The Payroll Source Section 12.4
    Certification Examination Content Outline Section IVE

    a. Evaluation Phase
    b. User Testing Phase
    c. Analysis Phase
    d. Conceptual Definition Phase

15. If the state law requires a minimum wage of $6.50 per hour, but federal law requires $5.85, what hourly minimum wage must be paid to employees who are covered by both state and federal law?
    The Payroll Source Section 2.2
    Certification Examination Content Outline Section IB

    a. $2.13
    b. $4.25
    c. $5.85
    d. $6.50

16. An employee who is paid $10.00 per hour works a 43-hour week. The employee is claiming married with 3 withholding allowances, is paid weekly, and has no voluntary or required deductions. The employee has year-to-date wages of $25,000.00 and lives and works in a state with no state income tax. Using the percentage method, calculate the employee's net pay.
    The Payroll Source Section 2.6-3 & 6.4-2
    Certification Examination Content Outline Sections IIIA; IIIB

    a. $381.86
    b. $391.75
    c. $402.05
    d. $415.90

17. An employer has received several attachments against an employee's wages. The attachments were received in the following order: Federal tax levy, consumer garnishment, and child support withholding order. In which order are the attachments applied against the employee's wages?
    The Payroll Source Section 9.1-1, 9.1-2 & 9.1-3
    Certification Examination Content Outline Section IIB

    a. Federal levy, child support payment, consumer garnishment
    b. Child support payment, consumer garnishment, federal levy
    c. Child support payment, federal levy, consumer garnishment
    d. Federal levy, consumer garnishment, child support payment

18. What are the maximum wages, if any, on which social security tax is withheld?
    The Payroll Source Section 6.7-2
    Certification Examination Content Outline Section IC

    a. $94,200
    b. $97,500
    c. $102,000
    d. There is no maximum

19. What action must occur for the employer to designate a worker as an independent contractor?
    The Payroll Source Section 1.2-1
    Certification Examination Content Outline Section IA

    a. The worker signs a contract of independent worker status.
    b. The worker meets the common law test of independent contractor status.
    c. The worker is part-time or temporary.
    d. The worker uses the employer's tools.

20. Payments made by a business to non-corporate independent contractors for services rendered must be reported to the IRS when the payments exceed:
    The Payroll Source Section 8.12-1
    Certification Examination Content Outline Section IIC

    a. $1,000.00 for the calendar year
    b. $600.00 in the last 12 months
    c. $600.00 for the calendar year
    d. $l,500.00 for the calendar year

21. A federal tax levy is received with the employee claiming married filing jointly with two exemptions on Form 668-W. The employee's biweekly gross pay is $1,000.00, and the employee claims married with two allowances on Form W-4. The employee has no other voluntary or involuntary deductions from pay and is not subject to state income tax. Using the wage-bracket method to calculate federal income tax withholding, what amount, if any, must be paid to the IRS biweekly for the federal tax levy?
    The Payroll Source Section 9.1-1
    Certification Examination Content Outline Section IIIB

    a. $688.46
    b. $344.23
    c. $192.04
    d. $0.00

22. What financial statement presents the financial position of a business entity by summarizing assets, liabilities, and owner's equity?
    The Payroll Source Section 11.7-1
    Certification Examination Content Outline Section VA

    a. Income Statement
    b. Trial Balance
    c. Balance Sheet
    d. Cash Flow Statement

23. All of the following duties would be included in the job description of an employee working in the payroll department EXCEPT:
    The Payroll Source Section 13.2-2
    Certification Examination Content Outline Section VIC

    a. Data entry of payroll input
    b. Review source documents for proper authorization
    c. Reconciliation of payroll bank account
    d. Distribution of payroll related reports

24. An employee is paid $1,500.00 biweekly. The employee's deductions are federal income tax $250.00, state income tax $75.00, Medicare tax $21.75, social security tax $93.00, credit union $75.00, union dues $50.00, medical insurance $150.00. What is the employee's disposable pay?
    The Payroll Source Section 9.1-2
    Certification Examination Content Outline Section IIB

    a. $1,010.25
    b. $1,135.25
    c. $1,060.25
    d. $910.25

25. What is a "Request for Proposal"?
    The Payroll Source Section 12.4-3
    Certification Examination Content Outline Section IVD

    a. A vendor's written bid to the prospective purchaser of the service or software
    b. A company's description of its structure, requirements and expectations of a new system prepared for the vendor
    c. The project team's recommendations to the appropriate approval committee
    d. The agreement between the company and vendor describing the software to be provided

## 15.19 Practice Test Number 2

1. Which of the following types of compensation is reported on Form W-2, but is NOT subject to federal income tax withholding?
    The Payroll Source Section 3.4-29
    Certification Examination Content Outline Section IIIB

    a. Dismissal pay
    b. Uniform allowances
    c. Value of group-term life insurance over $50,000.00
    d. Whole life insurance

2. Who, if anyone, is liable if an employer fails to respond to an IRS tax levy against an employee's wages?
    The Payroll Source Section 9.1-1
    Certification Examination Content Outline Section IIIB

    a. Employer only
    b. Employee only
    c. Both employee and employer
    d. No one is liable

3. An employee whose year-to-date wages are $60,000.00 receives a net bonus check of $100.00. The employee is not subject to state income tax. Using the supplemental flat rate, calculate the gross amount of the employee's bonus payment.
   The Payroll Source Section 3.4-11
   Certification Examination Content Outline Section IIIA

   a. $67.35
   b. $148.48
   c. $153.02
   d. $155.40

4. In which of the following situations may an employee claim to be exempt from federal income tax withholding on Form W-4?
   The Payroll Source Section 6.3-1
   Certification Examination Content Outline Section IIB

   a. Employee is not a United States citizen
   b. Employee pays estimated quarterly taxes
   c. Employee claims numerous exemptions and consequently will not incur a tax liability
   d. Employee did not incur tax liability in the preceding year and does not expect to incur tax liability in the current year

5. What are the three main areas regulated by the Fair Labor Standards Act?
   The Payroll Source Section 2.1
   Certification Examination Content Outline Section IB

   a. Minimum wage, overtime, garnishments
   b. Minimum wage, overtime, child labor
   c. Equal pay, child labor, garnishments
   d. Minimum wage, child labor, garnishments

6. What tax withholding, if any, is required when unpaid wages due an employee at death are paid to the employee's estate in a calendar year subsequent to the employee's death?
   The Payroll Source Section 3.4-30
   Certification Examination Content Outline Section IIIB

   a. Social security and Medicare taxes only
   b. Federal income tax only
   c. Social security and Medicare taxes and federal income tax
   d. No tax withholding is required

7. Which of the following payments is subject to social security tax?
   The Payroll Source Section 3.4-10
   Certification Examination Content Outline Section IIIA

   a. Workers' compensation benefit
   b. Wages paid in the year after the worker's death
   c. Payments to ministers of churches performing duties as such
   d. A back pay award as part of a settlement of a suit for unpaid overtime pay

8. All of the following payments are subject to social security tax EXCEPT:
   The Payroll Source Section 4.3-1
   Certification Examination Content Outline Section IIIA

   a. Dismissal payments
   b. Tips exceeding $20.00 per month
   c. Employee's elective deferral to a 401(k) plan
   d. Sick-leave payments after six calendar months of absence from work

9.  What is the penalty for failure to file Form W-2 electronically when required?
    The Payroll Source Section 8.13-1
    Certification Examination Content Outline Section IIE

    a. $5.00 per statement to a maximum of $100,000.00
    b. $5.00 per statement to a maximum of $200,000.00
    c. $5.00 per statement to a maximum of $20,000.00
    d. Penalty is dependent upon number of days correctly filed W-2s are late

10. Under the principles of double entry bookkeeping, what does a credit to an account signify?
    The Payroll Source Section 11.1
    Certification Examination Content Outline Section VB

    a. An increase in an asset account
    b. A decrease in a capital account
    c. A decrease in a liability account
    d. An increase in a liability account

11. What is the purpose of an accrual?
    The Payroll Source Section 11.5
    Certification Examination Content Outline Section VA

    a. To allow adjustments to budgets
    b. To spread large payments over twelve months
    c. To offset debits and credits as they are incurred
    d. To assign revenue and expenses to the period in which they are earned or incurred

12. All of the following transactions are recorded as an expense EXCEPT:
    The Payroll Source Section 11.1
    Certification Examination Content Outline Section VA

    a. Vacation pay
    b. Cost of employee benefits
    c. Employee portion of social security
    d. Employer portion of social security

13. In a computer system what is the organization of related data called?
    The Payroll Source Section 12
    Certification Examination Content Outline Section IVB

    a. Job
    b. Field
    c. File
    d. Record

14. How is an interface in a computerized payroll system defined?
    The Payroll Source Section 12.2-1
    Certification Examination Content Outline Section IVB

    a. A procedure to pass information from one system to another
    b. A diagram of how data flows between systems
    c. A piece of equipment that connects the terminal to the mainframe
    d. Written instructions for users which describe the system's functions

15. What is the PRIMARY purpose of internal audits?
    The Payroll Source Section 11.8
    Certification Examination Content Outline Section VIB

    a.  To balance all accounts
    b.  To avoid posting errors in expense accounts
    c.  To prepare manual entries to the general ledger
    d.  To comply with corporate and legal requirements

16. A $220 per month parking space provided by an employer to an employee is defined as a:
    The Payroll Source Section 3.2-1
    Certification Examination Content Outline Section IIB

    a.  De minimis fringe benefit
    b.  Qualified transportation fringe benefit
    c.  No-additional-cost fringe benefit
    d.  Qualified employee discount

17. On which form are household employees' payroll taxes reported?
    The Payroll Source Section 8.5-3
    Certification Examination Content Outline Section IIB

    a.  Form 1040, Schedule H
    b.  Form 941
    c.  Form 941-M
    d.  Form 945

18. All of the following wage payments are included when calculating the employee's regular rate of pay EXCEPT:
    The Payroll Source Section 2.6-3
    Certification Examination Content Outline Section IIIA

    a.  Nondiscretionary bonus
    b.  Shift differential
    c.  Paid time not worked
    d.  Premium pay less than one and one-half times the base rate

19. From which of the following taxes are cafeteria plan contributions generally exempt?
    The Payroll Source Section 4.5-8
    Certification Examination Content Outline Section IIB

    a.  Social Security and Medicare taxes, FIT, and FUTA only
    b.  Social Security and Medicare taxes, FIT, and SIT only
    c.  Social Security and Medicare taxes, FUTA, and SUTA only
    d.  SIT and FIT only

20. What is the maximum FUTA tax wage base per employee?
    The Payroll Source Section 7.1-4
    Certification Examination Content Outline Section IC

    a.  $7,000.00
    b.  $8,000.00
    c.  $15,500.00
    d.  $102,000.00

21. On which form are payments to independent contractors reported to the IRS?
    The Payroll Source Section 8.12-1
    Certification Examination Content Outline Section IIC

    a. W-2
    b. 1099-MISC
    c. SS-8
    d. 1099-INT

22. When must taxes advanced by an employer on behalf of employees during a calendar year be recovered so that the amount advanced is not included in the employee's income for the year?
    The Payroll Source Section 3.5-2
    Certification Examination Content Outline Section IIIA

    a. January 1 of the following calendar year
    b. January 31 of the following calendar year
    c. March 31 of the following calendar year
    d. April 1 of the following calendar year

23. All of the following accounts are asset accounts EXCEPT:
    The Payroll Source Section 11.1-1
    Certification Examination Content Outline Section VA

    a. Cash
    b. Accounts Receivable
    c. Inventory
    d. Accounts Payable

24. Which of the following workers would be considered an independent contractor?
    The Payroll Source Section 1.2-1
    Certification Examination Content Outline Section IA

    a. A life insurance agent
    b. A lawyer hired on a project-by-project basis with the company providing secretarial services and office space
    c. A lecturer who is paid a percentage of the money collected at fund raisers when speaking on behalf of a nonprofit clinic
    d. An outside salesperson who is paid by commission but is guaranteed a minimum salary

25. An employee who is paid $10.00 per hour works the following hours in a workweek. What must the employee be paid under the FLSA?
    The Payroll Source Section 2.6-3
    Certification Examination Content Outline Section IIIA

    | Sun | Mon | Tue | Wed | Thu | Fri | Sat |
    |-----|-----|-----|-----|-----|-----|-----|
    | 0 | 8 | 8 | 10 | 8 | 8 | 4 |

    a. $400.00
    b. $460.00
    c. $490.00
    d. $550.00

## 15.20 Practice Test Number 3

1. All of the following benefits are taxable compensation EXCEPT:
   The Payroll Source Section 3.2-1
   Certification Examination Content Outline Section IIB

   a. Personal use of a company car
   b. Noncash sales prizes and awards
   c. Business use of a company car
   d. Back pay award

2. What is the maximum elective deferral to a 401(k) plan during 2008 by an employee under 50 years of age which is not included in federal gross income?
   The Payroll Source Section 4.6-1
   Certification Examination Content Outline Section IIB

   a. $15,000.00
   b. $15,500.00
   c. $20,500.00
   d. $46,000.00

3. Which of the following deductions from an employee's pay has the highest priority?
   The Payroll Source Section 9.1-2
   Certification Examination Content Outline Section IIIB

   a. Credit union
   b. Child support
   c. Creditor garnishment
   d. Employee benefits

4. What amount would be included in the employee's income when the employer chooses to pay the taxes on a bonus of $800.00 and to use the supplemental flat rate for calculating the federal income tax? The employee's year to date earnings are $17,500.00 and the employee is not subject to any state income tax.
   The Payroll Source Section 3.4-11
   Certification Examination Content Outline Section IIIA

   a. $538.80
   b. $1,000.00
   c. $1,187.82
   d. $1,224.18

5. Documents relating to federal income, social security and federal unemployment taxes must be retained for a minimum of:
   The Payroll Source Section 10.2
   Certification Examination Content Outline Section IID

   a. 2 years
   b. 3 years
   c. 4 years
   d. 5 years

6. Which of the following requirements regulates the handling of unclaimed wages?
   The Payroll Source Section 5.5
   Certification Examination Content Outline Section IIA

   a. Internal Revenus Service
   b. State escheat laws
   c. The Walsh-Healy Act
   d. The Consumer Credit Protection Act

7. What is the federal minimum wage as of January 1, 2008?
   The Payroll Source Section 2.5
   Certification Examination Content Outline Section IB

   a. $4.25 per hour
   b  $5.15 per hour
   c. $5.50 per hour
   d. $5.85 per hour

8. Under what law are employers required to extend health care coverage to terminated employees?
   The Payroll Source Section 4.1-5
   Certification Examination Content Outline Section IIA

   a. OBRA '89
   b. TAMRA '88
   c. OBRA '87
   d. COBRA '85

9. Business expense advances not spent, but which are part of an accountable plan, must be returned to the employer within how many days to avoid taxation?
   The Payroll Source Section 3.3-5
   Certification Examination Content Outline Section IIB

   a. Within 120 days after the expenses were incurred
   b. Within 120 days after the advance was disbursed
   c. Within 60 days after the expenses were incurred
   d. Within 60 days after the advance was disbursed

10. If submitted electronically, Copy A of Form W-2 must be sent to the SSA no later than:
    The Payroll Source Section 8.14
    Certification Examination Content Outline Section IIC

    a. January 31
    b. February 15
    c. Last day of February
    d. March 31

11. Which form must be completed in addition to Form 941, when the employer is a semiweekly depositor?
    The Payroll Source Section 8.3-4
    Certification Examination Content Outline Section IIC

    a. Schedule B
    b. Schedule D
    c. Form 943
    d. Form 945

12. If payday for the last week in December falls in January, what date governs the year for which the wages are reported?
    The Payroll Source Section 6.1
    Certification Examination Content Outline Section IG

    a. The date in the year in which the wages were earned
    b. The date in the year in which the wages are recorded on the General Ledger
    c. The date in the year in which the pay was made available to employees
    d. The date in the year chosen at the employer's option

13. Which of the following amounts of employment tax liability in a lookback period allows the employer to deposit federal taxes monthly?
    The Payroll Source Section 8.2-1
    Certification Examination Content Outline Section IIC

    a. $25,000
    b. $52,000
    c. $98,000
    d. $105,000

14. A salesperson who lives and works in a state with no state income tax works for a salary plus a bonus. The employee receives a $2,000.00 bonus and has year-to-date wages of $54,000.00. Using the supplemental flat rate, calculate the net amount of the employee's bonus.
    The Payroll Source Section 6.4-2 & 6.7-1
    Certification Examination Content Outline Section IC

    a. $1,500.00
    b. $1,347.00
    c. $1,307.00
    d. $1,287.00

15. What entries are required to record $45,000.00 in salaries earned between March 27 and March 30 but not paid until April 6?
    The Payroll Source Section 11.5
    Certification Examination Content Outline Section VC

    a. Debit assets, credit salary expense
    b. Debit salary expense, credit salary payable
    c. Debit salary payable, credit payroll checking
    d. Debit salary payable, credit salary expense,

16. Which of the following entries would be posted as a credit?
    The Payroll Source Section 11.2
    Certification Examination Content Outline Section VA

    a. Increase in an asset account
    b. Decrease in a liability account
    c. Increase in an expense account
    d. Decrease in an asset account

17. In what document are financial transactions first posted?
    The Payroll Source Section 11.3
    Certification Examination Content Outline Section VC

    a. Chart of Accounts
    b. General Ledger
    c. Journal
    d. Balance Sheet

18. If a company closes its books on March 31, which of the following statements is true?
    The Payroll Source Section 11.4
    Certification Examination Content Outline Section VA

    a. The company's fiscal year is the calendar year.
    b. For corporate income tax purposes the company operates on a calendar year.
    c. The company's fiscal year is April 1 to March 31.
    d. The company has two overlapping fiscal years.

19. An employee enters data into the payroll system, where it is collected and later processed with similar data. This method is known as:
    The Payroll Source Section 12.3
    Certification Examination Content Outline Section IVB

    a. interfacing
    b. integration
    c. batch processing
    d. real-time processing

20. What is the exchange of information between two computer systems?
    The Payroll Source Section 12.2
    Certification Examination Content Outline Section IVB

    a. Integration
    b. Interface
    c. On-line
    d. Time sharing

21. Which of the following procedures is the BEST internal control procedure?
    The Payroll Source Section 11.8
    Certification Examination Content Outline Section VIB

    a. Cancelled checks are reviewed by payroll department, then passed on to the internal audit department
    b. The check signer is stored by the payroll department for safekeeping
    c. Payroll checks are signed and sealed by the cash management department
    d. The payroll department operates the check signer and mails all payroll checks

22. Which basic management skill focuses on communicating with top management?
    The Payroll Source Section 13.2-5
    Certification Examination Content Outline Section VIE

    a. Planning
    b. Organizing
    c. Reporting
    d. Directing

23. What is the IRS definition of wages?
    The Payroll Source Section 3.1
    Certification Examination Content Outline Section IIIA

    a. Monies received as benefits paid by the employer
    b. Regular pay plus overtime compensation
    c. Compensation received for services rendered
    d. Commissions and bonuses

24. An employee's hourly rate of pay is $8.00 per hour and the employee is paid 8 hours for a holiday during the week. What is the employee's gross pay for the week under FLSA if the employee works the following hours?
    The Payroll Source Section 2.6-3
    Certification Examination Content Outline Section IIIA

| Sun | Mon | Tue | Wed | Thu | Fri | Sat |
|-----|-----|-----|-----|-----|-----|-----|
| 0   | 8   | 0   | 8   | 8   | 8   | 4   |

    a. $288.00
    b. $352.00
    c. $368.00
    d. $384.00

25. The company pays employees who work on holidays at a double-time rate. A salaried nonexempt employee earning $48,000.00 per year who normally works a 40-hour workweek works 7 hours on a holiday. What is the additional pay due the employee?
    The Payroll Source Section 2.6-3
    Certification Examination Content Outline Section IIIA

    a. $161.54
    b. $242.31
    c. $323.12
    d. $369.28

# 15.21  Practice Test Number 4

1. Which of the following facts disqualifies an employee from the executive exemption from minimum wage and overtime?
    The Payroll Source Section 2.4-1
    Certification Examination Content Outline Section IB

    a. Having the authority to hire employees
    b. Being paid a salary of $600.00 per week
    c. Directing the work of one employee
    d. Spending more than 20% of time worked on nonexempt duties

2. Employers must provide Form W-2 to employees no later than:
    The Payroll Source Section  8.8-1
    Certification Examination Content Outline Section IIC

    a. December 31
    b. January 31
    c. February 28
    d. March 31

3. On what form is federal unemployment tax reported?
    The Payroll Source Section  7.1-7
    Certification Examination Content Outline Section IIC

    a. Form 940
    b. Form 941
    c. Form 945
    d. Form 944

4. What are the maximum earnings, if any, subject to Medicare tax?
   The Payroll Source Section 6.7-1
   Certification Examination Content Outline Section IC

   a. $135,000.00
   b. $102,000.00
   c. $97,500.00
   d. No limit

5. For federal tax purposes, what is the minimum retention period for records when the employer does not claim a refund, credit, or abatement?
   The Payroll Source Section 10.2
   Certification Examination Content Outline Section IID

   a. 4 years from the due date of the return or the date the tax is paid, whichever is later
   b. 4 years from the last IRS audit
   c. 7 years from the due date of the return or the date the tax is paid, whichever is later
   d. Indefinite

6. Employers must store records in what form?
   The Payroll Source Section 10.8-3
   Certification Examination Content Outline Section IID

   a. Paper
   b. Micromedia
   c. Computer media
   d. Any form is acceptable

7. Under the management theory of situational leadership, under which management style would a manager be likely to control the job and the procedures while relying on personal communication with employees to coach them in performing the job?
   The Payroll Source Section 13.1
   Certification Examination Content Outline Section VIC

   a. High task/high relationship
   b. Low task/high relationship
   c. Low task/low relationship
   d. High task/low relationship

8. All of the following skills are management skills EXCEPT:
   The Payroll Source Section 13.2
   Certification Examination Content Outline Section VIC

   a. Strategic planning
   b. Writing documentation
   c. Defining goals
   d. Defining subtasks

9. All of the following steps are taken when recruiting for a new employee EXCEPT:
   The Payroll Source Section 13.2-2
   Certification Examination Content Outline Section VIC

   a. Writing a job description
   b. Evaluating candidates
   c. Interviewing
   d. Introducing the candidate to all employees

10. Training can improve all of the following attributes of an employee EXCEPT:
    The Payroll Source Section 13.2-2
    Certification Examination Content Outline Section VIC

    a. Attitude
    b. Skills
    c. Knowledge
    d. Abilities

11. In which of the following situations would it be appropriate for a supervisor to counsel an employee?
    The Payroll Source Section 13.2-3
    Certification Examination Content Outline Section VIC

    a. When the employee has a dependency problem
    b. When the employee has family problems
    c. When the employer has a budget freeze on salary increases
    d. When the employee's parent has died

12. How much foreign earned income may an employee exclude from gross income in 2008?
    The Payroll Source Section 14.1-4
    Certification Examination Content Outline Section IIB

    a. $82,400.00
    b. $85,700.00
    c. $87,600.00
    d. The salary of a federal government employee grade GS-14, step 1

13. What does a totalization agreement allow an employee to do?
    The Payroll Source Section 14.2-4
    Certification Examination Content Outline Section IIB

    a. Pay social security tax in only one country
    b. Pay social security taxes in two countries
    c. Pay income tax in two countries
    d. Pay income tax in only one country

14. Under which of the following situations may all health insurance premiums paid be excluded from the employee's income?
    The Payroll Source Section 4.1-2
    Certification Examination Content Outline Section IIIA

    a. When the employee pays the premium directly to the insurance company
    b. When the employee and employer share the premium
    c. When the employer withholds the premium
    d. When the employer pays the premium

15. What is sick pay?
    The Payroll Source Section 4.3-1
    Certification Examination Content Outline Section IIIA

    a. Amounts paid when the employee has a doctor appointment
    b. Amounts paid when the employee's child has a doctor appointment
    c. Amounts paid due to sickness or illness
    d. Amounts paid due to job-related sickness or illness

16. What is a defined benefit pension plan?
    The Payroll Source Section 4.6-1
    Certification Examination Content Outline Section ID

    a. A plan in which benefits are based upon employee contributions
    b. A plan in which benefits are based upon employer contributions
    c. A plan in which employees are promised a certain level of benefits
    d. A plan in which employees are required to make contributions

17. What is a defined contribution pension plan?
    The Payroll Source Section 4.6-1
    Certification Examination Content Outline Section ID

    a. A plan in which benefits are based upon employee and/or employer contributions
    b. A plan in which benefits are based only upon employer contributions
    c. A plan in which employees are promised a certain level of benefits
    d. A plan in which employees are required to make contributions

18. A profit sharing pension plan is what type of pension plan?
    The Payroll Source Section 4.6-1
    Certification Examination Content Outline Section ID

    a. Defined Benefit Plan
    b. Defined Contribution Plan
    c. Cash or Deferred Arrangement
    d. Nonqualified Deferred Compensation

19. A governmental educational institution may offer qualified deferred compensation under what section of the Internal Revenue Code?
    The Payroll Source Section 4.6-3
    Certification Examination Content Outline Section ID

    a. 401(k)
    b. 403(b)
    c. 408(k)(6)
    d. 501(c)(18)(D)

20. An employee who uses a company car which is available for personal use and has a fair market value of $17,000.00 may value the personal use under what method?
    The Payroll Source Section 3.2-2
    Certification Examination Content Outline Section IIIA

    a. Cents-per-mile
    b. Commuting valuation
    c. Annual lease value
    d. Employee's estimate of value

21. All of the following items of information are needed to calculate the value of group-term life insurance EXCEPT:
    The Payroll Source Section 3.3-1
    Certification Examination Content Outline Section IIIA

    a. Employee's age at December 31
    b. Employer's cost of the group-term life insurance
    c. IRS table of group-term life insurance values
    d. Employee's after-tax group-term life insurance deduction

22. Which of the following requirements determines how soon employees must be paid after a pay period ends?
    The Payroll Source Section 5.1
    Certification Examination Content Outline Section IG

    a. Internal Revenue Service
    b. The ability of the payroll system to process pay
    c. State law
    d. Fair Labor Standards Act

23. What may employers require when implementing direct deposit?
    The Payroll Source Section 5.3-2
    Certification Examination Content Outline Section IG

    a. That participating employees authorize the deposit
    b. That participating employees deposit their net pay in their checking account
    c. That new employees must participate
    d. That all payroll and systems department employees must participate

24. What is the monthly maximum amount of employer-provided parking that is excluded from income as a qualified transportation fringe benefit?
    The Payroll Source Section 3.2-1
    Certification Examination Content Outline Section IIIA

    a. $200.00
    b $205.00
    c. $215.00
    d. $220.00

25. An employer provides an employee with the ability to use a company vanpool to come to work. How much is the value of each trip?
    The Payroll Source Section 3.2-2
    Certification Examination Content Outline Section IIIA

    a. $1.00
    b. $1.50
    c. $2.00
    d. $3.00

# GLOSSARY OF COMMON PAYROLL TERMS AND ACRONYMS

**ABC Test:** A set of criteria used by many states to determine the relationship of a worker to the organization for which services are performed. A worker meeting these criteria is considered an independent contractor under the state's unemployment insurance law.

**Accelerated Deposit Rule:** Also known as the one-day rule, it requires employers that accumulate a tax liability of $100,000 or more during a deposit period to deposit the withheld taxes within one banking day of the day the liability was incurred.

**Acceptance Agent:** A financial institution, college or university, federal agency, or professional tax return preparer that operates under an agreement with the IRS to aid aliens in processing their requests for Individual Taxpayer Identification Numbers.

**Account:** The representation of assets, expenses, liabilities, and revenues in the general ledger, to which debit and credit entries are posted to record changes in the value of the account.

**Accountable Plan:** An employer's business expense reimbursement plan that satisfies all IRS requirements regarding substantiation, business connection, and return of excess amounts in a reasonable period of time.

**Accounting Period:** The period covered by an income statement (e.g., month, year); also known as the business cycle.

**Accrual:** The recognition of assets, expenses, liabilities, or revenues after the cash value has been determined but before it has been transferred.

**AccuWage:** A software program available from the Social Security Administration that can be used to test electronic wage reports (Form W-2 information) for proper formatting before submittal to the SSA.

**ACH:** Automated Clearing House.

**ACP:** Actual Contribution Percentage.

**Actual Contribution Percentage (ACP):** The percentage of employer matching contributions and after-tax employee contributions made to an employee's account in a §401(k) plan. The IRS uses the ACP to determine whether the plan discriminates in favor of highly compensated employees.

**Actual Deferral Percentage (ADP):** The percentage of wages deferred by employees participating in a salary reduction plan (e.g., §401(k) plan). The IRS uses the ADP to determine whether the plan meets the agency's nondiscrimination requirements.

**ADA:** Americans With Disabilities Act of 1990.

**AD&D:** Accidental Death and Dismemberment Insurance.

**ADEA:** Age Discrimination in Employment Act of 1967.

**Adjusting Entry:** An entry made at the end of an accounting period to update or adjust an account before financial statements are prepared.

**Administrative:** Denotes regulations, interpretations, announcements, etc., issued by government agencies empowered to enforce laws, such as the Internal Revenue Service, the Department of Labor, the Social Security Administration, and the Equal Employment Opportunity Commission.

**Adoption Assistance:** Financial benefit provided by an employer to an employee to help with the child adoption process. Within certain limitations, it is excluded from federal income tax withholding, though not social security and Medicare taxes.

**ADP:** Actual Deferral Percentage.

**Advance Earned Income Credit (AEIC):** Payments of earned income credit during the year to employees who expect to be eligible for the credit. Employers make the payments out of federal income, social security, and Medicare taxes withheld from the employees' wages.

**AEIC:** Advance Earned Income Credit.

**After-tax Deduction:** A deduction from an employee's pay that does not reduce the employee's taxable wages. It is taken out only after all applicable taxes and other deductions have been withheld (e.g., union dues, garnishments, charitable contributions).

**Age Discrimination in Employment Act of 1967 (ADEA):** Federal law that prohibits employment discrimination on the basis of an individual's age (40 or older).

**AJCA:** American Jobs Creation Act of 2004.

**Alien:** A citizen of a country other than the U.S. or one of its territories or possessions.

**American Jobs Creation Act of 2004 (AJCA):** Federal law that created a second level of supplemental wage tax rates and stricter rules on the taxability of nonqualified deferred compensation.

**Americans With Disabilities Act of 1990 (ADA):** Federal law that broadly prohibits discrimination against individuals with disabilities who can perform the essential functions of a job with or without reasonable accommodation.

**Annual Wage Reporting (AWR):** The Social Security Administration's system of recording wages reported annually by employers on Forms W-2.

**APA:** American Payroll Association.

**Application Service Provider (ASP):** An outsourcing arrangement where the outsourcing company hosts each application at its location and the client gains access through the Internet.

**Approved RCH Provider:** A company that has been approved by the American Payroll Association to award Recertification Credit Hours (RCHs) for its payroll education curriculum.

**Archer MSA:** See Medical Savings Account.

**ASP:** Application Service Provider.

**Assets:** Resources acquired by a business that are consumed by the business.

**Assignment:** See "Wage Assignment."

**ATIP:** Attributed Tip Income Program.

**Attachment:** See "Wage Attachment."

# *Glossary*

**Attributed Tip Income Program:** A tip reporting procedure for the restaurant industry that attributes tip income to employees who participate by applying a "formula tip rate" to a restaurant's gross receipts over a certain period of time.

**Audit:** A review of a business's records and procedures to determine their accuracy and completeness.

**Authorization Agreement:** In general, a written agreement (entered into voluntarily) authorizing an employer to withhold and distribute a portion of an employee's wages to a party designated by the employee (e.g., direct deposit, union dues, savings bonds).

**Automated Clearing House (ACH):** A Federal Reserve Bank or private financial institution acting on behalf of an association operating a facility that serves as a clearinghouse for direct deposit transactions. Entries are received and transmitted by the ACH under the rules of the association.

**AWR:** Annual Wage Reporting.

**Back Pay Award:** A cash award made to an employee that generally results from legal action to remedy a violation of federal or state wage-hour or employment discrimination laws.

**Backup Withholding:** Income tax withholding required from nonemployee compensation when the payee fails to furnish the payer with a taxpayer identification number or the payer is notified by the IRS that the payee's TIN is incorrect.

**Balance:** The value of an account, as determined by calculating the difference between the debits and credits in the account.

**Balance Sheet:** A financial statement that presents a business's financial position in terms of its assets, liabilities, and owner's equity as of a certain date (generally the end of the company's fiscal year, but may be issued quarterly as well).

**Base Period:** When dealing with unemployment compensation, it generally consists of the first 4 of the last 5 quarters immediately preceding the claimant's benefit year.

**Base Period Wages:** Wages earned during the base period. The amount is generally one of several criteria used in determining a claimant's eligibility for unemployment compensation.

**Batch Processing:** Processing data as a group, either to increase controls or processing efficiency.

**Behavioral Control:** The right of a business to direct and control the details and means by which a worker performs the work to be done.

**Benefit Ratio:** In the context of unemployment compensation, it is a type of experience rating system that bases an employer's unemployment tax rate on the ratio of the employer's benefit charges to its taxable payroll for a specific period of time.

**Benefit Wage Ratio:** In the context of unemployment compensation, it is a type of experience rating system that bases an employer's unemployment tax rate on the ratio of the employer's benefit wages to its taxable payroll for a specific period of time.

**Benefit Wages:** In the context of unemployment compensation, an amount charged to an employer's account when a former employee receives unemployment benefits. The amount is determined by the base period wages paid by that employer to the claimant.

**Benefit Year:** In the context of unemployment compensation, the 52-week period beginning on the first day a claim for benefits is filed.

**BLS:** Bureau of Labor Statistics.

**Bona Fide:** Refers to actions taken in good faith, without pretense or fraud.

**BPO:** Business Process Outsourcing.

**BSO:** Business Services Online

**Business Process Outsourcing (BPO):** The outsourcing of end-to-end business processes and functions, including their required support services.

**Business Services Online (BSO):** Suite of electronic employer wage reporting and SSN verification options available through the Social Security Administration's website.

**Business Standard Mileage Rate:** A cents-per-mile figure issued annually by the IRS. Reimbursements for employee transportation expenses incurred while using their vehicles for business are not included in income up to the business standard mileage rate.

**CA:** U.S. Circuit Court of Appeals, generally preceded by a number identifying the circuit (e.g., 9th CA).

**Cafeteria Plan:** A plan that offers flexible benefits under IRC §125. Employees choose their benefits from a "menu" of cash and benefits, some of which can be paid for with pretax deductions from wages.

**Cash or Deferred Arrangement (CODA):** An arrangement under a retirement plan that allows employees to either receive cash or have the employer contribute an equivalent amount to the plan.

**Catch-up Contributions:** Elective deferrals by an employee to a defined contribution retirement plan or IRA above any statutory or plan-mandated limit

**CB:** Cumulative Bulletin.

**CCPA:** Consumer Credit Protection Act.

**Central Information File (CIF):** A file maintained by an Automated Clearing House (ACH) that contains depository financial institution names, routing numbers, addresses of contact persons, settlement and delivery information, and output medium requested.

**Check Clearing for the 21$^{st}$ Century Act:** See "Check 21."

**Check 21:** The Check Clearing for the 21st Century Act – allows banks to use "substitute" checks and electronic check imaging in clearing paper checks, thus reducing greatly the amount of paper used in the check clearing process.

**Child Support Withholding:** The process of withholding amounts from an employee's compensation to satisfy a child support order from a court or a state child welfare administrative agency. The employer is responsible for withholding the amounts and paying them over to the party named in the withholding order.

**Circular E:** IRS Publication 15, Employer's Tax Guide. This publication contains the basic rules, guidelines, and instructions for withholding, depositing, reporting, and paying federal employment taxes.

**Client/Server:** A method of computing where one computer is tied to another and each share a portion of the work load, with the main data storage being on the server.

**COBRA:** Consolidated Omnibus Budget Reconciliation Act of 1985.

**CODA:** Cash or deferred arrangement.

**COLA:** Cost-of-living adjustment.

# Glossary

**Common Law Employee:** A worker who is an employee under the common law test.

**Common Law Test:** A test that measures the control and direction that an employer has the authority to exercise over a worker. Where the employer has the right to direct the worker as to how, where, and when the work will be completed, in addition to controlling the result of the work, the worker is a common law employee.

**Common Paymaster:** One of two or more related corporations that pays employees who work concurrently for the related corporations. Under this arrangement, the related corporations are treated as a single employer for social security, Medicare, and FUTA tax purposes.

**Compensation:** All cash and noncash remuneration given to an employee for services performed for the employer.

**Compensatory Time:** Paid time off granted to an employee for working extra hours. The Federal Wage-Hour Law places severe restrictions on the use of compensatory time to avoid paying overtime, although special exemptions are allowed for public sector employees.

**Concurrent Employment:** Working for more than one related corporation under a common paymaster arrangement.

**Consolidated Omnibus Budget Reconciliation Act of 1985 (COBRA):** Federal law that requires employers with group health care coverage to offer continued coverage to separated employees and other qualifying beneficiaries.

**Constructive Payment:** An IRS rule that considers wages to have been paid to an employee when the employee has access to the wages without substantial limitations or restrictions.

**Consumer Credit Protection Act (CCPA):** Federal law that restricts the amount of an employee's earnings that can be garnished to pay creditor debts, including child support.

**Consumer Price Index (CPI):** A measure of the change in prices of certain basic goods and services (e.g., food, transportation, housing) developed and published by the Bureau of Labor Statistics (BLS).

**Control Group:** A group of key or highly compensated employees in a company whose proportion of benefits is limited under the qualification requirements of certain benefit plans (e.g., §125 or §401(k) plans). Also, employers may not use the commuting valuation method for such employees when determining the value of their personal use of a company-provided vehicle.

**Cost-of-Living Adjustment (COLA):** An adjustment of wages or benefit payments to account for changes in the cost of living, generally based on changes in the Consumer Price Index (CPI).

**Cost-of-Living Index:** See "Consumer Price Index."

**Covered Employees:** For each law affecting payroll and human resources, this term defines those workers who are subject to the law.

**CPA:** Certified Public Accountant.

**CPI:** Consumer Price Index.

**CPP:** Certified Payroll Professional.

**Credit:** An accounting entry that increases liabilities and revenues and decreases assets and expenses.

**Credit Reduction:** A reduction in the credit an employer receives against FUTA tax owed for state unemployment taxes paid, where the state has not repaid a federal loan under the joint federal/state unemployment compensation program.

**Critical Path:** Management strategy that maps out deadlines that must be met to finish a project within the time allowed.

**CSEA:** Child Support Enforcement Agency.

**Cumulative Bulletin (CB):** Bound volumes published annually by the IRS that contain information printed in that year's weekly Internal Revenue Bulletins.

**Dashboard:** A method of presenting payroll data using easy-to-comprehend charts and graphs showing current state, trend analysis, and future projections.

**De Minimis:** Anything that is too insignificant to merit legal scrutiny, such as a fringe benefit that is provided occasionally and is too small to justify accounting for or recording it. This does not apply to cash or cash equivalents except in very specific instances such as supper money.

**Death Indicator:** A code received by an employer using the Social Security Number Verification Service indicating whether the person associated with the SSN submitted for verification is deceased or not deceased.

**Debit:** An accounting entry that increases assets and expenses and decreases liabilities and revenues.

**Deduction:** An amount subtracted from an employee's gross pay to reach net pay, or an amount allowed to taxpayers as an offset against income.

**Deemed Substantiation:** Safe-harbor rules under which IRS requirements regarding the substantiation of amounts spent on employee business expenses are considered to have been met (e.g., per diem allowances).

**Deferred Compensation:** In general, the postponement of a wage payment to a future date. Usually describes a portion of wages set aside by an employer for an employee and put into a retirement plan on a pretax basis.

**Defined Benefit Plan:** A retirement plan that uses a formula (generally based on an employee's salary and length of service) to calculate an employee's retirement benefits and is not funded by employee contributions to the plan.

**Defined Contribution Plan:** A retirement plan with benefits determined by the amount in an employee's account at the time of retirement. The account may be funded by contributions from both the employer and the employee.

**Dependent Care Assistance Program:** An employer plan providing dependent care services or reimbursement for such services.

**Dependent Group-Term Life Insurance:** Term life insurance that gives an employee death benefits should the employee's spouse or other dependents die.

**Designated Roth Contribution:** A portion of an employee's elective deferrals that the employee elects to contribute to a Roth IRA rather than to the employee's §401(k) or §403(b) plan.

**Direct Deposit:** The electronic transfer of an employee's net pay directly into financial institution accounts designated by the employee, thus avoiding the need for a paycheck.

# *Glossary*

**Disaster Recovery:** A plan for keeping the payroll function operational after a shutdown of the system is caused by a natural or man-made disaster.

**Discrimination:** In the context of employee benefits, favorable treatment of highly compensated employees under an employer's plan.

**Dismissal Pay:** Amounts paid to employees who are terminated from employment, also known as payments in lieu of notice, termination pay, or severance pay.

**Disposable Earnings:** That part of an employee's earnings remaining after deductions required by law (e.g., taxes). It is used to determine the amount of an employee's pay that is subject to a garnishment, attachment, or child support withholding order.

**Donning and Doffing:** The act of putting on and taking off clothing, uniforms, protective wear, etc. at work, which may or may not be part of the employee's workday depending on how indispensable the donning and doffing is to the employee's principal work activity.

**Double-Entry Accounting:** The recording of equal debits and credits for every financial transaction.

**EACA:** Eligible Automatic Contribution Arrangement.

**Early Retirement Age:** The earliest age at which social security retirement benefits can be received—currently age 62. Individual company retirement plans may provide for benefits at an earlier retirement age.

**Earned Income Credit (EIC):** A tax credit that is available to low-income employees. It may be taken when the employee files his or her individual tax return, or partially paid in advance by the employer during the year.

**Economic Growth and Tax Relief Reconciliation Act of 2001 (EGTRRA):** Significant tax cut legislation enacted in 2001 that reduced income tax rates and increased pension plan elective deferrals.

**EDI:** Electronic Data Interchange.

**Educational Assistance Program:** An employer plan providing for payment or reimbursement of an employee's educational expenses.

**EEOC:** Equal Employment Opportunity Commission. This federal agency is responsible for administering and enforcing the Civil Rights Act of 1964, the Age Discrimination in Employment Act of 1967, the Americans With Disabilities Act of 1990, and the Equal Pay Act of 1963.

**EFT:** Electronic Funds Transfer.

**EFTPS:** Electronic Federal Tax Payment System.

**EFTPS-Direct:** An electronic tax payment method that allows an employer to access the Electronic Federal Tax Payment System directly by computer or phone to report its employment tax deposit information.

**EFTPS-Online:** An EFTPS-Direct payment option that allows employers to deposit taxes, monitor the status of current deposits, and check their recent payment history over the Internet.

**EFTPS-Through a Financial Institution:** An electronic payment method where an employer instructs its financial institution to originate a federal tax deposit through the ACH system to the U.S. Treasury.

**EFW2, EFW2C:** Sets of specifications for filing Forms W-2 and W-2c electronically with the Social Security Administration.

**EGTRRA:** Economic Growth and Tax Relief Reconciliation Act of 2001.

**EIC:** Earned Income Credit.

**EIN:** Employer Identification Number.

**e-IWO:** Electronic Income Withholding Order.

**Elective Deferral:** The amount of pretax dollars that an employee chooses to have the employer contribute to a qualified deferred compensation plan (e.g., a §401(k) plan) in the employee's behalf, also known as pretax contributions or employer contributions.

**Electronic Federal Tax Payment System (EFTPS):** System that allows employers to make federal tax deposits electronically through the ACH network.

**Electronic Filing:** The process of filing tax and information returns directly from one computer to another.

**Electronic Funds Transfer (EFT):** The transfer of money electronically from an account in one financial institution to an account in another financial institution (see Direct Deposit).

**Electronic Income Withholding Order (e-IWO):** An order to withhold child support from an employee's wages that is received by the employer electronically.

**Electronic Signature:** An electronic substitute for a paper signature that may carry the same legal effect in the payroll context; it may be accomplished using technologies such as personal identification numbers, biometrics, "click-to-accept" boxes, and electronic signature pads.

**Electronic Tax Application (ETA):** The term for the same-day settlement procedures for electronic tax deposits made through the Electronic Federal Tax Payment System.

**Electronic Vaulting:** A process by which an employer's data and processing applications are duplicated at a remote site to make it easier to continue payroll processing in the event of a disaster.

**Eligible Automatic Contribution Arrangement (EACA):** A non-safe-harbor method providing limited relief from distribution restrictions for deferred compensation plans with an automatic enrollment feature.

**Employee:** An individual who performs services for another individual or an organization in return for compensation. See also "Common Law Employee" and "Covered Employees."

**Employee Business Expenses:** Amounts spent by an employee for travel, lodging, meals, etc., while on the employer's business. Reimbursements for such expenses may be excluded from income if they are properly accounted for.

**Employee Retirement Income Security Act of 1974 (ERISA):** Federal law regulating the operation of private sector pension and benefit plans.

**Employee Self-Service:** An application that gives an employee access to personal and company data and allows the employee to review, print out, and/or update certain portions of that data. It can be accomplished by phone, at a centralized computer workstation, or on individual personal computers.

**Employee Stock Purchase Plan (ESPP):** An employer plan under which all employees are given the opportunity to buy the employer's stock at a discount, subject to strict limitations.

# *Glossary*

**Employee's Withholding Allowance Certificate:** The federal Form W-4 or an equivalent state or local form on which the employee states the number of withholding allowances he or she claims. The form is used by the employer to determine the amount of federal, state, and local income taxes to withhold from the employee's compensation.

**Employer:** An individual or organization that hires individuals to perform services in return for compensation, and that has the authority to control and direct the work of those individuals as part of the employer-employee relationship.

**Employer Identification Number (EIN):** The employer's account number with the Internal Revenue Service, it consists of nine digits (00-0000000).

**Employer's Supplemental Tax Guide**: IRS Publication 15-A. This publication provides more detailed information for employers than Circular E (Publication 15), especially in the areas of employee status determinations and sick pay taxation and reporting.

**Employer's Tax Guide to Fringe Benefits:** IRS Publication 15-B. This publication provides detailed information for employers on fringe benefits that are excluded from employees' income, as well as the valuation, taxation, and reporting requirements for taxable fringe benefits.

**Employment Tax e-file System:** The IRS's electronic filing system for Forms 941 and 940.

**Employment Verification:** The process of determining whether a newly hired employee is authorized to work in the United States under the Immigration Reform and Control Act.

**emTRAC:** Employer's Tip Reporting Alternative Commitment.

**Enterprise Coverage:** A test for determining whether an employer's entire operation is covered by the Fair Labor Standards Act. It is based on the employees' involvement in interstate commerce and the employer's annual volume of revenue.

**EPA:** Equal Pay Act.

**Equal Pay Act (EPA):** A federal law requiring equal pay for men and women performing work requiring equal skill, effort, and responsibility under similar working conditions. It was made part of the FLSA in 1963.

**ERISA:** Employee Retirement Income Security Act of 1974.

**Escheat:** In the context of payroll, the turning over of unclaimed wages to the state after a period of time determined by state law.

**ESPP:** Employee Stock Purchase Plan.

**ETA:** Electronic Tax Application.

**E-Verify:** A web-based system through which employers can match information provided by new employees on Form I-9 against information contained in the SSA's and USCIS's data bases to verify the employees' employment eligibility.

**Excess Deferral:** The amount of an employee's deferred compensation that exceeds the IRS's annual contribution limit.

**Exempt Employees:** While this term can refer to anyone not covered as an employee under a certain law, it generally means those employees who are exempt from the minimum wage, overtime pay, and certain recordkeeping requirements of the Fair Labor Standards Act.

**Exercise Price:** The price an employee pays for a stock when a stock option granted by an employer to an employee is exercised by the employee.

**Expatriate:** For U.S. payroll purposes, a U.S. citizen or resident alien who lives and works outside the U.S.

**Experience Rating:** In the context of unemployment compensation, it is the employer's past record of unemployment claims activity. This past record can then be used to determine the employer's unemployment tax rate (i.e., the higher the turnover rate, the higher the tax rate).

**Extended Benefits:** Unemployment benefits paid beyond the normal 20 or 26 weeks allowed by most states (authorized by federal legislation).

**External Audit:** An audit of an organization's financial statements by a disinterested third party (e.g., an outside accountant or accounting firm).

**Fair Labor Standards Act (FLSA):** See "Federal Wage-Hour Law."

**Family and Medical Leave Act of 1993 (FMLA):** Law guaranteeing 12 weeks' unpaid leave to most employees to care for newborn or newly adopted children, or to deal with a serious illness or injury suffered by the employee or an ailing child, spouse, or parent of the employee.

**FASB:** Financial Accounting Standards Board.

**FAVR:** Fixed and variable rate mileage allowance.

**Federal Wage-Hour Law:** The Fair Labor Standards Act of 1938, as amended. It regulates such areas as minimum wage, overtime pay, and child labor for employers and employees covered by the law.

**FICA:** Federal Insurance Contributions Act. It also describes the combined taxes levied for social security and Medicare.

**Field Service Advice (FSA):** Written advice to IRS field agents and examiners from the IRS Chief Counsel's office to guide them in handling particular factual situations.

**Filing Information Returns Electronically (FIRE):** The IRS's system for filing information returns (e.g., Forms 1099-MISC) electronically.

**Financial Accounting Standards Board (FASB):** Group that sets the standards for sound financial management.

**Financial Control:** The right of a business to direct and control the economic aspects of a worker's job.

**Financial Statements:** Reports that summarize a business's financial position and operating results (comprised of a balance sheet, income statement, and statement of cash flow).

**FIRE:** Filing Information Returns Electronically.

**FIT:** Federal Income Tax.

**FITW:** Federal Income Tax Withholding. FIT withheld from an employee's wages when they are paid.

**Flat Rate Withholding:** See "Supplemental Wages."

**Flexible Benefits:** The option to choose from a menu of benefits offered by an employer. See "Cafeteria Plan."

# Glossary

**Flexible Spending Arrangement (FSA):** An arrangement that allows an employee to have pretax dollars deducted from wages and put into an account to pay for health insurance deductibles and copayments and dependent care assistance (separate accounts for medical and dependent care FSAs).

**FLSA:** Fair Labor Standards Act (see Federal Wage-Hour Law).

**Fluctuating Workweek:** An arrangement between an employer and a nonexempt employee to pay the employee a fixed weekly salary even though the employee's hours may vary from week to week.

**FMLA:** Family and Medical Leave Act of 1993.

**FMV:** Fair market value. Used to determine the value of noncash, employer-provided benefits for payroll tax purposes, or the value of facilities provided to employees in lieu of wages.

**Foreign Country:** A country or territory not under the jurisdiction of the U.S. government.

**Foreign Earned Income Exclusion:** An election by a U.S. citizen or resident alien working abroad to exclude up to a certain amount of foreign earned income from the taxpayer's gross income.

**Foreign Housing Cost Exclusion:** An exclusion from income for reasonable foreign housing expenses exceeding a base housing amount that is available to U.S. employees working abroad whose tax home is not in the U.S.

**§401(k) Plan:** A cash or deferred arrangement that allows employees to authorize their employer to place pretax dollars in a retirement plan that invests the money. The contributions (including those matched by the employer) and any earnings on them are not subject to federal income tax (most state income taxes also) until they are withdrawn.

**§403(b) Annuity:** An annuity or mutual fund that provides retirement income for employees of public schools and certain tax exempt organizations.

**§457 Plan:** A deferred compensation plan that provides retirement income for employees of public sector employers (e.g., state and local governments) and certain tax exempt organizations.

**FPC:** Fundamental Payroll Certification.

**Fringe Benefits:** Compensation other than wages provided to an employee, such as health and life insurance, vacations, employer-provided vehicles, public transportation subsidies, etc., that may be taxable or nontaxable.

**FSA:** Flexible spending arrangement; Field Service Advice.

**FTD:** Federal tax deposit.

**Fundamental Payroll Certification (FPC):** A basic level of payroll certification offered by the American Payroll Association to those who pass a knowledge-based examination.

**FUTA:** Federal Unemployment Tax Act. It requires employers to pay a certain percentage of their employees' wages (up to a maximum wage limit) as a payroll tax to help fund unemployment compensation benefits for separated employees.

**GAAP:** Generally Accepted Accounting Principles.

**GAO:** General Accounting Office.

**Gap Analysis:** Comparison of the functionalities of old and new payroll systems to determine if there are any gaps in the functionality of the new system that need to be addressed before going live.

**Garnishee:** In a payroll context, an employer that receives an order requiring withholding from an employee's wages to satisfy a debt. A garnishee can also be a debtor against whom a creditor has brought a process of garnishment.

**Garnishment:** A legal proceeding authorizing an involuntary transfer of an employee's wages to a creditor to satisfy a debt.

**GASB:** Governmental Accounting Standards Board.

**GAW:** Guaranteed Annual Wage.

**General Ledger:** A ledger containing all the transactions in the debit and credit accounts of a business.

**Generally Accepted Accounting Principles (GAAP):** A set of rules and procedures set forth by the Financial Accounting Standards Board that outline accepted accounting practices broadly and in detail.

**Golden Parachute:** Payments made to business executives in excess of their usual compensation (e.g., stock options, bonuses) in the event the business is sold and the executives are terminated from employment.

**Governmental Accounting Standards Board (GASB):** Group that sets the standards for sound governmental financial management.

**Grace Period:** An extra time period provided for in a cafeteria plan that allows employees with a health FSA to be reimbursed for health care expenses incurred after the end of the plan year. It can be no longer than 2½ months.

**Graphical User Interface (GUI):** Software that interacts between the user and the application in a user friendly manner to simplify user tasks and shorten the learning curve. GUIs use a mouse to maneuver around a window.

**Green card:** INS Form I-551, Permanent Resident Card, which entitles the bearer to permanent resident status in the U.S. and provides proof of work authorization and identity under the Immigration Reform and Control Act (formerly known as the Alien Registration Receipt Card).

**Gross-up:** An IRS-approved formula that employers can use to determine the taxable gross payment when the employer wishes to pay the employee's share of tax.

**Group Legal Services Plan:** An employer plan providing for the advance provision or prepayment of personal legal services for employees and their dependents.

**Group-term Life Insurance (GTL):** Term life insurance that is provided to employees, with the cost being borne by the employer, the employee, or both.

**GTL:** Group-term life insurance.

**Guaranteed Annual Wage (GAW):** A plan guaranteeing employees their annual income (regardless of the work available) or that they will be kept on the payroll (although possibly at a lower wage).

**GUI:** Graphical User Interface.

**HCE:** Highly Compensated Employee.

# *Glossary*

**Health Insurance Portability and Accountability Act (HIPAA):** Law passed in 1996 restricting the right of group health plans to limit participation by newly hired employees and their dependents because of preexisting medical conditions and protecting the privacy of health care information.

**Health Reimbursement Arrangement (HRA):** An employer-funded arrangement under which the employer reimburses an employee and the employee's spouse and dependents for medical care expenses up to a maximum dollar amount for the coverage period.

**Health Savings Account (HSA):** Tax-exempt trusts or custodial accounts created exclusively to pay for the qualified medical expenses of the account holder (e.g., employee) and his or her spouse and dependents.

**HI:** Hospital Insurance (the Medicare component of FICA).

**High-Low Substantiation Method:** A safe-harbor method (deemed substantiation) for reimbursing lodging, meal, and incidental expenses incurred by an employee who is traveling overnight on the employer's business.

**Highly Compensated Employee (HCE):** In the context of certain fringe benefit plans, an employee who is an owner or officer of a business or whose salary exceeds a certain amount (indexed each year for inflation). Many benefits offered by employers do not qualify for favorable tax treatment if they discriminate in favor of highly compensated employees. And employers may also be restricted in their use of safe-harbor valuations of benefits provided to such employees. In the context of overtime requirements under the FLSA, an employee who earns more than $100,000 in annual compensation.

**HIPAA:** Health Insurance Portability and Accountability Act.

**Housing Allowance:** Payment made to a U.S. citizen or resident alien working abroad to make up the added cost of obtaining reasonable living quarters in a foreign country.

**HRA:** Health Reimbursement Arrangement.

**HRIS:** Human Resource Information System.

**HRMS:** Human Resource Management System.

**HSA:** Health Savings Account.

**ICE:** Immigration and Customs Enforcement.

**IIRIRA:** Illegal Immigration Reform and Immigrant Responsibility Act of 1996.

**Illegal Immigration Reform and Immigrant Responsibility Act of 1996:** Law enacted in 1996 that amends IRCA by reducing the number of documents that employers must accept to prove a new hire's identity and work authorization.

**ILM:** Internal Legal Memorandum.

**Immigration and Customs Enforcement (ICE):** Agency of the Department of Homeland Security that enforces the prohibition against the hiring of unauthorized aliens by U.S. employers.

**Immigration Reform and Control Act of 1986 (IRCA):** Law enacted in 1986 that prohibits employers from hiring persons who are not authorized to work in the U.S. and from discriminating against those who are based on their national origin or citizenship.

**Impute:** The addition of the value of cash/noncash compensation to an employee's taxable wages in order to properly withhold income and employment taxes from the wages.

**Incentive Stock Option (ISO):** A stock option plan that gives an employee the opportunity to buy the employer corporation's stock at a fixed price for a certain period of time, and that offers favorable tax treatment if certain conditions are met.

**Income Statement:** A financial statement showing a company's results of operations for an accounting period or fiscal year.

**Income Tax Treaties:** Treaties between the U.S. and foreign countries that may have provisions governing the tax treatment of U.S. employees working in those countries, as well as aliens from those countries working in the U.S.

**Indefinite Assignment:** See "Long-Term Assignment."

**Independent Contractor:** A nonemployee contracted by a business to perform services. Although the business specifies the result of the work to be performed, it has no right to control the details of when, how, or who will ultimately perform the work.

**Individual Retirement Arrangement (IRA):** A trust created or organized for the exclusive benefit of an individual or his or her beneficiaries.

**Individual Taxpayer Identification Number (ITIN):** A tax reporting identification number issued to aliens in the U.S. who cannot get a social security number but are required to file a tax or information return with the IRS.

**Information Return:** A return sent to the IRS (e.g., 1099 series) or the SSA (e.g., Form W-2, Copy A along with Form W-3) that indicates information relevant to tax liability.

**Information Statement:** A statement sent to a payee (e.g., 1099 series) or an employee (e.g., Form W-2) that indicates payments made and taxes withheld by the party issuing the statement.

**Interactive Voice Response (IVR):** In the employment context, a telephone system that allows employees to make changes by touch-tone phone to their payroll and personal data.

**Internal Audit:** An audit of a business's policies, procedures, operations, and records carried out by employees of the business as opposed to outside parties.

**Internal Control:** Measures used by a company to safeguard company assets by preventing errors, waste, embezzlement, and fraud.

**Internal Legal Memorandum (ILM):** An interpretation of a point of tax law designated for internal use by the IRS.

**Internal Revenue Bulletin (IRB):** Issued regularly (weekly except during the summer) by the IRS, the IRB contains recently issued regulations, revenue procedures, and other agency announcements.

**Internal Revenue Code (IRC):** Federal tax laws. Generally referred to as the Internal Revenue Code of 1986, which was the year of the latest major overhaul of the Code. The IRC also comprises Title 26 of the United States Code.

**Internal Revenue Service (IRS):** Federal agency charged with interpreting, implementing, and enforcing the tax laws of the U.S.

**Internal Revenue Service Restructuring and Reform Act of 1998:** Law enacted in 1998 to reform the governance structure of the IRS to make it more responsive to taxpayers and to promote electronic filing of information.

# Glossary

**Interstate Commerce:** The exchange of goods and/or services across state lines. It provides a basis for congressional and federal government agency regulation of wages and hours of work and other employment-related matters.

**IRA:** Individual Retirement Arrangement.

**IRB:** Internal Revenue Bulletin.

**IRC:** Internal Revenue Code.

**IRCA:** Immigration Reform and Control Act.

**IRS:** Internal Revenue Service.

**ISO:** Incentive Stock Option.

**ITIN:** Individual Taxpayer Identification Number.

**IVR:** Interactive Voice Response.

**Journal:** A record of financial transactions that debit or credit an account.

**KAC:** Knowledge Assessment Calculator

**Key Employee:** In the context of certain fringe benefit plans, an officer or owner (of all or a significant part) of a business whose annual pay exceeds a certain amount. Many benefits offered by employers do not qualify for favorable tax treatment if they discriminate in favor of key employees. In the context of the Family and Medical Leave Act, a high salaried employee who may not be entitled to reinstatement after FMLA leave if doing so would cause the employer serious economic injury.

**Kiosk:** A centrally located, specialized workstation located for easy employee access, where employees can inquire about and modify their payroll and personal data, as well as view company-provided information.

**Knowledge Assessment Calculator (KAC):** Patent-pending, online tool for employees and managers with payroll-related responsibilities to assess the employees' strengths and weaknesses and recommend training offerings from the American Payroll Association that address those shortcomings.

**LAN:** Local Area Network.

**Leased Employees:** Employees of a leasing agency who are hired and trained for the client firm through the agency. Withholding, depositing, and reporting responsibilities remain with the leasing agency.

**Leave-sharing Plan:** An arrangement allowing employees to donate paid leave days to a leave bank for use by employees who need to use the leave for medical emergencies or in the event of a natural disaster.

**Levy:** An attachment to satisfy a tax debt or a court judgment.

**Liabilities:** Debts of a business that have yet to be paid.

**Local Area Network (LAN):** A network in which all computers are physically attached to each other and data are transmitted at high speeds over short distances.

**Local National:** An employee who works in the country where his home base is located, even though the employee may actually be a citizen of another country.

**Lock-in Letter:** A notice sent by the IRS to an employer that tells the employer how many withholding allowances and what marital status an employee may claim on his or her Form W-4, *Employee's Withholding Allowance Certificate*.

**Long-Term Assignment:** A job assignment that is realistically expected to last more than 12 months.

**Long-Term Care Insurance:** An insurance contract providing for coverage of qualified long-term care services, including diagnostic, preventive, treating, mitigating and rehabilitative services, which is treated as an accident and health insurance contract for payroll tax purposes.

**Lookback Period:** The 12-month period running from July 1 of the second preceding calendar year through June 30 of the preceding calendar year, for employers filing Form 941. The employer's payroll tax liability during this period determines its depositor status for the current year. The period may be different for some employers.

**Mainframe:** Large, powerful computer that is generally used for companywide computing since it can handle multiple users and tasks at the same time.

**Matching Principle:** Matching revenue earned during an accounting period with the expenses incurred in generating the revenue.

**Medical Savings Account (MSA):** An arrangement through which an employer or an employee (but not both) can put tax-preferred contributions into an account for the payment of health care deductibles under a high deductible health insurance plan.

**Medical Support Withholding**: The process of withholding amounts from an employee's compensation to satisfy a medical support order from a court or a state child welfare administrative agency. The employer is responsible for withholding the amounts and paying them over to the party named in the medical support withholding order.

**Medicare:** A federal hospital insurance program for individuals age 65 or older and some disabled persons. It is funded through the hospital insurance (HI) component of FICA tax.

**Merit Rating:** See "Experience Rating."

**Minicomputer:** Smaller than a mainframe computer, but they can still handle multiple users and tasks on a more limited basis; often used to handle departmental computing needs in large organizations.

**Minimum Wage:** The lowest amount that an employer can pay its employees per hour under federal or state law.

**Monopolistic State:** A state that administers workers' compensation premiums and benefits solely through a state fund, prohibiting employers from purchasing insurance from a private insurance carrier.

**MQGE:** Medicare Qualified Government Employee, who only has the Medicare component of FICA, but not social security, withheld from wages.

**MSA:** Medical Savings Account.

**Multiple Worksite Report (MWR):** A report developed by the Bureau of Labor Statistics to help it collect statistical information on U.S. businesses with multiple worksites.

**MWR:** Multiple Worksite Report.

**NACHA:** NACHA, The Electronic Payments Association.

# *Glossary*

**National Council States:** For workers' compensation purposes, states that adhere to the uniform classification codes in the *Basic Manual for Workers' Compensation*, published by the National Council on Compensation Insurance.

**National Medical Support Notice (NMSN):** Document provided by a state child support agency to an employer requiring that an employee's child be enrolled in medical insurance coverage provided by the employer and that an amount be withheld from the employee's wages to pay premiums for the coverage.

**Negative Account Employer:** An employer whose state unemployment tax payments are less than the benefits charged to its unemployment reserve account.

**Negative Election:** A salary deferral to fund pre-tax employee benefits that is begun without the employee making an affirmative election to begin the deferral.

**Net Pay:** That part of an employee's wages that remains after all deductions have been subtracted (e.g., taxes, health insurance premiums, union dues, etc.).

**Network:** System connecting computers and applications that consists of the physical connection (topology) and the software.

**New Hire Reporting:** The reporting of newly hired and rehired employees to state agencies to facilitate the collection of child support and/or to uncover abuse in the state's unemployment compensation, workers' compensation, or public assistance programs.

**NLRB:** National Labor Relations Board.

**NMSN:** National Medical Support Notice

**No-Additional-Cost Services:** A tax-free fringe benefit for employees consisting of free services offered by an employer at no substantial additional cost to the employer.

**No-match Letter:** A letter sent by the SSA to an employer that informs the employer of employee names and social security numbers on Forms W-2 sent to SSA by the employer that do not match SSA's data base.

**Nonaccountable Plan:** An employer's business expense reimbursement plan that does not meet the requirements regarding business connection, substantiation, and returning excess amounts. Payments made under the plan are included in employees' income.

**Noncash Fringe Benefits:** Benefits provided to employees in some form other than cash (e.g., company car, health and life insurance, parking facility, etc.), which may be taxable or nontaxable.

**Nondiscrimination Testing:** Tests that determine whether benefit plans provided by an employer discriminate in favor of highly compensated or key employees. If such discrimination is found, the employer will lose its favorable tax treatment for the benefit. Benefits provided under the plan may be taxable to employees receiving them.

**Nonexempt Employees:** Employees who are covered by the minimum wage and overtime provisions of the Fair Labor Standards Act. They may be paid on an hourly or salary basis.

**Nonqualified Plan:** In the context of employee benefits, an employer retirement plan that does not meet IRS qualification requirements.

**Nonqualified Stock Option (NSO):** See "Nonstatutory Stock Option".

**Nonresident Alien:** An individual from a foreign country working in the U.S. who does not pass either the "green card" or "substantial presence" residency test, but is subject to federal income tax on U.S. source income.

**Nonstatutory Stock Option (NSO):** A stock option plan that gives an employee the opportunity to buy the employer corporation's stock at a fixed price for a certain period of time, without the conditions that apply to an incentive stock option.

**Normal Credit:** Amount of an employer's required contributions paid timely into a state unemployment insurance fund, to a maximum of 90% of the employer's basic federal unemployment tax rate, taken as a credit against the employer's federal unemployment tax.

**Normal Retirement Age:** Currently 65 and 2 months, the age at which retirees may receive unreduced social security benefits. Individual company retirement plans may use a different age.

**NSO:** Nonqualified Stock Option; Nonstatutory Stock Option.

**OASDI:** Old Age, Survivors and Disability Insurance, also known as social security.

**Obligee:** A person to whom a debt is owed.

**Obligor:** A person who owes a debt.

**OCSE:** Office of Child Support Enforcement.

**ODFI:** Originating Depository Financial Institution.

**OMB:** Office of Management and Budget.

**On-Call Time:** Nonwork time during which employees are required to be available to handle job-related emergencies.

**One-Day Deposit Rule:** See Accelerated Deposit Rule.

**Online Processing:** Processing performed under direct control of the computer (can be batch or realtime).

**Operating System:** The computer program that controls the basic operations of a computer (e.g., Windows, UNIX).

**Opportunity Wage:** A reduced minimum wage that can be paid to teenagers during their first 90 days at work.

**Originating Depository Financial Institution (ODFI):** A financial institution that is qualified to initiate deposit entries submitted by an employer as part of the direct deposit process.

**OSHA:** Occupational Safety and Health Administration.

**Other Compensation:** Compensation not subject to federal income tax withholding that an employer must report on an employee's W-2 in Box 1.

**Outplacement Services:** Services provided by employers to help employees find a new job after a layoff or reduction in force.

**Overtime:** Hours worked in excess of maximums set by federal or state law that must be compensated at a premium rate of pay (e.g., under the FLSA, all hours worked over 40 in a workweek must be paid at no less than 1½ times the employee's regular rate of pay).

# *Glossary*

**Owner's Equity:** The assets of a company minus its liabilities.

**Participating Depository Financial Institution (PDFI):** A financial institution that can accept direct deposits and transmit or receive entries.

**Paycards:** Stored value debit cards that are funded by employers with employees' net pay. Employees can access their net pay by using the cards to make purchases or withdraw cash.

**Payroll Period:** The period of service for which an employer pays wages to its employees.

**Payroll Register:** A report listing and summarizing the compensation paid and deductions taken from each employee's wages for the payroll period.

**Payroll Tax:** Any tax levied by a government agency on employees' wages, tips, and other compensation.

**PC:** Personal Computer.

**PDFI:** Participating Depository Financial Institution.

**PDS:** Private Delivery Service.

**Pearson VUE:** The company that administers the Certified Payroll Professional and Fundamental Payroll Certification examinations.

**PEO:** Professional Employer Organization.

**Per Diem:** A flat daily rate of reimbursement for business expenses (e.g., meals, lodging, and incidentals) incurred by employees while traveling overnight on business.

**Percentage Method of Withholding:** One allowable method for calculating federal income tax withholding from an employee's wages, most often used when the calculation is automated.

**Personal Computer (PC):** Computers that are designed for personal use by having all the computer functionality, operating systems, and applications self-contained.

**Positive Account Employer:** An employer whose state unemployment tax contributions are more than the benefits charged to its unemployment reserve account.

**Preliminary and Postliminary Activities:** Time spent by employees to get ready for work or to get ready to leave work, which is generally not compensable time unless the activities are essential to the employee's principal work activity.

**Premium Pay:** In a payroll context, it can have two meanings. It can be the extra pay above an employee's regular rate of pay that is paid for working overtime hours. Or it can be a special pay rate for work done on weekends, on holidays, during undesirable shifts, or for doing dangerous work.

**Pretax Deduction:** A deduction taken from gross pay that reduces taxable wages.

**Private Delivery Service (PDS):** A private sector company that delivers packages. If their services are "designated" by the IRS, materials delivered to them by a taxpayer for delivery to the IRS are considered postmarked on the date the delivery to the PDS is recorded on their database or marked on the package.

**Private Letter Ruling (PLR):** A ruling provided by the IRS when requested by a taxpayer who wants to know how the tax laws apply to a particular factual situation. The ruling applies only to the taxpayer requesting it, and cannot be relied on by other taxpayers.

**Professional Employer Organization (PEO):** An employee leasing firm that arranges with clients to lease their employees back to the client and handle all payroll and human resources functions for the client.

**Public Sector Employer:** An employer that is a state or local governmental unit (e.g., county, town, village) or a political subdivision of such a unit (e.g., school district, sewer district).

**QACA:** Qualified Automatic Contribution Arrangement.

**QETP:** Questionable Employment Tax Initiative.

**Qualified Automatic Contribution Arrangement (QACA):** A safe-harbor method for deferred contribution retirement plans that provide for automatic contributions to meet applicable nondiscrimination tests.

**Qualified Plan:** A benefit plan that meets IRS qualification requirements for tax-favored treatment (e.g., nondiscrimination).

**Qualified Retirement Planning Services:** Certain retirement planning advice or information provided by an employer, the value of which is excluded from employees' income if it is provided in a nondiscriminatory manner.

**Qualified Transportation Fringe:** Certain employer-provided transportation benefits that can be excluded from employees' income up to certain annually adjusted limits (i.e., transit passes, vanpools, parking).

**Qualifying Event:** One of several events that results in the loss of group health insurance coverage for employees or their dependents and entitles them to continued coverage under the Consolidated Omnibus Budget Reconciliation Act of 1985 (COBRA)

**Questionable Employment Tax Practice (QETP) Initiative:** A collaborative program involving the IRS, DOL, and state agencies to identify employment tax avoidance schemes and increase voluntary compliance.

**RDB:** Relational Data Base.

**RDFI:** Receiving Depository Financial Institution.

**Reasonable Basis Test:** A standard used to determine whether a worker can be treated as a independent contractor whether or not the common law test is met, based on prior court and administrative rulings, IRS audits, or longstanding practice in the industry.

**Receiving Depository Financial Institution (RDFI):** A financial institution that qualifies to receive direct deposit entries from an Automated Clearing House.

**Reciprocity:** In payroll, a relationship between states under which privileges granted by one are returned by the other (e.g., reciprocal enforcement of child support orders, reciprocal agreements not to tax non-residents working in a state).

**Reconciliation:** The process of ensuring that amounts withheld, deposited, paid, and reported by employers agree with each other and that if they do not, determining the reasons and making the necessary corrections.

**Regular Rate of Pay:** An hourly pay rate determined by dividing the total regular pay actually earned for the workweek by the total number of hours worked.

**Regulations:** The means by which government agencies administer and enforce laws (e.g., rules issued by the IRS to enforce the tax laws).

**Rehabilitation Act of 1973:** A federal law prohibiting discrimination against qualified disabled individuals by federal government contractors and grantees.

**Reimbursement Financing:** An unemployment insurance financing system that allows employers to pay back to the state unemployment trust fund any benefits paid to their former employees, rather than paying a tax based on their experience rating. This form of financing is most often used by nonprofit groups and public sector employers.

**Reimbursement Fund:** See "Flexible Spending Arrangement."

**Related Corporations:** A group of corporations meeting certain common ownership and concurrent employment requirements that may be treated as one employer for social security, Medicare, and FUTA purposes.

**Relational Data Base (RDB):** A file management system that organizes data into a series of tables, each containing a series of related data in columns and rows.

**Reserve Ratio:** In the context of unemployment compensation it is a type of experience rating system that bases an employer's unemployment tax rate on the ratio of taxes less benefits to taxable payroll.

**Resident Alien:** In the context of payroll, an individual who passes either the "green card" or "substantial presence" test for determining resident status in the U.S. Resident aliens are generally subject to federal income tax withholding and social security and Medicare taxes on the same basis as U.S. citizens.

**Revenue Procedures (Rev. Proc.):** Official statements from the IRS on how to carry out tax compliance.

**Revenue Rulings (Rev. Rul.):** Published decisions issued by the IRS that apply the tax laws to a particular set of facts. They can be used by taxpayers to determine their tax liability in similar factual situations.

**Roth IRA:** An individual retirement arrangement to which nondeductible contributions may be made (subject to certain AGI phase-outs), and the distributions from which are generally nontaxable.

**RRTA:** Railroad Retirement Tax Act.

**Safe-harbor:** An IRS-approved alternative method (usually a short-cut) for complying with IRS rules, regulations, and procedures (e.g., per diem allowances and high-low substantiation).

**Salary Reduction Arrangement:** See "Cash or Deferred Arrangement."

**Sarbanes-Oxley Act:** Law passed in response to corporate financial scandals that imposes requirements on publicly held companies designed to restore investor and public confidence in corporate financial management.

**Savings Incentive Match Plans for Employees of Small Employers (SIMPLE Plans):** Retirement plans for employees of small employers (no more than 100 employees) that have simpler administrative and nondiscrimination requirements than other retirement plans.

**SCA:** Service Center Advice.

**SDI:** State Disability Insurance.

**SDU:** State Disbursement Unit.

**SECA:** Self-Employment Contributions Act.

**Segregation of Duties:** A basic principle of internal control that prevents individuals from having responsibility for all phases of a job process, thus guarding against misuse or misappropriation of company assets.

**Self-Employment Contributions Act (SECA):** This law requires self-employed individuals to pay both the employer and employee share of social security and Medicare taxes.

**SEP:** Simplified Employee Pension.

**Service Center Advice (SCA):** An opinion on a point of tax law as applied to a specific set of facts provided to an IRS service center from the IRS Chief Counsel's ofice.

**Service Provider:** An independent company that processes its clients' payrolls for a fee, or that handles one or more parts of its clients' payroll process (i.e., tax filing, garnishments).

**Severance Pay:** A payment offered by some employers to terminated employees (usually those who are terminated through no fault of their own) that is designed to tide them over until new employment is secured.

**Shared Services:** The consolidation of related functions and integration of the processes involved with them throughout an entire organization.

**Shift Differential:** Extra pay received by employees for working a less-than-desirable shift (e.g., evenings or late nights).

**Short-Term Assignment:** A job assignment that is realistically expected to and in fact does last less than 12 months.

**SIFL:** Standard Industry Fare Level.

**SIMPLE Plans:** Savings Incentive Match Plans for Employees of Small Employers.

**Simplified Employee Pension (SEP):** An Individual Retirement Arrangement (IRA) with special participation requirements that is available to certain small employers.

**SIT:** State Income Tax.

**Social Security:** The Old Age, Survivors, and Disability Insurance (OASDI) component of FICA.

**Social Security Administration (SSA):** The federal government agency that administers social security.

**Social Security Number (SSN):** An individual's taxpayer identification number, it consists of nine digits (000-00-0000).

**Social Security Number Verification Service (SSNVS):** An Internet-based service that allows employers to verify employees' names and social security numbers by keying them in or uploading a file.

**Social Security Statement:** The earnings and benefit verification statement sent by the Social Security Administration annually to employees over age 24 in the U.S. who are not currently receiving social security benefits.

**Special Accounting Rule:** A safe-harbor rule that allows employers to treat certain noncash fringe benefits provided to employees in November or December as received in the following year. If an employer uses the special accounting rule, the employee must also report the benefit for the same period.

**Special Wage Payments**: Payments made to employees or former employees for services performed in an earlier year. These payments require special reporting by employers so that retirees' social security benefits are not reduced under the annual earnings test because of amounts earned in prior years.

**Split-dollar Life Insurance:** An arrangement where an employer pays that part of an annual life insurance premium representing the increase in the cash surrender value of the policy during the year, while the employee pays the remainder of the premium.

**Split Shifts:** A workday that is divided into two parts separated by a spread of hours longer than the conventional rest or meal period.

**SSA:** Social Security Administration.

**SSN:** Social security number.

**SSNVS:** Social Security Number Verification Service.

**Standard Industry Fare Level (SIFL):** A cents-per-mile rate used to value non-commercial flights for purposes of including the personal use of corporate aircraft in an employee's income.

**State Disbursement Unit (SDU):** A centralized location for the collection and disbursement of withheld child support payments throughout a state.

**Statement on Auditing Standards (SAS)-70 Report:** A report from a third-party vendor written by an independent auditor that describes the vendor's internal control procedures and their effectiveness after testing.

**Statute of Limitations:** A period of time established by law during which parties can take legal action to enforce their rights.

**Statutory Employees:** Special groups of employees identified by law (e.g., full-time life insurance salespeople, certain homeworkers) whose wages are not subject to FITW, but are subject to FICA and FUTA.

**Statutory Nonemployees:** Special groups of workers who may qualify as common law employees but are treated under the law as independent contractors (e.g., qualified real estate agents and direct sellers) whose compensation is not subject to federal income tax withholding or employment taxes.

**Statutory Stock Option:** An Incentive Stock Option or an option exercised under an Employee Stock Purchase Plan.

**Straight Time:** The standard number of work hours during a workweek for which an employee's regular rate of pay will be paid.

**SUB:** Supplemental Unemployment Benefits.

**Substantiation:** In the context of reimbursed employee business expenses, the requirement that employees keep records of the time, place, and business purpose of reimbursable expenses they incur, including receipts (also used to track business use of company-provided vehicles).

**Substitute Forms:** Tax forms that are printed by private printers rather than the Internal Revenue Service. They must meet certain specifications to be acceptable for filing.

**SUI:** State Unemployment Insurance.

**Supper Money:** The irregular and occasional payment of amounts to employees who work late to cover the cost of meals eaten during that extra working time.

**Supplemental Military Pay:** Payments made by an employer to an employee who is serving in the U.S. armed forces to make up the difference between the employee's military pay and his or her regular wages.

**Supplemental Unemployment Benefits (SUB):** Employer plans that provide supplements to state unemployment compensation benefits.

**Supplemental Wages:** Compensation received by employees other than their regular pay, such as bonuses, commissions, and severance pay. Income tax may be withheld from such payments at a flat rate under certain circumstances.

**SUTA Dumping:** An illegal practice of manipulating state unemployment insurance rates to achieve a lower employer tax rate, generally by forming a new company and transferring employee to that company, which has a lower, "new employer" UI rate.

**Table I:** Refers to IRS Uniform Premium Table I, which is used to calculate the value of group-term life insurance over $50,000.

**Take-Home Pay:** In the context of a federal tax levy, the amount of an employee's wages that remains after all normal deductions in effect at the time of the levy have been subtracted.

**TAMRA '88:** Technical and Miscellaneous Revenue Act of 1988.

**Tax Equalization Plan:** A plan offered by an employer to an employee working abroad that would provide the employee with the same take-home pay he or she would have in the U.S.

**Tax Protection Plan:** A plan offered by an employer to an employee working abroad that would guarantee the employee a foreign tax obligation no larger than he or she would have in the U.S.

**Tax Reform Act of 1986 (TRA '86):** Sweeping tax reform legislation that lowered tax rates and sought to eliminate many of the loopholes in the tax laws.

**Taxable Wage Base:** The maximum amount of employee compensation subject to social security, FUTA, and state unemployment insurance taxes.

**Taxpayer Identification Number (TIN):** A social security number or employer identification number, which serves as the taxpayer's account number with the IRS.

**TEFRA:** Tax Equity and Fiscal Responsibility Act of 1982.

**Temporary Assignment:** See "Short-Term Assignment."

**Temporary Help Agency Employees:** Workers hired through temporary help agencies who are screened and trained by the agency to provide services for client firms. They are employees of the agency, rather than the client firm.

**TFA:** Treasury Financial Agent.

**Third-Country National:** In the context of U.S. payroll, someone who is a non-U.S. citizen working in a country other than the U.S.

**Third-Party Sick Pay:** Payments made by a third party, such as a state or private insurer, to employees because of nonjob-related illness or injury.

**Third-Party Designee:** An individual authorized by an employer to correspond with the IRS regarding the completion and processing of an employment tax return (e.g., Form 940, 941, 945).

**Time-and-a-Half:** Payment of 1½ times an employee's regular rate of pay for hours worked over 40 in a workweek, as required by the Federal Wage-Hour Law (for nonexempt employees only).

**TIN:** Taxpayer Identification Number.

**Tip Credit:** A reduction in the minimum wage allowed for tipped employees (e.g., 50% of the federal minimum wage).

**Tip Rate Determination Agreement (TRDA):** An agreement by an employer with the IRS on a certain tip percentage and a requirement that 75% of the tipped employees agree to report at least the tip percentage found in the agreement.

**Tip Reporting Alternative Commitment (TRAC):** An agreement between a hospitality employer and the IRS that bases FICA assessments on employee audits and requires the employer to educate its employees on tip reporting.

**Title VII:** The employment discrimination portion of the Civil Rights Act of 1964, which prohibits job bias based on race, sex, color, religion, or national origin.

**Totalization Agreements:** Agreements between the U.S. and foreign countries that prevent double social security and Medicare taxation of U.S. employees working abroad and aliens working in the U.S.

**TRA '86:** Tax Reform Act of 1986.

**TRAC:** Tip Reporting Alternative Commitment.

**TRDA:** Tip Rate Determination Agreement.

**Treasury Financial Agent (TFA):** One of two banks chosen to implement the Electronic Federal Tax Payment System for depositing federal taxes electronically.

**Trust Fund Taxes:** The amounts withheld by employers from employees' pay for federal income, social security, and Medicare taxes. They are referred to as trust fund taxes because the money is held in a special trust fund for the U.S. government. Amounts withheld for state and local income taxes are held in trust for the state or local government.

**§218 Agreement:** An agreement between a state or local government employer and the state social security agency under which the employees are subject to social security and Medicare coverage.

**UC:** Unemployment Compensation.

**UI:** Unemployment Insurance.

**UIFSA:** Uniform Interstate Family Support Act.

**Uniform Interstate Family Support Act (UIFSA):** Model state child support enforcement law under which employers must put into effect a child support withholding order from another state's child support enforcement agency if the order appears "regular on its face."

**Uniform Premium Table:** See "Table I".

**Uniformed Services Employment and Reemployment Rights Act of 1994 (USERRA):** Federal law guaranteeing, among other things, the right of U.S. veterans to make additional elective deferrals under their employer's §401(k) plan for the time they spent in military service.

**Universal Availability:** A requirement that employers provide an equal opportunity for employees to make elective deferral catch-up contributions.

**USC:** United States Code, where federal laws are compiled.

**USCIS:** U.S. Citizenship and Immigration Services

**U.S. Citizenship and Immigration Services (USCIS):** A federal government agency, part of the Homeland Security Department, to which the employment eligibility functions of the Immigration and Naturalization Service were transferred in 2003.

**USERRA:** Uniformed Services Employment and Reemployment Rights Act of 1994.

**Voluntary Contribution:** Advance payments of unemployment tax that can reduce an employer's state unemployment tax rate.

**Wage Assignment:** A voluntary agreement by an employee to transfer portions of future wage payments (e.g., insurance premium deductions, credit union deductions).

**Wage Attachment:** An involuntary transfer of an employee's wage payment to satisfy a debt.

**Wage-bracket Withholding Method:** A procedure for calculating the amount of federal income tax to be withheld from an employee's wages based on wage-bracket tables classified by the employee's marital status and payroll period.

**Wage Continuation Sheet:** A periodic report (e.g., quarterly) from employers to state unemployment agencies containing employees' names, total wages, and unemployment taxable wages.

**Wage-Hour Law:** See "Federal Wage-Hour Law."

**Wage Orders:** State agency directives that set wage and hour standards, usually for specific industries.

**WAN:** Wide Area Network.

**WC:** Workers' Compensation.

**Web-Enabled Application:** An application that uses the Internet as another means of accessing an organization's data and the HRMS application logic itself.

**White Collar Employees:** In the context of the Federal Wage-Hour Law, these are executive, administrative, professional (including computer-related professionals), or outside sales employees who are exempt from the law's minimum wage, overtime pay, and certain recordkeeping requirements.

**Wide Area Network (WAN):** A network in which information is transmitted over long distances at relatively slower speeds using telephone lines.

**Withholding:** Subtracting amounts from an employee's wages for taxes, garnishments or levies, and other deductions (e.g., medical insurance premiums, union dues). These amounts are then paid over to the government agency or other party to whom they are owed.

**Work-sharing Plan:** An agreement to reduce some employees' hours to avoid laying off other employees. Those employees whose hours were reduced receive partial unemployment benefits.

**Worker Classification:** The process of determining whether an individual performing services for a business is either an employee or an independent contractor.

# *Glossary*

**Worker Classification Settlement Program:** A process that allows IRS agents and businesses to resolve worker classification cases as early in the enforcement process as possible with a settlement of past liabilities and an agreement to treat the workers as employees in the future.

**Workstation:** In the context of computers, a powerful personal computer that is generally faster than a standard PC.

**Workweek:** The basis for determining an employee's regular rate of pay and overtime pay due under the Fair Labor Standards Act. It can be any consecutive 7-day (168-hour) period chosen by the employer (e.g., Saturday through Friday, Wednesday through Tuesday).

# INDEX

as employees of leasing agency, 1-13
benefit plan issues, 1-13—1-14
training, 1-13
who controls, 1-13
**Leave sharing plans,** 3-78
**Levy,** see Federal tax levy
**Liabilities,** 11-4, 11-9
**Life insurance:**
group-term life insurance, 3-26—3-28
split-dollar life insurance, 3-29—3-32
whole-life insurance, 3-28—3-29
**Life insurance salespersons,** 1-10—1-11
**Line of business requirement,** 3-6
**Loans:**
below market, 3-79—3-80
draws against commission as, 3-80
repayment, effect on minimum wage, 9-49
student, 9-46—9-47
to employees, 3-79—3-80
**Local Area Network,** 12-7
**Lock-in letter,** 6-15—6-16
**Lodging,** see Employee business expenses,
Meals and lodging
**Long-term assignments,** see Indefinite
assignments
**Long-term care insurance,** 4-11
**Lookback period,** 8-5—8-8
**Loose-leaf services,** 13-32

-M-

**Magnetic media reporting:**
multiple worksite report, 7-38—7-41
state unemployment reporting, 7-33—7-38
state W-2 reporting, 8-103—8-106
**Management theories,** 13-2—13-5
**Manager self-service,** 12-31
**Managing a payroll department:**
coaching, 13-13
controlling performance, 13-14—13-16
counseling, 13-13—13-14
crisis management, 13-19—13-20
customer service, 13-26—13-29
delegating, 13-9
directing employees, 13-11—13-14
feedback, 13-11—13-13
hiring, 13-6—13-9
listening, 13-12—13-13
meetings, 13-17—13-18
performance evaluations, 13-24—13-26
reporting, 13-16—13-17
research needs, 13-28—13-35
situational leadership, 13-2—13-3
staffing, 13-6—13-11
strategic planning, 13-5—13-6
team building, 13-22—13-24
time management, 13-21—13-22
training, 13-9—13-10
**Matching principle,** 11-3

**Meals and lodging:**
deductions below minimum wage, 9-48—9-49
employee business travel expense,
3-40—3-55
furnished by employer, 2-35—2-36, 3-56
moving expenses, 3-33—3-37
substantiation of, 3-44
**Medical expenses, reimbursement for,**
4-4—4-8
**Medical insurance,** see Health and accident
insurance
**Medical savings accounts**
as part of pilot project, 4-11
eligible employers and employees, 4-9
reporting requirements, 4-10, 8-67
tax treatment, 4-9—4-10
**Medical support orders,** 9-23—9-27
**Medicare tax:**
calculating withholding, 6-45—6-46
common paymaster, 6-47—6-48
coverage and exemptions, see Social
security tax
employee works for more than one employer,
6-46
employees of foreign affiliates, 14-5
public sector application, 6-50—6-53
successor employers, 6-47
tax rate, 6-44
totalization agreements, 14-4—14-5,
14-35
wage limit eliminated, 6-44
**Meetings,** 13-17—13-18
**Mergers and acquisitions,** 6-47, 7-8—7-9, 8-5,
8-28—8-29
**Mileage rates:**
cents-per-mile valuation method, 3-21—3-22
moving expenses, 3-33
standard business, 3-51
**Military pay,** 3-80—3-81
**Minimum wage,** see Fair Labor Standards Act
**MMREF,** See Magnetic Media Reporting and
Electronic Filing
**Monopolistic states,** 4-47
**Motion picture theater employees,** 2-34
**Motor carrier employees,** 2-33
**Moving expenses:**
deductibility of, 3-33—3-34
distance test, 3-33
foreign moves, 14-13
Form 3903, 3-35, A-346
household goods, transportation of, 3-33
meals, treatment of, 3-33
military personnel, 3-36—3-37
pre-move househunting costs, 3-34
real estate expenses, 3-34
reimbursements for, 3-34
reporting on Form W-2, 3-35—3-36, 8-67
temporary living quarters, 3-34
time test, 3-33

# *Index*